Guitar Tab White Pages

Volume 3

Also Available!

HL00690471

HL00699557

HL00699590

HL00690508

ISBN 1-4234-0005-4

7777 W. Bluemound Rd. P.O. Box 13819 Milwaukee, WI 53213

Visit Hal Leonard Online at
www.halleonard.com

Alphabetical Song Listing

Ain't Talkin' 'Bout Love 6
Van Halen

Ain't Too Proud to Beg 13
The Temptations

Alive 16
Pearl Jam

All Along the Watchtower............24
Jimi Hendrix

All for You......................................36
Sister Hazel

American Pie 43
Don McLean

Aqualung 57
Jethro Tull

Are You Gonna Be My Girl 69
Jet

Babe, I'm Gonna Leave You 78
Led Zeppelin

Back in Black................................92
AC/DC

Bang a Gong (Get It On)..............99
T. Rex

Bark at the Moon........................106
Ozzy Osbourne

Big City Nights 114
Scorpions

Black Velvet 126
Alannah Myles

Blaze of Glory 135
Jon Bon Jovi

Blue Collar Man (Long Nights)....143
Styx

Blue Sky..152
The Allman Brothers Band

Born to Be Wild 162
Steppenwolf

The Boys Are Back in Town 166
Thin Lizzy

Breakdown....................................175
Tom Petty & The Heartbreakers

Brown Eyed Girl 179
Van Morrison

Buddy Holly 186
Weezer

Burning for You 193
Blue Oyster Cult

Carry On..202
Crosby, Stills & Nash

Carry on Wayward Son 213
Kansas

Catfish Blues 221
Jimi Hendrix

Cherry Pie 233
Warrant

Cherub Rock 240
Smashing Pumpkins

Cold Shot 250
Stevie Ray Vaughan

Cold Sweat, Pt. 1 256
James Brown

Creep 260
Radiohead

Cuts Like a Knife..........................270
Bryan Adams

Damn Right, I've Got the Blues ..280
Buddy Guy

Dear Mr. Fantasy 287
Traffic

Deuce 299
Kiss

Don't Stand So Close to Me......305
The Police

Don't Tell Me You Love Me 309
Night Ranger

Dream Police 321
Cheap Trick

Dreams..325
Fleetwood Mac

Empire 334
Queensryche

Everyday 344
Dave Matthews Band

Evil Ways 351
Santana

Evil Woman 354
Electric Light Orchestra

Fall to Pieces 362
Velvet Revolver

Fat Lip..370
Sum 41

Fight for Your Right (To Party)....376
Beastie Boys

Fly 379
Sugar Ray

Free..385
Phish

Funk #49..395
The James Gang

Get Ready......................................398
Rare Earth

Gone Away....................................402
The Offspring

Grace 406
Jeff Buckley

Gypsy Road 415
Cinderella

Hand in My Pocket 422
Alanis Morissette

A Hard Day's Night 429
The Beatles

Hard to Handle............................432
The Black Crowes

Heartbreaker 442
Pat Benatar

Heaven 451
Los Lonely Boys

Heaven Tonight 463
Yngwie Malmsteen's Rising Force

Here I Go Again............................472
Whitesnake

Highway Star 481
Deep Purple

Hold On Loosely 490
38 Special

Hollywood Nights 506
Bob Seger & The Silver Bullet Band

Hot Legs..515
Rod Stewart

The House of the Rising Sun....525
The Animals

Hurts So Good..............................531
John "Cougar" Mellencamp

I Am the Highway 537
Audioslave

I Can't Explain 543
The Who

I Can't Help Myself 545
The Four Tops

I Get Around..................................548
The Beach Boys

I Heard It Through the Grapevine ..555
Marvin Gaye

I Want to Hold Your Hand 559
The Beatles

I Wish 564
Stevie Wonder

I'd Love to Change the World....569
Ten Years After

If You're Gone..............................576
Matchbox Twenty

It's Your Thing 582
The Isley Brothers

Jane Says....................................585
Jane's Addiction

Jeremy 589
Pearl Jam

Jessie's Girl 596
Rick Springfield

Just a Girl...................................603
No Doubt

Keep Away 610
Godsmack

Killer Queen 616
Queen

Kryptonite 624
3 Doors Down

Land of Confusion 631
Genesis

Last Child....................................636
Aerosmith

Lay It on the Line...........................643
Triumph

Le Freak 652
Chic

Lightning Crashes............................657
Live

Lights Out 662
Michael Schenker

Like the Way I Do...........................676
Melissa Etheridge

Lithium 687
Nirvana

Long Cool Woman (In a Black Dress) 691
The Hollies

Lost in Germany 698
King's X

Lovesong 703
The Cure

Magic Man 709
Heart

Mas Tequila 720
Sammy Hagar

Midnight Train 729
Buddy Guy (with Jonny Lang)

My Sharona 739
The Knack

No More Mr. Nice Guy......................750
Alice Cooper

No Rain.......................................758
Blind Melon

Nookie 767
Limp Bizkit

Oh Well Part 1 773
Fleetwood Mac

Once Bitten Twice Shy 782
Great White

One Step Closer 792
Linkin Park

One Way or Another 796
Blondie

Panama.......................................805
Van Halen

Peg 815
Steely Dan

Photograph 820
Def Leppard

Pornograffitti 828
Extreme

Practice What You Preach.................837
Testament

Pretending 848
Eric Clapton

Rock This Town 856
Stray Cats

Rock'n Me 866
Steve Miller Band

Rocky Mountain Way.......................871
Joe Walsh

Santeria 878
Sublime

Saturday Night's Alright (For Fighting)........................882
Elton John

Secret Agent Man 890
Johnny Rivers

Seven Bridges Road 895
Eagles

Sharp Dressed Man.........................899
ZZ Top

Shimmer.....................................907
Fuel

Should I Stay or Should I Go 912
The Clash

Somebody Told Me 916
The Killers

Space Lord...................................923
Monster Magnet

Stay...928
Lisa Loeb & Nine Stories

Stupid Girl 937
Garbage

Sweet Home Alabama.....................940
Lynyrd Skynyrd

Talk Dirty to Me 948
Poison

Texas Flood 960
Stevie Ray Vaughan

That Thing You Do! 968
The Wonders

This Love 972
Maroon5

Time 980
Hootie & The Blowfish

(So) Tired of Waiting for You......990
The Kinks

Too Rolling Stoned 993
Robin Trower

The Trooper 1006
Iron Maiden

Turn Me Loose.............................1017
Loverboy

Turn the Page..............................1025
Metallica

25 or 6 to 4................................1047
Chicago

Up All Night 1057
Slaughter

Wanted Dead or Alive 1064
Bon Jovi

The Warrior................................1071
Scandal

We Built This City 1081
Starship

We're Ready 1089
Boston

What's My Age Again? 1098
blink-182

Whip It 1103
Devo

White Rabbit 1106
Jefferson Airplane

White Wedding............................1112
Billy Idol

Wish You Were Here 1122
Incubus

Yankee Rose 1127
David Lee Roth

Ziggy Stardust 1139
David Bowie

Zombie 1146
The Cranberries

Guitar Notation Legend 1151

Artist Listing

AC/DC
Back in Black 92

BRYAN ADAMS
Cuts Like a Knife 270

AEROSMITH
Last Child 636

THE ALLMAN BROTHERS BAND
Blue Sky 152

THE ANIMALS
The House of the Rising Sun 525

AUDIOSLAVE
I Am the Highway 537

THE BEACH BOYS
I Get Around 548

BEASTIE BOYS
Fight for Your Right (To Party) 376

THE BEATLES
A Hard Day's Night 429
I Want to Hold Your Hand 559

PAT BENATAR
Heartbreaker 442

THE BLACK CROWES
Hard to Handle 432

BLIND MELON
No Rain 758

BLINK-182
What's My Age Again? 1098

BLONDIE
One Way or Another 796

BLUE OYSTER CULT
Burning for You 193

BOB SEGER & THE SILVER BULLET BAND
Hollywood Nights....506

BON JOVI
Wanted Dead or Alive 1064

JON BON JOVI
Blaze of Glory 135

BOSTON
We're Ready 1089

DAVID BOWIE
Ziggy Stardust 1139

JAMES BROWN
Cold Sweat, Pt. 1....256

JEFF BUCKLEY
Grace....406

CHEAP TRICK
Dream Police 321

CHIC
Le Freak 652

CHICAGO
25 or 6 to 4 1047

CINDERELLA
Gypsy Road....415

ERIC CLAPTON
Pretending....848

THE CLASH
Should I Stay or Should I Go 912

ALICE COOPER
No More Mr. Nice Guy....750

THE CRANBERRIES
Zombie 1146

CROSBY, STILLS & NASH
Carry On 202

THE CURE
Lovesong....703

DAVE MATTHEWS BAND
Everyday 344

DEEP PURPLE
Highway Star....481

DEF LEPPARD
Photograph 820

DEVO
Whip It....1103

EAGLES
Seven Bridges Road 895

ELETRIC LIGHT ORCHESTRA
Evil Woman 354

MELISSA ETHERIDGE
Like the Way I Do 676

EXTREME
Pornograffitti 828

FLEETWOOD MAC
Dreams 325
Oh Well Part 1 773

THE FOUR TOPS
I Can't Help Myself 545

FUEL
Shimmer 907

GARBAGE
Stupid Girl 937

MARVIN GAYE
I Heard It Through the Grapevine 555

GENESIS
Land of Confusion....631

GODSMACK
Keep Away....610

GREAT WHITE
Once Bitten Twice Shy 782

BUDDY GUY
Damn Right, I've Got the Blues....280
Midnight Train (with **JONNY LANG**)....729

HOOTIE & THE BLOWFISH
Time 980

SAMMY HAGAR
Mas Tequila 720

HEART
Magic Man....709

JIMI HENDRIX
All Along the Watchtower 24
Catfish Blues....221

THE HOLLIES
Long Cool Woman (In a Black Dress) 691

BILLY IDOL
White Wedding 1112

INCUBUS
Wish You Were Here 1122

IRON MAIDEN
The Trooper....1006

THE ISLEY BROTHERS
It's Your Thing 582

THE JAMES GANG
Funk #49 395

JANE'S ADDICTION
Jane Says 585

JEFFERSON AIRPLANE
White Rabbit 1106

JET
Are You Gonna Be My Girl 69

JETHRO TULL
Aqualung....57

ELTON JOHN
Saturday Night's Alright (For Fighting)....882

KANSAS
Carry on Wayward Son 213

THE KILLERS
Somebody Told Me 916

KING'S X
Lost in Germany 698

THE KINKS
(So) Tired of Waiting for You 990

KISS
Deuce 299

THE KNACK
My Sharona....739

LED ZEPPELIN
Babe, I'm Gonna Leave You 78

LIMP BIZKIT
Nookie 767

LINKIN PARK
One Step Closer 792

LISA LOEB & NINE STORIES
Stay 928

LIVE
Lightning Crashes 657

LOS LONELY BOYS
Heaven 451

LOVERBOY
Turn Me Loose 1017

LYNYRD SKYNYRD
Sweet Home Alabama 940

MAROON5
This Love 972

MATCHBOX TWENTY
If You're Gone 576

DON McLEAN
American Pie 43

JOHN "COUGAR" MELLENCAMP
Hurts So Good 531

METALLICA
Turn the Page 1025

MONSTER MAGNET
Space Lord 923

ALANIS MORISSETTE
Hand in My Pocket 422

VAN MORRISON
Brown Eyed Girl 179

ALANNAH MYLES
Black Velvet 126

NIGHT RANGER
Don't Tell Me You Love Me 309

NIRVANA
Lithium 687

NO DOUBT
Just a Girl 603

THE OFFSPRING
Gone Away 402

OZZY OSBOURNE
Bark at the Moon 106

PEARL JAM
Alive 16
Jeremy 589

PHISH
Free 385

POISON
Talk Dirty to Me 948

THE POLICE
Don't Stand So Close to Me 305

QUEEN
Killer Queen 616

QUEENSRYCHE
Empire 334

RADIOHEAD
Creep 260

RARE EARTH
Get Ready 398

JOHNNY RIVERS
Secret Agent Man 890

DAVID LEE ROTH
Yankee Rose 1127

SANTANA
Evil Ways 351

SCANDAL
The Warrior 1071

MICHAEL SCHENKER
Lights Out 662

SCORPIONS
Big City Nights 114

SISTER HAZEL
All for You 36

SMASHING PUMPKINS
Cherub Rock 240

RICK SPRINGFIELD
Jessie's Girl 596

SLAUGHTER
Up All Night 1057

STARSHIP
We Built This City 1081

STEELY DAN
Peg 815

STEPPENWOLF
Born to be Wild 162

STEVE MILLER BAND
Rock'n Me 866

ROD STEWART
Hot Legs 515

STRAY CATS
Rock This Town 856

STYX
Blue Collar Man (Long Nights) 143

SUBLIME
Santeria 878

SUGAR RAY
Fly 379

SUM 41
Fat Lip 370

T. REX
Bang a Gong (Get It On) 99

THE TEMPTATIONS
Ain't Too Proud to Beg 13

TEN YEARS AFTER
I'd Love to Change the World 569

TESTAMENT
Practice What You Preach 837

THIN LIZZY
The Boys Are Back in Town 166

38 SPECIAL
Hold On Loosely 490

3 DOORS DOWN
Kryptonite 624

TOM PETTY & THE HEARTBREAKERS
Breakdown 175

TRAFFIC
Dear Mr. Fantasy 287

TRIUMPH
Lay It on the Line 643

ROBIN TROWER
Too Rolling Stoned 993

VAN HALEN
Ain't Talkin' 'Bout Love 6
Panama 805

STEVIE RAY VAUGHAN
Cold Shot 250
Texas Flood 960

VELVET REVOLVER
Fall to Pieces 362

JOE WALSH
Rocky Mountain Way 871

WARRANT
Cherry Pie 233

WEEZER
Buddy Holly 186

WHITESNAKE
Here I Go Again 472

THE WHO
I Can't Explain 543

STEVIE WONDER
I Wish 564

THE WONDERS
That Thing You Do! 968

YNGWIE MALMSTEEN'S RISING FORCE
Heaven Tonight 463

ZZ TOP
Sharp Dressed Man 899

Ain't Talkin' 'Bout Love

Words and Music by David Lee Roth, Edward Van Halen, Alex Van Halen and Michael Anthony

Am F G5
Yeah, you may have all you want, ___ ba - by, ___ but I got some - thin' you need, _
Oh, yeah, you think you're real - ly cook - in', ba - by. ___ You bet - ter find your - self a
Chorus
Gtr. 1: w/ Rhy. Fig. 1 (4 times)
Am F G5 Am G5
friend, oh, yeah. ___ my friend. ___ Ain't talk - in' 'bout love.
Gtr. 1
P.M.
P.S.
Am G5 Am G5
My love is rot - ten to the core. ___ Ain't talk - in' 'bout love.
1.
Am G5
Just like I told you be - fore, ___ yeah, be - fore. ___ 2. You know you're sem - i good -
2.
Guitar Solo
Am G5 Am G5
Just like I told you be - fore, ___ be - fore, _ uh, be - fore, ___ uh, be - fore, _ be - fore.
Gtr. 1
w/ bar
P.M.
P.M.
*Hold bend while sliding.
Riff B
**Gtr. 2
mf
**Elec. sitar arr. for gtr.

Am
G5
w/ bar
let ring
Am
G5
Am
G5
End Riff B
grad. release
Chorus
Gtr. 1: w/ Rhy. Fig. 1 (3 times)
Gtr. 2 tacet
Am
G5
Am
G5
Ain't talk-in' 'bout love. Babe, it's a rot-ten to the core. __
w/ bar

Am
G5
Ain't talk - in' 'bout love.
Just like I told you be - fore,
Interlude
Am
G5
Am
F
G5
uh, be - fore.
I been to the edge,
an' there I stood an' looked
Gtr. 1
Riff C
End Riff C
P.M.
let ring
mp
flanger off
*Back volume down 1/2 way.
Gtr. 1: w/ Riff C (2 times)
down.
You know I lost a lot of friends there, ba - by,
I got no time to mess a -
round.
Mmm, so if you want it, got to bleed for it, ba - by.
Yeah, got to, got to
8va
f
w/ flanger
Harm.
Pitches: D G B
bleed, ba - by.
Mmm, you got to, got to bleed, ba - by.
Hey, got to, got to
loco
w/ bar

Chorus

Gtr. 1: w/ Rhy. Fig. 1
Am
G5
Am
G5
bleed, ba - by. Ain't talk - in' 'bout love. My love is rot - ten to the
loco
8va
mp
f
let ring
Harm.
loco
f

Gtr. 1: w/ Rhy. Fig. 2
Am
G5
Gtr. 1: w/ Rhy. Fig. 1
Am
G5
core. Ain't talk - in' 'bout love. Just like I told you be - fore,

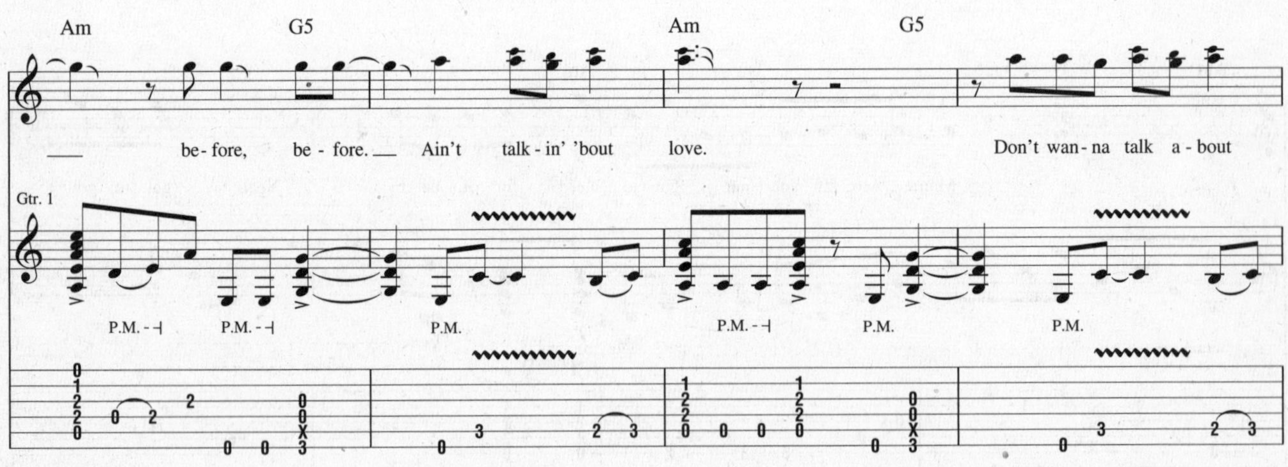

Am
G5
Am
G5
be - fore, be - fore. Ain't talk - in' 'bout love. Don't wan - na talk a - bout
Gtr. 1
P.M.
P.M.
P.M.
P.M.
P.M.
P.M.

Am
G5
Am
G5
love. Don't need to talk a - bout love. Ain't gon - na talk a - bout
8va
loco
P.M.
P.M.
P.M.
P.M.
P.M.

Guitar Solo
Gtr. 2: w/ Riff B
Am
G5
love
no more,
no more.
Ah!
P.M.
w/ bar
Gtr. 1
w/ bar
grad. dive
Hey! Hey! Hey!
Gtr. 2
grad. release
Outro
Gtr. 1: w/ Rhy. Fig. 1 (2 times)
Gtr. 2 tacet
Hey! Hey! Hey!

Am
G5
Hey! Hey! Hey!
Gtr. 1
P.M.
P.M.
Hey! Hey! Hey!
Am
G5
Am
G5
C5
Play 4 times
Hey! Hey! Hey!
Hey! Hey! Hey!
P.M.
P.M.
P.M.
P.M.
P.M.
P.M.
A5
B5
C
A5
B5
E5
Am
B5
C
w/ bar
slack
A5
B5
Em7
Free time
E9
N.C.
P.M.
w/ bar
grad. dive
-4 1/2
-2

Ain't Too Proud to Beg

Words and Music by Edward Holland and Norman Whitfield

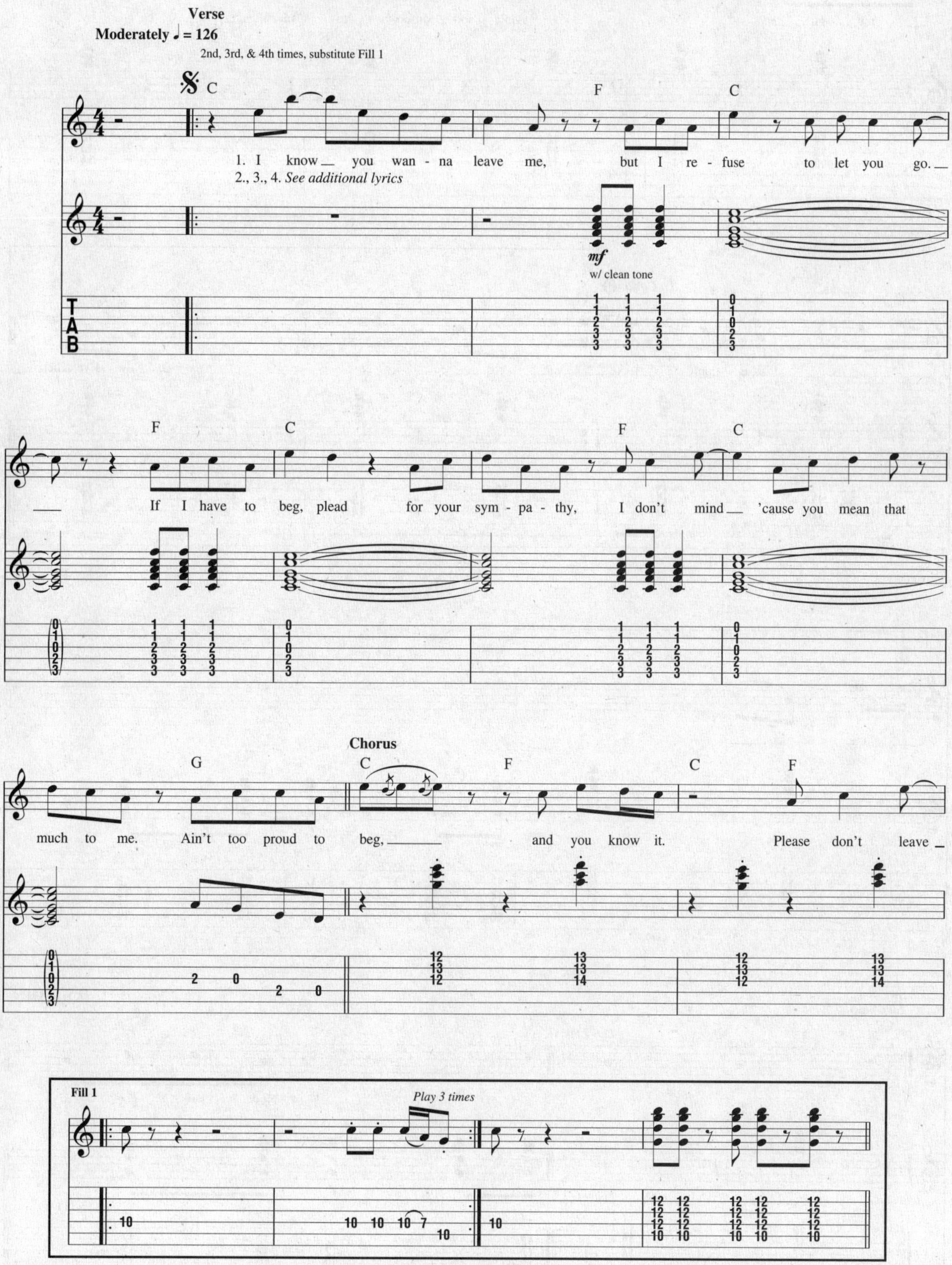

Verse

Moderately ♩ = 126

2nd, 3rd, & 4th times, substitute Fill 1

C F C

1. I know you wan - na leave me, but I re - fuse to let you go.

2., 3., 4. *See additional lyrics*

mf

w/ clean tone

F C F C

If I have to beg, plead for your sym - pa - thy, I don't mind 'cause you mean that

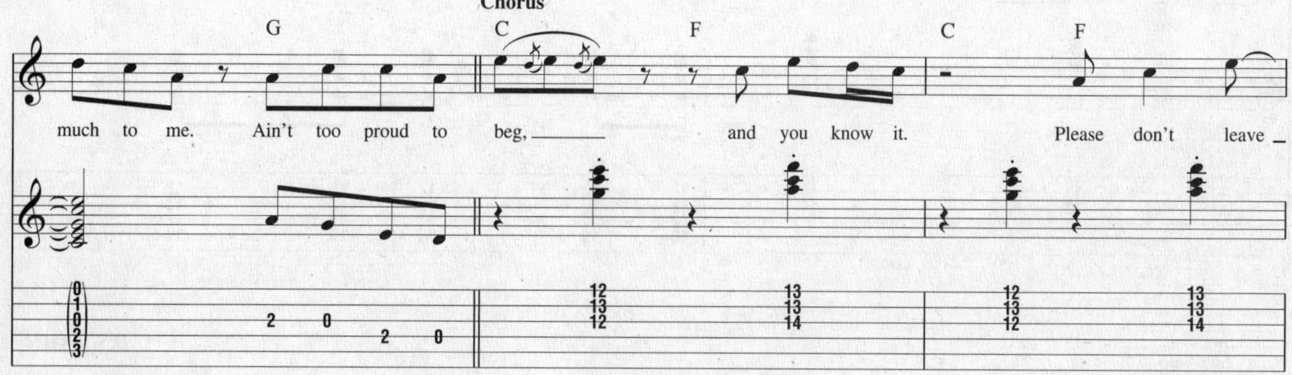

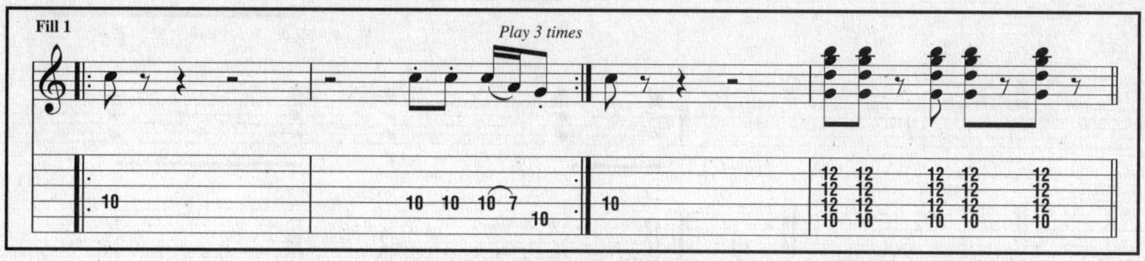

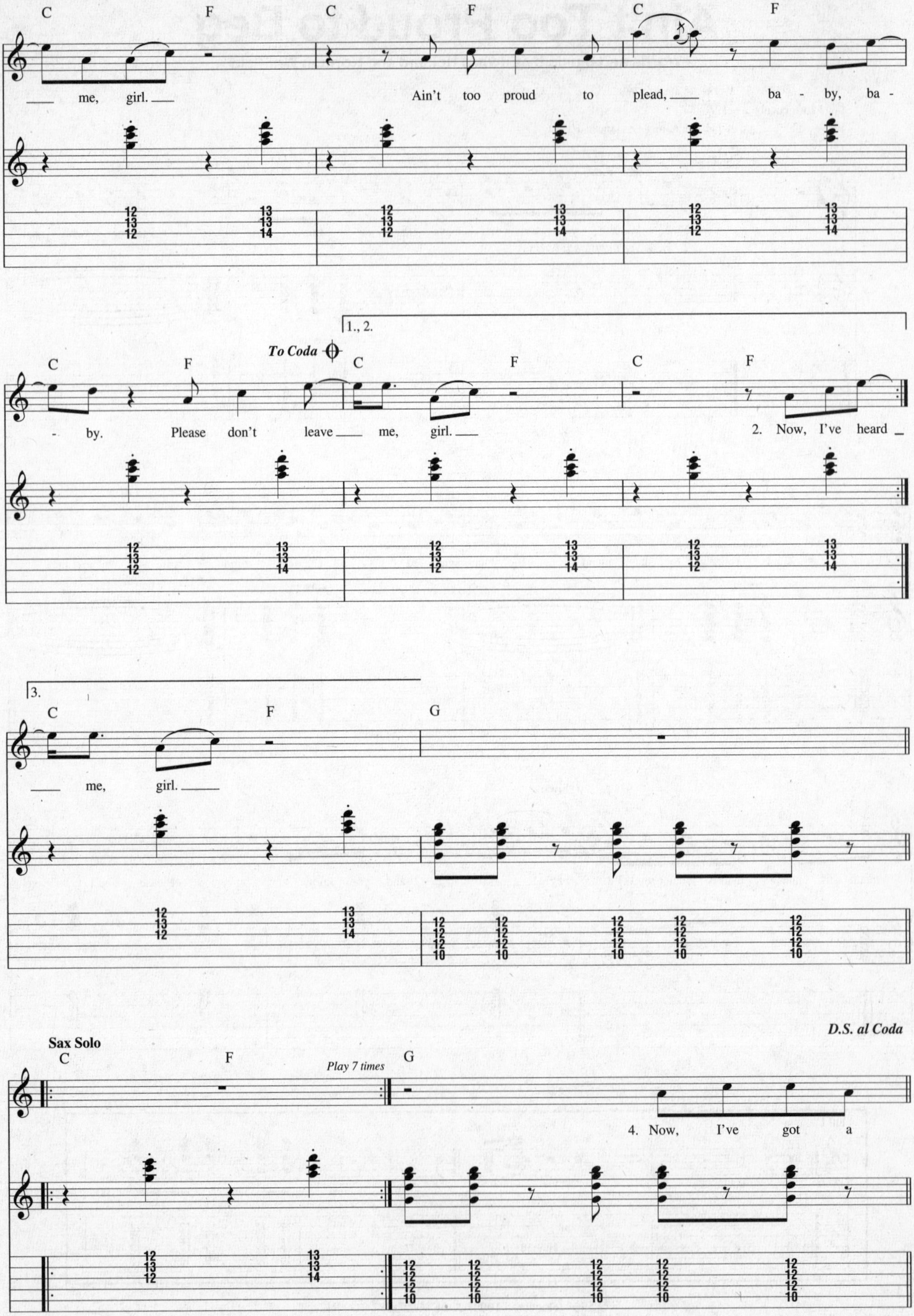

C F C F C F

___ me, girl. ___ Ain't too proud to plead, ___ ba - by, ba -

1., 2.

To Coda 𝄌

C F C F C F

- by. Please don't leave ___ me, girl. ___ 2. Now, I've heard ___

3.

C F G

___ me, girl. ___

D.S. al Coda

𝄌 Coda

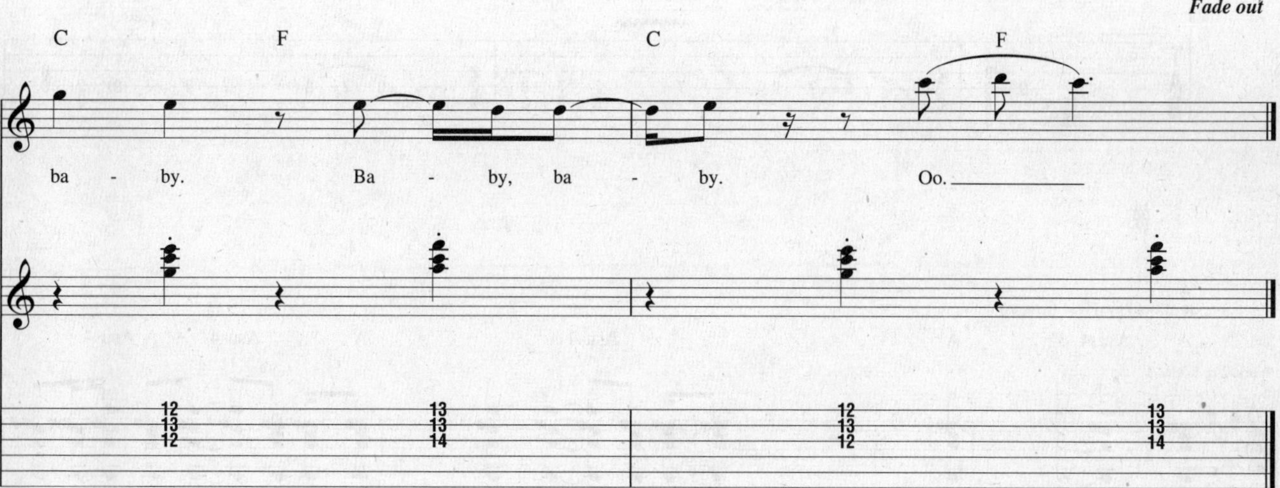

Additional Lyrics

2. Now, I've heard a cryin' man is half a man,
   With no sense of pride.
   But if I have to cry to keep you, I don't mind weepin'
   If it'll keep you by my side.

3. If I have to sleep on your doorstep all night and day
   Just to keep you from walking away.
   Let your friends laugh, even this I can stand,
   'Cause I wanna keep you any way I can.

4. Now, I've got a love so deep in the pit of my heart,
   And each day it grows more and more.
   I'm not ashamed to call and plead to you, baby,
   If pleading keeps you from walking out that door.

Alive

Music by Stone Gossard
Lyric by Eddie Vedder

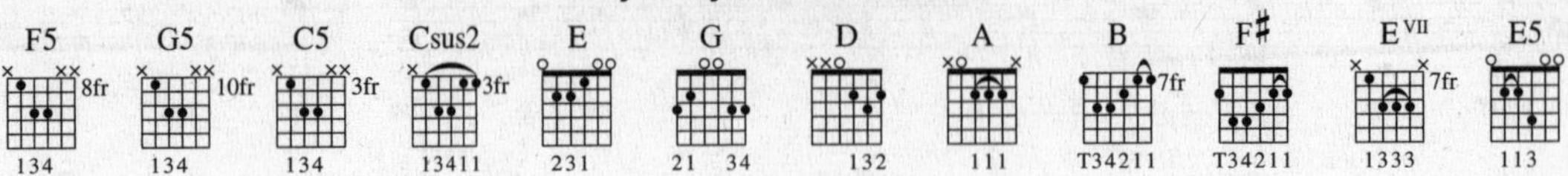

Intro

Moderately slow Rock ♩ = 76

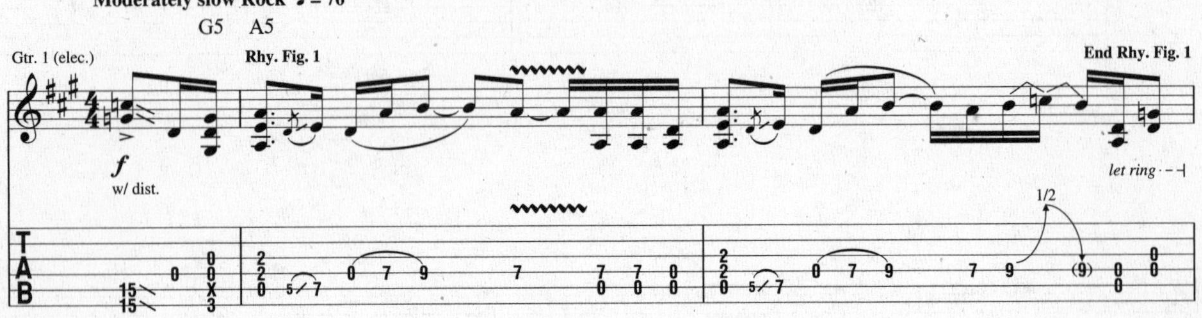

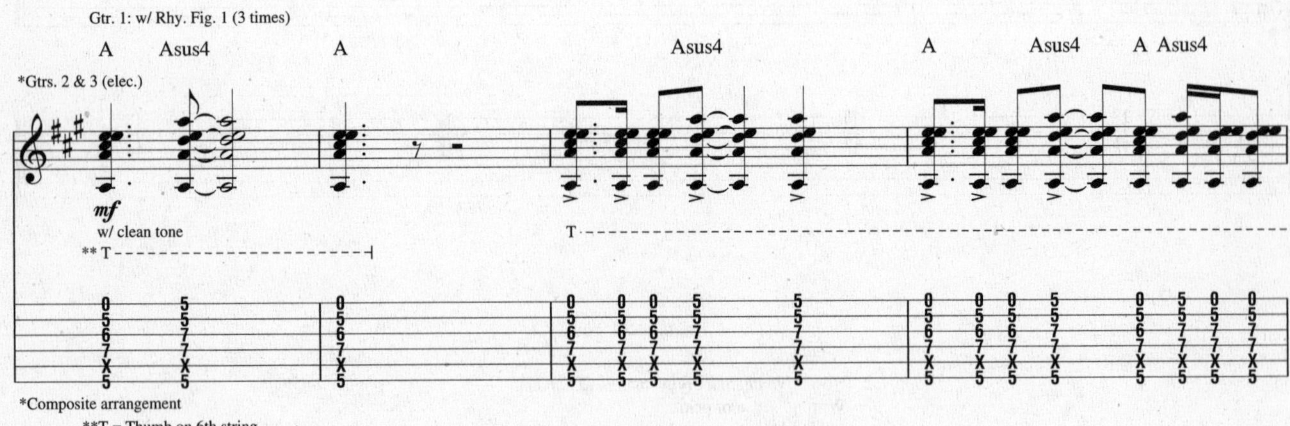

Verse
Gtr. 1: w/ Rhy. Fig. 1 (2 times)
2nd time, Gtr. 4 tacet
A
Asus4
1. "Son," she said, "Have I got a lit - tle sto - ry for you.
2. While she walks slow - ly a - cross a young man's room,
Rhy. Fig. 2
End Rhy. Fig. 2
Gtrs. 2 & 3: w/ Rhy. Fig. 2 (3 times)
what you thought was your dad - dy was noth - in' but a... While you were sit - ting
she said, "I'm read - y for you." I can't re - mem - ber
Gtr. 1
P.M.
Gtr. 1: w/ Rhy. Fig. 1 (2nd meas.)
Gtr. 1: w/ Rhy. Fig. 1
home a - lone at age thir - teen, your real dad - dy was dy - ing; Sor - ry you did - n't
an - y - thing to this ver - y day, 'cept the love, the love. Oh,
F5
G5 C5
Csus2
(cont. in notation)
see him. But I'm glad we talked." Oh,
you know where, now I can see. I just
Gtrs. 2 & 3
(cont. in slashes)

Chorus
3rd time, Gtr. 1: w/ Rhy. Fig. 5 (4 times)
E G D A
Rhy. Fig. 3A
End Rhy. Fig. 3A
*Gtrs. 2, 3 & 4
I'm oh, I'm still a - live. Aay,
stare, I, I'm still a - live. Aay,
Gtr. 1
Rhy. Fig. 3
End Rhy. Fig. 3
let ring
*Gtr. 4 (acous.) played f, Composite arrangement
1st time, Gtr. 1: w/ Rhy. Fig. 3
1st time, Gtrs. 2, 3 & 4: w/ Rhy. Fig. 3A (2 times)
2nd time, Gtr. 1: w/ Rhy. Fig. 3 (2 times)
2nd & 3rd times, Gtrs. 2, 3 & 4: w/ Rhy. Fig. 3A (3 times)
E G D A
I'm oh, I'm still a - live. Aay,
I'm oh, I'm still a - live. Aay,
1.
E G D A B
Gtrs. 2 & 3
I'm oh, I'm still a - live, aay, oh, oh.
Gtr. 1
Rhy. Fig. 4
End Rhy. Fig. 4
let ring
2., 3.
E G D A
I'm oh, I'm still a - live. Aay,
Rhy. Fig. 5
Gtr. 1
let ring

To Coda
1st time, Gtr. 1: w/ Rhy. Fig. 4
E
G
D
A
1. I'm oh, I'm still a - live, aay.
2. I'm oo, I'm still a - live, yeah, yeah, yeah, yeah, yeah, yeah.
Bridge
B
F♯
B
Gtrs. 2 & 3
Gtr. 4
w/ dist.
Gtr. 1
F♯
B
Gtrs. 2 & 3
*Gtrs. 1 & 4
(cont. in notation)
*Composite arrangement
F♯
B
F♯
Gtrs. 1 & 4
Gtrs. 2 & 3
mp
dist. off
let ring

Gtr. 1 tacet
A7 A7sus2 Dsus2
A7 A7sus2 D5(add6)
"Is some-thing wrong?" she said.
Of course there is.
"You're still a-
*Gtrs. 2, 3 & 4
mf
let ring
*Composite arrangement
B7 B7sus2 Esus2
B7 B7sus2 E6sus2
live," she said.
Oh, and do I de-serve to be?
Is that the ques-tion?
And if so,
D.S. al Coda
(take 1st lyrics)
Gtr. 1
if so,
who an-swers?
Who an-swers?
*w/ dist.
(cont. in slashes)
*Gtrs. 2 & 3
Coda
Guitar Solo
Gtr. 1: w/ Rhy. Fig. 5 (4 times)
Gtrs. 3 & 4: w/ Rhy. Fig. 3A (17 1/2 times)
E
G
D
A
Gtr. 2
w/ wah-wah

E
G
D
A
8va
loco
Harm.
Gtr. 2
Gtr. 1
Gtr. 1: w/ Rhy. Fig. 3A (11 1/2 times)
wah-wah off
let ring

D
A
E
G
let ring
1 hold bend

E
G
D
A
grad. bend
1/2
let ring
P.M.
Free time
Gtr. 3 tacet
E5
Gtrs. 3 & 4
Gtr. 4
rit.
Gtr. 2
Gtr. 1
rake

All Along the Watchtower

Words and Music by Bob Dylan

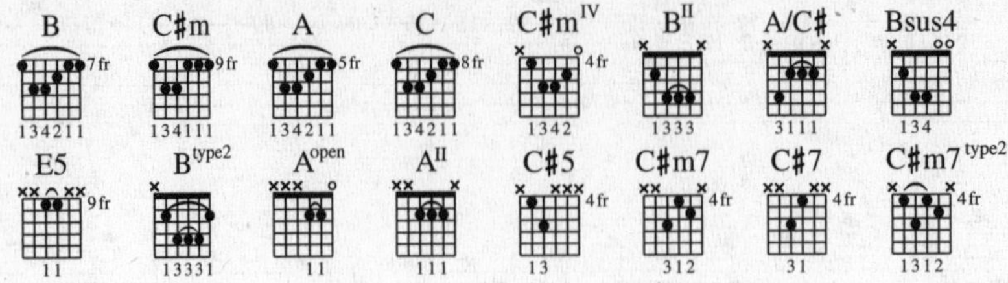

Tune Down 1/2 Step:
① = E♭ ④ = D♭
② = B♭ ⑤ = A♭
③ = G♭ ⑥ = E♭

Intro

Moderately ♩ = 112

B C#m B A B C#m B A

*Gtr. 1 (12-str. acous.)

mf

* Two gtrs. arranged for one.

B C C#m B A B

Gtr. 2 (elec.)

f

w/ dist.

full full full full full

C#m B A B C

Verse

C#m IV B II

1. There must be some kind a way

full full full full

p *mp*

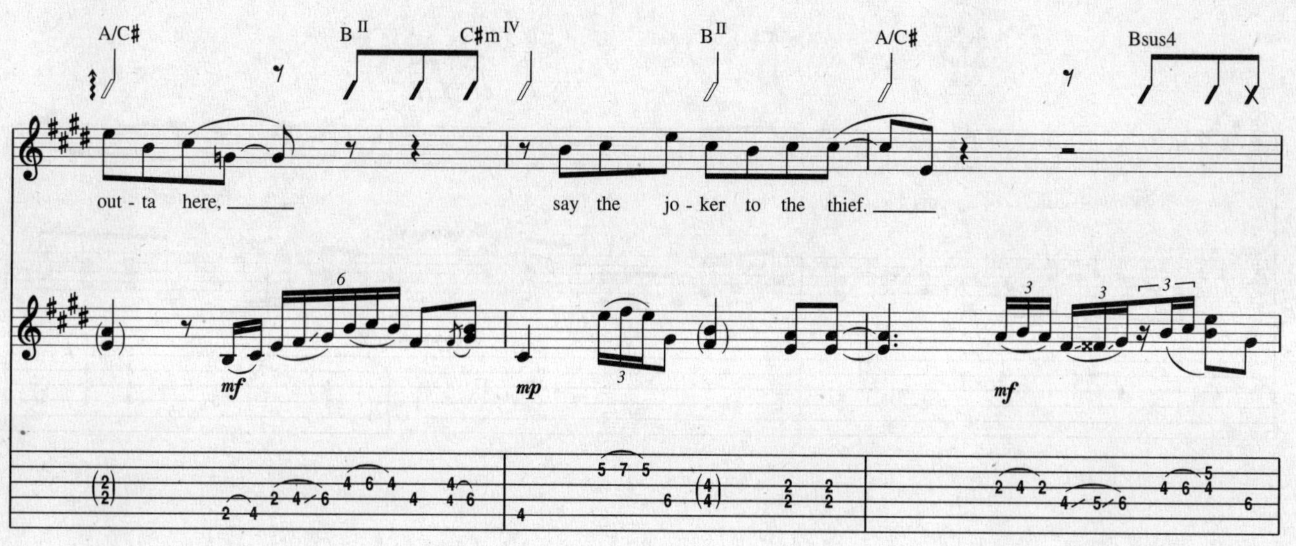
A/C#
B II
C#m IV
B II
A/C#
Bsus4
out - ta here,
say the jo - ker to the thief.
mf
mp
mf

C#m IV
B II
A/C#
B II
C#m IV
B II
A/C#
There's too much con - fu - sion,
na.
I can't get no re - lief.
mp

E5
F#
G#
E5
C#m IV
B II
A/C#
B II
C#m IV
9fr
11fr
Busi - ness men, they ah,
ah, drink my wine.
mf
mp
mf

B II
A/C#
B type2
C#m IV
Plow man, dig my earth, uh.
None will lev - el on
mp
mf
A/C#
A open
the line, uh,
no - bod - y of it is worth.
Hey, hey!
A II
C#
4fr
full
Guitar Solo
f w/ tape delay
full 1/2
hold bend
semi - harm.
1 1/2

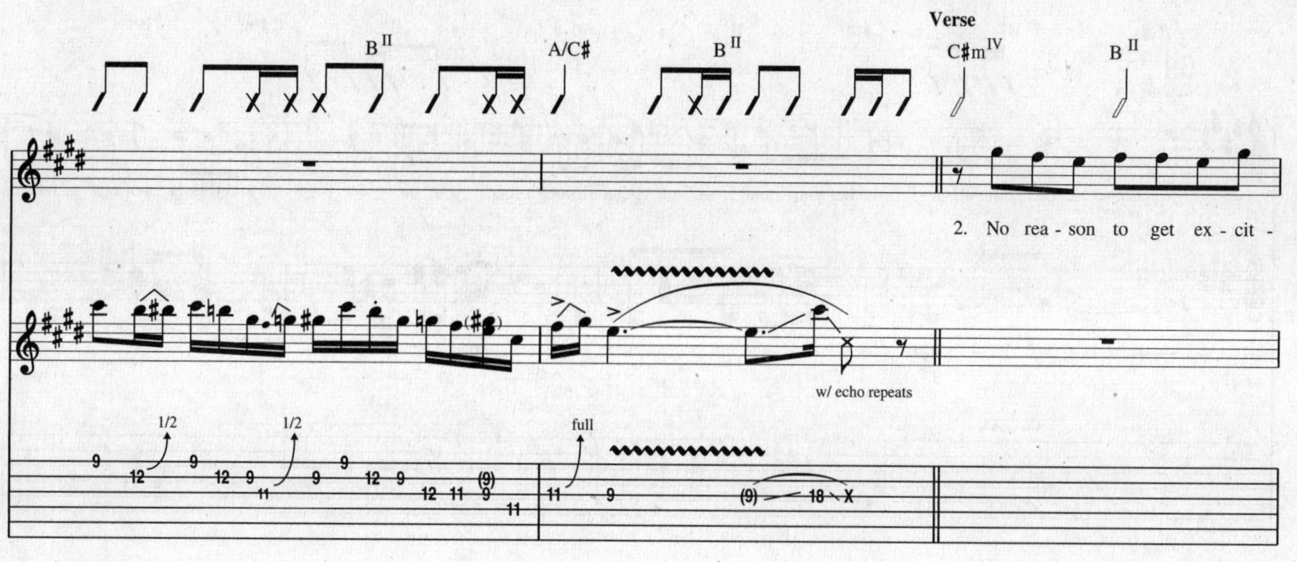
Verse
B II
A/C#
B II
C#m IV
B II
2. No rea - son to get ex - cit -
w/ echo repeats
1/2
1/2
full

A/C#
B II
C#m IV
B II
A/C#
B II
ed, uh, heh, the thief, he kind - ly spoke.
mf
mp
mf

C#m IV
B II
A/C#
B II
C#m IV
B II
There are man - y here a - mong us
who feel that life is but a joke.
mp
mf
mp

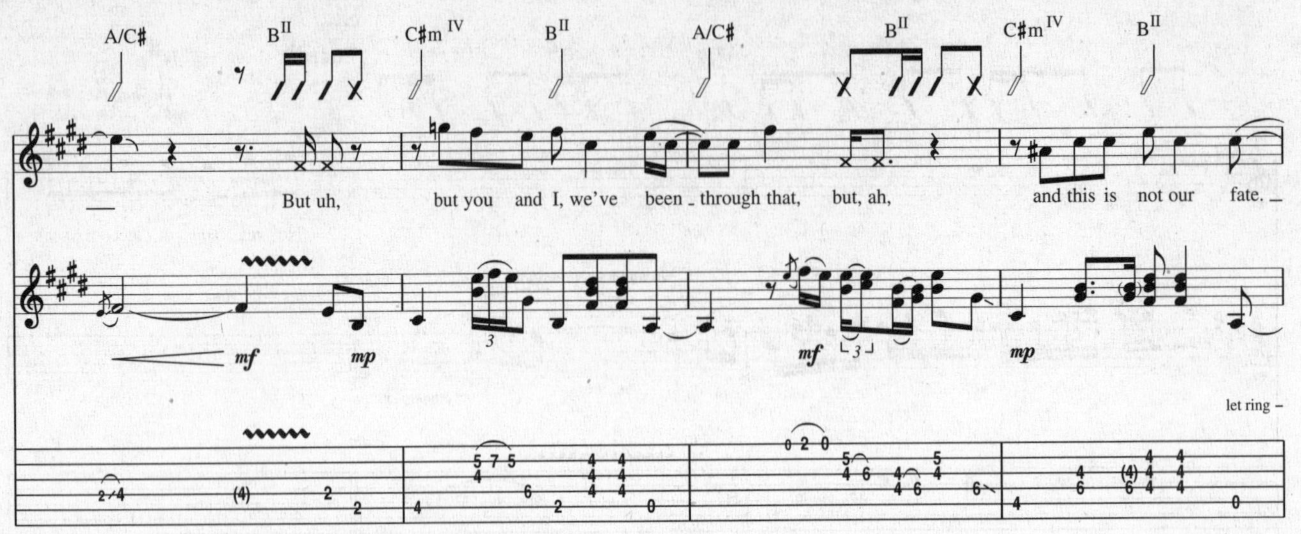

* Played ahead of the beat.

Guitar Solo

C♯m^IV
B^II
A/C♯
full
Interlude
Gtr. 2 tacet
Gtr. 3 (12-str. elec.)
mf w/ delay
w/ slide
steady gliss.
rake
Hey!
echo repeat

Guitar Solo
Gtr. 3 tacet
C♯m IV
B II
A/C♯
Gtr. 2
f * w/ wah-wah
echo repeat
full
* + = closed
○ = open
let ring
hold bend
wah-wah & echo off

B^II
A^II
A/C#
B^II

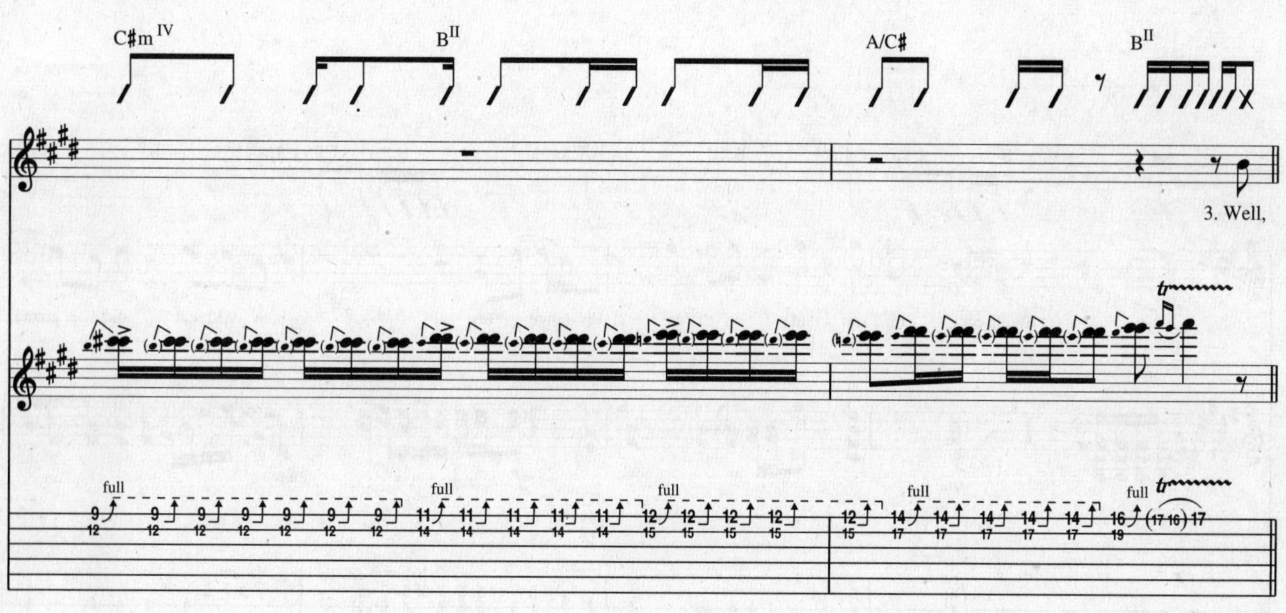

C#m^IV
B^II
A/C#
B^II
3. Well,
full
full
full
full
full

Verse

C#m^IV
B^II
A/C#
B^II
C#5
C#m^IV
B^II
A/C#
B^II
C#5
all a - long _ the watch - tow-er,
prin-ces kept the view. _
p
mp
mf
mp
mf

C♯m IV
B II
A/C♯
B II
C♯5
C♯m IV
B II
While all the wo-men came ___ and went,
bare feet ser-vants too. ___
mp
mf
mp

A/C♯
B II
C♯5
C♯m IV
B II
A/C♯
B II
C♯5
C♯m IV
B II
Well, ah, oh, out-side in the cold dis-tance, _ uh, a wild cat did _ growl._
static
mf
mp
*T
*T = Thumb on ⑥

A/C♯
B II
C♯5
C♯m IV
B II
A/C♯
B II
Two rid-ers were ap-proach-in' ___ and the
mf
mp
mf

Outro
C♯m IV
B II
C♯ A/C♯ C♯ A/C♯ C♯ A/C♯ B II
A/C♯
wind be - gan to howl.
Hey!
Ah.
mp
mf
f
full
C♯m7
C♯7
All a-long the watch-tow -
1 1/2
er
they say come

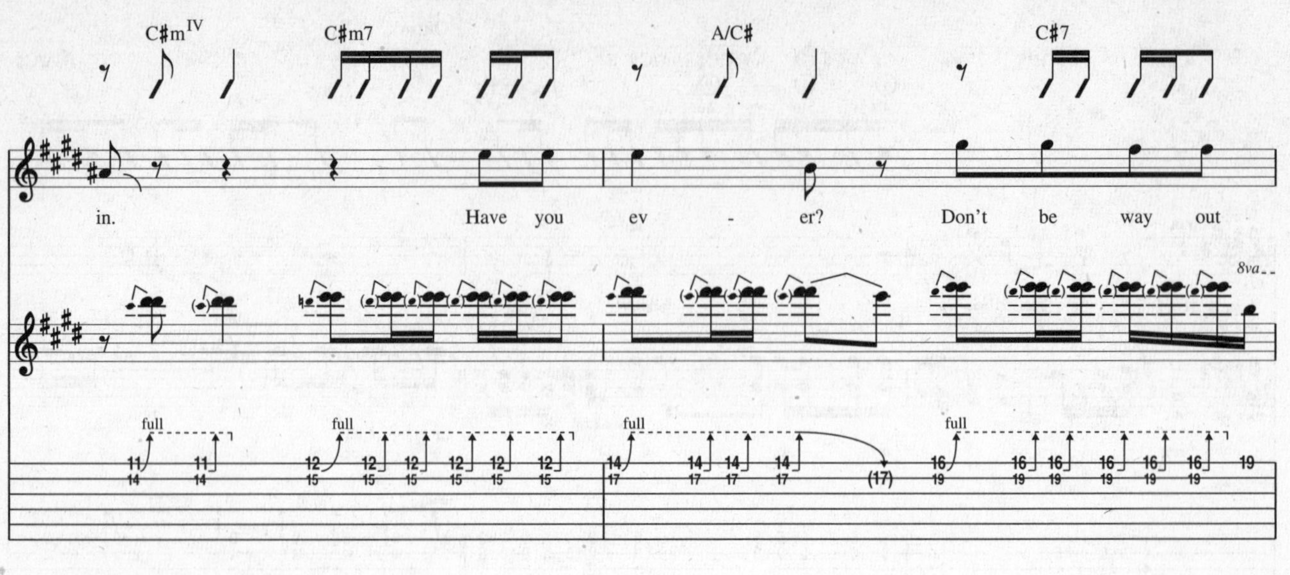

C#m^IV
C#m7
A/C#
C#7
in.
Have
you
ev
-
er?
Don't
be
way
out
8va
full
full
full
full

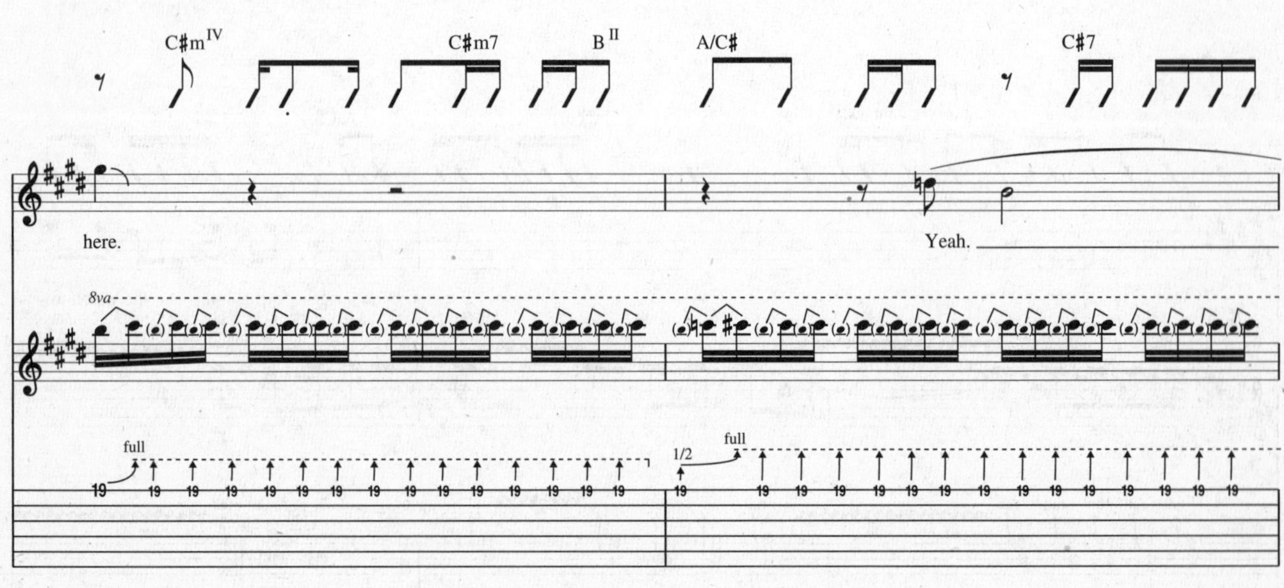

C#m^IV
C#m7
B^II
A/C#
C#7
here.
Yeah.
8va
full
1/2
full

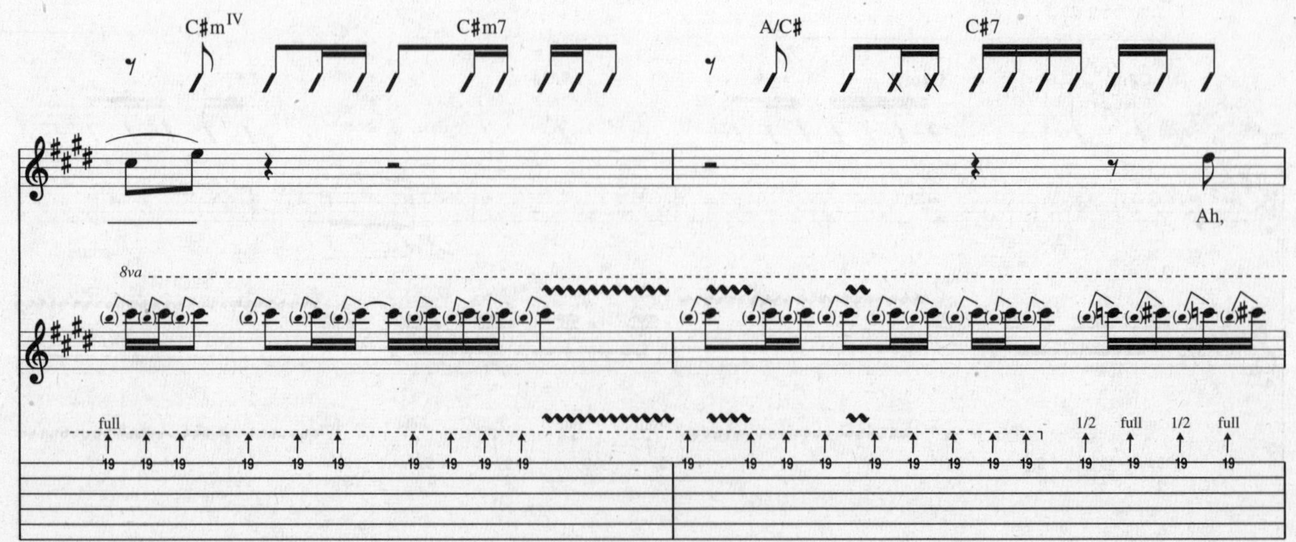

C#m^IV
C#m7
A/C#
C#7
Ah,
8va
full
1/2
full
1/2
full

C#m IV
C#7
A/C#
C#7
babe.
8va
full
3/4
1/2
19
C#m7 type2
C#m7
A/C#
C#7
Well, all a - long the watch-tow -
C#m7 type2
C#m7
A/C#
Fade Out
- er.
full 1/2

All for You

Words and Music by Ken Block, Jeff Beres, Andrew Copeland, Ryan Newell and Mark Trojanowski

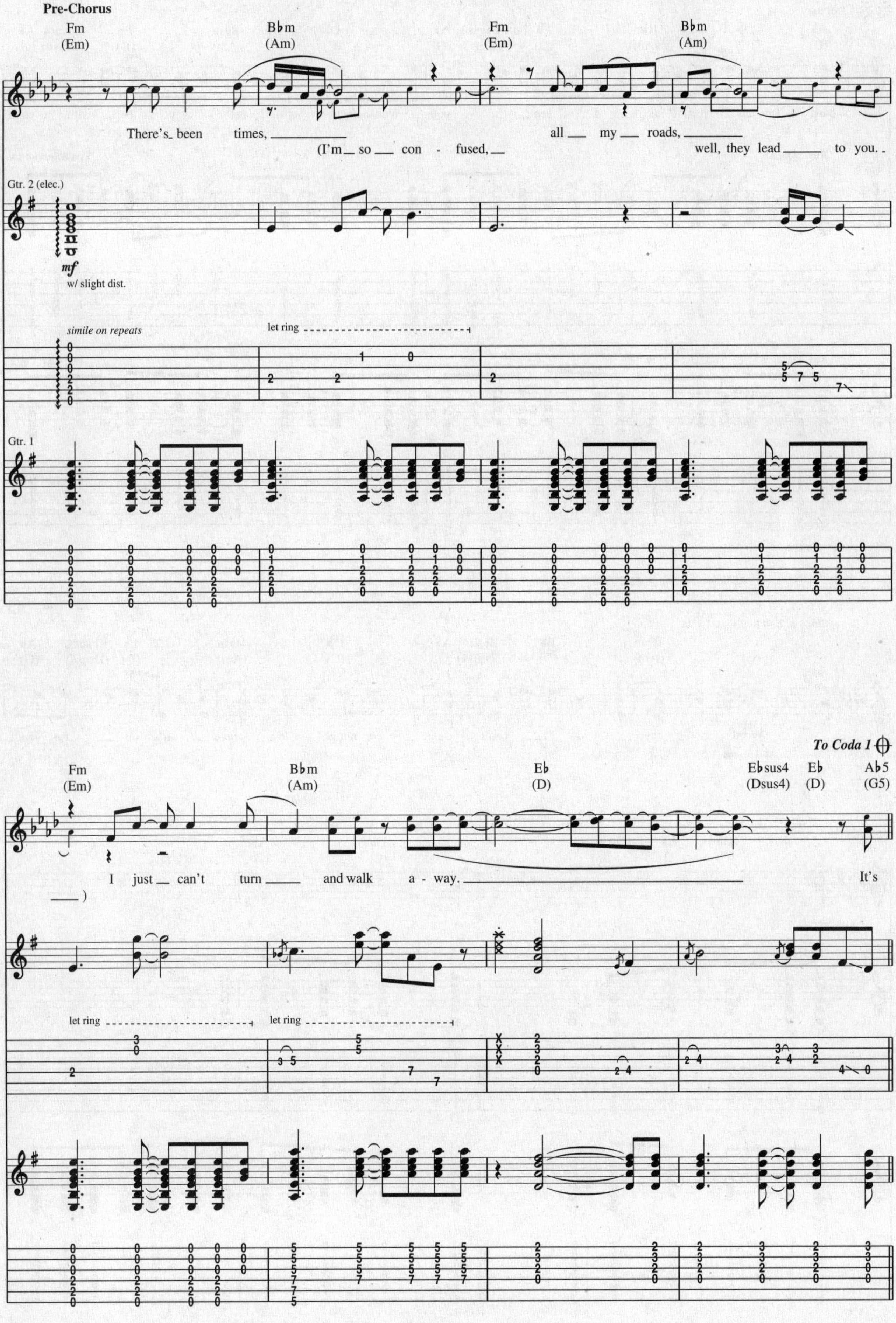

Pre-Chorus

Fm (Em) | B♭m (Am) | Fm (Em) | B♭m (Am)

There's been times, all my roads,
(I'm so con - fused, well, they lead to you.

Gtr. 2 (elec.)

mf

w/ slight dist.

simile on repeats

let ring

Gtr. 1

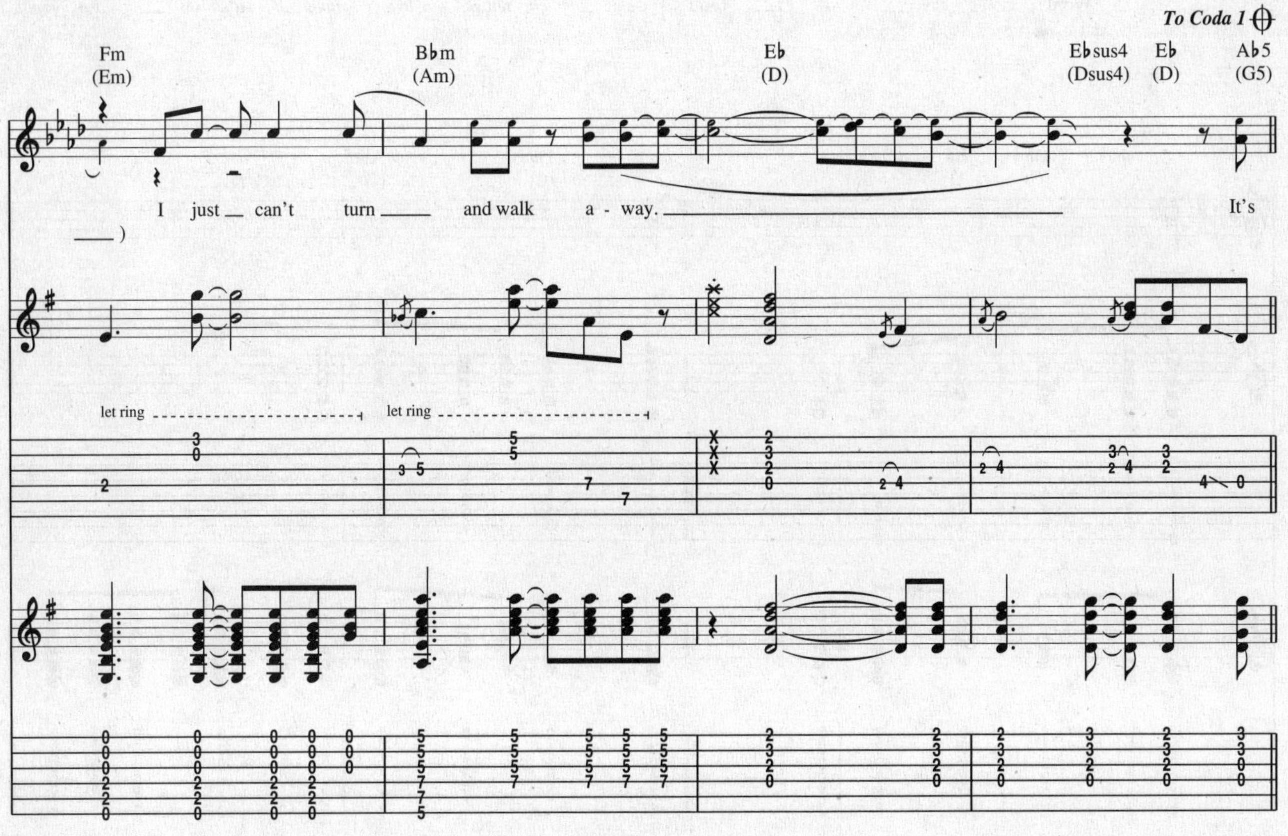

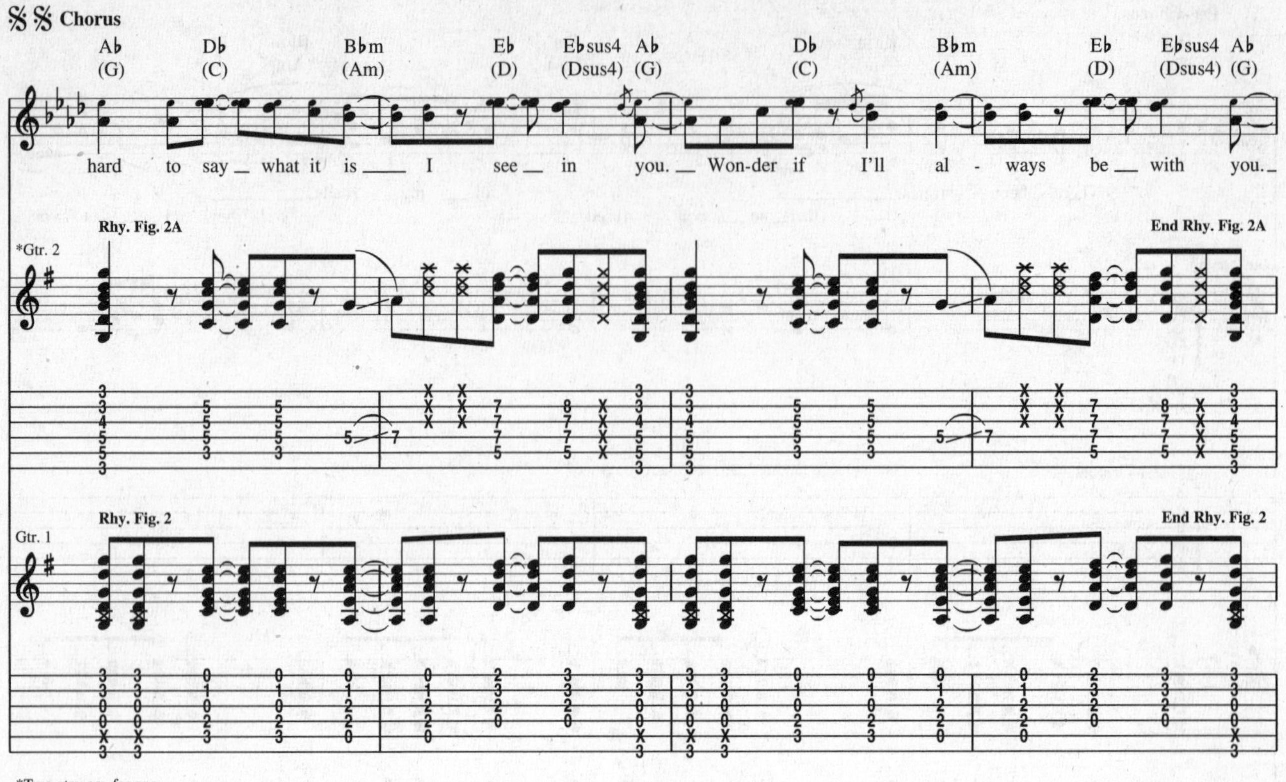

*Two gtrs. arr. for one.

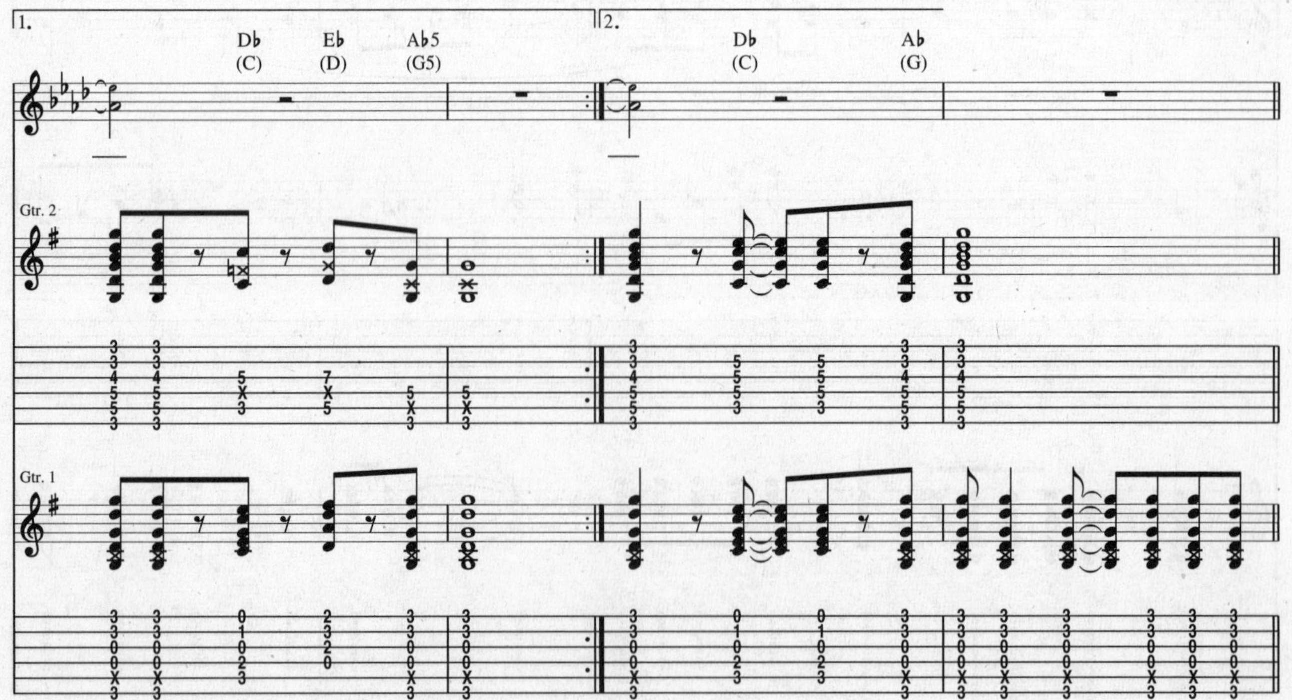

Bridge
Half-Time Feel
D♭add9
(Cadd9)
Fm
(Em)
Rain __ comes pour - ing down, __ fall - ing from __ blue skies. __
(Pour - ing down. __ Fall -
*Gtrs. 1 & 2
let ring throughout
*composite arrangement
- ing from __ blue skies. __)
Words __ with - out a sound __
End Half-Time Feel
E♭
(D)
com - in' from __ your eyes. __
Guitar Solo
Gtrs. 1 & 2: w/ Rhy. Figs. 2 & 2A, 3 1/2 times
A♭
(G)
D♭
(C)
B♭m
(Am)
E♭sus4
(Dsus4)
Gtr. 3
(elec.)
w/ dist.
P.M.

Db
(C)
Bbm
(Am)
Eb
(D)
Ebsus4
(Dsus4)
Ab
(G)
full
D.S. al Coda 1
Gtr. 1: w/ Rhy. Fill 1
Gtr. 2: w/ Rhy. Fill 2
1/2
Rhy. Fill 1
Gtr. 1
Rhy. Fill 2
Gtr. 2

Coda 2

Chorus

Coda 2

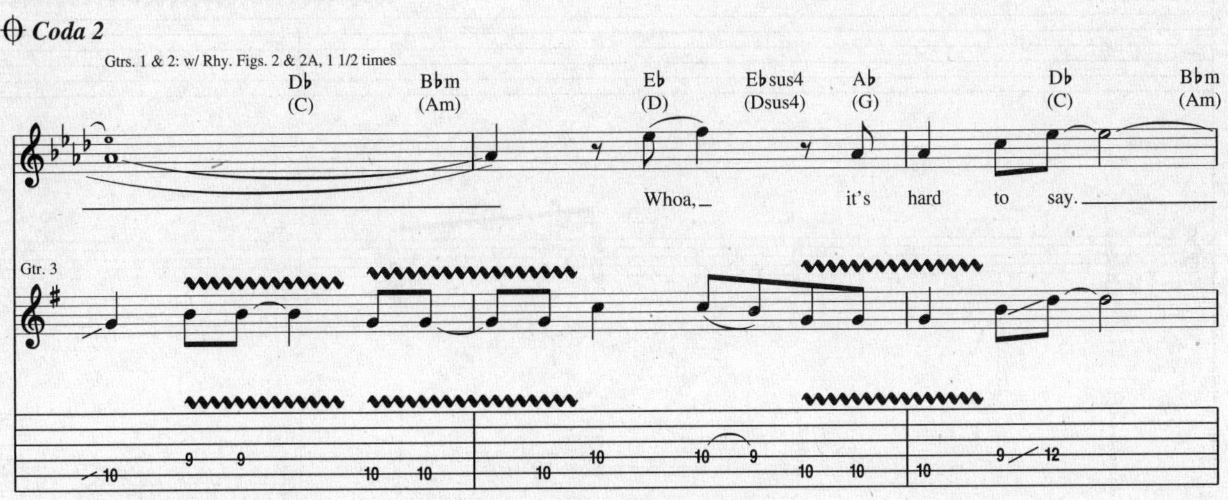

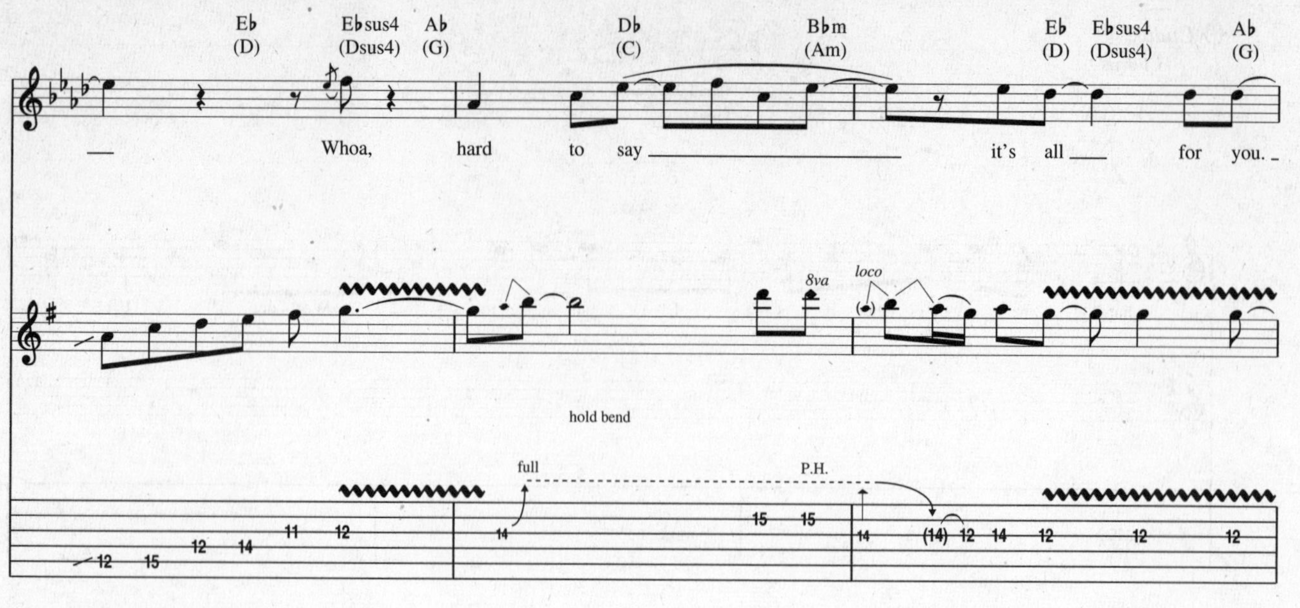

(G5) (C) (D) (G5)

Gtr. 1

Gtr. 3

full full

Gtr. 2

American Pie

Words and Music by Don McLean

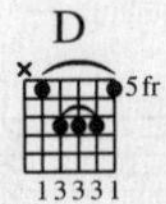

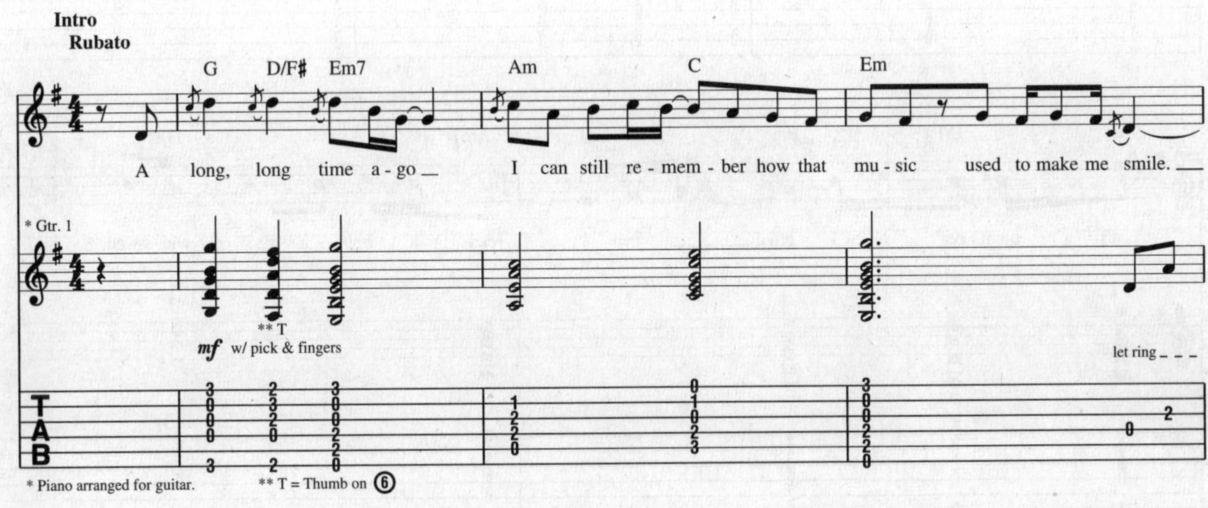

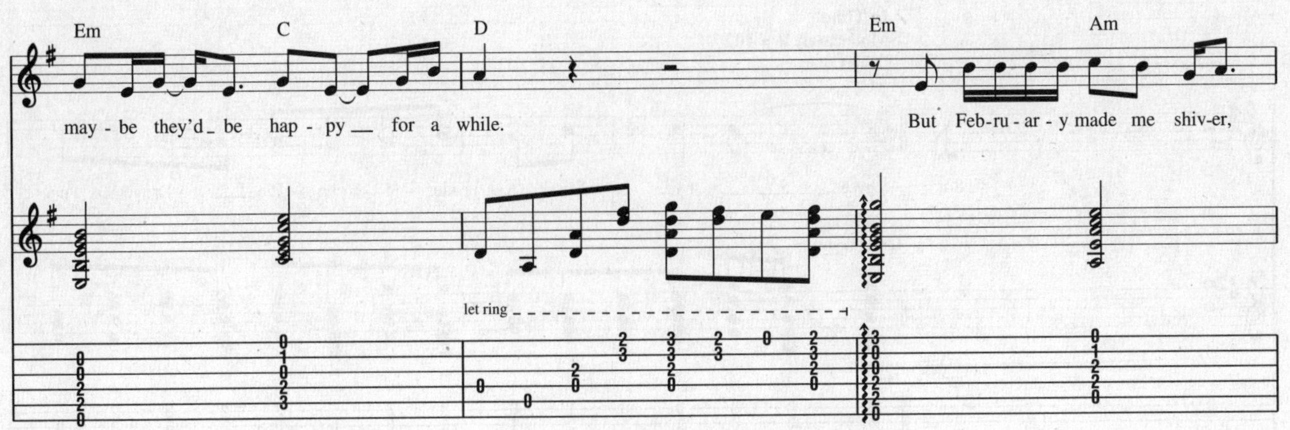

Em
Am
C
G/B
Am
C
D
with ev - 'ry pa - per I'd de - liv - er. Bad news on the door - step, I could - n't take one more step. I
G
D/F#
Em
Am7
D
can't re - mem - ber if I cried when I read a - bout his wid - owed bride.
G
D/F#
Em
C
D
G
Some - thing touched me deep in - side, the day the mu - sic died.
let ring
Chorus
In Time
Moderately ♩ = 102
Gtr. 1 tacet
G
C
G
D
So, bye, bye, Miss A - mer - i - can Pie. Drove my
Rhy. Fig. 1
Gtr. 2 (acous.)
mp w/ pick

G C G D G C
Chev - y to the lev - ee, but the lev - ee was dry. An' them good ol' boys were drink - in'
G D Em A7
whis - key an' rye, sing - in', "This - 'll be the day that I die,
Faster ♩ = 142
Em D7 D9 D7 D7sus4 D7 D9 D7
this - 'll be the day that I die."
End Rhy. Fig. 1
mf
let ring
Verse
G Am C
1. Did you write the book of love and do you have faith in
ten years we've been on our own, an' moss grows fat on
Rhy. Fig. 2

Am
Em
D7
D9
D7
God a - bove, if the Bi - ble tells you so?
a roll - ing stone. But, that's not how it used to be.
D7sus4 D7
D9
D7
G
D/F#
Em
Now, do you be - lieve in rock 'n' roll? Can
When the jest - er sang for the king an' queen in a
T
Am7
C
Em
mu - sic save your mor - tal soul? An' can you teach me
coat he bor - rowed from James Dean. An' a voice that came
A7
A9
A7
D7
D9
D7
D7sus4 D7
how to dance real slow? Well, I
from you and me. Oh, an'

Em
D
Em
know that you're in love with him, 'cause I saw you danc - in'
while the king was look - ing down, the jest - er stole his
D7
C
G
Am
Asus2
Am
in the gym. You both kicked off your shoes. Man, I
thorn - y crown. The court - room was ad - journed. No
C
D7
G
D/F#
dig those rhy - thm - ic blues. I was a lone - ly teen - age
ver - dict was re - turned. And while Len - in read a book
Em
Am
C
bronc - in' buck with a pink car - na - tion an' a pick - up truck. But
on Marx, a quar - tet prac - ticed in the park. And

G D/F# Em C
I knew I was out of luck, the day the mu-
we sang dir - ges in the dark, the day the mu-
D7 G C G D
- sic died. I start - ed sing - in', "Bye,
- sic died. We were sing - in', "Bye,
End Rhy. Fig. 2
Chorus
Gtr. 2: w/ Rhy. Fig. 1, simile
G C G D G C
bye, Miss A - mer - i - can Pie. Drove my Chev - y to the lev - ee, but the
G D G C G D
lev - ee was dry. Them good ol' boys were drink - in' whis - key an' rye, an' sing - in'
Em A7 Em
this - 'll be the day that I die, this - 'll be the day that I die."
1.
D7 D9 D7 D7sus4 D7 D9 D7
2. Now for
2.
D7 D9 D7 D7sus4 D7 D9 D7
die.
Verse
Gtr. 2: w/ Rhy. Fig. 2, simile
G Am
3. Hel - ter, skel - ter in the sum - mer swel - ter. The birds
Gtr. 3 (elec.)
mf w/ clean tone
w/ pick & fingers

C Am Em D7 D9 D7
flew off with a fall-out shel - ter, eight miles high an' fall-in' fast.
D7sus4 D7 D9 D7 G D/F# Em Am7
It land - ed foul out on the grass. The play-ers tried for a
C Em A7 A9 A7 D7 D9 D7
for-ward pass, with the jest - er on the side - lines in a cast.
D7sus4 D7 Em D Em
Now, the half - time air was sweet per-fume, while the ser - geants played a
mf

D7
C
G
Am
Asus2
Am
C
march - in' tune.
We all got up to dance, oh, but we nev - er got the chance.
full
full
mp
full
D7
G
D/F#
Em
'Cause the play - ers tried to take the field,
full
Am
C
G
D/F#
Em
the march - ing band re - fused to yield.
Do you re - call what was re - vealed the day
C
D7
G
C
G
D
the mu - sic died?
We start - ed sing - in', "Bye

Chorus
Gr. 2: w/ Rhy. Fig. 1, simile
G C G D G C G D
bye, Miss A - mer - i - can Pie. Drove my Chev - y to the lev - ee, but the lev - ee was dry. Them
let ring
G C G D Em A7
good ol' boys were drink - in' whis - key an' rye, an' sing - in' this - 'll be the day that I die,
let ring
Em D7 D9 D7 D7sus4 D7 D9 D7
this - 'll be the day that I die."
4. Oh, an' there we were all
Verse
Gtr. 2: w/ Rhy. Fig. 2, simile
G
Am C Am Em
in one place, a gen - er - a - tion lost in space, with no time left to start

D7 D9 D7 D7sus4 D7 D9 D7 G D/F# Em
a - gain. So, come on, Jack be nim-ble, Jack be quick.
let ring
hold bend
full
full
full
Am7 C Em A7 A9 A7
Jack Flash sat on a can- dle stick, 'cause fire is the dev-il's on - ly friend.
D7 D9 D7 D7sus4 D7 Em D
Oh, and as I watched him on the stage my
Em D7 C G Am Asus2 Am
hands were clenched in fists of rage. No an - gel born in Hell could
let ring

C
D7
G
D/F#
Em
break that Sa-tan's spell. And as the flames climbed high in - to the night to
Am
C
G
D/F#
Em
light the sac - ri - fi-cial rite, I saw Sa - tan laugh-ing with de-light, the day
C
D7
G
C
G
D
the mu - sic died. He was sing-in', "Bye,
let ring
Chorus
Gtr. 2: w/ Rhy. Fig. 1, 1st 9 meas., simile
G
C
G
D
G
C
G
D
bye, Miss A - mer - i - can Pie. Drove my Chev-y to the lev-ee, but the lev-ee was dry. Them
mf
let ring throughout

G C G D Em A7
good ol' boys were drink-in' whis-key an' rye, an' sing-in' this-'ll be the day that I die,
mf
Em D
Gtr. 3
this-'ll be the day that I die."
Gtr. 1
mf
let ring
(cont. in slash)
Verse
Rubato (Half-Time Feel)
Gtr. 3 tacet
G D/F# Em Am C Em
5. I met a girl who sang the blues and I asked her for some hap-py news. But she just smiled and turned a-
Gtr. 1
D G D/F# Em G/B Am G/B C
way. I went down to the sa-cred store where I'd heard the mu-sic years be-fore. But the

Em C D Em7 A7sus4
man there said the mu-sic would-n't play. And in the streets the chil-dren screamed, the
let ring
Em Am C G/B Am Bm7 C D
lov-er's cried an' the po-ets dreamed. But not a word was spo-ken, the church bells all were bro-ken. An' the
let ring
let ring
G D/F# Em G/B C D D7 G D/F# Em
three men I ad-mire most, the Fa-ther, Son and the Ho-ly Ghost, they caught the last train for the coast, the
T
C D G
day the mu - sic died. An' they were sing - in', "Bye,

Chorus
In Time ♩ = 90
Gtr. 2: w/ Rhy. Fig. 1, 1st 7 meas., simile
Gtr. 1 tacet
G C G D G C G D
bye, Miss A - mer - i - can Pie. Drove my Chev - y to the lev - ee, but the lev - ee was dry. An' them
G C G D Em
good ol' boys were drink - in' whis - key an' rye, sing - in' this - 'll be the day that I

A7 A9 Em D7 D9 D7 D7sus4 D7 D9 D7 D9
die, this - 'll be the day that I die." They were sing - in',
Gtr. 2

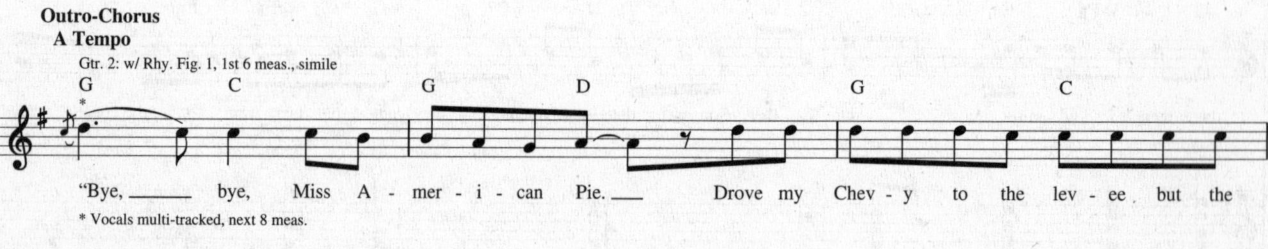
Outro-Chorus
A Tempo
Gtr. 2: w/ Rhy. Fig. 1, 1st 6 meas., simile
G C G D G C
"Bye, bye, Miss A - mer - i - can Pie. Drove my Chev - y to the lev - ee but the
* Vocals multi-tracked, next 8 meas.

G D G C G D
lev - ee was dry. Them good ol' boys were drink - in' whis - key an' rye, sing - in',

C D G C G
this - 'll be the day that I die."
Gtr. 2

Aqualung

Music by Ian Anderson
Lyrics by Jennie Anderson

Gtr. 1: w/ Riff A (3 times)
Gtr. 2: w/ Rhy. Fig. 1
Rhy. Fill 1
End Rhy. Fill 1
Gtr. 2
Snot's run - ning down his nose, greas - y fin - gers smear - ing shab - by clothes
*Symbols in parentheses represent chord names respective to capoed guitar. Symbols above reflect actual sounding chords.
Gtr. 2: w/ Rhy. Fill 1
Hey, Aq - ua - lung. Dry - ing in the cold sun,
Gtr. 2: w/ Rhy. Fig. 1
watch - ing as the fril - ly pant - ies run.
Riff A1
Gtr. 3 (elec.)
w/ dist.
Hey, Aq - ua - lung.
End Riff A1
Gtr. 2: w/ Rhy. Fill 1
Gtr. 3 tacet
Gtr. 2: w/ Rhy. Fig. 1 (1st 5 meas.)
Gtr. 3: w/ Riff A1
Feel - ing like a dead duck, spit - ting out pie - ces of his

F (D)
Eb (C) F (D)
Eb (C) F (D) Gb (Eb) Db (Bb)
Eb (C)
Db (Bb) Gb (Eb)
bro - ken luck.
Oh, Hey,
Aq - ua - lung.
To Coda
Bridge
E (Db) B (Ab)
D (B)
Gm (Em)
Fsus2/4 (Dsus2/4) F (D)
Sun streak - ing cold, an
Gtr. 2
Rhy. Fig. 2
*Capoed fret is "0" in tab.
**w/ tone filter, next 43 1/2 meas.
Fsus4 (Dsus4) F (D) Fsus2/4 (Dsus2/4) C (A)
C7sus2/4 (A7sus2/4) C (A)
C7sus2/4 (A7sus2/4) Cm (Am)
Csus2 (Asus2) Cm (Am) C7sus2/4 (A7sus2/4)
old man wand' - ring lone - ly.
Tak - ing time the
Gm (Em)
Gm7 (Em7) Gm (Em)
Fsus4 (Dsus4) F (D) Gm7 (Em7)
on - ly way he knows.
End Rhy. Fig. 2

Gtr. 2: w/ Rhy. Fig. 2
Gm (Em) Fsus2/4 (Dsus2/4) F (D) Fsus2/4 F (Dsus2/4) (D) Fsus2/4 F (Dsus2/4) (D) Fsus4 F Fsus2/4 C (Dsus4) (D) (Dsus2/4) (A) C7sus2/4 C (A7sus2/4) (A) C7sus2/4 (A7sus2/4)
Leg hurt - ing bad, as he bends to pick a dog - end. He
*Sung behind the beat.
Cm (Am) Csus2 Cm C7sus2/4 Gm (Asus2) (Am) (A7sus2/4) (Em) Gm7 Gm (Em7) (Em) F (D) Fsus2/4 F (Dsus2/4) (D) Fsus2/4 F (Dsus2/4) (D) Fsus4 F Gm7 (Dsus4) (D) (Em7)
goes down to the bog and warms his feet.
Fsus2/4 F (Dsus2/4) (D) Fsus2/4 F (Dsus2/4) (D) Fsus2/4 F (Dsus2/4) (D) Gm7 (Em7)
Gtr. 2
Gtr. 2: w/ Rhy. Fig. 2 (2 times)
Gm (Em) Fsus2/4 (Dsus2/4) F (D) Fsus2/4 F (Dsus2/4) (D) Fsus2/4 F (Dsus2/4) (D) Fsus4 F Fsus2/4 (Dsus4) (D) (Dsus2/4)
Feel - ing a - lone, the ar - my's up the road.
C (A) C7sus2/4 C (A7sus2/4) (A) C7sus2/4 Cm (A7sus2/4) (Am) Csus2 Cm C7sus2/4 Gm (Asus2) (Am) (A7sus2/4) (Em) Gm7 Gm (Em7) (Em)
Sal - va - tion a la mode and a cup of
F (D) Fsus2/4 F (Dsus2/4) (D) Fsus2/4 F (Dsus2/4) (D) Fsus4 F Gm7 Gm (Dsus4) (D) (Em7) (Em) Fsus2/4 (Dsus2/4)
tea. Aq - ua - lung, my
F (D) Fsus2/4 F (Dsus2/4) (D) Fsus2/4 F (Dsus2/4) (D) Fsus4 F Fsus2/4 C (Dsus4) (D) (Dsus2/4) (A) C7sus2/4 C (A7sus2/4) (A) C7sus2/4 (A7sus2/4)
friend, don't you start a - way un - eas - y. You

Cm (Am) Csus2 (Asus2) Cm (Am) C7sus4 (A7sus4) Gm (Em) Gm7 (Em7) Gm (Em) F (D) Fsus2/4 (Dsus2/4) F (D) Fsus2/4 (Dsus2/4) F (D) Fsus4 (Dsus4) F (D) Gm7 (Em7)
poor old sod, you see it's on - ly me.
Fsus2/4 (Dsus2/4) F (D) Fsus2/4 (Dsus2/4) F (D) Gm7 (Em7)
Gtr. 2
Fast ♩ = 176
Gm (Em) F (D) Fsus2/4 (Dsus2/4) F (D) Gm (Em) Gm11 (Em11)
Do you still re - mem - ber De - cem - ber's fog - gy freeze, when the
Rhy. Fig. 3
End Rhy. Fig. 3
Gtr. 2: w/ Rhy. Fig. 3
Gm (Em) F (D) Fsus2/4 (Dsus2/4) F (D) Gm (Em) Gm11 (Em11)
ice that clings on to your beard was scream - ing ag - o - ny? Hey! Then you
*w/ out tone filter
Gm (Em) F (D) Fsus2/4 (Dsus2/4) F (D) Gm (Em)
snatch your rat - tl - ing last breaths with deep sea div - er sounds and the
Gtr. 2

Cm
(Am)
F
(D)
Fsus2/4
(Dsus2/4)
flow - ers bloom _ like ___ mad - ness in ___ the ___ spring.
F
(D)
Fsus4 F Fsus2/4
(Dsus4) (D) (Dsus2/4)
Gm7 Gm
(Em7) (Em)
Sun ___ streak - ing
Rhy. Fig. 4
C
(A)
C7sus2/4
(A7sus2/4)
cold, _ an old man wand' - ring lone - ly, tak - ing time _ the
Gm
(Em)
on - ly way ___ he ___ knows.
End Rhy. Fig. 4
62

Gtr. 2: w/ Rhy. Fig. 4
Gm (Em) F (D) Fsus2/4 (Dsus2/4) F (D) C (A) C7sus2/4 (A7sus2/4)
Leg hurt - ing bad, as he bends to pick a dog - end. He
Cm (Am) Gm (Em) F (D) Fsus2/4 (Dsus2/4) F (D) Fsus4 (Dsus4) F (D) Fsus2/4 (Dsus2/4)
goes down to the bog and warms his feet.
F (D) Fsus4 (Dsus4) F (D) Fsus2/4 (Dsus2/4) Gm (Em)
Whoa, ho, ho, no. Feel - ing a - lone,
Gtr. 2
Rhy. Fig. 5
F (D) Fsus2/4 (Dsus2/4) F (D) C (A) C7sus2 (A7sus2)
the ar - my's up the road. Sal -
End Rhy. Fig. 5
Gtr. 2: w/ Rhy. Fig. 4 (last 4 meas.)
Cm (Am) Gm (Em) F (D) Fsus2/4 (Dsus2/4)
va - tion a la mode and a cup of tea.
Gtr. 2: w/ Rhy. Fig. 5
F (D) Fsus4 (Dsus4) F (D) Fsus2/4 (Dsus2/4) Gm (Em) F (D) Fsus2/4 (Dsus2/4)
Aq - ua - lung, my friend, don't you
Gtr. 2: w/ Rhy. Fig. 4 (last 4 meas.)
F (D) C (A) C7sus2 (A7sus2) Cm (Am)
start a - way un - eas - y. You poor old sod, you

Gm
(Em)
F
(D)
Fsus$^2_4$
(Dsus$^2_4$)
F
(D)
Fsus4 F Fsus$^2_4$
(Dsus4) (D) (Dsus$^2_4$)
see it's on - ly me,
me.
(D^{open})
Gtr. 2
Oh, ho, ho, ho, oh,
Gtr. 1
Interlude
(Em)
(D^{open})
no.
(A)
*Gtrs. 1 & 3
*Composite arrangement
(Am)
(Em)
fdbk.
let ring
fdbk.

Gtr. 3 tacet
(D open)
Gtr. 1
let ring
Guitar Solo
(Em)
(C open)
(D open)
(Em)
Rhy. Fig. 6
End Rhy. Fig. 6
Gtr. 2: w/ Rhy. Fig. 6 (2 times)
Gm
(Em)
E♭
(C)
F
(D)
Gm
(Em)
fdbk.
Pitch: G
E♭
(C)
F
(D)
Gm
(Em)
let ring
(Em)
(C open)
(D open)
(Dsus4) (D open) (Dsus4) (D open)(Dsus2/4)
Gtr. 2
Gtr. 1
let ring
let ring
let ring

Gtr. 2: w/ Rhy. Fig. 6 (3 1/2 times)
(D open)
(Dsus4)
(D open)
Gm
(Em)
E♭
(C)
let ring
F
(D)
Gm
(Em)
E♭
(C)
let ring
F
(D)
Gm
(Em)
E♭
(C)
F
(D)
Gm
(Em)
E♭
(C)
let ring
(D open)
(Dsus4) (D open) (Dsus4) (D open)
Gtr. 2
Gtr. 1
let ring
let ring

Bridge
A tempo
Gtr. 1 tacet
Gtr. 2: w/ Rhy. Fig. 2 (1 1/2 times)
Dee, dee, dee, dee, dee, dee, dee, dee, dee, dee.
Dee, dee, dee, dee, dee, dee, dee, dee, dee, dee.
Aq - ua - lung, my
friend, don't you start a - way un - eas - y. You
poor old sod, you see it's on - ly me, yeah.
Gtr. 2
Hmm.

D.S. al Coda

Interlude
Gtr. 2 tacet
Gm
N.C.
Gm
N.C.
Gtr. 1
5 3 6 3 4 3
5 3 6 3 4 3

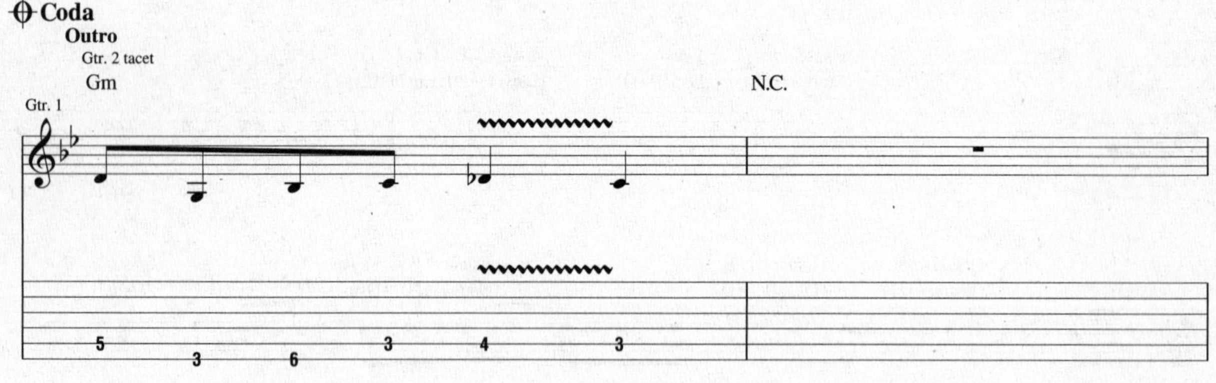
Coda
Outro
Gtr. 2 tacet
Gm
N.C.
Gtr. 1
5 3 6 3 4 3

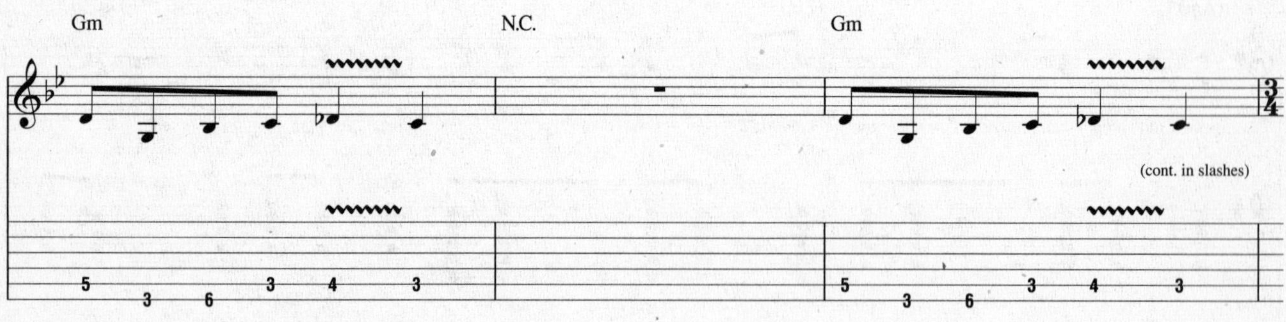
Gm
N.C.
Gm
(cont. in slashes)
5 3 6 3 4 3
5 3 6 3 4 3

Free time
D♭5
E♭5
F5
Gtr. 1
Whoa, oh, oh, Aq - ua - lung.
Gtr. 3
8
10
12

Are You Gonna Be My Girl

Words and Music by Nic Cester and Cameron Muncey

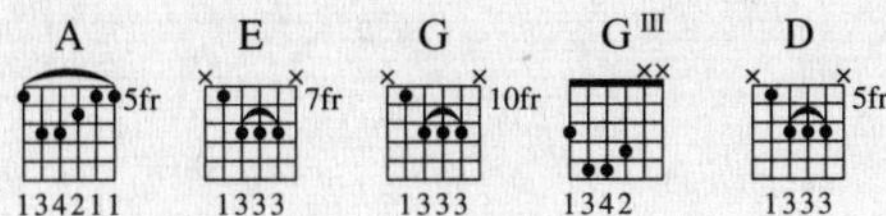

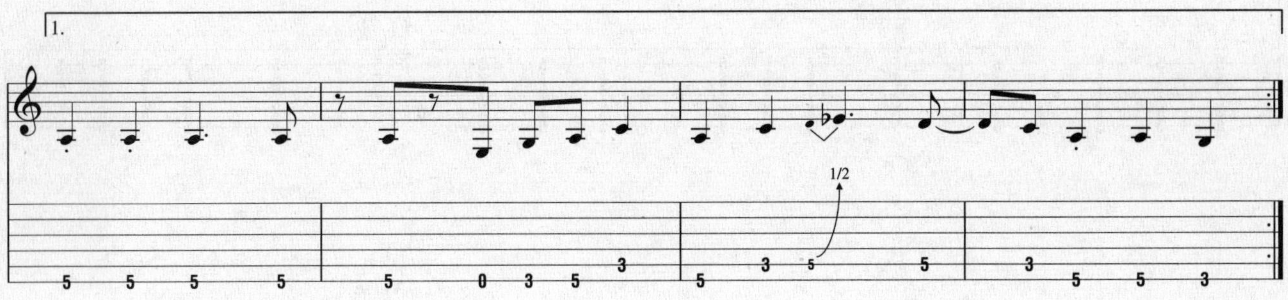

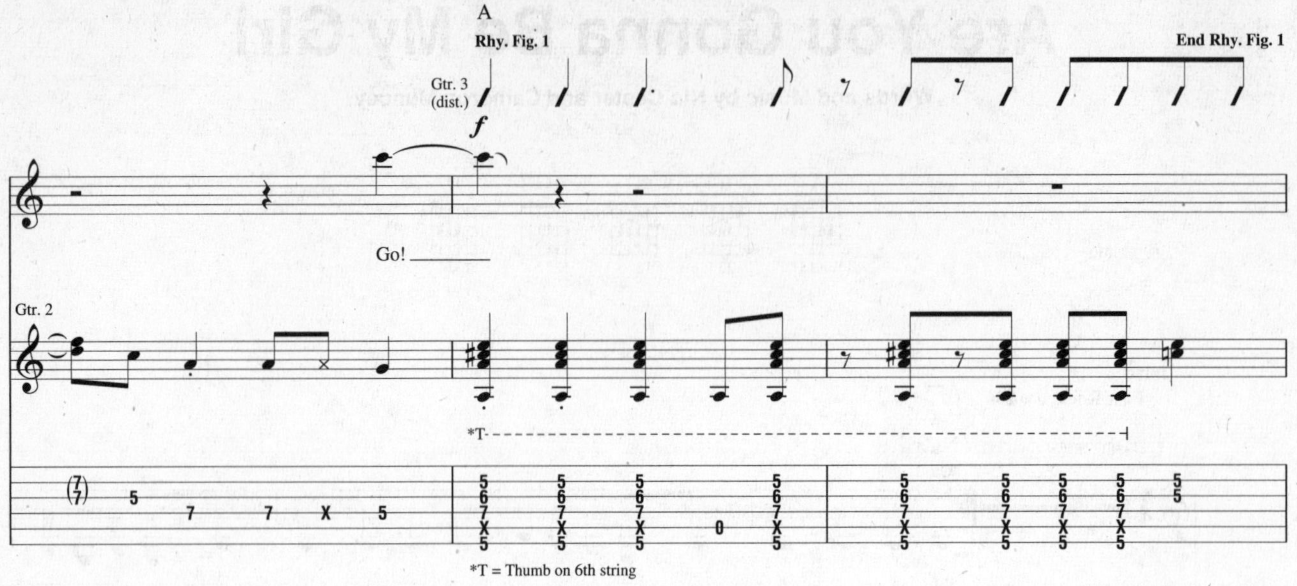
A
Rhy. Fig. 1
End Rhy. Fig. 1
Gtr. 3
(dist.)
f
Go!
Gtr. 2
*T
*T = Thumb on 6th string

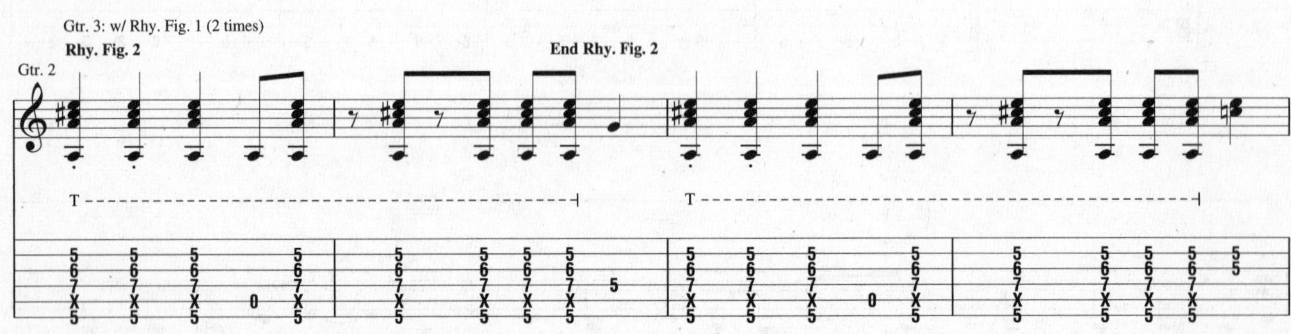
Gtr. 3: w/ Rhy. Fig. 1 (2 times)
Rhy. Fig. 2
End Rhy. Fig. 2
Gtr. 2
T
T

N.C.
Verse
A
N.C.
1. So, one, two, three, take my
Riff A
End Riff A
Gtr. 3
1/2
Gtr. 2
1/2

Gtrs. 2 & 3 tacet
hand and come with me be - cause you look so fine and I real - ly want to make you mine.

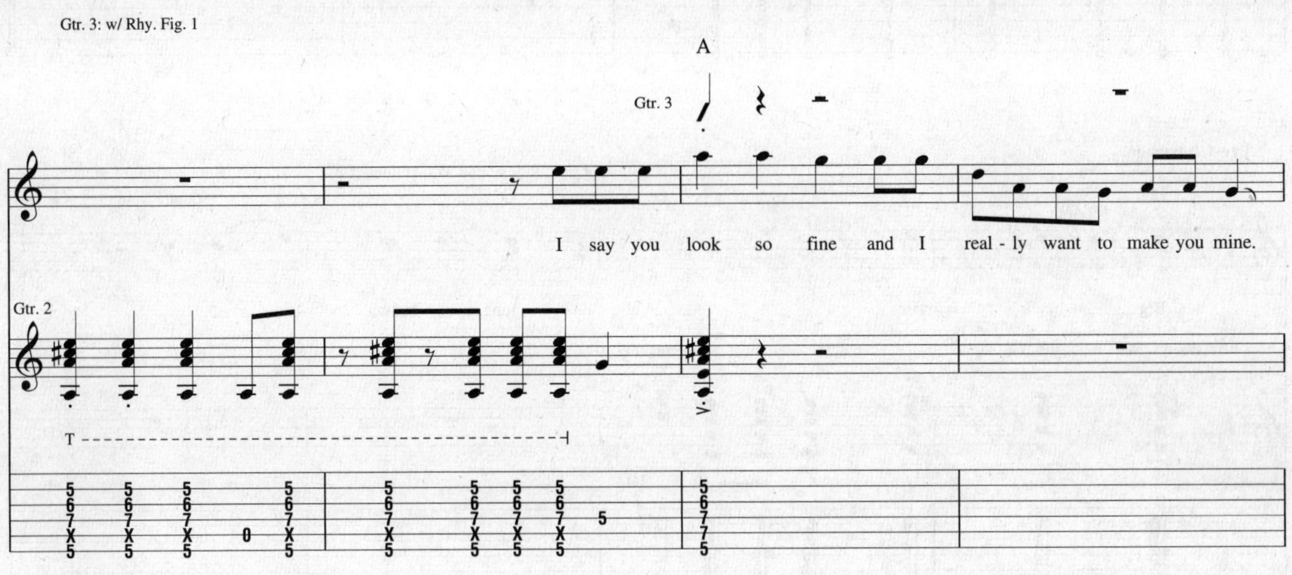
Gtr. 3: w/ Rhy. Fig. 1
A
Gtr. 3
I say you look so fine and I real - ly want to make you mine.
Gtr. 2
T

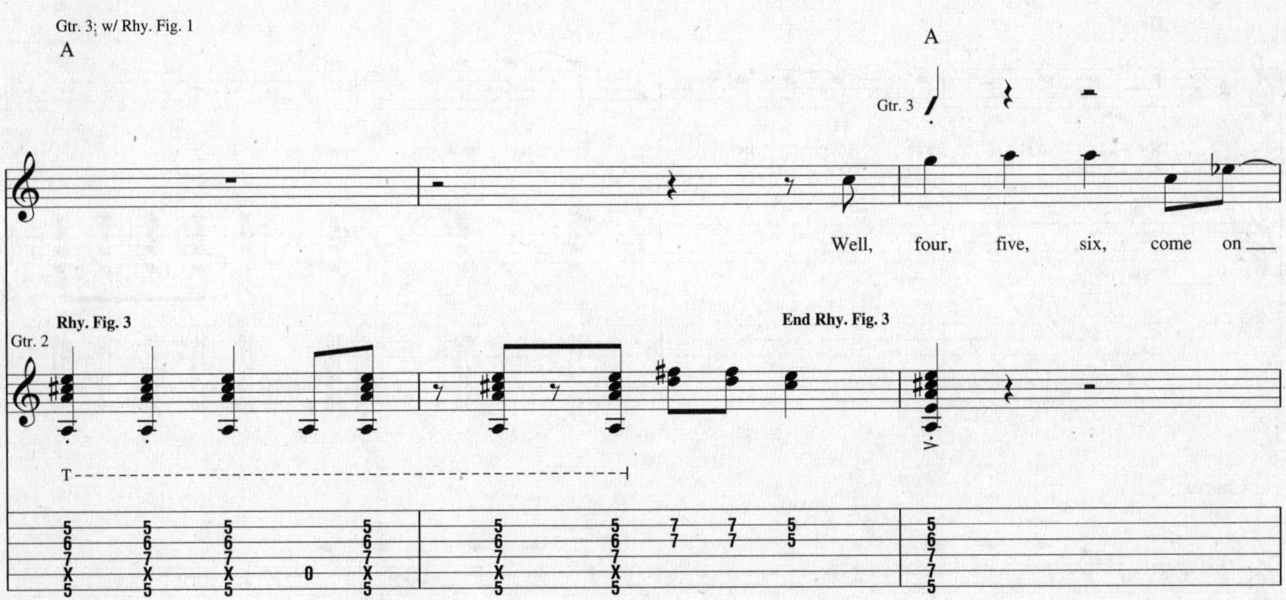
Gtr. 3: w/ Rhy. Fig. 1
A
A
Gtr. 3
Well, four, five, six, come on
Rhy. Fig. 3
End Rhy. Fig. 3
Gtr. 2
T

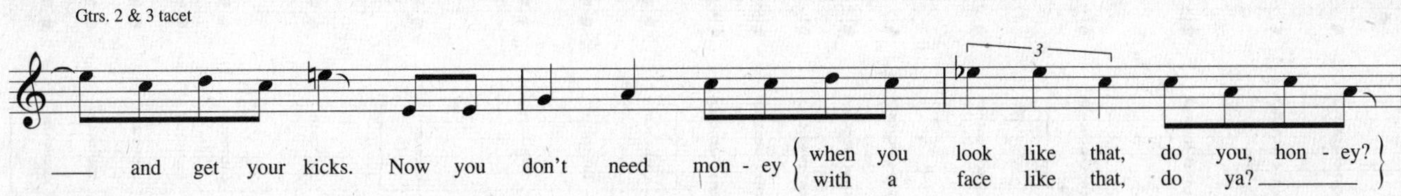
Gtrs. 2 & 3 tacet
and get your kicks. Now you don't need mon - ey when you look like that, do you, hon - ey?
with a face like that, do ya?

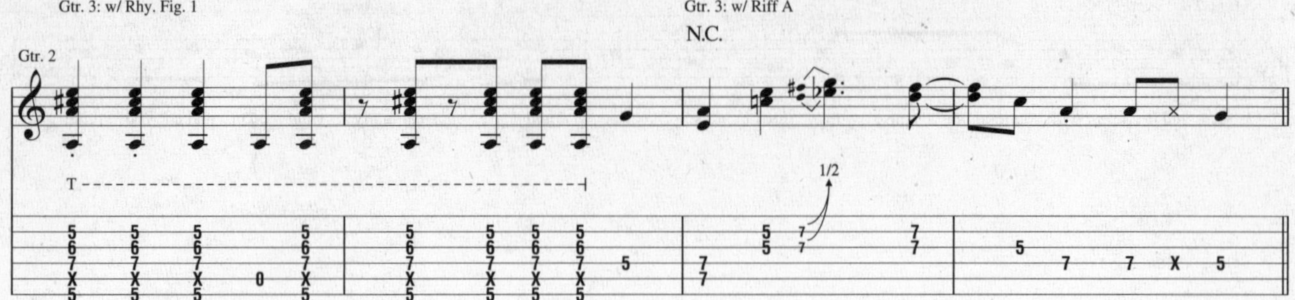

Pre-Chorus

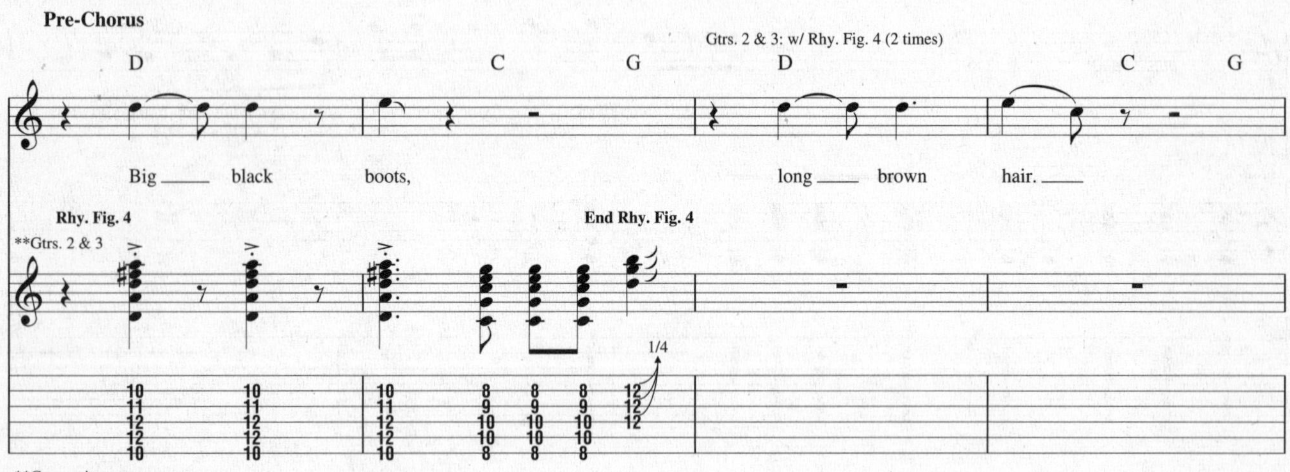

**Composite arrangement

Chorus

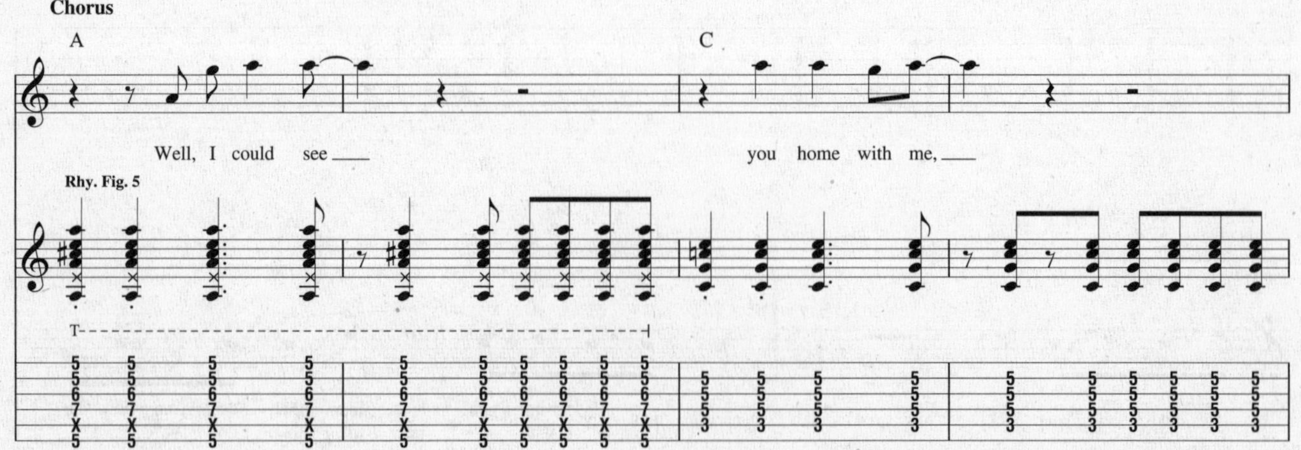

D
A
but you were with an - oth - er man, yeah.
End Rhy. Fig. 5
Gtrs. 2 & 3: w/ Rhy. Fig. 5
C
I know we ain't got much to say
D
A
be - fore I let you get a - way, yeah.
E
Gtr. 3
Gtr. 2
1.
G
I said, "Are you gon - na be my girl?"

Gtr. 3: w/ Rhy. Fig. 1 (3 times)
A

Gtr. 3: w/ Riff A
N.C.
2. Well, it's a -
1/2

2.
G
I said, "Are you gon - na be my girl?"

Gtr. 2: w/ Rhy. Fig. 2 (4 times)
Gtr. 3 tacet
A5

Ah,
Gtr. 3

Guitar Solo

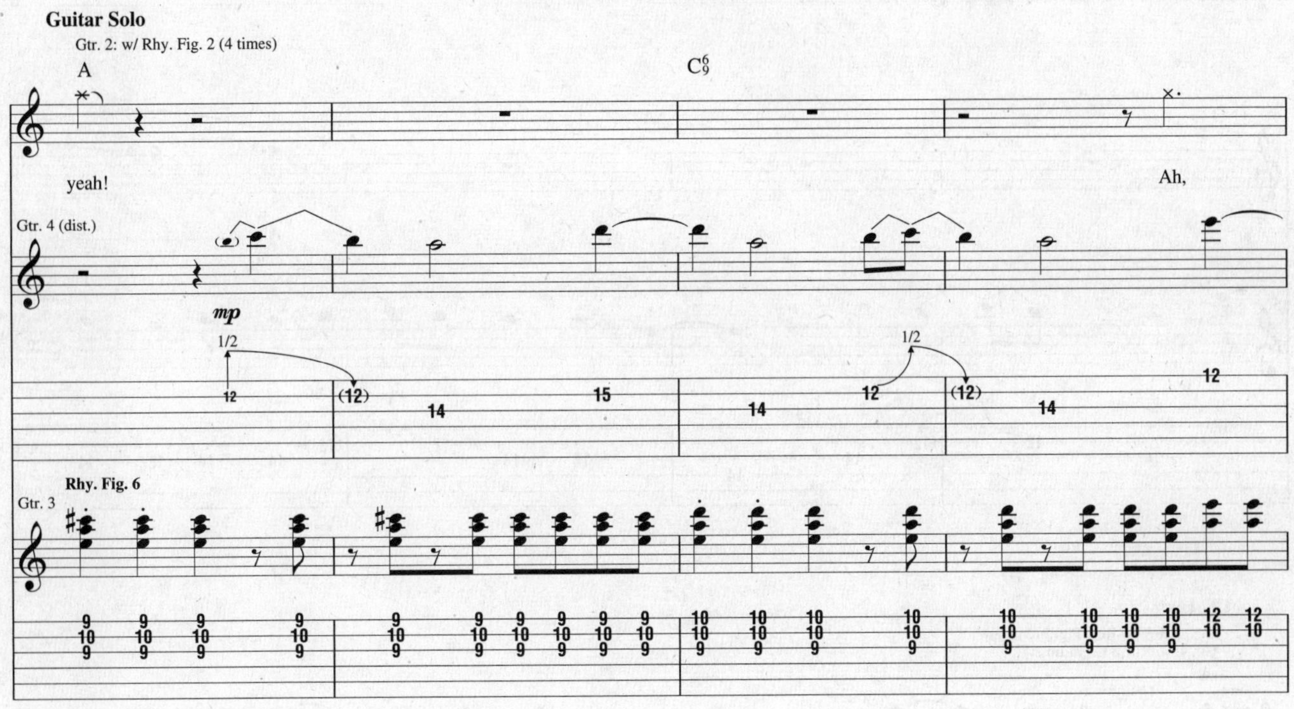
Gtr. 2: w/ Rhy. Fig. 2 (4 times)
A
yeah!
Ah,
Gtr. 4 (dist.)
mp
Rhy. Fig. 6
Gtr. 3

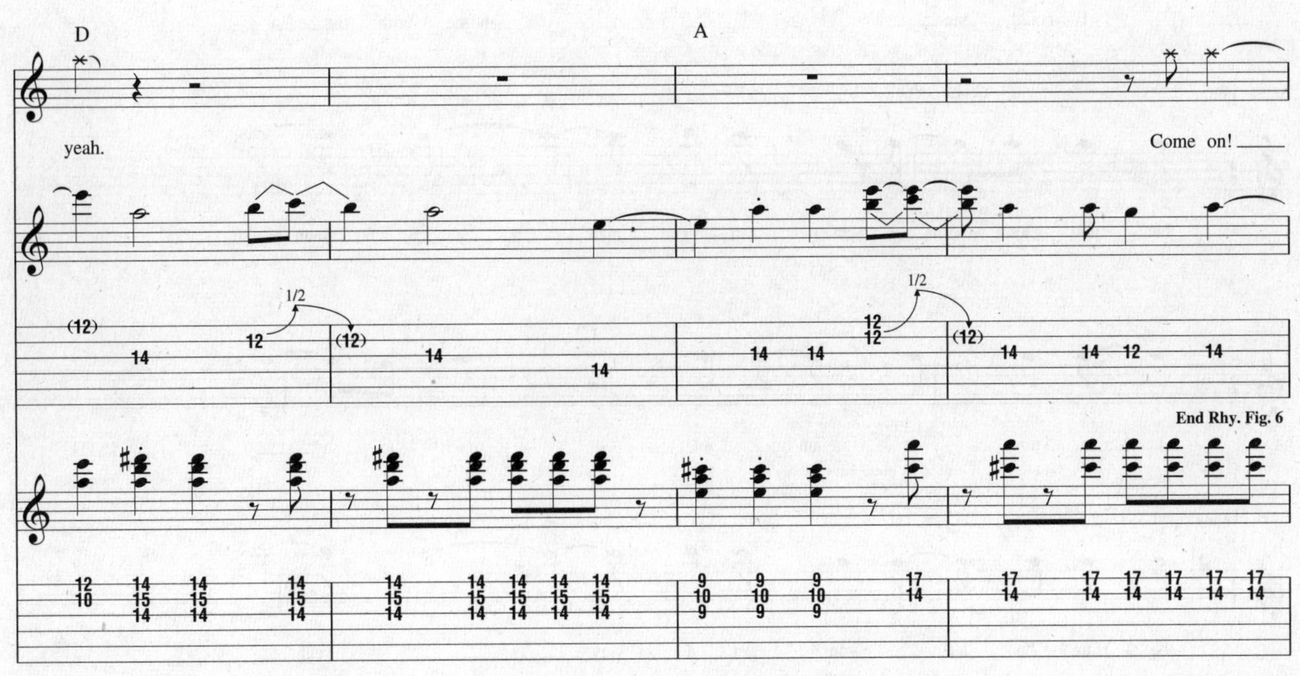
D
A
yeah.
Come on!
End Rhy. Fig. 6

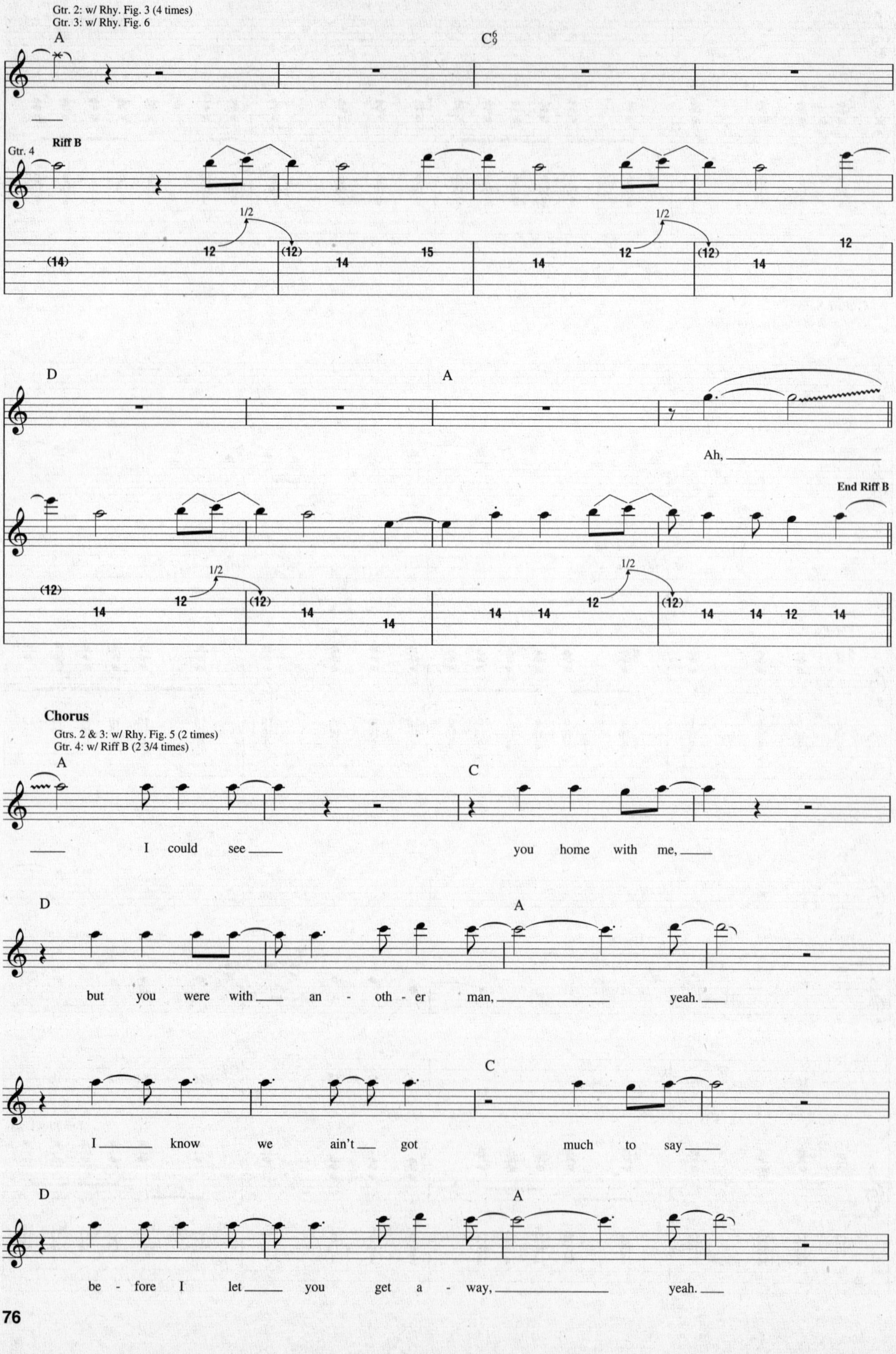

Gtr. 2: w/ Rhy. Fig. 3 (4 times)
Gtr. 3: w/ Rhy. Fig. 6

A C6/9

Riff B

Gtr. 4

1/2 1/2

(14) 12 (12) 14 15 14 12 (12) 14 12

D A

Ah,

End Riff B

1/2 1/2

(12) 14 12 (12) 14 14 14 14 12 (12) 14 14 12 14

Chorus

Gtrs. 2 & 3: w/ Rhy. Fig. 5 (2 times)
Gtr. 4: w/ Riff B (2 3/4 times)

A C

I could see you home with me,

D A

but you were with an - oth - er man, yeah.

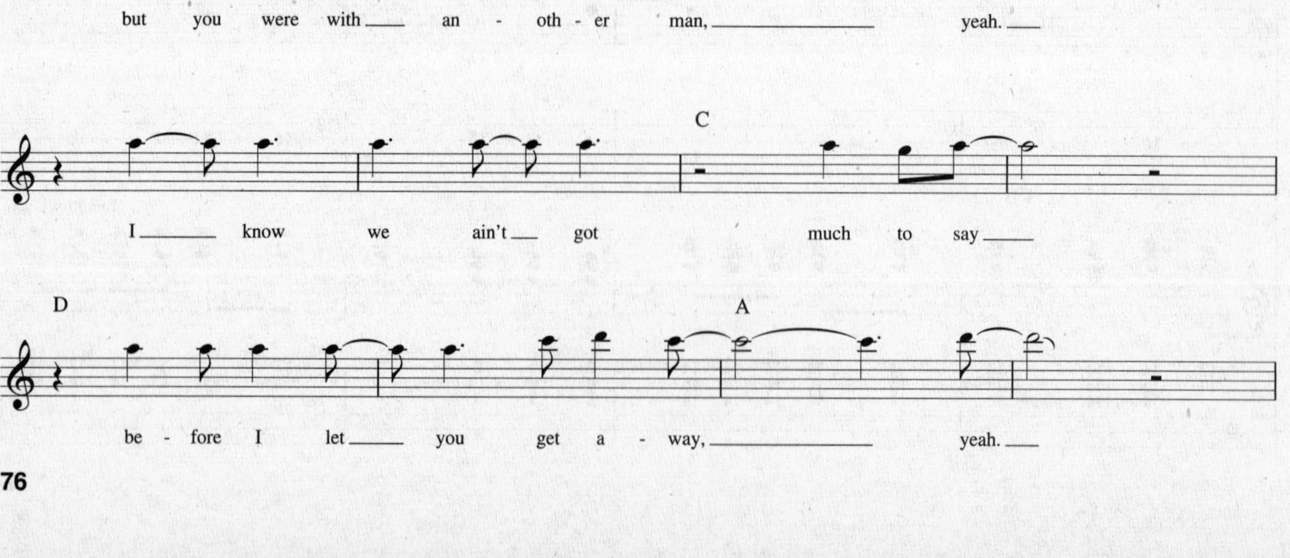

Gtr. 3: w/ Rhy. Fig. 5 (1st 6 meas.)
C
Uh, be my girl.
Be my
Gtr. 2

D
girl.
Are you gon - na be my
(cont. in slashes)

A
E GIII E GIII E D
open open open
Gtrs. 2 & 3
girl?
Yeah!
Gtr. 4

Babe, I'm Gonna Leave You

Words and Music by Anne Bredon, Jimmy Page and Robert Plant

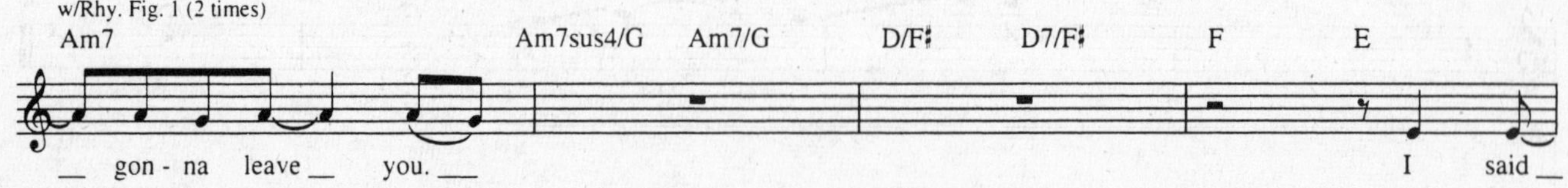

Am7
Am7/G
D/F♯
D7/F♯
F
E
na leave you. I'll
F6
F
E7
E
F6
F
E7
E
leave you when the sum-mer-time, leave you when the sum - mer comes
Am
Am7/G
D7/F♯
F
E
a-roll - in,' leave you when the sum-mer comes
Am
Am7 Dm(add9)
Am
Am7 Dm(add9)
a - long.
Rhy. Fig. 2
mf

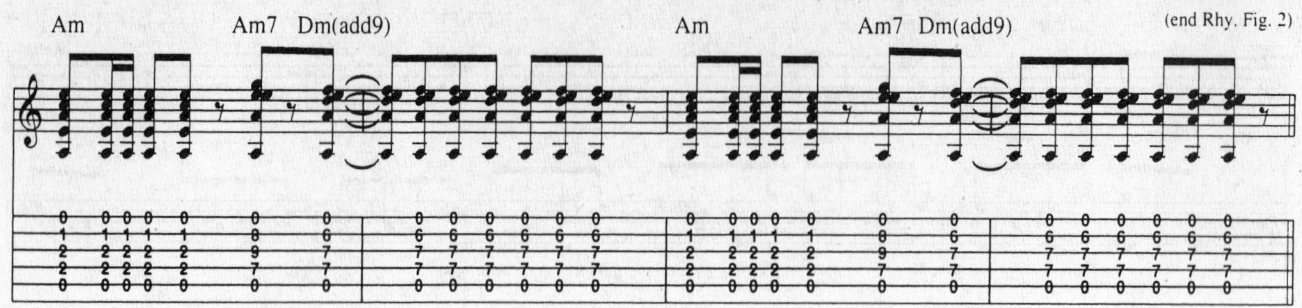
Am
Am7
Dm(add9)
Am
Am7
Dm(add9)
(end Rhy. Fig. 2)

Am
Am7sus4/G
Am7/G
D7/F♯
F
E
Babe, babe, __ babe, ____ babe, __ babe, ____ babe, __ ba - by, mm, ba- by I ___
mp

Am7
Am7sus4/G
Am7/G
D/F♯
D7/F♯
F
E
wan - na leave __ you. ___ I ain't jok - in' __ wom-an, I've got to ___

Am7
Am7sus4/G
Am7/G
D7/F♯
F
E
__ ram - ble. __ Oh, yeah. ___

w/Fill 1
Am7
Am7sus4/G
Am7/G
D/F♯
D7/F♯
F
E
Ba - by, ba - by, I will leave you. (I've) real - ly got to
F6
F
E7
E
F6
F
E7
E
ram - ble.
(pp:) (I can hear it call - in' me.)
I can hear it call - in' me the way it
Am
Am7sus4/G
Am7/G
D7/F♯
F
E
used to do.
I can hear it call - in' me back home.
w/Rhy. Fig. 2
Am
Am7
Dm(add9)
Am
Am7
Dm(add9)
Am
Am7
Dm(add9)
Am
Am7
Dm(add9)
Fill 1 (Gtr. 2 acous.)

Am7add9 Dm(sus4)/A Dm/A Am7add9 Dm(sus4)/A Dm/A
mp
Am7add9 Dm(sus4)/A Dm/A Am7add9 Dm(sus4)/A Dm/A
Am Am7/G D7/F♯ F E
Ba - by, oh, babe, I'm gon - na
Rhy. Fig. 3A (Gtr. 3-elec.)
(end Rhy. Fig. 3A)
f
Rhy. Fig. 3 (Gtr. 1)
(end Rhy. Fig. 3)
f
w/Rhy. Figs. 3 & 3A (both 3 times)
Am Am7/G D7/F♯ F E
leave you. Oh,
Am Am7/G D7/F♯ F E
ba - by, you know I've real - ly
Am Am7/G D7/F♯ F E
got to leave you. Oh.

F
E
F
E
I could hear it call - in' me,
I said don't you hear it call - in' me the way it
Gtr. 3
(Gtr. 3 out)
Gtr. 1
w/Rhy. Fig. 2
Am
Am7
Dm(add9)
used to do?
Oh.
Am7sus4/G
Am7/G
D/F♯
D7/F♯
Gtr. 2
mp

Am7
Am7(sus4)/G
Am7/G
D/F♯
D7/F♯
F
E

Am7
Am(add6)
G7
G6
D(add9)/F♯
D/F♯
Fmaj7
E
I know, ___ I know, ___ I know I nev- er, nev- er, nev-er, nev- er, nev- er gon-na
(Gtr. 2 out)

Am
C/G
D7/F♯
F
E
leave you babe, _ but I got- ta go a-way from this place. _

Am7 Am(add6) G6 G7 D(add9)/F# D/F# Fmaj7/E E
I got- ta quit you, yeah. Oh,
Am C/G D7/F# F E
ba - by, ba - by, ba - by, ba - by,
cresc.
w/Rhy. Figs. 3 & 3A (both 2 times)
Am Am7/G D7/F# F E
ba - by, ba - by, ba - by. Oh.
Am Am7/G D7/F# F E
Don't you hear it call - in' me?
Am Am7(sus4)/G Am7/G D7/F# F E
Oh. Wom - an.
Gr. 1
mp

Am7 Am(add6) G7 G6 D(add9)/F♯ D/F♯ Fmaj7 E

Wom - an. I know. I know. Feels

Gtr. 3

8va

mp

full full full full full full full full

Am7 Am(add6) G6 G7 D(add9)/F♯ D/F♯ Fmaj7 E
grow, yes it is. We gon-na go walk-in' through the park ev-'ry day.
w/Rhy. Figs. 3 & 3A (both 2 times)
Am Am7/G D7/F♯ F E
Oh, my babe. Ev-'ry day. Oh.
Am Am7/G D7/F♯ F E
My, my, my, my, my, my, babe, I'm gon-na leave you,
Am Am7(sus4)/G Am7/G D/F♯ D7/F♯
go a-way.
Gtr. 2
mp

F E Am7 Am(add6) G7 G6 D(add9)/F♯ D/F♯

Oh, ___ huh.

hold bend

full full 1/2

Fmaj7 E Am7 Am(add6) G7 G6

So good, sweet ba - by. ___

Dadd9/F♯ D/F♯ Fmaj7 E Am

It was real - ly, real - ly good. ___

C/G D7/F♯ F E

You made me hap- py ev- 'ry __ sin- gle

Am
Am7(sus4)/G
Am7/G
D7/F♯
F
E
day,
but now
I've got to go a -
(Gtr. 2 out)
w/Rhy. Figs. 3 & 3A (both 4 times)
Am
Am7/G
D7/F♯
F
E
Am
way.
Oh,
oh,
oh.
Am7/G
D7/F♯
F
E
Am
Am7/G
D7/F♯
F
E
Am
Am7/G
D7/F♯
F
E
Ba - by,
ba - by,
ba - by,
Free time
F
E7
that's
when it's
call - in' me,
Gtr. 1

F
E7
I said that's when it's call - in' me back home.
A/C♯
Cm6
Bm7
B♭maj7
Gtr. 2
(Gtr. 2 out)
Gtr. 1
(pick w/fingers)
Am(add9)
Gtr. 3

Back in Black

Words and Music by Angus Young, Malcolm Young and Brian Johnson

Chorus
A5
E5
B5
B5
G5
D
back.
Yes, I'm
back.
Well, I'm
Gtrs. 1 & 2
Rhy. Fig. 2
1/4
back,
Well, I'm
back in
black.
Yes, I'm
back
in
black.
Oh!
To Coda
End Rhy. Fig. 2

Guitar Solo

E5
E7
E6
E5
Gtr. 1
P.M.
P.M.
P.M.
Gtr. 2
Rhy. Fig. 3
E7
E6
E5
A
E5
A
P.M.
P.M.
P.M.
End Rhy. Fig. 3
Gtr. 2: w/Rhy. Fig. 3, 2½ times
E5
E7
E6
E5
full
full
full
P.M.
1/4
1/4
E7
E6
E5
A
E5
A
full
full
full
full

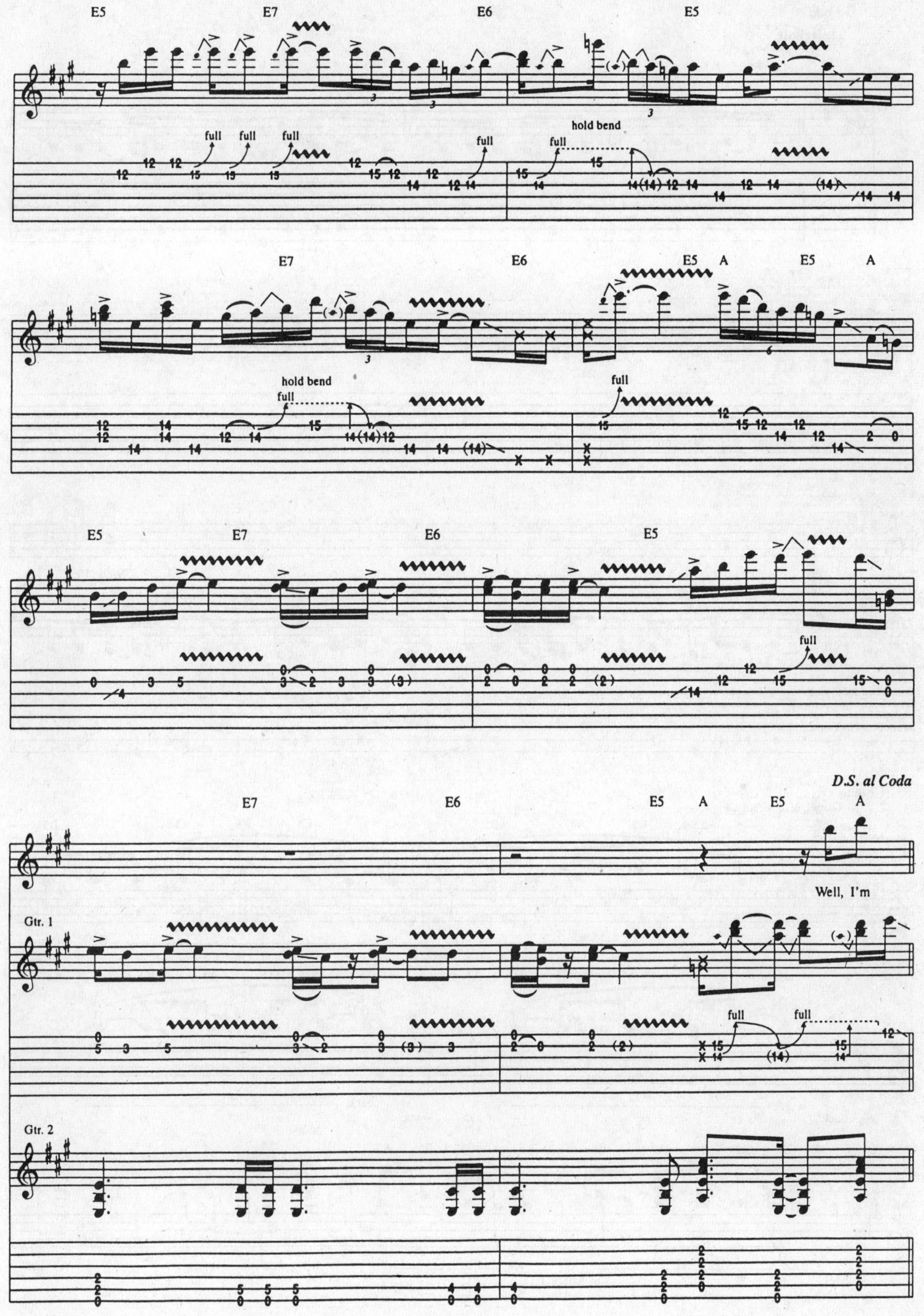
E5
E7
E6
E5
full
full
full
full
full
hold bend
E7
E6
E5
A
E5
A
hold bend
full
full
E5
E7
E6
E5
full
D.S. al Coda
E7
E6
E5
A
E5
A
Well, I'm
Gtr. 1
full
full
Gtr. 2

Coda
Interlude
w/Voc. ad lib.
N.C.(E5)
(A5)
(E5)
Well, I'm
Chorus
Gtrs. 1 & 2: w/Rhy. Fig. 2
A5 E5 B5 A5 B5 A5 E5 B5 A5 B5
back, back. Well, I'm
(I'm back. I'm
G5 D A5 G5 A5 G5 D A5 G5 A5
back, back,
back. I'm back. I'm
E5 B5 A5 B5 A5 E5 B5 A5 B5 G5
back, back. It's back in black. Yes, I'm
back. I'm back.)

D
A5
back in— black.—
I wan-na say it.
Gtr. 3 (dist.)
mf
full
f
3/4
Gtrs. 1 & 2
Outro/Guitar Solo
Gtrs. 1 & 2: w/Rhy. Fig. 3, till fade
Gtr. 3
E5
E7
E6
E5
1/4
E7
E6
E5
A
E5
A
full
full
Begin Fade
E5
E7
E6
E5
1/2
full
1/2
full
1/2
full
1/2
full
full
1/2

E7
E6
E5
A
8va
15ma
full
1/4
P.H.
hold bend
Fade Out

Bang a Gong (Get It On)

Words and Music by Marc Bolan

End Rhy. Fig. 3
dirt - y and sweet, oh yeah.
wind - y and wild, oh yeah.
Well, you're
Well, you're built
End Rhy. Fig. 2

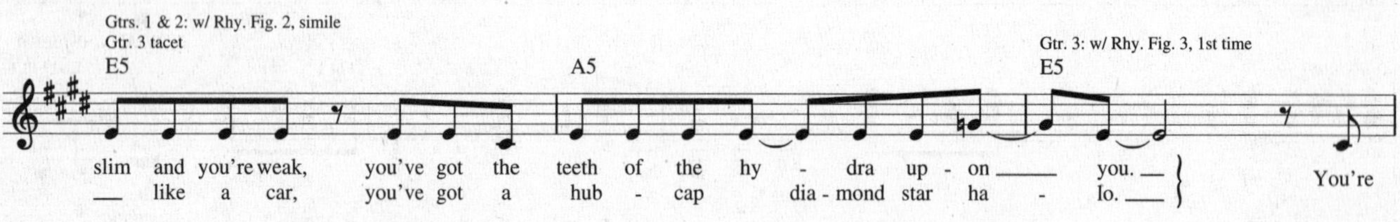
Gtrs. 1 & 2: w/ Rhy. Fig. 2, simile
Gtr. 3 tacet
E5
A5
Gtr. 3: w/ Rhy. Fig. 3, 1st time
E5
slim and you're weak, you've got the teeth of the hy - dra up - on you.
like a car, you've got a hub - cap dia - mond star ha - lo.
You're

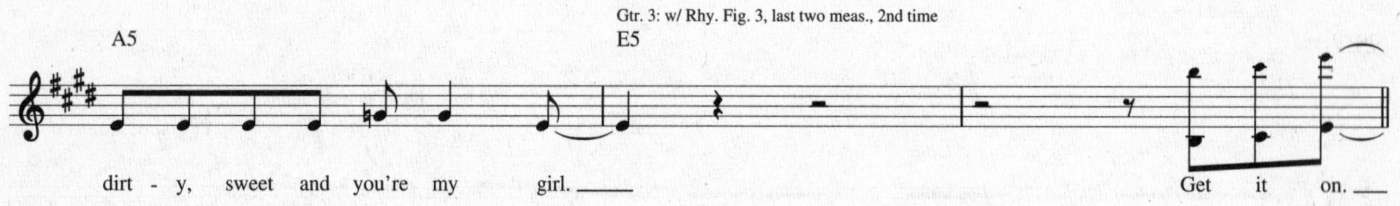
A5
Gtr. 3: w/ Rhy. Fig. 3, last two meas., 2nd time
E5
dirt - y, sweet and you're my girl.
Get it on.

Chorus
G5
A5
E5/B
Rhy. Fig. 4A
Gtr. 3
Bang a gong. Get it on.
Get it on.
Gtrs. 1 & 2
Rhy. Fig. 4

To Coda
G5
A5
E5/B
(cont. in notation, 2nd time)
Bang a gong. Get it on.
Verse
Gtr. 1: w/ Rhy. Fig. 2, 2 times, simile
End Rhy. Fig. 4A
Gtr. 3
A7/C# (no root)
2. Well, you're built like a car, you've got a hub - cap dia-mond star ha -
(Ooh.)
(Ooh.
End Rhy. Fig. 4
Rhy. Fig. 5
Gtr. 2
slight P.M.
P.M.
- lo.
You're built like a car, oh yeah.
Ooh.
slight P.M.
slight P.M. throughout

Gtr. 2: w/ Rhy. Fig. 5, simile
E5
A5
(cont. in notation)
Well, you're an un - tamed youth, that's the truth, with your cloak full of ea -
Ooh.
End Rhy. Fig. 5
Gtr. 3
E5
A5
E5
- gles. You're dirt - y, sweet and you're my girl. Get it on.
)
Chorus
Gtrs. 1, 2 & 3: w/ Rhy. Figs. 4 & 4A, simile
G5
A5
E5
G5
Bang a gong. Get it on. Get it on. Bang a gong.
D.S. al Coda
Gtr. 3: w/ Fill 1
A5
E5
Get it on. Ow. 3. Well, you're wind -
(Ooh.)
Coda
Interlude
Gtr. 1: w/ Rhy. Fig. 1, 2 times
Gtr. 2 tacet
E5 E6 E5 E6 E5 E6 E5 E6 E5 E6 E5 E6 E5 E6 E5 E6 E5
Ah.
Gtr. 3

Gtr. 2: w/ Rhy. Fig. 1
E6 E5 E6 E5 E6 E5 E6 E5 E6 E5 E6 E5 E6 E5 E6 E5
(Ooh. Ooh.)
4. Well, you're dirt -
1/2
* fade in
Verse
Bkgd. Voc.: w/ Voc. Fig. 2, 2 times
Gtr. 1: w/ Rhy. Fig. 2, 2 times, simile
Gtr. 2: w/ Rhy. Fig. 5, simile
Gtr. 3: w/ Rhy. Fig. 3, simile
E5 A5 E5
- y and sweet, clad in black, don't look back, and I love you. You're
A5 E5
Gtr. 2: w/ Rhy. Fig. 2, simile
dirt - y and sweet, oh yeah. Well, you dance when you walk, so let's dance,
Gtr. 3: w/ Rhy. Fig. 3
A5 E5 A5 E5
take a chance, un - der - stand me. You're dirt - y, sweet an you're my girl.
Chorus
Gtrs. 1 & 2: w/ Rhy. Fig. 4, 1st 8 meas., simile
Gtr. 3: w/ Rhy. Fig. 4A, 1st 6 meas., simile
G5 A5 E5
Get it on. Bang a gong. Get it on. Get it on.
Gtr. 3: w/ Fill 2
Gtrs. 1, 2 & 3: w/ Rhy. Figs. 4 & 4A, 1st 4 meas.
G5 A5 E5 G5
Bang a gong. Get it on. Ow! Get it on. Bang a gong.
Voc. Fig. 2
(Ooh. Ooh.)

Interlude
Gtr. 1: w/ Rhy. Fig. 1
A5
E5
E5 E6 E5 E6 E5
E6 E5 E6 E5
Get it on.
Ow!
(Get it on.)
Sax Break
Gtrs. 1 & 2: w/ Rhy. Fig. 1
Gtr. 3
E6 E5 E6 E5
E6 E5 E6 E5
E5 E6 E5 E6 E5
E6 E5 E6 E5
Chorus
Gtr. 1: w/ Rhy. Fig. 4, 1st 8 meas., 2 times
Gtr. 2: w/ Rhy. Fig. 4, 1st 8 meas., 1st time; 1st 6 meas., 2nd time
E6 E5 E6 E5
E6 E5 E6 E5
G5
A5
Get it on.
Bang a gong.
Get it on.
Fill 3
End Fill 3
Gtr. 3: w/ Fill 3, 2nd time, simile
E5
G5
Uh, uh, uh, uh, uh, uh.
Get it on.
Bang a gong.
* 1st time
Fill 2
Gtr. 3
T
A
B

1.
A5
E5
Get it on.
Uh, uh, uh, uh, uh. Get it on.
2.
Gtr. 3: w/ Fill 3, simile
E5
Take me.
Gtr. 2
grad. release
1 1/2
(cont. in slash)
Outro
G5
Gtrs. 1 & 2
A5
Gtr. 3
full
full
full
Gtrs. 1 & 2: w/ Rhy. Fig. 6, 7 times, simile
E5 E6 E5 E6 E5 E5 E6 E5 E6 E5 E6 E5 E6 E5 E6 E5 E6 E5
Rhy. Fig. 6
End Rhy. Fig. 6
Well, mean-
1/2
Begin Fade
E6 E5 E6 E5 E6 E5 E6 E5 E6 E5 E6 E5 E6 E5 E6 E5
Fade Out
-while I'm still think-in'.
(Ah.)

Bark at the Moon

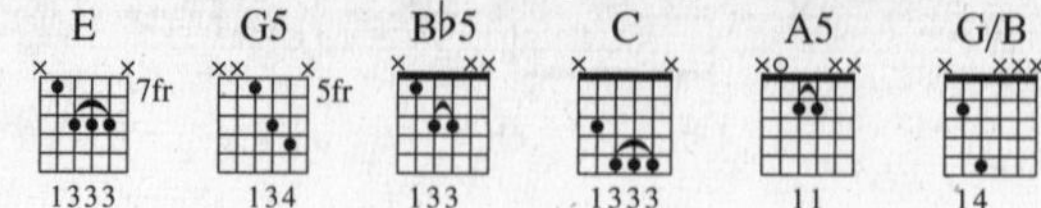

Intro

Moderate Rock ♩ = 148

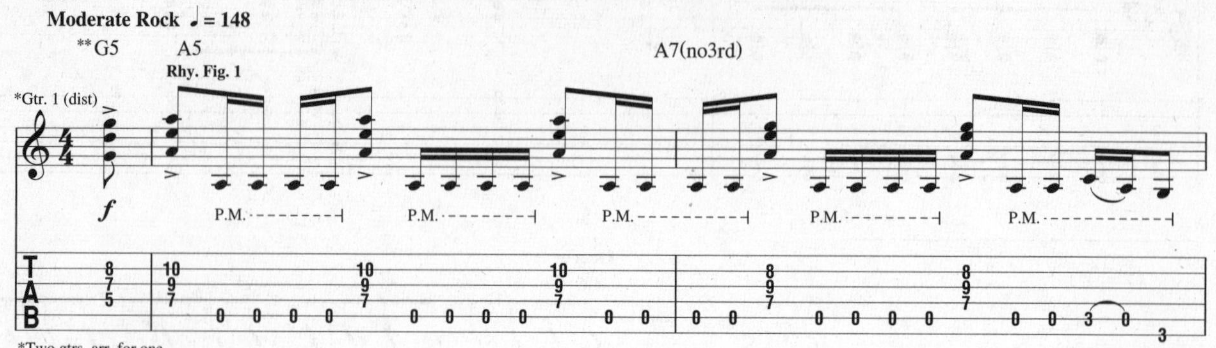

*Two gtrs. arr. for one

**Chord symbols reflect basic harmony.

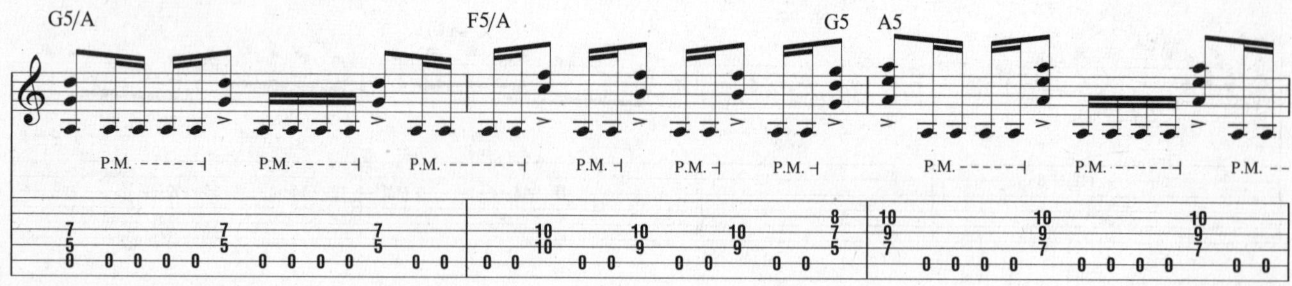

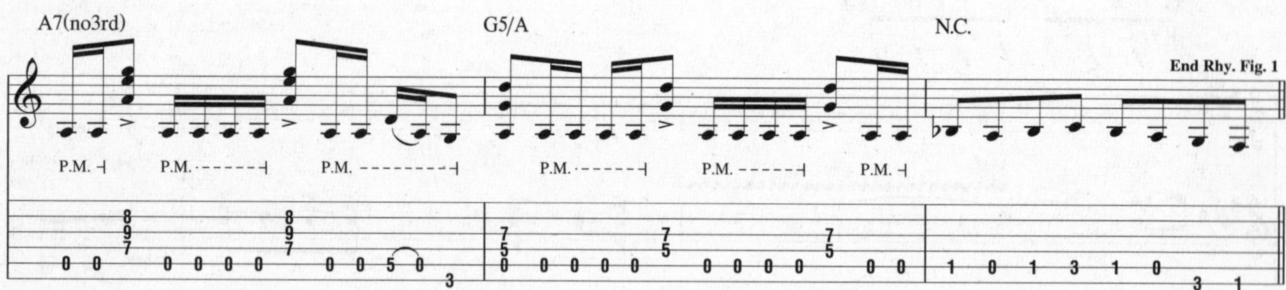

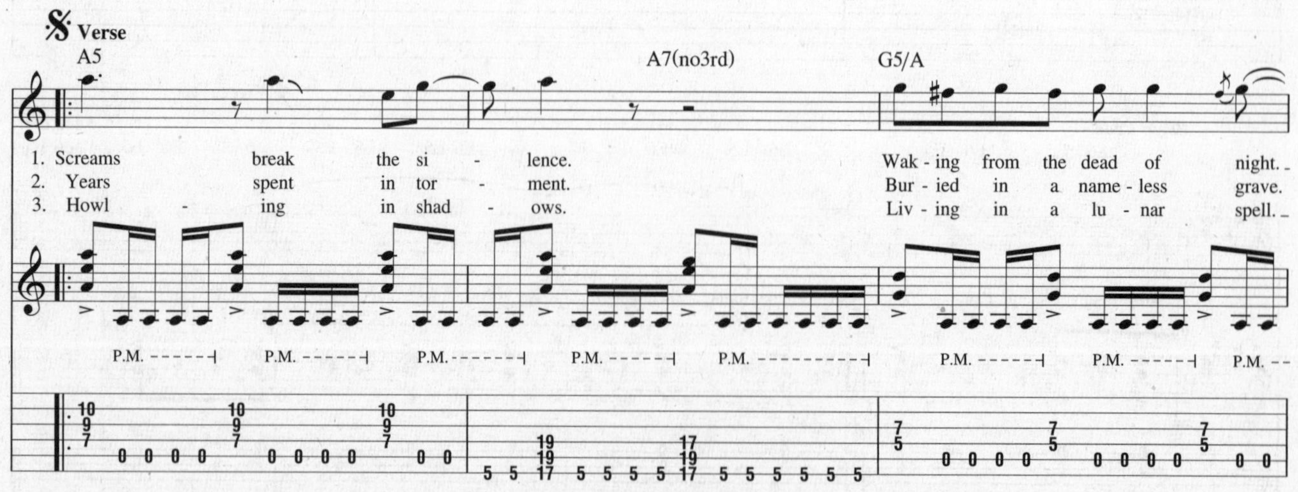

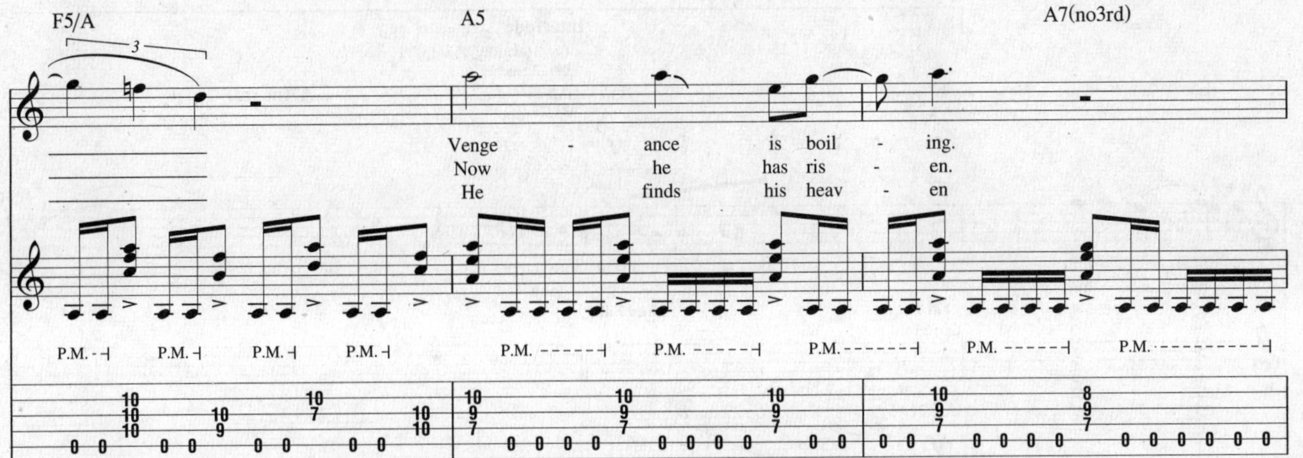
F5/A
A5
A7(no3rd)
3
Venge - ance is boil - ing.
Now he has ris - en.
He finds his heav - en
P.M.

Pre-Chorus
G5/A
N.C.
F♯m
*D5/F♯
He's re - turned to kill the light.
Mir - a - cles would have to save.
spew - ing from the mouth of hell.
1. Then when he's found who he's
2., 3. Those that the beast is
P.M.
*Bass plays note to right of slash in chord symbol, next 2 meas.

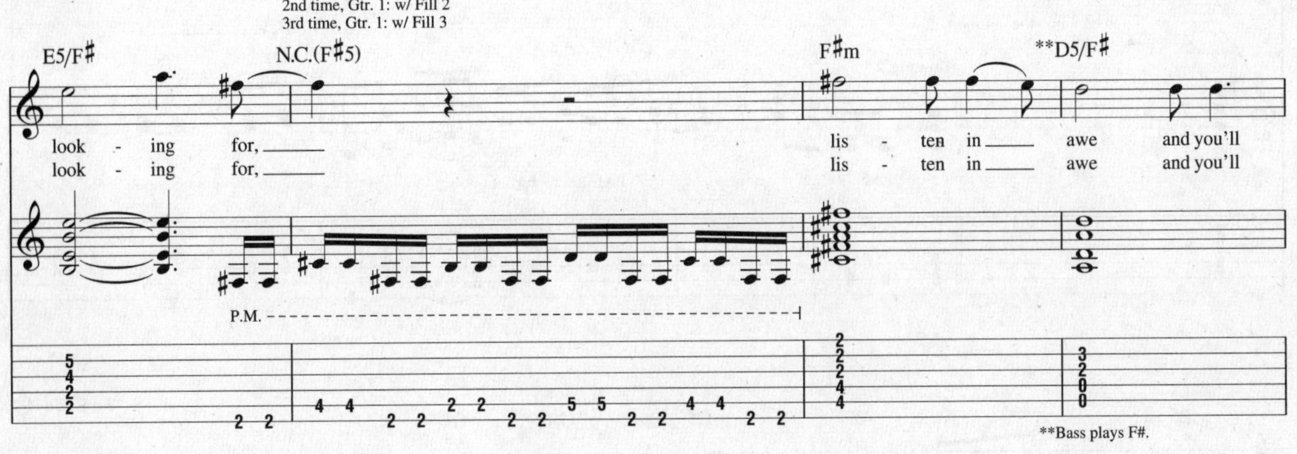
2nd time, Gtr. 1: w/ Fill 2
3rd time, Gtr. 1: w/ Fill 3
E5/F♯
N.C.(F♯5)
F♯m
**D5/F♯
look - ing for,
look - ing for,
lis - ten in awe and you'll
lis - ten in awe and you'll
P.M.
**Bass plays F#.

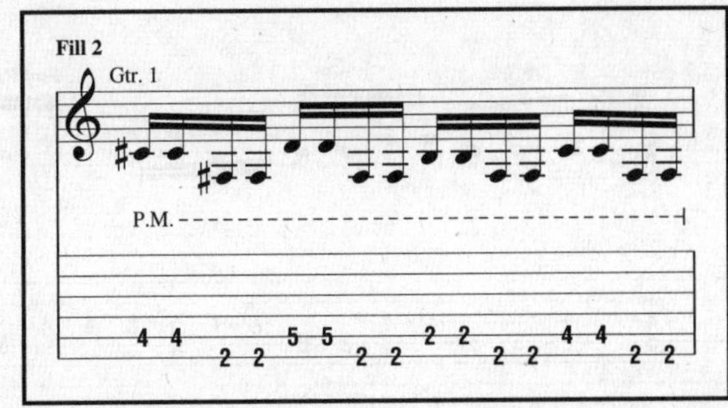
Fill 2
Gtr. 1
P.M.

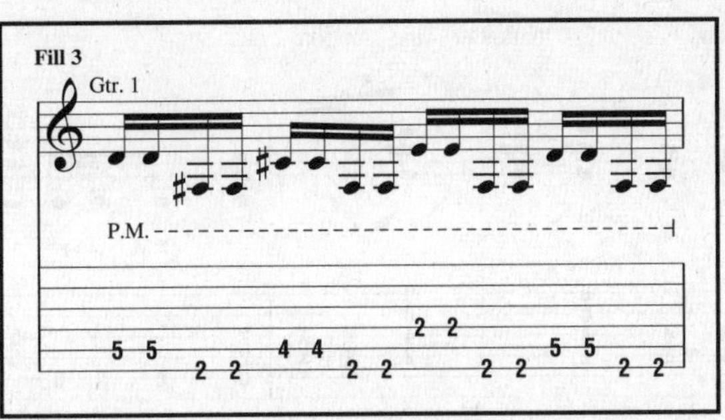
Fill 3
Gtr. 1
P.M.

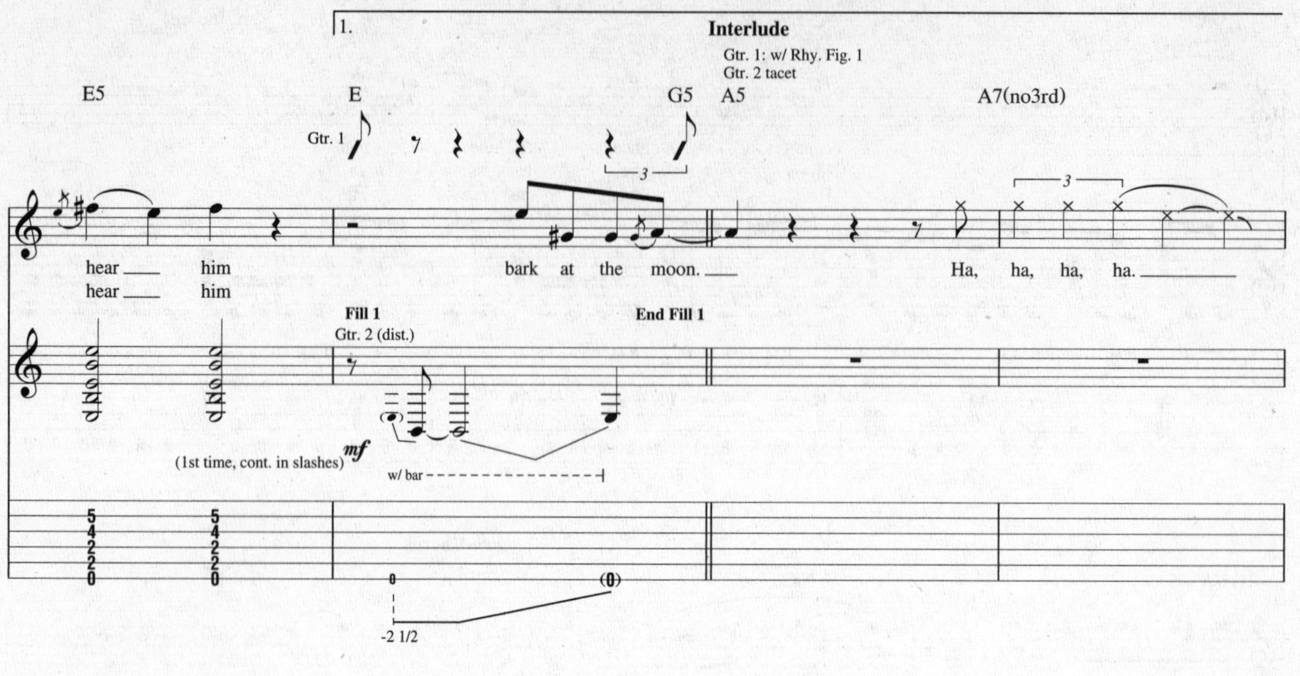
1.
Interlude
Gtr. 1: w/ Rhy. Fig. 1
Gtr. 2 tacet
E5
E
G5
A5
A7(no3rd)
Gtr. 1
hear him bark at the moon.
hear him
Ha, ha, ha, ha.
Fill 1
Gtr. 2 (dist.)
End Fill 1
mf
(1st time, cont. in slashes)
w/ bar
-2 1/2

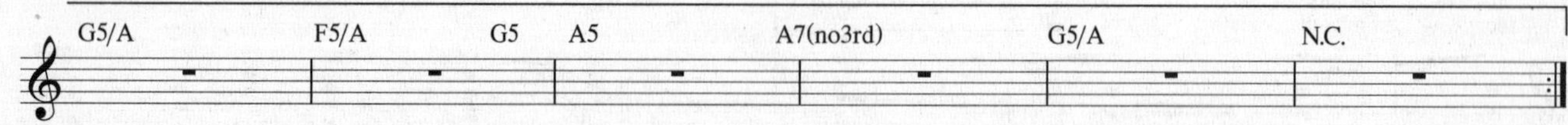
G5/A
F5/A
G5
A5
A7(no3rd)
G5/A
N.C.

2.
Chorus
Gtr 2: w/ Fill 1
E N.C.
A5
C5 D5
G/B G
G F
bark at the moon.
Hey,
Rhy. Fig. 2
P.M.
P.M.
P.M.

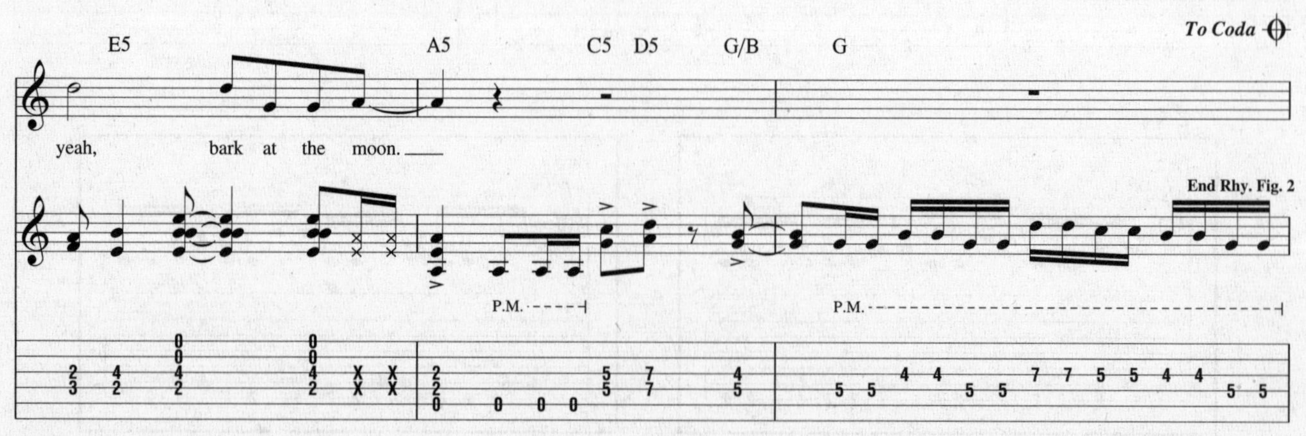
To Coda
E5
A5
C5 D5
G/B
G
yeah, bark at the moon.
End Rhy. Fig. 2
P.M.
P.M.

Bridge
Half-time feel
G F
E5
F5
E5 F5
G5
They cursed and bur - ied him, a - long with shame.
*Gtrs. 1 & 2
Rhy. Fig. 3
8va
loco
w/ bar
P.M.
P.H.
-1 1/2
*Composite arrangement; starts on beat 4 1/2 before Bridge.
E5 F5
E5 F5
G5
E5
And thought his time - less soul had gone, gone.
End Rhy. Fig. 3
w/ bar grad. dive
w/ bar steady gliss.
+2 1/2
Gtrs. 1 & 2: w/ Rhy. Fig. 3
F5
E5 F5
G5
E5
In emp - ty burn - ing hell un - ho - ly one.
F5
E5 D5
C5 B♭5
But he's re - turned to prove them wrong, so wrong.
Gtr. 2
Gtr. 1
let ring

Guitar Solo
End half-time feel
C5
Dm
C5
Ooh yeah, ba - by.
mf
f
rake
Rhy. Fig. 4
let ring
P.M.
Dm
15ma
loco
C5
A5
B♭5
End Rhy. Fig. 4
8va
A5
G5
B♭5
A5

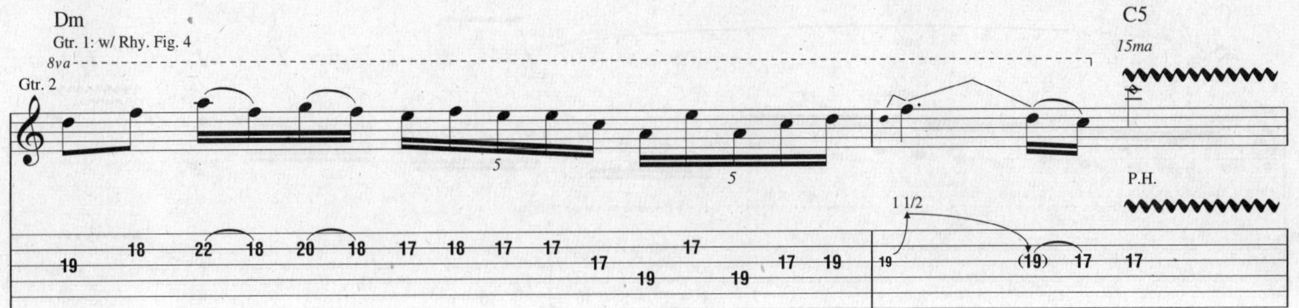
Dm
Gtr. 1: w/ Rhy. Fig. 4
8va
Gtr. 2
C5
15ma
P.H.
1 1/2

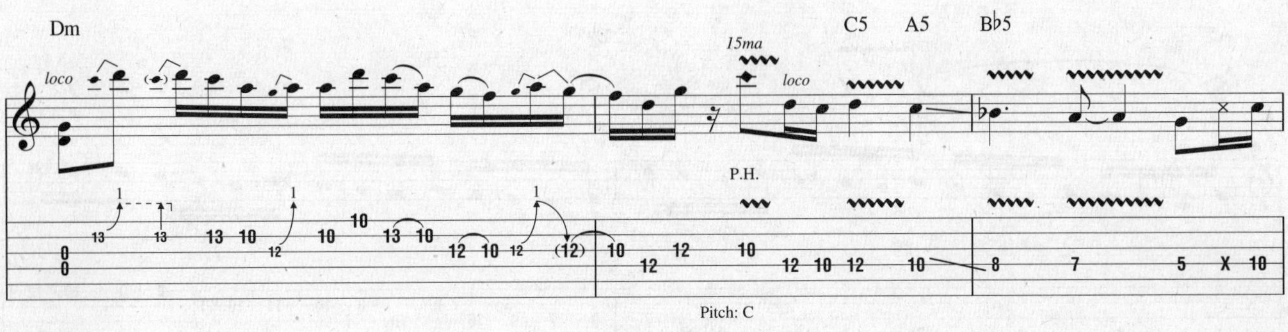
Dm
loco
15ma
loco
C5
A5
B♭5
P.H.
Pitch: C

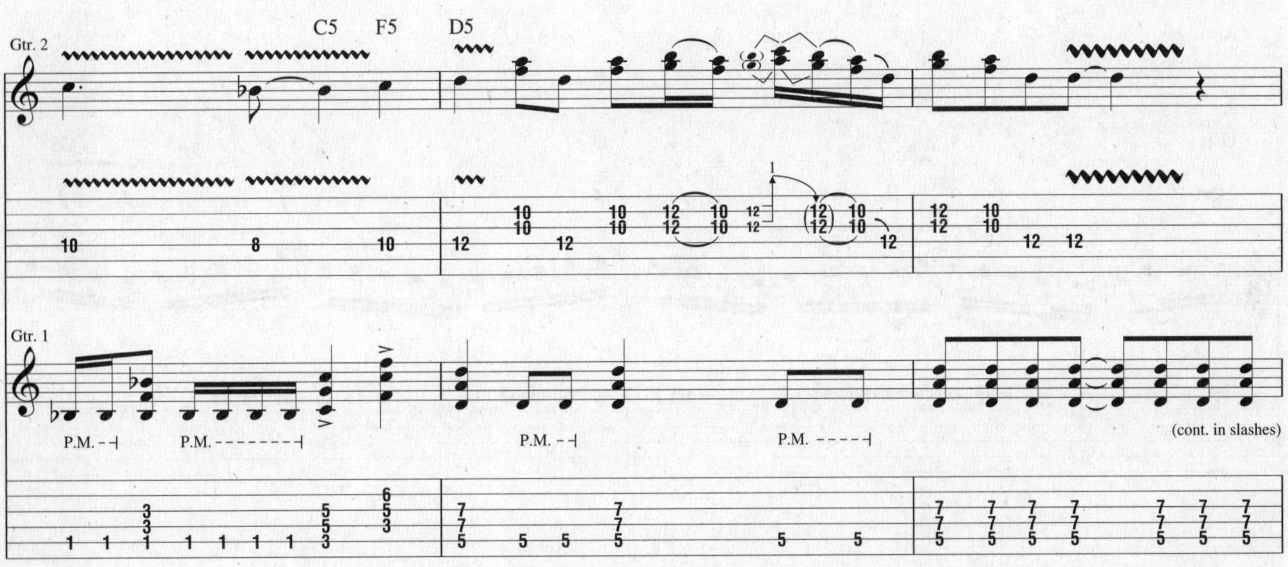
Gtr. 2
C5
F5
D5
Gtr. 1
P.M.
(cont. in slashes)

B♭5
Gtr. 1
P.M.

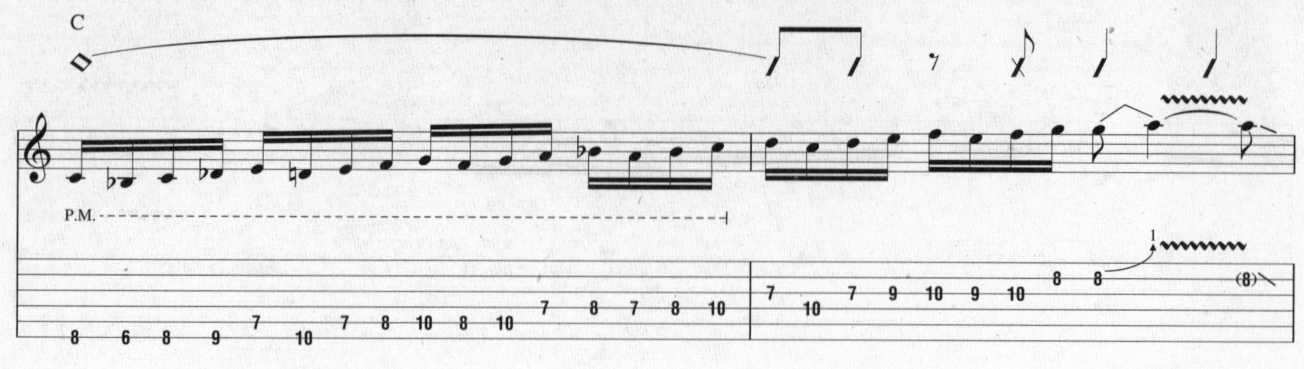
C
P.M.

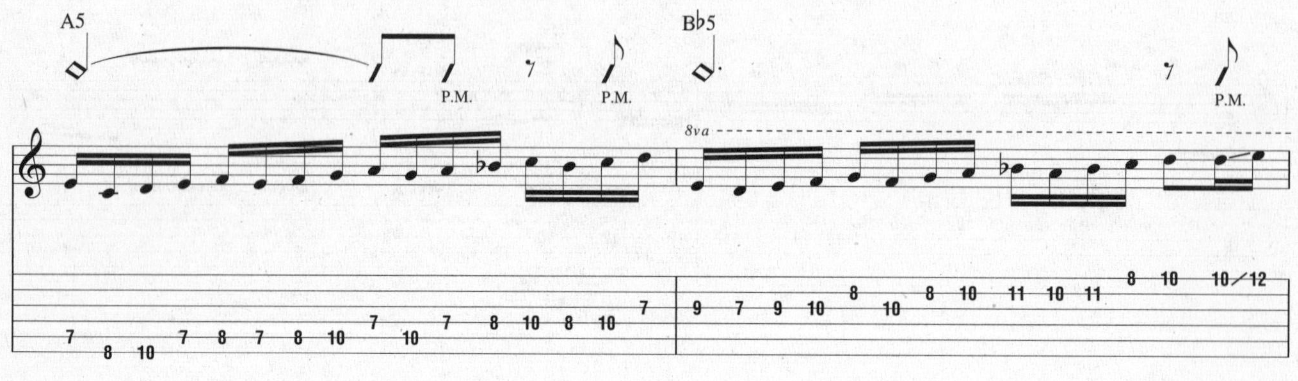
A5
P.M.
P.M.
B♭5
P.M.
8va

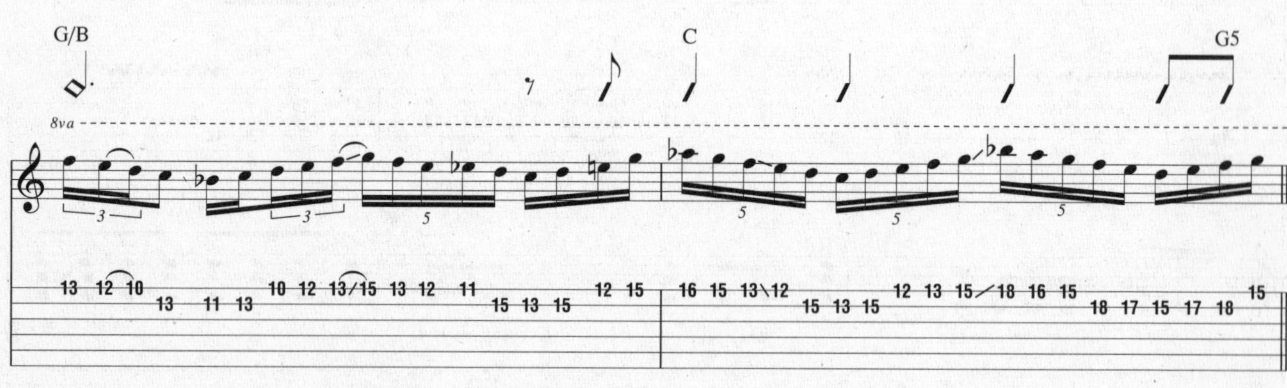
G/B
C
G5
8va

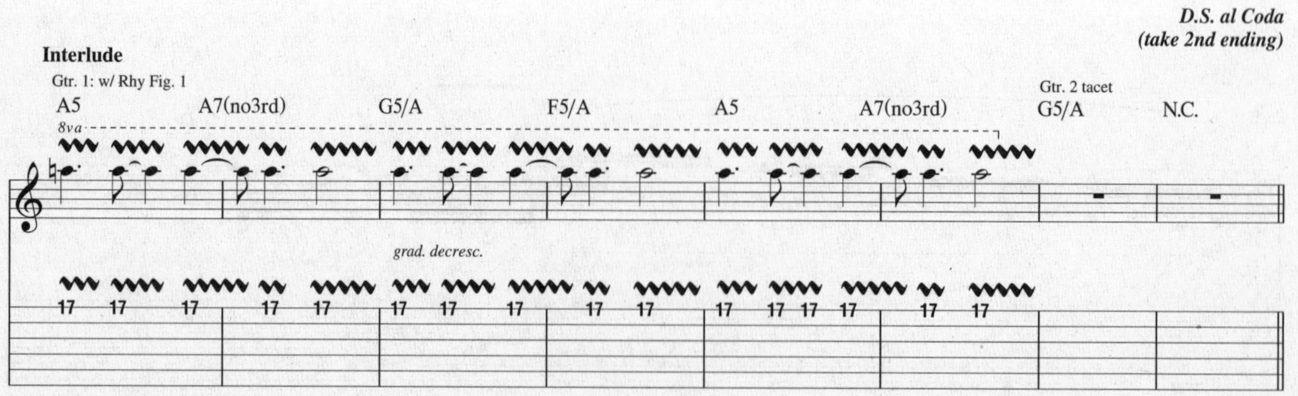
D.S. al Coda
(take 2nd ending)
Interlude
Gtr. 1: w/ Rhy Fig. 1
Gtr. 2 tacet
A5
A7(no3rd)
G5/A
F5/A
A5
A7(no3rd)
G5/A
N.C.
8va
grad. decresc.

Coda
Gtr. 1: w/ Rhy. Fig. 2
G F
E5
A5 C5 D5 G/B G
G F
Hey,
yeah,
bark at the moon.
Oh
Rhy. Fig. 5
End Rhy. Fig. 5
Gtr. 1: w/ Rhy. Fig. 5
E5
A5
C5 D5 G/B G
G F
E5
yeah,
bark at the moon.
Ow!
Outro
Gtr. 1: w/ Rhy. Fig. 1
A5
C5
D5/A
G/B
G
Gtr. 2
G F
E5
A5
C5
D5
G/B
G
Gtr. 1: w/ Rhy. Fig. 5
G F
E5
A5
Gtr. 1

Big City Nights

Words and Music by Klaus Meine and Rudolf Schenker

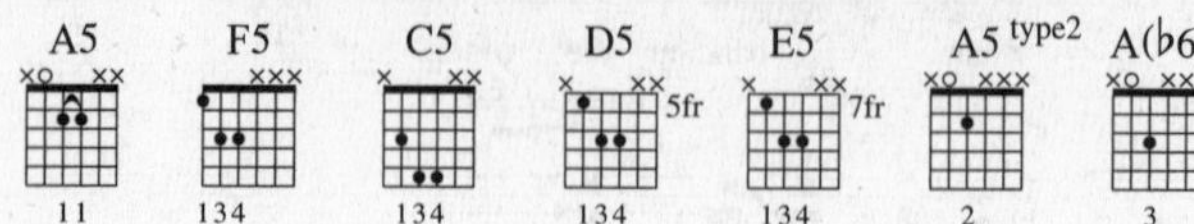

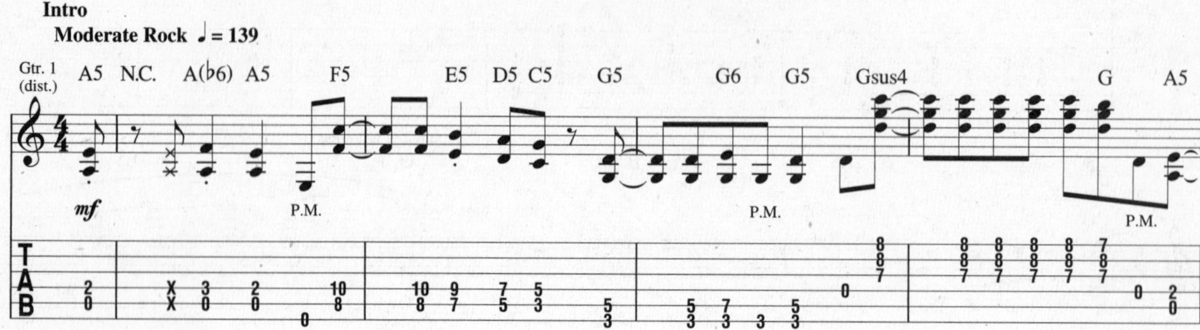

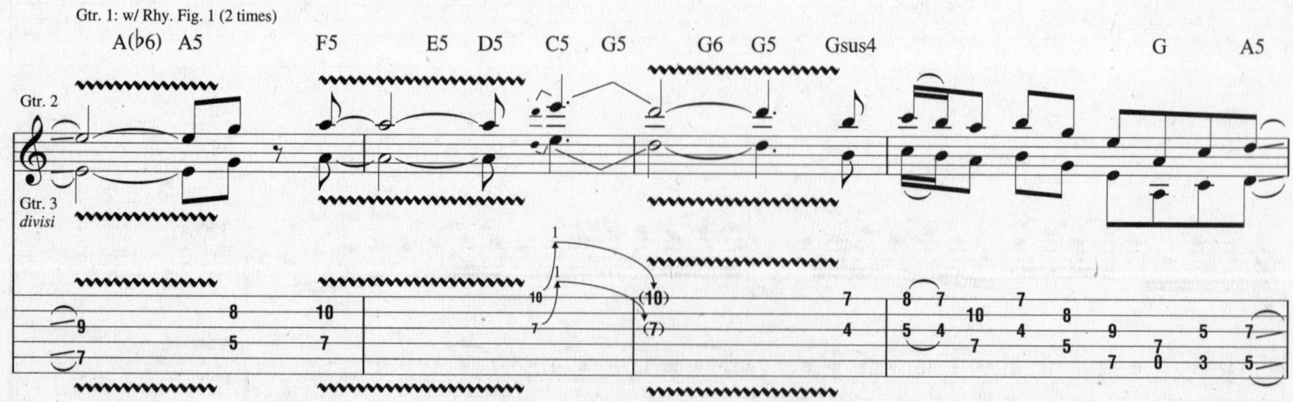

* Chord symbols reflect overall harmony.

F C Csus4 C Esus4 E Esus4 E Asus4
try to cut a big piece out of life, it feels al -
Gtr. 4
P.M. P.M. P.M. P.M.
Gtr. 1
End Rhy. Fig. 2
P.M. P.M. P.M. P.M.
(cont. in slashes)
A5 F5 C5 D5 A5
Rhy. Fig. 3
Gtr. 1
- right to go out to catch an out - ra - geous thrill. But it's more
Gtr. 4
Rhy. Fig. 3A
let ring
F5 C5 E5
like spin - ning wheels of for - tune, which nev - er stand still.
End Rhy. Fig. 3A

Chorus
G A5type2 A(♭6) A5 F5 E5 D5 C5 G5
⑥
3 fr
End Rhy. Fig. 3
Gtr. 1: w/ Rhy. Fig. 1 (2 times)
Big city, big city nights.
P.M.
G6 G5 Gsus4 G A5 A(♭6) A5 F5
You keep me burning. Big city,
P.M.
P.H.
* Move pickhand up & down string to achieve random harmonics.
E5 D5 C5 G5 G6 G5 Gsus4 G A5
big city nights. 2. When the sun-
8va
loco
P.H.
1/2
Pitches: D D A A♭ G F# F
Verse
Gtr. 1: w/ Rhy. Fig. 2
A5 F5 C5 Csus4 C Dsus4 D D5 A5
light is rising up in my eyes, and the long
P.M.

F5 C5 Csus4 C Esus4 E Esus4 Asus4
night has left me back at some-bod-y's side, it feels al-
P.M. P.M. P.M.
Gtrs. 1 & 4: w/ Rhy. Figs. 3 & 3A
Am F6 F C5 Csus4 C D D5 Asus4
right for a long sweet min-ute like hours be-fore. But it's more
Am F6 F C5 Csus4 C E
like look-ing out for some-thing can't find an-y-more.
Chorus
Gtr. 1: w/ Rhy. Fig. 1 (3 ¾ times)
A5type2 A(♭6) A5 F5
Big cit-y,
Gtr. 4
let ring
C
loco
P.H.
P.M.
E5 D5 C5 G5 G6 G5 Gsus4 G A5
big cit-y nights. You keep me burn-ing.

A(♭6) A5 F5 E5 D5 C5 G5 G6 G5 Gsus4
Big cit - y, big cit - y nights.
P.M.
1/2
G A5 A(♭6) A5 F5 E5 D5 C5 G5
Al - ways yearn - ing. Big cit - y, big cit - y nights.
P.M.
G6 G5 Gsus4 G A5
You keep me burn - ing.
C
loco
P.H.
A(♭6) A5 F5 E5 D5 C5 G5 G6 G5 Gsus4
Big cit - y, big cit - y nights.

Bridge
Half - time feel
G Gsus4 N.C. N.C. E5 G5 C5
There is no dream that you can't make true
Gtrs. 1 & 4
B5 N.C. E5 G5 C5
if you're look - ing for love.
But there's no girl's burn - ing the ice
End half - time feel
D5 (D5) A5type2
Gtr. 1
a - way from my heart,
may - be to - night.
Gtrs. 1 & 4
Gtr. 4
(Gtr. 1 cont. in slashes)
P.M.
(cont. in slashes)
Gtr. 2
Gtr. 3
divisi
* w/ delay repeats

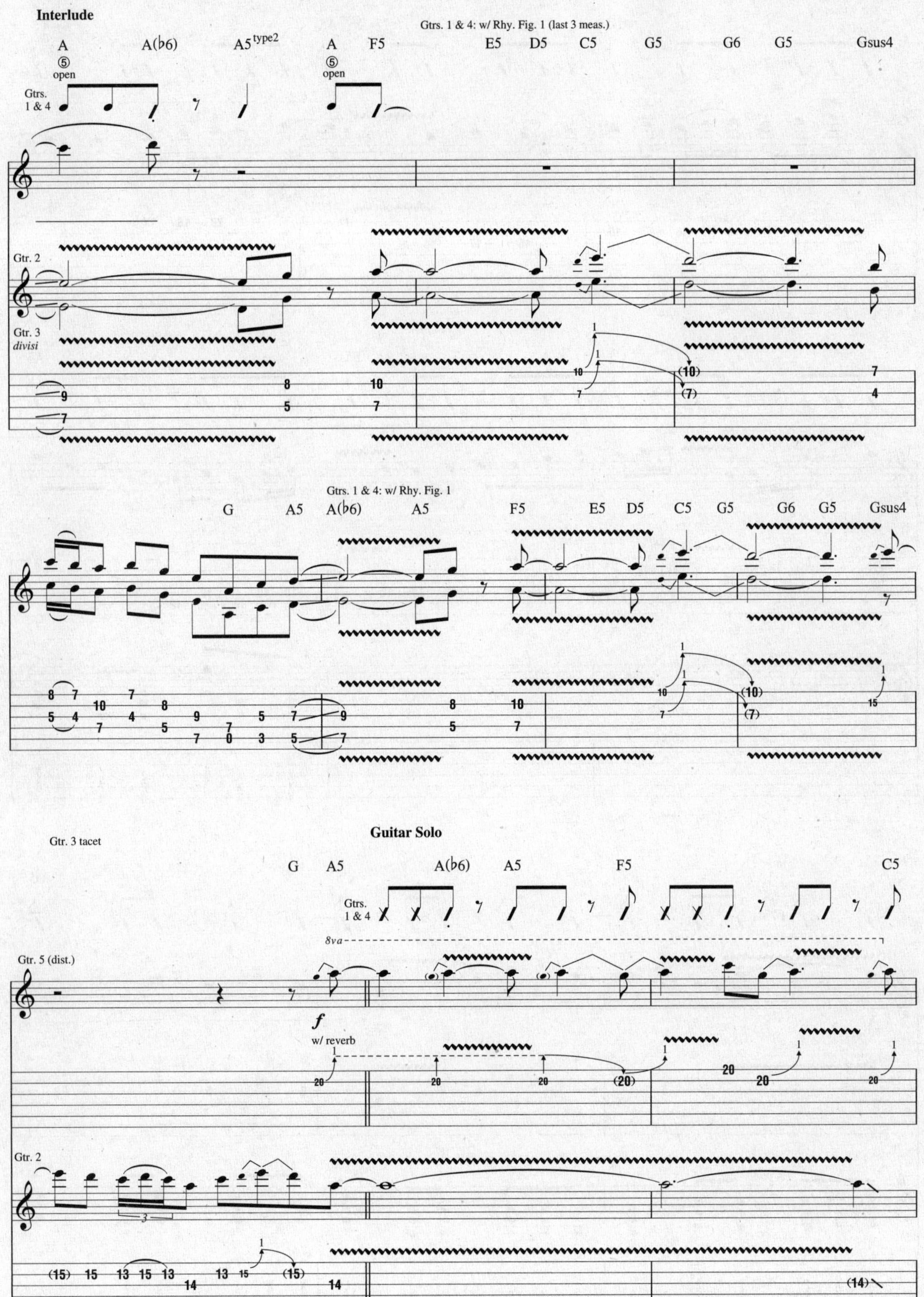
Interlude
Gtrs. 1 & 4: w/ Rhy. Fig. 1 (last 3 meas.)
A
A(♭6)
A5type2
A
F5
E5
D5
C5
G5
G6
G5
Gsus4
open
open
Gtrs. 1 & 4
Gtr. 2
Gtr. 3
divisi
Gtrs. 1 & 4: w/ Rhy. Fig. 1
G
A5
A(♭6)
A5
F5
E5
D5
C5
G5
G6
G5
Gsus4
Gtr. 3 tacet
Guitar Solo
G
A5
A(♭6)
A5
F5
C5
Gtrs. 1 & 4
8va
Gtr. 5 (dist.)
f
w/ reverb
Gtr. 2

Gtr. 2 tacet
D5
A5
F5
Gtr. 5
loco
8va
C5
E5
Gtr. 1
(Gtr. 4 cont. in notation)
Gtr. 4
F5
C5
D5

A5
F5
C5
8va
grad. bend
1/2
E5
A5type2
loco
Chorus
Gtr. 1: w/ Rhy. Fig. 1 (4 times)
Gtr. 5 tacet
A5 A(♭6) A5 F5 E5 D5 C5 G5 G6 G Gsus4 G A5
Big cit - y, big cit - y nights.
You keep me burn - ing.
P.M.

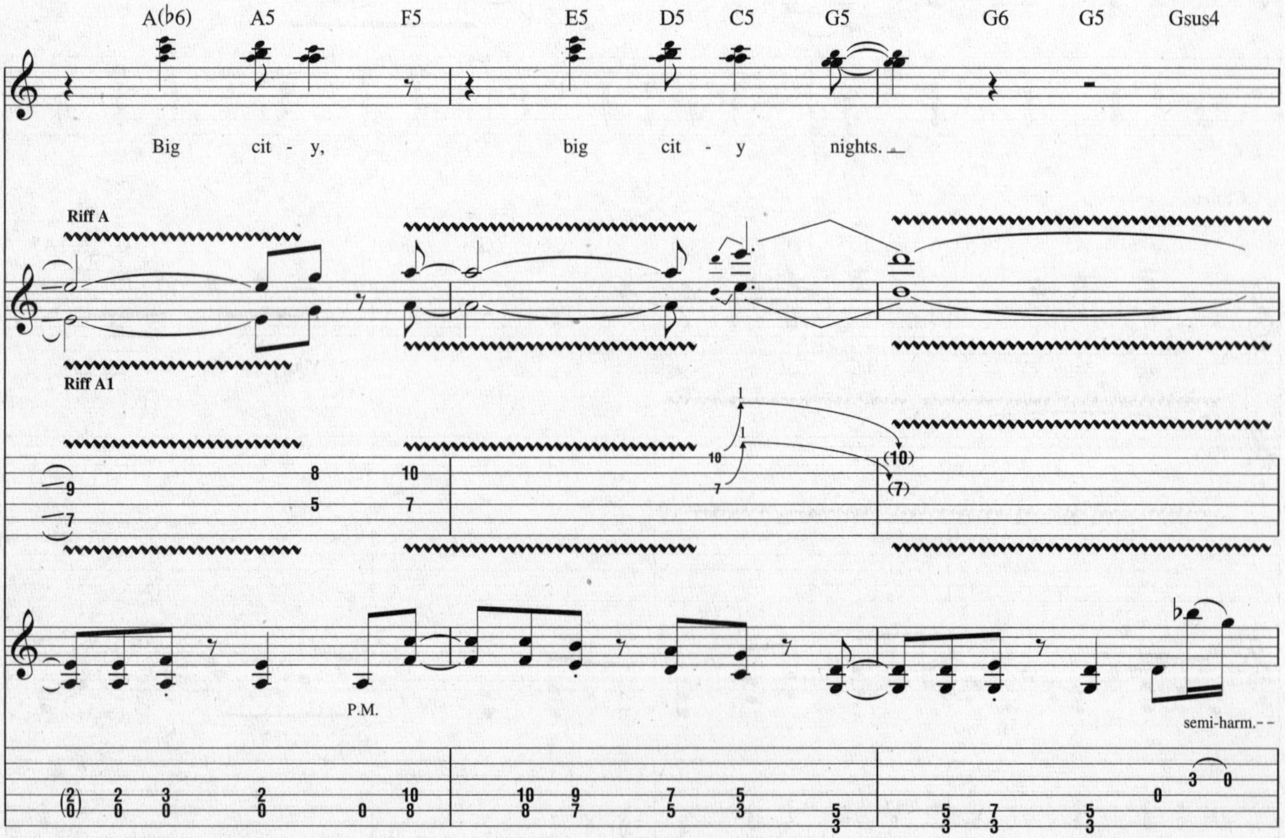

A(♭6) A5 F5 E5 D5 C5 G5 G6 G5 Gsus4

Big cit - y, big cit - y nights.

Riff A

Riff A1

P.M.

semi-harm.

G A5 A(♭6) A5 F5 E5 D5 C5 G5
You keep me burn - ing. Big cit - y, big cit - y nights.
semi-harm.
P.M.
P.M.
G6 G5 Gsus4 G A5
Al - ways yearn - ing.
End Riff A
End Riff A1
Outro
Gtrs. 1 & 4: w/ Rhy. Fig. 1 (till fade)
Gtrs. 2 & 3: w/ Riffs A & A1 (till fade)
A(♭6) A5 F5 E5 D5 C5 G5 G6 G5 Gsus4 G A5
Big cit - y, big cit - y nights. You keep me burn - ing.
Play 2 Times & Fade out
A(♭6) A5 F5 E5 D5 C5 G5 G6 G5 Gsus4 G A5
Big cit - y, big cit - y nights. Al - ways yearn - ing.

Black Velvet

Words and Music by David Tyson and Christopher Ward

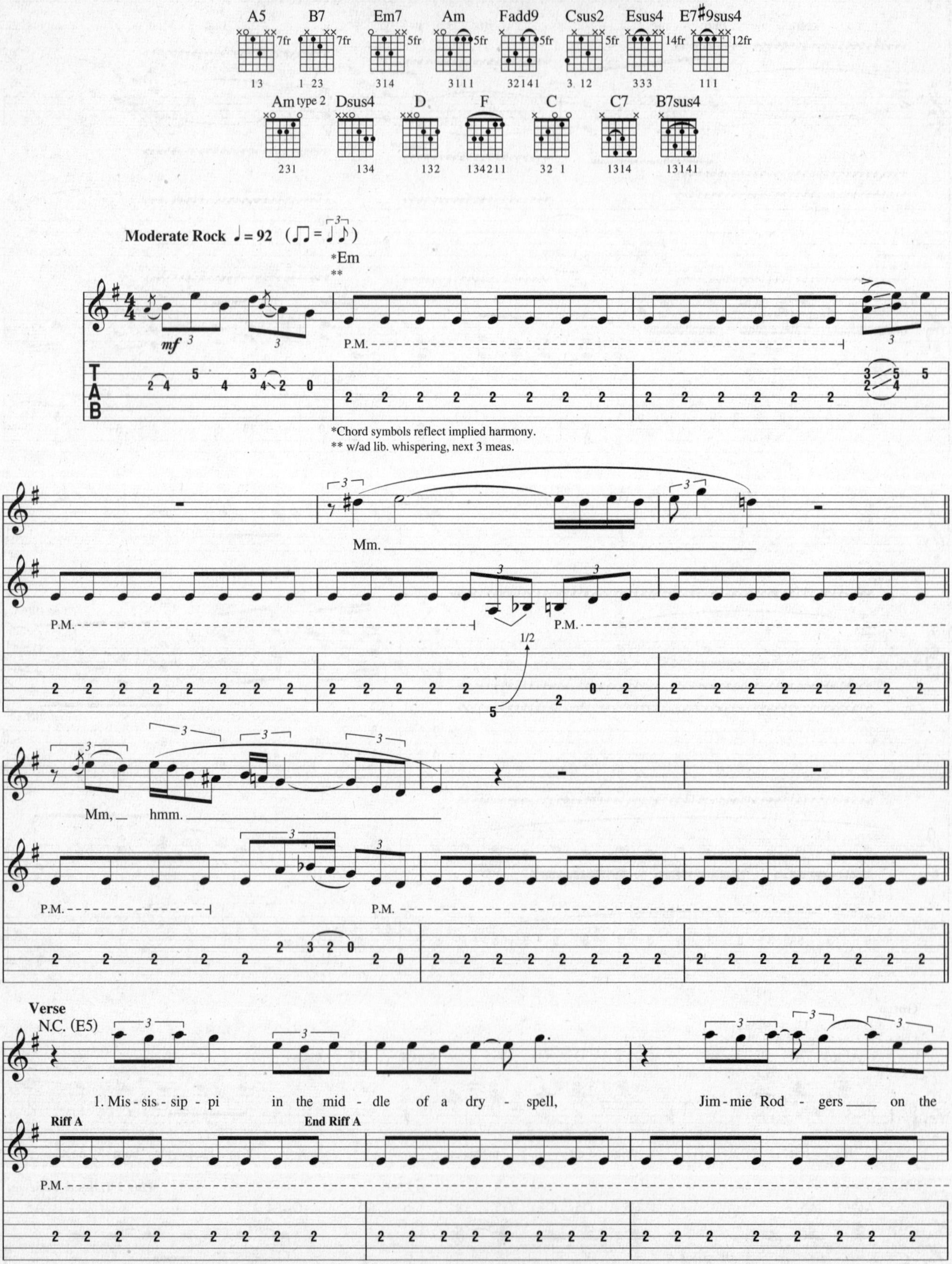

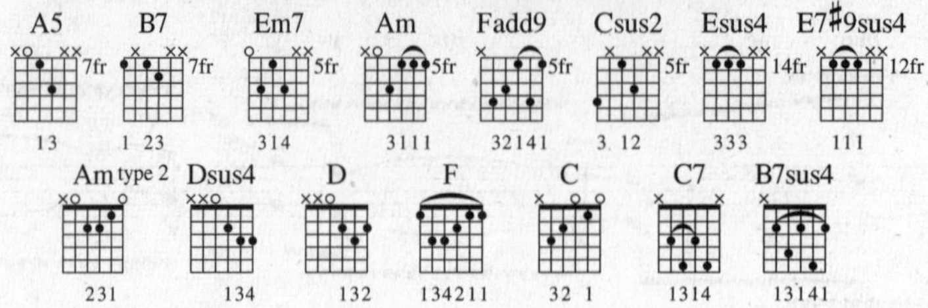

Moderate Rock ♩ = 92

*Em

**

mf

P.M.

*Chord symbols reflect implied harmony.
** w/ad lib. whispering, next 3 meas.

Mm.

P.M.

1/2

Mm, hmm.

P.M.

Verse

N.C. (E5)

1. Mis - sis - sip - pi in the mid - dle of a dry - spell, Jim - mie Rod - gers on the

Riff A

End Riff A

P.M.

Vic - tro - la up high.
Ma-ma's danc - in' with a ba - by on her shoul - der,
P.M.
rake
P.M.

Pre-Chorus
Bsus4
B
the sun is set - tin' like mo - las - ses in the sky.
That boy could sing, knew how to
Rhy. Fig. 1
let ring
P.M.

Asus4
A
Gsus4
G
Dsus2
move ev - 'ry - thing.
Al - ways want ing more,
he'll leave you long - ing for
End Rhy. Fig. 1
let ring
let ring
let ring

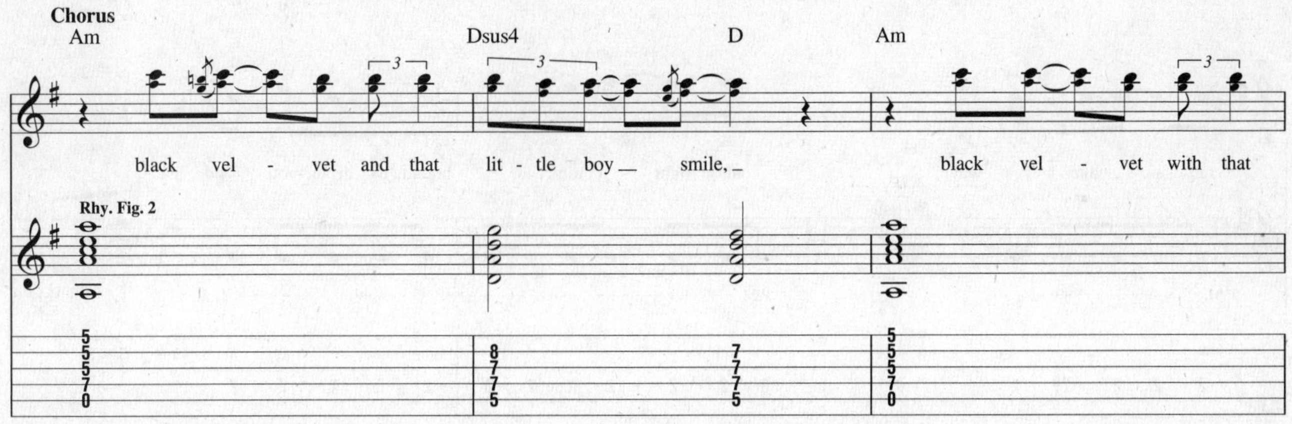
Chorus
Am
Dsus4
D
Am
black vel - vet and that lit - tle boy smile,
black vel - vet with that
Rhy. Fig. 2

F
C
Am
Dsus4
D
slow, South - ern style,
A new re - lig - ion ___ that - 'll bring you ___ to your knees,
End Rhy. Fig. 2
C7
B7
Em
black vel - vet, if you please.
P.M.
Verse
Em
2. Up in Mem - phis, the
mu - sic's ___ like a heat wave,
white light - nin',
bound to drive you wild. ___
1/2

Pre-Chorus

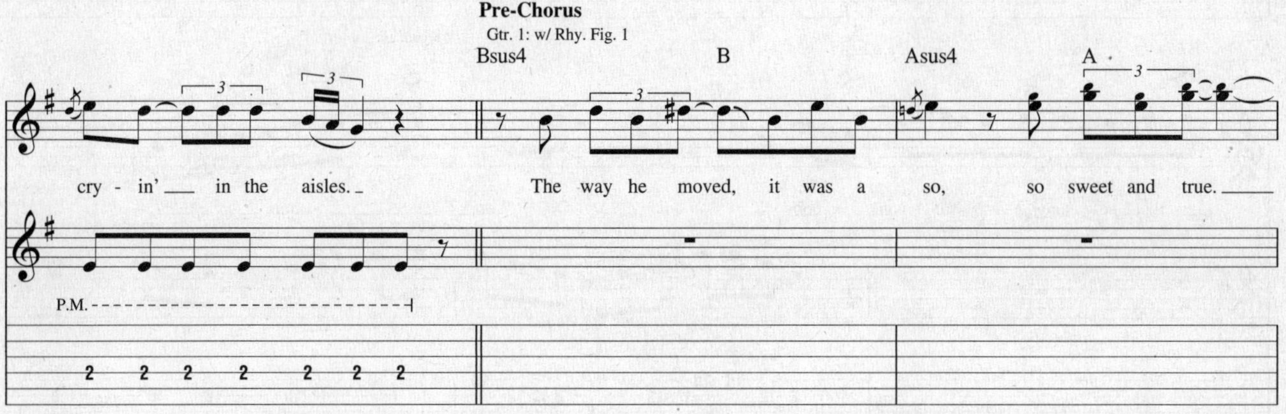

Chorus

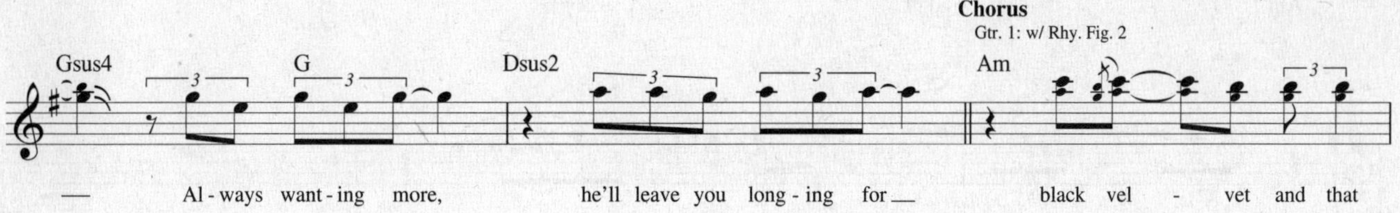

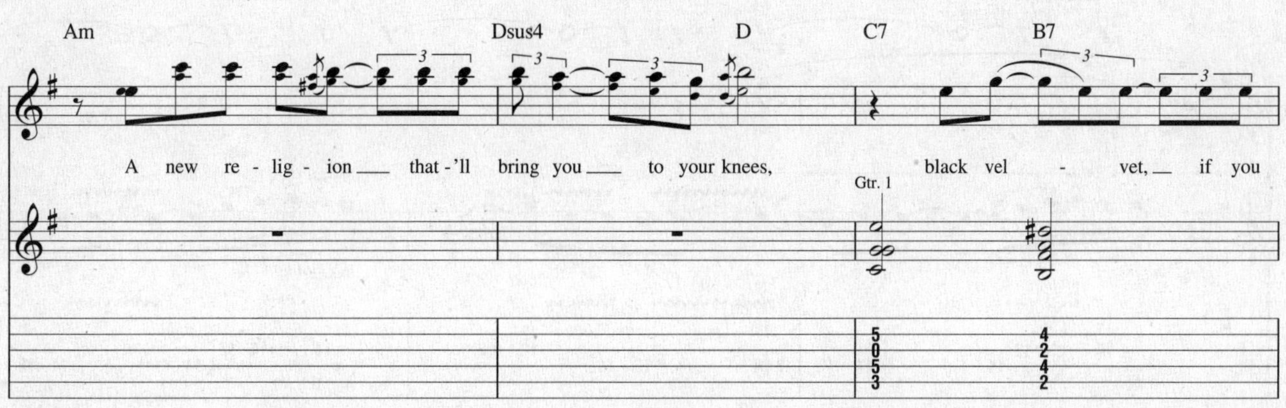

Bridge
Em
Gtr. 1 w/ Riff A (2 times)
A5
* Gtr. 3
please.
Ev - 'ry word of ev - 'ry song
Gtr. 2 (elec.)
P.M.
rake
P.M.
rake
Harm.
P.M.
* Kybd. arr. for gtr.
B7
Em7
that he sang was for you, hoo.
Oo, hoo, hoo.
let ring
Am
Fadd9
Csus2
B
9 fr.
In a flash, he was gone, it hap - pened so soon.
What could you do?
Guitar Solo
Gtr. 1: w/ Riff A (7 times)
Esus4
E7♯9sus4
Esus4
E7♯9sus4
rake
rake

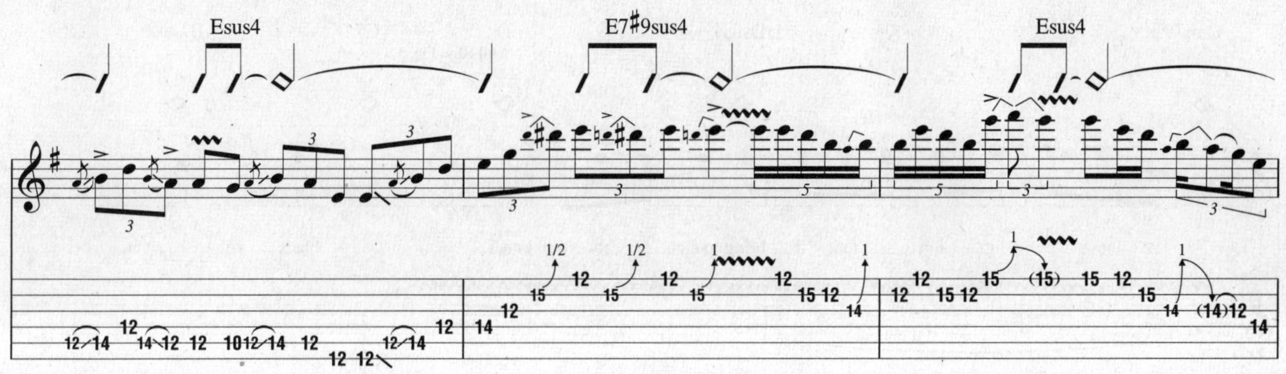
Esus4
E7#9sus4
Esus4

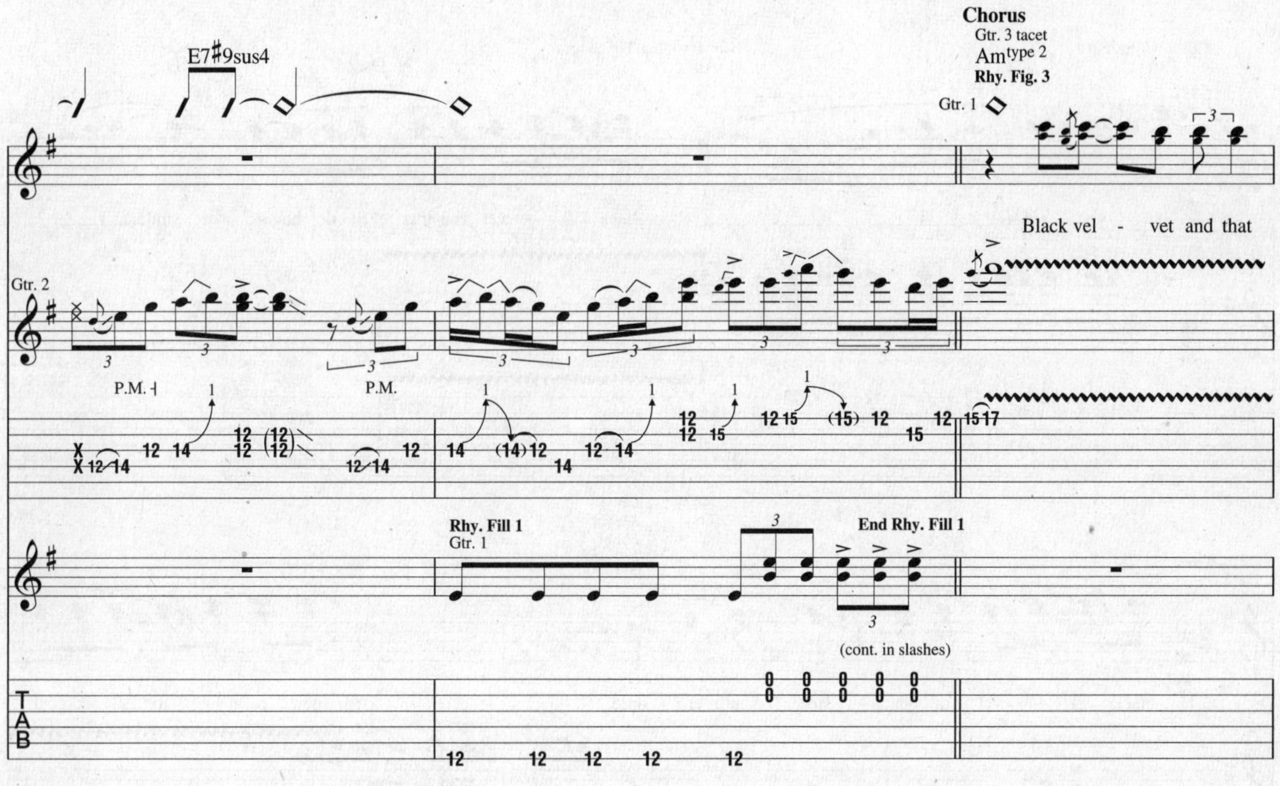
E7#9sus4
Chorus
Gtr. 3 tacet
Am type 2
Rhy. Fig. 3
Gtr. 1
Black vel - vet and that
Gtr. 2
P.M.
Rhy. Fill 1
Gtr. 1
End Rhy. Fill 1
(cont. in slashes)

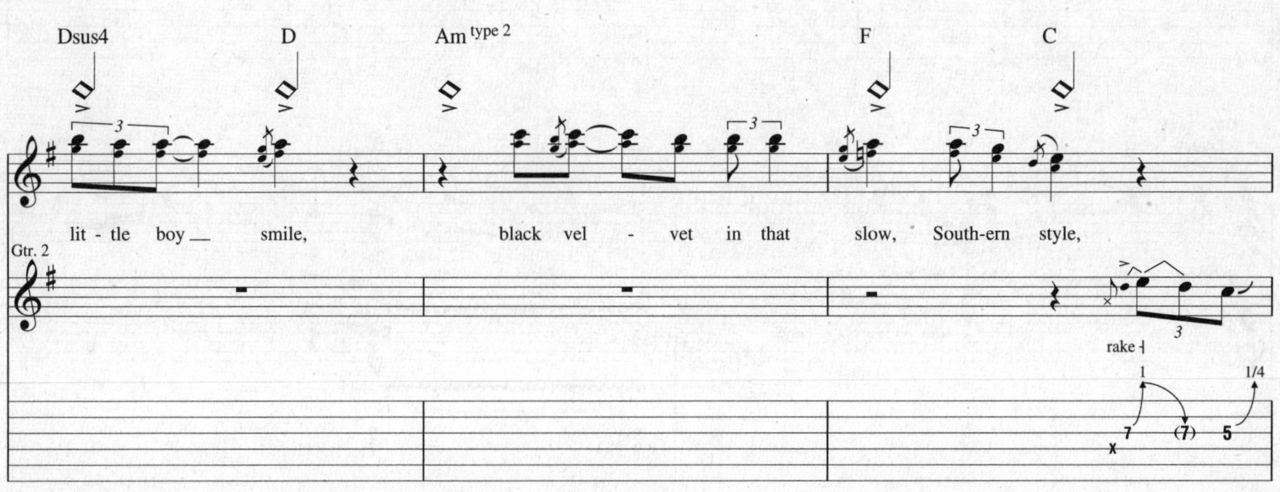
Dsus4
D
Am type 2
F
C
lit - tle boy smile,
black vel - vet in that
slow, South-ern style,
Gtr. 2
rake

Am type2
Dsus4
D
End Rhy. Fig. 3
C7
B7sus4
A new re - lig - ion that -'ll bring you to your knees,
black vel - vet,
Gtr. 1: w/Rhy. Fill 1
Em
Gtr. 1: w/ Rhy. Fig. 3
Am
Dsus4
D
if you please!
Black vel - vet and that lit-tle boy's smile,
Am
F
C
Am
black vel - vet in that slow, South-ern style.
A new re - lig - ion that -'ll
rake
Gtr. 2 tacet
Dsus4
D
C7
B7
bring you to your knees,
black vel - vet...
if
Gtr. 1

Outro
Gtr. 3: w/ Rhy. Fig. 4 (3 times)
Esus4 E7#9sus4
Esus4
E7#9sus4
Rhy. Fig. 4
End Rhy. Fig. 4
Gtr. 3
you please.
P.M.
Esus4
E7#9sus4
Esus4
If you please.
E#9sus4
Esus4
Em
If you please.
grad. release
If you

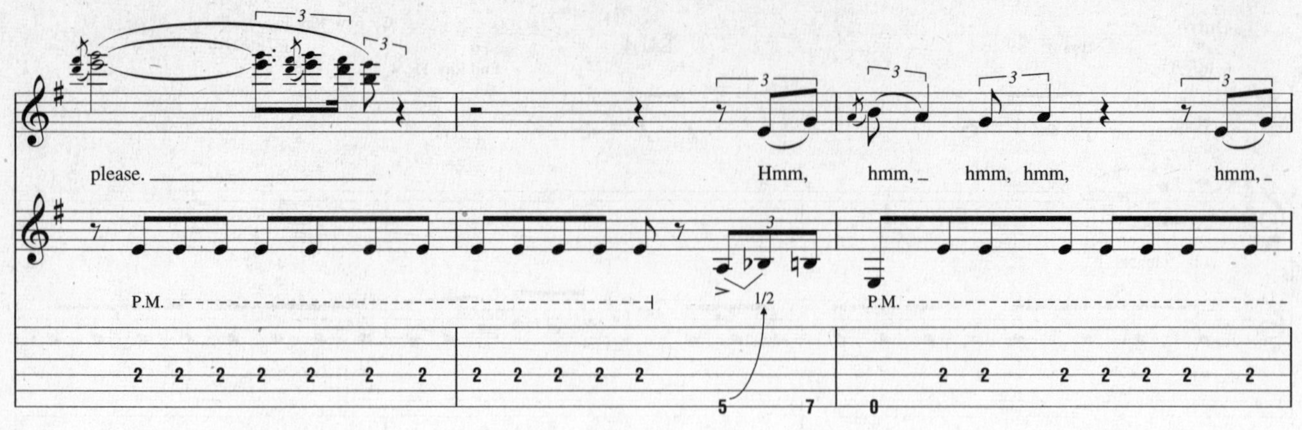

Begin Fade

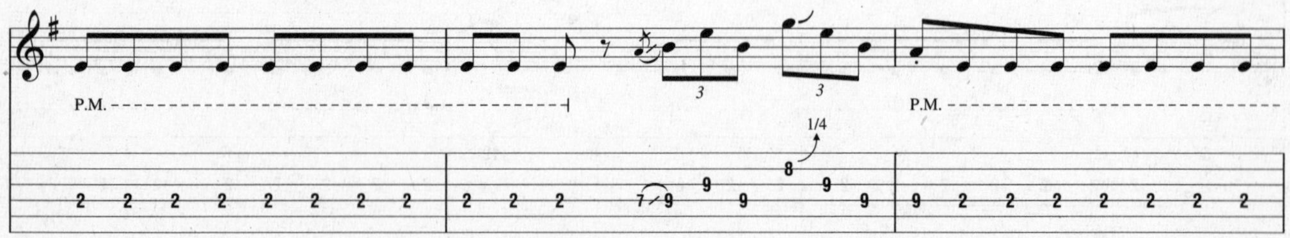

Fade out

Blaze of Glory

Words and Music by Jon Bon Jovi

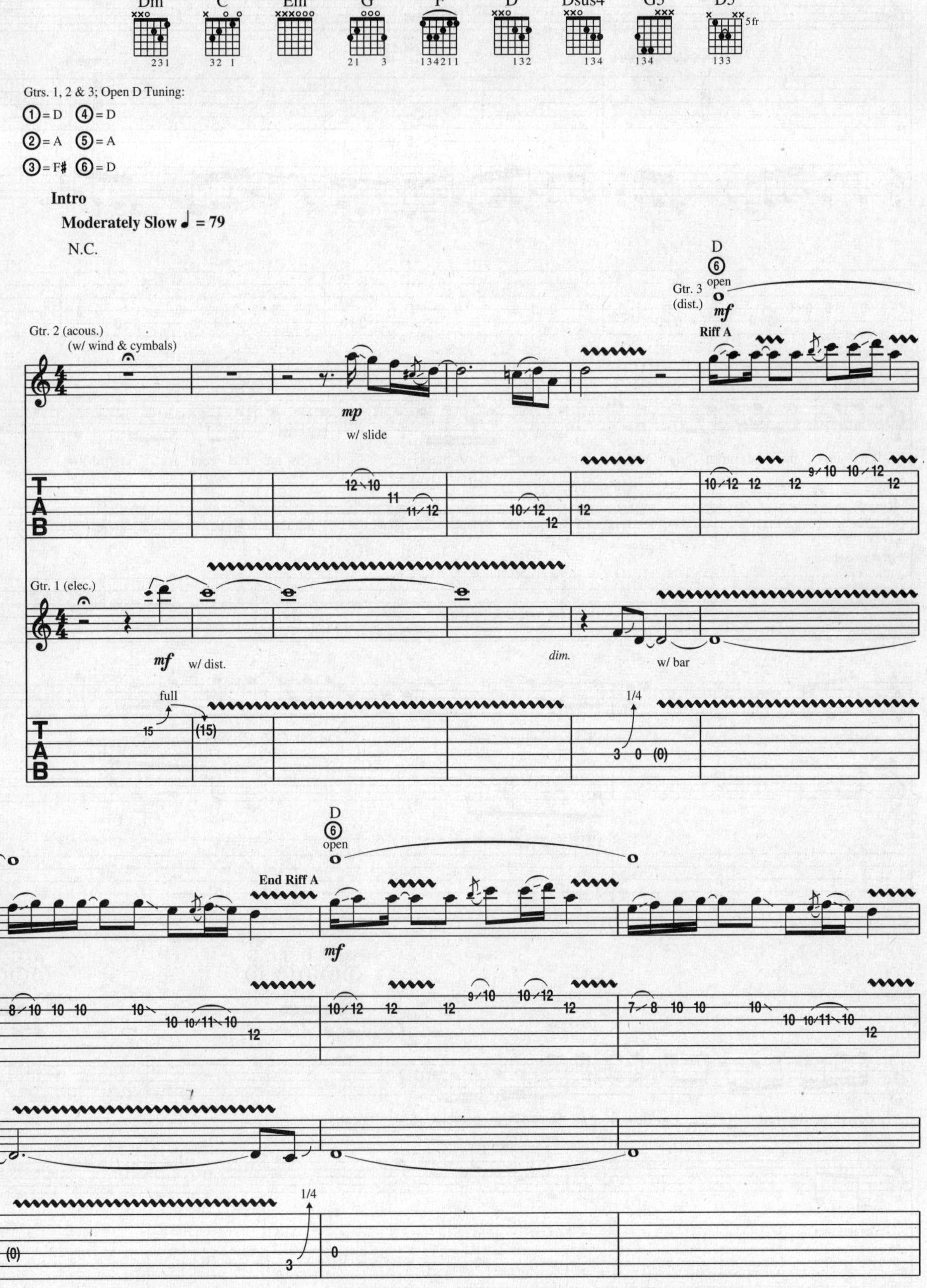

D
6
open
full
Verse
Gtrs. 1 & 3 tacet
*Dm
C
G
1. Wake up in the morn - ing and I raise my wea-ry head. I've got an old coat for a pil-low, and the
Gtr. 2
pp w/ o slide
Dm
F
C
earth was last night's bed. I don't know where I'm go-ing. On-ly God knows where I've been. I'm a
let ring
let ring
Gtr. 2: w/ Riff A, 2 times
A C D F
D
open 3fr open 3fr
open
G
Gtr. 1
dev-il on the run, a six-gun lov-er, a can-dle in the wind. Yeah!
let ring
let ring

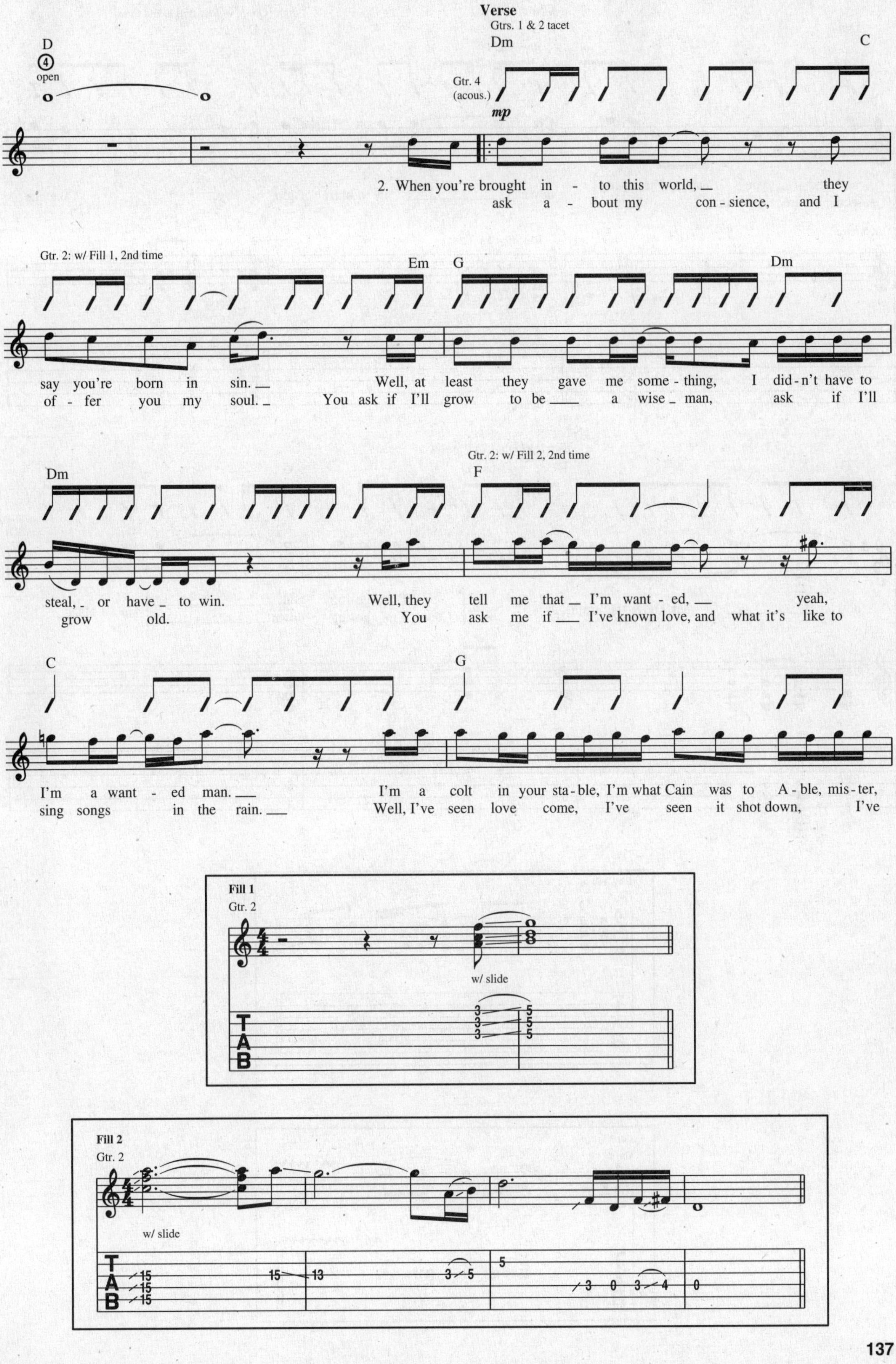

Verse

Gtrs. 1 & 2 tacet

D ④ open | Dm | C

Gtr. 4 (acous.) *mp*

2. When you're brought in - to this world, __ they
ask a - bout my con - science, and I

Gtr. 2: w/ Fill 1, 2nd time

Em G Dm

say you're born in sin. __ Well, at least they gave me some - thing, I did - n't have to
of - fer you my soul. __ You ask if I'll grow to be __ a wise _ man, ask if I'll

Gtr. 2: w/ Fill 2, 2nd time

Dm F

steal, _ or have _ to win. Well, they tell me that _ I'm want - ed, __ yeah,
grow old. You ask me if __ I've known love, and what it's like to

C G

I'm a want - ed man. __ I'm a colt in your sta - ble, I'm what Cain was to A - ble, mis - ter,
sing songs in the rain. __ Well, I've seen love come, I've seen it shot down, I've

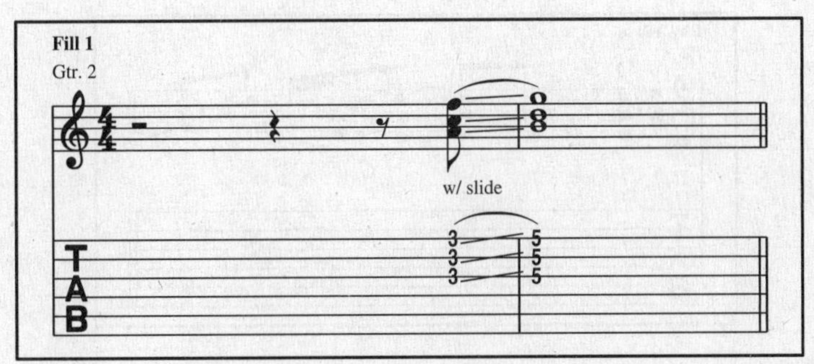

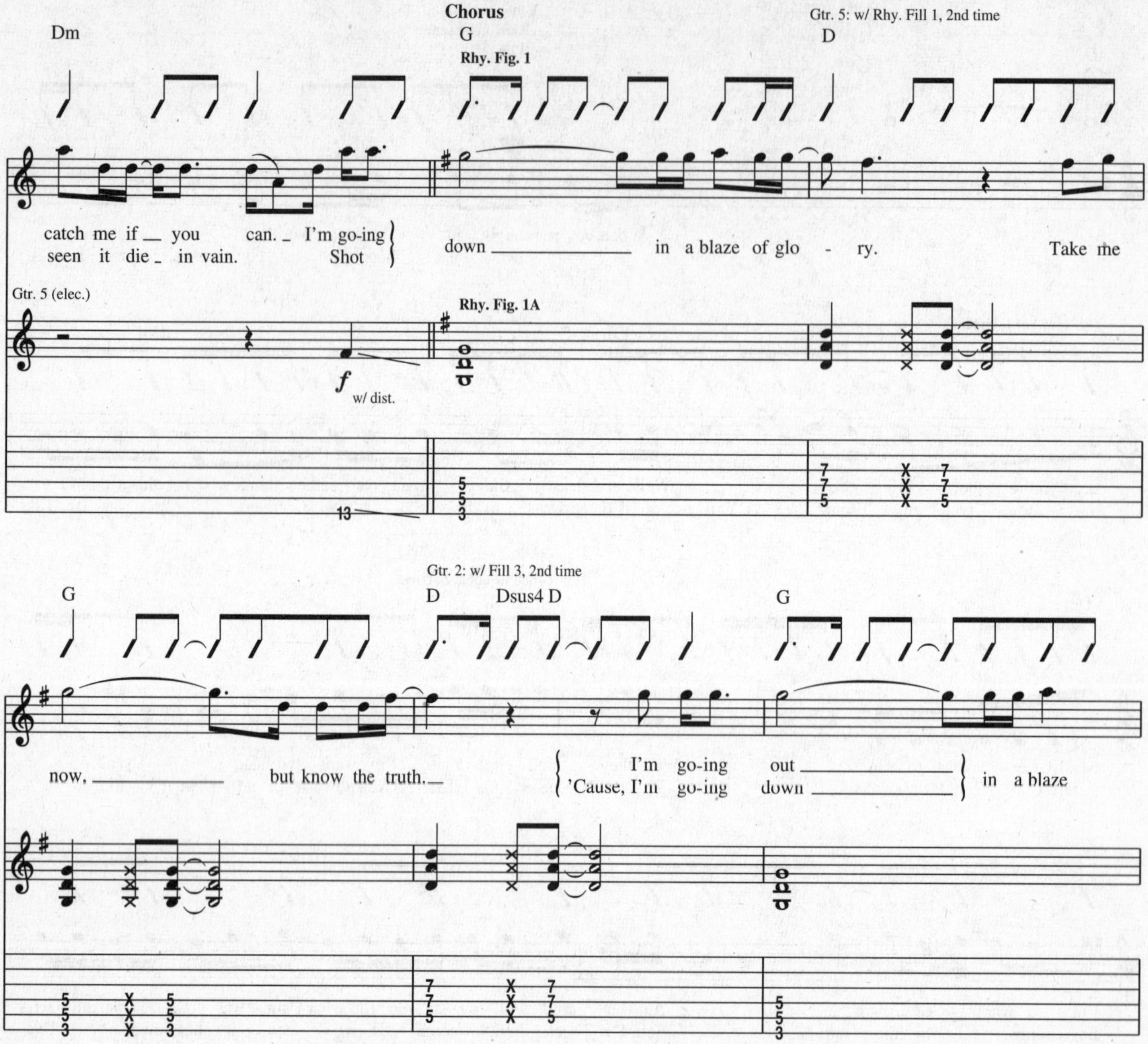

Chorus

Gtr. 5: w/ Rhy. Fill 1, 2nd time

Dm G D

Rhy. Fig. 1

catch me if _ you can. _ I'm go-ing
seen it die _ in vain. Shot
down _ in a blaze of glo - ry. Take me

Gtr. 5 (elec.)

Rhy. Fig. 1A

f w/ dist.

Gtr. 2: w/ Fill 3, 2nd time

G D Dsus4 D G

now, _ but know the truth. _
I'm go-ing out _
'Cause, I'm go-ing down _
in a blaze

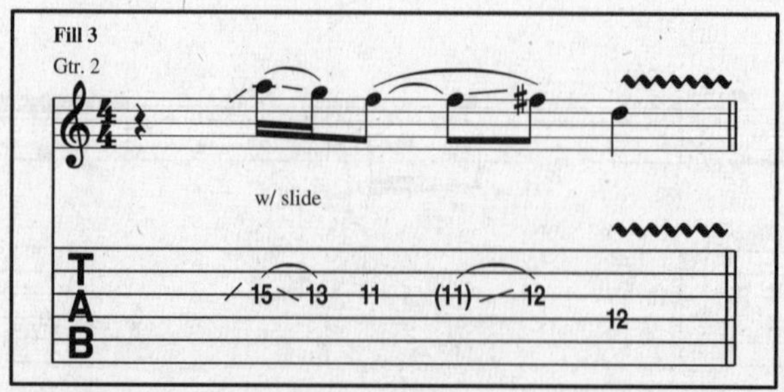

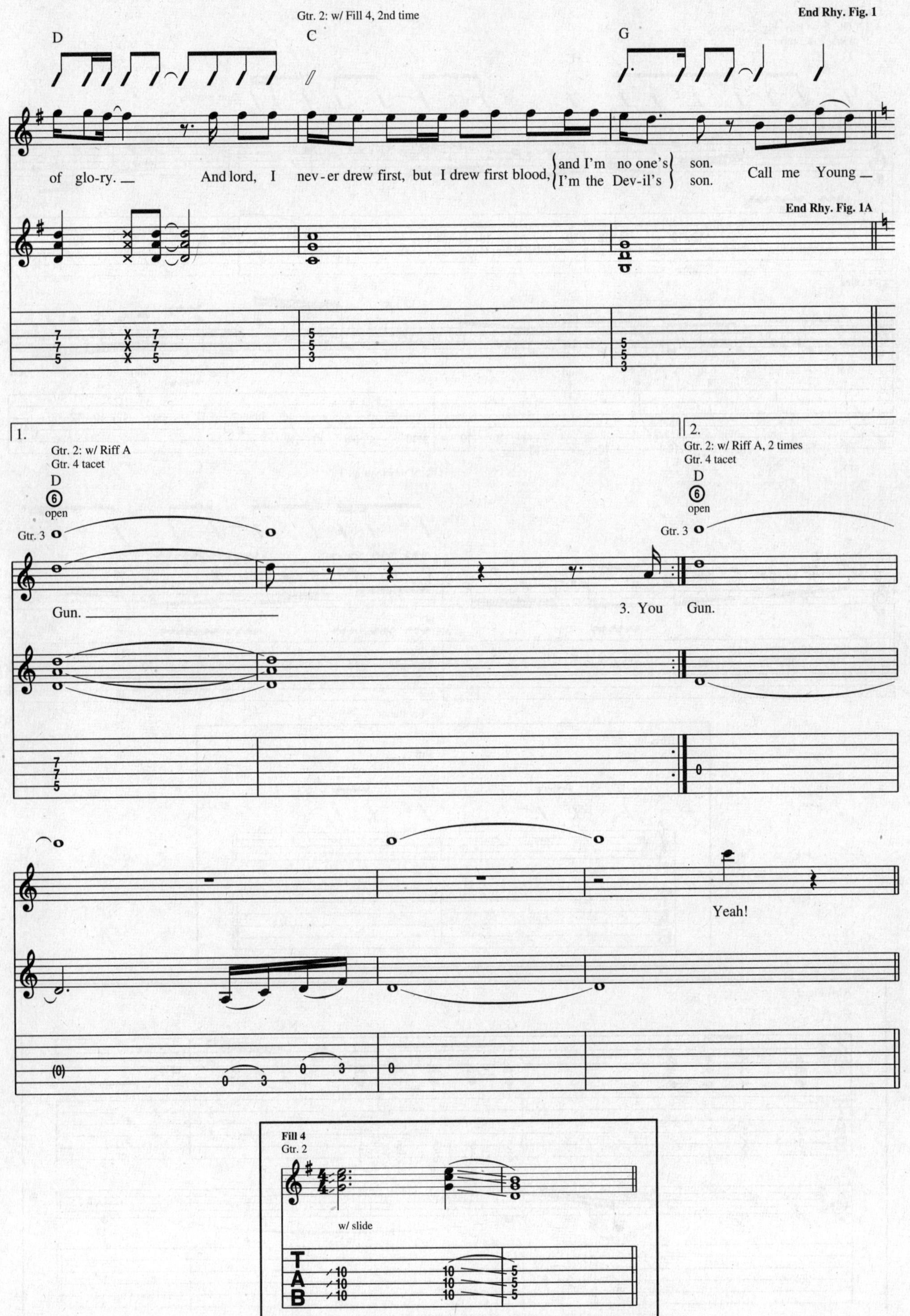

Gtr. 2: w/ Fill 4, 2nd time
End Rhy. Fig. 1
D
C
G
of glo-ry. And lord, I nev-er drew first, but I drew first blood, and I'm no one's son.
I'm the Dev-il's son.
Call me Young
End Rhy. Fig. 1A
1.
Gtr. 2: w/ Riff A
Gtr. 4 tacet
D
open
Gtr. 3
Gun.
2.
Gtr. 2: w/ Riff A, 2 times
Gtr. 4 tacet
D
open
Gtr. 3
3. You
Gun.
Yeah!
Fill 4
Gtr. 2
w/ slide

Guitar Solo
Gtr. 5: w/ Rhy. Fig. 2, 3 times
Gtrs. 2 & 3 tacet
G
D
G
Gtr. 4
cont. simile
*Gtr. 6
8va
loco
w/ slide
*clean elec.
D
G
full
D
Gtr. 5: w/ Rhy. Fig. 3
F
Gtr. 4
*bar flutter
Rhy. Fig. 2
G5
D5
Gtr. 5
Rhy. Fig. 3
Gtr. 5
F5
G5
N.C.

Gtr. 2: w/ Riff A, 2 times
Gtr. 4 tacet
Gtr. 6 tacet
G
N.C.
8va
Verse
Gtrs. 2 & 5 tacet
*Dm
C
G
4. Each night I go to bed, I pray the Lord my soul to keep. No, I ain't look-ing for for-give-ness, but be-
*Chords implied by kybd.
Dm
F
C
fore I'm six feet deep. Lord, I got to ask a fa - vor, and I hope you'll un-der-stand. 'Cause, I've
G
Dm
G
Dm
lived life to the ful-lest, let this boy die like a man. Star-ing down a bul-let, let me make my fi - nal stand.
Chorus
Gtr. 4 & 5: w/ Rhy. Figs. 1 & 1A
N.C.
G
D
G
D
Shot down in a blaze of glo - ry. Take me now, but know the truth. I'm go-ing
Gtr. 2
w/ slide
G
D
C
G
out in a blaze of glo-ry. Lord, I nev-er drew first, but I drew first blood, and I'm no one's son. Call me Young

Gtr. 2 tacet
D
C
G
D
Rhy. Fig. 4
End Rhy. Fig. 4
Gtr. 4
Gun.
I'm a young gun.
Yeah.
Young
Gtr. 6
w/ slide
Gtr. 5
Rhy. Fig. 4A
End Rhy. Fig. 4A
Outro
Gtrs. 4 & 5: w/ Rhy. Figs. 4 & 4A
Gtrs. 4, 5 & 6 tacet
open
Gtr. 3
gun.
Yeah, yeah, yeah. Young
Gun.
Ah.
Gtr. 2
Free Time
dim.
rit.
let ring

Blue Collar Man (Long Nights)

Words and Music by Tommy Shaw

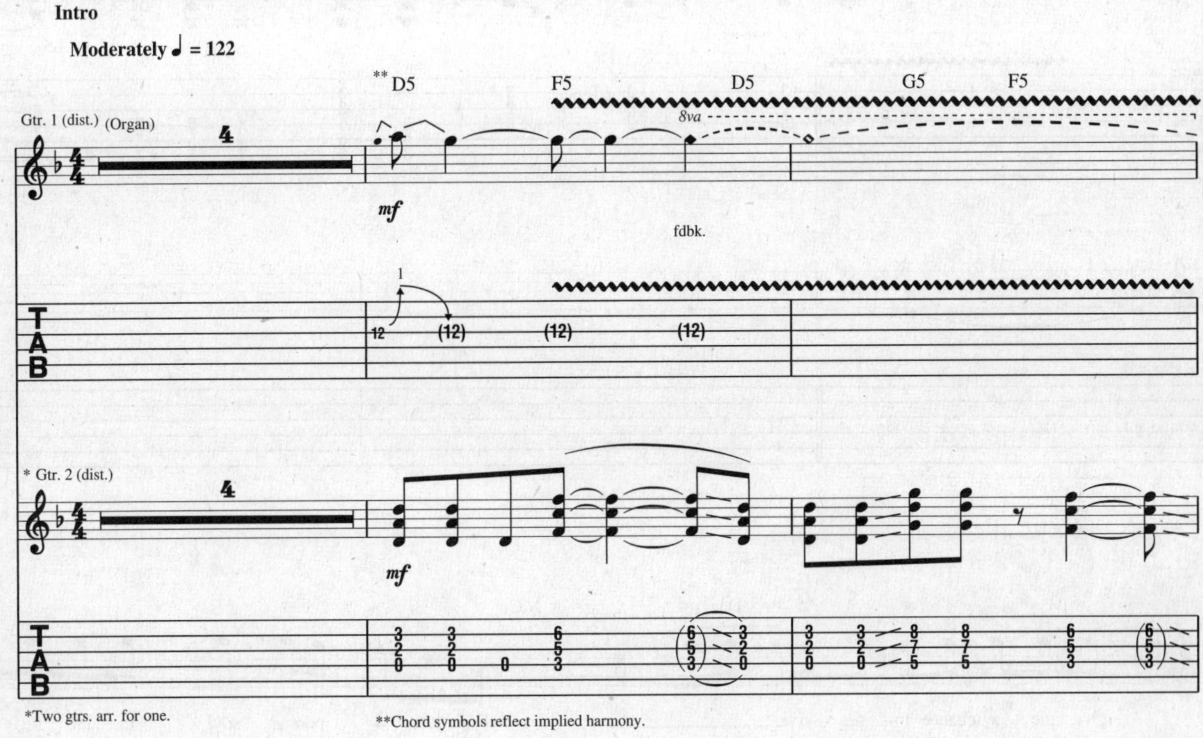

*Two gtrs. arr. for one.

**Chord symbols reflect implied harmony.

Verse
Gtr. 1 tacet
D5
G5
Gm
G5
Bb5
C5
1. Give me a job, give me se - cu - ri - ty,
Rhy. Fig. 1
* w/ wah-wah
P.M.
*Used as a filter

A5
D5
N.C.
D5
give me a chance to sur - vive. I'm just a poor soul in the un - em -
Gtr. 2
semi-harm.

Gm
Bb5
C5
Cb5
Bb5
N.C.
ploy - ment line, my God I'm hard - ly a - live. 2. My
End Rhy. Fig. 1

Verse
1st time, Gtr. 2: w/ Rhy. Fig. 1
2nd time, Gtr. 2: w/ Rhy. Fig. 1, 1st 3 meas.
D5
G5
Gm
G5
B♭5 C5
moth - er and fath - er, my wife and my friends,
3. Make me an of - fer that I can't re - fuse.
2nd time, Gtr. 2: w/ Rhy. Fill 1
2nd time, Gtr. 2: w/ Rhy. Fig. 1, last 4 meas.
A5 D5 N.C. D5
I see them laugh in my face. But I've got the pow - er, and I've
Make me a re - spect - ab - le man. This is my last time in the un - em -
Gm B♭5 C5 C♭5 B♭5 N.C.
got the will. I'm not a cha - ri - ty case.
ploy - ment line, so like it or not.
I'll take those...
Chorus
3rd time, Gtr. 1; w/ Fill 1
D5 B♭/D C5/D D5 B♭ C5
Voc. Fig. 1
End Voc. Fig. 1
(Long nights, im - pos - si - ble odds.)
1. Keep - in' my eye to the key -
2., 3. Keep - in' my back to the
Gtr. 2 Rhy. Fig. 2
P.M.
D5 D5 B♭/D C5/D D5
Voc. Fig. 2
To Coda
End Voc. Fig. 2
hole. If it takes...
wall. If it takes...
(All 1., 3. that 2., 4. night to be just what I am.)
Well, I'm
End Rhy. Fig. 2
P.M.
Rhy. Fill 1
Gtr. 2
Fill 1
Gtr. 1

1.

N.C. D5 N.C.

gon - na be a blue col - lar man.

Gtr. 1

Gtr. 2

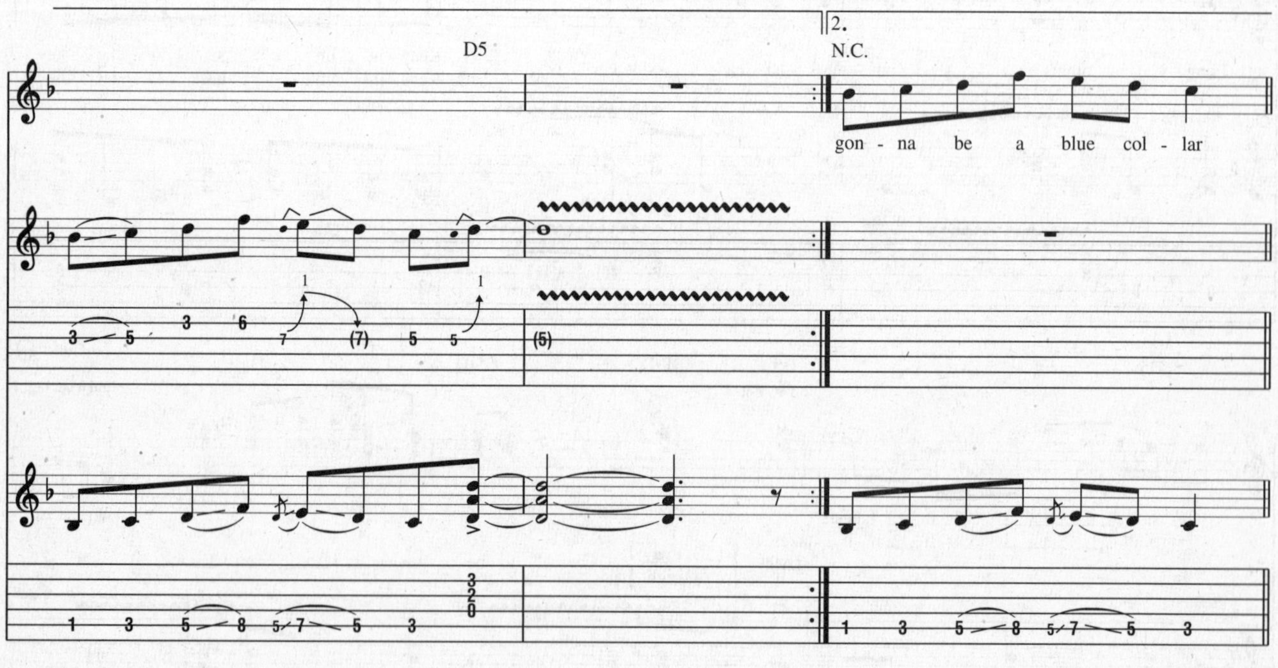

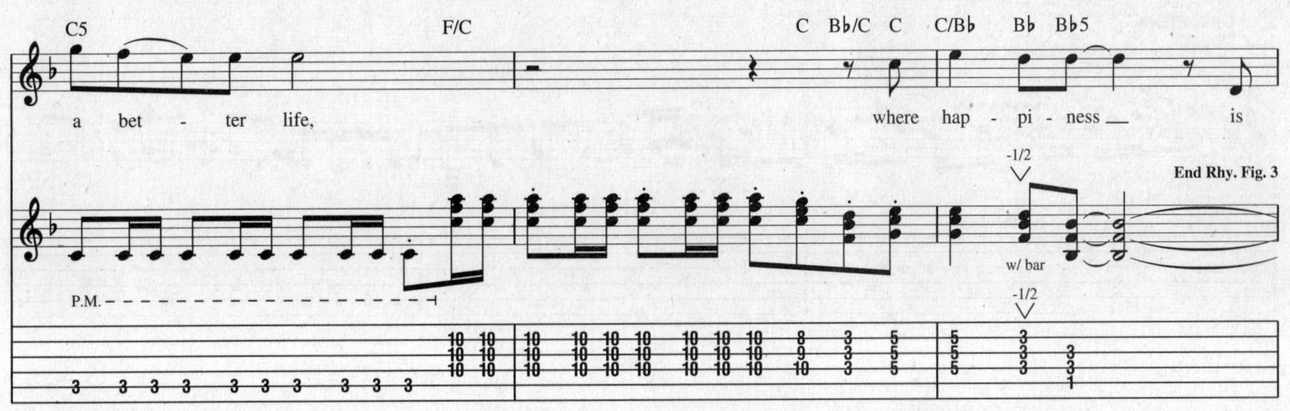

*Harmonic located six-tenths the distance between the 3rd & 4th frets.

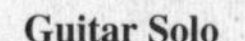
Guitar Solo

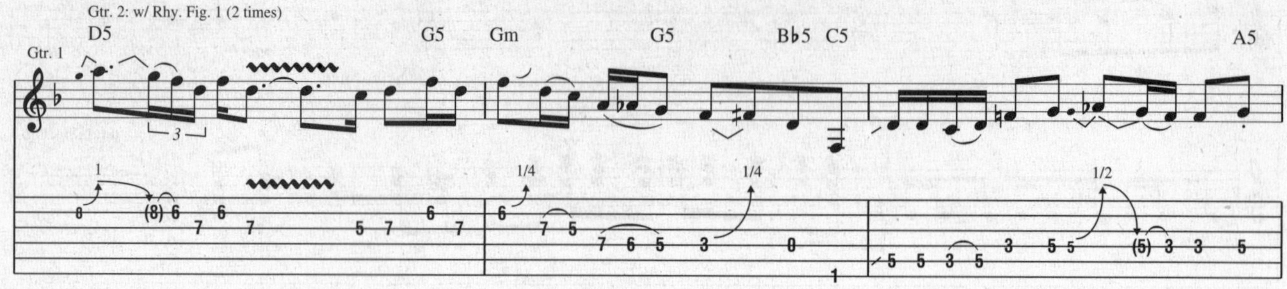
Gtr. 2: w/ Rhy. Fig. 1 (2 times)
D5
G5
Gm
G5
B♭5
C5
A5
Gtr. 1
1
1/4
1/4
1/2

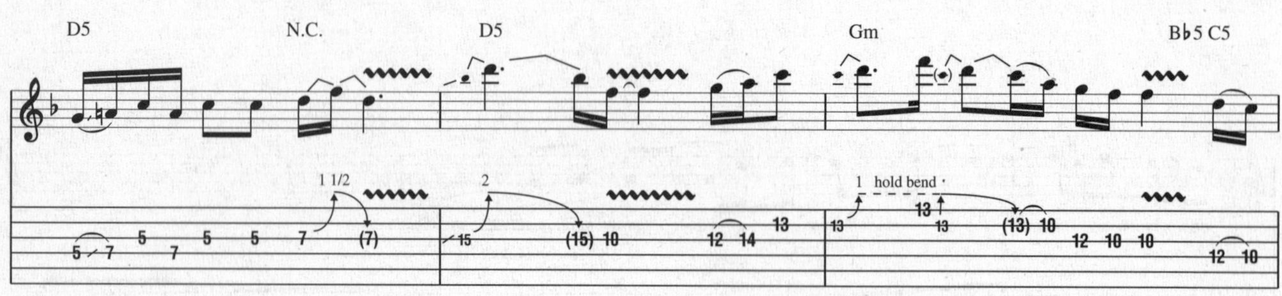
D5
N.C.
D5
Gm
B♭5 C5
1 1/2
2
1 hold bend

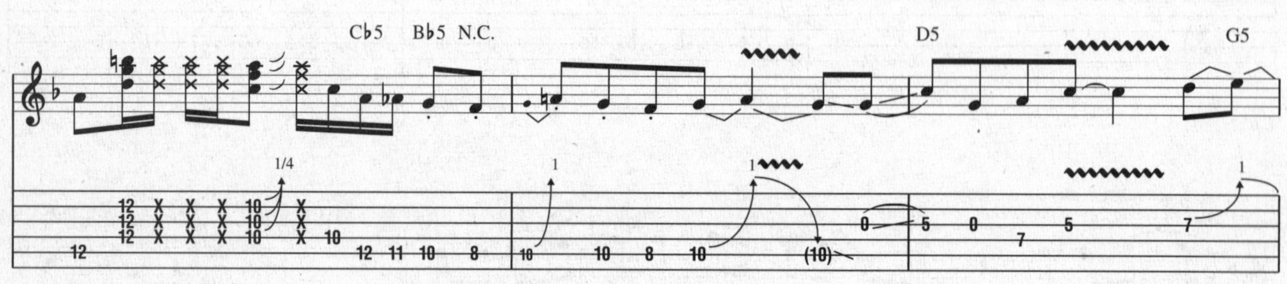
C♭5
B♭5
N.C.
D5
G5
1/4
1
1
1

Gm
G5
B♭5
C5
A5
D5
N.C.
1 1/2
1

D5
Gm
B♭5
C5
P.M.

Cb5 Bb5 N.C.

I'll take those...

P.M. 1 1/2 1

5 0 7 10 14 (14) 10 12 10 12 10 12 | 12 10 10 10 13 10 13 13 10 12 10 12 12 12 10 8

Coda

Interlude

Bb5 Bb C/Bb Bb

Voc. Fig. 3

gon - na be a blue col - lar man.

(Do, do, do, do, do,

8va

Gtr. 2

fdbk.

1 3 5 8 7 5 8 6 8 8 | | (8) |

pitch: C

Gtr. 2 tacet

Bkdg. Voc.: w/ Voc. Fig. 3 (3 times)

C/Bb Bb C/Bb B C/Bb Bb C/Bb Bb

End Voc. Fig. 3

You don't un-der - stand.

do, do, do.)

Gtr. 1

loco

steady gliss. P.M.

1 6 6 6 6 6 6 6 6 6 6 6 6 8 8 8 6 8 8 8 6

C/Bb F5 Bb5 C5

I'll take those...

8va loco

steady gliss. P.H.

8 8 8 6 8 8 8 6 8 8 8 6 8 8 8 6 8 8 6 8 8 6 8 8 6 3 3 1 3 3 1 | 8 8 8 6 8 8 8 6 8 8 8 6 8 8 8 6 8 8 8 6 8 8 8 6 X X X 6 8 8 8 6 | 6 8 8 6 8 8 8 6 10 10 8

pitch: D

Chorus
Bkgd. Voc.: w/ Voc. Fig. 1
Gtr. 2: w/ Rhy. Fig. 2
D5 B♭/D C5/D D5 B♭5 C5
Keep - in' my eye to the key -
Bkgd. Voc.: w/ Voc. Fig. 2
D5 D5 B♭/D C5/D D5 N.C.
- hole. If it takes... Well I'd
D5
rath - er be a blue col - lar, rath - er be a blue col - lar, gon - na be a blue col - lar man.
Gtr. 1
Gtr. 2
8va
loco
fdbk.
pitch: A
fdbk.
pitch: A

Outro
D5
F5
F5 G5
F
Al - right.
8va
loco
fdbk.
P.S.
pitch: G
w/ wah-wah
let ring
N.C.
Spoken: Be - lieve it.
rit.
pitch: A

Blue Sky

Words and Music by Dickey Betts

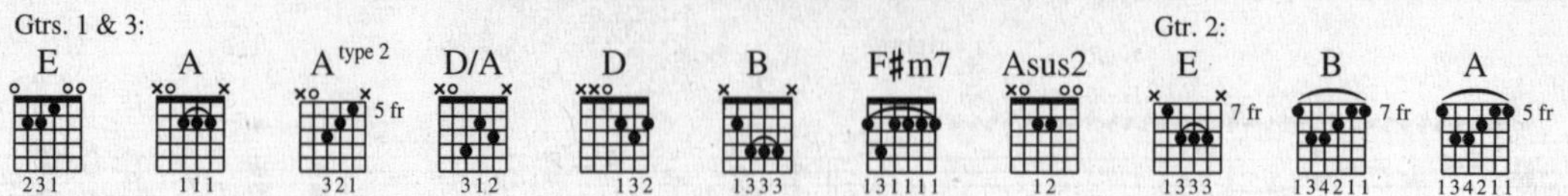

Intro

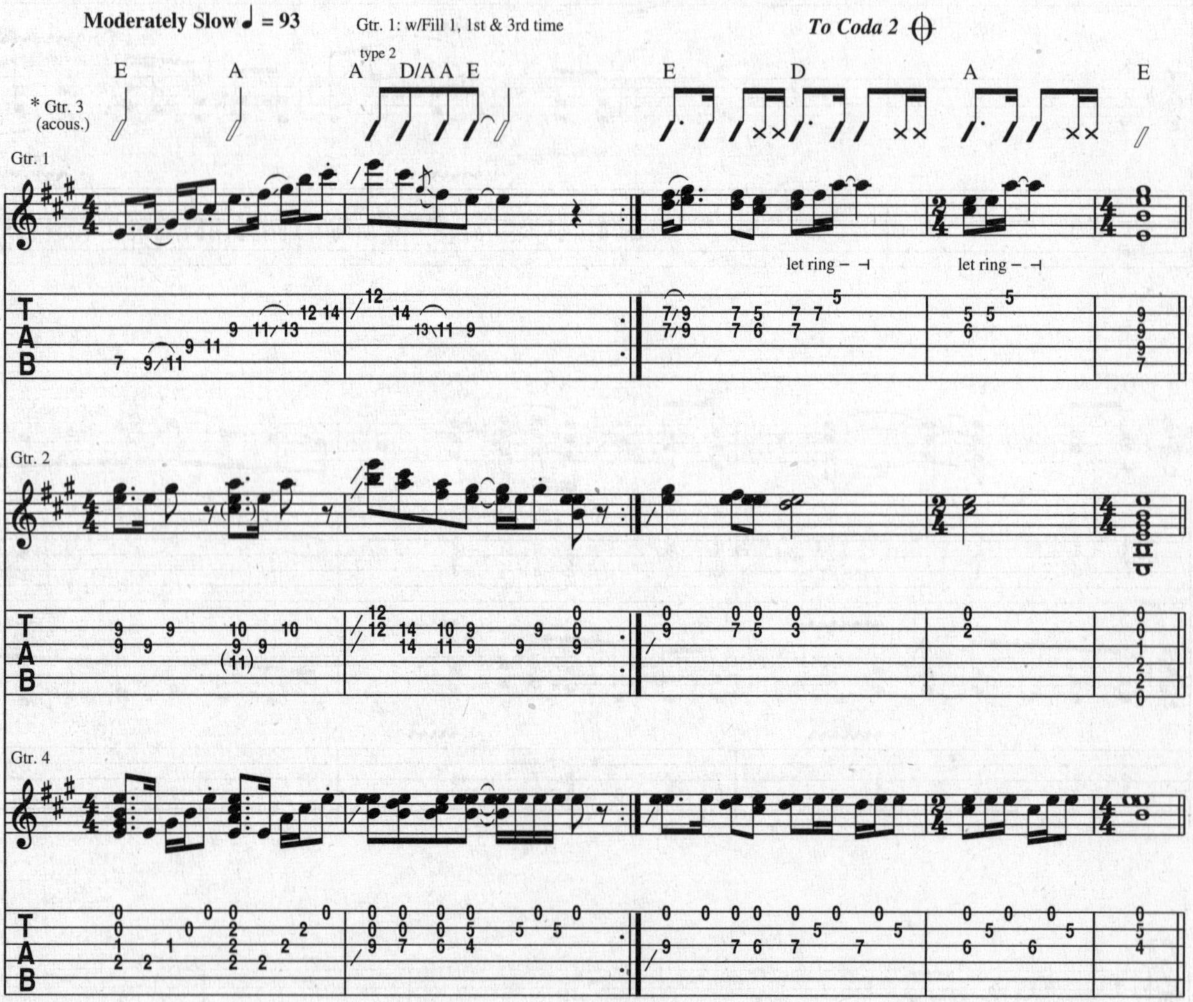

Moderately Slow ♩ = 93

Gtr. 1: w/Fill 1, 1st & 3rd time

To Coda 2 ⊕

E A A type 2 D/A A E E D A E

* Gtr. 3 (acous.)

Gtr. 1

let ring

let ring

Gtr. 2

Gtr. 4

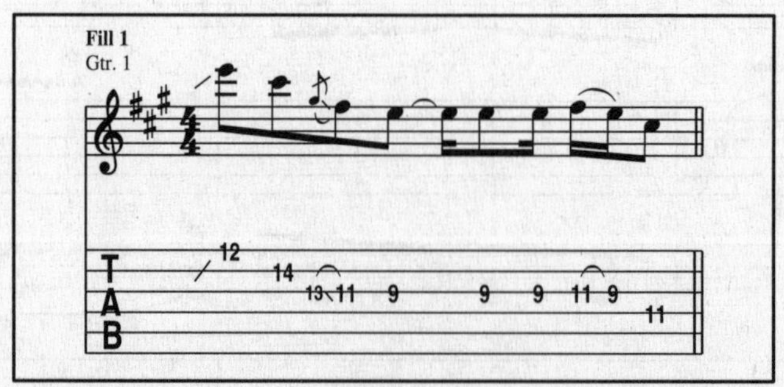

Verse

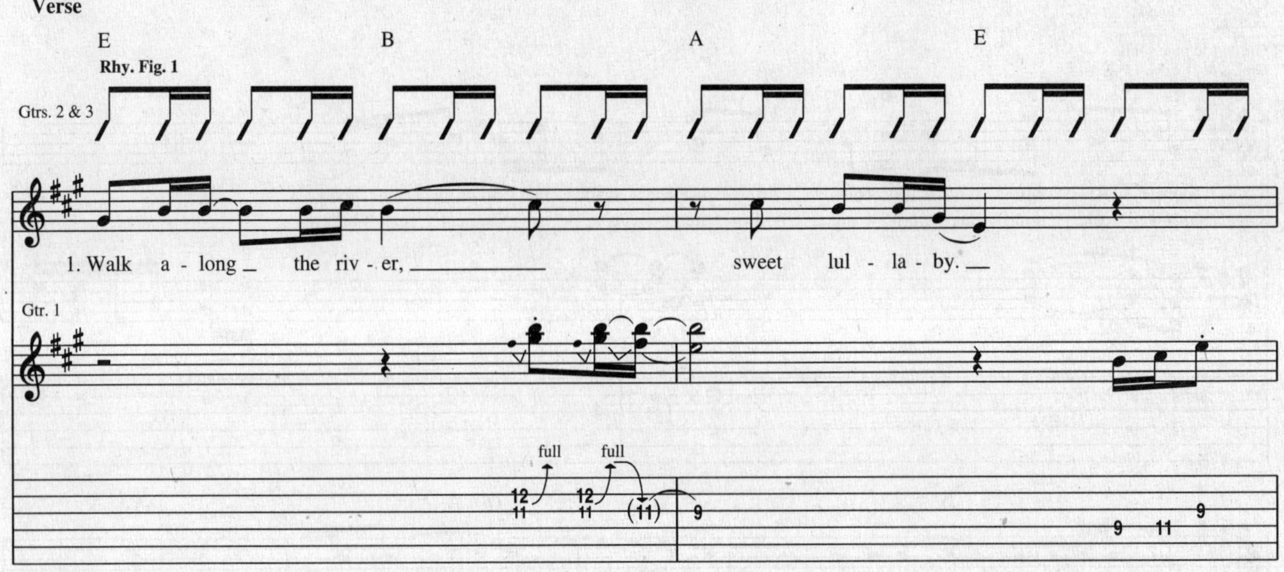
E
B
A
E
Rhy. Fig. 1
Gtrs. 2 & 3
1. Walk a - long _ the riv - er, ___ sweet lul - la - by. __
Gtr. 1
full
full
12 11
12 11
(11)
9
9 11 9

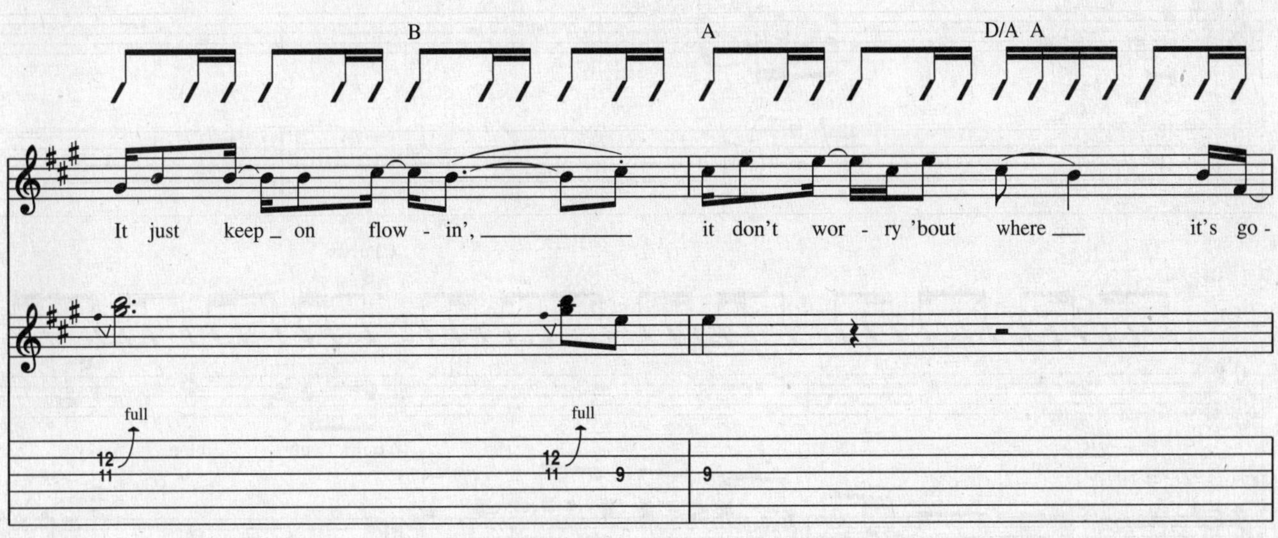
B
A
D/A A
It just keep _ on flow - in', ___ it don't wor - ry 'bout where __ it's go -
full
full
12 11
12 11 9
9

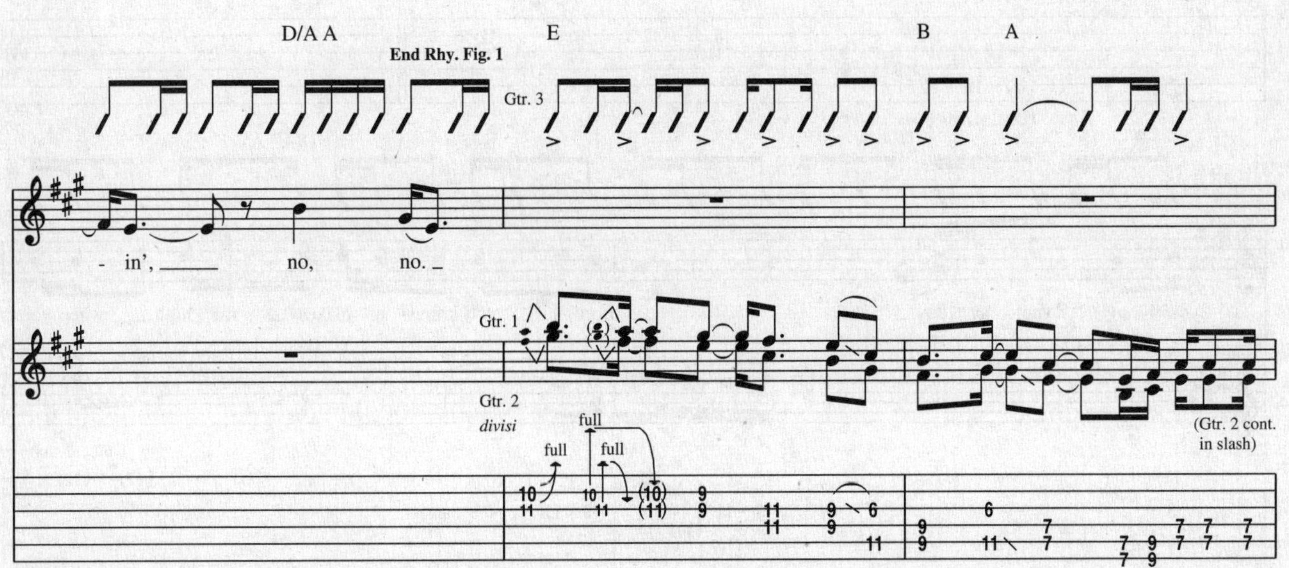
D/A A
End Rhy. Fig. 1
E
B A
Gtr. 3
- in', ___ no, no. _
Gtr. 1
Gtr. 2
divisi
full
full
full
(Gtr. 2 cont. in slash)

Gtr. 1: 2nd time simile
Gtrs. 2 & 3: w/Rhy. Fig. 1
E B A E
Don't fly Mis - ter Blue - bird, I'm just walk - in' down the road.
2. Good old Sun - day morn - ing, bells are ring - in' ev - ery where.
Gtr. 1
8va
full
B A D/A A D/A A
Ear - ly morn - in' sun - shine tell me all I need to know, know.
Goin' to Car - o - lin - na, won't be long and I'll be there.
8va
full full full
Chorus
E A B A
Gtr. 3
You're my blue sky,
Gtr. 1
Gtr. 2
divisi
full full
Gtr. 2 cont. in slash (simile)
full full
*Gtr. 2 to right of slash in TAB.
E D/A A B D/A A
Gtr. 2 & 3
you're my sun - ny day. Lord, you know it makes me high when you
Gtr. 1
1 1/2 full

Guitar Solo

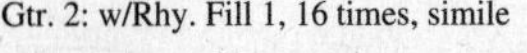

Gtr. 2: w/Rhy. Fill 1, 16 times, simile

Gtr. 3: cont. rhythm simile

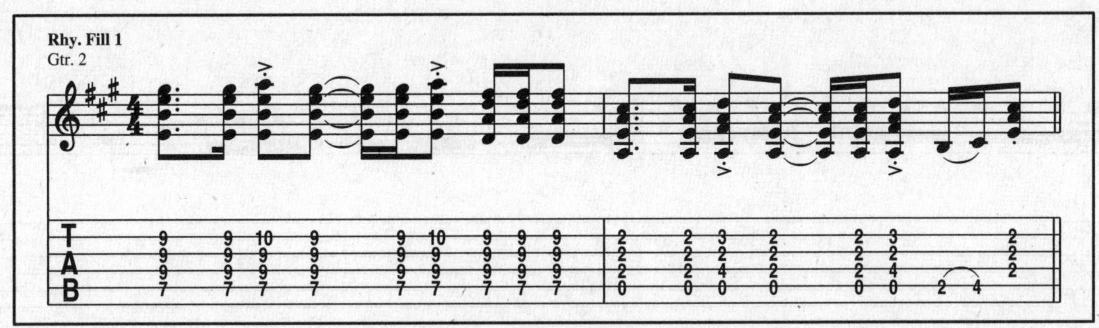

A
E
A
1 1/2
full
E
A
full
full
full
1 1/2
slow release
full
E
A
E
full
full
full
1 1/2
full
A
E
8va
full
full
A
E
8va
loco
A
E

A
E
8va
A
E
A
E
8va
8va
A
E
loco
A
full
E
full
full
full 1/2
A
8va
E
8va
full
A

*Gtr. 2 to right of slash in TAB.

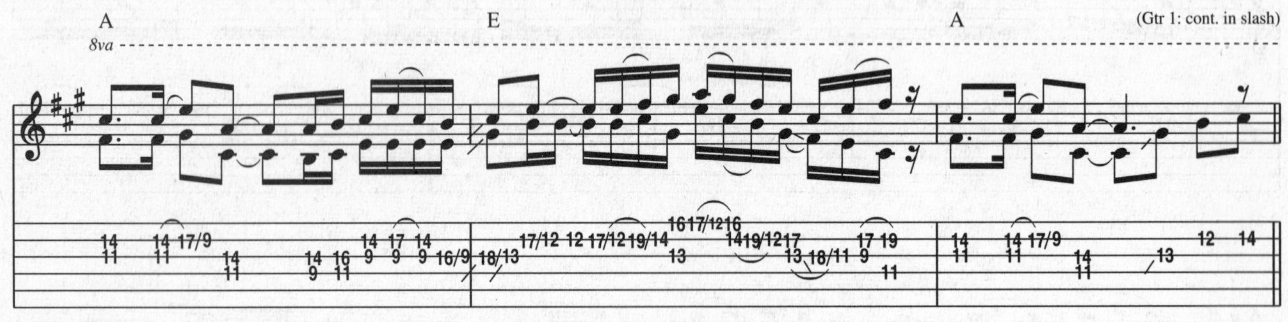

Guitar Solo

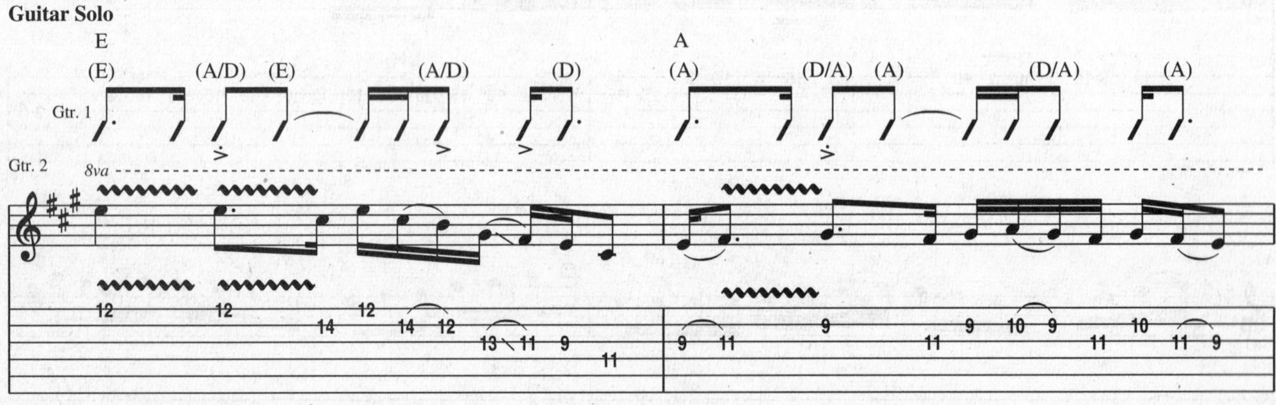

Gtr 1: cont. rhythm simile

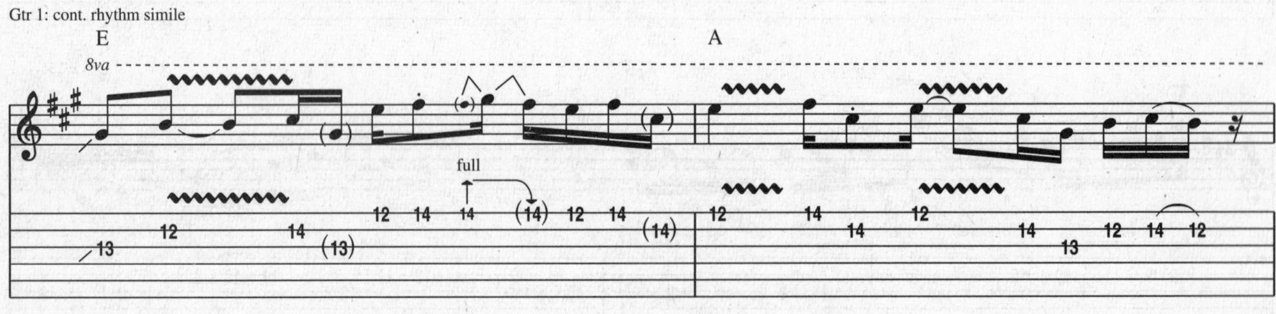

E
8va
A
E
A
E
A
full
E
A
E
A
E
A
E
A
E
A
E
A

E
A
8va

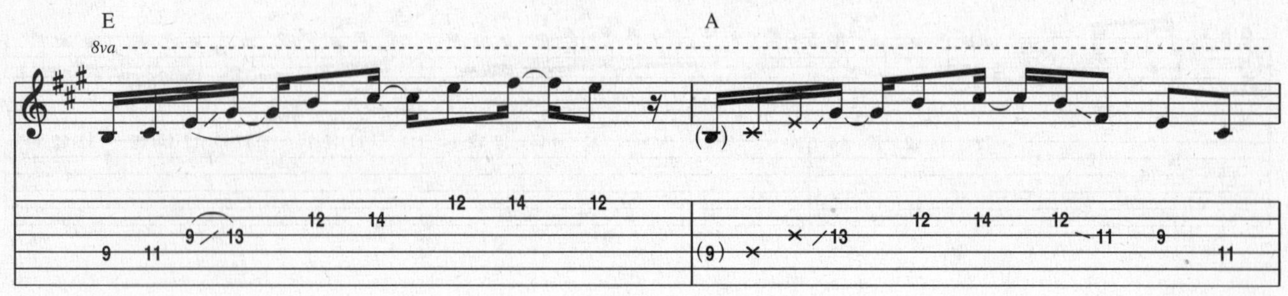
E
A
8va

E
A
8va

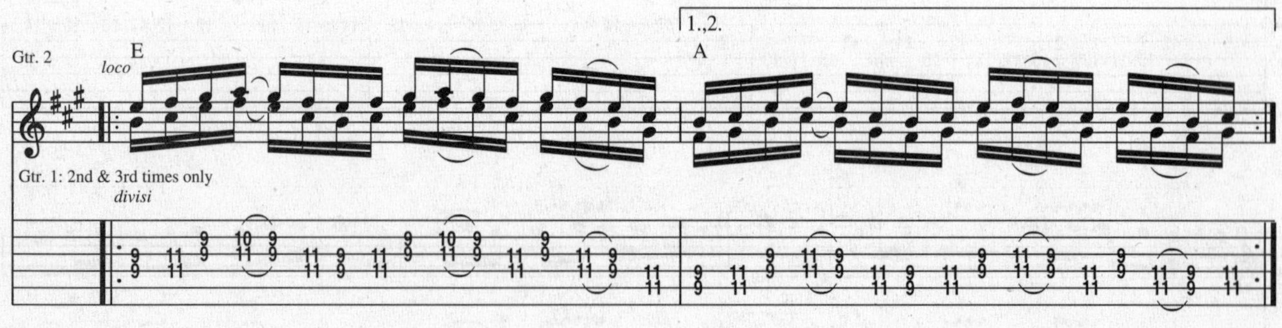
1.,2.
Gtr. 2
E
loco
A
Gtr. 1: 2nd & 3rd times only
divisi

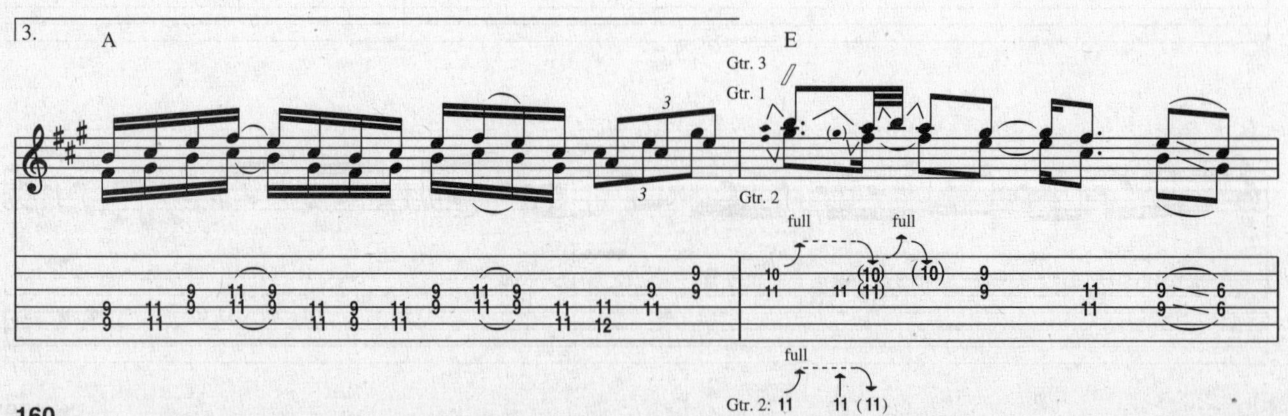
3.
A
E
Gtr. 3
Gtr. 1
Gtr. 2
full
full
full
Gtr. 2: 11 11 (11)

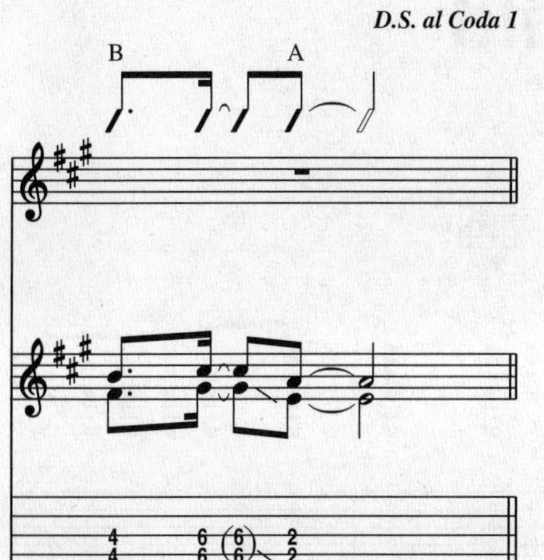

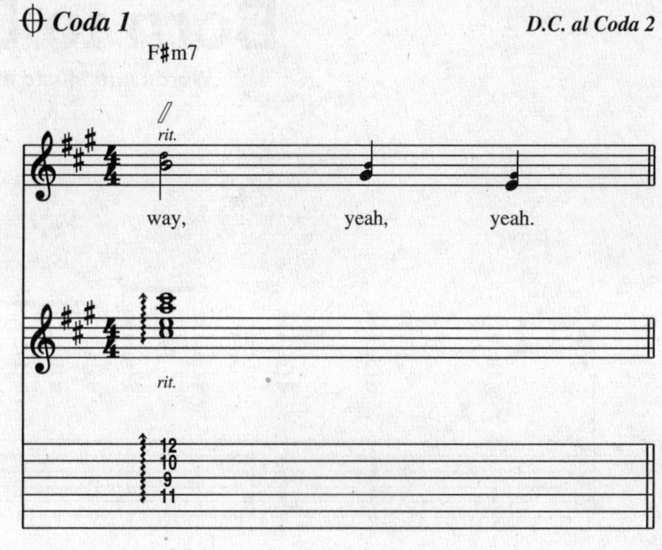

Coda 2

A

Asus2

E

Gtr. 3

Gtr. 1

Gtr. 2

Gtr. 4

Born to Be Wild

Words and Music by Mars Bonfire

Pre-Chorus
Gtr. 1: w/ Fill 1, 2nd time
G A E G A E
Yeah, darlin' go make it hap - pen, take the world in a love em - brace.
let ring
let ring
3/4
let ring
let ring
full

Gtr. 1: w/ Fill 2, 2nd time
Gtr. 1: w/ Fill 3, 3rd time
1.
G A E G A E5
Fire all of your guns at once and ex - plode in - to space.
let ring
let ring
let ring
let ring

2., 3.
E G
Like a true na - ture's child we were born, born to be wild.

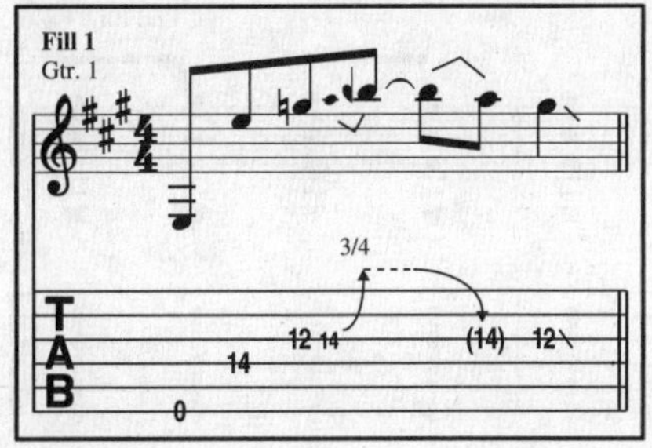
Fill 1
Gtr. 1
3/4

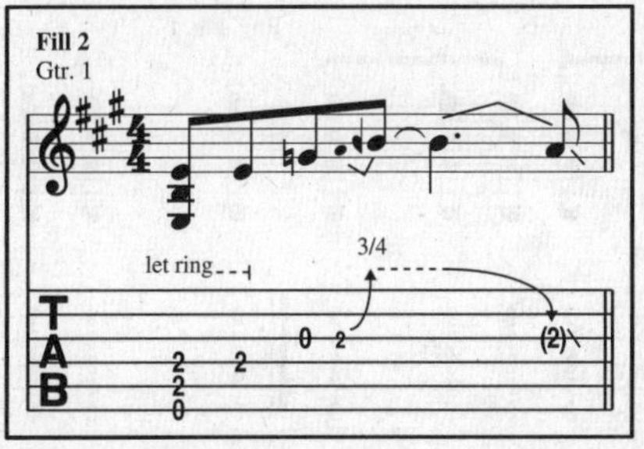
Fill 2
Gtr. 1
let ring
3/4

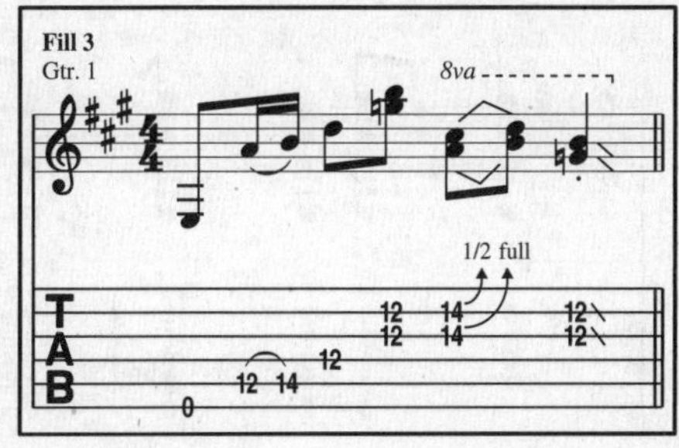
Fill 3
Gtr. 1
8va
1/2 full

Chorus

To Coda

Organ Solo

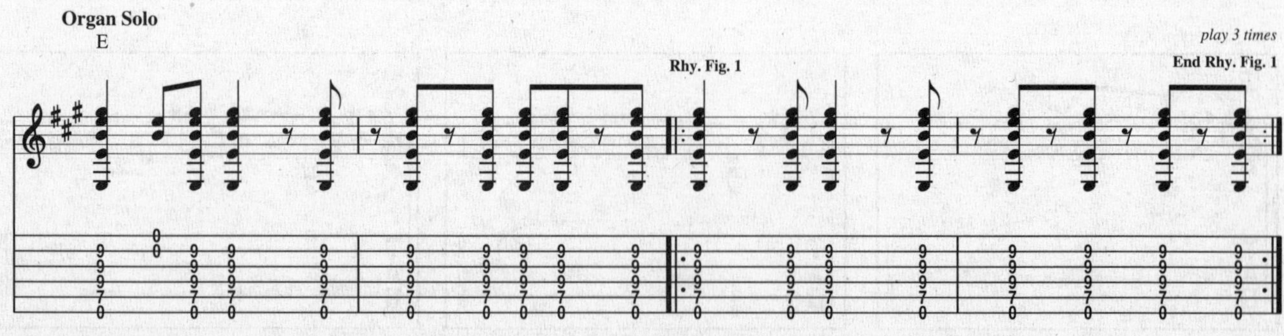

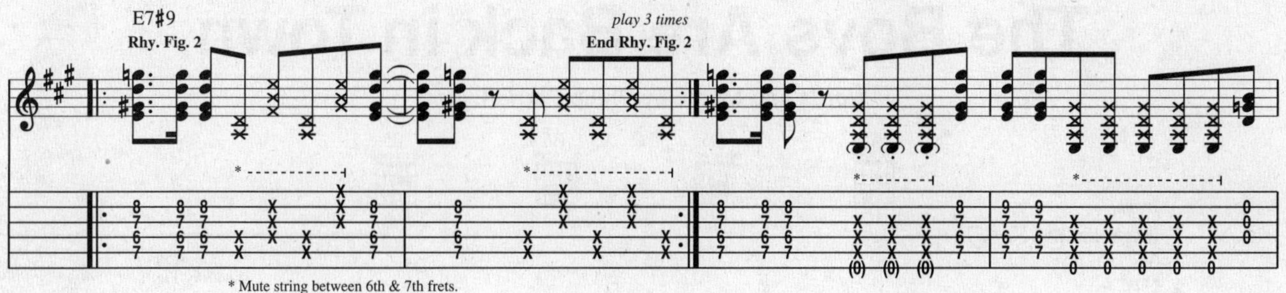
E7#9
Rhy. Fig. 2
play 3 times
End Rhy. Fig. 2
* Mute string between 6th & 7th frets.

D.S. al Coda
E
Gtr. 1
Gtrs. 1 & 2 tacet
Gtr. 2
8va
p
w/ slide
Coda
Outro
Gtr. 1: w/ Rhy. Fig 1, 4 times, simile
Gtr. 1: w/ Rhy. Fig. 2, 1 1/2 times
E
E7#9
Gtr. 2
w/ slide

Fade Out
8va
Gtr. 1: w/ Fill 4

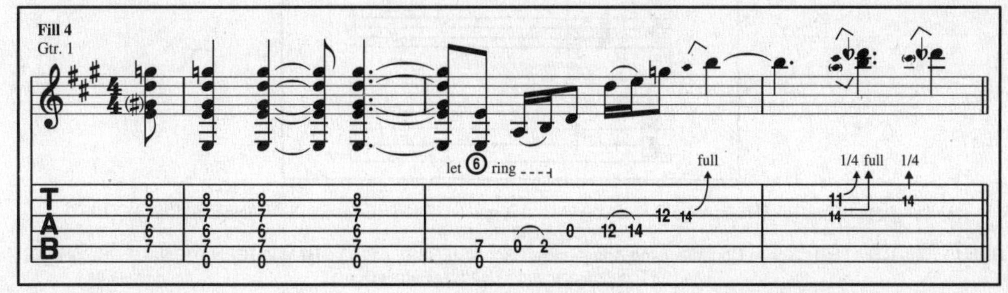
Fill 4
Gtr. 1
let ⑥ ring
full
1/4 full
1/4
T
A
B

The Boys Are Back in Town

Words and Music by Philip Parris Lynott

F#7 sus 4
Bm7
Bm7/E
Gtr 3: w/ fill 2, 2nd time
A5
Have - n't changed, had - n't much _ to say, but man, I still think them _ cats are cra - zy.
Man, when I tell you she was cool, she was red hot! I mean she was steamin'!
The drink will flow and blood will spill, and if the boys wan - na fight you better let'em.
*for Bm7/E mute A string w/1st finger of left hand.
Gtr 2: 3rd time w/ Fill 4
let ring
C#m7
D
F
C#m7
They were ask - in' if you were a - round, how you was, _ where you could _ be found.
And that time over at Johnny's place, well this chick _ got up and she slapped Johnny's face.
That juke-box in the corner blastin' out my favorite song. The nights are getting warm and it won't be long.
let ring
Fill 2
Gtr 3
1/2
Fill 4
Gtr 2
let ring

F#7sus4
Bm7
Bm7/E
A5
Told them you were liv-in' down - town, driv-in' all the old men cra - zy. The
Man, we just fell a-bout the place. If that chick don't wan - na know, forget her.
Won't be long 'till sum-mer comes, now that the boys are here again.
Gtrs. 1&3: continue above
let ring
Gtr 2: 3rd time w/ Fill 5.
Chorus
Gtrs. 1&3: w/ Rhy. Fig. 1 (3 times)
B5
D5
A5
boys are back in town. The boys are back in town. I said the
Gtr. 2
to Coda
boys are back in town. The boys are back in town. The
Fill 5
Gtr 2:

B5
D5
boys are back in town. The boys are back in town. The boys are back in town.
The boys
Gtr. 3 tacet
N.C.
are back in town.
Gtr. 1
Rhy. Fig. 3
Gtr. 2
Rhy. Fig. 4
End Rhy. Fig. 3
A5
End Rhy. Fig. 4
Gtr. 2: w/ Fill 3, 2nd time
full
Fill 3
Gtr. 2:

Bridge

Dsus4 D C#m7 F#7sus4 Bmin7

Spread the word __ a-round.

Gtrs 1&3:

Rhy. Fig. 2

E9sus4 F#7sus4

Guess who's back in town. _

P.M.

End Rhy. Fig. 2

Dsus4 D C#m7 F#7sus4 Bm7

You _ spread the word a-round.

Gtrs. 1&3

Gtr. 2: w/ Rhy. Fig. 2

E9sus4 F#7sus4 *D.S. al Coda*

End Rhy. Fig. 2

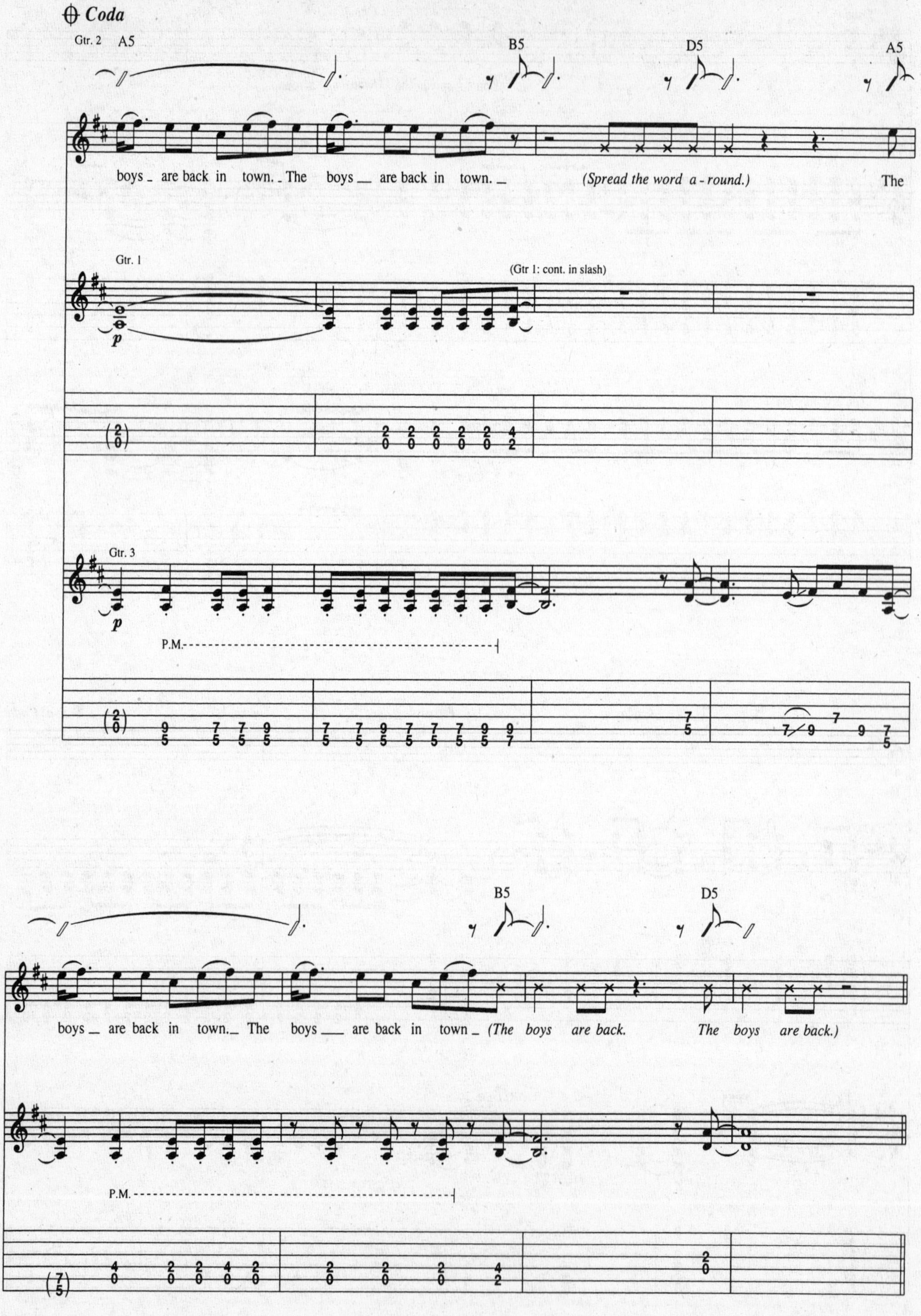

𝄌 *Coda*

Gtr. 2 A5 B5 D5 A5

boys _ are back in town. _ The boys __ are back in town. _ *(Spread the word a - round.)* The

Gtr. 1

(Gtr 1: cont. in slash)

p

Gtr. 3

p

P.M.

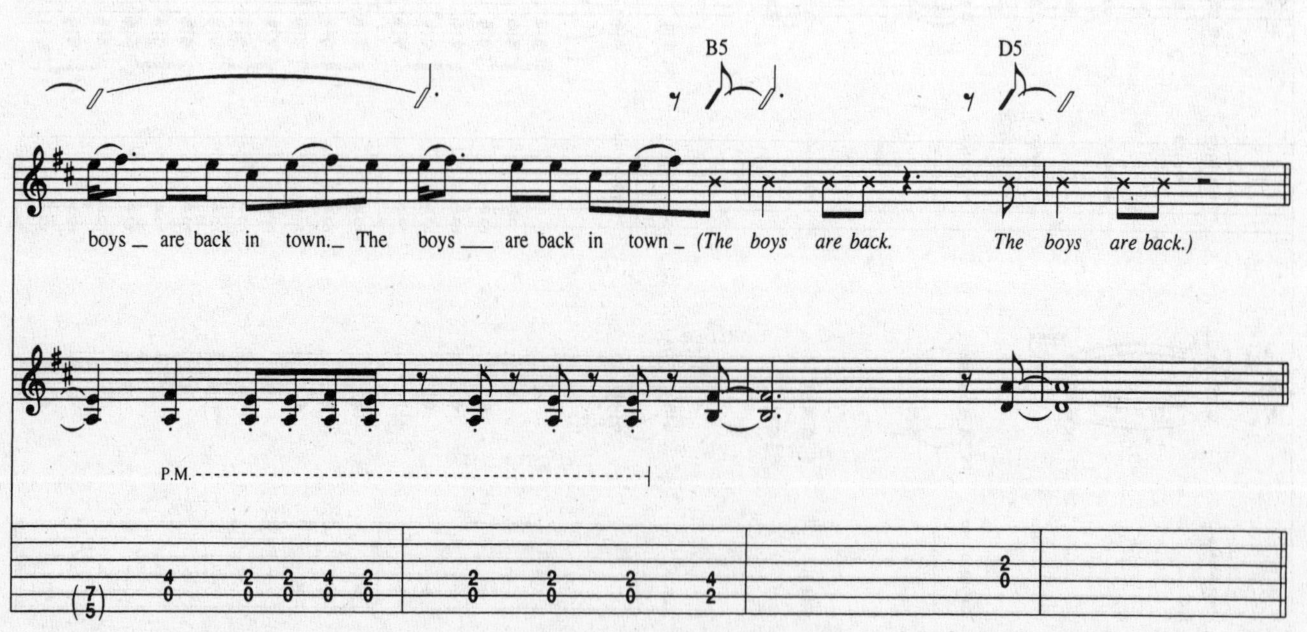

Gtr. 1 N.C.
Gtr. 2
D5
Gtr. 3:
E5
(Gtr. 1: play chords w/ Gtr. 3, 2nd time)
2nd time only
2nd time only
Gtr. 1: w/ Rhy. Fig. 3 (7 times)
Gtr. 2: w/ Rhy. Fig. 4 (7 times)
N.C.
Gtr. 3: w/ Fill 6 (2 times)
The boys are back in town a - gain.
Gtr. 4: w/ Fill 7
'Been hang - in' down at Di - no's
Fill 6
Gtr.3
Fill 7
Gtr. 4

The boys are back_ in town_ a-gain._
Gtr. 3
Gtr. 4
hold bend
full
fade

Breakdown

Words and Music by Tom Petty

Intro

Moderate Rock ♩ = 110

* Fender Rhodes elec. piano arr. for gtr.

** Chord symbols reflect overall harmony.

Verse
Gtr. 1: w/ Rhy. Fig. 1 (3 1/2 times)
Gtr. 2 tacet
Am G Am G Am G Am G Am G
1. It's al - right if you love me, it's al - right if you don't. I'm not a - fraid of you
2. There is no sense in pre - tend-ing; your eyes give you a - way. Some - thin' in - side you is
Gtr. 3 (clean)
Rhy. Fig. 2
mf
w/ echo
Am G Am G
1.
Gtr. 3 tacet
F F6 Famj7 F6
run - nin' a - way, hon - ey, I get the feel - ing you won't.
feel - in' like I do. We've said all there is to
Whispered: (I said...)
End Rhy. Fig. 2 Rhy. Fig. 3
Gtr. 1
End Rhy. Fig. 3
2.
Gtr. 1: w/ Rhy. Fig. 3
F F6 Famj7 F6
Chorus
2nd time, Gtr. 5: w/ Fill 1
A5 G5 F5 G5
say. Ba - by. Break - down, go a - head, give it to me.
Gtr. 4 (fuzz)
Rhy. Fill 1A
End Rhy. Fill 1A Rhy. Fig. 4
Gtrs. 2 & 4
End Rhy. Fig. 4
f
Fill 1
Gtr. 5
w/ bar

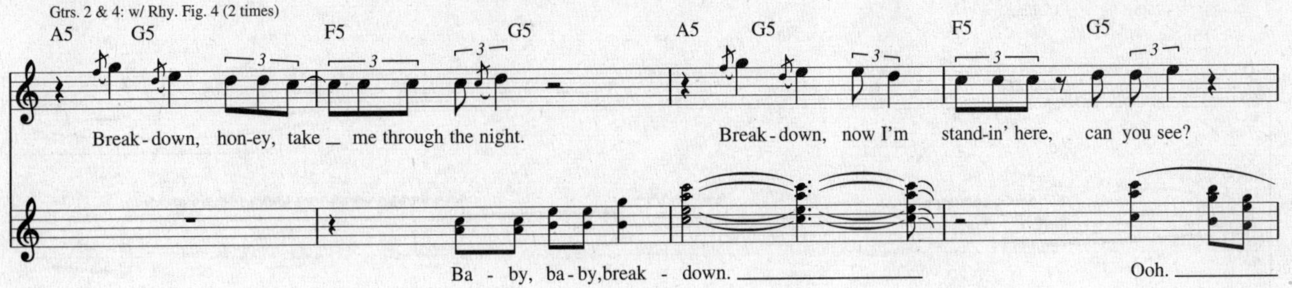
Gtrs. 2 & 4: w/ Rhy. Fig. 4 (2 times)
A5 G5 F5 G5 A5 G5 F5 G5
Break - down, hon - ey, take _ me through the night. Break - down, now I'm stand - in' here, can you see?
Ba - by, ba - by, break - down. Ooh.
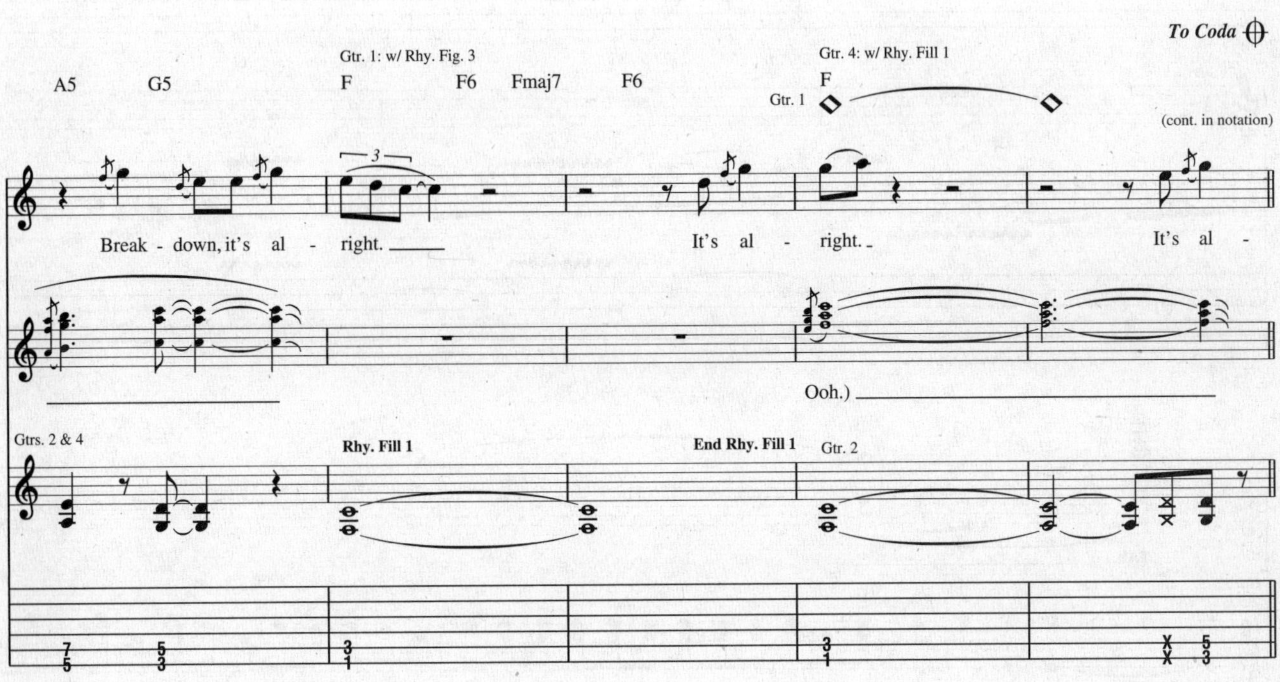
To Coda
A5 G5
Gtr. 1: w/ Rhy. Fig. 3
F F6 Fmaj7 F6
Gtr. 4: w/ Rhy. Fill 1
F
Gtr. 1
(cont. in notation)
Break - down, it's al - right. It's al - right. It's al -
Ooh.)
Gtrs. 2 & 4
Rhy. Fill 1
End Rhy. Fill 1
Gtr. 2

Interlude
Am G Am G Am G Am G
right. Ah.
Gtr. 1
8va
loco
Gtr. 2

Gtr. 1: w/ Rhy. Fig. 1 (3 1/2 times)
Am G Am G Am G
(Ah.)
Gtrs. 2 & 4
Gtr. 4
Gtr. 2
divisi
Gtrs. 2 & 4
D.S. al Coda
Gtrs. 2 & 4: w/ Rhy. Fill 1A
F
Gtr. 1
Gtr. 5
(fuzz)
Gtrs. 2 & 4
divisi
let ring
Coda
Outro
Gtr. 1: w/ Rhy. Fig. 1 (till fade)
Gtr. 3: w/ Rhy. Fig. 2 (till fade)
right.
Gtr. 2
Riff A
End Riff A
Gtr. 2: w/ Riff A (till fade)
Repeat and fade

Brown Eyed Girl

Words and Music by Van Morrison

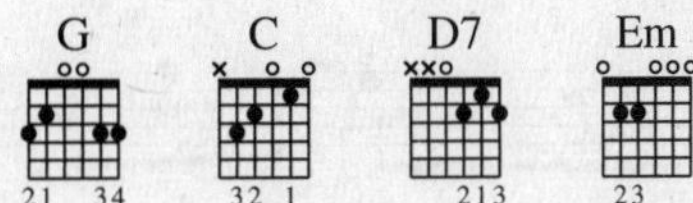

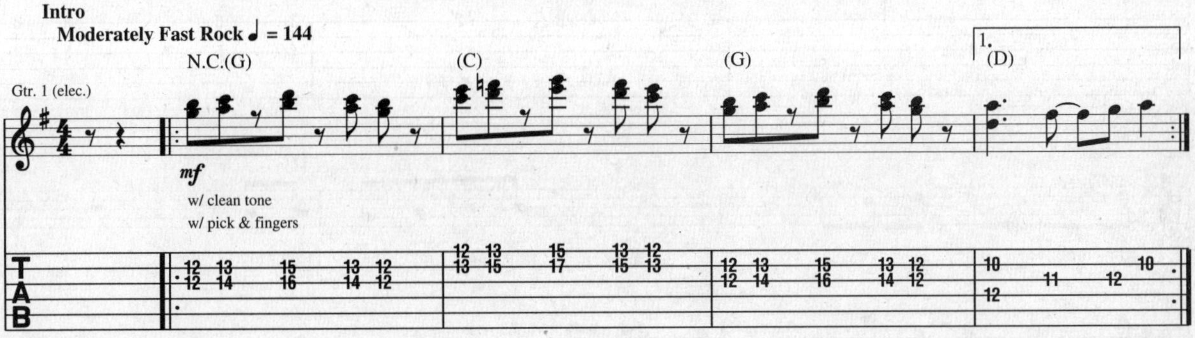

Intro

Moderately Fast Rock ♩ = 144

N.C.(G) (C) (G) 1. (D)

Gtr. 1 (elec.)

mf

w/ clean tone

w/ pick & fingers

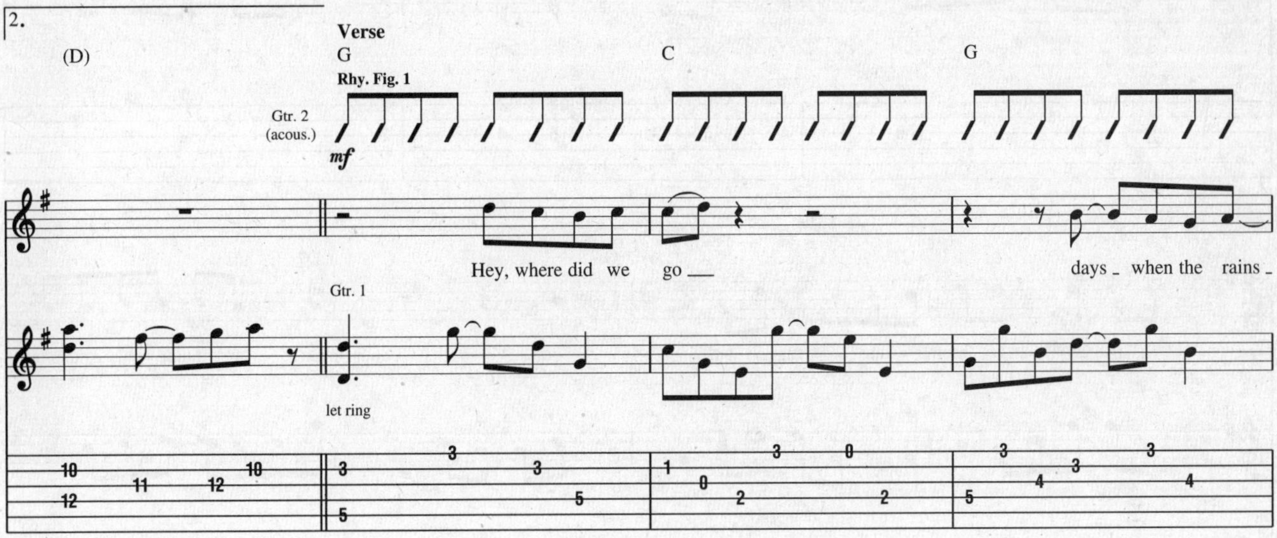

2. (D)

Verse

G C G

Rhy. Fig. 1

Gtr. 2 (acous.)

mf

Hey, where did we go — days — when the rains —

Gtr. 1

let ring

G
D7
G
play - in' a new game.
Laugh - ing and a
C
G
D7
run - ning, hey, hey,
skip - ping and a jump - ing,
G
C
G
D7
in the mis - ty morn - ing fog with our, our hearts a thump - in'. And you,
C
D7
G
Em
Rhy. Fig. 2
Gtr. 2
my brown - eyed girl.
Gtr. 1

C
D7
G
D7
End Rhy. Fig. 2
Yeah, you, my brown-eyed girl.
Verse
Gtr. 2: w/ Rhy. Fig. 1, 4 times
G
C
G
D7
2. Now, what-ev-er hap-pened to Tues-day and so slow?
G
C
G
D7
Go-ing down the old mine with a tran-sis-tor ra-di-o.
G
C
G
Stand-ing in the sun-light laugh-ing, hid-ing be-hind a

D7 G C
rain - bow's wall. Slip - ping and a slid - ing
Gtr. 2: w/ Rhy. Fig. 2
G D7 C D7
all a - long the wa - ter - fall with you, my brown - eyed girl.
G Em C D7
You, my brown - eyed girl.
G D7 D7
Gtr. 2
Do you re - mem - ber when we used to sing?
Gtr. 1

Chorus
Gtr. 2: w/ Rhy. Fig. 1, 2 times
G
C
G
Sha, la, la, la, la, la, la, la, la, la, la, la, te, da.
Rhy. Fig. 3
D7
G
C
Just like that.
Sha, la, la, la, la, la, la, la,
End Rhy. Fig. 3
G
D7
G
Gtr. 2
la, la, la, te, da.
La, te, da.
Gtr. 1
Bass Interlude
Gtrs. 1 & 2 tacet
N.C.(G)
(C)
(G)
(D7)

Verse

Gtr. 2: w/ Rhy. Fig. 1, 4 times
G
C
G
D7
3. So hard to find my way now that I'm all on my own.
Gtr. 1
G
C
G
D7
I saw you just the oth-er day; my, how you have grown.
G
C
G
Cast my mem-'ry back there, Lord. Some - times I'm o -
D7
G
C
ver - come think - in' 'bout it. Laugh - ing and a run - ning, hey, hey,

Gtr. 2: w/ Rhy. Fig. 2
G
D7
C
D7
be - hind the sta - di - um with you,
my brown - eyed girl.
G
Em
C
D7
A you, my brown - eyed girl.
G
D7
D7
Gtr. 2
Do you re - mem - ber when a we used to sing?
Gtr. 1
Chorus
Play 4 Times & Fade
w/ Lead Voc. ad lib.
Gtr. 1: w/ Rhy. Fig. 3, simile
Gtr. 2: w/ Rhy. Fig. 1
G
C
G
D7
Sha, la, la, la, la, la, la, la, la, la, la, te, da.

Buddy Holly

Words and Music by Rivers Cuomo

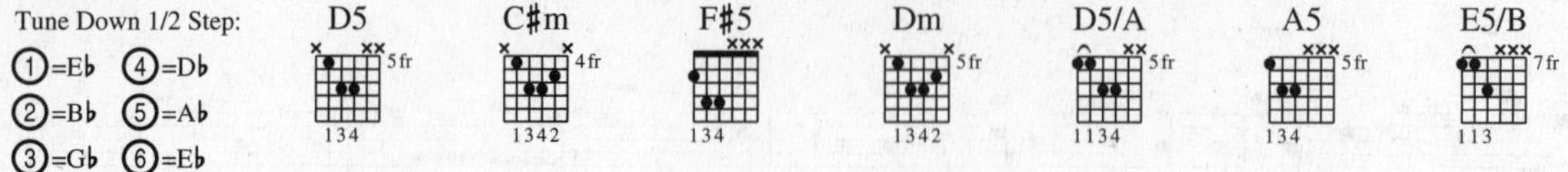

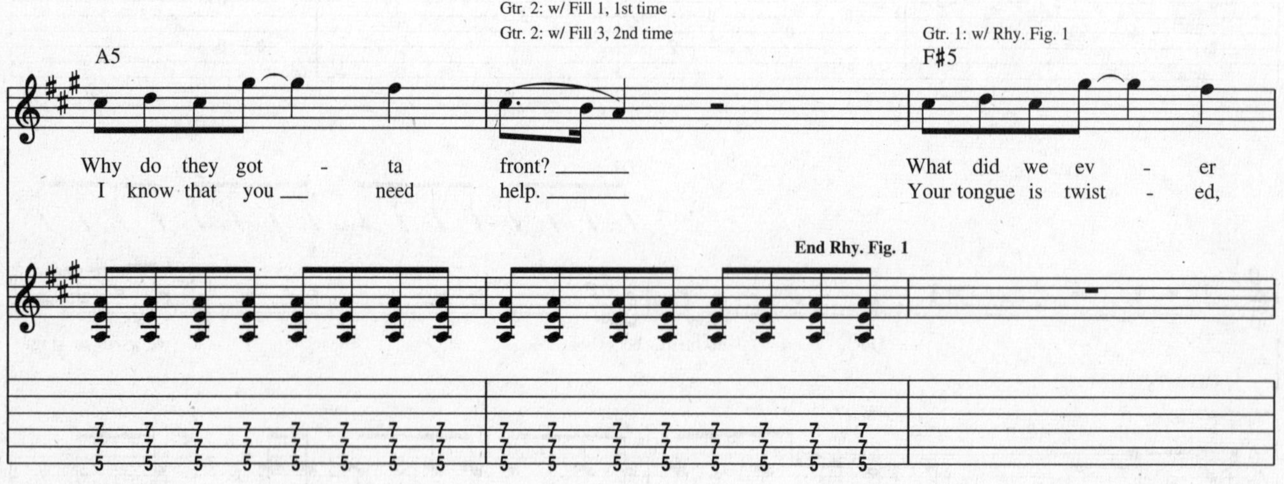

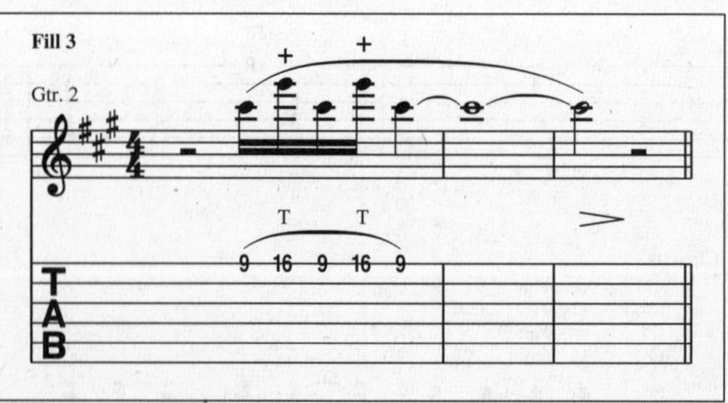

Gtr. 3: w/ Fill 2, 1st time
Gtr. 3: w/ Fill 4, 2nd time
E/G#
A5
do to these guys that made them so vi - o - lent?
your eyes are slit. You need a guard - i - an.
Pre-Chorus
D5
C#m
F#5
D5
Rhy. Fig. 2
Gtr. 1
(Woo - hoo.) But/And you know I'm yours. (Woo - hoo.) And I know
Gtr. 3
let ring throughout
C#m
F#5
D5
Dm
End Rhy. Fig. 2
(cont. in notation)
you're mine. (Woo - hoo, and that's for all time.
Fill 2
Gtr. 3 (dist.)
vol. swell
Fill 4
Gtr. 3
vol. swell

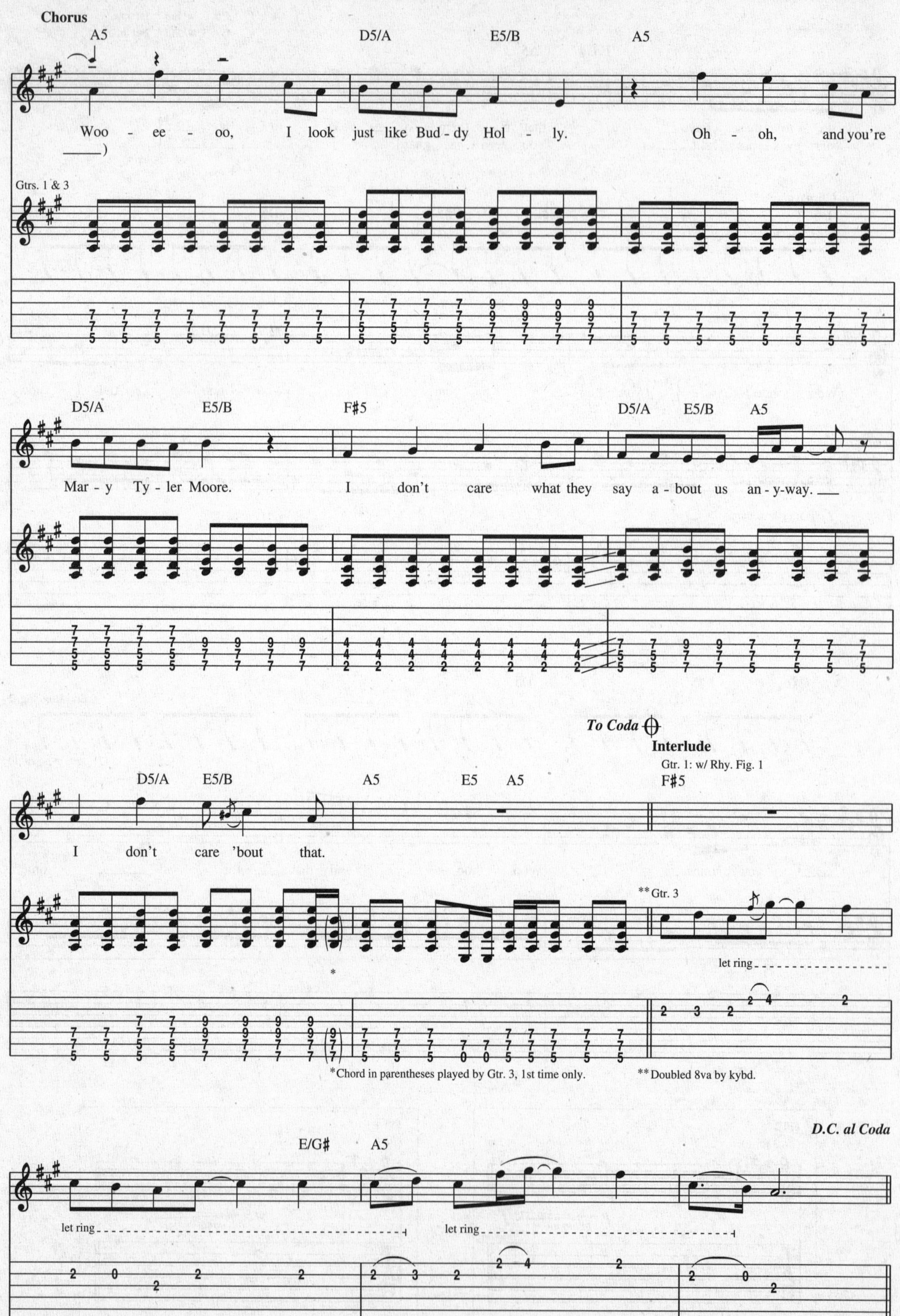
Chorus
A5
D5/A
E5/B
A5
Woo - ee - oo, I look just like Bud - dy Hol - ly. Oh - oh, and you're
Gtrs. 1 & 3
D5/A
E5/B
F♯5
D5/A
E5/B
A5
Mar - y Ty - ler Moore. I don't care what they say a - bout us an - y - way.
To Coda
Interlude
Gtr. 1: w/ Rhy. Fig. 1
D5/A
E5/B
A5
E5
A5
F♯5
I don't care 'bout that.
**Gtr. 3
let ring
*Chord in parentheses played by Gtr. 3, 1st time only.
**Doubled 8va by kybd.
D.C. al Coda
E/G♯
A5
let ring
let ring

Coda
A5 D5/A E5/B A5 E5 A5
I don't care 'bout that.
Gtrs. 1 & 3
Bridge
A5 N.C. F#5 N.C. F#5 N.C. F#5 A6 B5 C#5 B5 N.C.
Bang, bang, knock on the door, 'noth-er big bang, you're down _ on the floor.
8va
15ma
loco
Harm.
Harm.
pitch: D (C#) A
*All notes in parentheses played by Gtr. 3.
A5 N.C. F#5 N.C. F#5 N.C. F#5 A6 B5 C#5 B5 N.C.
Oh no, what do I do? __ Don't look now, but I lost my shoe.
15ma
loco
Harm.
pitch: C♮ (G♮)
A5 N.C. F#5 N.C. F#5 N.C. F#5 A6 B5 C#5 B5 N.C.
I can't run and I ___ can't kick. What's a mat-ter babe, are you feel - in' sick?
15ma
loco
Harm.
pitch: C♮ (A)

A5 N.C. F#5 N.C. F#5 N.C. F#5 A6 B5 C#5 B5 N.C.
What's a mat-ter, what's a mat-ter, what's a mat-ter you? What's a mat-ter babe, are you feel - in' blue? Oh,
15ma
loco
Gtr. 4 (dist.)
mf
Gtrs. 1&3 divisi
Harm.
pitch: C♮ (D) A (D)
Guitar Solo
Gtrs. 1 & 3: w/ Rhy. Fig. 2, simile
D5 C#m F#5 D5
oh, oh, oh, oh, oh, oh, oh.
Gtr. 4
8va
full
C#m F#5 D5
8va
loco
And that's
full
Dm D5/A
Gtrs. 1 & 3
for all time.
(And that's for all time.)
tr
1/2

Outro-Chorus
N.C.
A5
D5/A
E5/B
Woo - ee - oo, I look just like Bud - dy Hol - ly.
Gtrs. 1 & 3
8va
loco
Gtr. 4
full
fdbk.
*Doubled 8va by kybd.
Gtr. 4 tacet
F#5
Oh - oh, and you're Mar - y Ty - ler Moore. I don't care what they
say a - bout us an - y - way. I don't care 'bout that.
Rhy. Fig. 3

Gtrs. 1 & 3: w/ Rhy. Fig. 3, 2 times
A A5 E5 A5 D5/A E5/B
I don't care 'bout that.
Gtrs. 1 & 3
End Rhy. Fig. 3
Gtr. 4
A A5 E5 A5 D5/A E5/B
I don't care 'bout that.
Gtr. 4
A A5 E5 A5 A5 D5/A E5/B A5 E F#5 E F#5
open
open
Gtrs. 1 & 3
I don't care 'bout that.

Burning for You

Words and Music by Donald Roeser and Richard Meltzer

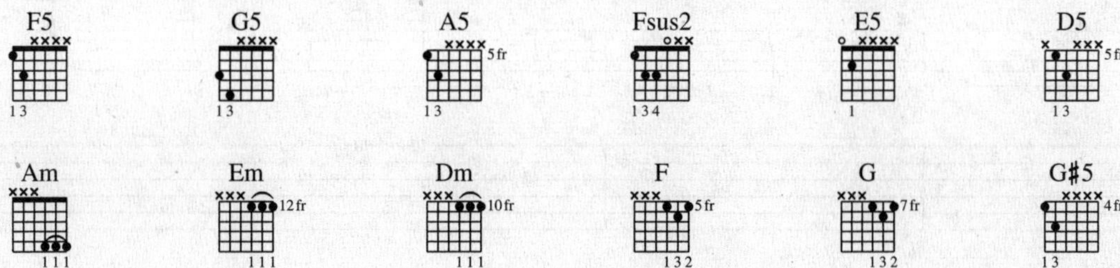

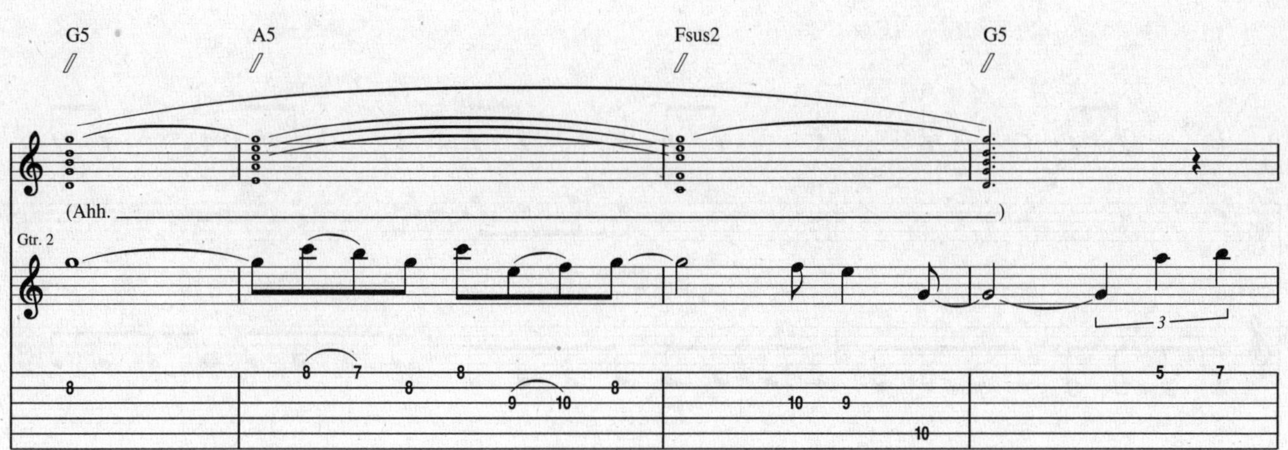

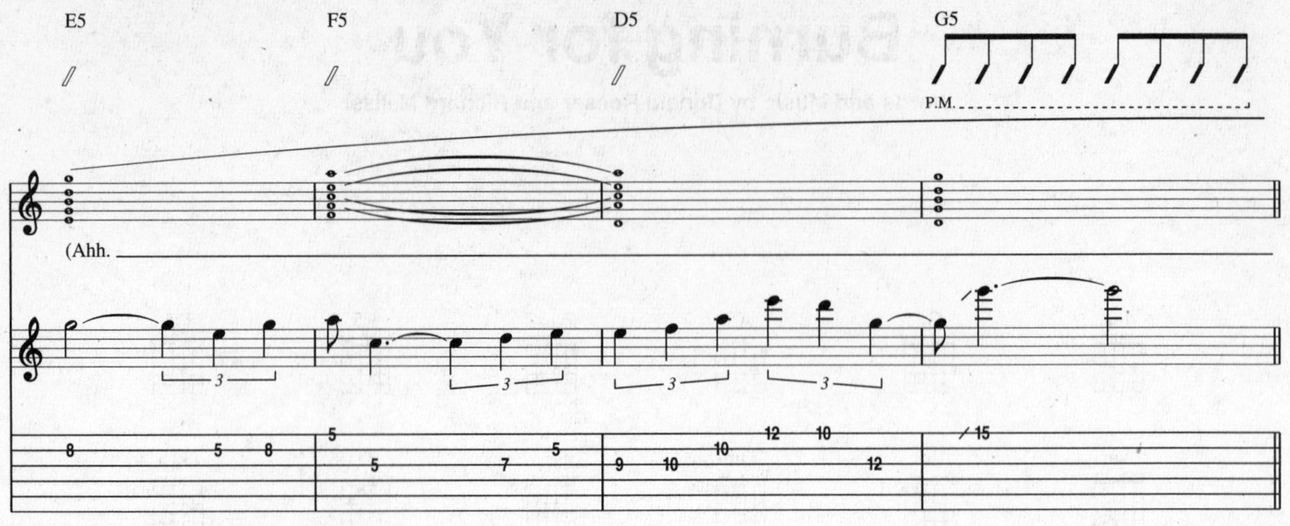
E5
F5
D5
G5
P.M.
(Ahh.

Verse
Am
Em
Dm
Rhy. Fig. 1A
—)
1. Home in the val - ley, home in the cit -
2. Time is the es - sence, time is the sea -
Rhy. Fig. 1
P.M.

F
G
Am
Em
y. Home is - n't pret - ty,
son. Time ain't no rea - son,
P.M.

Gtr. 1: w/ Rhy. Fig. 1A
Gtr. 2: w/ Rhy. Fig. 1, 1st 7 meas. only
Dm
F
G
Am
End Rhy. Fig. 1A
ain't no home for me.
got no time to slow.
Home in the dark-
Time ev-er-last-
End Rhy. Fig. 1
P.M.
full
Em
Dm
F
G
ness,
ing,
home on the high-way.
time to play, "B sides."
Am
Em
Dm
Home is-n't my way,
Time ain't on my side,
home I'll nev-er be.
time I'll nev-er know.
Chorus
Gtr. 2 tacet
F
* G
A5 G#5 A5
G5
F5
G5
Burn out the day,
Gtr. 2
Rhy. Fill 1
End Rhy. Fill 1
Rhy. Fig. 2
Gtr. 1
P.M.
* Bass plays E
A5 G#5 A5
G5
F5
G5
N.C. (C)
burn out the night.
I can't see no
I'm not the one to

Gtr. 2: w/ Fill 1, 2nd time
F5
G5
rea - son to put up a fight.
tell you what's wrong or what's right.

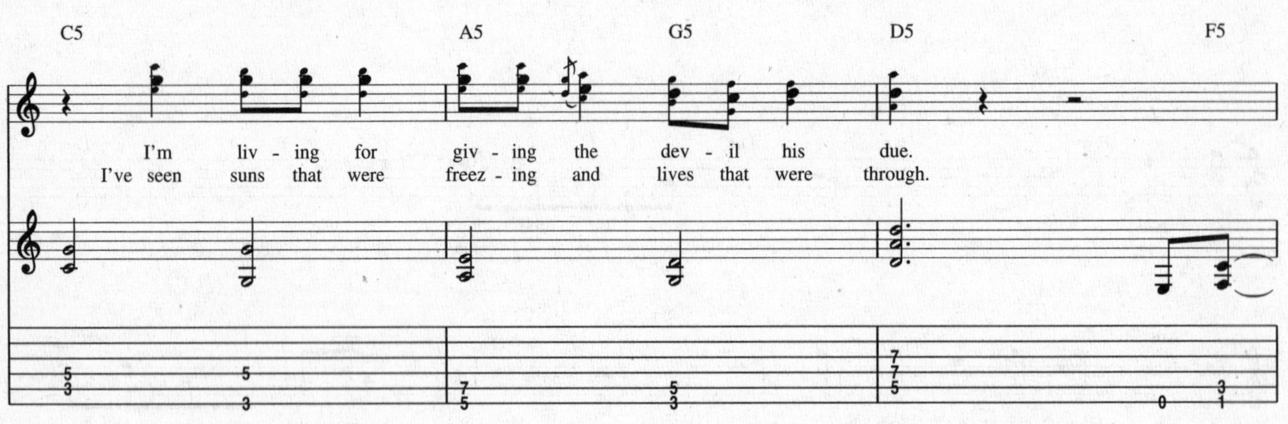
C5
A5
G5
D5
F5
I'm liv - ing for giv - ing the dev - il his due.
I've seen suns that were freez - ing and lives that were through.

G5
A5
G♯5
A5
G5
F5
G5
And I'm burn - in', I'm burn - in', I'm burn - in' for you.
(But)

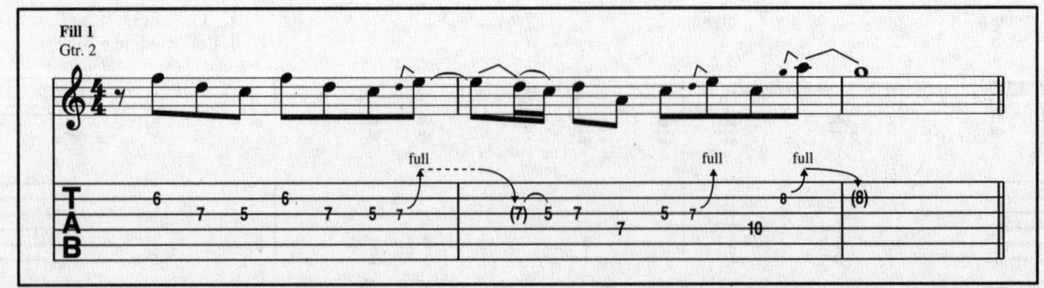
Fill 1
Gtr. 2
full
full
full

A5 G#5 A5 G5 F5 G5 A5 G#5 A5 G5 F5
I'm burn - in', I'm
End Rhy. Fig. 2
To Coda
Interlude
G5 F5
Gtr. 1
burn - in', I'm burn - in' for you.
Rhy. Fig. 3
Gtr. 2
(cont. in slash)
G5
(Ahh.
End Rhy. Fig. 3
A5 Fsus2 G5 E5
(Ahh.
full

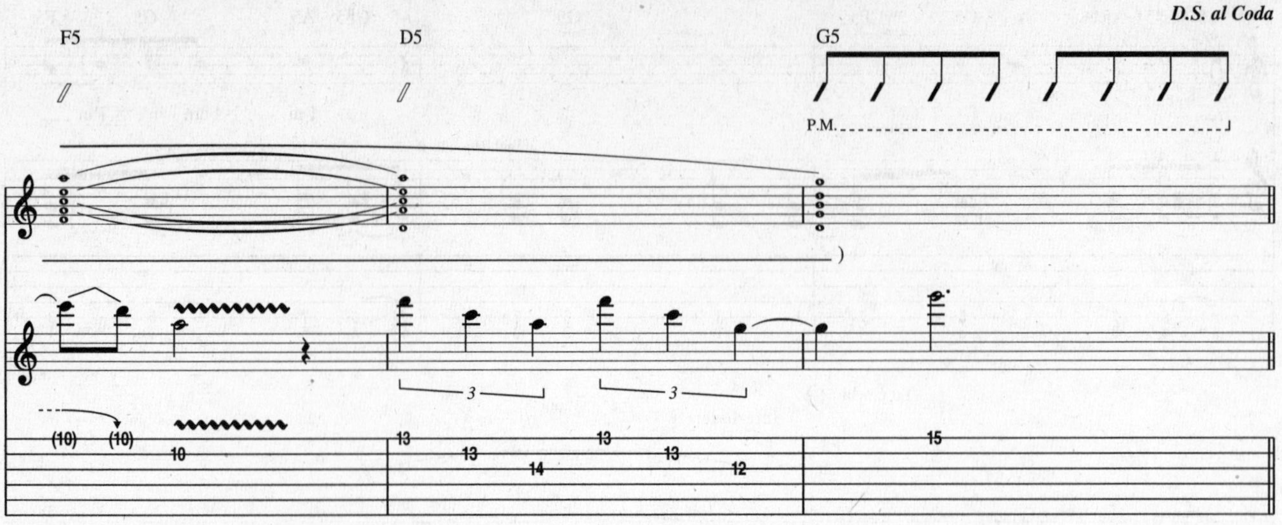
F5
D5
G5
P.M.

Coda
Gtr. 2: w/ Rhy. Fig. 3
Gtr. 3 (elec.)
w/ slight dist.
full

Guitar Solo

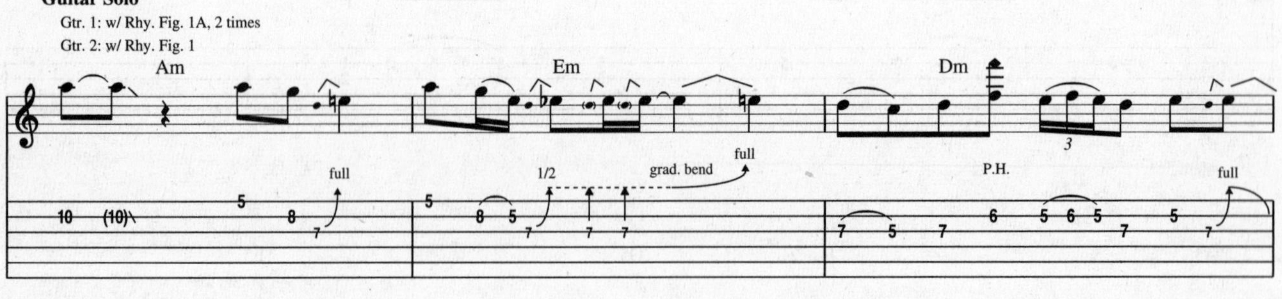
Gtr. 1: w/ Rhy. Fig. 1A, 2 times
Gtr. 2: w/ Rhy. Fig. 1
Am
Em
Dm
full
1/2
grad. bend
P.H.

F
G
Am
Em
full
1/4

Gtr. 2: w/ Rhy. Fig. 1, 1st 7 meas. only
Dm
F
G
Am
8va
full
Em
Dm
F
G
loco
Am
Em
Dm
Chorus
Gtr. 2: w/ Rhy. Fill 1
F
* G
Gtr. 1: w/ Rhy. Fig. 2
A5 G#5 A5
G5
F5
Gtrs. 2 & 3 tacet
G5
Burn out the day,
* Bass plays E
A5 G#5 A5
G5
F5
G5
N.C. (C)
burn out the night.
I can't see no
F5
G5
rea - son to put up a fight.
Gtr. 3

C5 A5 G5 D5 F5
I'm liv - ing for giv - ing the dev - il his due.
G5 A5 G♯5 A5 G5 F5 G5
And I'm burn - in', I'm burn - in', I'm burn - in' for you.
Gtr. 1: w/ Rhy. Fig. 2, 1st 2 meas. only, 4 times
A5 G♯5 A5 G5 F5 G5 A5 G♯5A5 G5 F5
I'm burn-in', I'm
Gtr. 3
full
full
1/2
G5 A5 G♯5 A5 G5 F5 G5
burn-in', I'm burn-in' for you.
1/2
full
A5 G♯5 A5 G5 F5 G5 A5 G♯5 A5 G5 F5
I'm burn-in', I'm burn-in', I'm burn-in' for you.

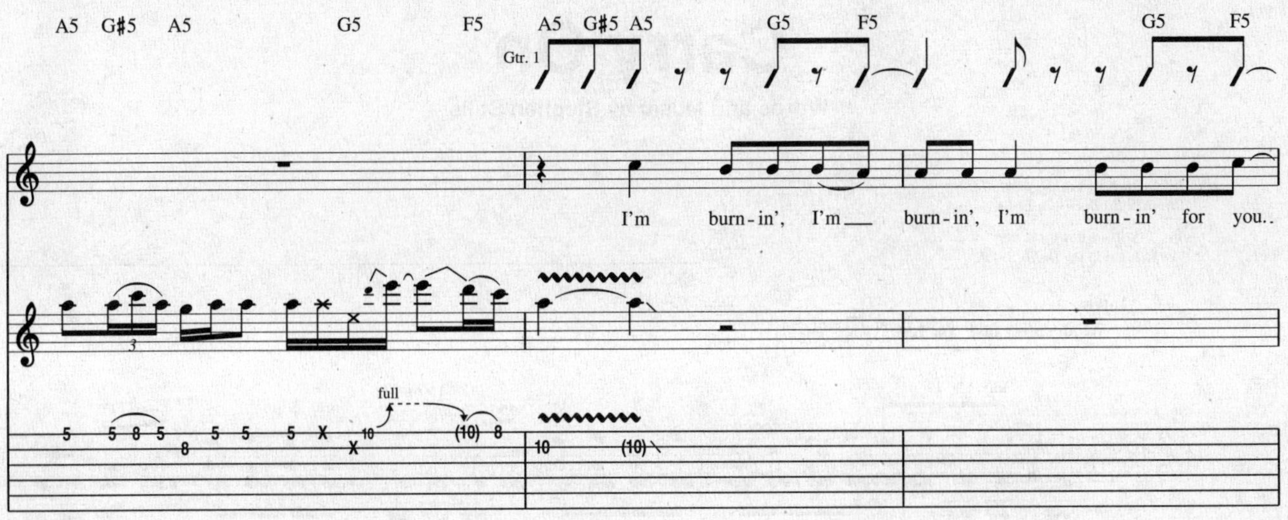
A5 G#5 A5 G5 F5 A5 G#5 A5 G5 F5 G5 F5
Gtr. 1
I'm burn-in', I'm burn-in', I'm burn-in' for you..
full

Gtr. 2: w/ Rhy. Fig. 3
Gtr. 3 tacet
8va
full

A5
rit.
(Ahh.)
Gtr. 2
loco
rit.

Carry On

Words and Music by Stephen Stills

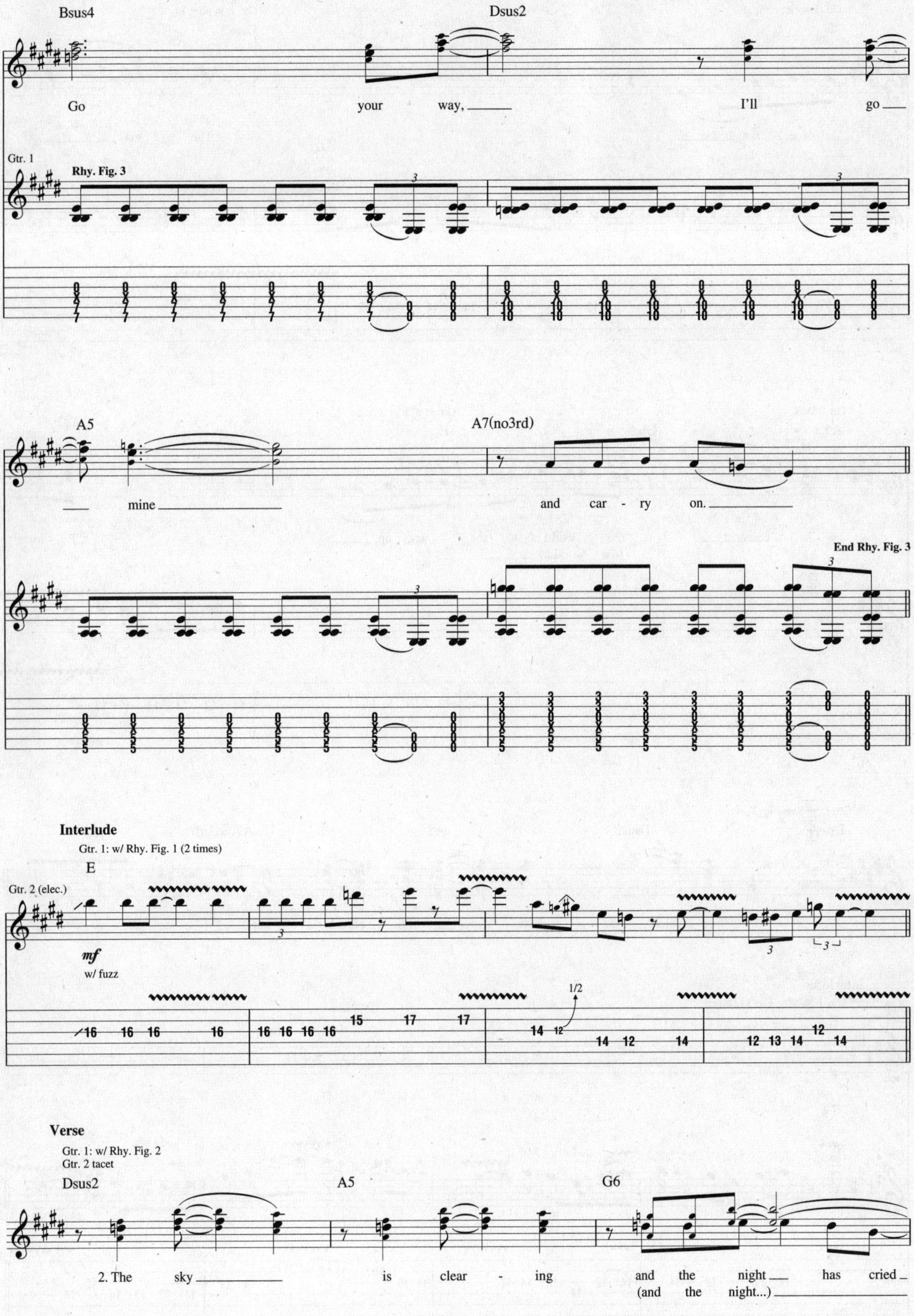

Bsus4 Dsus2

Go your way, I'll go

Gtr. 1

Rhy. Fig. 3

A5 A7(no3rd)

mine and car - ry on.

End Rhy. Fig. 3

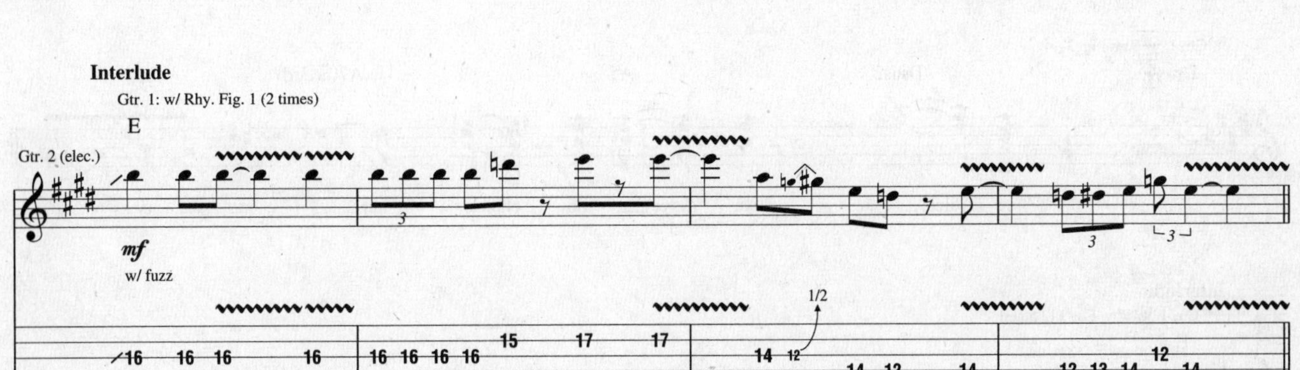

Gtr. 1: w/ Rhy. Fig. 1
E
Gtr. 1: w/ Rhy. Fig. 2
Dsus2
e - nough.
The sun,
Gtr. 2
3
13
14 14 14 14 14 12 14

Gtr. 2 tacet
A5
G6
Gtr. 1: w/ Rhy. Fig. 1
E
he come,
the world to sof - ten up.
(the world...)
Re - joice,
3
14 12 14 14 12 12

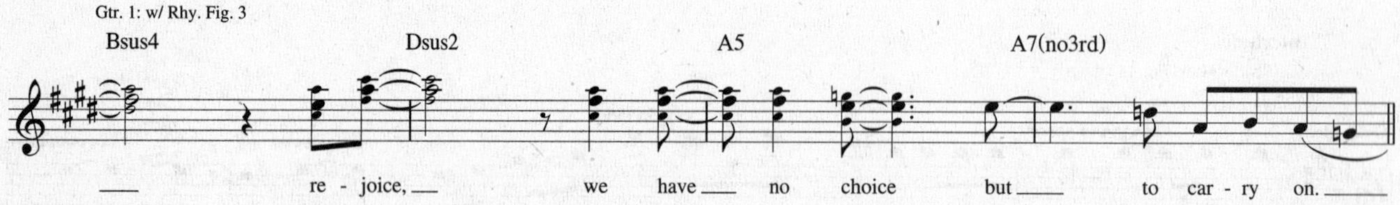
Gtr. 1: w/ Rhy. Fig. 3
Bsus4
Dsus2
A5
A7(no3rd)
re - joice,
we have no choice but to car - ry on.

Interlude

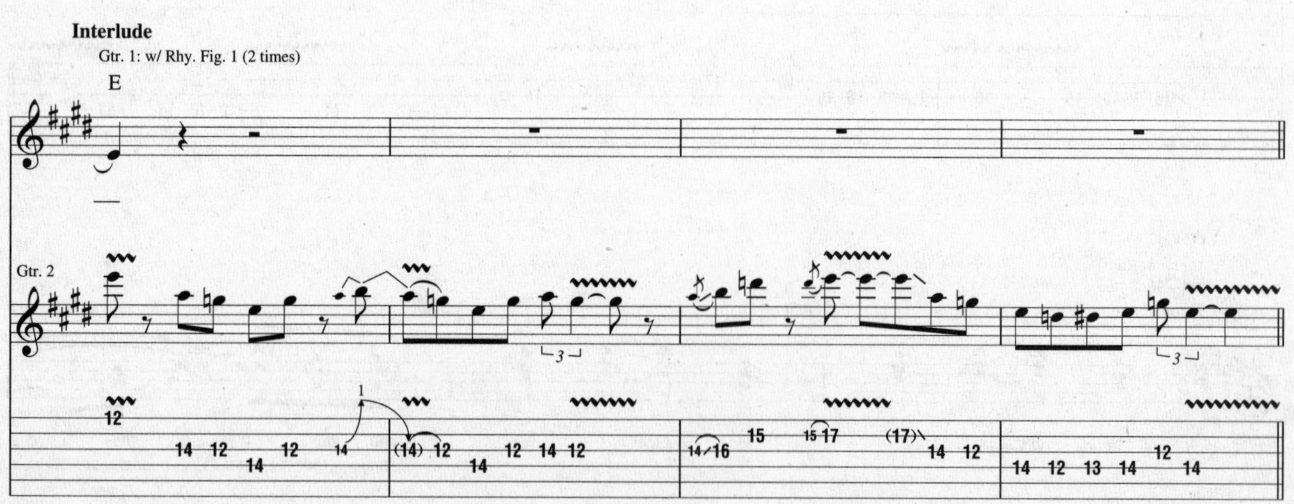
Gtr. 1: w/ Rhy. Fig. 1 (2 times)
E
Gtr. 2
3
3
3
1
12
14 12 14 12 14
(14) 12 14 12 14 12
14 16 15 15 17 (17) 14 12
14 12 13 14 12 14

Verse
Gtr. 1: w/ Rhy. Fig. 2
Dsus2
A5
G6
3. The for - tunes of fa - bles are a - ble to
(are a - ble...)
1/2

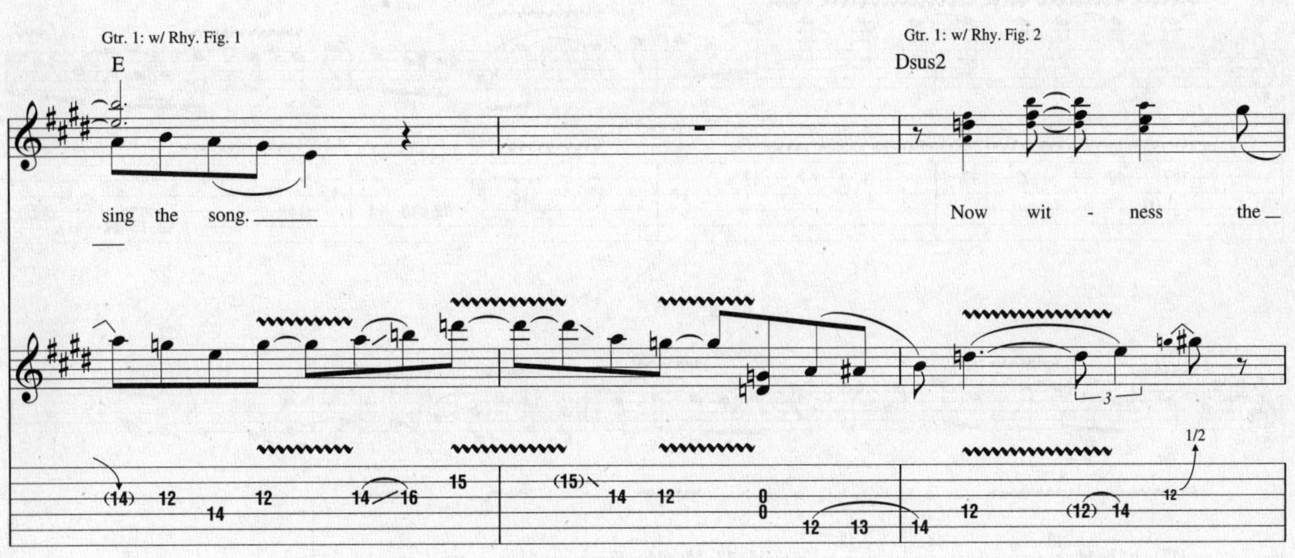
Gtr. 1: w/ Rhy. Fig. 1
E
Gtr. 1: w/ Rhy. Fig. 2
Dsus2
sing the song.
Now wit - ness the
1/2

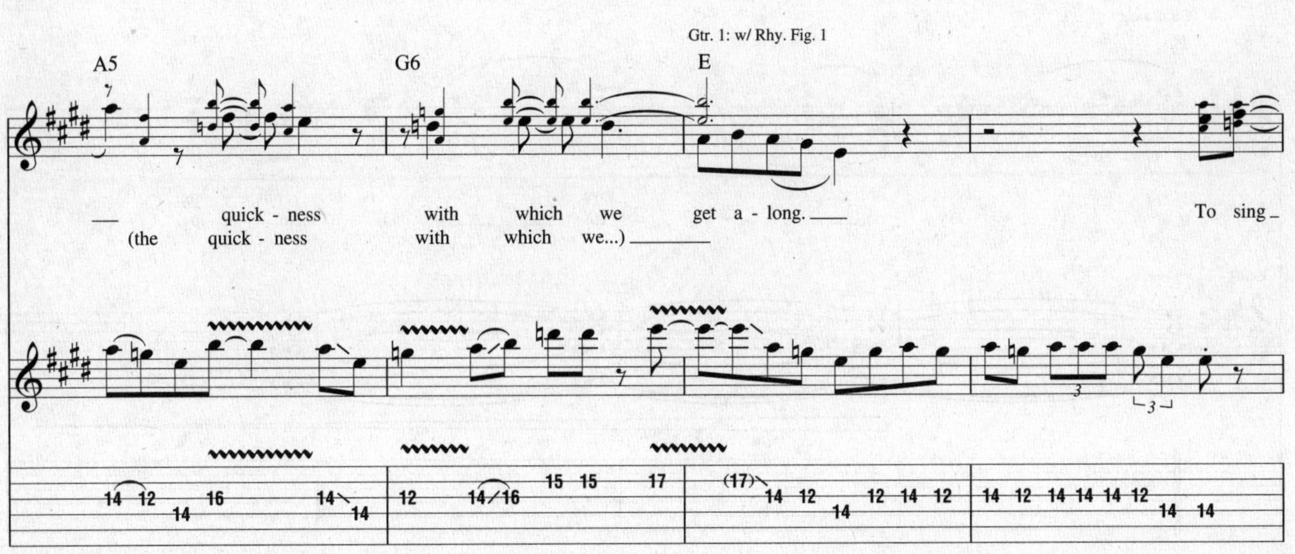
A5
G6
Gtr. 1: w/ Rhy. Fig. 1
E
quick - ness with which we get a - long.
(the quick - ness with which we...)
To sing

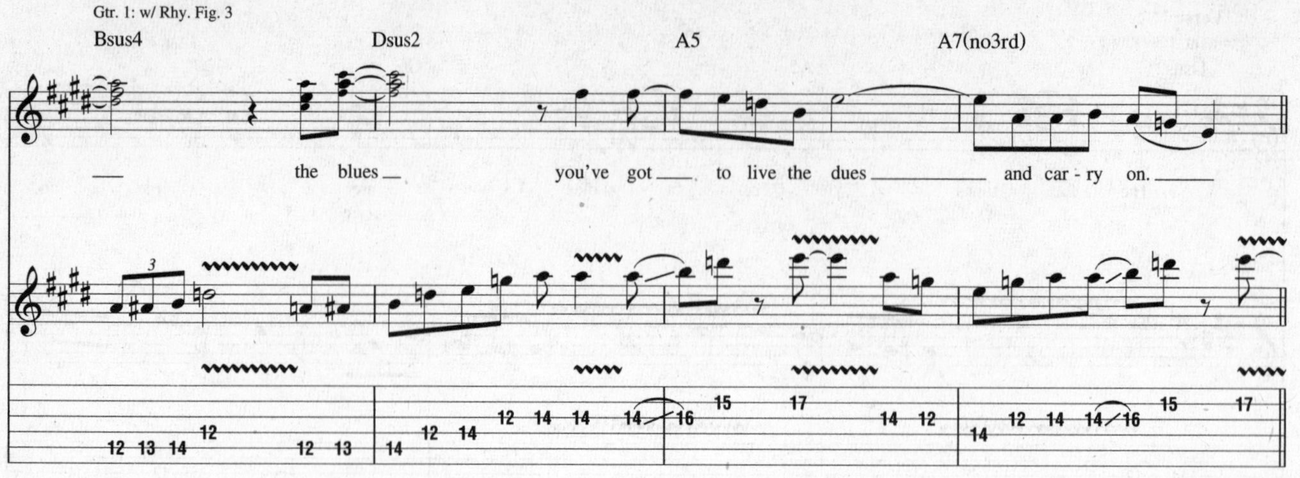
Gtr. 1: w/ Rhy. Fig. 3
Bsus4
Dsus2
A5
A7(no3rd)
the blues you've got to live the dues and car - ry on.

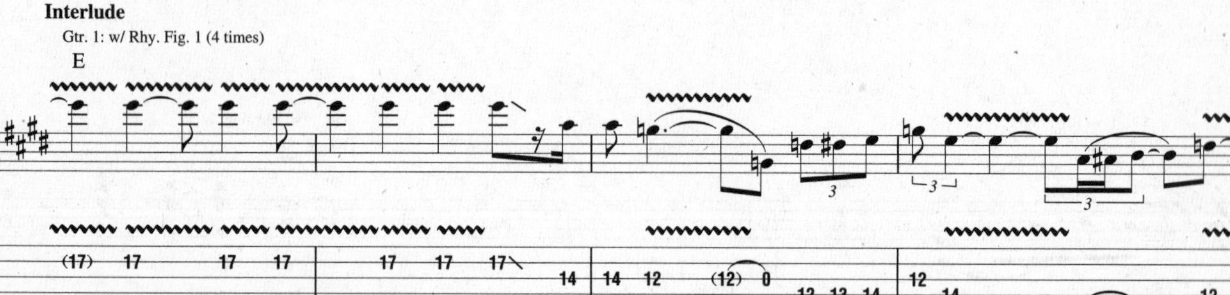
Interlude
Gtr. 1: w/ Rhy. Fig. 1 (4 times)
E

1/2

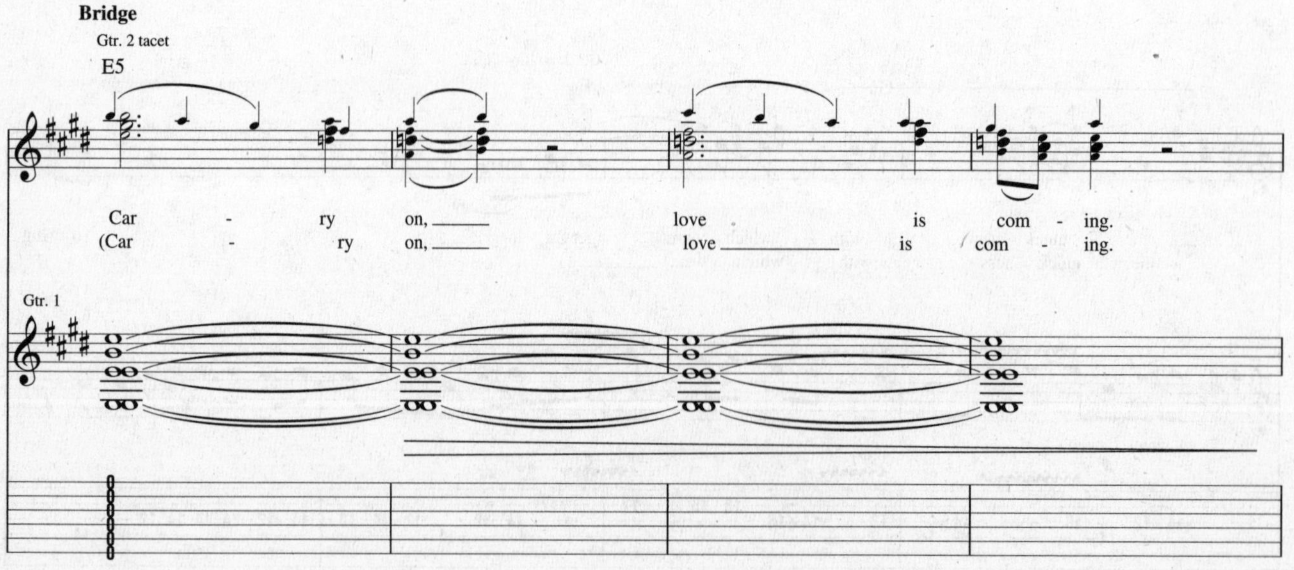
Bridge
Gtr. 2 tacet
E5
Car - ry on, love is com - ing.
(Car - ry on, love is com - ing.
Gtr. 1

Organ Solo

*Organ arr. for gtr.

Guitar Solo

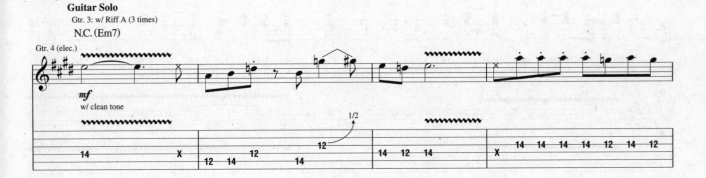

Verse

Verse
E Bm D N.C. (Em7)
4. Where are you go - ing now, my love? Where will you be to - mor - row?
Rhy. Fig. 4
End Rhy. Fig. 4
Gtr. 3: w/ Rhy. Fig. 4
E Bm D N.C. (Em7)
Will you bring me hap - pi - ness? Will you bring me sor - row? Oh, the
Gtr. 4
Chorus
E D Bm A E D Bm
ques - tions of a thou - sand dreams, what you do and what
Gtr. 4
Gtr. 3
Rhy. Fig. 5

Gtr. 4 tacet
A
E
D
A
G
you see.
Lov - er, can you talk to me?
End Rhy. Fig. 5
Guitar Solo
Gtr. 3: w/ Riff A (3 times)
N.C. (Em7)
Gtr. 5 (elec.)
mf
w/ clean tone & wah-wah
Gtr. 3: w/ Riff B
Verse
Gtr. 3: w/ Rhy. Fig. 4 (2 times)
Gtr. 5 tacet
E
Bm
D
N.C. (Em7)
5. Girl, when I was on my own chas - ing you down,
Gtr. 4

E
Bm
D
N.C. (Em7)
what was it made you run?
Try-ing your best just to get a-round the ques-
Chorus
Gtr. 3: w/ Rhy. Fig. 5
E
D
Bm
A
E
D
Bm
tions of a thou-sand dreams,
what you do and what
Gtr. 2
Gtr. 4
A
E
D
A
G
you see.
Lov-er, can you talk to me?
1/2
(cont. on lower staff)

Outro-Guitar Solo
Gtr. 3: w/ Riff A (till end)
Gtr. 4 tacet
N.C. (Em7)
Gtr. 5
Gtr. 2
Begin fade

Gtr. 5

Gtr. 2

Gtr. 4

Fade out

Carry on Wayward Son

Words and Music by Kerry Livgren

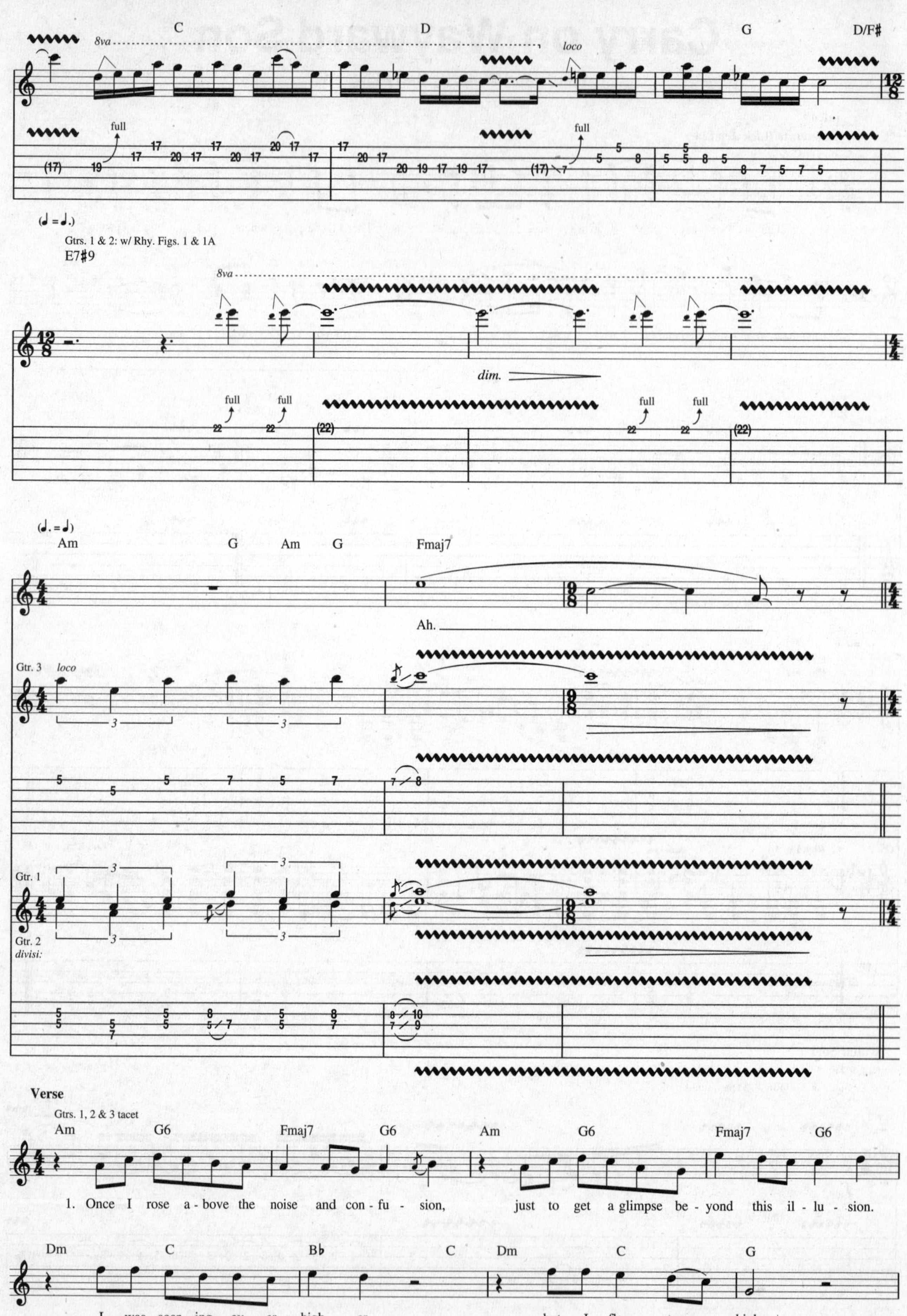
C
D
G
D/F#
8va
loco
full
(♩ = ♩.)
Gtrs. 1 & 2: w/ Rhy. Figs. 1 & 1A
E7#9
dim.
(♩. = ♩)
Am
G
Am
G
Fmaj7
Ah.
Gtr. 3
Gtr. 1
Gtr. 2
divisi:
Verse
Gtrs. 1, 2 & 3 tacet
Am G6 Fmaj7 G6 Am G6 Fmaj7 G6
1. Once I rose a - bove the noise and con - fu - sion, just to get a glimpse be - yond this il - lu - sion.
Dm C B♭ C Dm C G
I was soar - ing ev - er high - er, but I flew too high.

Am G6 Fmaj7 G6 Am G6 Fmaj7 G6
'Though my eyes could see, I still was a blind man. 'Though my mind could think, I still was a mad - man.
Gtr. 4 Rhy. Fig. 2
(acous.)
mf
let ring throughout
Dm C B♭ C Dm C G
I hear the voi - ces when I'm dream - ing. I can hear them say:
End Rhy. Fig. 2
Chorus
Gtr. 4 tacet
Am C G Fsus2 Am C G
"Car - ry on, my way - ward son, There'll be peace when you are done.
Gtr. 1 Rhy. Fig. 3
w/ clean tone
let ring throughout
Am C G Fadd9 F N.C.
Lay your wear - y head to rest. Don't you cry no
End Rhy. Fig. 3

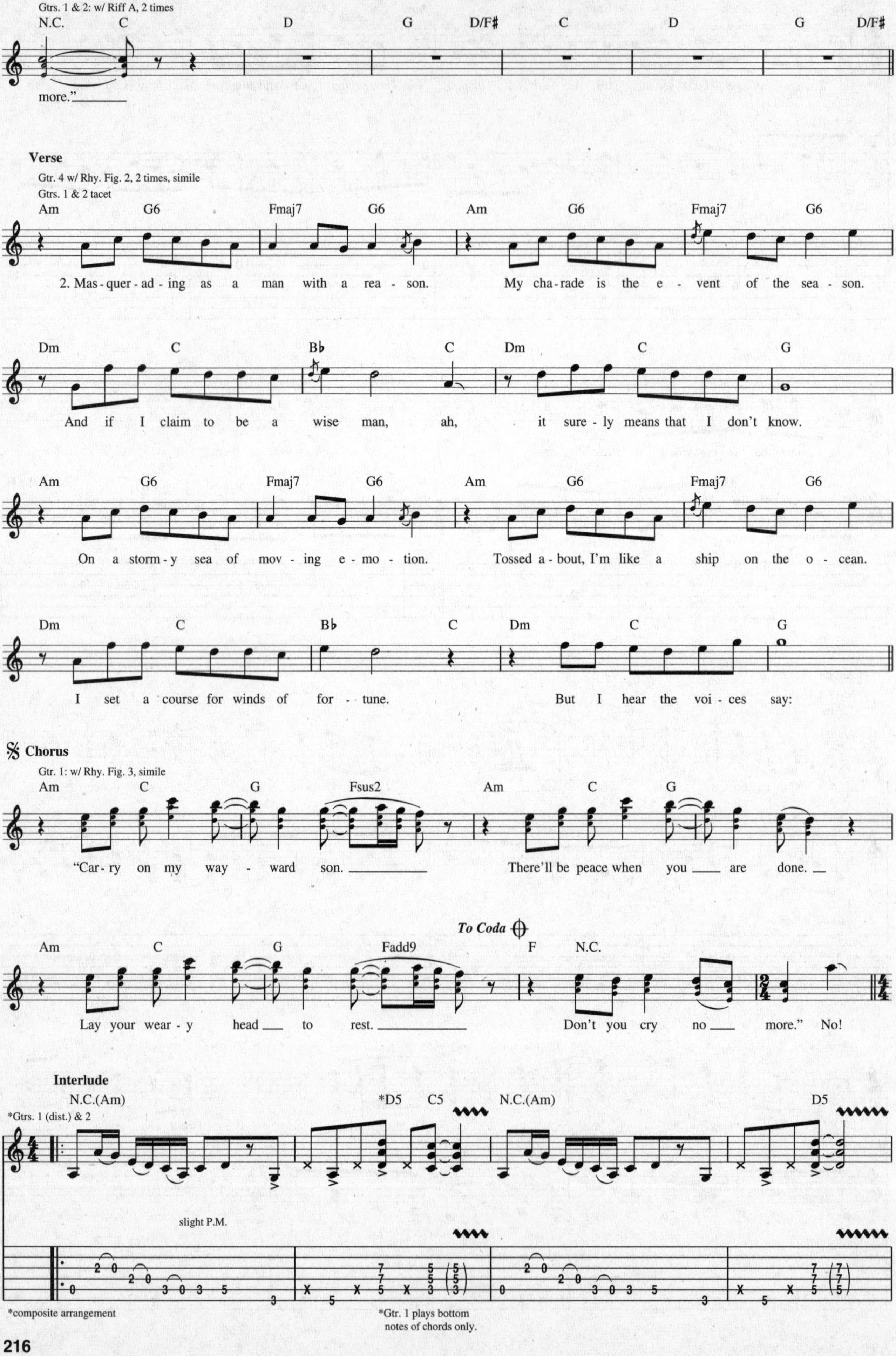

Gtrs. 1 & 2: w/ Riff A, 2 times

N.C. C D G D/F# C D G D/F#

more."

Verse

Gtr. 4 w/ Rhy. Fig. 2, 2 times, simile
Gtrs. 1 & 2 tacet

Am G6 Fmaj7 G6 Am G6 Fmaj7 G6

2. Mas - quer - ad - ing as a man with a rea - son. My cha - rade is the e - vent of the sea - son.

Dm C B♭ C Dm C G

And if I claim to be a wise man, ah, it sure - ly means that I don't know.

Am G6 Fmaj7 G6 Am G6 Fmaj7 G6

On a storm - y sea of mov - ing e - mo - tion. Tossed a - bout, I'm like a ship on the o - cean.

Dm C B♭ C Dm C G

I set a course for winds of for - - tune. But I hear the voi - ces say:

𝄋 Chorus

Gtr. 1: w/ Rhy. Fig. 3, simile

Am C G Fsus2 Am C G

"Car - ry on my way - ward son. There'll be peace when you are done.

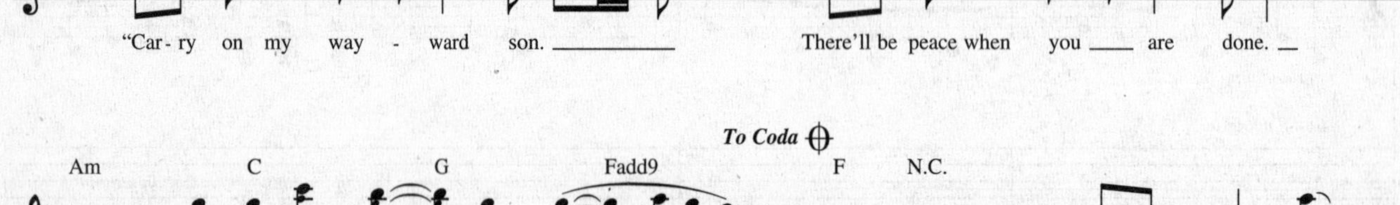

Interlude

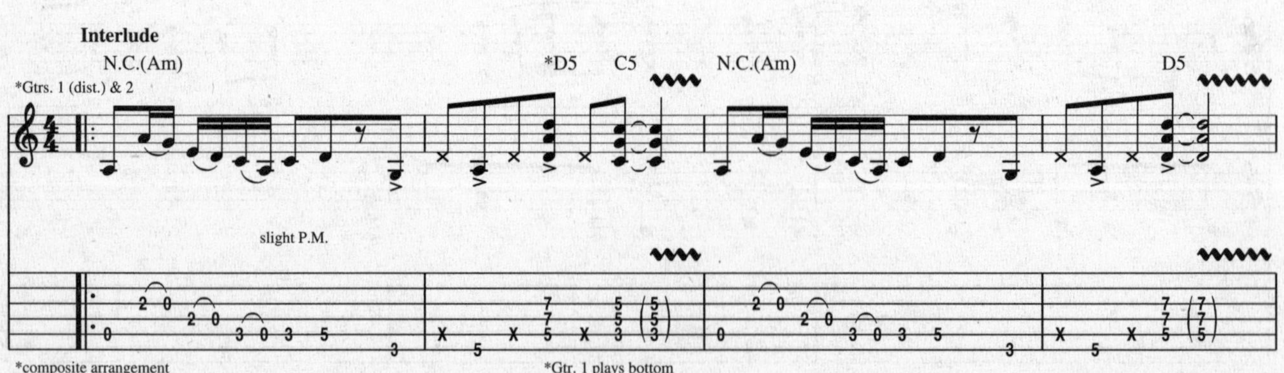

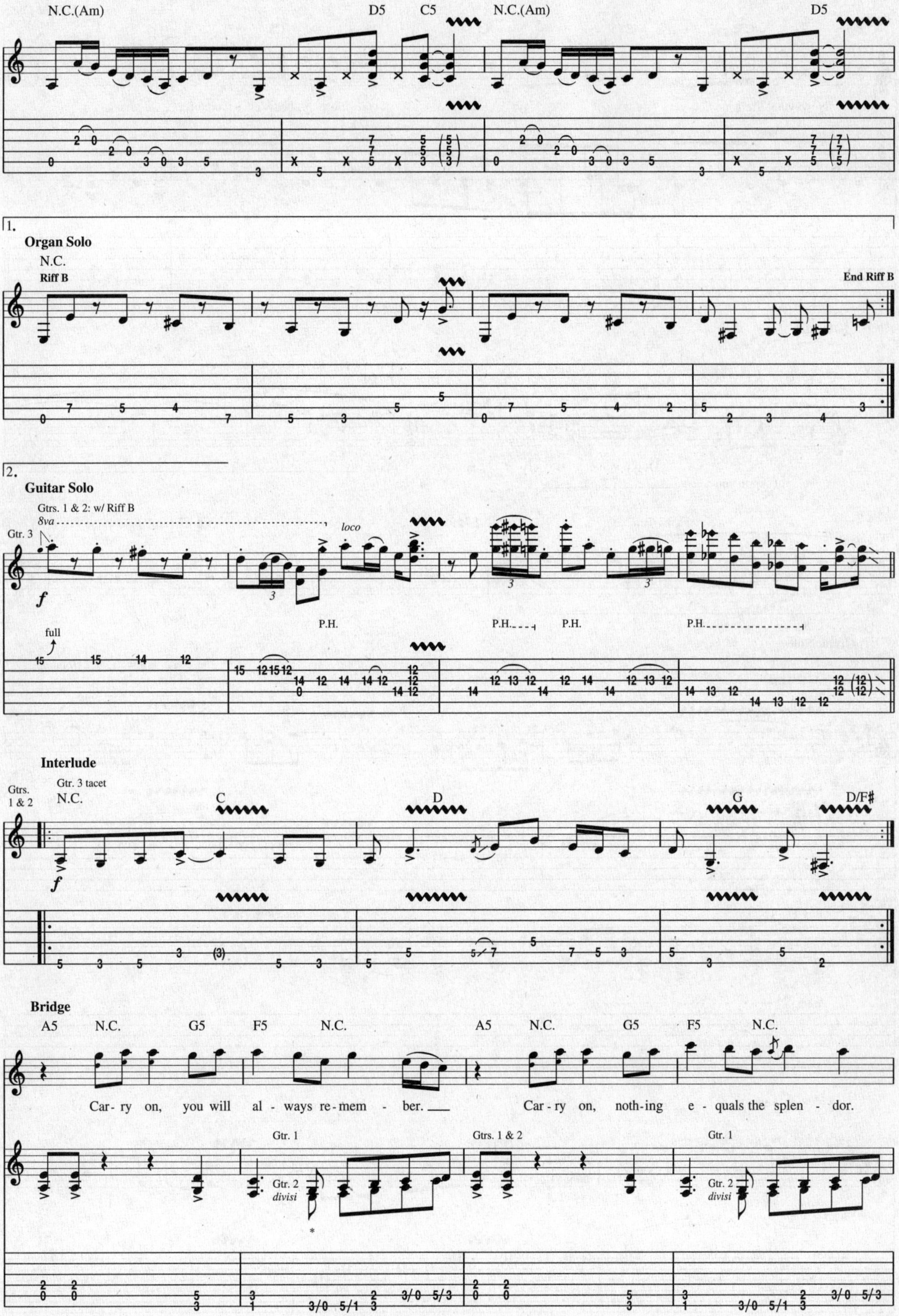

N.C.(Am) D5 C5 N.C.(Am) D5

1.

Organ Solo

N.C.

Riff B

End Riff B

2.

Guitar Solo

Gtrs. 1 & 2: w/ Riff B

Gtr. 3

8va

loco

f

full

P.H. P.H. P.H. P.H.

Interlude

Gtrs. 1 & 2

Gtr. 3 tacet

N.C. C D G D/F#

f

Bridge

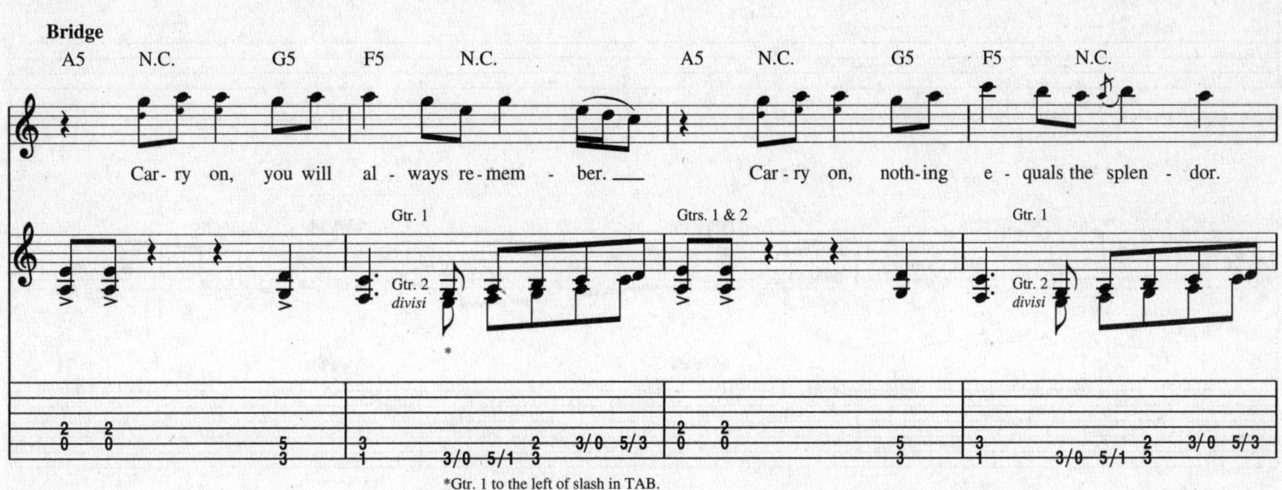

*Gtr. 1 to the left of slash in TAB.

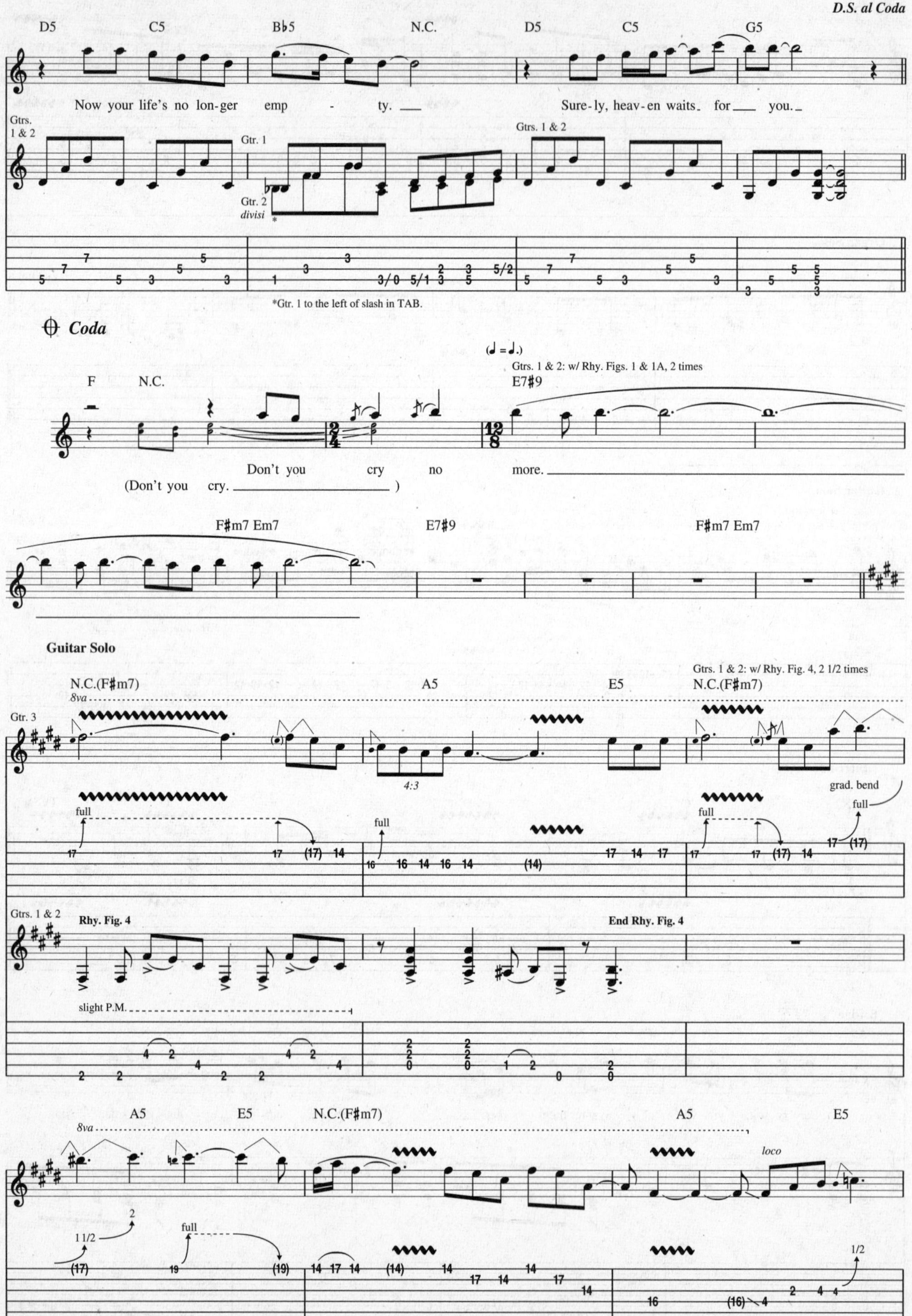
D.S. al Coda
D5 C5 B♭5 N.C. D5 C5 G5
Now your life's no lon-ger emp - ty.
Sure-ly, heav-en waits for you.
Gtrs. 1 & 2
Gtr. 1
Gtr. 2 divisi
*Gtr. 1 to the left of slash in TAB.
Coda
(♩ = ♩.)
Gtrs. 1 & 2: w/ Rhy. Figs. 1 & 1A, 2 times
F N.C. E7♯9
Don't you cry no more.
(Don't you cry.)
F♯m7 Em7 E7♯9 F♯m7 Em7
Guitar Solo
Gtrs. 1 & 2: w/ Rhy. Fig. 4, 2 1/2 times
N.C.(F♯m7) A5 E5 N.C.(F♯m7)
8va
Gtr. 3
grad. bend
full
Gtrs. 1 & 2
Rhy. Fig. 4
End Rhy. Fig. 4
slight P.M.
A5 E5 N.C.(F♯m7) A5 E5
loco
218

N.C. (F♯m7)
A
Gtr. 3 tacet
E7♯9
No more!
Gtr. 1
Gtr. 2
slight P.M.
Gtr. 3: w/ Fill 1
F♯m7 Em7
Gtr. 3 tacet
E7♯9
slight P.M.
P.M.

Gtr. 3: w/ Fill 1
F♯m7 Em7
Gtrs. 1 & 2: w/ Rhy. Fig. 4, 4 times
N.C. (F♯m7)
A5
E5
Gtr. 3
P.M.
full
hold bend
1/4
1/2
8va
Am
G
Fmaj7
loco
dim.
Gtr. 1
Gtr. 2
divisi
Fill 1
w/ echo repeats

Catfish Blues

Words and Music by Robert Petway

Tune Down 1/2 Step:

①= E♭ ④= D♭

②= B♭ ⑤= A♭

③= G♭ ⑥= E♭

Intro

Slowly ♩. = 66

Freely

N.C. (E7)

let ring

let ring

A tempo

* semi-harm

* semi-harm achieved by partially muting between 2nd and 3rd frets

drums enter

even bend

P.M.

rake

Verse
N.C. (E7)
1. Well, I wish I was a cat - fish
swim-min' in, Lord, the deep blue
sea. I have, ah, all you pret - ty wom-an(s)
fish - in' af - ter me, fish - in' af - ter me,
P.M.
let ring
snap
full
1/2
1/4

fish - in' af - ter me, yeah! Oh yeah!
mp
P.M.
mf
f
Oh yeah! Oh yeah!
Oh yeah.
mf P.M.
Yeah! 2. Well, now I went down
P.M.
mp

Verse
N.C. (E7)
my girl - friend's house, an' I
sat down, Lord, on her front step. But she said, ah,
"Come in now, Ji - mi, my hus - band just now left,
ah, just now left." Whoa yeah!
mf
mp
f
P.M.
let ring
full
1/2
1/4

Oh, yeah!
Oh yeah!
fuzz on
Oh yeah.
let ring
even gliss.
Guitar Solo
E
D7 D#7 E7
lay back
E E7 A (E7)
loco
8va

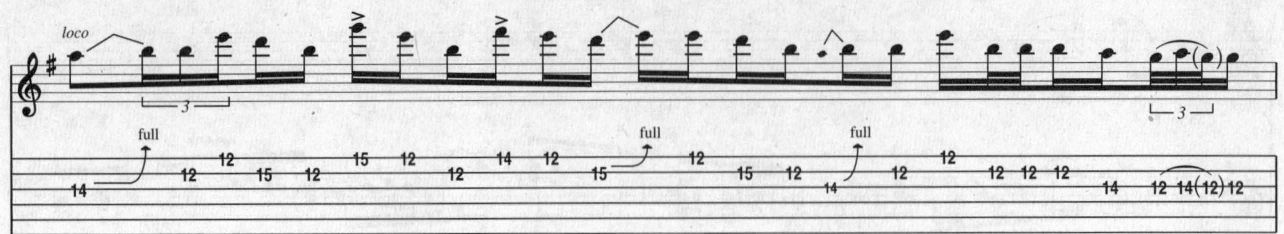
loco
full
full
full

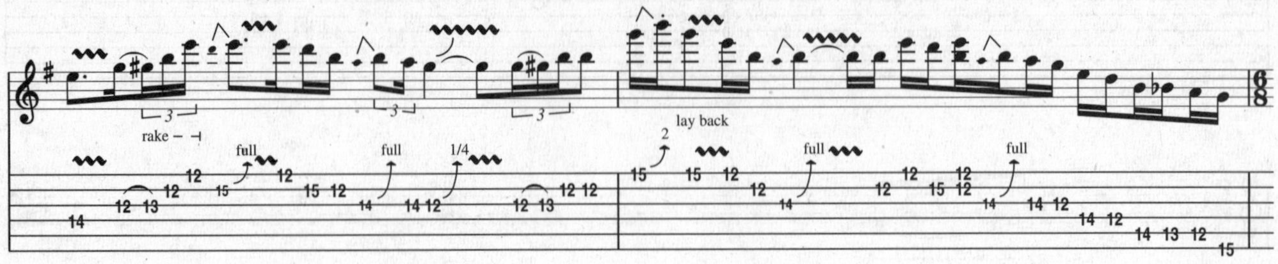
rake
full
full
1/4
lay back
2
full
full

5:3
let ring
full
full
full
full
full
full

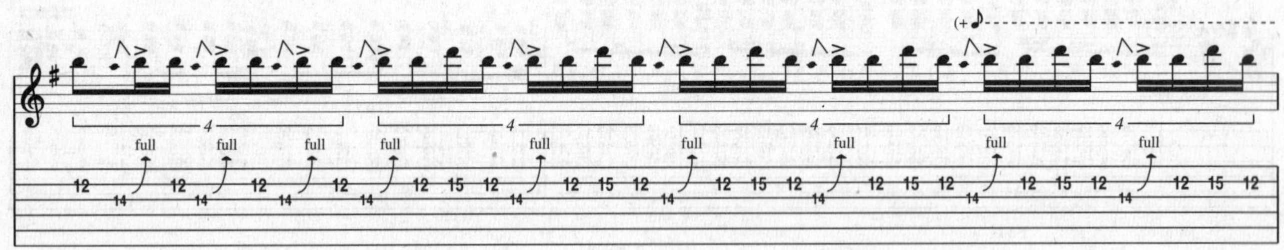
full
full
full
full
full
full
full
full
full

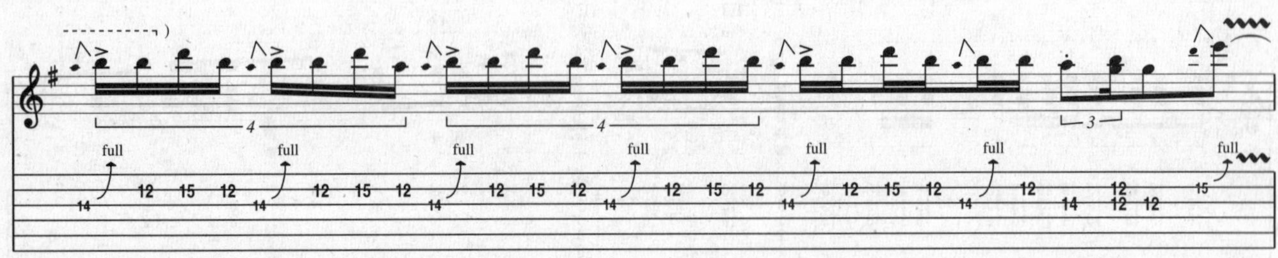
full
full
full
full
full
full
full

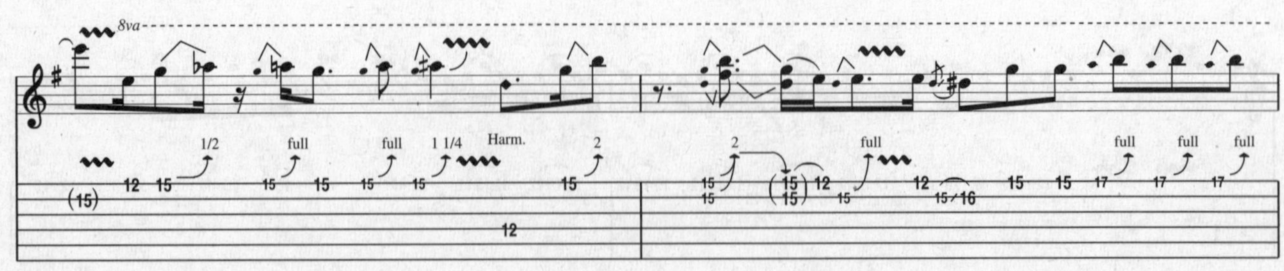
8va
1/2
full
full
1 1/4
Harm.
2
2
full
full
full
full

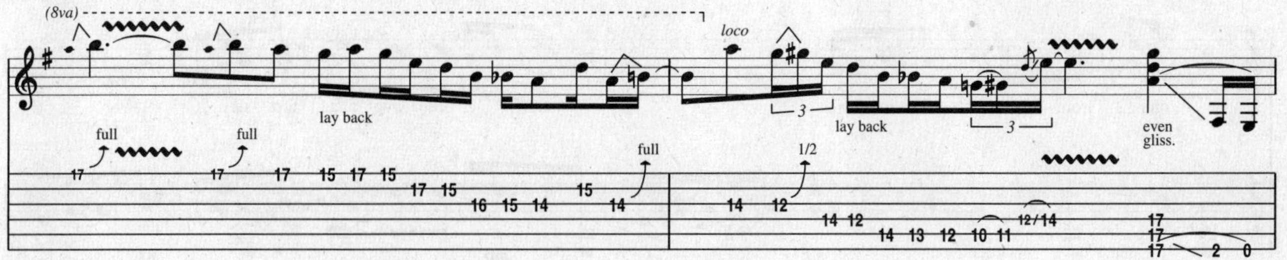
(8va)
loco
full
full
lay back
lay back
3
3
1/2
even gliss.

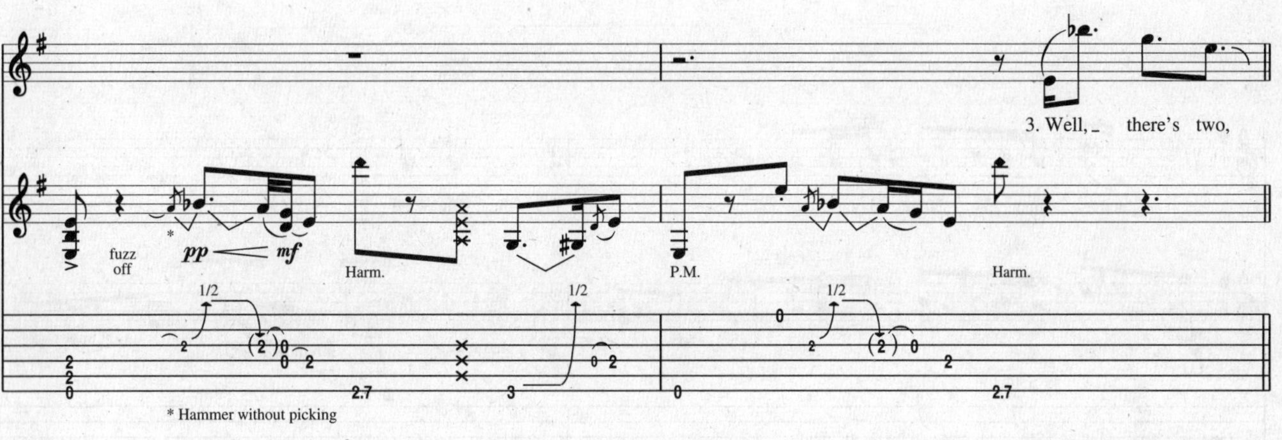
3. Well, there's two,
fuzz off
pp
mf
Harm.
P.M.
Harm.
1/2
1/2
1/2
* Hammer without picking

Verse

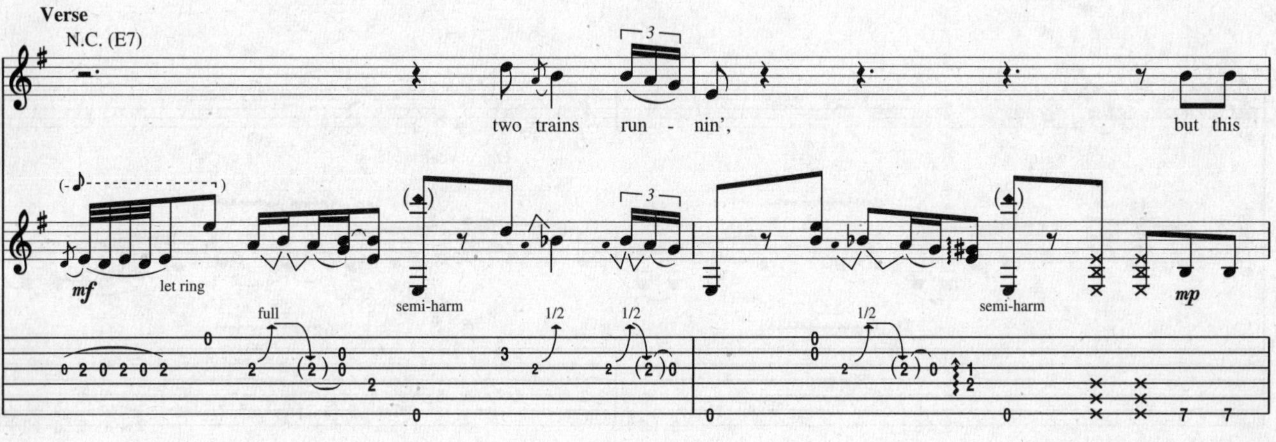
N.C. (E7)
two trains run - nin', but this
mf
let ring
semi-harm
semi-harm
mp
full
1/2
1/2
1/2

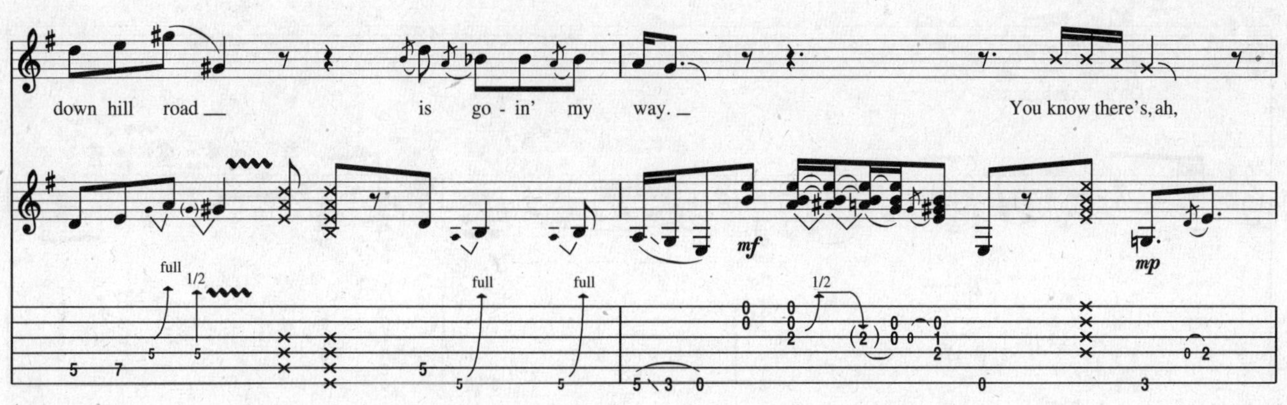
down hill road is go - in' my way. You know there's, ah,
mf
mp
full
1/2
full
full
1/2

one _ train run at mid - night, _
oth - er one leave just - 'fore day, _
mf
mp
mf
P.M.
1/2
1/2
1/2

leave _ just _ 'fore day. ____
Oh well.
mp
P.M.
P.M.
p
mp
rake
1/2
1/2

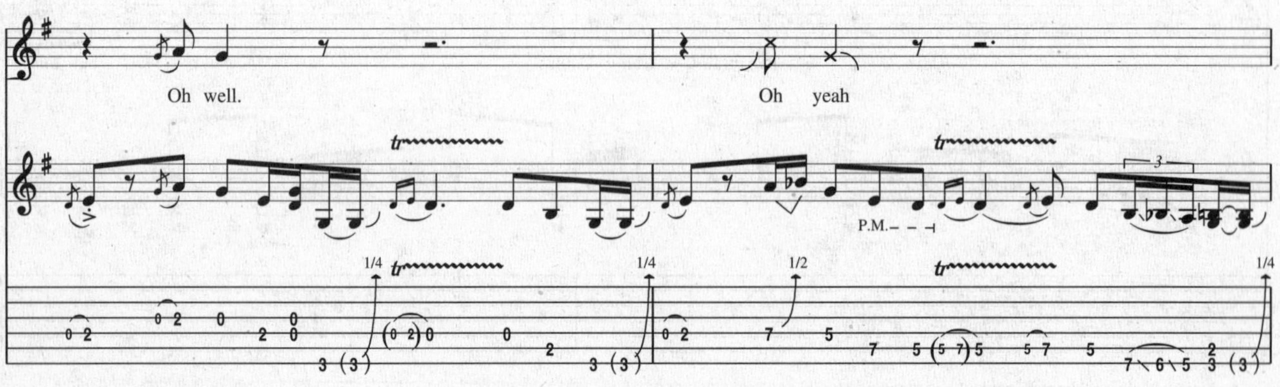

Oh well.
Oh yeah
P.M.
1/4
1/4
1/2
1/4

Oh _ yeah. _
let ring
f
1/2
1/4
full
full

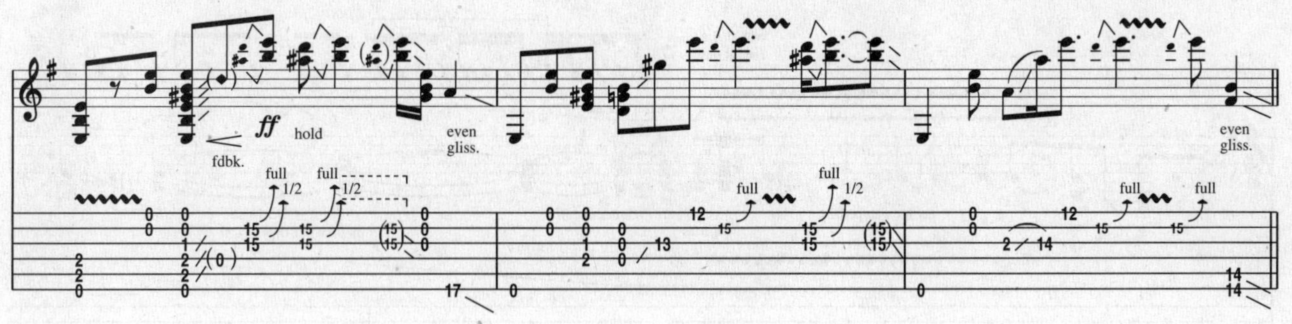
fdbk.
ff
hold
even
gliss.
full
1/2
even
gliss.

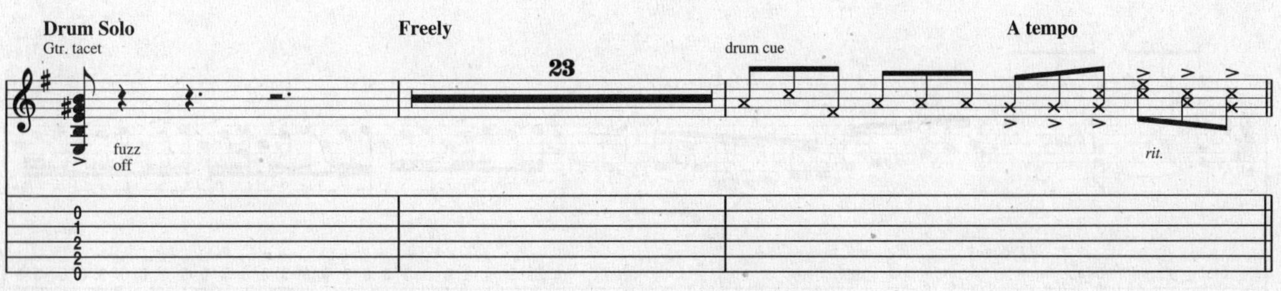
Drum Solo
Gtr. tacet
Freely
23
drum cue
A tempo
fuzz
off
rit.

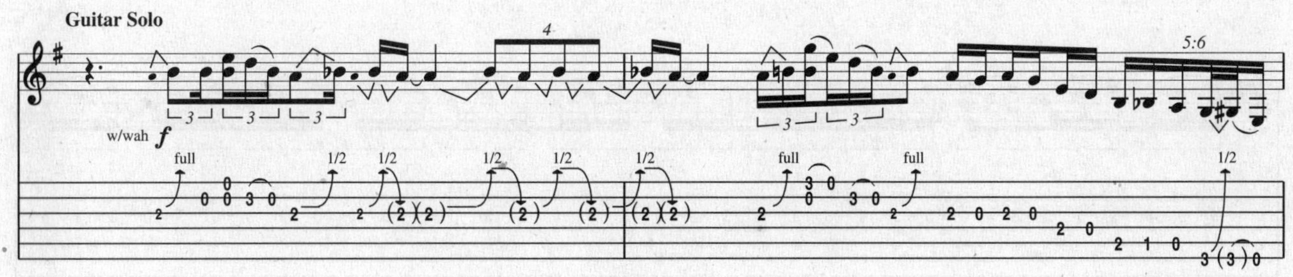
Guitar Solo
w/wah
f
full
1/2

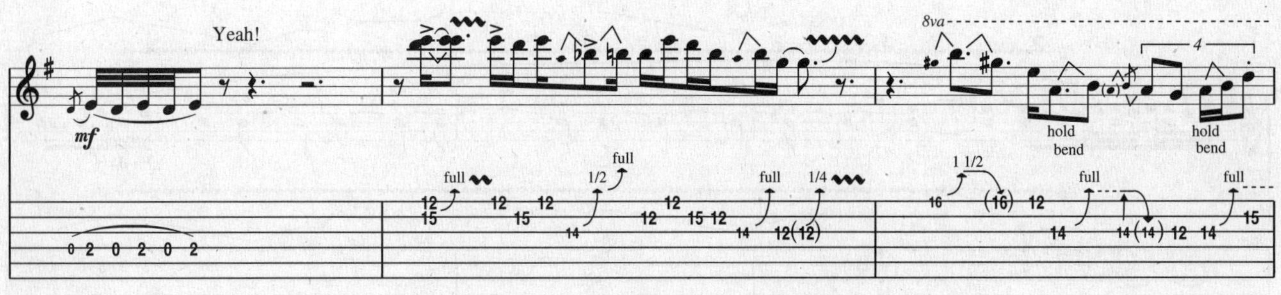
Yeah!
mf
8va
hold
bend
hold
bend
full
1/2
1/4
1 1/2

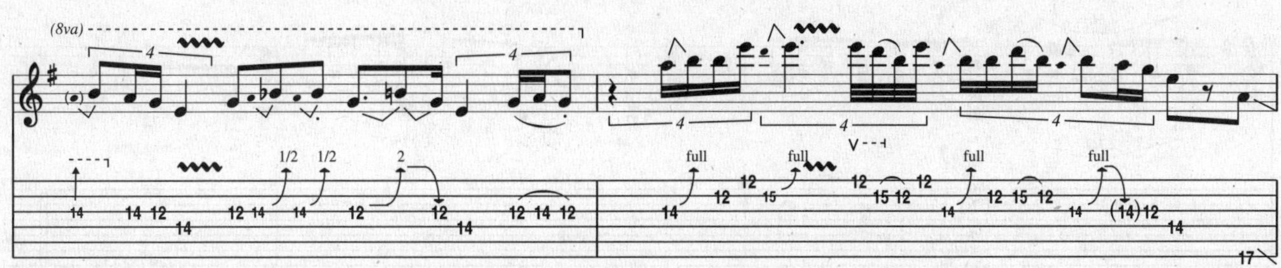
(8va)
full
1/2
2

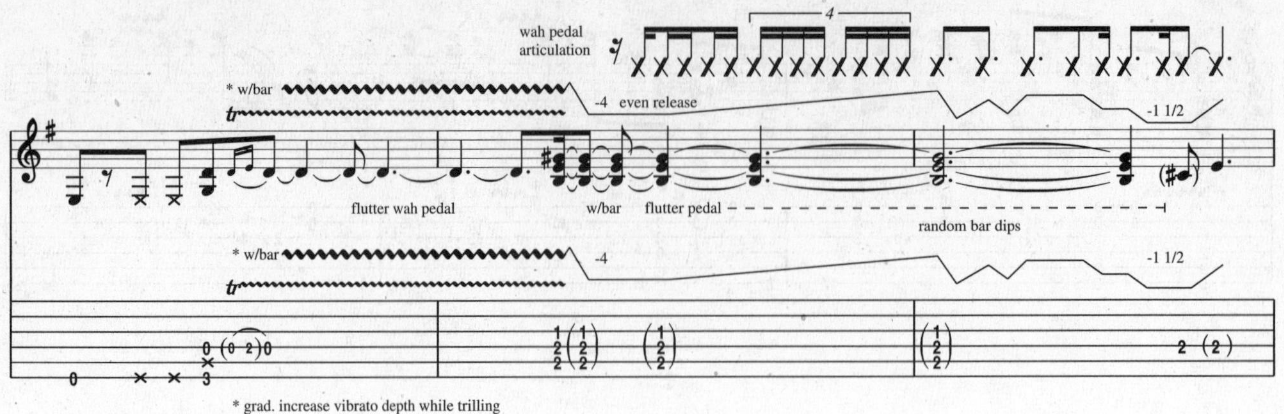
wah pedal articulation
* w/bar
-4 even release
-1 1/2
flutter wah pedal
w/bar
flutter pedal
random bar dips
* grad. increase vibrato depth while trilling

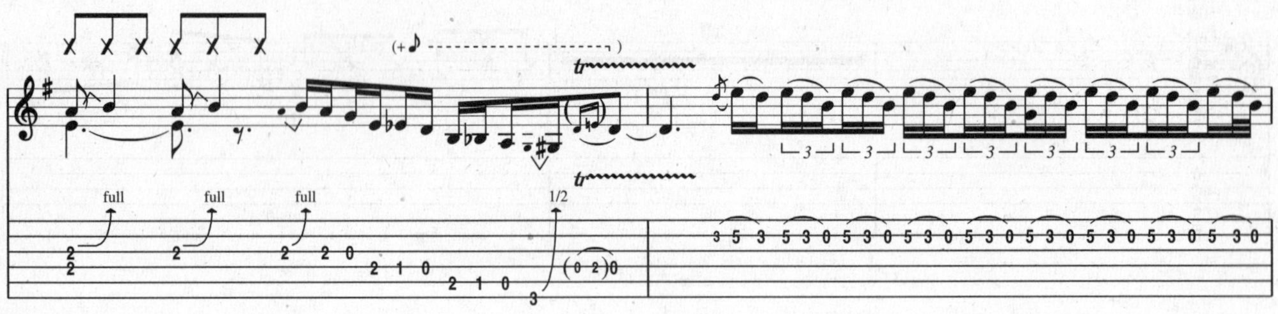
full
full
full
1/2

w/bar

full
full
P.M.
mf
mp
string noise

Tempo 2
= ca. 188
f
hold bend
full
hold bend
full
full
full
full
full
full
full

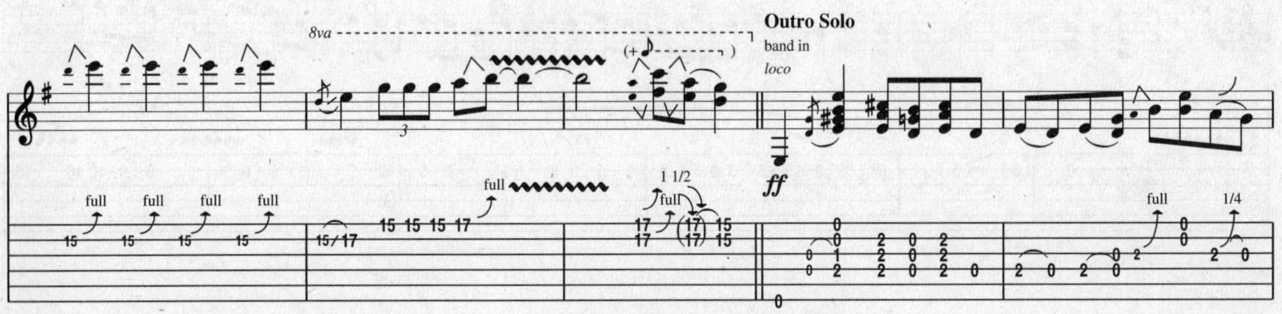
8va
Outro Solo
band in
loco
ff
full
full
full
full
full
1 1/2
full
full
1/4

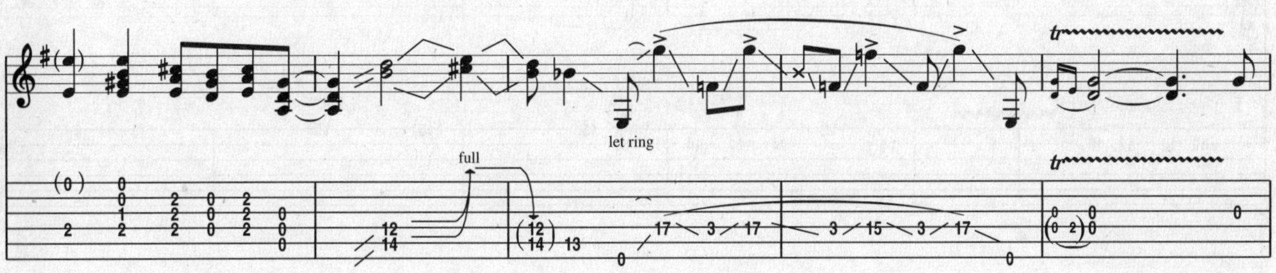
let ring
tr
full
tr

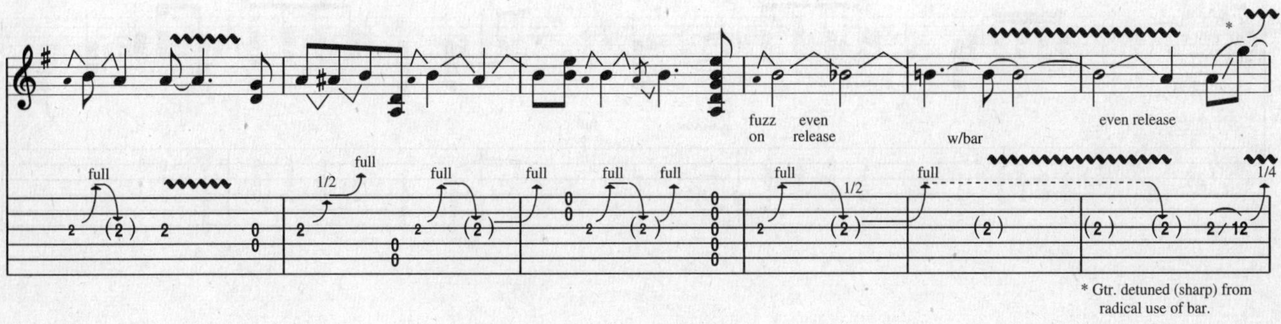
fuzz
on
even
release
w/bar
even release
full
1/2
full
full
full
full
full
full
1/2
full
1/4
* Gtr. detuned (sharp) from
radical use of bar.

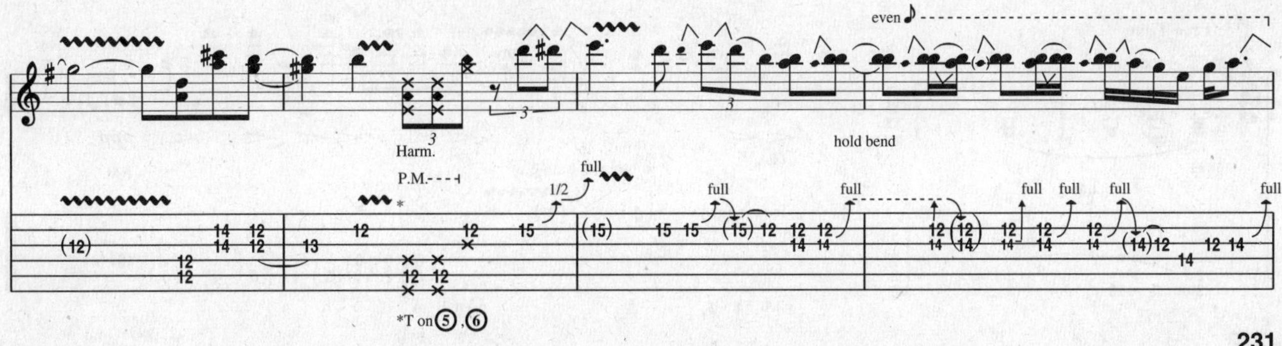
even
Harm.
P.M.
hold bend
1/2
full
full
full
full
full
full
full
*T on 5, 6

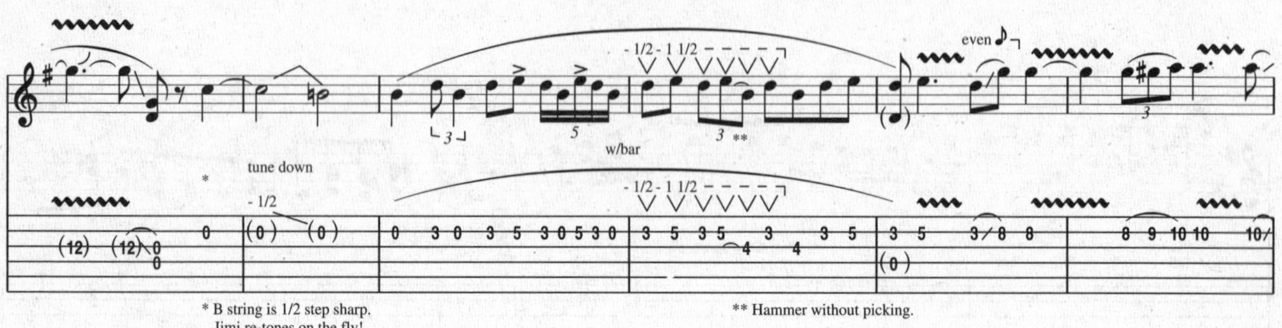

* B string is 1/2 step sharp.
Jimi re-tones on the fly!

** Hammer without picking.

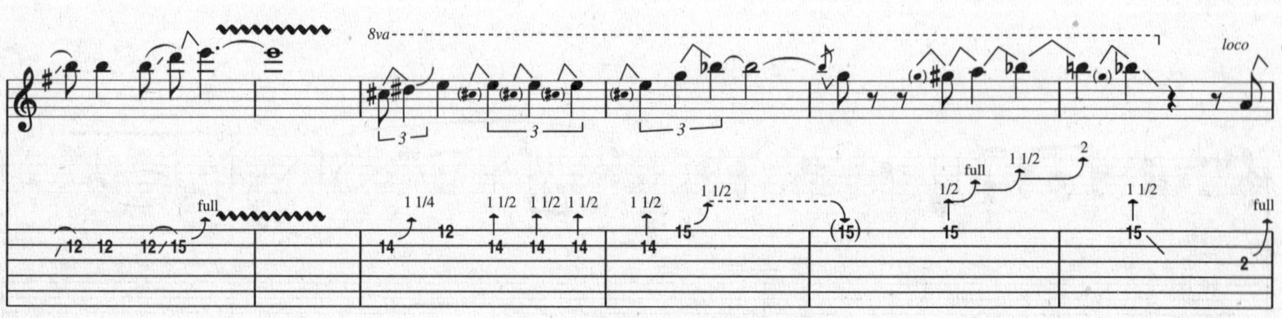

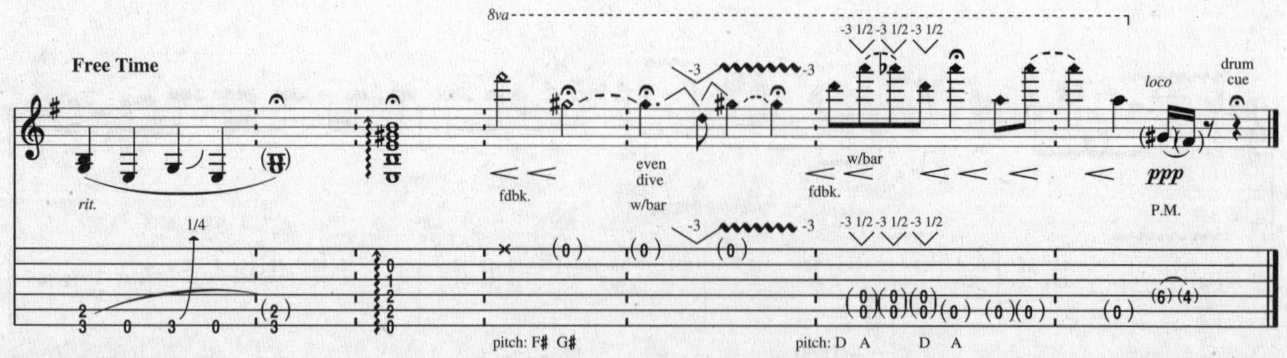

Cherry Pie

Words and Music by Jani Lane

N.C. (E)
G5
A5
Heh, heh.
Well, _
Both gtrs.
P.M.
1/4
Verse 1:
E5
D5
A
swing - in' on the front porch, swing - in' on the lawn, swing - in' where we want 'cause there ain't no - bod - y home. _
E
Swing - in' to the left and swing - in' to the right, I think a - bout base - ball, I'll swing all night, yeah. _
Yeah, yeah, _
huh!

Verse 2 & 3:
E5
Gtrs. rest for 1st six beats (2nd time only)
D5
A5
2. Swing - in' in the liv - in' room, swing - in' in the kitch - en, most folks don't 'cause they're too bus - y bitch - in'.
3. See additional lyrics
Swing - in' in there 'cause she want - ed me to feed her so I mixed up the bat - ter and she _ licked the beat - er.
Chorus:
A5
C5
D5
F5
G5
E5
G5
I scream, you scream, we all scream for her. Don't e - ven try 'cause you can't ig - nore _ her. She's my cher - ry pie; _
P.M.
w/Fill 1 (1st time only)
A
Csus2
D5
E5
G5
D5
A
cool drink of wa - ter such a sweet sur - prise, _ tastes so good make a grown man cry. Sweet cher - ry pie. _ Oh yeah!
Fill 1
Gtr. II
G5
D5
A5
T
A
B

E5
G5
A
Csus2
D5
She's my cher - ry pie, put a smile on your face ten miles wide.
E5
G5
To Coda
D5
A
D.S. al Coda
Looks so good, bring a tear to your eye. Sweet cher - ry pie, yeah.
Coda
D5
A
6 12fr.
E
Sweet cher - ry pie yeah, hi.
Guitar solo:
A5 B5 A5 B5 A5 B5
A5 B5 A5 B5 A5
6 4fr.
G♯
Yeah, swing it all night long.
Gtr. 1
hold
semi-harm.
grad. bend
full
A5 B5 A5 B5 A5 B5
A5 B5 A5 B5 A5
6 4fr.
G♯
Swing it. Hey, hey, ow!
8va
-21/2
full
w/bar
1½

N.C.
D5 C5
8va
Gtr. I
full
1/2
1
Gtr. II
P.M.
1/4
C5
D5
I'm a trained pro - fes - sion - al.
Verse 4:
E5
E5
D5
A
Swing - in' in the bath - room, swing - in' on the floor, swing - in' so hard_ for - got to lock the door._
loco
Both gtrs.

E5
In walks her dad - dy stand - in' six foot four, said, "You ain't gon - na swing with my daugh - ter no more."
Chorus:
A5 C5 D5 F5 G5
She's my cher - ry pie, cool drink of wa - ter, such a sweet sur - prise.
A5 C5 G5 D5 Dsus4 D
Tastes so good make a grown man cry. Sweet cher - ry pie. Oh yeah!
A5 C5 D5 F5 G5
She's my cher - ry pie, put a smile on your face ten miles wide.

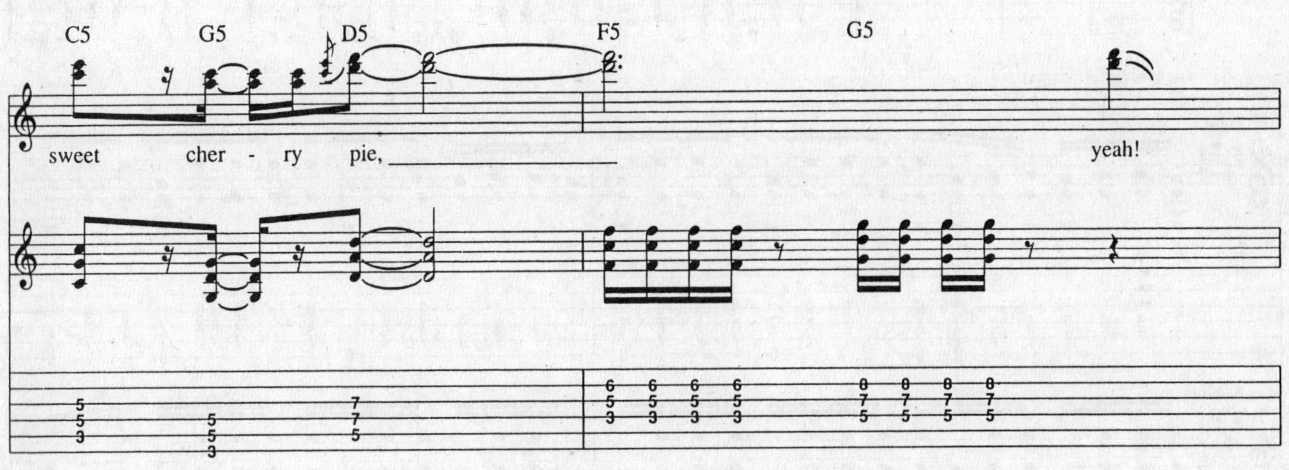

Verse 3:
Swingin' to the drums,
Swingin' to guitar,
Swingin' to the bass,
In the back of my car.

Ain't got money,
Ain't got no gas,
But we'll get where we're going
If we swing it real fast.

Cherub Rock

Words and Music by Billy Corgan

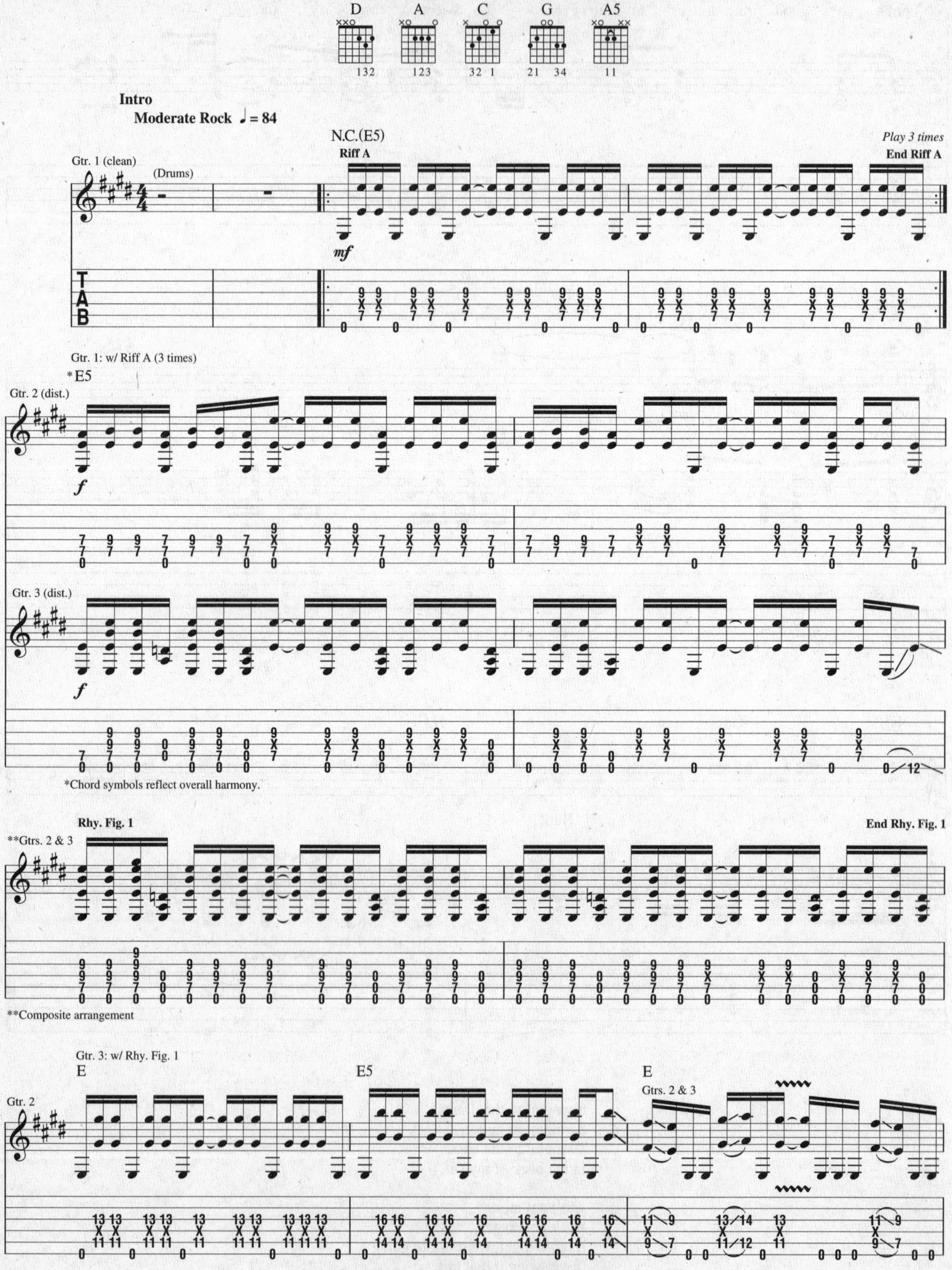

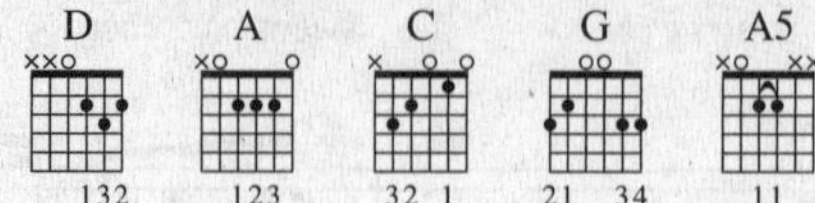

Intro
Moderate Rock ♩ = 84

N.C.(E5)
Riff A
Play 3 times
End Riff A
Gtr. 1 (clean)
(Drums)
mf

Gtr. 1: w/ Riff A (3 times)
*E5
Gtr. 2 (dist.)
f

Gtr. 3 (dist.)
f

*Chord symbols reflect overall harmony.

Rhy. Fig. 1
End Rhy. Fig. 1
**Gtrs. 2 & 3

**Composite arrangement

Gtr. 3: w/ Rhy. Fig. 1
E
E5
E
Gtr. 2
Gtrs. 2 & 3

D A E
Gtr. 3
Rhy. Fill 1A
End Rhy. Fill 1A
Riff B
T=Thumb on 6th string
Gtr. 2
Rhy. Fill 1
End Rhy. Fill 1
Riff B
Gtrs. 2 & 3
Verse
E
1. Freak out, (and) give in, does-n't mat-
sters u - nite; come a - lign
End Riff B
Riff C
End Riff C
Gtrs. 2 & 3: w/ Rhy. Fills 1 & 1A
Gtrs. 2 & 3: w/ Riff C
D A E
- ter what you be - lieve in. Stay cool, and be
for the big fight to rock for you. (But) be - ware, all those an-

Gtrs. 2 & 3: w/ Rhy. Fills 1 & 1A
D
A
Gtrs. 2 & 3: w/ Riff C
E
— some - bod - y's fool — this year.
- gels with their wings glued on,
'Cause they know who is right -
'cause deep down they are fright -
D
A
C
G
- eous, what is bold, ——
- ened and they're scared ——
so —— I'm told. ——
if you — don't stare. ——
Rhy. Fig 2A
Gtr. 3
End Rhy. Fig. 2A
Rhy. Fig. 2
Gtr. 2
End Rhy. Fig. 2
Chorus
Gtrs. 2 & 3: w/ Rhy. Figs. 2 & 2A
D
A
C
G
Who —— wants — hon - ey, — as
Rhy. Fig. 3
Gtr. 4 (dist.)
mf
End Rhy. Fig. 3
Gtr. 4: w/ Rhy. Fig. 3
D
A
C
G
long —— as — there's some mon - ey? ——
(Mon, mon - ey.) ——

1.
D
A
C
Rhy. Fig. 4B
End Rhy. Fig. 4B
Gtr. 4
Who wants that hon -
Rhy. Fig. 4A
End Rhy. Fig. 4A
Gtr. 3
Rhy. Fig. 4
End Rhy. Fig. 4
Gtr. 2
Interlude
Gtrs. 2 & 3: w/ Riff B
Gtr. 4 tacet
E
ey? Ah, oh. Ah, oh. 2. Hip -
2.
C
G A5
Interlude
E
D5 A C G5
Gtr. 4
(cont. in notation)
- ey? Let me out.
Rhy. Fig. 5
End Rhy. Fig. 5
Gtr. 3
Rhy. Fig. 5A
End Rhy. Fig. 5A
Gtr. 2
Gtrs. 2 & 4
1/2

Gtrs. 2, 3 & 4: w/ Rhy. Figs. 5 & 5A (3 times)
E D5 A C G5 E D5
Yeah, let me out. Yeah, let me
A C G5 E D5 A C G5
out. Yeah, let me out!
Interlude
Gtrs. 3 & 4: w/ Riff A (2 times)
E5 E
Gtr. 2
Gtr. 5 (dist.)
E5 E7 E5
w/ chorus & flanger
Guitar Solo
D5 A5 E D5 A5
8va
Gtr. 5
P.H.
Gtrs. 2 & 3

E
8va
loco
D5
A5
P.H.
1/2
1
E
D5
A5
C
G5
grad. bend
1
1
1/2
1
1/2
1
Bridge
Gtrs. 2 & 3: w/ Rhy. Figs. 2 & 2A (4 times)
D
A
Gtr. 5 tacet
C
G
D
A
Tell me all of your se - crets. Can-not help but be -
Gtr. 6 (dist.)
fdbk.
p
mp
Gtr. 7 (dist.)
mp

C G D A C G
lieve this is true. Tell me all of your se - crets. I know,
1/4
8 7 (7) 7 (7) 2 4 2
1
15 (15)
5 4 5 5 7 5
1
7 (7)
D A C G
I know, I know (I) should have lis - tened to what I was told.
Gtr. 6
fdbk.
don't pick
(15) (14)
Gtr. 7
fdbk.
(7) (7)
Pitch: A
Gtr. 5
fdbk.
don't pick
f
(7)

Chorus

Gtrs. 2 & 3: w/ Rhy. Figs. 2 & 2A (2 times)
Gtr. 4: w/ Rhy. Fig. 3 (2 times)
Gtrs. 6 & 7 tacet

Gtr. 5

*Set for one octave above

Gtrs. 2, 3 & 4: w/ Rhy. Figs. 4, 4A & 4B

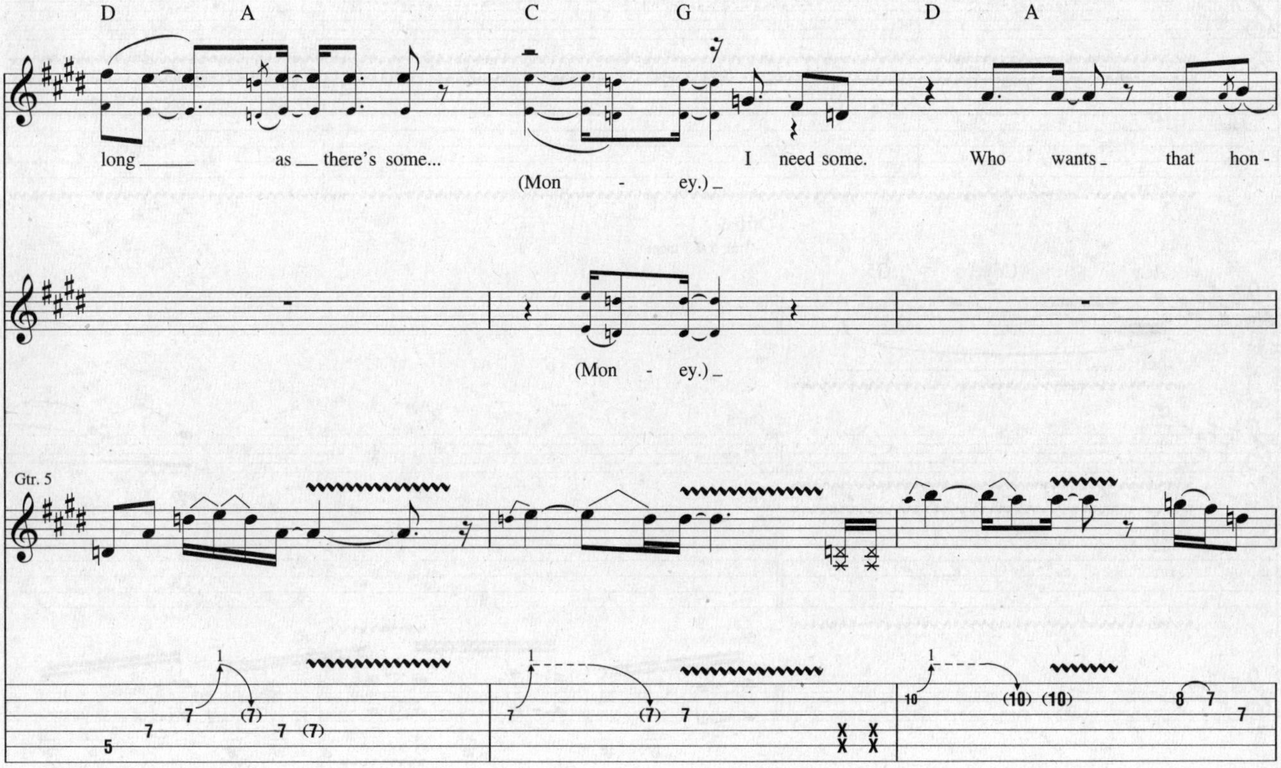

D A C G D A

long ___ as _ there's some... I need some. Who wants _ that hon -
(Mon - ey.) _

(Mon - ey.) _

Gtr. 5

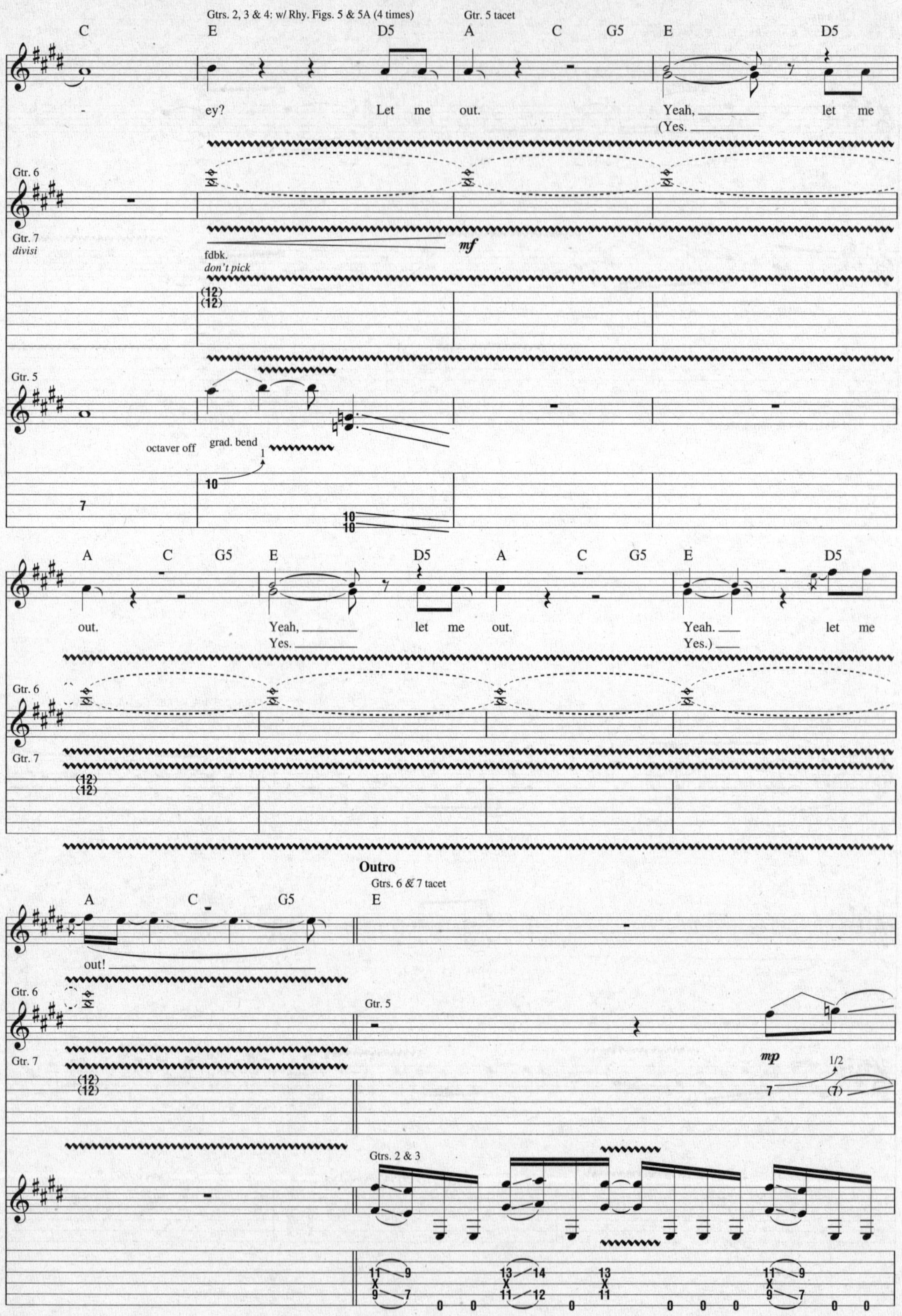

Gtrs. 2, 3 & 4: w/ Rhy. Figs. 5 & 5A (4 times)
Gtr. 5 tacet
C
E
D5
A
C
G5
E
D5
- ey? Let me out. Yeah, let me
(Yes.
Gtr. 6
Gtr. 7
divisi
fdbk.
don't pick
mf
Gtr. 5
octaver off
grad. bend
1
A
C
G5
E
D5
A
C
G5
E
D5
out. Yeah, let me out. Yeah. let me
Yes. Yes.)
Gtr. 6
Gtr. 7
Outro
Gtrs. 6 & 7 tacet
A
C
G5
E
out!
Gtr. 6
Gtr. 5
Gtr. 7
mp
1/2
Gtrs. 2 & 3

(Oh.
Oh.
Oh.)
1/2
D5
E5
E

Cold Shot

Words and Music by Mike Kindred and Wesley Clark

Tune Down 1/2 Step:
① = E♭ ④ = D♭
② = B♭ ⑤ = A♭
③ = G♭ ⑥ = E♭

Intro

Moderate Shuffle ♩ = 120

N.C. (Am7)

Gtr. 1

f w/ slight dist.

(enter band)

picking cont. simile

Verse

Am N.C.
And now I reach to kiss your lips, my touch don't mean a thing.
And now I see you out some - where, you won't give me the time of day.
Chorus
(Dm7)
(Am7)
And that's a cold shot, ba - by, yeah, that's a drag.
And that's a cold shot, darl - in', yeah, that's a drag.
ba - by, yeah, that's a drag.
8va loco
1/4
(Dm7)
Gtr. 1: w/ Fill 1, 2nd time only
E7#9
A cold shot, ba - by, I let our love go
'n' that's a cold shot, ba - by, we've let our love go
'n' that's a cold shot, ba - by, we've let our love go
Fill 1
Gtr. 1
T
A
B

(Am7)
To Coda
1.
bad.
bad.
bad.
2.
Guitar Solo
N.C. (Am7)
* T = Thumb on 6
(D5)
(Am7)
rake

(D5)

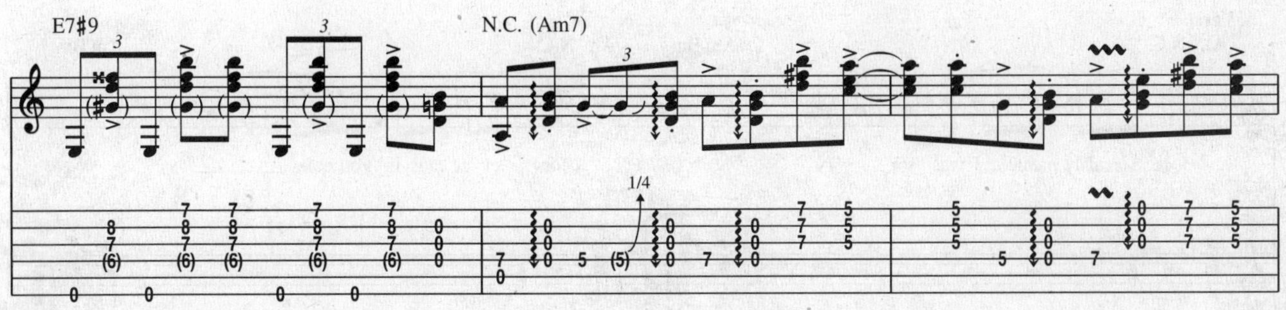
E7#9
N.C. (Am7)

even

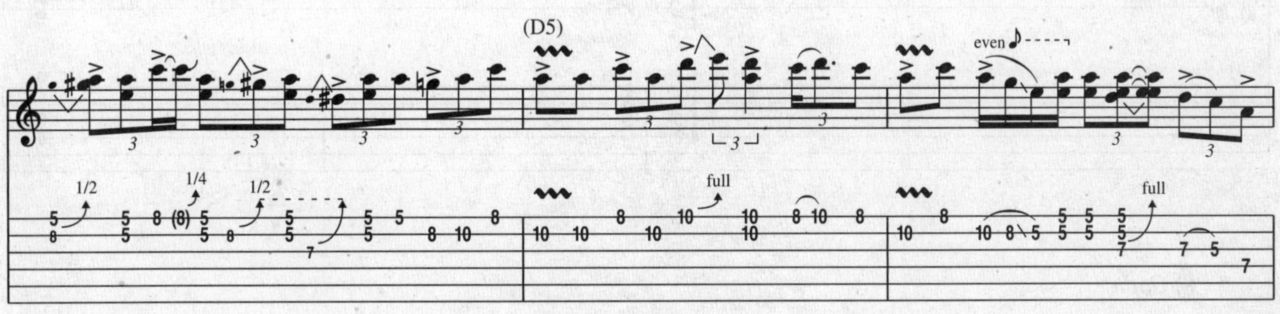
(D5)
even

(Am7)
(E5)
let ring
hold bend
hold bend
rake

(D5)
(Am7)
full
1/4

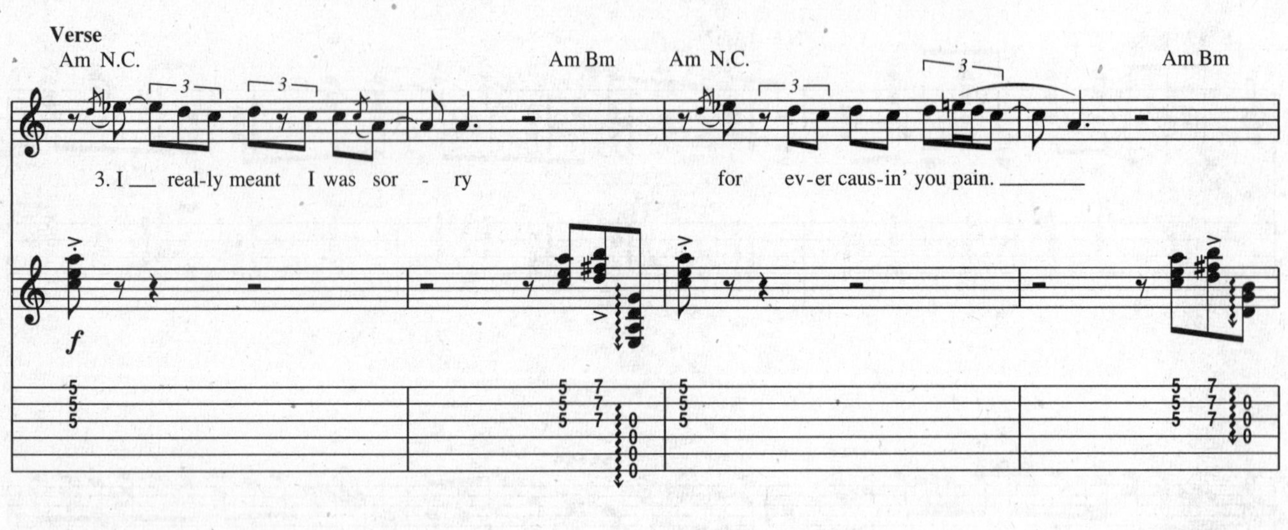

Verse
Am N.C.
Am Bm
3. I real-ly meant I was sor - ry
for ev-er caus-in' you pain.
f

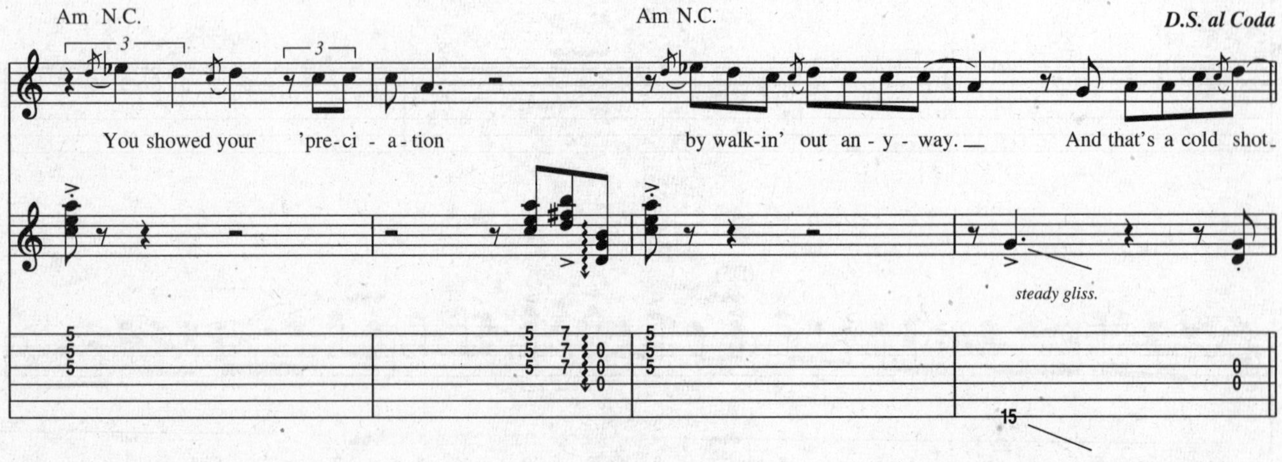

Am N.C.
D.S. al Coda
You showed your 'pre-ci - a-tion
by walk-in' out an - y - way.
And that's a cold shot
steady gliss.

Coda
1/4

Outro
N.C.(Am7)
End shot, too bad,
cold shot.
E7#9
E9
Am N.C.
(drums fill)
A7#9
Am7
Spoken: Don't let our true love run cold.
On cue:
On cue:

Cold Sweat, Pt. 1

Words and Music by James Brown and Alfred James Ellis

last. Uh. I don't care, dar - lin',
a - bout your thoughts. Ha, uh. I just
want to sat - is - fy your thoughts. Oh.
Gtr. 1: w/ Fill 1
Chorus
C9
F9
When ya kiss me,
Rhy. Fig. 2
Gtr. 1
End Rhy. Fig. 2
Rhy. Fig. 2A
Gtr. 2
End Rhy. Fig. 2A
Gtr. 1: w/ Rhy. Fig. 2, 4 times
Gtr. 2: w/ Rhy. Fig. 2A, 4 times, simile
when ya miss me.
Hold
You hold
my hand, make me un - der - stand.
me tight. Make ev - 'ry - thing al - right.
I break out
Fill 1
Gtr. 1
P.M.
T
A
B

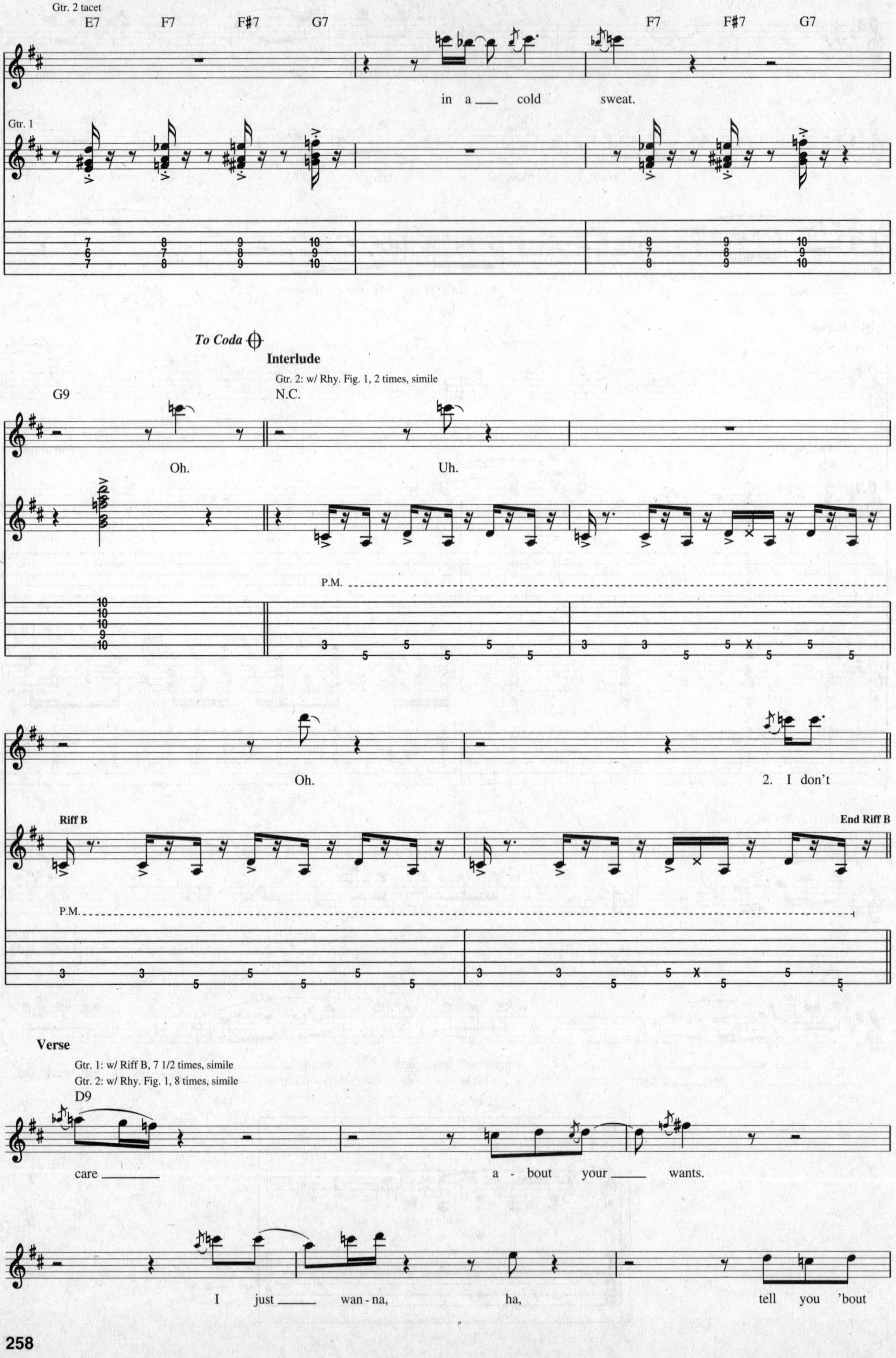

To Coda 𝄌

Interlude

Gtr. 2: w/ Rhy. Fig. 1, 2 times, simile

G9

N.C.

Oh. Uh.

P.M.

Oh. 2. I don't

Riff B

End Riff B

P.M.

Verse

Gtr. 1: w/ Riff B, 7 1/2 times, simile

Gtr. 2: w/ Rhy. Fig. 1, 8 times, simile

D9

care a - bout your wants.

I just wan - na, ha, tell you 'bout

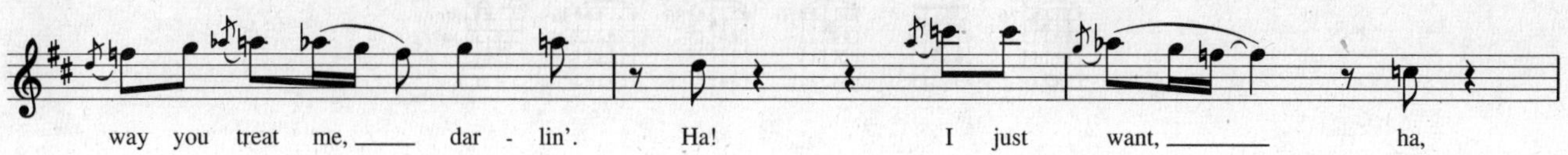

Coda

Outro

Gtr. 1: w/ Riff B, till fade, simile
Gtr. 2: w/ Rhy. Fig. 1, till fade, simile

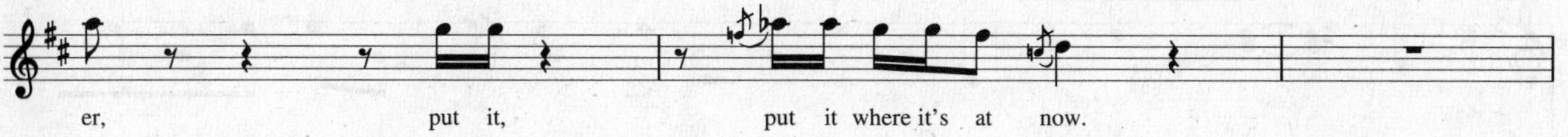

Begin Fade

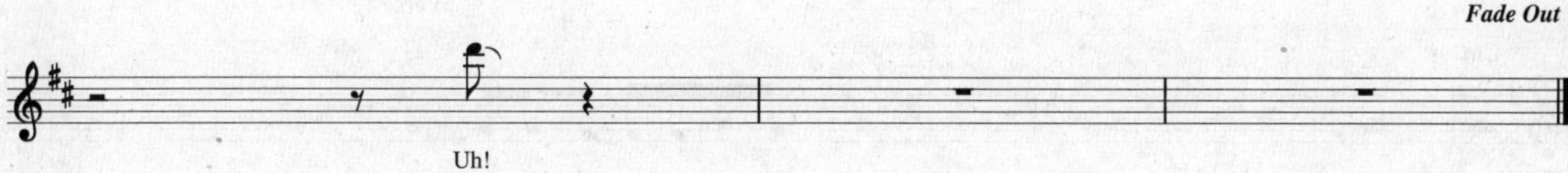

Creep

Words and Music by Albert Hammond, Mike Hazlewood, Thomas Yorke,
Richard Greenwood, Philip Selway, Colin Greenwood and Edward O'Brian

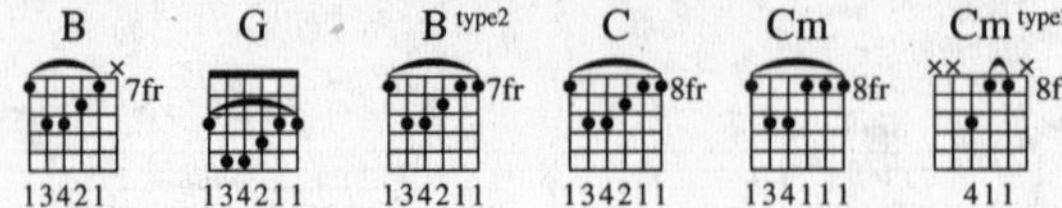

Intro
Moderately slow ♩ = 80

Gtr. 2 tacet

B

Gtr. 2 (clean)

could-n't look you in the eye. You're just like an an-

C Cm

-gel. (Your) skin makes me cry.

G

You float like a feath - er in a beau-ti-ful world.

End Riff A Riff B

B C

I wish I was spe - cial. You're so fuck-ing spe-

Chorus
Gtr. 1 tacet
Cm
G
Gtr. 3
- cial,
but I'm a
creep.
Gtr. 1
End Riff B
Gtr. 3 (dist.)
(cont. in slashes)
Gtr. 4 (dist.)
15ma
loco
mf
*fdbk.
let ring
*Microphonic fdbk., not caused by string vibration.
B type2
(cont. in notation)
I'm a
weird - o.
1. What
2. What
the hell am I do-ing here?
Gtr. 4
let ring
let ring

To Coda
C
I don't be - long
Gtr. 3
Gtr. 4
let ring
Cm
here.
2. I don't care if it hurts,
let ring
steady gliss.

Verse

Gtr. 1: w/ Riff A
Gtrs. 2 & 3 tacet
Gtr. 4 tacet
G
B
I wan - na have con - trol.
Gtr. 3
ppp
Gtr. 4
ppp
Gtr. 2
let ring
C
Cm
I want a per - fect bod - y.
I want a per - fect soul.
Gtr. 1: w/ Riff B
G
I want you to no - tice
when I'm not a - round.
B
C
You're so fuck - ing spe - cial.
I wish I was spe -

D.S. al Coda

*Microphonic fdbk, not caused by string vibration.

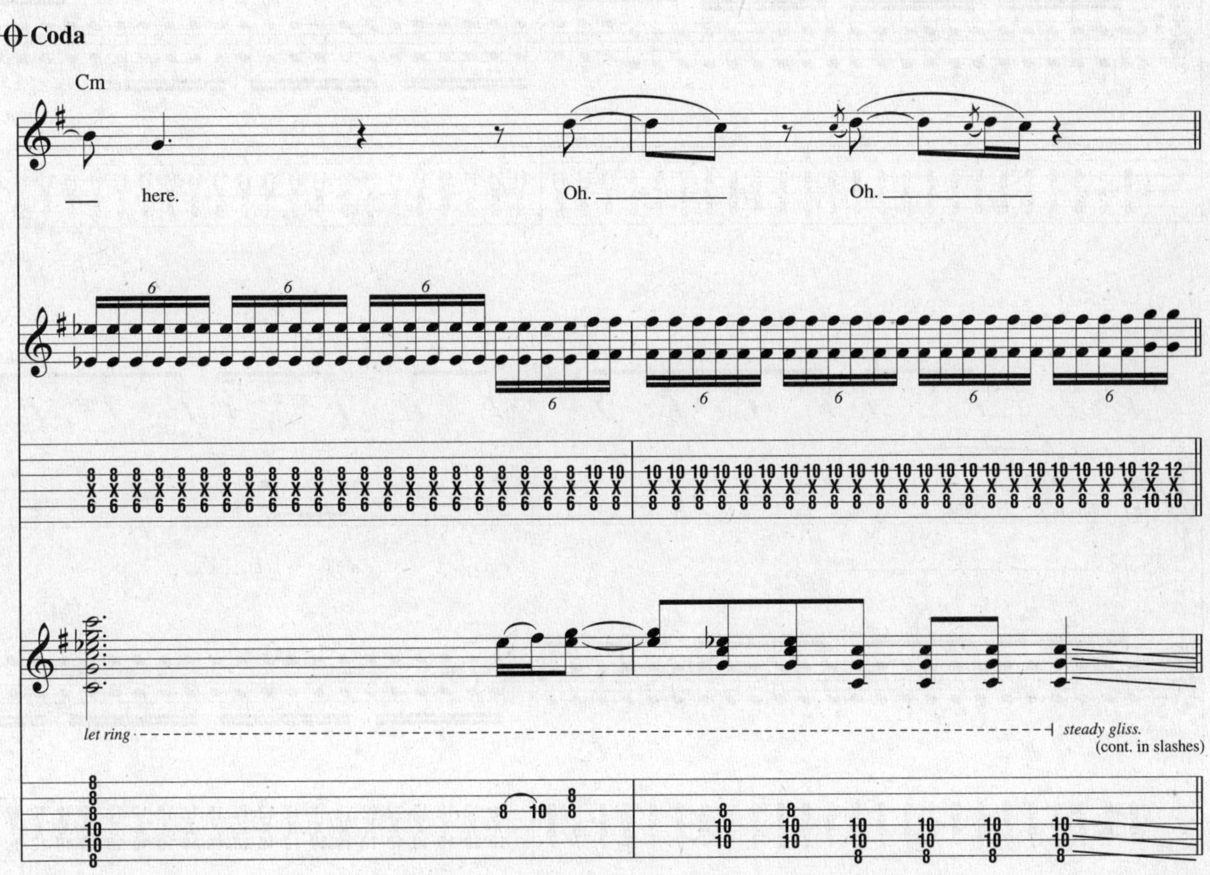

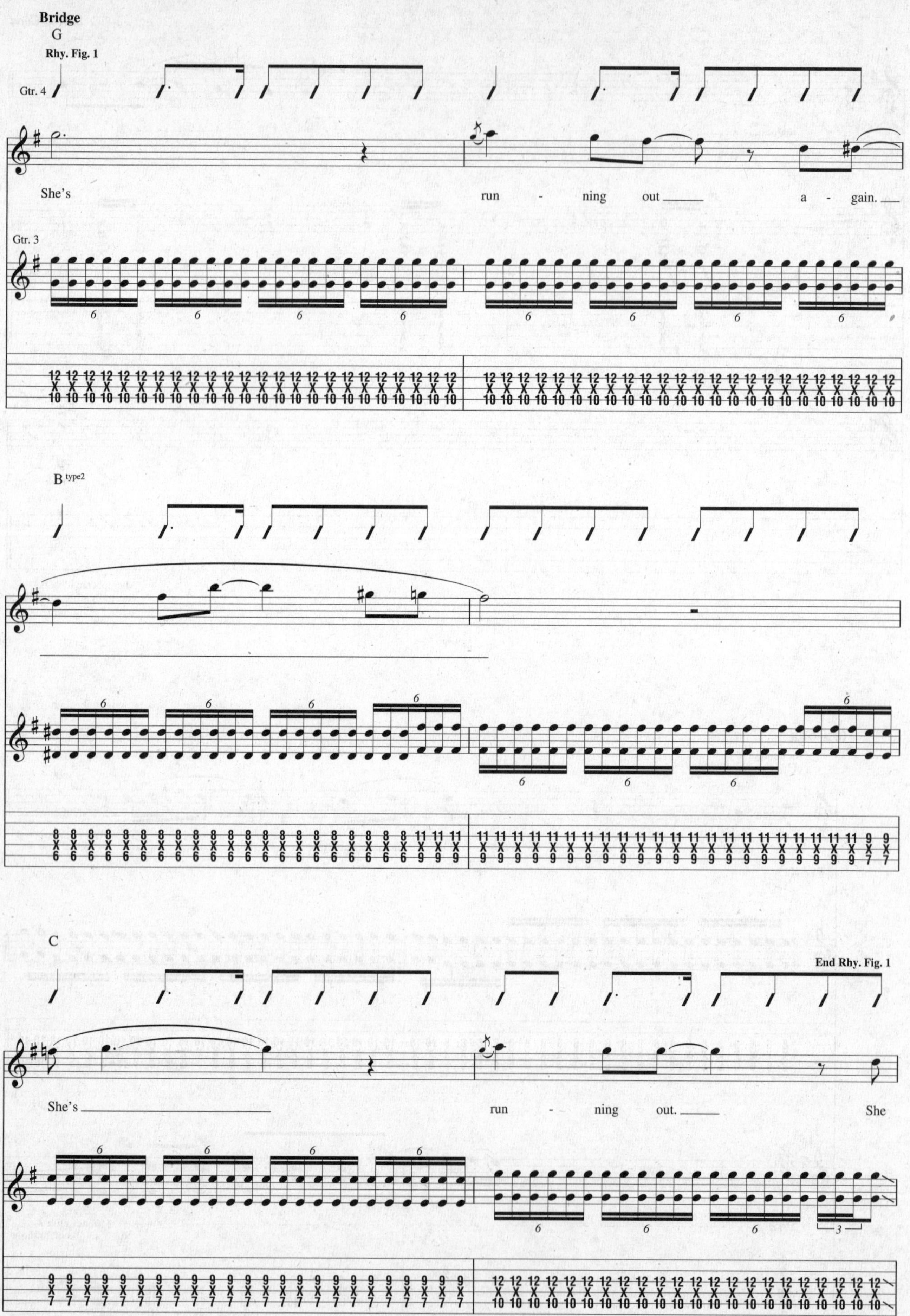
Bridge
G
Rhy. Fig. 1
Gtr. 4
She's
run - ning out a - gain.
Gtr. 3
B type2
C
End Rhy. Fig. 1
She's
run - ning out.
She

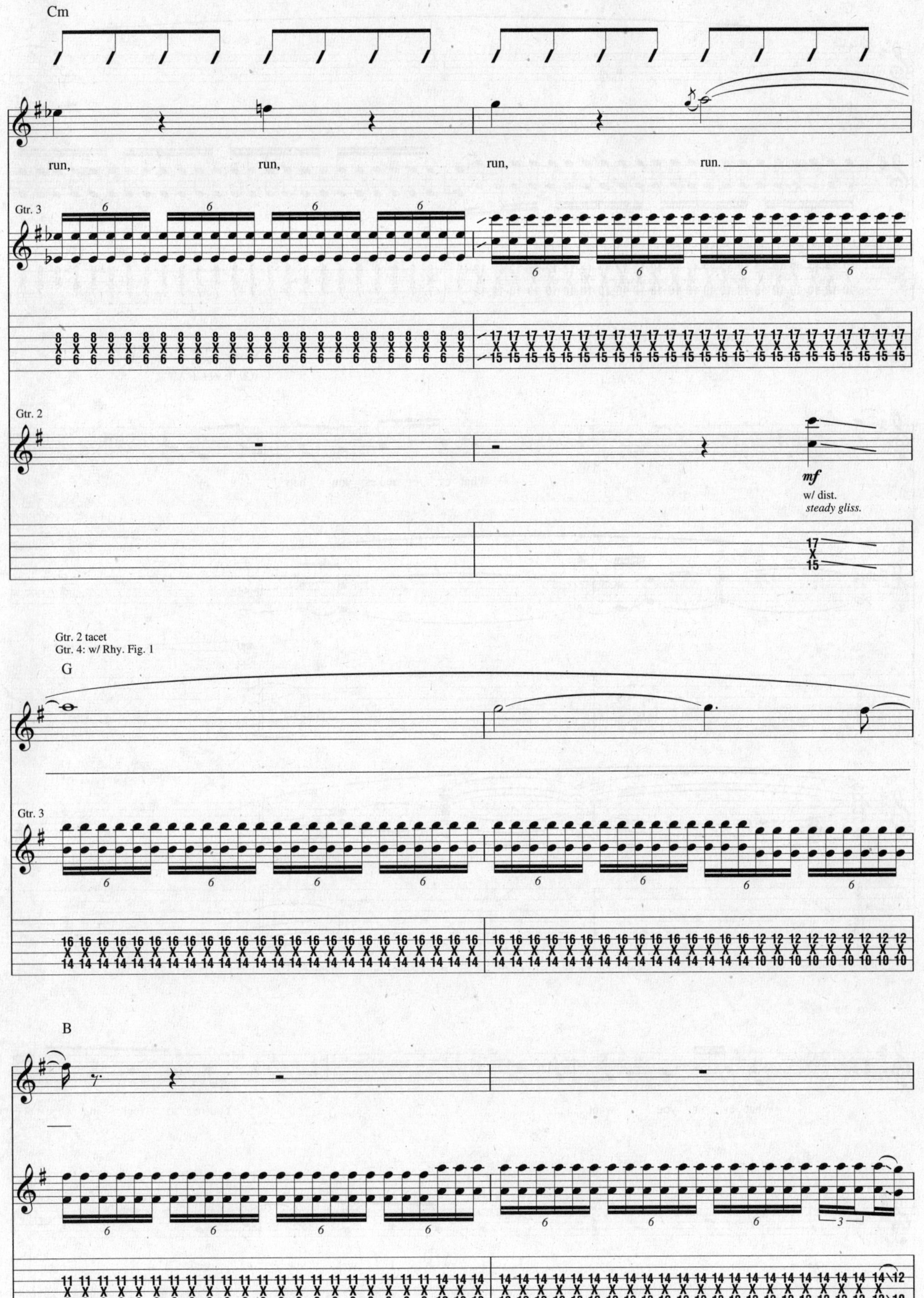
Cm
run,
run,
run,
run.
Gtr. 3
Gtr. 2
mf
w/ dist.
steady gliss.
Gtr. 2 tacet
Gtr. 4: w/ Rhy. Fig. 1
G
B

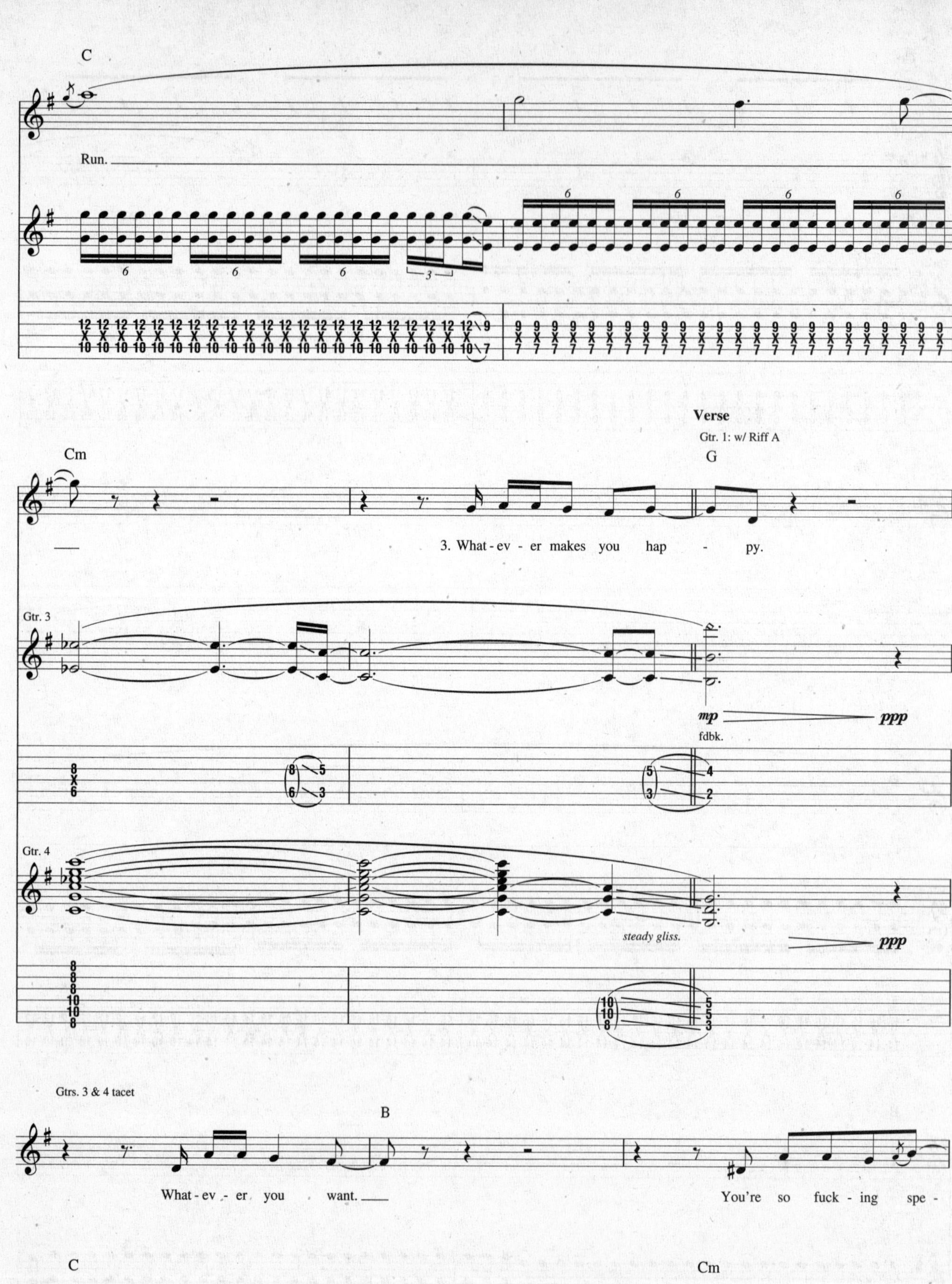
C
Run.
Cm
Verse
Gtr. 1: w/ Riff A
G
3. What-ev-er makes you hap-py.
Gtr. 3
mp
ppp
fdbk.
Gtr. 4
steady gliss.
ppp
Gtrs. 3 & 4 tacet
B
What-ev-er you want.
You're so fuck-ing spe-
C
-cial.
Cm
I wish I was spe-cial,

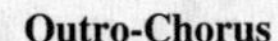
Outro-Chorus

Gtr. 1: w/ Riff B (1st 6 meas.)
G
but I'm a creep.
I'm a weird -
8va
loco
Gtr. 4
pp
*fdbk.
*Microphonic fdbk., not caused by string vibration.

B
C
- o.
What the hell am I do - ing here?
p

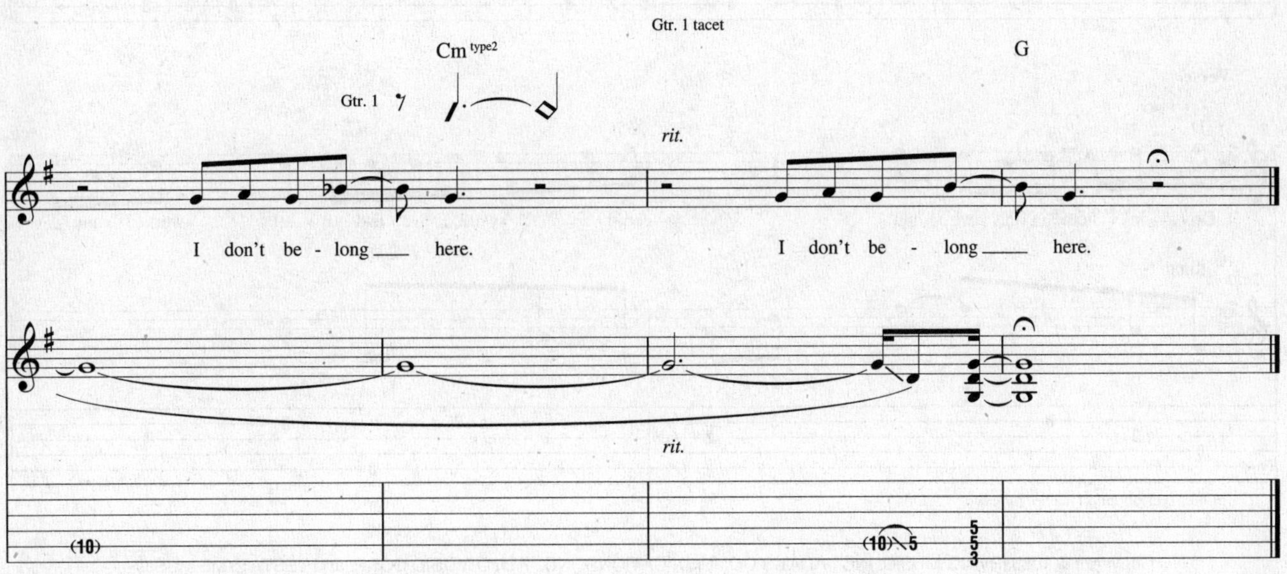
Gtr. 1 tacet
Cm type2
G
Gtr. 1
rit.
I don't be - long here.
I don't be - long here.

Cuts Like a Knife

Words and Music by Bryan Adams and Jim Vallance

*Chord symbols reflect implied harmony.

Gtr. 2: w/ Riff B (1 3/4 times)
D
G5
Csus2
You had this boy _ be-liev - in'
End Riff B
way be - yond _ the sha - dow _ of a doubt, _
yeah. _ Well, I
heard it on the street, _ I heard you might have found _ some - bod - y new,
Gtr. 1
f
p
yeah. Well, who _ is he, ba - by? Who is he and tell me what he means to
Gtr. 2
Riff C
Rhy. Fig. 2

Pre-Chorus
D
D5
A
Rhy. Fig. 3
Gtr. 1
you,
oh yeah. __
I took it all for grant - ed,
but
End Riff C
Rhy. Fig. 3A
mp
mf
End Rhy. Fig. 2
f
(cont. in slashes)

Bm
Csus2
G5
End Rhy. Fig. 3
(cont. in notation)
how was I to know ___
that you'd be let - ting go?
Now it cuts like a
Gtr. 2
End Rhy. Fig. 3A

Chorus
Gtr. 2: w/ Rhy. Fig. 1
D
G5
Csus2
D
G5
Csus2
knife,
but it feels so
right. __
Yeah, __
cuts like a
Riff D
Gtr. 1
End Riff D

D
G5
Csus2
knife,
oh, but it feels so right.
2. There's
Riff D
Verse
Gtr. 1 tacet
Gtr. 2: w/ Riff B
times I've been mis-tak - en,
there's times I've thought I've been mis-un-der-stood,
ooh yeah.
Gtrs. 1 & 2: w/ Rhy. Fig. 2 & Riff C
So wait a min-ute, dar - lin'.
Can't you see we did the best we could?
Pre-Chorus
Gtrs. 1 & 2: w/ Rhy. Figs. 3 & 3A
D5
A
Ooh, we could.
This would-n't be the first time that
Bm
things have gone a - stray,
now you've thrown it all a - way.
Now it cuts like a
Chorus
Gtr. 1: w/ Riff D
knife,
yeah, but it feels so right.
Oh, it cuts like a
Rhy. Fig. 4
End Rhy. Fig. 4
Gtr. 2

Gtr. 1: w/ Riff A (2 times)
Gtr. 2: w/ Rhy. Fig. 4 (1st 2 meas.)
D
G5
Csus2
Gtr. 2: w/ Rhy. Fig. 4 (2 times)
D
* Voc. Fig. 1
knife,
yeah, ___ but it feels so right.
(Na, na, na, ___ na, na,
*Pertains to bkgd. vocs. only
G5
Csus2
End Voc. Fig. 1
D
G5
Csus2
Oh, ___ and it cuts like a knife, _
but it feels so right, ba - by.
na, na, na, ___ na, na.)
Gtr. 3 (dist.)
f
1/4
Bkgd. Voc.: w/ Voc. Fig. 1
D
G5
Csus2
D
G5
Csus2
Oh, _ it cuts like a knife, _
yeah. ___
Gtr. 3
Gtr. 1
Guitar Solo
Gtrs. 1 & 2: w/ Rhy. Fig. 4 (1 1/2 times)
D
G5
Csus2
D
Gtr. 3
w/ bar

G5
Csus2
D
G5
Csus2
8va
Pre-Chorus
Gtrs. 1 & 2: w/ Rhy. Figs. 3 & 3A
D
A
I took it all for grant - ed, but
8va
Gtr. 3
Gtrs. 1 & 2
Gtr. 3 tacet
Bm
Csus2
G5
how was I to know that you'd be let - ting go? Now it cuts like a
Interlude
D
Gtr. 1 tacet
knife, yeah, but it feels so right.
Gtr. 2
mp
Gtr. 1
pp

Uh.
Now it cuts like a knife,
yeah,
but it feels so
Gtr. 2

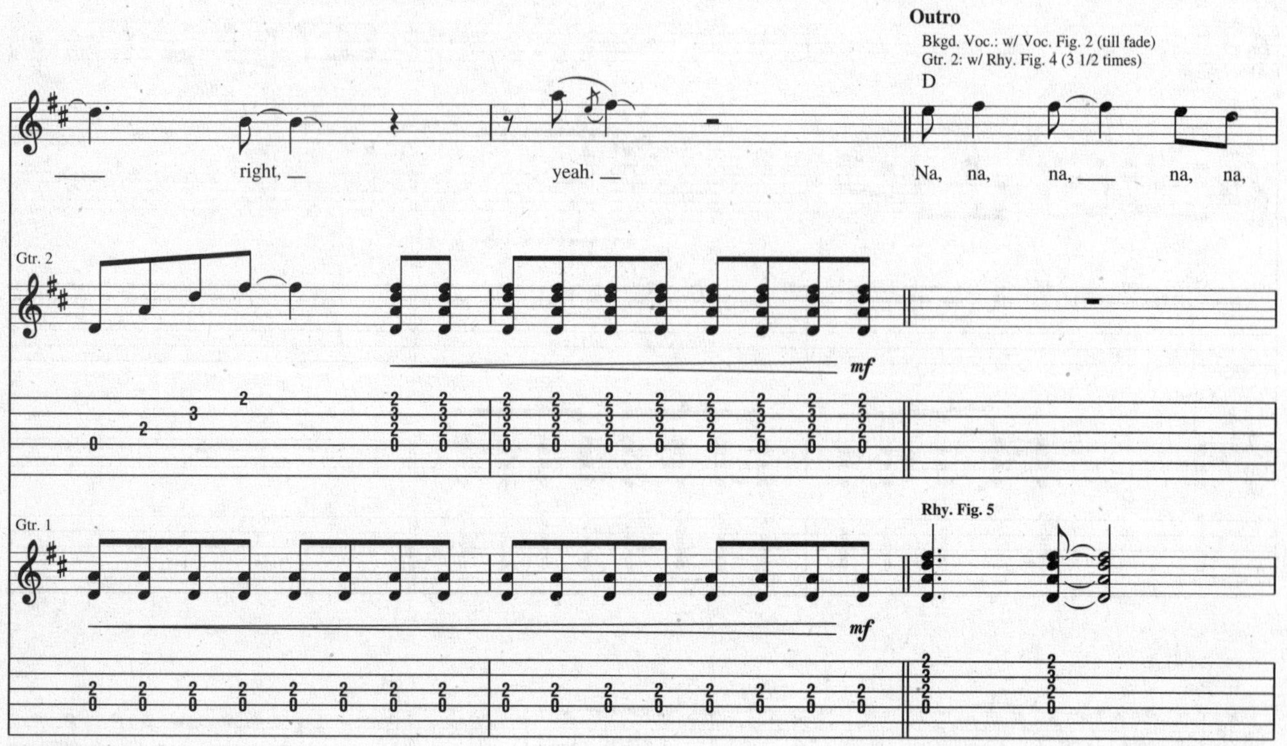
Outro
Bkgd. Voc.: w/ Voc. Fig. 2 (till fade)
Gtr. 2: w/ Rhy. Fig. 4 (3 1/2 times)
D
right,
yeah.
Na, na, na, na, na,
Gtr. 2
mf
Gtr. 1
Rhy. Fig. 5
mf

G5
Csus2
D
G5
Csus2
na, na, na, na, na.
Oh, it cuts like a knife.
Gtr. 1
End Rhy. Fig. 5

Voc. Fig. 2
(Na, na, na, na, na, na, na, na, na, na.)

Gtr. 1: w/ Rhy. Fig. 5 (2 1/2 times)
D
G5
Csus2
D
G5
Csus2
Oh, yeah, yeah, but it feels so right, baby.
Gtr. 3
Outro-Guitar Solo
Lead Voc.: ad Lib. (till fade)
Rhy. Fig. 6
End Rhy. Fig. 6
Gtr. 2
open
w/ bar
Riff E
End Riff E
Gtr. 1

Gtrs. 1 & 2: w/ Rhy. Figs. 4 & 5 (3 1/2 times)
D
G5
Csus2
D
Gtr. 3
8va
G5
Csus2
D
G5
Csus2
loco
D
8va
loco
G5
Csus2
D
P.H.
w/ bar
pitch: E
D#
Begin fade
G5
Csus2
D
G5
Csus2
D
8va

Gtrs. 1 & 2: w/ Riff E & Rhy. Fig. 6
G5
Csus2
D
8va
loco
P.H.
pitch: G
Gtrs. 1 & 2: w/ Rhy. Figs. 4 & 5 (till fade)
w/ bar
Fade out
Harm.
pitch: D G

Damn Right, I've Got the Blues

By Buddy Guy

A7
hold bend
full
E7
1/2
D7
You're
End Rhy. Fig. 1

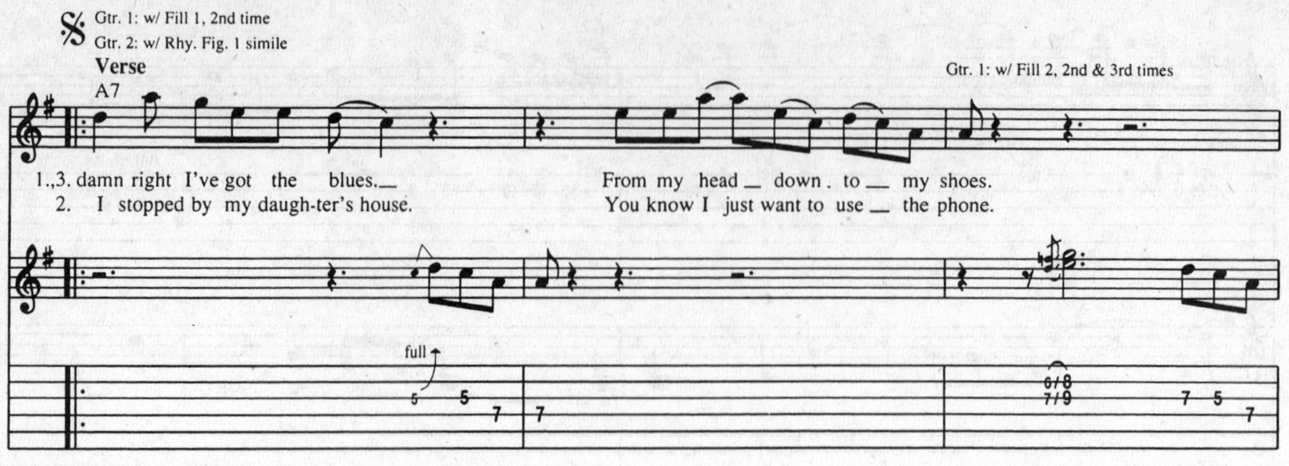
Gtr. 1: w/ Fill 1, 2nd time
Gtr. 2: w/ Rhy. Fig. 1 simile
Verse
A7
Gtr. 1: w/ Fill 2, 2nd & 3rd times
1.,3. damn right I've got the blues.
2. I stopped by my daugh-ter's house.
From my head down to my shoes.
You know I just want to use the phone.
full

Gtr. 1: w/ Fill 1, 2nd time
D7
You damn right I got the blues.
I stopped by my daugh - ter's house.
From my head down to my
You know I just want to use the

Gtr. 1: w/ Fill 3, 2nd time; w/ Fill 5, 3rd time
A7
E7#9
shoes.
phone.
I can't win
You know my new grand - ba - by came
full
let ring
1/2

Fill 1
Gtr. 1
full
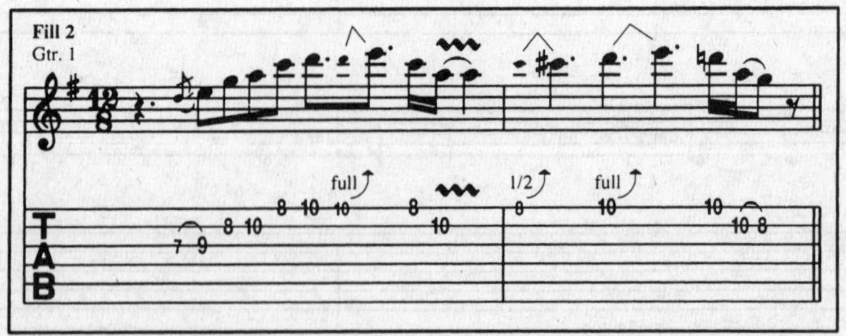
Fill 2
Gtr. 1
full
1/2

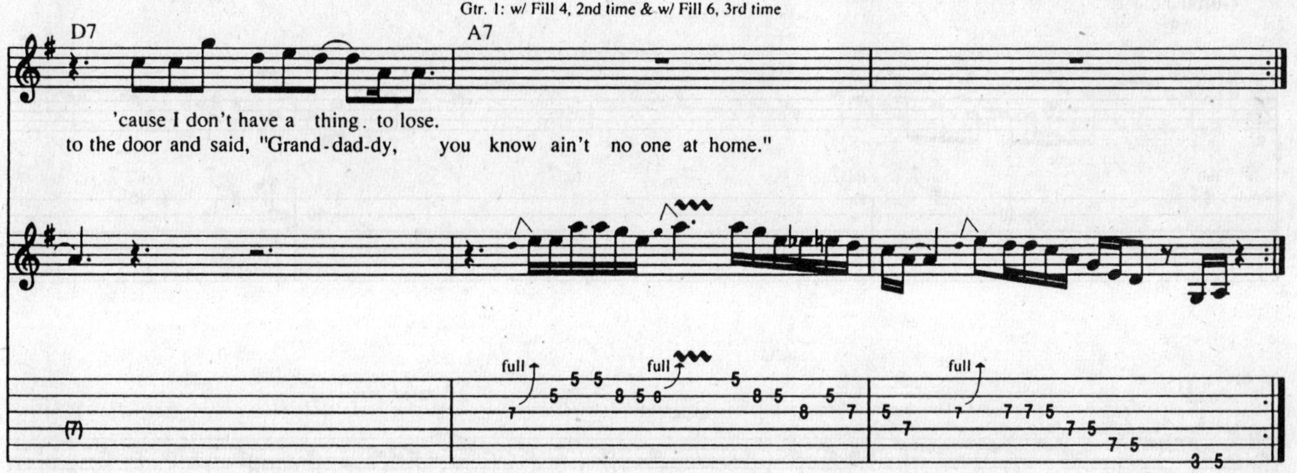
Gtr. 1: w/ Fill 4, 2nd time & w/ Fill 6, 3rd time
D7
A7
'cause I don't have a thing. to lose.
to the door and said, "Grand-dad-dy, you know ain't no one at home."
full
full
full

Fill 3
Gtr. 1
full
full

Fill 4
Gtr. 1
full
full

Fill 5
Gtr. 1
full
1/2
1/2
full

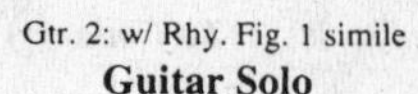
Gtr. 2: w/ Rhy. Fig. 1 simile

Guitar Solo

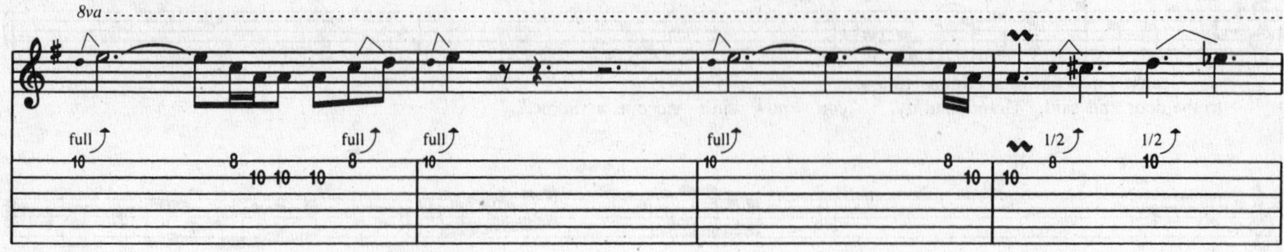
A7
8va
full
full
full
full
1/2
1/2

D7
8va
A7
full
-1/2
1/2
1/2
1/2
1/2
full
full
full
full
full
full

8va
E7
D7
full
full
full

A7
D.S. al Coda
You're
8va
loco
1/2

Fill 6
Gtr. 1
full
full

Coda

Gtr. 2: Cont. w/ Fill 7

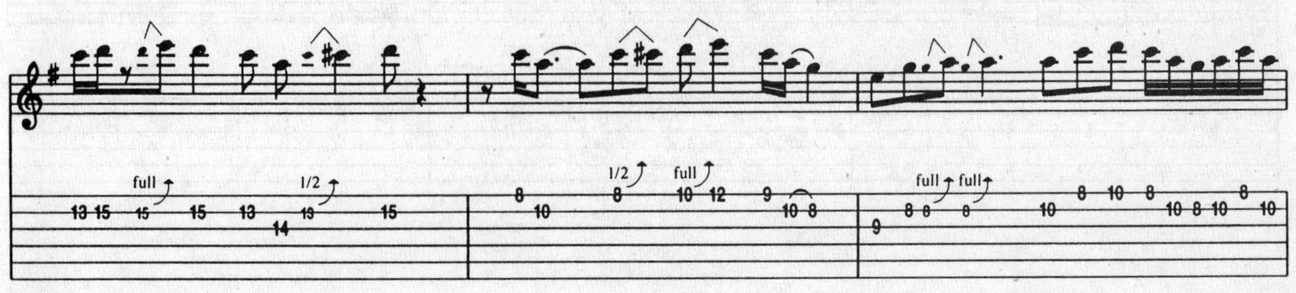

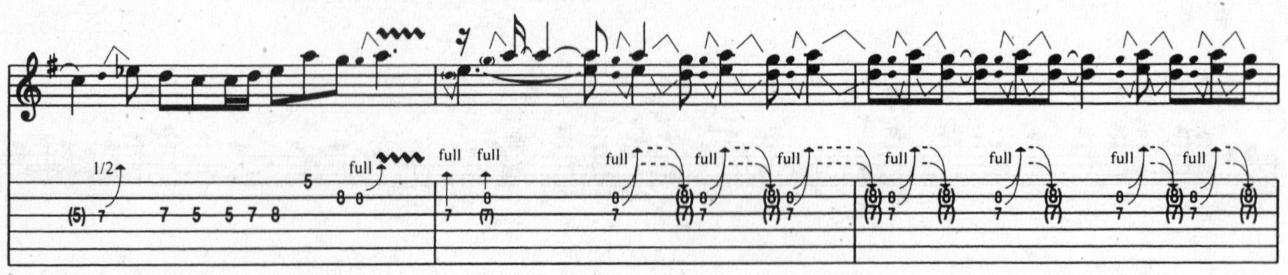

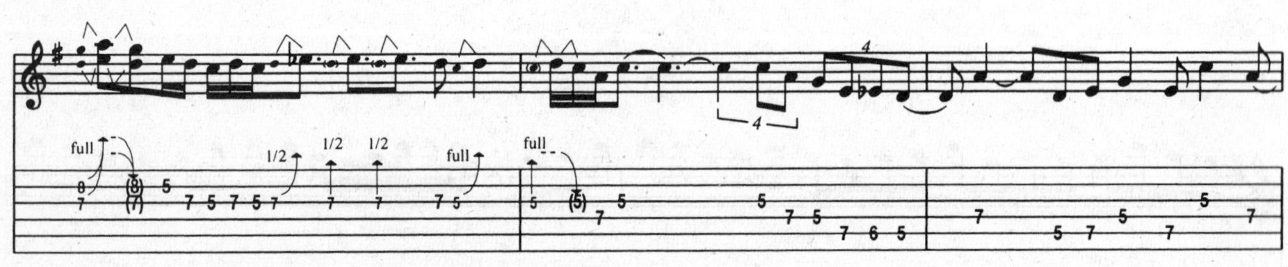

* Gtrs. 1 & 2 continue in unison 5th time

Dear Mr. Fantasy

Words and Music by James Capaldi, Chris Wood and Steve Winwood

G
Do an - y - thing, take us out of this gloom. Sing a song,
D
A
play gui - tar, make it snap - py.
G
You are the one who can make us all laugh, but
D
A
do - ing that, you break out in tears.
*Roll up vol. pedal to add dist.

G
Please don't be sad if it was a straight mind you had, we
D
A
would - n't have known you all those years.
Bridge
F#m
A
Oo, ah.
*T = Thumb on 6th string
F#m
A
Oo, ah.

F♯m
A
Oo, ah.
F♯m
G
E7
Oo, ah, ah.
Verse
A
G
2. Dear Mis - ter Fan - ta - sy, play us a tune,
D
A
some - thing to make us all hap - py.

G
Do an - y - thing take us out of this gloom. Sing a song,
D
A
play gui - tar, make it snap - py. Yeah, yeah.
*Roll up vol. pedal to add dist.
Guitar Solo
A
G
D
grad. bend
A

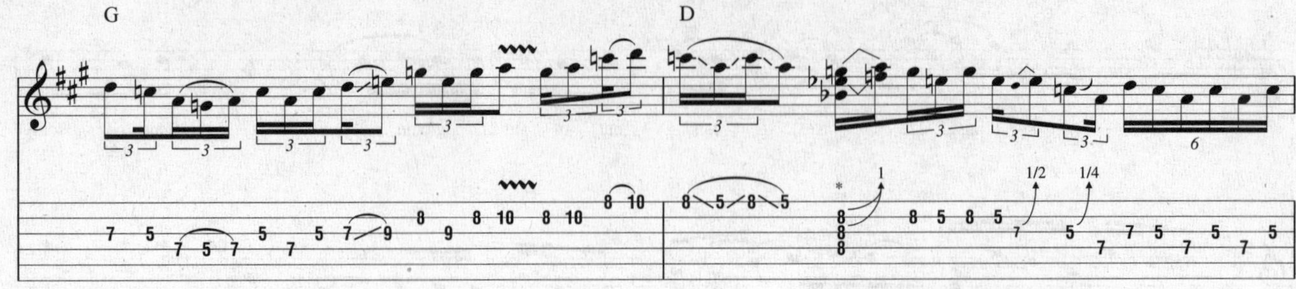

*3rd & 4th strings slip under 3rd finger of left hand while bending 2nd string.

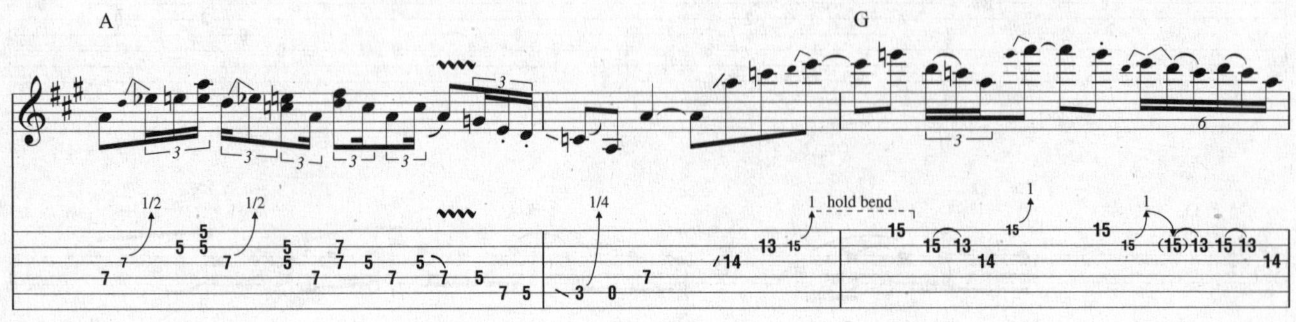

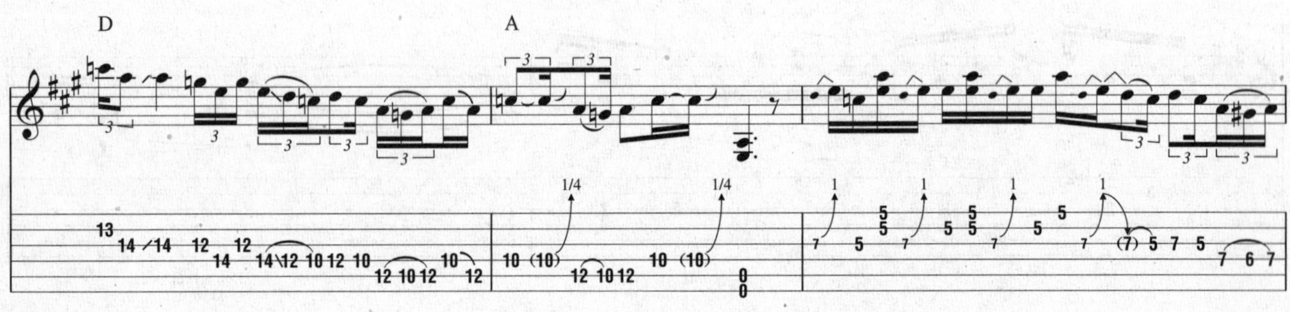

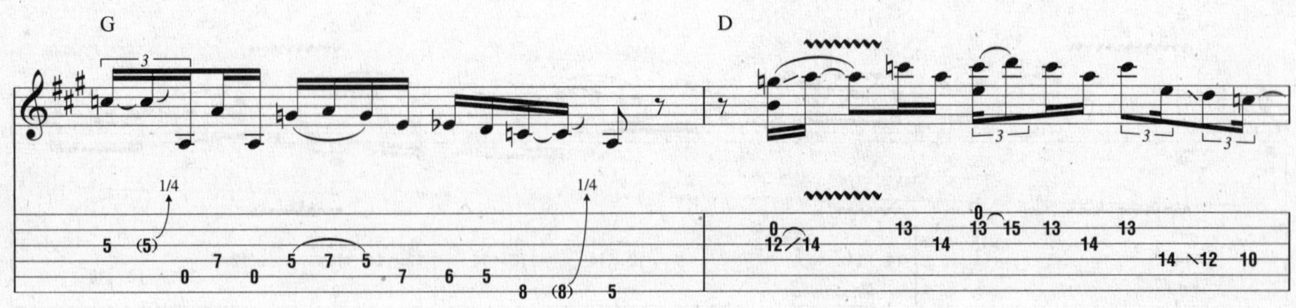

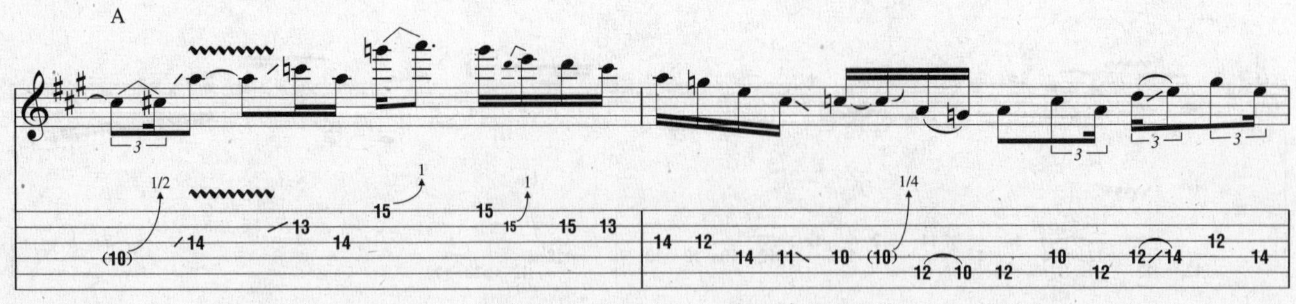

G
D

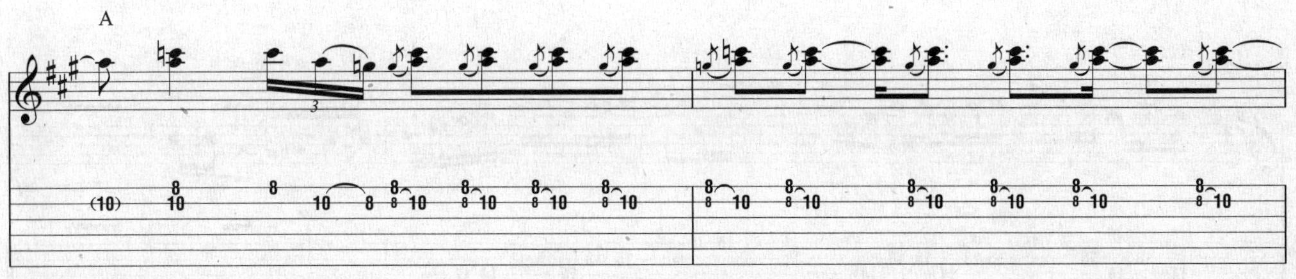
A

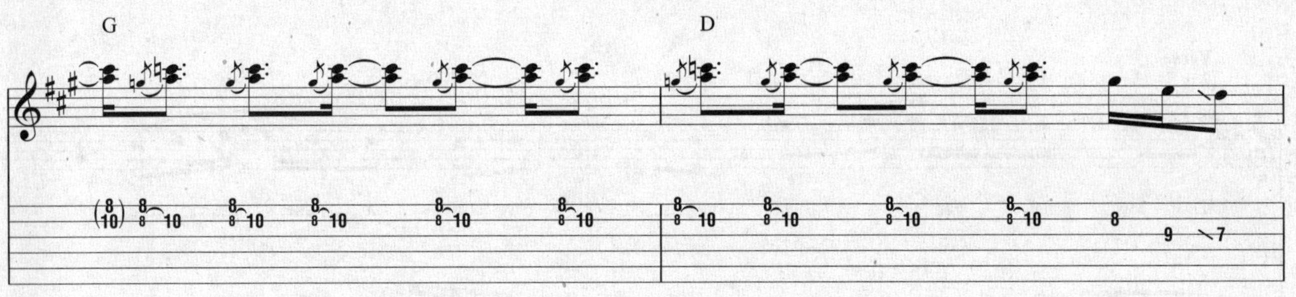
G
D

A

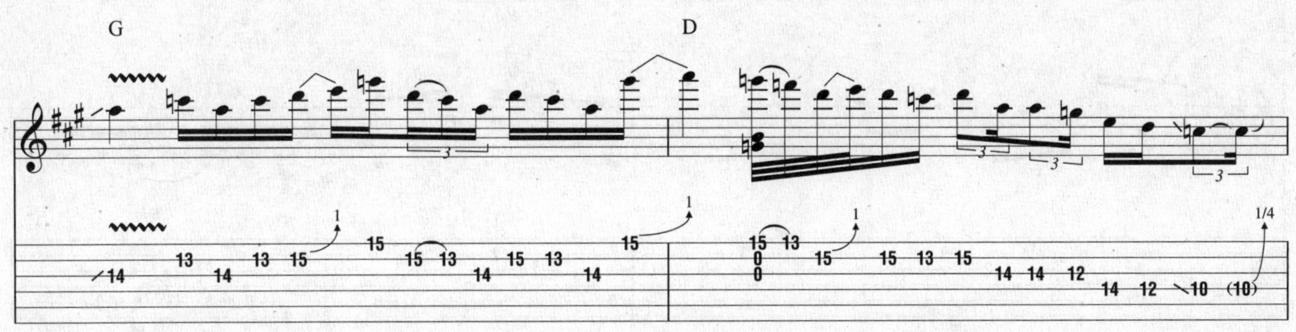
G
D

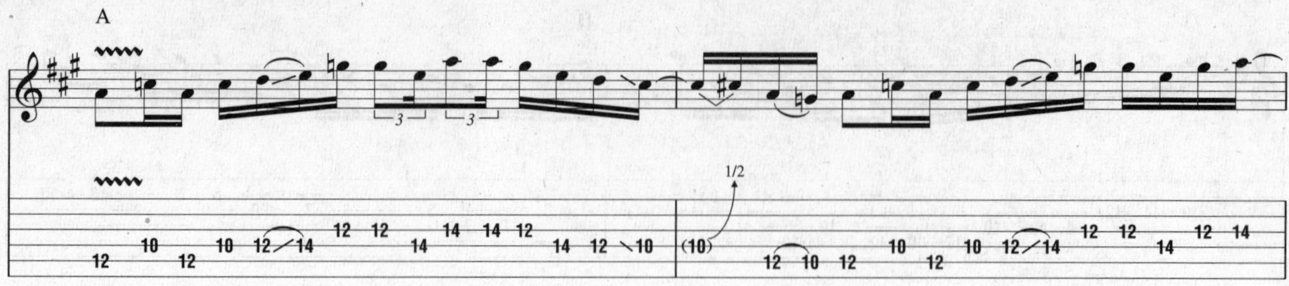
A
1/2

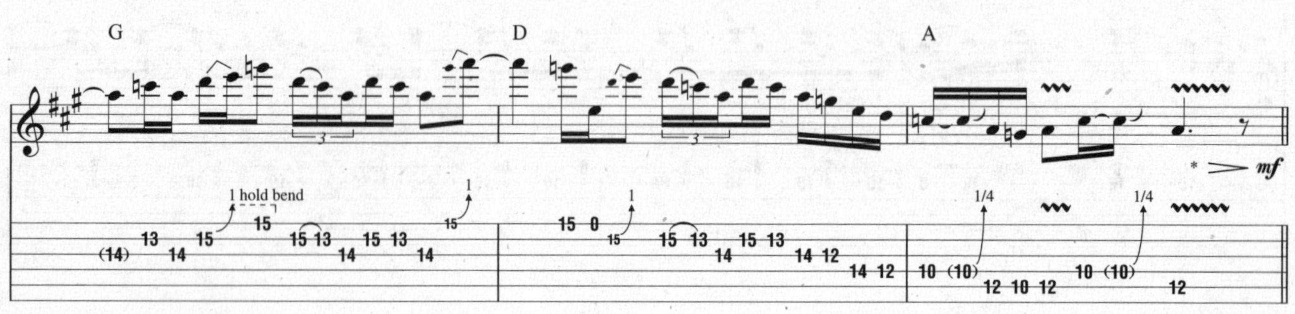
G
D
A
1 hold bend
1/4
*Roll back vol. pedal to produce clean tone.

Verse

A
G
3. Dear Mis - ter Fan - ta - sy, play us a tune,

D
A
some-thing to make us all hap - py.
1/4

G
Do an - y - thing, take us out of this gloom. Sing a song,
D
A
play gui - tar, make it snap - py.
1/4
1/4
G
You are the one who can make us all laugh, but
1/4
D
A
do - ing that, you break out in tears.

A
G
Please don't be sad if it was a straight mind you had, we
*Roll up vol. pedal to add dist.
D
A
would-n't have known you all these years.
Please, Mis-ter Fan-ta-sy.
Outro
A
G
D/F♯
A
G
D

A
G

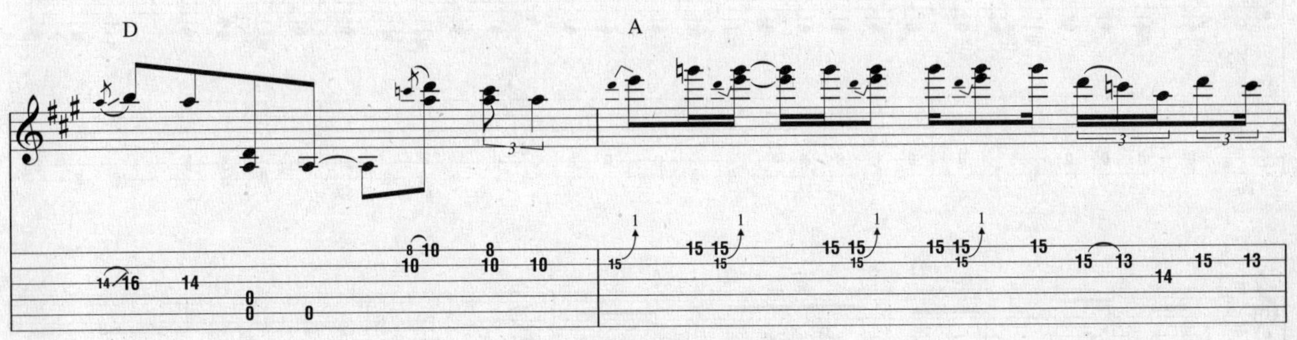
D
A

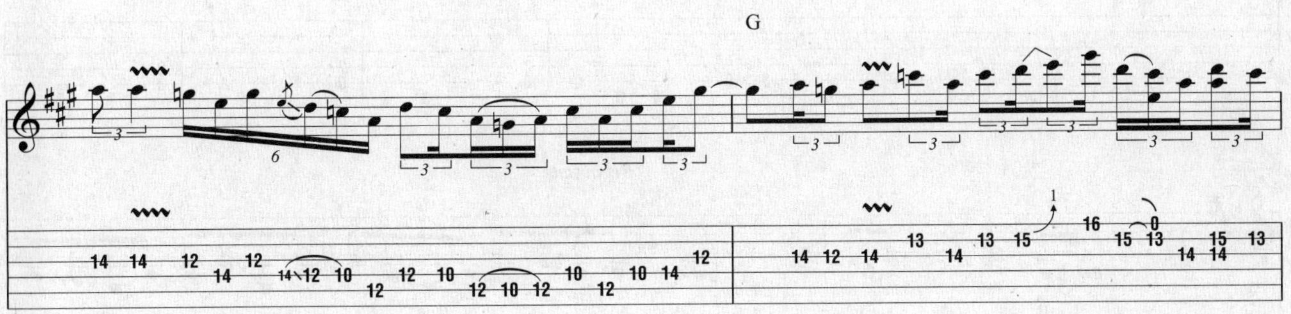
G

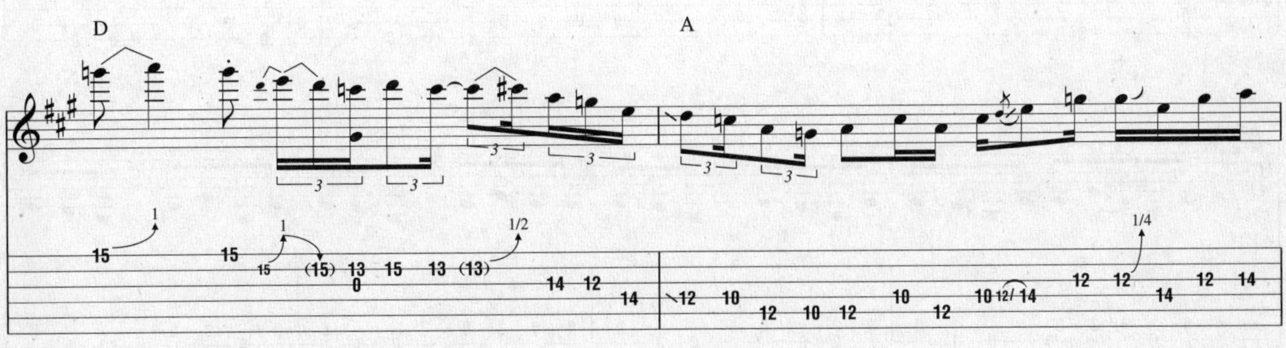
D
A

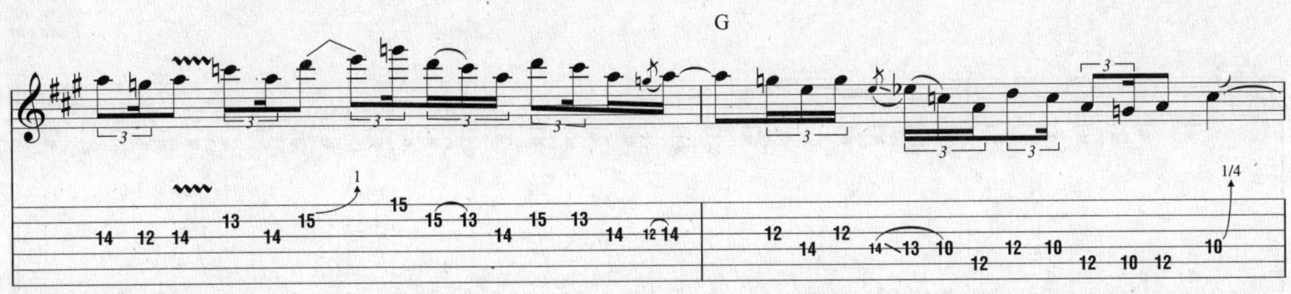
G

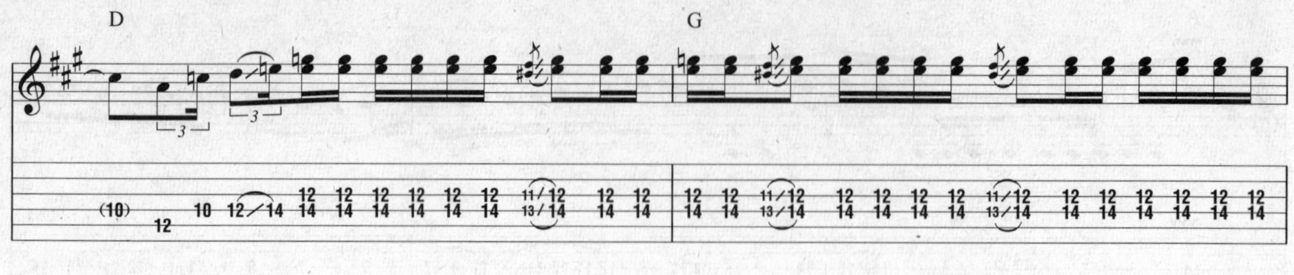

Double-time feel

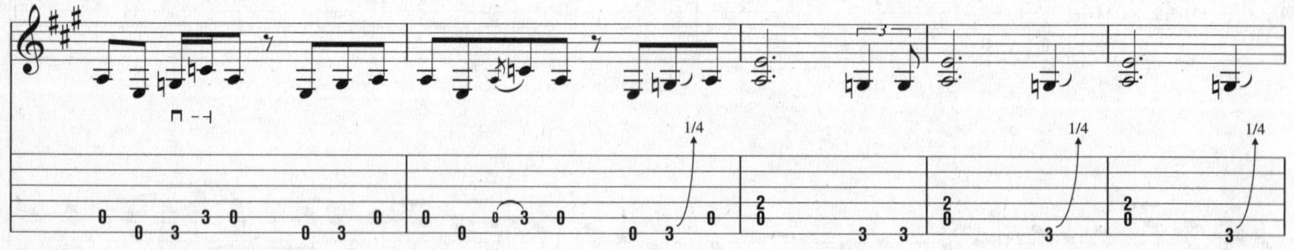

Begin fade

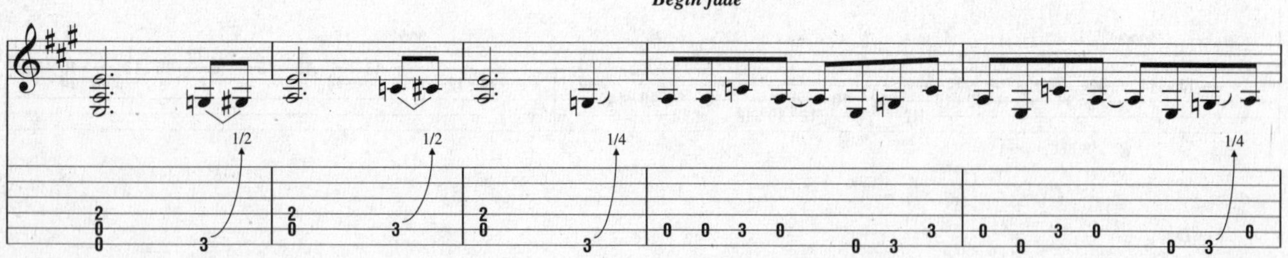

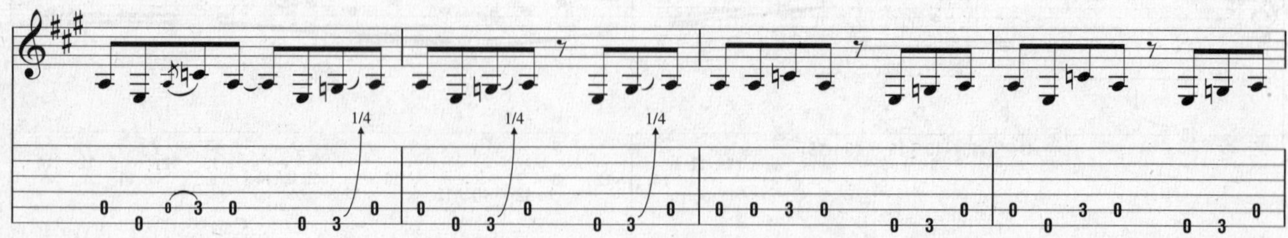

Fade out

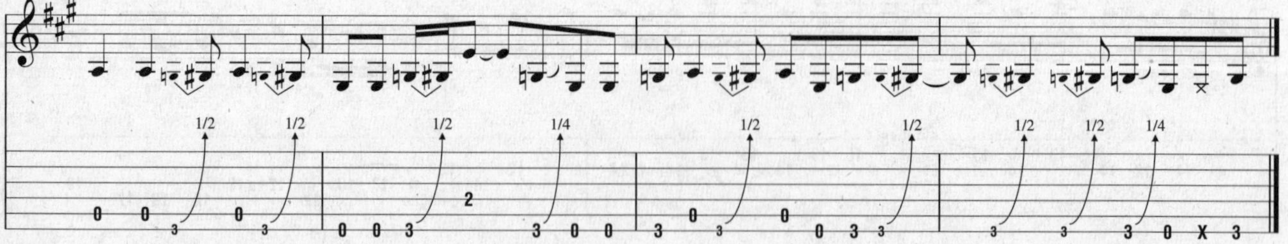

Deuce

Words and Music by Gene Simmons

Chorus
Am
C5
D5
C5
A5
N.C.
ba-by, do the things he says _ to do.
Ba-by, if you're feel-in' good, and
End Rhy. Fig. 2
Rhy. Fig. 3
C5
C#5
D5 G5 G#5 A5
F
G
ba-by, if you're feel-in' nice,
you know your man is work-in' hard.
He's worth a deuce!
Gtr. 1
Gtr. 2
(Both notes vib.)
Gtrs. 1 & 2:
End Rhy. Fig. 3
Gtrs. 1 & 2: w/Rhy. Fig. 1, 2 times
N.C.
Gtr. 3
full
grad. release
Verse
Gtrs. 1 & 2: w/Rhy. Fig. 2
Am
C5
D5
Hon - ey, ______ don't push your man be - hind _ his years. _
Fdbk.
(8va)
Fdbk.

N.C.
Am
C5
D5
And ba - by, stop cry - in' all your tears.
N.C.
Am
C5
D5
C5
A5
Ba-by, do the things he says to do. Do it!
Chorus
Gtrs. 1 & 2: w/Rhy. Fig. 3
N.C.
C5
C#5
Ba - by, if you're feel - in' good, yes, ba - by, if you're feel - in' nice,
D5 G5 G#5 A5
F
G
you know your man is work - in' hard. He's worth a deuce!
Guitar solo
Gtrs. 1 & 2: w/Rhy. Fig. 1, 4 times
Gtr. 3
N.C.
f
full
grad. bend

grad. bend
full
tr
1 1/2
Chorus
Gtrs. 1 & 2: w/Rhy. Fig. 3, 1st 5 bars only
N.C.
C5
C♯5
And ba-by, if you're feel-in' good,
yes, ba-by if you're feel-in' nice,
mf
D5 G5 G♯ A5
F
G
Gtrs. 1 & 2
you know your man is work-in' hard!

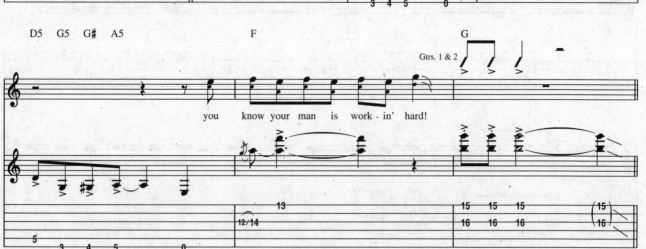

(Gtr. 2 tacet)
A5
F/A
G/B
A5
Gtr. 1
(w/Phase shifter)
Outro
Gtrs. 1 & 2: w/Rhy. Fig. 1, 4 times
N.C.
F5
A
12 fr.
Gtr. 2
Gtr. 3
(Phase shifter off)
full
Ah!
8va
(8va)

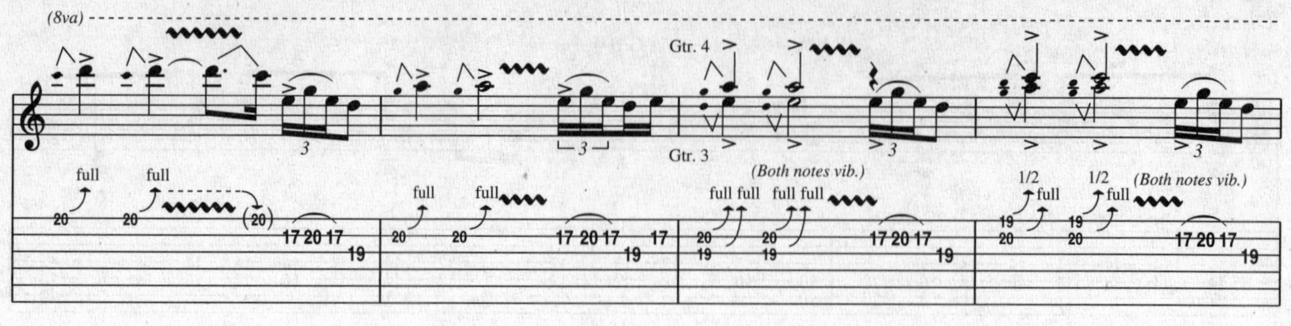
(8va)
Gtr. 4
Gtr. 3
full
(Both notes vib.)
1/2

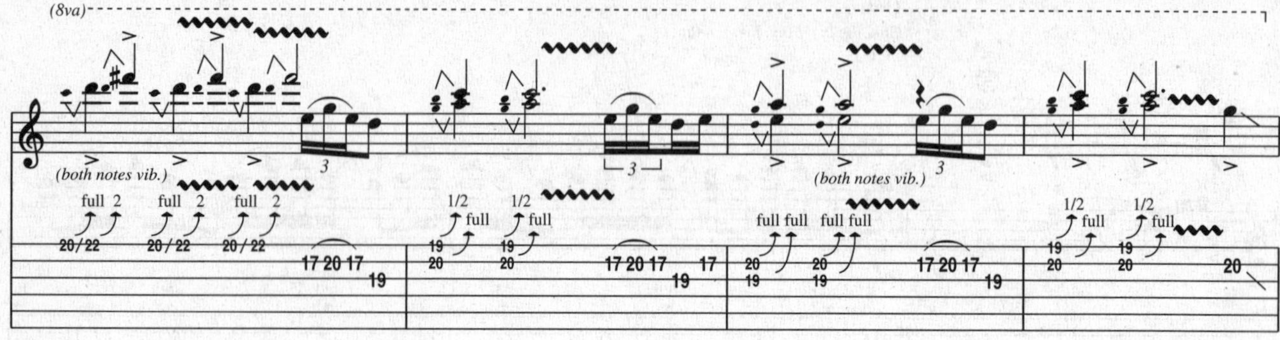
(8va)
(both notes vib.)
full
1/2

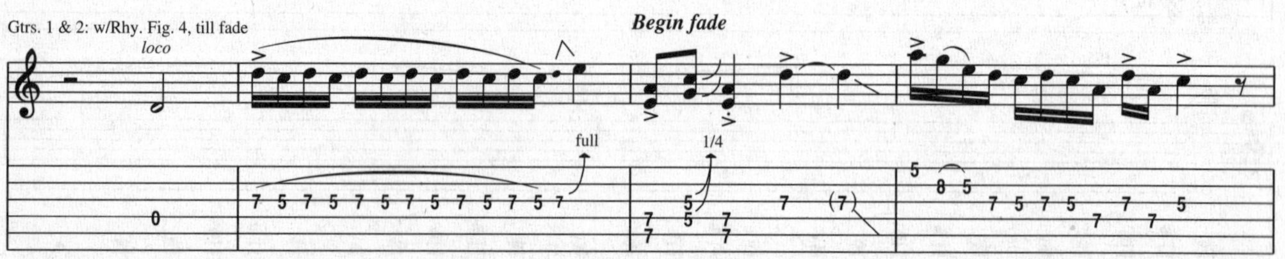
Gtrs. 1 & 2: w/Rhy. Fig. 4, till fade
loco
Begin fade
full
1/4

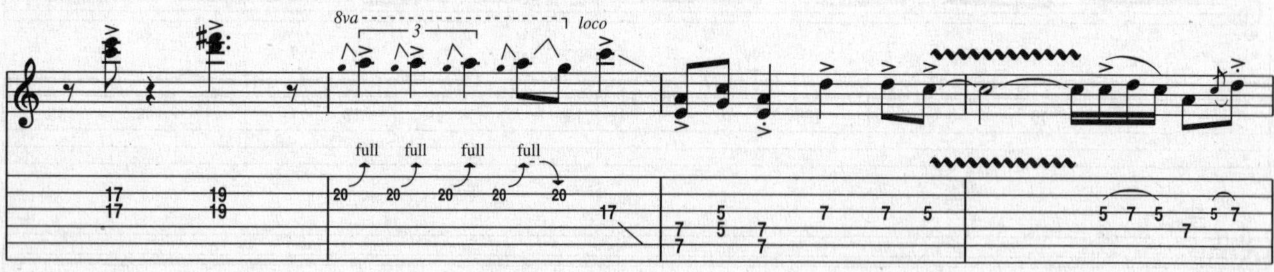
8va
loco
full

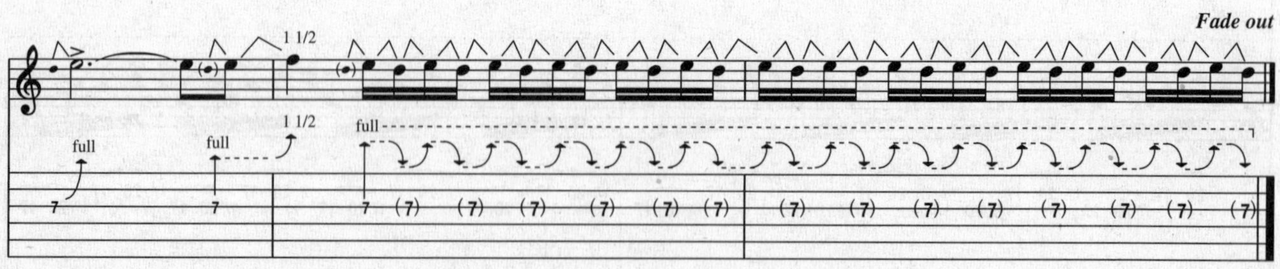
Fade out
1 1/2
full

Rhy. Fig. 4
Gtrs. 1 & 2
N.C.

Don't Stand So Close to Me

Music and Lyrics by Sting

E♭
Gm
She wants him so bad - ly, knows what she wants to be.
Some - times it's not so eas - y to be the teach - er's pet.
Strong words in the staff - room, the ac - cu - sa - tions fly.
End Rhy. Fig. 1
End Rhy. Fig. 1A
P.M.

Gtrs. 1, 2 & 3: w/Rhy. Figs. 1 & 1A
Gtr. 1: w/Rhy. Fig. 2, 4th time
E♭
Gm
In - side her there's long - ing, this girl's an o - pen page.
Temp - ta - tion, frus - tra - tion, so bad it makes him cry.
It's no use, he sees her. He starts to shake and cough
Gtr. 1: 2nd & 3rd times
P.M.

To Coda
E♭
Gm
Book mark - ing, she's so close now. This girl is half his age.
Wet bus stop, she's wait - ing, his car is warm and dry.
just like the old man in that book by Nab - o - kov.
Rhy. Fig. 2
End Rhy. Fig. 2

Chorus

Gtr. 1: w/ Fill 1, 2nd time

D A D A Bm Bm/A Am/F♯ Em/F♯

Bkgd. Voc. Fig. 1 **End Bkgd. Voc. Fig. 1**

Don't stand, don't stand so, don't stand so close to me.

Gtr. 1 **Rhy. Fig. 3** **End Rhy. Fig. 3**

mf w/chorusing

Gtr. 2 **Rhy. Fig. 3A** **End Rhy. Fig. 3A**

mf

P.M.

Gtr. 3 **Rhy. Fig. 3B** **End Rhy. Fig. 3B**

mf

Gtr. 1: w/ Fill 1, 2nd time
D
A
D
A
Bm
Bm/A
Am/F#
Em/F#
Don't stand, don't stand so, don't stand so close to me.
P.M.
1., 2.
3.
D.S. al Coda
Am/F#
Em/F#
P.M.
Coda
Play 6 times and Fade
Gtrs. 1, 2 & 3: w/Rhy. Figs. 3, 3A & 3B
w/ Bkgd. Voc. Fig. 1
Please don't stand so close to me.

Don't Tell Me You Love Me

Words and Music by Jack Blades

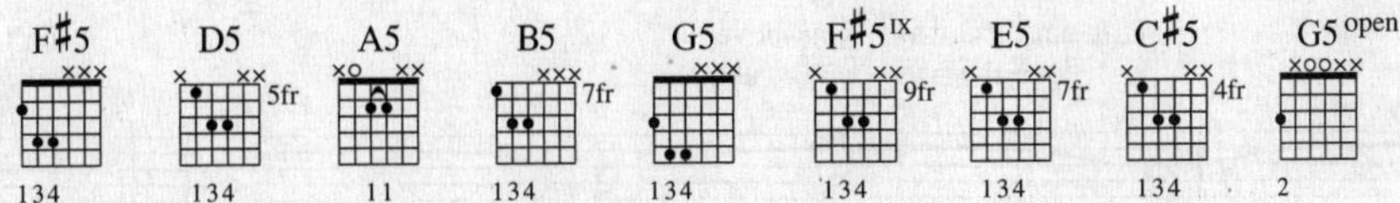

* Chord symbols reflect implied harmony, next 4 meas.

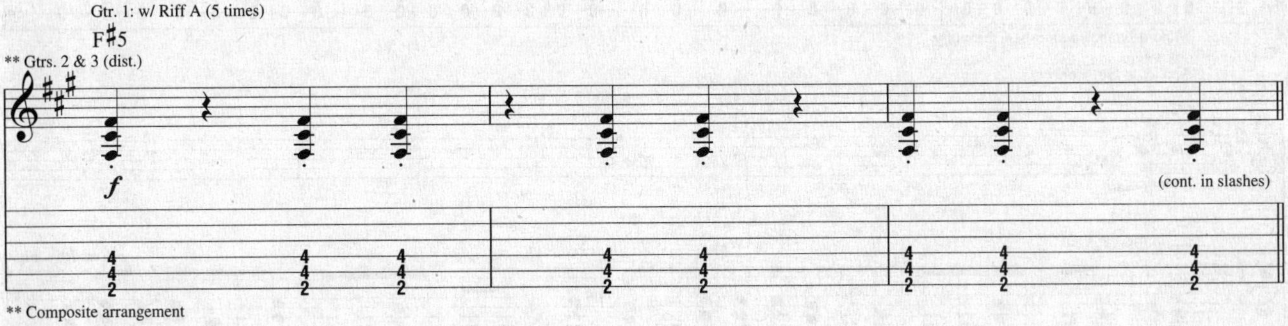

Gtr. 1: w/ Riff A (5 times)

F#5

** Gtrs. 2 & 3 (dist.)

f

(cont. in slashes)

** Composite arrangement

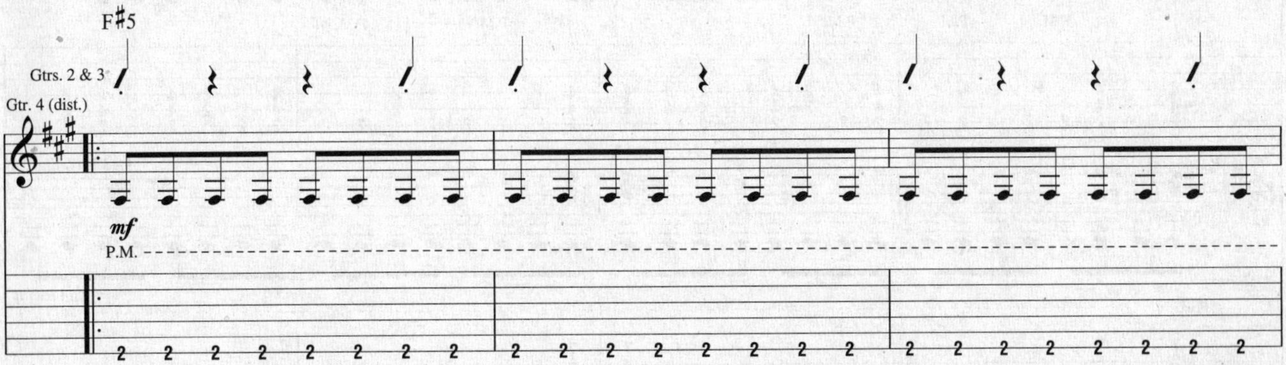

F#5

Gtrs. 2 & 3

Gtr. 4 (dist.)

mf

P.M.

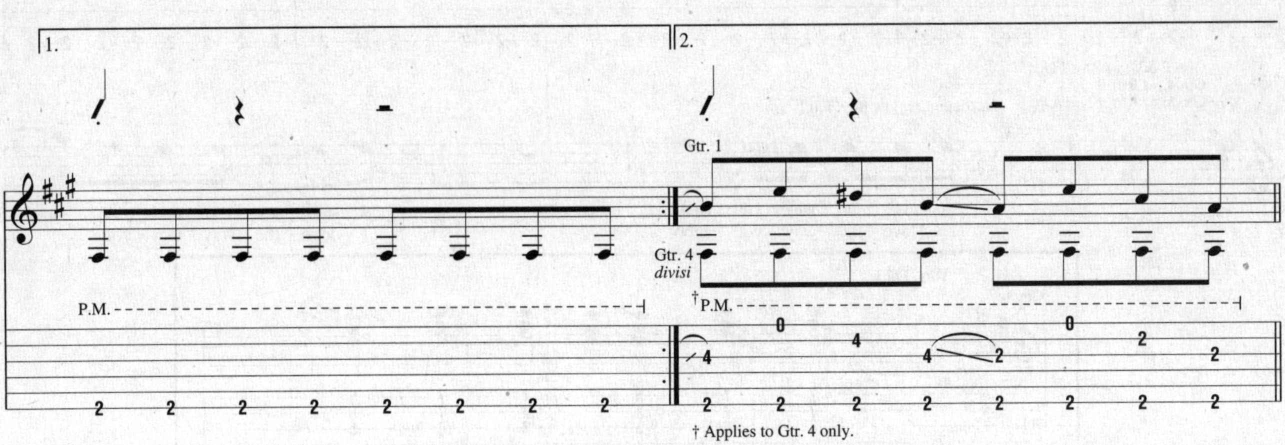

1. P.M.

2. Gtr. 1

Gtr. 4 *divisi*

†P.M.

† Applies to Gtr. 4 only.

Verse
Gtr. 1 tacet
*A5
1. It ain't the way you move, it ain't the way that you move
2. I love the way you use, I love the way that you use
Gtrs. 2 & 3
Rhy. Fig. 1
** Gtr. 5
Rhy. Fig. 1A
mf
Gtr. 4
divisi
Riff B
†P.M.
* Chord symbols reflect basic harmony.
** Synth. arr. for gtr.
† Applies to Gtr. 4 only.
F#5
me.
me.
Oh, no.
Aw, yeah.
End Rhy. Fig. 1
P.M.
End Rhy. Fig. 1A
End Riff B
Gtrs. 2 & 3: w/ Rhy. Fig. 1
Gtr. 4: w/ Riff B
Gtr. 5: w/ Rhy. Fig. 1A
2nd time: Gtr. 3 w/ Rhy. Fill 1
A5
It ain't the way you shake, it ain't the way that you shake
I love the way you shoot, I love the way that you
Rhy. Fill 1
Gtr. 3

F♯5
me.
shoot to kill me.
Oh, no.
Oh, yeah.
I've lived
It's tak-en

Pre-Chorus
D
Bm
N.C.
twen-ty-five years, I'm a kid on the run. I've got a pis-tol for ac-tion. Don't
miles and lines to learn the right from the wrong. I keep you hang-ing on. So don't
tell me you love
Gtrs. 2 & 3

Chorus
Half-time feel
End half-time feel
F♯m
D
E
C♯
me. Don't tell me you love me. Don't tell me,
(Gtr. 2, cont. in slashes)

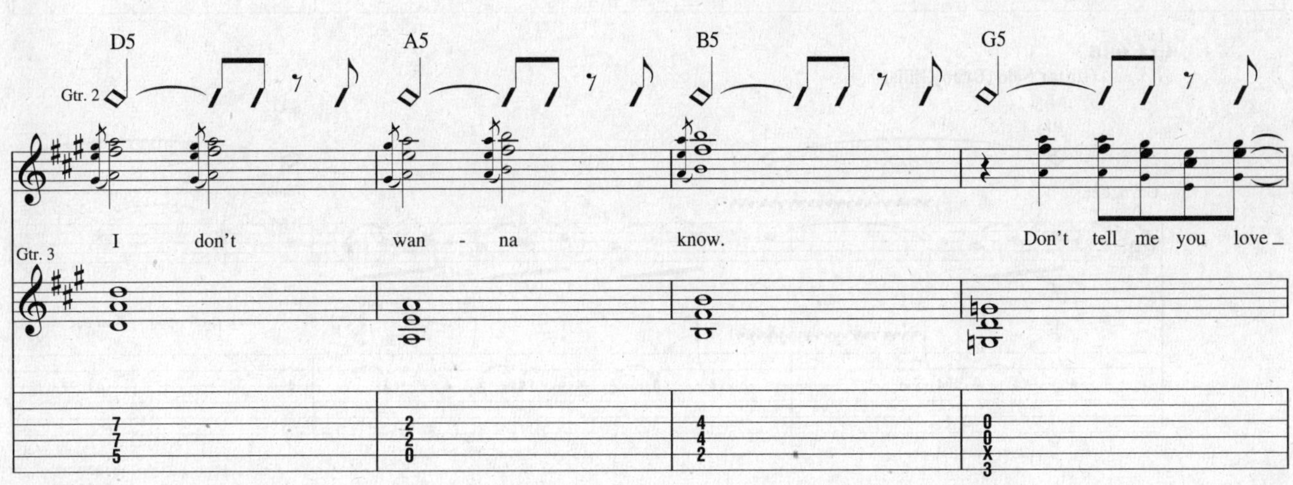
D5
A5
B5
G5
Gtr. 2
I don't wan - na know. Don't tell me you love
Gtr. 3

F♯5IX
D5
E5
C♯5
me.
Don't tell me you love me.
Don't tell me,
Rhy. Fig. 2
D5
A5
B5
N.C.
To Coda
(cont. in notation)
I don't wan - na know.
Gtrs. 2 & 3
End Rhy. Fig. 2
(cont. in slashes)
Interlude
D.S. al Coda
Gtr. 4: w/ Riff B (last 4 meas.)
Gtrs. 2 & 3
P.M.
Gtr. 1
(cont. in notation)
let ring
Coda
Guitar Solo (Brad Gillis)
Rhy. Fig. 3
Gtr. 6 (dist.)
15ma
P.H.
* w/ bar
* Hold bend while depressing vibrato bar.

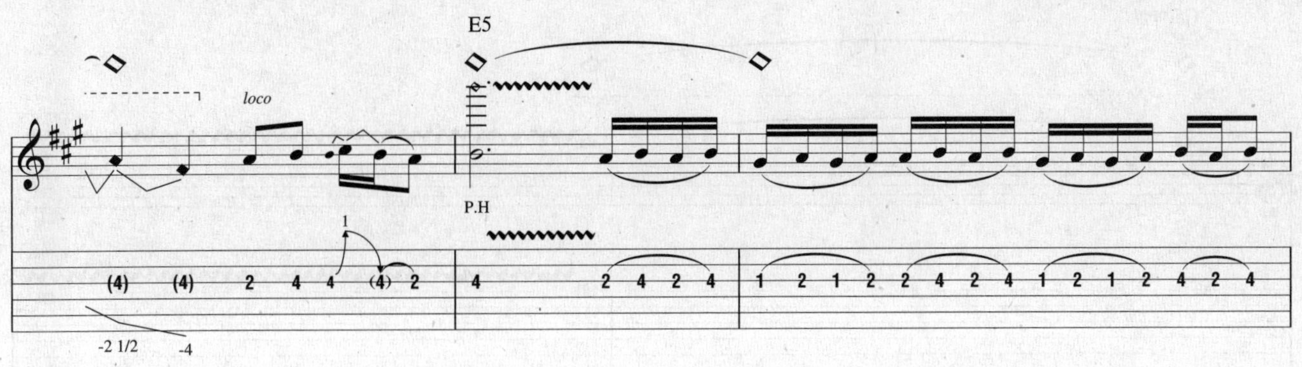

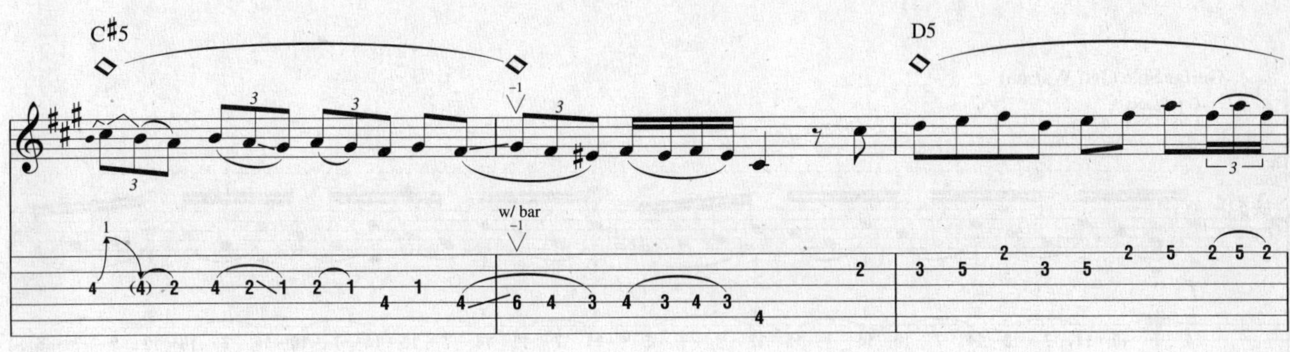

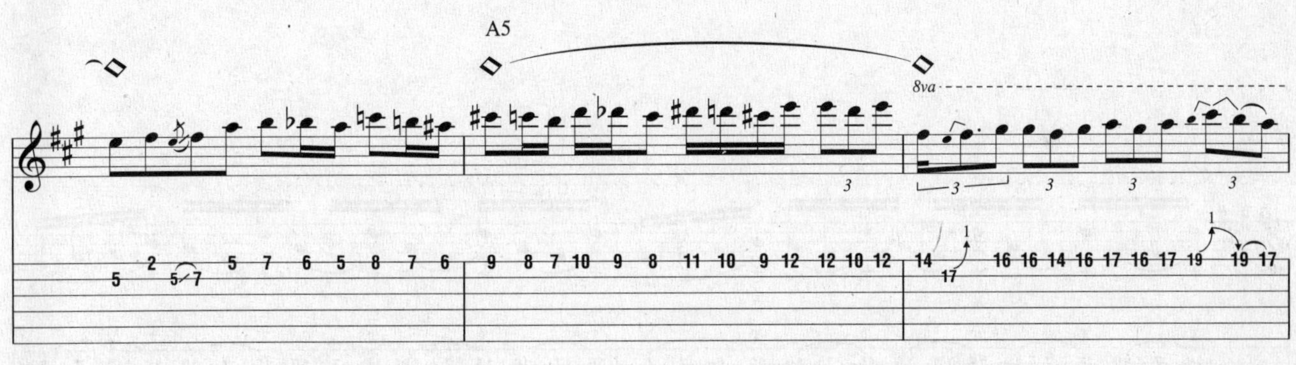

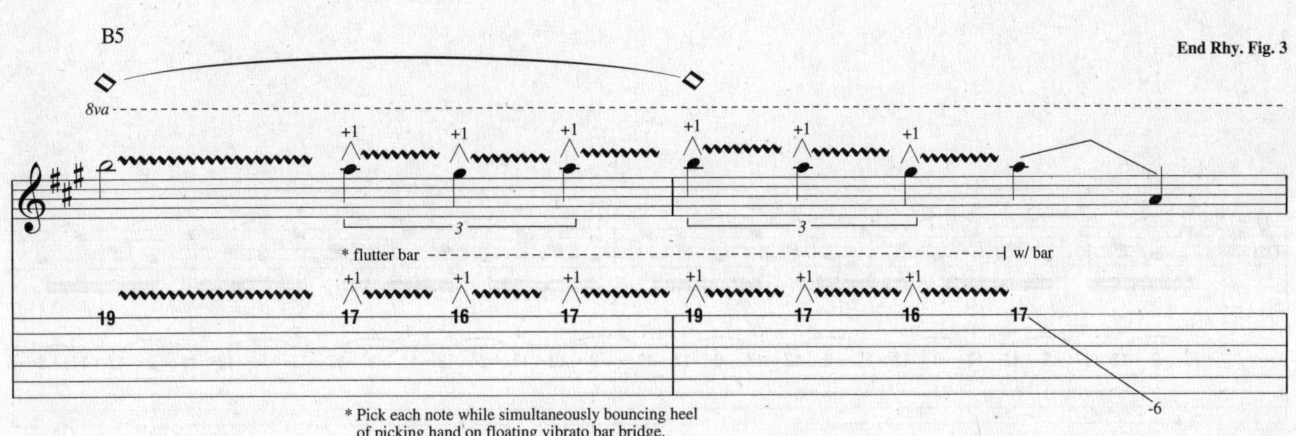

* Pick each note while simultaneously bouncing heel of picking hand on floating vibrato bar bridge.

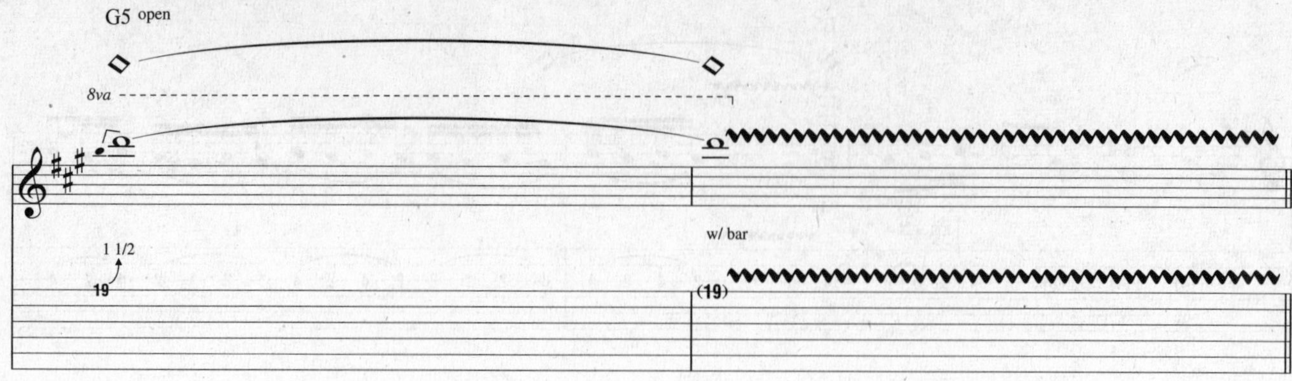
G5 open
8va
1 1/2
w/ bar

Guitar Solo (Jeff Watson)
Gtr. 6 tacet
Gtrs. 2 & 3: w/ Rhy. Fig. 3
F♯5
Gtr. 7 (dist.)
8va
f

D5
8va

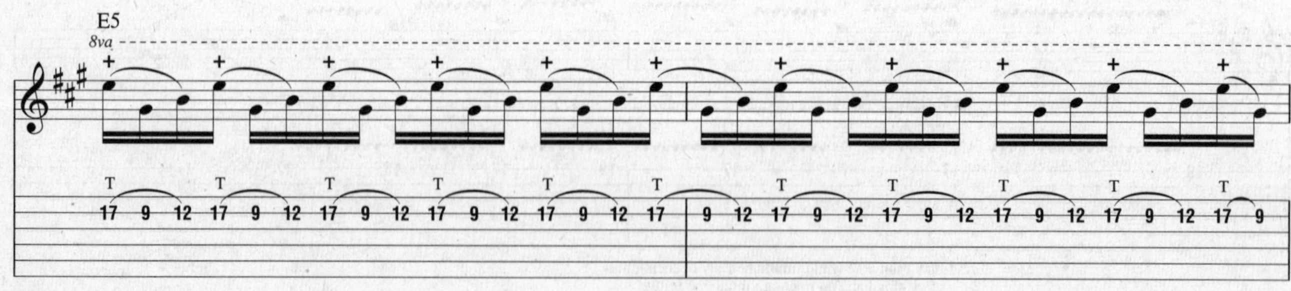
E5
8va

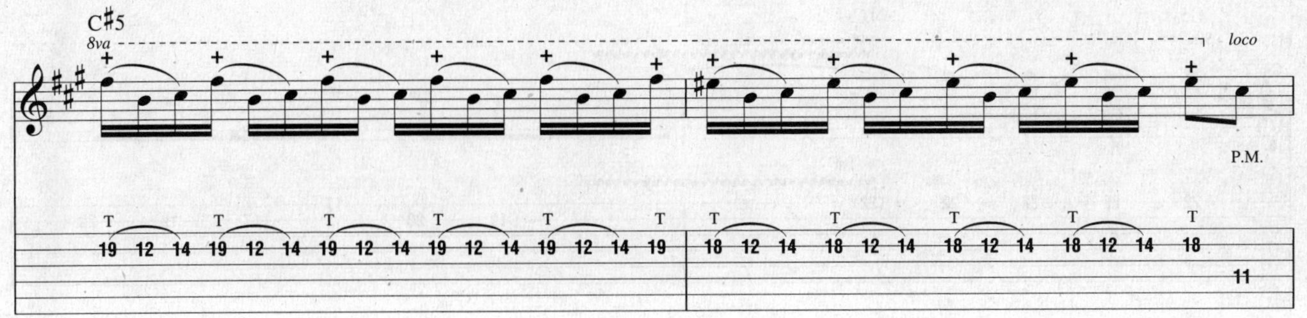
C♯5
8va
loco
P.M.
T
19 12 14 19 12 14 19 12 14 19 12 14 19 12 14 19 18 12 14 18 12 14 18 12 14 18 12 14 18
11

D5
P.M.
12 11 12 14 15 12 14 15 14 12 15 14 12 15 14 12 15 14 12 14

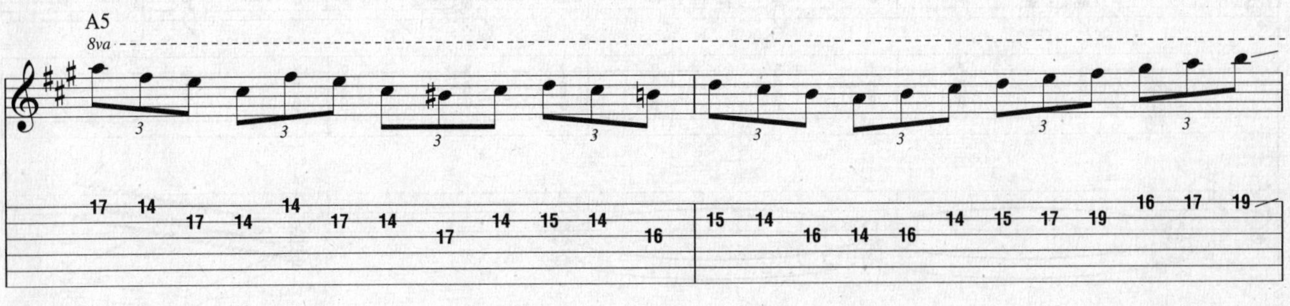
A5
8va
17 14 17 14 14 17 14 17 14 15 14 16 15 14 16 14 16 14 15 17 19 16 17 19

B5
8va
21 19 17 21 19 17 21 19 17 21 19 17 19 21 17 19 21 19 17 21 19 17 21 19 17 21 19 17 19 21 17 19 21

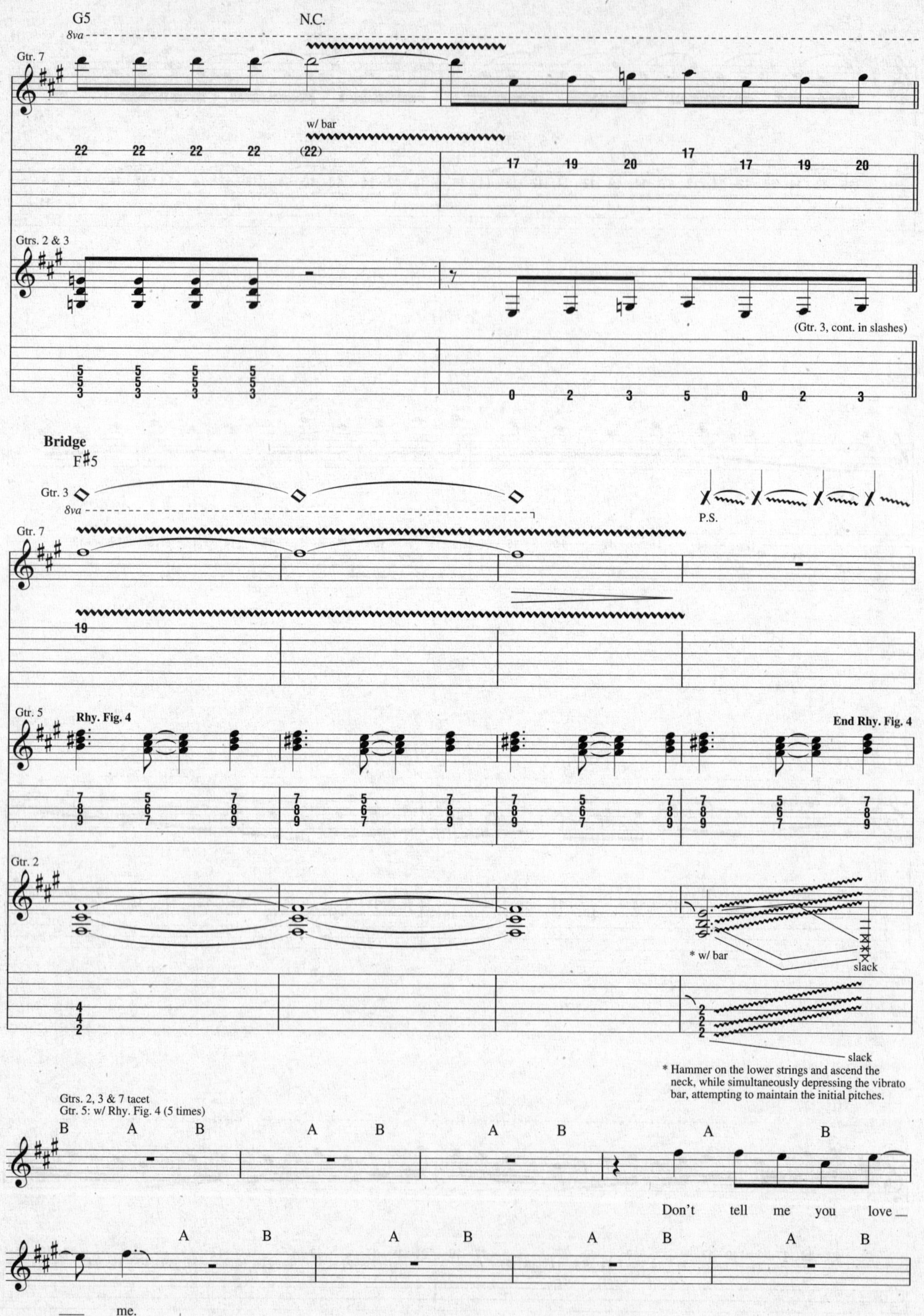
G5
N.C.
8va
Gtr. 7
w/ bar
Gtrs. 2 & 3
(Gtr. 3, cont. in slashes)
Bridge
F#5
Gtr. 3
P.S.
Gtr. 5
Rhy. Fig. 4
End Rhy. Fig. 4
Gtr. 2
* w/ bar
slack
* Hammer on the lower strings and ascend the neck, while simultaneously depressing the vibrato bar, attempting to maintain the initial pitches.
Gtrs. 2, 3 & 7 tacet
Gtr. 5: w/ Rhy. Fig. 4 (5 times)
B A B A B A B A B
Don't tell me you love
A B A B A B A B
me.

A B A B A B A B
Don't tell me you love me.
Don't tell me you love me. Don't tell me you love
(Love me, you love me, you love me, you love me, you
me. Don't tell me you love me, love me, love me, yeah.
love me, you love me, you love me, you love me.)
Interlude
F♯5 D5 E5 C♯5
Gtrs. 2 & 3
Gtr. 6
Gtr. 7
divisi
D5 A5 B5 G5open
Don't tell me you love
Gtr. 6
Gtr. 7

Chorus
Gtrs. 6 & 7 tacet
F#5
D5
E5
C#5
Gtrs. 2 & 3
me. Don't tell me you love me. Don't tell me,
D5
A5
B5
G5 open
I don't wan - na know. Don't tell me you love
Gtrs. 2 & 3: w/ Rhy. Fig. 2
F#5
D5
E5
C#5
me. Don't tell me you love me. Don't tell me,
Gtr. 6
P.H.
Gtr. 7
D5
A5
B5
N.C.
I don't wan - na know.

Outro - Guitar Solo

F♯5

8va

w/ bar

14 14 (14) (14) 14 (14) (14) 14 (14) (14) 14 (14) (14)

-2 1/2 -1 -2 1/2 -1 -2 1/2 -1 -2 1/2 -1

8va

w/ bar

14 14 (14) (14) 14 (14) (14) 14 (14) (14) 14 (14) (14)

-3 1/2 -1 -3 1/2 -1 -3 1/2 -1 -3 1/2 -1

Dream Police

Words and Music by Rick Nielsen

Verse
Gtr. 1
E5 B5
talk is cheap, and those ru-mors ain't nice. And when I
can't tell lies, 'cause they're lis-ten-ing to me. And when I
E5 B5 E5
fall a - sleep I don't think I'll sur - vive the night, the
fall a - sleep, bet they're spy-ing on me to - night, to -
Pre-Chorus
B5 E5 E E5 E F♯5 E5 D♯5 E5 E E8 E E8 E E8 E
open
night. 'Cause they're wait-ing for me. They're look-ing for me. Ev - 'ry sin -
E8 E E8 E E8 E E5/B D5/A C5/G B5 A A
gle night they're driv - ing me in - sane.
To Coda
A B C B A G F♯ F E5 D5 C5 B5
open 2fr 3fr 2fr open 3fr 2fr 1fr
(cont. in notation, 3rd time)
mp mf
Those men in - side my brain.
Gtr. 1: w/ Rhy. Fill 1, 2nd time
1.
Chorus
Gtr. 1: w/ Rhy. Fig. 1, simile
B E B A E
The dream po - lice, they live in - side of my head. The dream po - lice, they come to
(Live in - side of my head.
Rhy. Fill 1
Gtr. 1
(cont. in slash)
T
A
B

B A E B A E5
me in my bed. _ The dream po - lice, _ they're com-in' to ar - rest _ me, oh no. _____ 2. Well, I
Come to me in my bed. __)
2.
Bridge
E5 A5 E5
Gtr. 1
I try to sleep, they're wide a - wake, they won't leave me a - lone. _ They don't get paid to take va - ca-tions, or let me a - lone. _
A5
(cont. in notation)
They spy on me, I try - to - hide, they won't let me a - lone. _ They per - se - cute me, they're the judge and ju - ry all in one.
Gtr. 1
let ring
Guitar Solo
N.C. E5
1/2
1.
B5
let ring
2.
B5 E5 B5
D.S. al Coda
'Cause they're
Coda
Interlude
B Bsus4 B(♭5) B5
brain.
Gtr. 1
let ring
let ring
let ring

G° G#° A° A#° B° C° C#° D° Eb° E° F° F#° G°
F#(b5) Gmaj7 G#7 G/B C(b5) C#maj7
let ring throughout
D5 D#maj7 E(b5) G(b5) G#5 Amaj7
A#maj7 A(b5) A#maj7 A(b5)
play 3 times
The
Outro Chorus
Gtr. 1: w/ Rhy. Fig. 1, 1st 6 meas., simile
E B A E B A
dream po - lice, they live in - side of my head. The dream po - lice, they come to me in my bed. The
(Live in - side of my head. Come to me in my bed.
E B A
dream po - lice they're com - in' to ar - rest me. The
)
Play 6 Times and Fade
Gtr. 1: w/ Rhy. Fig. 1, 1st 2 meas., simile
E B A
dream po - lice. (Po - lice, po - lice.) The

Dreams

Words and Music by Stevie Nicks

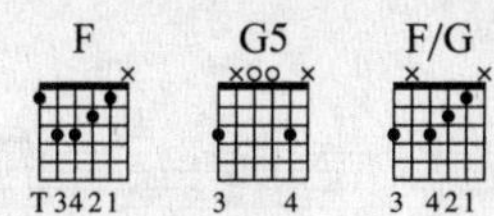

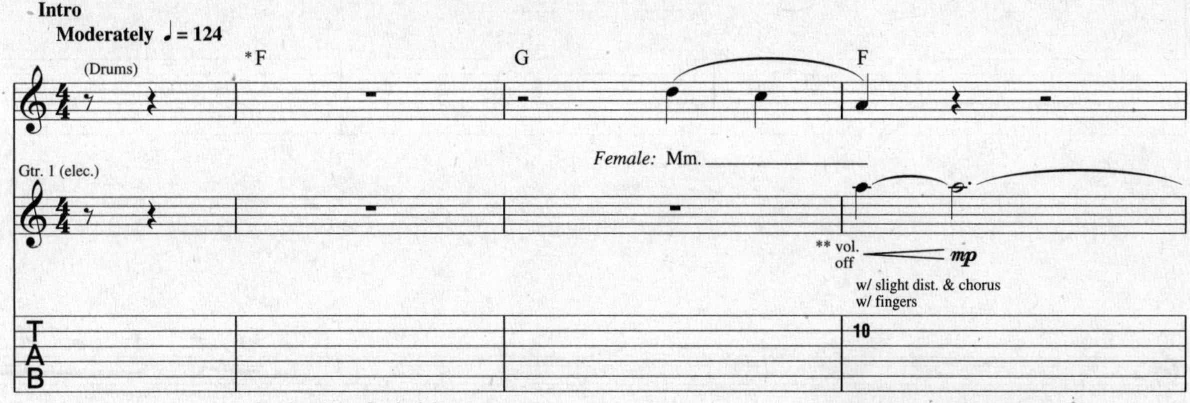

* Chord symbols reflect basic harmony.

** Indicates vol. swell throughout (performed w/ vol. pedal on recording). Begin w/ vol. off unless otherwise indicated.

*** T = Thumb on 6th string

† Rock vol. knob or pedal back and forth in rhythm indicated, thereby creating a tremolo effect.

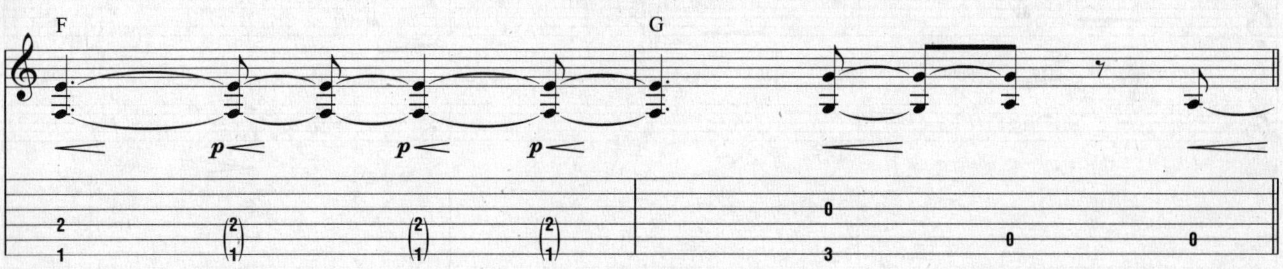

G
F
G
- dom. Well, who am I to keep you down?
let ring

F
G
F
It's on - ly right

G
F
G
that you should play the way you feel it. But

F
G
F
lis - ten care - ful - ly to the sound of your lone -

Pre-Chorus
G
Fmaj7
G7
- li - ness, like a heart - beat, drives you mad in the still -
Female: (Heart - beat.
let ring

Fadd9
G7
Fmaj7
- ness of re - mem - ber - ing what you had
Still - ness. Lone - ly.
let ring
sim.
let ring sim.

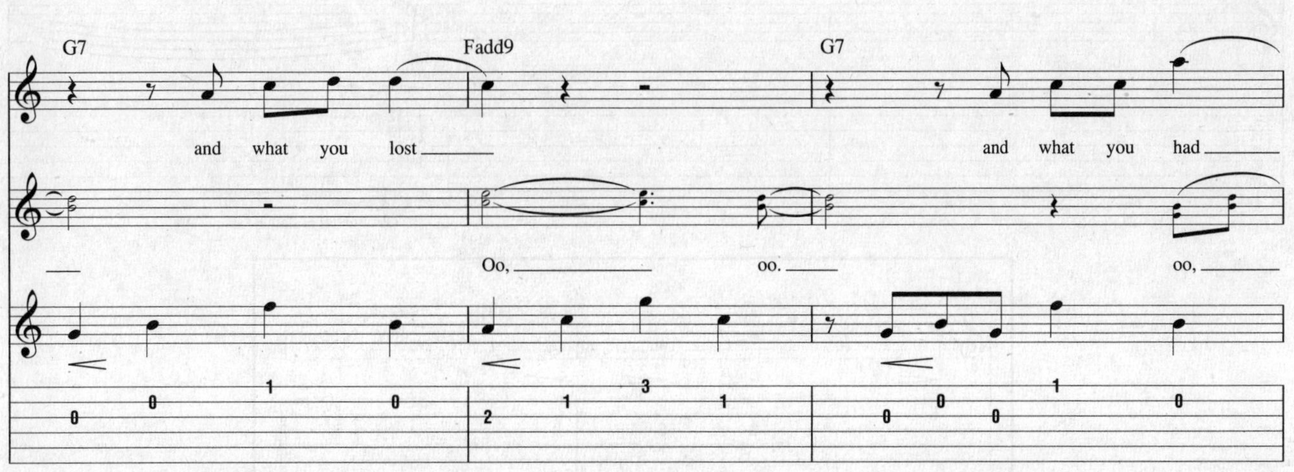

G7
Fadd9
G7
and what you lost and what you had
Oo, oo. oo,

Fmaj7
G7
2nd time, Gtr. 1: w/ Fill 1
Fadd9
and what you lost.
oo, what you lost.
Female: (Oo.)
oo.
Ah,
ah.)
Chorus
F
Gtr. 2 (acous.)
*G5
G7
mp
Male & Female: Oh, thun - der on - ly hap - pens when it's rain -
Thun - der on - ly hap - pens when it's rain -
* 2nd time, play F/G.
F
*G5
F
Rhy. Fig. 1
- ing.
- ing.
Play - ers on - ly love
Play - ers on - ly love
† Gtr. 3 (elec.)
Gtr. 1
divisi
mf
† clean tone & chorus
** Gtr. 1 to left of slash in tab.
Fill 1
Gtr. 1

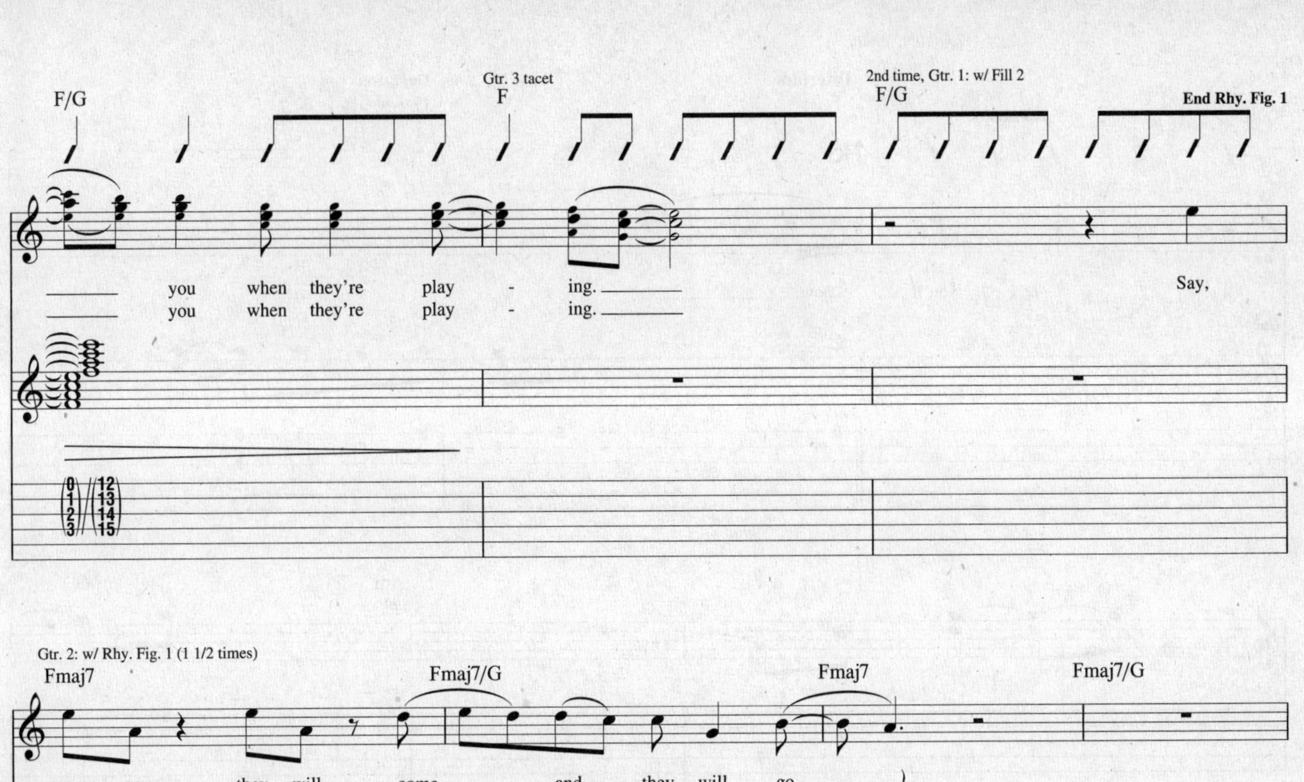
Gtr. 3 tacet
2nd time, Gtr. 1: w/ Fill 2
F/G
F
F/G
End Rhy. Fig. 1
you when they're play - ing.
you when they're play - ing.
Say,

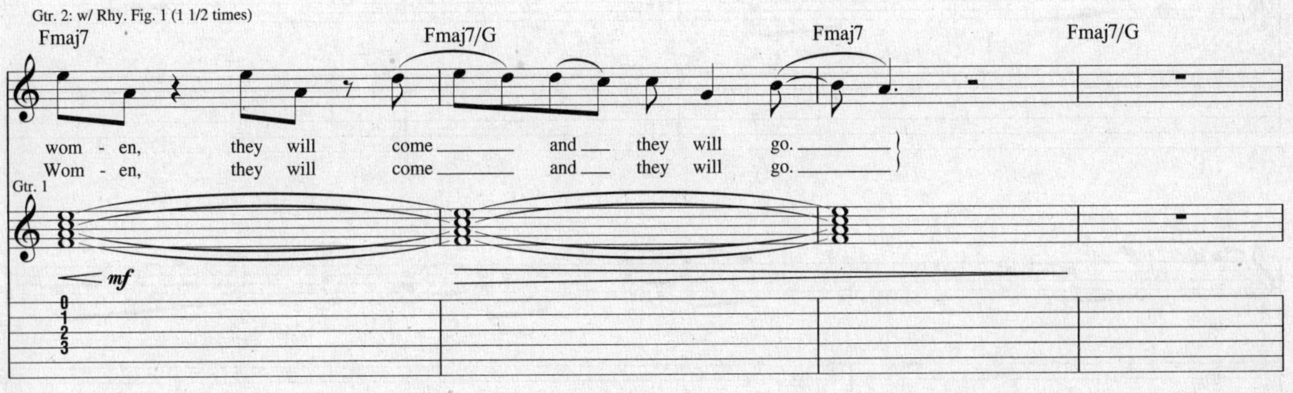
Gtr. 2: w/ Rhy. Fig. 1 (1 1/2 times)
Fmaj7
Fmaj7/G
Fmaj7
Fmaj7/G
wom - en, they will come and they will go.
Wom - en, they will come and they will go.
Gtr. 1
mf

To Coda
Gtr. 3 tacet
Fmaj7
Fmaj7/G
F
Gtr. 2
When the rain wash - es you clean, you'll know,
Gtr. 3
Gtr. 1
divisi
mp

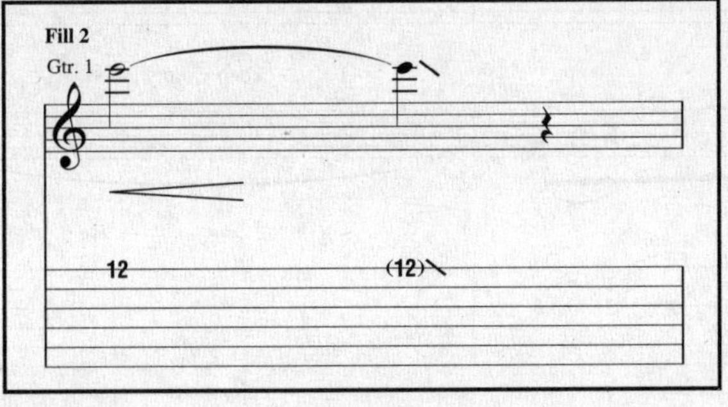
Fill 2
Gtr. 1

Interlude
F/G
F
Gtr. 2 tacet
G
you'll
know.
Gtr. 1
F
Am
G
F
let ring
Verse
F
G
F
2. Now here I go a - gain, I see the crys - tal vi -
let ring
G
F
G
- sion. I keep my vi - sions to my - self.

F
G
F
It's on - ly me

G
F
G
who wants to wrap a - round your dreams. And

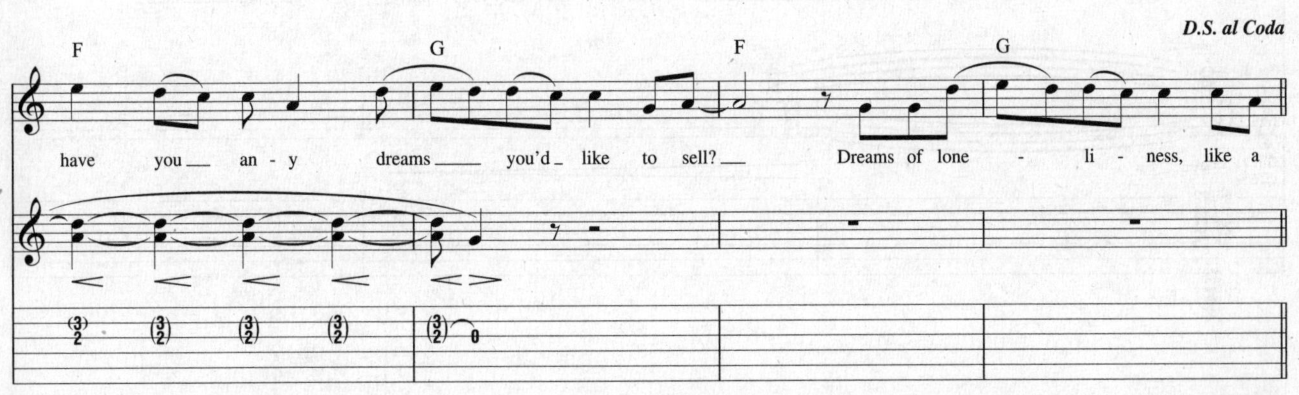
D.S. al Coda
F
G
F
G
have you an - y dreams you'd like to sell? Dreams of lone - li - ness, like a

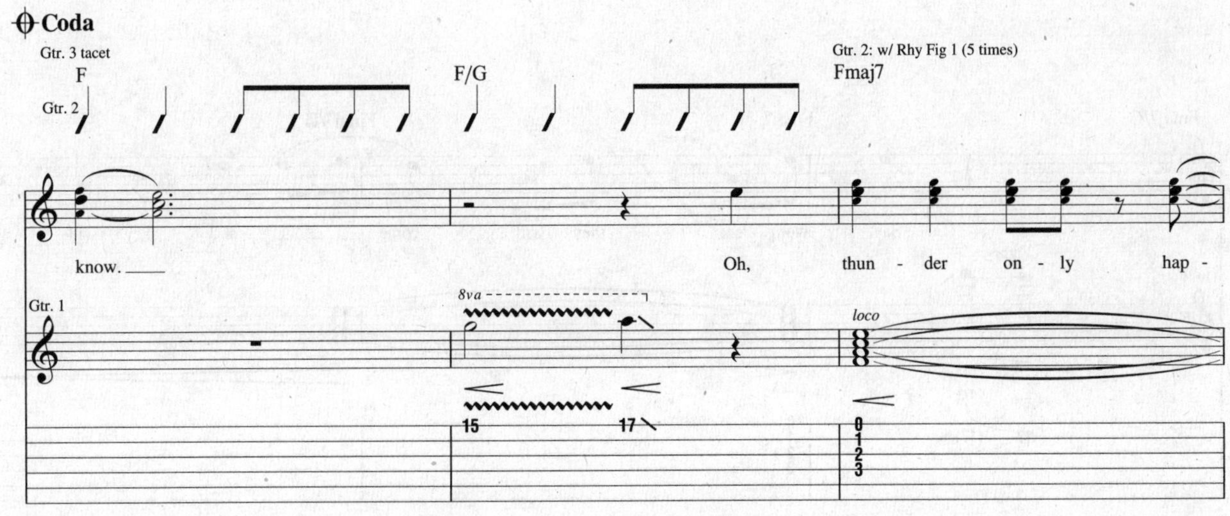
Coda
Gtr. 3 tacet
F
Gtr. 2
F/G
Gtr. 2: w/ Rhy Fig 1 (5 times)
Fmaj7
know. Oh, thun - der on - ly hap -
Gtr. 1
8va
loco

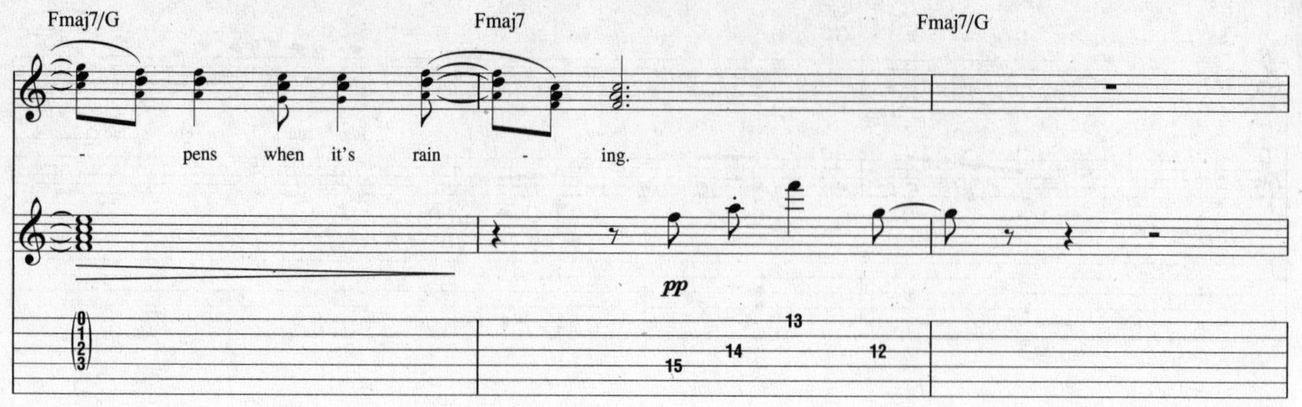
Fmaj7/G
Fmaj7
Fmaj7/G
- pens when it's rain - ing.
pp
13
15 14 12
0
1
2
3

Fmaj7
Fmaj7/G
Gtr. 3 tacet
Fmaj7
Play - ers on - ly love you when they're play - ing.
Gtr. 3
Gtr. 1
divisi
0 12
1 13
2 14
3 15

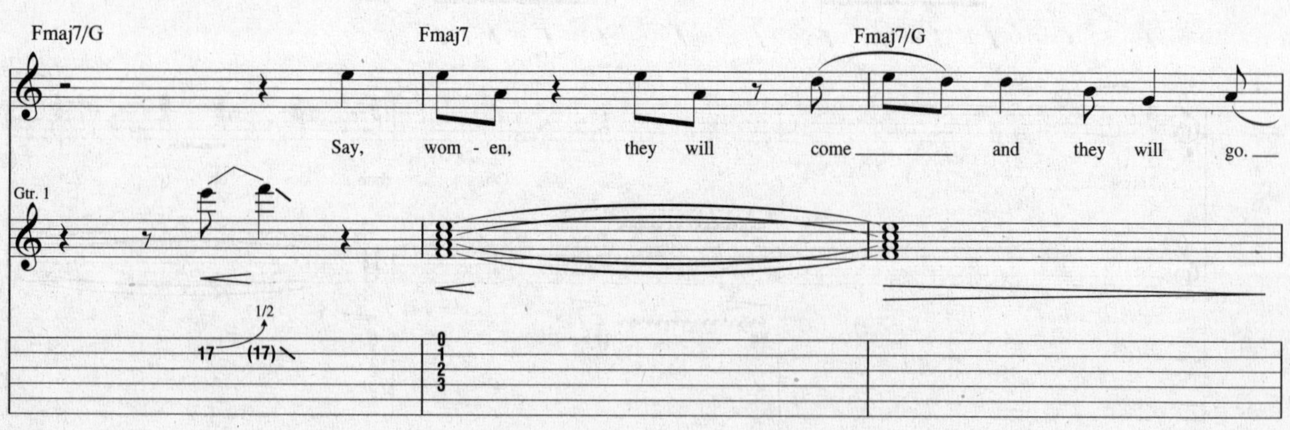
Fmaj7/G
Fmaj7
Fmaj7/G
Say, wom - en, they will come and they will go.
Gtr. 1
1/2
17 (17)
0
1
2
3

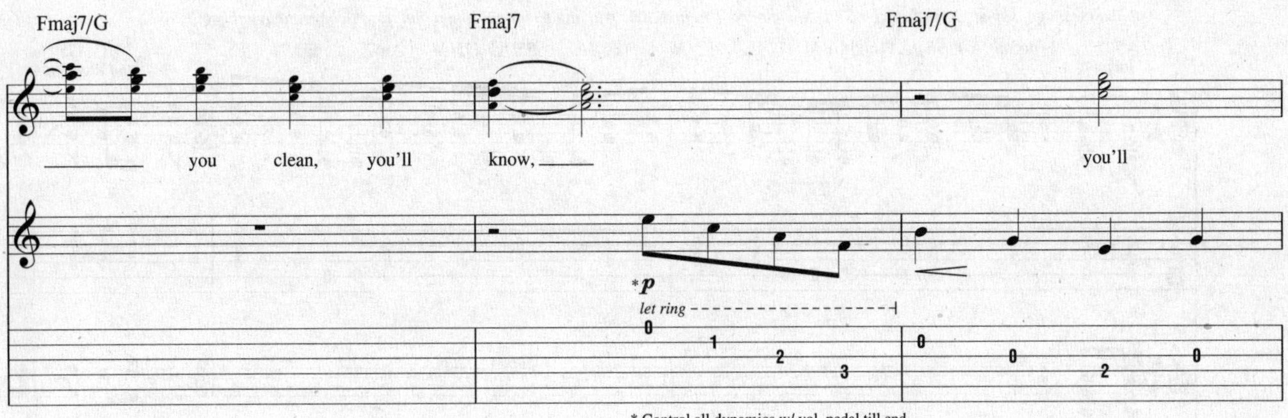

* Control all dynamics w/ vol. pedal till end.

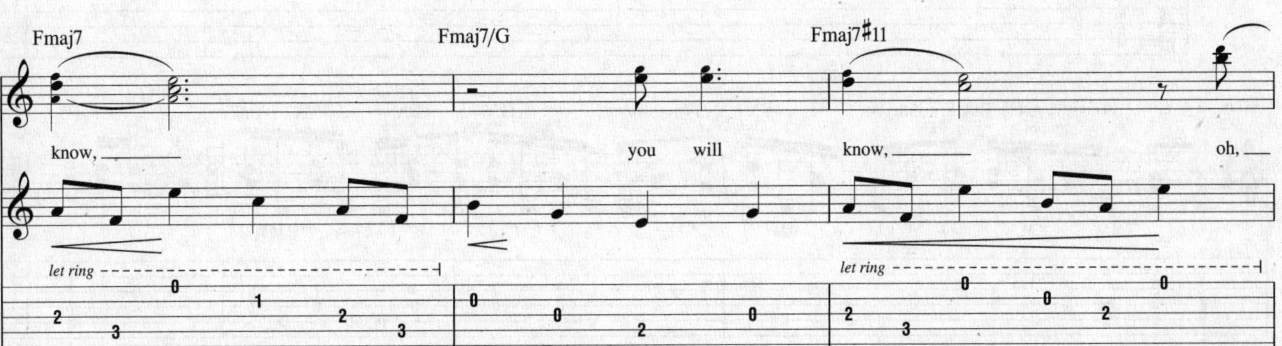

Empire

Words and Music by Geoff Tate and Michael Wilton

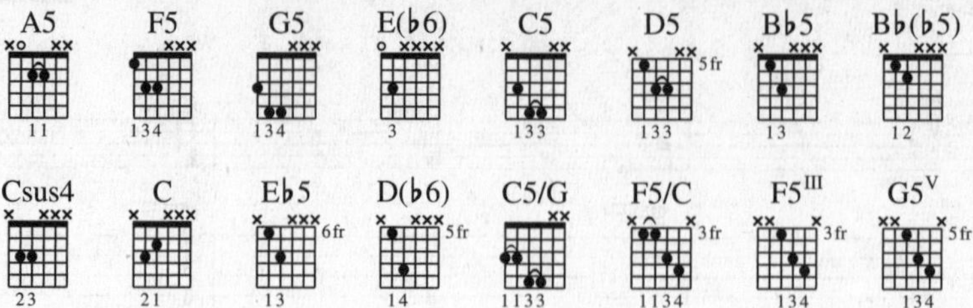

Intro

Moderately slow rock ♩ = 80

Next message, saved, Saturday at 9:24 P.M. "Sorry, I'm just...it's starting to hit me like a, um, um, two ton heavy thing."

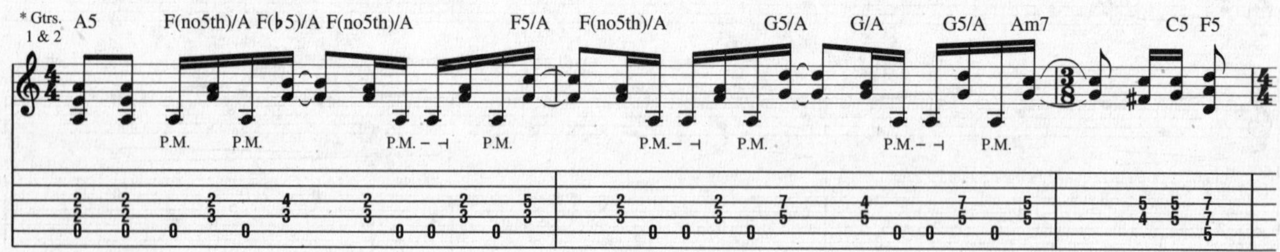

* Composite arrangement

A5
F(no5th)/A
F(♭5)/A
F(no5th)/A
F5/A
F(no5th)/A
C5
G5
C5
Gtr. 4 (dist.)
f
1/2
Gtr. 3 (dist.)
Riff A
End Riff A
1
Gtrs. 1 & 2
P.M.
Verse
A5
G5
C5
1. Last night the word came down, ten dead in Chi - na - town.
(Gtr. 2 cont. in slashes)

Gtrs. 3 & 4 tacet
A5
G
3fr
F5
Gtr. 2
In - no - cent, their on - ly - crime was be - ing the wrong place at the wrong time
Gtr. 1
A5
G5
C5
(cont. in notation)
Too bad, peo - ple say, what's wrong with the kids to - day?
Gtrs. 1 & 2
A5
G5
F5
I tell you right now they've got noth - in' to lose. They're build - ing em - pire.
Verse
A5
2. John - ny used to work af - ter school
Rhy. Fig. 3
Gtr. 3
Gtrs. 1 & 2
divisi
fdbk.

G5
C5
A5
Gtr. 2
at the cin - e - ma show.
Got - ta hus - tle if he wants an ed - u - ca - tion,
Gtrs. 1 & 2
Gtr. 1
(Gtr. 2 cont. in slashes)
G
3fr
F5
A5
(cont. in notation)
yeah, he's got - ta long way to go.
Now he's out on the streets all day sell - ing
crack to the peo - ple who pay.
Got an A - K - for - ty - sev - en for his best friend,
Gtrs. 1 & 2
Pre-Chorus
F5
D5
G5
D5
busi - ness the A - mer - i - can way.
East - side meets
Rhy. Fig. 4
End Rhy. Fig. 3

F5
D5
E5
C5
F5
D5
G5
D5
West - side __ down - town. __ No time, __ the
F5
D5
G5
F5
G5
Chorus
A5
F(no5th)/A
F(♭5)/A
F(no5th)/A
F5/A
walls fall, __ down.
(Down.
Can't you
End Rhy. Fig. 4
P.M.
F(♭5)/A
F5/A
G5/A
Am7
G5
A5
F(no5th)/A
F(♭5)/A
F(no5th)/A
F5/A
Voc. Fig. 1
feel it com - ing? __
Em - pire.)
Can't you
End Voc. Fig. 1
F(no5th)/A
G5
G/A
Am7
G5
D5
C5
A5
hear it call - ing? __
3. Black man, black man, black man, black

Verse
Gtrs. 1 & 2: w/ Rhy. Fig. 3
G5 C5
man, black man, trapped a - gain, holds his chains in his hand.
A5 G F5
Broth - er kill - ing broth - er for the prof - it of an - oth - er, game point, no - bod - y wins.
A5 G5 C5
De - clines right on time. What hap - pened to the dream sub - lime?
A5 G5 F5
Tear it all down we'll build it up a - gain. An - oth - er em - pire?
Pre-Chorus
Gtrs. 1 & 2: w/ Rhy. Fig. 4
F5 D5 G5 D5 F5 D5 E5 C5 F5 D5 G5 D5 F5 D5 G5 F5 G5
East - side meets West - side down - town. No time, (No time.) the walls fall, down.
(Down.)
Chorus
Gtrs. 1 & 2: w/ Rhy. Fig. 2 (2 times)
Bkgd. Voc.: w/ Voc. Fig. 1 (2 times)
A5 F(no5th)/A F(♭5)/A F(no5th)/A F5/A F(♭5)/A F5/A G5/A Am7 G5 A5 F(no5th)/A F(♭5)/A F(no5th)/A F5/A
Can't you feel it com - ing? Can't you
Gtrs. 1 & 2: w/ Rhy. Fig. 1
F(♭5)/A F5/A G5/A Am7 G5 A5 F(no5th)/A F(♭5)/A F(no5th)/A F5/A F(♭5)/A F5/A G5/A Am7 G5/A F5 C G5
hear it com - ing? Can't some - one here stop it?
Interlude
Gtrs. 1 & 2
C5 G5 C5 G5 C5 D5

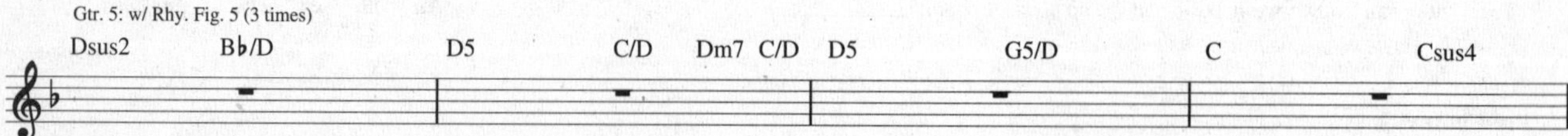

Spoken: In fiscal year 1986 to '87 the local, state, and federal governments spent a combined total of 60.6 million dollars on law enforcement.

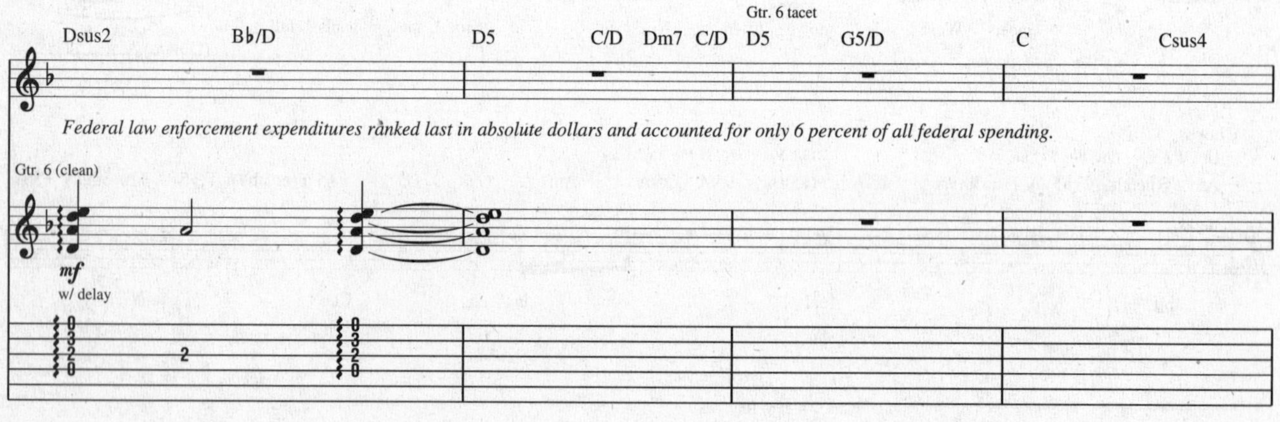

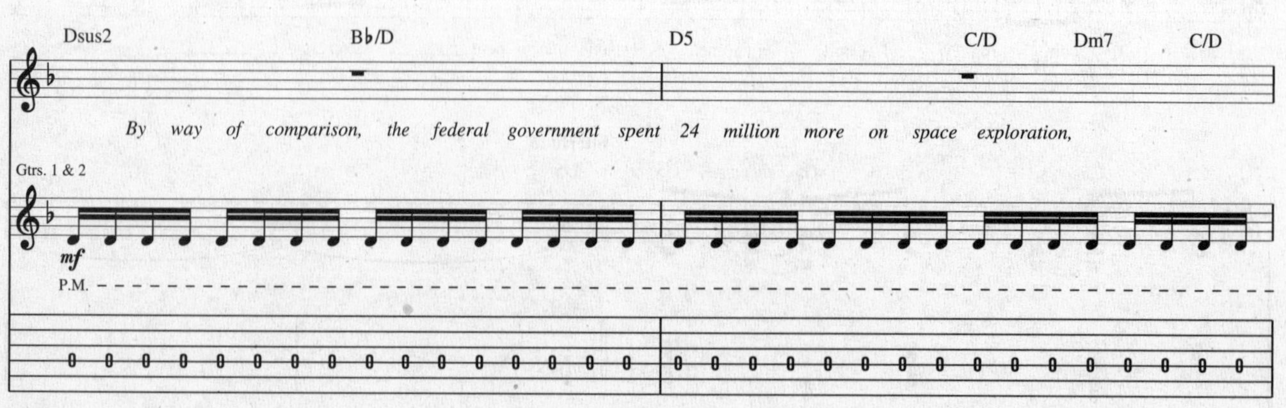

D5
G5/D
C
Csus4
and 43 times more on national defense and international relations than on law enforcement.
P.M.
(cont. in slashes)
Guitar Solo
A5
G5
F5
E(♭6)
C5
Gtrs. 1 & 2
8va
Gtr. 3
loco
D5
Bb5
Bb(b5)
Gtr. 2: w/ Fill 1
Csus4
Gtr. 1
Fill 1
Gtr. 2

Bb5 Bb(b5) Bb5 Bb(b5) Bb5
Eb5 D(b6) C5/G
Gtrs. 1 & 2
Eb5 D(b6) C5/G
Eb5 D(b6) C5/G
8va
Chorus
Gtrs. 1 & 2: w/ Rhy. Fig. 2 (4 times)
* Bkgd. Voc.: w/ Voc. Fig. 1 (4 times)
Gtr. 3 tacet
Eb5 D(b6) F5/C F5 III G5 V
A5 F(no5th)/A F(b5)/A F(no5th)/A F5/A F(b5)/A F5/A G5/A Am7 G5
Voc. Fig. 2
Can't you feel it com - ing?
(Em -
loco
w/ bar
* w/ delay
Bkgd. Voc.: w/ Voc. Fig. 2 (2 1/2 times)
A5 F(no5th)/A F(b5)/A F(no5th)/A F5/A F(b5)/A F5/A G5/A Am7 G5 A5 F(no5th)/A F(b5)/A F(no5th)/A F5/A
End Voc. Fig. 2
Can't you hear it com - ing? Can't you
pire.)
F(b5)/A F5/A G5/A Am7 G5 A5 F(no5th)/A F(b5)/A F(no5th)/A F5/A F(b5)/A F5/A G5/A Am7 G5
feel it com - ing? Can't you hear it com - ing?
Gtr. 3

Outro

Bkgd. Voc.: w/ Voc. Fig. 2 (last meas.)
Gtrs. 1 & 2: w/ Rhy. Fig. 2 (4 times)
Gtr. 3: w/ Riff A (2 times)

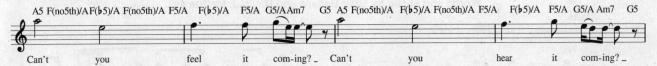

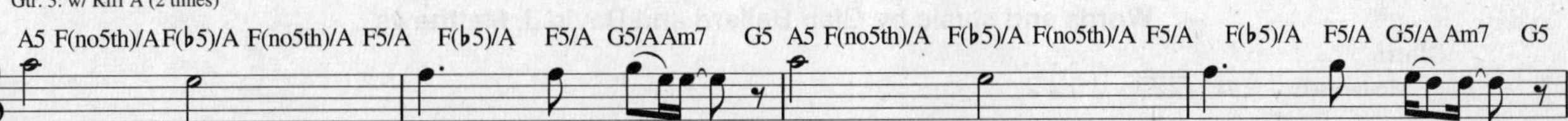

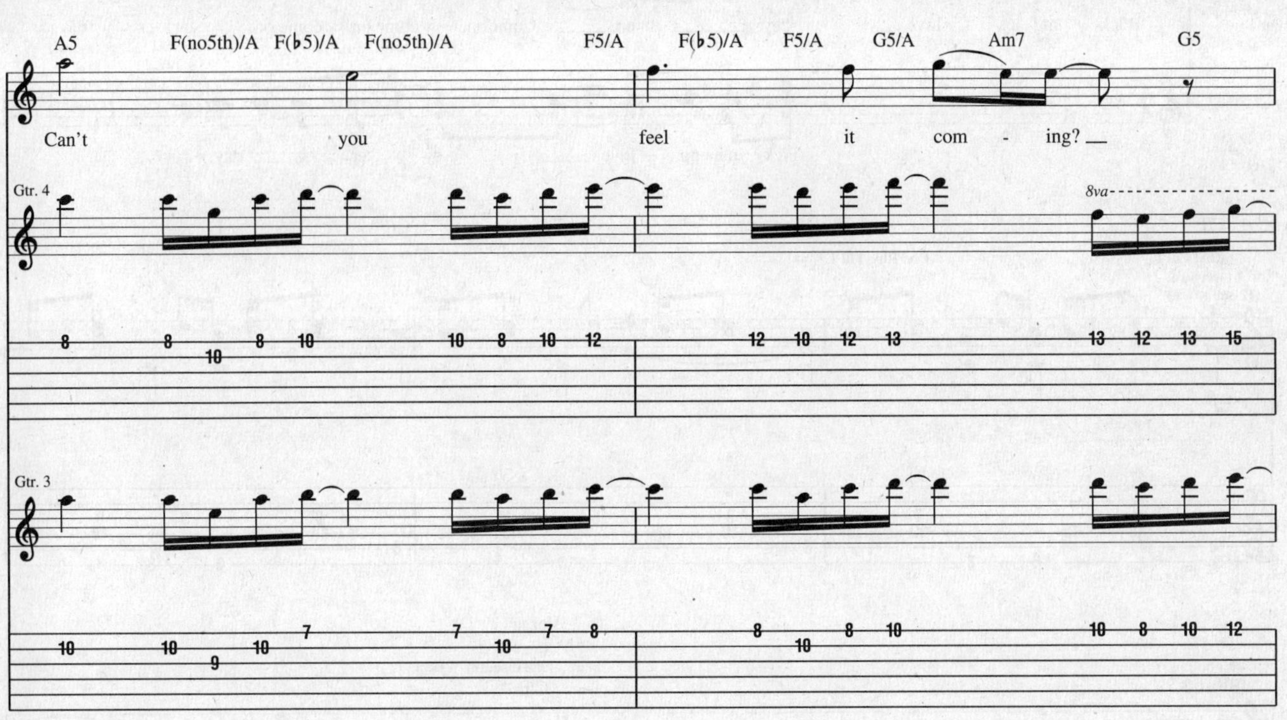

Everyday

Words and Music by Glen Ballard and David J. Matthews

Gtr. 1: w/ Rhy. Fig. 1 (2 3/4 times)
C/F C C/F C C/F C
Pay no mind to taunts or ad - vanc - es. I take my chanc - es on
Pay no mind to taunts or ad - vanc - es. I'm gon-na take my chanc - es on

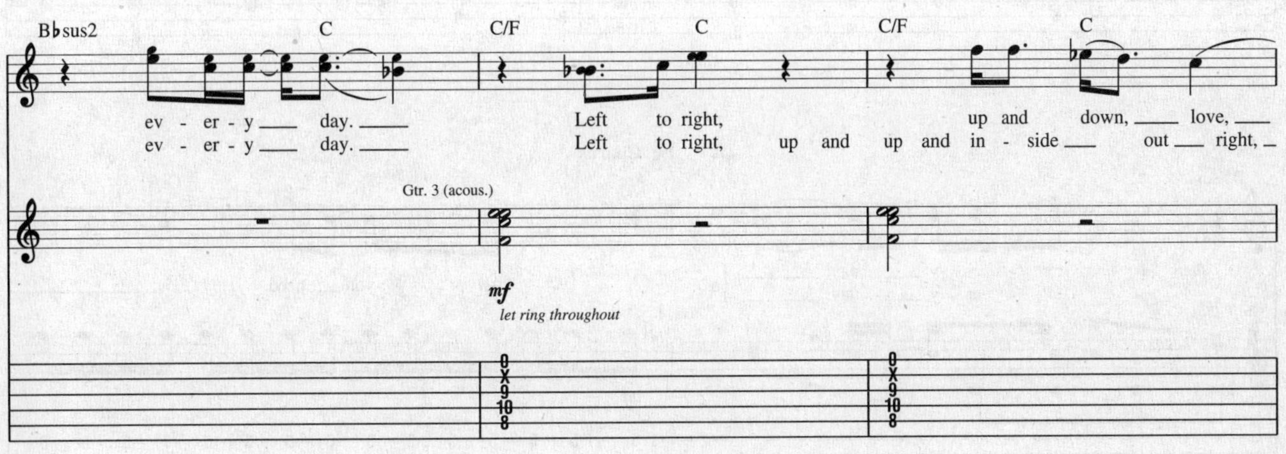
B♭sus2 C C/F C C/F C
ev - er - y day. Left to right, up and down, love,
ev - er - y day. Left to right, up and up and in - side out right,
Gtr. 3 (acous.)
mf
let ring throughout

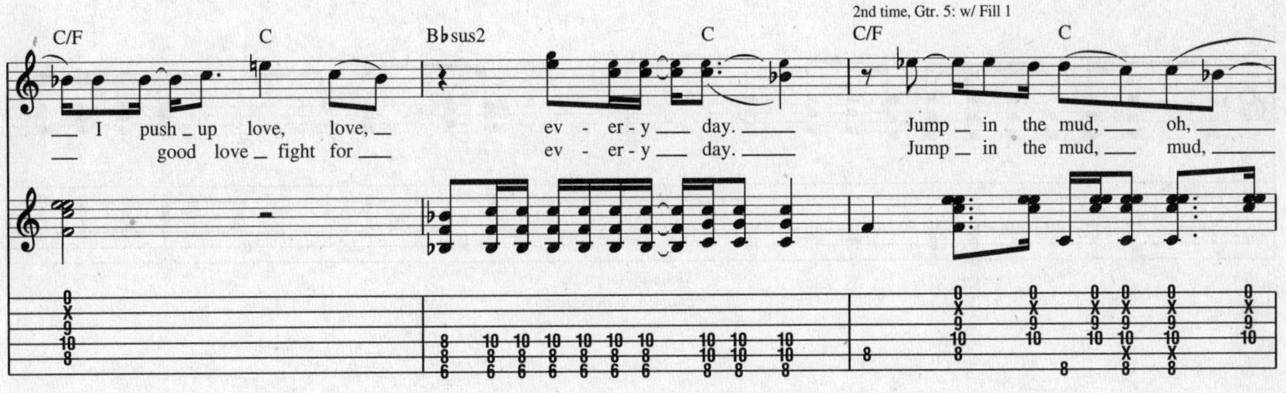
C/F C B♭sus2 C
2nd time, Gtr. 5: w/ Fill 1
C/F C
I push up love, love, ev - er - y day. Jump in the mud, oh,
good love fight for ev - er - y day. Jump in the mud, mud,

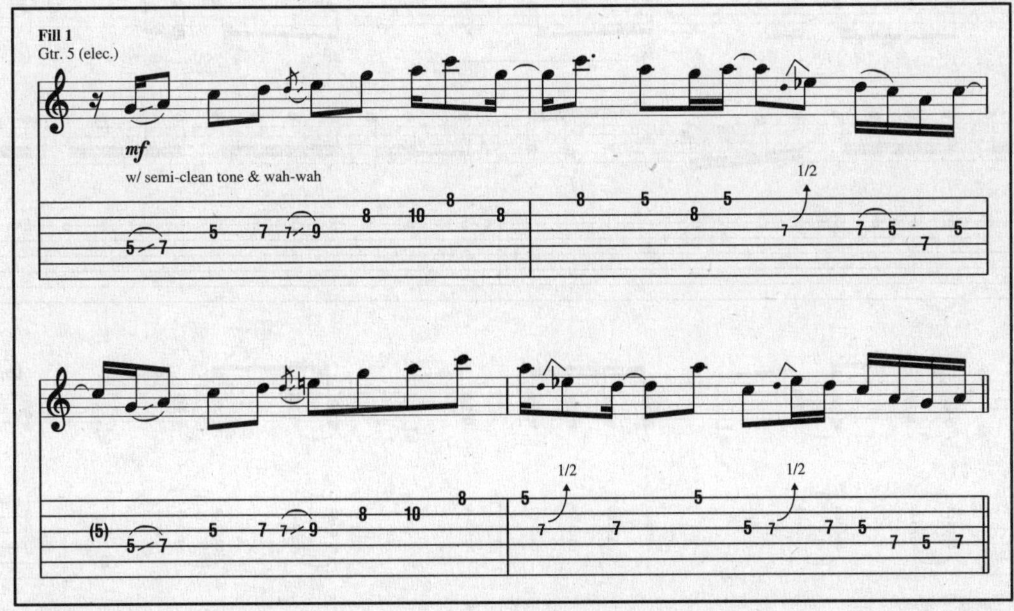
Fill 1
Gtr. 5 (elec.)
mf
w/ semi-clean tone & wah-wah
1/2

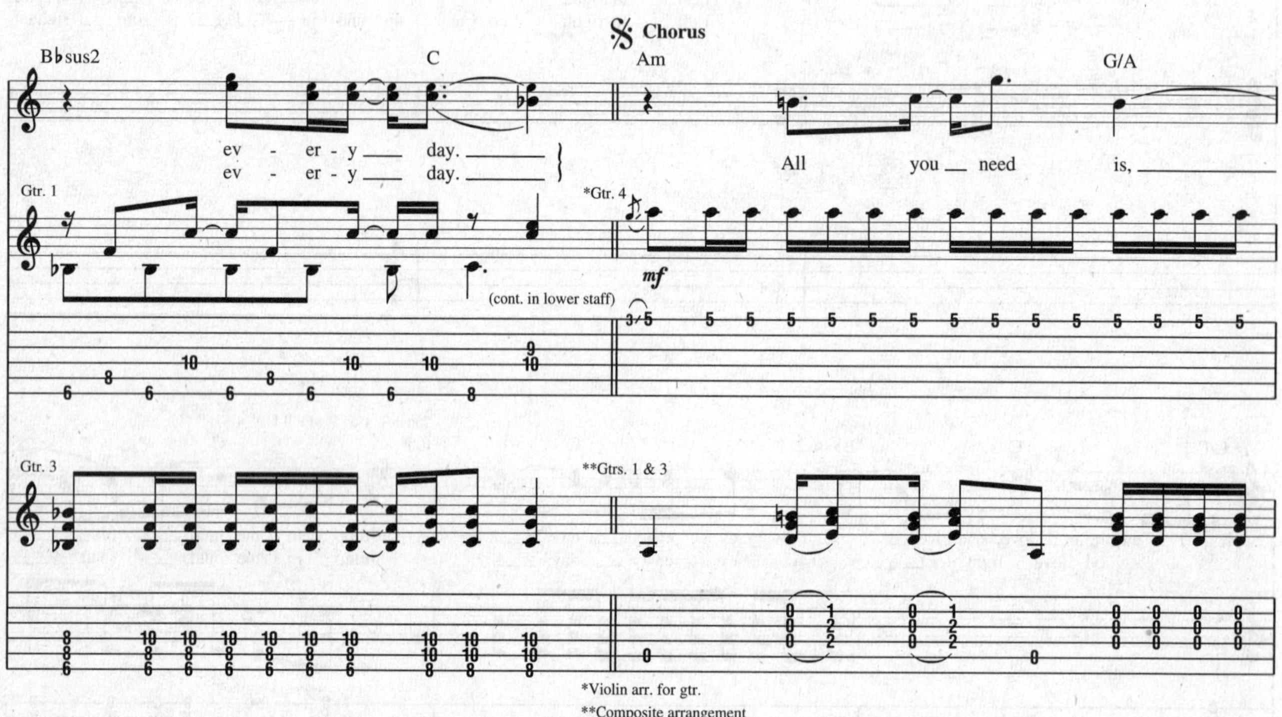

*Violin arr. for gtr.

**Composite arrangement

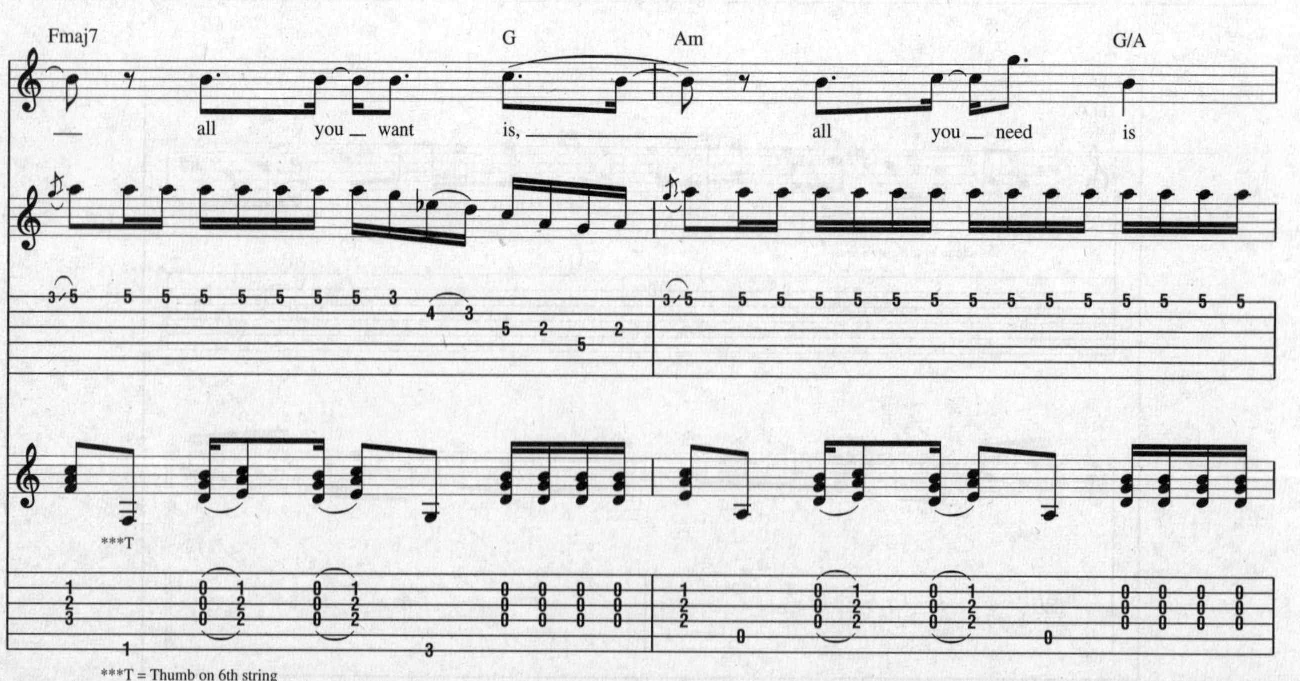

***T = Thumb on 6th string

Fmaj7
G
Am
G/A
love.
All you need is,
T
Fmaj7
G/F
Fmaj7
To Coda
1.
G
what you want is,
all you need is love.
Oo,
Fill 2
Rhy. Fill 2
End Rhy. Fill 2
Gtrs. 1 & 2: w/ Rhy. Fill 1
Gtr. 3 tacet
* Gtrs. 1 & 2: w/ Rhy. Fig. 1 (last 3 meas.)
C/F
C
C/F
C
C/F
C
B♭sus2
C
ev - 'ry day,
ev - 'ry day.
Oh, ev - 'ry day.
End Fill 2
Gtr. 4
*Last note of Rhy. Fig. 1 is played by Gtr. 1 only.

2.
Gtr. 4 tacet
Bridge
G
Bb sus2
Db/Ab
Ab sus2
C5
C5/G
love.
Oo.
What you've got,
Rhy. Fig. 2
*Gtr. 5 (elec.)
End Rhy. Fig. 2
mf
w/ dist.
Rhy. Fig. 2A
End Rhy. Fig. 2A
*Two gtrs. arr. for one.
Gtrs. 1 & 3: w/ Rhy. Fig. 2A (2 1/2 times)
Gtr. 5: w/ Rhy. Fig. 2 (2 1/2 times)
lay it down on me.
What you've got,
D.S. al Coda
lay it down on me.
Gtr. 5
Gtrs. 1 & 3
Coda
Gtrs. 1 & 3: w/ Rhy. Fill 2
Gtr. 4: w/ Fill 2
Gtrs. 1 & 2: w/ Rhy. Fill 1
**Gtrs. 1 & 2: w/ Rhy. Fig. 1 (last 3 meas.)
C/F
C
love.
Oo,
ev - 'ry day,
ev - 'ry
**Last note of Rhy. Fig. 1 is played by Gtr. 1 only.

Outro
w/ Bkgd. Voc. ad lib (till end)
Gtr. 1: w/ Rhy. Fig. 1 (6 3/4 times)
C/F
C
Bbsus2
day.
Oh, ev - 'ry day.
Mm, mm, pick me up, love.
Pick me up, love, hey, oh,
Voc. Fig. 1
(Pick me up, love.
Mm, lift me up, love, oh, oh, to,
oo, ev - er - y day.
Lift me up, love.
Pick me up, love,
w/ Lead Voc. ad lib (till end)
Bkgd. Voc.: w/ Voc. Fig. 1 (till end)
to the top ev - er - y day.
Come on, come on, come on, ev - er - y - day.
End Voc. Fig. 1
ev - er - y day.
Gtr. 5
1/2
1

B♭sus2
C
C/F
C
C/F
C
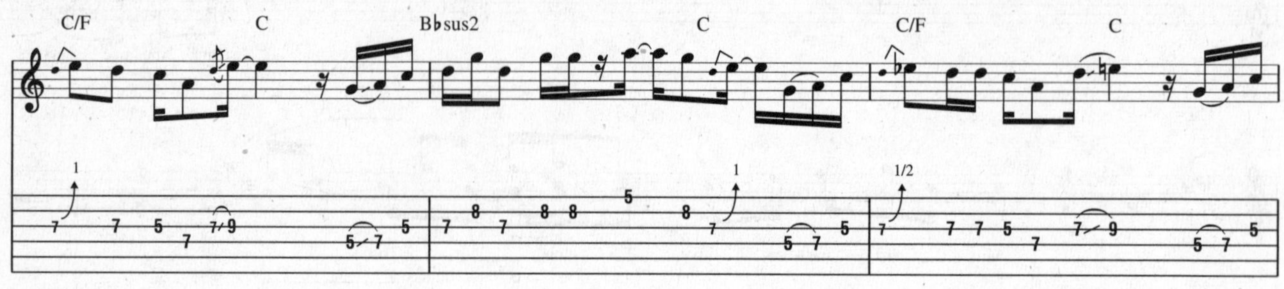
C/F
C
B♭sus2
C
C/F
C

C/F
C
C/F
C
B♭sus2
C

C/F
C
C/F
C
C/F
C
B♭sus2
C

C/F
C
C/F
C
C/F
C
B♭sus2
C
Gtr. 1

Evil Ways

Words and Music by Sonny Henry

Verse
Gtr. 1: w/ Rhy. Fill 1, 2nd time
C Gm C Gm C Gm C
- by. 2. When I come home, ba - by, my house is dark and my

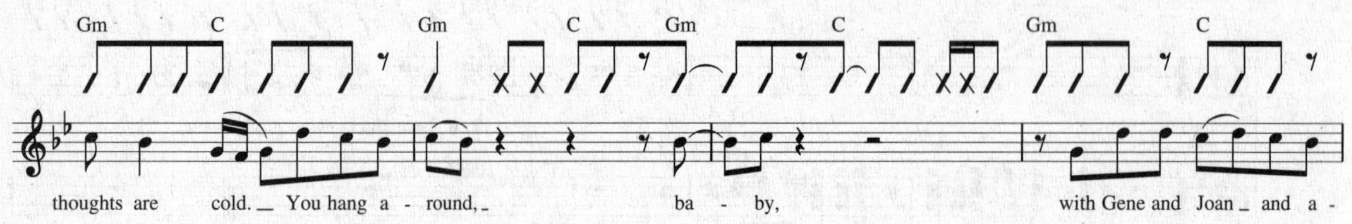
Gm C Gm C Gm C Gm C
thoughts are cold. You hang a - round, ba - by, with Gene and Joan and a -

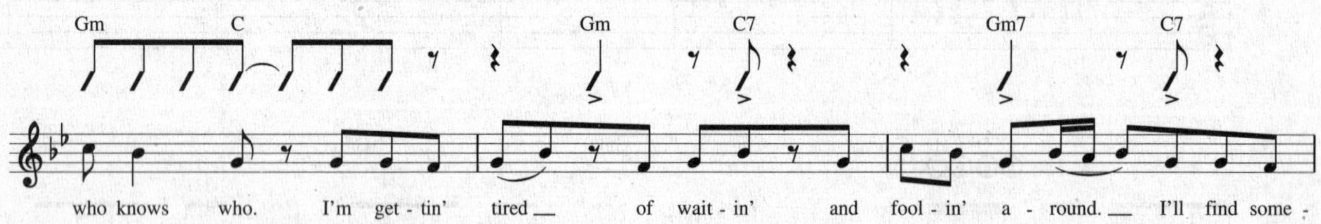
Gm C Gm C7 Gm7 C7
who knows who. I'm get - tin' tired of wait - in' and fool - in' a - round. I'll find some -

To Coda
Gtr. 1: w/ Rhy. Fill 2, 2nd time
Gm C7 Gm7 C7 D7
bod - y that won't make me feel like a clown. This can't go on.

Organ Solo
play 8 times
Gm C Gm C Gm C Gm C Gm
simile on repeats
*(cont. in notation)
Lord knows you got to change.
*Last time

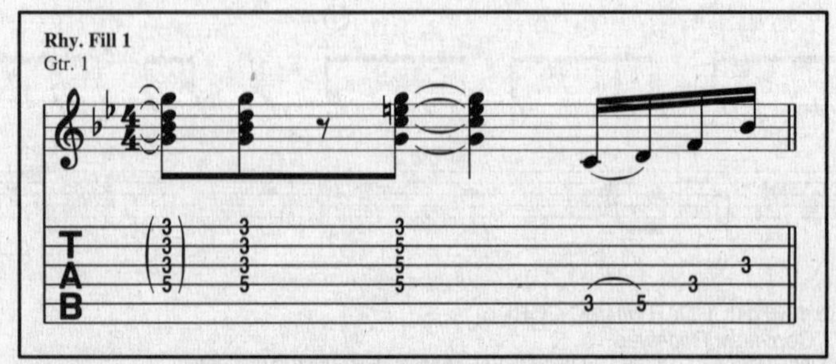
Rhy. Fill 1
Gtr. 1

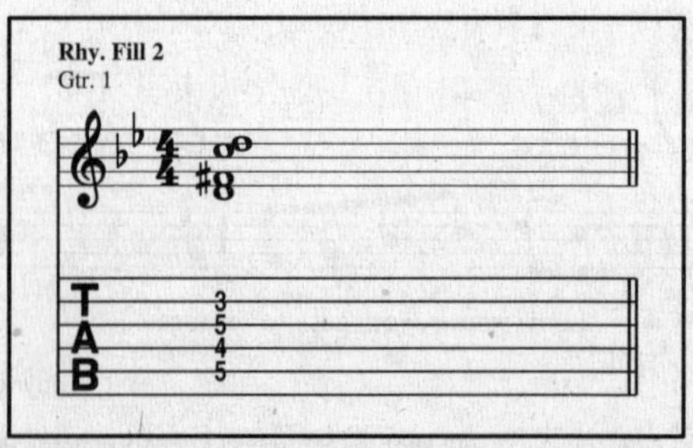
Rhy. Fill 2
Gtr. 1

D.S. al Coda
Gm C N.C. Gm C N.C.
3. When I come
Gtr. 1
Coda
N.C. Gm C7 Gm C7
Yeah, yeah, yeah!
Gm C7 Gm C7
Hey, hey.
Outro Guitar Solo
*Gm C
* Chords implied by organ and bass.
Begin Fade
Gm C Gm C Gm C
full
Fade Out

Evil Woman

Words and Music by Jeff Lynne

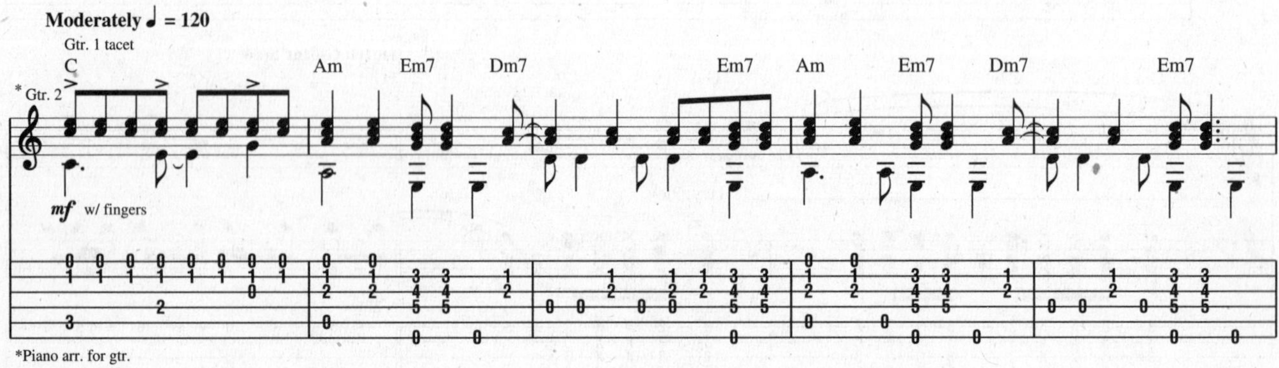

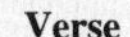
Verse

Gtrs. 2 & 3: w/ Rhy. Figs. 1 & 1A (3 times)
Em7
Dm7
Em7
Am
Em7
Dm7
1. Hey wom - an, you got the blues. Guess you ain't got no one else

Em7
Am
Em7
Dm7
Em7
to use. There's an o - pen road that leads no - where, so just

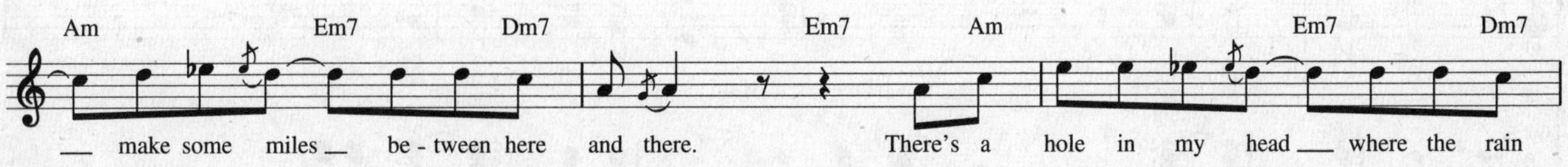
Am
Em7
Dm7
Em7
Am
Em7
Dm7
make some miles be - tween here and there. There's a hole in my head where the rain

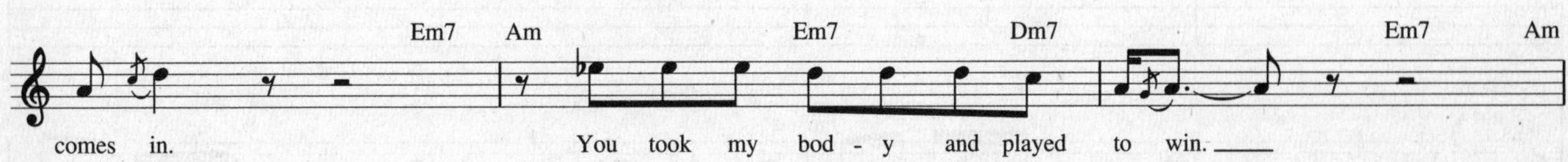
Em7
Am
Em7
Dm7
Em7
Am
comes in. You took my bod - y and played to win.

Em7
Dm7
Em7
Ha, ha, wom - an it's a cry - in' shame. But you
Gtr. 3
Rhy. Fig. 2A
End Rhy. Fig. 2A
Gtr. 2
Rhy. Fig. 2

Gtr. 3 tacet
Fmaj7
G
C
ain't got no - bod - y else to blame.
End Rhy. Fig. 2
Gtr. 2
Chorus
Gtr. 2: w/ Rhy. Fig. 1 (2 times)
2nd time, Gtr. 3: w/ Rhy. Fig. 4 (2 times)
Am Em7 Dm7 Em7 Am Em7 Dm7 Em7 Am
E - vil wom - an, e - vil wom - an.
Gtr. 3
Gtr. 4 (fuzz)
Riff A
f
* w/ octave pedal
*Set one octave lower & one octave higher.
To Coda
Em7 Dm7 Em7 Am Em7 Dm7 Em7 Am
E - vil wom - an, e - vil wom - an.
Rhy. Fig. 3
End Rhy. Fig. 3

Verse
Gtrs. 2 & 3: w/ Rhy. Figs. 1 & 1A (3 times)
Gtr. 4 tacet
Am
Em7
Dm7
2. Rolled in from an - oth - er town, hit some
Gtr. 1
Gtr. 4
End Riff A
gold too hot to set-tle down. But a fool and his mon - ey soon go
Riff B
sep- 'rate ways. You found a fool ly-in' in a daze.
End Riff B
Gtr. 1: w/ Riff B
Ha, ha, wom-an what you gon-na do? You de - stroyed all the vir-tues that the Lord

Gtr. 2: w/ Rhy. Fig. 2
Gtr. 3: w/ Rhy. Fig. 2A
Em7 Am Em7 Dm7 Em7
gave you. It's so good that you're feel-in' pain, but you
Gtr. 1
10 10 10 10 8 10 10 10 10 10 8 10 8 10
Fmaj7 G C
Gtr. 1 tacet
bet-ter get your face on board the ver-y next train.
(Train.)
10 8 8 8 8 9
Chorus
Gtrs. 2 & 3: w/ Rhy. Figs. 1 & 3 (2 times)
Gtr. 4: w/ Riff A
Am Em7 Dm7 Em7 Am Em7 Dm7 Em7 Am
E - vil wom - an, e - vil wom - an.
Em7 Dm7 Em7 Am Em7 Dm7 Em7 Am
E - vil wom - an, e - vil wom - an.
(You're an e - vil wom - an.)
String Solo
Gtr. 3: w/ Rhy. Fig. 1A (3 1/2 times)
Em7 Dm7 Em7 Am Em7 Dm7 Em7 Am Em7 Dm7 Em7
(Hey, hey, hey, hey!)
Gtr. 1
5 5 5 8 7 7 5 5 5 7 5 5 5 10 8 10 10

Am
Em7
Dm7
(Hey, hey, hey, hey!)
Fmaj7
G
Em9
(Hey, hey, hey.)
Chorus
Gtr. 1 tacet
Gtr. 2: w/ Rhy. Fig. 1 (2 times)
Gtr. 4: w/ Riff A
E - vil wom - an,
e - vil wom - an.
E - vil wom -
Gtr. 1
Gtr. 3
w/ heavy flanger
8va
loco
Rhy. Fig. 4

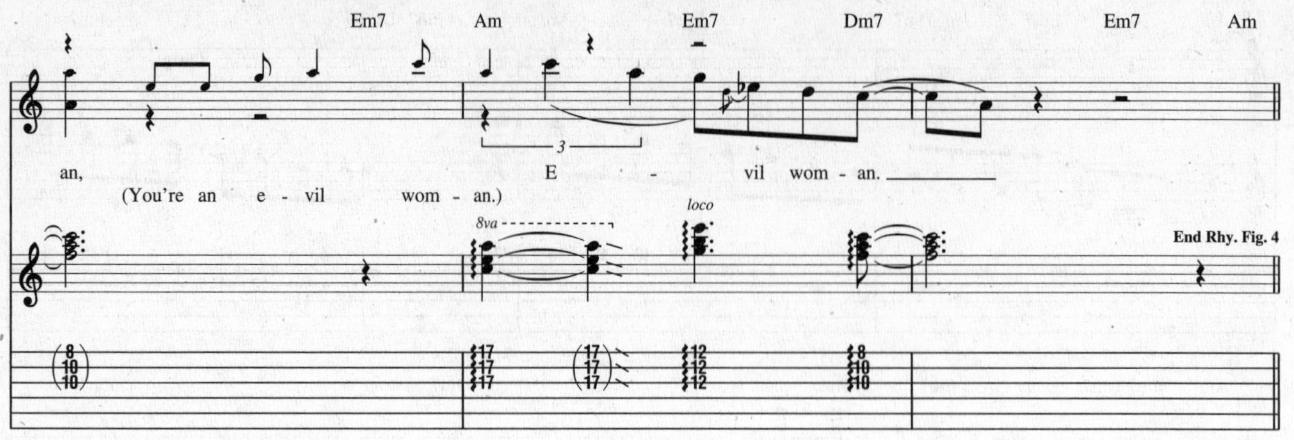
Em7 Am Em7 Dm7 Em7 Am
an, E - vil wom - an.
(You're an e - vil wom - an.)
8va
loco
End Rhy. Fig. 4

Verse

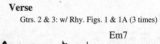

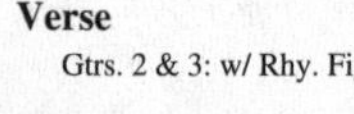
Gtrs. 2 & 3: w/ Rhy. Figs. 1 & 1A (3 times)

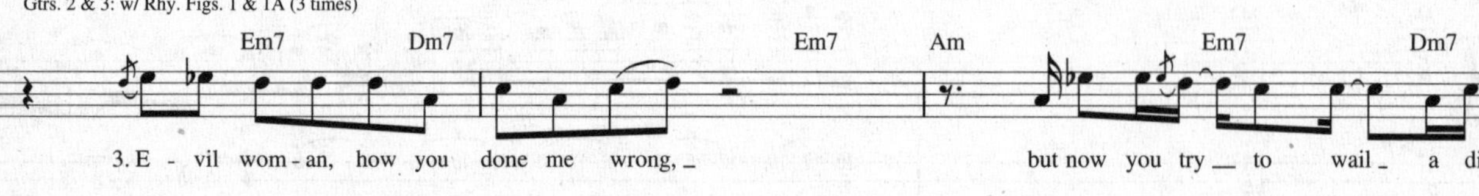
Em7 Dm7 Em7 Am Em7 Dm7
3. E - vil wom - an, how you done me wrong, but now you try to wail a dif -

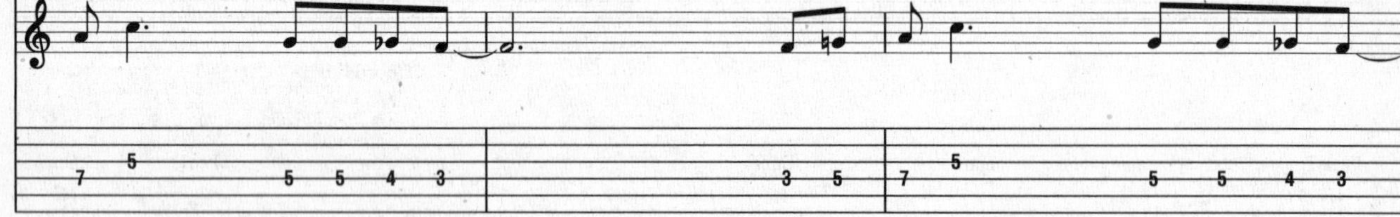
Gtr. 1

Em7 Am Em7 Dm7 Em7
- 'rent song. Ha, ha, fun - ny how you broke me up.

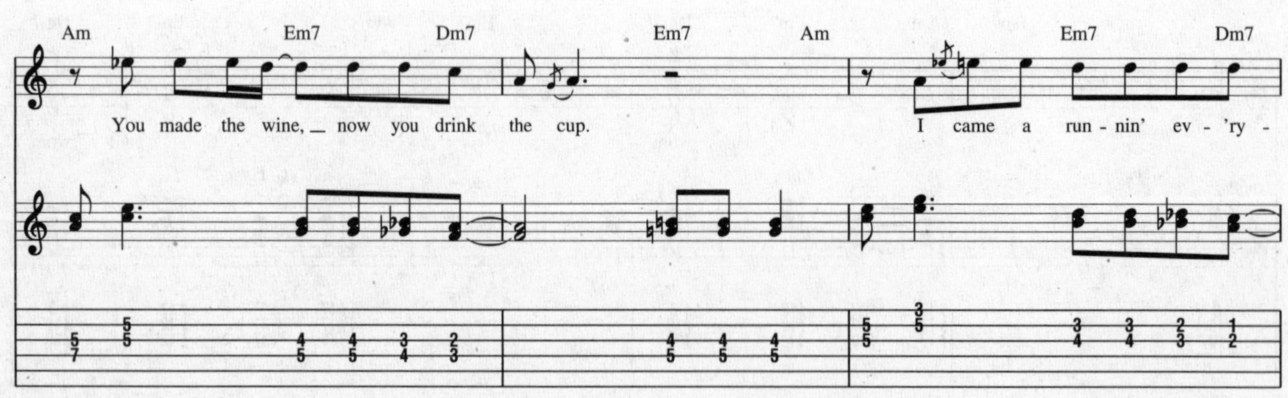
Am Em7 Dm7 Em7 Am Em7 Dm7
You made the wine, now you drink the cup. I came a run - nin' ev - 'ry -

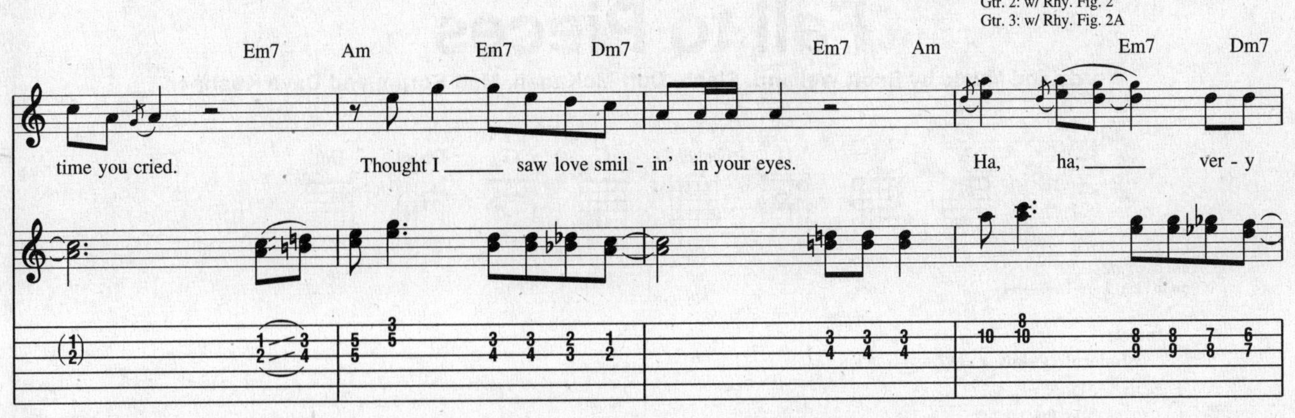
Gtr. 2: w/ Rhy. Fig. 2
Gtr. 3: w/ Rhy. Fig. 2A
Em7 Am Em7 Dm7 Em7 Am Em7 Dm7
time you cried. Thought I saw love smil - in' in your eyes. Ha, ha, ver - y

D.S. al Coda
Em7 Fmaj7 G C
nice to know that you ain't got no place a left to go.
(Go.)

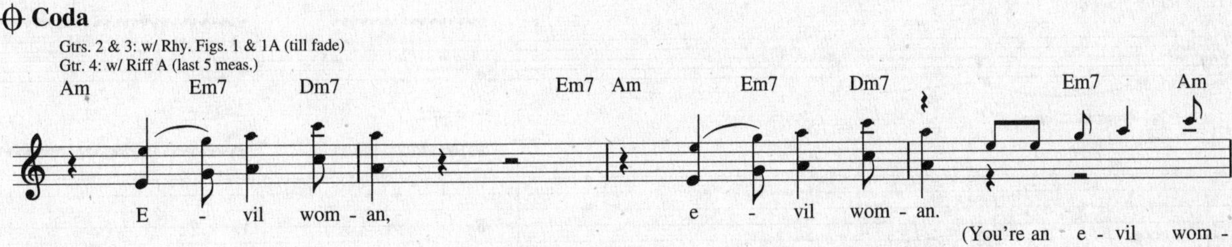
Coda
Gtrs. 2 & 3: w/ Rhy. Figs. 1 & 1A (till fade)
Gtr. 4: w/ Riff A (last 5 meas.)
Am Em7 Dm7 Em7 Am Em7 Dm7 Em7 Am
E - vil wom - an, e - vil wom - an.
(You're an e - vil wom -

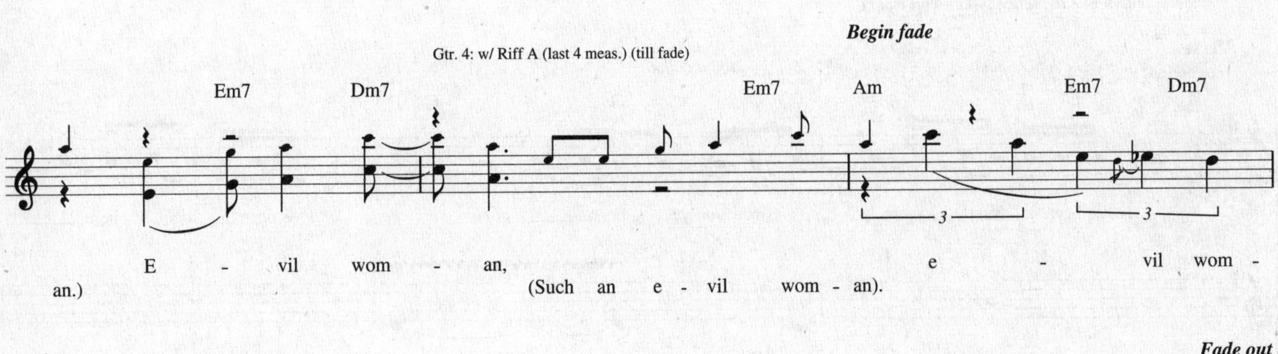
Begin fade
Gtr. 4: w/ Riff A (last 4 meas.) (till fade)
Em7 Dm7 Em7 Am Em7 Dm7
E - vil wom - an, e - vil wom -
an.) (Such an e - vil wom - an).

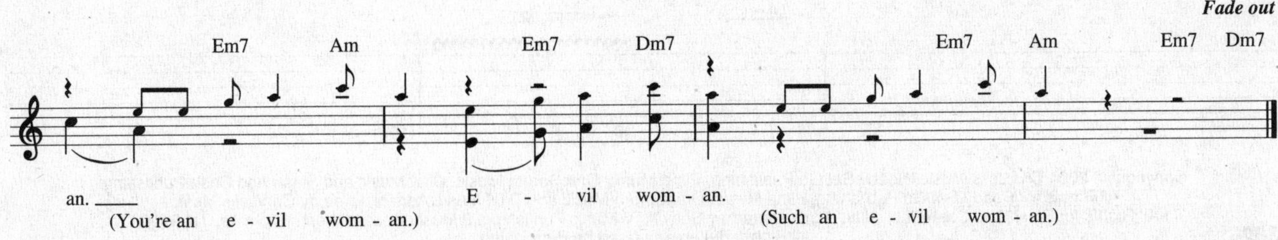
Fade out
Em7 Am Em7 Dm7 Em7 Am Em7 Dm7
an. E - vil wom - an.
(You're an e - vil wom - an.) (Such an e - vil wom - an.)

Fall to Pieces

Words and Music by Scott Weiland, Slash, Duff McKagan, Matt Sorum and Dave Kushner

Tune down 1/2 step:
(low to high) Eb-Ab-Db-Gb-Bb-Eb

C G C D C G C
I've grown old.
Fall to piec - es, I'm fall - in'.
Pre-Chorus
Gtrs. 1 & 2 tacet
D C G A
Fell to piec - es, and I'm still fall - in'.
Ev-'ry time, I'm
Rhy. Fig. 2
End Rhy. Fig. 2
Gtr. 1
Gtr. 3 (dist.)
Rhy. Fig. 3
Gtr. 2
Gtr. 4 (dist.)
G5 D G5 A G5 A G5
fall - in' down.
All a-lone I fall to piec - es.
End Rhy. Fig. 3

Interlude
D
C
G5
Riff A
Gtr. 5 (dist.)
End Riff A
1/2
Rhy. Fig. 4
Gtr. 3
End Rhy. Fig. 4
Rhy. Fig. 4A
Gtr. 4
End Rhy. Fig. 4A
D
C
G5
1/2
Rhy. Fig. 5
End Rhy. Fig. 5
Rhy. Fig. 5A
End Rhy. Fig. 5A

Verse
Gtr. 1: w/ Rhy. Fig. 1 (3 times)
Gtrs. 3-5 tacet
D C G C D
2. I keep a jour - nal of mem - o - ries. I'm feel-in' lone - ly,
Gtr. 2
C G C D C G C
I can't breathe. Fall to piec - es, I'm fall - in'.
Gtr. 1: w/ Rhy. Fig. 2
D C G
Fell to pie - es and I'm still fall - in'.
Pre-Chorus
Gtr. 2 tacet
Gtr. 4: w/ Rhy. Fig. 3
A
Ev-'ry time, I'm
Gtr. 3
G5 D G5 A G5 A G5
fall - in' down. All a - lone I fall to piec - es.

Chorus
Gtrs. 3 & 4: w/ Rhy. Figs. 4 & 4A (3 times)
D C G5 D C G5
Ev-'ry time, I'm fall - in' down. All a-lone I fall to piec - es.
D C G5
Gtrs. 3 & 4: w/ Rhy. Figs. 5 & 5A
D C G5
Ev-'ry time, I'm fall - in' down. All a-lone I fall to piec - es.
Bridge
Bm G
All the years I've tried with more to go.
Gtr. 6 (clean)
mf
w/ chorus
let ring throughout
Gtr. 3
Bm G
And will the mem-'ries die? I'm wait - ing.
let ring

Bm
A
Gtr. 3
And will I find you?
And can I find you?
(cont. in slashes)
G5
G
15 fr
We're fall - ing down, I'm fall - ing.
Gtr. 6
Guitar Solo
Gtr. 4: w/ Rhy. Fig. 4A (3 times)
Gtr. 6 tacet
D
Rhy. Fig. 6
Cadd9/D D
C
G
End Rhy. Fig. 6
Gtr. 5

Gtr. 3: w/ Rhy. Fig. 6
D
Cadd9/D D
C
G
8va
loco
let ring
hold bend
D
Dsus4 D
C
G
G
15 fr
Gtr. 3
(cont. in notation)
let ring
Em
G5
A
G5
Gtr. 4
Gtr. 5
Gtr. 3
slight P.M.
Chorus
Gtr. 3: w/ Rhy. Fig. 4 (3 times)
Gtr. 4: w/ Rhy. Fig. 4A (7 times)
Gtr. 5 tacet
D
C
G5
D
Ev - 'ry time, I'm
fall - in' down.
All a - lone I fall
Gtr. 5
8va
loco

C
G5
D
C
G5
to piec - es.
Ev - 'ry time, I'm
fall - in' down.
D
C
G5
All a - lone I fall
to piec - es.
Gtr. 3
Gtr. 3: w/ Rhy. Fig. 4A (3 times)
Gtr. 5: w/ Riff A (3 times)
D
C
G5
D
Ev - 'ry time, I'm
fall - in' down.
All a - lone I fall
C
G5
D
C
G5
to piec - es.
Ev - 'ry time, I'm
fall - in' down.
D
Cadd9/D
D
C
G5
Gtr. 3
All a - lone I fall
to piec - es.
Gtr. 5
1/2
Gtr. 4

Fat Lip

Words and Music by Sum 41

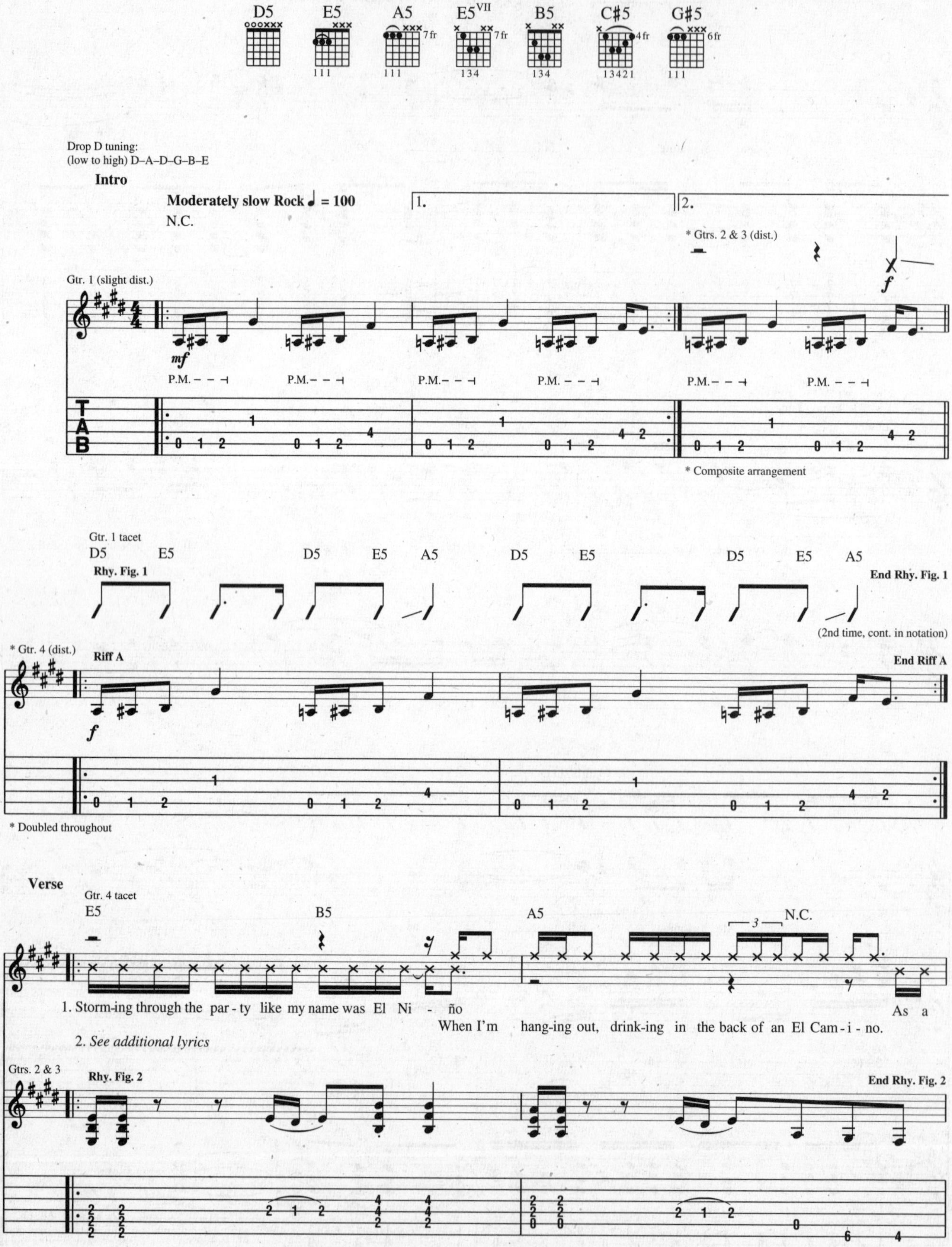

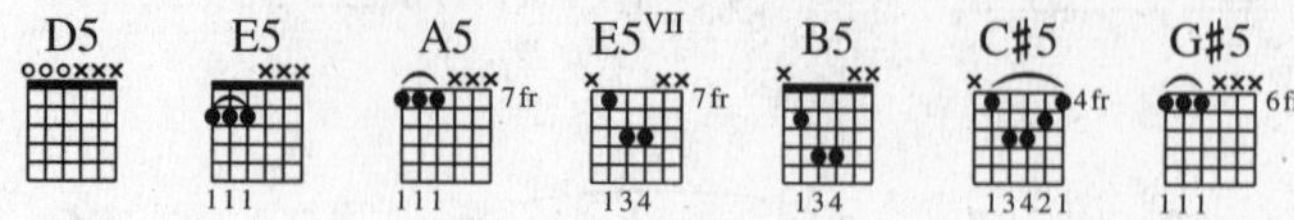

Drop D tuning:
(low to high) D–A–D–G–B–E

Intro

Moderately slow Rock ♩ = 100

N.C.

1. 2.

* Gtrs. 2 & 3 (dist.)

Gtr. 1 (slight dist.)

mf

P.M. P.M. P.M. P.M. P.M. P.M.

* Composite arrangement

Gtr. 1 tacet

D5 E5 D5 E5 A5 D5 E5 D5 E5 A5

Rhy. Fig. 1 **End Rhy. Fig. 1**

(2nd time, cont. in notation)

* Gtr. 4 (dist.)

Riff A **End Riff A**

f

* Doubled throughout

Verse

Gtr. 4 tacet

E5 B5 A5 N.C.

1. Storm-ing through the par - ty like my name was El Ni - ño When I'm hang-ing out, drink-ing in the back of an El Cam - i - no. As a

2. *See additional lyrics*

Gtrs. 2 & 3

Rhy. Fig. 2 **End Rhy. Fig. 2**

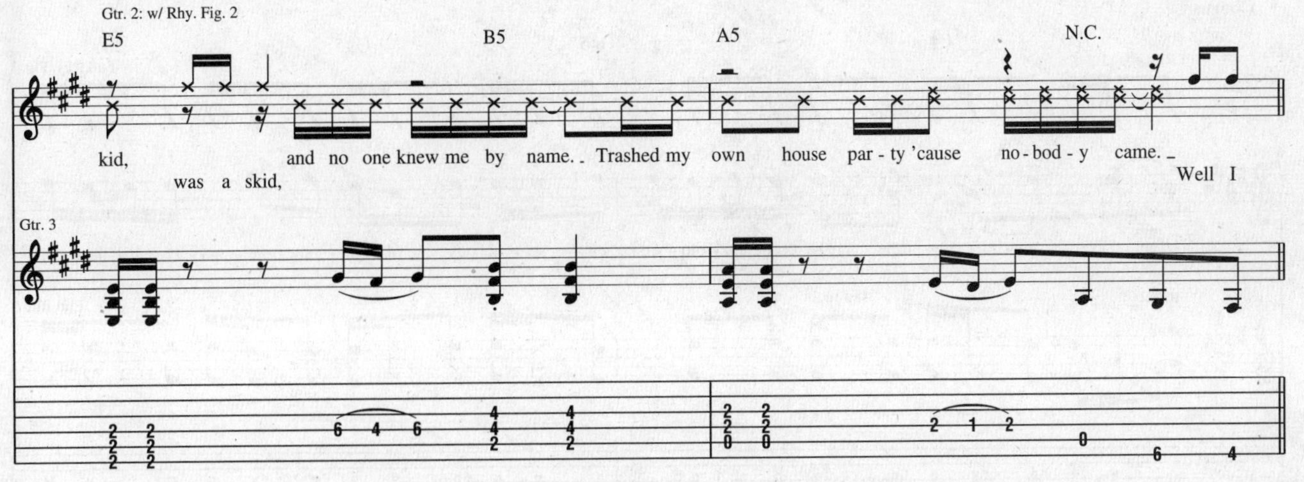
Gtr. 2: w/ Rhy. Fig. 2
E5
B5
A5
N.C.
kid, and no one knew me by name. Trashed my own house par-ty 'cause no-bod-y came.
was a skid,
Well I
Gtr. 3

Pre-Chorus
Double-time feel
E5
C#5
A5
know I'm not the one you thought you knew back in high school, nev-er go-ing, nev-er show-ing up when we had to. (Is it) at-
2. See Additional lyrics
Gtrs. 2 & 3
P.M.

E5
C#5
N.C.
ten-tion that we crave? Don't tell us to be-have. I'm sick of al-ways hear-ing "Act your age." I don't want to
Gtrs. 2 & 3
P.M.
P.S.
steady gliss.
(cont. in slashes)
Gtr. 4

Chorus
E5VII B5 C#m G#5 A5 G#5 A5
Rhy. Fig. 3
End Rhy. Fig. 3
Gtrs. 2 & 3
waste my time, be-come an-oth-er ca-su-al-ty of so-ci-e-ty. I'll nev-er
Gtr. 4
Riff B
End Riff B
1.
End double-time feel
Gtrs. 2 & 3: w/ Rhy. Fig. 3
E5 B5 C#m G#5 A5 G#5 A5
fall in line, be-come an-oth-er vic-tim of your con-form-i-ty and back
Riff C
End Riff C
Interlude
Gtrs. 2 & 3: w/ Rhy. Fig. 1 (2 times)
Gtr. 4: w/ Riff A (2 times)
D5 E5 D5 E5 A5 D5 E5 D5 E5 A5 D5 E5 D5 E5 A5 D5 E5 D5 E5 A5 N.C.
down.
2. Be-cause you don't
* w/ delay repeats
2.
End double-time feel
Interlude
Gtr. 4 tacet
G#5 A5 G#5 A5 E5 A5
vic-tim of your con-form-i-ty and back down.
* w/ delay repeats

Bridge
Gtrs. 2 & 3 tacet
E5
E5/D#
Don't count on me
Gtr. 5 Riff D
(clean)
mp
let ring
C#m
A5
to let you know when. Don't count on me, I'll do it a - gain.
End Riff D
Gtr. 5: w/ Riff D
it's the point your miss - ing. Don't count on me,
Gtr. 6 (clean)
Bridge
Gtr. 6 tacet
D5
Gtrs. 2 & 3
(cont. in notation)
Well, I'm a no - good nick, low - er mid - dle class brat
'cause I'm not lis - t'ning. back -
Gtr. 6

D5 E5 D5 E5 A5 N.C.
and I don't give a shit a-bout noth-ing.
packed,
You be stand-ing on the corn-er talk-ing all that ku-fuf-fin.
But you
D5 E5 D5 E5 A5 D5 E5 D5 E5
don't make sense from all the gas you be huff-ing.
'Cause if the egg don't stain,
you'll be ring-ing off the
hook!
You're on the
D5 E5 D5 E5 A5 D5 E5 D5 E5 A5
hit list,
want-ed
in the tel-e-phone book. I like songs with dis-tor-tion,
to drink in pro-por-tion.
The
N.C.
doc-tor said my mom should have had an a-bor-tion.
* w/ delay repeats.

Gtr. 4

I don't want to

Gtrs. 2 & 3

P.M.

w/ phaser

Chorus

Double-time feel

Gtrs. 2 & 3: w/ Rhy. Fig. 3 (4 times)
Gtr. 4: w/ Riff B (3 times)

E5 B5 C♯m G♯5 A5 G♯5 A5

waste __ my __ time, be-come an-oth-er ca - su - al - ty of so - ci - e - ty. I'll nev - er

End double-time feel

E5 B5 C♯m G♯5 A5 G♯5 A5 E5 B5 C♯m

fall __ in __ line, be-come an-oth-er vic - tim of your con-form - i - ty and back down.

(Waste my time with them. __

Gtr. 4: w/ Riff C

G♯5 A5 G♯5 A5 E5 B5 C♯m G♯5 A5 G♯5 A5

Ca - su - al - ty of so - ci - e - ty. Vic - tim of your con-form - i - ty and back

__ Waste my time __ a - gain.) __

Outro

Gtrs. 2 & 3: w/ Rhy. Fig. 1 (1 1/2 times)
Gtr. 4: w/ Riff A (2 times)

D5 E5 D5 E5 A5 D5 E5 D5 E5 A5 D5 E5 D5 E5 A5

down.

* w/ delay repeats

Gtrs. 2 & 3 D5 E5 D5 E5 A5 E5

Additional Lyrics

2. Because you don't
Know us at all, we laugh when old people fall.
But what would you expect with a conscience so small?
Heavy Metal and mullets, it's how we were raised.
Maiden and Priest were the gods that we praised.

2nd Pre-Chorus:
'Cause we like having fun at other people's expense and
Cutting people down is just a minor offense then.
It's none of your concern, I guess I'll never learn.
I'm sick of being told to wait my turn.
I don't want to...

Fight for Your Right (To Party)

Words and Music by Rick Rubin, Adam Horovitz and Adam Yauch

Tune down 1/2 step:
(low to high) Eb–Ab–Db–Gb–Bb–Eb

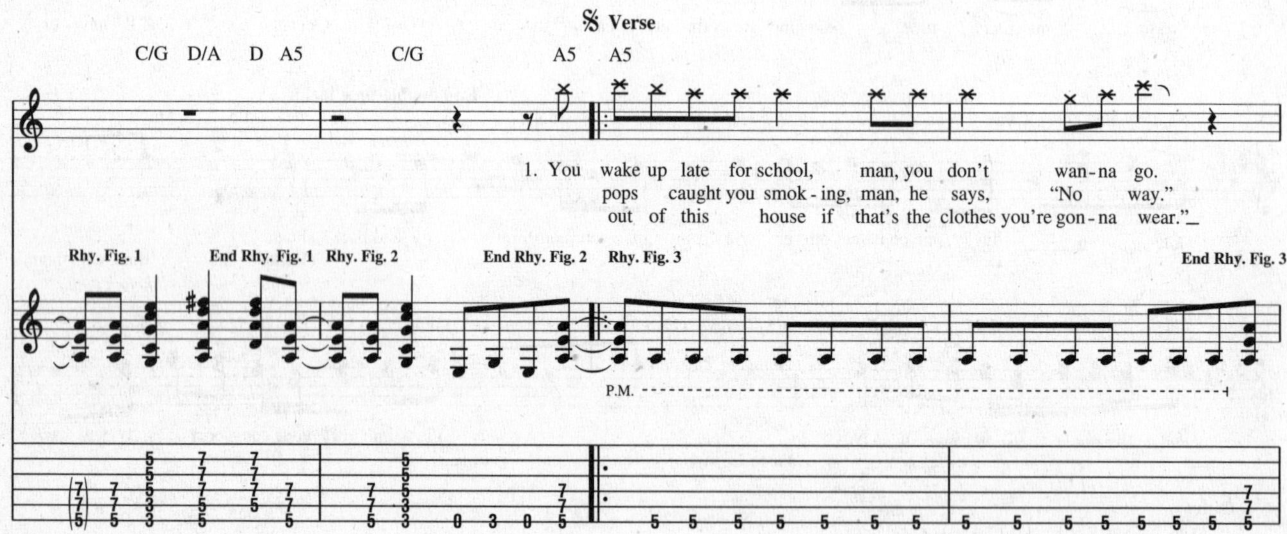

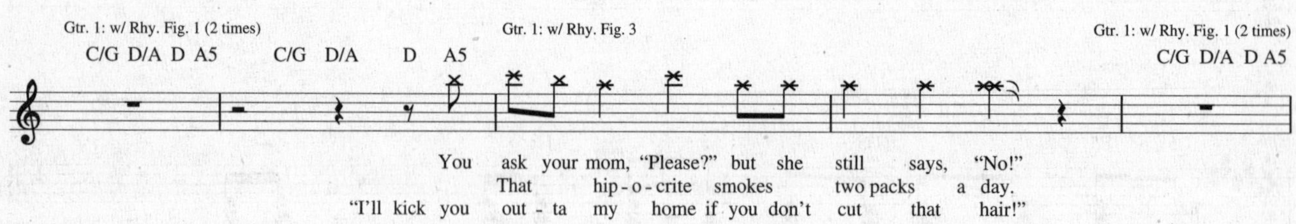

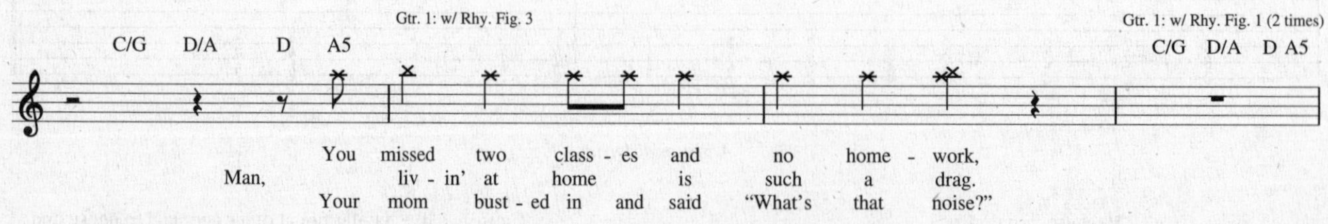

Gtr. 1: w/ Rhy. Fig. 3
Gtr. 1: w/ Rhy. Fig. 1
C/G D/A D A5
but your teach - er preach - es class like you're some kind of jerk.
Now, your mom threw a - way your best por - no mag.
Oh, mom you're just jeal - ous, it's the Beast - ie Boys!
Spoken: Bust it.
Chorus
N.C. D/A N.C. D A5
You got - ta fight for your right to par -
Gtr. 1
To Coda 1
Gtr. 1: w/ Rhy. Fig. 1 (3 times)
Gtr. 1: w/ Rhy. Fig. 2
ty.
2. Your
Interlude
To Coda 2
C/G D/A D E5
You got-ta fight.
Gtr. 2 (dist.)
w/ bar
Rhy. Fill 1
End Rhy. Fill 1

Guitar Solo
Gtr. 1: w/ Rhy. Fig. 1 (7 times)
A5 C/G D/A D A5 C/G D/A D A5 C/G D/A D A5 C/G D/A D A5
8va
Gtr. 2
w/ bar
grad. release
loco
1/2
D.S. al Coda 1
Gtr. 1: w/ Rhy. Fig. 2
C/G D/A D A5 C/G D/A D A5 C/G D/A D A5 C/G A5
3. "Don't step
8va
f
w/ bar
Coda 1
D.S.S. al Coda 2
(take 2nd ending)
C/G D/A N.C.
You got-ta fight
Gtr. 1
Coda 2
Outro
Gtr. 1: w/ Rhy. Fill 1
Gtr. 1: w/ Rhy. Fig. 1 (7 times)
A5 C/G D/A D A5 C/G D/A D A5
Par - ty.
C/G D/A D A5 C/G D/A D A5 C/G D/A D A5 C/G G/A D A5 C/G D/A D A5
Par - ty.
Gtr. 1
C/G G5 A5

Fly

Words and Music by William Maragh, Alan Shacklock, Mark McGrath, Rodney Sheppard, Joseph Nichol, Stan Frazier and Murphy Karges

Verse 1:
A D/F♯ A D/F♯
1. All a - round the world stat - ues crum - ble for me. Who knows
Gtr. 3
Rhy. Fig. 2
P.M.
A D/F♯ A D/F♯
how long I've loved you?
end Rhy. Fig. 2
w/Rhy. Fig. 2 (Gtr. 3)
w/Rhy. Fill 1 (Gtr. 4)
A D/F♯ A D/F♯ A D/F♯ A D/F♯
Ev-'ry-where I go, peo-ple stop and they see. Twen-ty-five years old, my moth - er, God rest her soul.
Chorus:
w/Rhy. Fig. 3 (Gtr. 3) 4 times
A D A D
I just wan - na fly. Put your arms
Rhy. Fig. 4
Gtr. 4
Rhy. Fill 1
Gtr. 4 (Elec.)
mf
w/clean tone
Rhy. Fig. 3
Gtr. 3

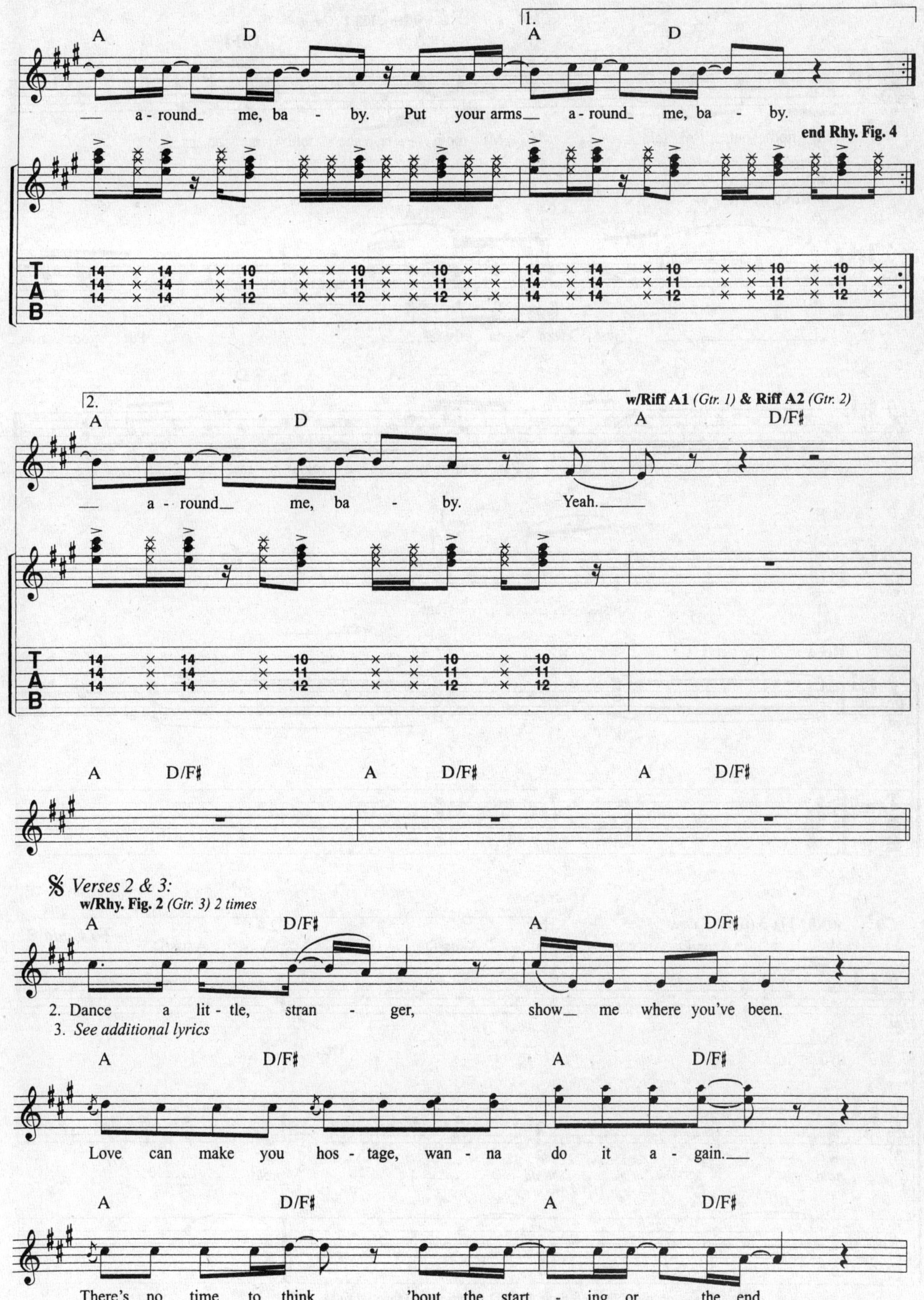
1.
A D A D
— a - round_ me, ba - by. Put your arms__ a - round_ me, ba - by.
end Rhy. Fig. 4
14 14 10 10 10 14 14 10 10 10
14 14 11 11 11 14 14 11 11 11
14 14 12 12 12 14 14 12 12 12
2.
w/Riff A1 (Gtr. 1) & Riff A2 (Gtr. 2)
A D A D/F♯
— a - round__ me, ba - by. Yeah.____
14 14 10 10 10
14 14 11 11 11
14 14 12 12 12
A D/F♯ A D/F♯ A D/F♯
Verses 2 & 3:
w/Rhy. Fig. 2 (Gtr. 3) 2 times
A D/F♯ A D/F♯
2. Dance a lit - tle, stran - ger, show_ me where you've been.
3. See additional lyrics
A D/F♯ A D/F♯
Love can make you hos - tage, wan - na do it a - gain.___
A D/F♯ A D/F♯
There's no time to think__ 'bout the start - ing or___ the end.__

*Bass gtr. plays D each time Asus/D is indicated (throughout).

Interlude:
A5
Gtr. 1
f w/dist.
P.M.
Gtr. 2
*Gtr. 4
* w/chorus and compression (next 4 bars).

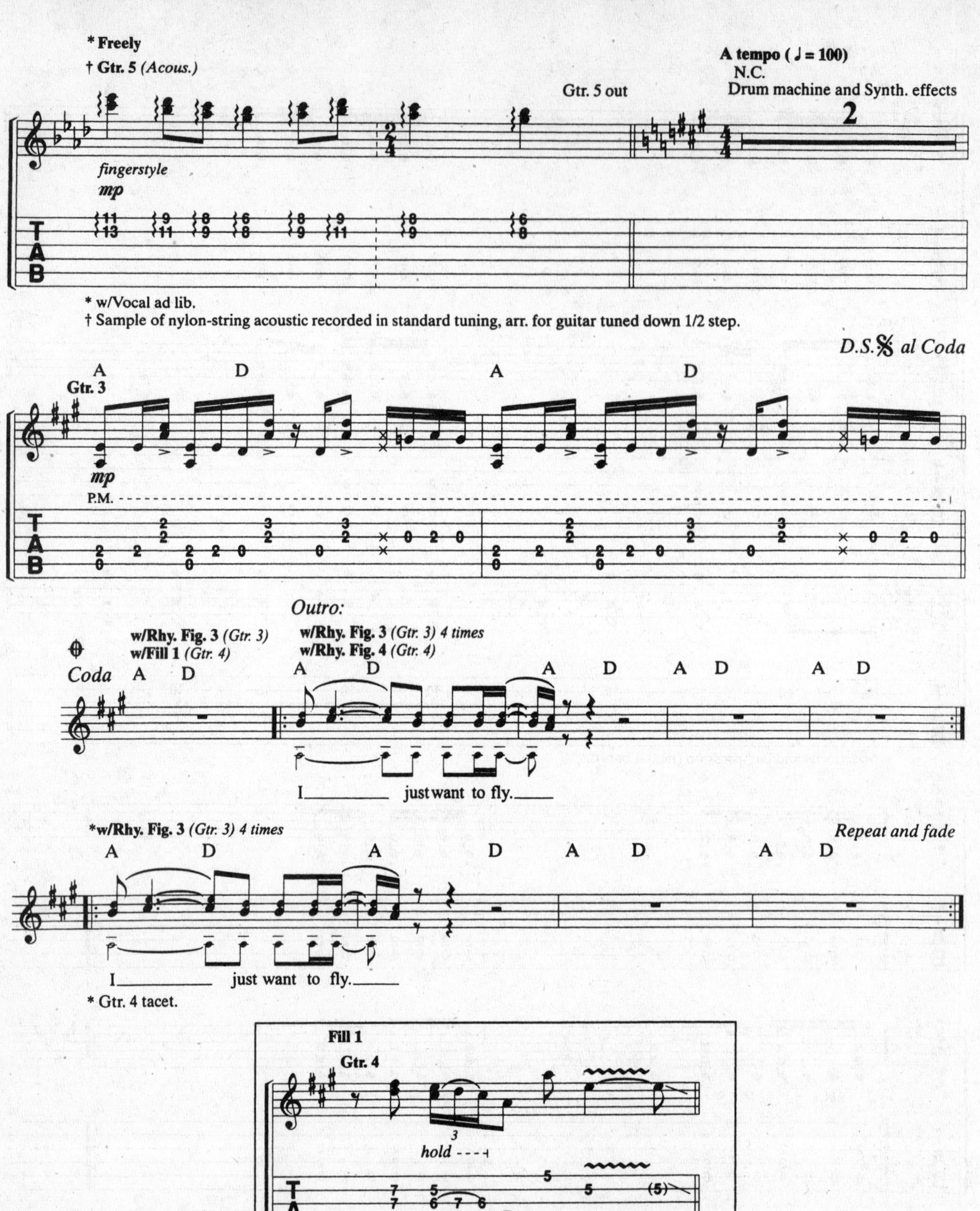

Verse 3:
All around the world statues crumble for me.
Who knows how long I've loved you?
Everyone I know has been so good to me.
Twenty-five years old,
My mother, God rest her soul.
(To Chorus:)

Free

Written by Trey Anastasio and Tom Marshall

Gtrs. 1, 2 & 3; Tune Up 1/2 Step:
① = F ④ = E♭
② = C ⑤ = B♭
③ = A♭ ⑥ = F

Gtr. 4; Drop D Tuning, Up 1/2 Step:
① = F ④ = E♭
② = C ⑤ = B♭
③ = A♭ ⑥ = E♭

*Key Signature denotes D Mixolydian.
**Tap on back of neck.

*Piano arr. for gtr.

Verse
D
C
*G
F
D
Cadd9
float - ing in the blimp a lot. I feel the feel-ing I for-got
(Feel.)
Gtr. 4
let ring
let ring
Gtr. 1
mp
mf
w/ slight dist.
*Chord symbols reflect implied tonality.
G
F
*G/D
F/D
D
of swim-ming weight - less in the womb or bounc - ing gent -
Rhy. Fig. 1
*bass plays D
G/D
F/D
D
G/D
F/D
D
- ly 'round the room. In a min-ute I'll be free and you'll be

Verse

G/D F D D

splash - ing in — the sea. — 2. I feel — no — cur - i -

(Feel, —

End Rhy. Fig. 1

f

fdbk.

C G F D Cadd9 G F G/D F/D

os - i - ty. — I see — the path a-head of me. In a min-ute I'll — be free —

see. —)

mf

*fdbk.

fdbk.

*vol. swell

pitch: D

Gtr. 4: w/ Rhy. Fig. 1
D G/D F/D D G/D F/D D G/D F/D
and you'll be splash - ing in the sea. We'll hear a ti - ny cry as the ship goes slid-ing by. .
Gtr. 1
fdbk.
mp
mf
pitch: F#
Chorus
Gtr. 2 tacet
D D C/D Em/D D G/D D
Free.
Gtr. 4
Riff A1
End Riff A1
Gtr. 1
Riff A
End Riff A
1/2
Gtr. 1: w/ Riff A, 1st 5 meas.
Gtr. 4: w/ Riff A1
C/D Em/D D G/D D
Free.
Guitar Solo
Gtr. 4 tacet
C G F
Gtr. 2
f w/ wah-wah
full
Gtr. 1

D
C
G
F
D
full
1/2
F/D
G/D
D
F/D
G/D
8va
D
F/D
G/D
D
F/D
G/D
8va
Gtr. 2
Gtr. 1

Chorus
Gtr. 3 tacet
Gtr. 4: w/ Riff A1, 1st 4 meas.
D
D
C
Em/D
D
G
loco
Free.
P.H.
pitch: F#
Riff A
Interlude
D5
Gtr. 4 tacet
full
1/4
Gtr. 2
1/2 full
Gtr. 3
w/ bar
Gtr. 1

Bridge
D
I'm float - ing in the
(Float.
full
full
fdbk.
Bb7
blimp a lot.
full
P.H.
p f p
fdbk.

D
I
feel
Feel.
full
full
full
w/ bar
B♭7
the feel - ing I for - got.

Gtr. 3 tacet
D
I'm
float
Float
P.H.
1/2
full
full
1/4
pitch: B
mp
mf
fdbk.
-1
B♭7
B♭7♯5
D
ing in the
blimp a lot.
I
feel
)
Gtr. 2
full
full
full
1/4
1/2
1/2
1/4
Gtr. 1

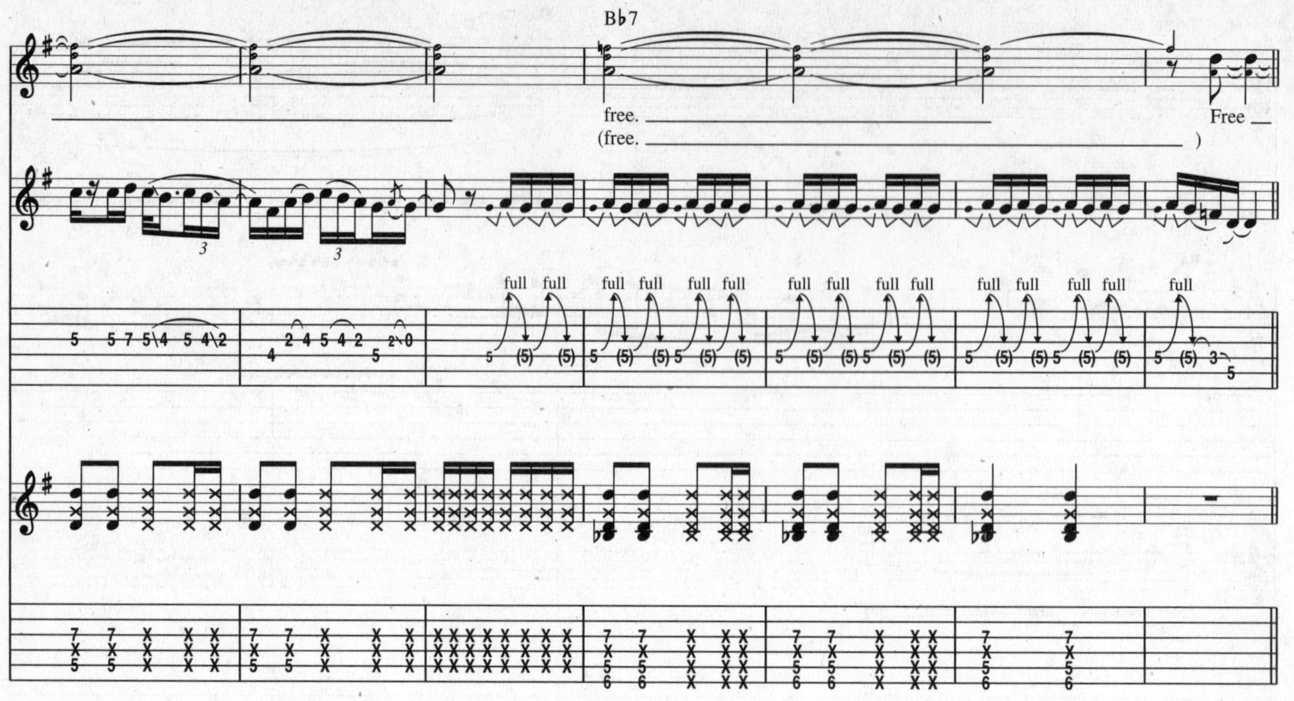

Outro-Chorus

Gtr. 1: w/ Riff A
Gtr. 2 tacet

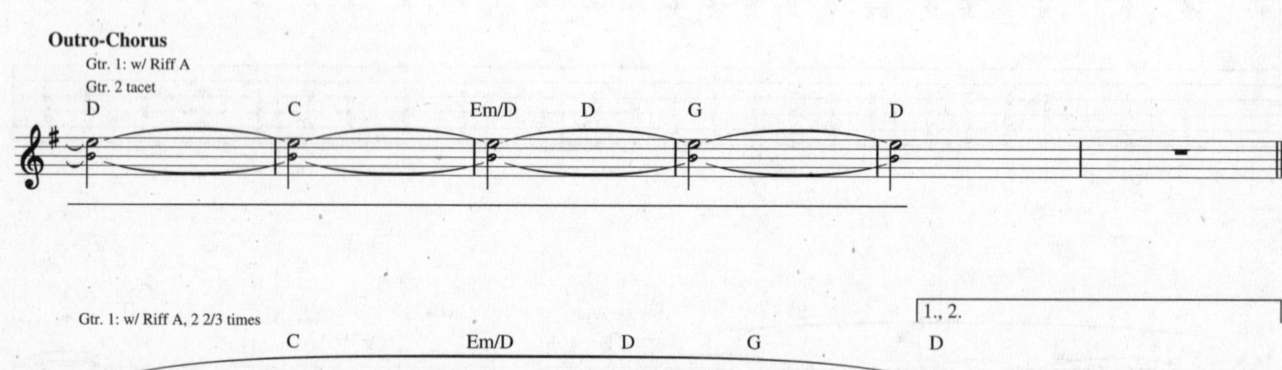

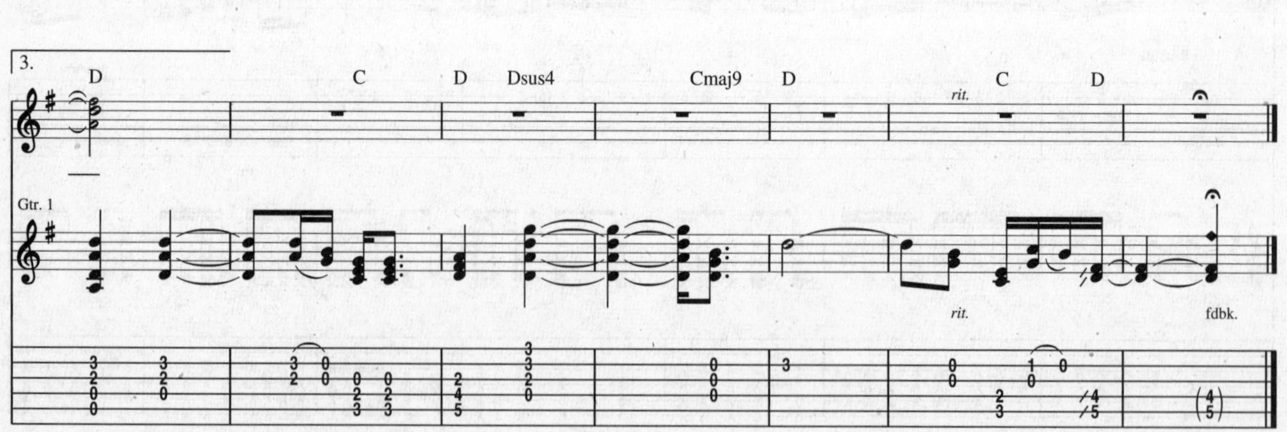

Funk #49

Words and Music by Joe Walsh, Dale Peters and James Fox

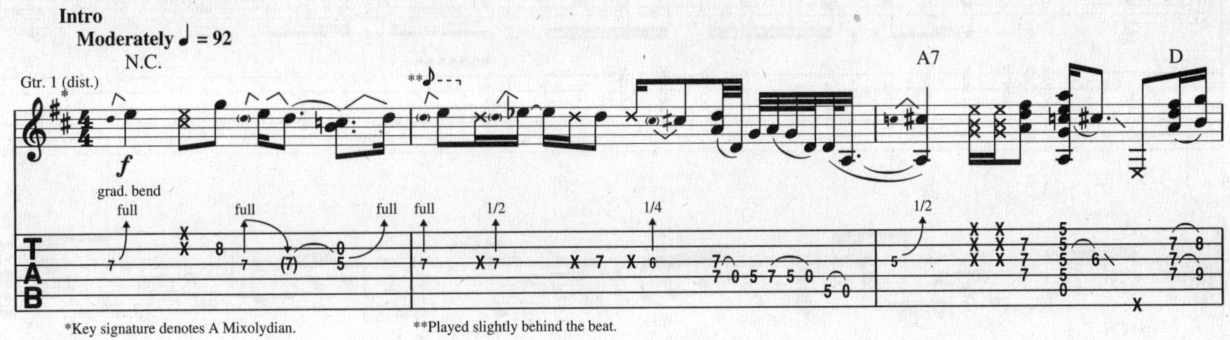

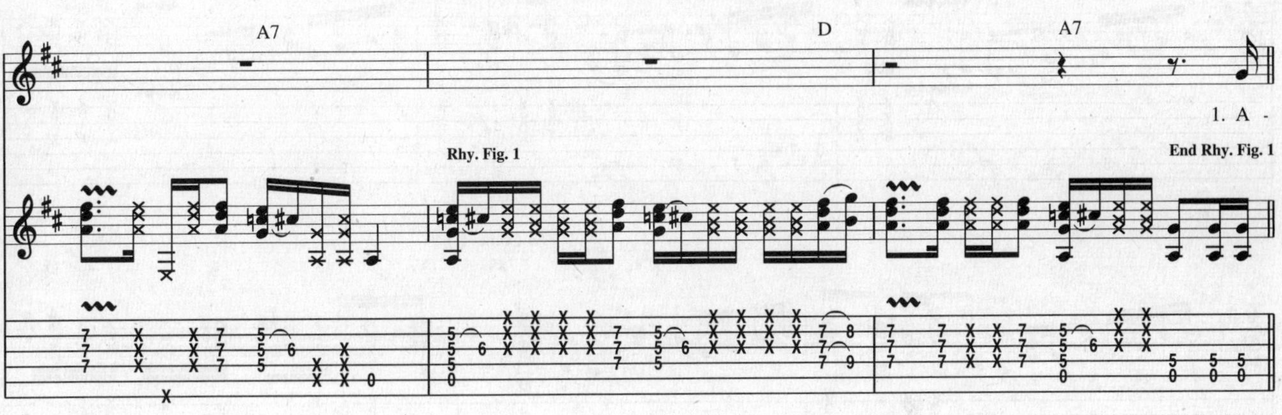

D
A7
I don't think that's act - in' right, you don't think it's show - in'.
You don't think that I know your plan; what you try'n' to hand me?
If you're gon - na act this way, I think there's trou - ble brew - in'.
A5
* slight P.M.
* next 8 meas.
** Note in parenthesis added at random
B5
To Coda
E7#9
A7
D
1.
2.
A7
A7
Drum Solo
Gtr. 1 tacet
15
Interlude
N.C.(A)
rake
1/4
1/2
1/4

A
D
A7
D
A7
A7
Rhy. Fig. 2
D
A7
D.S. al Coda
End Rhy. Fig. 2
Coda
Outro
Gtr. 1: w/ Rhy. Fig. 1, 4 times
A7
D
A7
D
A7
D
A7
D
A7
Gtr. 1: w/ Rhy. Fig. 2, 2 times
D
A7
Begin Fade
D
A7
Gtr. 1
P.M.
D
A7
D/A
A7
P.M.
Fade Out
D/A
A7
D/A
A7
D/A
A7
D

Get Ready

Words and Music by William "Smokey" Robinson

my dreams real, I tell them you do. You're out - ta sight. Well,
12 12 10 12 12 10 10 12 12 10 12 10 10 12 12 10 12 12 10 10

twee - dle - e - dee, twee - dle - e - dum. Look out, ba - by, 'cause

Chorus

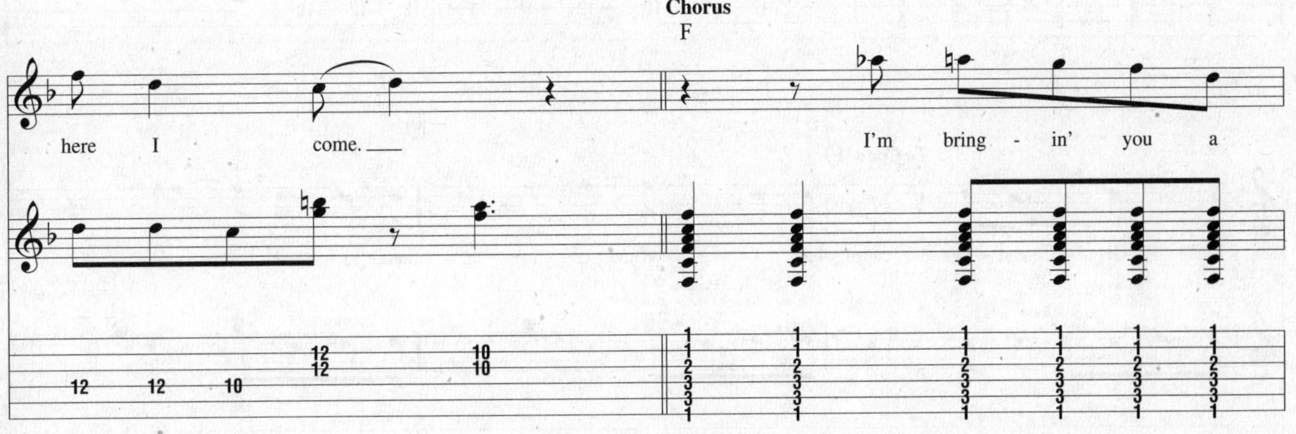
F
here I come. I'm bring - in' you a

B♭
Gm
C
love that's true. (Get read - y, get read - y.)

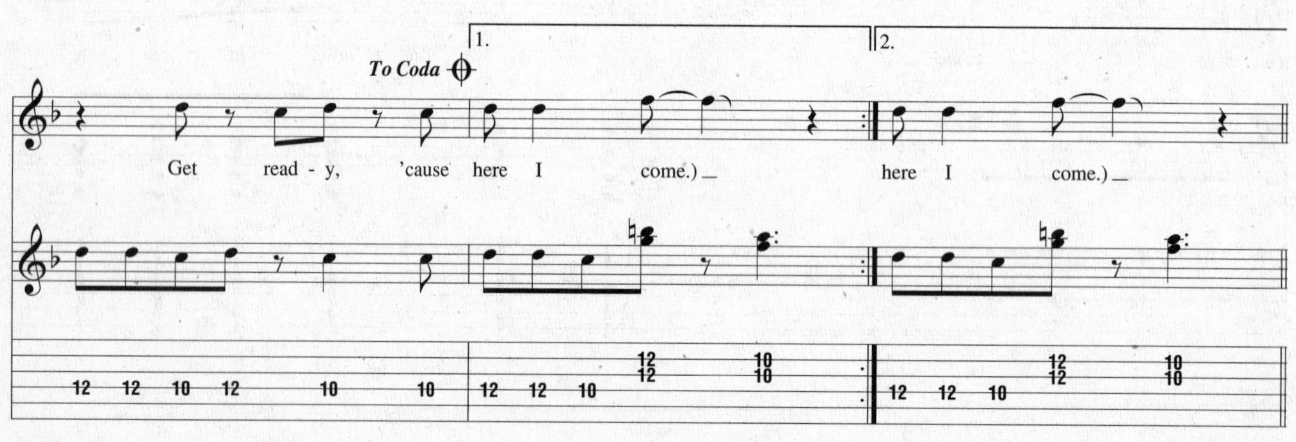

Saxophone Solo

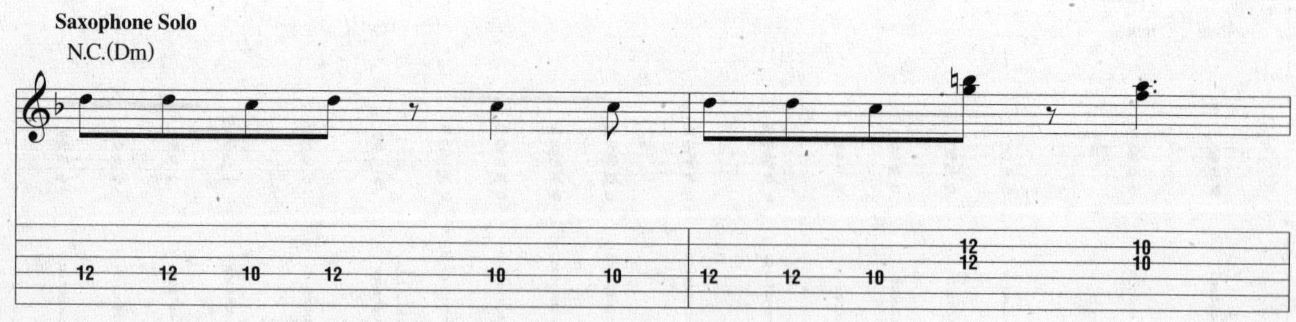

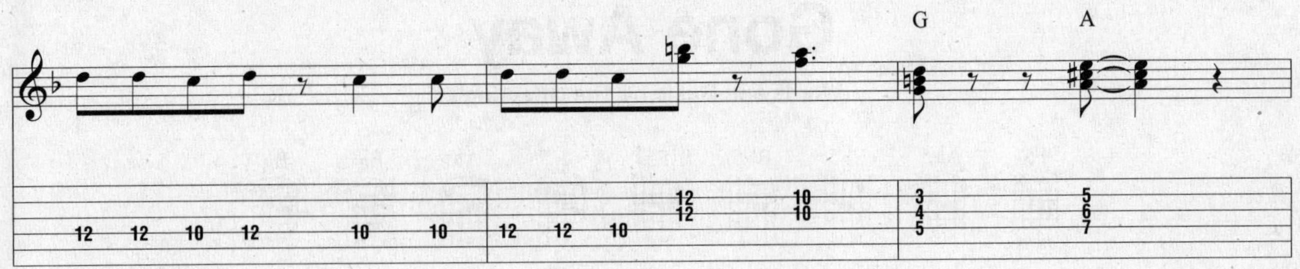

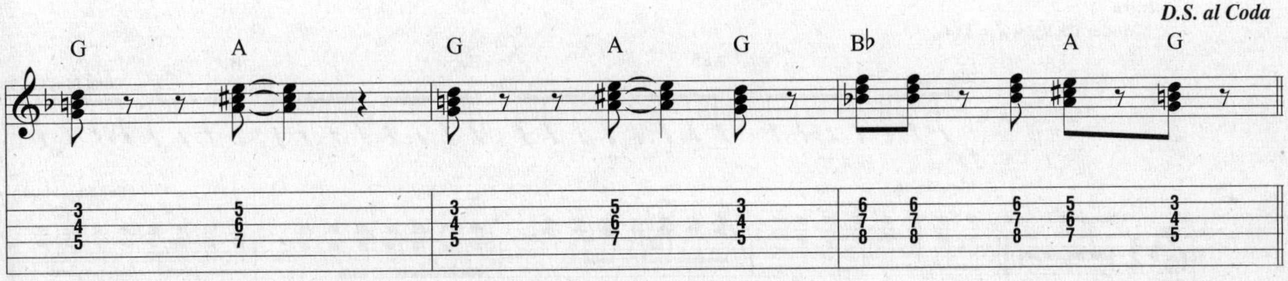

Additional Lyrics

2. You wanna play hide and seek with love,
   Let me remind ya,
   Lovin', you're gonna miss
   And the time it takes to find ya.
   Well, fee, fi, fo, fum.
   Look out, baby, now, here I come.

3. If all my friends should want me to,
   I think I'll understand.
   Hope I get to you before they do,
   'Cause that's how I planned it.
   Well, tweedle-e-dee, now, tweedle-e-dum.
   Look out, baby, now, here I come.

Gone Away

Words and Music by The Offspring

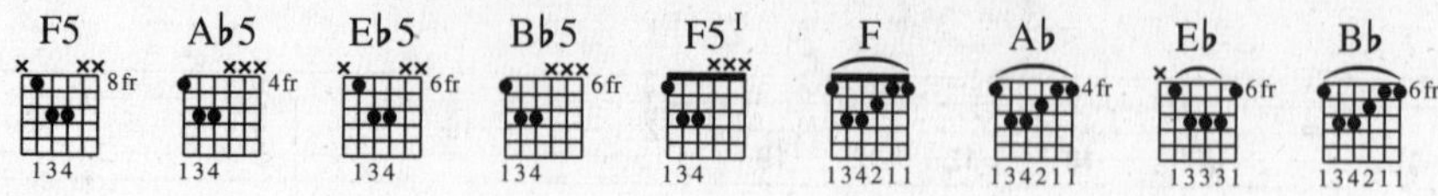

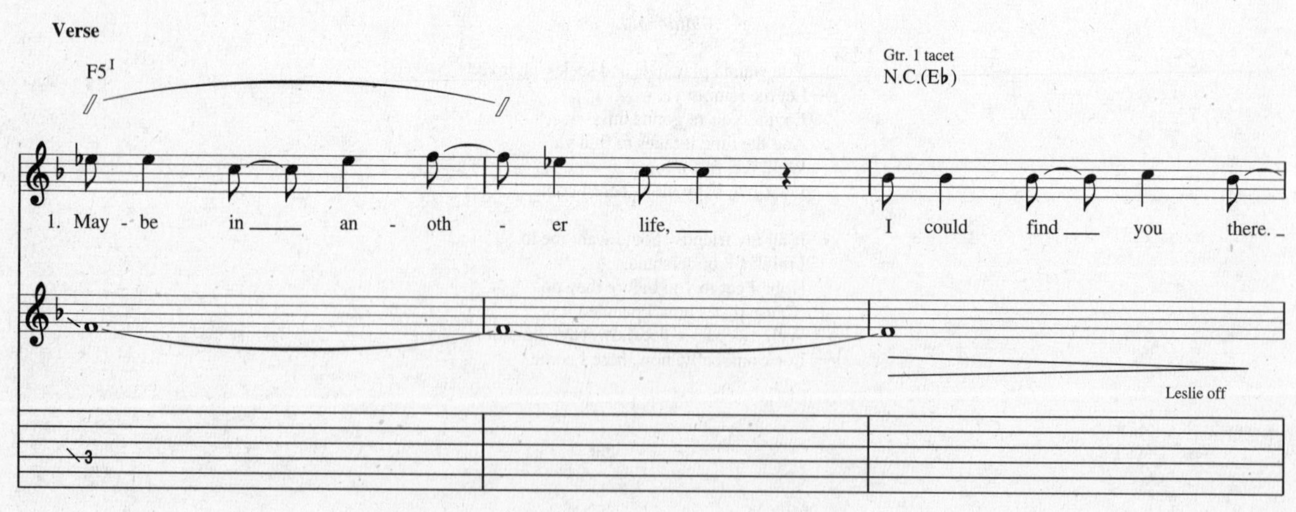

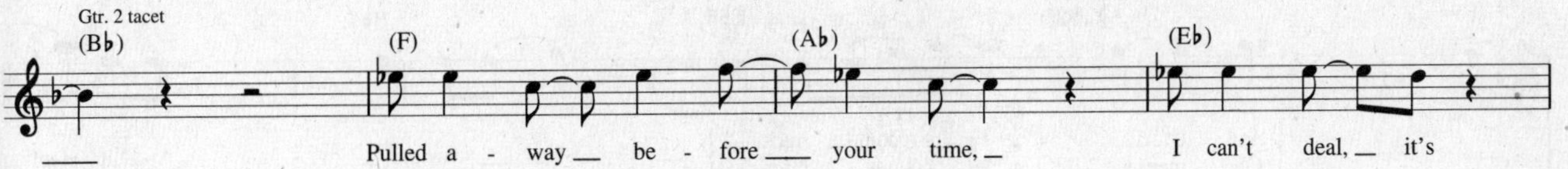
Gtr. 2 tacet
(Bb) (F) (Ab) (Eb)
Pulled a - way be - fore your time, I can't deal, it's

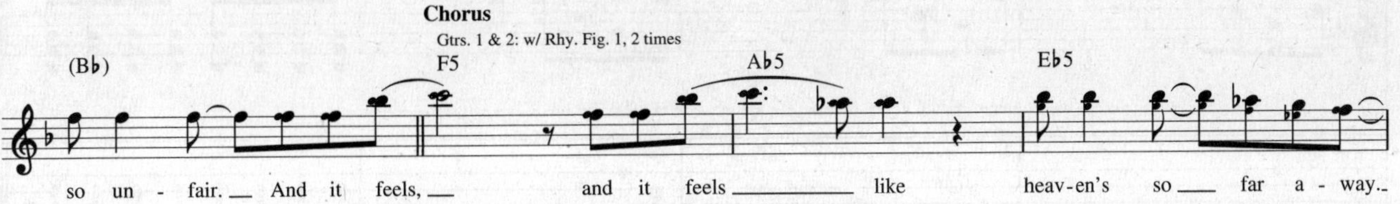
Chorus
Gtrs. 1 & 2: w/ Rhy. Fig. 1, 2 times
(Bb) F5 Ab5 Eb5
so un - fair. And it feels, and it feels like heav-en's so far a - way.

Bb5 F5 Ab5 Eb5
And it feels, yeah, it feels like the world has grown cold

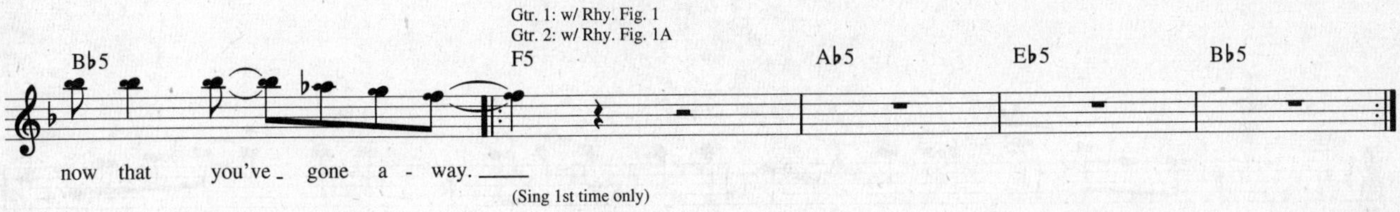
Gtr. 1: w/ Rhy. Fig. 1
Gtr. 2: w/ Rhy. Fig. 1A
Bb5 F5 Ab5 Eb5 Bb5
now that you've gone a - way.
(Sing 1st time only)

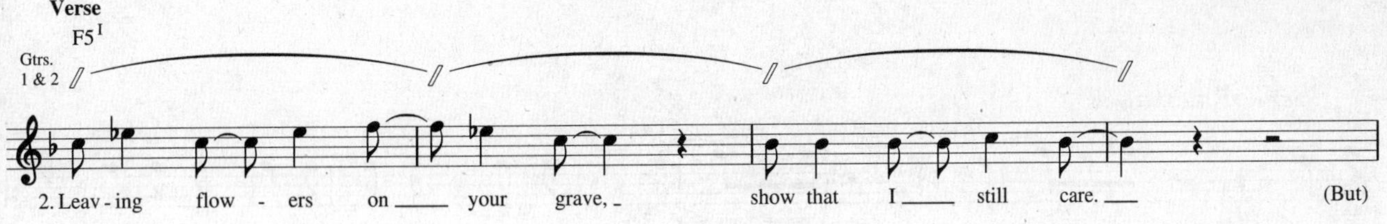
Verse
F5
Gtrs. 1 & 2
2. Leav - ing flow - ers on your grave, show that I still care. (But)

Gtrs. 1 & 2 tacet
N.C.(F) (Ab) (Eb) (Bb)
black ros - es and Hail Mar - y's can't bring back what's tak - en from me.

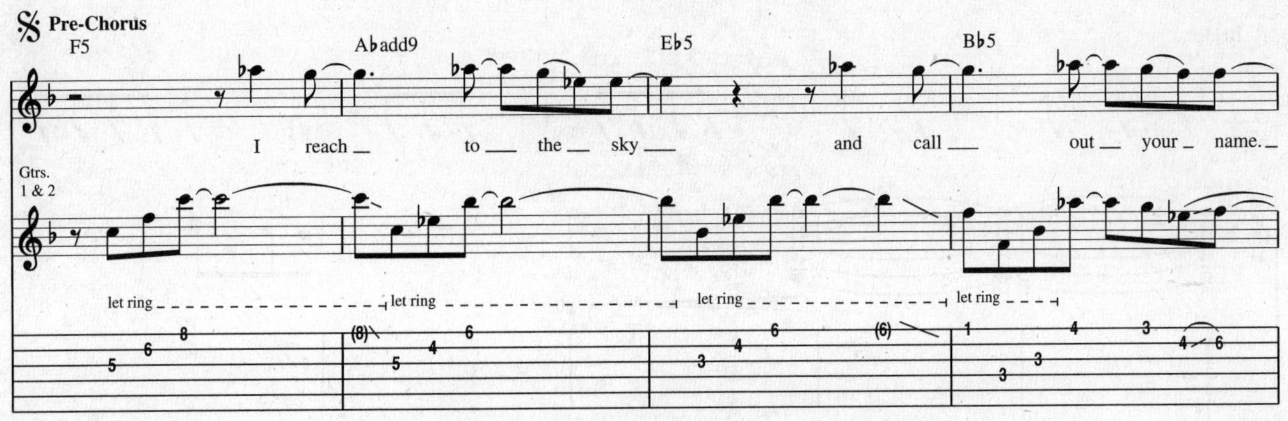
Pre-Chorus
F5 Abadd9 Eb5 Bb5
I reach to the sky and call out your name.
Gtrs. 1 & 2
let ring
5 6 8 (8) 5 4 6 3 4 6 (6) 1 3 4 3 3 4 6

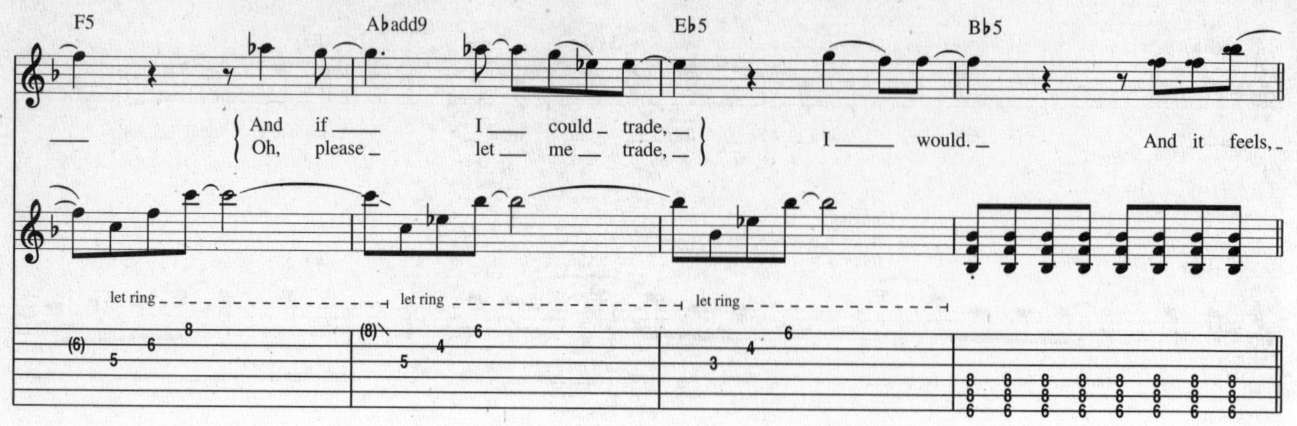

F5
Abadd9
Eb5
Bb5
And if I could trade,
Oh, please let me trade,
I would.
And it feels,
let ring
let ring
let ring

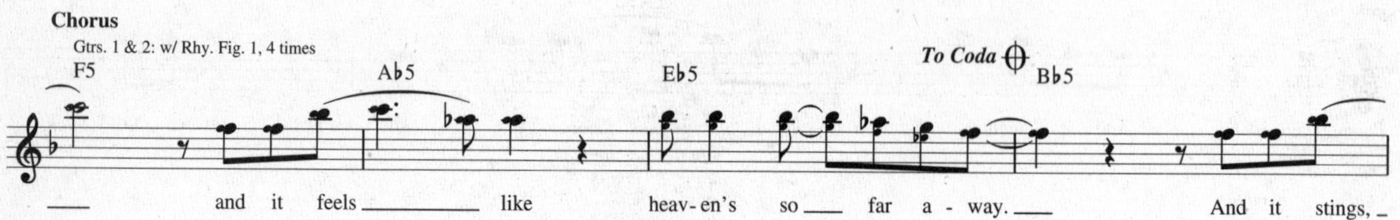

Chorus
Gtrs. 1 & 2: w/ Rhy. Fig. 1, 4 times
To Coda
F5
Ab5
Eb5
Bb5
and it feels like heav-en's so far a-way. And it stings,

F5
Ab5
Eb5
Bb5
yeah, it stings now. The world is so cold now that you've gone a-way,

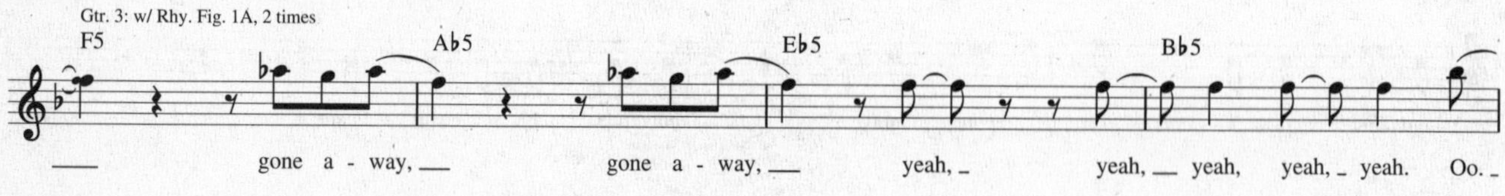

Gtr. 3: w/ Rhy. Fig. 1A, 2 times
F5
Ab5
Eb5
Bb5
gone a-way, gone a-way, yeah, yeah, yeah, yeah, yeah. Oo.

F5
Ab5
Eb5
Bb5
Well, oo, whoa, yeah.
Bridge
F
Ab
Eb
Gtr. 1 tacet
Bb
F
Gtr. 3 (clean)
f
Gtrs. 1 & 2
Gtr. 2
w/ Leslie

Ab
Eb
Gtr. 3 tacet
Bb
Gtr. 1
*P.M.
I say yeah so...
Gtr. 2
(Leslie off)
Interlude
Gtr. 1: w/ Rhy. Fig. 1, 2 times
Gtr. 2: w/ Rhy. Fig. 1A, 2 times
F5
Ab5
Eb5
Bb5
Whoa, yeah, yeah, yeah, oh.
D.S. al Coda
Mm.
Coda
And it feels, yeah, it feels like the
world has grown cold now that you've gone a - way,
Gtr. 2: w/ Rhy. Fig. 1A, 2 3/4 times
gone a - way,
gone a - way, yeah, yeah, yeah, yeah, yeah. Oo.
Well, ooh, whoa, yeah. Well, oo,
1.
2.

Grace

Words and Music by Jeff Buckley and Gary Lucas

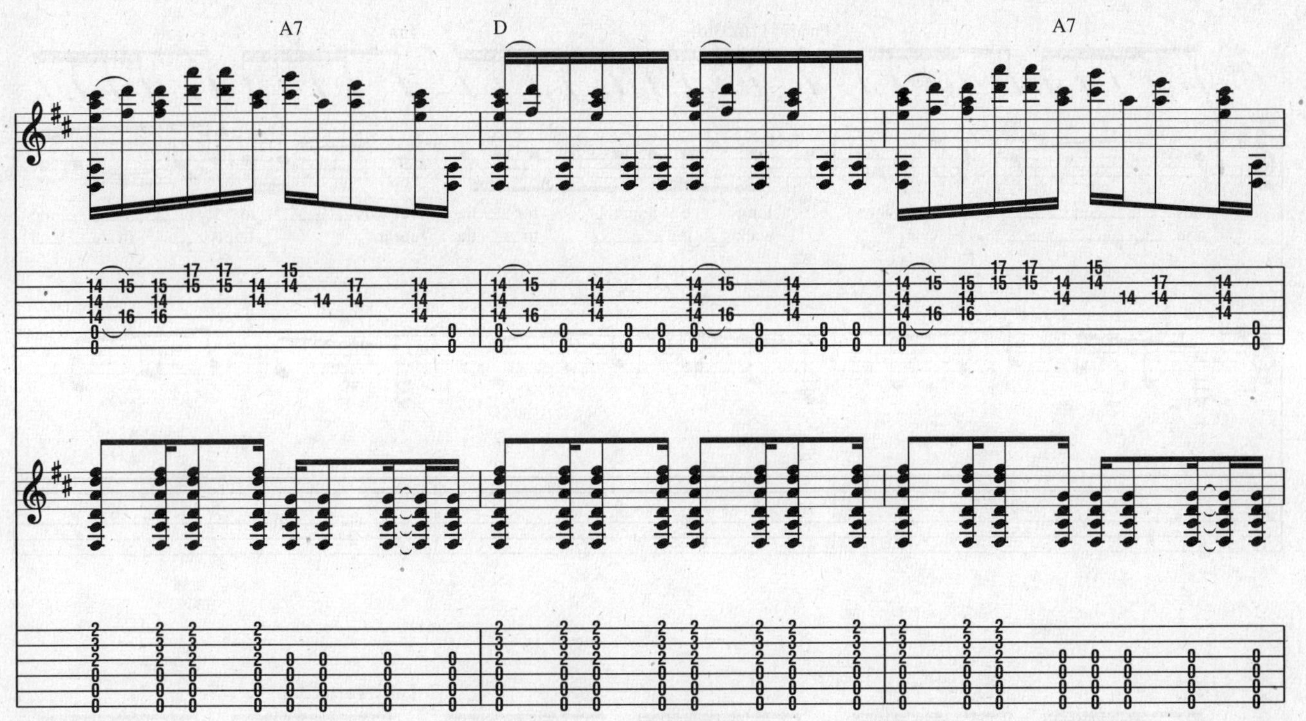

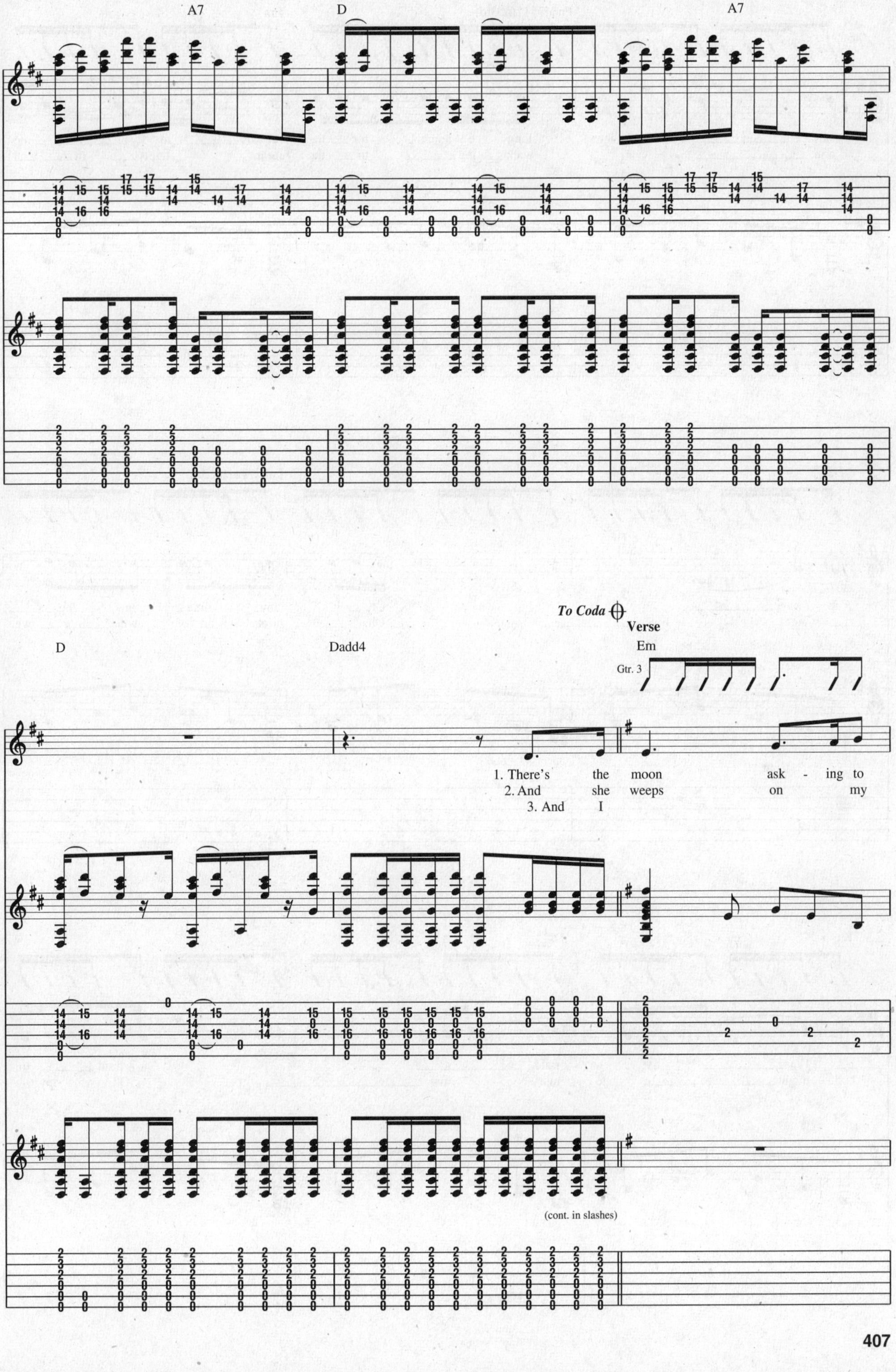

To Coda ⊕

Verse

D

Dadd4

Em

Gtr. 3

1. There's the moon ask - ing to
2. And she weeps on my
3. And I

(cont. in slashes)

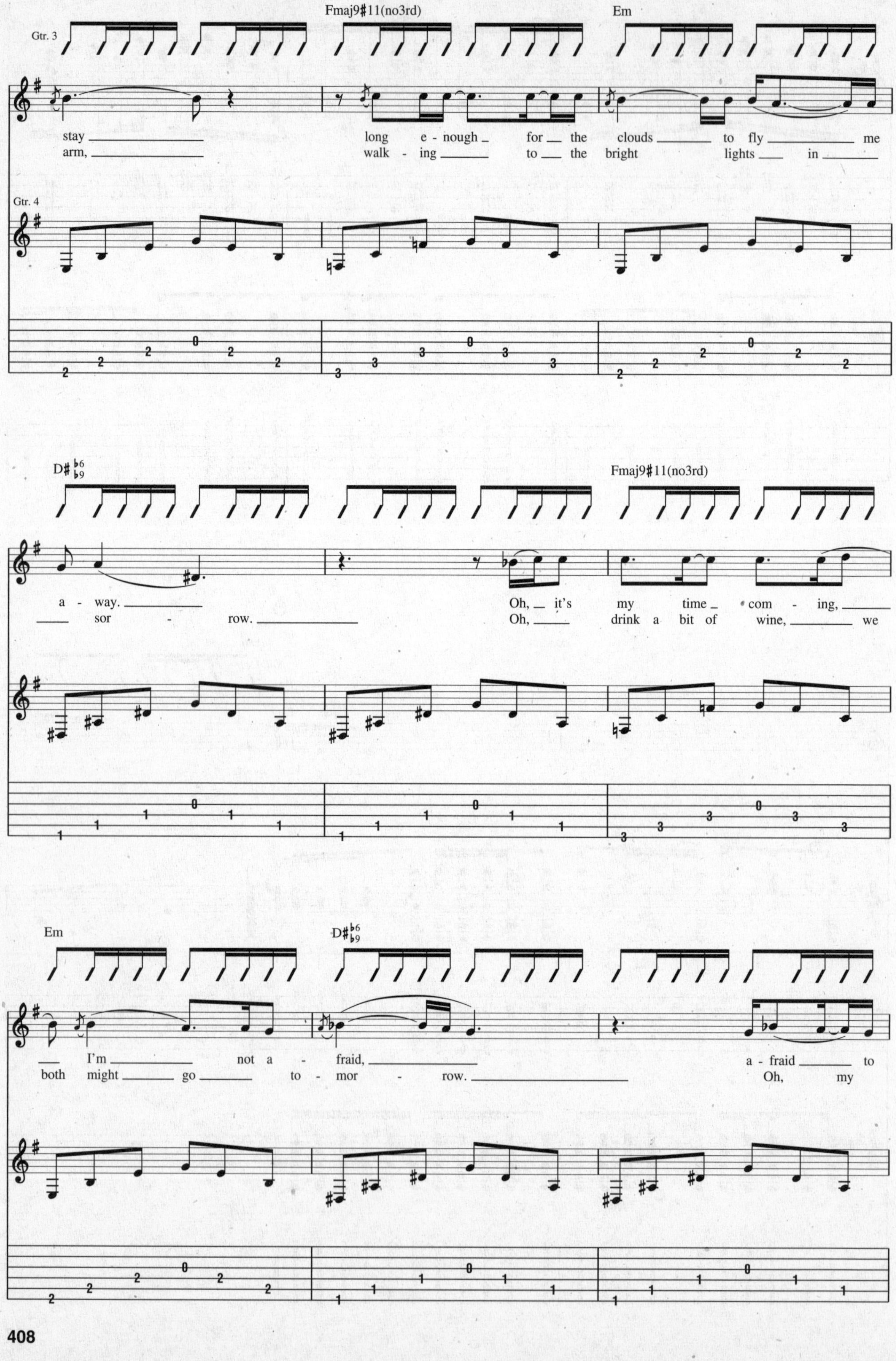

Fmaj9#11(no3rd) Em

Gtr. 3

stay long e - nough for the clouds to fly me

arm, walk - ing to the bright lights in

Gtr. 4

D#♭6♭9 Fmaj9#11(no3rd)

a - way. Oh, it's my time com - ing, we

sor - row. Oh, drink a bit of wine, we

Pre-Chorus
Em
Em
B7/F#
(cont. in notation)
die.
love.
1. My fad - ing voice
2. And the rain is fall -
Rhy. Fig. 1
Gtrs. 3 & 4
Em/G
A6
Bm(add4)
Aadd9
sings of love.
ing and I be - lieve my time has
End Rhy. Fig. 1
Em
B7/F#
come.
But she cries to the
It re - minds me of the
Rhy. Fig. 2

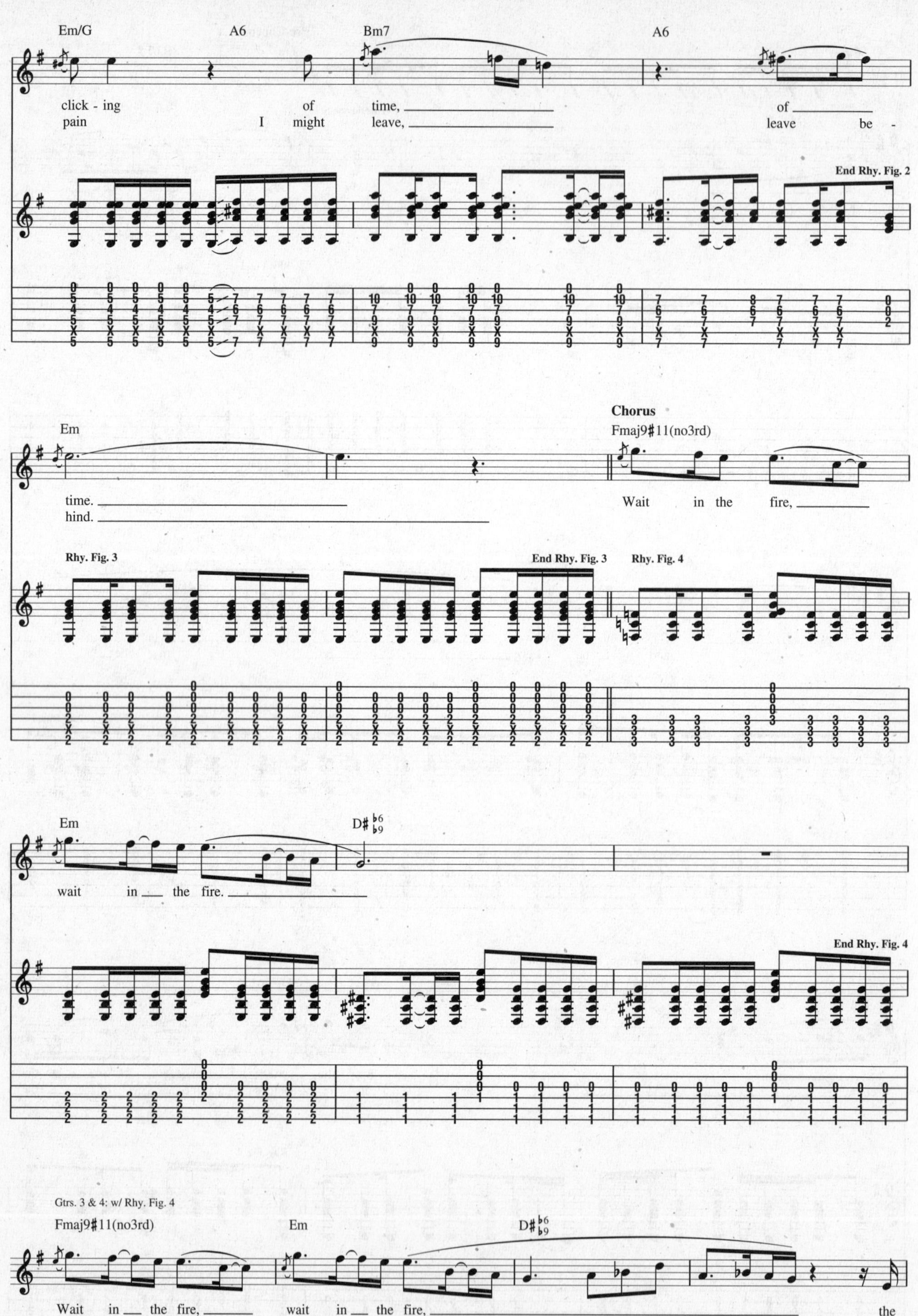
Em/G
A6
Bm7
A6
click - ing of time,
of
pain I might leave,
leave be -
End Rhy. Fig. 2
Em
Chorus
Fmaj9#11(no3rd)
time.
hind.
Wait in the fire,
Rhy. Fig. 3
End Rhy. Fig. 3
Rhy. Fig. 4
Em
D# b6 b9
wait in the fire.
End Rhy. Fig. 4
Gtrs. 3 & 4: w/ Rhy. Fig. 4
Fmaj9#11(no3rd)
Em
D# b6 b9
Wait in the fire,
wait in the fire,
the

1.
Interlude
Gtr. 1: w/ Riff A
Em
Fm
fire.
Gtrs. 3 & 4
p
2.
Bridge
Gtr. 4 tacet
Gm
Em
B♭sus2/E♭
Csus2/F
Ho.
Oh,
Gtr. 3
mf
* rasgado
Rhy. Fig. 5
End Rhy. Fig. 5
-1/2
Gtr. 2
w/ bar
Gtrs. 3 & 4
f
* Rapidly strum w/ right hand fingers
Dsus2/G
D♭sus2/G♭
oh,

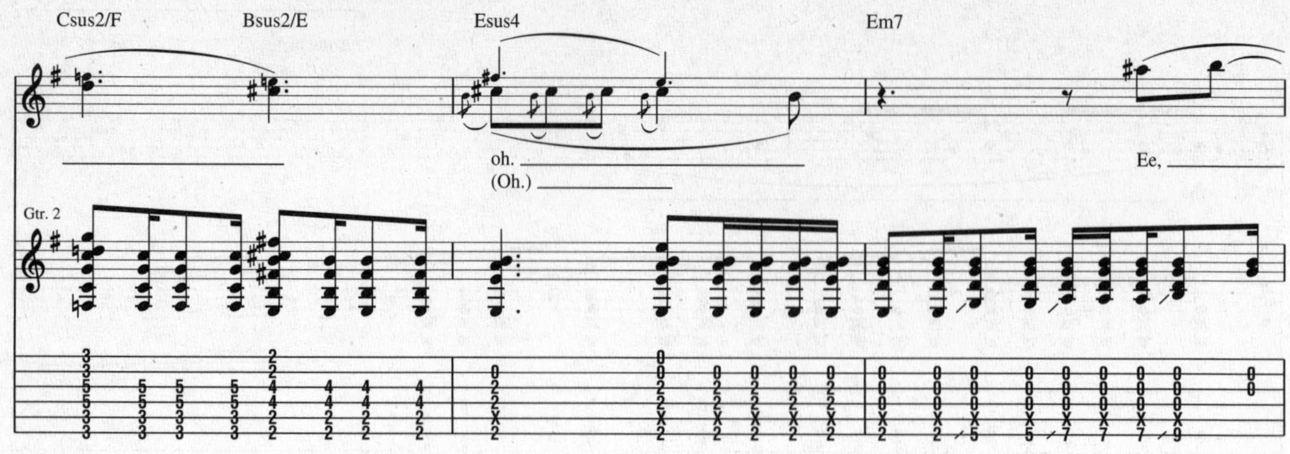
Csus2/F
Bsus2/E
Esus4
Em7
oh.
(Oh.)
Ee,
Gtr. 2

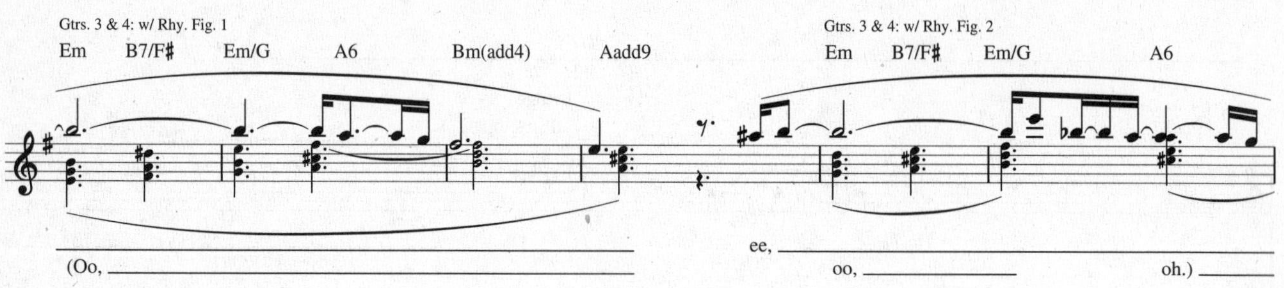
Gtrs. 3 & 4: w/ Rhy. Fig. 1
Em B7/F♯ Em/G A6 Bm(add4) Aadd9
Gtrs. 3 & 4: w/ Rhy. Fig. 2
Em B7/F♯ Em/G A6
ee,
(Oo,
oo,
oh.)

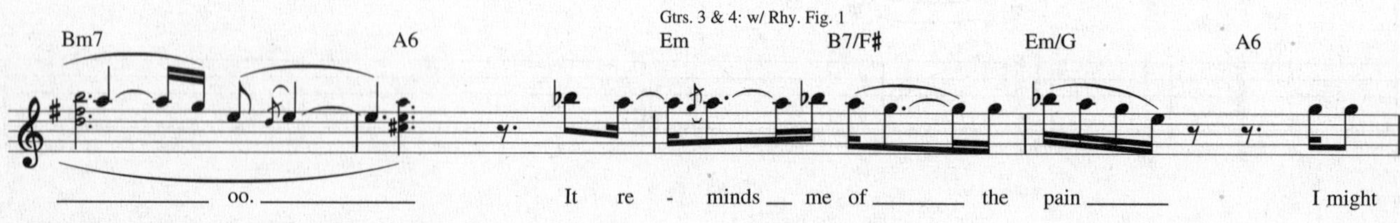
Bm7 A6
Gtrs. 3 & 4: w/ Rhy. Fig. 1
Em B7/F♯ Em/G A6
oo.
It re - minds me of the pain I might

Bm(add4) Aadd9
Gtrs. 3 & 4: w/ Rhy. Fig. 3
Em
leave,
leave be - hind.

Interlude

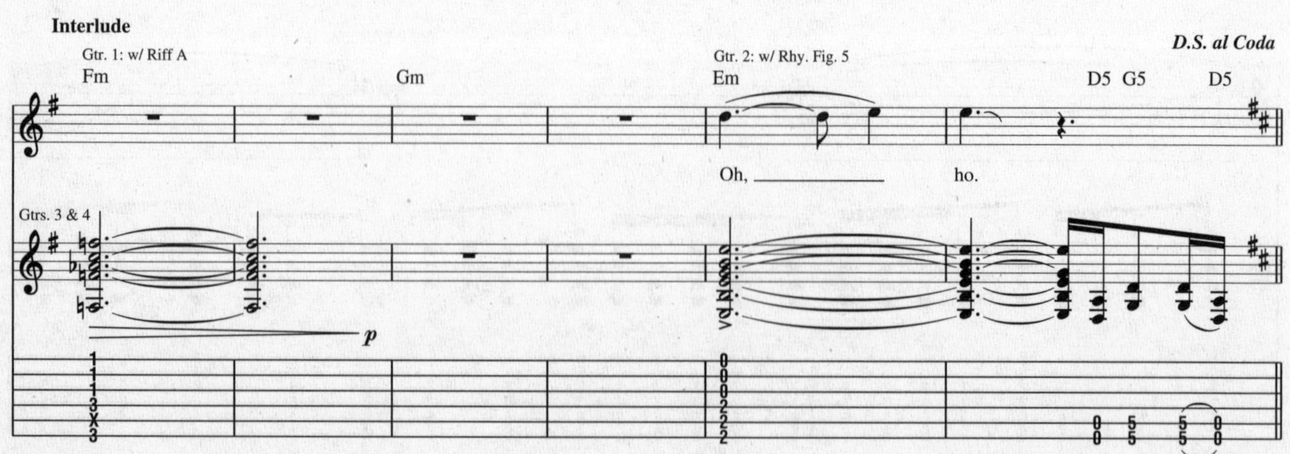
Gtr. 1: w/ Riff A
Fm Gm
Gtr. 2: w/ Rhy. Fig. 5
Em
D.S. al Coda
D5 G5 D5
Oh,
ho.
Gtrs. 3 & 4
p

Coda
Verse
Em
Fmaj9#11(no3rd)
Em
feel them drown my name, so eas - y to know and for -
Gtrs. 3 & 4
D#♭6♭9
Fmaj9#11(no3rd)
- get with this kiss. I'm not a - fraid to
Em
D#♭6♭9
go, but it goes so slow.
Outro
Gtrs. 3 & 4: w/ Rhy. Fig. 4 (6 1/2 times)
Fmaj9#11(no3rd)
Em
D#♭6♭9
Fmaj9#11(no3rd)
Oh,

Em
D♯♭6♭9
oh, yeah, yeah.
Fmaj9♯11(no3rd)
Em
D♯♭6♭9
Wait in the fire, wait in the fire. Oh, ah, ah.
Gtr. 5 (elec.)
Rhy. Fig. 6
End Rhy. Fig. 6
w/ clean tone & heavy flanger
Gtr. 5: w/ Rhy. Fig. 6 (3 1/2 times)
Lead Voc.: cont. ad Lib.
Wait in the fire,
wait in the fire.
Wait in the fire,
wait in the fire.
Wait in the fire,
Free time
wait in the fire.
Oh, ah.
Gtrs. 3, 4 & 5

Gypsy Road

Words and Music by Tom Kiefer

Gtrs. 1 & 2: w/ Rhy. Figs. 2 & 2A
Gtr. 3: w/ Rhy. Fill 1
A
B
seems all those dreams have come true but they're pass - ing me by.
wish and a prayer, cross my fin-gers 'cause I al - ways get by.
Some
Some

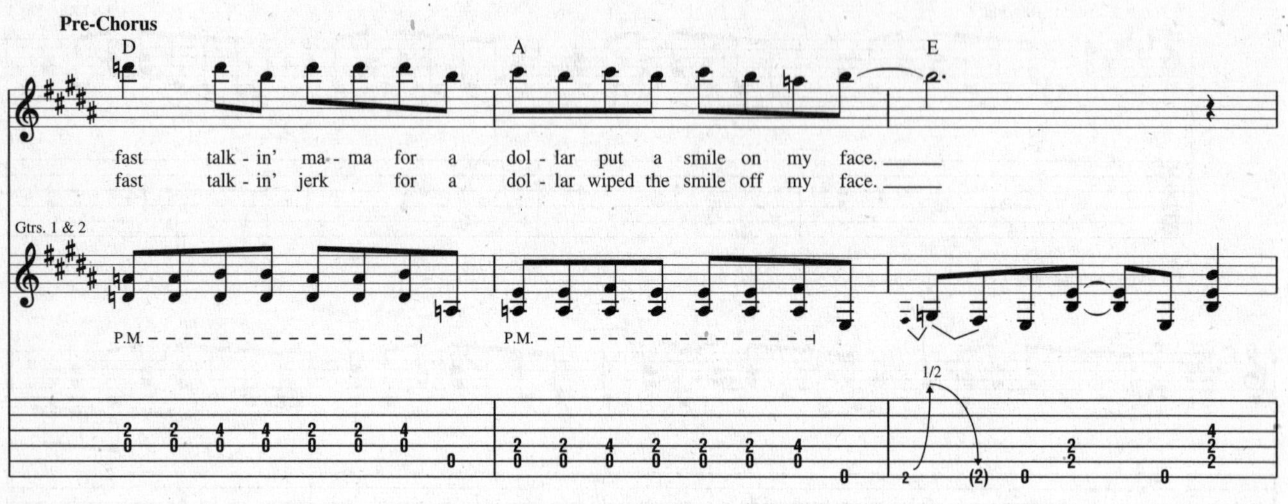
Pre-Chorus
D
A
E
fast talk - in' ma - ma for a dol - lar put a smile on my face.
fast talk - in' jerk for a dol - lar wiped the smile off my face.
Gtrs. 1 & 2
P.M.
P.M.
1/2

D
A
I'm driv - in' all night, I end up in the same old place.
I'm driv - in' all night just to keep the rat in the race.
P.M.
P.M.

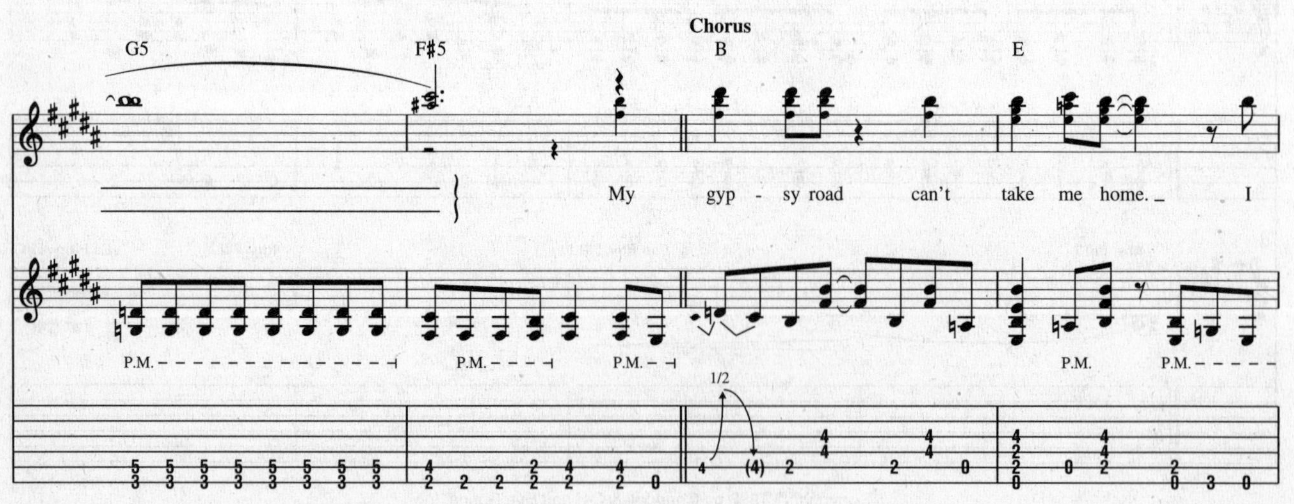
G5
F#5
Chorus
B
E
My gyp - sy road can't take me home. I
P.M.
P.M.
P.M.
1/2
P.M.
P.M.

A
E
B
drive all night just to see the light. My gyp - sy road can't
P.M.
P.M.
1/2
E
A
E
take me home. I keep on push - ing 'cause it feels al -
P.M.
P.M.
P.M.
1/2
Gtrs. 1 & 2: w/ Rhy. Fig. 1
B
1st time, Gtr. 3: w/ Rhy. Fill 2
right.
Bridge
C♯m
A
E
B
Some-times I feel so old. Got my lights burn-in' bright, but I'm a look-in' pret - ty sold.
Gtrs. 1 & 2
P.M.
Gtr. 3

C♯m
A
Gtr. 3 tacet
B
Some-times I feel so cold, so cold. Let's go!
P.M.
Guitar Solo
D
A
E
Gtr. 4 (dist.)
Gtrs. 1 & 2

Interlude
B5
Break of day!
1/2
1/2
1
grad. release
1/2
P.M.
P.M.
P.M.
B
Gtr. 4 tacet
E
A
E
Mmm. Got to
1/4
Rhy. Fig. 3
End Rhy. Fig. 3
let ring
Gtrs. 1 & 2: w/ Rhy. Fig. 3 (2 1/2 times)
get on home.
Woo!
One time! My gyp - sy road
can't take me home.
My gyp - sy road
can't

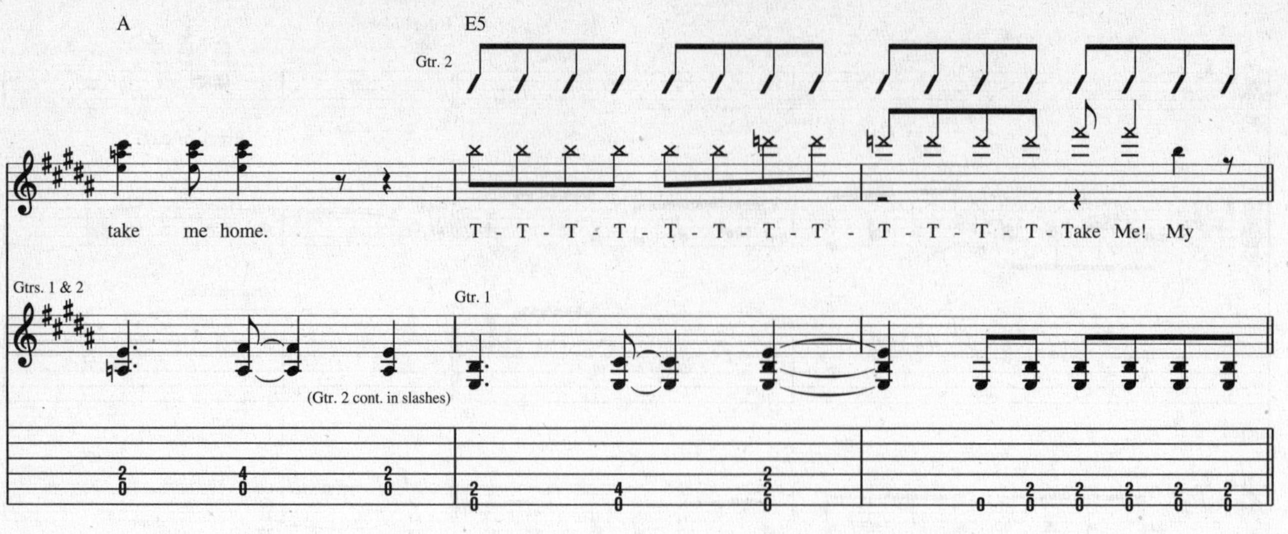

Outro-Chorus

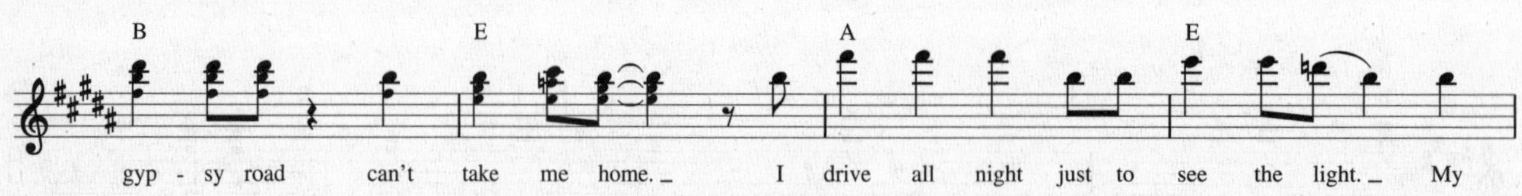

Begin fade
B
E
A
gyp - sy road.
My gyp - sy road.
Gtr. 4
semi-harm.
E
B
E
Ah, yeah! My gyp - sy road.
My
A
E
B
gyp - sy road.
My gyp - sy road can't
8va
hold bend
Fade out
E
A
E
B
take me home. I drive all night just to see the light. My gyp - sy road can't
8va

Hand in My Pocket

Lyrics by Alanis Morissette

Music by Alanis Morissette and Glen Ballard

sane but I'm o - ver - whelmed, I'm lost but I'm hope - ful, ba -
brave but I'm chick - en - shit, I'm sick but I'm pret - ty, ba -

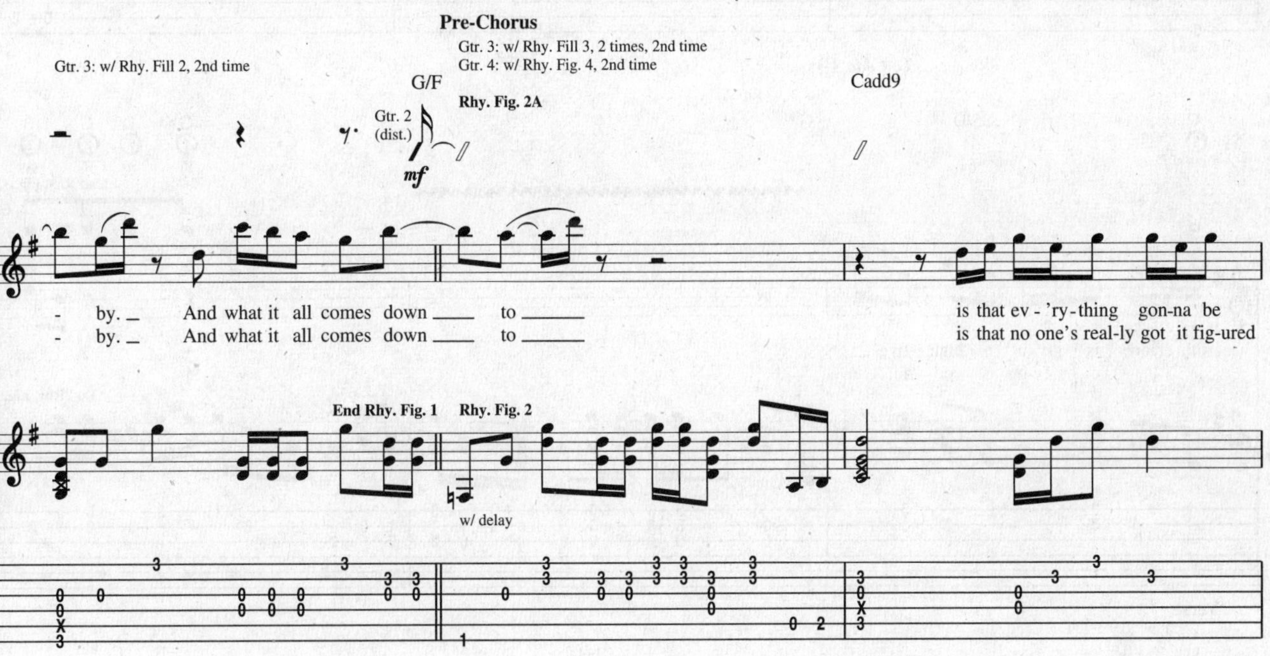
Pre-Chorus
Gtr. 3: w/ Rhy. Fill 2, 2nd time
Gtr. 3: w/ Rhy. Fill 3, 2 times, 2nd time
Gtr. 4: w/ Rhy. Fig. 4, 2nd time
G/F
Cadd9
Gtr. 2 (dist.)
Rhy. Fig. 2A
mf
- by. And what it all comes down to is that ev - 'ry-thing gon-na be
- by. And what it all comes down to is that no one's real-ly got it fig-ured
End Rhy. Fig. 1
Rhy. Fig. 2
w/ delay

Rhy. Fill 2
Gtr. 3
slight P.M.

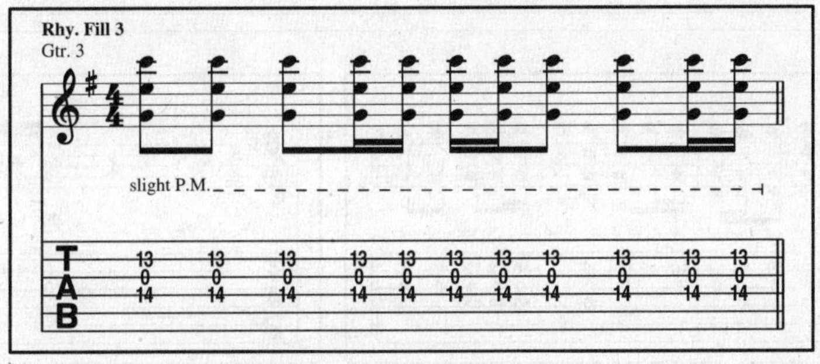
Rhy. Fill 3
Gtr. 3
slight P.M.

Chorus
Gtr. 3: w/ Riff A, 1st time; w/ Rhy. Fill 4, 2nd time
Gtr. 3: w/ Rhy. Fill 3, 2 times, 2nd time
* w/ bar
End Rhy. Fig. 2A
Rhy. Fig. 3A
End Rhy. Fig. 2
Rhy. Fig. 3
fine, fine, fine,
out just yet
'cause I've got a one hand in my pock - et and the
To Coda
Gtr. 3: w/ Riff A
End Rhy. Fig. 3A
End Rhy. Fig. 3
oth-er one is giv-in' a high five.
play-in' a pi - an - o.
2. I feel
Verse
Gtr. 1: w/ Rhy. Fig. 1
drunk but I'm so - ber, I'm young and I'm un - der - paid. I'm
Gtr. 4 (slight dist.)
Riff B
End Riff B
mf
let ring
Rhy. Fill 4
Gtr. 3
slight P.M.
Riff A
Gtr. 3 (slight dist.)
mf w/ delay

Gtr. 4: w/ Riff B, 3 times
Gtype2
C
3fr
Gtr. 3: w/ Riff A
G/B
G D G
3fr 3fr open
Gtype2
tired but I'm work - in', a - yeah.
I care but I'm rest - less, I'm
C
3fr
G/B
G/F
here but I'm real-ly gone.
I'm wrong and I'm sor - ry, ba - by.
And what it all comes down
Pre-Chorus
Gtrs 1 & 2: w/ Rhy. Figs. 2 & 2A, simile
G/F
Cadd9
Gtr. 3: w/ Riff A
G
to
is that ev-'ry-thing's gon-na be quite al - right.
Gtr. 4
Rhy. Fig. 4
let ring
Chorus
Gtrs. 1 & 2: w/ Rhy. Figs. 3 & 3A
G/F
C
G5/D
'cause I've got-a one hand in my pock-et and the oth-er one is flick-in' a cig-a-rette.
End Rhy. Fig. 4
Rhy. Fig. 5
End Rhy. Fig. 5
let ring
let ring
let ring

Solo
Gtr. 1: w/ Rhy. Fig. 1
G
Gtype2
E
2fr
Gtype2
Gtr. 2
Gtr. 5
8va
* Harmonica arr. for gtr.
Gtr. 3
Gtr. 4
let ring
G/B
C
Gtype2
E
2fr
D
open
D
open
C
8va

G/B
E
2fr
G type2
C
G type2
And what it all comes down
8va
Pre-Chorus
Gtr. 5 tacet
Gtrs. 1 & 2: w/ Rhy. Figs. 2 & 2A
Gtr. 4: w/ Rhy. Fig. 4
G/F
Cadd9
to
is that I have - n't got it all fig - ured
Gtr. 3
let ring
Gtr. 3 tacet
G
Chorus
Gtrs. 1 & 2: w/ Rhy. Figs. 3 & 3A
Gtr. 4: w/ Rhy. Fig. 5
G/F
out just yet
'cause I've got - a one hand in my pock - et and the
D.S. al Coda
C
G5/D
G
oth - er one is giv - in' a peace sign.
3. I'm

Coda
Gtr. 3: w/ Rhy. Fill 1
Gtr. 3: w/ Rhy. Fill 2
Pre-Chorus
Gtr. 4: w/ Rhy. Fig. 4
Gtype3
G/F
Gtr. 2
And what it all comes down to my friends, yeah,
Gtr. 1
Cadd9
Gtype3
is that ev-'ry-thing's just fine, fine, fine. 'Cause I've got-a
Gtr. 4: w/ Rhy. Fig. 5
F G/F
C Cadd9 G
Gtype2
one hand in my pock - et and the oth-er one is hail-ing a tax - i - cab.
Outro
Gtype3
play 7 times
Gtype3

A Hard Day's Night

Words and Music by John Lennon and Paul McCartney

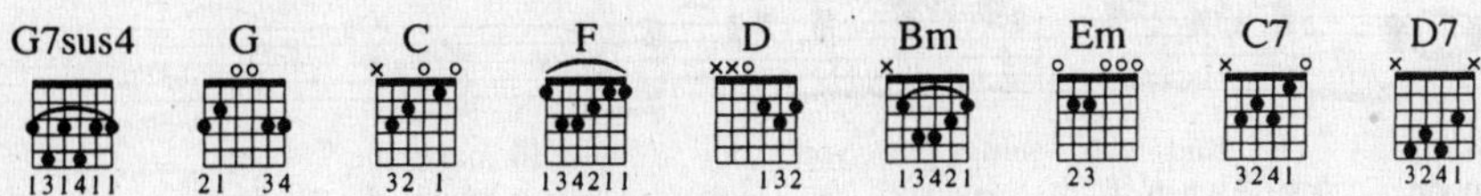

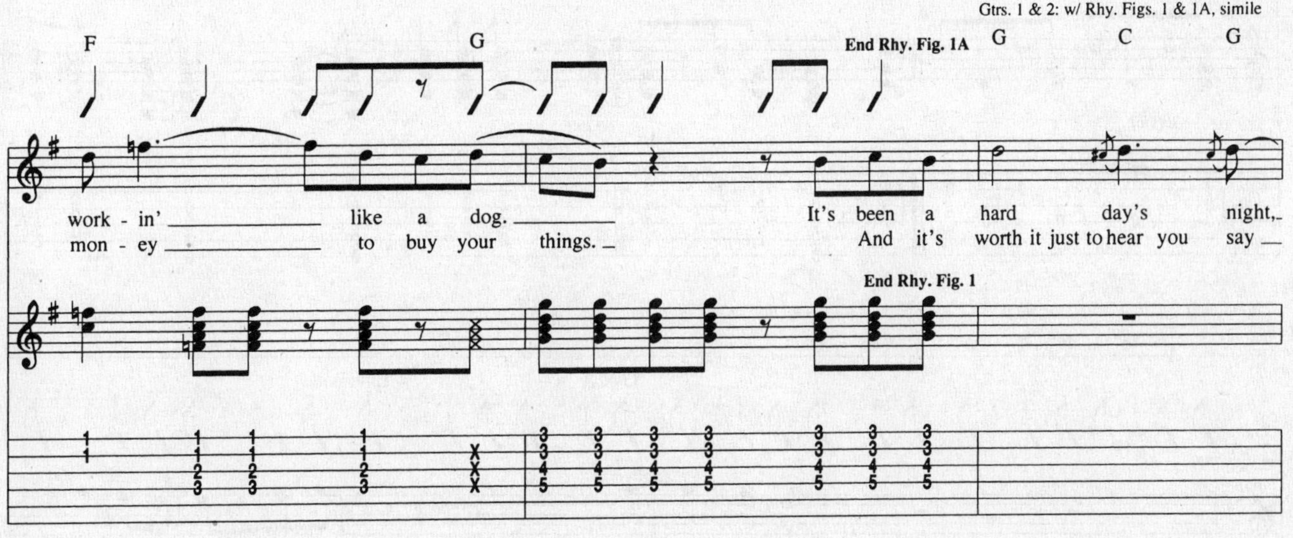

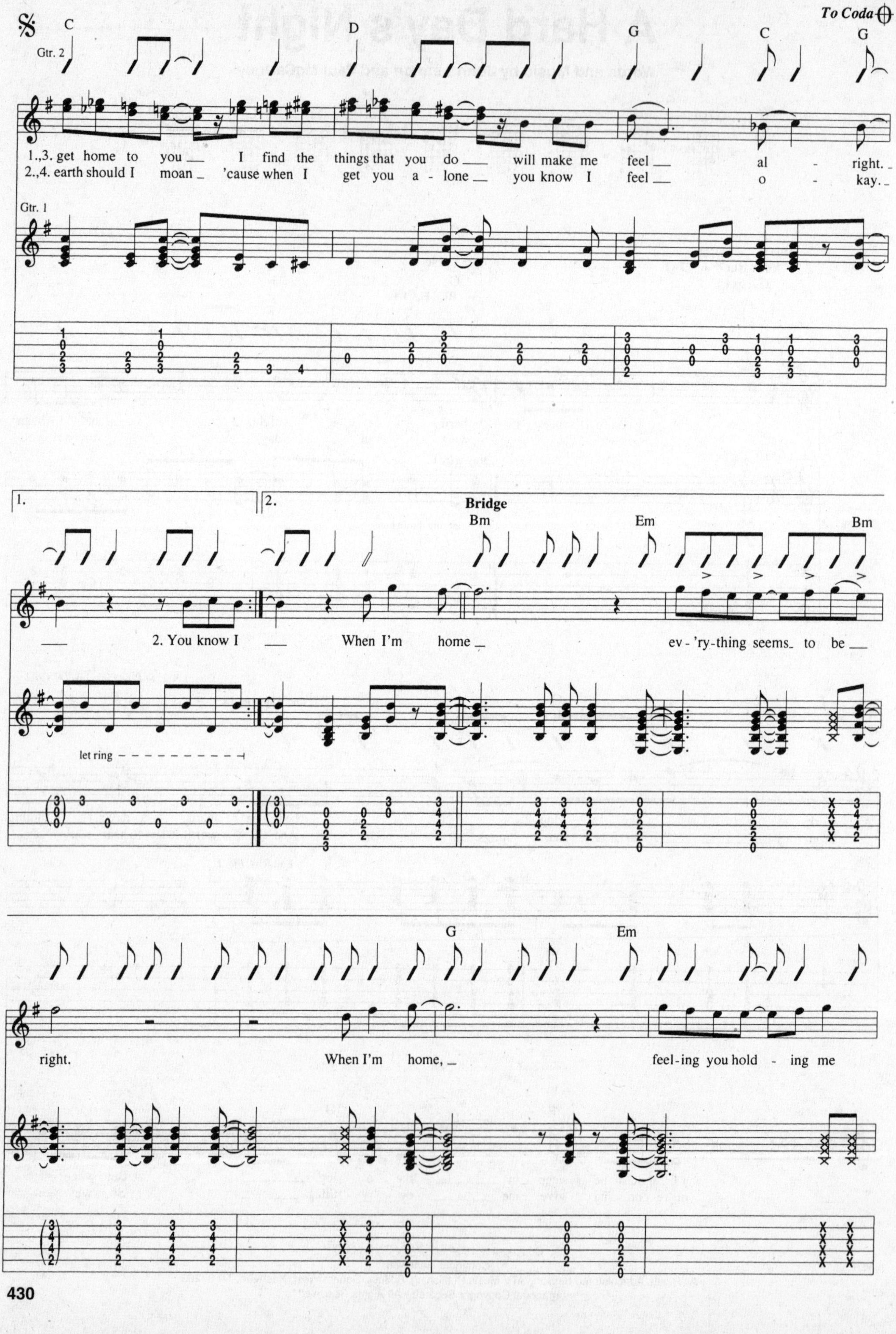

1. 2.

Bridge

Bm Em Bm

2. You know I When I'm home ev - 'ry-thing seems to be

let ring

G Em

right. When I'm home, feel-ing you hold - ing me

C7
D7
(2nd time) D.S.S. al Coda
3.
tight, tight, yeah. 3., 5. It's been a Ow!
Guitar Solo
Gtrs. 1 & 2: w/ Rhy. Figs. 1 & 1A, simile
G C G F G
D.S. al 2nd Ending
Coda
C
sing 2nd time only
4. So why on
You know I
*Gtr. 3 (12-str. acous.)
*Doubled by clavichord an octave lower.
Tag
G C G C G C F
Play 3 Times and Fade
feel al - right. You know I feel al - right.
Gtr. 4 (12-str. elec.)
let ring
w/ slight dist.

Hard to Handle

Words and Music by Allen Jones, Alvertis Bell and Otis Redding

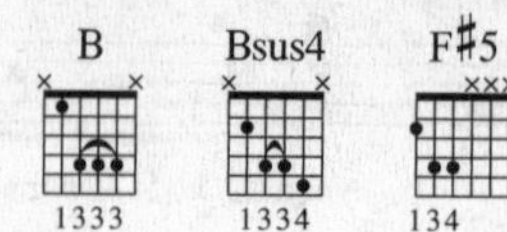

Gtr. 1: Open G tuning:
(low to high) D-G-D-G-B-D

Intro

Moderate Rock ♩ = 102

N.C.

(Drums)

Gtr. 1 (slight dist.)

mf

Verse

B Bsus4 B Bsus4

Rhy. Fig. 1A

*Gtr. 2 (dist.)

mf

1. Ba - by, here I am, I'm a man on the scene.

Gtr. 1

Rhy. Fig. 1

P.M.

*w/ slide on middle finger.

B Bsus4 B Bsus4

I can give you what you want, but you got to come home with me.

P.M.

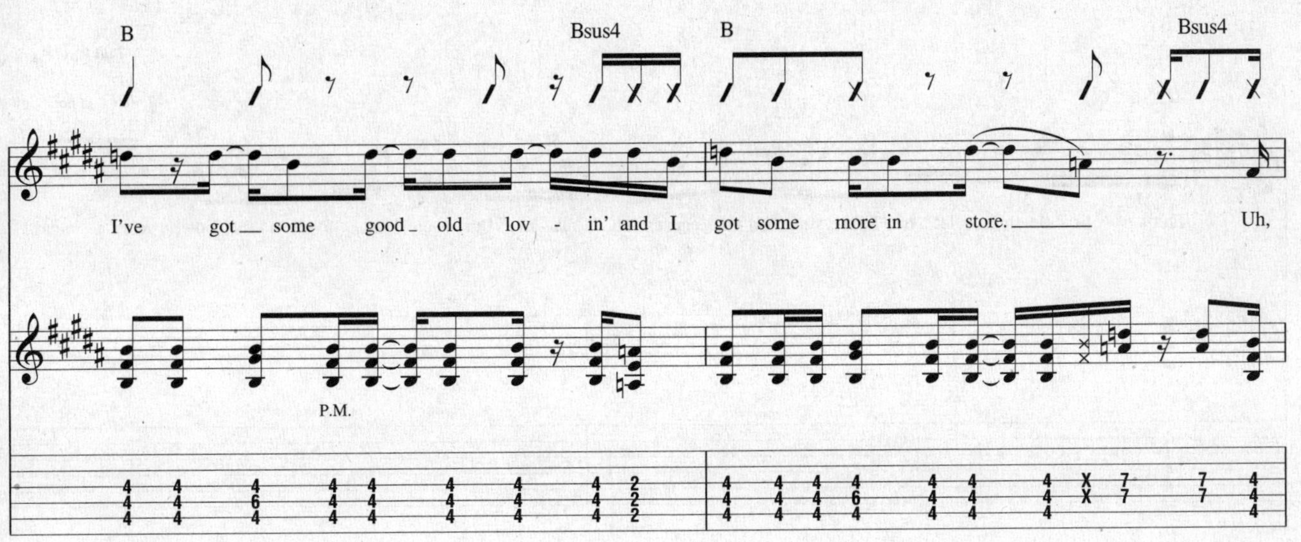
B
Bsus4
B
Bsus4
I've got some good old lov - in' and I got some more in store. Uh,
P.M.

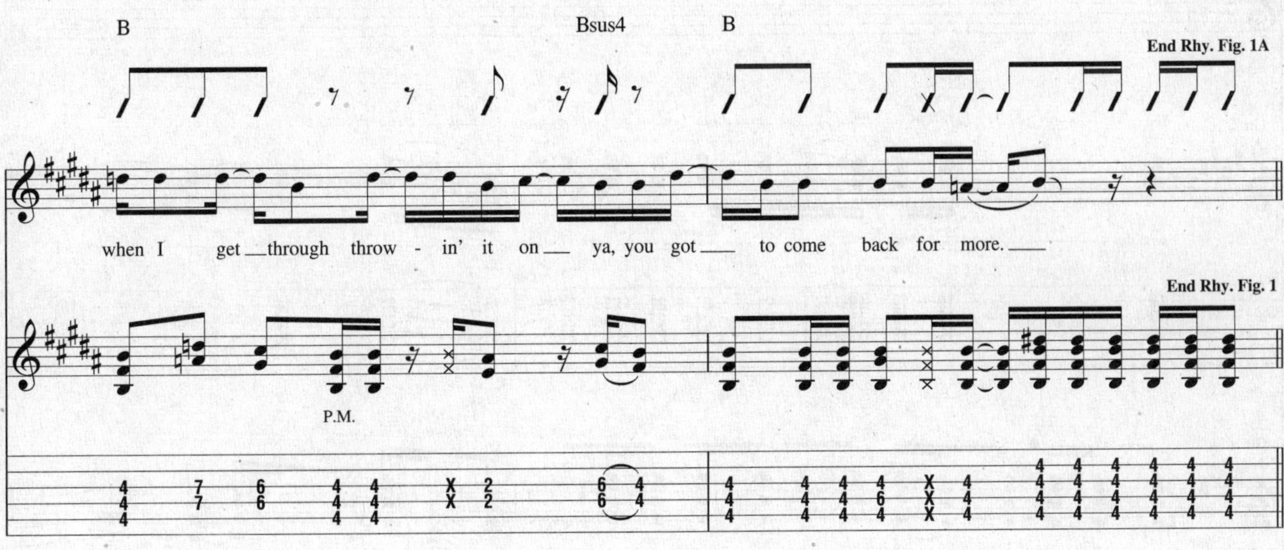
B
Bsus4
B
End Rhy. Fig. 1A
when I get through throw - in' it on ya, you got to come back for more.
End Rhy. Fig. 1
P.M.

Chorus

F♯5
Rhy. Fig. 2
Boys have things that come by the doz - en. That ain't noth - in' but drug - store lov - in'.

B
End Rhy. Fig. 2
(cont. in notation)
Pret - ty lit - tle thing, let me light your can - dle 'cause, uh, ma - ma, I'm sure hard to han - dle now, yes, a - round.

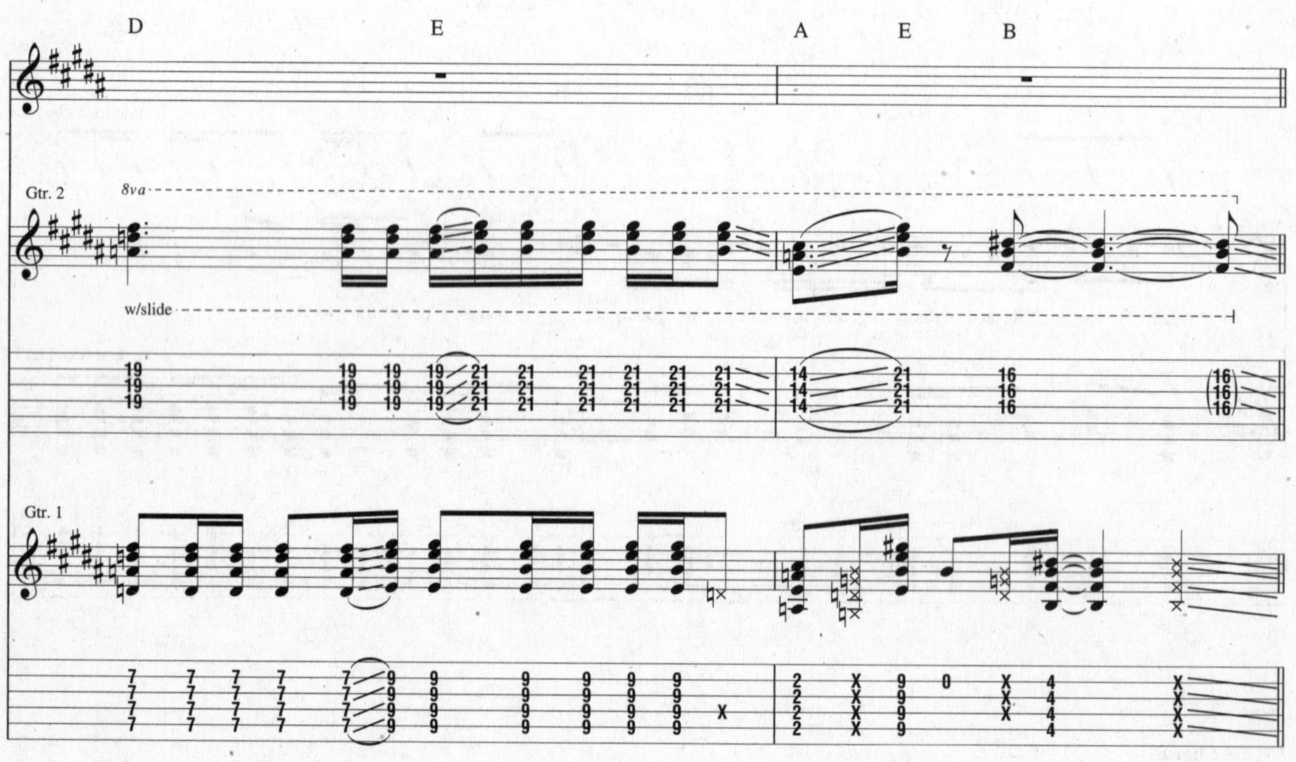
D
E
A
E
B
Gtr. 2
8va
w/slide
Gtr. 1

Verse

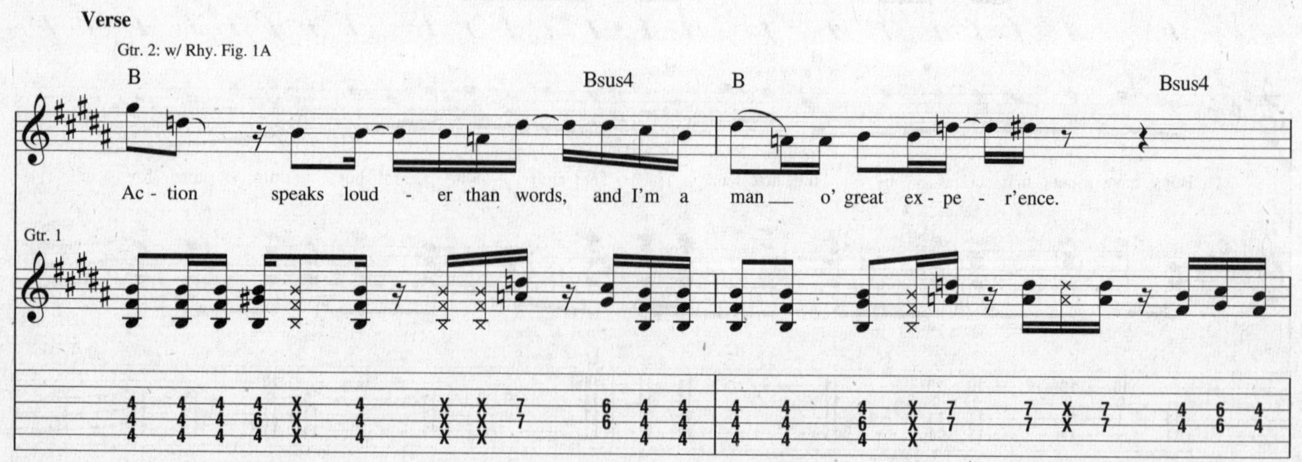
Gtr. 2: w/ Rhy. Fig. 1A
B
Bsus4
B
Bsus4
Ac - tion speaks loud - er than words, and I'm a man o' great ex - pe - r'ence.
Gtr. 1

B
Bsus4
B
Bsus4
I know you got an-oth - er man, but I can love you bet-ter than him. Take
B
Bsus4
B
Bsus4
my hand, don't be a - fraid. I'm gon-na prove ev-'ry word I say. I'm
B
Bsus4
B
ad-ver-tis - in' love for free, so you can place your ad with me.
Chorus
Gtr. 2: w/ Rhy. Fig. 2
F#5
Boys that come a - long, a dime by the doz-en. That ain't noth - in' but ten cent lov-in'.

B N.C.
Pret - ty lit - tle thing, let me light your can - dle 'cause, uh, ma - ma, I'm sure hard to han - dle now, yes, a - round.
A E B A E B A B
Yeah. Hard to han - dle now.
8va
Gtr. 2
Rhy. Fig. 3
w/slide
Gtr. 1
A E B A E B A5
Oh, ba - by.
8va
End Rhy. Fig. 3
w/slide

Verse

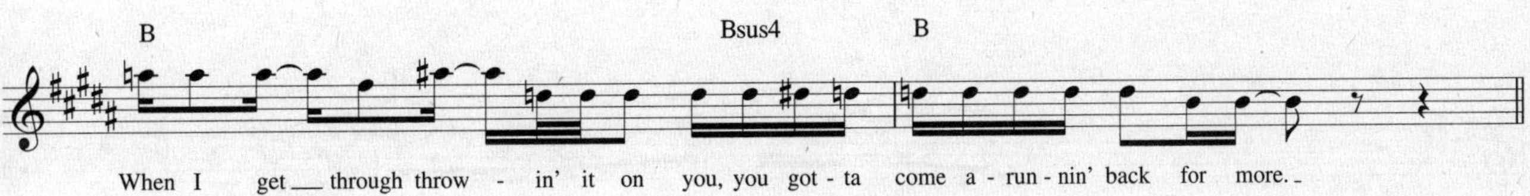

Chorus

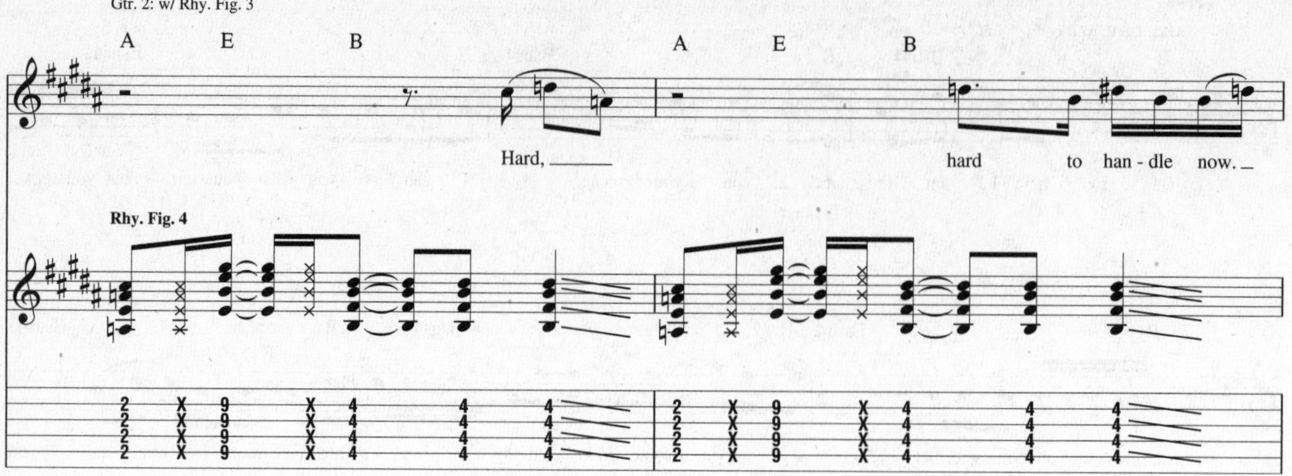
Gtr. 2: w/ Rhy. Fig. 3
A E B A E B
Hard, hard to han - dle now.
Rhy. Fig. 4

A E B A E B
Oh, yeah, yeah, yeah, yeah, ooh, yeah.
Gtr. 3 (dist.)
Gtr. 1
End Rhy. Fig. 4

Guitar Solo

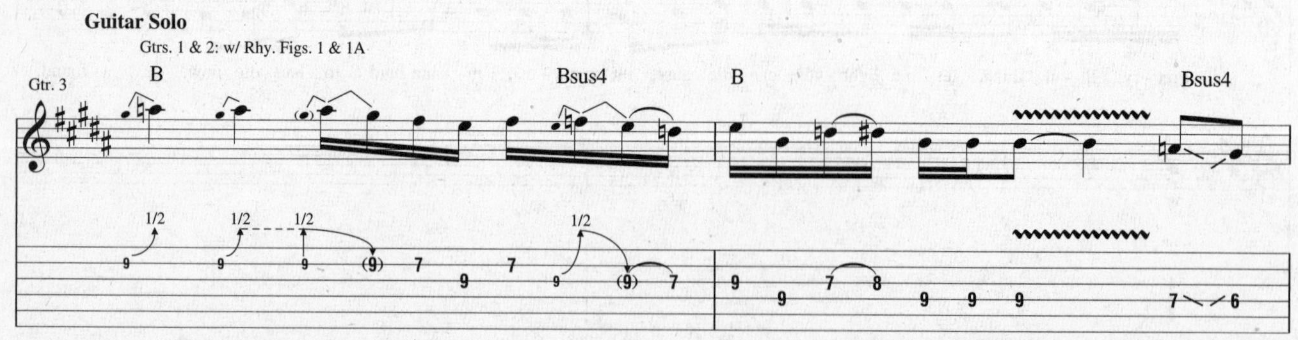
Gtrs. 1 & 2: w/ Rhy. Figs. 1 & 1A
Gtr. 3
B Bsus4 B Bsus4

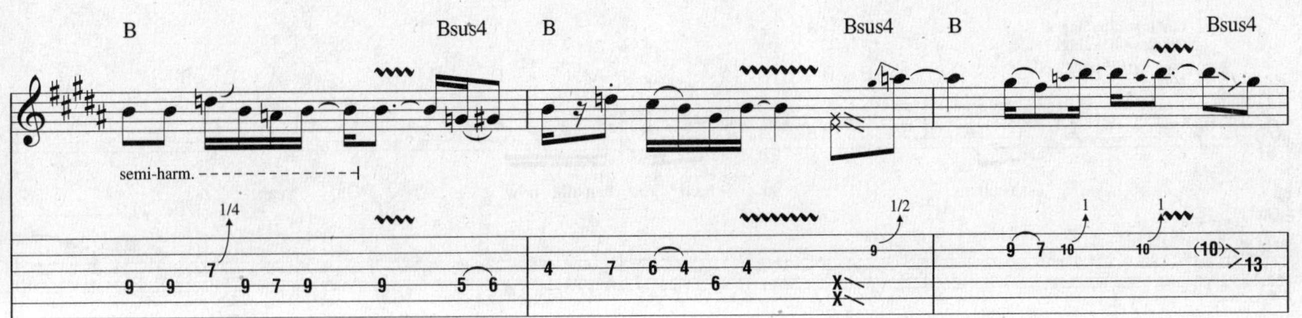

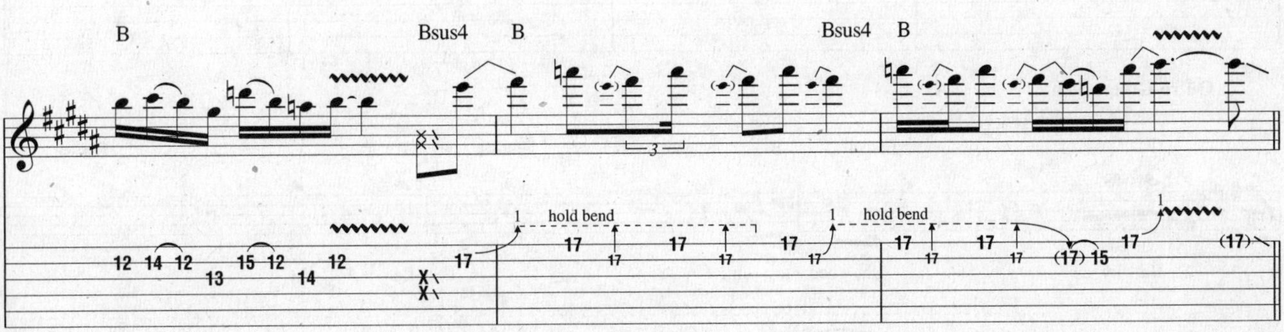

Chorus

Gtr. 2: w/ Rhy. Fig. 2
Gtr. 3 tacet

Gtr. 1: w/ Rhy. Fig. 4
Gtr. 2: w/ Rhy. Fig. 3
A E B
Yeah. So hard to han-dle now. Oh, yeah.
Gtr. 3
8va
rake
Outro-Guitar Solo
Gtrs. 1 & 2: w/ Rhy. Figs. 1 & 1A
B Bsus4
Ba - by. Uh, good lov - in'. Ba - by.
hold bend
Ba - by, oh, oh, good lov - in'. I need good
lov - in'. I got to

Gtr. 1: w/ Rhy. Fig. 4 (1st 3 meas.)
Gtr. 2: w/ Rhy. Fig. 3 (1st 3 meas.)
B
A
E
B
have it.
Oh,
yeah.
Yeah.
loco
1/2
1/4
A
E
B
A
E
B
So
hard
to
han - dle
now.
Yeah.
Free time
A
E
B
Mm,
mm.
Gtr. 3
Gtr. 2
8va
w/slide
Gtr. 1

Heartbreaker

Words and Music by Cliff Wade and Geoff Gill

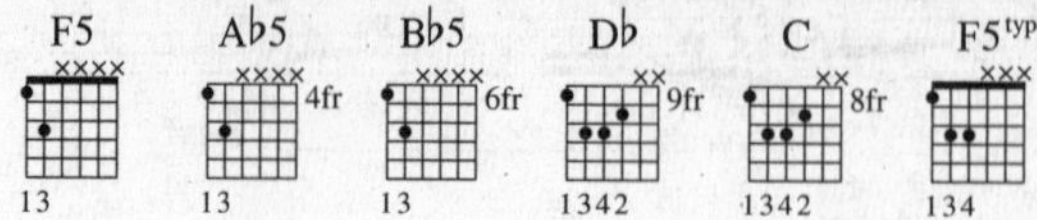

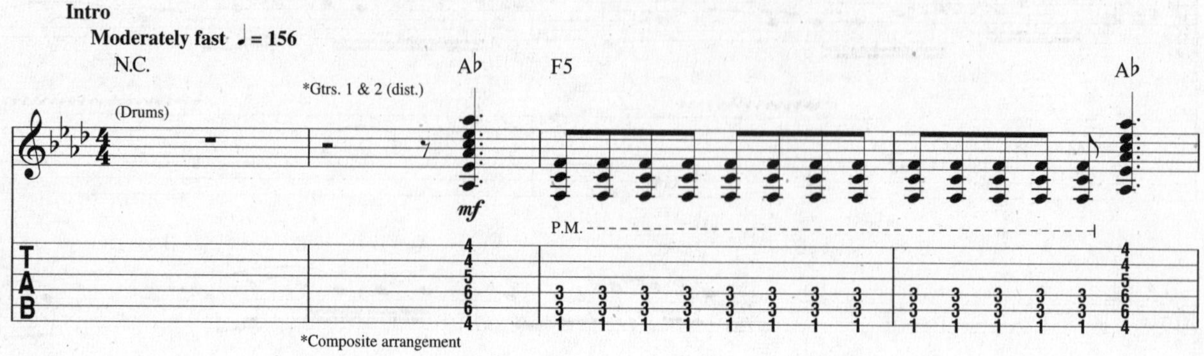

F5
E♭5
D♭5
Drown - in' me in your prom - is - es
bet - ter left un - said.
You taught me the ways of de - si - re,
now it's tak - in' its toll.
P.M.
B♭5
C
E♭5
Fm
E♭
D♭
You're the right kind of sin - ner to re - lease
P.M.
B♭5
C5
Fm
E♭
my in - ner fan - ta - sy.
The in - vin - ci - ble win -
P.M.
D♭
B♭5
C5
- ner, and you know that you were born to be...
P.M.

To Coda
Chorus
Half-time feel
N.C. F5 G5 A♭ N.C. B♭ C5
You're a heart - break - er, dream mak - er, love tak - er, don't you
Rhy. Fig. 2

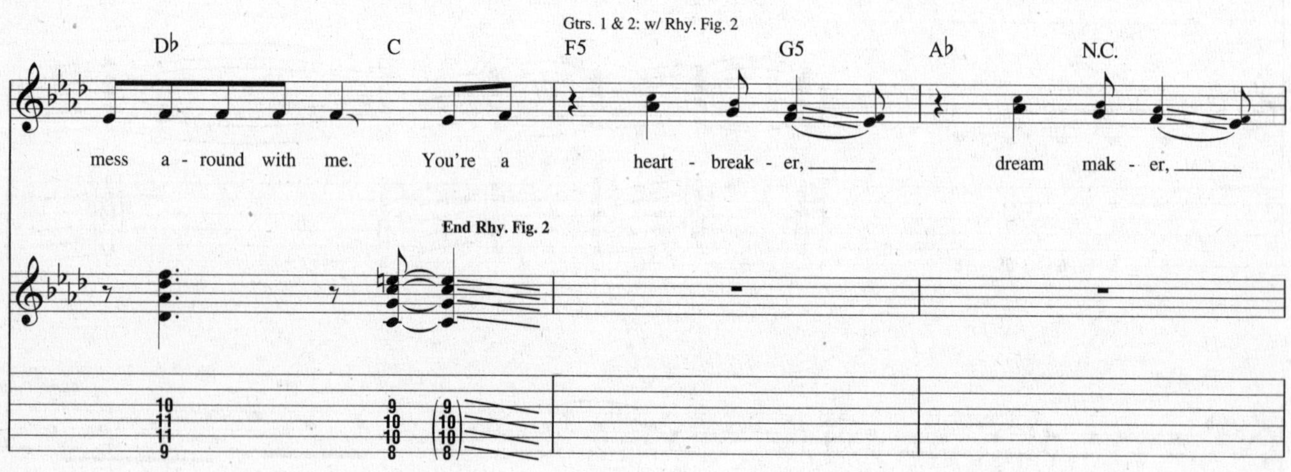
Gtrs. 1 & 2: w/ Rhy. Fig. 2
D♭ C F5 G5 A♭ N.C.
mess a - round with me. You're a heart - break - er, dream mak - er,
End Rhy. Fig. 2

Interlude
End half-time feel
Gtrs. 1 & 2: w/ Rhy. Fig. 1
B♭ C5 D♭ C F5
love tak - er, don't you mess a - round, no, no, no.

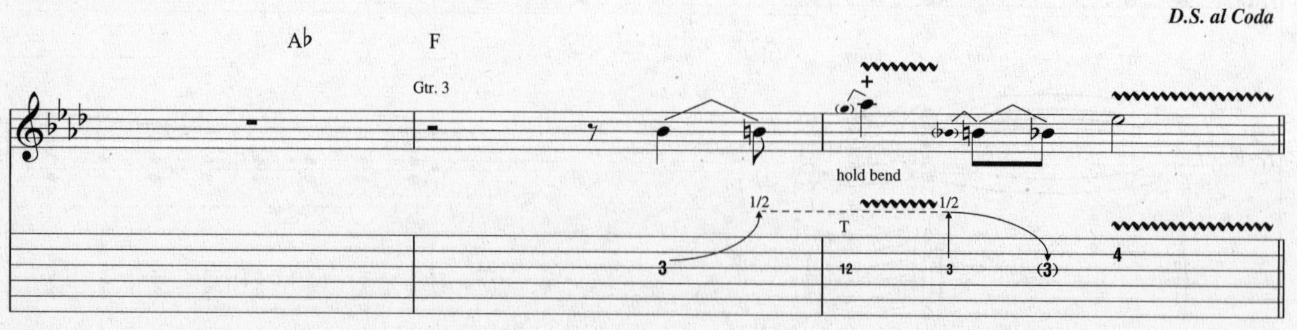
D.S. al Coda
A♭ F
Gtr. 3
hold bend
1/2
T
1/2

Coda
Chorus
Half-time feel
F5 G5 A♭ N.C. B♭ C
heart - break - er, dream mak - er, love tak - er, don't you
Gtrs. 1 & 2
Rhy. Fig. 3

Gtrs. 1 & 2: w/ Rhy. Fig. 3
D♭ C F5 G5 A♭ N.C. B♭ C
mess a - round with me. You're a heart - break - er, dream mak - er, love tak - er, don't you
End Rhy. Fig. 3

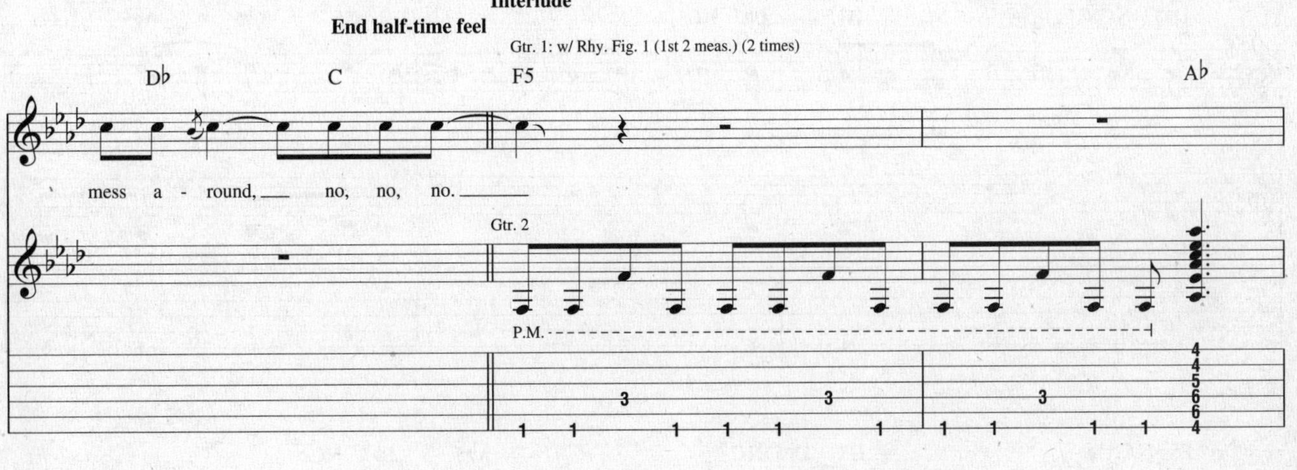
Interlude
End half-time feel
Gtr. 1: w/ Rhy. Fig. 1 (1st 2 meas.) (2 times)
D♭ C F5 A♭
mess a - round, no, no, no.
Gtr. 2
P.M.

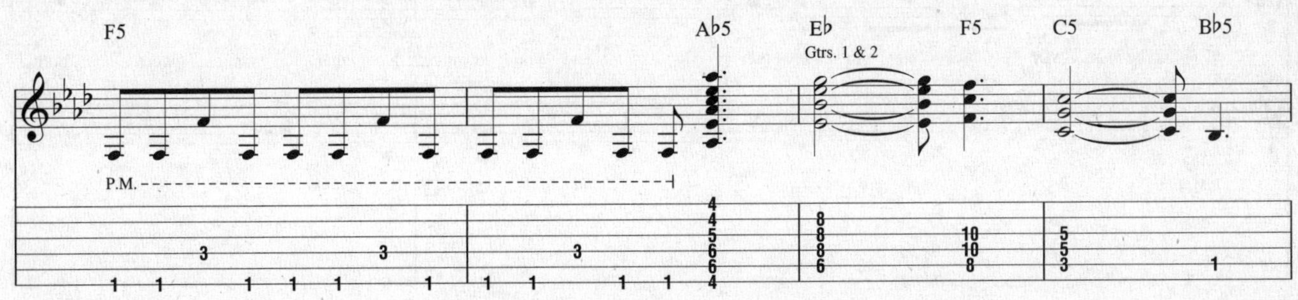
F5 A♭5 E♭ F5 C5 B♭5
Gtrs. 1 & 2
P.M.

Ab5
G5
F5
Eb5
D5
Eb5
F5
C5
Bb5
Ab5
Eb5
Bb5
G5
F5
C5
P.M.
Bridge
F5 N.C.
C5
You're the right kind of sin -
Db5 N.C.
Ab5
Bb5 N.C.
C5
Bb5
Ab5
G5
- ner to re - lease my in - ner fan - ta - sy.
F5 N.C.
C5
Db5 N.C.
Ab5
Bb5 N.C.
The in - vin - ci - ble win - ner and you know that you were born

Chorus
Gtrs. 1 & 2 tacet
C5
N.C.
to be...
You're a heart - break - er,
P.M.
dream mak - er,
love tak - er, don't you mess a - round with me. You're a
F5 G5 A♭5 B♭5 C5
heart - break - er,
dream mak - er,
love tak - er, don't you
Gtr. 2
D♭5 C5 F5 A♭5
mess a - round with me. You're a heart - break - er, dream mak - er,
Gtr. 1
Rhy. Fig. 4
P.M.
Gtr. 2
P.M.

Outro - Guitar Solo

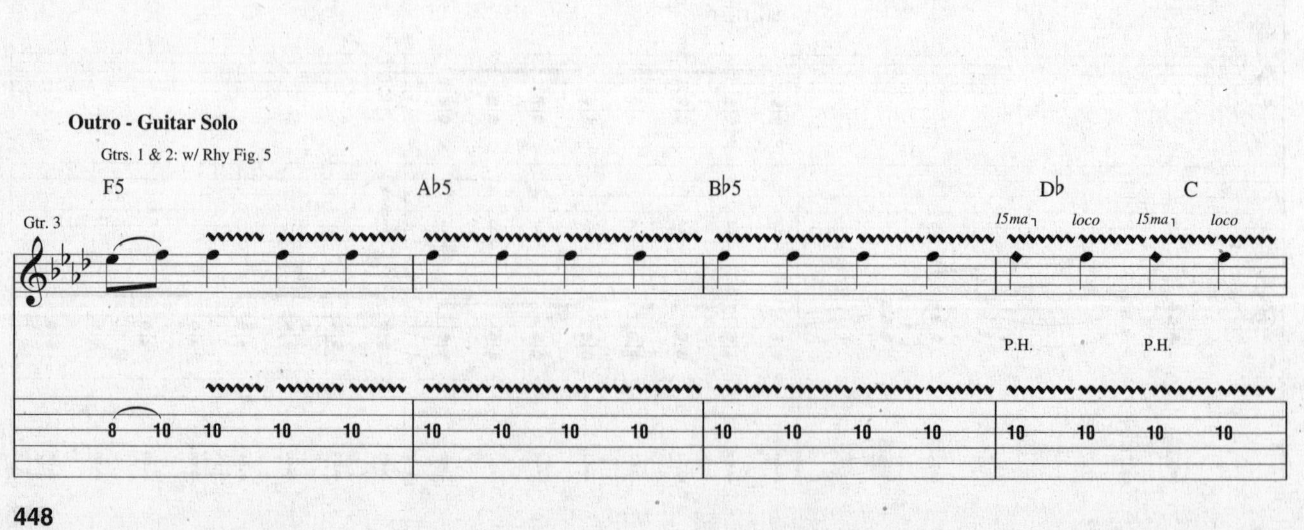

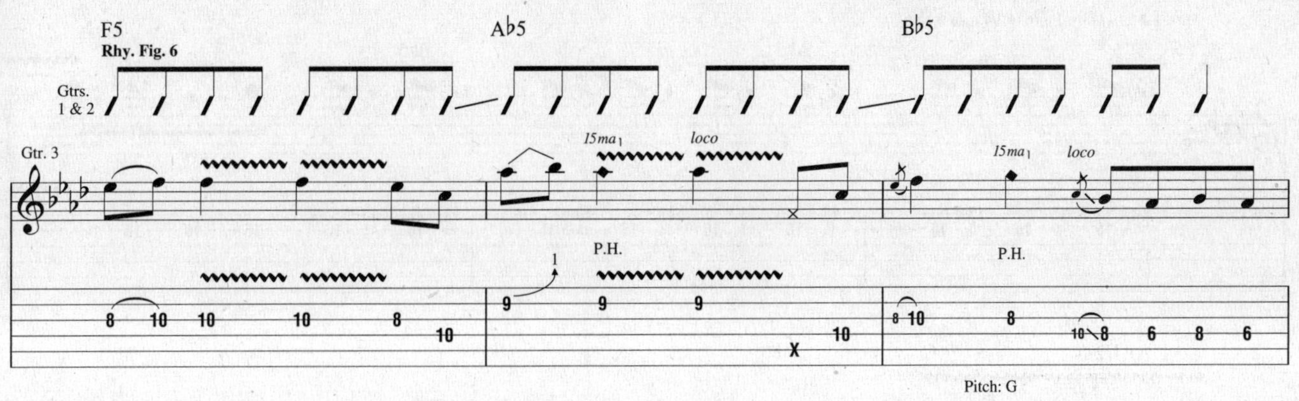
F5
Rhy. Fig. 6
Gtrs. 1 & 2
A♭5
B♭5
Gtr. 3
15ma
loco
P.H.
Pitch: G

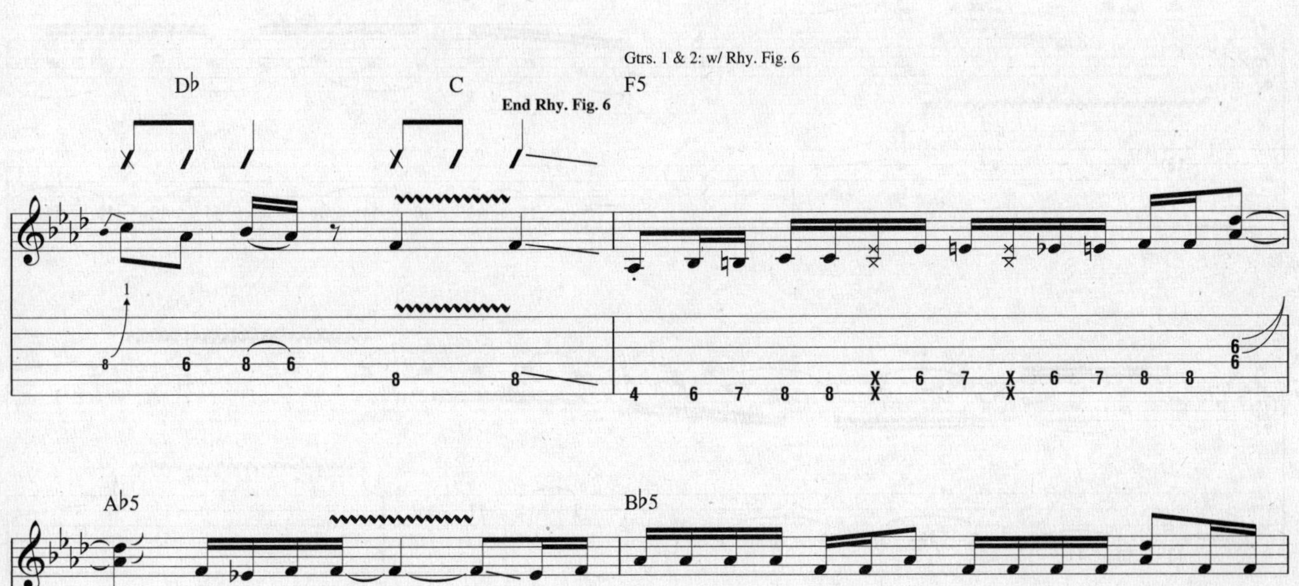
D♭
C
End Rhy. Fig. 6
Gtrs. 1 & 2: w/ Rhy. Fig. 6
F5

A♭5
B♭5

D♭
C
Gtrs. 1 & 2: w/ Rhy. Fig. 5
F5
A♭5
P.H.
Pitches: D E D E D E

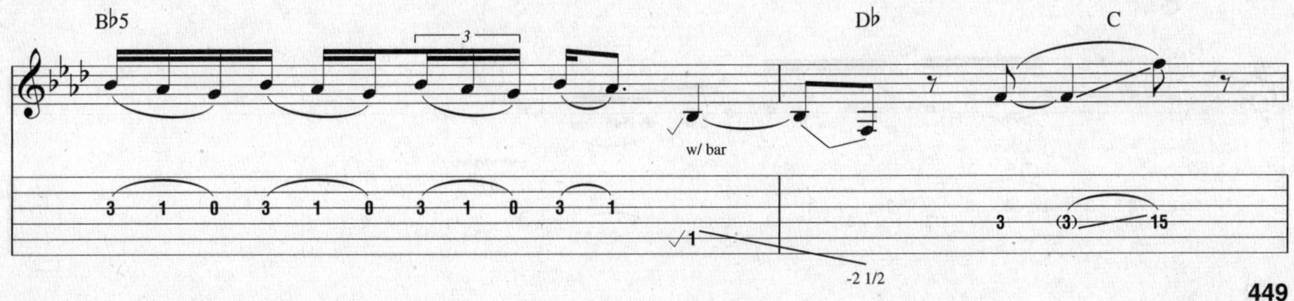
B♭5
D♭
C
w/ bar
-2 1/2

Gtrs. 1 & 2: w/ Rhy. Fig. 6 (1 3/4 times)

F5 Ab5 Bb5

Db C F5

Ab5 Bb5

Free time

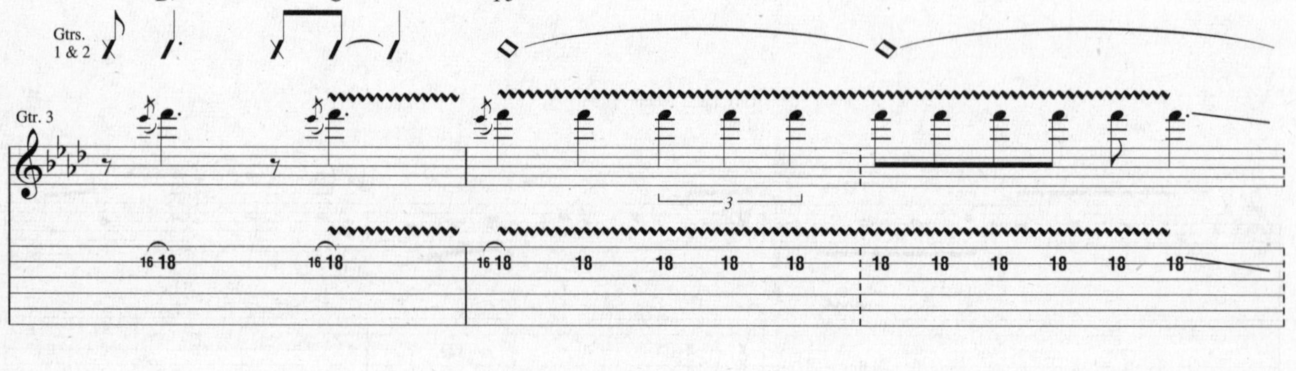

Heaven

Words and Music by Henry Garza, Joey Garza and Ringo Garza

Tune down 1/2 step:
(low to high) E♭-A♭-D♭-G♭-B♭-E♭

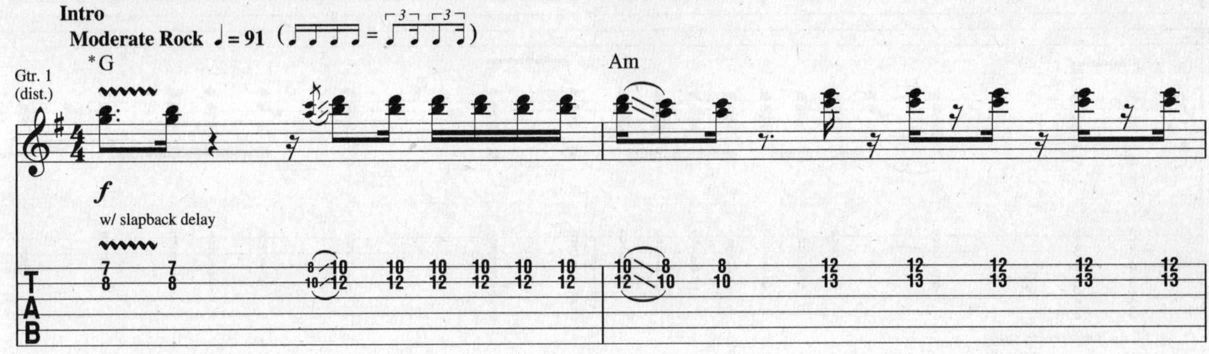

*Chord symbols reflect implied harmony.

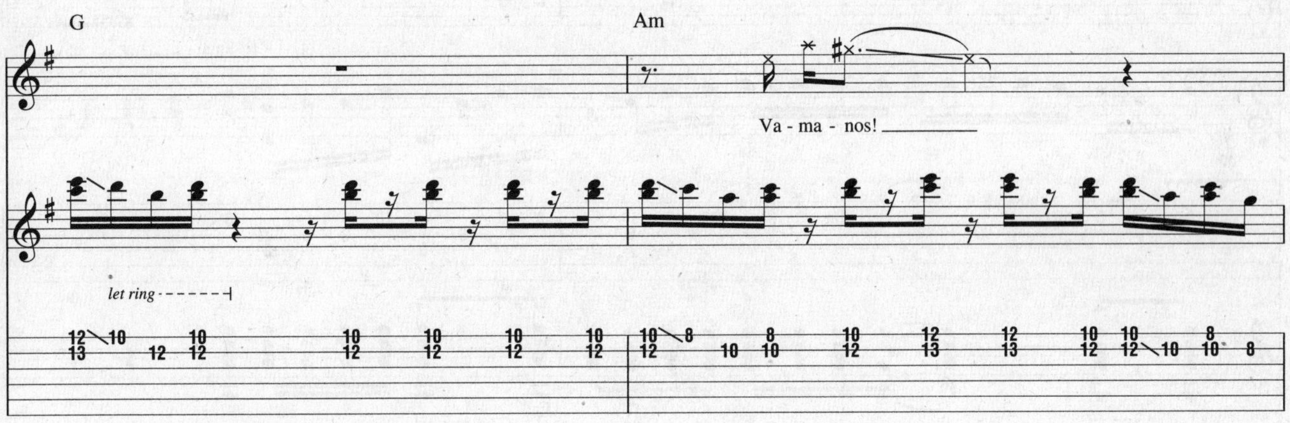

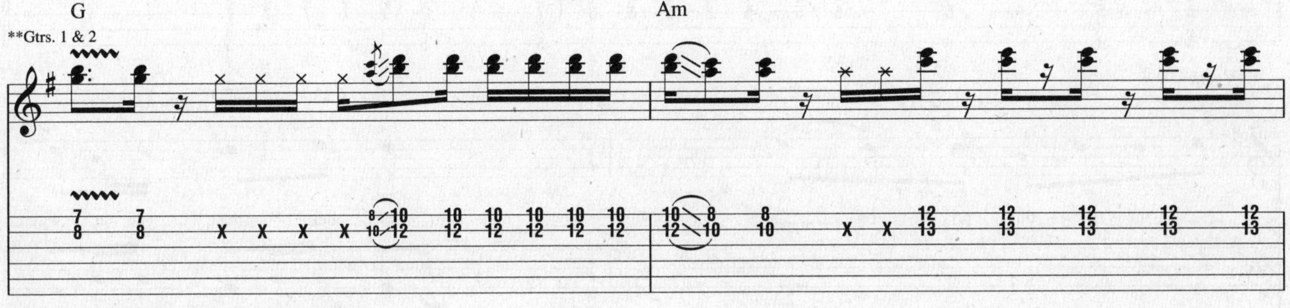

**Composite arrangement, Gtr. 2 (clean) played *mf*.

G
Gsus4 G
Am
Asus4 Am
Asus4 Am
Gtr. 1
rake
Gtr. 2
*T = Thumb on 6th string
N.C.
1. Save
Verse
me from this pris - on,
Lord, help me get a - way.
Am7 Am
P.M.
Rhy. Fig. 1
End Rhy. Fig. 1

G
Gsus4 G
Am
'cause on
Riff A
End Riff A
P.M.
T
Gtr. 1: w/ Riff A
Asus4 Am Am7
ly you can save me now
from this mis - er - y.
Gtr. 2
N.C.
2. I've
Gtr. 1
Rhy. Fig. 2
End Rhy. Fig. 2

Verse
G
Gsus4 G
Am
Asus4
Am
been lost in my own place
and I'm get - tin' wear - y.
Riff B
End Riff B
P.M.
T
Gtr. 1: w/ Riff B (2 times)
*Voc. Fig. 1
End Voc. Fig. 1
(How far is heav - en?)
And I
Gtr. 2
*Applies to upstemmed part only.
Am(add9)
know that I need to change
my ways of liv - in'.

Bkgd. Voc.: w/ Voc. Fig. 1
G
Gsus4 G
Am
N.C.
Lord, can you tell me?
Gtr. 1
P.M.
Gtr. 2
T
Interlude
Gtr. 2: w/ Rhy. Fig. 2
let ring
Verse
Gtr. 2: w/ Rhy. Fig. 1 (2 times)
Am7 Am
3. I've been locked up way too long in this cra - zy world.
mf

Bkgd. Voc.: w/ Voc. Fig. 1
G
Gsus4 G
Am
Am7 Am
And I'll
Riff C
End Riff C
P.M.
Gtr. 1: w/ Riff C (2 times)
just keep on pray - in', Lord,
and just keep on liv - in'.
Rhy. Fig. 3
Gtr. 2
Bkgd. Voc.: w/ Voc. Fig. 1 (3 times)
Asus4
Yeah,
Lord, can you tell me?
End Rhy. Fig. 3
Gtr. 2: w/ Rhy. Fig. 3
'Cause I just got to know how far,
Gtr. 1

G
Gsus4 G
Am
yeah.
Yeah,
Lord, can you tell me?
P.M.
P.M.

Guitar Solo

G
Gsus4 G
Am
Asus4
Am
Asus4
Am
Gtr. 1
Gtr. 2

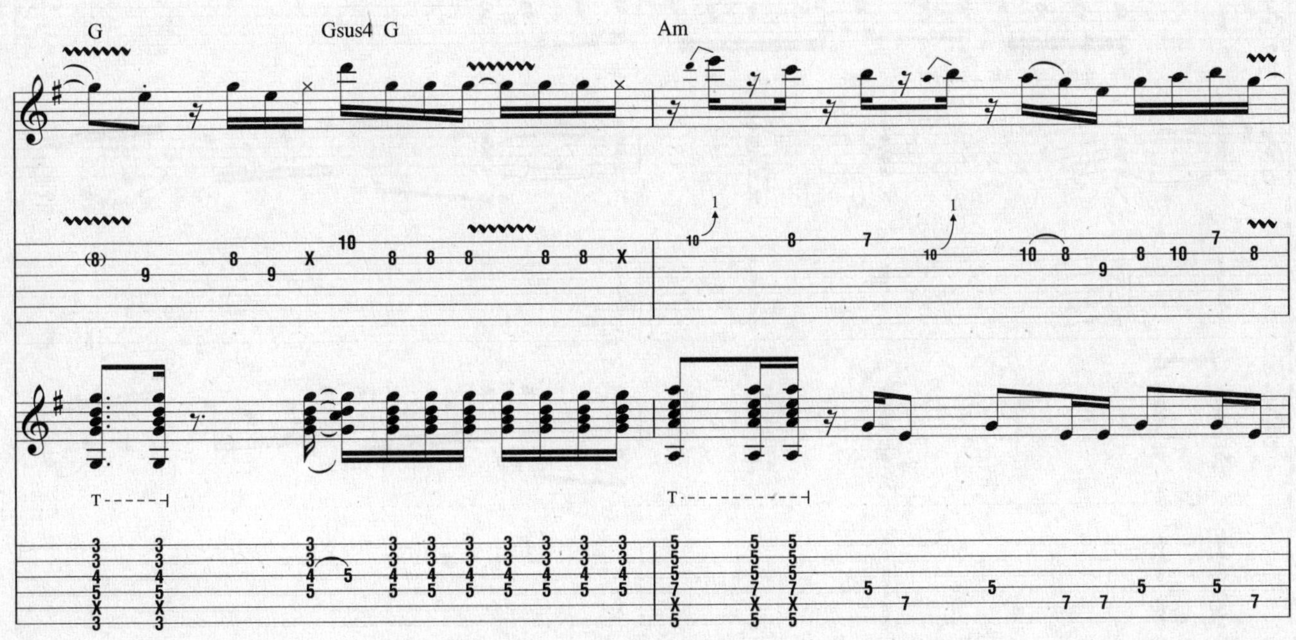

G
Gsus4 G
Am

G
Gsus4
Am
rake
Asus4
Bridge
A#m
Bm
Tú que es - tás en - trad - o al ci - el - o,
Gtr. 1
Gtr. 2
let ring

Gtr. 2 tacet
F C D N.C.
he - cha - me tu ben - di - ci - ón. 4. 'Cause I
Gtrs. 1 & 2
Gtr. 1
rake
Verse
G Am Asus4 Am Asus4 Am
know there's a bet - ter place than this place I'm liv - in'.
Gtr. 1
Riff D
mf
P.M.
Gtr. 2
Bkgd. Voc.: w/ Voc. Fig. 1
G Am
And I
End Riff D
P.M.

Gtr. 1: w/ Riff D (2 times)
Gtr. 2: w/ Rhy. Fig. 3 (2 1/2 times)
G
Gsus4 G
Am
just got to have some faith, and just keep on giv - ing.
Bkgd. Voc.: w/ Voc. Fig. 1 (4 times)
G
Gsus4 G
Am
G
Gsus4 G
Yeah, Lord, can you tell me?
Am
G
Gsus4 G
Am
'Cause I just got to know how far, yeah.
Yeah, Lord, can you tell me?
G
Gsus4 G
Am
'Cause I just got - ta know how far.
(Oh.)
(Oh.)
Gtr. 1
P.M.
Outro
G
Gsus4 G
Am
I just wan - na know how far.
Gtr. 1
f
let ring
Gtr. 2
T
T

G Gsus4 G Am Am(add9) Am Asus4 Am

T

T

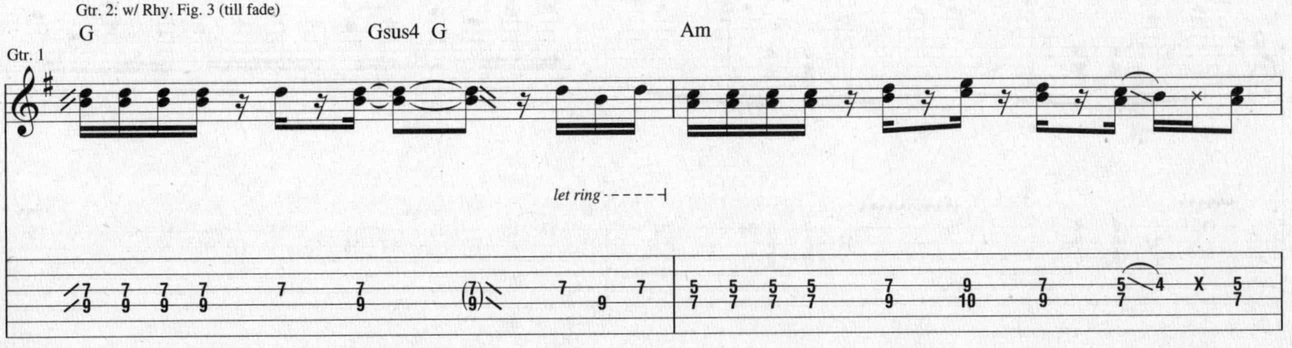

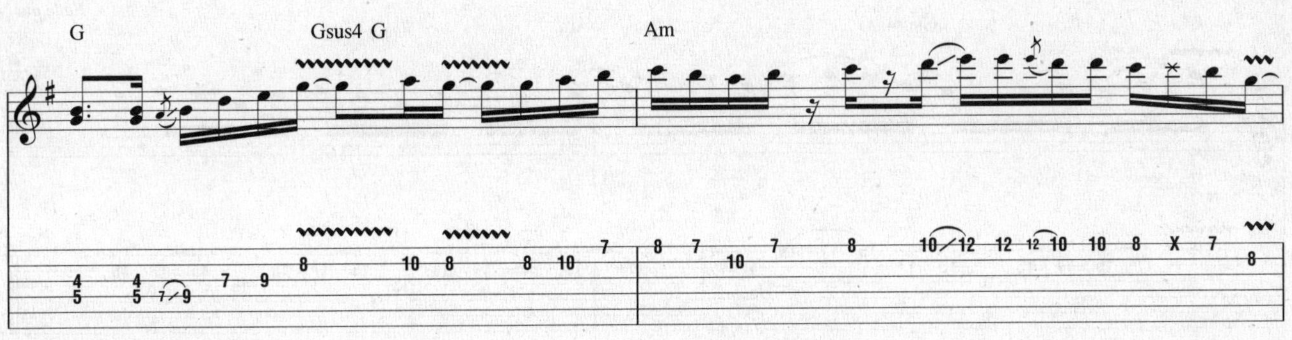

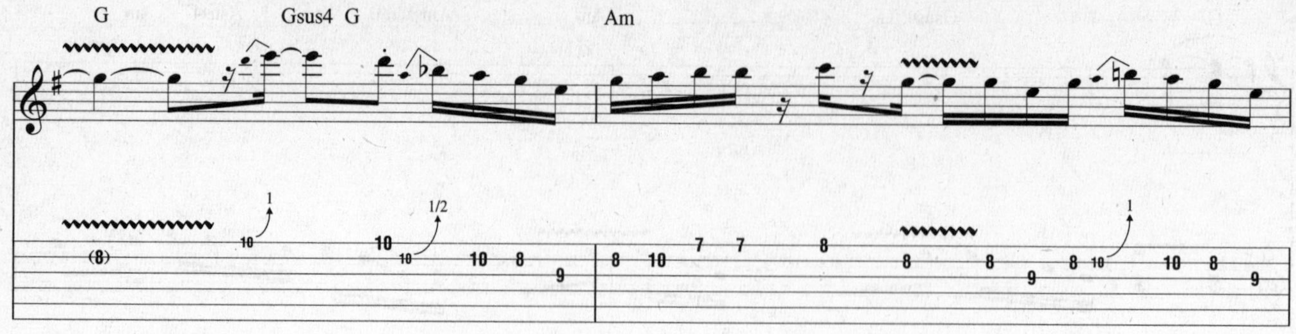
G
Gsus4 G
Am

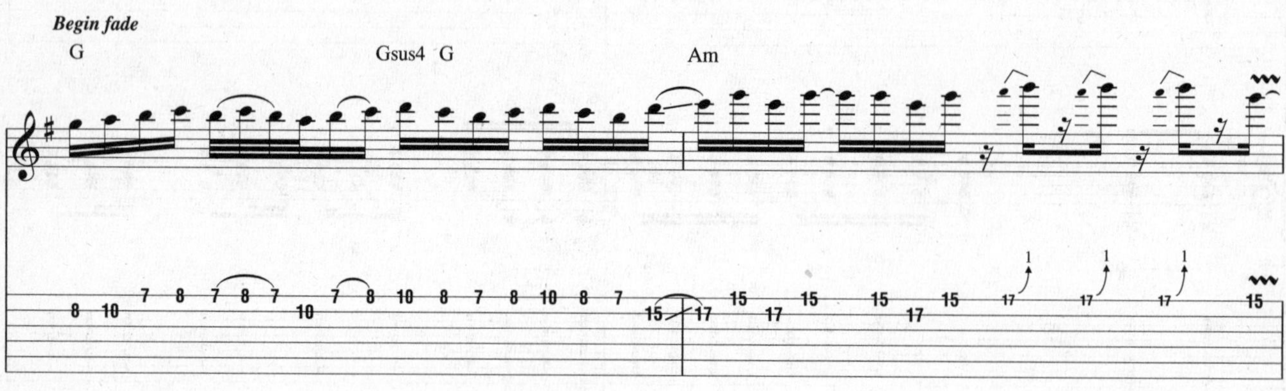
Begin fade
G
Gsus4 G
Am

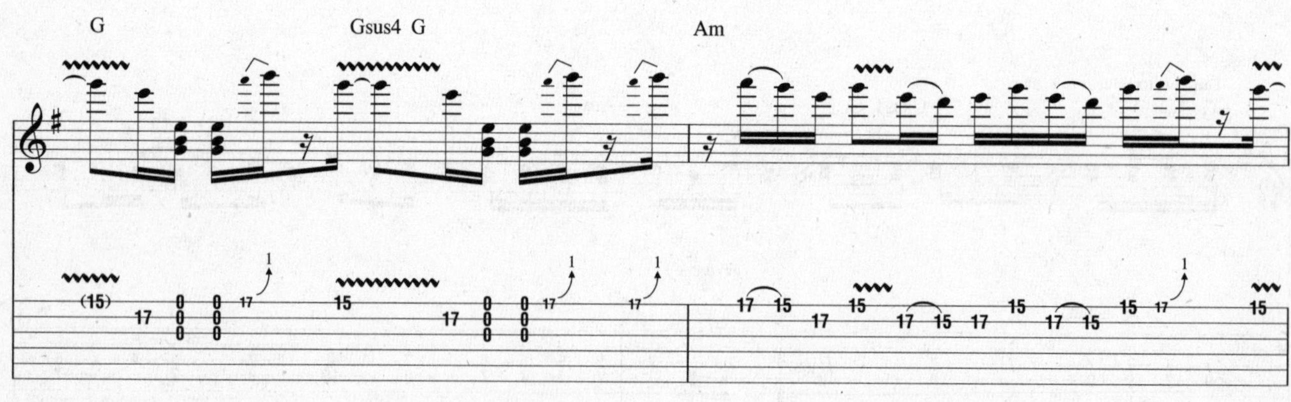
G
Gsus4 G
Am

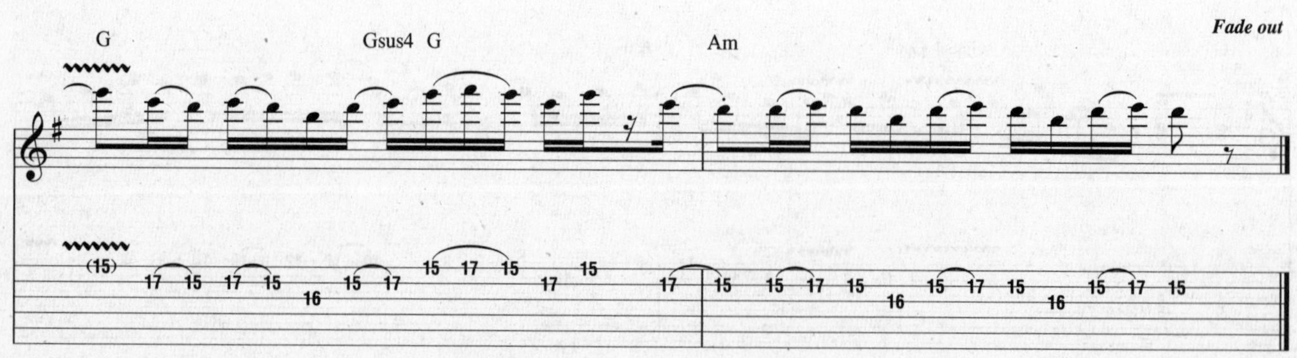
Fade out
G
Gsus4 G
Am

Heaven Tonight

Words and Music by Yngwie Malmsteen and Joe Lynn Turner

Verse
* F#m
D/F#
F#m
1. Lost in a dream in the arms of the night, two lone - ly pris - 'ners of our
* Chord symbols reflect overall harmony.
D/F#
F#m
A
E
own de - vice. Don't let me go, hold on to - geth -
let ring
C#/E#
F#m
er. You wan - na know if love
let ring
D/F#
F#m
D/F#
can be real. I wan - na take ev - 'ry - thing I can steal.

F#m A E C#/E#
Love on the line, it's now or nev - er.
P.M.
Pre-Chorus
D A/C# Bm A E/G# D/F#
Why can't the night last for - ev - er?
* Riff A
Gtr. 1
Gtr. 2 (dist.) divisi
f
1/2
* Includes Gtrs. 1 & 2
** Gtr. 2 to right of slash in tab.
Chorus
C#/E# C# Gtr. 2 tacet E Dsus#4/E
This could be par -
Gtrs. 1 & 2
End Riff A
Gtr. 1
Rhy. Fig. 1
*** P.M.
*** P.M. on ⑥, next 8 meas.
D/E C/E D/E
- a - dise, hold - ing you here by my side.

E
Dsus#4/E
D/E
C/E
D/E
If we just close our eyes, we'll be in heav -
- en to - night.
Verse
F#m
D/F#
2. Run through the night down streets of de - sire.
End Rhy. Fig. 1
P.M.
F#m
D/F#
F#m
A
E
Burn - in' my soul, my heart's on fire.
Give up the fight, it's sweet sur - ren -
w/ bar
C#/E#
F#m
- der.
With trem - bling hands, we reach
P.M.

D/F# F#m D/F# F#m A
for it all. Two des-p'rate hearts wait - in' to fall. I need you now,
E C#/E#
now more than ev - er.
w/ bar
let ring
w/ bar
Pre-Chorus
Gtrs. 1 & 2: w/ Riff A
D A/C# Bm A E/G# D/F# C#/E# C#
Why can't the night last for - ev - er?
Chorus
Gtr. 1: w/ Rhy. Fig. 1
E Dsus#4/E D/E C/E D/E
This could be par - a - dise, hold - ing you here
Gtr. 2
mf

E
Dsus♯4/E
D/E
— by my side. If we — just close — our eyes,
(Heav - en to -
P.M.
P.M.
P.M.
Harm.

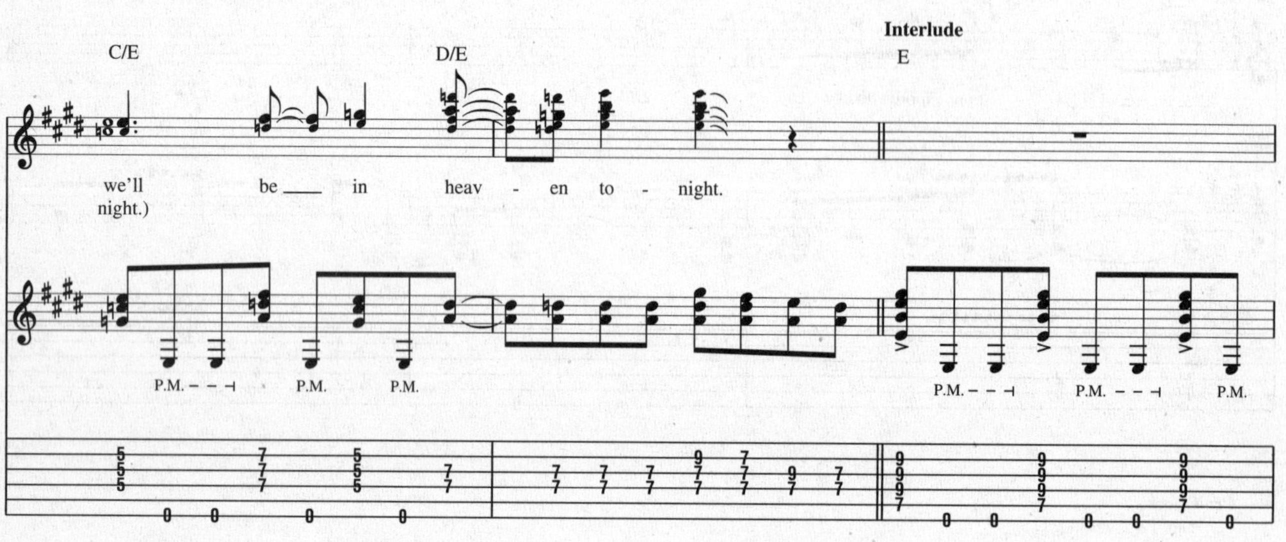
C/E
D/E
Interlude
E
we'll be — in heav - en to - night.
night.)
P.M.
P.M.
P.M.
P.M.
P.M.
P.M.

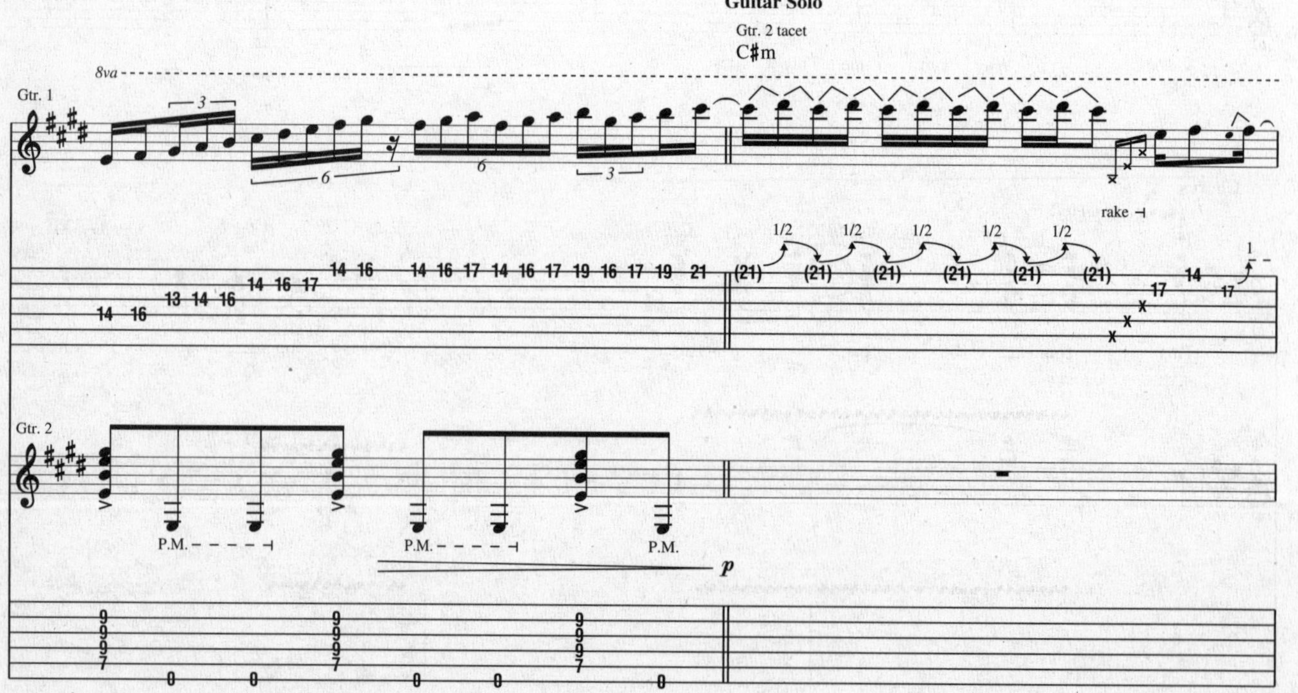
Guitar Solo
Gtr. 2 tacet
C♯m
8va
Gtr. 1
rake
Gtr. 2
P.M.
P.M.
P.M.
p

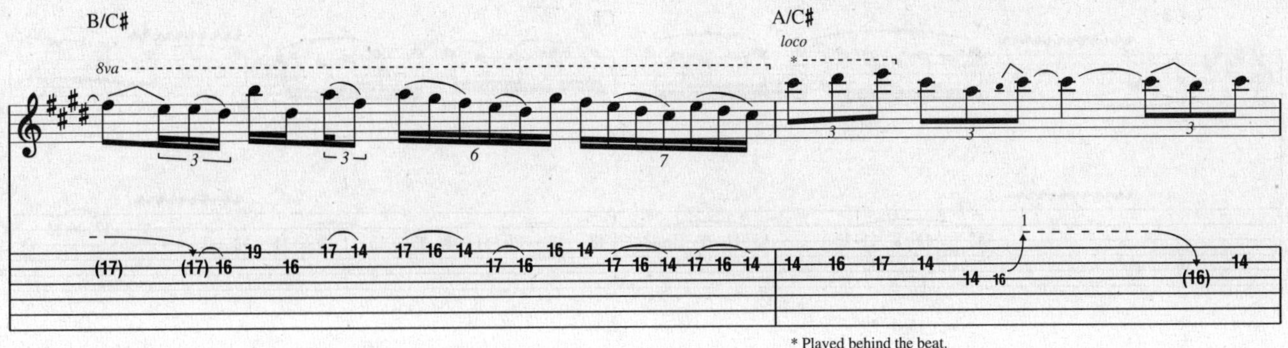

* Played behind the beat.

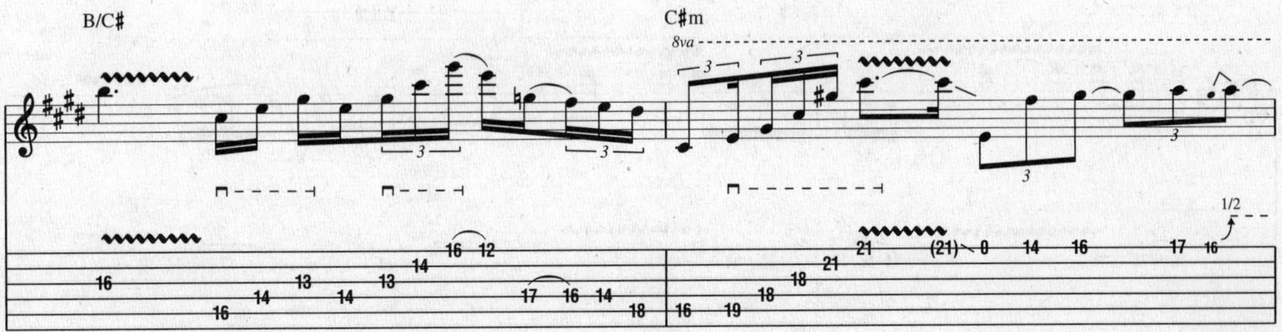

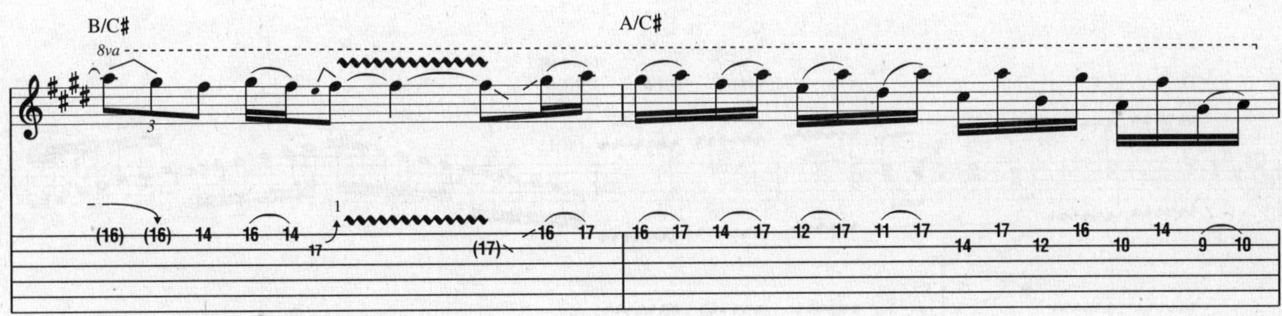

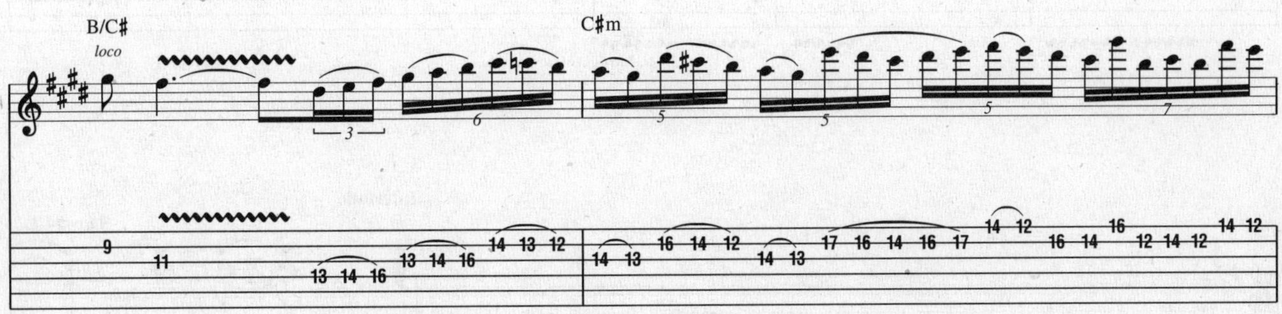

** Played behind the beat.

B/C#
C#m

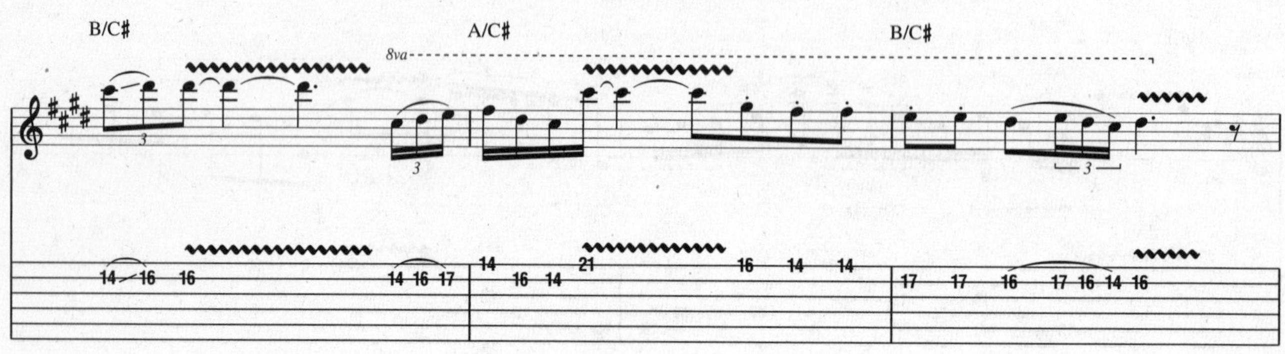
B/C#
A/C#
8va
B/C#

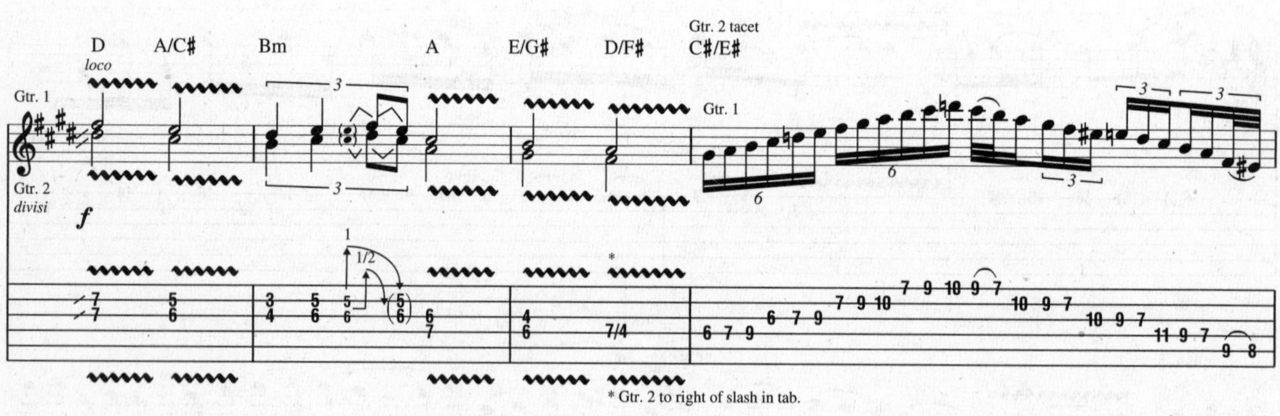
Gtr. 2 tacet
D
A/C#
Bm
A
E/G#
D/F#
C#/E#
loco
Gtr. 1
Gtr. 2
divisi
f
* Gtr. 2 to right of slash in tab.

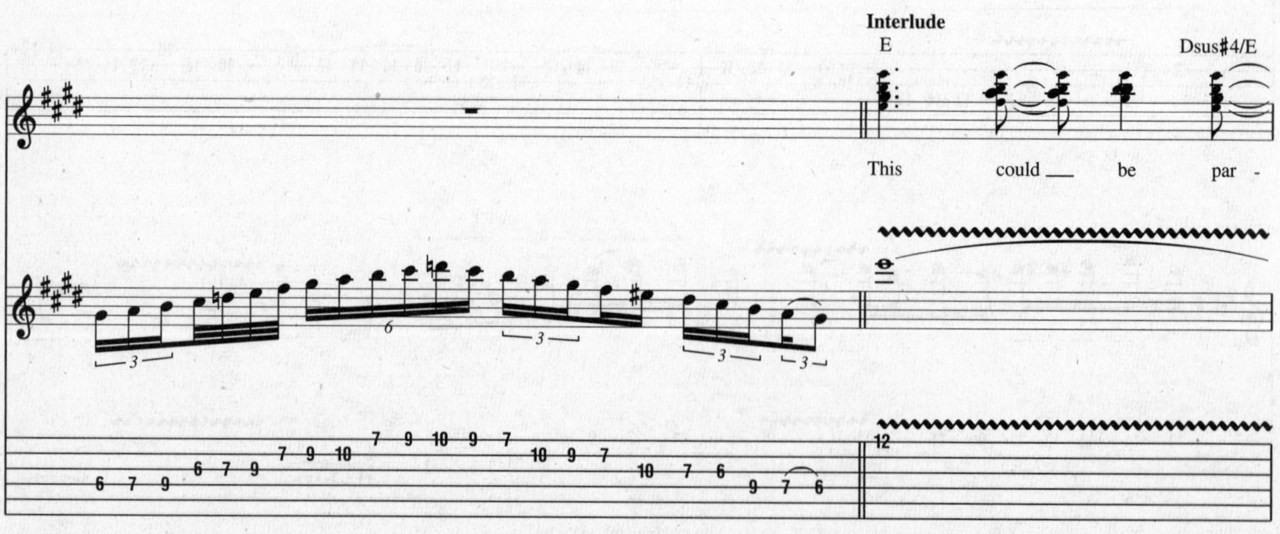
Interlude
E
Dsus#4/E
This could ___ be par -

Gtr. 1 tacet
D/E
C/E
D/E
- a - dise,
hold - ing ___ you here ___ by my side.
(12)
Dsus#4/E
D/E
C/E
D/E
If we ___ just close ___ our eyes,
we'll be ___ in heav -
- en to - night.
Gtr. 1
* steady gliss.
17 16 15 14 13 12 11 10 9 8 7 6 5 4 3 2
* Slide L.H. finger down string.
Outro-Chorus
Gtr. 1: w/ Rhy. Fig. 1 (till fade)
w/ Voc. ad Lib (till fade)
E
Dsus#4/E
D/E
C/E
D/E
This could _ be par - a - dise,
hold - ing ___ you here ___ by my side.
This feels _ like par - a - dise,
I see ___ the world ___ in your eyes.
(Heav - en to - night.)
E
Dsus#4/E
D/E
C/E
D/E
If we ___ just close ___ our eyes, hold ___ on tight,
we'll be ___ in heav - en to - night.
(Heav - en to - night.)
Play 3 times and fade
E
Dsus#4/E
D/E
C/E
D/E
This feels _ like par - a - dise,
we'll be ___ in heav - en to - night.
(Heav - en to - night.)

Here I Go Again

Words and Music by Bernie Marsden and David Coverdale

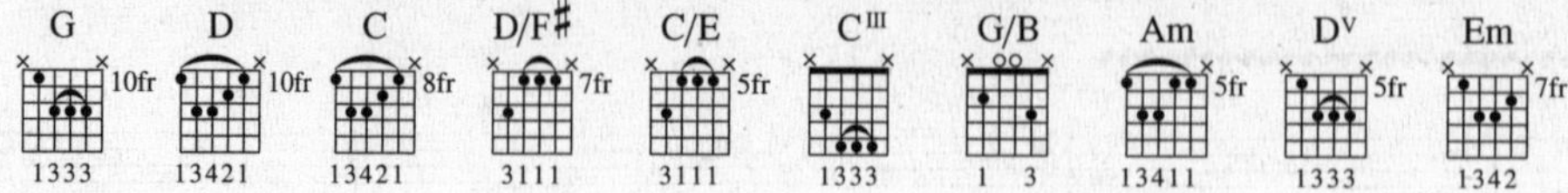

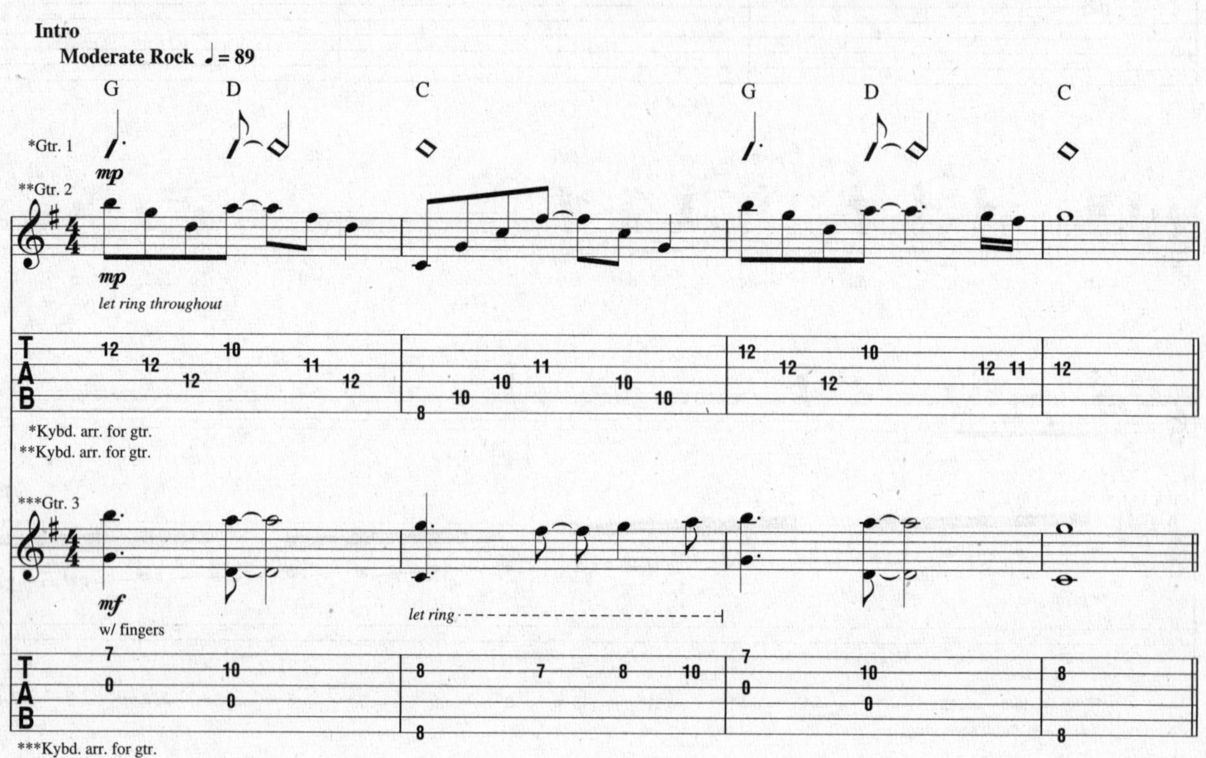

C G D/F# C/E D C^III G/B
5fr
been. Hang-in' on the prom-is-es and the songs of yes-ter-day,
let ring
Am D^V C B Am
8fr 7fr
and I've made up my mind, I ain't wast-in' no more time.
let ring
D^V Em Am C
Gtr. 2 tacet
End Rhy. Fig. 1
Gtr. 1
Here I go a-gain, here I go a-gain.
Gtr. 2
let ring
Gtr. 3
End. Rhy. Fig. 1A

Verse
Gtr. 1: w/ Rhy. Fig. 1
Gtr. 3: w/ Rhy. Fig. 1A (1st 9 meas.)
G Em Am C D *G D
Gtr. 1
2. Though I keep search - ing for an an -
Gtr. 3
Gtr. 2
*Chord symbols reflect overall harmony.
C G D C
- swer, I nev - er seem to find what I'm look - in' for.
G D/F# C/E C G/B Am
Oh, Lord, I pray you'll give me strength to car - ry on. 'Cause I know what it means
D Am D C D
to walk a - long the lone - ly street of dreams. And
Gtr. 3
*Gtrs. 4 & 5 (dist.)
divisi
mf
*Composite arrangement

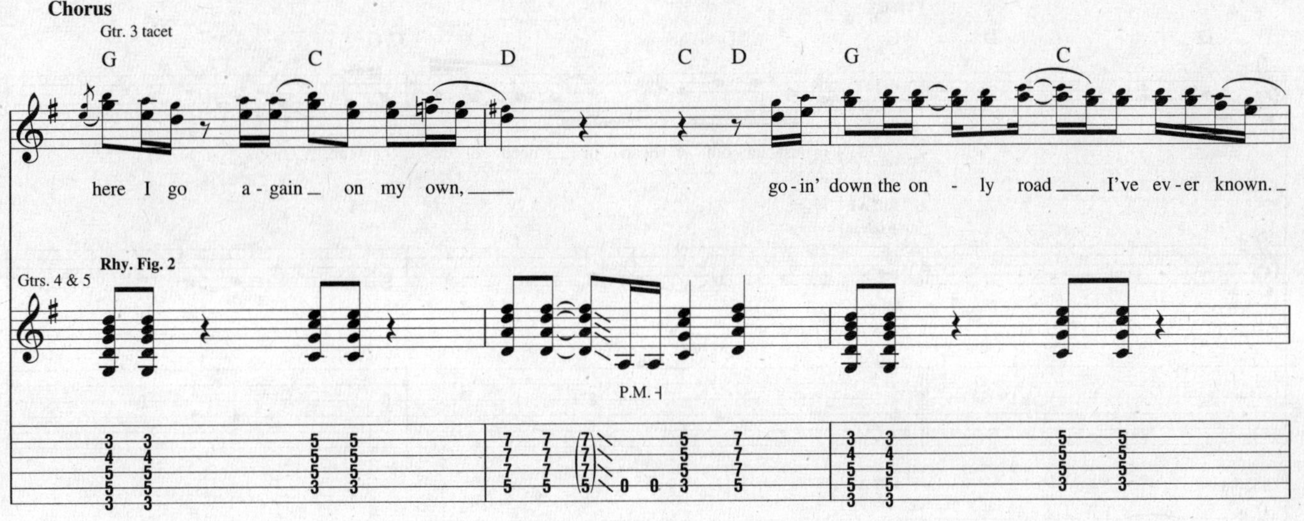
Chorus
Gtr. 3 tacet
G C D C D G C
here I go a-gain on my own, go-in' down the on-ly road I've ev-er known.
Rhy. Fig. 2
Gtrs. 4 & 5
P.M.

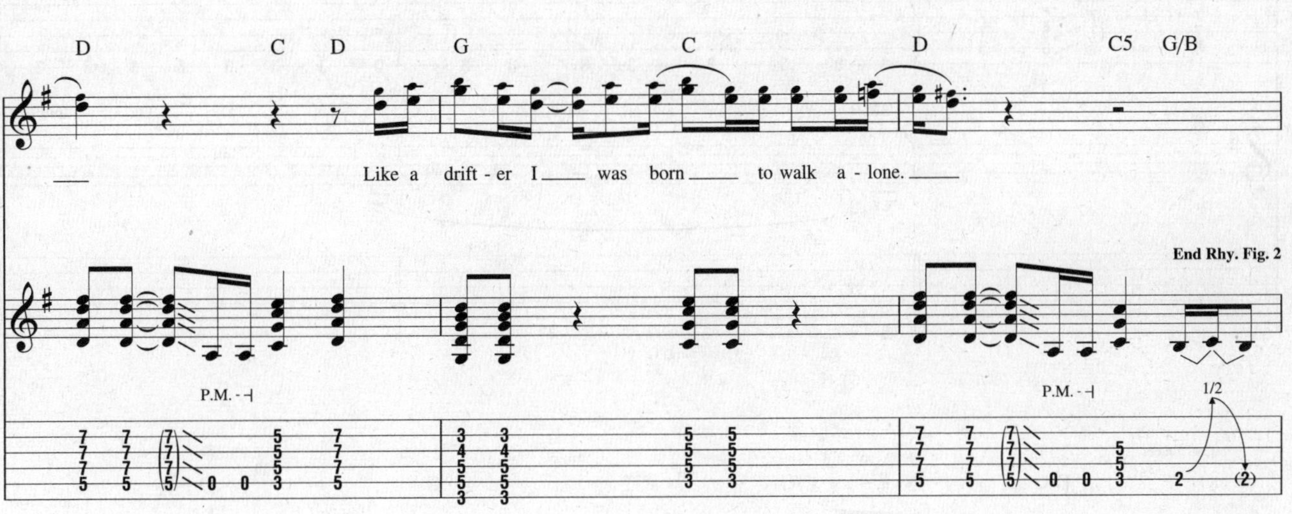
D C D G C D C5 G/B
Like a drift-er I was born to walk a-lone.
End Rhy. Fig. 2
P.M.
P.M.
1/2

Am7 D Am7
And I've made up my mind, I ain't wast-in' no more time.
P.M.
P.M.
P.M.

Verse
D
C
D
G
*D/G
C/G
3. I'm just an-oth-er heart in need of res - cue,
Riff A1
Gtr. 6 (clean)
mf
w/ reverb & chorus
let ring
Gtrs. 4 & 5
Riff A
Gtr. 4
P.M.
Riff B
Gtr. 5
End Riff B
*Bass plays G.
Gtr. 5 tacet
G
D/G
C/G
G
D/F♯
wait-in' on love's sweet char-i - ty.
And, I'm gon-na hold on for the
Gtr. 6
let ring
Gtr. 4
P.M.

Pre-Chorus
Gtr. 6 tacet
C/E C5 G/B Am7 D
rest of my days. 'Cause I know what it means to
Gtr. 6
End Riff A1
let ring
Gtr. 4
Gtrs. 4 & 5
End Riff A
Rhy. Fig. 3
P.M.
1/2

Am7 D C5 D5
walk a - long the lone - ly street of dreams. And
Gtrs. 4 & 5
End Rhy. Fig. 3
P.M.

Chorus
Gtrs. 4 & 5: w/ Rhy. Fig. 2
G C D C D G C
here I go a - gain on my own, go - in' down the on - ly road I've ev - er known.
D C D G C D C5 G/B
Like a drift - er I was born to walk a - lone.

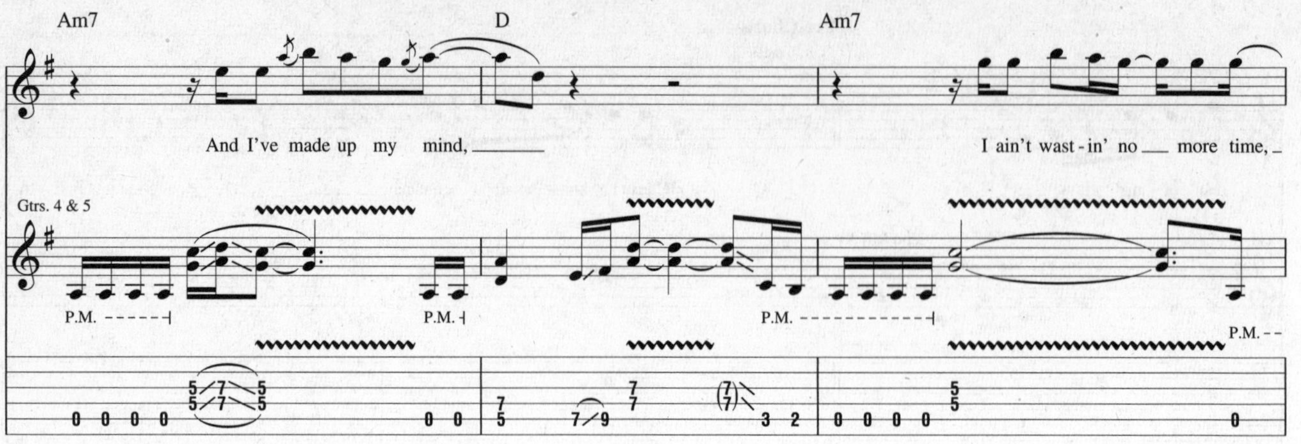

Am7
D
Am7
And I've made up my mind,
I ain't wast-in' no more time,
Gtrs. 4 & 5
P.M.
P.M.
P.M.
P.M.

Bridge

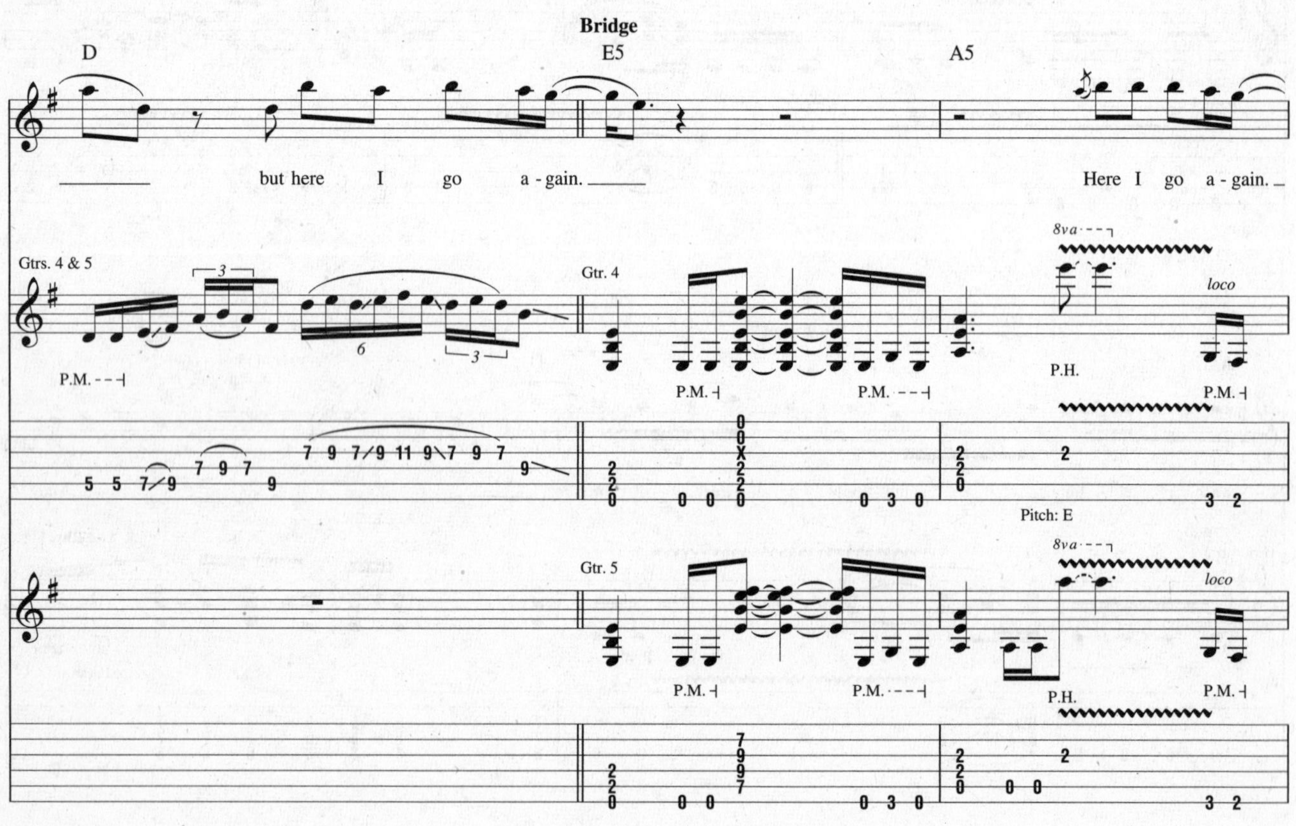

D
E5
A5
but here I go a-gain.
Here I go a-gain.
Gtrs. 4 & 5
P.M.
Gtr. 4
8va
loco
P.M.
P.M.
P.H.
P.M.
Pitch: E
Gtr. 5
8va
loco
P.M.
P.M.
P.H.
P.M.

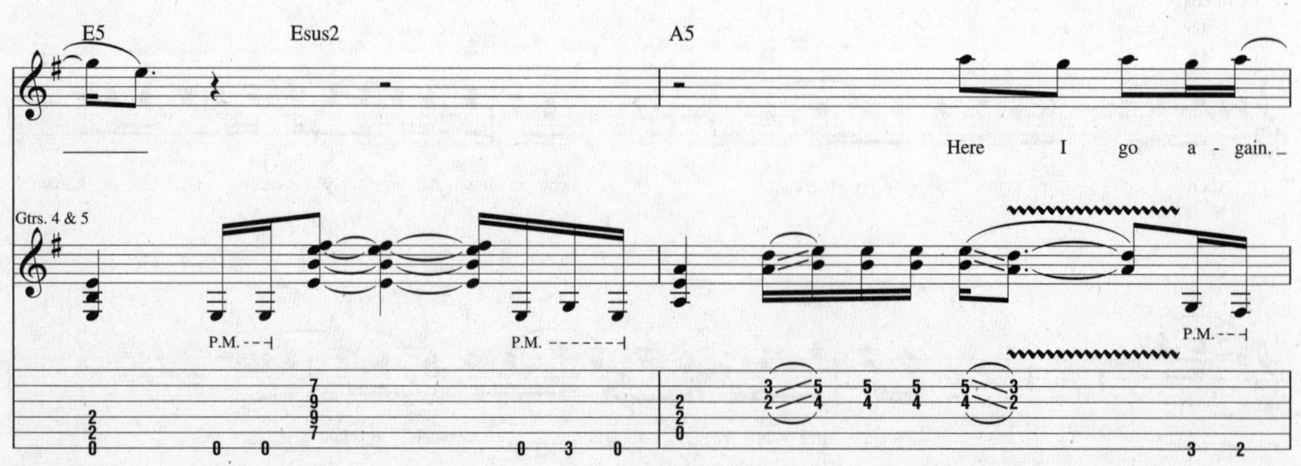

E5
Esus2
A5
Here I go a-gain.
Gtrs. 4 & 5
P.M.
P.M.
P.M.

Guitar Solo

Gtrs. 4 & 6: w/ Riffs A & A1
Gtr. 5: w/ Riff B

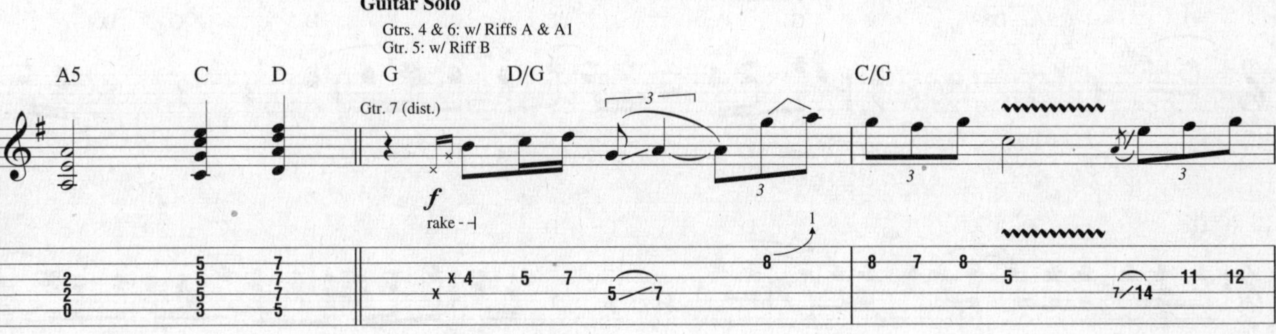

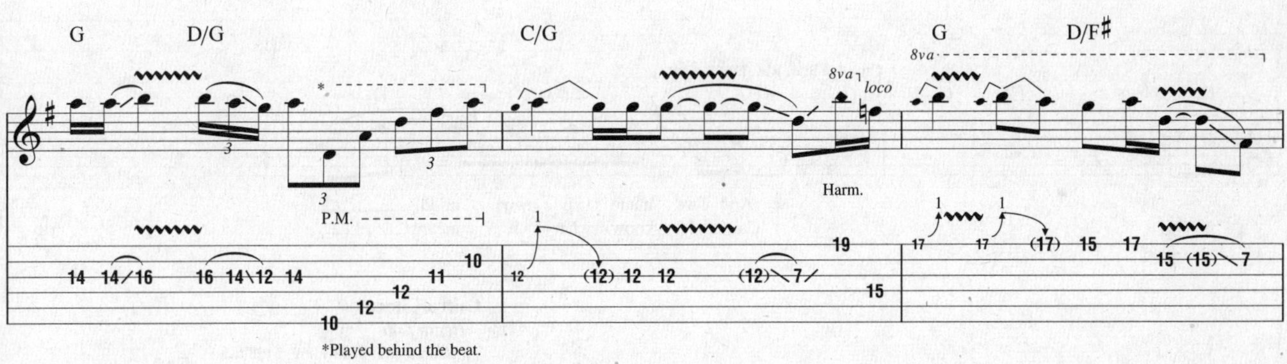

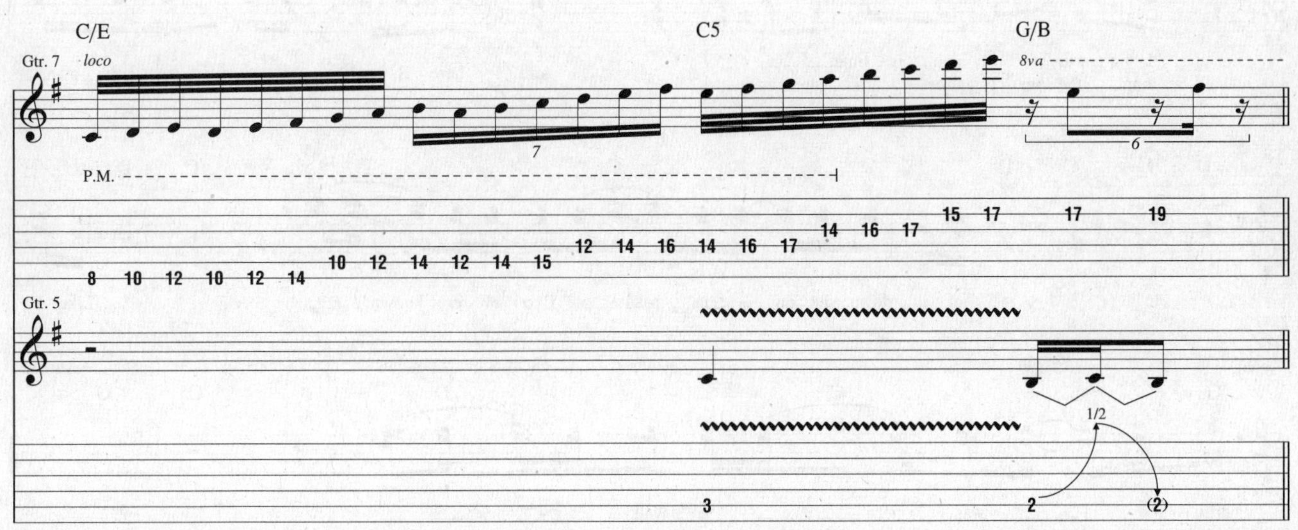

Pre-Chorus
Gtrs. 4 & 5: w/ Rhy. Fig. 3
Gtr. 7 tacet
Am7 D Am7
8va
'Cause I know what it means to walk a - long the lone - ly street of dreams.
Gtr. 7
1/2
19
Chorus
Gtrs. 4 & 5: w/ Rhy. Fig. 2
D C5 D5 G C D C D
And here I go a - gain on my own, go - in'
G C D C D G C
down the on - ly road I've ev - er known. Like a drift - er I was born to walk a - lone.
Gtrs. 4 & 5: w/ Rhy. Fig. 3
D C5 G Am7 D
And I've made up my mind,
'Cause I know what it means to
Outro-Chorus
Begin fade
Gtrs. 4 & 5: w/ Rhy. Fig. 2 (till fade)
Am7 D C5 D5 G C
I ain't wast - in' no more time.
walk a - long the lone - ly street of dreams.
And here I go a - gain on my own,
D C D G C D C D
go - in' down the on - ly road I've ev - er known. Like a
Fade out
G C D C5 G
drift - er I was born to walk a - lone.

Highway Star

Words and Music by Ritchie Blackmore, Ian Gillan, Roger Glover, Jon Lord and Ian Paice

F5
Ooh, it's a kill - in' ma - chine, it's got a ev - 'ry - thing.
Ooh, she's a kill - in' ma - chine, she's got a ev - 'ry - thing.
Ooh, I'm in heav - en a - gain, I got a ev - 'ry - thing.
Gtr. 1
slight P.M.
N.C.
D
Like a driv - in' pow - er, big fat tires and ev -
Like a mov - in' mouth, bod - y con - trol and ev -
Like a mov - in' ground, throt - tle con - trol and ev -
slight P.M.
let ring
A5
Am7
'ry - thing. I love it! And I need it! I bleed it!
'ry - thing. I love her! And I need her! I seed her!
'ry - thing. I love it! And I need it! I seed it!
slight P.M.
P.M.
N.C.(C)
(D)
(C)
Yeah, it's a wild hur - ri - cane!
Yeah, she turns me on!
Eight cylinders, all mine!
All right! Hold

To Coda 2
(D)
(C)
(D)
(F)
(G)
(A5)
tight!
I'm
a
high
-
way
star!
1.
2.
To Coda 1
Keyboard Solo
N.C.
(D5)
play 4 times
(cont. in slash, 3rd time)
P.M. throughout
play 3 times
(A5)
(E)
(Gm)
(D)
(F)
Gtr. 1
(Dm)
(Am)
let ring throughout

slight P.M.

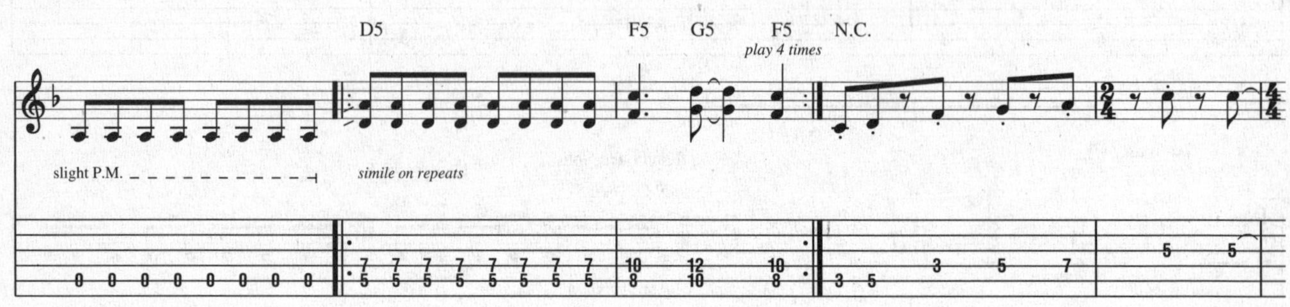
D5
F5
G5
F5
play 4 times
N.C.
slight P.M.
simile on repeats

D.S. al Coda 1
C5
B♭5

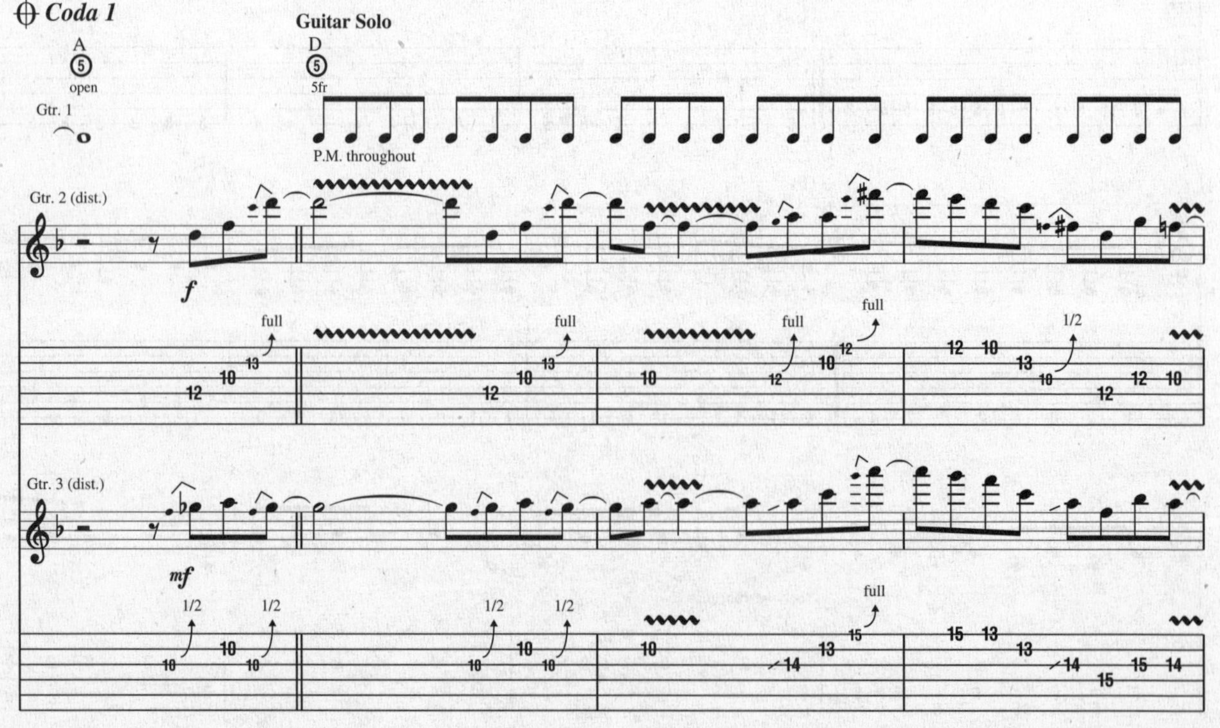
Coda 1
Guitar Solo
A
open
D
5fr
Gtr. 1
P.M. throughout
Gtr. 2 (dist.)
Gtr. 3 (dist.)

full
full
full
1/2
full
full
full
A
open
steady gliss.
full
full
1/2
1/2
full
full
1/2
steady gliss.
full
full
full
full
full
full
1/2
1/2
1/4
1/2
1/2
1/2
1/2
1/2
full
full
full
1/2
1/2
1/2
1/2
1/2
1/2
full
full
full

D
5
5fr
Rhy. Fig. 3
G
6
3fr
full
End Rhy. Fig. 3
C
5
3fr
let ring
G
4
5fr
C
3
5fr
A
6
5fr
P.M. throughout

Gtr. 1: w/ Rhy. Fig. 3, 2nd time, simile
let ring
full

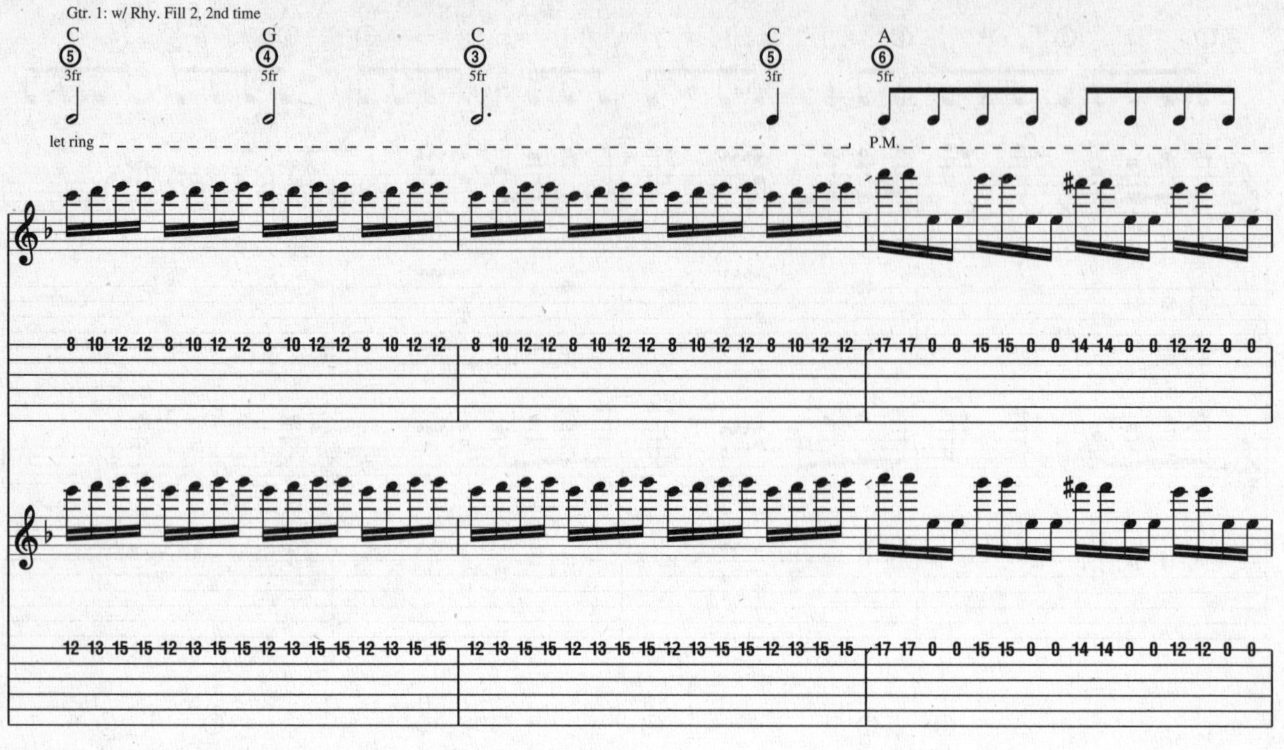

Gtr. 1: w/ Rhy. Fill 2, 2nd time
C
5
3fr
G
4
5fr
C
3
5fr
C
5
3fr
A
6
5fr
let ring
P.M.
8 10 12 12 8 10 12 12 8 10 12 12 8 10 12 12
8 10 12 12 8 10 12 12 8 10 12 12 8 10 12 12
17 17 0 0 15 15 0 0 14 14 0 0 12 12 0 0
12 13 15 15 12 13 15 15 12 13 15 15 12 13 15 15
12 13 15 15 12 13 15 15 12 13 15 15 12 13 15 15
17 17 0 0 15 15 0 0 14 14 0 0 12 12 0 0

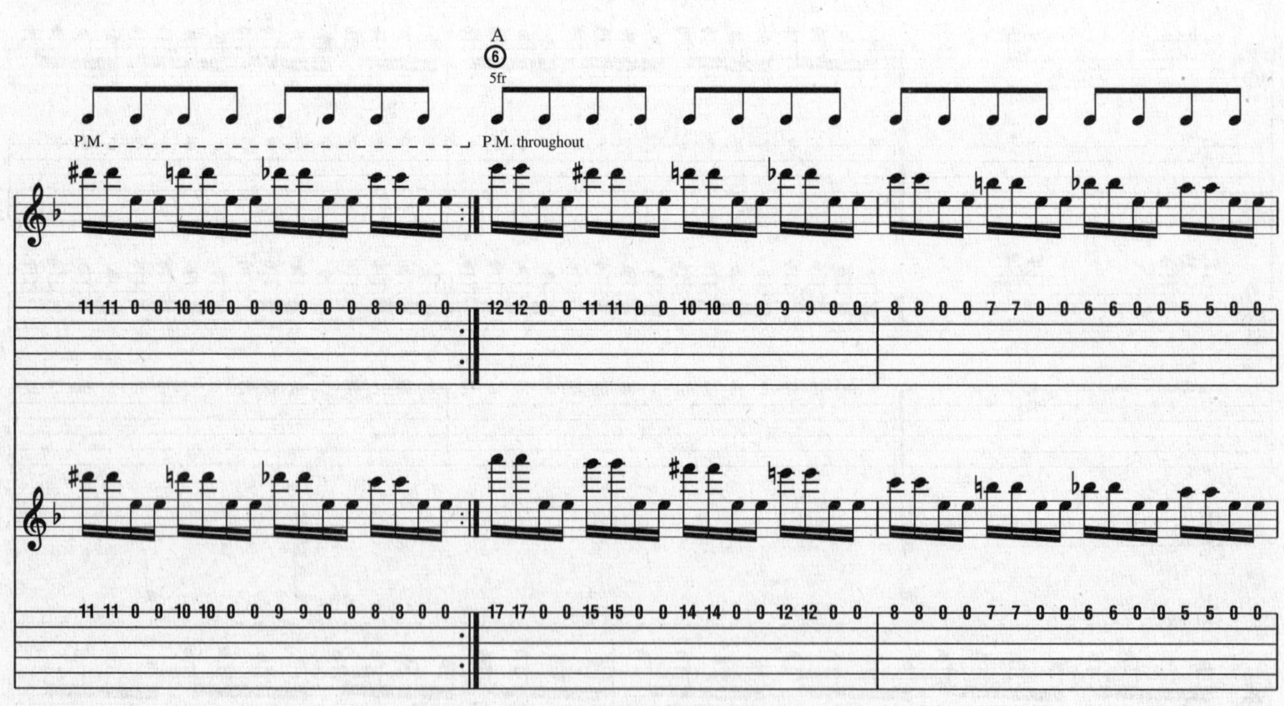

A
6
5fr
P.M.
P.M. throughout
11 11 0 0 10 10 0 0 9 9 0 0 8 8 0 0
12 12 0 0 11 11 0 0 10 10 0 0 9 9 0 0
8 8 0 0 7 7 0 0 6 6 0 0 5 5 0 0
11 11 0 0 10 10 0 0 9 9 0 0 8 8 0 0
17 17 0 0 15 15 0 0 14 14 0 0 12 12 0 0
8 8 0 0 7 7 0 0 6 6 0 0 5 5 0 0

Rhy. Fill 2
Gtr. 1
P.M.
T
A
B
3 3 3 3 3 3 3 3
3 3 3 3 3 3 3 3

full
D.S. al Coda 2
(1st lyrics)
Gtr. 1: w/ Rhy. Fill 1
C
B♭
w/ bar
Coda 2
N.C. (G)
(A)
(C)
(D)
(F)
(G)
(A)
(C)
- way star! I'm a high - way star! I'm
Free Time
(D)
(F)
(G)
(A)
a high - way star!
rit.
3/4
1/2

Hold On Loosely

Words and Music by Don Barnes, Jeff Carlisi and James Michael Peterik

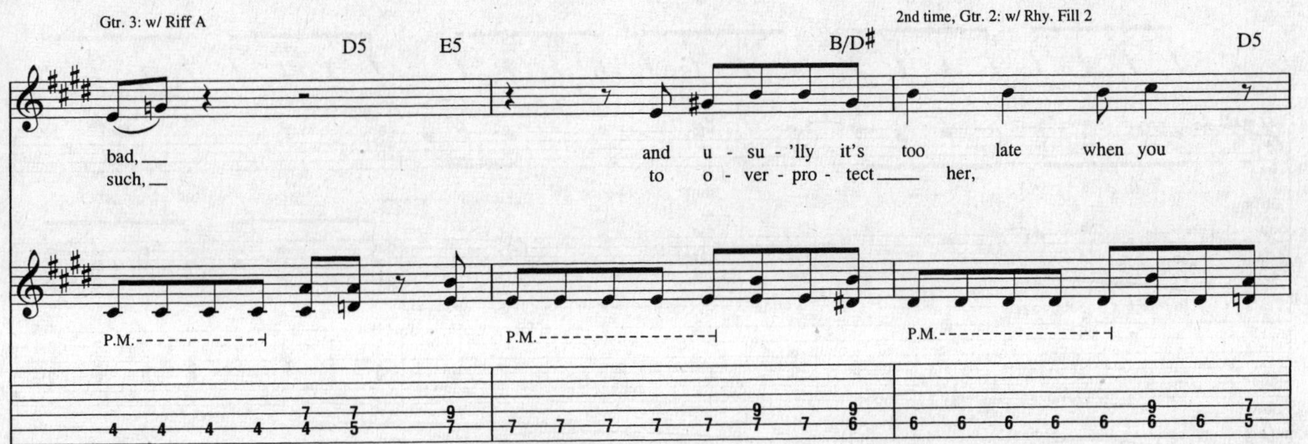

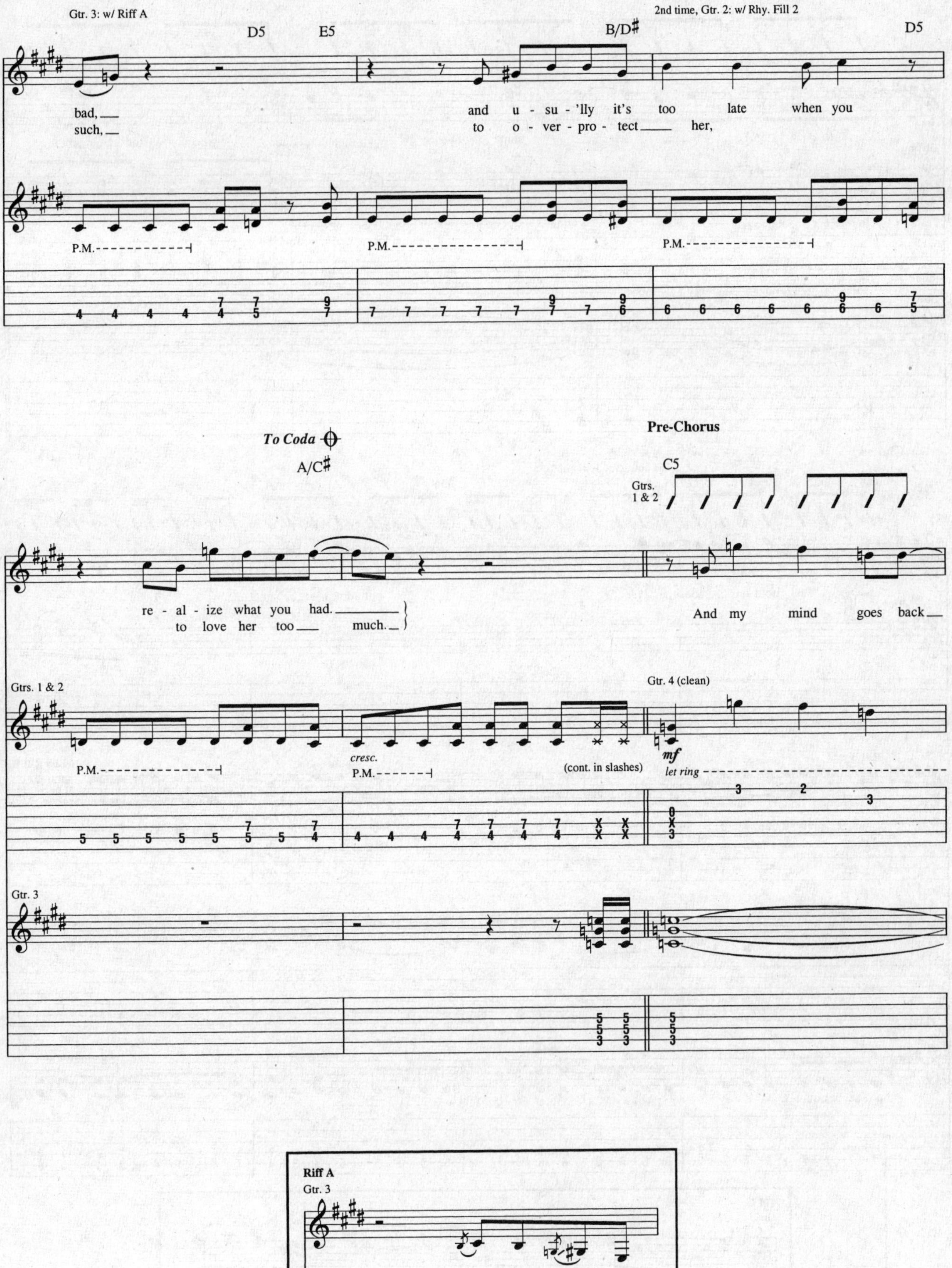

To Coda

Pre-Chorus

A/C♯

C5

Gtrs. 1 & 2

re - al - ize what you had. ___
to love her too ___ much. __

And my mind goes back __

Gtrs. 1 & 2

cresc.

P.M.

P.M.

(cont. in slashes)

Gtr. 4 (clean)

mf

let ring

Gtr. 3

D5
(Gtr. 2, cont. in notation)
to a girl I left some years a - go who told me,
Gtr. 4
let ring
Gtr. 3
Chorus
2nd time, Gtr. 5: w/ Fill 1
E5
B/D#
D5
A/C#
D5
Gtr. 1
"Just hold on loose - ly,
but don't let go.
Gtr. 5 (dist.)
Gtr. 4
Riff B
End Riff B
let ring
Gtr. 3
Gtr. 2
P.M.
Fill 1
Gtr. 5

Gtr. 4: w/ Riff B
E5
B/D♯
D5
A/C♯
(cont. in notation)
If you cling too tight - ly,
you're gon-na lose con - trol."
Gtr. 5
Gtr. 3
Gtr. 2
P.M.
(cont. in slashes)
F♯5
B5type2
Gtr. 5 tacet
A5type2
1.
Rhy. Fig. 1A
End Rhy. Fig. 1A
(2nd time, Gtr. 2 cont. in notation)
Your ba - by needs some - one to be - lieve in,
and a whole lot of space to breathe in.
Gtr. 4
Rhy. Fig. 1C
End Rhy. Fig. 1C
let ring
Rhy. Fig. 1B
End Rhy. Fig. 1B
(2nd time, Gtr. 3 cont. in slashes)
Gtr. 1
Rhy. Fig. 1
End Rhy. Fig. 1

2.

Bridge

Gtr. 3

dim.

to breathe in.

Don't let her slip a-

Gtr. 4

dim.

Gtr. 2

Gtrs. 1 & 2

let ring

Gtr. 1

*Chord symbols reflect overall harmony.

D.S. al Coda

D/A
G/A
D/A
G6/A
D/A
A5
A♯5
B5
don't let your heart get in her way,
yeah,
yeah,
yeah.
Gtr. 3
Gtrs. 1 & 2

Coda
Chorus
Gtr. 4: w/ Riff B (2 times)
D5
E5
E5
B/D♯
Gtr. 1
So, hold on loose - ly,
Gtr. 3
Gtrs. 1 & 2
Gtr. 2
P.M.
(Gtr. 1 cont. in slashes)
P.M.
P.M.
P.M.

D5 A/C♯ D5 E5 B/D♯

Gtr. 1

but don't let go.

If you cling too tight - ly,

Gtr. 5

Gtr. 3

Gtr. 2

P.M.

D5 A/C♯

Gtrs. 1, 2, 3 & 4: w/ Rhy. Figs. 1, 1A, 1B & 1C

F♯m B

you're gon - na lose con - trol.

Your ba - by needs some -

P.M.

Outro

Gtr. 4: w/ Riff B

E5 B/D# D5 A/C# A5 B5

Gtr. 1

So, hold on loose - ly, but don't let go.

Gtr. 5

Gtr. 3

Gtr. 2

P.M. P.M. P.M. P.M.

E5
B/D♯
D5
A/C♯
D5 D♯5 E5
Gtr. 1
If you cling too tight - ly,
you're gon-na lose it,
you're gon-na lose con - trol.
Gtr. 5
8va
loco
P.H.
Gtr. 4
let ring
let ring
Gtr. 3
Gtr. 2
P.M.
P.M.

*Gtr. 4: w/ Riff B (till end)

Rhy. Fig. 2

B/D♯ D5 A/C♯

Gtr. 1

Gtr. 5

Gtr. 3

Gtr. 2

P.M. P.M. P.M. P.M.

*1st time, 1st note of Riff B is tied, not struck.

D5 E5 B/D♯ D5

End Rhy. Fig. 2

Yeah, yeah, yeah, yeah.

P.M. P.M. P.M.

E5
Rhy. Fig. 3
B/D♯
D5
A/C♯

So, hold on loose - ly, but don't let go.

hold bend

Riff C

Rhy. Fig. 4

P.M. P.M. P.M.

A5
B5
E5
B/D♯
D5
End Rhy. Fig. 3
If you cling too tight - ly,
P.M.
Gtr. 1: w/ Rhy. Fill 4
N.C.
E5
you're gon - na lose con - trol.
Rhy. Fill 4
Gtr. 1

Gtr. 1: w/ Rhy. Fig. 2

B/D♯ D5 A/C♯

Hold ___ on loose - ly, ___ but don't let ___ go. ___

P.M. P.M. P.M.

D5 E5 B/D♯

If you cling too tight -

P.M. P.M.

Gtr. 1: w/ Rhy. Fill 4

D5 N.C. E5

-ly to___ her,___ you're gon - na lose___ con - trol,___ yeah,___ yeah,___ yeah.___

End Riff C

End Rhy. Fig. 4

P.M. P.M.

*Gtr. 1: w/ Rhy. Fig. 3
Gtr. 2: w/ Rhy. Fig. 4 (till end)
**Gtr. 3: w/ Riff C (till end)

*1st note of Rhy. Fig. 3 is tied, not struck.
**1st note of Riff C is tied, not struck (till end).

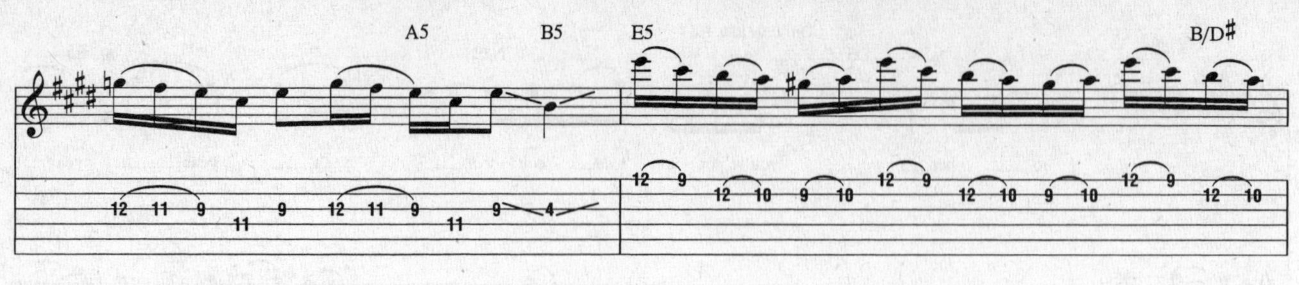
A5
B5
E5
B/D♯

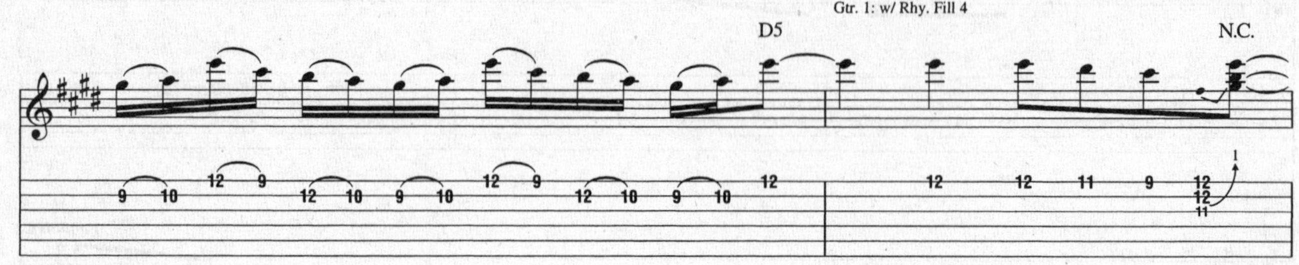
Gtr. 1: w/ Rhy. Fill 4
D5
N.C.

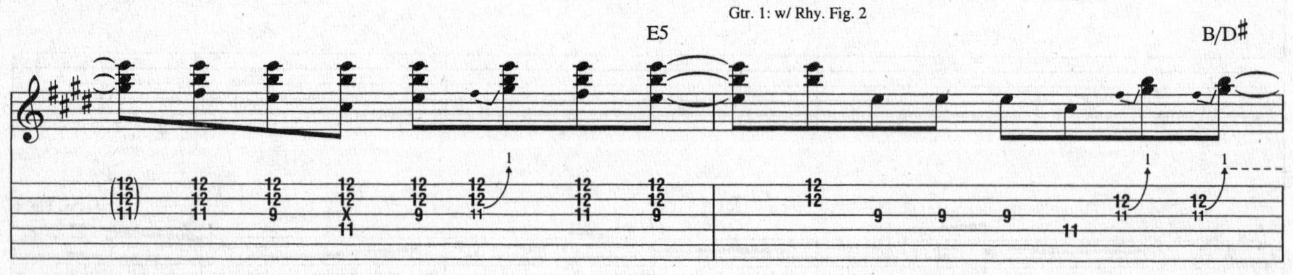
Gtr. 1: w/ Rhy. Fig. 2
E5
B/D♯

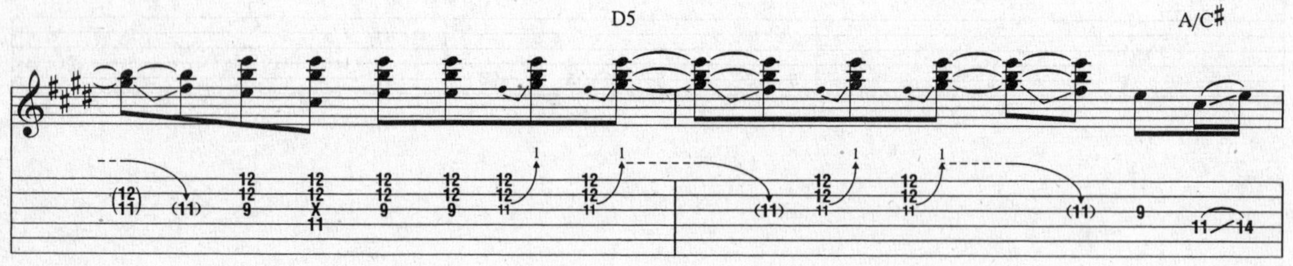
D5
A/C♯

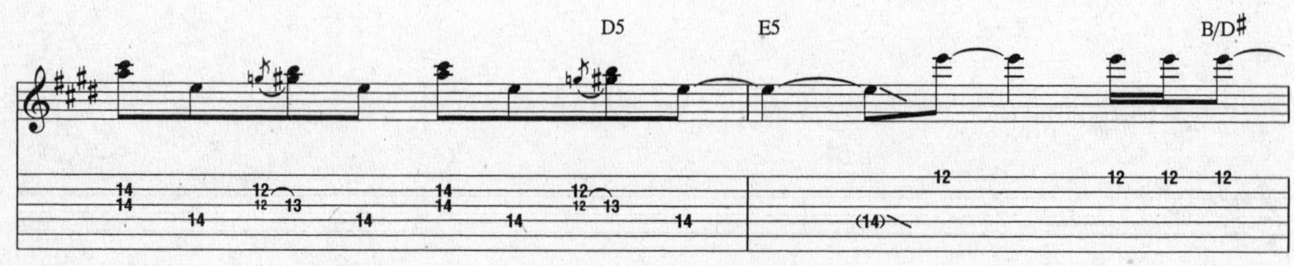
D5
E5
B/D♯

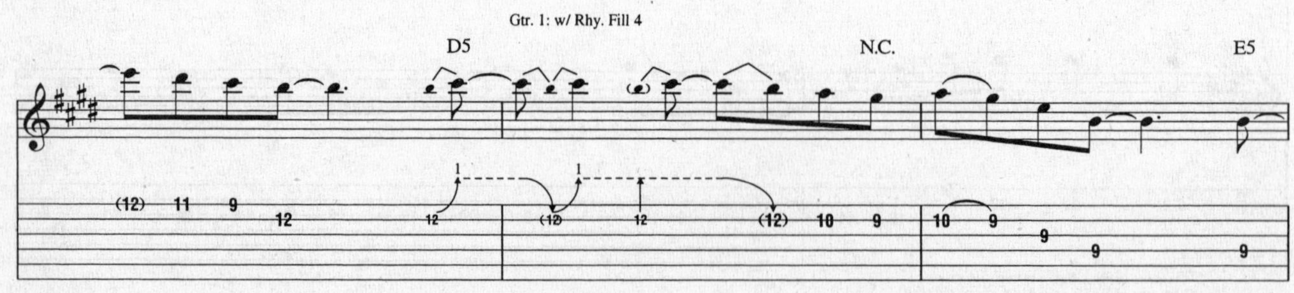
Gtr. 1: w/ Rhy. Fill 4
D5
N.C.
E5

*Gtr. 1: w/ Rhy. Fig. 3
B/D♯
D5
*1st note of Rhy. Fig. 3 is tied, not struck.
A/C♯
A5
B5
E5
B/D♯
Begin fade
Gtr. 1: w/ Rhy. Fill 4
D5
N.C.
Gtr. 1: w/ Rhy. Fig. 2
E5
8va
B/D♯
D5
A/C♯
D5
E5
B/D♯
Fade out
D5

Hollywood Nights

Words and Music by Bob Seger

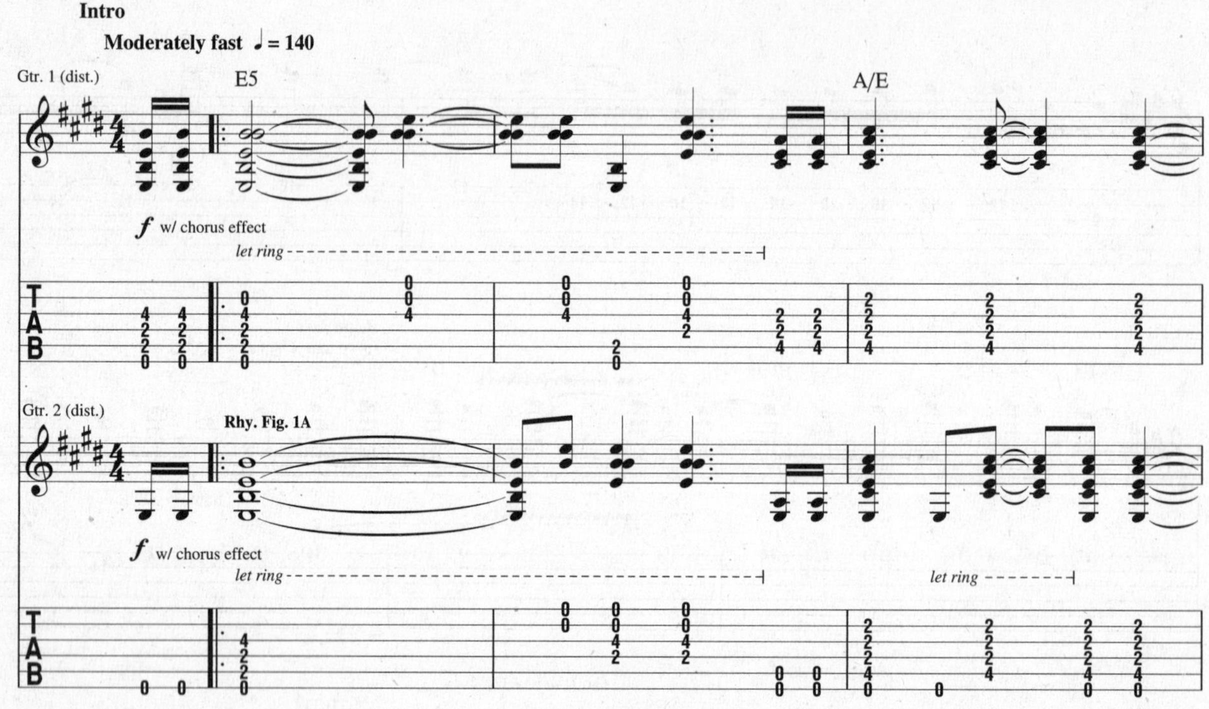

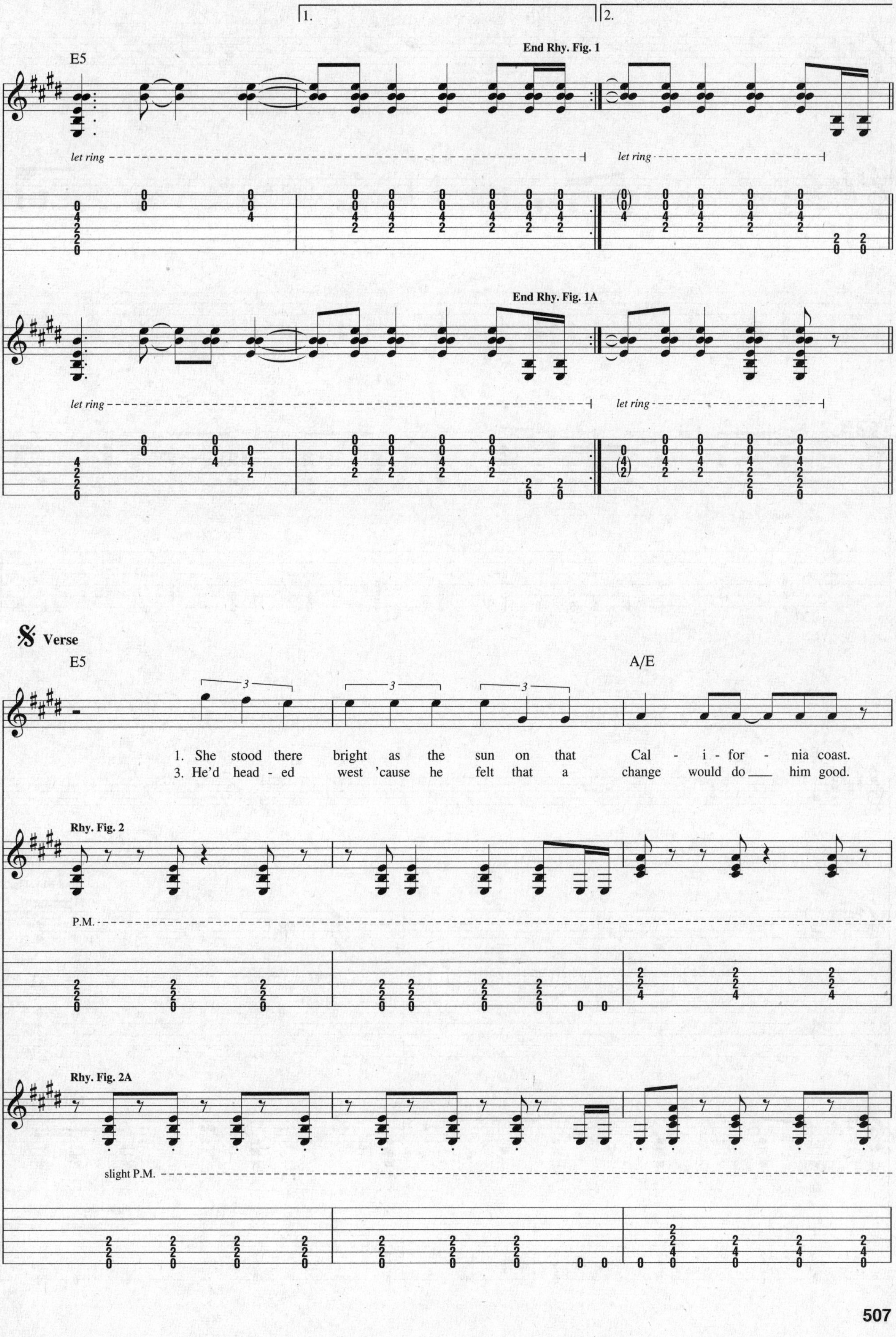

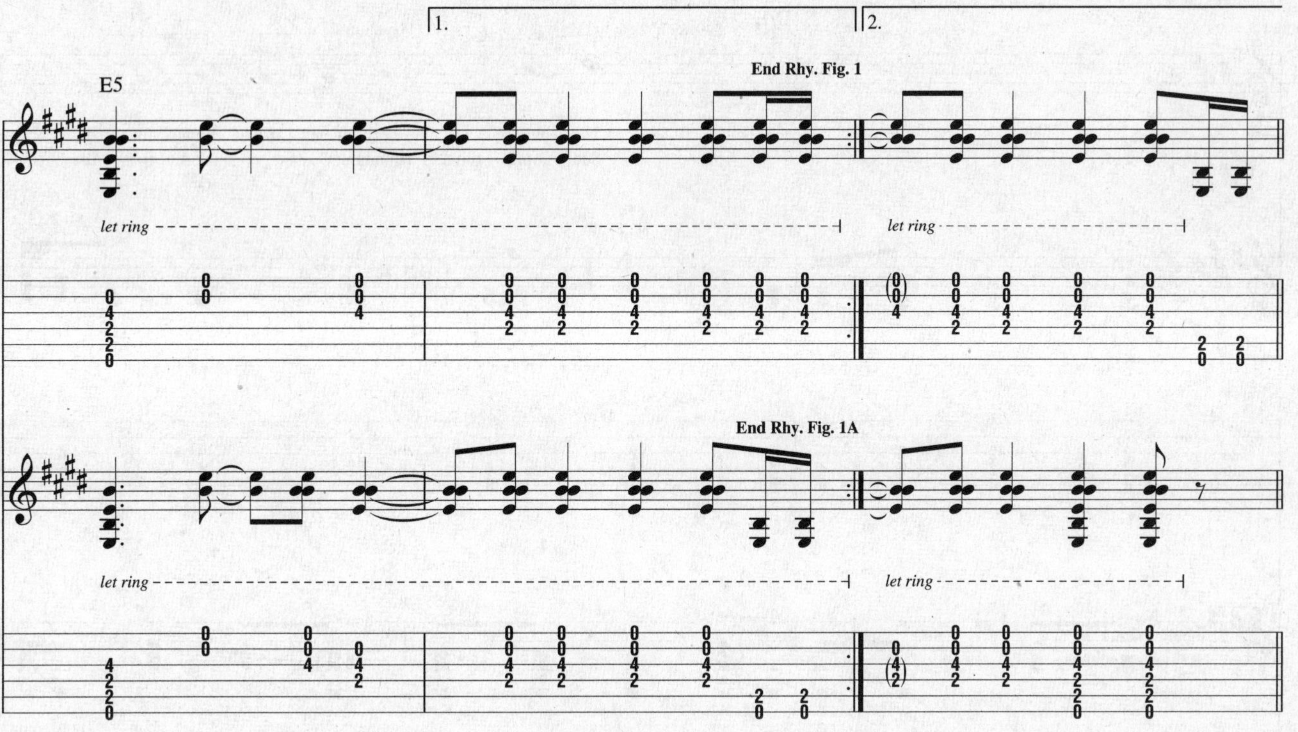

Verse

E5 A/E

1. She stood there bright as the sun on that Cal - i - for - nia coast.
3. He'd head - ed west 'cause he felt that a change would do___ him good.

Rhy. Fig. 2

P.M.

Rhy. Fig. 2A

slight P.M.

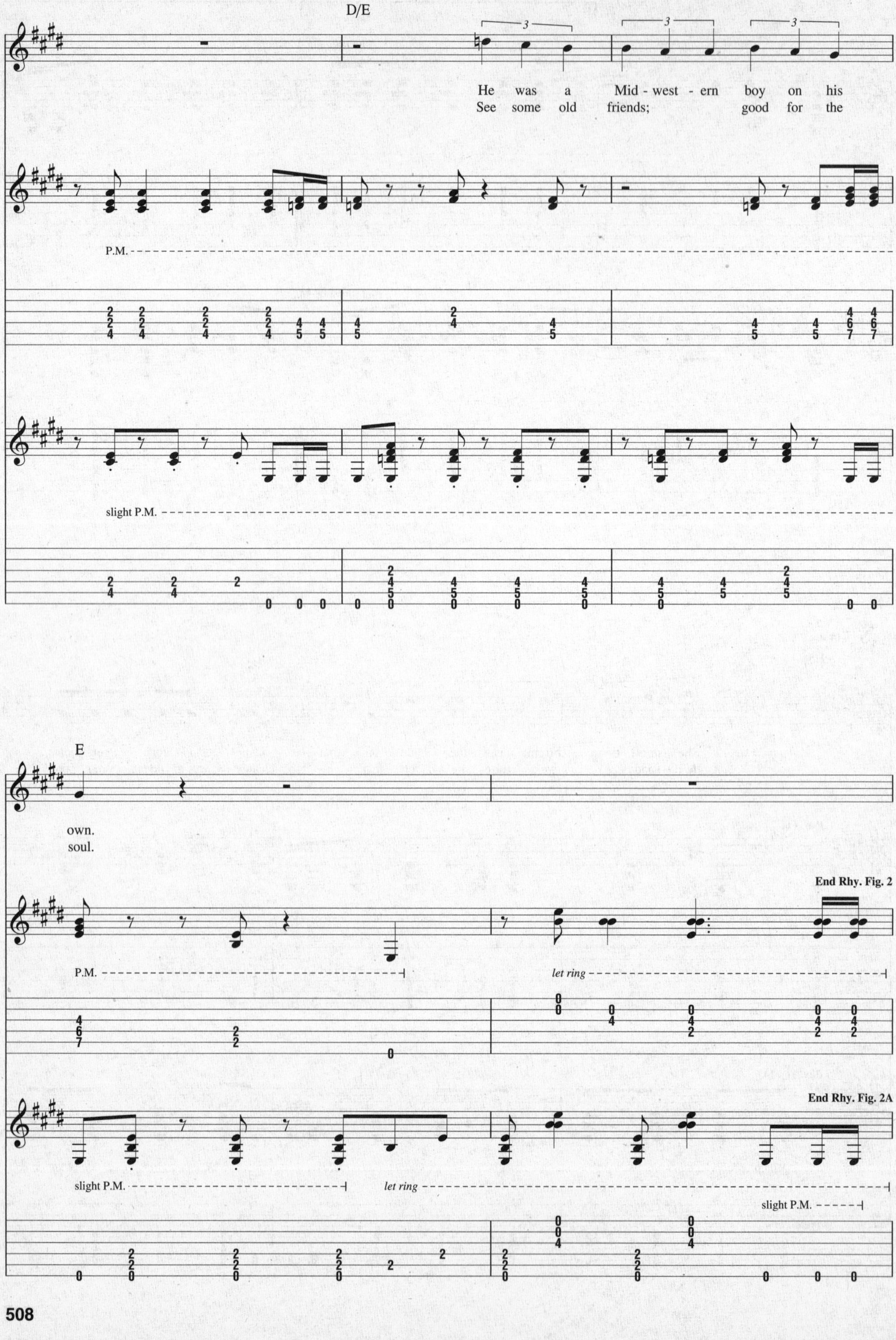

D/E

He was a Mid - west - ern boy on his
See some old friends; good for the

P.M.

slight P.M.

Gtrs. 1 & 2: w/ Rhy. Figs. 2 & 2A
E5
A/E
She looked at him with those soft eyes, so in - no - cent and blue.
She had been born with a face that would let her get her way.
D/E
E
He knew right then he was too far from home.
He saw that face and he lost all con - trol.
Interlude
Gtrs. 1 & 2: w/ Rhy. Figs. 1 & 1A
E5
A/E
Oo,
Yeah,
he was too far
he had lost all
D/E
E5
Verse
Gtrs. 1 & 2: w/ Rhy. Figs. 2 & 2A (2 times)
E5
from home.
con - trol.
2. She took his
4. Night af - ter
A/E
hand and she led him a - long that gold - en beach.
night and day af - ter day, it went on and on.
D/E
E
They watched the waves tum - ble o - ver the sand.
Then came that morn - ing he woke up a - lone.
E5
A/E
They drove for miles and miles up those twist - ing, turn - ing roads.
He spent all night star - ing down at the lights of L. A.,
To Coda
D/E
E
High - er and high - er and high - er they climbed.
won - der - ing if he could ev - er go home.
And those Hol -

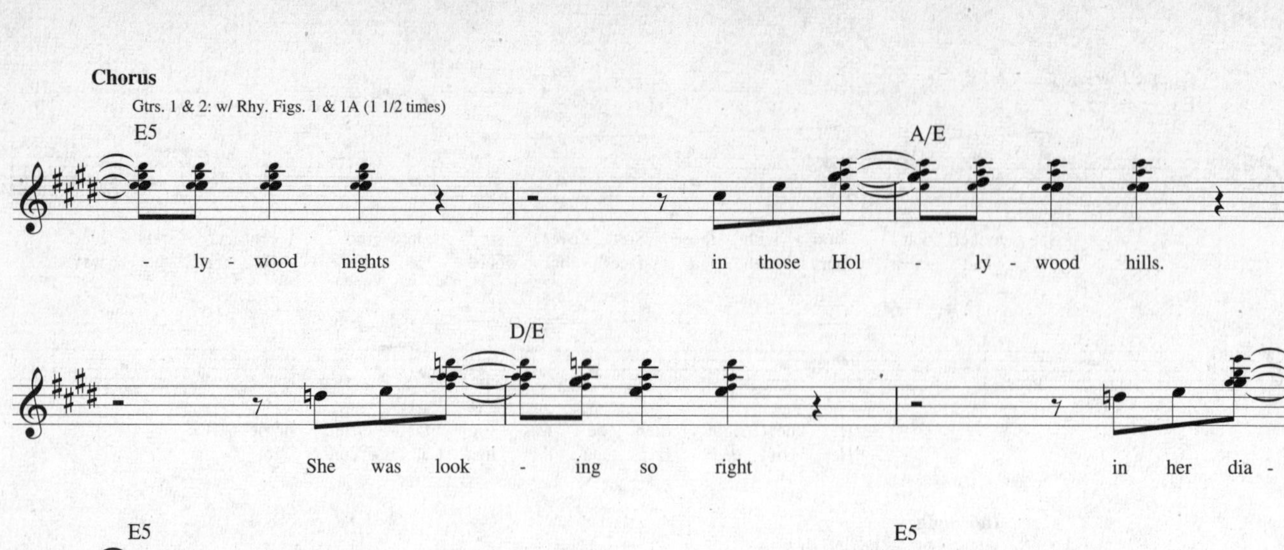
Chorus
Gtrs. 1 & 2: w/ Rhy. Figs. 1 & 1A (1 1/2 times)
E5
A/E
- ly - wood nights in those Hol - ly - wood hills.
D/E
She was look - ing so right in her dia -

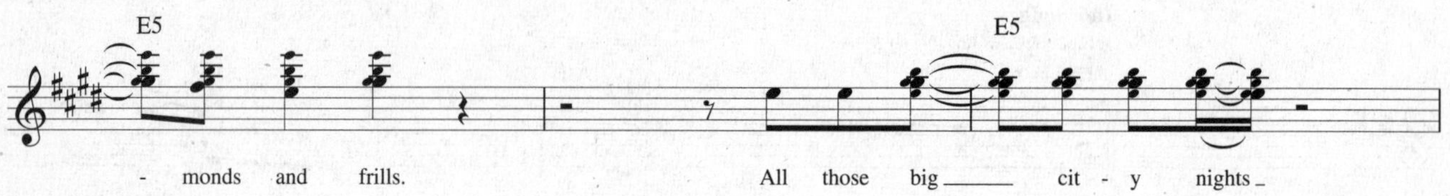
E5
E5
- monds and frills. All those big cit - y nights

A/E
in those high, roll - ing hills;

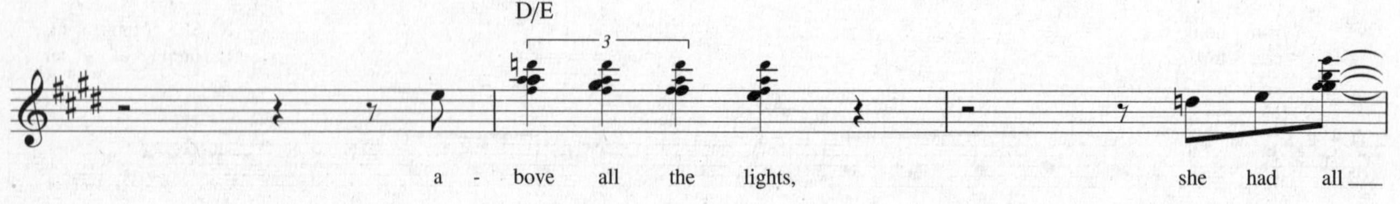
D/E
3
a - bove all the lights, she had all

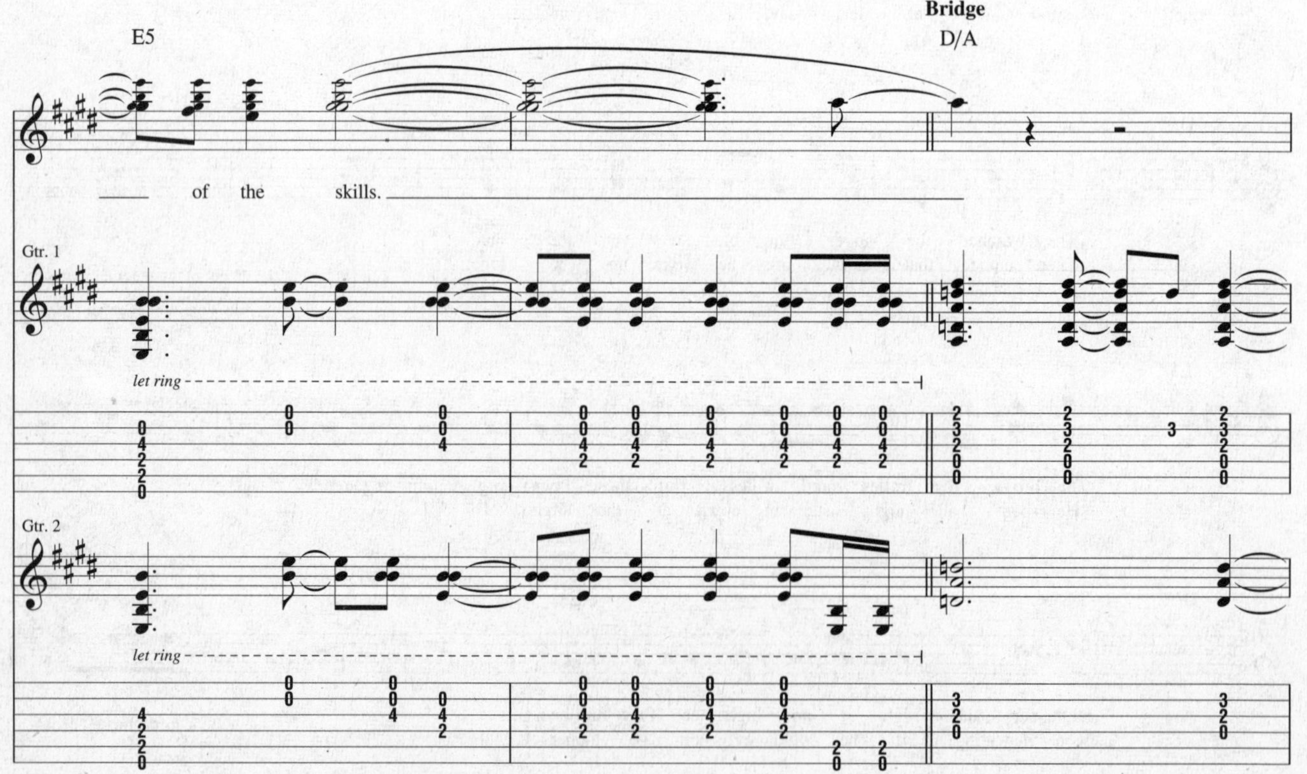
Bridge
E5
D/A
of the skills.
Gtr. 1
let ring
Gtr. 2
let ring

E5 A/E

Yeah!

let ring

E5

Ow.

let ring

P.M.

let ring

slight P.M.

D.S. al Coda

Mm.

P.M.

slight P.M.

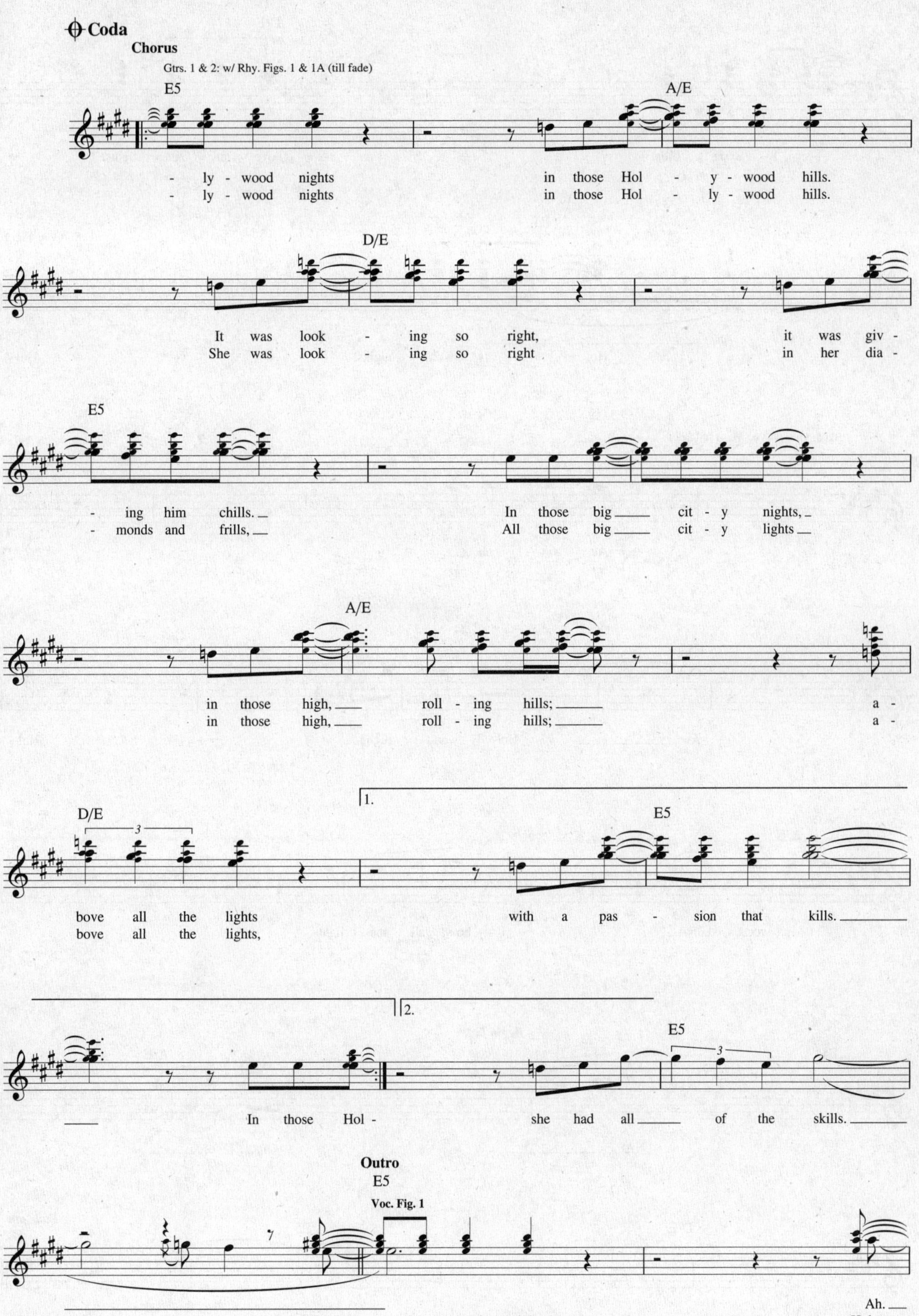
Coda
Chorus
Gtrs. 1 & 2: w/ Rhy. Figs. 1 & 1A (till fade)
E5
A/E
- ly - wood nights in those Hol - y - wood hills.
- ly - wood nights in those Hol - ly - wood hills.
D/E
It was look - ing so right, it was giv -
She was look - ing so right in her dia -
E5
- ing him chills. In those big cit - y nights,
- monds and frills, All those big cit - y lights
A/E
in those high, roll - ing hills; a -
in those high, roll - ing hills; a -
D/E
1.
E5
bove all the lights with a pas - sion that kills.
bove all the lights,
2.
E5
In those Hol - she had all of the skills.
Outro
E5
Voc. Fig. 1
Ah.
(Hol - ly - wood nights. Hol -

A/E
D/E
- ly - wood hills.
A - bove all the lights.

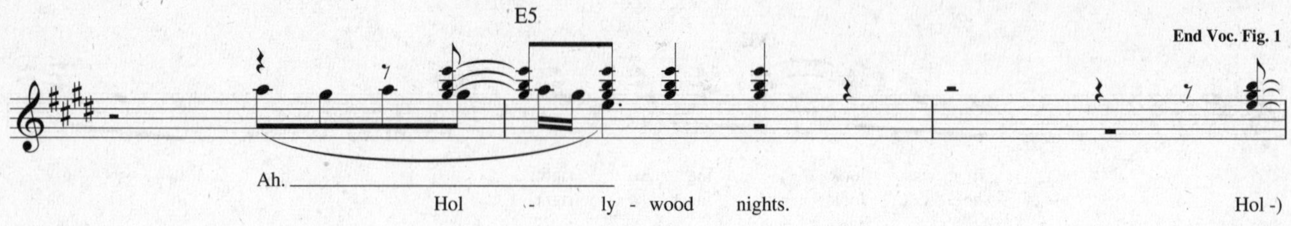
E5
End Voc. Fig. 1
Ah.
Hol - ly - wood nights.
Hol -)

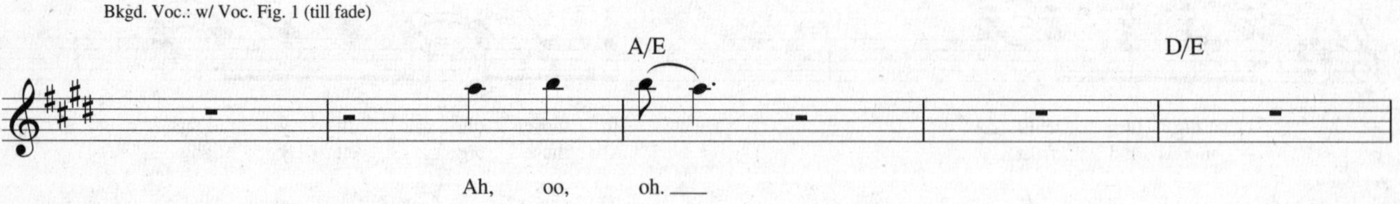
Bkgd. Voc.: w/ Voc. Fig. 1 (till fade)
A/E
D/E
Ah, oo, oh.

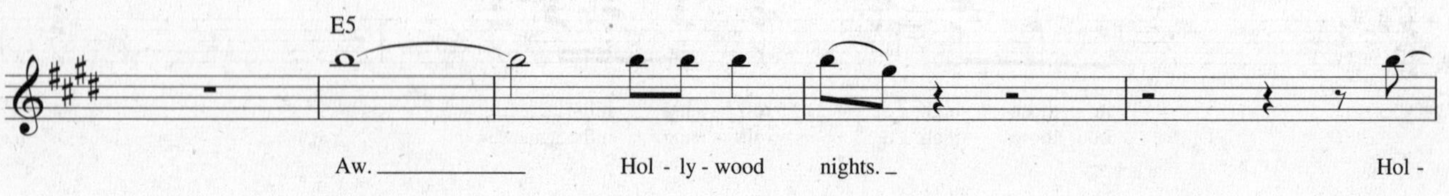
E5
Aw.
Hol - ly - wood nights.
Hol -

A/E
D/E
- ly - wood hills.
A - bove all the lights.

Begin fade
E5
A/E
Ah.
Oh, oh.

Fade out
D/E
E5
Ah.

Hot Legs

Words and Music by Rod Stewart

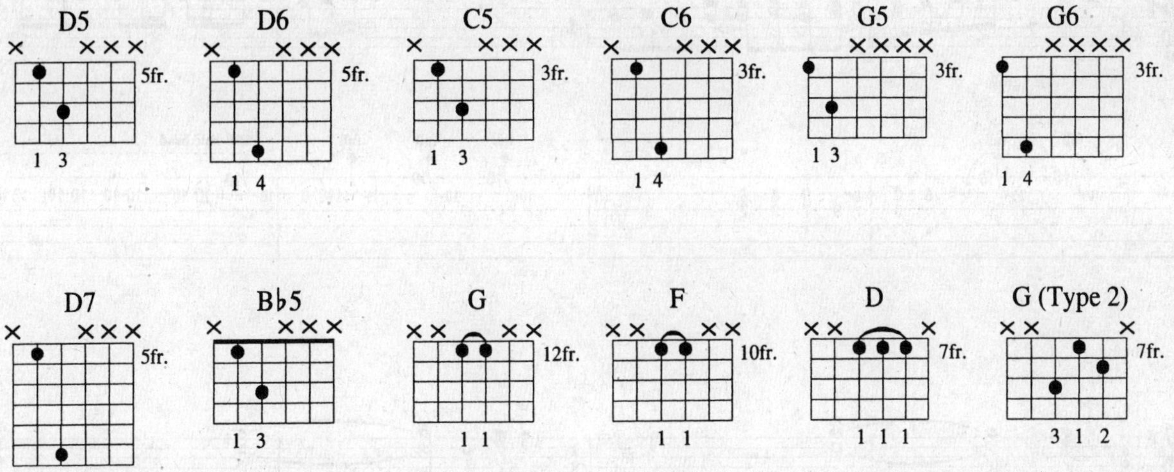

Introduction

Moderate Rock ♩ = 116

D5 D6 D5 D6 D5 D6 D5 D6 D5 C5 C6 C5 C6 C5 C6 C5 C6

Gtr. 1

Gtr. 2

Drums

f

let ring

w/dist.

full full full full full full full full full

Gtr 3

f

w/dist.

(Gtr. 1 out)

G5 G6 G5 G6 G5 G6 G5 G6 G5 G6 G5 G6 G5 G6 G5 G6 G5

full full full full full full hold bend

N.C.
(G5)
Fill 1

full full full full full full

Fill 2

full full full full full full

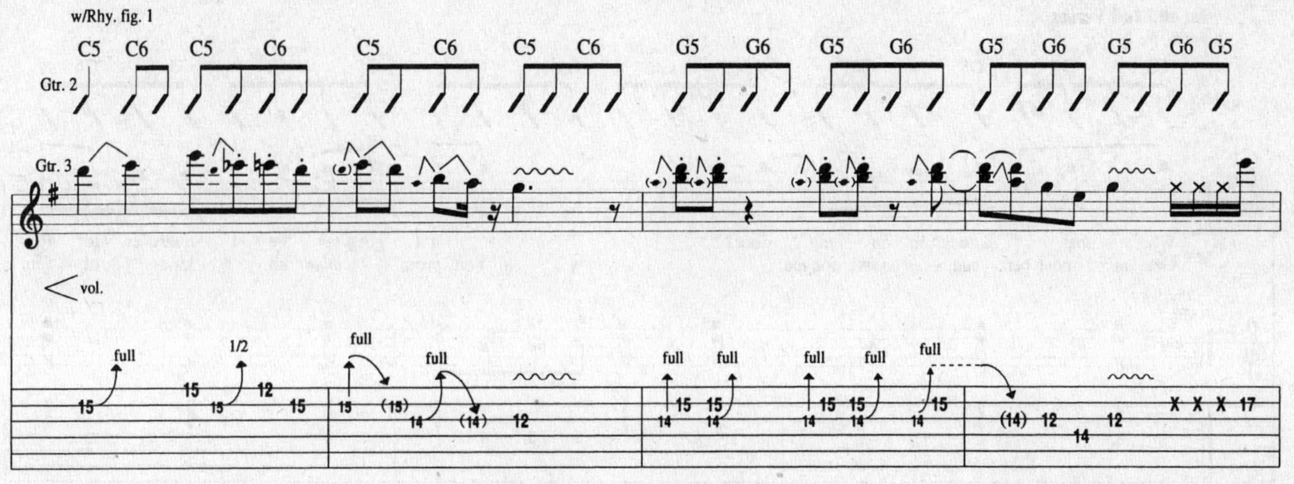

w/Rhy. fig. 1
C5 C6 C5 C6 C5 C6 C5 C6 G5 G6 G5 G6 G5 G6 G5 G6 G5
Gtr. 2
Gtr. 3
vol.
full
1/2

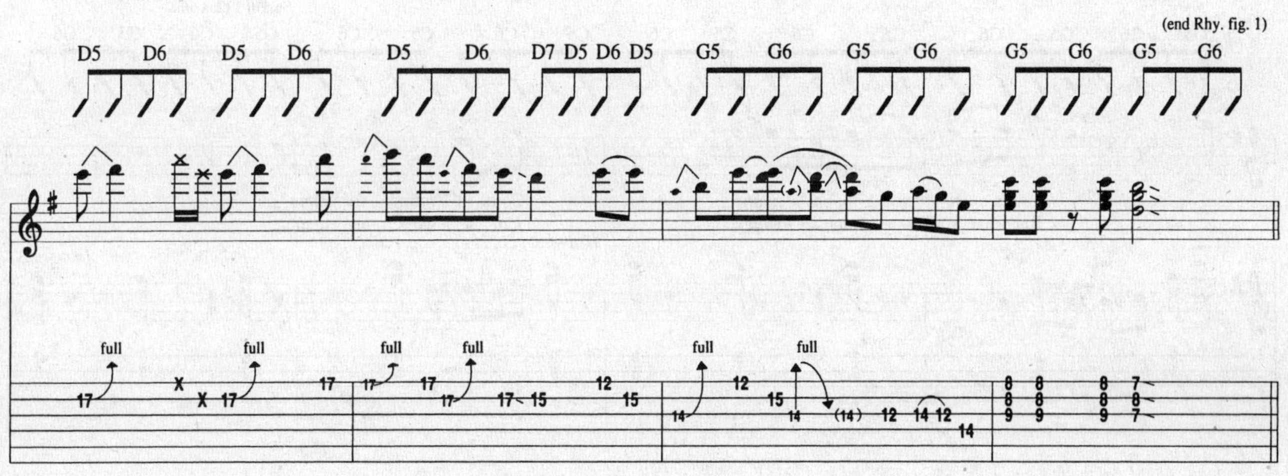

(end Rhy. fig. 1)
D5 D6 D5 D6 D5 D6 D7 D5 D6 D5 G5 G6 G5 G6 G5 G6 G5 G6
full

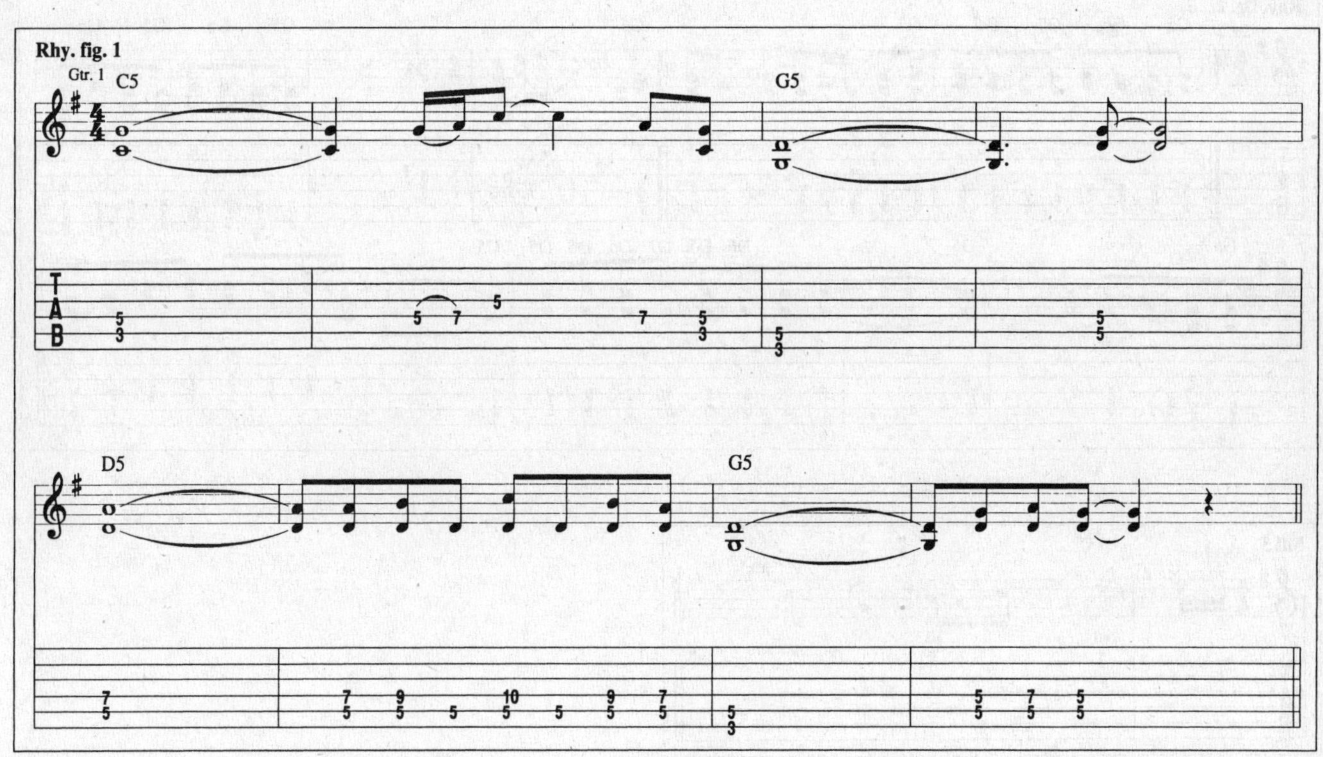

Rhy. fig. 1
Gtr. 1
C5
G5
D5
G5

1st and 2nd Verses

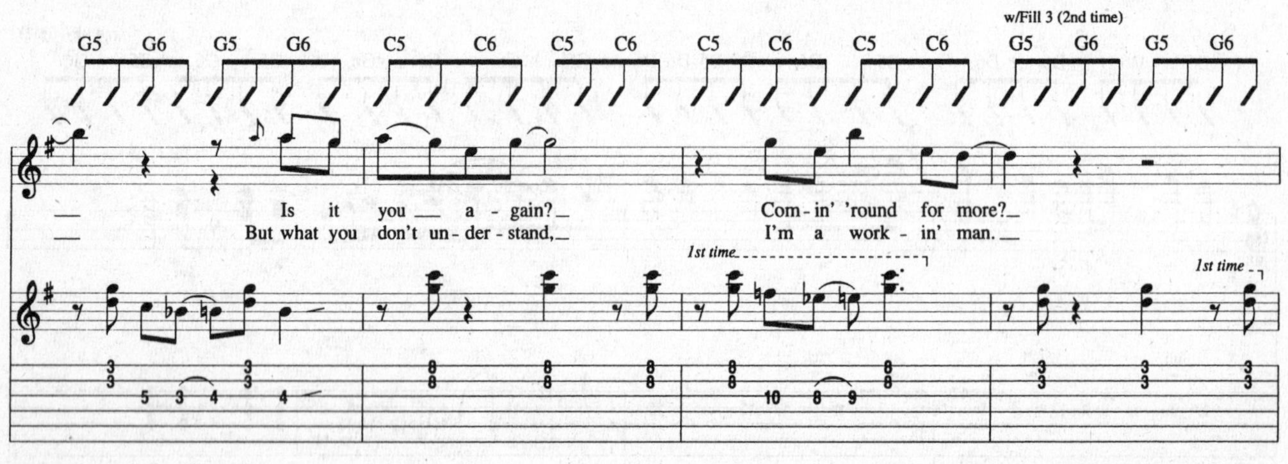

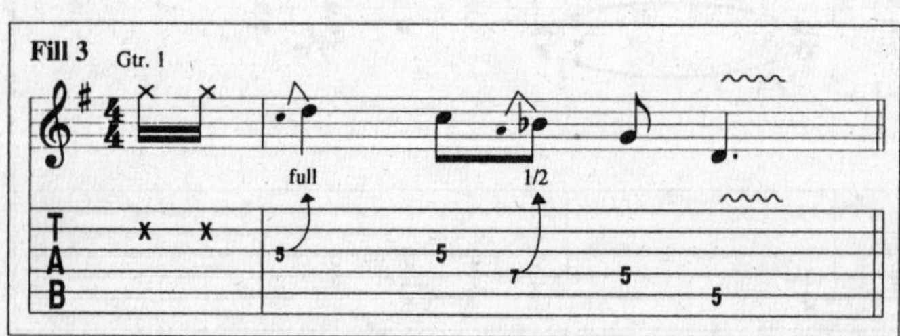

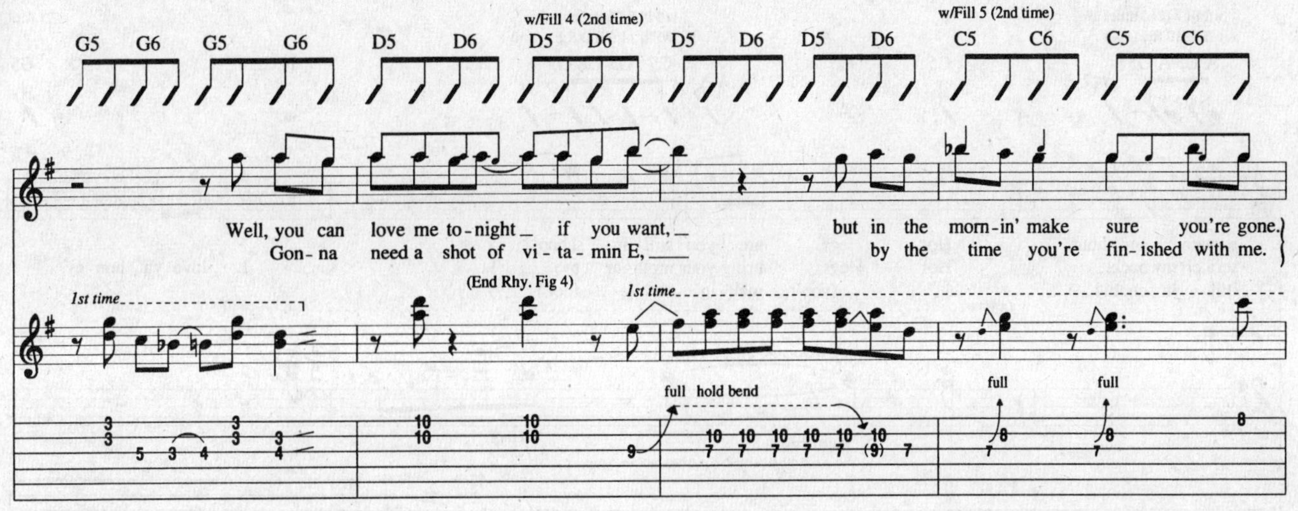
w/Fill 4 (2nd time)
w/Fill 5 (2nd time)
G5 G6 G5 G6 D5 D6 D5 D6 D5 D6 D5 D6 C5 C6 C5 C6
Well, you can love me to-night__ if you want,__ but in the morn-in' make sure you're gone.
Gon-na need a shot of vi-ta-min E,___ by the time you're fin-ished with me.
1st time
(End Rhy. Fig 4)
full hold bend
full
full

(end Rhy. figs. 4, 2 and 3)
Chorus
Rhy. fig. 5
Gtr. 2
w/Fill 9 (on D.S.)
w/Fill 6 (2nd time)
C5 C6 C5 C6 C5 G5 C5 G5 C5 G5 C5 G5
I'm talk-in' to ya'.
Hot legs, you're wear-in' me out.__ Hot legs, you can
Hot legs, you're an al - ley cat.__ Hot legs, you can
D.S.: (in your sat - in shoes.__) (are you
1st time
Gtr. 1
full
both notes vib.
full

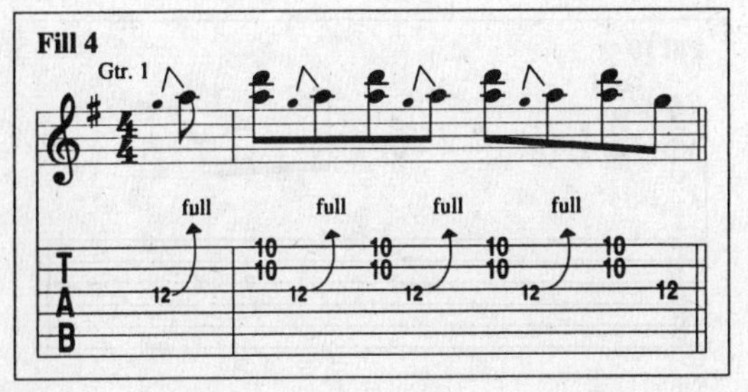
Fill 4
Gtr. 1
full
full
full
full

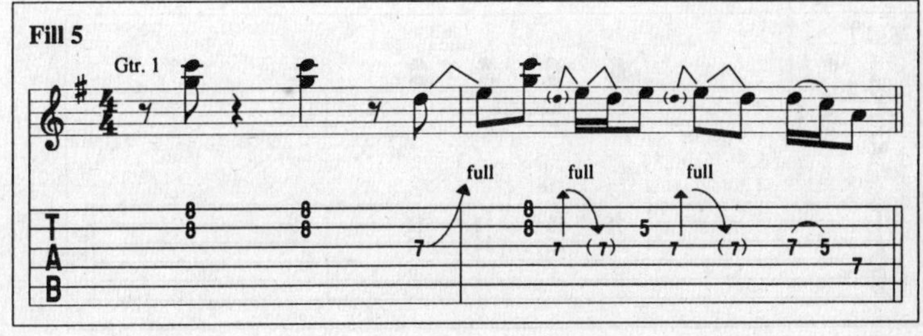
Fill 5
Gtr. 1
full
full
full

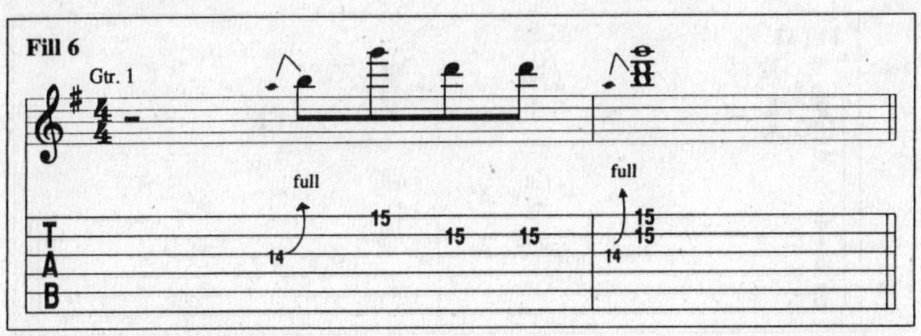
Fill 6
Gtr. 1
full
full

Fill 9
Gtr. 1

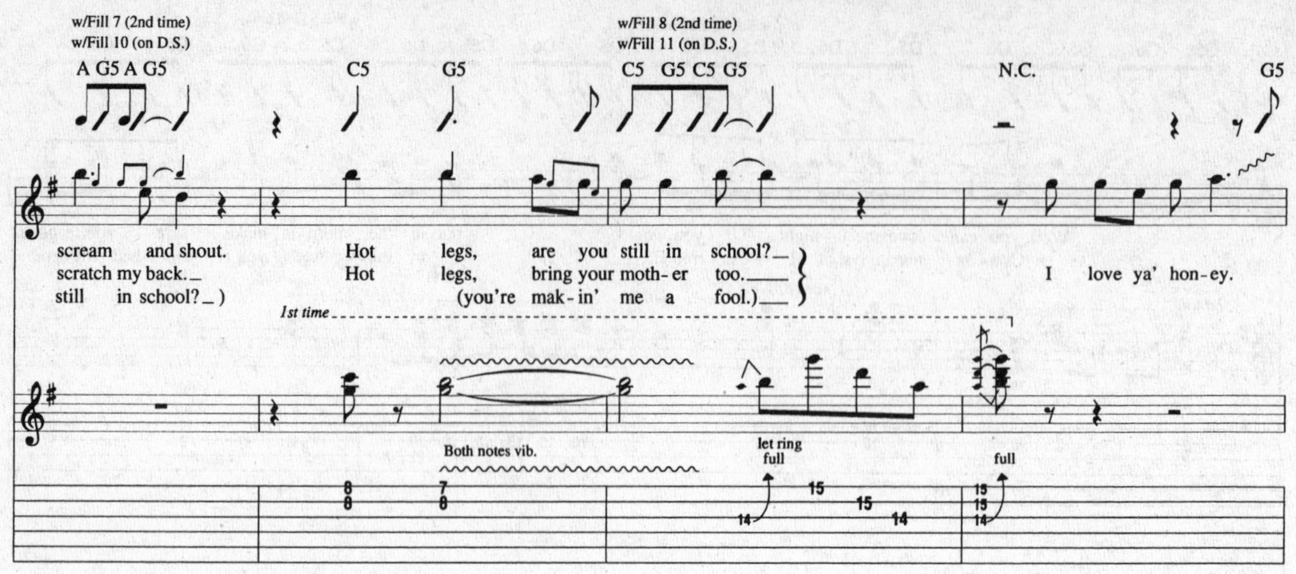
w/Fill 7 (2nd time)
w/Fill 10 (on D.S.)
w/Fill 8 (2nd time)
w/Fill 11 (on D.S.)
A G5 A G5
C5
G5
C5 G5 C5 G5
N.C.
G5
scream and shout.
scratch my back.
still in school?
Hot legs, are you still in school?
Hot legs, bring your moth-er too.
(you're mak-in' me a fool.)
I love ya' hon-ey.
1st time
Both notes vib.
let ring
full
full

To Coda
(end Rhy. fig. 5)
*Bass Solo
Band Out (except drums)
N.C.
(G5)
2nd time:
C5 G5 C5 G5
Ooh ya.
Gtr. 2
1st time
*arr. for Gtr.

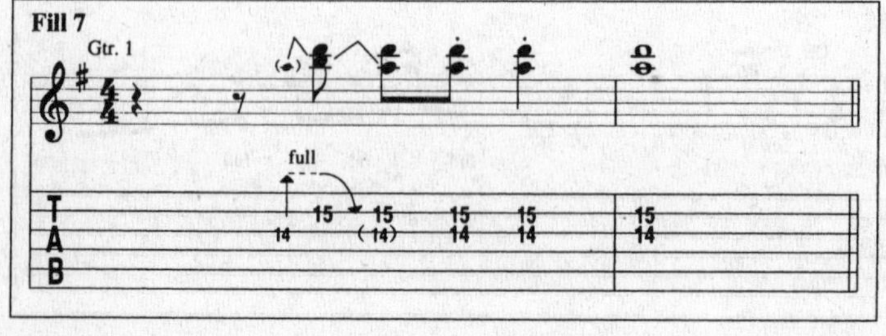
Fill 7
Gtr. 1
full

Fill 10
Gtr. 1

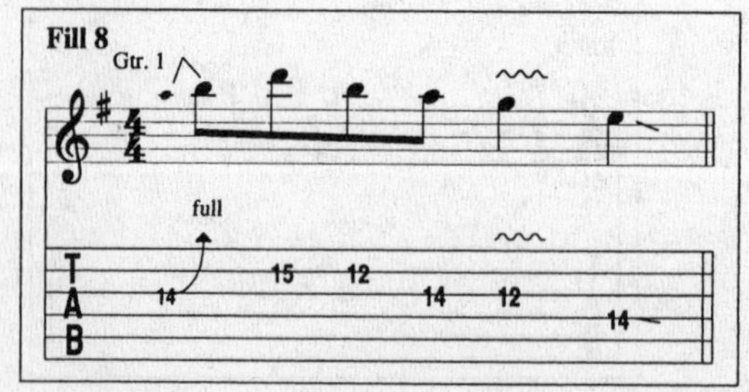
Fill 8
Gtr. 1
full

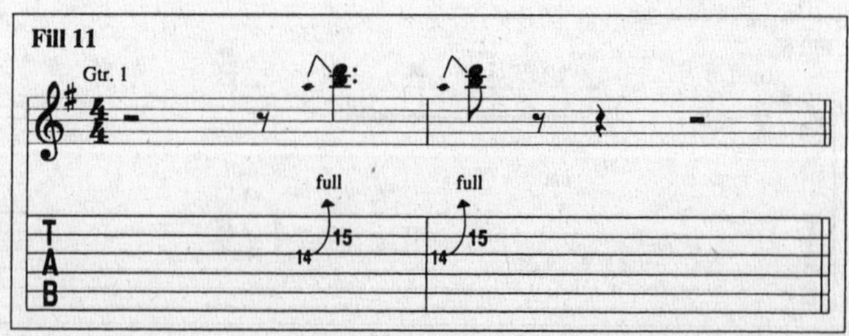
Fill 11
Gtr. 1
full
full

Guitar Solo
Band in
w/Fills 1 and 2
Gtr. 2
Gtr. 1
C5
Bb5
G
F
D
G (type 2)
G5
E
full
1/4
w/bar
slowly release bend
3fr.
5fr.
2fr.

3rd Verse

w/Rhy. figs. 3 and 4

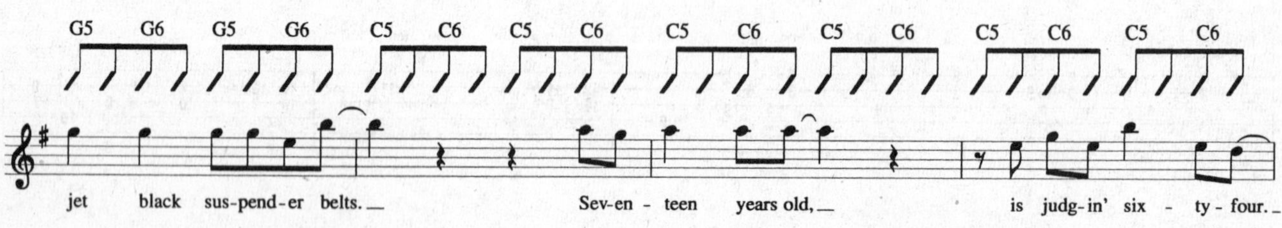

(end Rhy. fig. 4)

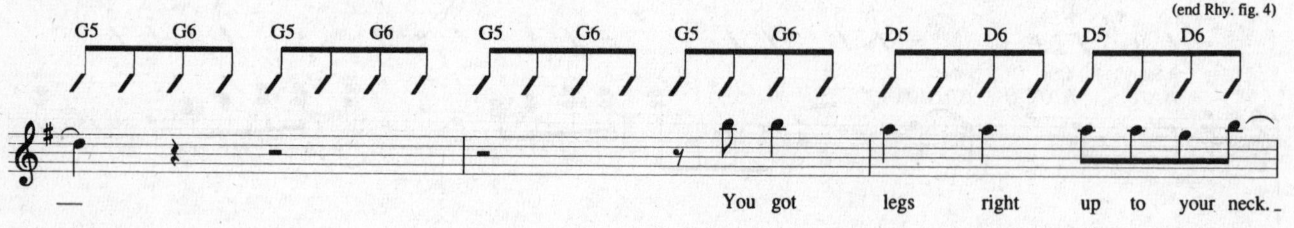

D.S. al Coda

(end Rhy. fig. 3)

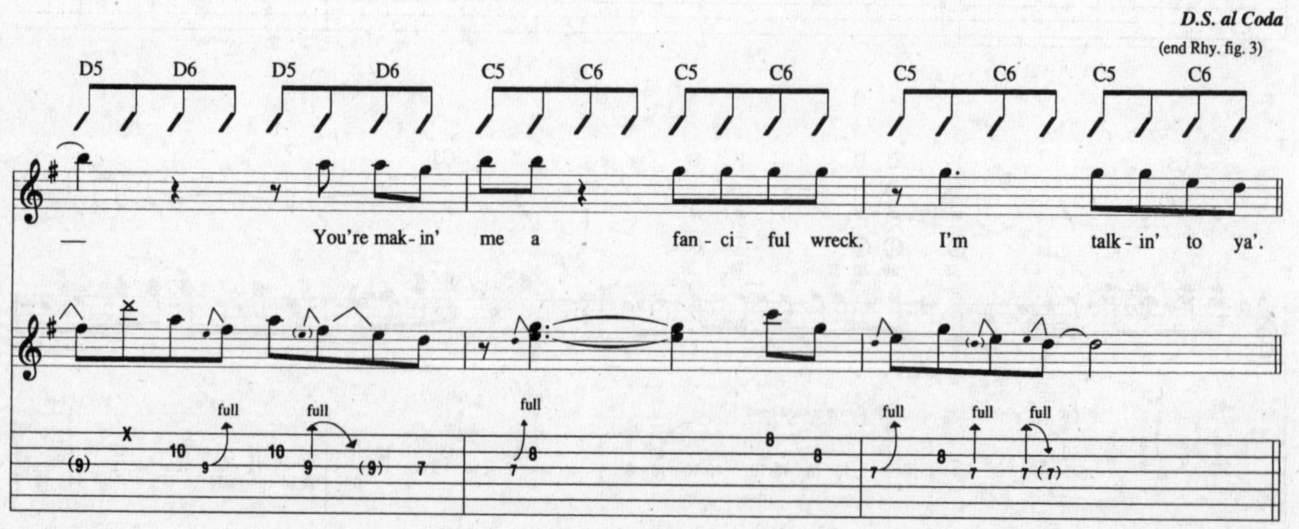

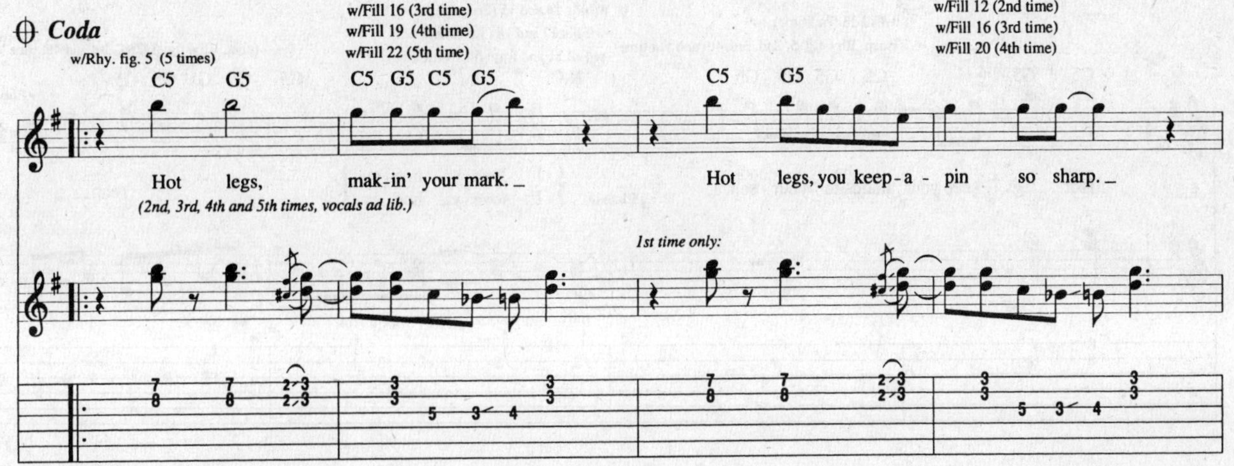
Coda
w/Rhy. fig. 5 (5 times)
w/Fill 16 (3rd time)
w/Fill 19 (4th time)
w/Fill 22 (5th time)
w/Fill 12 (2nd time)
w/Fill 16 (3rd time)
w/Fill 20 (4th time)
C5 G5 C5 G5 C5 G5 C5 G5
Hot legs, mak-in' your mark. _ Hot legs, you keep-a - pin so sharp. _
(2nd, 3rd, 4th and 5th times, vocals ad lib.)
1st time only:

Fill 12
Gtr. 1

Fill 16
Gtr. 1

Fill 19
Gtr. 1
full

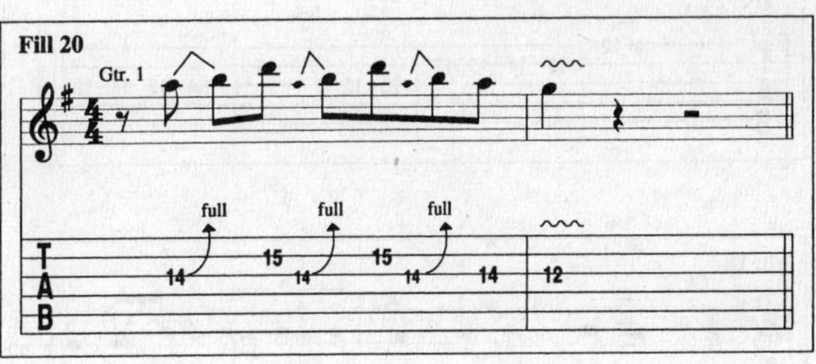
Fill 20
Gtr. 1
full

Fill 22
Gtr. 1
full

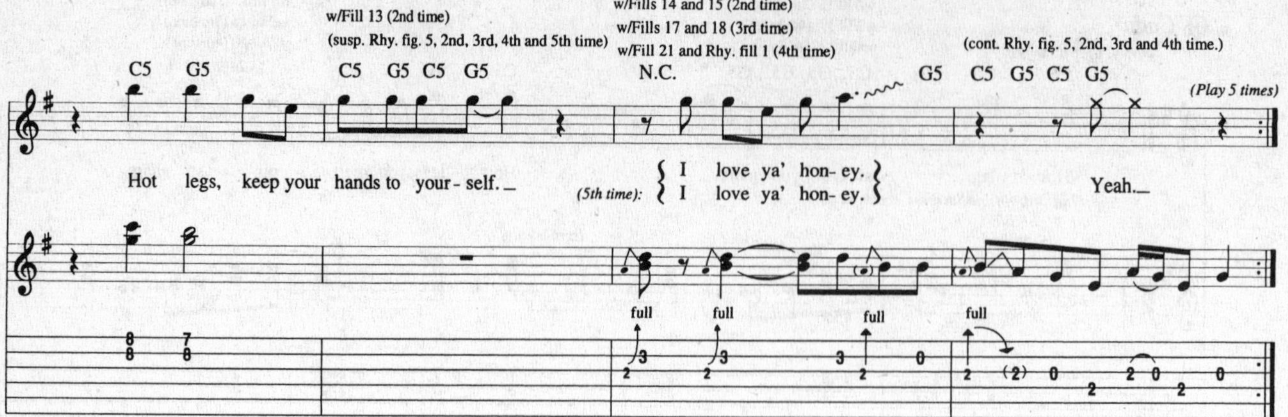
w/Fill 13 (2nd time)
(susp. Rhy. fig. 5, 2nd, 3rd, 4th and 5th time)
w/Fills 14 and 15 (2nd time)
w/Fills 17 and 18 (3rd time)
w/Fill 21 and Rhy. fill 1 (4th time)
(cont. Rhy. fig. 5, 2nd, 3rd and 4th time.)
C5 G5 C5 G5 C5 G5 N.C. G5 C5 G5 C5 G5
(Play 5 times)
Hot legs, keep your hands to your-self.
I love ya' hon-ey.
(5th time): I love ya' hon-ey.
Yeah.
full

Fill 13
Gtr. 1

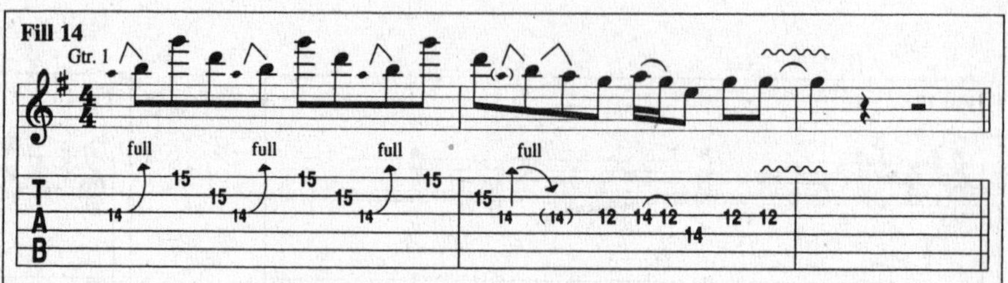
Fill 14
Gtr. 1
full

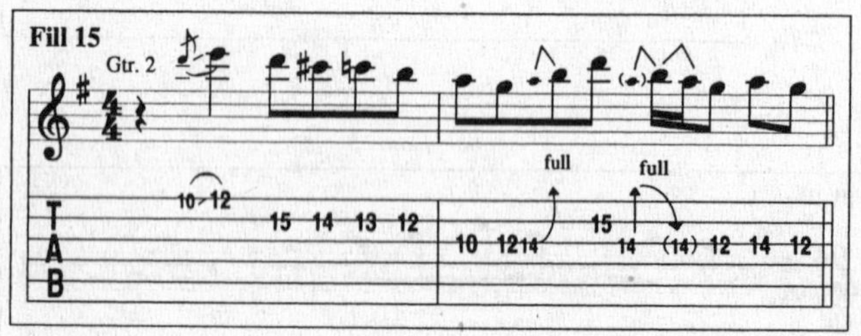
Fill 15
Gtr. 2
full

Fill 17
Gtr. 1

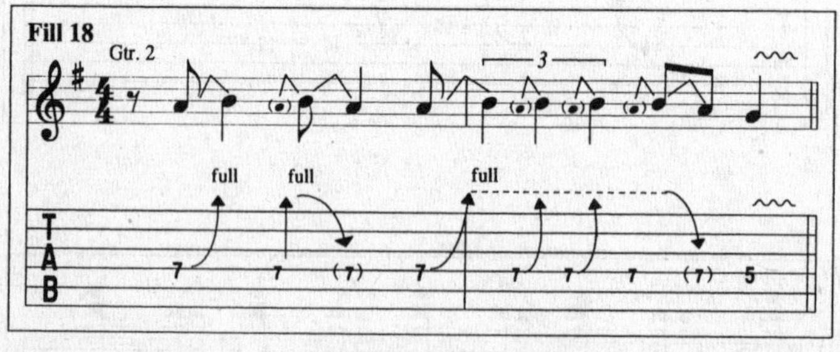
Fill 18
Gtr. 2
full

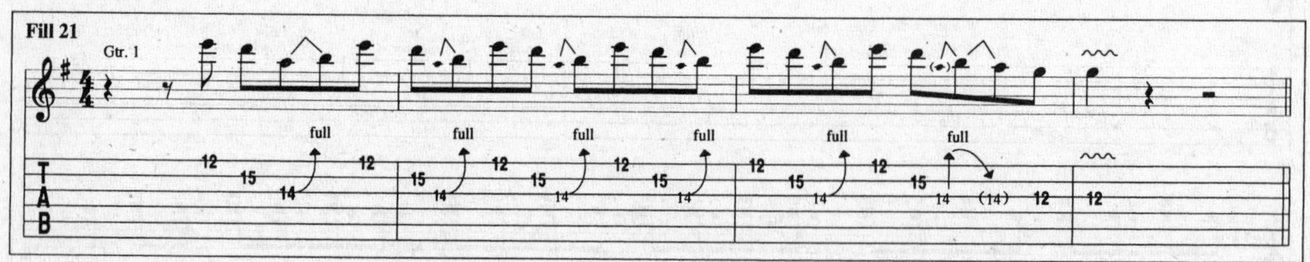
Fill 21
Gtr. 1
full

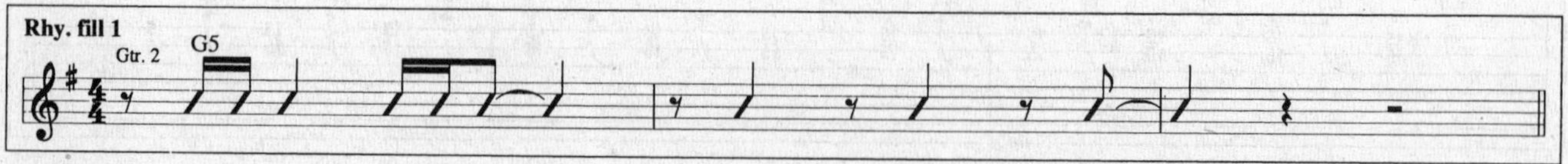
Rhy. fill 1
Gtr. 2
G5

The House of the Rising Sun

Words and Music by Alan Price

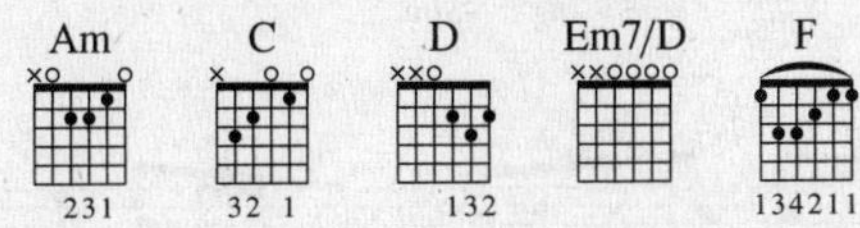

Intro

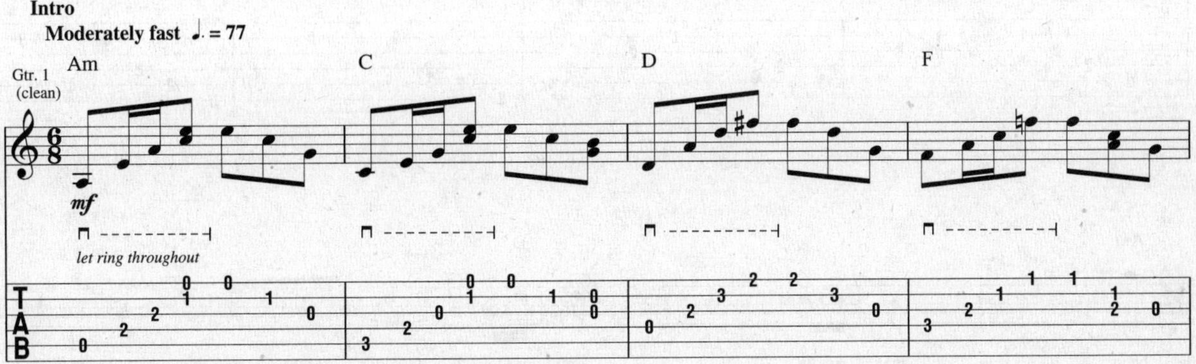

Verse

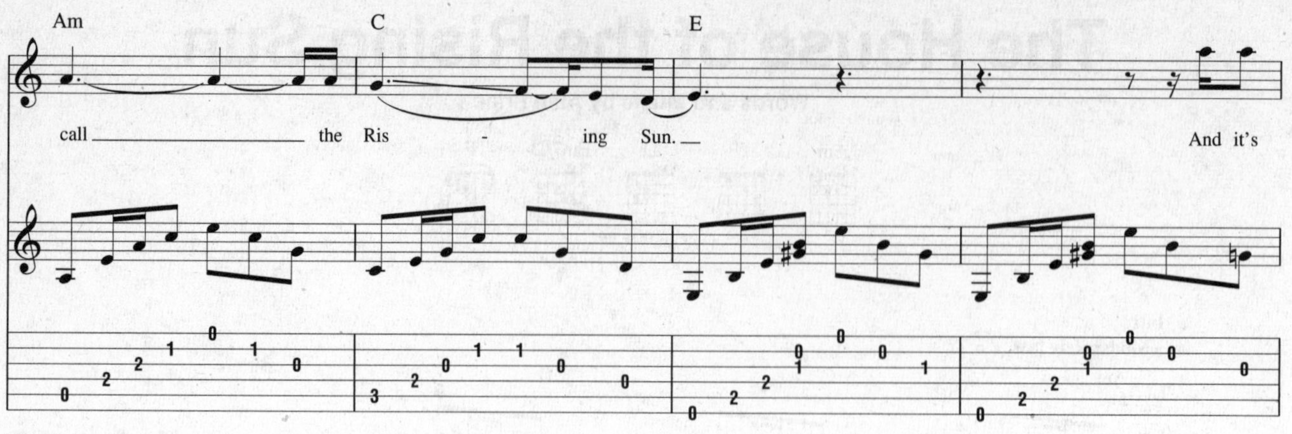
Am
C
E
call the Ris - ing Sun.
And it's

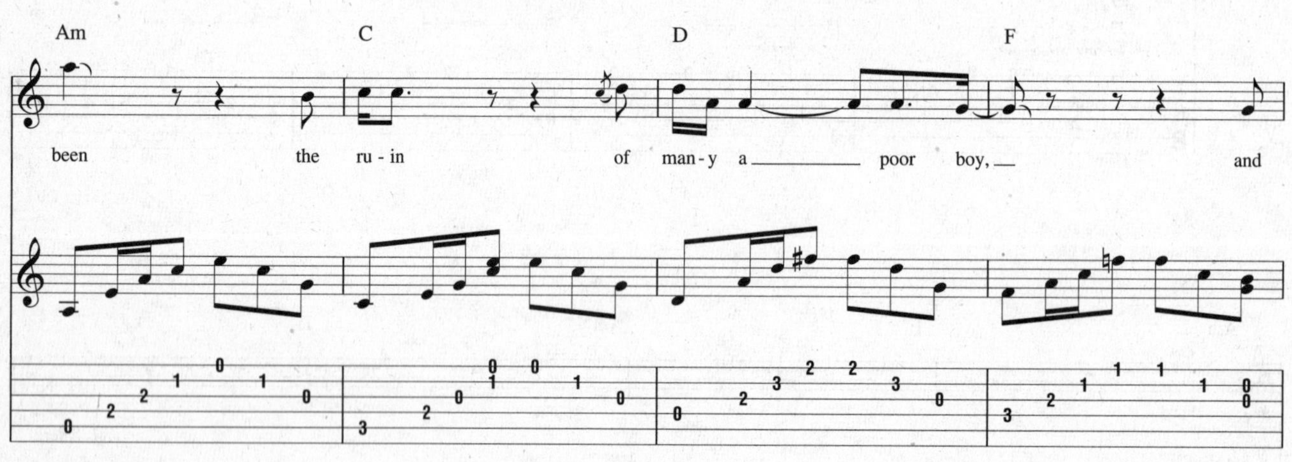
Am
C
D
F
been the ru - in of man - y a poor boy, and

Interlude

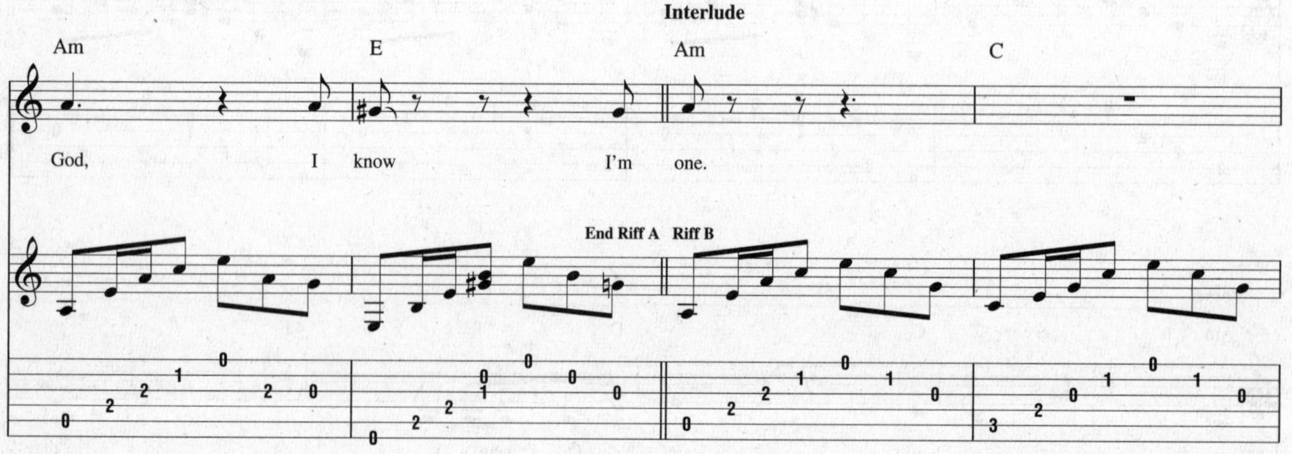
Am
E
Am
C
God, I know I'm one.
End Riff A
Riff B

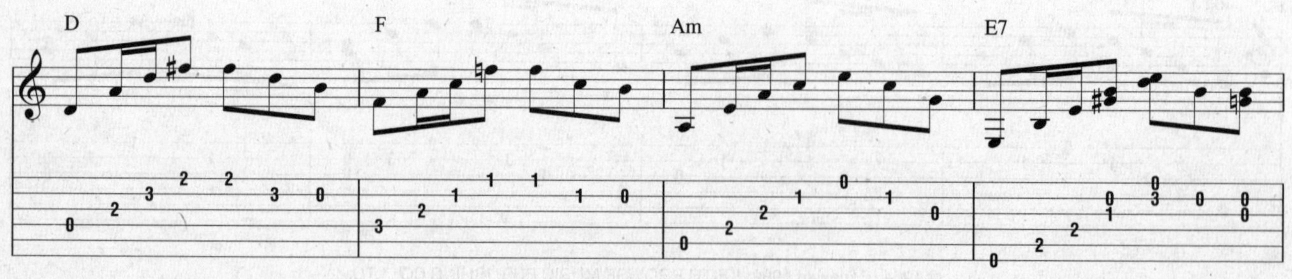
D
F
Am
E7

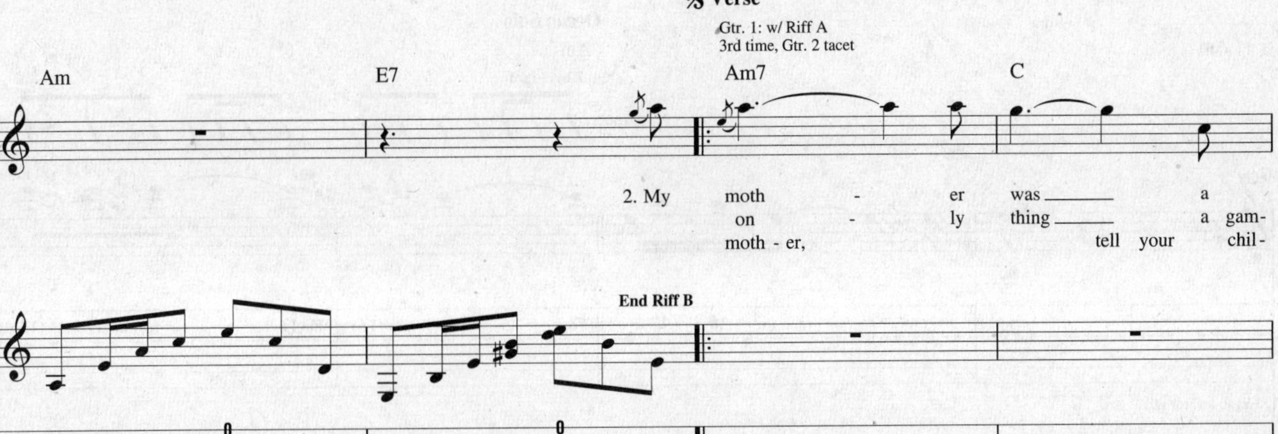
Verse
Gtr. 1: w/ Riff A
3rd time, Gtr. 2 tacet
Am E7 Am7 C
2. My moth - er was a
on - ly thing a gam-
moth - er, tell your chil-
End Riff B

D F Am C
tai - lor, she sewed my new blue jeans.
- bler needs is a suit - case and a truck.
dren not to do what I have done,

E Am C
My fa - ther was a
And the on - ly time he's
spend your lives in

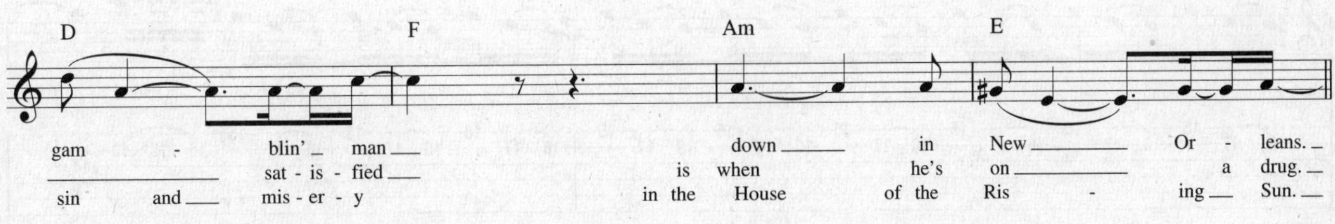
D F Am E
gam - blin' man down in New Or - leans.
sat - is - fied is when he's on a drug.
sin and mis - er - y in the House of the Ris - ing Sun.

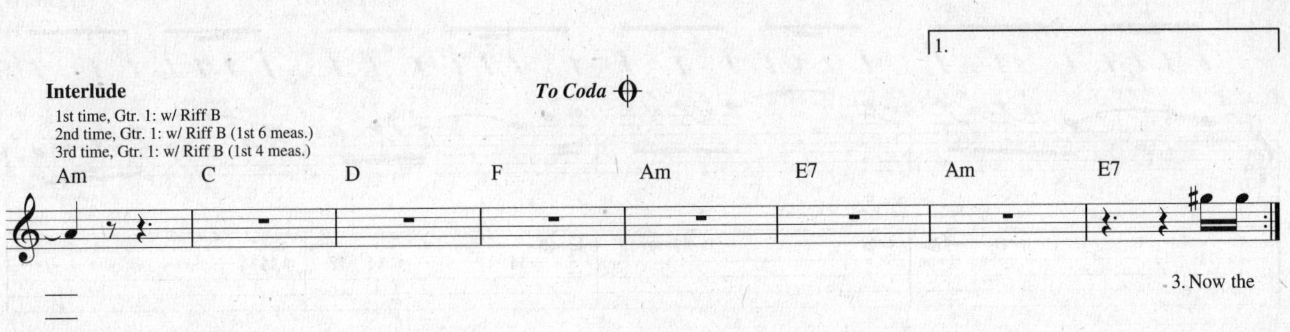
Interlude
1st time, Gtr. 1: w/ Riff B
2nd time, Gtr. 1: w/ Riff B (1st 6 meas.)
3rd time, Gtr. 1: w/ Riff B (1st 4 meas.)
To Coda
1.
Am C D F Am E7 Am E7
3. Now the

2.
Organ Solo
Am
E
Am
C
Rhy. Fig. 1
Gtr. 1
*Gtr. 2
mf
*Organ arr. for gtr.
Gtr. 1
(cont. in slashes)
D
Em7/D
F
Em7/D
Am
C
Em7/D
Gtr. 1
Gtr. 2
8va
E
8va
loco
Am
C
D
Em7/D
F
Em7/D

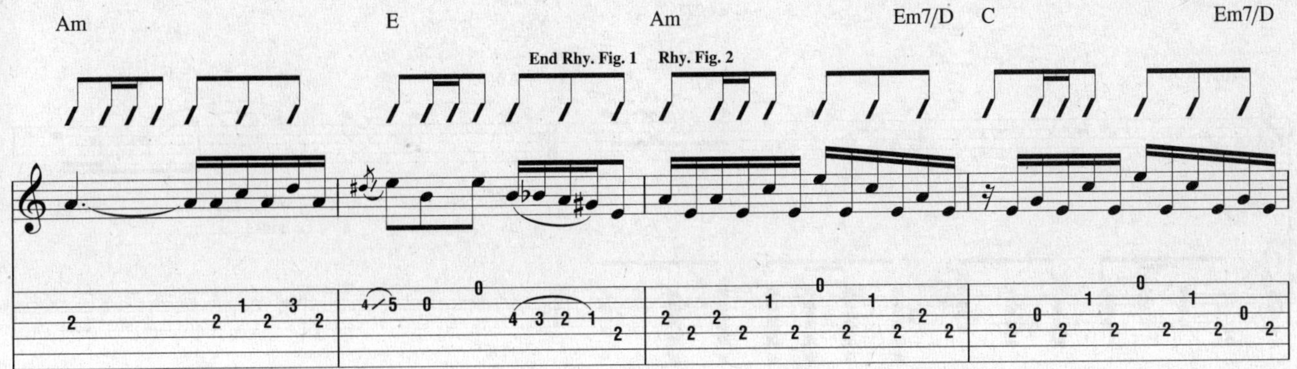
Am
E
Am
Em7/D
C
Em7/D
End Rhy. Fig. 1
Rhy. Fig. 2

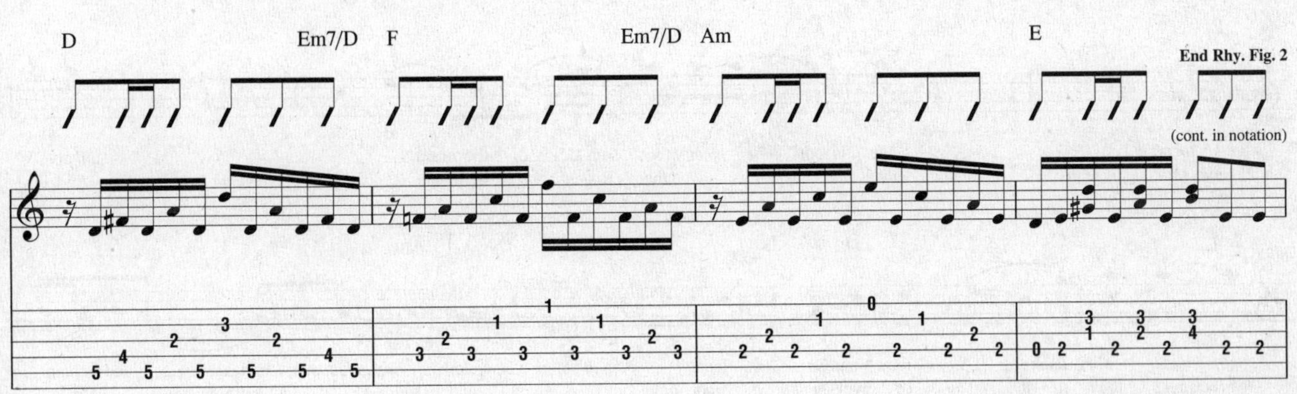
D
Em7/D
F
Em7/D
Am
E
End Rhy. Fig. 2
(cont. in notation)

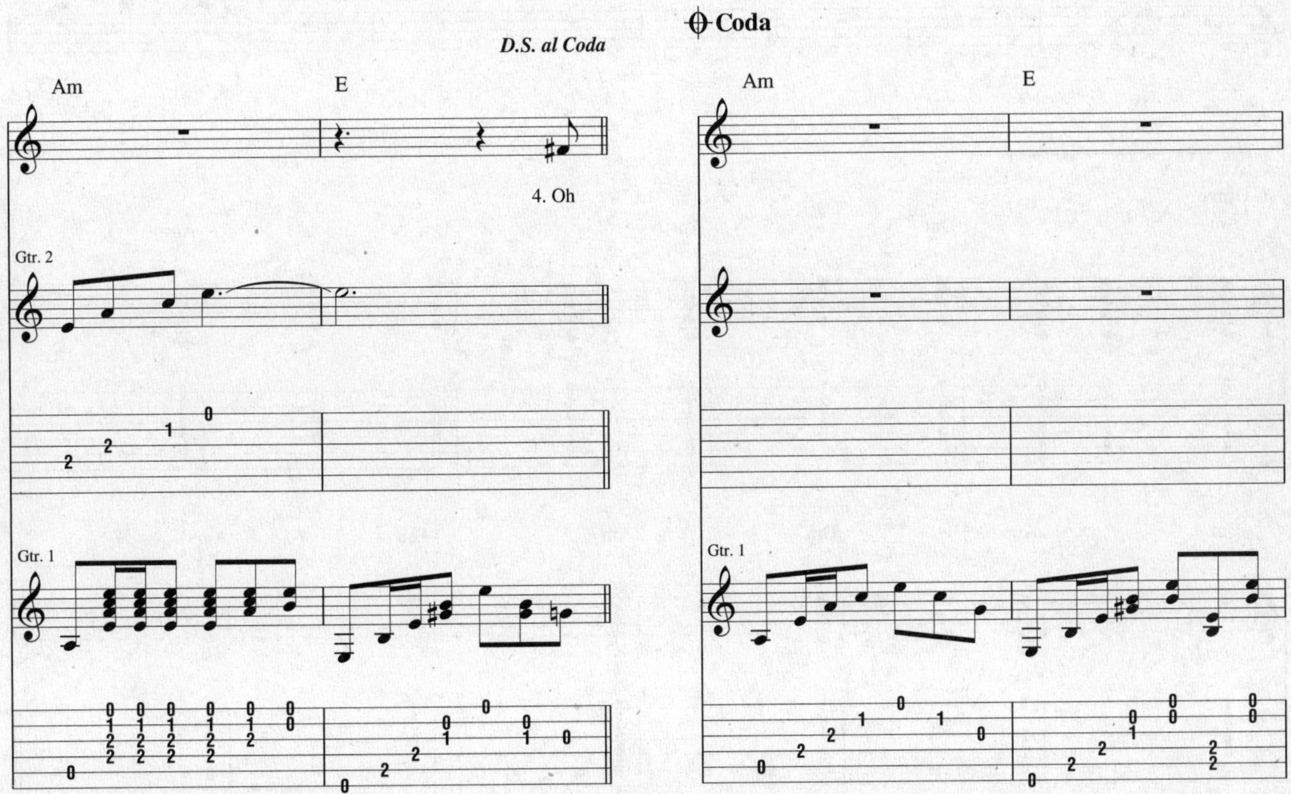
Coda
D.S. al Coda
Am
E
Am
E
4. Oh
Gtr. 2
Gtr. 1
Gtr. 1

Verse
Gtr. 1: w/ Rhy. Fig. 1
Am E Am C
5. Well, I got one foot on the plat -
is a house in
D F Am C E
- form, the oth - er foot on the train. I'm
New Or - leans they call the Ris - ing Sun. And it's
Am C D F Am E
go - in' back to New Or - leans to wear that ball and chain.
been the ru - in of man - y a poor boy, and God, I know I'm
Interlude
1st time, Gtr. 1: w/ Rhy. Fig. 2
2nd time, Gtr. 1: w/ Rhy. Fig. 2 (1st 6 meas.)
Am C D F Am E Am E
one.
1.
6. Well, there
2.
Outro
Gtr. 1
Am Dm Am Dm Am
Dm Am Dm Am Dm Am9
slight rit.

Hurts So Good

Words and Music by John Mellencamp and George Green

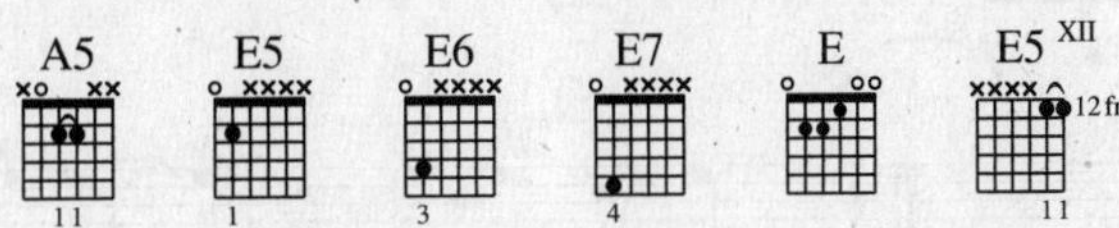

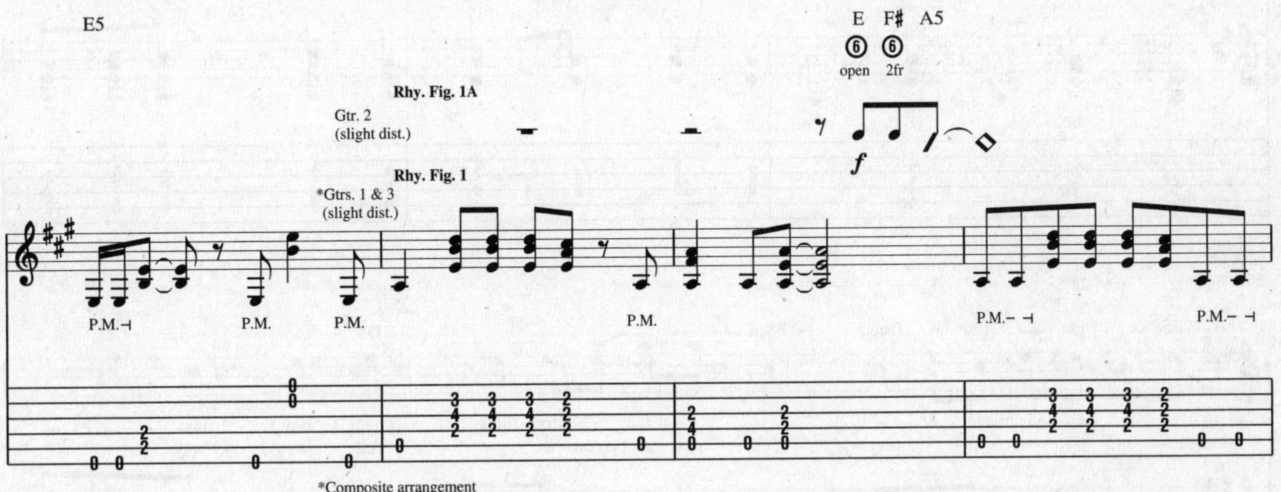

Verse

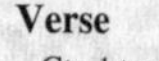

Gtr. 1 tacet
E F♯ A5
open 2fr
Gtr. 2 tacet
E5 E6 E6 E5
1. When I was a young boy,
2. Don't have to be so ex-cit-ing.
Gtr. 3

F♯m D5 A
said put a-way those young boy ways. Now that I'm get-tin' old-
Just try-in' to give my-self a lit-tle bit of fun, yeah. You al-ways look so
P.M.

E5 E6 E5 Esus2 F♯m D5
-er, so much old-er I long for those young boy days
in-vit-ing. You ain't as green as you are young.

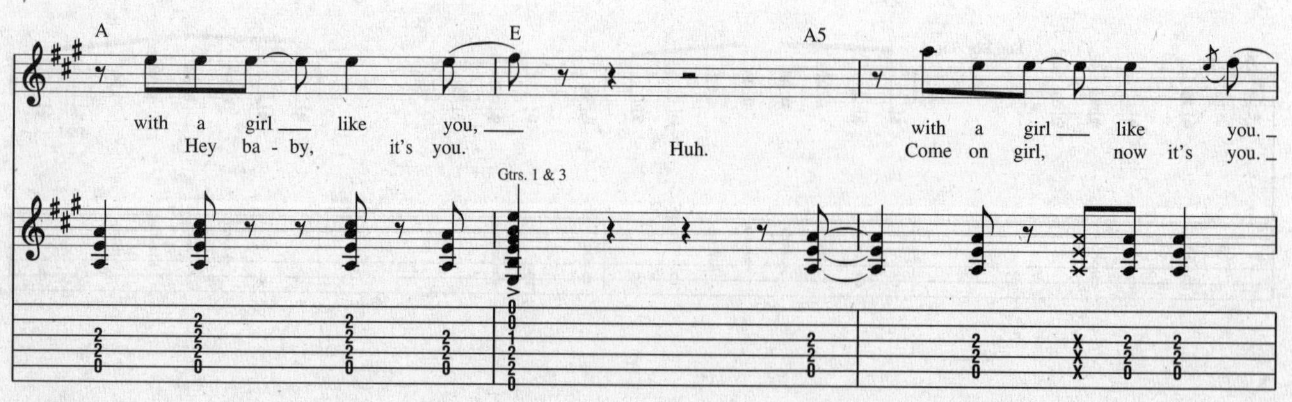

A E A5
with a girl like you, with a girl like you.
Hey ba-by, it's you. Huh. Come on girl, now it's you.
Gtrs. 1 & 3

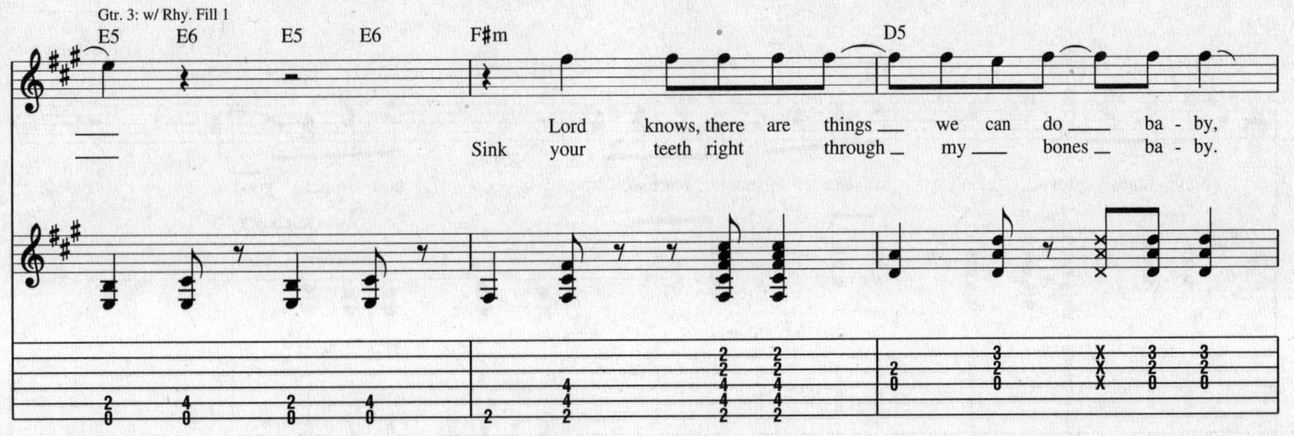
Gtr. 3: w/ Rhy. Fill 1
E5
E6
E5
E6
F#m
D5
Lord knows, there are things ___ we can do ___ ba - by,
Sink your teeth right through _ my ___ bones _ ba - by.

Chorus

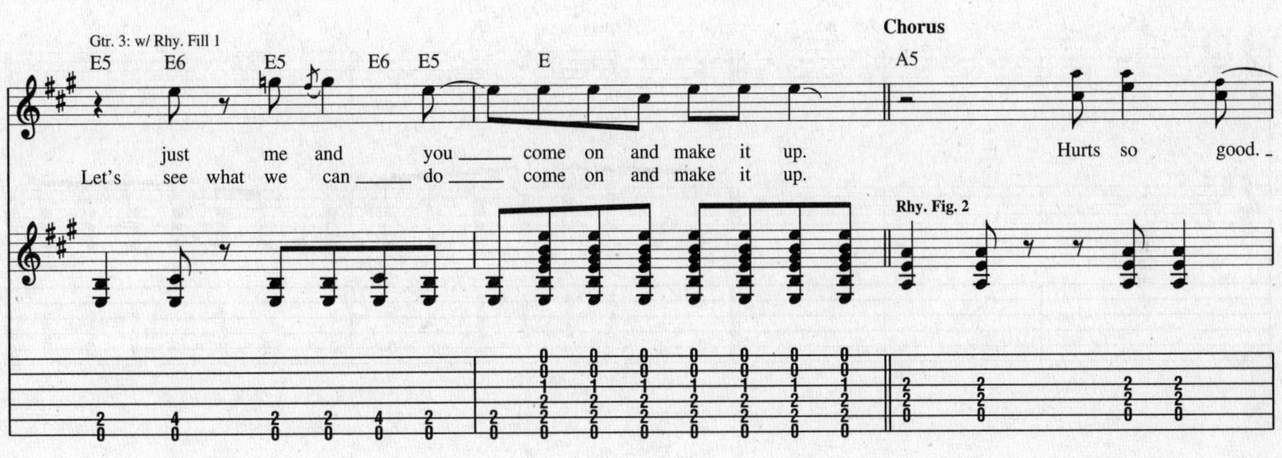
Gtr. 3: w/ Rhy. Fill 1
E5
E6
E5
E6
E5
E
A5
just me and you ___ come on and make it up.
Let's see what we can ___ do ___ come on and make it up.
Hurts so good. _
Rhy. Fig. 2

E5
E6
E5
E6
A5
E5
E6
E5
E6
Come on ba - by, make it hurt so good.

Rhy. Fill 1
Gtr. 3

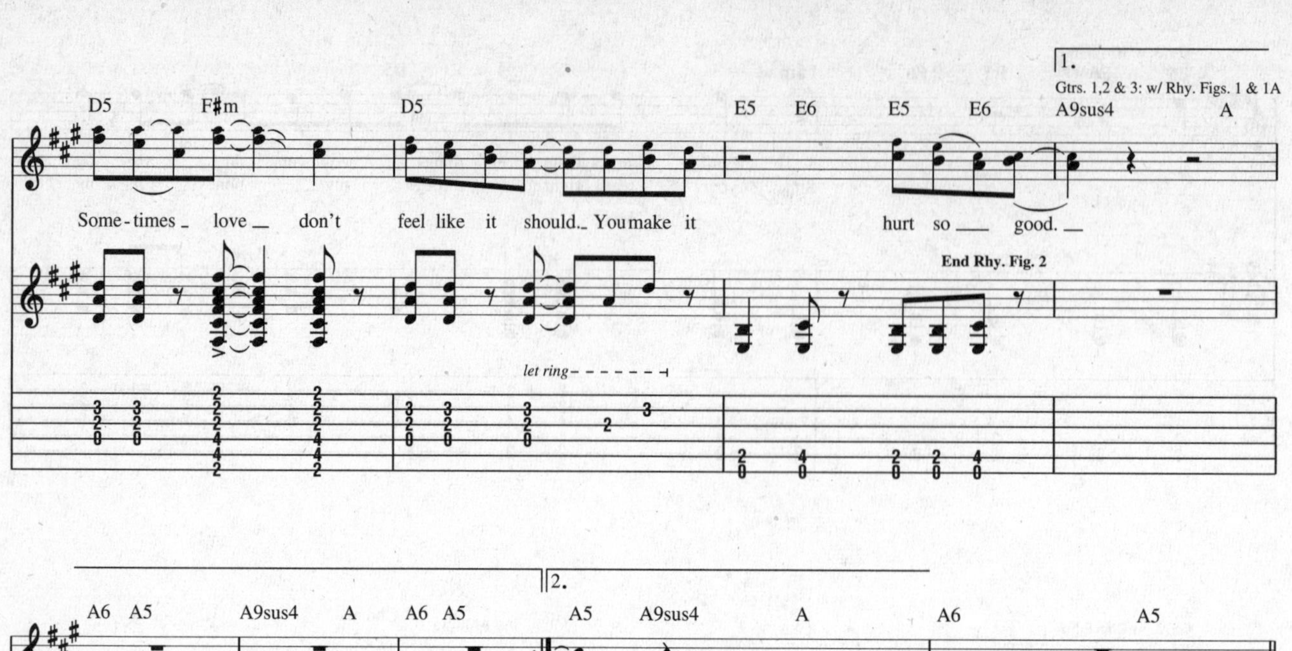
1.
Gtrs. 1,2 & 3: w/ Rhy. Figs. 1 & 1A
D5
F♯m
D5
E5
E6
E5
E6
A9sus4
A
Some-times love don't feel like it should. You make it hurt so good.
End Rhy. Fig. 2
let ring
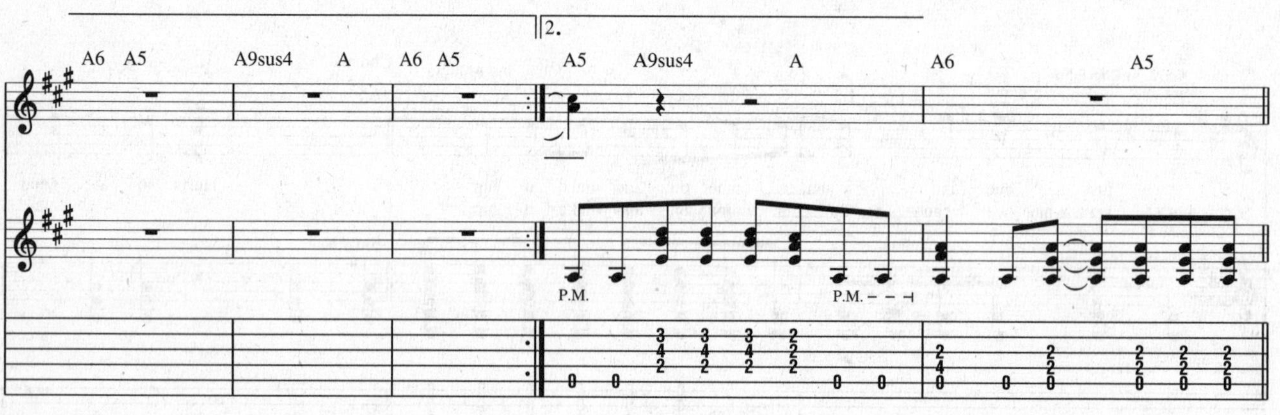
2.
A6
A5
A9sus4
A
A6
A5
A5
A9sus4
A
A6
A5
P.M.
P.M.
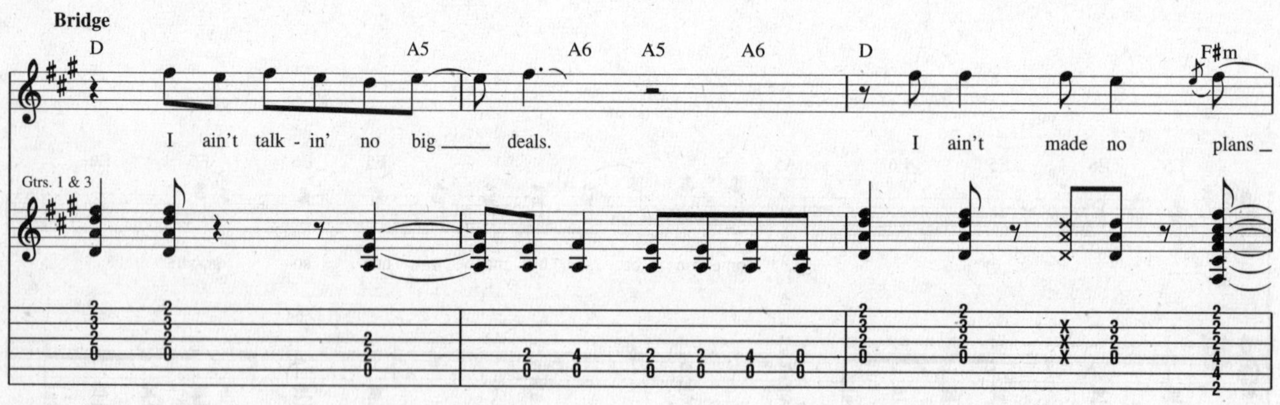
Bridge
D
A5
A6
A5
A6
D
F♯m
I ain't talk-in' no big deals. I ain't made no plans
Gtrs. 1 & 3

A5
D
A5
A6
A5
A6
by my-self. I ain't talk-in' no high heels. Ba-by, we could
(Gtr. 3, cont. in slashes)

E5
E6
E7
E5
Gtr. 3
walk a - round all day long. Walk a - round, all
Gtr. 1
Gtr. 2: w/ Rhy. Fill 2
day long.
Uh!
E
A5
Rhy. Fill 2
Gtr. 2
f

Chorus

Gtrs. 1 & 3: w/ Rhy. Fig. 2
Gtrs. 1 & 3: w/ Rhy. Fig. 2 (1st 6 meas., 2nd time)

A5 E5 E6 E5 E6 A5 E5 E6 E5 E6 D5 F♯m

Hurts so good. _ Come on ba - by, make it hurt so good. Some-times _ love _ don't

D5 | 1. E5 E6 E5 E6 A5 A9sus4 A A6 A

feel like it should, _ you make it hurt so _ good. _

Gtrs. 1 & 3

3 3 3 2 2
4 4 4 2 2
2 2 2 2 4 2
0 0 0 0 0 0 0

2. E5 XII | Gtrs. 1, 2 & 3: w/ Rhy. Figs. 1 & 1A
A9sus4 A A6 A5 A9sus4 A A6 A5

Gtrs. 1 & 3

hurt so _ good. _ Ay! Ay!

Outro

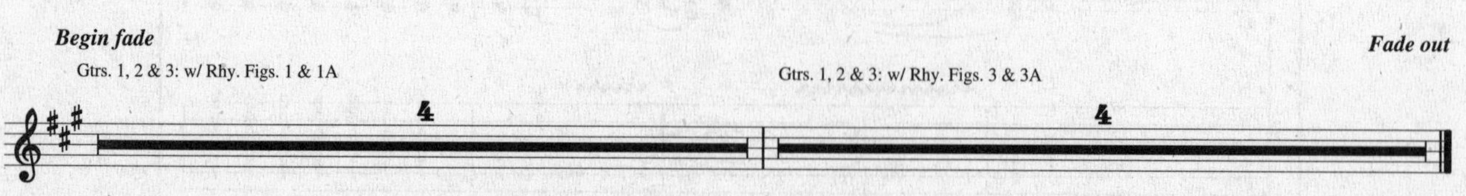

I Am the Highway

Lyrics by Chris Cornell
Music written and arranged by Audioslave

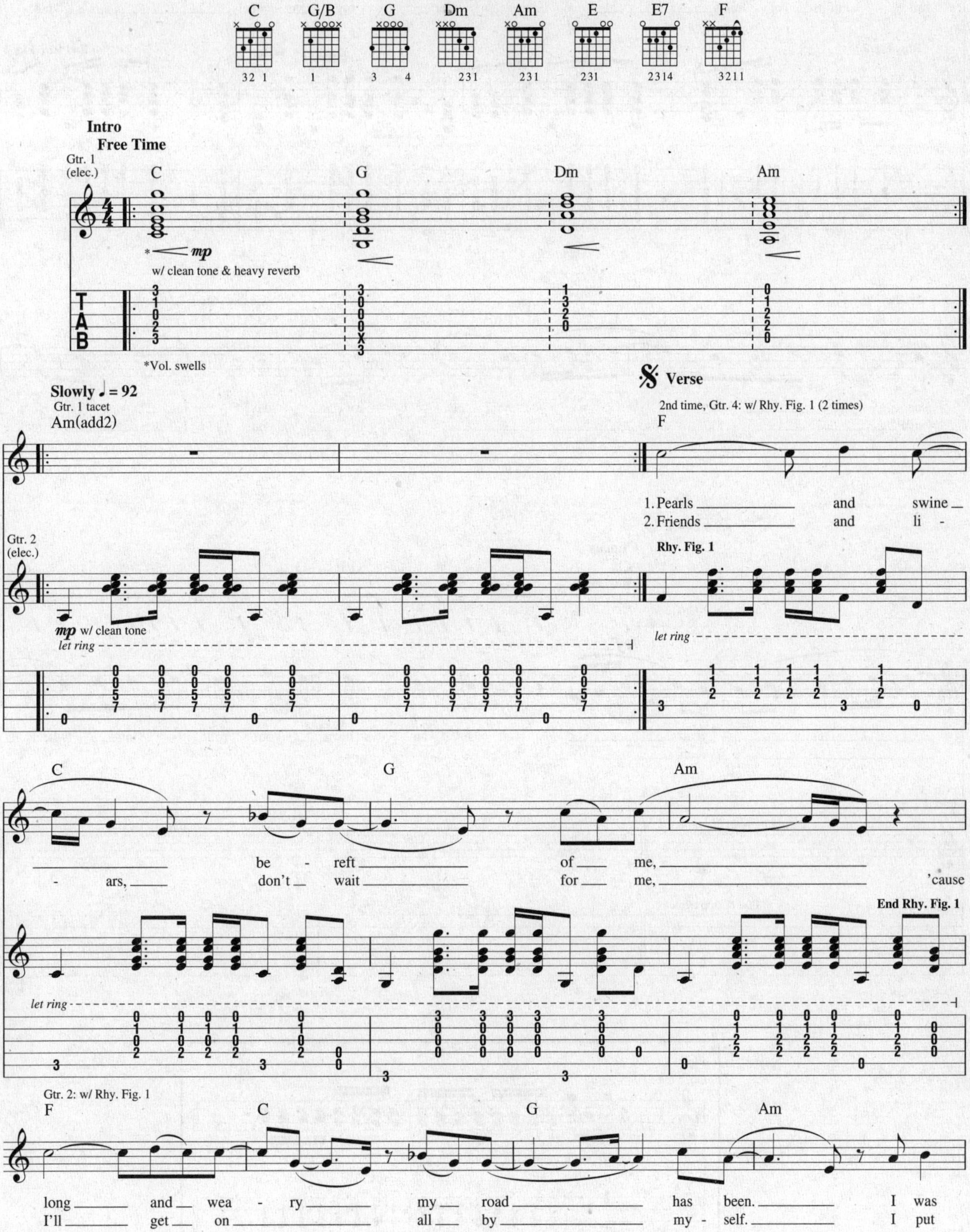

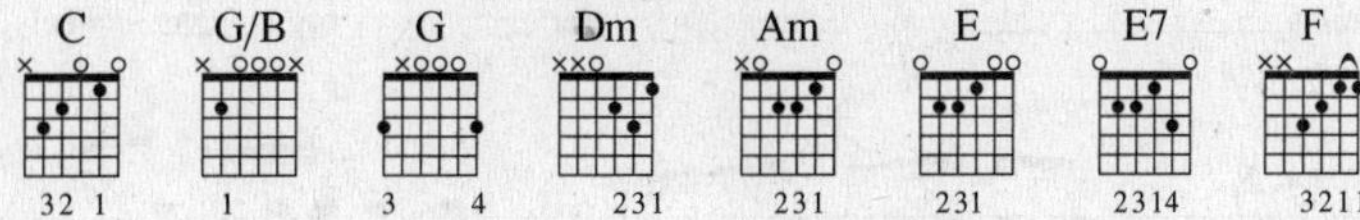

Intro
Free Time

Gtr. 1 (elec.)

C G Dm Am

mp

w/ clean tone & heavy reverb

*Vol. swells

Slowly ♩ = 92

Gtr. 1 tacet

Am(add2)

Gtr. 2 (elec.)

mp w/ clean tone

let ring

𝄋 **Verse**

2nd time, Gtr. 4: w/ Rhy. Fig. 1 (2 times)

F

Rhy. Fig. 1

let ring

1. Pearls and swine
2. Friends and li-

C G Am

bereft of me,
-ars, don't wait for me, 'cause

let ring

End Rhy. Fig. 1

Gtr. 2: w/ Rhy. Fig. 1

F C G Am

long and wea - ry my road has been. I was
I'll get on all by my - self. I put

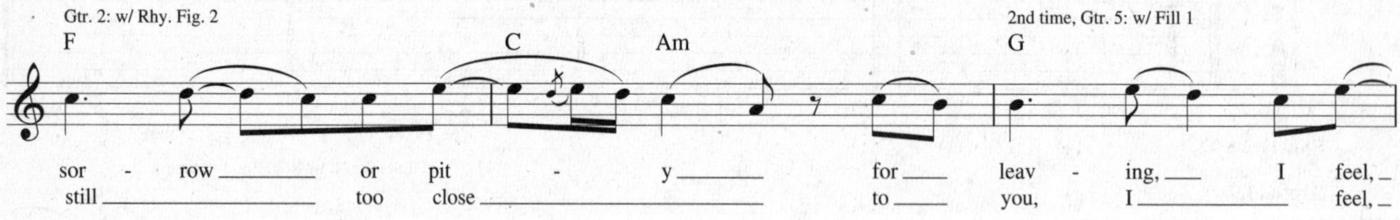

*Baritone gtr.

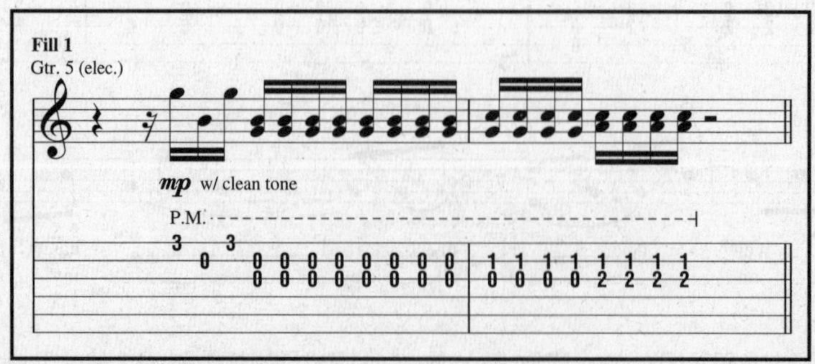

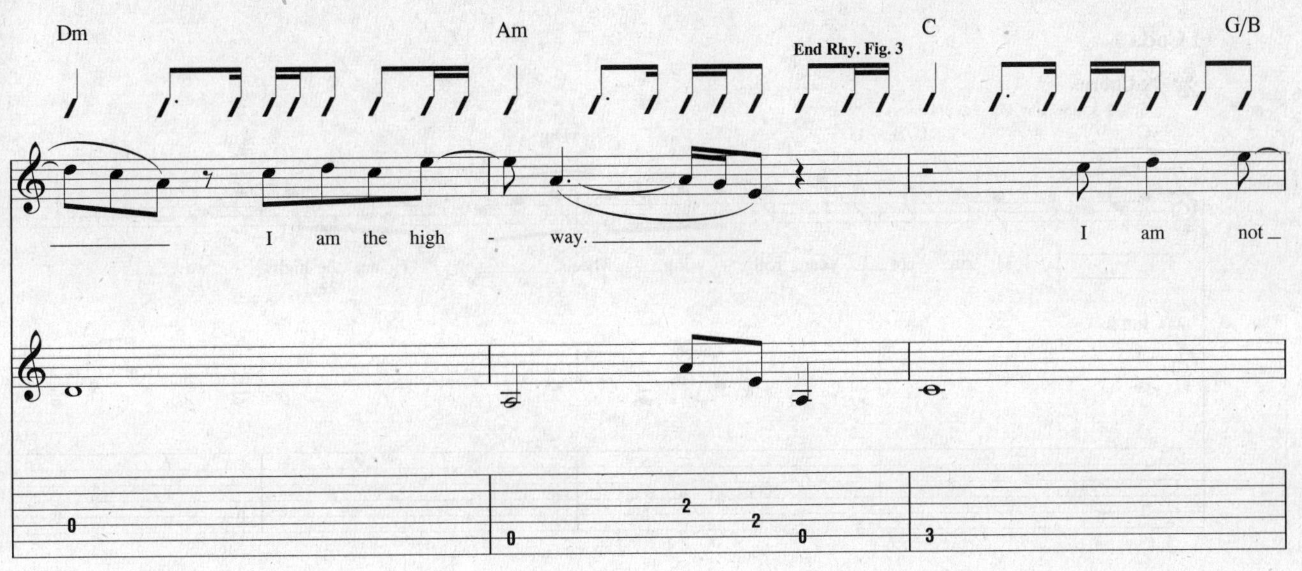

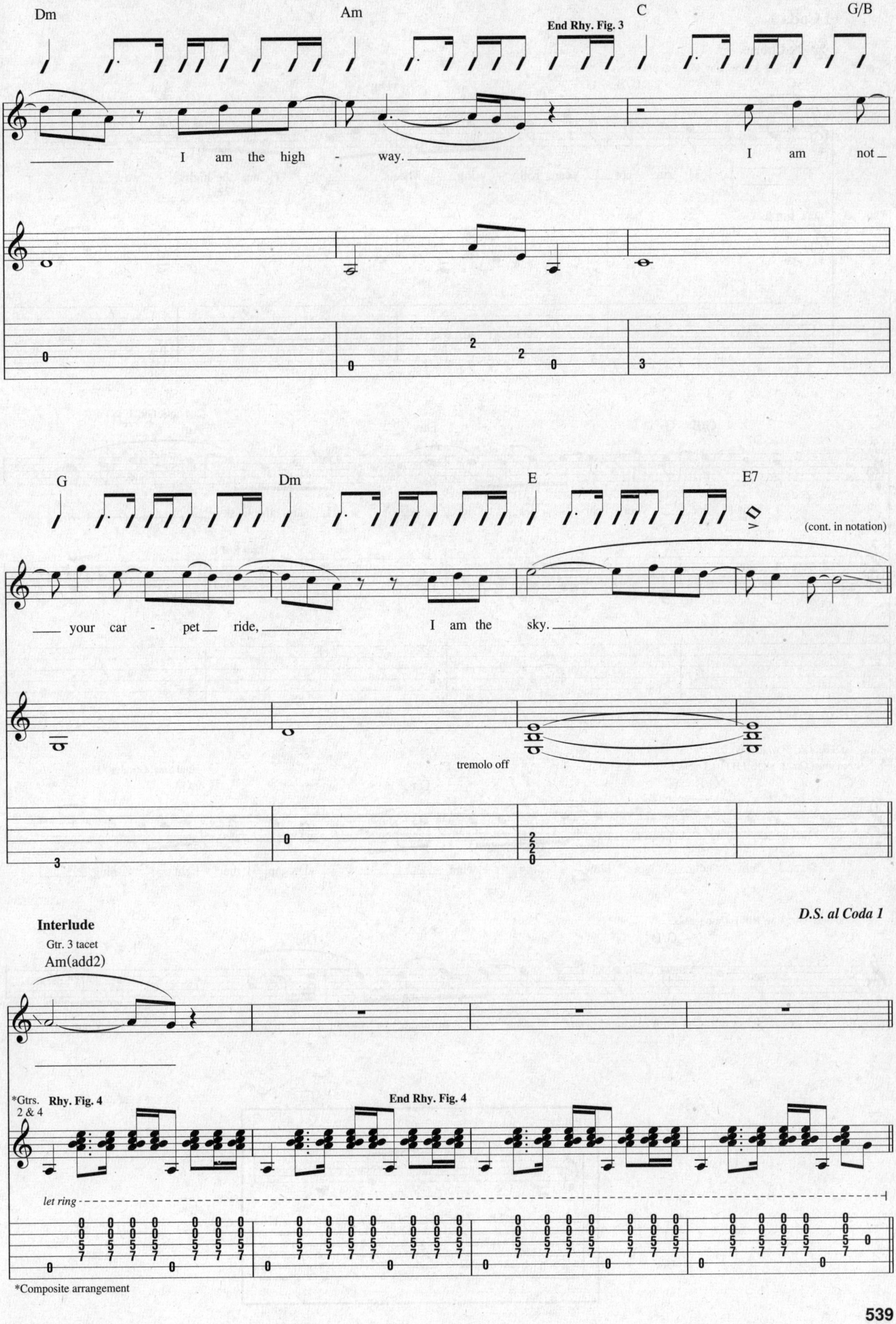

G Dm E E7

(cont. in notation)

your car - pet ride, I am the sky.

tremolo off

Interlude

Gtr. 3 tacet

Am(add2)

D.S. al Coda 1

*Gtrs. 2 & 4 **Rhy. Fig. 4** **End Rhy. Fig. 4**

let ring

*Composite arrangement

Coda 1

Chorus

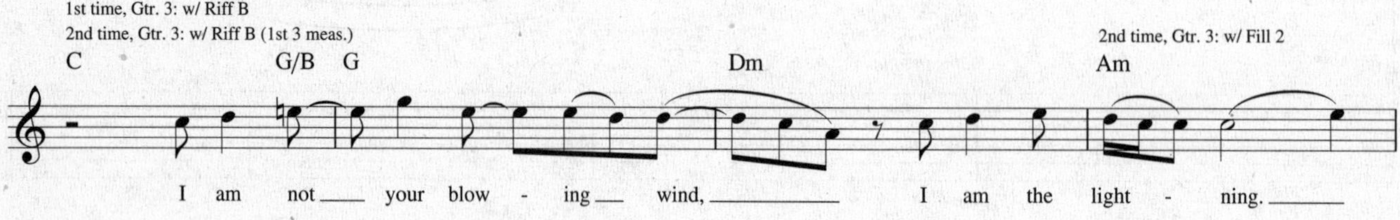

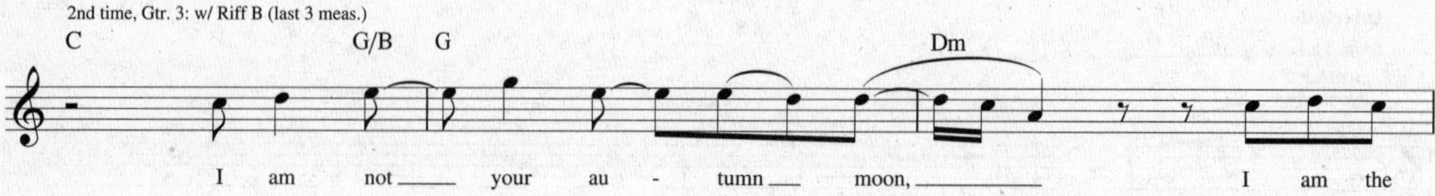

To Coda 2
E
Gtrs. 2 & 4
night,
the night.
Gtr. 3
tremolo off
Guitar Solo
Gtr. 3 tacet
F
C
G
Am
Rhy. Fig. 5
End Rhy. Fig. 5
Gtr. 6 (elec.)
mp
w/ clean tone & *delay
*Set for eighth note regeneration w/ 1 repeat.
Gtrs. 2 & 4: w/ Rhy. Fig. 5 (3 times)
Harm.

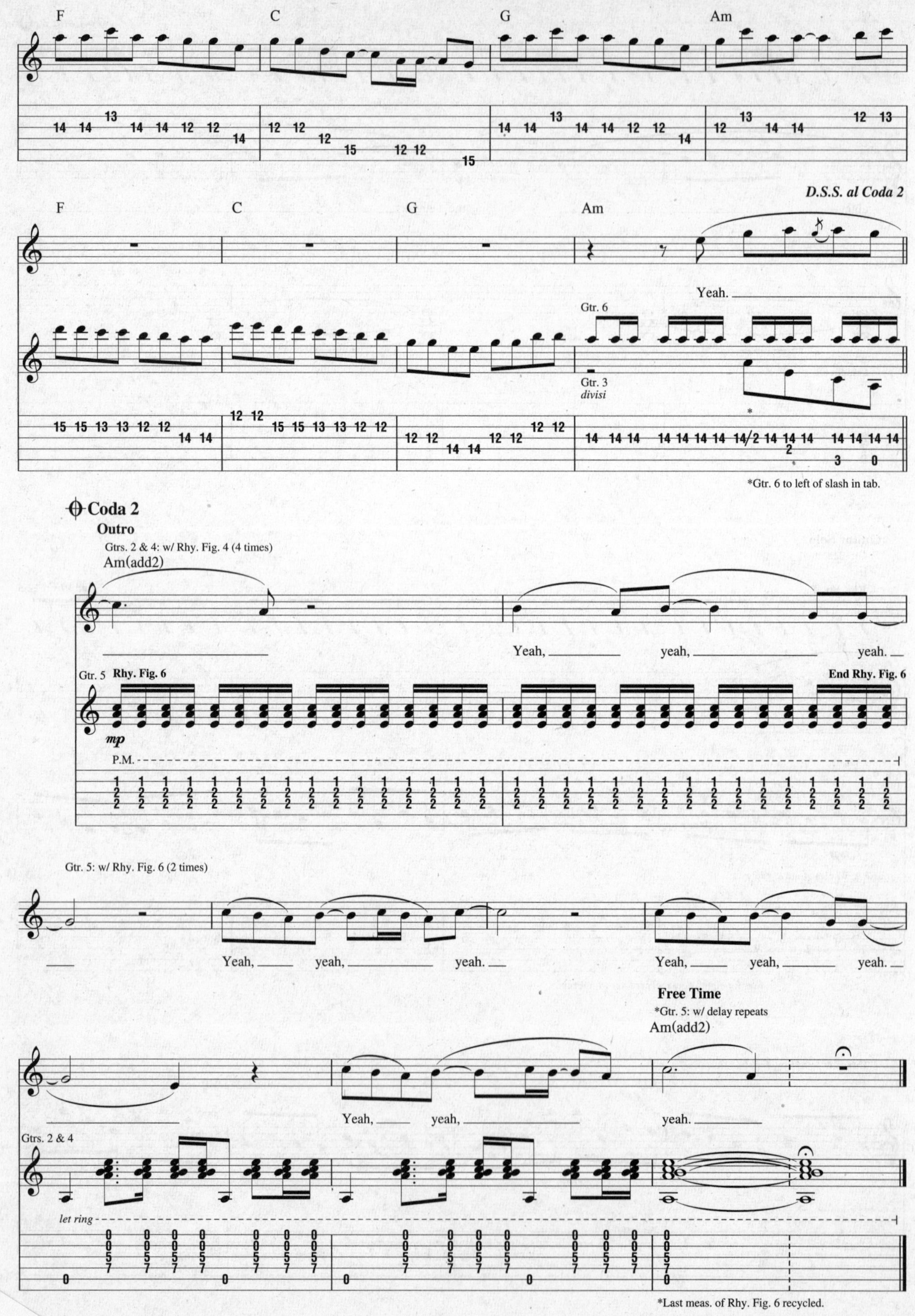
F
C
G
Am
D.S.S. al Coda 2
Yeah.
Gtr. 6
Gtr. 3
divisi
*Gtr. 6 to left of slash in tab.
Coda 2
Outro
Gtrs. 2 & 4: w/ Rhy. Fig. 4 (4 times)
Am(add2)
Yeah, yeah, yeah.
Gtr. 5
Rhy. Fig. 6
End Rhy. Fig. 6
mp
P.M.
Gtr. 5: w/ Rhy. Fig. 6 (2 times)
Yeah, yeah, yeah.
Yeah, yeah, yeah.
Free Time
*Gtr. 5: w/ delay repeats
Am(add2)
Yeah, yeah, yeah.
Gtrs. 2 & 4
let ring
*Last meas. of Rhy. Fig. 6 recycled.

I Can't Explain

Words and Music by Peter Townshend

Chorus
Gtr. 1: w/Rhy. Fig. 1, 2 times
E D A E D A E
can't ex - plain, can't ex - plain. Yeah, hear what I'm say - in' girl. Can't ex - plain.
(Ooh. Can't ex - plain. Ooh. Can't ex - plain.)
1st Guitar Solo
D.S. al Coda
N.C.(E) (D) (A) (E) (D) (A) (E)
Coda
Gtr. 1: w/Rhy. Fig. 1, 2 times
E D A E D A E
Can't ex - plain. Please give me one more try now. Can't ex - plain.
(Ooh. Can't ex - plain. Ooh. Can't ex - plain.)
2nd Guitar Solo
N.C.(E) (D) (A) (E) (D) (A) (E)
* Gtr. 2
* 12 str. electric
(E) (D) (A) (E) (D) (A) (E)
full
Chorus
Gtr. 1: w/Rhy. Fig. 1, 2 times
E D A E D A E
Said, I can't ex - plain it. You drive me out of my mind.
(Ooh. Can't ex - plain. Ooh. Can't ex - plain.
E D A E E D A E
Tell me what its got me, yeah. I said I can't ex - plain.
Ooh. Can't ex - plain. Ooh. Can't ex - plain.)
Gtr. 1

I Can't Help Myself (Sugar Pie, Honey Bunch)

Words and Music by Brian Holland, Lamont Dozier and Edward Holland

G F G C6
End Rhy. Fig. 1
I love you and nobody else. In
End Riff B
Gtrs. 1 & 2: w/ Riff B & Rhy. Fig. 1
C G
and out my life, you come and you go
(In and out my life, come and you go.
Sug-ar pie hon-ey bunch, do an-y-thing you ask me to.
(Sug-ar pie hon-ey bunch,
Dm G
Voc. Fig. 1
leav-ing just your pic-ture be-hind. And I kissed it a
Oo,
Can't help my-self, I want you and
ask me to.)
Verse
Gtrs. 1 & 2: w/ Riff B & Rhy. Fig. 1
F G C6 C
End Voc. Fig. 1
thou-sand times. 2. When you snap your fin-ger or
oo.) 5. Sug-ar pie hon-ey bunch,
no-bod-y else. Oo.
To Coda
G
wink your eyes, I come a run-nin' to you. I'm tied to your
(Can't
you know that I love you. Can't
(Sug-ar pie hon-ey bunch. Love you.)
Dm G F G C6
a-pron string and there's noth-ing that I can do. Oo.
help my-self. Oo.)
Saxophone Solo
Gtrs. 1 & 2: w/ Riff B & Rhy. Fig. 1
C G
Can't

Bkgd. Voc.: w/ Voc. Fig. 1
Dm G F G C6
help my - self, no, I can't help my - self. 3. 'Cause sug -
Verse
Gtrs. 1 & 2: w/ Riff B & Rhy. Fig. 1, 2 times
C G
- ar pie hon - ey bunch, I'm weak - er than a man should be.
(Sug - ar pie hon - ey bunch.)
Dm G
I can't help my - self. I'm a fool in
F G C6 C
love, you see. Wan - na tell you I don't love you, tell
G
you that we're through. And I've tried, but ev - 'ry time I
(Can't
Dm G F G C6
see your face I get all choked up in - side. When
help my - self.)
Interlude
Gtr. 1: w/ Riff A
N.C. (C)
I call your name, girl, it starts to flame. (Burn - in' in my heart, tear'n'
D.S. al Coda
it all a - part.) No mat - ter how I try, my love I can - not hide. 4. 'Cause
Coda
Begin Fade
Dm G F G C6
help my - self, no I can't help my - self. Oo.
Fade Out
Gtrs. 1 & 2: w/ Riff B & Rhy. Fig. 1, 1st 2 meas.
C
Sug - ar pie hon - ey bunch. (Sug - ar pie hon - ey bunch.)

I Get Around

Words and Music by Brian Wilson and Mike Love

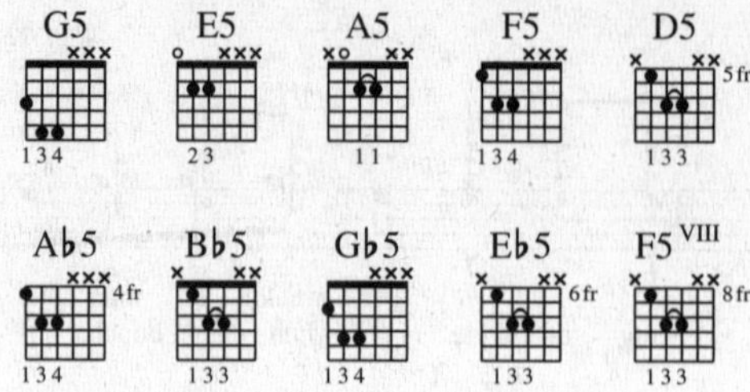

A5
I'm a real cool head.
I'm mak - in' real good bread.
I get a - round.
Get a - round, round, round
I get a - round.

Verse
Gtr. 2 tacet
N.C.
F5
D5
End Rhy. Fig. 1
1. I'm get - tin' bugged driv - in' up and down the
End Voc. Fig. 1
Get a - round, round, round I get a - round.)
End Riff A
Riff B

same old strip. I got - ta find a new place where the kids are hip.
Gtr. 2
mf
End Riff B
Gtr. 1
divisi
*Gtr. 1 to the right of slash in tab.

Chorus

Bkgd. Voc.: w/ Voc. Fig. 1
Gtr. 1: w/ Rhy. Riff A
Gtr. 2: w/ Rhy. Fig. 1

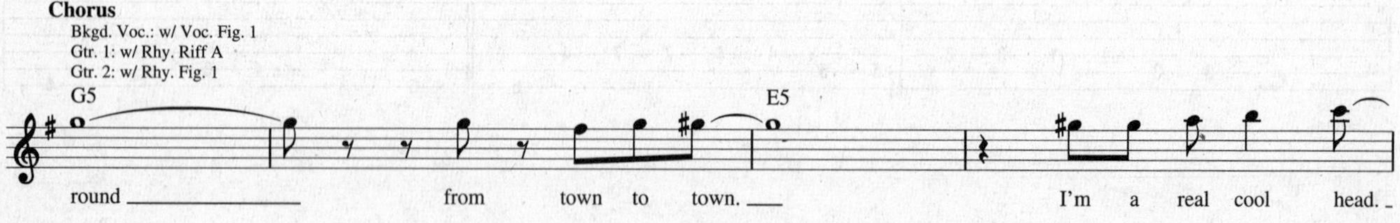

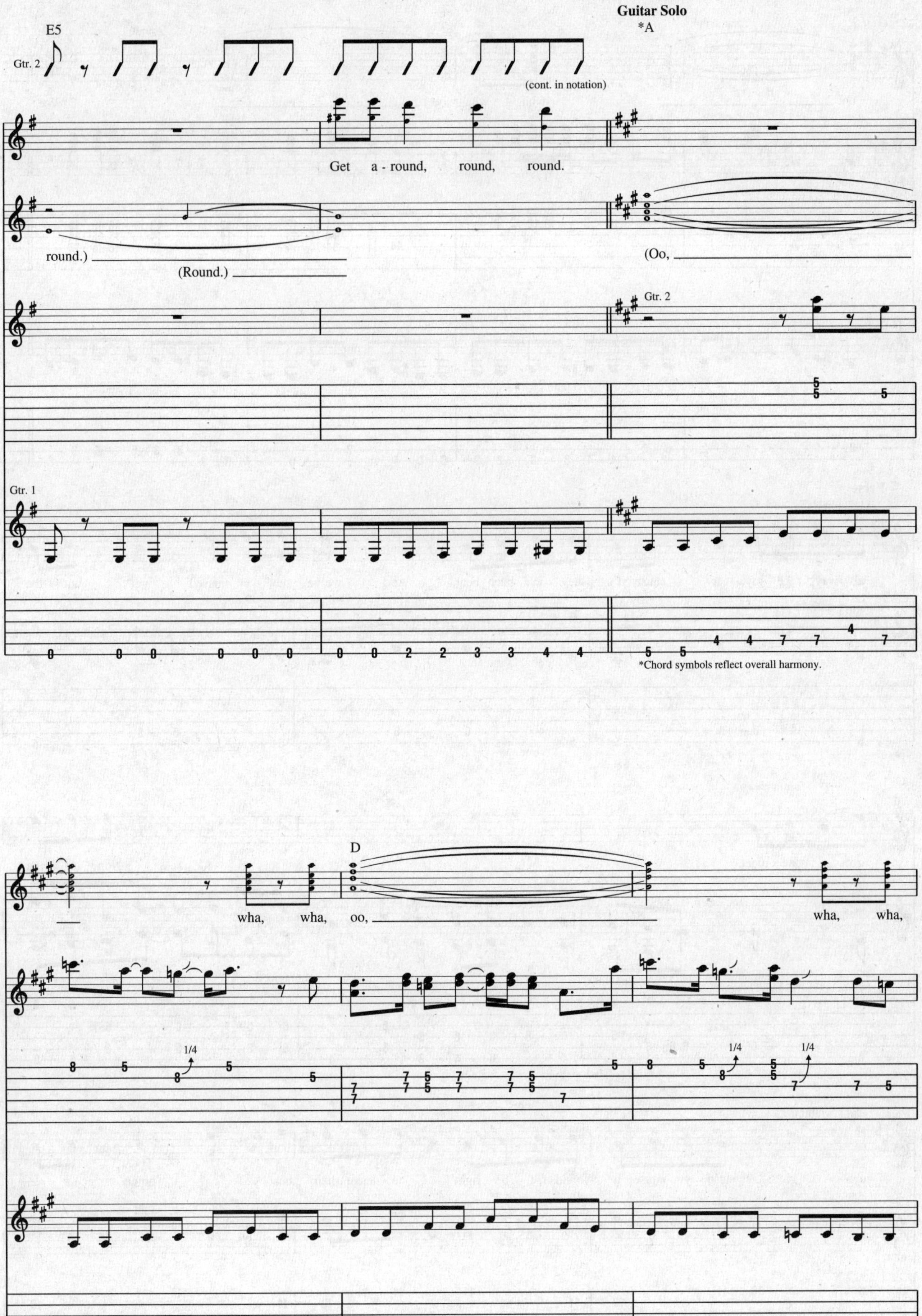

Guitar Solo

*A

E5

Gtr. 2

(cont. in notation)

Get a - round, round, round.

round.) (Round.) (Oo,

Gtr. 2

Gtr. 1

*Chord symbols reflect overall harmony.

A
E
F
oo, wha, wha, oo.) 2. We
Verse
Gtr. 2 tacet
N.C.
al - ways take my car cause it's nev - er been beat. And we've nev - er missed yet with the
Gtr. 1
Riff C
girls we meet. None of the
Gtr. 2
Gtr. 1
divisi
End Riff C
*Gtr. 1 to right of slash in tab.
Gtr. 1: w/ Riff C
guys go stead - y 'cause it would - n't be right to leave their best girl home on a
Gtr. 2

Chorus
Ab5
Rhy. Fig. 2
Gtr. 2
Sat - ur - day night. I get a - round from town to town.
Voc. Fig. 2
(Get a - round, round, round I get a - round.
Riff D
Gtr. 1
(cont. in slashes)
F5
Bb5
I'm a real cool head.
Get a - round, round, round I get a - round. Get a - round, round, round
Gb5
Eb5
End Rhy. Fig. 2
I'm mak - in' real good bread.
End Voc. Fig. 2
I get a - round. Get a - round, round, round I get a - round.
(I get a - round. I get a -
End Riff D

F5VIII
Eb5
Interlude
Ab5
Oo.
Round.)
round.)
(Round, round, get a-round,
Gtrs. 1 & 2 tacet
N.C.
Oo,
I get a - round.
(I get a - round, yeah.)
Get a - round, round, round
I get a - round.)
Outro-Chorus
Bkgd. Voc.: w/ Voc. Fig. 2 (till fade)
Gtr. 1: w/ Riff D (till fade)
Gtr. 2: w/ Rhy. Fig. 2 (till fade)
Ab5
F5
Begin fade
Bb5
wha, wha, oo.
Oo.
Gb5
Eb5
Ab5
Oo.
Honk-in' on,
down, on the town.
F5
Bb5
Gb5
Eb5
Fade out
Oo.
Oo.

I Heard It Through the Grapevine

Words and Music by Norman J. Whitfield and Barrett Strong

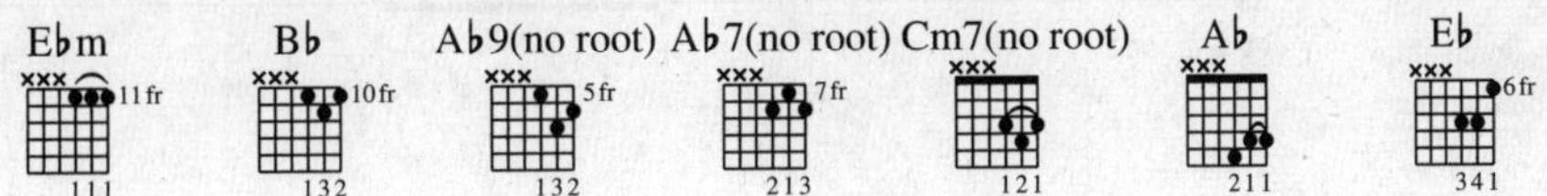

*Kybd. arr. for gtr.

**Key Signature denotes Eb Dorian

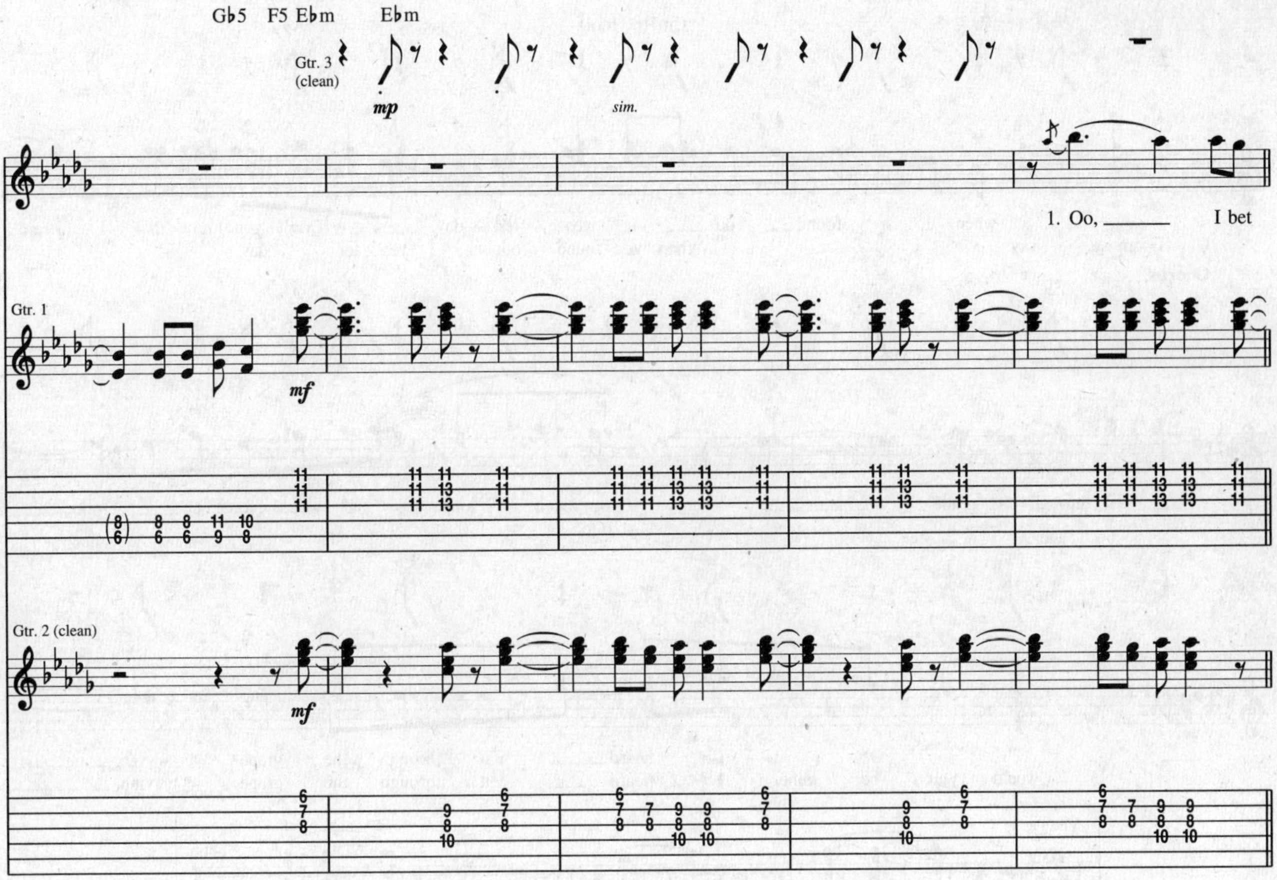

Gb5 F5 Ebm Ebm

Gtr. 3 (clean)

mp

sim.

1. Oo, _____ I bet

Gtr. 1

mf

Gtr. 2 (clean)

mf

Verse
Gtr. 2 tacet
Gtr. 1 tacet
Bkgd. Voc.: w/ Voc. Fig. 1, 2nd & 3rd times
Ebm
Bb
Ab9(no root)
Gtr. 3
you, won-dered how I knew 'bout your plans to make me blue
2., 3. See Additional Lyrics
Gtr. 1
*Bkd. Voc. 2nd time
Ab7(no root)
Ebm
with some oth-er guy you knew be-fore. Be-tween the two of us guys,
Bb
Ab9(no root)
Cm7(no root)
you know I love you more. It took me by sur-prise, I must say,
(Took me by sur-prise,
Ab
Cm7(no root)
Ab
when I found out yes-ter-day. Don't you know that I heard
I must say. When you found out yes-ter-day.)
Chorus
Eb
Ab
it through the grape-vine? Not much long-er would you be mine.
(Oo,
Eb
Oh, I heard it through the grape-vine.
would you be mine. I heard it through the grape-vine.
Voc. Fig. 1
(Oo. Oo, oo. Oo.)

Ab
(cont. in notation)
Oh, I'm just a - bout to lose my mind.
Oo.
To Coda
N.C.
Eb5
Gb5
Eb5
Gtr. 3 tacet
Gb5 F5 Eb5
Hon - ey, hon - ey, well.
Heard it through the grape - vine, not much long - er would you be my ba -
Gtr. 3
Gtr. 1
1.
2.
Gb5
Eb5
Gb5 F5
Ebm
Gb5 F5
Ebm
2. I know a man do, do, do, do.
- by. Do, do, do, do, do.
Gtr. 1
Interlude
D.S. al Coda
Ebm
Gtr. 3
)
3. Peo - ple say be - lieve half
Gtr. 1

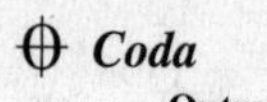

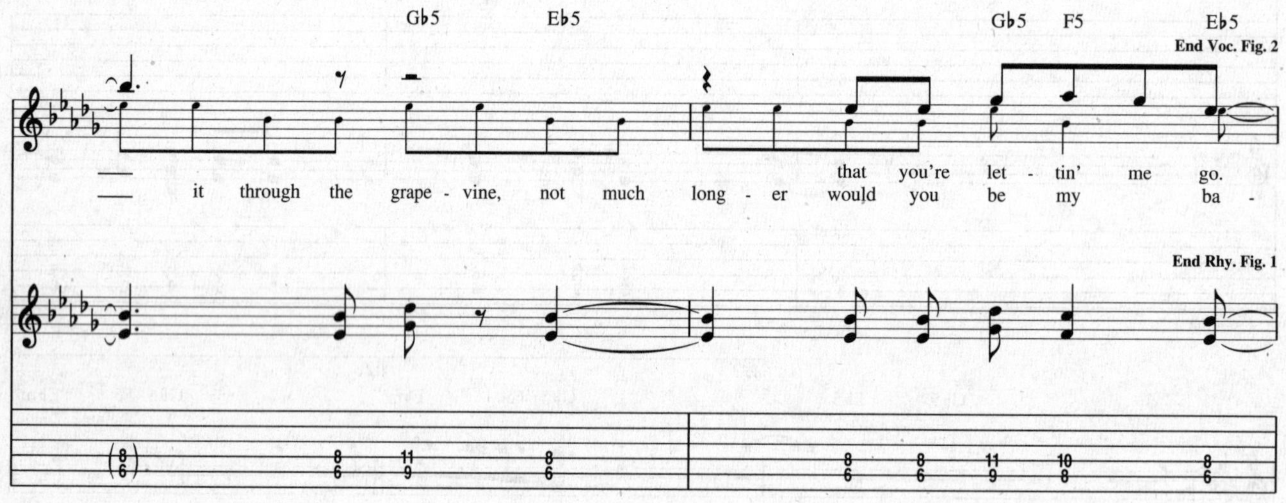

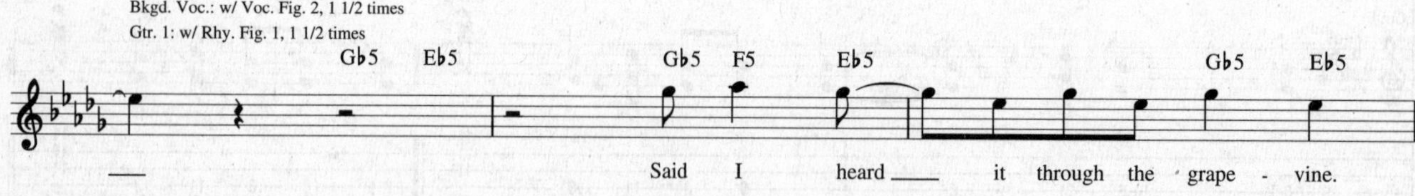

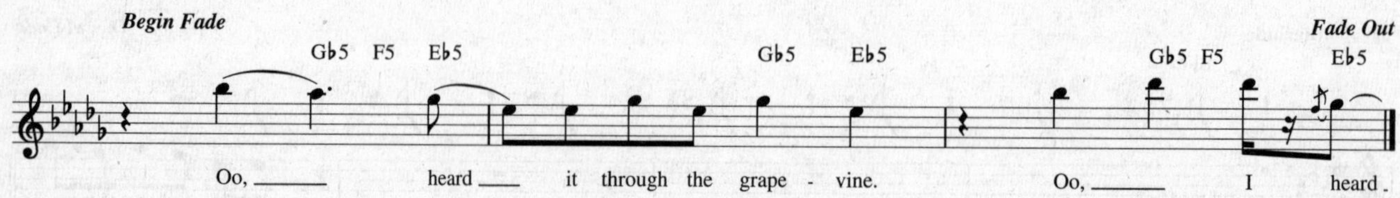

Additional Lyrics

2. I know a man ain't supposed to cry,
But these tears, I can't hold inside.
Losing you would end my life, you see.
'Cause you mean that much to me.
You could've told me yourself that you love someone else.
Instead, I heard...

3. People say believe half of what you see.
Some and none of what you hear.
But I can't help from being confused.
If it's true, please tell me dear.
Do you plan to let me go for the other guy you loved before?

I Want to Hold Your Hand

Words and Music by John Lennon and Paul McCartney

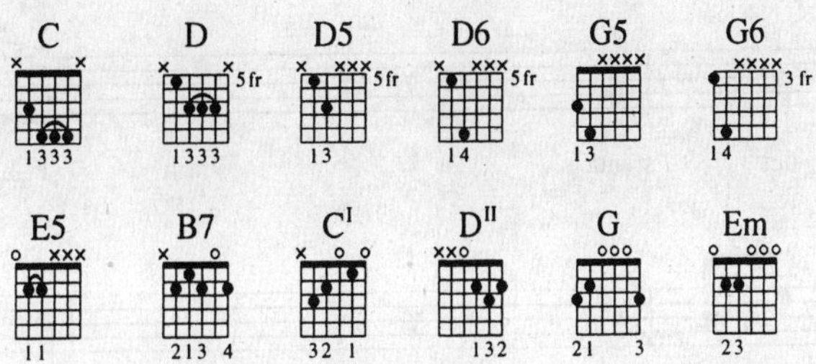

Intro

Moderately Fast ♩ = 136

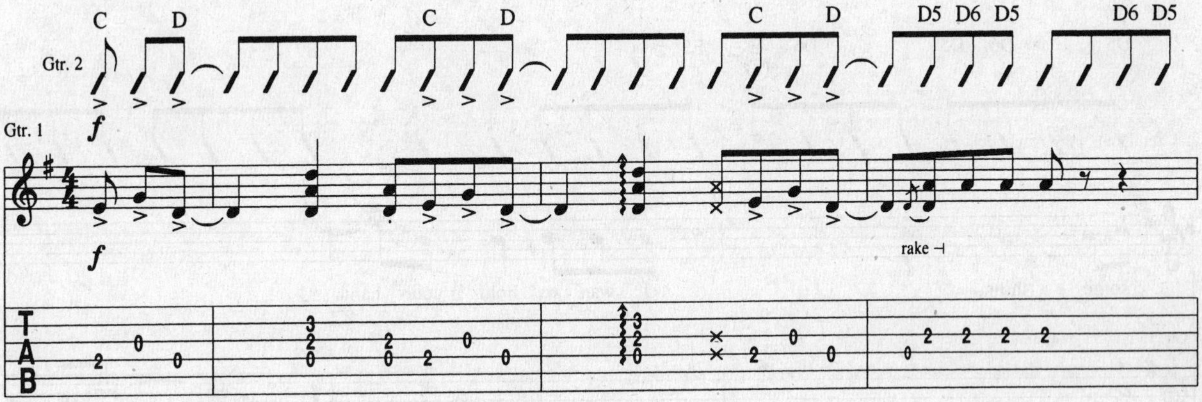

C D C D C D D5 D6 D5 D6 D5

Gtr. 2

Gtr. 1

f

rake

Verse

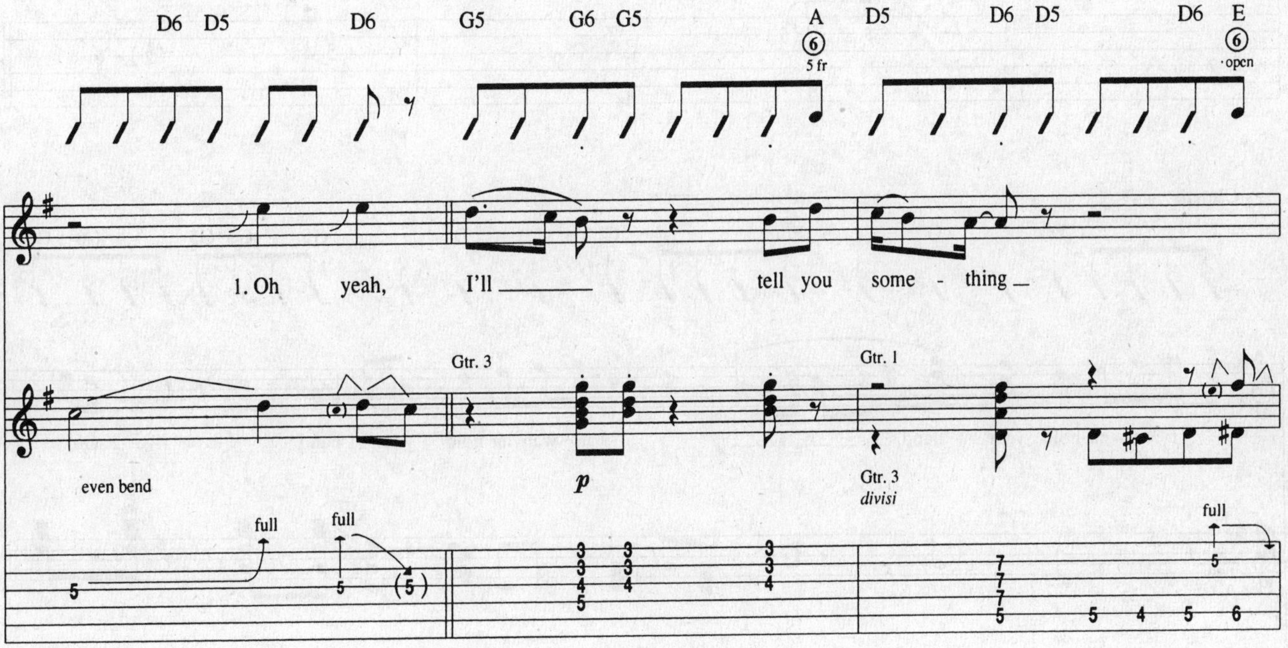

D6 D5 D6 G5 G6 G5 A D5 D6 D5 D6 E

⑥ 5 fr

⑥ open

1. Oh yeah, I'll ___ tell you some - thing ___

even bend

Gtr. 3

p

Gtr. 1

Gtr. 3 *divisi*

full full full

E5 B7 E G5 G6 G5
I think you'll un - der - stand. When I say that
Gtr. 3
D5 D6 D5 D6 E E5 B7 C
some - thing, I wan - na hold your hand.
Gtr. 1
Gtr. 3
divisi
1 1/2
full
Chorus
C D G Em C D G5 G6 G5 G6 G5
I wan - na hold your hand. I wan - na hold your hand. 2. Oh,

Verse
G5 G6 G5 D5 D6 D5 D6 E E5
open
please
3., 4. you
say to
got that
me
some - thin',
you'll let me be your
I think you'll un - der -
Gtr. 1
Gtr. 3
divisi
full
* Play D# 2nd time only (omit B).
B7 E G5 G6 G5 D5 D6 D5 D6 E
man.
stand.
And
When
please
I
say to
say that
feel that
me
some - thing,
some - thing,
*Play C 2nd time only (omit B).
Gtr. 1: w/ Fill 1, 2nd time
Gtr. 1: w/ Fill 2, 3rd time
To Coda
Chorus
E5 B7 C D
you'll let me hold your hand.
I wan - na hold your hand.
Now, let me hold your
I wan - na hold your
Fill 1
Gtr. 1
full
Fill 2
Gtr. 1
full

G
Em
C I
D II
G5
G6
G5
hand.
I wan - na hold your _ hand.

Bridge

Gtr. 2 tacet
Dm
Upper part tacet 1st time
G
C
Am
And when I touch you I feel hap - py in - side. _
let ring
let ring simile

Dm
G
Gtr. 2
C
D
C
D
It's such a feel - ing that my love,
I can't hide, _
I can't hide, _

1.
2.
D.S. al Coda
C
D
D5 D6 D5
D6 D5
D6 D5
D6 D5
I can't hide.
3. Yeah,
4. Yeah,
full
Coda
Chorus
C^I
D^II
G
Em
C^I
D^II
I wan - na hold your hand.
I wan - na hold your
B7
C^I
D^II
C^I
G
hand.
I wan - na hold your hand.

I Wish

Words and Music by Stevie Wonder

Gtr. 1: w/ Fill 1, 2nd time

Bb7 C7 Fm7 Abm7 Bb7 C7

E - ven though we some - time - would not get a thing, we were hap - py with the
Ma - ma gives you mon - ey for Sun-day school, you trade just for can - dy

Gtr. 1

simile on repeat

Fm7 Bb+7 Ebm7 Ab7

joy the day would bring. Sneak - in' out the back door, to
af - ter church is through. Smok - in' cig - a - rettes and

Ebm7 Ab7 Ebm7 Ab7

hang out with those hood - lum friends of mine, ooh.
writ - in' some - thing nas - ty on the wall. (You nas - ty boy.)

E♭m7
A♭7
Greet - ed at the back door with, "Boy, I
Teach - er sends you to the
Riff B
Gtr. 1: w/ Riff A, 2nd meas., 2nd time
Gtr. 1: w/ Riff B, 1st meas., 2nd time
thought I told you not to go out - side."
prin - ci - pal's of - fice down the hall.
End Riff B
B♭7
C7
Gtr. 1: w/ Fill 1, 2nd time, simile
Fm7
A♭m7
Try'n' your best to bring the wa - ter to your eyes,
You grow up and learn that kind of thing ain't right,
B♭+7
think - in' it might stop her from whoop - in' your be - hind.
but while you were do - in' it, it sure felt out - ta sight.
I wish those

Chorus
Gtr. 1: w/ Riff B, 2 times
Ebm7
Ab7
days could come back once more. Why did those
days ev - er have to go? I wish those
To Coda
days could come back once more. Why did those days ev -
Gtr. 1
er have to go? 'Cause I loved them so.
(Do, do, do, do, do,
D.S. al Coda
do, do, do, do, do, do, do.
Do, do, do, do, do, do, do, do, do, do.)

Coda
Ebm7
Ab7
Ebm7
Ab7
er have to go? Ooh, hoo.

Ebm7
Ab7
Ebm7
Ab7
Ebm7
Ab7

Outro

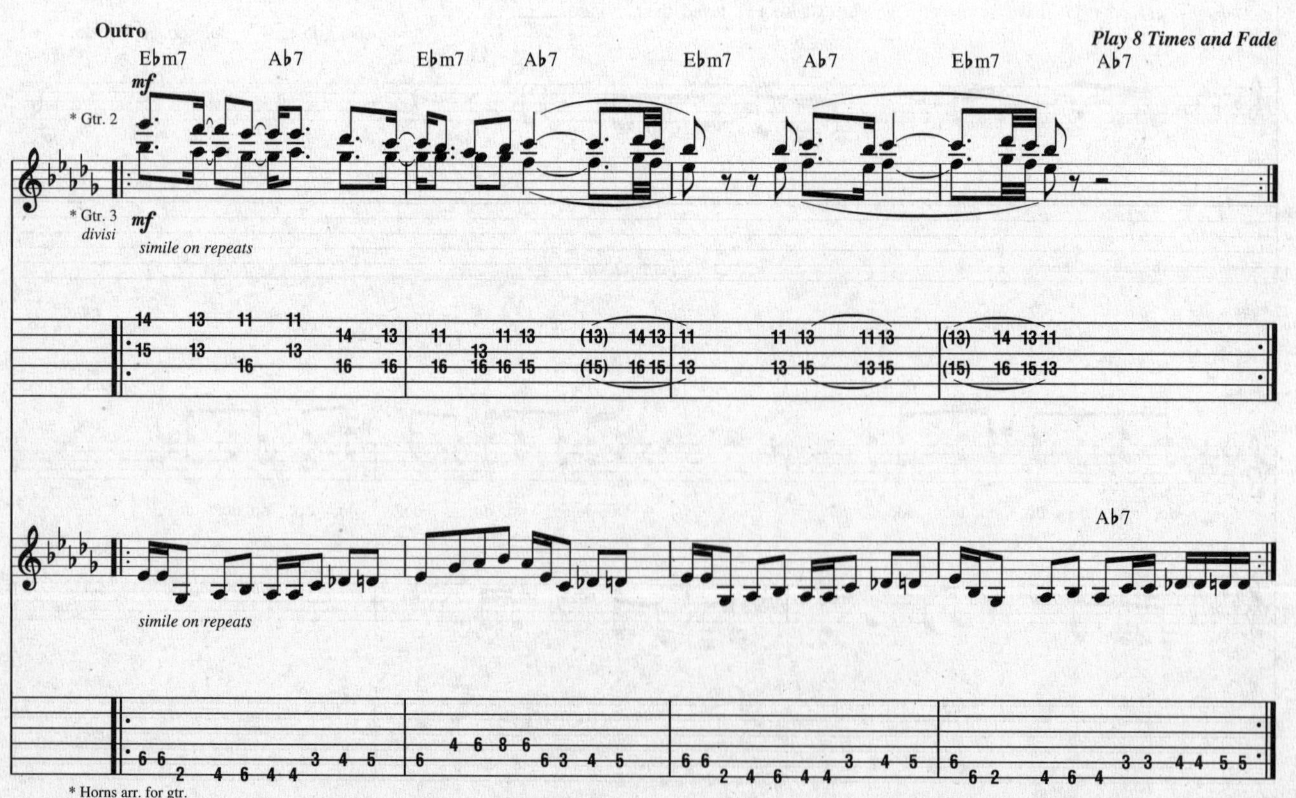
Play 8 Times and Fade
Ebm7
Ab7
Ebm7
Ab7
Ebm7
Ab7
Ebm7
Ab7
mf
* Gtr. 2
* Gtr. 3
divisi
mf
simile on repeats
simile on repeats
Ab7
* Horns arr. for gtr.

I'd Love to Change the World

Words and Music by Alvin Lee

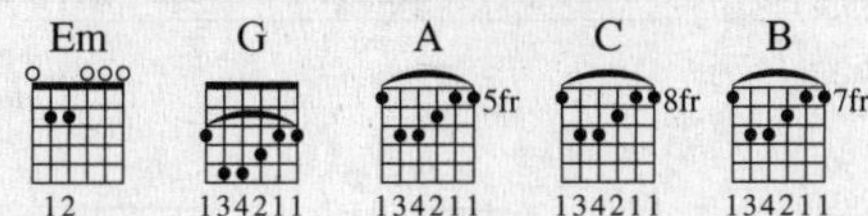

Intro

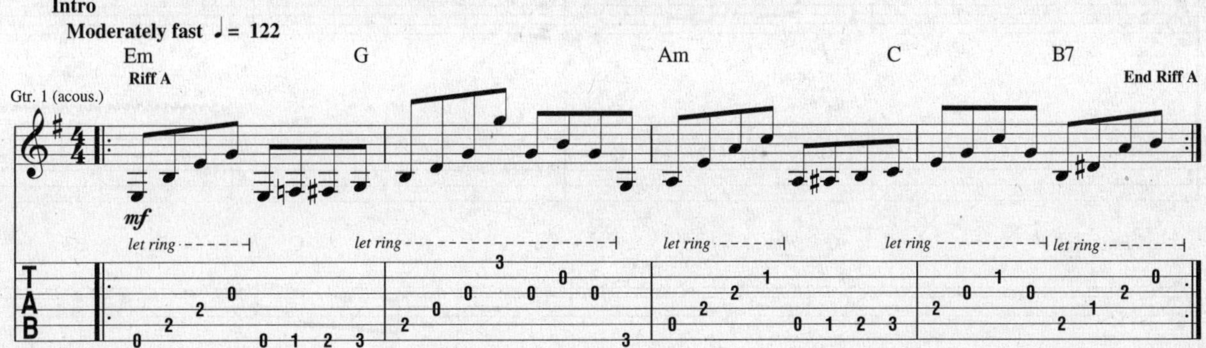

Verse

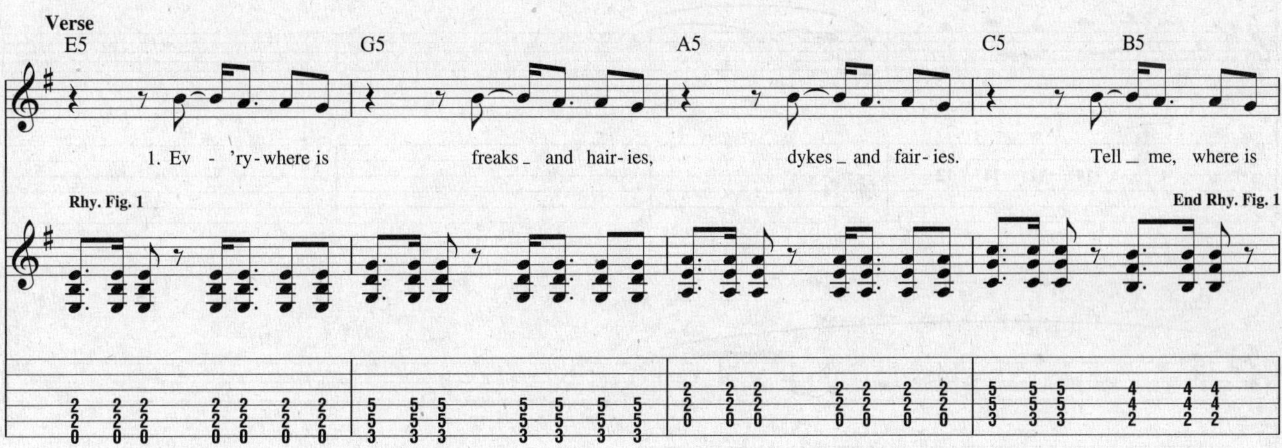

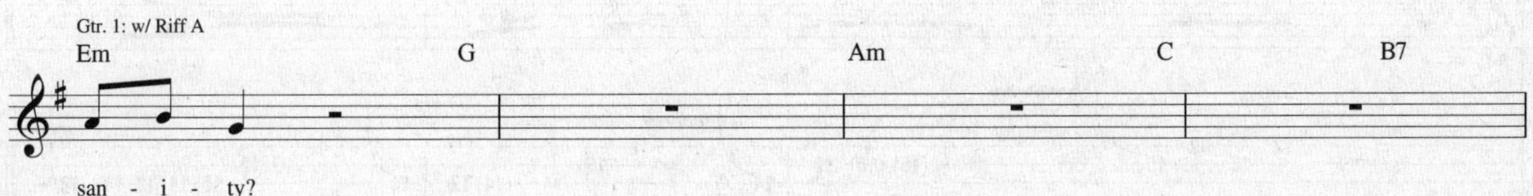

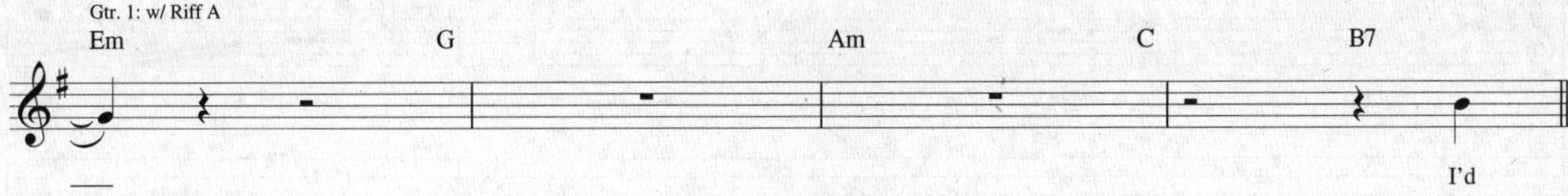

Chorus
Gtr. 1: w/ Riff A (3 times)
Em G Am C B7
love to change the world, but I don't know what to do.
Gtr. 2 (elec.)
f
w/ dist.
Em G Am C B7
So I leave it up to you.
Em G Am C B7
let ring
Verse
Gtr. 1: w/ Rhy. Fig. 1
E5 G5 A5 C5 B5
2. Pop - u - la - tion keeps on breed - ing. Na - tion bleed - ing, still more feed - ing

Gtr. 1: w/ Riff A
Em
G
Am
C
B7
e - con - o - my.
hold bend
hold bend
Gtr. 1: w/ Rhy. Fig. 1
E5
G5
A5
C5
B5
Life is fun-ny.
Skies are sun-ny.
Bees make hon-ey.
Who needs mon-ey?
Gtr. 1: w/ Riff A
Em
G
Am
C
B7
Mon-o-pol-y.
I'd
8va
Chorus
Gtr. 1: w/ Riff A (3 times)
Em
G
Am
C
B7
love to change the world,
but I don't know what to do.
loco
let ring

Em
G
Am
C
B7
So I leave it up to you.
8va
loco
Whoa, yeah!
Guitar Solo
Rhy. Fig. 2
End Rhy. Fig. 2
Gtr. 1
Gtr. 2
A
B
Gtr. 1: w/ Rhy. Fig. 2 (3 times)

Em
loco
G
A
8va
C
loco
B
Em
G
A
C
B
Verse
Gtr. 1: w/ Rhy. Fig. 2 (2 times)
Em
G
A
C
B
3. World _ pol-lu - tion
is no so-lu - tion.
In - sti-tu - tion,
e-lec - tro-cu - tion.
Em
G
A
C
B
There's black or white, _
rich or poor. __
Gov-er - nors, _
stop the war. _

Guitar Solo

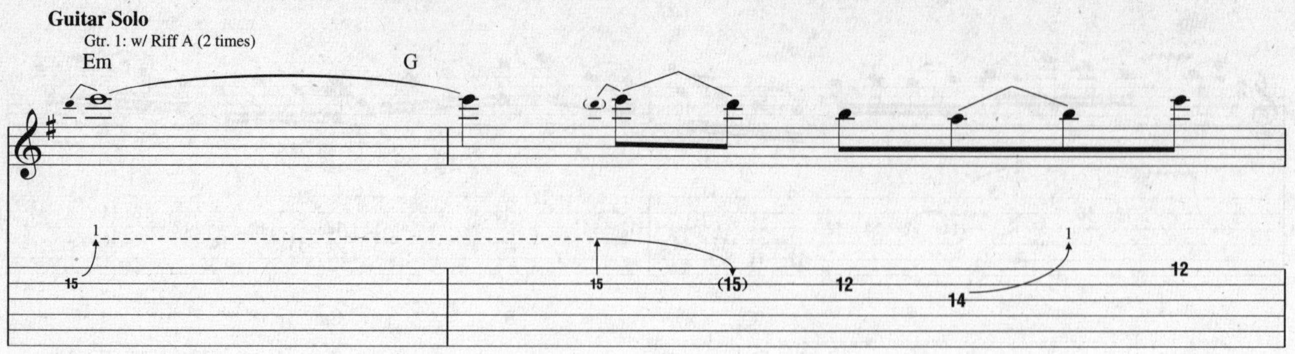

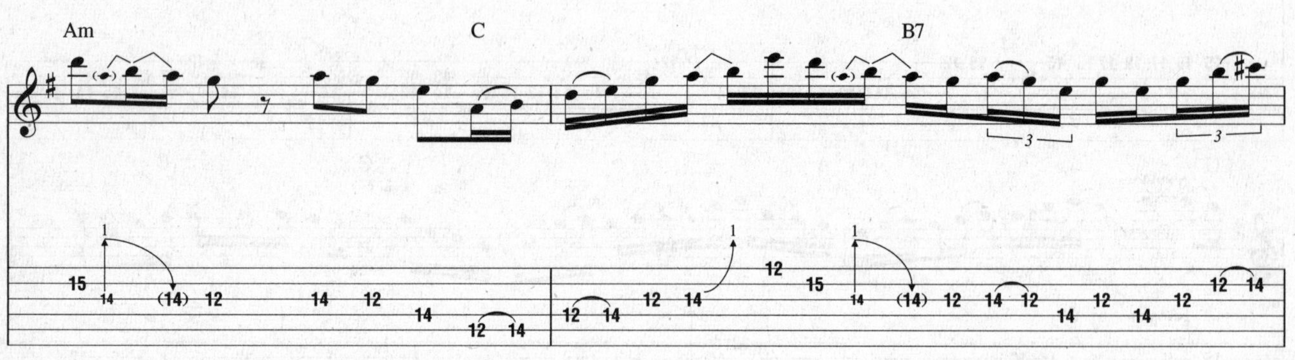

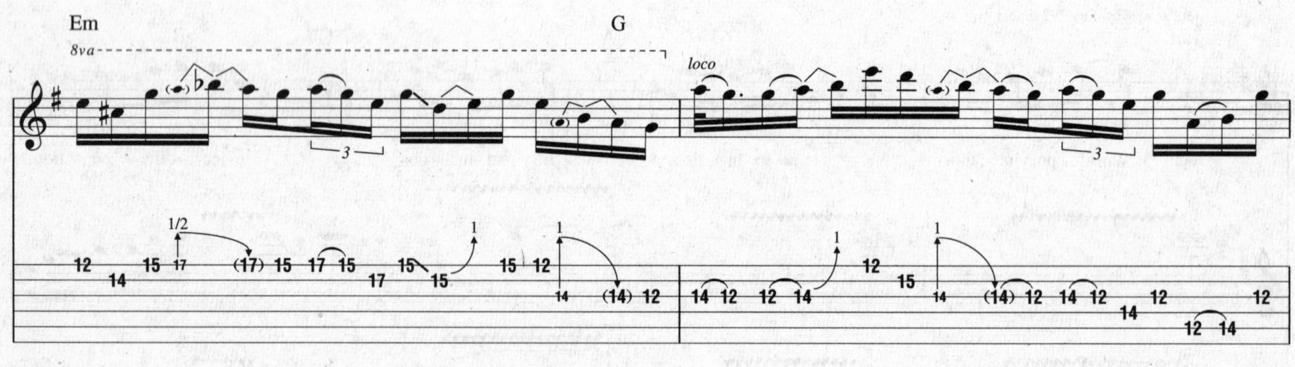

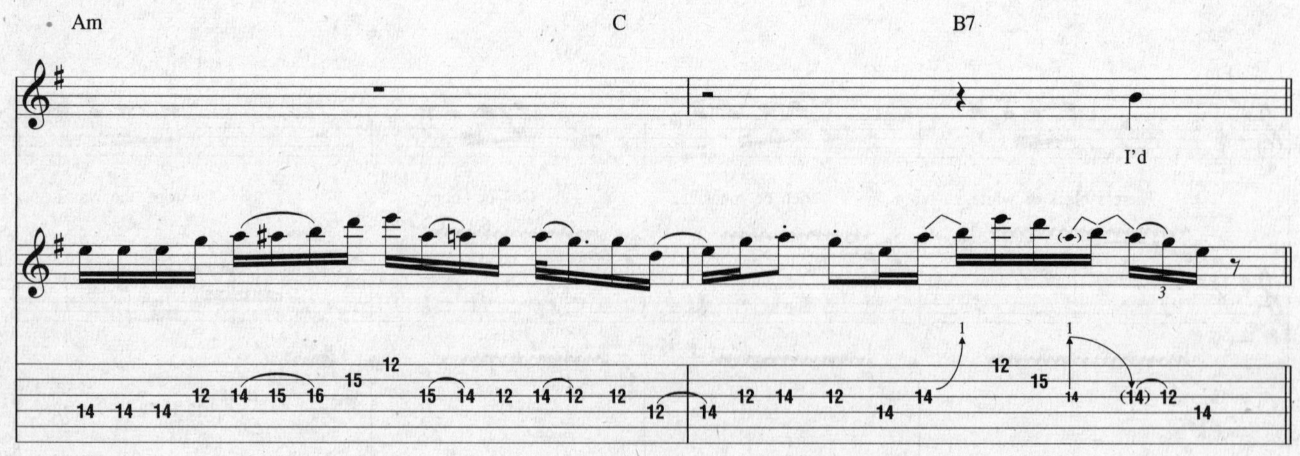

Outro-Chorus
Gtr. 1: w/ Riff A (3 times)
Em G Am C
love to change the world, but I don't
hold bend
B7 Em G
know what to do.
Am C B7 Em G
So I leave it up to you.
Am C B7 Em
Gtr. 1
Whispered: What's go - ing on?
8va
loco
fdbk.
Pitch: G♯

If You're Gone

Written by Rob Thomas

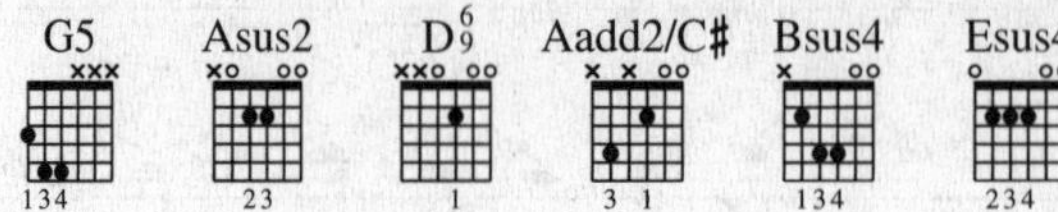

* Symbols in parentheses represent chord names respective to capoed guitars. Symbols above reflect actual sounding chords. Capoed fret is "0" in tab. Chord symbols reflect overall tonality and are implied.

Verse
Gtrs. 1 & 2 tacet
A (D) D (G) F♯m (Bm) E (A) D (G)
1. I think I've al - read - y lost ___ you, I think you're al - read - y gone. ___
2. I think you're al - read - y leav - ing, feels like your hand is on the door. ___
3. I bet you're hard to get o - ver, I bet the room just won't shine.
Gtr. 3 (elec.)
mp w/ clean tone & Leslie
let ring throughout
A (D) A/C♯ (D/F♯) D (G) A/C♯ (D/F♯) Bm (Em) 1. E (A)
I think I'm fi - nal - ly scared now. You think I'm weak, I think you're wrong.
I thought this place was an em - pire, now I'm re - laxed, I can't be sure.
I bet my hands I can stay here and I bet you need more than you mind.
let ring
2. E (A)
Pre-Chorus
Gtr. 3 tacet
Bm (Em)
And I think you're so mean, I think we should try.
Riff A
Gtr. 1
let ring throughout
E (A) A (D) D (G) A/C♯ (D/F♯) Bm (Em)
I think I could need this in my life and I think I'm scared,
this in my life. I think I'm just

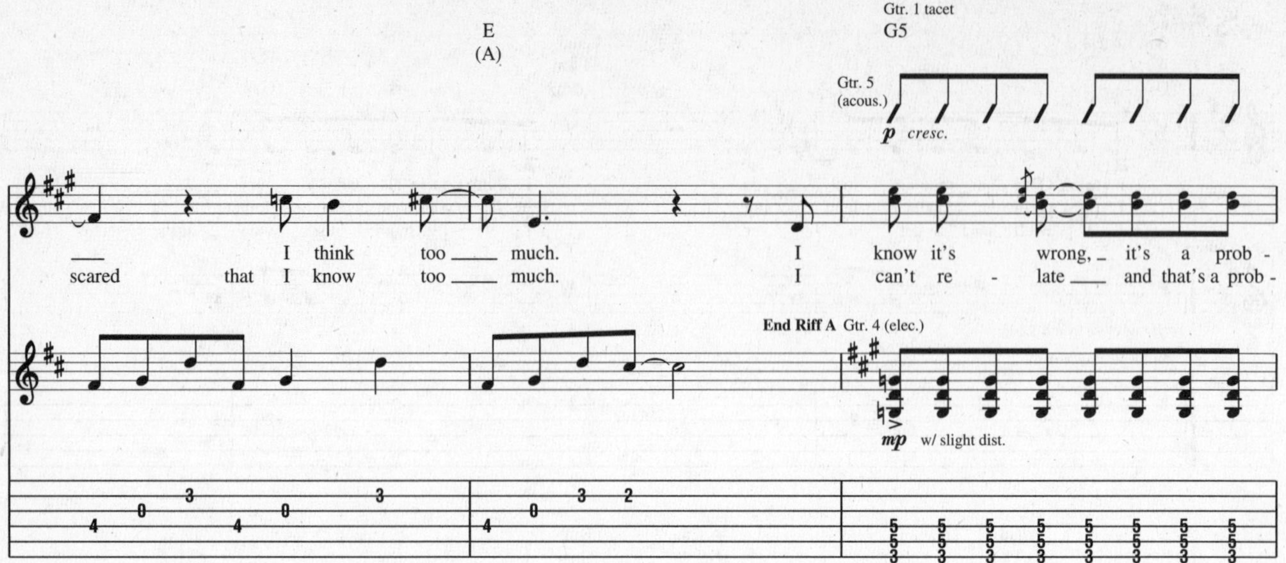
E
(A)
Gtr. 1 tacet
G5
Gtr. 5
(acous.)
p cresc.
I think too much.
scared that I know too much.
I know it's wrong, it's a prob -
I can't re - late and that's a prob -
End Riff A
Gtr. 4 (elec.)
mp w/ slight dist.

Chorus
Gtr. 4 tacet
Asus2
Rhy. Fig. 1
mf
lem I'm deal - ing.
lem I'm feel - ing.
If you're gone,
may - be it's time to come home.
Gtr. 6
(elec.) Riff B
mf
w/ clean tone

Aadd2/C♯
Bsus4
There's an aw - ful lot of breath - ing room,

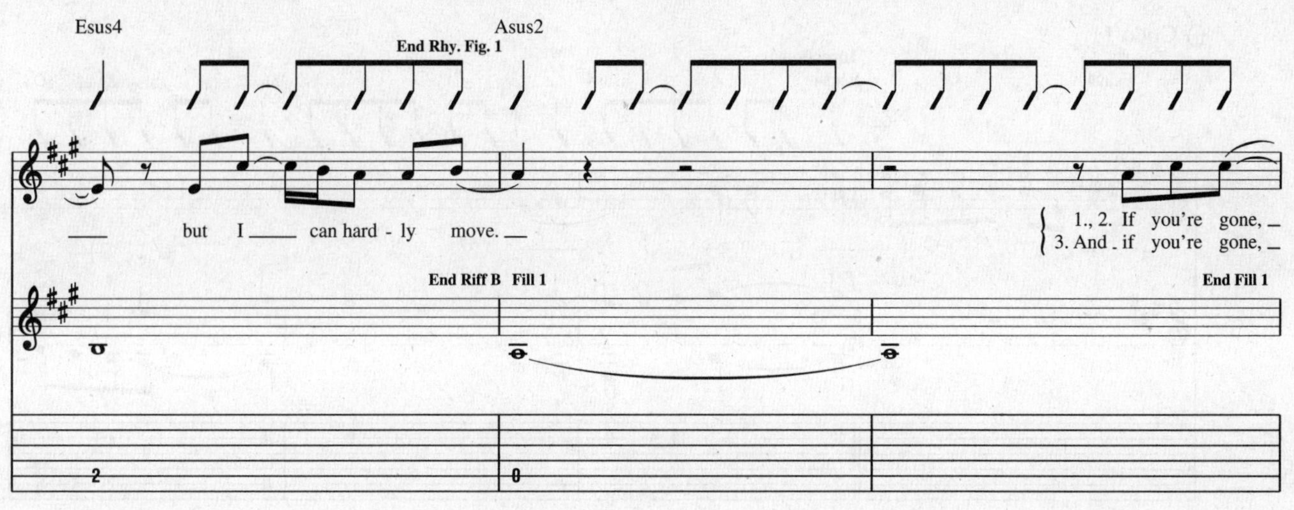
Esus4
Asus2
End Rhy. Fig. 1
but I can hard - ly move.
1., 2. If you're gone,
3. And if you're gone,
End Riff B Fill 1
End Fill 1

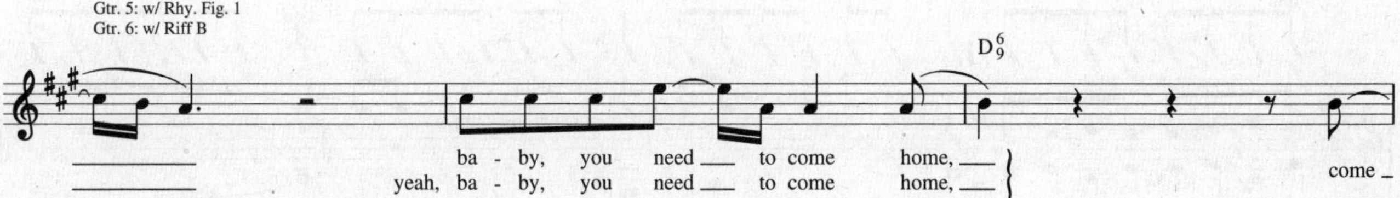
Gtr. 5: w/ Rhy. Fig. 1
Gtr. 6: w/ Riff B
D6/9
ba - by, you need to come home,
yeah, ba - by, you need to come home,
come

To Coda 1
To Coda 2
Aadd2/C♯
Bsus4
Esus4
home. There's a lit - tle bit of some - thing me in ev - 'ry - thing in

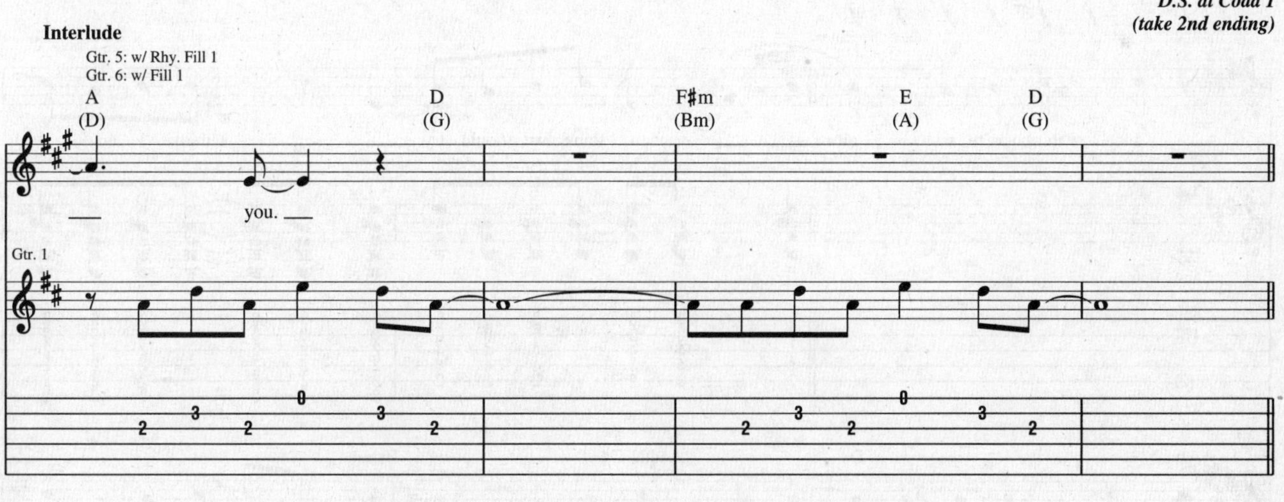
D.S. al Coda 1
(take 2nd ending)
Interlude
Gtr. 5: w/ Rhy. Fill 1
Gtr. 6: w/ Fill 1
A
(D)
D
(G)
F♯m
(Bm)
E
(A)
D
(G)
you.
Gtr. 1

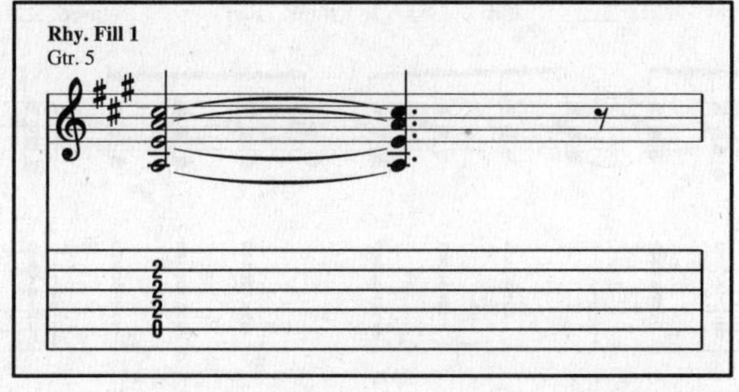
Rhy. Fill 1
Gtr. 5

Coda 1
Interlude
Esus4
Bsus4
Esus4
Asus2
Gtr. 5
in ev - 'ry-thing in, in you.
* Gtr. 7
Gtr. 4
divisi
* Horns arr. for gtr.
Aadd2/C#
Bsus4
Esus4
Asus2
Pre-Chorus
Gtr. 1: w/ Riff A
Gtrs. 4 & 7 tacet
Bsus4
Esus4
(cont. in notation)
I think you're so mean, I think we should try. I think I could need
Gtr. 5
Asus2
Aadd2/C#
Bsus4
this in my life and I think I'm scared. Do I talk too

D.S.S. al Coda 2

Esus4
G6/9
much?
I know it's wrong. It's a prob - lem I'm deal - ing. If you're gone,

Coda 2
Outro
Bm (Em)
E (A)
Gtr. 8: w/ Rhy. Fill 2
you.
(Some - thing in me,
Ev - 'ry-thing in,
Gtr. 1
mp
let ring throughout

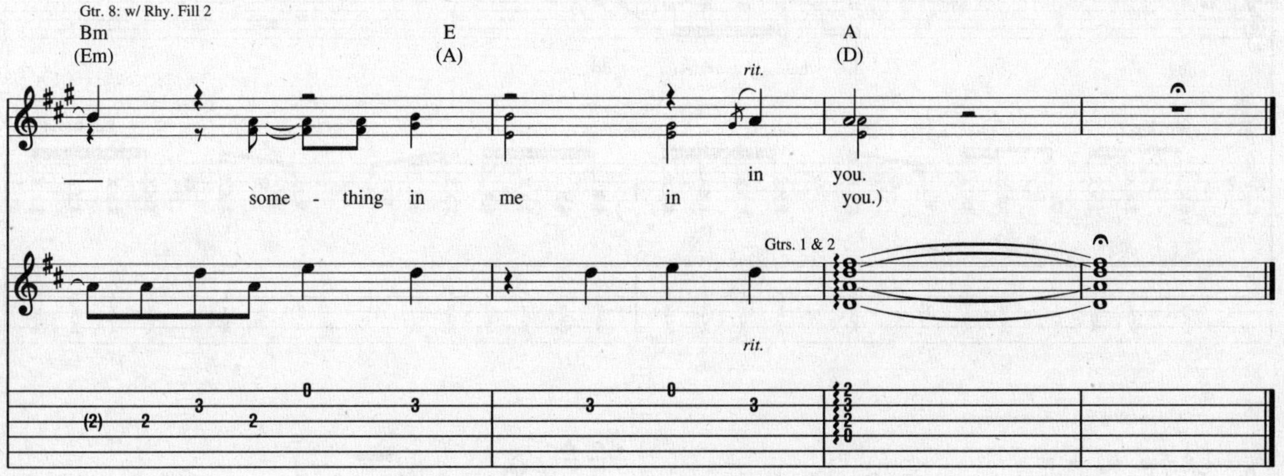
Gtr. 8: w/ Rhy. Fill 2
Bm (Em)
E (A)
A (D)
rit.
some - thing in me in you.)
in you.
Gtrs. 1 & 2

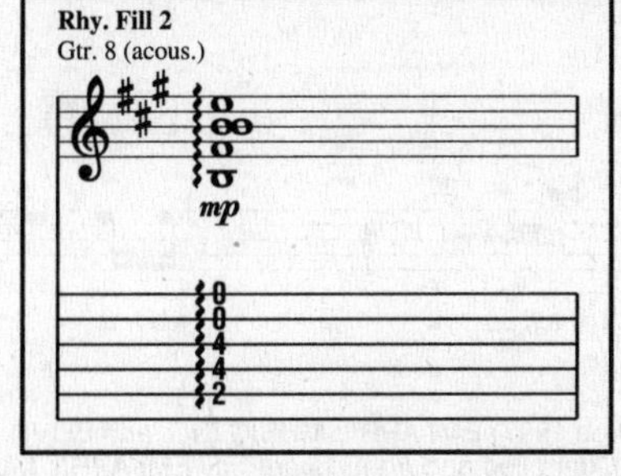
Rhy. Fill 2
Gtr. 8 (acous.)
mp

It's Your Thing

Words and Music by Rudolph Isley, Ronald Isley and O'Kelly Isley

Verse
F7
love ya, may-be I will, ha. If I need me a wom-
Gtr. 1
Rhy. Fig. 2
-an, it ain't no big deal. Ah, you need love
(Doo, wop.) (Doo, wop.)
now just the same as I do. Makes me no dif-
(Doo, wop.) (Doo, wop.)
-'rence now who ya give your thing to. Oh, it's your
(Doo, wop.) (Doo, wop.)
End Rhy. Fig. 2
Chorus
Gtr. 1: w/ Rhy. Fig. 1, 4 times, simile
N.C.(F)
thing, do what you wan-na do. I can't tell ya who to
(It's your thing.)

To Coda 2
sock it to. It's your thing, do what you wan-na do, now.
(It's your thing.)
Interlude
Gtr. 1: w/ Rhy. Fill 1
Gtr. 1: w/ Rhy. Fig. 2, simile
F7
I can't tell you who to sock it to. Oh, yeah. Al - right.
D.S. al Coda 1
Spoken: Lord, have mer-cy. Oh, it's your
Coda 1
Verse
Gtr. 1: w/ Rhy. Fill 1
Gtr. 1: w/ Rhy. Fig 2, simile
F7
sock it to. I'm not try - in' to run your life. I know you
wan - na do what's right. Oh, give your love, girl, to who-ev - er you
(Doo, wop.) (Doo, wop.)
D.S.S. al Coda 2
choose. How can you lose with the stuff you use, now? It's your
(Doo, wop.) (Doo, wop.) (Doo, wop.)
Coda 2
Begin Fade
do. Don't let me tell ya who to sock it to. Let me know ya say it's my
Chorus
Gtr. 1: w/ Rhy. Fig. 1, till fade, simile
N.C.(F)
Fade Out
thing. I do what I wan-na do. I can't tell ya who to sock it to.
(It's your thing.)
Rhy. Fill 1
Gtr. 1
T
A
B

Jane Says

Words and Music by Perry Farrell, Dave Navarro, Stephen Perkins and Eric Avery

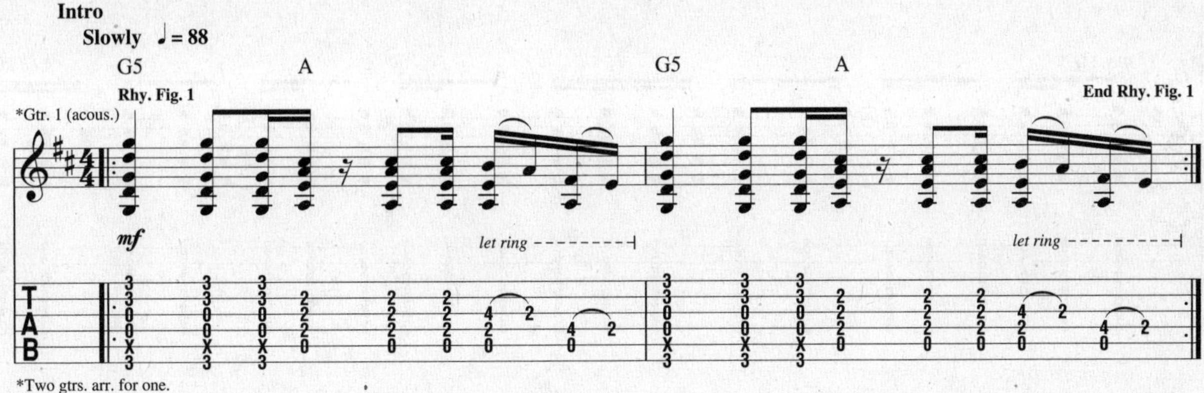

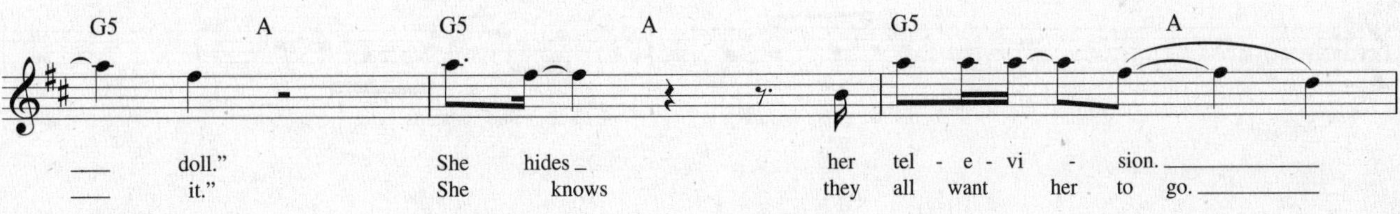

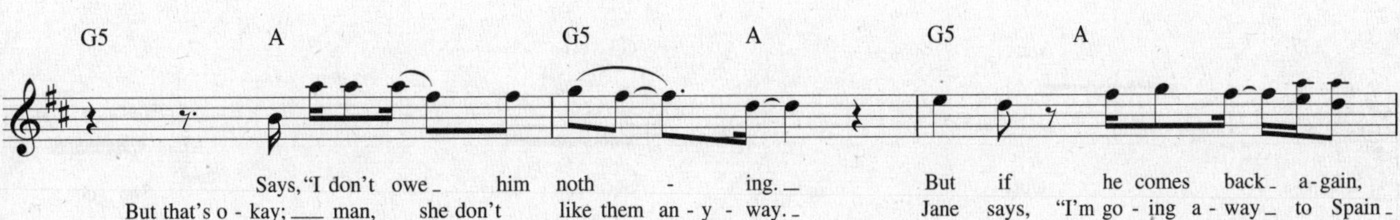

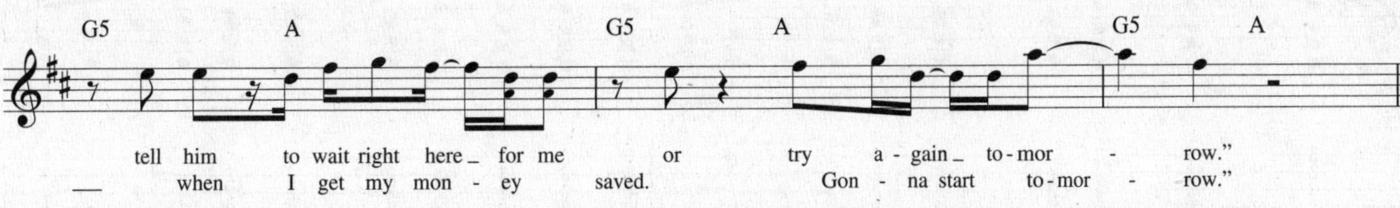

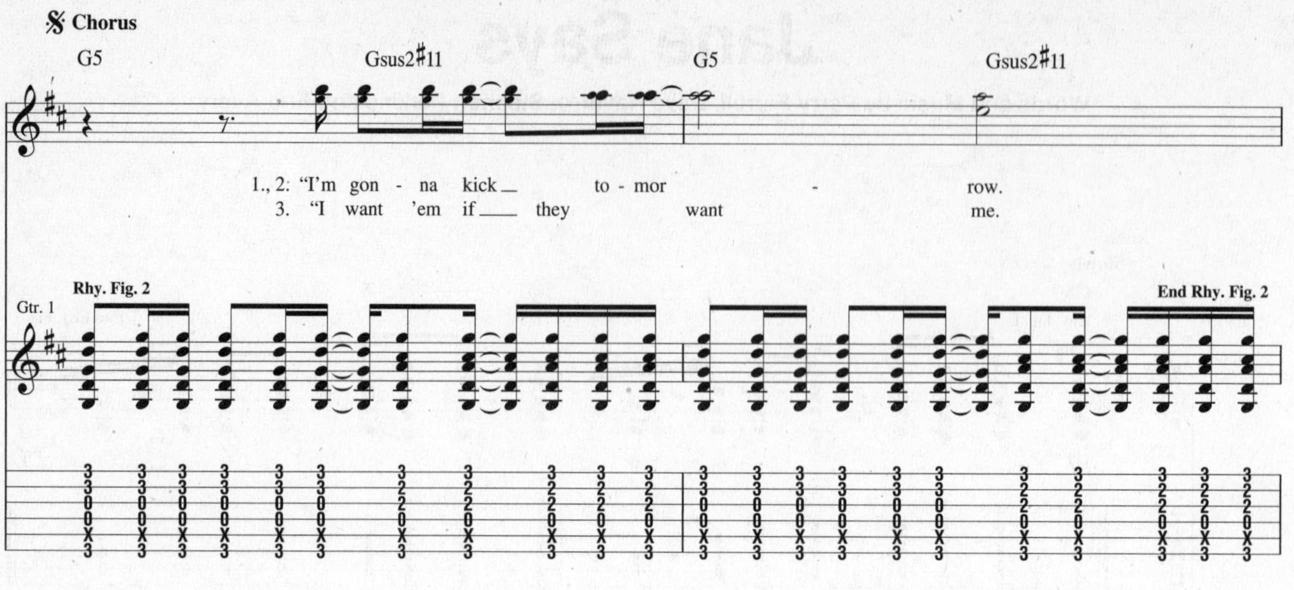

Chorus
G5
Gsus2♯11
G5
Gsus2♯11
1., 2: "I'm gon - na kick to - mor - row.
3. "I want 'em if they want me.
Rhy. Fig. 2
Gtr. 1
End Rhy. Fig. 2

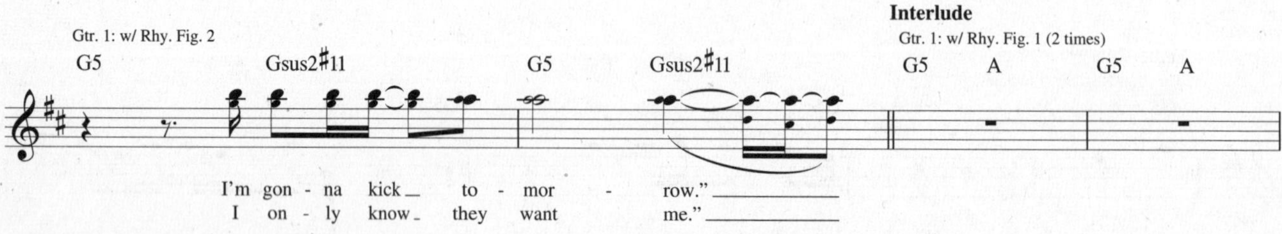

Interlude
Gtr. 1: w/ Rhy. Fig. 2
Gtr. 1: w/ Rhy. Fig. 1 (2 times)
G5 Gsus2♯11 G5 Gsus2♯11 G5 A G5 A
I'm gon - na kick to - mor - row."
I on - ly know they want me."

Verse
Gtr. 1: w/ Rhy. Fig. 1
G5 A G5 A G5 A G5 A
3., 5. She gets mad and she starts to cry. She

G5 A G5 A
takes a swing, man. She can't hit! She don't
Gtr. 1
let ring
let ring

1st time, Gtr. 1: w/ Rhy. Fig. 1 (2 times)
2nd time, Gtr. 1: w/ Rhy. Fig. 1 (2 1/2 times)

Verse

Gtr. 1: w/ Rhy. Fig. 1 (6 times)

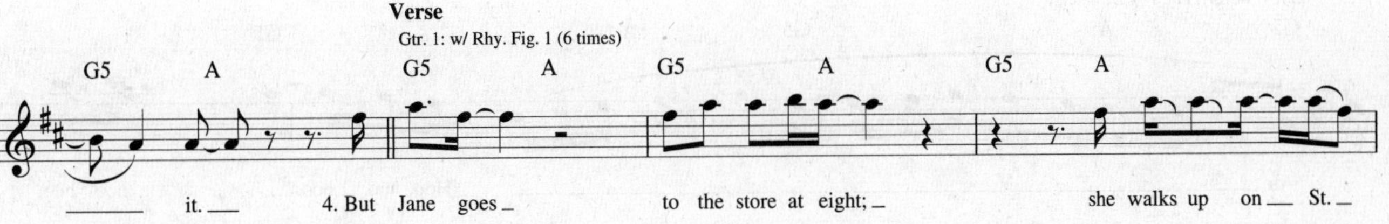

D.S. al Coda

𝄌 Coda

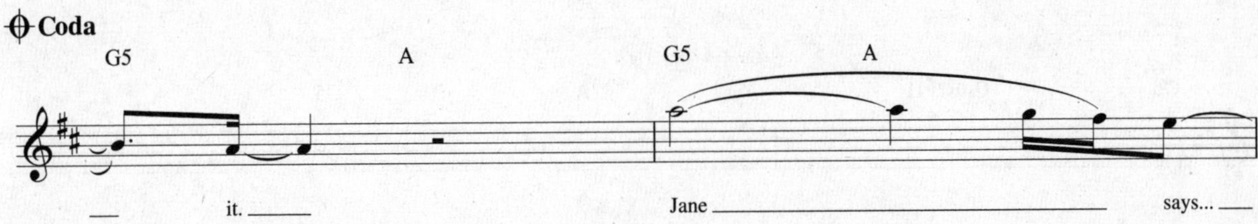

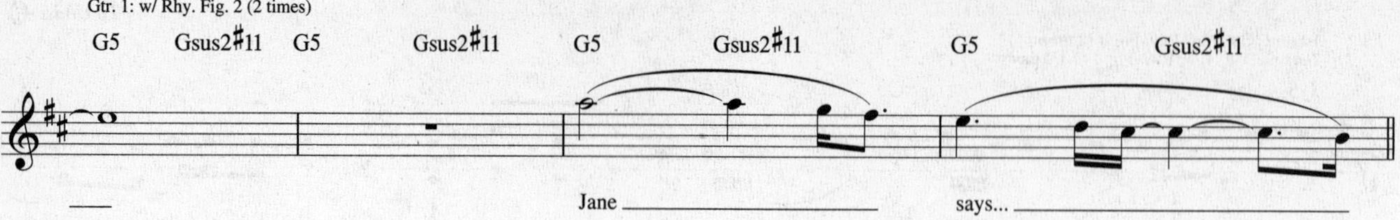
Gtr. 1: w/ Rhy. Fig. 2 (2 times)
G5 Gsus2♯11 G5 Gsus2♯11 G5 Gsus2♯11 G5 Gsus2♯11
Jane
says...

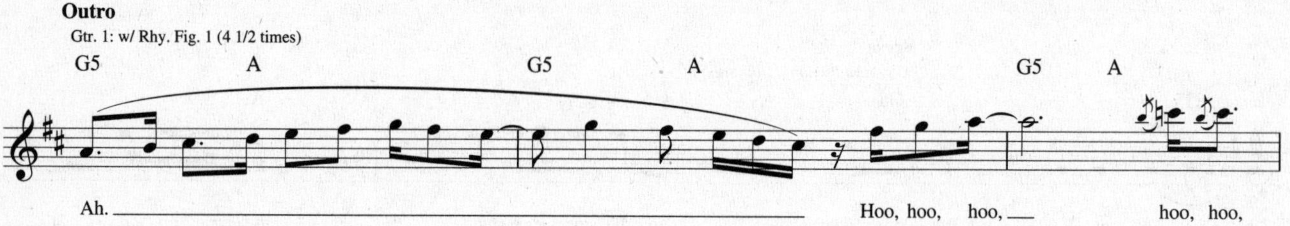
Outro
Gtr. 1: w/ Rhy. Fig. 1 (4 1/2 times)
G5 A G5 A G5 A
Ah.
Hoo, hoo, hoo,
hoo, hoo,

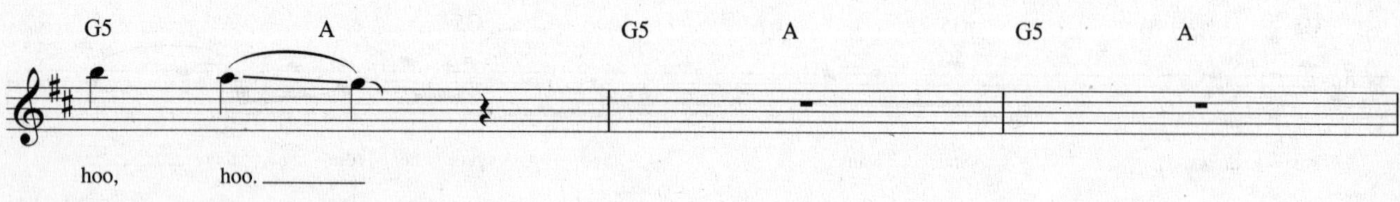
G5 A G5 A G5 A
hoo,
hoo.

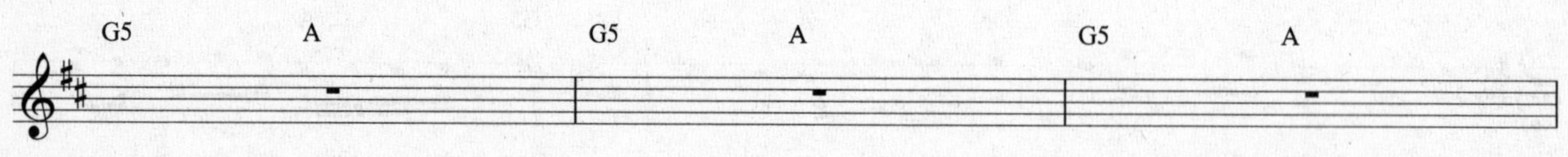
G5 A G5 A G5 A

Begin fade
Gtr. 1: w/ Rhy. Fig. 2 (2 times)
G5 Gsus2♯11 G5 Gsus2♯11 G5 Gsus2♯11

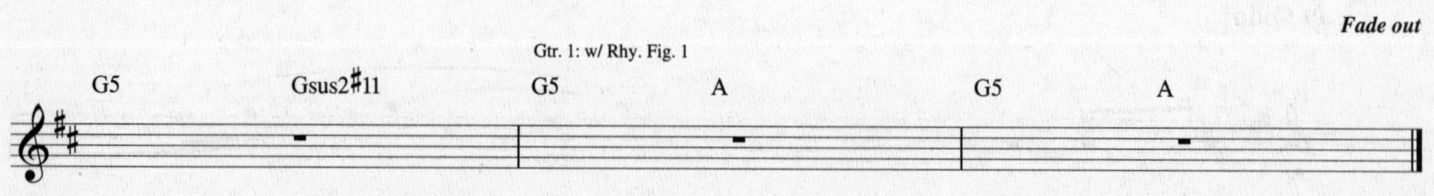
Fade out
Gtr. 1: w/ Rhy. Fig. 1
G5 Gsus2♯11 G5 A G5 A

Jeremy

Music by Jeff Ament
Lyric by Eddie Vedder

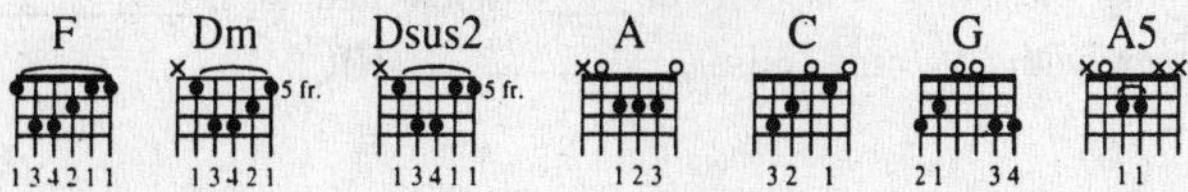

Verse
w/Rhy. Fill 1 (2nd time only)
1. At home drawing pictures of mountain tops, with him on
2. get? And he hit me with a surprise, left my jaw left hurtin,
Rhy. Fig. 1
Gtr. 1
w/Rhy. Fig. 1
w/Rhy. Fill 1 (2nd time only)
top. Lemon yellow sun; arms raised in a V.
ooh dropped wide open. Just like the day, oh
(end Rhy. Fig. 1)
A5 D5/A
The dead lay in pools of maroon below. Daddy didn't
like the day I heard. Daddy didn't
Rhy. Fig. 2
Gtrs. 3 & 4
(w/distortion)
let ring
let ring
Rhy. Fill 1
Gtr. 1

G5/A
D5/A
A5
w/Rhy. Fill 2
give at - ten - tion, oh, to the fact that mom - my did - n't
give af - fec - tion, no, and the boy was some - thing that mom - my would - n't
(end Rhy. Fig. 2)
let ring
w/Rhy. Fig. 2
A5
D5/A
G5/A
D5/A
A5
w/Rhy. Fill 2
care. King Jer - e - my the wick - ed oh ruled his world.
wear. King Jer - e - my the wick - ed oh ruled his world.
w/Rhy. Fill 3 (3rd time only)
F
Dm
Dsus2
Dm
A
Gtr. 5
Rhy. Fig. 3B
(end Rhy. Fig. 3B)
mf
(acoustic)
Jer- e- my spoke in class to - day.
Rhy. Fig. 3A
Gtr. 3
(end Rhy. Fig. 3A)
Rhy. Fig. 3
Gtr. 4
(end Rhy. Fig. 3)
let ring
Rhy. Fill 2
Gtr. 4
let ring
Rhy. Fill 3
Gtr. 3
T
A
B

w/Rhy. Fig. 3 (1st 3 bars)
w/Rhy. Fill 4 (2nd & 3rd time)
w/Rhy. Fill 5 (2nd & 3rd time)
To Coda
w/Rhy. Fill 6 (1st time only)
F Dm Dsus2 C A
Jer - e - my spoke in class to - day.
Gtrs. 3 & 4
* 2nd & 3rd times Rhy. Fill 4 implies F(add9)
1. Verse
w/Rhy. Fig. 1 (twice)
N.C.
2. Clear - ly I re - mem - ber pick - ing on the boy, seemed a harm - less
lit - tle fuck. Ooh but we un - leashed a li - on. Gnashed
2.
w/Rhy. Figs. 3, 3A & 3B
F
his teeth and bit the re - cess la - dies breast. How could I for - Jer - e - my spoke in
Rhy. Fill 4
Gtrs. 3 & 4
Rhy. Fill 6
Gtr. 1
Rhy. Fill 5
Gtrs. 4
let ring
let ring

w/Rhy. Fill 5
Dm
Dsus2
Dm
A
class
day.
N.C.
Ooh, ooh, ooh, ooh, ooh, ooh, ooh, ooh, ooh, ooh, ooh, ooh,
Rhy. Fig. 4
w/Rhy. Fig. 4
ooh, ooh. Try to for-get this.
Try to e-rase
(Try to for-get this.
(end Rhy. Fig. 4)
w/Rhy. Fill 7
D.S. al Coda
this
from the black
Try to e-rase this,)
CODA
w/Rhy. Fig. 3, 3A & 3B
F
Dm
Dsus2
Dm
w/Rhy. Fill 5
A
Jer-e-my spoke in class to-day.
Rhy. Fill 7
Gtrs. 3 & 4
P.M.
T
A
B

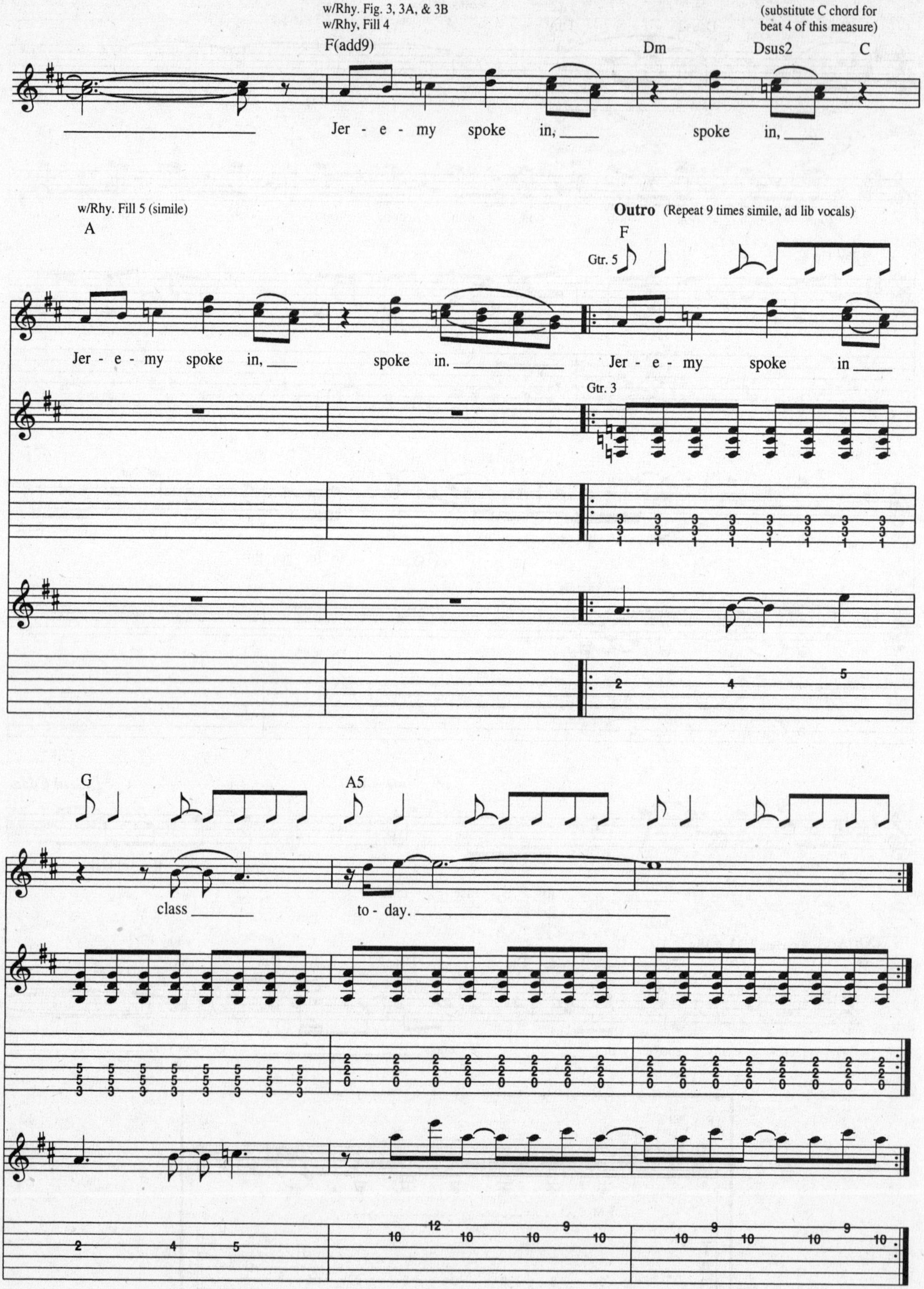

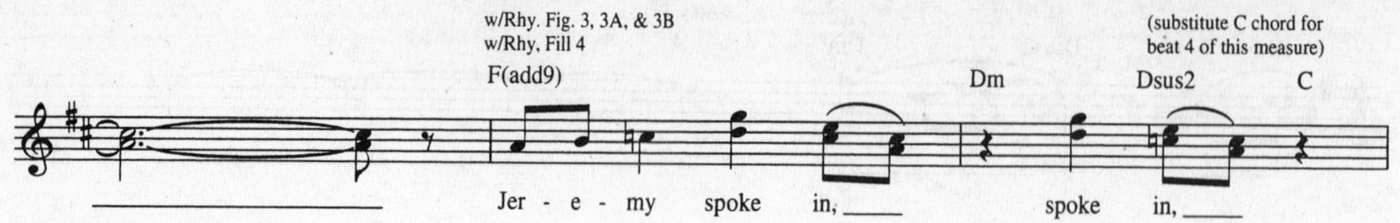

w/Rhy. Fill 5 (simile)

Outro (Repeat 9 times simile, ad lib vocals)

A

F

Gtr. 5

Jer - e - my spoke in,

spoke in.

Jer - e - my spoke in

Gtr. 3

G

A5

class

to - day.

Ah - ha,
ah - ha,
ah - ha
Gtr. 5
Gtr. 3
harm
w/bar
harm
rit.
ah - ha.
Gtr. 5
harm.
harm.

Jessie's Girl

Words and Music by Rick Springfield

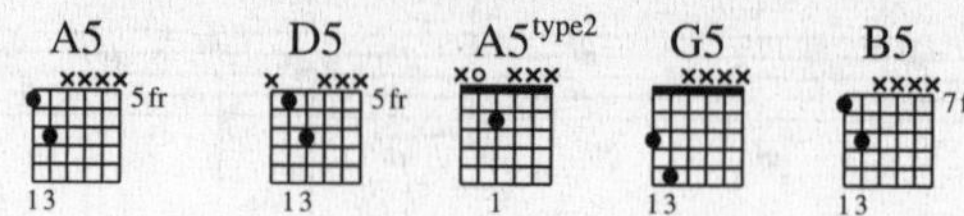

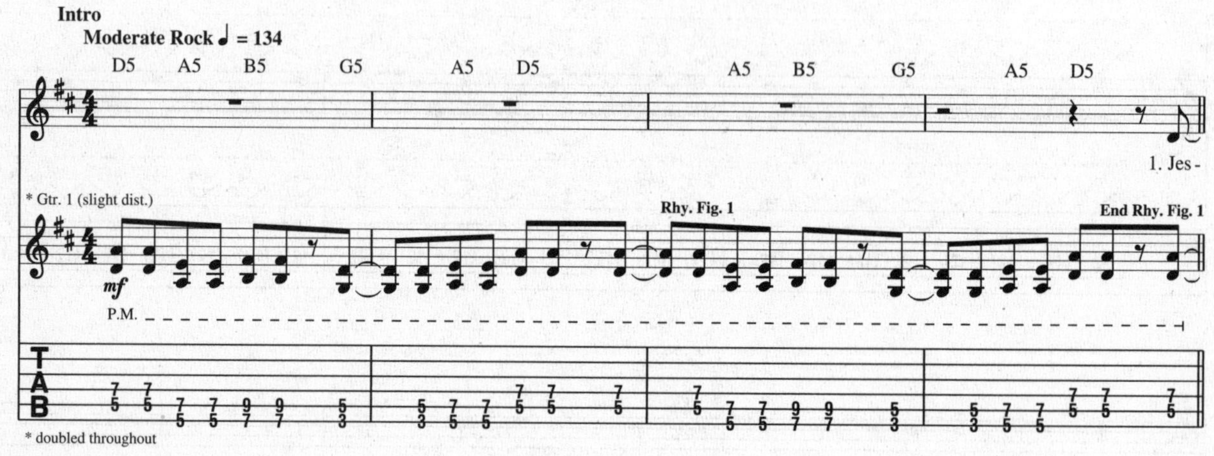

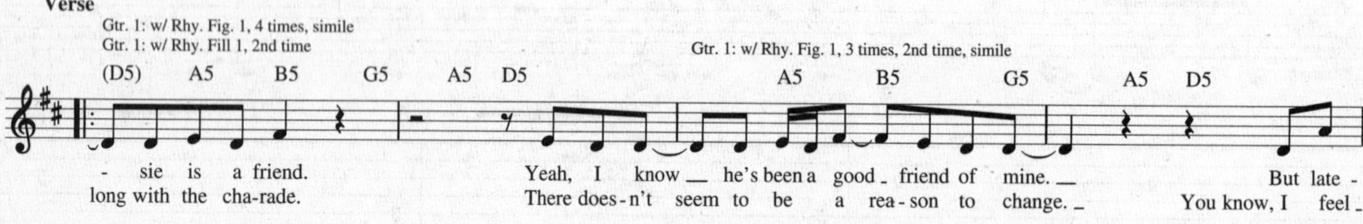

* Gtr. 1: w/ Rhy. Fig. 1, 2 1/2 times, simile
A5
D5
A5
B5
G5
A5
D5
to make her mine. And she's watch - in' him with those eyes.
is prob - 'ly moot. 'Cause she's watch - in' him with those eyes.
And she's
Gtr. 2 (dist.)
f
* w/ dist.
A5
B5
G5
A5
D5
lov - in' him with that bod - y, I just know it. And he's hold -
A5
B5
G5
Gtr. 1
A5
D5
A5 type 2
P.M.
(cont. in notation)
- ing her in his arms late, late at night. You know, I wish that I had

* Chord symbols reflect combined tonality.

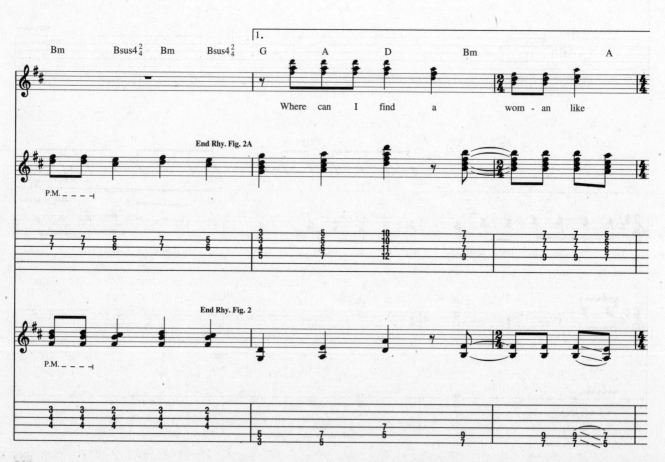

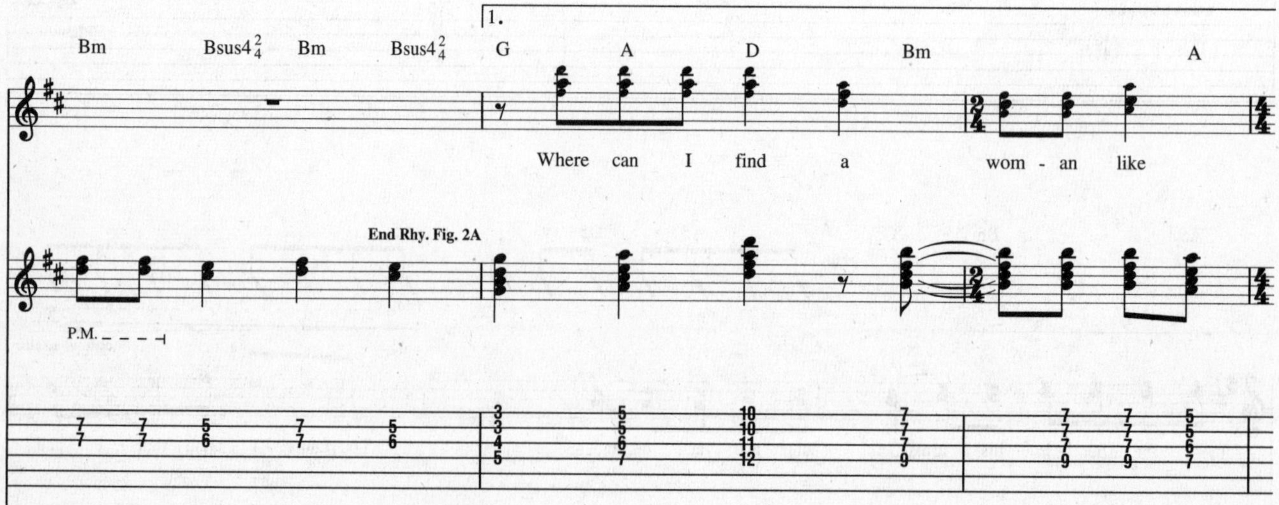

1.

Bm Bsus4$\frac{2}{4}$ Bm Bsus4$\frac{2}{4}$ G A D Bm A

Where can I find a wom - an like

End Rhy. Fig. 2A

P.M.

End Rhy. Fig. 2

P.M.

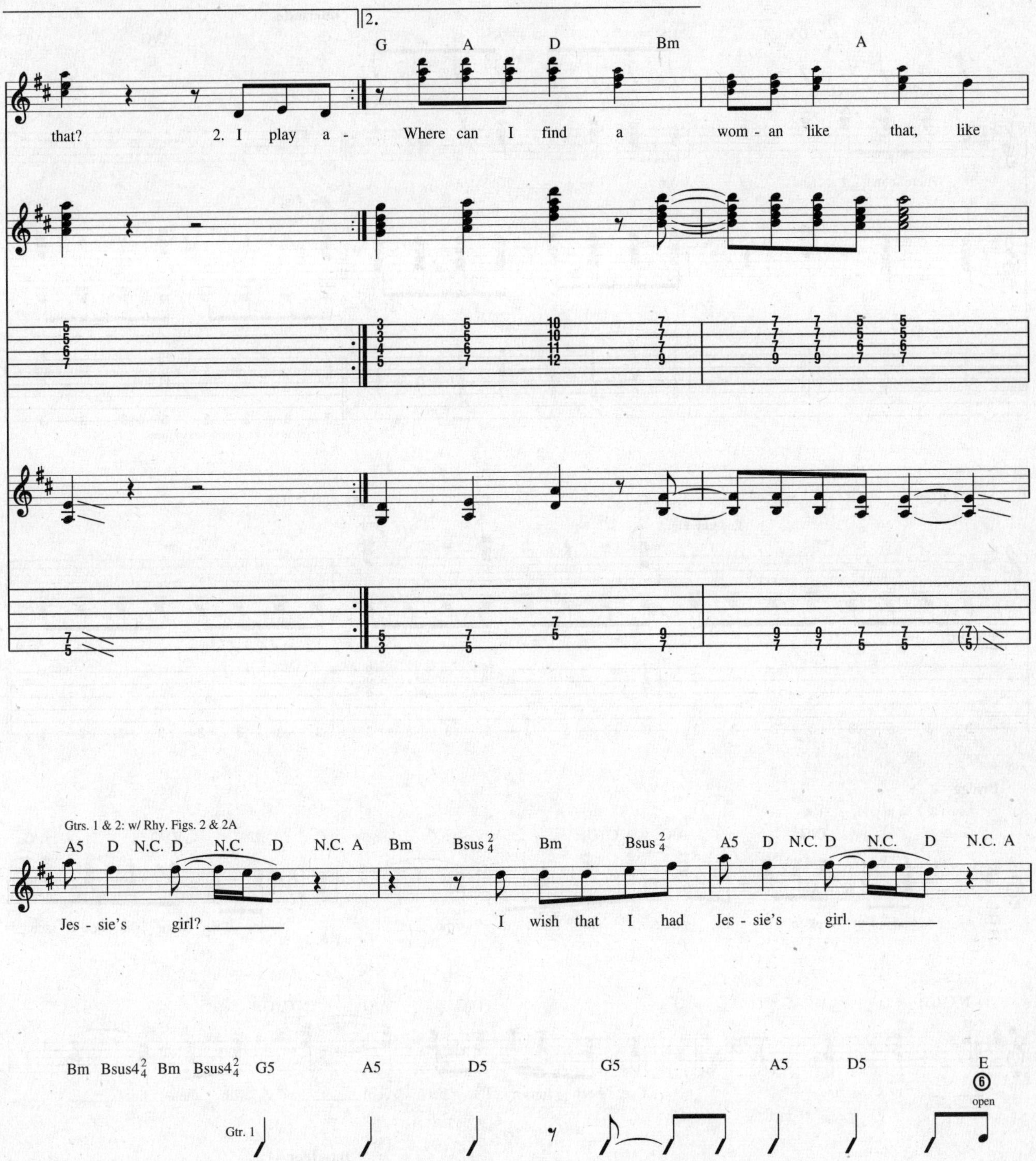

2.

G A D Bm A

that? 2. I play a- Where can I find a wom - an like that, like

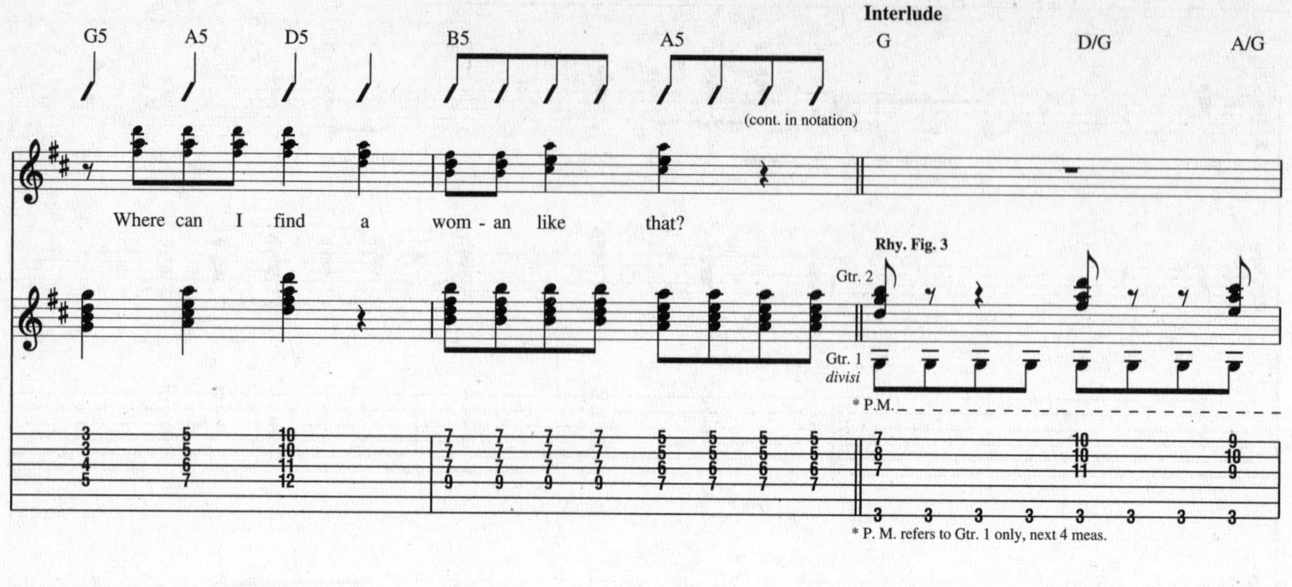
Interlude
G5 A5 D5 B5 A5 G D/G A/G
(cont. in notation)
Where can I find a wom - an like that?
Rhy. Fig. 3
Gtr. 2
Gtr. 1
divisi
* P.M.
* P. M. refers to Gtr. 1 only, next 4 meas.

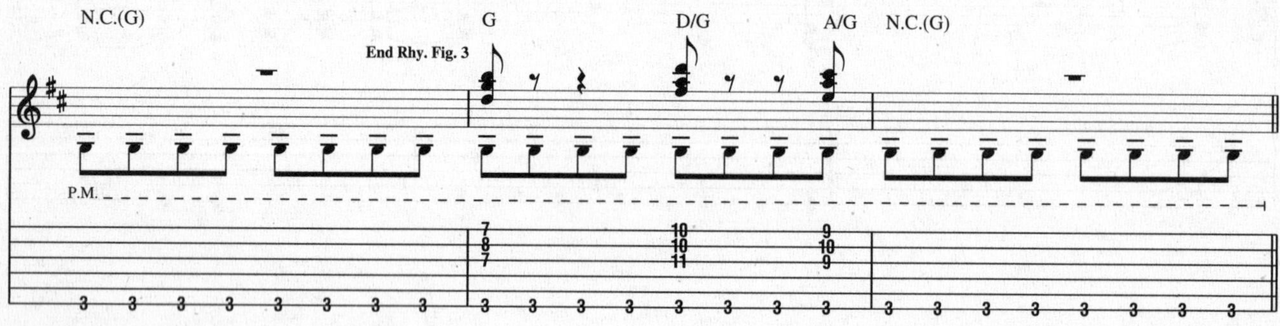
N.C.(G) G D/G A/G N.C.(G)
End Rhy. Fig. 3
P.M.

Bridge

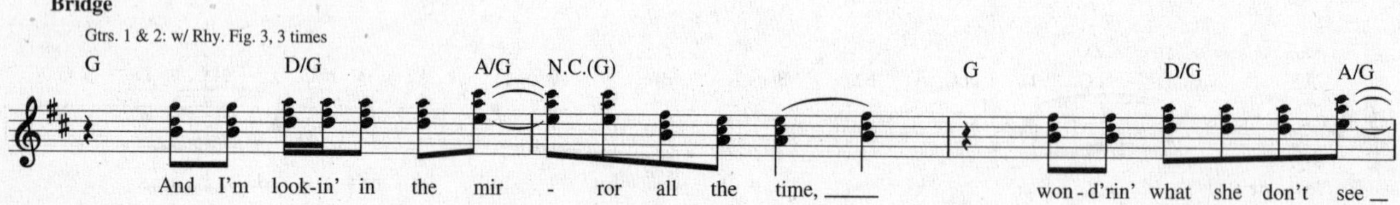
Gtrs. 1 & 2: w/ Rhy. Fig. 3, 3 times
G D/G A/G N.C.(G) G D/G A/G
And I'm look-in' in the mir - ror all the time, won - d'rin' what she don't see

N.C.(G) G D/G A/G N.C.(G)
in me. I've been fun - ny, I've been cool with the lines.

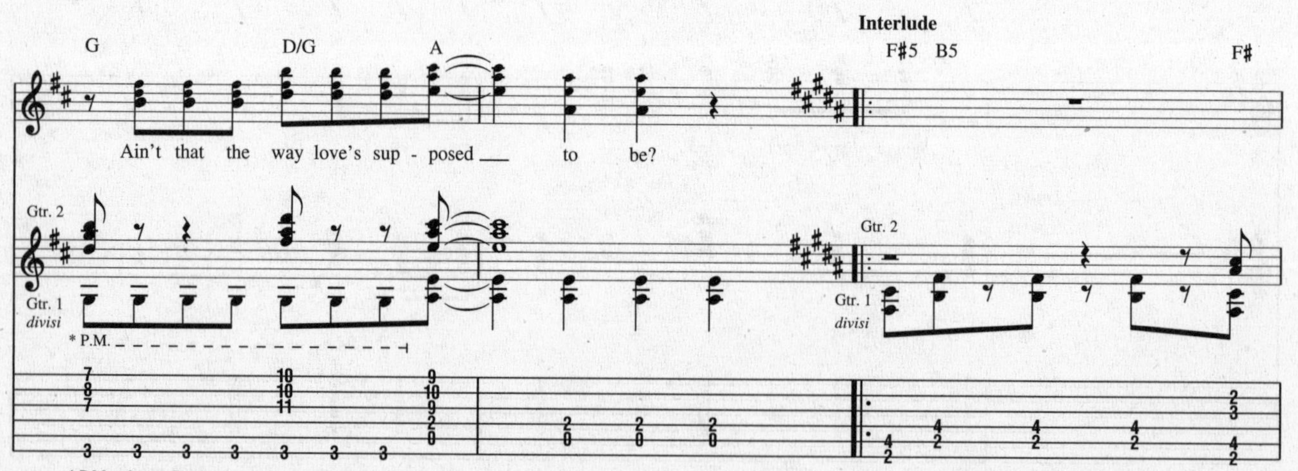
Interlude
G D/G A F♯5 B5 F♯
Ain't that the way love's sup - posed to be?
Gtr. 2
Gtr. 1
divisi
* P.M.
* P.M. refers to Gtr. 1 only.

1., 2., 3.
4.
G#m
G#sus 2/4
G5
A5
D5
B5
Tell me...
Where can I find a
Guitar Solo
Gtr. 1
wom-an like that?
Gtr. 2
(cont. in slash)
Harm.
w/ bar
full
hold bend
w/ pick & fingers

A5 B5 G5 A5 D5 A5 type 2
P.M.
You know, I wish that I had
steady gliss.
Chorus
Gtrs. 1 & 2: w/ Rhy. Figs. 2 & 2A, 1 1/2 times
A5 D N.C. D N.C. D N.C. A Bm Bsus 2/4 Bm Bsus 2/4 A5 D N.C. D N.C. D N.C. A
Jes - sie's girl. I wish that I had Jes - sie's girl.
Jes - sie's girl? I wish I had Jes - sie's girl.
* Sing harmony 2nd time only, next 5 meas.
Bm Bsus 2/4 Bm Bsus 2/4 A5 D N.C. D N.C. D N.C. A Bm Bsus 2/4 Bm Bsus 2/4
I want Jes - sie's girl.
I want, I want Jes - sie's girl.
1.
2.
G5 A5 D5 B5 A5
A D/A A D/A A G D5
Gtr. 1
(cont. in notation)
Where can I find a wom-an like that, like
Gtr. 2
rit.
Gtr. 1
rit.

Just a Girl

Words and Music by Gwen Stefani and Thomas Dumont

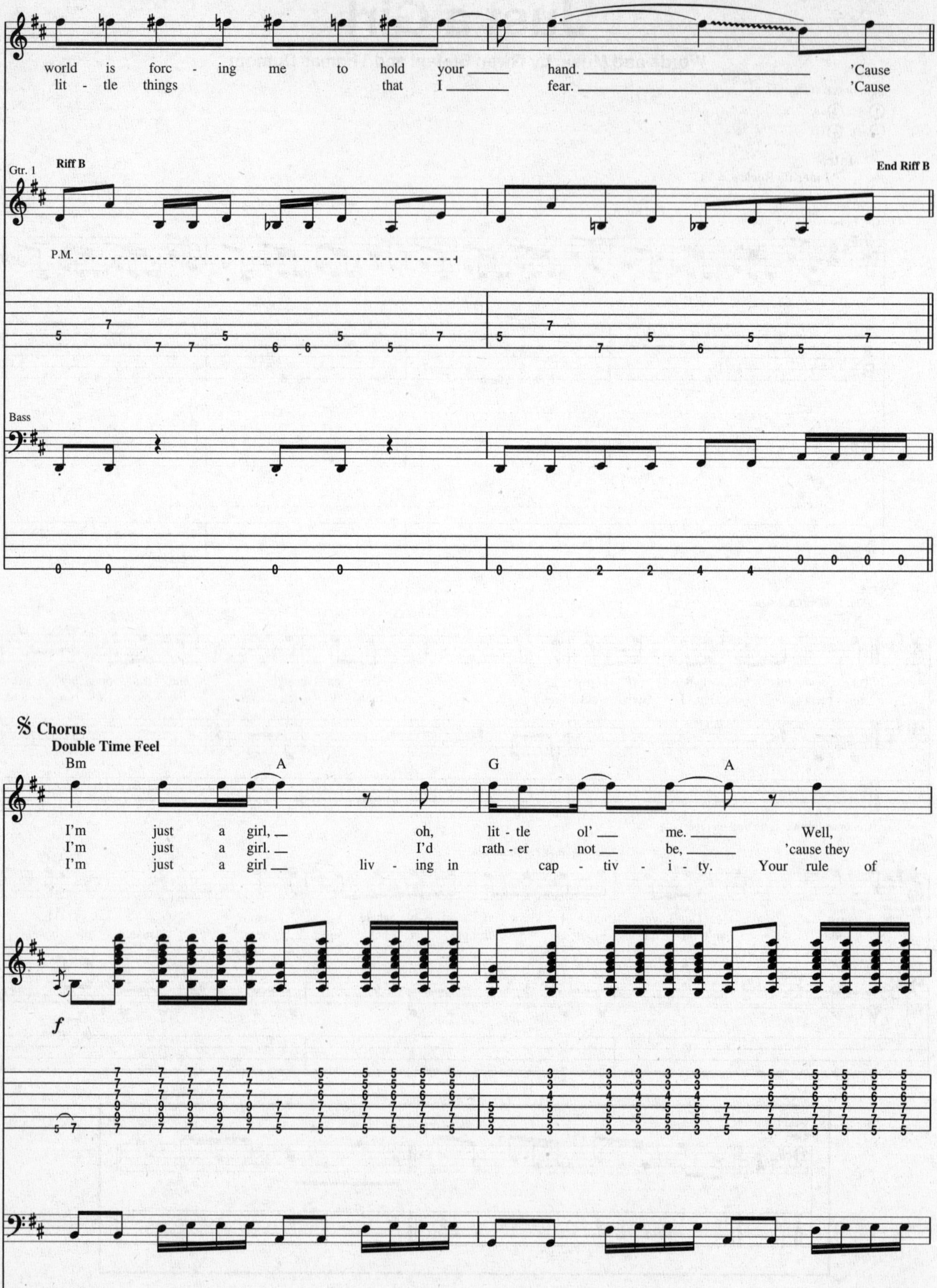

𝄋 Chorus
Double Time Feel

Bm A G A

I'm just a girl, ___ oh, lit - tle ol' ___ me. ___ Well,
I'm just a girl. ___ I'd rath - er not ___ be, ___ 'cause they
I'm just a girl ___ liv - ing in cap - tiv - i - ty. Your rule of

f

Bass: w/ Bass Fill 1, 1st time

Bm A G A

don't let me out of ___ your ___ sight. Oh,
won't let me drive late ___ at ___ night. _ Oh,
thumb makes me wor - ry some. ___ Oh,

Bm A G A

I'm just a girl, ___ all pret - ty and pe - tite. ___ So don't_
I'm just a girl. ___ Guess I'm some kind of freak, ___ 'cause they all ___
I'm just a girl. ___ What's my des - ti - ny? What I've suc -

Rhy. Fig. 1

End Rhy. Fig. 1

Bass Fig. 1

1.

Bm A G A

___ let me have an - y ___ rights. ___

___ sit and stare with ___ their ___

cumbed to is mak - ing ___ me ___

Rhy. Fig. 2 End Rhy. Fig. 2

End Bass Fig. 1

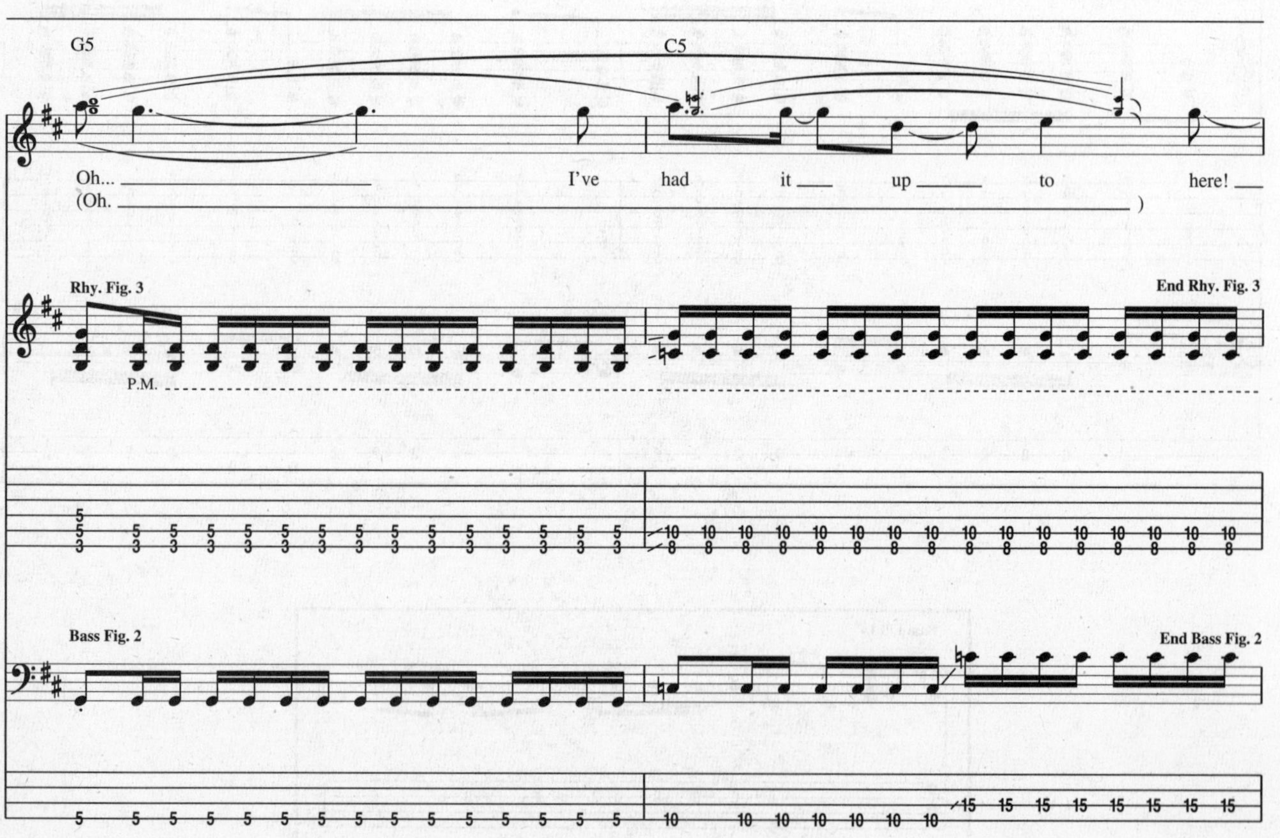

2.,3.
To Coda
Bass: w/ Bass Fill 2, 2nd time
N.C.
G
A
2. The
eyes.
numb.
Oh,
Oh,
mf
P.M.
8va
loco
Harm.
Gtr. 1: w/ Rhy. Fig. 1
Bass: w/ Bass Fig. 1, simile
Bm
A
G
A
Gtr. 1: w/ Rhy. Fig. 2
Bm
A
I'm just a girl. Take a good look at me, just your typ - i - cal pro - to - type.
G
A
Bass: w/ Bass Fig. 2
Gtr. 1: w/ Rhy. Fig. 3
G5
C5
Oh... I've had it up to here!
(Oh.)
Interlude
Gtr. 1: w/ Rhy. Fig. 1, 4 times, simile
Bm
A
G
A
Bm
A
*Gtr. 2
Riff C
Bass
*synth. arr. for gtr.
Bass Fill 2
Bass

G
A
End Riff C
Bm
A
G
A
Bm
A
G
A
Gtr. 1: w/ Rhy. Fig. 3
Gtr. 2 tacet
Bass: w/ Bass Fig. 2
G5
Oh... am I
(Oh.
End Double Time Feel
C5
Gtr. 1: w/ Riff A, 2 times
N.C.
mak - ing my - self clear?
)
I'm just a girl.
Bass
8va
loco
Harm.
Verse
Gtr. 1: w/ Riff A
Gtr. 1: w/ Riff B
D.S. al Coda
(take 2nd ending)
3. I'm just a girl in the world.
That's all that you'll let me be!
Oh,

Coda
Gtr. 1: w/ Rhy. Fig. 1, 3 times
Gtr. 2: w/ Riff C, 2 times
Bass: w/ Bass Fig. 1, simile
Bm A G A Bm A
I'm just a girl, my a - pol - o - gies. What I've be - come is so bur - den -
Bass: w/ Bass Fill 3
G A Bm A G A
- some. Oh, I'm just a girl, luck - y me. Twid - dle - dum,
Gtr. 1: w/ Rhy. Fig. 2
Bass: w/ Bass Fig. 1, 1st 2 meas.
Gtr. 1: w/ Rhy. Fig. 3, 2 times
Bass: w/ Bass Fig. 2, 2 times, simile
Bm A G A G5
there's no com - par - i - son. Oh... I've
(Oh.
End Double Time Feel
C5 G5 C5
had it up to! Oh... I've had it up to!!
Oh.
Slower ♩ = 92
Freely
w/ synth effects
G5 C5 rit. Bm
Oh... I've had it up to here.
Oh.)
Gtr. 1
rit.
Bass
rit.
Bass Fill 3
Bass

Keep Away

Words and Music by Sully Erna

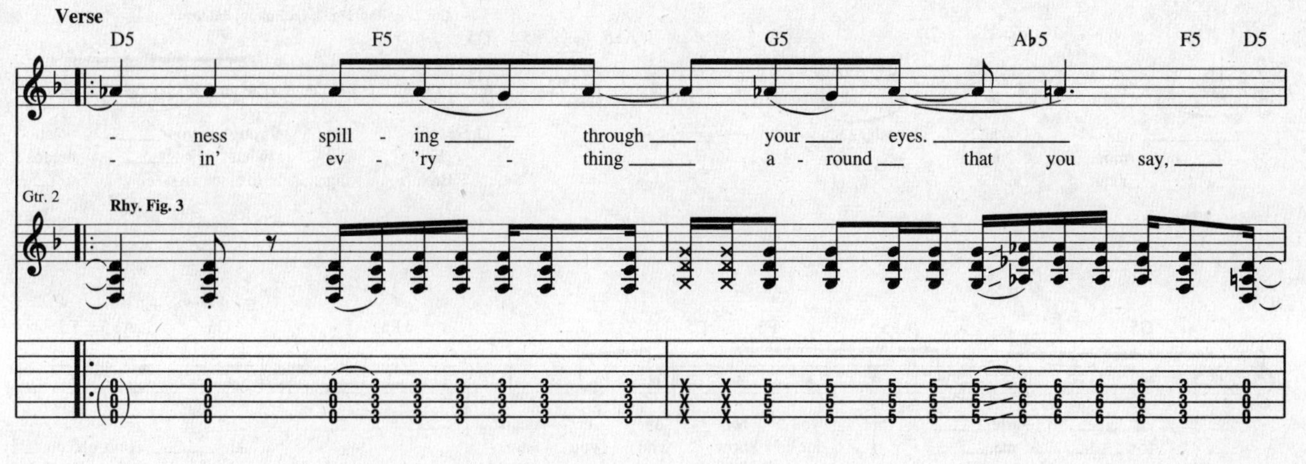
Verse
D5 F5 G5 A♭5 F5 D5
- ness spill - ing through your eyes.
- in' ev - 'ry - thing a - round that you say,
Gtr. 2
Rhy. Fig. 3

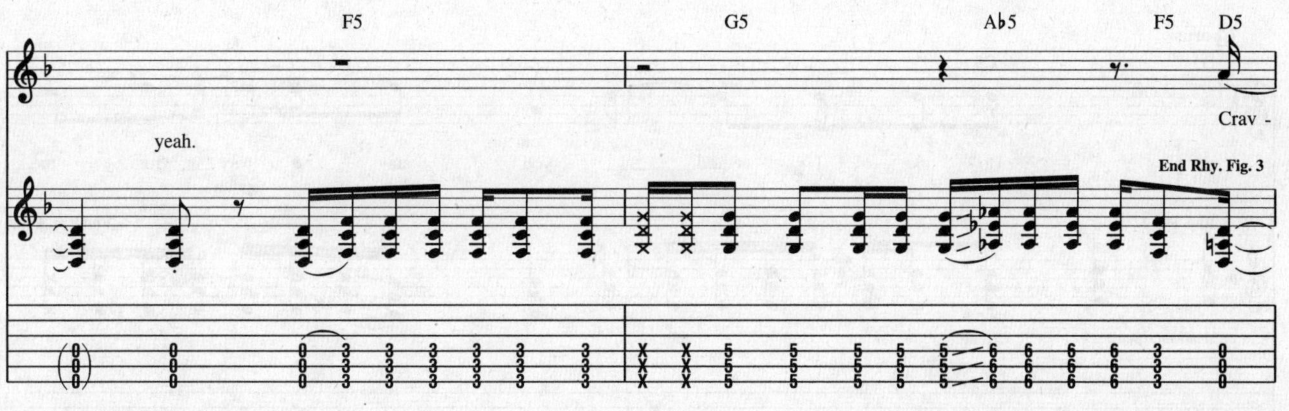
F5 G5 A♭5 F5 D5
yeah.
Crav -
End Rhy. Fig. 3

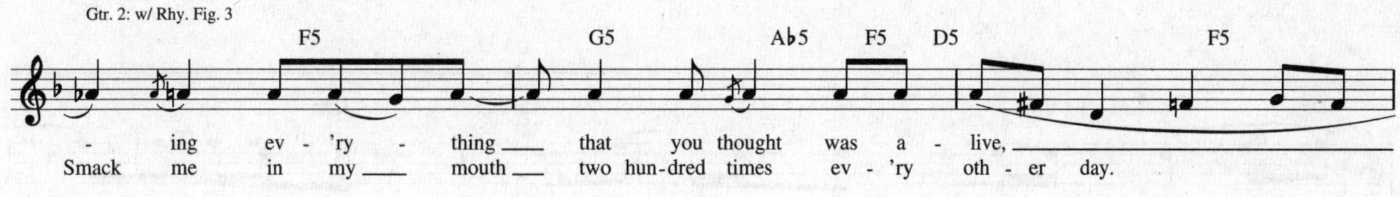
Gtr. 2: w/ Rhy. Fig. 3
F5 G5 A♭5 F5 D5 F5
- ing ev - 'ry - thing that you thought was a - live,
Smack me in my mouth two hun - dred times ev - 'ry oth - er day.

Verse
Gtr. 2: w/ Rhy. Fig. 3, 1 3/4 times
Gtr. 2: w/ Rhy. Fill 2, 3rd time
Gtr. 2: w/ Rhy. Fig. 3, last 3 meas., 3rd time
G5 A♭5 F5 D5 D5 F5 G5 A♭5 F5 D5
yeah.
Oh.
2. Stab me, uh, in my heart a - gain,
4. Rag me, uh, I don't hear you an -
5. Drag - gin' on so lone - ly, aren't you tired, ba - by?

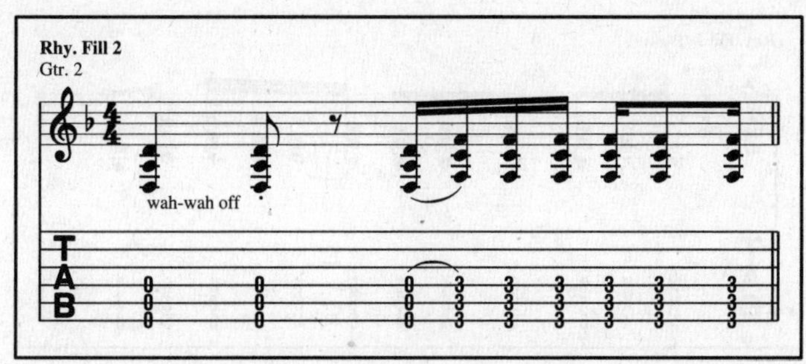
Rhy. Fill 2
Gtr. 2
wah-wah off

Gtr. 2: w/ Rhy. Fig. 3, 1st 3 meas., 3rd time
F5 G5 Ab5 F5 D5 F5
ah yeah. Drag me through your wast-
-y-more, not yet. Find out what it means
Yeah. Breath-ing life in-to
G5 Ab5 F5 D5 F5
Gtr. 2: w/ Rhy. Fill 1
G5 Ab5 F5
-ed life, are you for-ev-er dead?
to me, I don't know who you are.
your lungs, are you im-mune to me?
Ah, ooh, oh, oh.
Ah, yeah, yeah, yeah, yeah,
Chorus
D5 C5 A5 Bb5
yeah.
Do like I told you, stay a-way from me.
Rhy. Fig. 4
End Rhy. Fig. 4
simile on repeats
D5 C5
1.
A5 D5
Nev-er mis-un-der-stand me, keep a-way from
steady gliss.
Rhy. Fill 1
Gtr. 2

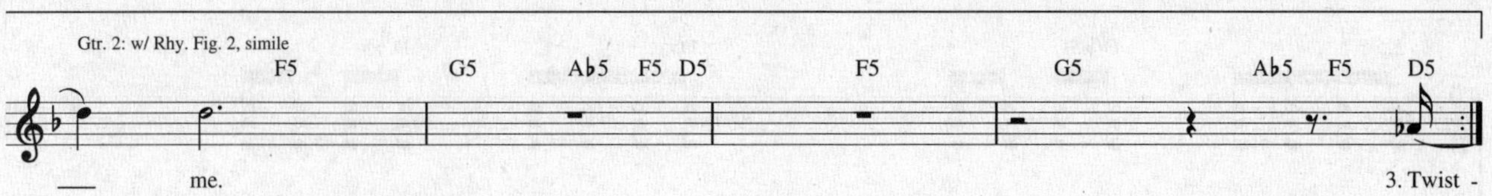
Gtr. 2: w/ Rhy. Fig. 2, simile
F5
G5
A♭5
F5
D5
F5
G5
A♭5
F5
D5
me.
3. Twist -

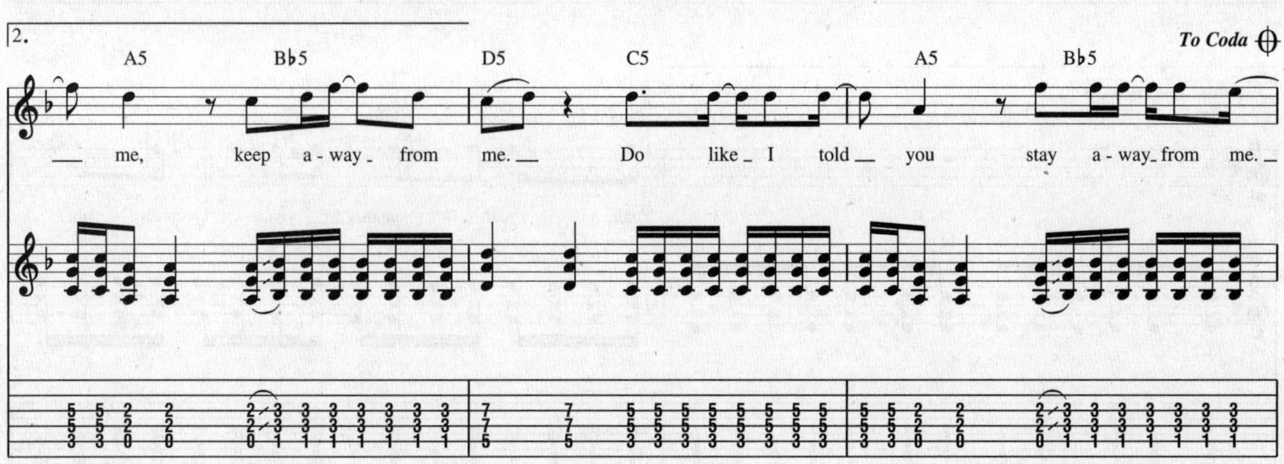
2.
To Coda
A5
B♭5
D5
C5
A5
B♭5
me, keep a - way from me. Do like I told you stay a - way from me.

D5
C5
A5
B♭5
C5
D5
Nev-er mis - un - der-stand me.
(Yeah, yeah.)

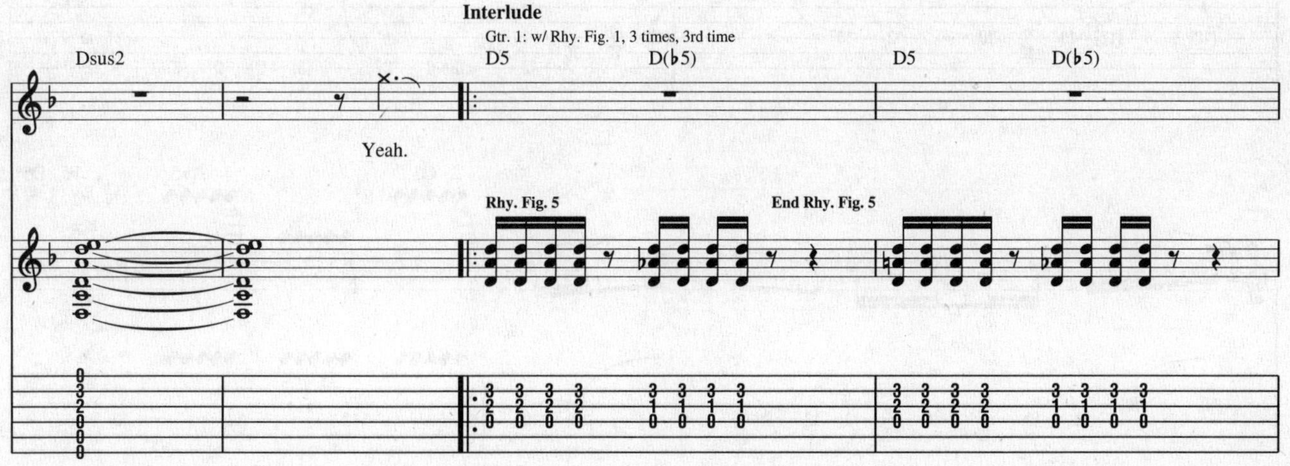
Interlude
Gtr. 1: w/ Rhy. Fig. 1, 3 times, 3rd time
Dsus2
D5
D(♭5)
D5
D(♭5)
Yeah.
Rhy. Fig. 5
End Rhy. Fig. 5

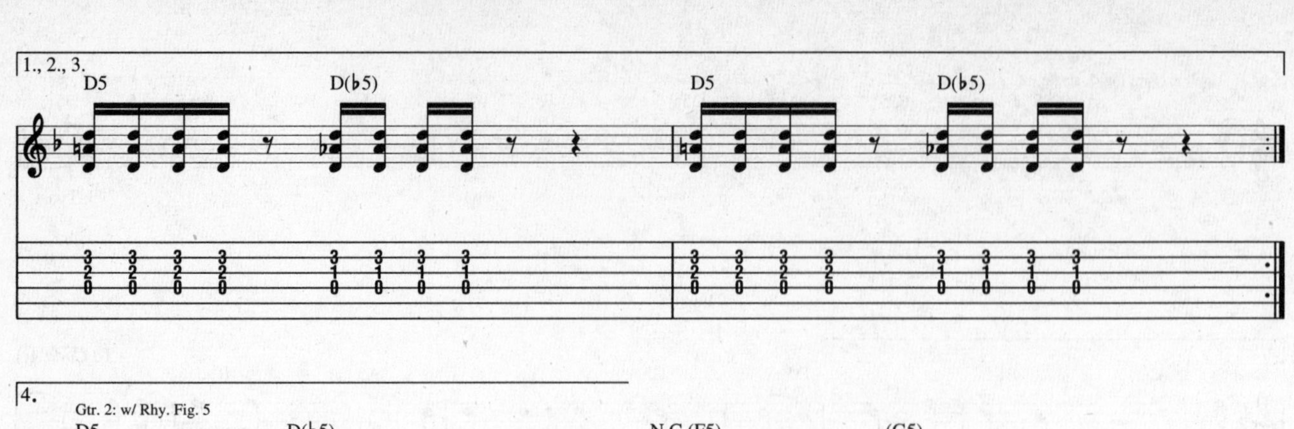

Guitar Solo

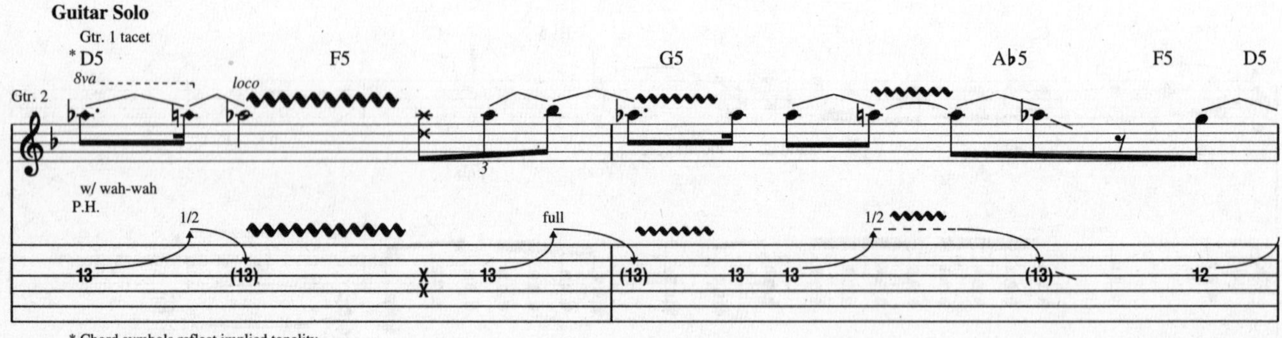

* Chord symbols reflect implied tonality.

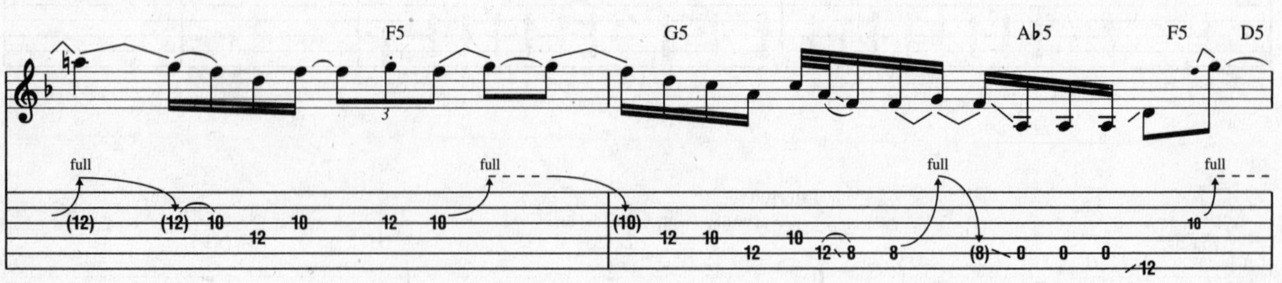

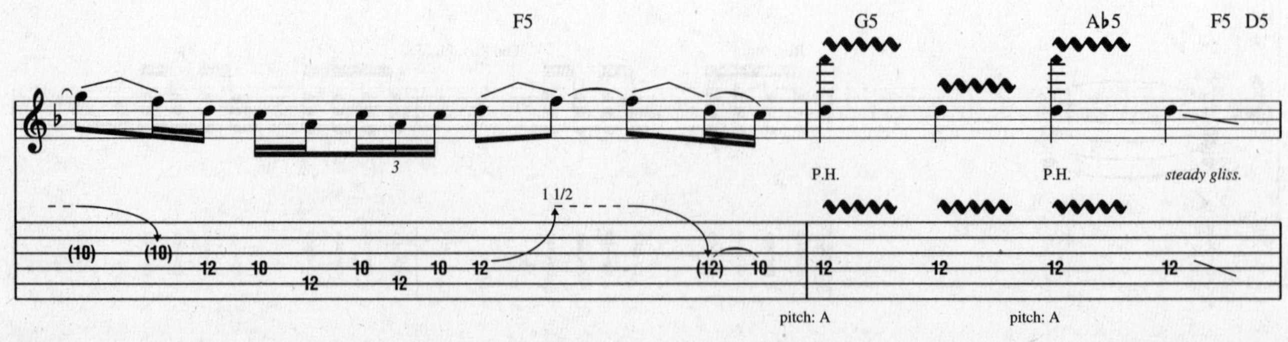

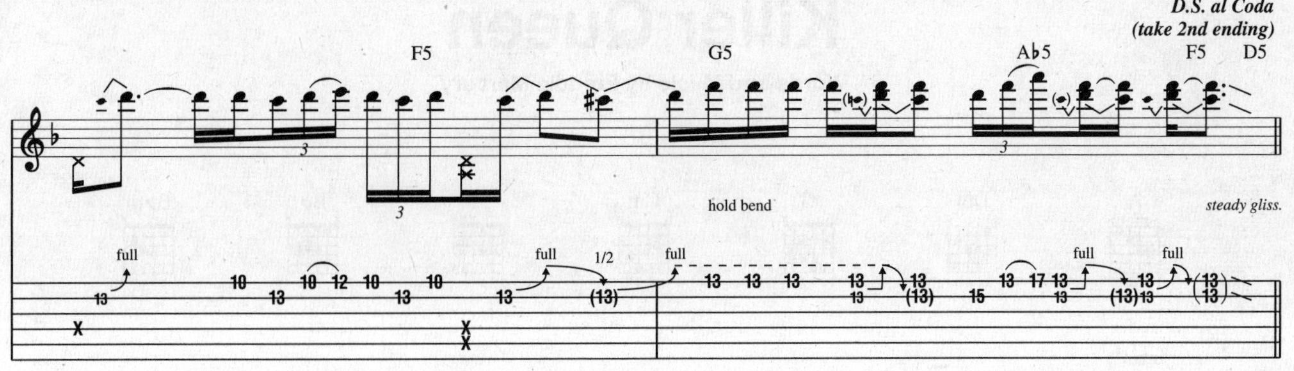
D.S. al Coda
(take 2nd ending)
F5 G5 A♭5 F5 D5
hold bend
steady gliss.
full full 1/2 full full full

Coda
Gtr. 2: w/ Rhy. Fig. 4, 4 times, simile
D5 C5 A5 B♭5 D5 C5
Nev-er mis-un-der-stand me. I,

A5 B♭5 D5 C5 A5 B♭5
yeah. Keep a-way from me, yeah. Nev-er mis-un-der-stand

D5 C5 A5 B♭5
me, nev-er mis-un-der-stand me, nev-er mis-un-der-stand

D5 C5 A5 B♭5 C5 D5
me, ah, yeah, yeah, yeah, yeah, yeah.
Gtr. 2
8va
fdbk.
fdbk.
pitch: E

Killer Queen

Words and Music by Freddie Mercury

Gtr. 2 tacet
Ab/Bb
Bb7
G7
Cm
Bb
Eb
you can't de - cline.
oo, oo.)
Ca - vi - ar and cig - ar - ettes,
well versed in et - i-quette, ex -
End Riff A
D7
Gm
F
Chorus
Bb
Dm
Gm
Dm
tr'or - din - ar - i - ly nice. She's a kill - er queen, gun - pow - der, gel - a - tine,
Gm
A7
Dm
G7
F/A
G7/B
C
dy - na - mite with a la - ser beam. An' guar - an - teed to blow your mind.
(Ba, ba, ba, ba.
Bb
A
Dm
Oo. Rec - om - mend - ed at the price, in -
An - y - time!)
let ring
Gtrs. 3, 4, 5 & 6: w/ Riff B (see next page)
G
C
Bb
F
Bb/F F11
Bb/F F11
sa - tia - ble an ap - pe - tite.
Wan - na try?
let ring

Verse

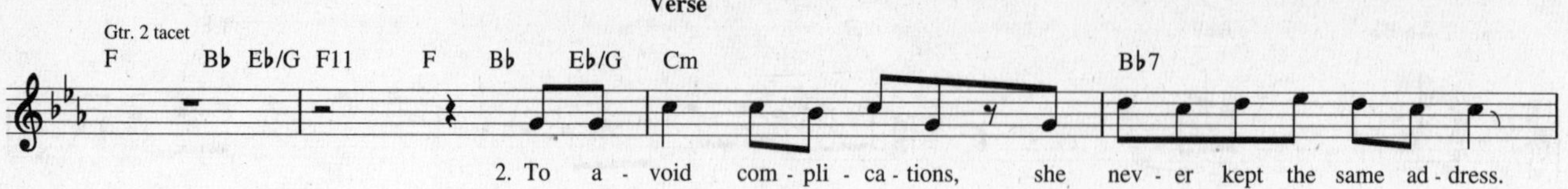
Gtr. 2 tacet
F Bb Eb/G F11 F Bb Eb/G Cm Bb7
2. To a - void com - pli - ca - tions, she nev - er kept the same ad - dress.

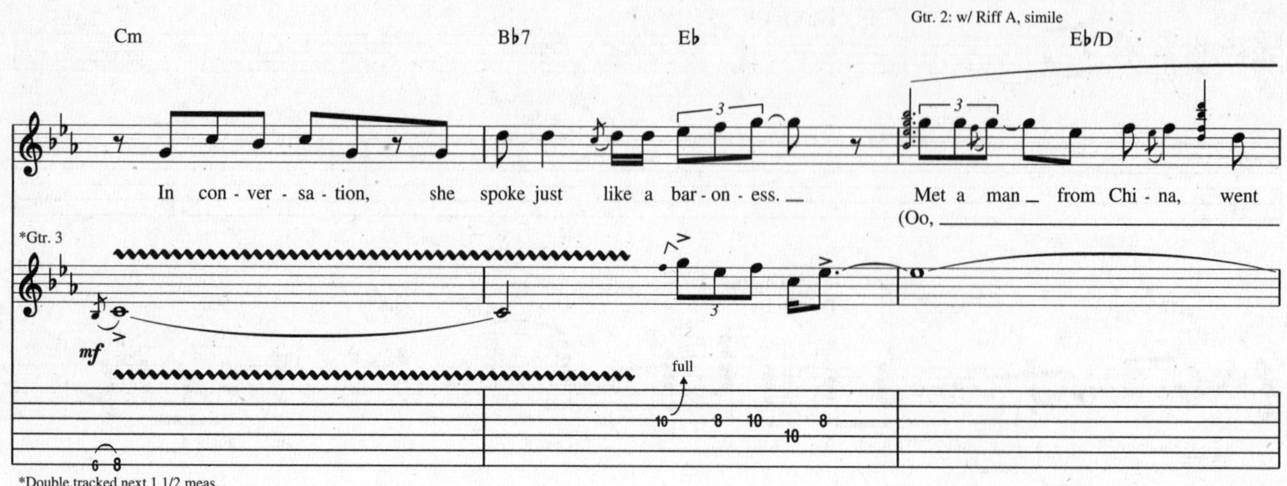
Gtr. 2: w/ Riff A, simile
Cm Bb7 Eb Eb/D
In con - ver - sa - tion, she spoke just like a bar - on - ess. Met a man from Chi - na, went
(Oo,
*Gtr. 3
mf
full
*Double tracked next 1 1/2 meas.

Gtr. 3 tacet
Eb7/Db Ab Abm Eb/Bb
down to Gei - sha Mi - nah, then a - gain in - ci - den - t'ly if you're
a kill - er, kill - er, she's a

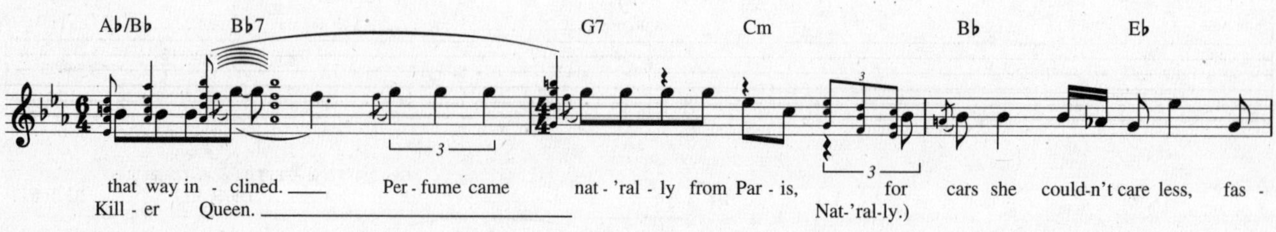
Ab/Bb Bb7 G7 Cm Bb Eb
that way in - clined. Per - fume came nat - 'ral - ly from Par - is, for cars she could - n't care less, fas -
Kill - er Queen. Nat - 'ral - ly.)

Riff B
*Gtrs. 3, 4, 5 & 6 (dist.)
mf
full
1/2
*One gtr. arr. per string.

Chorus

D7 Gm F B♭ Dm Gm Dm

tid - i - ous and pre - cise. _ She's a kill - er queen, _ gun - pow - der, gel - a - tine, _

Gm A7 Dm G7 F/A G7/B C B♭

dy - na - mite _ with a la - ser beam. _ An' guar - an - teed _ to blow your _ mind. _

(Bah, bah, bah, bah. An - y - time. _)

mf grad. bend full

Guitar Solo

A ⑥ 6fr A A ⑥ 6fr D ⑤ 6fr Dm A ⑥ 6fr A A ⑥ 6fr D ⑤ 6fr Dm G ⑥ 4fr G G ⑥ 4fr C ⑤ 4fr Cm

full full full

Gtrs. 4, 5, & 6: w/ Riff C

G ⑥ 4fr G Cm F5

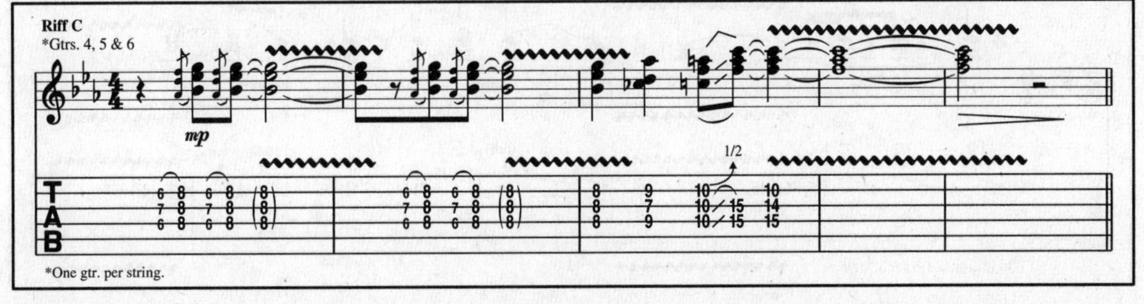

Gtr. 2 tacet

Cm Bb7

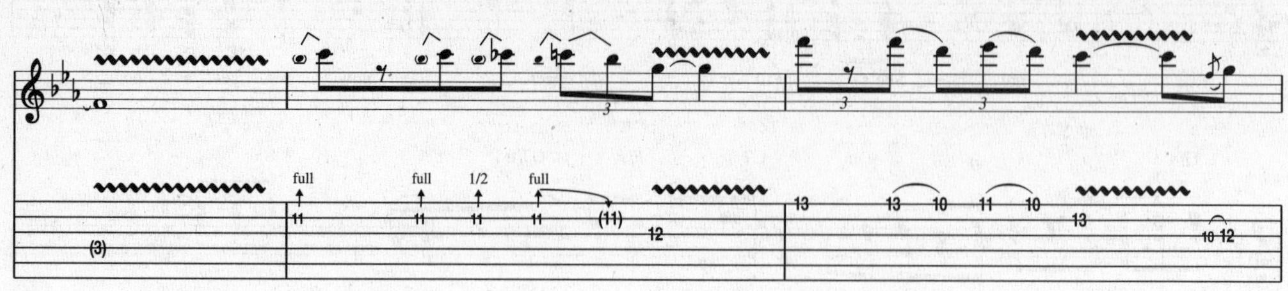

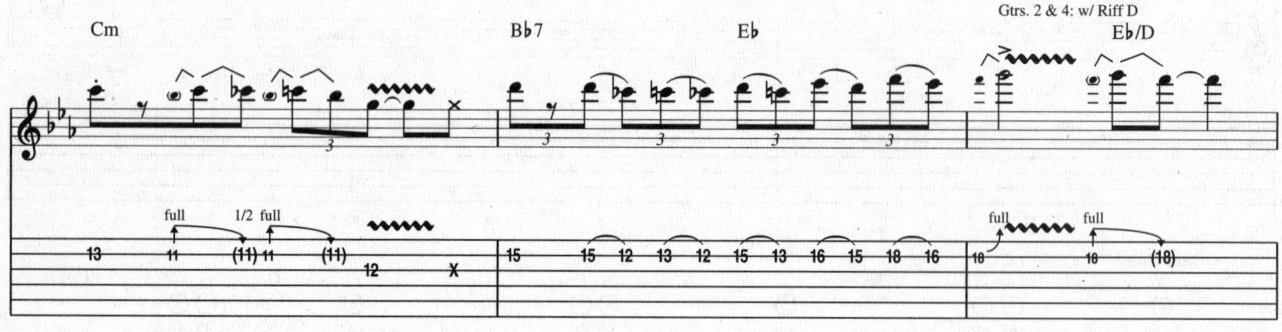

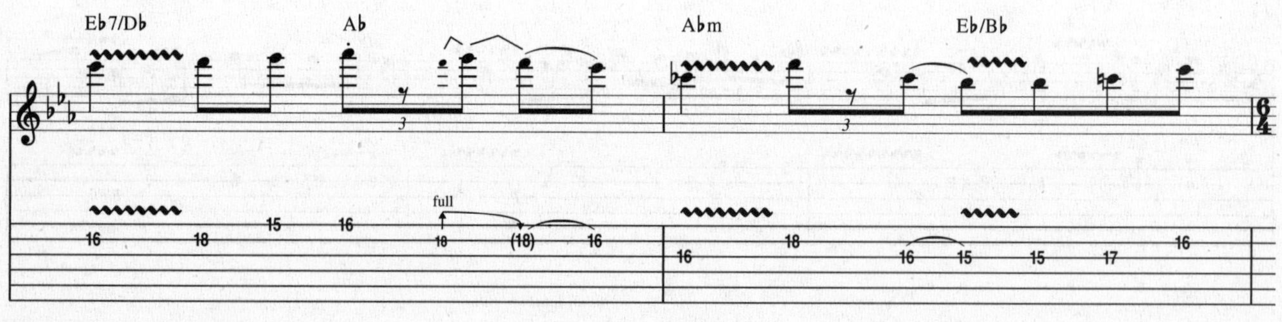

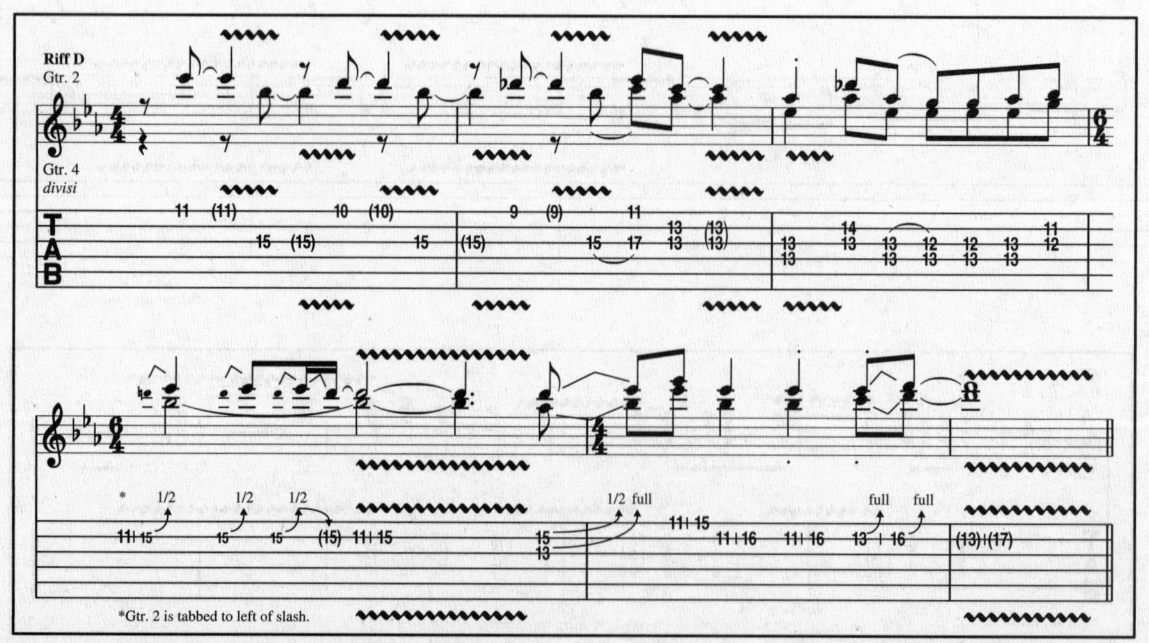

Ab/Bb Bb7 Eb/Bb Ab/Bb Bb7

3. Drop of a

full full full (18) (18) (18) 16 18 full full full full 1 1/2 (18)

Verse

Gtrs. 3 & 4: w/ Fill 1

G Cm G Cm Bb Eb

hat she's as will-ing as, play-ful as a puss-y cat then mo-ment-tar-i-ly out of ac-tion,

(Oo,

Gtr. 2

mf w/ wah-wah *mp*

1/2

Bb Eb D G5 F5 Bb F5

Gtr. 3

tem-po-rar-i-ly out of gas to ab-so-lute-ly drive.

oo, da, da, drive you wild,

rake 1/2

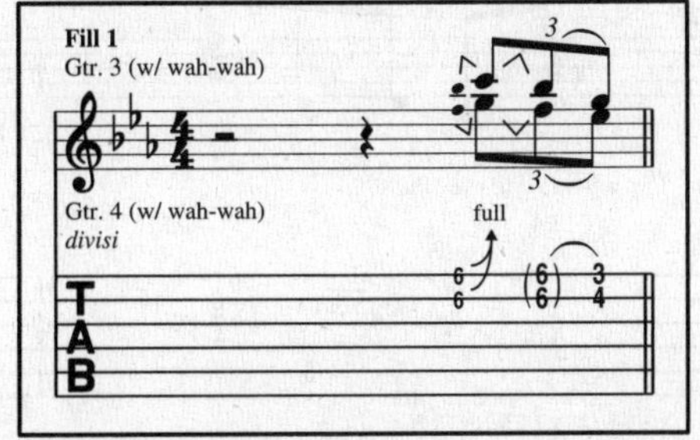

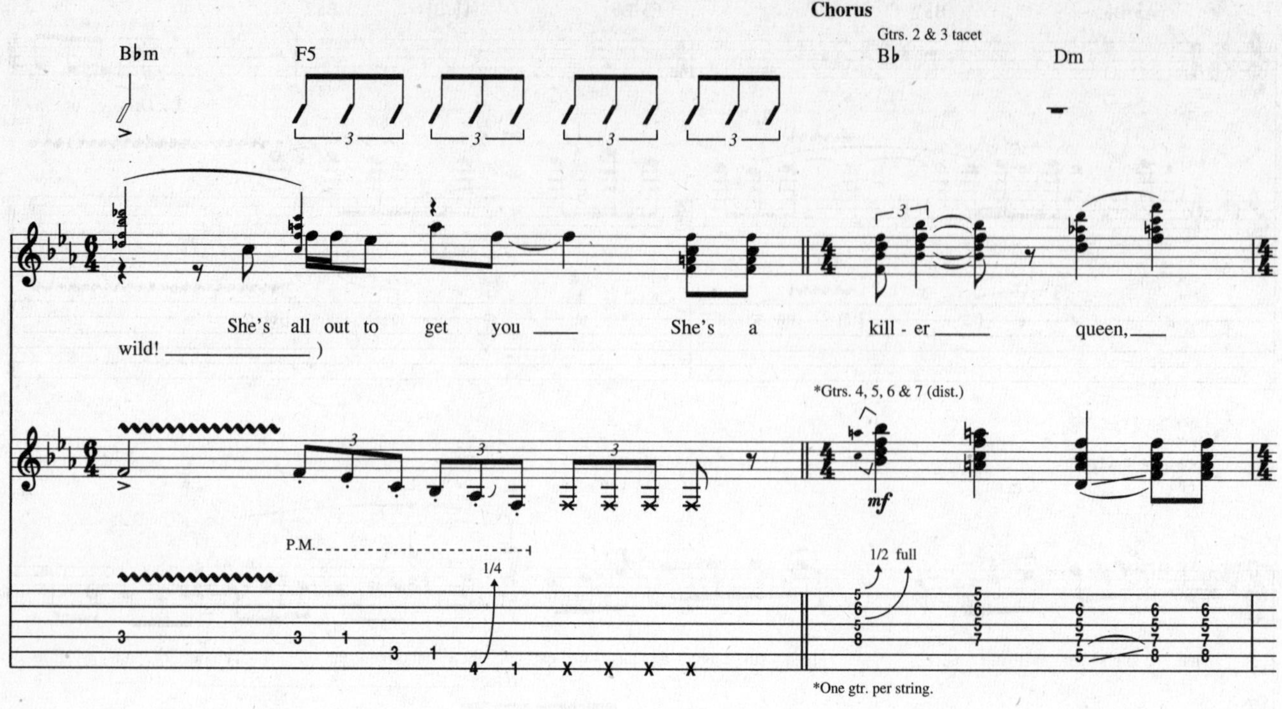
Chorus
Gtrs. 2 & 3 tacet
B♭m
F5
B♭
Dm
She's all out to get you ___ She's a kill - er ___ queen, ___
wild! ___)
*Gtrs. 4, 5, 6 & 7 (dist.)
mf
P.M.
1/4
1/2 full
*One gtr. per string.

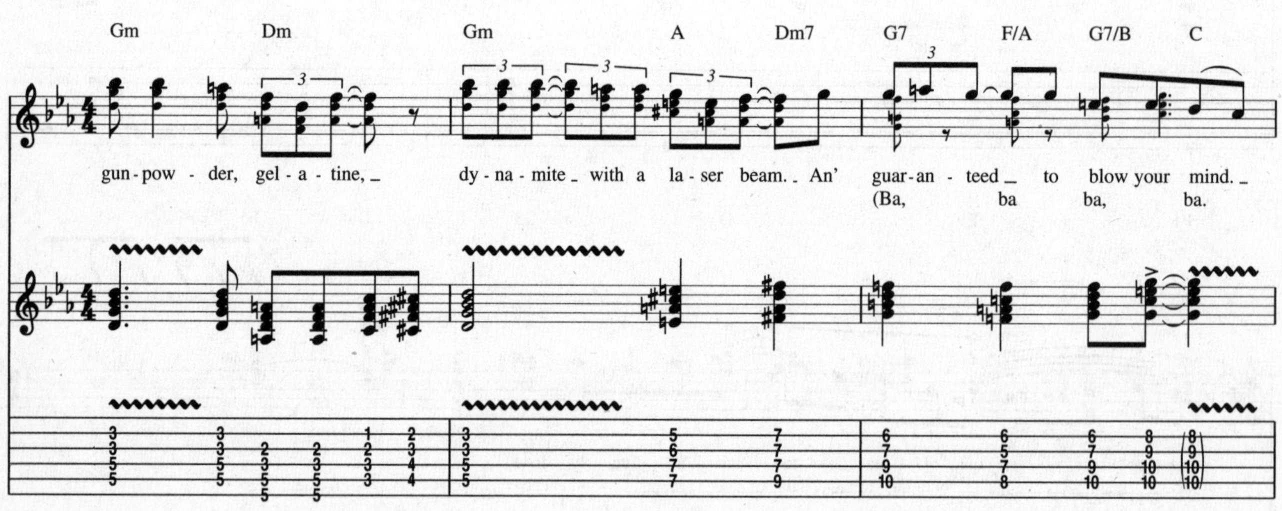
Gm
Dm
Gm
A
Dm7
G7
F/A
G7/B
C
gun-pow - der, gel - a - tine, _ dy - na - mite _ with a la - ser beam. _ An' guar - an - teed _ to blow your mind. _
(Ba, ba ba, ba.

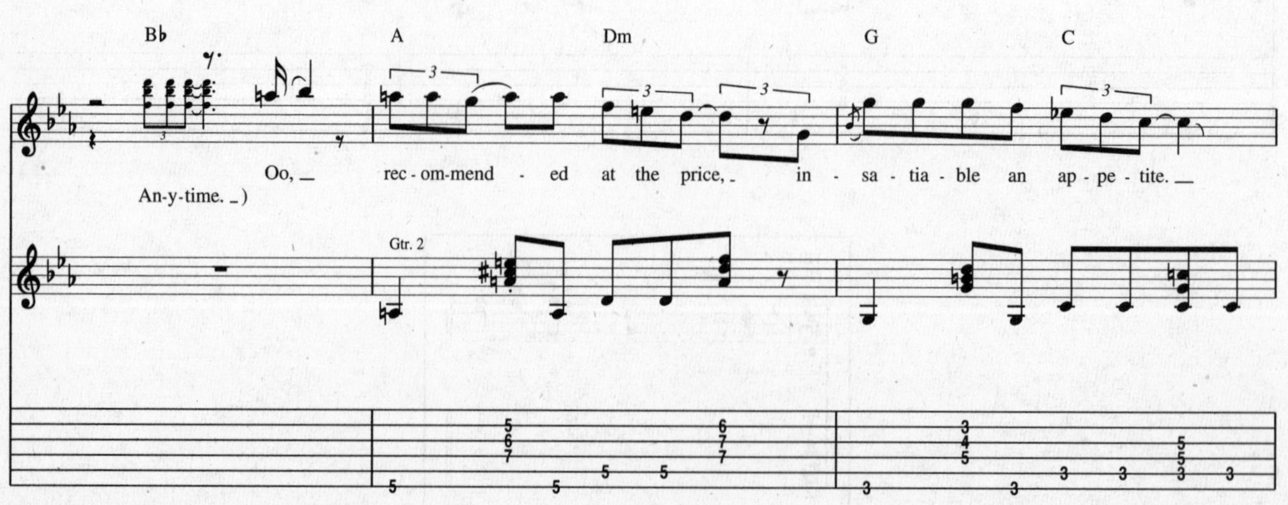
B♭
A
Dm
G
C
Oo, _ rec - om - mend - ed at the price, _ in - sa - tia - ble an ap - pe - tite. _
An - y - time. _)
Gtr. 2

Bb5
Gtr. 2 tacet
F
Bb/F
F11
F
Bb
Eb/G
Wan - na try?
You wan - na try?
Gtrs. 4, 5, 6 & 7
grad. bend
full 1/2 full
Outro
F11
F
Bb
Eb/Gb
Gtr. 3: w/ Fill 2, till end
Eb7
Riff E
End Riff E
Gtrs. 4, 5 & 6
Gtrs. 4, 5 & 6: w/ Riff E, till end
8va
Gtr. 2
Repeat and Fade
Fill 2
Gtr. 3
mp

Kryptonite

Words and Music by Matt Roberts, Brad Arnold and Todd Harrell

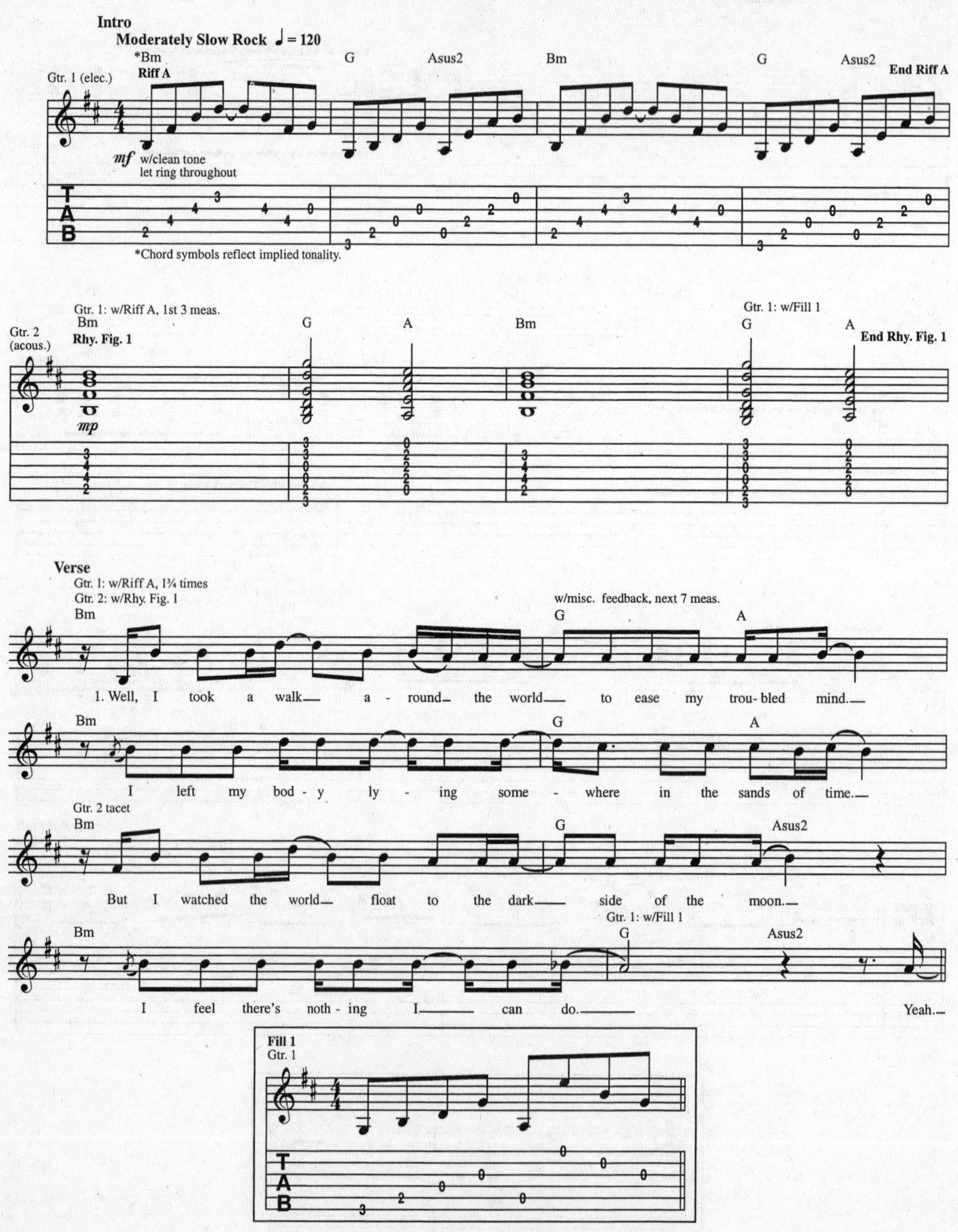

Interlude

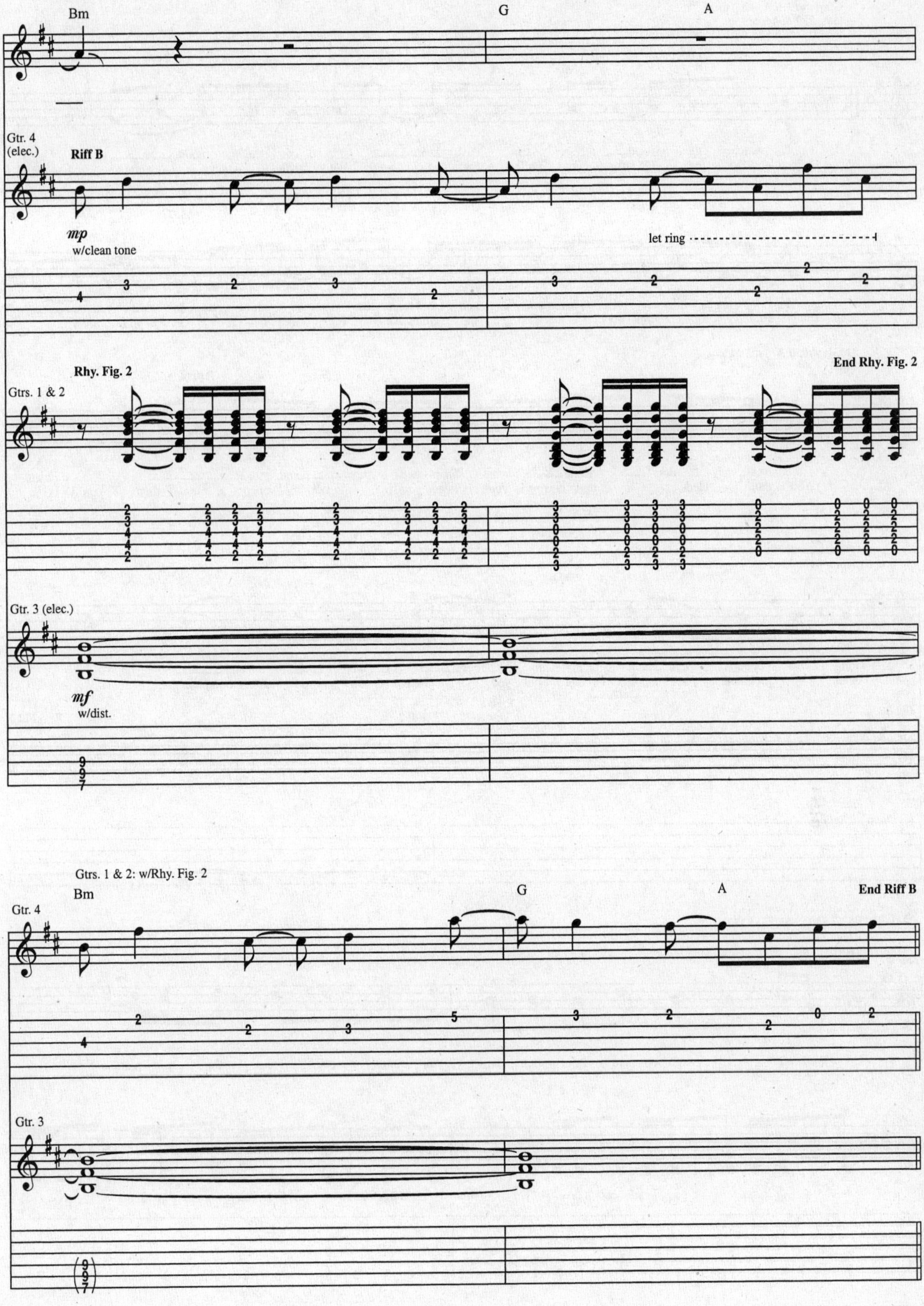

Bm G A

Gtr. 4 (elec.)

Riff B

mp

w/clean tone

let ring

Rhy. Fig. 2

End Rhy. Fig. 2

Gtrs. 1 & 2

Gtr. 3 (elec.)

mf

w/dist.

Verse
Gtr. 1: w/Riff A, 1st 3 meas.
Gtrs. 2, 3 & 4 tacet
w/misc. feedback, next 2 meas., 1st time
Bm
G
Asus2
2. I watched the world float to the dark side of the moon.
3. You called me strong, you called me weak, but still your se-crets I will
Gtr. 1: w/Fill 1
Af - ter all, I knew it had to be some - thing to do with you.
keep. You took for grant-ed all the times I nev - er let you down.
I real - ly don't mind what hap-pens now and then, as
You stum - bled in and bumped your head. If not for me, then you'd be
w/misc. feedback, next 2 meas.
long as you'll be my friend at the end.
dead. I picked you up and put you back on sol - id ground.
Gtr. 3
Fill 2
End Fill 2
Chorus
Gtr. 1 tacet
B5
G5
A5
Well, if I go cra - zy, then will you still call me Su - per - man?
P.M.

B5
E5
N.C.(F♯5)
If I'm a - live and, well, will you be there hold - ing my hand?
P.M.
B5
G5
A5
I'll keep you by my side with my su - per - hu - man might.
Gtr. 5: w/Fill 3, 2nd & 3rd times
F♯5
Kryp - to - nite.
Fill 3
Gtr. 5 (elec.)
f
w/dist.
TAB
22

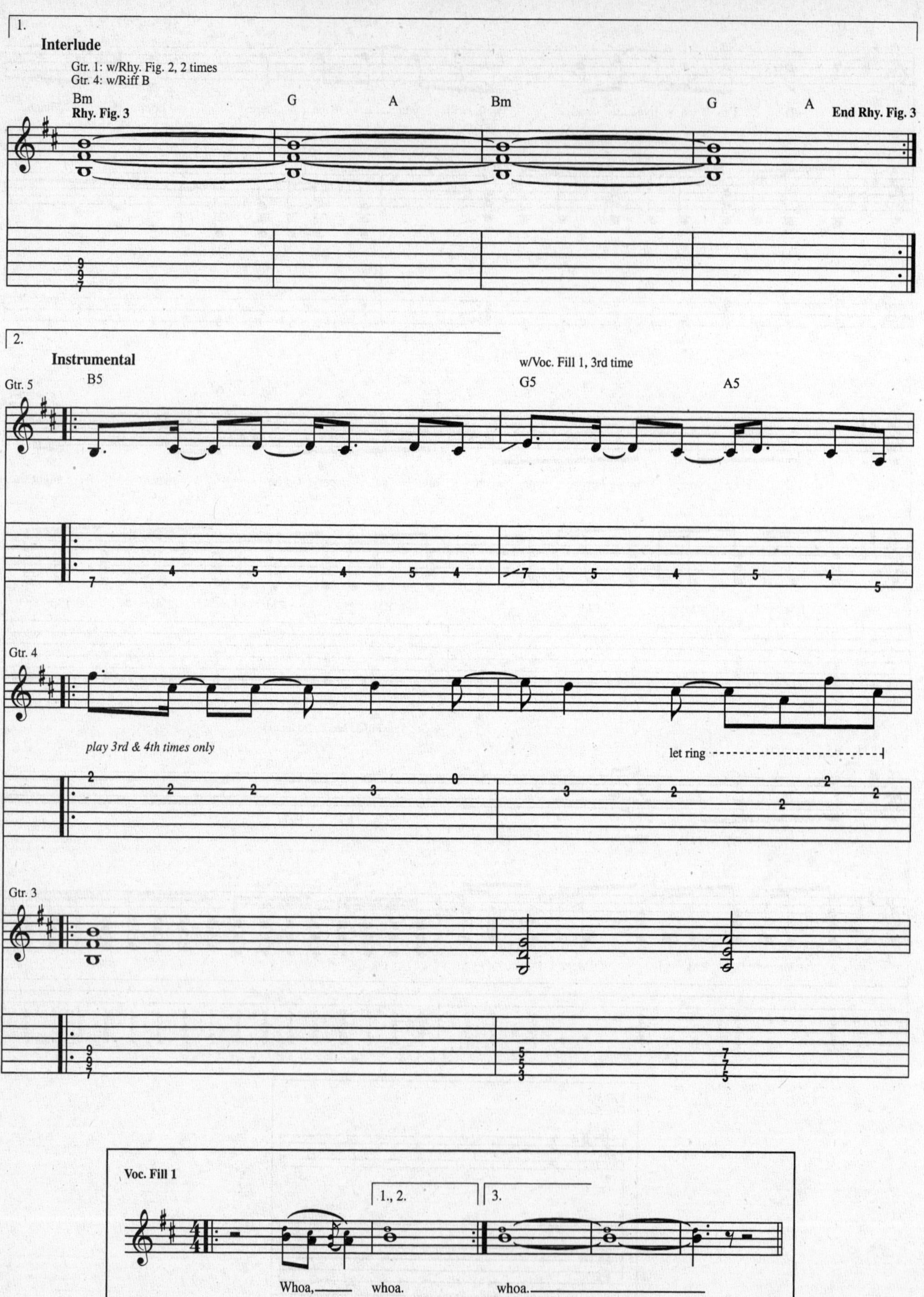
1.
Interlude
Gtr. 1: w/Rhy. Fig. 2, 2 times
Gtr. 4: w/Riff B
Bm
Rhy. Fig. 3
G
A
Bm
G
A
End Rhy. Fig. 3
2.
Instrumental
Gtr. 5
B5
w/Voc. Fill 1, 3rd time
G5
A5
Gtr. 4
play 3rd & 4th times only
let ring
Gtr. 3
Voc. Fill 1
1., 2.
3.
Whoa,
whoa.
whoa.

To Coda
B5
E5
F♯5
P.M.
Interlude
Gtr. 3: w/Rhy. Fig. 3
Gtr. 5 tacet
Bm
A
G
Riff C
Gtr. 4
Gtr. 1
Rhy. Fig. 4
End Rhy. Fig. 4
Gtr. 1: w/Rhy. Fig. 4
Bm
A
G
Gtr. 4
End Riff C

Chorus
Gtr. 1: w/Rhy. Fig. 4
Gtr. 4: w/Riff C, 2 times
Gtr. 3 tacet
Bm
A
G
If I go cra - zy, then will you still call me Su - per - man?
Bm
A
G
If I'm a - live and well will you be there hold - ing my hand?
Gtrs. 1 & 2 Riff D
End Riff D
let ring
let ring
let ring
Gtrs. 1 & 2: w/Riff D, 2 times
Bm
A
G
I'll keep you by my side with my sup - er - hu - man might.
D.S al Coda
(take 2nd ending, w/repeat)
Gtr. 3: w/Fill 2
Bm
A
G
Kryp - to - nite. Yeah!
Coda
Gtrs. 4 & 5 tacet
Gtr. 1
B5
w/heavy chorus
Gtr. 3

Land of Confusion

Words and Music by Tony Banks, Phil Collins and Mike Rutherford

Verse
Gtr. 1: w/ Rhy. Fig. 1
E5
G
2. Now, did you read the news to - day?
3. Ooh, Sup - er - man where are you now?
4. See additional lyrics
A
C
D
They say the dan - ger's gone a - way. But I can see the
Well, ev - 'ry - thing's gone wrong some - how. The men of steel,
D5/E
E5
fires still a - light. They're burn - ing in - to the night. 1., 3. There's
men of pow - er. They're los - ing con - trol by the hour.
Pre-Chorus
*D
Em
G
A
too man - y men, too man - y peo - ple mak - ing too man - y prob - lems,
2. This is the time, this is the place. So we look for the fu - ture,
*Chords implied by synthesizer (next 8 meas.)
and, not much love to go a - round. Can't you see this is a
but there's not much love to go a - round. Tell me why this is a
Chorus
E5
C5
D5
B5
land of con - fu - sion? Well, this is the world we live in
land of con - fu - sion. (Oh.
Rhy. Fig. 2
End Rhy. Fig. 2

Gtr. 1: w/ Rhy. Fig. 2 (3 times)
E5 C5 D5 B5 E5 C5
and these are the hands we're giv - en Use them and
Oh.

To Coda
D5 B5 E5 C5 D5 B5
let's start try - ing to make it a place worth liv - ing
Oh.)

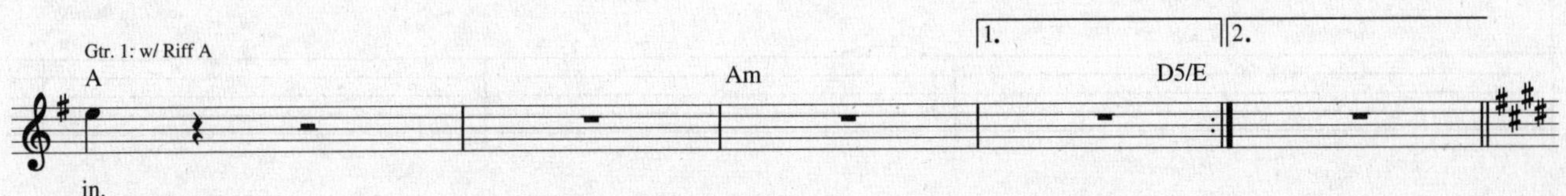
Gtr. 1: w/ Riff A
A Am D5/E
1. 2.
in.

Bridge

C♯m F♯/C♯
Riff B

A/C♯ E E/D♯ C♯m F♯
I re-mem - ber long a -
End Riff B

Gtr. 1: w/ Riff B
C♯m F♯/C♯
go. Mm, when the sun was shin - ing. The shine, the

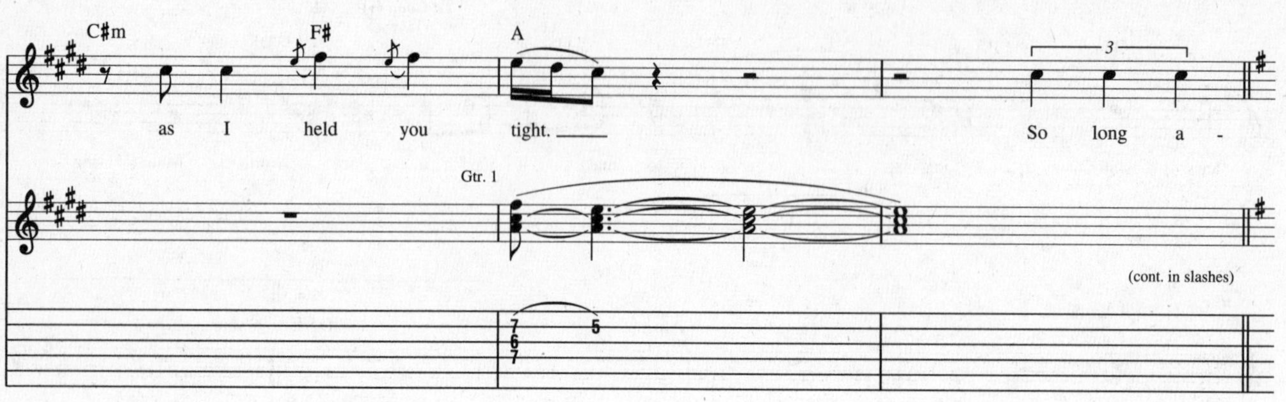

Interlude

*Synth. arr. for gtr.

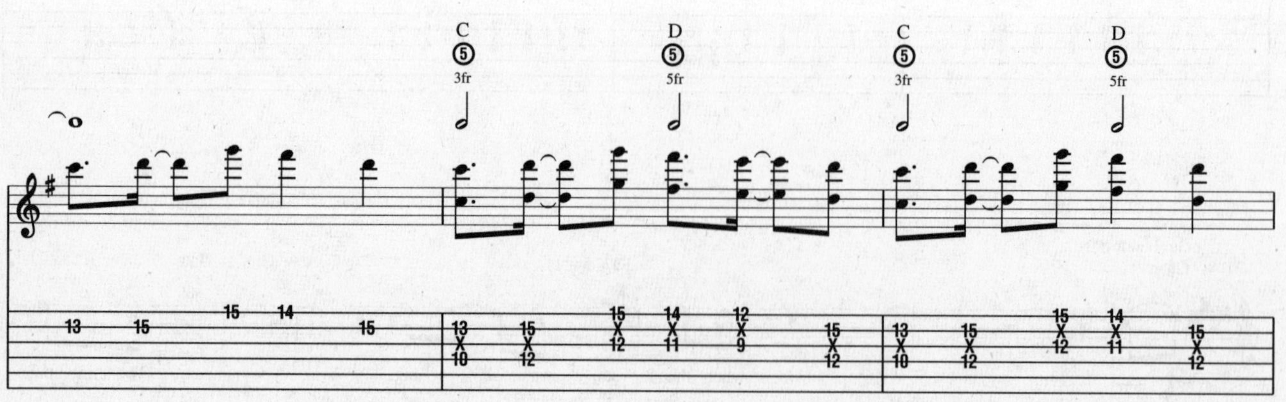

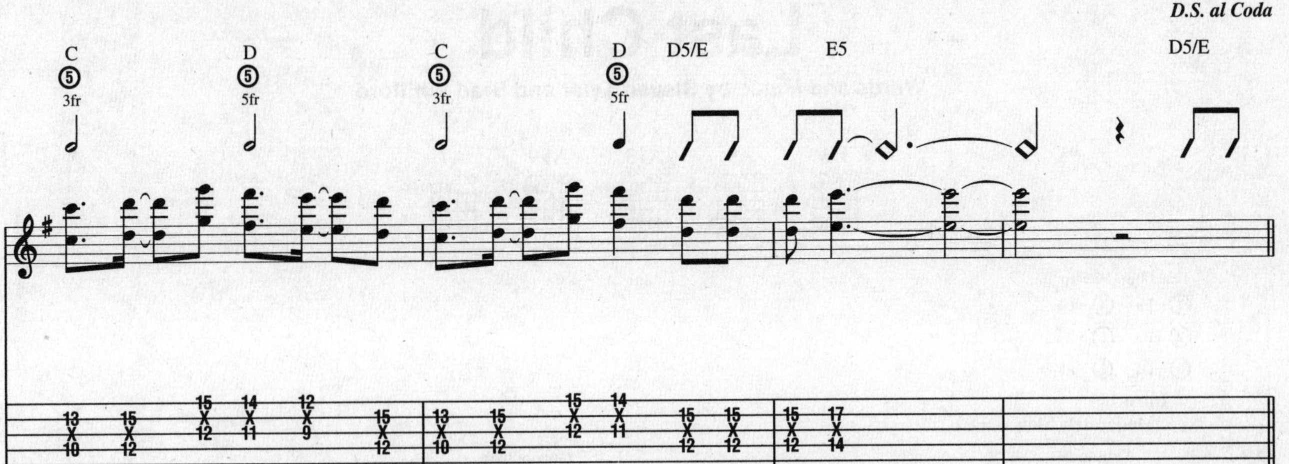

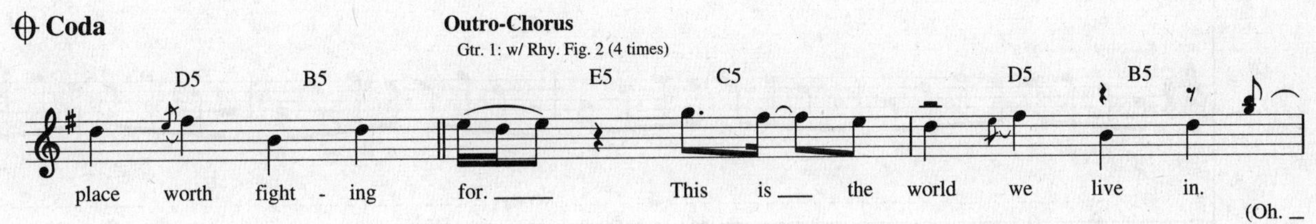

Additional Lyrics

4. I won't be coming home tonight.
My generation will put it right.
We're not just making promises,
That we know we'll never keep.

Last Child

Words and Music by Steven Tyler and Brad Whitford

End Rhy. Fig. 1
Yeah, ya, ya, yeah.
1. Take
End Riff A
0 2 4 5 4 2 4 5 2
0 2 4 5 4 2/0 4 5 2
0 2 4 5 4 2/0 4 0 5 2
End Rhy. Fig. 1A
Verse
Gtr. 1: w/ Riff A, 4 times
Gtrs. 3 & 4: w/ Rhy. Figs. 1 & 1A, 4 times
E9
me back to a South Tal - la - has - see,
in the field, put the mule in the sta - ble.
Gtr. 2
simile 2nd time
0 2 4 5 4 0 4 0 5 2
0 2 4 5 4 0 4 5 2
down 'cross the bridge to my sweet sas - sa - fras - see.
Ma, she's a - cook - in' put the eats on the ta - ble.
Can't
Hate's
0 2 4 5 4 2 4 0 5 2
0 2 4 5 4 0 4 5 2

* Gtr. 4 tabbed to the right of slash.

A9
A13
Ab9
A9
A13
*Ab9
tail poon - tang sweet - heart sweat who could make silk purse from a J. Paul Get and his ear,
their throats for pap - er notes and their ba - bies cry while cit - ies lie at their feet,
*A7, 2nd time
E9
with her face in her beer.
when you're rock - in' the streets.
Gtr. 1
Gtr. 2
Gtr. 4

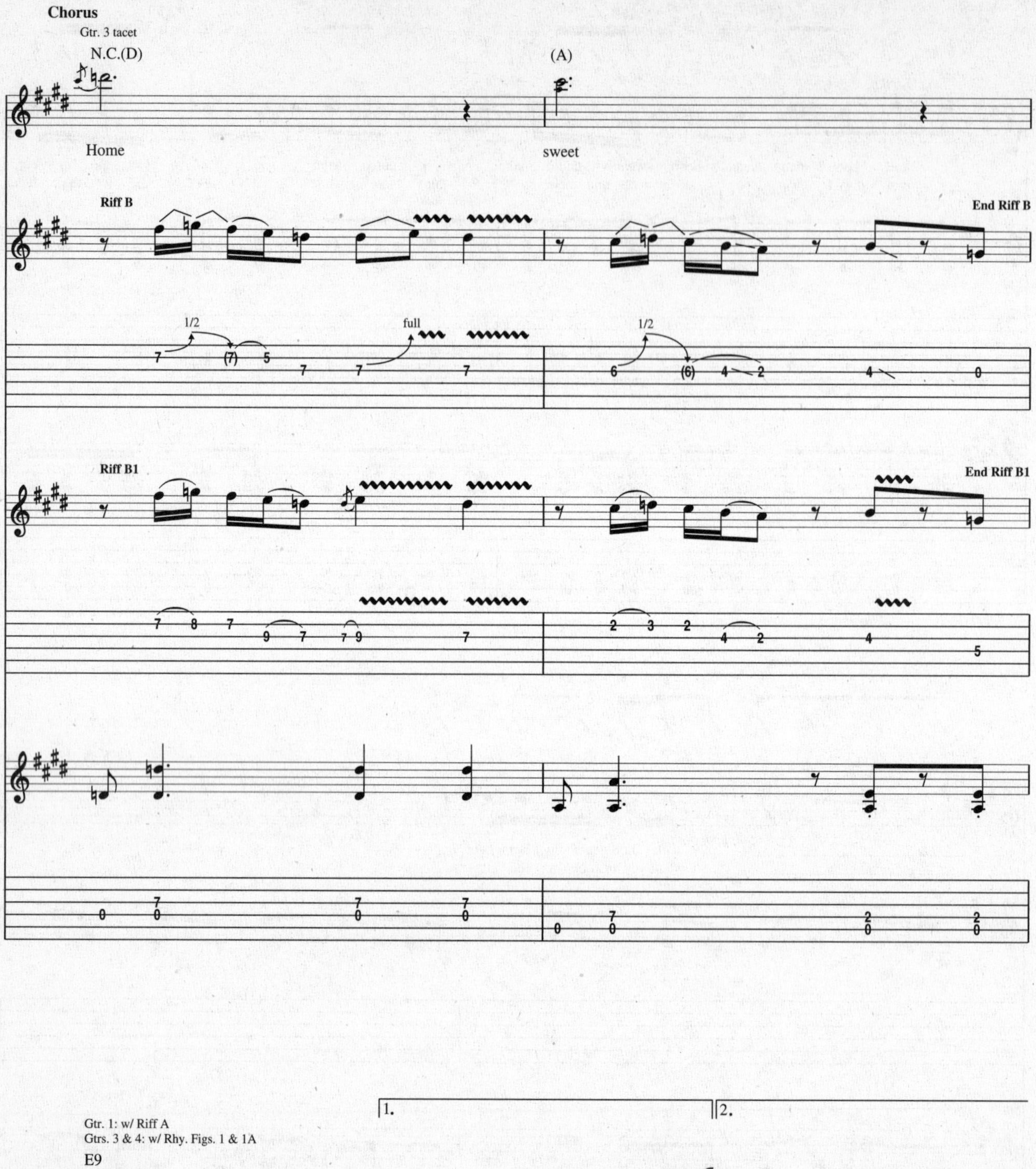

Chorus

Gtr. 3 tacet

N.C.(D) (A)

Home sweet

Riff B — End Riff B

1/2 full 1/2

Riff B1 — End Riff B1

Guitar Solo
Gtrs. 1 & 2: w/ Riffs C & C1, 2 times
N.C.(E5)
Gtr. 3
P.M.
full
Gtrs. 1 & 2: w/ Riff C, 4 times
Gtr. 1: w/ Riff B
Gtr. 2: w/ Riff D
(D)
(A)
Gtrs. 1 & 2: w/ Riff C, 2 times
N.C.(E5)
1/4
Gtr. 2: w/ Riff B1
Gtr. 1: w/ Riff B
Riff C
Gtr. 1
Riff C1
Gtr. 2
slight P.M.
Riff D
Gtr. 2

Outro
Gtr. 1: w/ Riff A, till fade
Gtr. 2: w/ Rhy. Fig. 1, till fade
E9
Gtr. 3 tacet
E9
Gtr. 2
Ma - ma take me home sweet home. I was the last child, just a punk in the streets.
Gtr. 1
Gtr. 3
* Vocals 8va till end.
I was the last child, just a punk in the streets. I was the
full
1/4
last child, just a punk in the streets. I was the last child, just a punk in the streets.
Begin Fade
full
I was the last child, just a punk in the streets.
Fade Out
I was the last child, just a punk in the streets.
full
full
full

Lay It on the Line

Words and Music by Mike Levine, Gil Moore, Rik Emmett and Ralph Santer

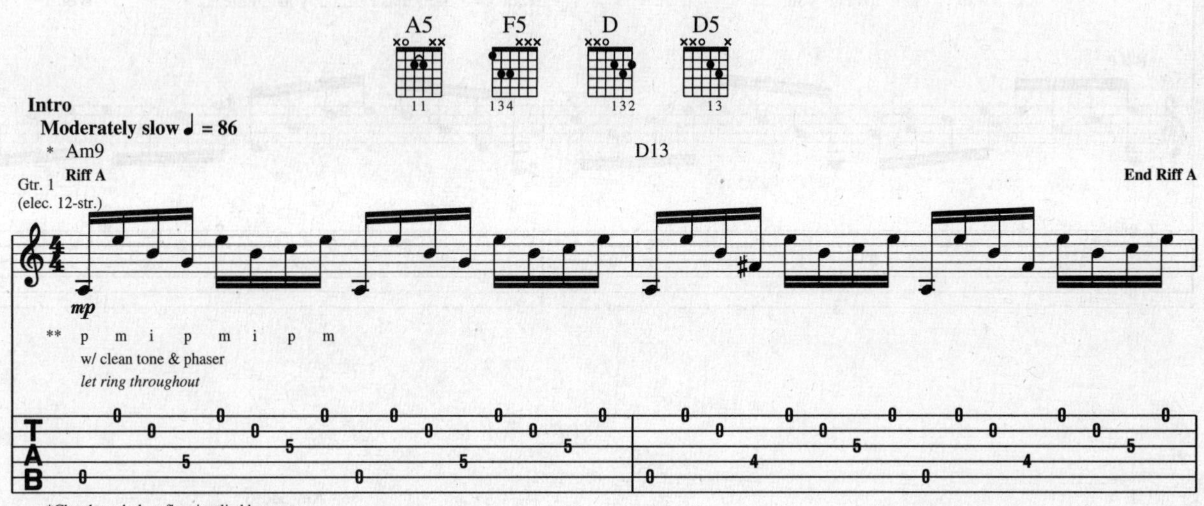

*Chord symbols reflect implied harmony.

**p = thumb (pick high octave string only), m = middle finger, i = index finger.

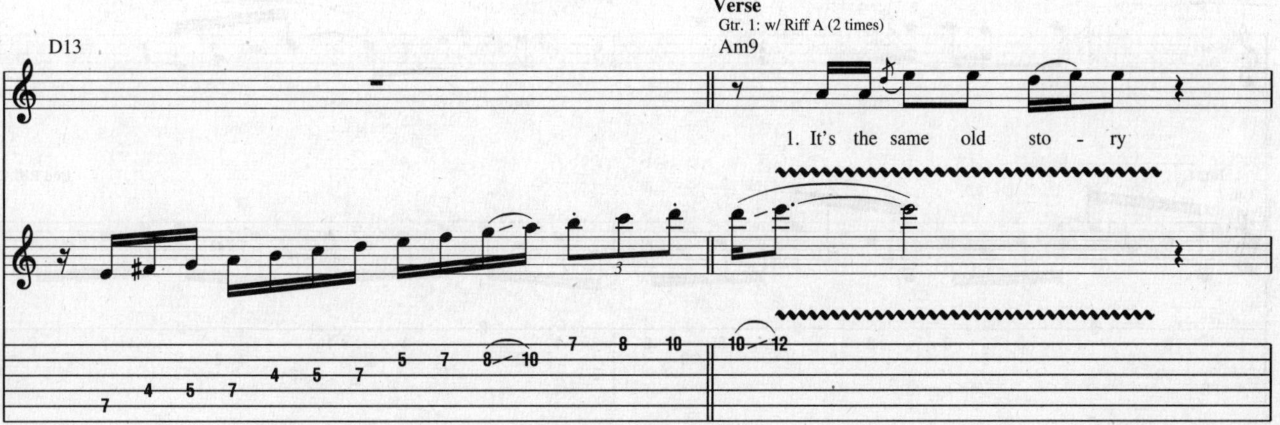

Am
Am7/G
Dsus2/F#
D
Dsus2
I wan - na love _ you. I wan - na make ___ you mine. _ Won't you
Riff B
Gr. 1

F
G
Am(add9)
lay it on ___ the line? ___
End Riff B

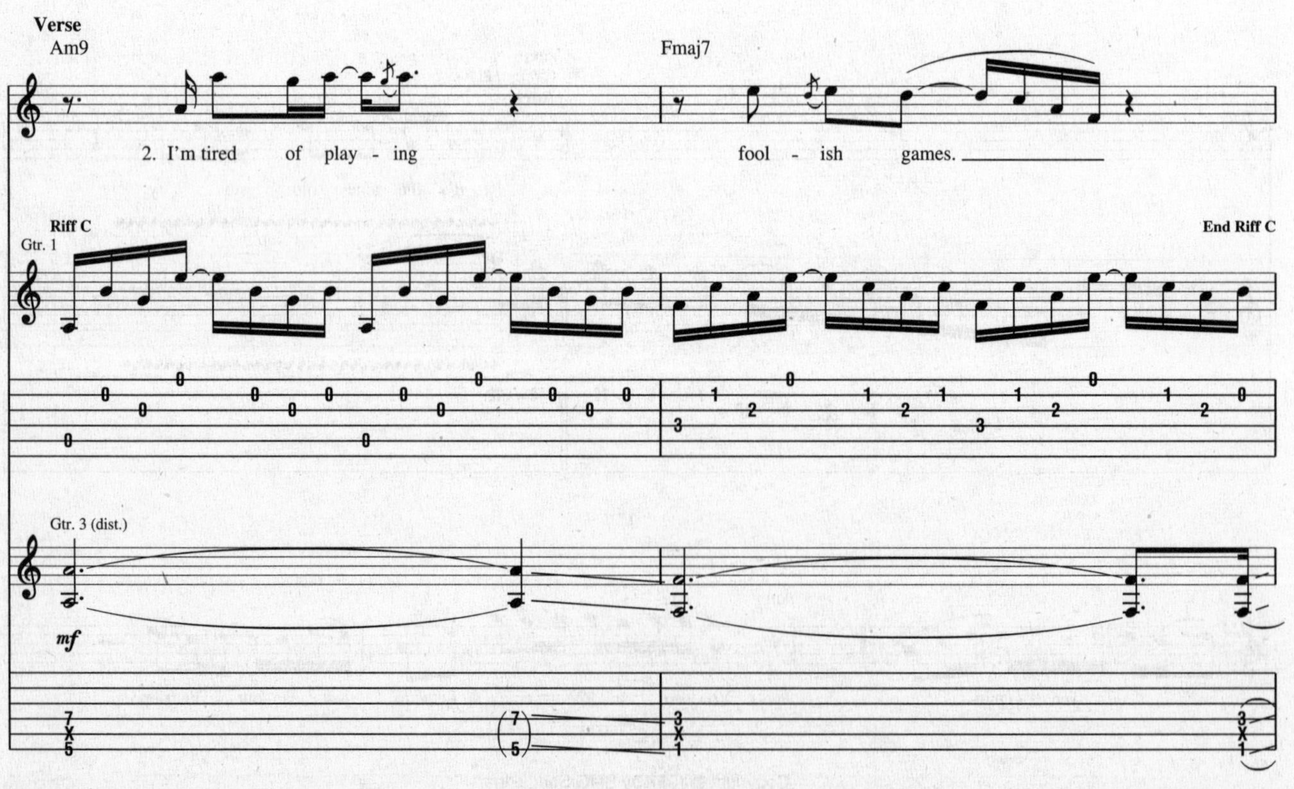
Verse
Am9
Fmaj7
2. I'm tired of play - ing fool - ish games. ___
Riff C
Gtr. 1
End Riff C
Gtr. 3 (dist.)
mf

Gtr. 1: w/ Riff C
Am9
Fmaj7
Gtr. 1: w/ Riff B
2nd time, Gtrs. 2 & 6: w/ Fill 1
Am
Am7/G
I'm tired of all __ of your __ lies making me in - sane. __
Well, I don't ask __ for much, the truth will do __ just __ fine.
I nev - er ev-er thought you could be so __ un - kind.
Riff D1
Gtr. 4 (dist.)
Gtr. 5 (dist.) divisi
mf
Riff D2
Gtr. 3
Riff D
Dsus2/F#
D
Dsus2
F
G
Am(add9)
Won't you lay __ it on __ the __ line? ____
End Riff D1
End Riff D2
End Riff D
Fill 1
Gtr. 2
Gtr. 6 divisi

Chorus
Gtr. 4 & 5 tacet
F5
G5
A5
Lay it on the line.
* Gtr. 3 & 6 (dist.)
*Composite arrangement
F5
G5
A5
G5
Lay it on the line.
Rhy. Fig. 1
End Rhy. Fig. 1
To Coda
F5
G5
F5
Lay it on the line.
(Line.)
Don't waste my
(cont. in slashes)
Guitar Solo
A5
F5
A5
Gtrs. 3 & 6
time.
Gtr. 2
mf
w/ dist.
P.H.

Verse
Gtr. 1: w/ Riff C
F5
A5
F5
D
Gtr. 6
(Gtr. 3, cont. in notation)
3. You've got no right to make me wait.
Gtr. 2
Gtr. 3
divisi
grad. bend
D.S. al Coda
A5
F5
D5
Bet - ter talk girl, be - fore it gets too late.
Coda
Interlude
A5
F5
A5
F5
Gtrs. 3 & 6
(cont. in notation)
time.
Gtr. 2
w/ delay
delay off

Guitar Solo

Dm G C G/B Am G

Gtr. 2

Gtr. 4

Gtr. 3

F E5 Am G/B A/C# A/E

P.M.

P.M.

P.M.

Dm G C G/B Am G

8va

let ring

let ring

1 1/2

F E Am Am/G

8va

loco

grad. release

D/F# F G Am C

P.M.

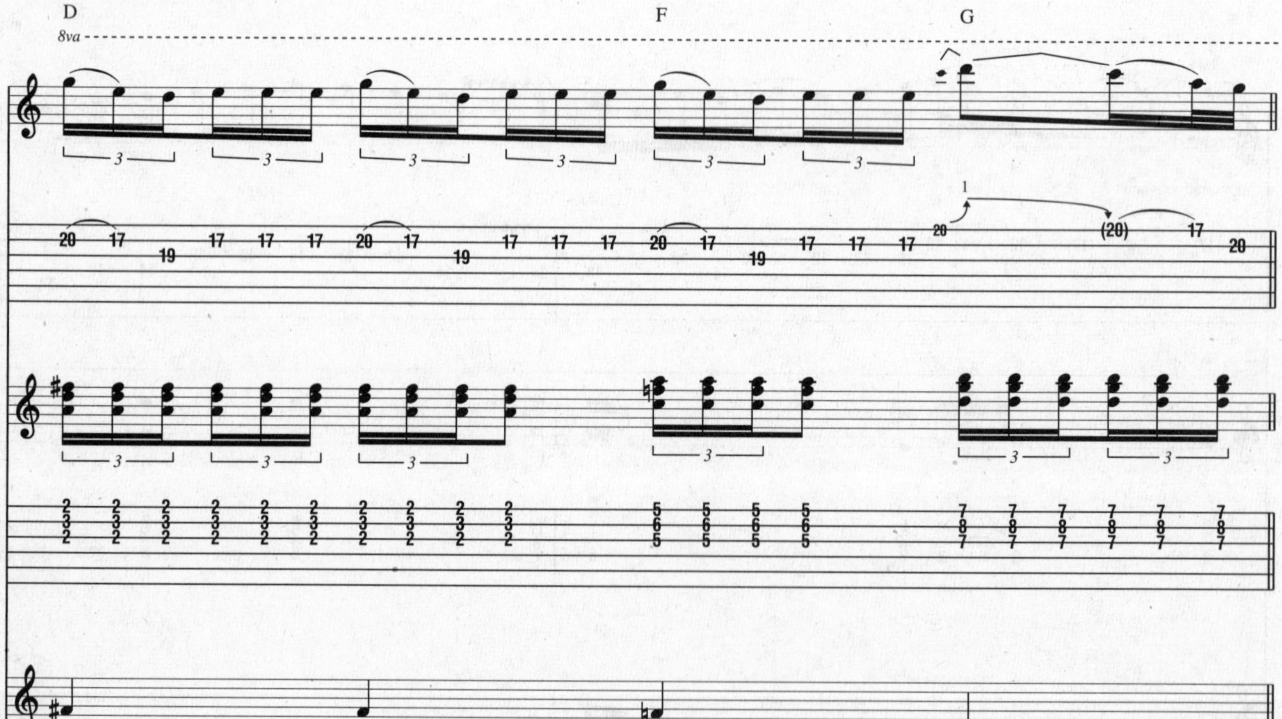

D F G

8va

(cont. in slashes)

Verse
A5
Gtrs. 2 & 4 tacet
F5
D5
Gtrs. 3 & 6
4. You know I love you, you know it's true.
(You know I love you, you know it's
8va
A5
F5
D5
Gtrs. 3, 4 & 5: w/ Riffs D, D1 & D2
Am
Am7/G
It's up to you girl, now what-'ve I got to do?
Don't hold me up girl, don't
true.)
Dsus2/F#
D
Dsus2
F
G
Am(add9)
waste my pre-cious time. Won't you lay it on the line?
Outro-Chorus
Play 4 times and fade
Gtr. 3 & 6: w/ Rhy. Fig. 1 (till fade)
w/ Voc. ad lib (till fade)
F5
G5
A5
G5
F5
G5
A5
G5
Lay it on the line. Lay it on the line.

Le Freak

Words and Music by Nile Rodgers and Bernard Edwards

Chorus

Moderately ♩ = 124

N.C. *C/G Am D C

One, two... Ah, ___ freak out! Le Freak, c'est Chic. Freak

Gtr. 1 (clean)

Riff A ... End Riff A

f

*Bass plays G.

Am | 1. D C | 2. D C

out! Ah, ___ freak

Verse

Gtr. 1: w/ Riff A (5 times)

Am
D
C
Am
It's up to you, it surely can be done. Young and old are
Come on along and have a real good time. Like the days of
2nd & 3rd times, Gtr. 1: w/ Riff A (2nd meas.)
D
C
Am
D
C
doin' it I'm told. Just one try and you too will be sold.
stompin' at the Savoy, now we're free, oh, what a joy.
Gtr. 1
Riff B
End Riff B
Gtr. 1: w/ Riff A (2 times)
Am
D
C
Am
It's called "Le Freak," they're doin' it night and day. Allow us, we'll
Just come on down to Fifty-four, find a spot out
To Coda
Chorus
1st time, Gtr. 1: w/ Riff A (2 times)
2nd time, Gtr. 1: w/ Riff A (1 1/2 times)
D
C
Am
D
C
show you they way.
on the floor.
Ah, freak out! Le Freak, c'est Chic. Freak
1.
2.
Am
D
C
D
Am
out!
Now
Gtr. 1

Interlude
Am
D
Freak!
Am
D
Am
D
Am7

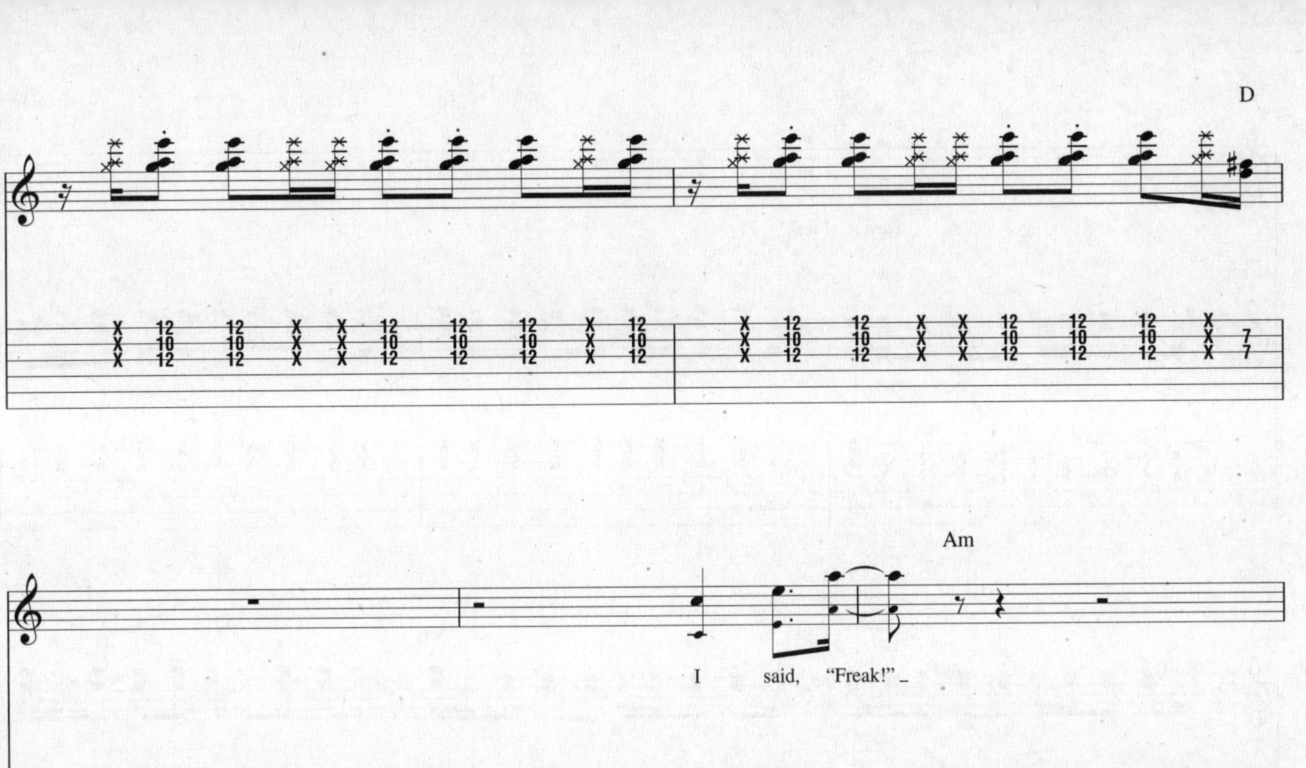
D

Am
I said, "Freak!"

D
Am
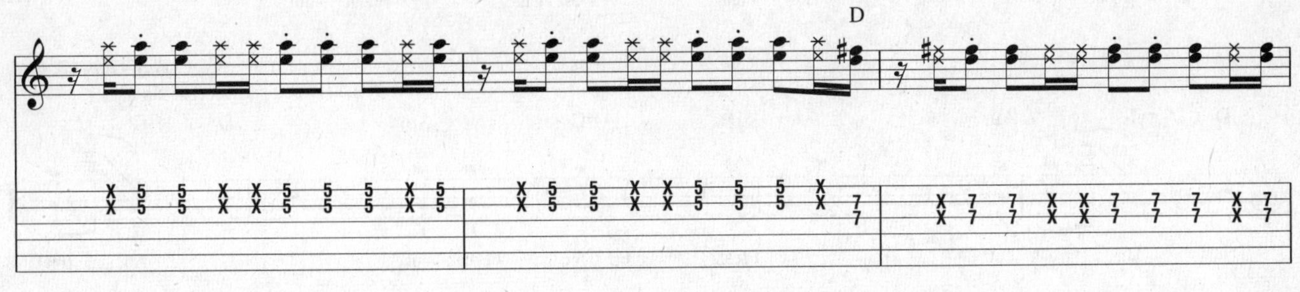
D

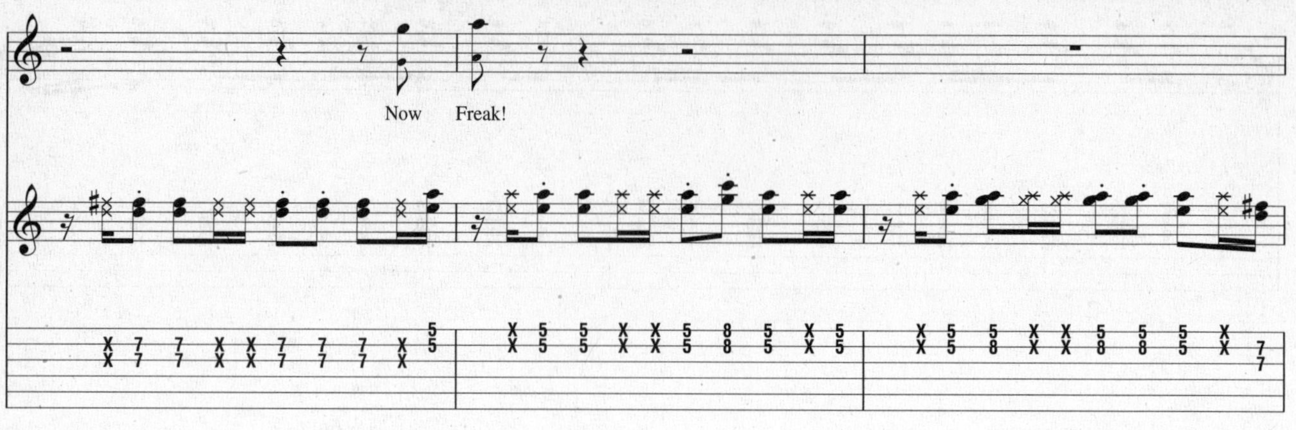

Coda

Outro-Chorus

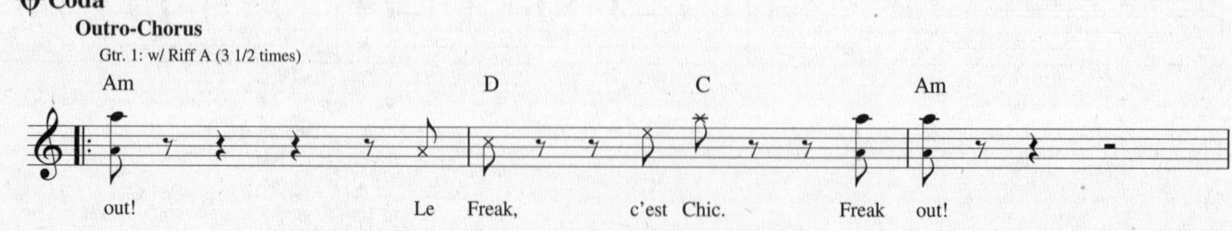

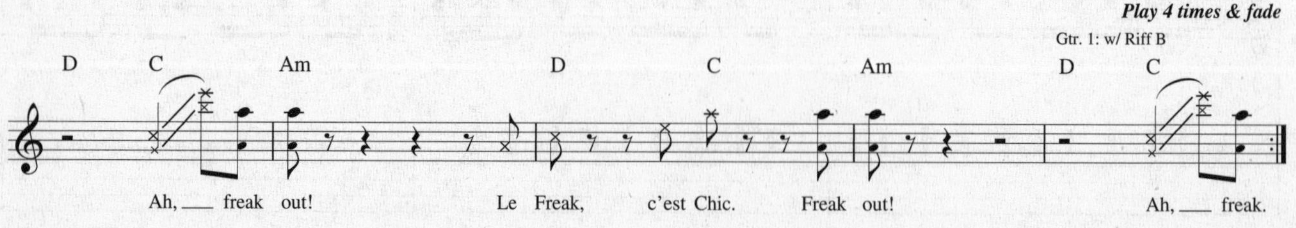

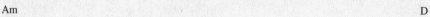

Lightning Crashes

Words and Music by Edward Kowalczyk, Chad Taylor, Patrick Dahlheimer and Chad Gracey

F
Csus2
G
Her in - ten - tions fall to the floor.
This mo - ment she's been - wait - ing for
F
Csus2
The an - gel clos - es her eyes.
The an - gel o - pens her eyes
G
F
The con - fu - sion that was hers, be - longs now,
a pale blue col - ored i - ris, pre - sents the cir -
Csus2
G
to the ba - by down - the hall.
- cle, and puts the glor - y out to hide, hide

Chorus
* Gtr. 2: w/ Rhy. Fig. 3A, 5 times, 2nd time only
Gtr. 1: w/ Rhy. Fig. 3, 2 times, simile
F Csus2 G F Csus2
Rhy. Fig. 3
End Rhy. Fig. 3
Gtr. 1
mf
Oh, now feel it com - in' back a - gain like a roll - in'
* amp tremolo off
G F Csus2 G
thun - der chas - ing the wind Forc - es pull - in' from the cen - ter of the Earth a - gain
1.
F Csus2 G E G D G
6 open 5 5fr
Gtr. 1
I can feel it
2.
F Csus2
Gtr. 1
f
I can feel it
G F Csus2 G
*
I can feel it
* with added gain
Interlude
Am Em7 F
Gtr. 1
play 3 times
Gtr. 2
Gtr. 3
3
Rhy. Fig. 3A
Gtr. 2
Fadd9 Csus2 G

Am Em7 F G

Chorus
Gtr. 3 tacet
Gtrs. 1 & 2: w/ Rhy. Figs. 3 & 3A, 14 times
F Csus2 G F Csus2
Oh, now feel it com - in' back a - gain like a roll - in'
G F Csus2
thun - der chas - ing the wind Forc - es pull - in' from the
G F Csus2 G
cen - ter of the Earth a - gain I can feel it.
Outro-Chorus
F Csus2 G
Oh, now feel it com - in' back a - gain
F Csus2 G F Csus2
like a roll - in' thun - der chas - ing the wind Forc - es pull - ing from the
1.
G F Csus2 G
cen - ter of the Earth a - gain I can feel it
2.
G F Csus2 G
I can feel it
(yeah yeah
F Csus2 G F Csus2 G
Gtrs. 1 & 2
mp rit.
I can feel it
yeah)

Lights Out

Words and Music by Michael Schenker, Phil Mogg, Andy Parker and Pete Way

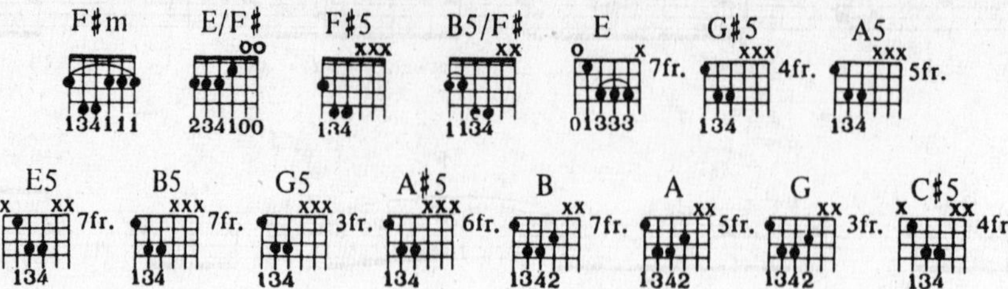

Intro **Medium Rock beat**

Verse
F♯5
E/F♯
B5/F♯
1. When love's back and the bat - tle's charg - ing, runs all the way.
Bkgd. Guitar
F♯5
E/F♯
Up to the front, I'm not go - in'.
P
F♯5
B5/F♯
E
May - be now your time's come.
(slightly muted)

F#5
Sl.

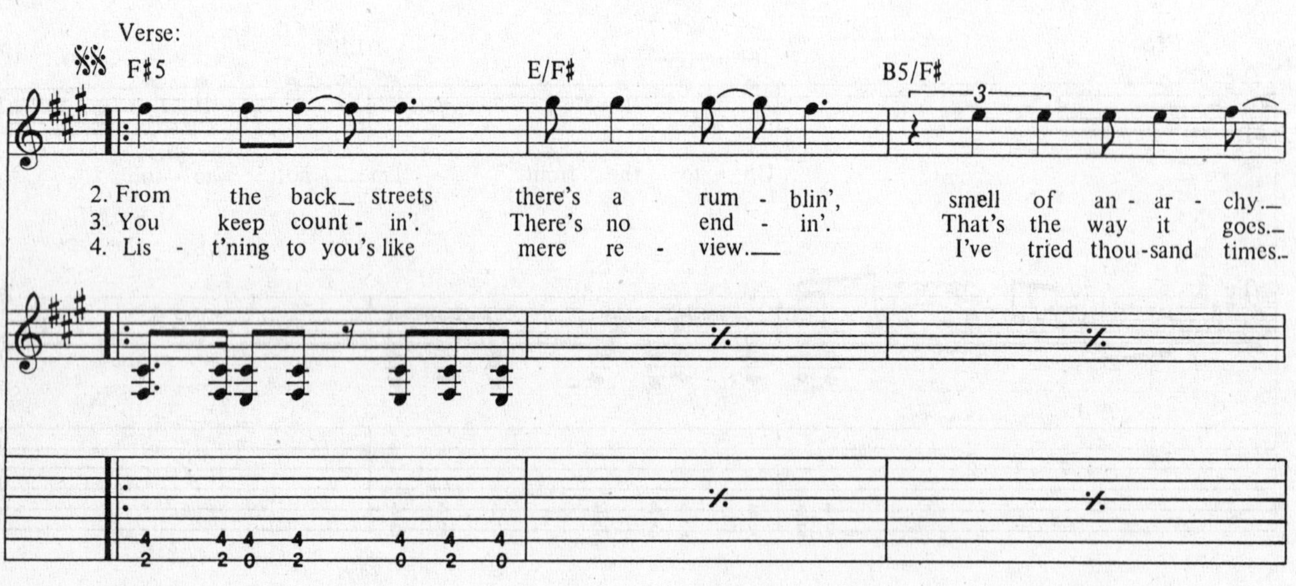
Verse:
F#5
E/F#
B5/F#
2. From the back streets there's a rum - blin', smell of an - ar - chy.
3. You keep count - in'. There's no end - in'. That's the way it goes.
4. Lis - t'ning to you's like mere re - view. I've tried thou - sand times.

F#5
E/F#
No more nice time black boy shoe shine
Fright-'ning thoughts what's been taught
Un - der your feet grass is grow - in'.
Full
1/2

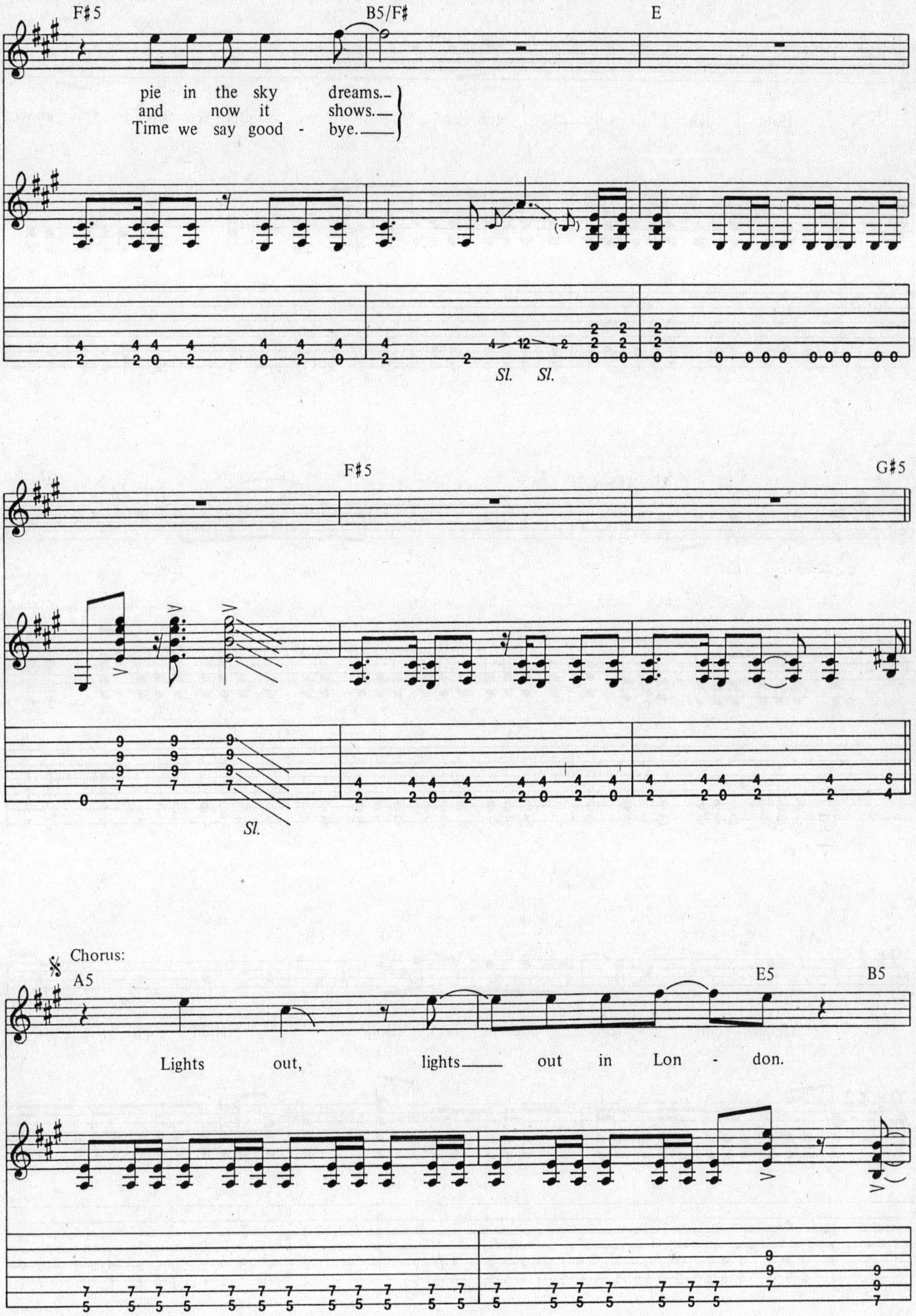

F♯5 B5/F♯ E

pie in the sky dreams.
and now it shows.
Time we say good - bye.

Sl. Sl.

F♯5 G♯5

Sl.

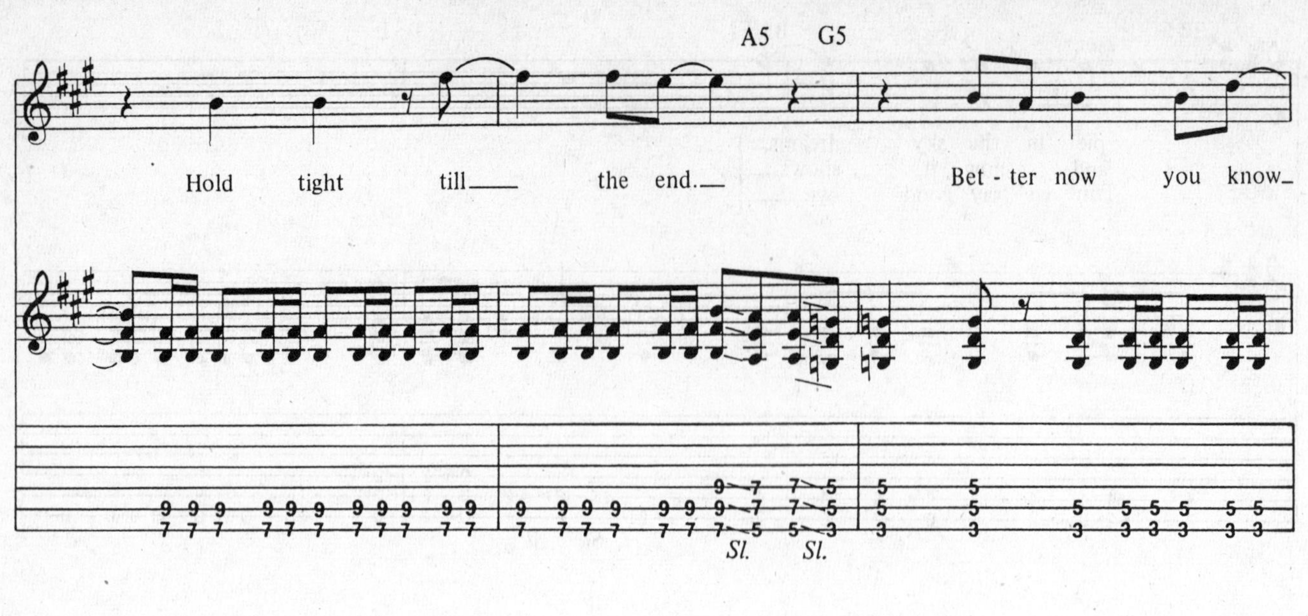
A5 G5
Hold tight till the end. Bet - ter now you know
Sl. Sl.

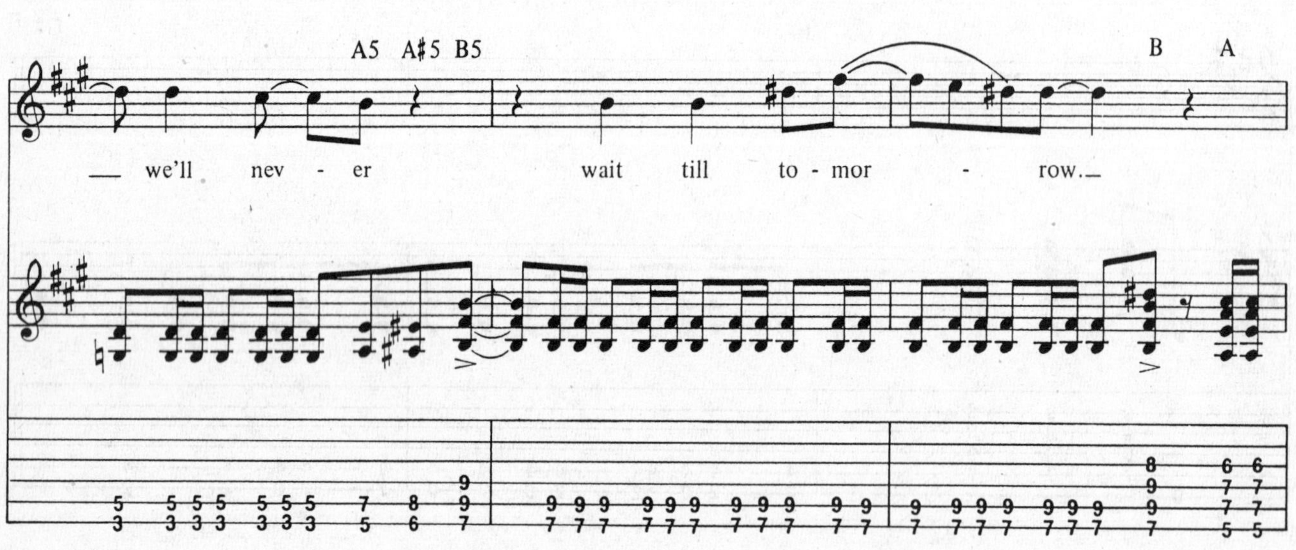
A5 A♯5 B5 B A
we'll nev - er wait till to - mor - row.

A5 E B5
Lights out, lights out in Lon - don. Hold tight till

To Coda I and II
1.
A5
G5
the end.
God knows when I'm com-in' on my run.
Sl.
Sl.
F♯5(m)
E/F♯
F♯5(m)
P H
2.
Guitar solo No. 1
F♯m
com-in' on my run.
8va
Full
Sl.

8va
5
5
5
P
H P
P
P
P
P
P
P
14
17 14
14 17 14
14
17 14
17 14
14
17 14
17 14
17 14
14
17 14

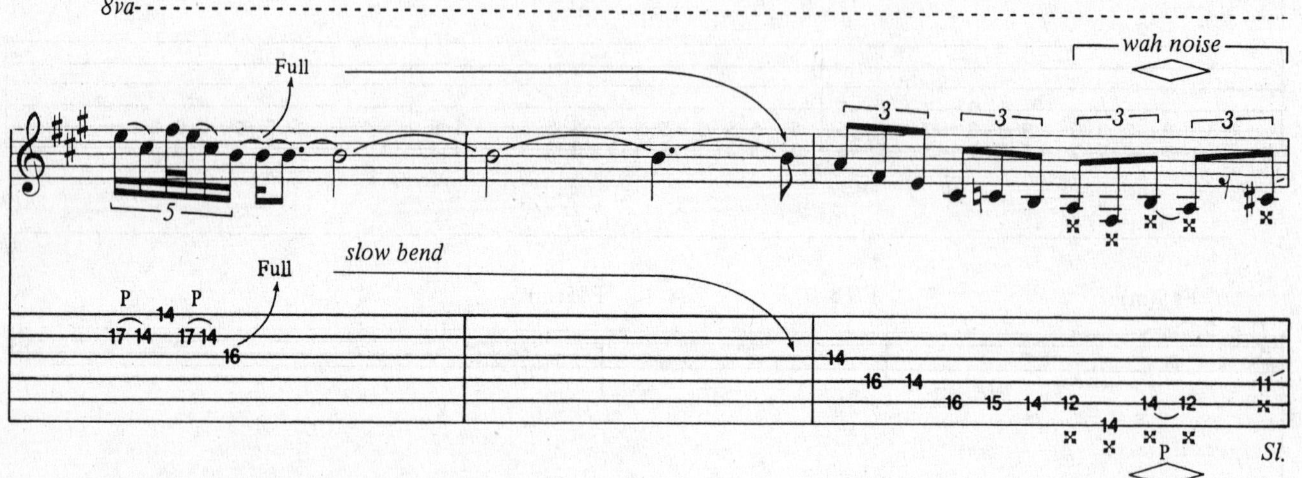
8va
Full
wah noise
3
3
3
3
5
slow bend
Full
P
14
P
17 14
17 14
16
14
16 14
16 15 14 12
14
14 12
11
P
Sl.

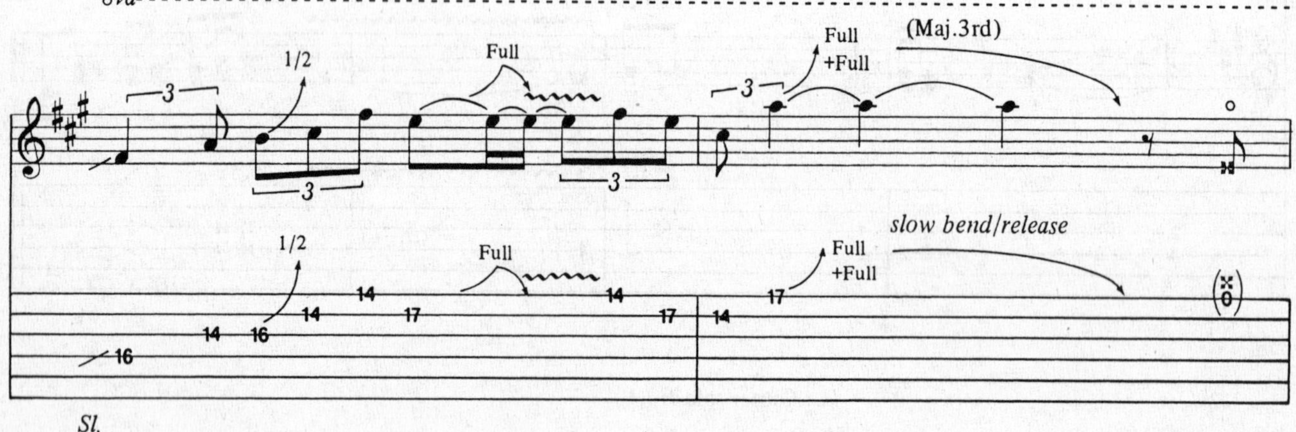
8va
1/2
Full
Full
+Full
(Maj.3rd)
3
3
3
3
slow bend/release
1/2
Full
Full
+Full
16
14 16 14
14
17
14
17
14
17
0
Sl.

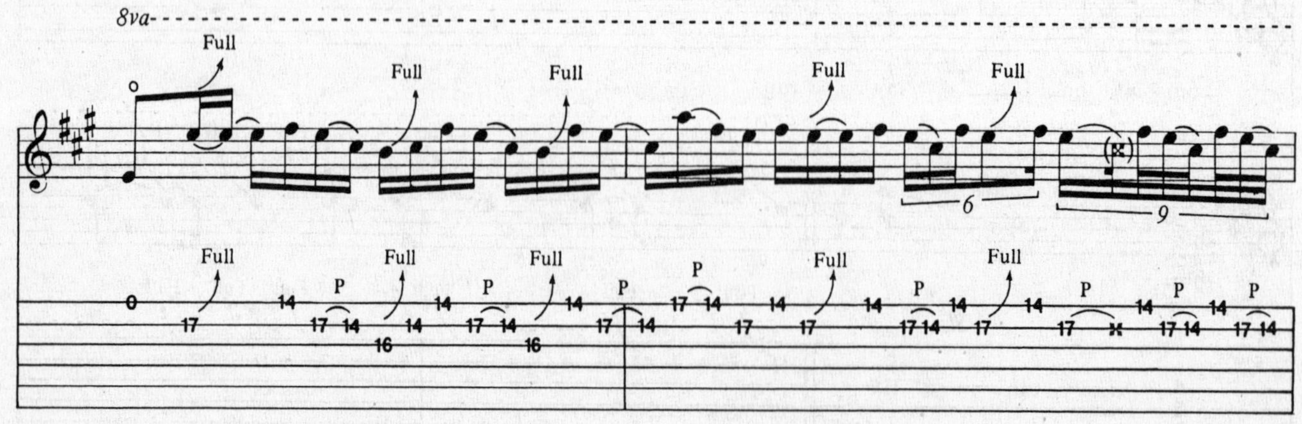
8va
Full
Full
Full
Full
Full
6
9
Full
Full
Full
Full
Full
P
P
P
P
P
P
P
P
0
17
14
17 14
16
14
14
17 14
16
14
17 14
17 14
14
17
14
17
14
17 14
14
17
14
17
14
17 14
14
17 14

8va
7
7
7
7
P P
P
P
P
P
P
P
P

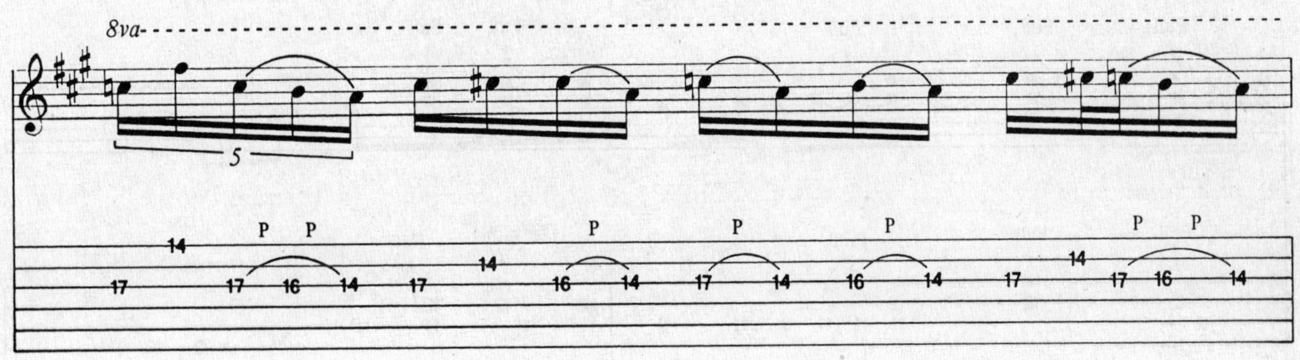
8va
5
P P
P
P
P
P P

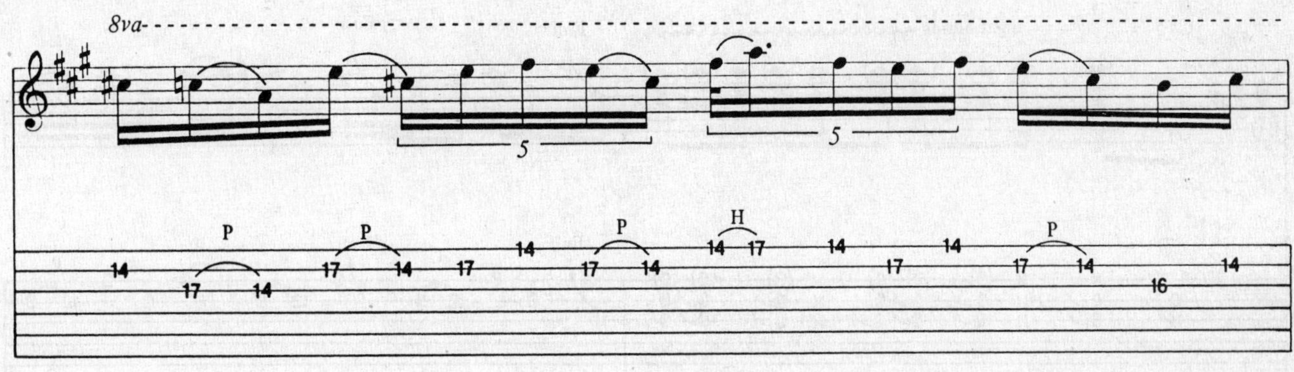
8va
5
5
P
P
P
H
P

8va
Rake
6
5
Sl.
Sl.
Sl.
Rake
Sl. P
Sl. P
Sl. P

8va-

(slightly rushed)-

Full

P

Full

H

Sl. P

Sl.

C♯5

loco

Full Full Full Full Full

F♯5

Full Full Full P Full Full

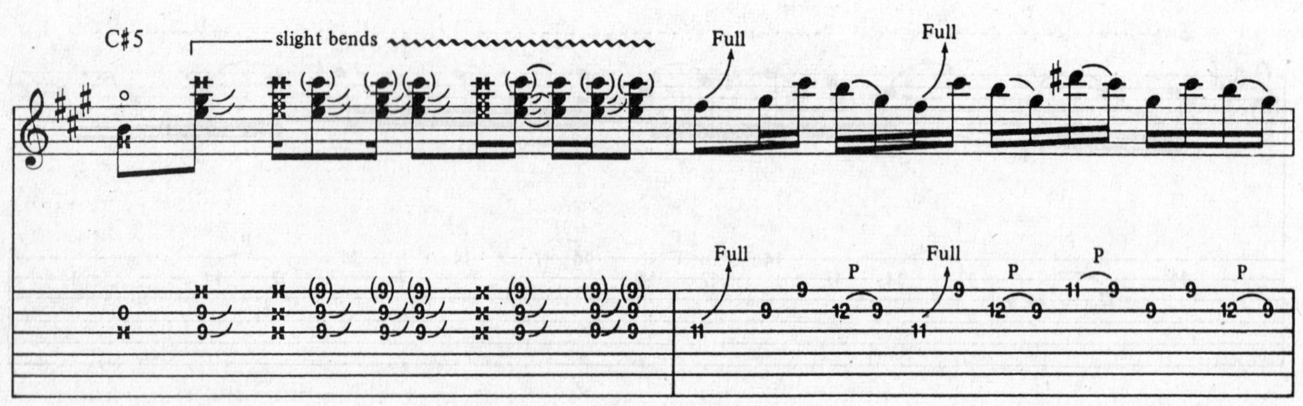

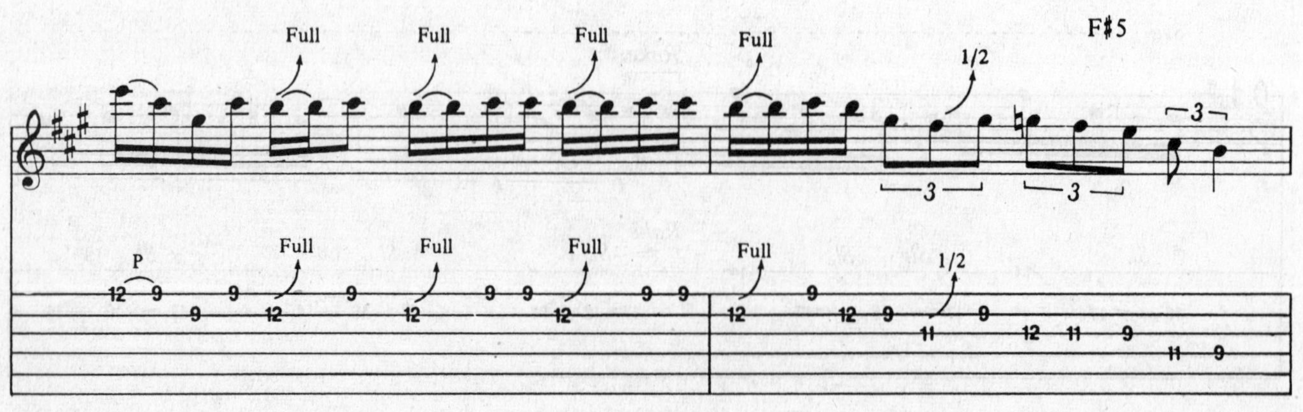

C#5
D.S. al Coda I
B5
3
(sustain into Chorus for 1½ bars)
P
P P
12 11 9 11 9
12 11
9
12 11 9 11 9
11 9
12 11 9
11
11 9
11 9 9 7

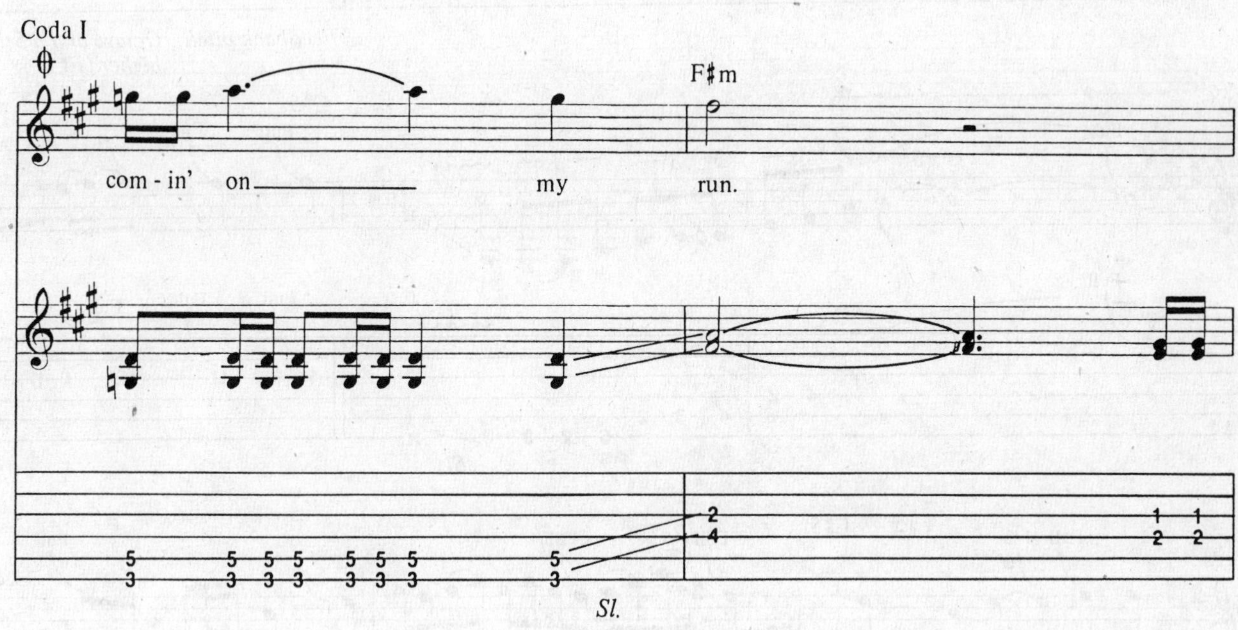
Coda I
F#m
com - in' on my run.
Sl.

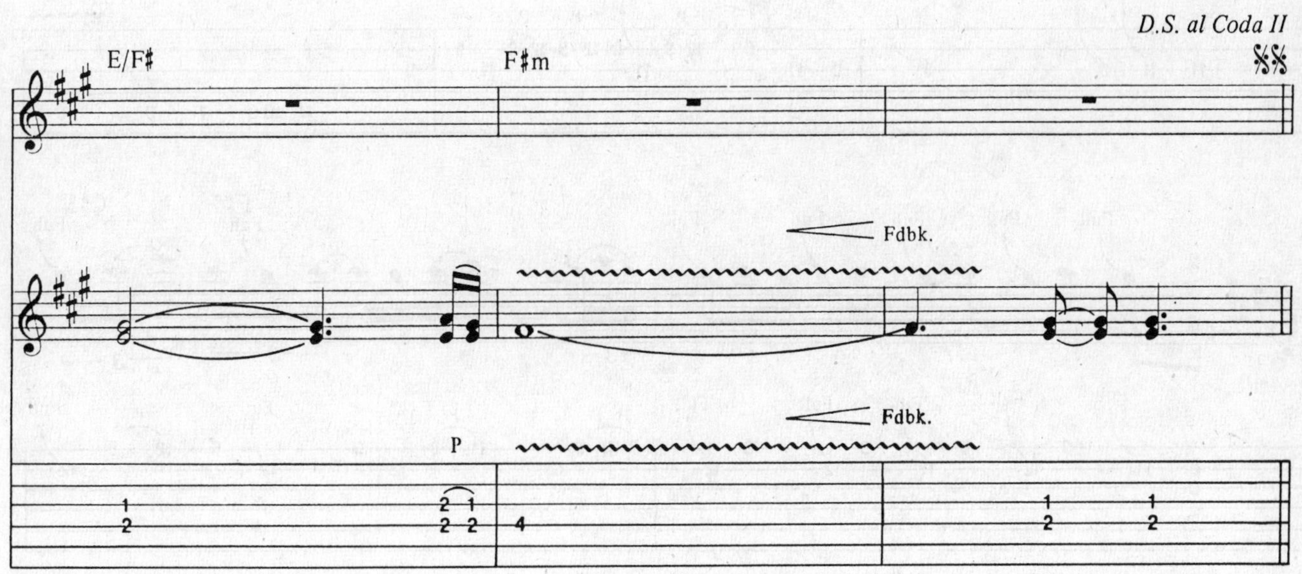
D.S. al Coda II
E/F#
F#m
Fdbk.
Fdbk.
P

Coda II
Guitar solo No.2
F♯5(m)
com - in' on my run.
Fdbk.
Full
slow bend
Feedback pitch: Octave and a 5th higher (F♯)
C♯5
Sl.
F♯5
C♯5
Rake
1/2

B5
A5
E5
B5
C♯5
F♯5
C♯5
Full
P
H P
1/2
Sl.

F♯5
C♯5

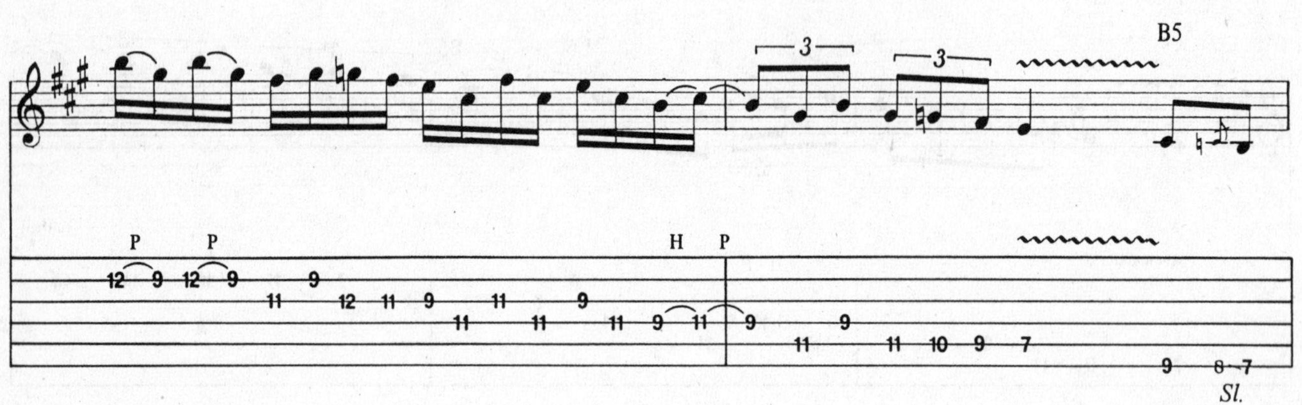
B5
Sl.

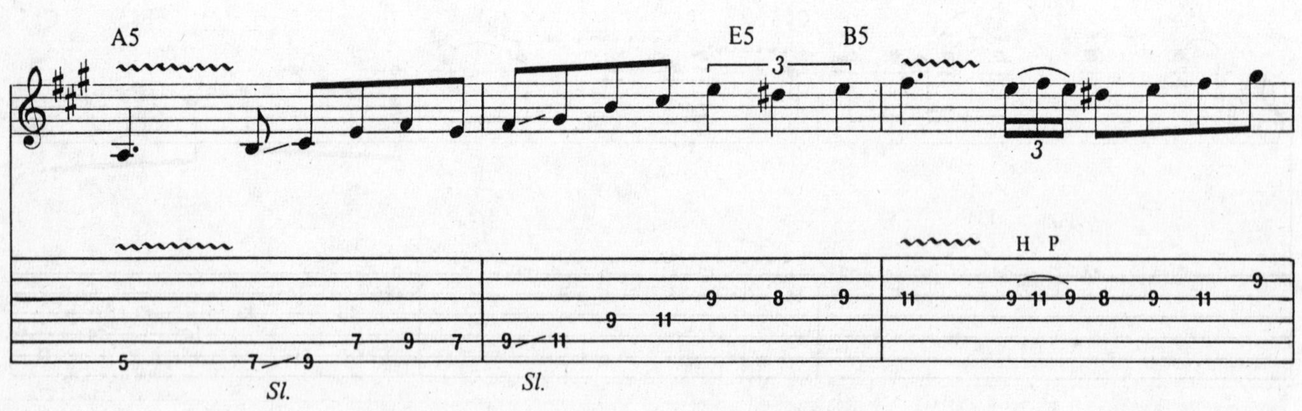
A5
E5
B5
Sl.
Sl.

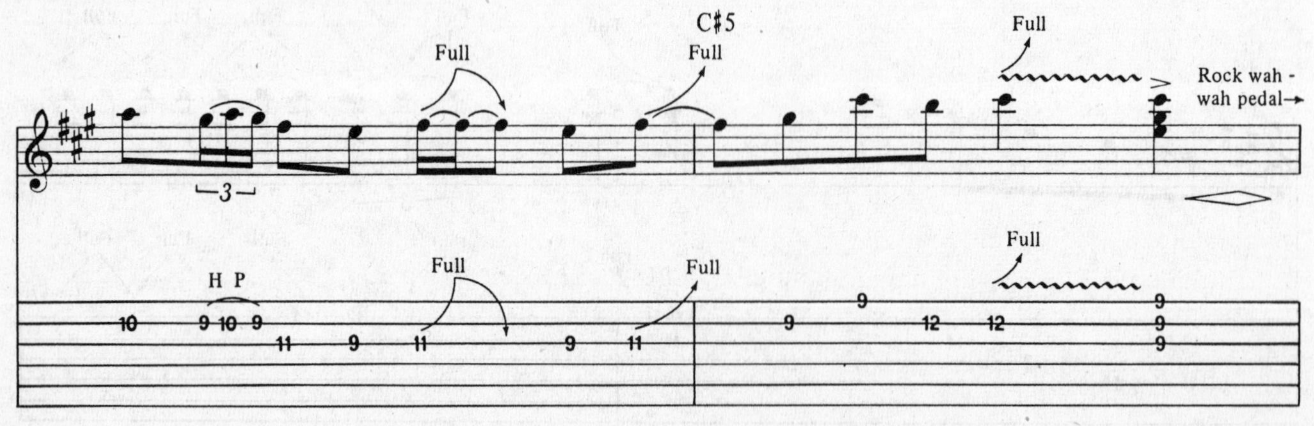
C♯5
Full
Full
Full
Rock wah - wah pedal

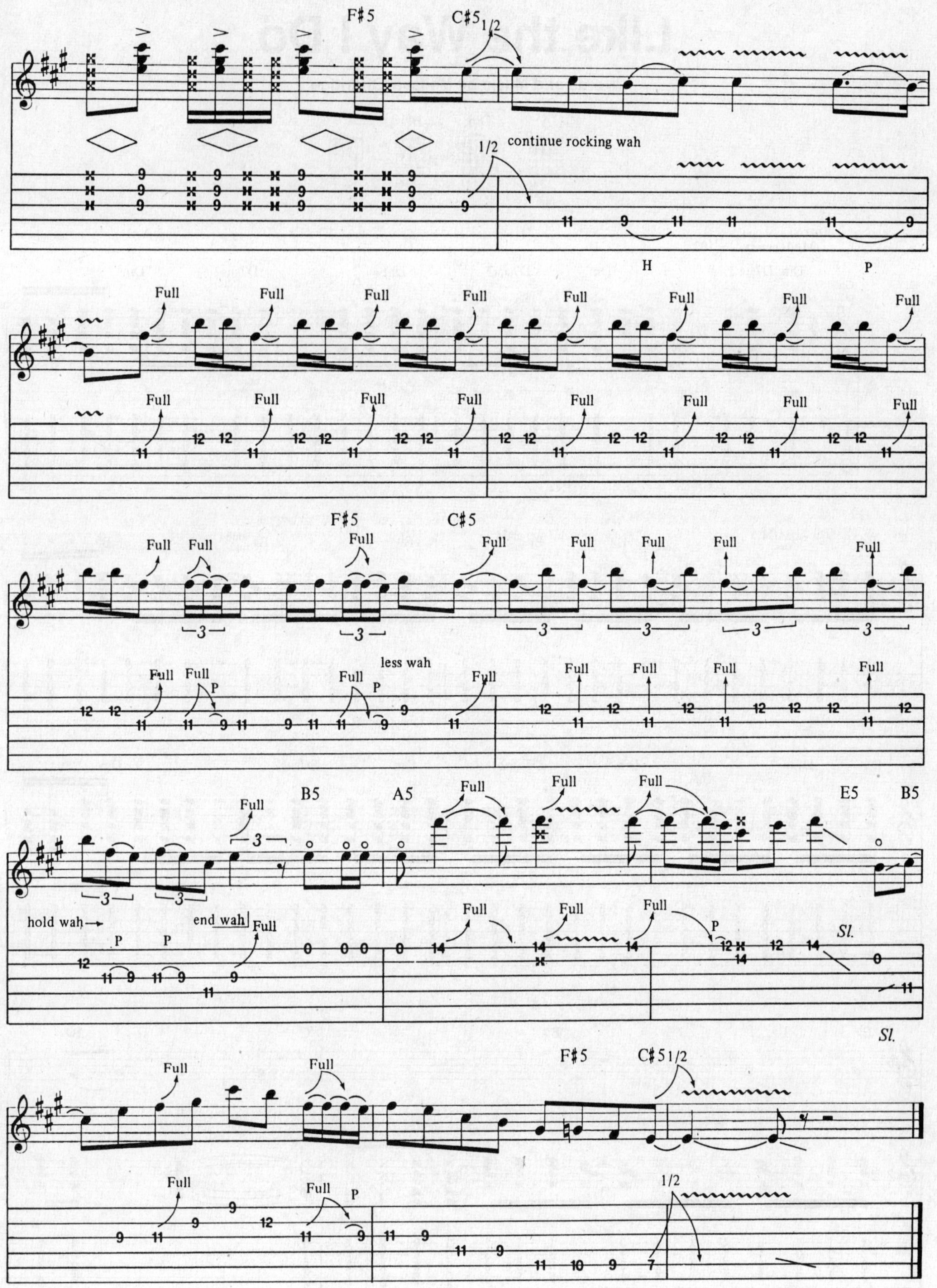

F#5
C#5
1/2
continue rocking wah
H
P
Full
less wah
hold wah
end wah
B5
A5
E5
Sl.

Like the Way I Do

Words and Music by Melissa Etheridge

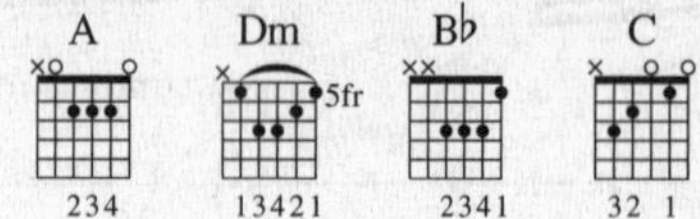

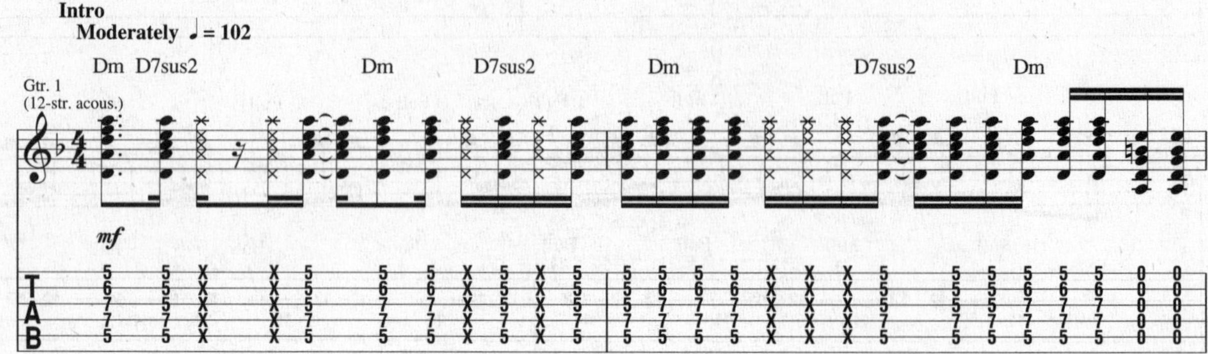

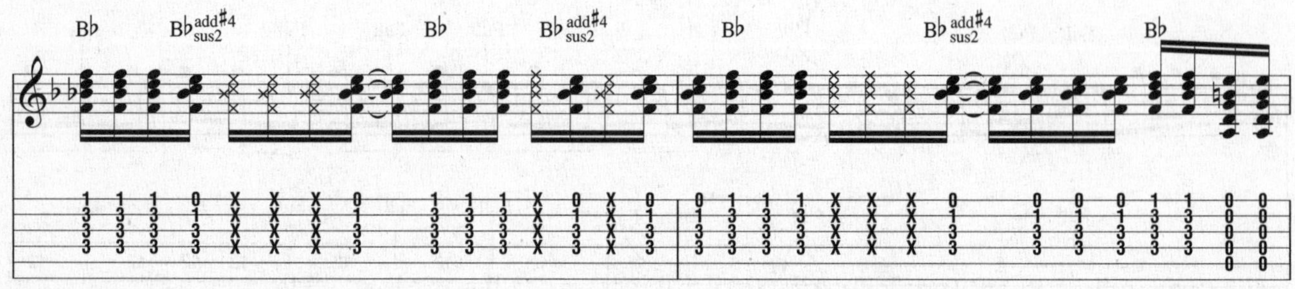

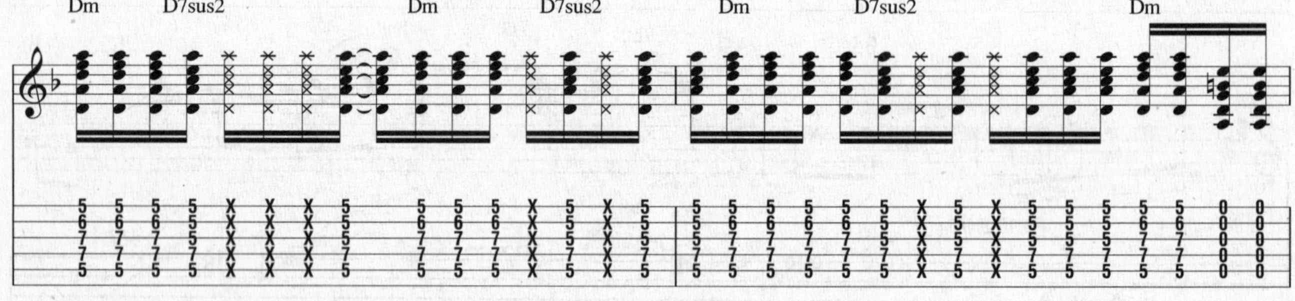

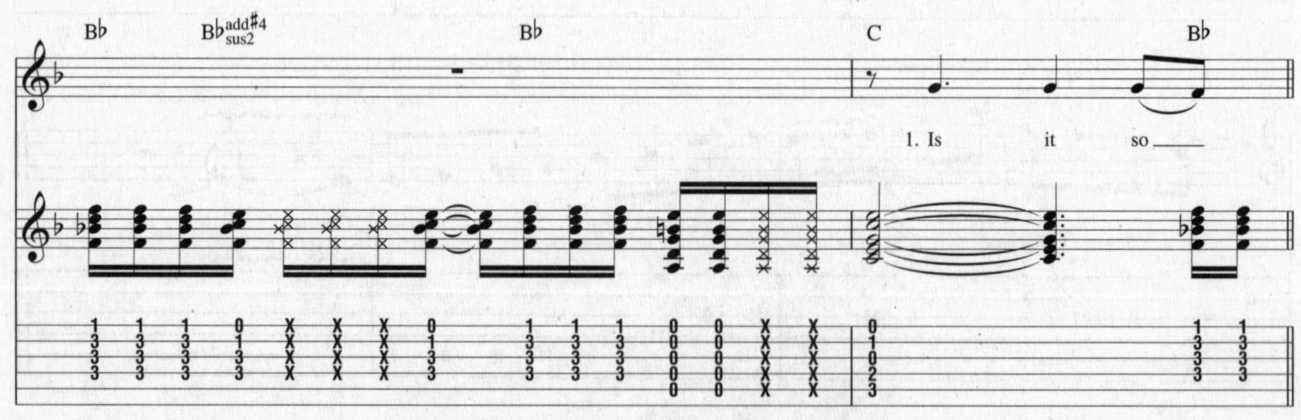

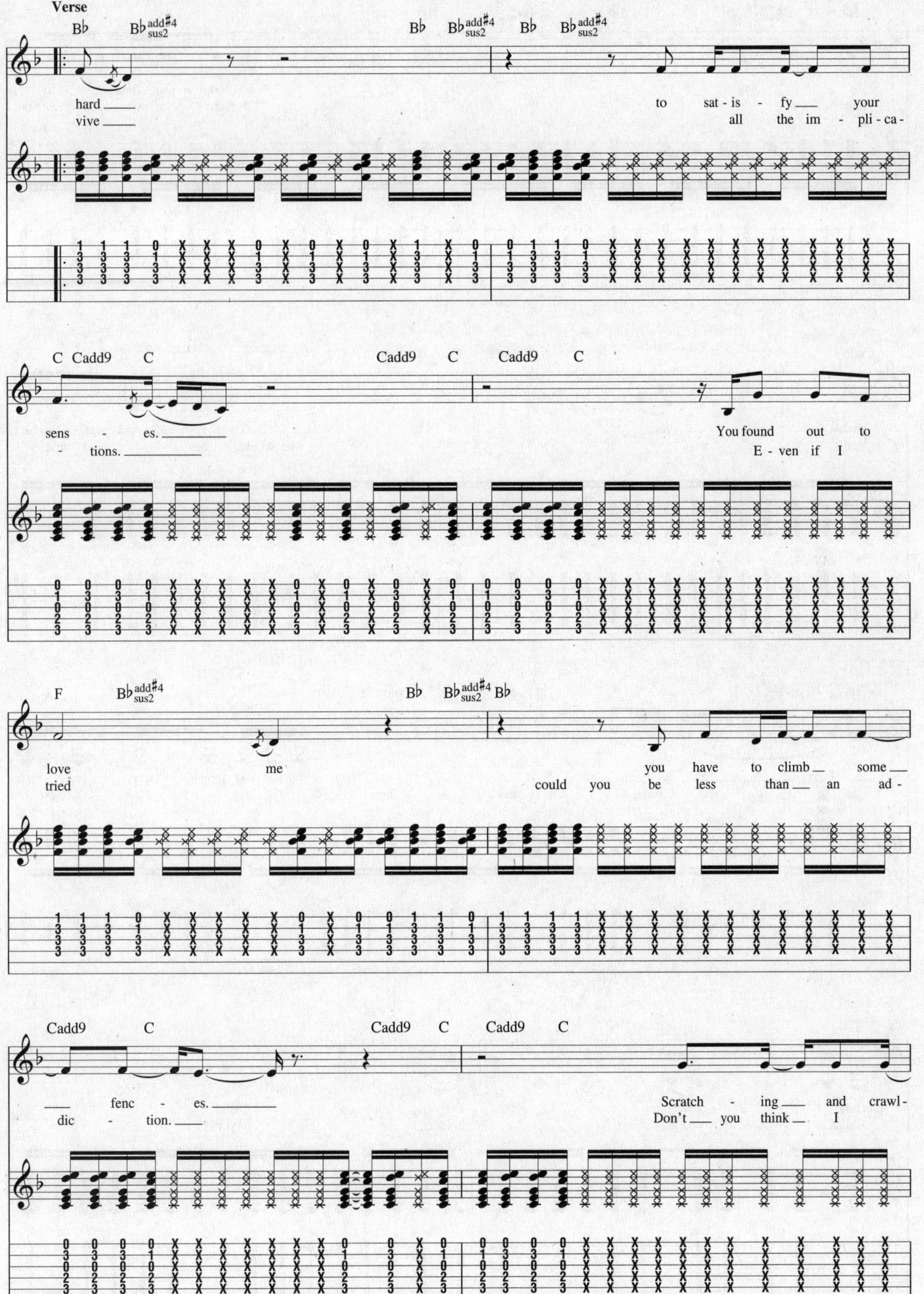
Verse
hard ___ to sat - is - fy ___ your
vive ___ all the im - pli - ca -
sens - es. ___
- tions. ___
You found out to
E - ven if I
love me you have to climb ___ some ___
tried could you be less than ___ an ad -
___ fenc - es. ___
dic - tion. ___
Scratch - ing ___ and crawl -
Don't ___ you think ___ I

B♭ B♭sus2add♯4 B♭ B♭sus2add♯4 B♭
- ing a - long the floor to
know there's so man - y oth -
Cadd9 C Cadd9 C Cadd9 C
touch you. And just when it
ers who would beg, steal and
B♭ B♭sus2add♯4 B♭ B♭sus2add♯4 B♭ A
feels right, you say you found some - one to
lie and fight, kill, and die, just to
hold you. Does she
hold you, hold you

like I do. Ba - by, tell me does she
like I do.
Chorus
Dm D7sus2 Dm D7sus2 Dm D7sus2 Dm
love you like the way I love you. Does she stim - u - late
Gtr. 1
Rhy. Fig. 1
B♭ B♭add♯4 sus2 B♭ B♭add♯4 sus2 B♭ B♭add♯4 sus2 B♭
you, at - tract and cap - ti - vate you. Tell me does she miss
Cadd9 C Cadd9 C Cadd9 C
you, ex - ist - ing just to kiss you, like the way I

Dm D7sus2 Dm D7sus2 Dm D7sus2 Dm D7sus2
do. Tell me does she
End Rhy. Fig. 1
Gtr. 1: w/ Rhy. Fig. 1 (1st 6 meas.)
Dm D7sus2 Dm D7sus2 Dm D7sus2 Dm
want you, in - fat - u - ate and haunt you. Does she know just how to shock
B♭ B♭add♯4sus2 B♭ B♭add♯4sus2 B♭ B♭add♯4sus2 B♭
you, e - lec - tri - fy and rock you. Does she in - ject
Cadd9 C Cadd9 C Cadd9 C
you, se - duce you and af - fect you, like the way I
1.
D7sus2 Dm D7sus2 Dm D7sus2 Dm Cadd9
do. Like the way I
Gtr. 2 (elec.)
mf w/ dist.
let ring
Gtr. 1
let ring
let ring

Gtr. 2: w/ Riff A
D7sus2 Dm
D7sus2
Dm
D7sus2
Dm
do.
2. Can I sur -
let ring
let ring
let ring
2.
D7sus2 Dm
D7sus2
Dm D7sus2
Dm
D7sus2 Dm
do.
Oh, no - bod - y
Gtr. 1
let ring
let ring
Bridge
B♭
B♭add♯4 sus2
B♭
B♭add♯4 sus2
B♭
B♭add♯4 sus2
loves you
like the way I
Gtr. 2
let ring
Gtr. 1
Rhy. Fig. 2

Gtr. 1: w/ Rhy. Fig. 2 (2½ times)
D7sus2 Dm
D7sus2 Dm D7sus2 Dm
D7sus2 Dm
B♭ B♭sus2add♯4 B♭
do.
No - bod-y wants you
let ring
End Rhy. Fig. 2
B♭sus2add♯4 B♭ B♭sus2add♯4 D7sus2 Dm
D7sus2 Dm D7sus2 Dm
D7sus2 Dm
like the way I do.
No - bod - y
B♭ B♭sus2add♯4 B♭
B♭sus2add♯4 B♭ B♭sus2add♯4 D7sus2 Dm
D7sus2 Dm D7sus2
needs you
like the way I
do.
No - bod - y
Dm D7sus2 Dm
B♭ B♭sus2add♯4 B♭
B♭sus2add♯4 B♭ B♭sus2add♯4
aches,
no - bod - y aches just to hold you
like the way I

A
Gtr. 1
do. No, no, no.
Gtr. 2
let ring
Tell me does she
let ring
Chorus
Gtr. 1: w/ Rhy. Fig. 1 (2 times)
Dm D7sus2 Dm D7sus2 Dm D7sus2 Dm
love you like the way I love you. Does she stim - u - late
Gtr. 2
Rhy. Fig. 3
P.M.
P.M.
B♭ B♭sus2add♯4 B♭ B♭sus2add♯4 B♭ B♭sus2add♯4 B♭
you, at - tract and cap - ti - vate you. Ba - by, ba - by, tell me does she miss
P.M.
P.M.

Cadd9 C Cadd9 C Cadd9 C
you, ex - ist - ing just to kiss you like the way I
End Rhy. Fig. 3
P.M.
P.M.
Dm D7sus2 Dm D7sus2 Dm D7sus2 Dm D7sus2
do. No, tell me does she
P.M.
Gtr. 2: w/ Rhy. Fig. 3
Dm D7sus2 Dm D7sus2 Dm D7sus2 Dm
want you, in - fat - u - ate and haunt you. Does she know just how to shock
B♭ B♭sus2add♯4 B♭ B♭sus2add♯4 B♭ B♭sus2add♯4 B♭
you, e - lec - tri - fy and rock you. Does she in - ject
Cadd9 C Cadd9 C Cadd9 C
you, se - duce you and af - fect you, ba - by, like the way I
D7sus2 Dm Dsus2 Dm D7sus2 Dm D7sus2
do. No, like the way I
Gtr. 2
let ring

Outro-Guitar Solo

C
Dm
let ring
let ring
let ring

Begin fade

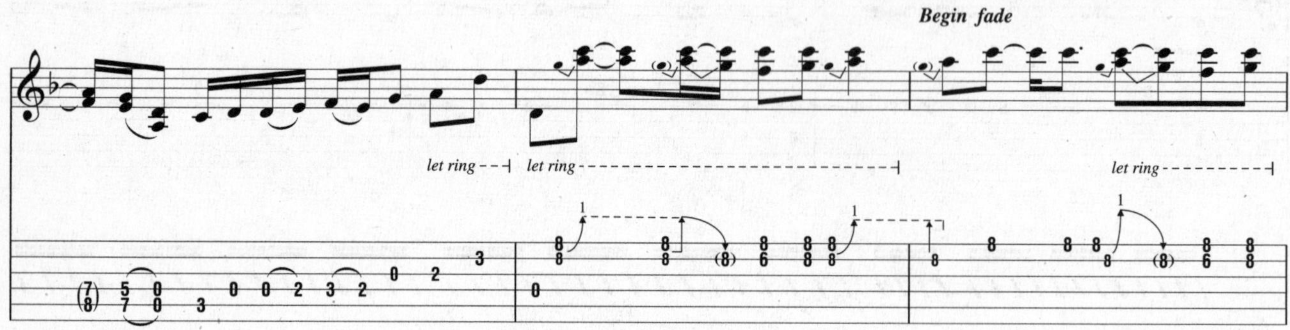
let ring
let ring
let ring

B♭
let ring
let ring

C
let ring
let ring
let ring

Dm
Fade out
let ring
let ring

Lithium

Words and Music by Kurt Cobain

Tune down 1 step:
(low to high) D-G-C-F-A-D

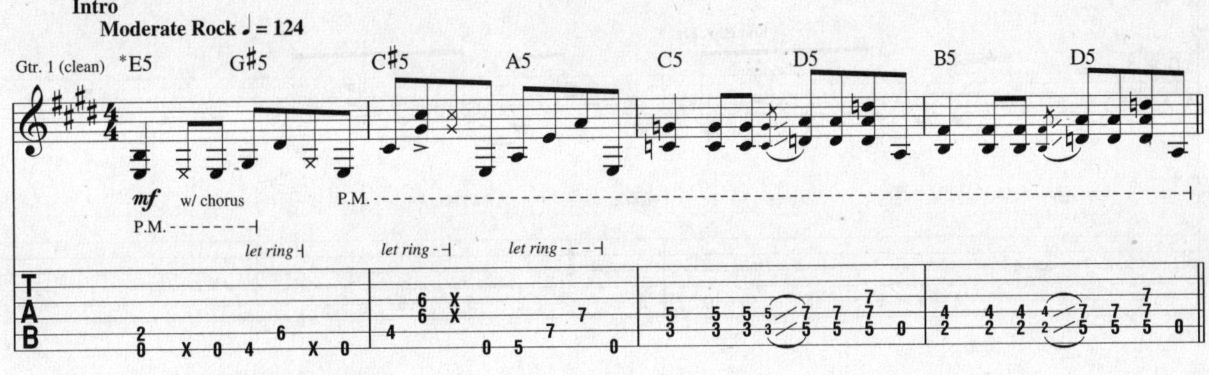

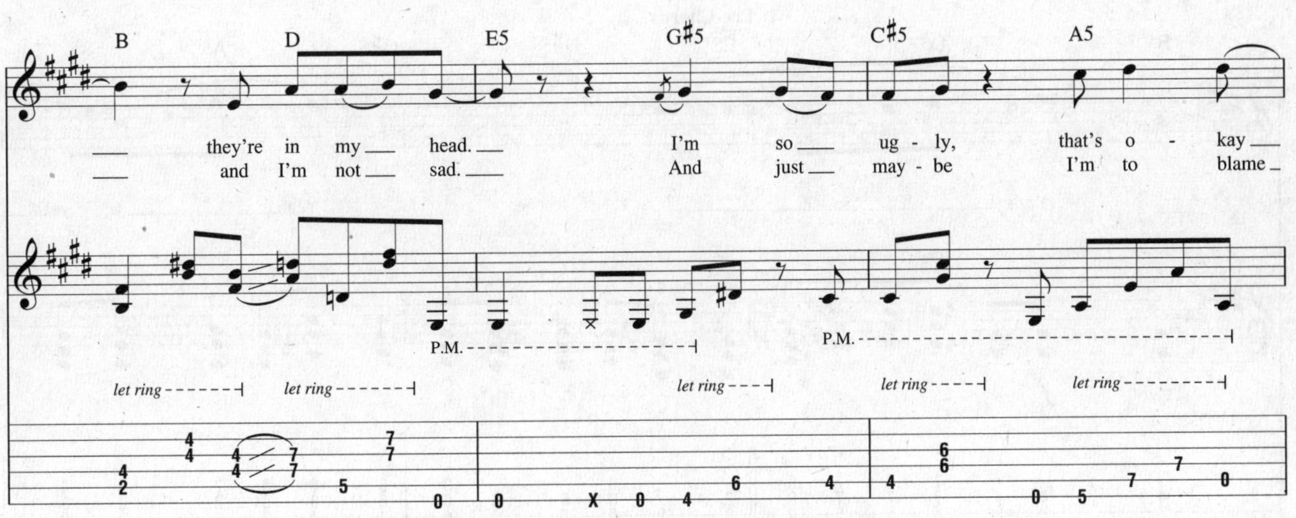

Gtr. 1: w/ Rhy. Fig. 1
C5
D5
B
D5
E5
G♯5
'cause so are you, broke our mirr's. Sunday
for all I've heard, but I'm not sure. I'm so ex-
End Rhy. Fig. 1
P.M.
let ring
let ring
let ring
let ring

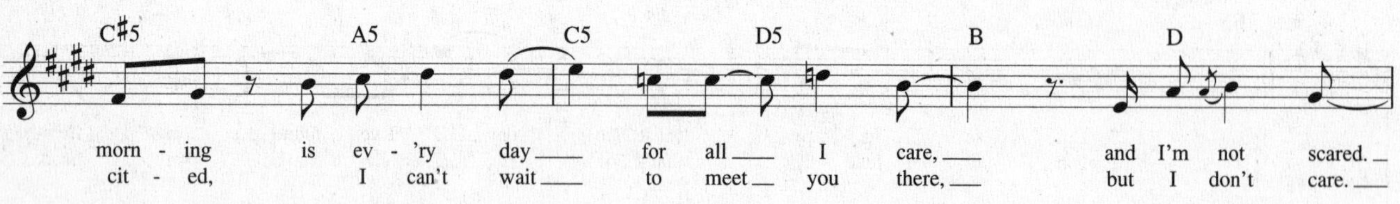
C♯5
A5
C5
D5
B
D
morn - ing is ev - 'ry day for all I care, and I'm not scared.
cit - ed, I can't wait to meet you there, but I don't care.

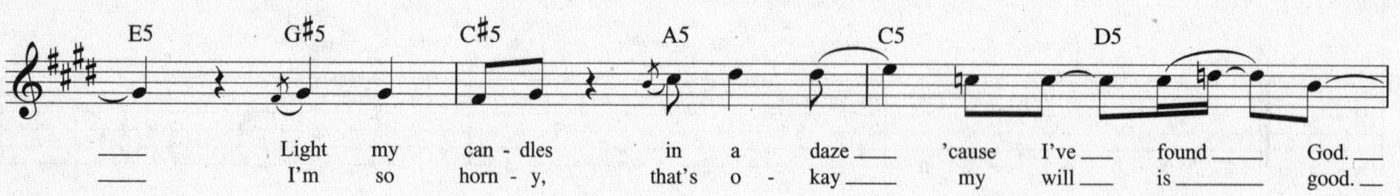
E5
G♯5
C♯5
A5
C5
D5
Light my can - dles in a daze 'cause I've found God.
I'm so horn - y, that's o - kay my will is good.

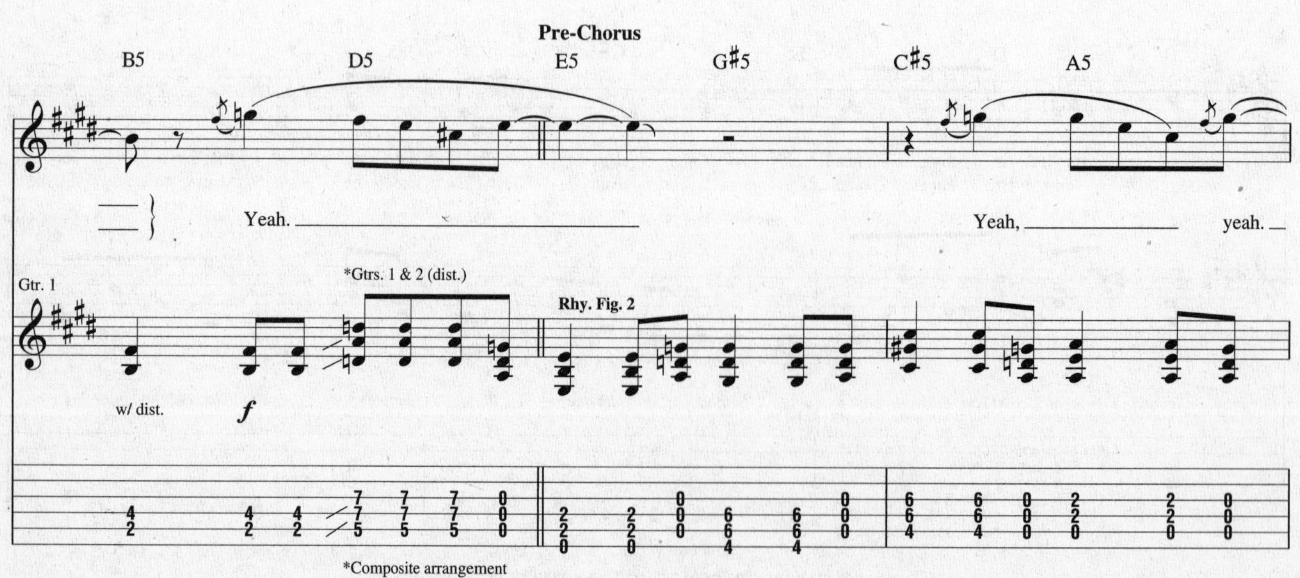
Pre-Chorus
B5
D5
E5
G♯5
C♯5
A5
Yeah.
Yeah, yeah.
Gtr. 1
*Gtrs. 1 & 2 (dist.)
Rhy. Fig. 2
w/ dist.
f
*Composite arrangement

Gtrs. 1 & 2: w/ Rhy. Fig. 2 (1 3/4 times)
C5 D5 B5 D5 E5 G#5
Yeah.
End Rhy. Fig. 2
C#5 A5 C5 D5 B5 D5
Yeah, yeah. Yeah.
E5 G#5 C#5 A5 C5 D5
Yeah, yeah.
Chorus
B5 D5 A5 C5 A5 C5 N.C.
Yeah.
1. I like you,
2., 3., 4. I like it,
I'm not gon - na crack.
Gtrs. 1 & 2
A5 C5 A5 C5 A5 C5
I miss you, I'm not gon - na crack. I love you,

1.
A5
C5
N.C.
I'm not gon - na crack. I'd kill you, I'm not gon - na crack.
2.
To Coda
D5
B5
I'm not gon - na crack.
(cont. in slashes)
Interlude
E
open
Gtrs. 1 & 2
Gtrs. 1 & 2 tacet
*Gtr. 3
mf
*Bass arr. for gtr.
D.S. al Coda
(with repeats)
Coda
E5
** mp
**Back off vol. knob

Long Cool Woman (In a Black Dress)

Words and Music by Allan Clarke, Roger Cook and Roger Greenaway

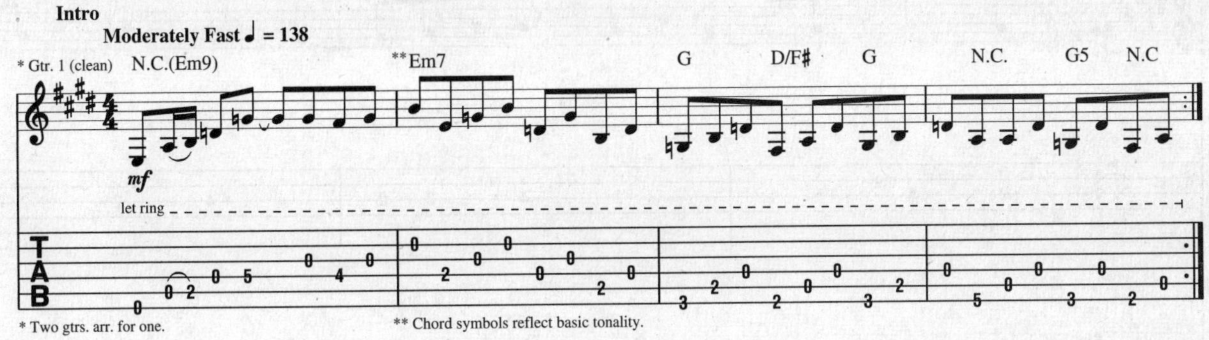

Verse
E7
G
A5
1. Sat - ur - day night I was down - town, work - in' for the F. B. I.
Rhy. Fig. 2A
Rhy. Fig. 2
E7
Sit - tin' in a nest of bad men, whis -

G
A5
E7
- key bot - tles pi - in' up high.
Boot -
End Rhy. Fig. 2A
End Rhy. Fig. 2
Gtrs. 1 & 2: w/ Rhy. Figs. 2 & 2A, simile
E7
G
A5
- leg - gin' booz - er on the west side, full of peo - ple who were do - in' wrong.
E7
Just a - bout to call up the D. A. man, when I heard
G
A5
E7
this wom - an sing - in' a song.
A
Pre-Chorus
A5
B5
pair of fort - y fives made me o - pen my eyes my tem - p'ra - ture start - ed to rise.
Gtr. 1

Chorus
A5
She was a long cool wom - an in a
simile on repeat
G5
E5
black dress, just a five nine beau - ti - ful tall. With
A5
G5
To Coda
just one look I was a bad mess, 'cause that long cool wom - an had it
Interlude
E7
all.
w/ pick & fingers
let ring
let ring

let ring
let ring
E7
Woo!
Gtr. 1: w/ Rhy. Fig. 1, simile
2. I
Gtr. 2
Verse
Gtr. 1: w/ Rhy. Fig. 2, 1st 8 meas., simile
E7
G
A5
E7
saw her head up to the ta - ble, well, a tall walk-in' big black cat. My
Rhy. Fig. 3
End Rhy. Fig. 3

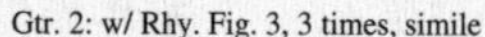
Gtr. 2: w/ Rhy. Fig. 3, 3 times, simile

G
A5
Char - lie said, "I hope that you're a - ble boy. 'cause I'm tell - in' you she knows where it's at."
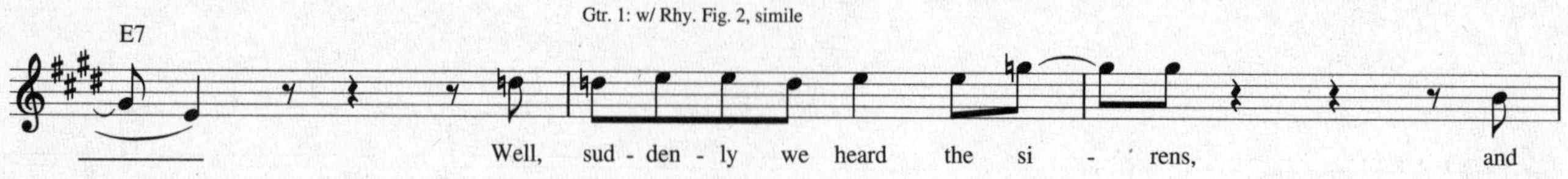
E7
Gtr. 1: w/ Rhy. Fig. 2, simile
Well, sud - den - ly we heard the si - rens, and

G
A5
E7
ev - 'ry - bod - y start - ed to run. A jump - in' out of doors and ta -
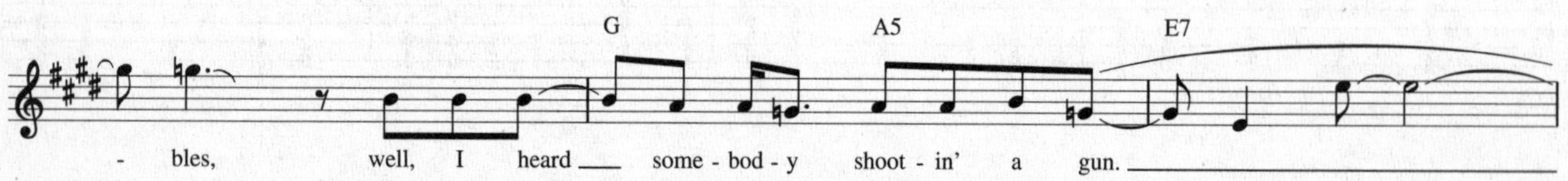
G
A5
E7
- bles, well, I heard some - bod - y shoot - in' a gun.
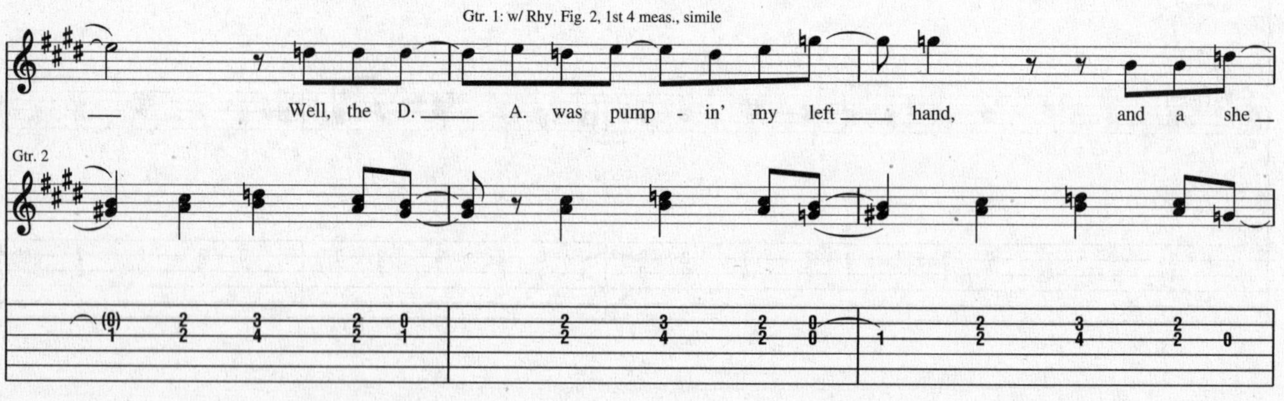
Gtr. 1: w/ Rhy. Fig. 2, 1st 4 meas., simile
Well, the D. A. was pump - in' my left hand, and a she
Gtr. 2
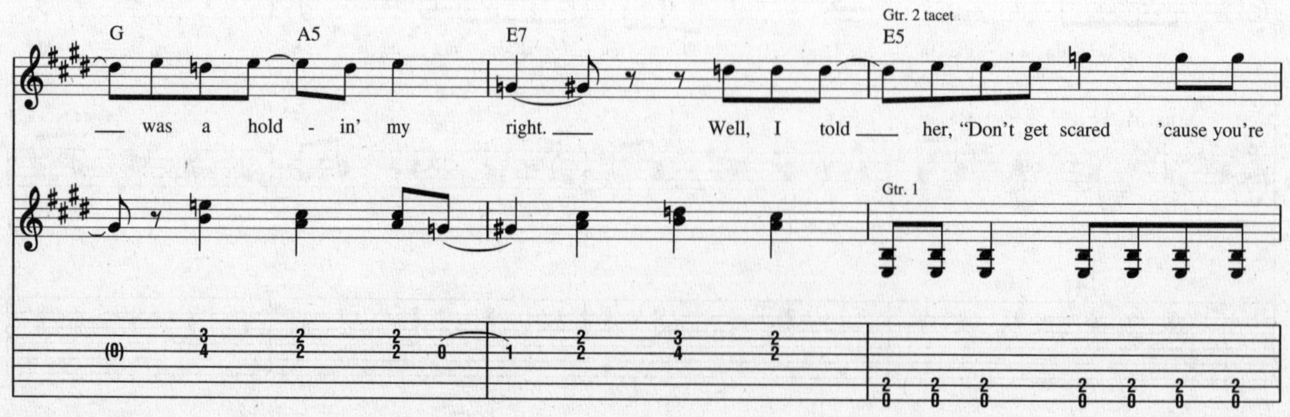
G
A5
E7
Gtr. 2 tacet
E5
was a hold - in' my right. Well, I told her, "Don't get scared 'cause you're
Gtr. 1

D.S. al Coda
G5
A5
gon - na be spared." Well, I got - ta be ___ for - giv - en if I'm wan - na spend my liv - in' with a
Coda
Outro
E5
all. ___ Had it all. ___
Gtr. 2
Gtr. 1
divisi
Outro
Gtr. 1: w/ Rhy. Fig. 1, simile, till fade
Gtr. 2: w/ Rhy. Fig. 3, 1st 2 meas., simile, till fade
E7
Had it all. ___ Had it all!
Had it all! Had it all!
Begin Fade
Ooh, ___ had it all!
Fade Out
Ah, she had it all. Yeah.

Lost in Germany

By Doug Pinnick, Ty Tabor, Jerry Gaskill and Sam Taylor

Pre-Chorus
E5
F#5
E5
A5
Like a pol - i - ti-cian in dis - guise. You know I
(Oh, woe is me.)
P.M.
D5
E5
F#5
N.C.(G)
had to look you in the eyes and smile, while I crawled an-oth - er mile in
Chorus
N.C.
To Coda
D5
1.
N.C.
Ger-man-y.
Lost in Ger-man-y.
D5
2.
N.C.
Ger-man-y.
D5

N.C.
D5
N.C.
Ger-man-y.
Lost in
Ger-man-y.
P.M.

N.C.
Rhy. Fig. 2
Gtr. 2 (elec.)
mf w/ clean tone
let ring throughout
Gtr. 1

End Rhy. Fig. 2
f

Interlude
Gtr. 2: w/ Rhy. Fig 2
N.C.
Dit, dit, dit, dit, dit, dit, dit, dit, dit, dit, dit, dit.
Gtr. 1
D.S. al Coda
(A5)
D5
Da.
(Na, na, na.)
Coda
N.C.
Ger-man-y.
G5 F5 D5 N.C.
Ger-man-y.
P.M.
D5 N.C.
Lost in Ger-man-y.
G5 F5 D5

Outro

Additional Lyrics

2. Swimming in an ocean of your feelings.
Counting every moment go one by one.
Laughing to keep from crying out in anger.
Praying that I can make it through this night.

(Oh, woe is me.)
It was like a never-ending week.
But I learned to turn the other cheek and smile,
While I ran for one more mile in...*(To Chorus)*

3. Shooting at a target that eludes me.
Hammering on a nail that just won't go in.
Biting on a tongue that wants to speak out.
Searching for a light that I can shine.

(Oh, woe is me.)
But now I have crossed that borderline.
And I wonder if I'll ever find your hand,
'Cause I did not understand in...*(To Chorus)*

Lovesong

Words and Music by Robert Smith, Laurence Tolhurst, Simon Gallup, Paul S. Thompson, Boris Williams and Roger O'Donnell

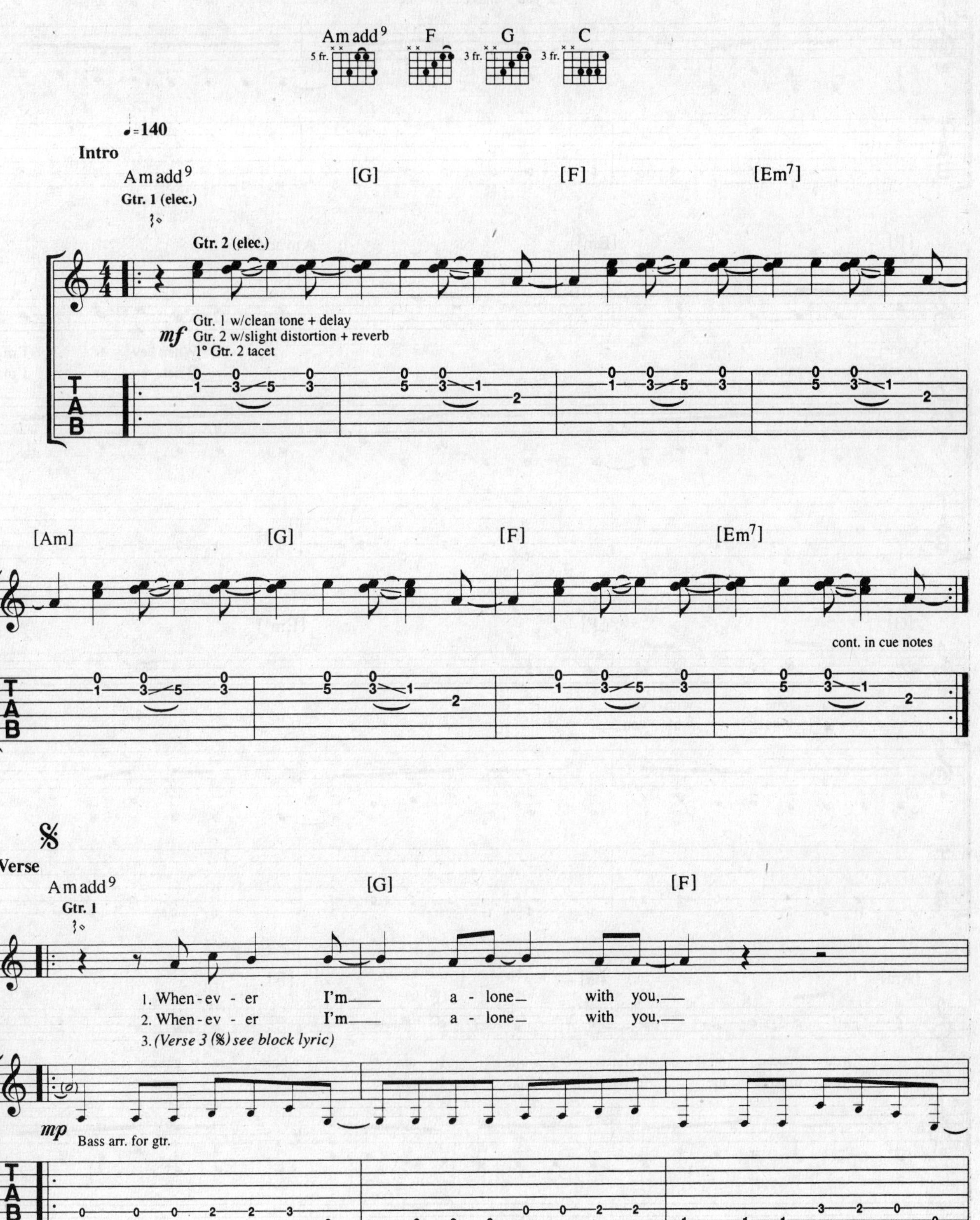

[Em7]
[Am]
[G]
you make me feel like I am
you make me feel like I am
[F]
[Em7]
Am add9
Gtr. 1
home a-gain.
young a-gain.
When-ev-er I'm
When-ev-er I'm
[G]
[F]
[Em7]
a-lone with you,
a-lone with you,
[Am]
[G]
[F]
you make me feel like I am whole a-gain.
you make me feel like I am fun a-gain.
T
A
B

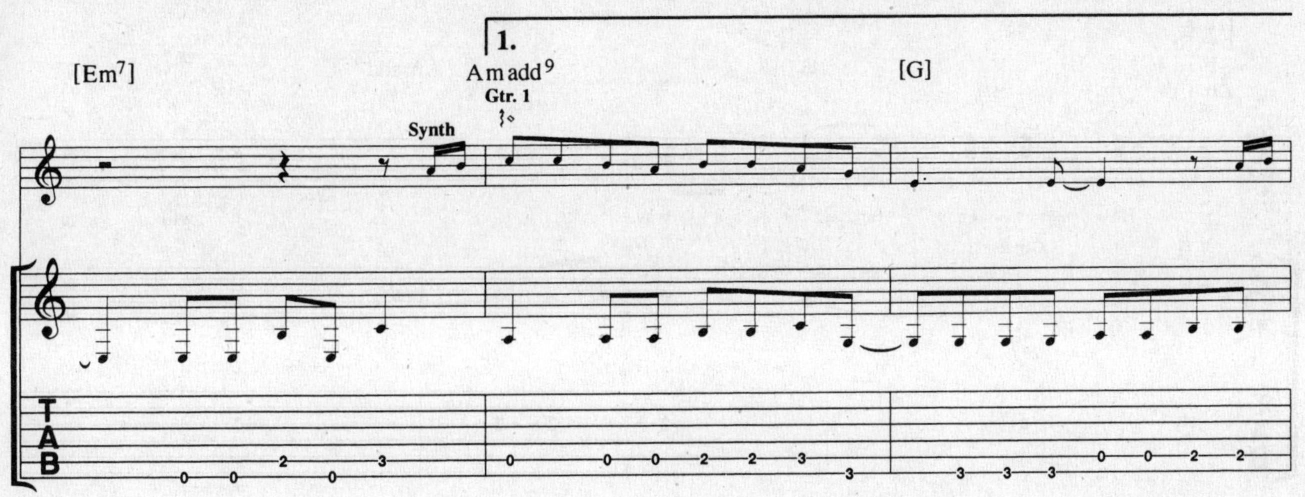
1.
[Em7]
Am madd9
Gtr. 1
Synth
[G]

[F]
[Em7]
[Am]

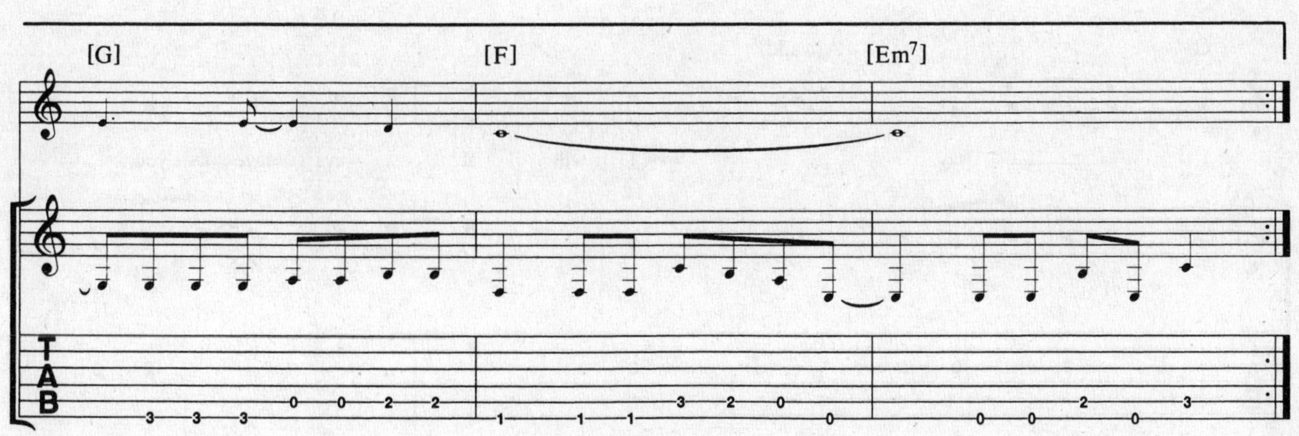
[G]
[F]
[Em7]

2. %.
F
G
Amadd9
C
Gtr. 1
How ever far a - way,
I will al -
Gtr. 2
mf
- ways love you.
However long I stay,
I will al - ways love you.
What - ev - er words
I say,
I will al - ways love you,
T
A
B

F
Gtr. 1
G
To Coda
I will al - ways love you.

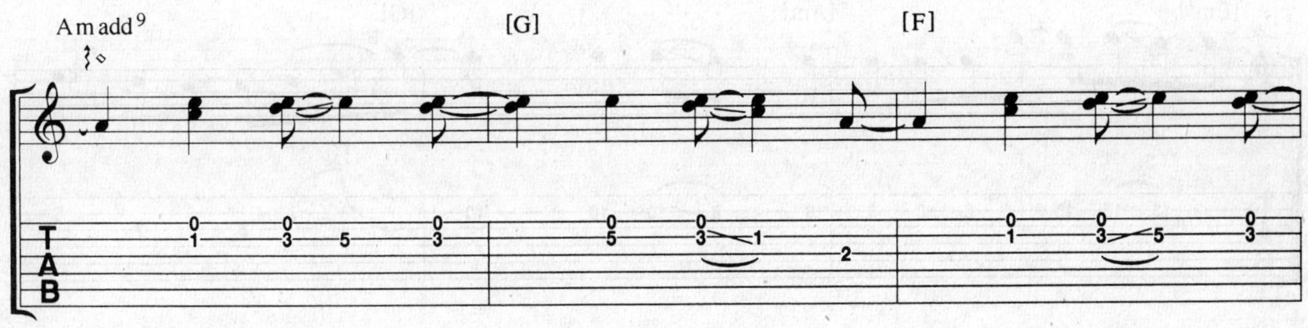
Am add9
[G]
[F]

[Em7]
[Am]
[G]
Fig. 1...

[F]
[Em7]
Fly me to the moon.
Gtr. 3 (elec.)
...Fig. 1 ends

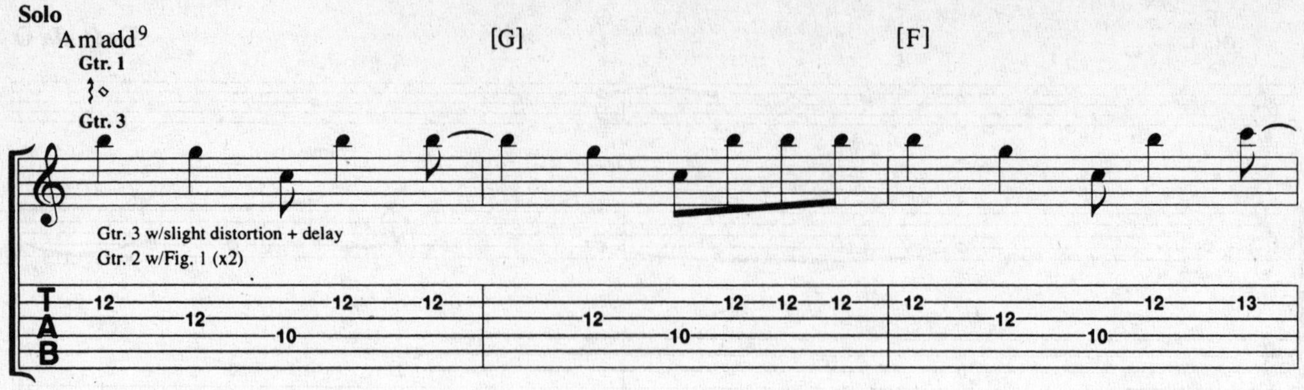

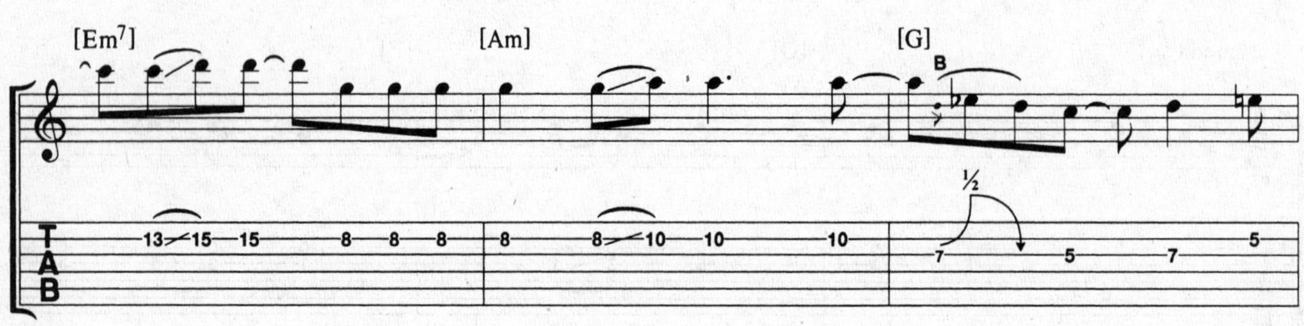

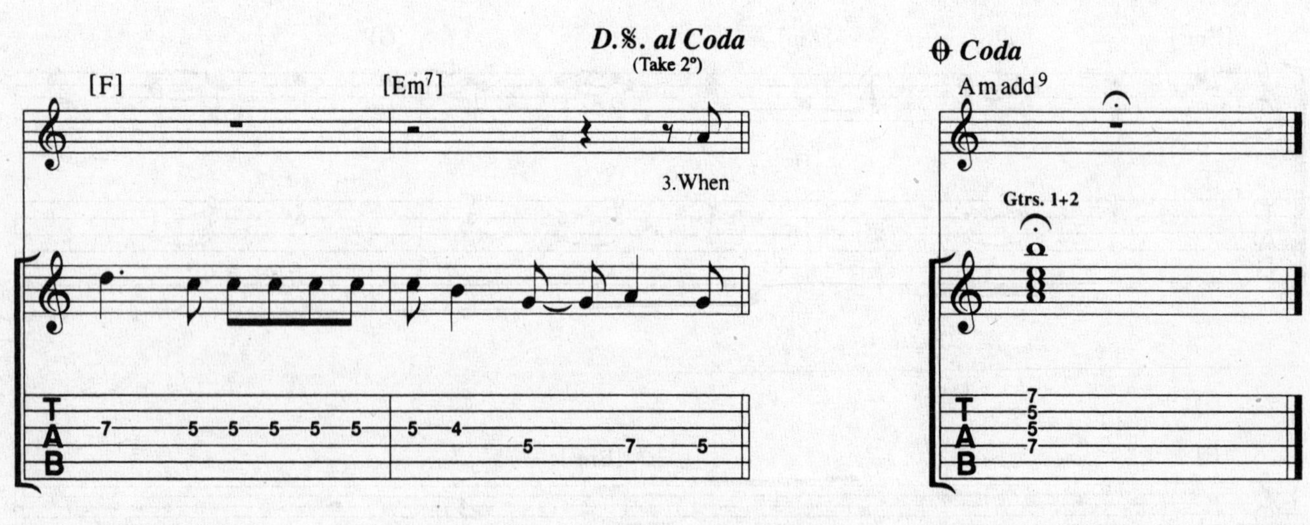

Verse 3:
Whenever I'm alone with you
You make me feel like I am free again
Whenever I'm alone with you
You make me feel like I am clean again.

Magic Man

Words and Music by Ann Wilson and Nancy Wilson

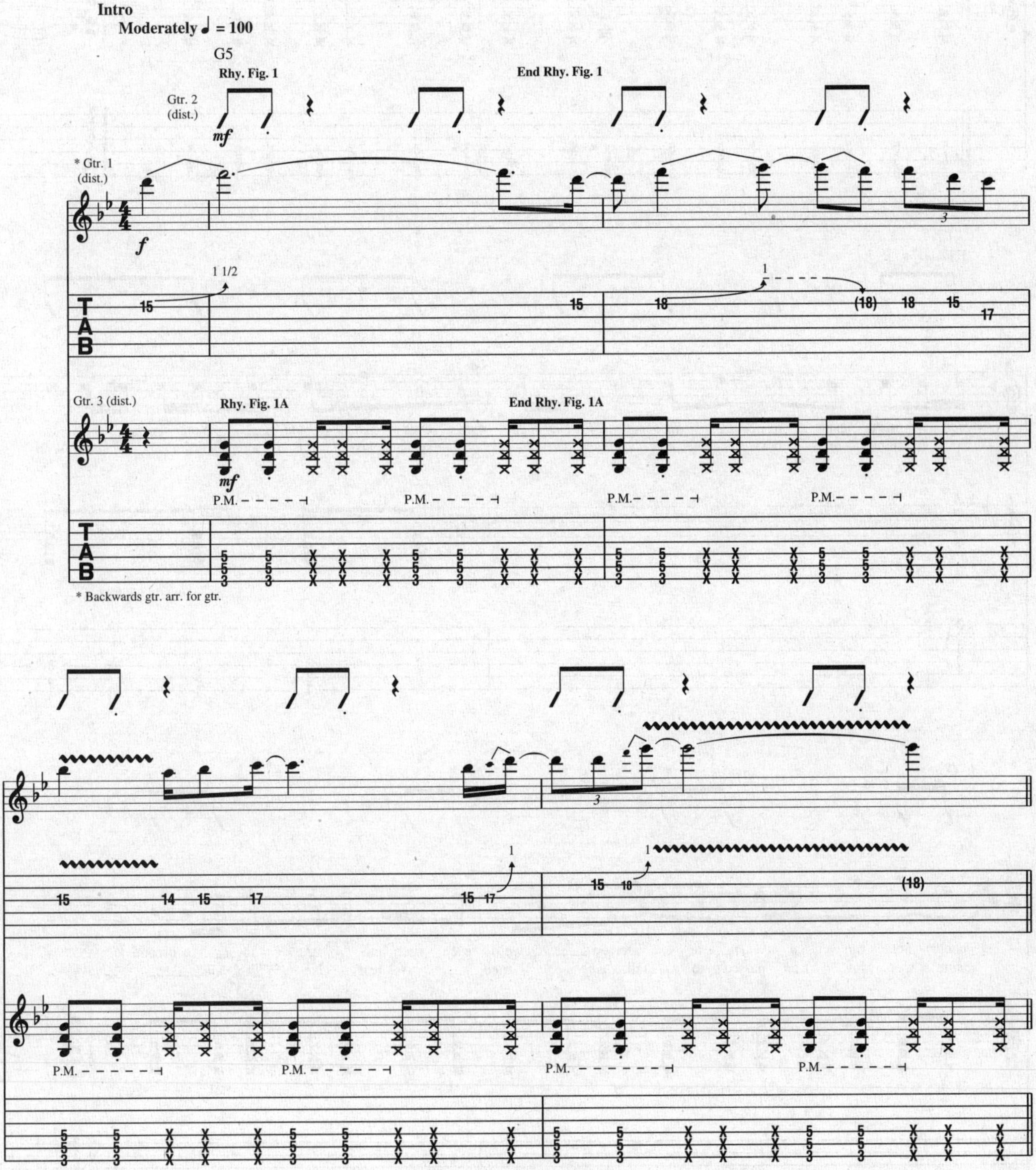

Intro

Moderately ♩ = 100

G5

Rhy. Fig. 1

End Rhy. Fig. 1

Gtr. 2 (dist.)

mf

* Gtr. 1 (dist.)

f

1 1/2

15 15 18 1 (18) 18 15 17

Gtr. 3 (dist.)

Rhy. Fig. 1A

End Rhy. Fig. 1A

mf

P.M.

* Backwards gtr. arr. for gtr.

15 14 15 17 1 15 17 15 18 1 (18)

P.M.

Verse
Gtr. 1 tacet
G5
1. Cold late night so long a - go, when I was not so strong, you know, a
2. Win - ter nights we sang in tune, played in - side the months of moon.
Gtr. 3
P.M.
F5
pret - ty man came to me. Nev - er seen eyes so blue. You know, I
Nev - er think of nev - er, let the spell last for - ev - er. Well,
G5
could not run a - way; it seemed we'd seen each oth - er in a dream.
sum - mer lov - er passed to fall, tried to real - ize it all.

F5
G5
Seemed like he knew me; he looked right through me. Yeah.
Ma-ma says she's wor-ried, grow-ing up in a hur-ry. Yeah.
P.M.
P.M.
Chorus
Gtr. 1: w/ Rhy. Fig. 1
Gtr. 4 (acous.)
B♭
B♭
F
G5
B♭
Rhy. Fig. 2
1. "Come on home, girl," he said with a smile.
2. "Come on home, girl," ma-ma cried on the phone. "Too
* Gtrs. 2 & 3
Rhy. Fig. 2A
* Composite arrangement
B♭
F
G5
"You don't have to love me yet, let's get high a-while. But
soon to lose my ba-by yet; my girl should be at home." But

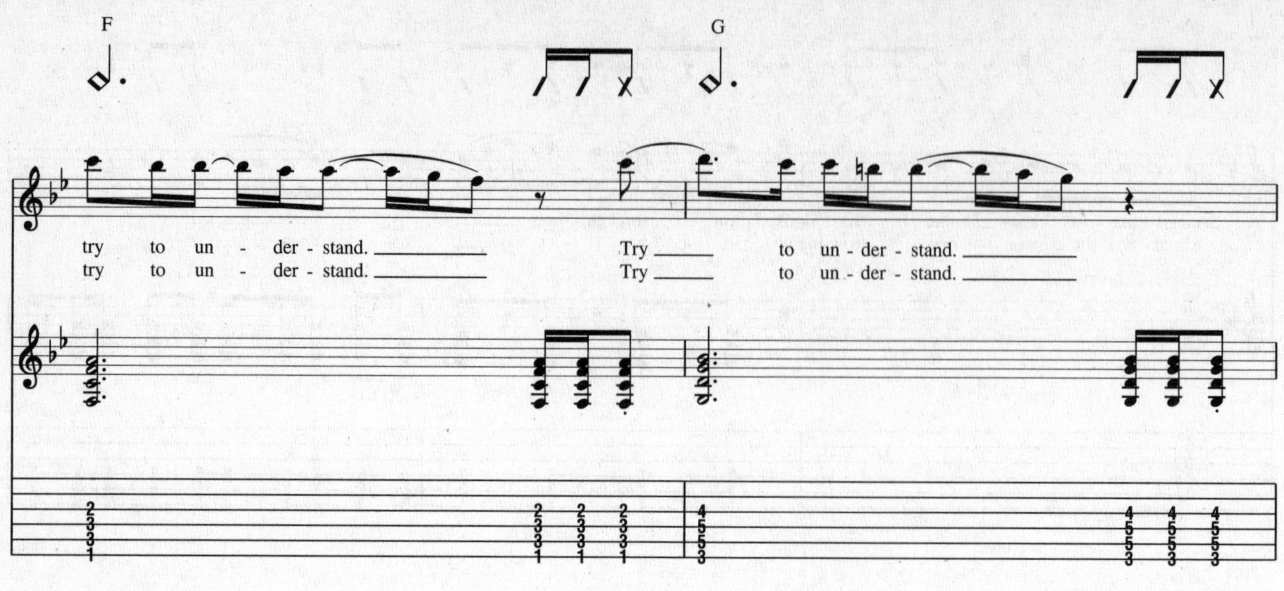
F
G
try to un - der - stand.
try to un - der - stand.
Try to un - der - stand.
Try to un - der - stand.

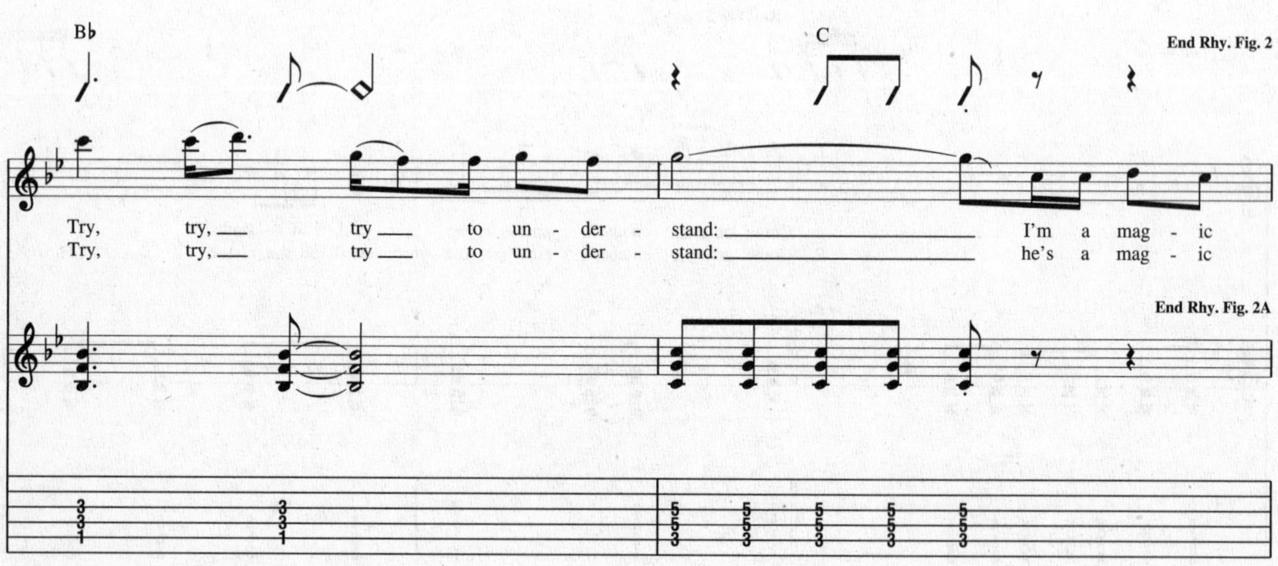
B♭
C
End Rhy. Fig. 2
Try, try, try to un - der - stand: I'm a mag - ic
Try, try, try to un - der - stand: he's a mag - ic
End Rhy. Fig. 2A

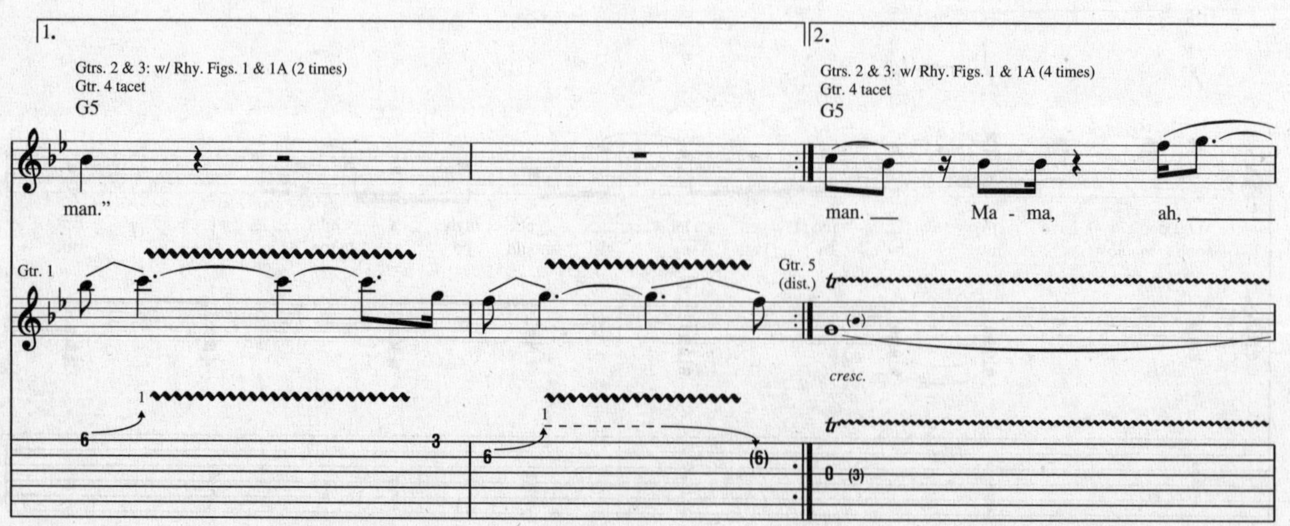
1.
2.
Gtrs. 2 & 3: w/ Rhy. Figs. 1 & 1A (2 times)
Gtr. 4 tacet
G5
Gtrs. 2 & 3: w/ Rhy. Figs. 1 & 1A (4 times)
Gtr. 4 tacet
G5
man."
man. Ma - ma, ah,
Gtr. 1
Gtr. 5
(dist.)
cresc.

Interlude

Chorus

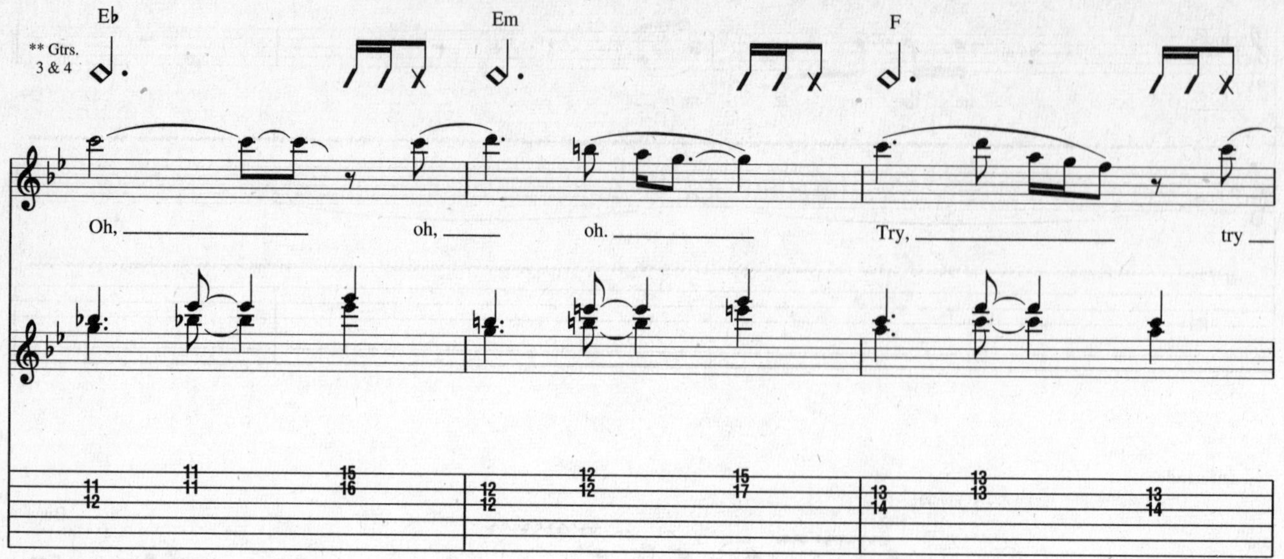

* Composite arrangement

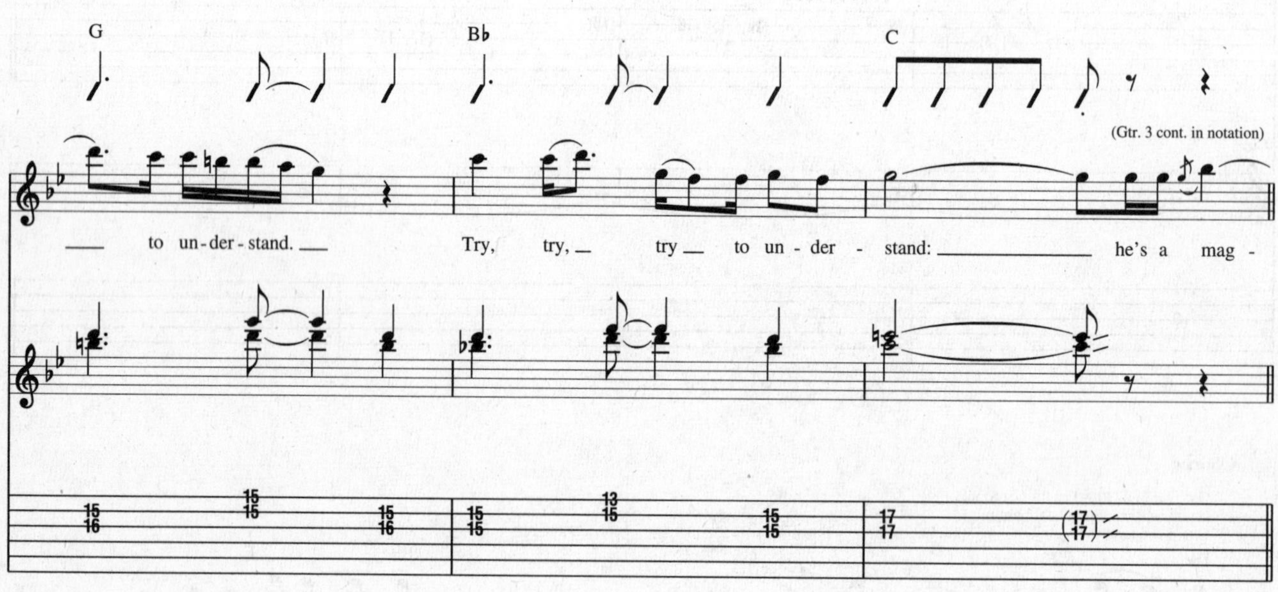

Interlude

** Composite arrangement

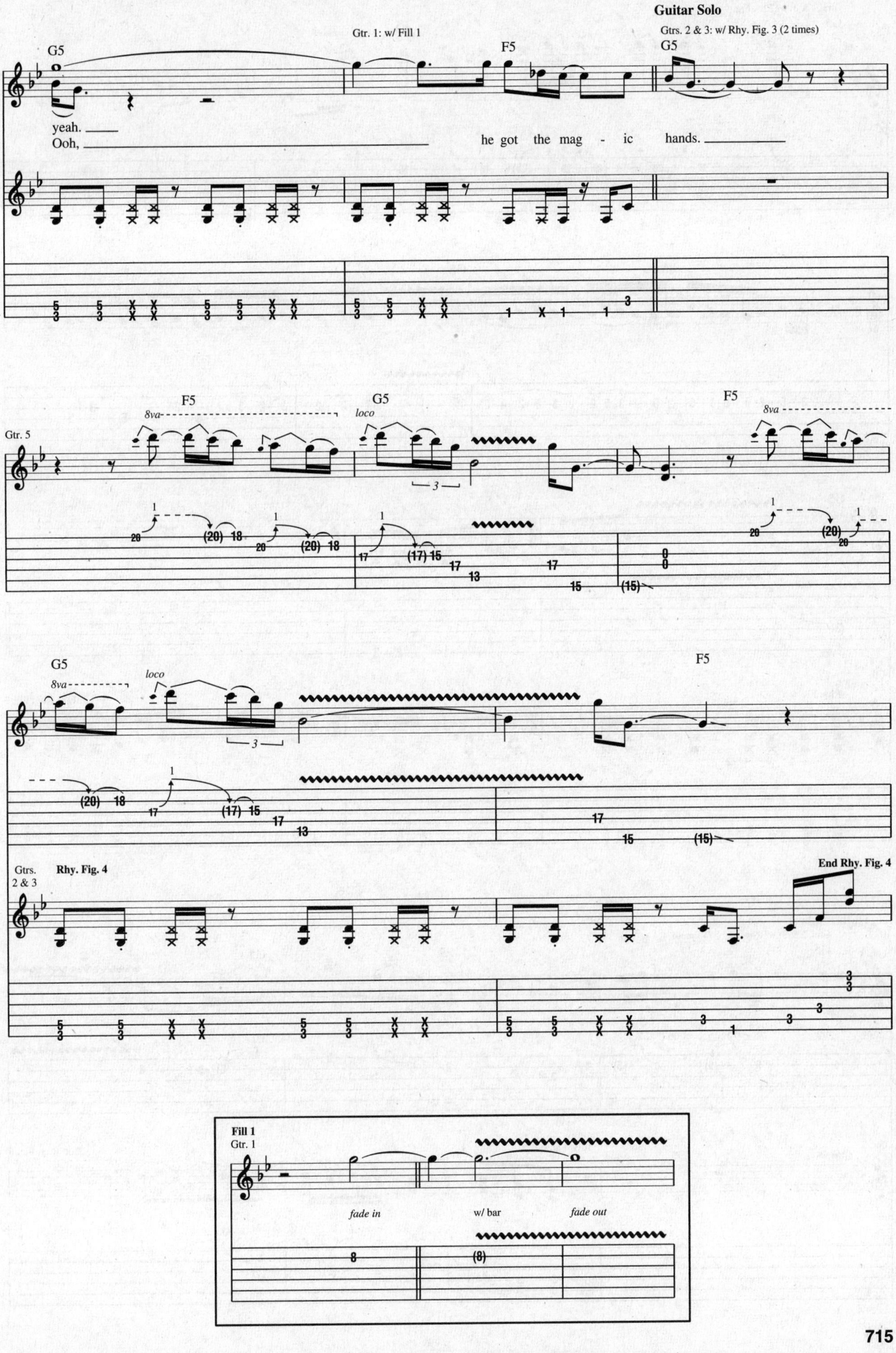

Guitar Solo

Gtr. 1: w/ Fill 1

Gtrs. 2 & 3: w/ Rhy. Fig. 3 (2 times)

G5 F5 G5

yeah.
Ooh, he got the mag - ic hands.

Gtr. 5

F5 G5 F5

8va *loco* *8va*

G5 F5

8va *loco*

Gtrs. 2 & 3 **Rhy. Fig. 4** **End Rhy. Fig. 4**

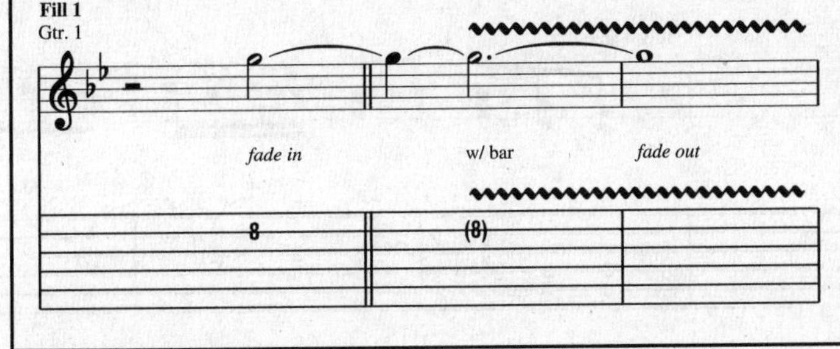

Gtrs. 2 & 3: w/ Rhy. Fig. 4 (3 times)
G5
F5
G5
hold bend
F5
G5
F5
P.M.
Gtr. 5
G5
N.C.
Gtrs. 2 & 3
Rhy. Fig. 5
End Rhy. Fig. 5
Guitar Solo
Gtrs. 2 & 3: w/ Rhy. Fig. 3 (4 times)
Gtr. 6
G5
F5
G5
mf
Gtr. 5
Rhy. Fig. 6
End Rhy. Fig. 6

Gtr. 5: w/ Rhy. Fig. 6 (3 times)
Gtr. 6
F5
G5
F5
G5
1/2
1/2
1/2
1/2

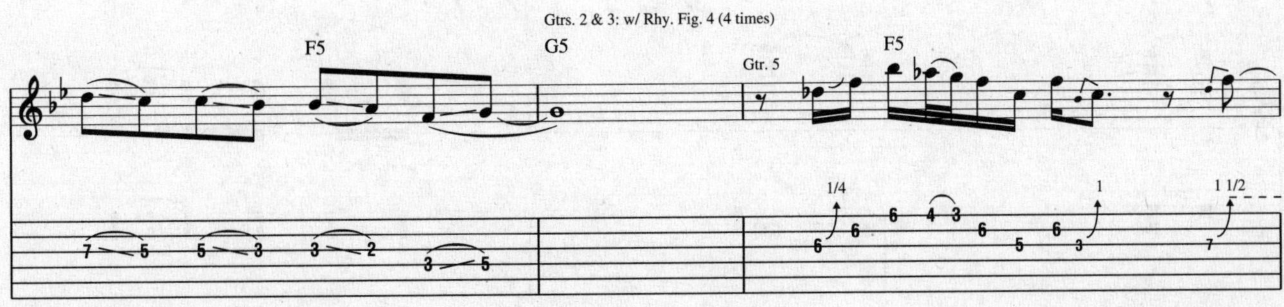
Gtrs. 2 & 3: w/ Rhy. Fig. 4 (4 times)
F5
G5
Gtr. 5
F5
1/4
1
1 1/2

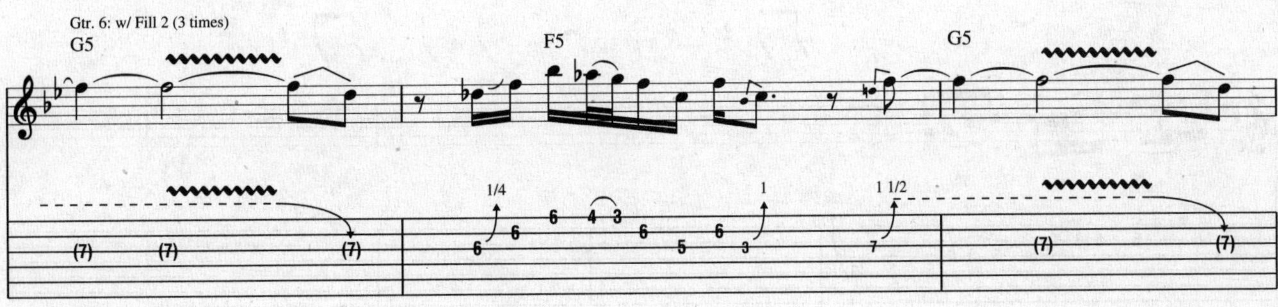
Gtr. 6: w/ Fill 2 (3 times)
G5
F5
G5
1/4
1
1 1/2

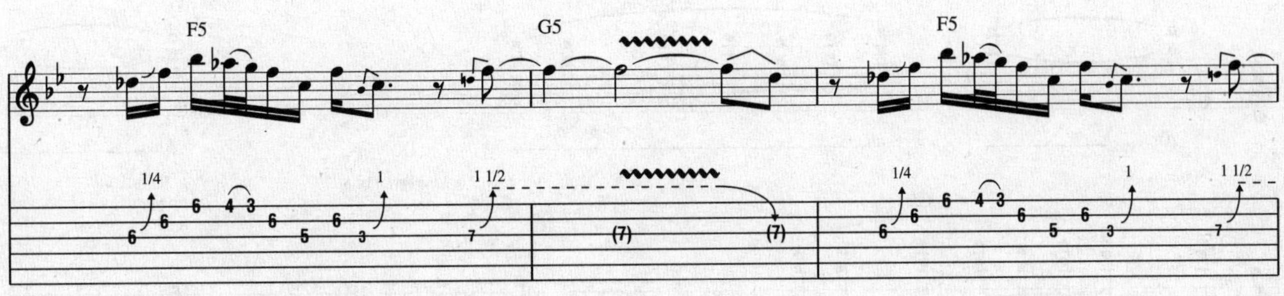
F5
G5
F5
1/4
1
1 1/2
1/4
1
1 1/2

Fill 2
Gtr. 6
1

Gtrs. 2 & 3: w/ Rhy. Fig. 5
Gtr. 6: w/ Fill 3
G5
N.C.
Gtrs. 2 & 3
G5
F5
F#5
G5
1 1/2
P.M.
Gtr. 5 tacet
(w/ synth)
G5
F5
F#5
G5
1/4
Interlude
Gtrs. 2 & 3: w/ Rhy. Fig. 3 (4 times)
Gtrs. 2 & 3: w/ Rhy. Fig. 4 (4 times)
G5
F5
G5
F5
G5
Ah,
ah,
Ah,
F5
G5
F5
Gtrs. 2 & 3: w/ Rhy. Fig. 5
G5
N.C.
ah,
Fill 3
Gtr. 6
1

Gtrs. 2 & 3
F5
Gtr. 4
F
Gtrs. 2 & 4
Gtr. 3
(Gtr. 2 cont. in slashes)
Chorus
Gtrs. 2 & 3: w/ Rhy. Fig. 2A
Gtr. 4: w/ Rhy. Fig. 2
B♭
F5
G5
"Come on home, girl," he said with a smile.
"You don't have to love me yet, let's get high a-while."
But try to un-der-stand. Try to un-der-stand.
Try, try, try to un-der-stand: he's a mag-ic man, yeah, oh.
G
C
N.C.

Mas Tequila

Lyrics by Sammy Hagar
Music by Sammy Hagar, Mile Leander and Gary Glitter

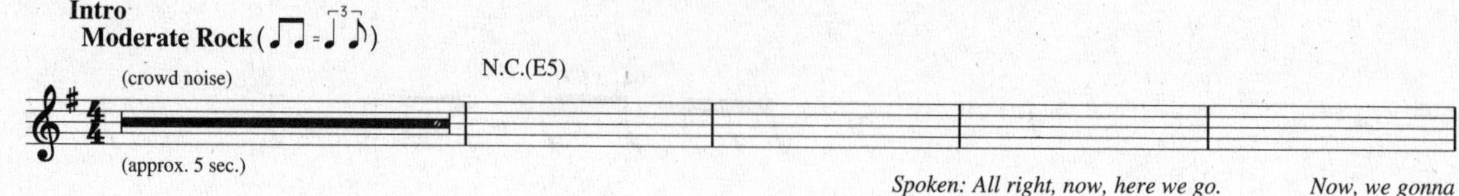

E5
D5
C#5
C5
B5
1/4
E5
G5
A5
E5
A5
G5
Uh!
Gtr. 3 (dist.)
mf
Gtrs. 1 & 2
P.M.
P.M.
P.M.
E5
G5
A5
E5
Gtr. 3 tacet
N.C.
1. I'm go - in'
Rhy. Fig. 1
End Rhy. Fig. 1
P.M.
P.M.
P.M.

Verse

E5
D5
A5
G5
way down south where the big blue a - ga - ve grow. __ Tak - in' a
Gtrs. 1 & 2
Rhy. Fig. 2
End Rhy. Fig. 2

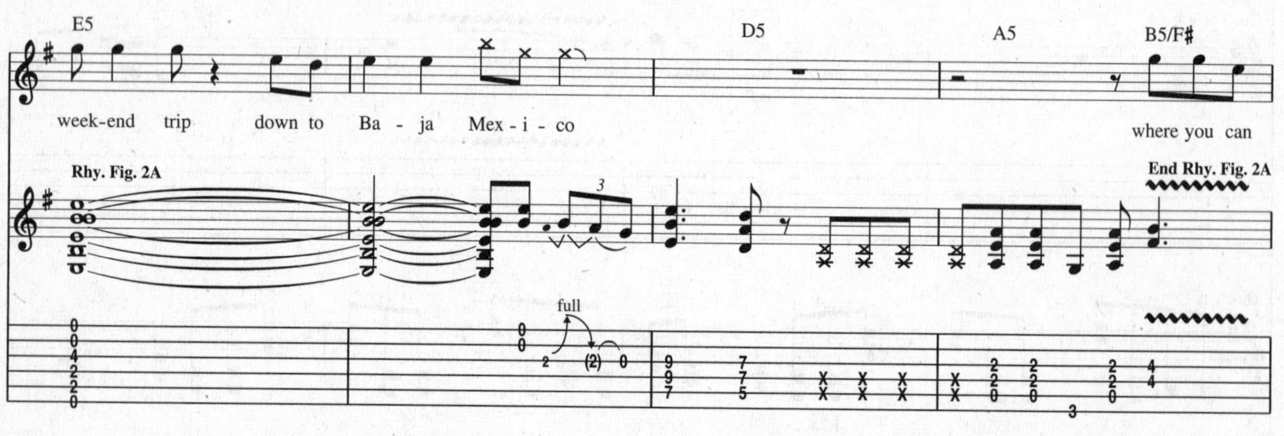
E5
D5
A5
B5/F#
week-end trip down to Ba - ja Mex - i - co where you can
Rhy. Fig. 2A
End Rhy. Fig. 2A
full

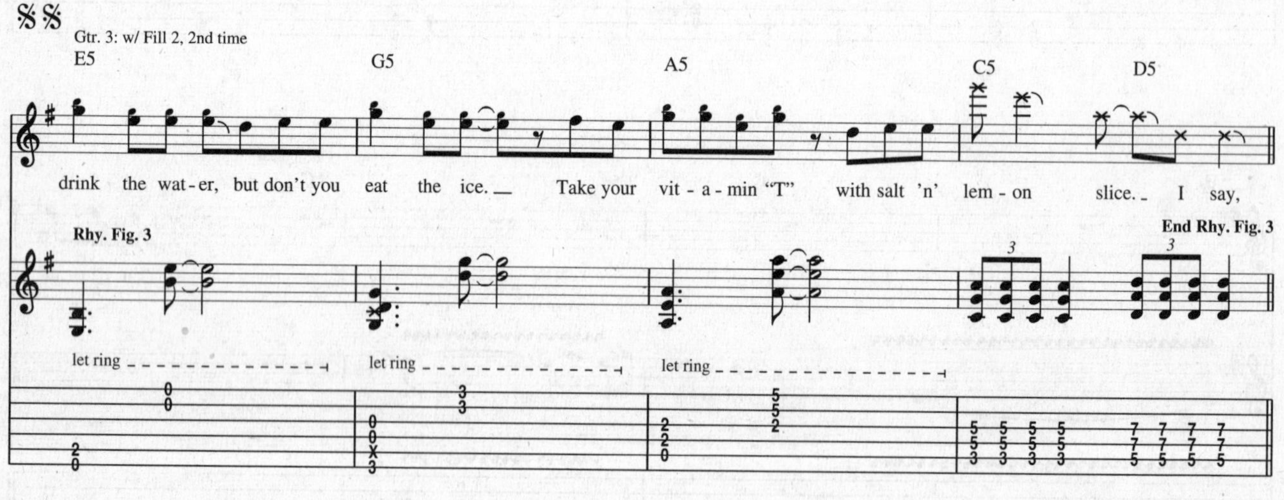
Gtr. 3: w/ Fill 2, 2nd time
E5
G5
A5
C5
D5
drink the wat - er, but don't you eat the ice. __ Take your vit - a - min "T" with salt 'n' lem - on slice. _ I say,
Rhy. Fig. 3
End Rhy. Fig. 3
let ring
let ring
let ring

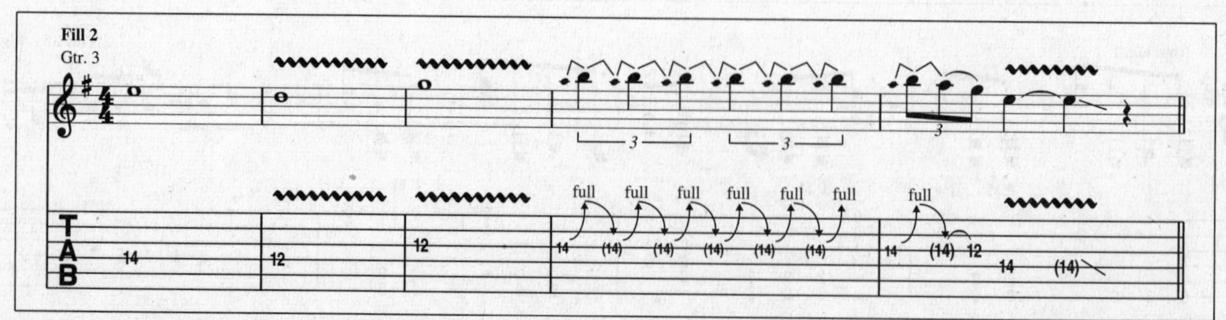
Fill 2
Gtr. 3
full
full
full
full
full
full
full

Chorus
D5
E5
A5
B5/F#
(One shot, hey!
Mas te - qui - la!
Two shots, hey, hey!
Que ve - ne - no.
Rhy. Fig. 4
To Coda 1
To Coda 2
C#5
C5
B5
N.C.
Three shots, hey!
Ar - ri - ba!
Hey! Hey! Hey!)
Mas te - qui - la!
End Rhy. Fig. 4
1/4
Interlude
Gtrs. 1 & 2: w/ Rhy. Fig. 1
Gtrs. 3: w/ Fill 1
G5
Whoa!
2. She did a
Verse
Gtrs. 1 & 2: w/ Rhy. Fig. 2A
mean Mac - ar - en - a to the "Funk - y Cold Me - din - a"
be - hind the
Fill 1

Gtrs. 1 & 2: w/ Rhy. Fig. 2
E5
D5
A5
G5
bod - y shot and three mar - ga - ri - tas. She'll drink it

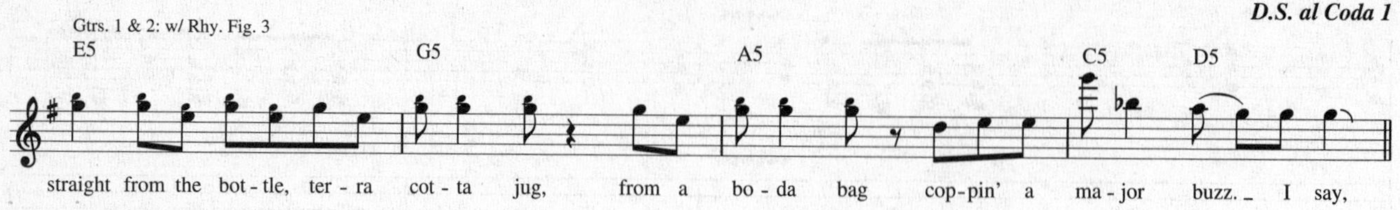
Gtrs. 1 & 2: w/ Rhy. Fig. 3
D.S. al Coda 1
E5
G5
A5
C5
D5
straight from the bot - tle, ter - ra cot - ta jug, from a bo - da bag cop - pin' a ma - jor buzz. I say,

Coda 1
Guitar Solo
B5
N.C.
N.C.(F#5)
(D5)
Mas te - qui - la!
(Hey! Hey!)
full
fdbk.

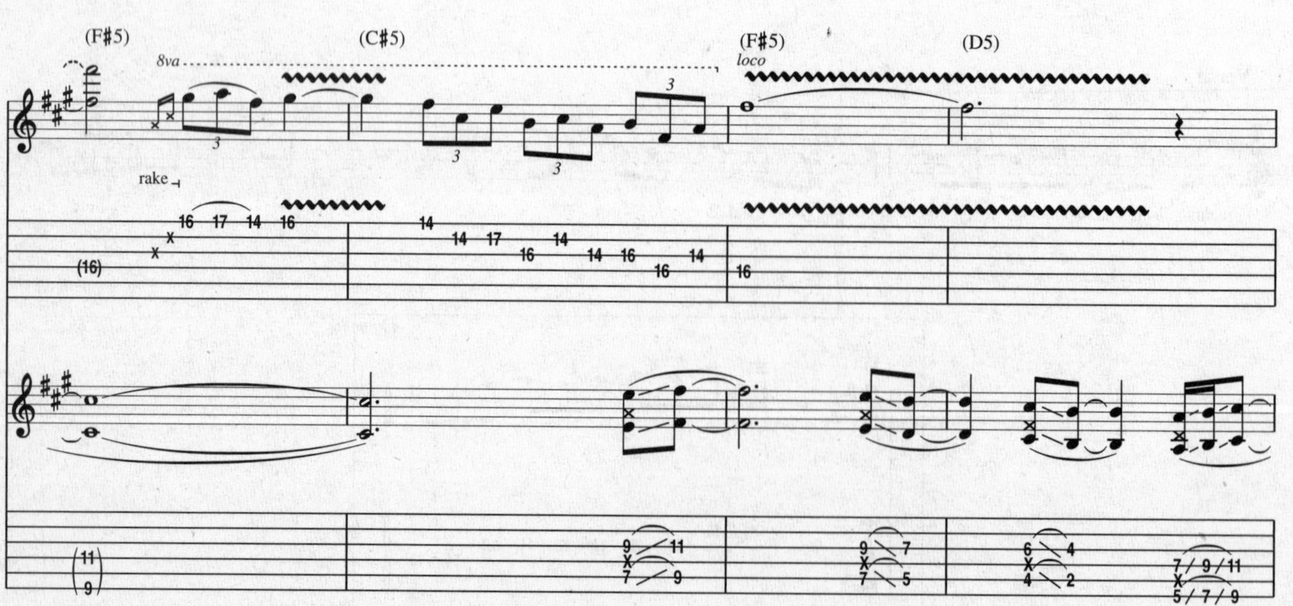
(F#5)
(C#5)
(F#5)
(D5)
8va
loco
rake

(C#5)
(B5)
(F#5)
8va
w/ bar
rake
full
1/2
(D5)
-1/2
loco
B5
Un-o mas,
bar - tend-er!

Gtr. 3 tacet
E5
D5
N.C.
Whoo, gim-me one more! Mas te - quil - a!
8va
Gtr. 4 (dist.)
full
1 1/2
2
P.M.
E5
D5
N.C.
loco
B5
1/2
1/4

Interlude
Gtr. 4 tacet
E5
N.C.
Crowd: Hey!
Hey!
Gtrs. 1 & 2
w/ wah-wah
D.S.S. al Coda 2
Hey!
Hey!
Hey!
Yeah, you can
wah-wah off
Coda 2
Outro-Chorus
Gtrs. 1 & 2: w/ Rhy. Fig. 4
Gtr. 3 tacet
B5
D5 E5
A5
B5/F#
Hey!
Hey!)
Mas te - qui - la!
(One shot, hey!
More te - qui - la!
Gtr. 3
Gtrs. 1 & 2
D5 E5
A5
B5/F#
E5 D5
C#5
C5
Two shots, hey, hey!
Que ve - ne - no.
Three shots, hey!
Ay, yi, yi, yi, yi,
Hey!

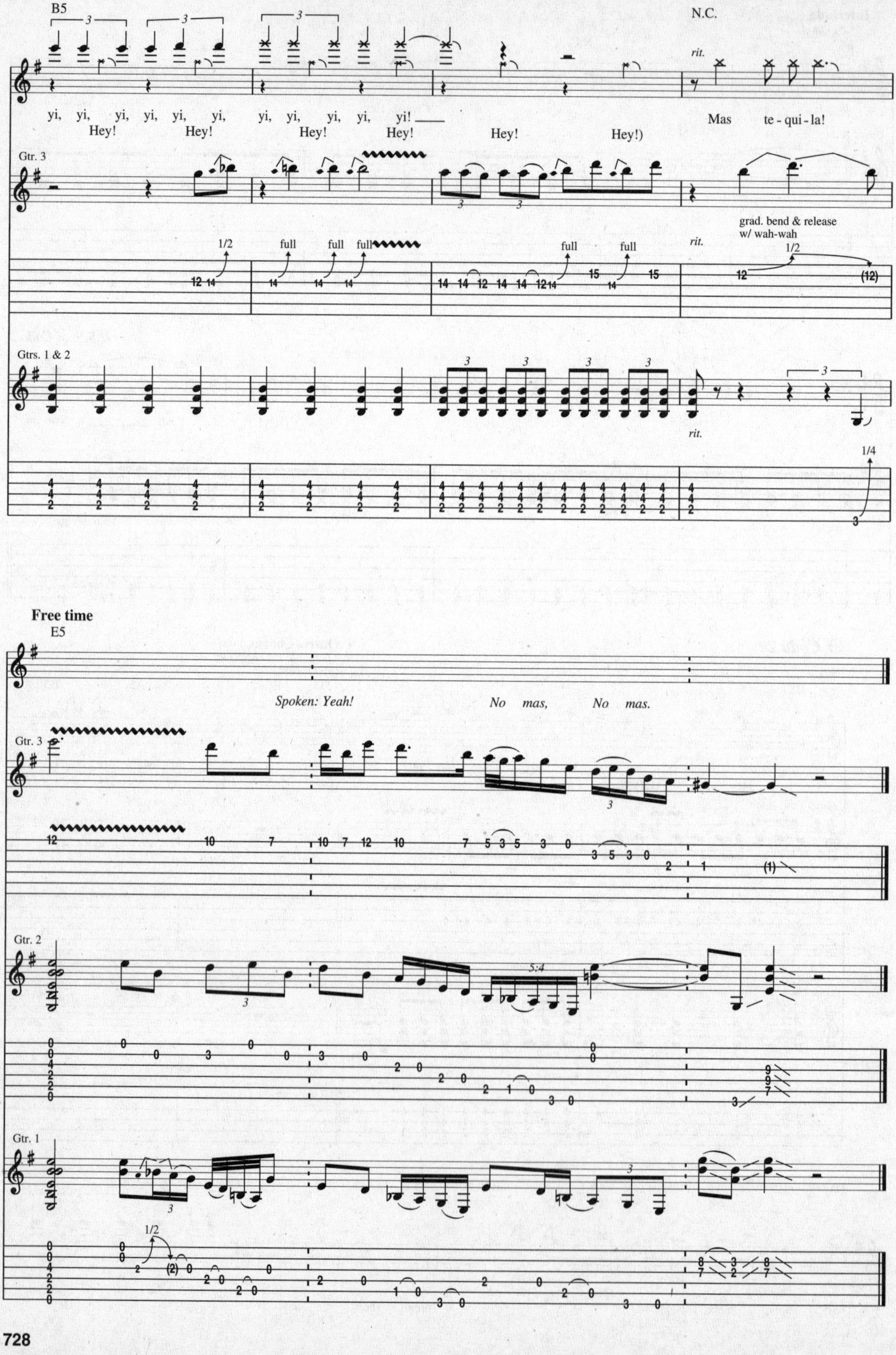

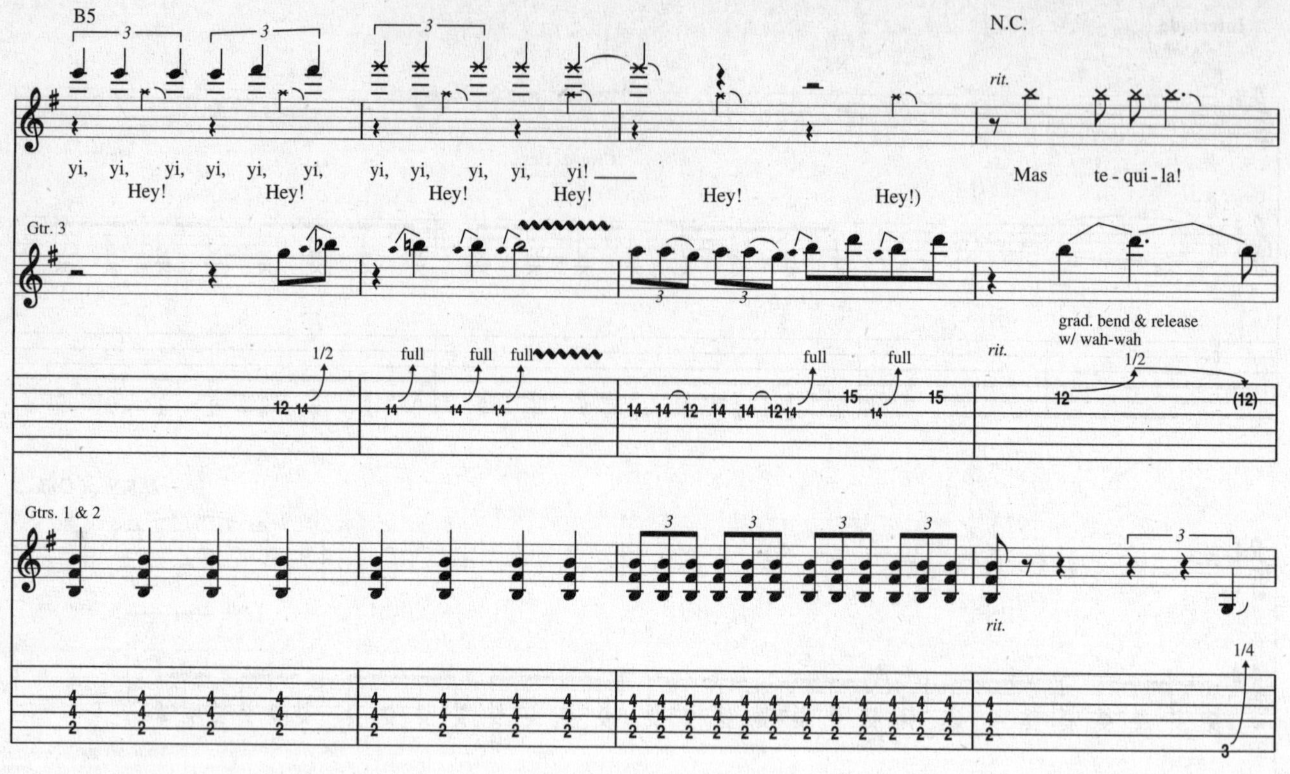

Free time

E5

Spoken: Yeah!

No mas, No mas.

Gtr. 3

Gtr. 2

Gtr. 1

1/2

Midnight Train

Words and Music by Jon Tiven and Roger Reale

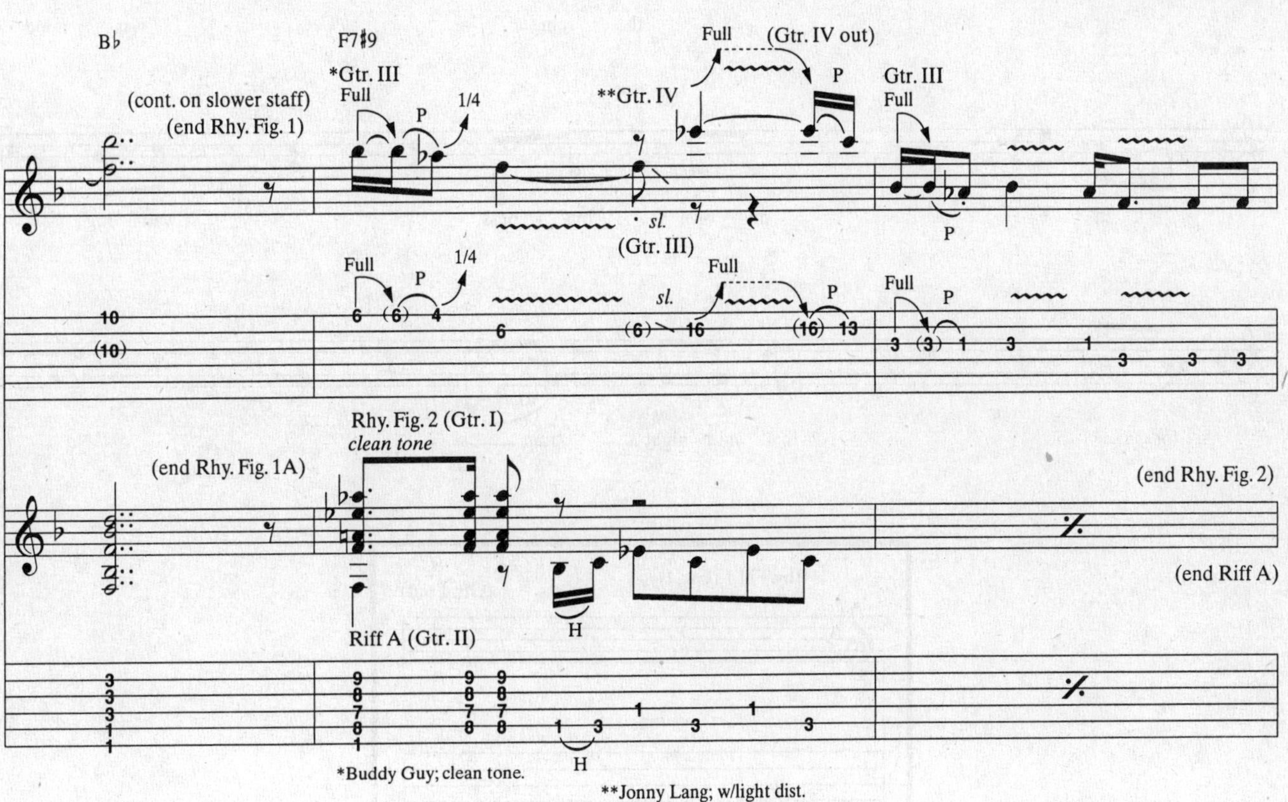

*Buddy Guy; clean tone.

**Jonny Lang; w/light dist.

w/Rhy. Fig. 2 & Riff A

(Gtr. I out)

1. I was

Full

Gtr. IV

(Gtrs. III & IV out)

sl. sl.

Gtr. III

Full

1 13 15 3/5 4 3 1 3 15 15 1 3

sl. sl. sl.

1st, 2nd Verses
w/Riff A (8 times)
2nd time w/Rhy. Fill 1
N.C.(F7)

stand - in' at the sta - tion, ten to mid -
2. *See additional lyrics*

night, in the rain. I was mind -

in' my own bus' - ness wait - ing

for that mid - night train. No -

Rhy. Fill 1 (Gtr. I)

(Gtr. I out)

1

2nd time Gtr. II substitute Riff A1 (4 times)
2nd time w/Fill 1
bod - y in— sight,—
star - in' at— my shoes.—
I took out my pa - per
to
Gtr. III
1/2
*Play 1st time only
P
*Next 5 bars.

find me some— good news,——
mind - in' my own bus' - ness,
sl.
Full
P
(Gtr. III out)

Riff A1 (Gtr. II)
H

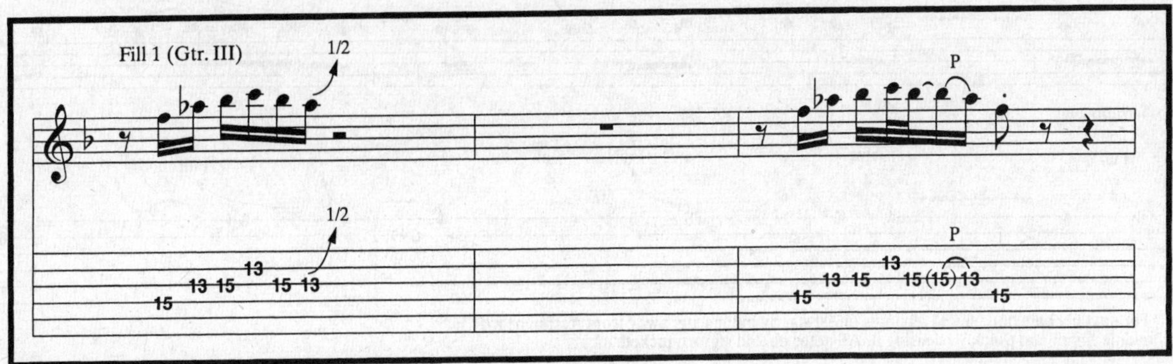
Fill 1 (Gtr. III)
1/2
P

*For next 6¾ bars only, sound all notes on 1st stg. by pulling stg. away from fretboard w/R.H. middle finger and quickly releasing it. All notes on 2nd stg. are picked.

Guitar solo
w/Rhy. Fig. 2 and Riff A (both 8 times)
B♭
F7♯9
grad. bend
(Gtr. III out)
Gtr. IV
w/heavier dist.
8va
loco
semi-harm.

(Gtrs. I & II out)
3rd Verse
N.C.
3. So I stood___ for for - ty min - utes. It was rain-
Gtr. IV
(Gtr. IV out)
*Gtr. V
*Distorted bass arr. for gtr.
in' and it was cold.___ When the ex - press rolled down the track,_
Gtr. V
I did not care where___ it was gon - na go.___
I did - n't care where___ ...gon - na go.___

Chorus
w/*Rhy. Fig. 2 and Riff A (both 4 times)
F7♯9
Yeah, yeah.
He said, "There ain't no mid - night train,
(Gtr. V out)
*Gtr. I w/rhythmic variations ad lib one bar before Outro solo.
there ain't no mid - night train,
there
ain't no mid - night train
com - in' down the line."
Outro solo
w/Rhy. Fig. 2 and Riff A (both till end)
F7♯9
Gtr. IV
Full
P
1/2
8va
sl.
loco
*Both stgs. bent w/ring finger.

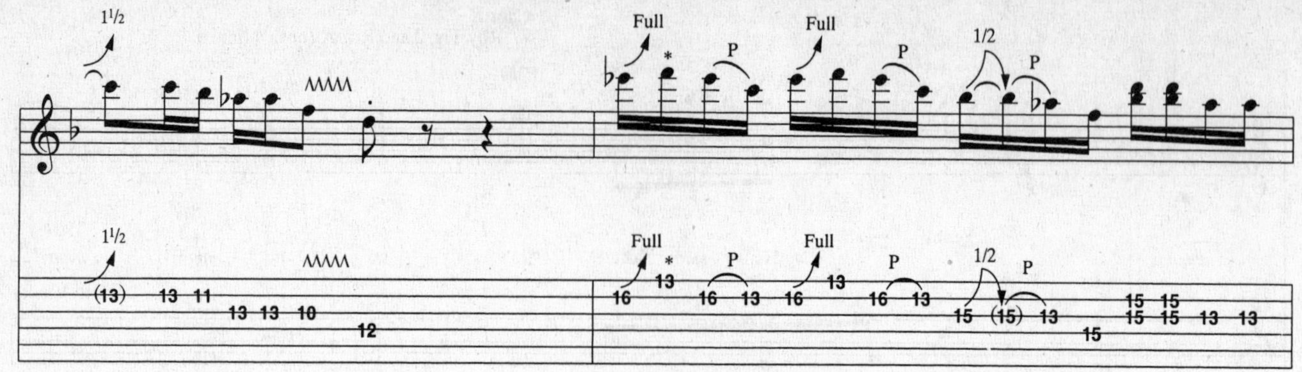

*Beginning at beat 1¼, this bar is played behind the beat.

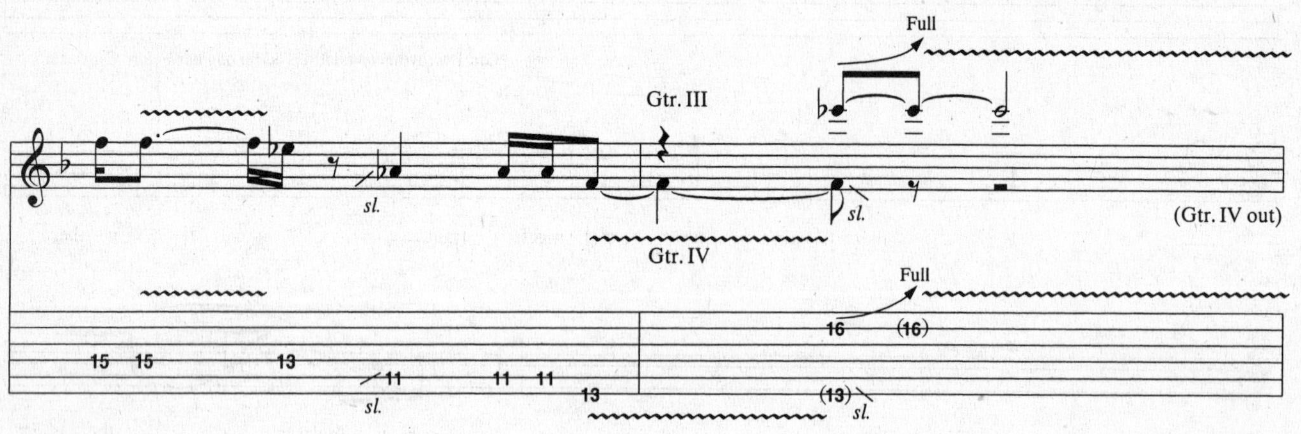

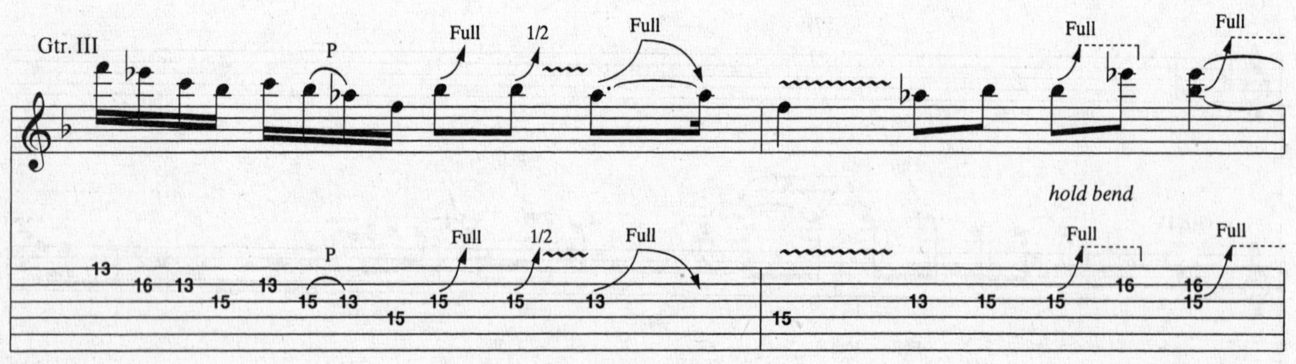

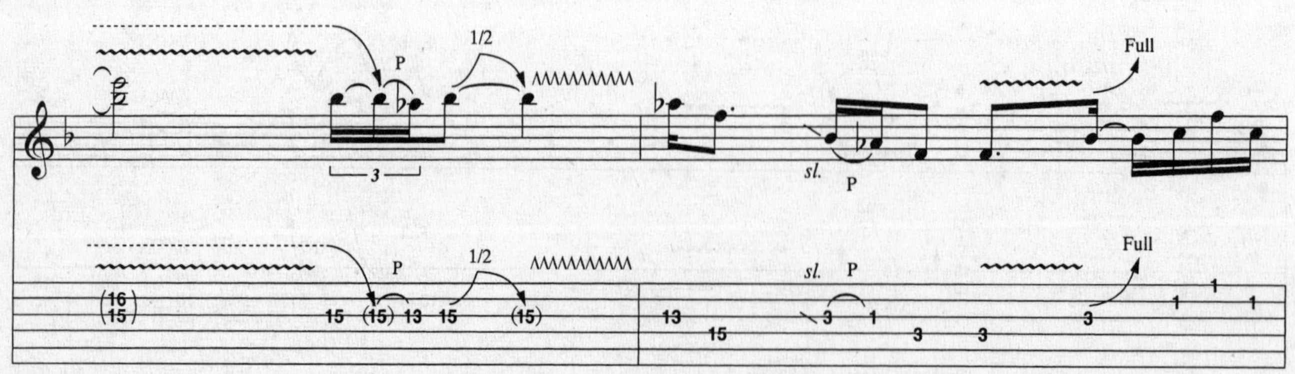

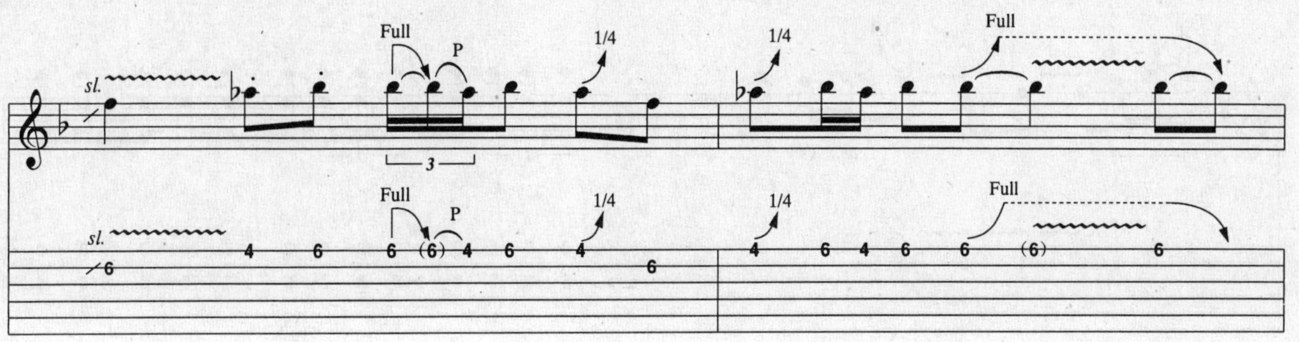

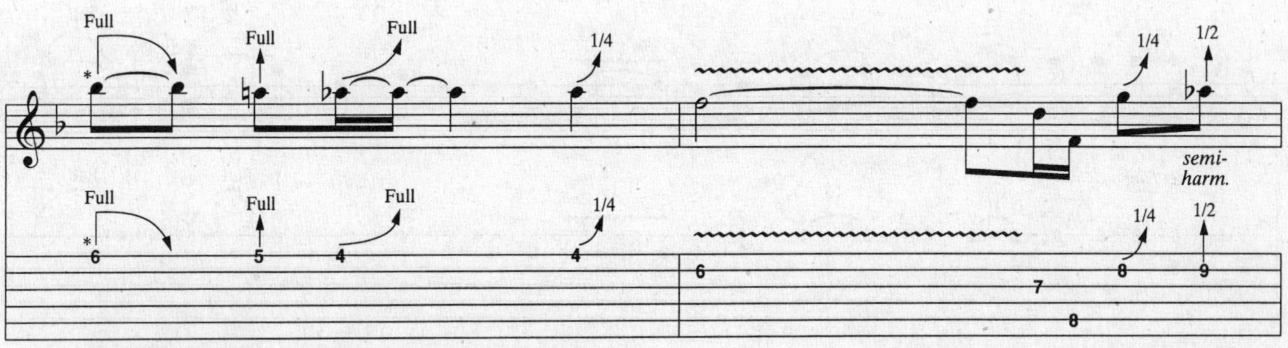

*Pull 1st stg. w/R.H. middle finger as before (next 3 bars only).

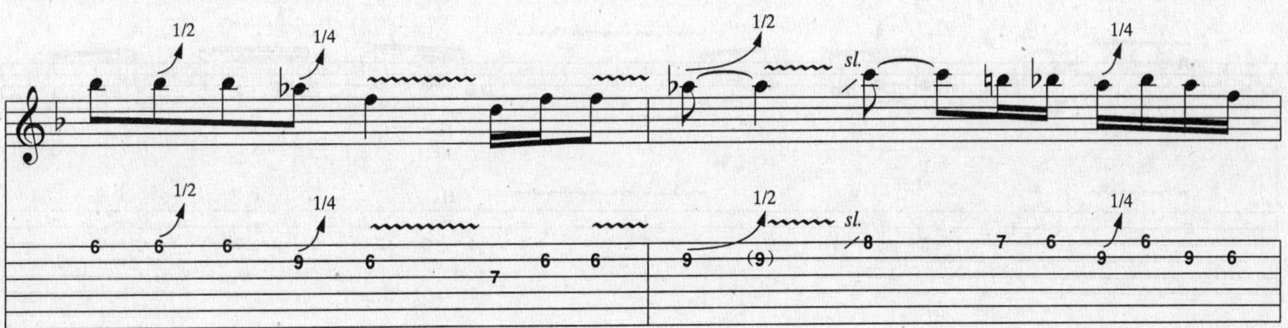

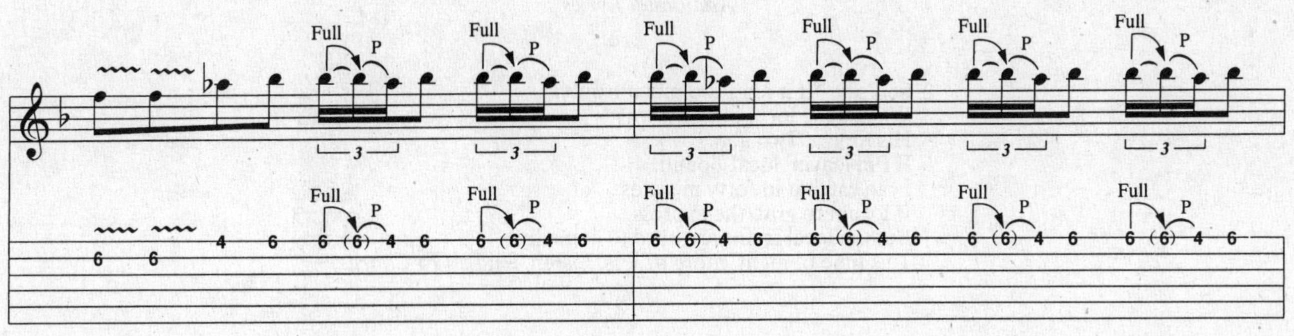

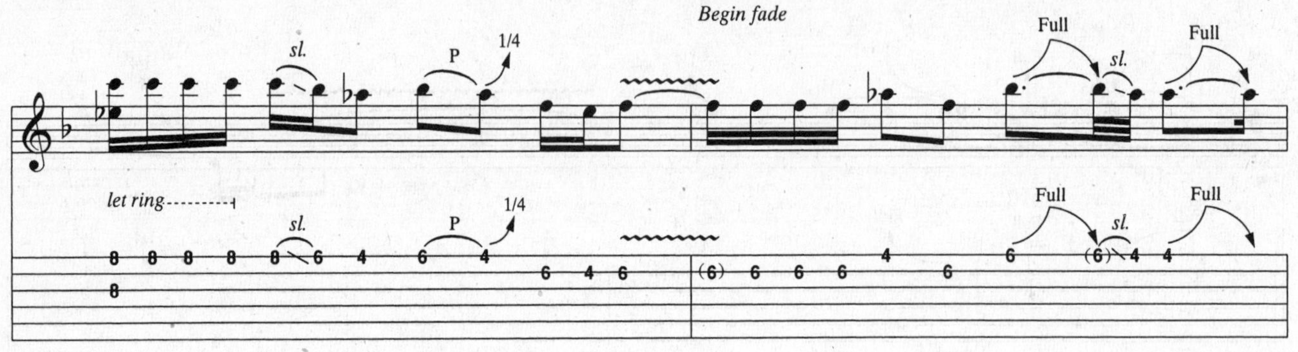

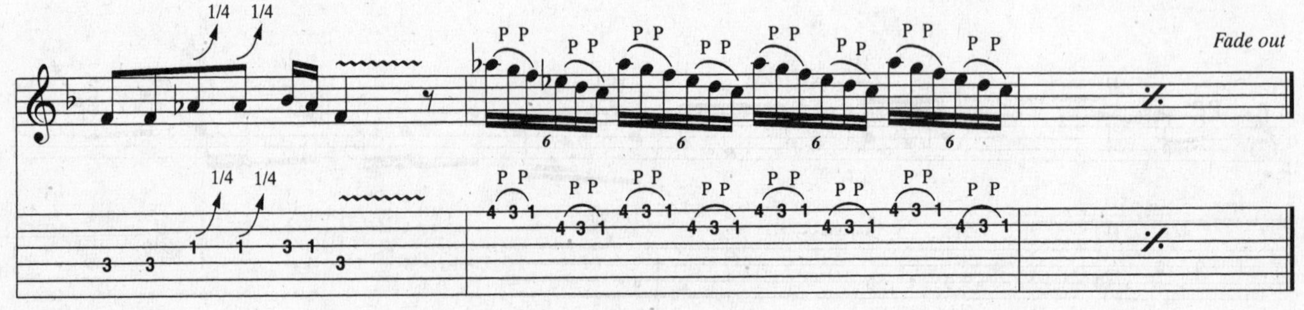

Additional Lyrics

2. So I say, "If it ain't too much trouble,
When's the local out of town?"
His reply: "Two a.m.,"
If I'm leavin' local-bound.
I can catch it in forty minutes
If I want to grab the express,
But the local trains are hard to come by
This time of night, more or less. Listen. Said... *(To Chorus)*

My Sharona

Words and Music by Doug Fieger and Berton Averre

Gtr. 1 tacet
C
B♭
F5
G5
time, Sha - ro - na? Oo, you make my mo - tor run,
eyes, Sha - ro - na? Keep - in' it a mys - ter - y.
time, Sha - ro - na? Is it d - d - des - ti - ny,
Gtrs. 1 & 2
Gtr. 2
my mo - tor run. Gun it com - in' off of the line, Sha - ro - na.
It gets to me. Run - nin' down the length of my thigh, Sha - ro - na. Nev -
d - des - ti - ny, or is it just a game in my mind, Sha - ro - na?
Chorus
G5
B♭
- ver gon - na stop; give it up. Such a dirt - y mind. I al - ways get it up for the touch of the young - er kind.
Gtr. 1
Gtr. 2

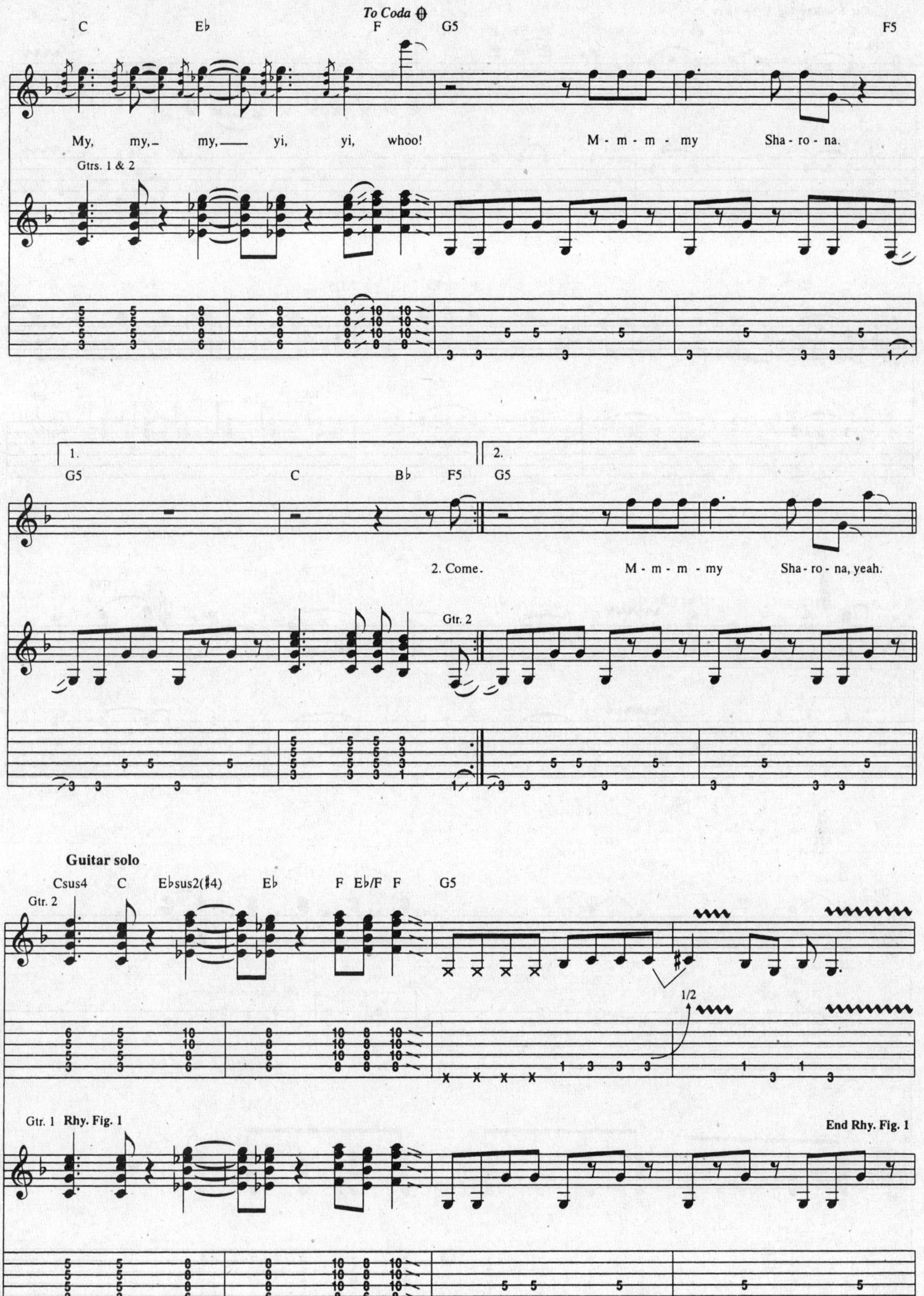
To Coda
C
E♭
F
G5
F5
My, my, my, yi, yi, whoo!
M - m - m - my Sha - ro - na.
Gtrs. 1 & 2
1.
2.
G5
C
B♭
F5
G5
2. Come.
M - m - m - my Sha - ro - na, yeah.
Gtr. 2
Guitar solo
Csus4
C
E♭sus2(♯4)
E♭
F
E♭/F
F
G5
Gtr. 2
1/2
Gtr. 1
Rhy. Fig. 1
End Rhy. Fig. 1

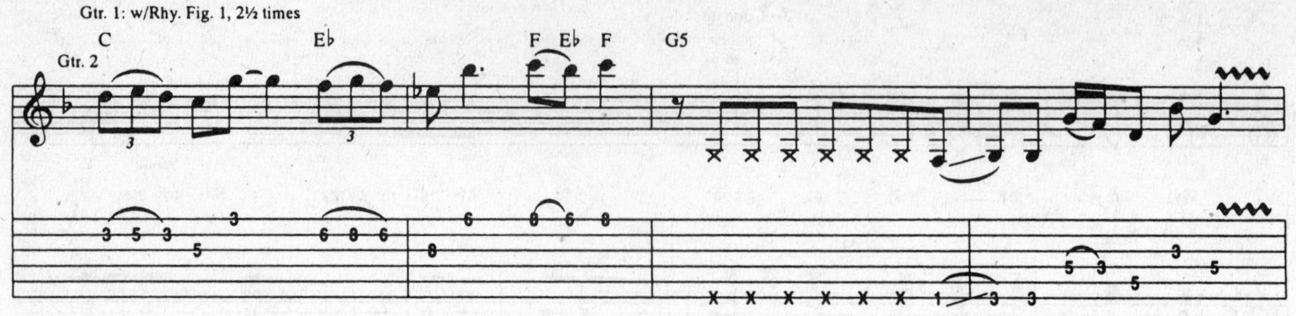

Gtr. 1: w/Rhy. Fig. 1, 2½ times
C
E♭
F E♭ F
G5
Gtr. 2

C
E♭
F E♭ F
G5
full
full

15ma
loco
C
E♭
F E♭ F
P.M.

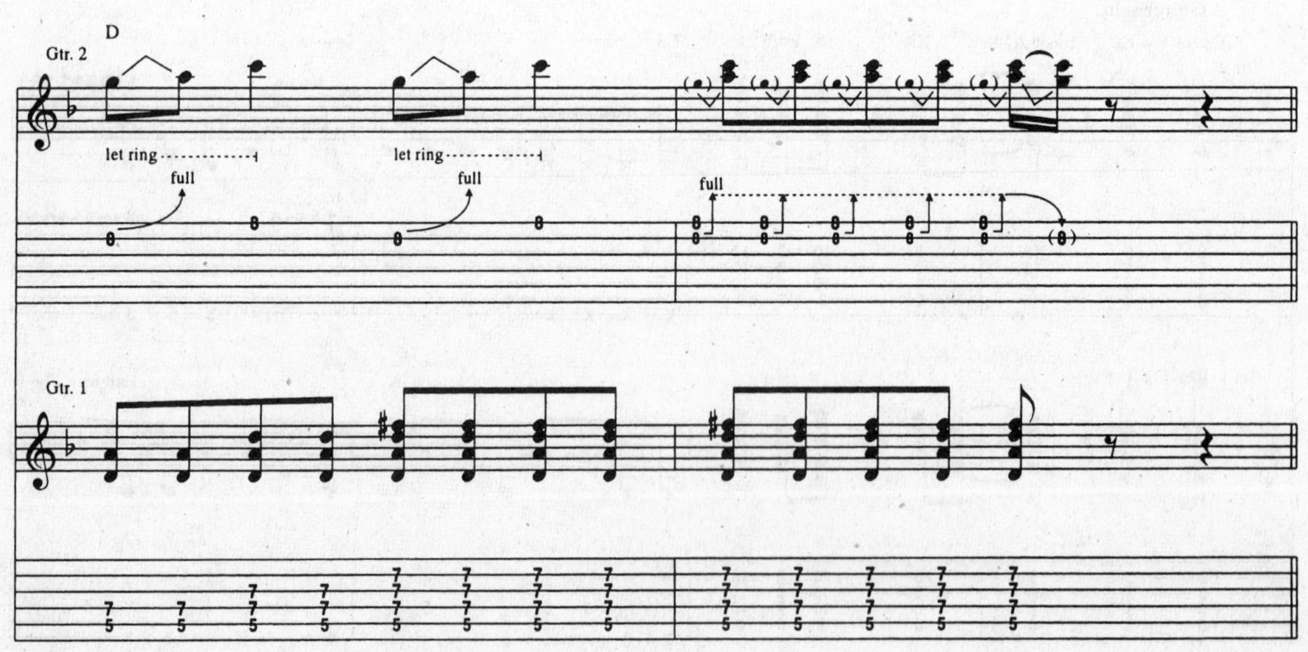

D
Gtr. 2
let ring
let ring
full
full
full
Gtr. 1

Interlude
G5
Gtrs. 1 & 2
F5
C
B♭
D.S. al Coda
3. When
Gtr. 2
Coda
E♭
F
M - m - m - m - m - m - m - my, my, my yi, yi whoo!
play 3 times
M - m - m - my Sha - ro - na.
M - m - m - my Sha - ro - na.

Interlude
C
G/C
F/C
G/C
C
G/C
F/C
G/C
Gtr. 1
Gtr. 2

Guitar Solo
C
G
F
G
C
G
F
G
Gtr. 2
full
Gtr. 1 Rhy. Fig. 2
End Rhy. Fig. 2

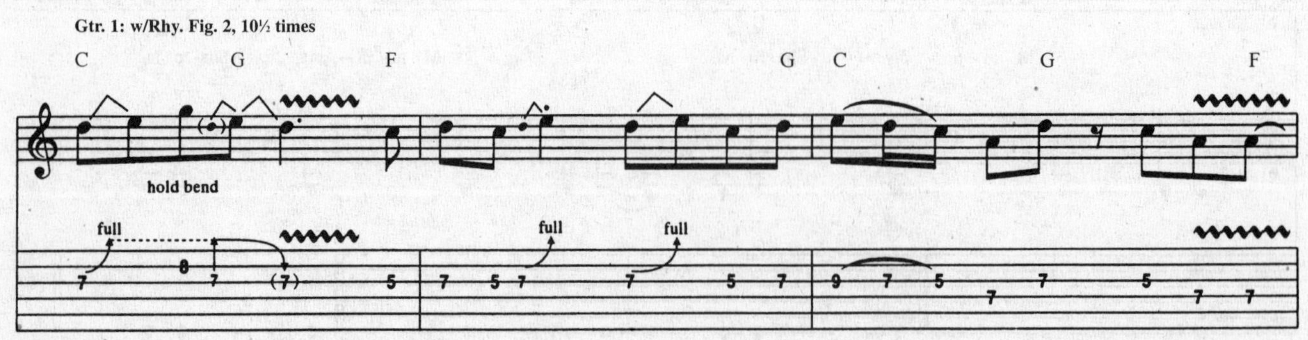
Gtr. 1: w/Rhy. Fig. 2, 10½ times
C
G
F
G
C
G
F
hold bend
full
full
full

F
G
C
G
F
let ring
full
hold bend

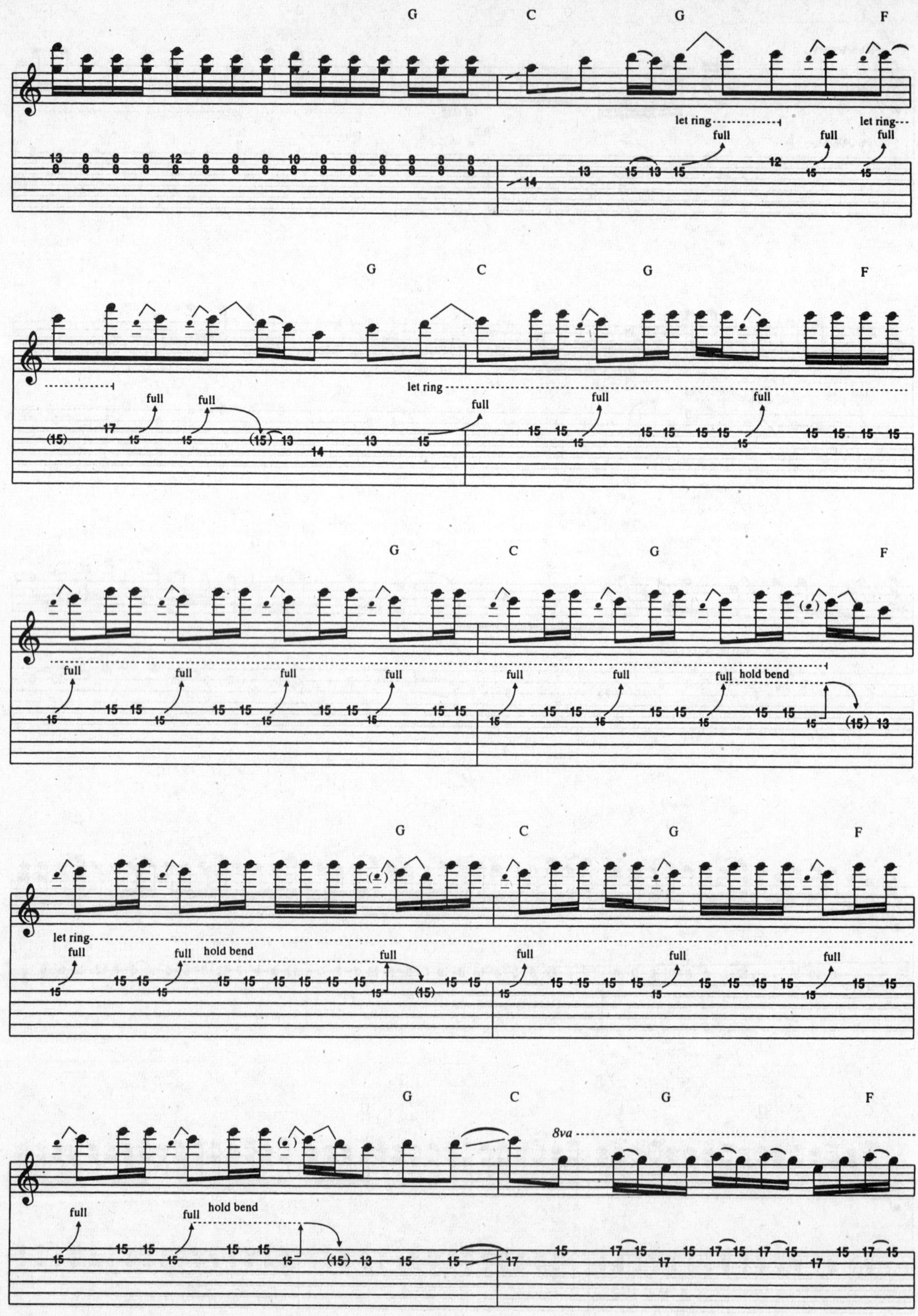
G
C
G
F
let ring
full
let ring
hold bend
8va

8va
G
C
G
F
G
full
17 15 17 15 15 17 15 17 15 15 17 15 17 15 17 15
18 18 18 18 18 18 18 18
C
G
F
G
C
G
F
8va
(18) 18 18 18 18 18 18 18 (18)
full
15 15 13 14 13
G
C
loco
G
full
15 13 14 13 15 15 12 15
12 12 15 12 10 12 10 8 10 8 7 8
7 5 6 5 6 5 8 7 6 5
3
3
C
G
F
G
C
G
F
full
full
full
full
full
full
7 5 8 7 9 7 9 7
(7) 5 7 5 5 7 5 7
(7) 5 5 7 5 5 7 5 5 7 5 5
G
C
G
F
full
G
C
G
F
G

C G F C G F
Gtr. 2
full
Gtr. 1
G C G F
C G F G

D
Interlude
G5
Gtrs. 1 & 2
F5 G5
play 3 times
F5
Outro
G5
F5 G5
Oo,
ah,
1., 2.
C
B♭
F5
3.
C
B♭
my Sha - ro - na.
my Sha - ro - na

No More Mr. Nice Guy

Words and Music by Alice Cooper and Michael Bruce

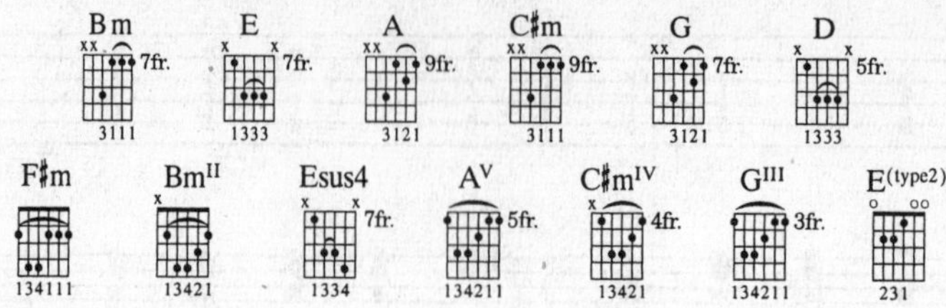

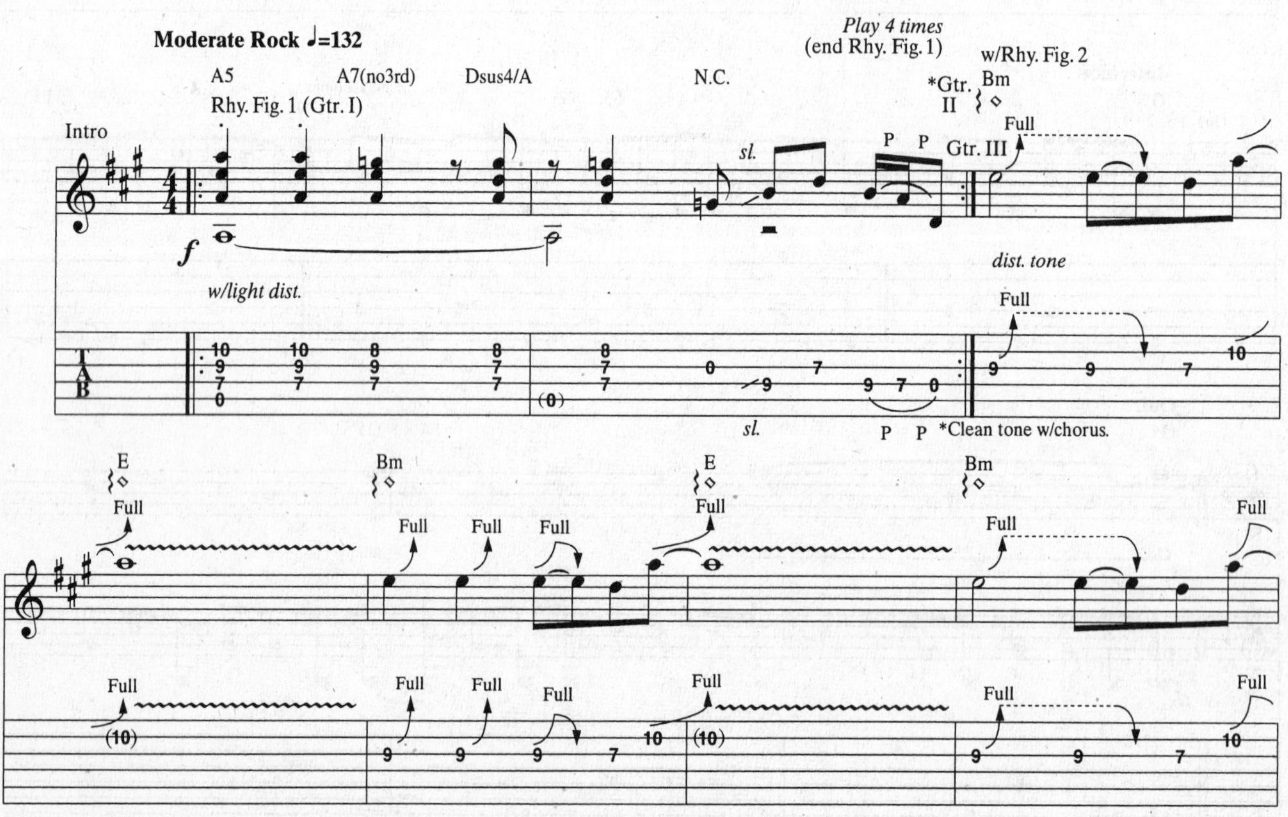

1st Verse
w/Rhy. Fig. 3
E
A
*C♯m
I used to be such a sweet, sweet thing— till they
Full
sl.
*Bass plays G♯ (this bar only).
G
Bm
D
E
A
got a hold of me.—
I o - pened doors for lit - tle -
(cont. in notation)
C♯m
G
Bm
D
E
— old la - dies;
I helped the blind to see.—
(Gtr. II out)
Rhy. Fig. 3 (Gtr. I)
1.
2.
(cont. in slashes)

Rhy. Fig. 4 (Gtr. I)
Pre-chorus
F♯m
BmII
D
E
sl.
I got no friends 'cause they read the pa - pers. They can't be seen-
Rhy. Fig. 4A (Gtr. II)
Esus4 E
with me And I'm get- tin' real shot down and I'm feel- in' mean.
H
*This bar doubled by Gtr. III.
(cont. in notation)
(end Rhy. Fig. 4)
Chorus
E5
D5
No more Mis - ter Nice Guy.
Gtr. III
Full
Gtr. II
(end Rhy. Fig. 4A)
*Rhy. Fig 5
*Gtr. I plays Rhy. Fig. 5 w/slight variations ad lib (throughout).

w/Rhy. Fig. 5
F♯m
N.C.
F♯m
E5
No more Mis - ter Clean.
No more Mis - ter Nice
Full
(end Rhy. Fig. 5)
(Gtr. II out)
D5
F♯m
N.C.
Guy. They say, "He's sick, he's ob - scene."
(Gtr. III out)
w/Rhy. Fig. 1 (4 times)
A5
A7(no3rd)
Dsus4/A
N.C.
(Ooh.)
1/2

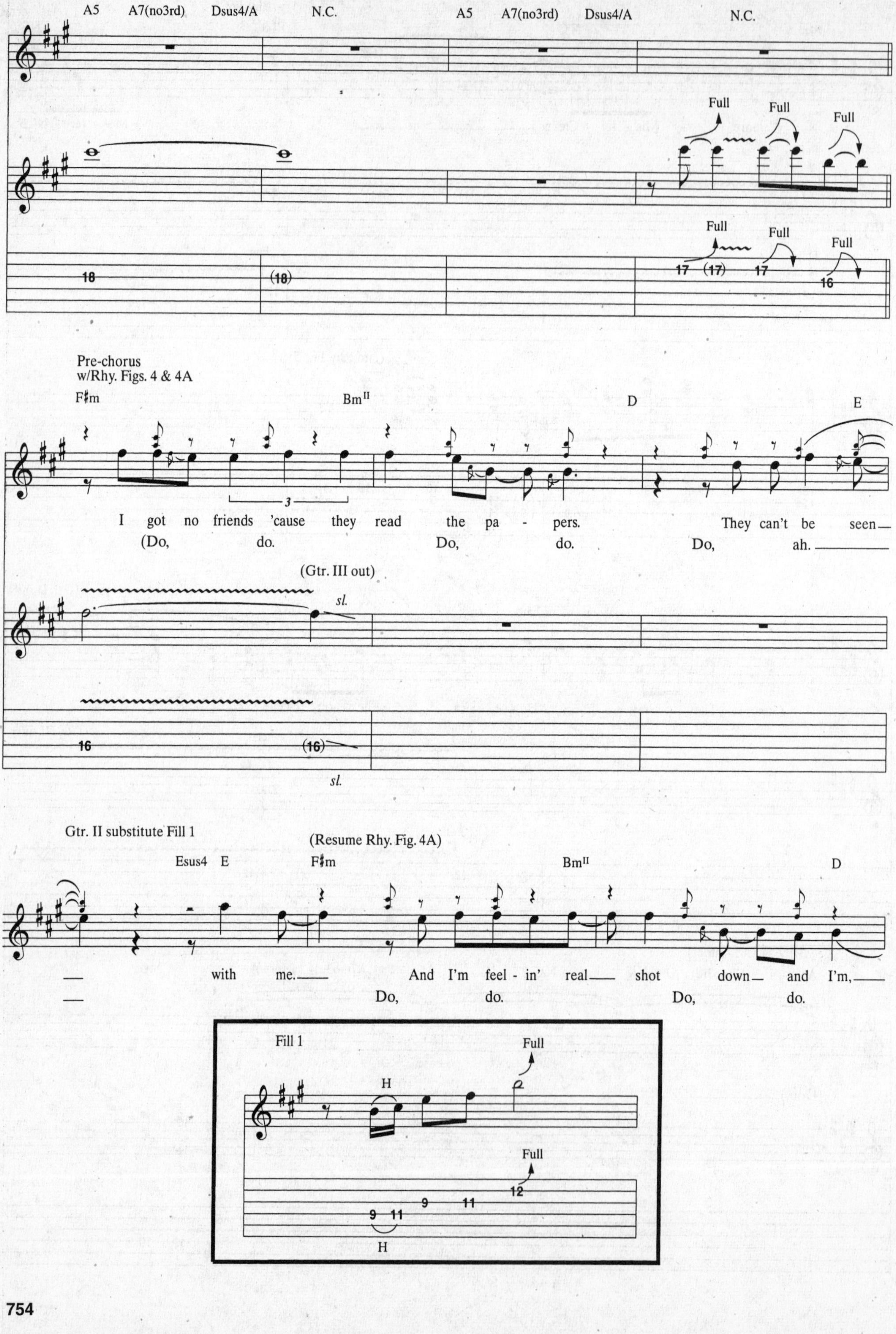

A5 A7(no3rd) Dsus4/A N.C. A5 A7(no3rd) Dsus4/A N.C.

Full Full Full

Full Full Full

18 (18) 17 (17) 17 16

Pre-chorus
w/Rhy. Figs. 4 & 4A

F♯m Bm[II] D E

I got no friends 'cause they read the pa - pers. They can't be seen —
(Do, do. Do, do. Do, ah. —

(Gtr. III out)

sl.

16 (16)

sl.

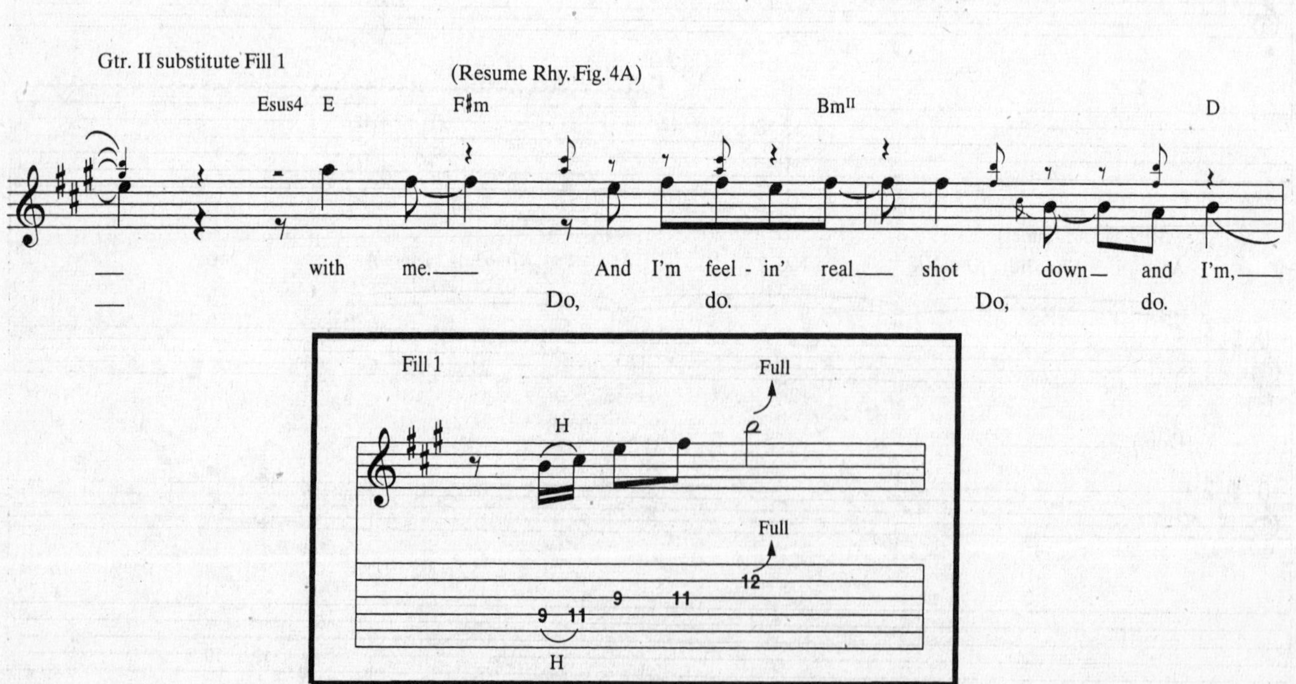

Chorus
w/Rhy. Fig. 5 (2 times)
E
D
F♯m
E5
I'm get - tin' mean.
Do, ah.)
No more Mis - ter Nice
Gtr. III
H
Full
semi-harm.
D5
F♯m
N.C.
Guy.
No more Mis - ter Clean.
Fill 2
Full
(end Fill 2)
F♯m
E5
D5
F♯m
N.C.
No more Mis - ter Nice Guy. They say, "He's sick, he's ob - scene."
(Gtr. III out)
2nd Verse
*Gtr. I
My dog bit me on the leg to - day.
Rhy. Fig. 6 (Gtr. II)
let ring
*Clean tone

G III
Bm II
E (type 2)
w/Rhy. Fig. 6
A V
My cat clawed my eyes.
My mom's been thrown out of the
C♯m IV
so - cial cir - cle and Dad has to hide.
Gtr. III
Full
sl.
Gtrs. I & II
*C♯m IV
*w/light dist.
I went to church in - cog - ni - to.
When ev - 'ry - bod - y rose,
D
*Bass plays G♯ (this bar only).
the Rev - 'rend Smith, he, he rec - og - nized me

Chorus
w/*Rhy. Fig. 5 (4 times) and Fill 2 (8 times)
GIII Bm II D E F♯m E5 D5
and punched me in the nose. He said, "No more Mis-ter Nice Guy.
sl.
sl.
*w/slight variations ad lib (both gtrs.)
F♯m N.C. F♯m E5
No more Mis-ter Clean. No more Mis-ter Nice
D5 F♯m N.C.
Guy." He said, "You're sick, you're ob-scene."
w/Bkgd. Voc. Fig. 1
F♯m E5 D5 F♯m N.C.
No more Mis-ter Nice Guy. No more Mis-ter Clean.
(Gtr. III out)
F♯m E5 D5 F♯m N.C.
No more Mis-ter Nice Guy. He said, "You're sick, you're ob-scene."
*A/E
Ooh.
Gtrs. I & II
*E played by bass.
Bkgd. Voc. Fog. 1
No more Mis-ter Nice Guy.

No Rain

Words and Music by Blind Melon

Chorus
E
E
⑥
open
D
D open
④
open
Dsus4
D
Rhy. Fig. 4
Gtr. 2
All I can say is that my life is pret - ty plain; I
Gtr. 1
Riff C
A
A
⑤
open
G5
E
E
⑥
open
E7
E
E7
E
End Rhy. Fig. 4
like watch - in' the pud - dles gath - er rain. And
End Riff C
Gtr. 2: w/ Rhy. Fig. 4
D
Dsus4
D
all I can do is just pour some tea for two and
Gtr. 1

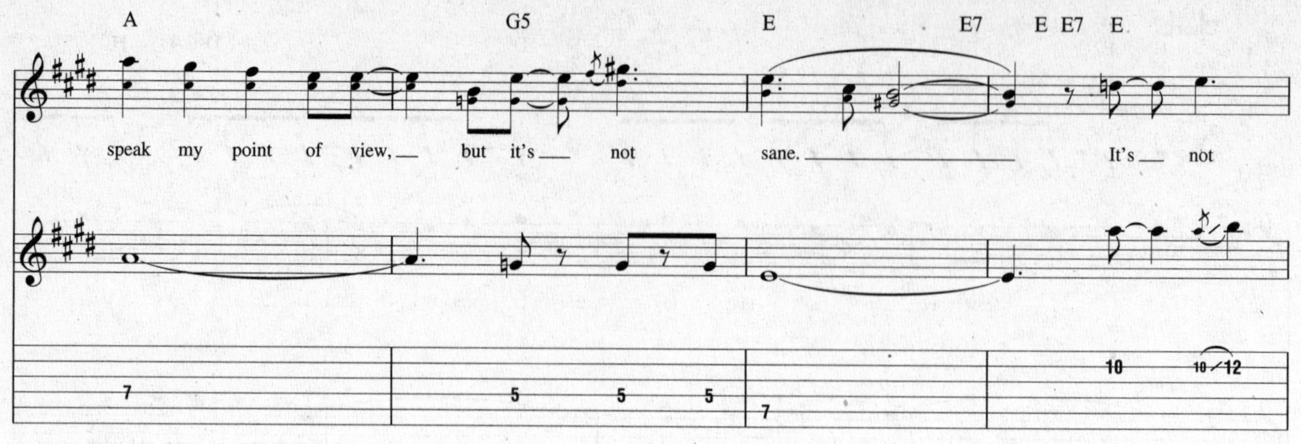
A
G5
E
E7
E E7 E
speak my point of view, __ but it's __ not sane. __ It's __ not
10
10 12
7
5 5 5
7

Verse
Gtr. 1: w/ Riff A
Gtr. 2: w/ Rhy. Fig. 2
Gtr. 1: w/ Riff B (1 3/4 times)
Gtr. 2: w/ Rhy. Fig. 3 (4 times)
E
D
sane. __ 1., 2. I just want some - one to

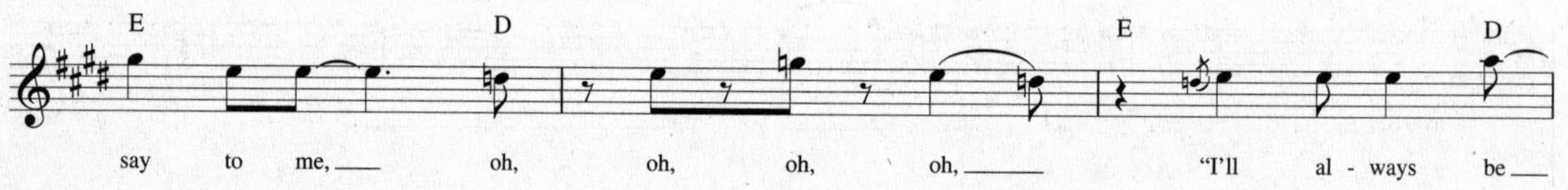
E
D
E
D
say to me, __ oh, oh, oh, oh, __ "I'll al - ways be __

E
D
__ there when __ you wake." __ Oh, yeah. __

E
D
E
D
Ya know I'd like to keep __ my cheeks __ dry to - day, __ hey. __

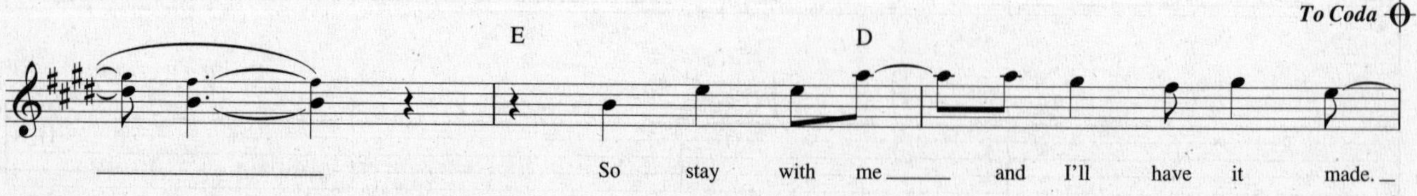
To Coda
E
D
So stay with me __ and I'll have it made. __

Chorus
Gtr. 1: w/ Riff C
Gtr. 2: w/ Rhy. Fig. 4 (1 1/2 times)
E
D
E
And I don't un - der - stand why I
(I'll have it made. And I...)
Gtr. 1
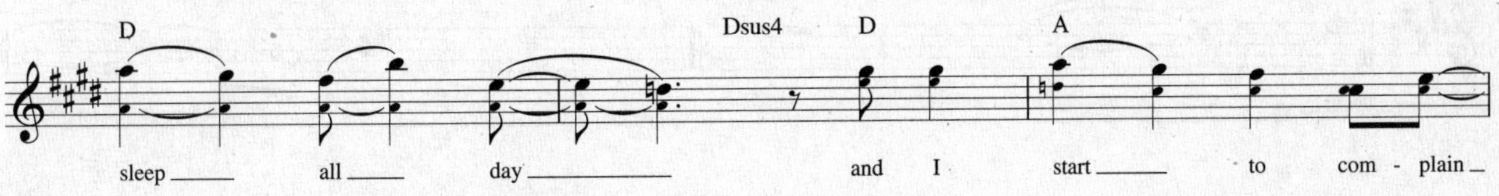
D
Dsus4
D
A
sleep all day and I start to com - plain

G5
E
E7
E E7 E
that there's no rain. And

D
Dsus4
D
all I can do is read a book to stay a - wake. And it
Gtr. 1
let ring
let ring

A
G5
E
E
⑥
open
Gtr. 2
rips my life a - way, ___ but it's a great es - cape, ___ es -
Gtr. 1
let ring
12
5 5 5
7
10 10 12

Gtr. 1: w/ Riff A (3 times)
Gtr. 2: w/ Rhy. Fig. 1
Gtr. 2: w/ Rhy. Fig. 2
cape, ___ es - cape. ___

Guitar Solo

Gtr. 2: w/ Rhy. Fig. 3 (4 times)
E
D
E
D
Go, yeah! ___
Gtr. 1
f
let ring

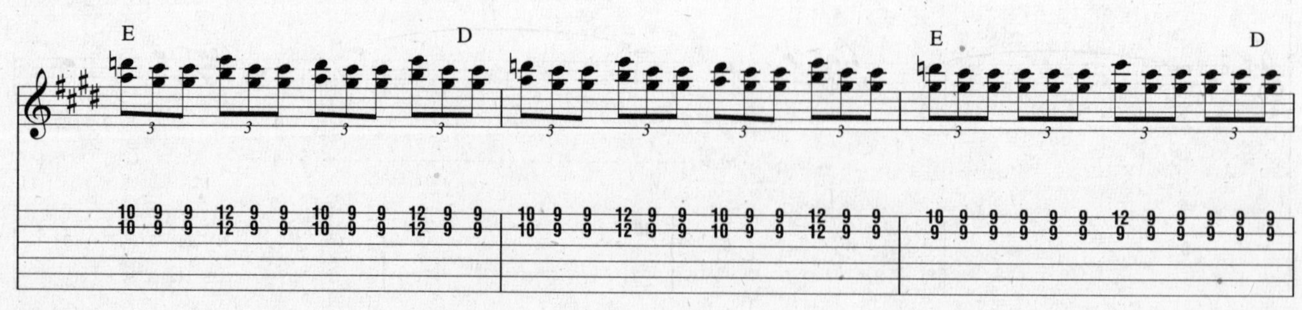
E
D
E
D

E
D
Oo,
hoo,
hoo.
Oh!

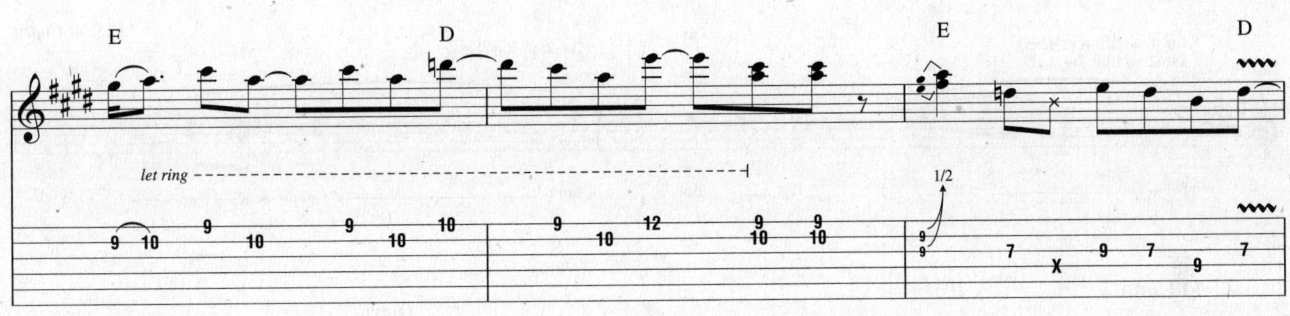
E
D
E
D
let ring
1/2

E
D
1/2
1

Chorus

E
D open
Gtr. 2
mp
All I can say is that my life is pret - ty plain. You don't
Gtr. 1
mp

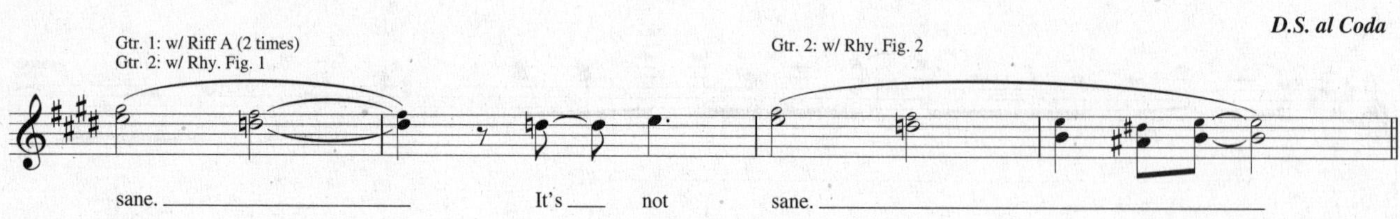

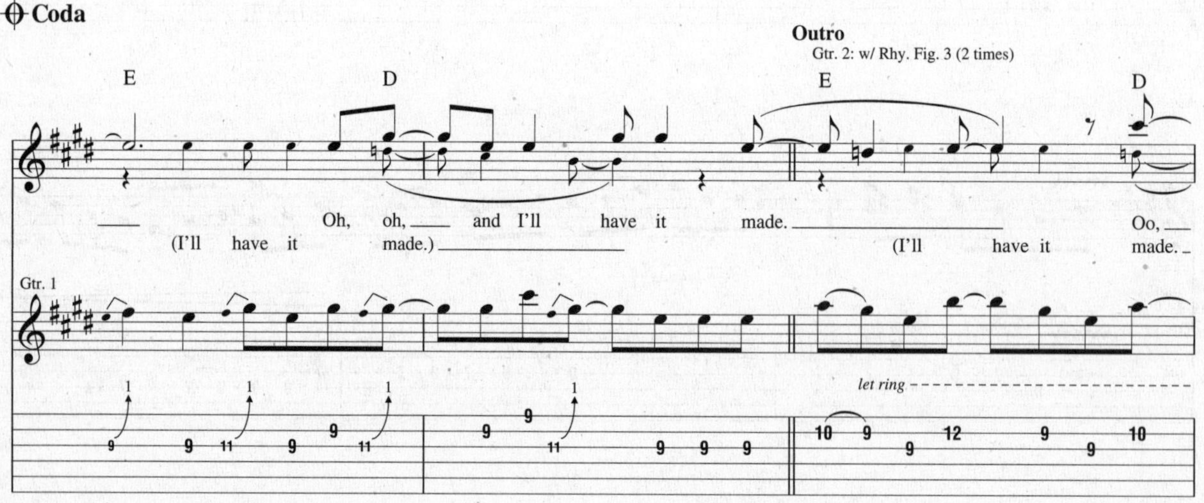

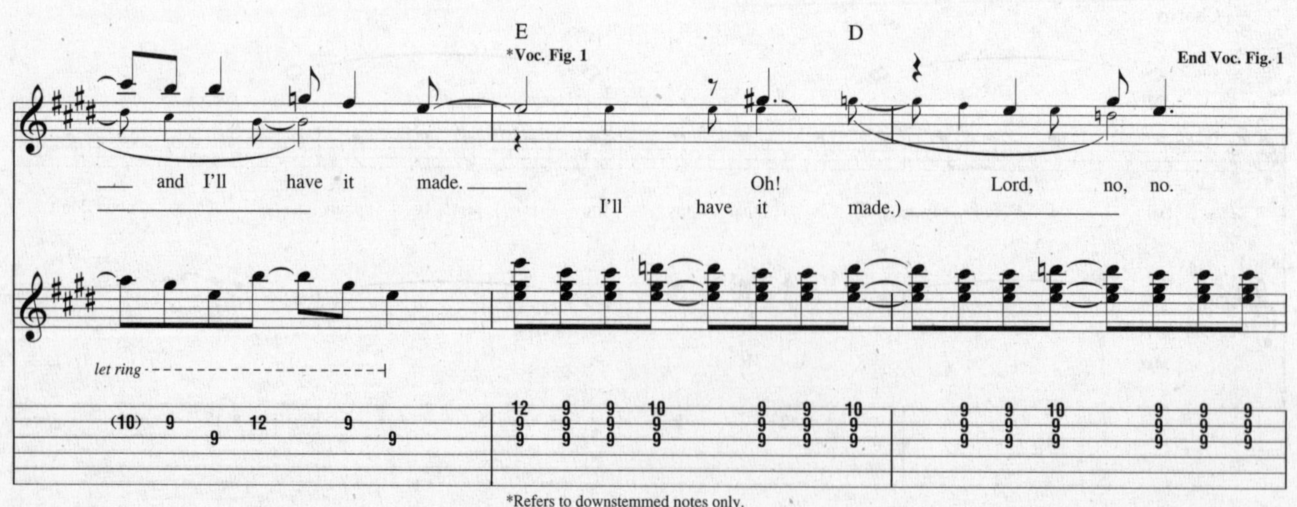

*Refers to downstemmed notes only.

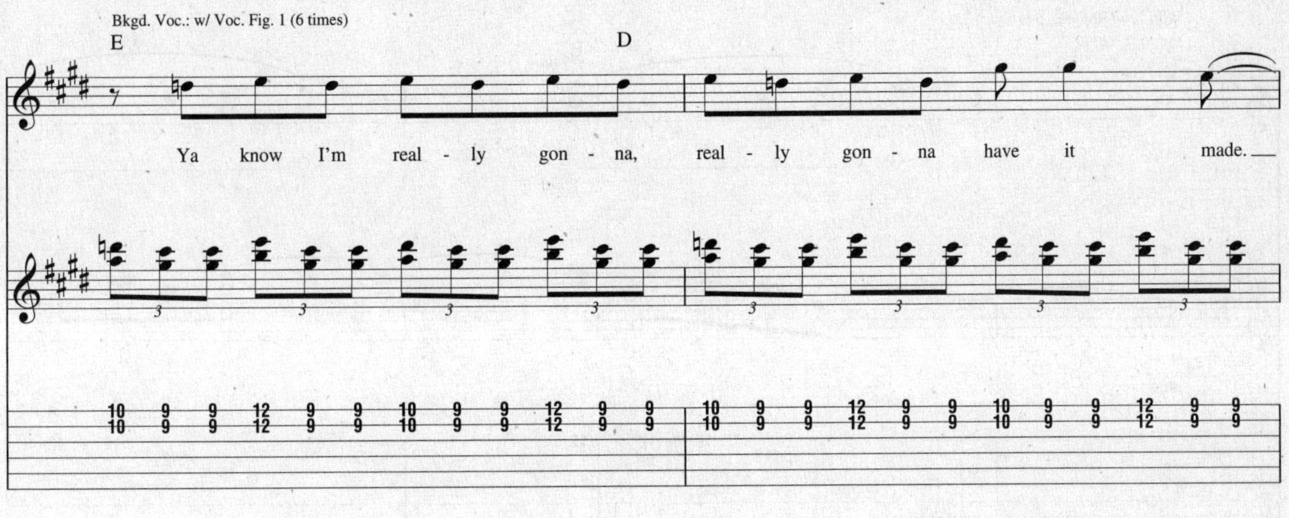
Bkgd. Voc.: w/ Voc. Fig. 1 (6 times)
E
D
Ya know I'm real - ly gon - na, real - ly gon - na have it made.

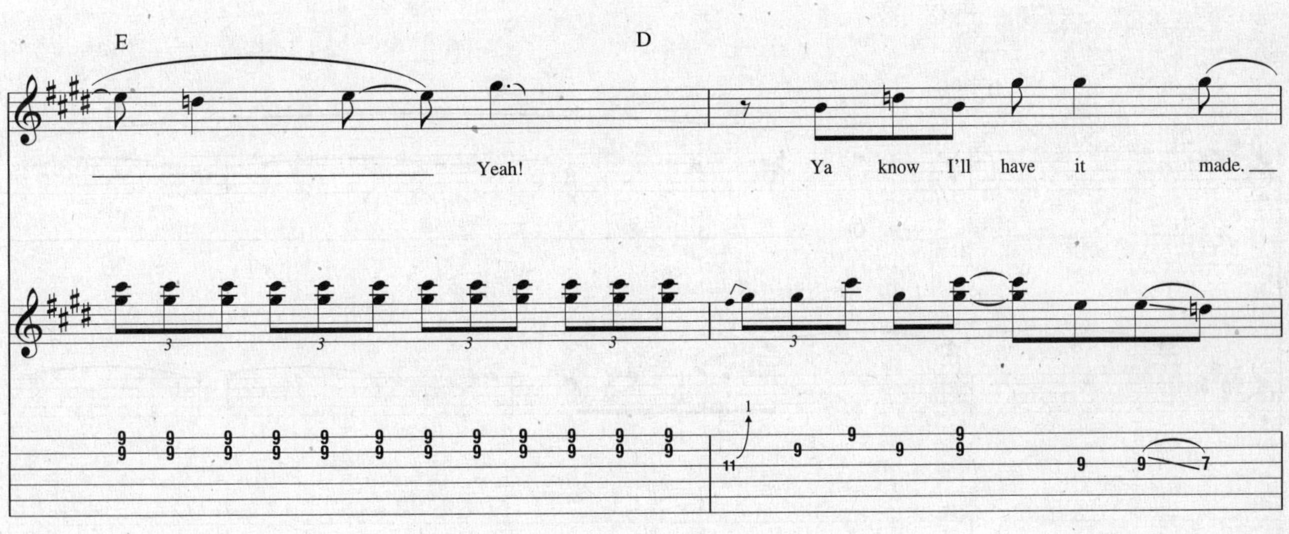
E
D
Yeah!
Ya know I'll have it made.

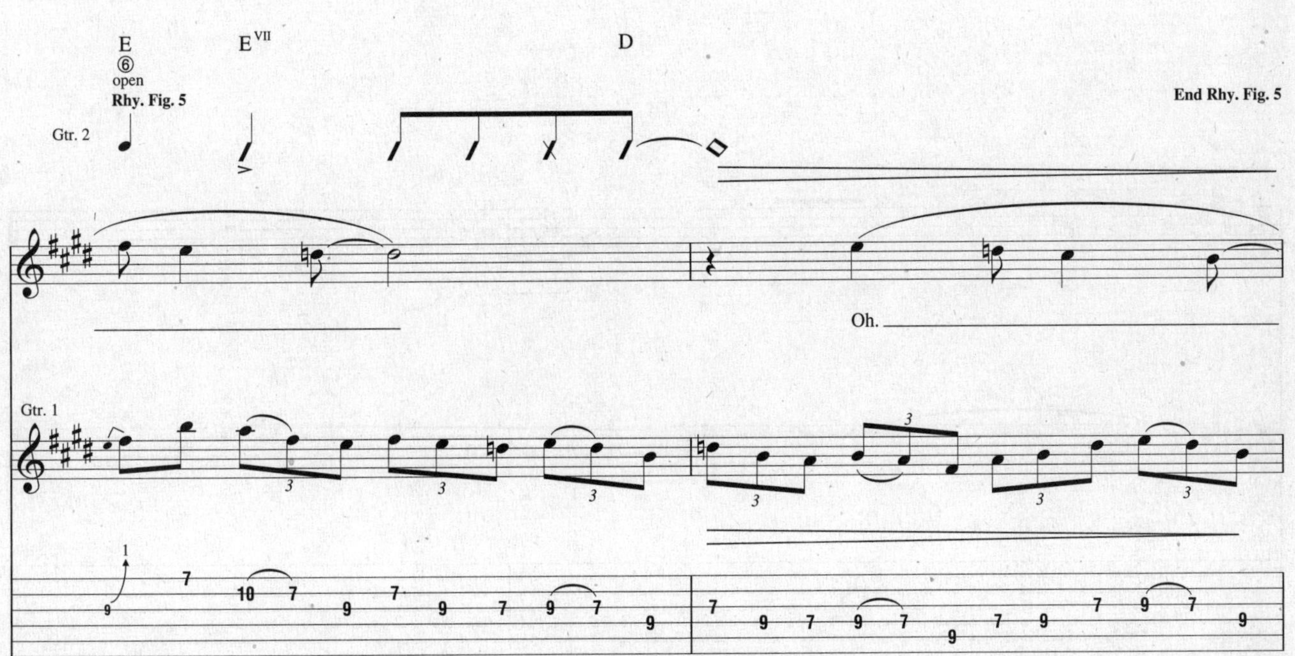
E
E VII
D
open
Rhy. Fig. 5
End Rhy. Fig. 5
Gtr. 2
Oh.
Gtr. 1

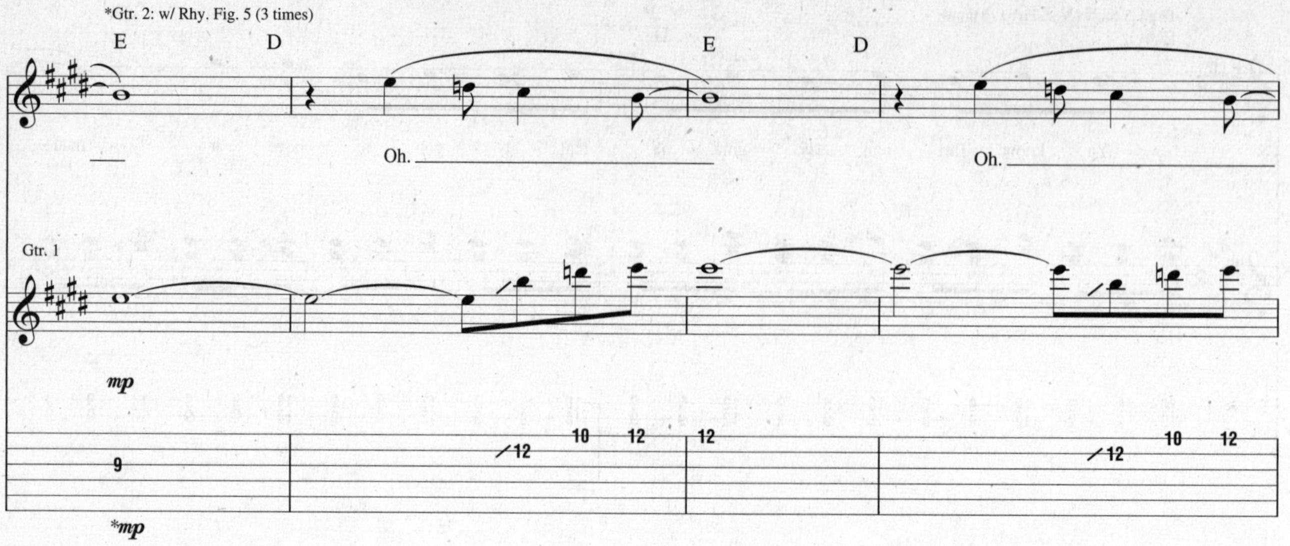
*Gtr. 2: w/ Rhy. Fig. 5 (3 times)
E
D
E
D
Oh.
Oh.
Gtr. 1
mp
*mp

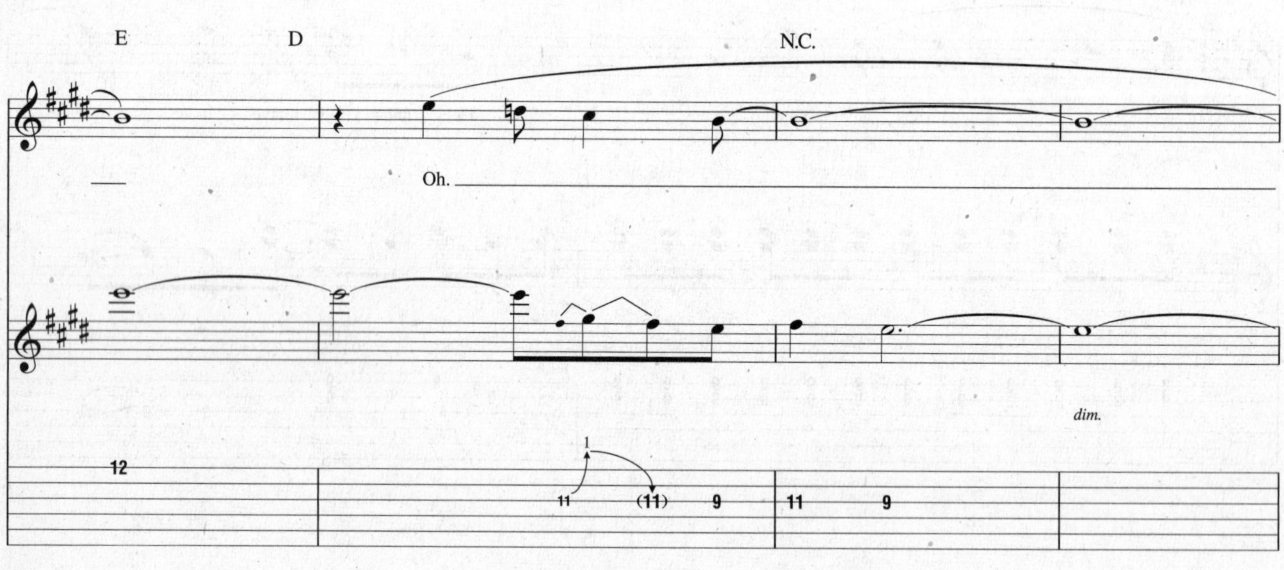
E
D
N.C.
Oh.
dim.

Oh,
oh,
oh,
oh,
oh.

Nookie

Words and Music by Fred Durst, Wesley Borland, Sam Rivers, John Otto and Leor Dimant

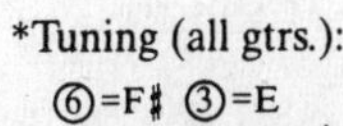

Play 4 times

*Wes Borland uses a custom 4-string guitar. You can use a standard 6- or 7-string, remove the top strings, and tune the bottom 4 strings as indicated using heavy gauge strings (the 6th is a .65 bass string).

**Music sounds a minor 3rd lower than written.

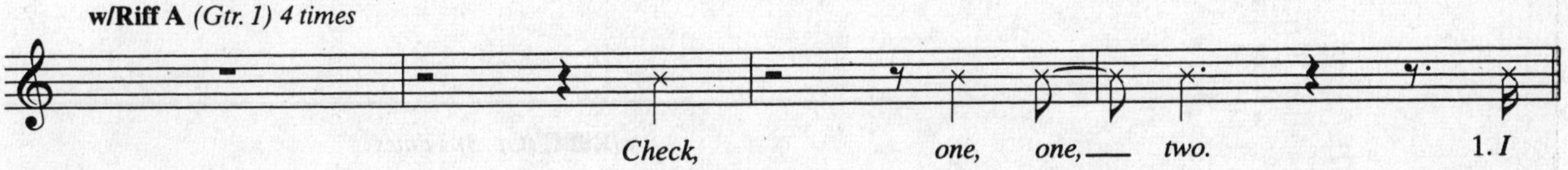

w/Riff A (Gtr. 1) 4 times

Check, one, one, two. 1. *I*

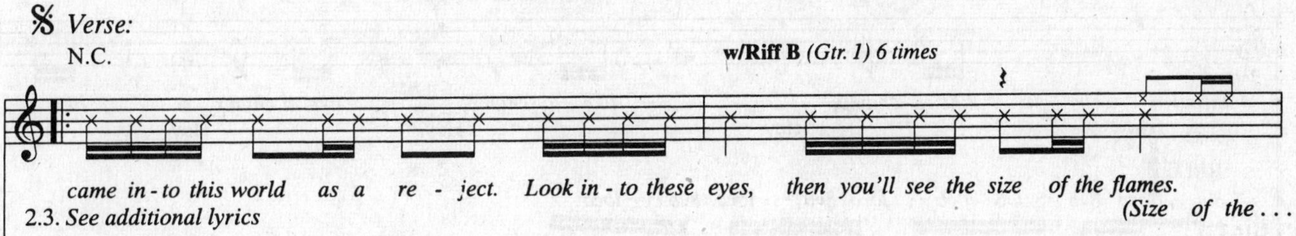

𝄋 *Verse:*

N.C.

w/Riff B (Gtr. 1) 6 times

came in-to this world as a re-ject. Look in-to these eyes, then you'll see the size of the flames.

(Size of the...

2.3. *See additional lyrics*

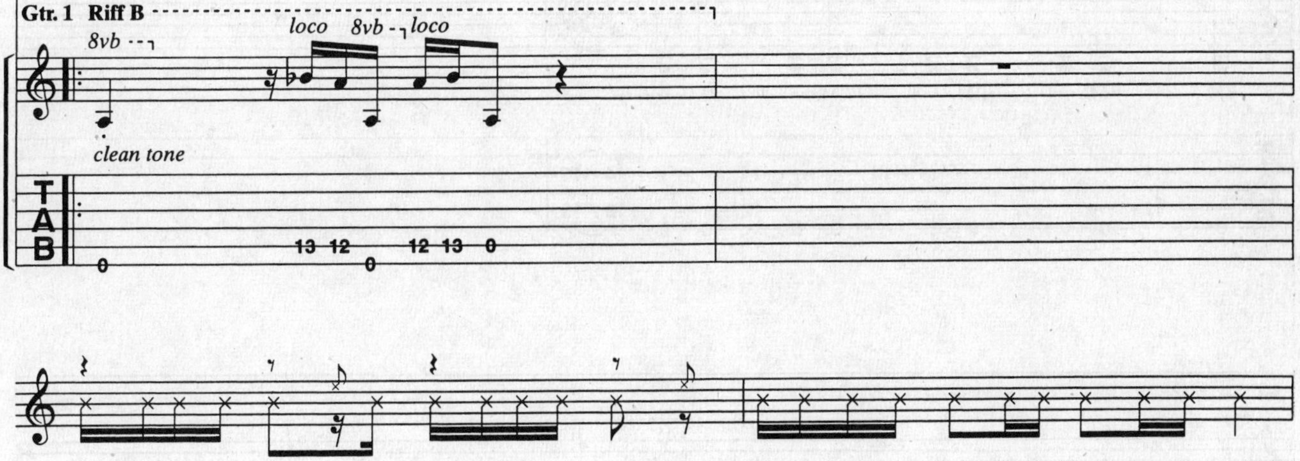

Gtr. 1 Riff B

8vb loco 8vb loco

clean tone

T A B 0 13 12 0 12 13 0

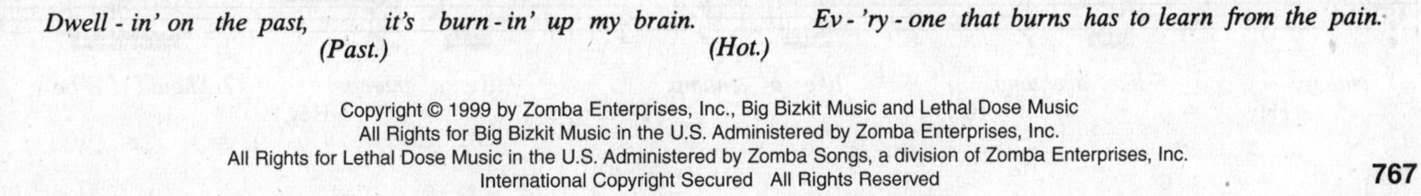

Dwell-in' on the past, it's burn-in' up my brain. Ev-'ry-one that burns has to learn from the pain.

(Past.) (Hot.)

Hey, I think a-bout the day my girl-ie ran a-way with my pay when fel-las came to
(Days.)

w/Fill 1 (Gtr. 2)
1.
play. Now she's stuck with my hom-ies that she f***ed, and I'm just a suck-er with a lump in my
(Play.)
(Ooh.)
Gtr. 1
Rhy. Fill 1
8vb
loco
8vb
13 12 0 12 13 0
0

w/Riff C (Gtr. 3) 3 times
throat like a chump, like a chump, like a chump, like a
(Hey. Hey. Hey. Hey.
Riff C
8vb loco 8vb loco 8vb loco 8vb loco 8vb loco
Gtr. 1
P.M. P.M. P.M. P.M. P.M.
14 14 14 14 14 15
12 12 12 12 12 13
0 0 0 0 0 0 0 0 0

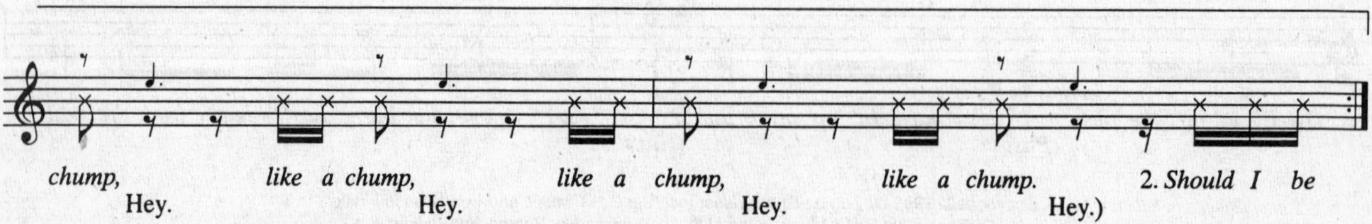
chump, like a chump, like a chump, like a chump. 2. Should I be
Hey. Hey. Hey. Hey.)

2.
To Next Strain
w/Riff B (Gtr. 1)
I won't lie that I can't de-ny.
3.
w/Rhy. Fill 1 (Gtr. 1)
heart in a blend-er and still I sur-ren-dered
w/Riff C (Gtr. 1) 4 times
like a chump, like a
(Hey. Hey.
chump, like a chump, like a chump, like a chump, like a chump, like a chump.
Hey. Hey. Hey. Hey. Hey.)
Chorus:
w/Riff A (Gtr. 1) 8 times
I did it all for the nook-ie, come on, the nook-ie, come on. So you can take that cook-ie and
Gtr. 2
Fill 2
end Fill 2
dist. tone
1
1/2
w/Fill 2 (Gtr. 2) 4 times
stick it up your. . .Yeah! Stick it up your. . .Yeah! Stick it up your. . .Yeah! Stick it up your. . .
I did it all for the nook-ie, come on, the nook-ie, come on. So you can take that cook-ie and
To Coda
1.
D.S.
stick it up your. . .Yeah! Stick it up your. . .Yeah! Stick it up your. . .Yeah! Stick it up your. . .
2.
Bridge:
N.C.(A5)
Stick it up your. . .Yeah! Stick it up your. . .
I'm on-ly hu-
Riff D
8vb
mf
clean tone

w/Bkgd. vcl. ad lib. (next 14 bars)
G5
C5
B♭5
man.
It's so eas - y for your friends
to give you their ad - vice.
8vb
loco
end Riff D
w/Riff D (Gtr. 1) 3 times
A5
They'll tell you just let it go.
It's
G5
C5
B♭5
A5
eas - i - er said than done.
I ap - pre - ci - ate it.
G5
C5
B♭5
I do, but just leave me a - lone.
G5
C5
B♭5
Leave me a - lone.
Just leave me a - lone,
A5
C5
Ain't noth - ing gon - na change,
'cause you can go a - way
a - lone,
a - lone,
Riff E
8vb
loco
Gtr. 1
f dist. tone

D5
B♭5
A5
and I'm just gon - na stay here and al - ways be the same.
a - lone, a - lone,
8vb loco
8vb loco
end Riff E
f
T
A
B
w/Riffs E (Gtr. 1) 2 times & E1 (Gtr. 2) 1 1/2 times
C5
Ain't noth - ing gon - na change, 'cause you can go a - way
a - lone, a - lone,
D5
B♭5
A5
and I'm just gon - na stay here and al - ways be the same.
a - lone.
C5
Ain't noth - ing gon - na change, 'cause you can go a - way
Al - ways be the same, al ways be the same,
D.S.S. %% al Coda
D5
E5
G5
and I'm just gon - na stay here and al - ways be the same.
you'll al - ways be the same.
Gtr. 2
T
A
B
*Hold note into Chorus.

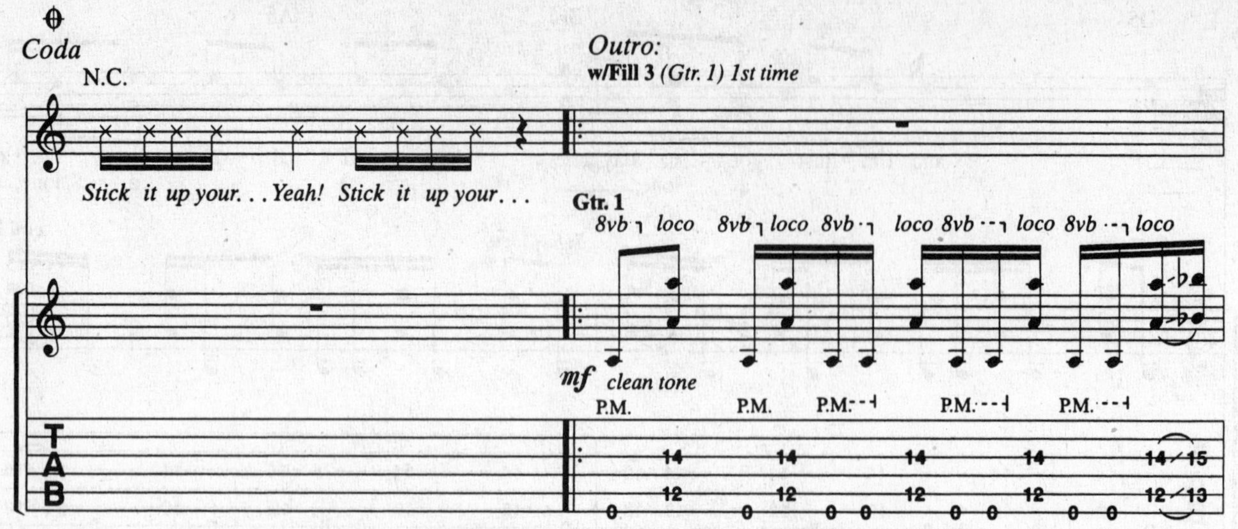

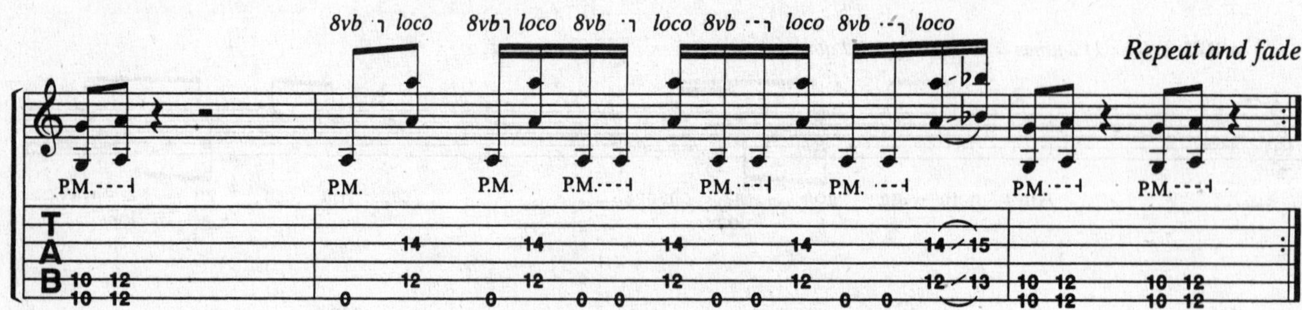

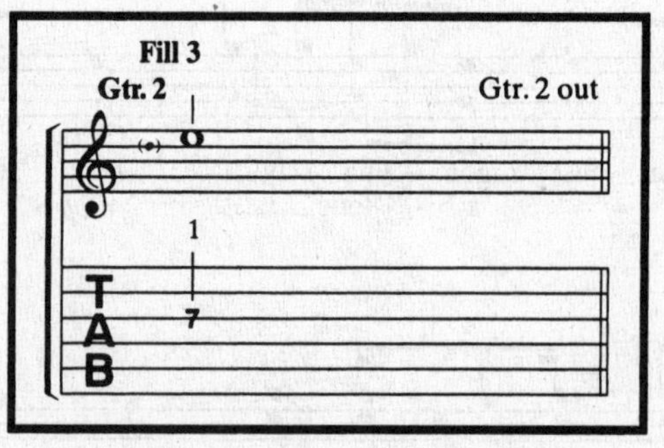

Verse 2:
Should I be feelin' bad? (No.) Should I be feelin' good? (No.)
It's kinda sad, I'm the laughin' stock of the neighborhood.
And you would think that I'd be movin' on, (Movin'.)
*But I'm a sucker like I said, f***-up in the head. (Not.)*
Maybe she just made a mistake and I should give her a break.
My heart'll ache either way.
Hey, what the hell. What you want me to say?
I won't lie, that I can't deny.
(To Chorus:)

Verse 3:
Why did it take so long?
Why did I wait so long, huh, to figure it out?
But I didn't.
And I'm the only one underneath the sun who didn't get it.
I can't believe that I could be deceived (But you were.) by my so-called girl,
But in reality had a hidden agenda.
She put my tender heart in a blender,
And still I surrendered
(Hey.) like a chump, etc.
(To Chorus:)

Oh Well Part 1

Words and Music by Peter Alan Green

*Chord symbols reflect overall harmony.

**Play 2nd time only (next 3 bars).

2.
Fill 1
End Fill 1
Gtr. 3 (elec.)
w/ dist.
f
1/4
Gtrs. 1 & 2
Rhy. Fig. 1

End Rhy. Fig. 1
Verse
Gtrs. 1 & 2 tacet
N.C.(Em)
Gtr. 3 tacet
1. I can't help a - bout the shape I'm in. I can't sing, I ain't pret - ty and my legs are thin.

But don't ask me what I think of you. I might not give the an-swers that you want me to.
Gtr. 1
Fill 2
End Fill 2
0 3 0

Gtr. 1: w/ Riff A (1st 3 meas.)
Em
Gtr. 1: w/ Fill 1
Mm.
Oh, well.
Gtr. 2

Gtr. 3
Gtrs. 1 & 2

Gtr. 3
Gtr. 2
Gtr. 1
divisi
Guitar Solo
Double-time feel
Em
Gtr. 3
Gtr. 4
Gtr. 2
Gtr. 1

Gtr. 1 tacet
Gtr. 2 tacet
Gtr. 3
Gtr. 4
Gtr. 2
Gtrs. 3 & 4 tacet
Verse
N.C.(Em)
2. Now, when I talked to God I knew He'd un - der - stand. He said,
stick by me and I'll be your guid-ing hand.
But don't ask me what I think of you. I might
Gtr. 1: w/ Fill 2
Gtr. 1: w/ Riff A (1st 3 meas.)
Em
not give the an-swer that you want me to.
Mm.
Gtr. 2

Gtr. 1: w/ Fill 1
Well.
Gtrs. 1 & 2: w/ Rhy. Fig. 1
Gtr. 3
Gtr. 4

Gtrs. 3 & 4
Play 4 times
Gtrs. 1 & 2
Outro
Gtrs. 2, 3 & 4 tacet
Gtr. 1
D
Em
Bm
f
let ring throughout
Gtr. 2
divisi
Am
Repeat and fade

Once Bitten Twice Shy

Words and Music by Ian Hunter

D5
C5
o - ver God's world.
You can't re - mem - ber when you got your last meal
P.M.
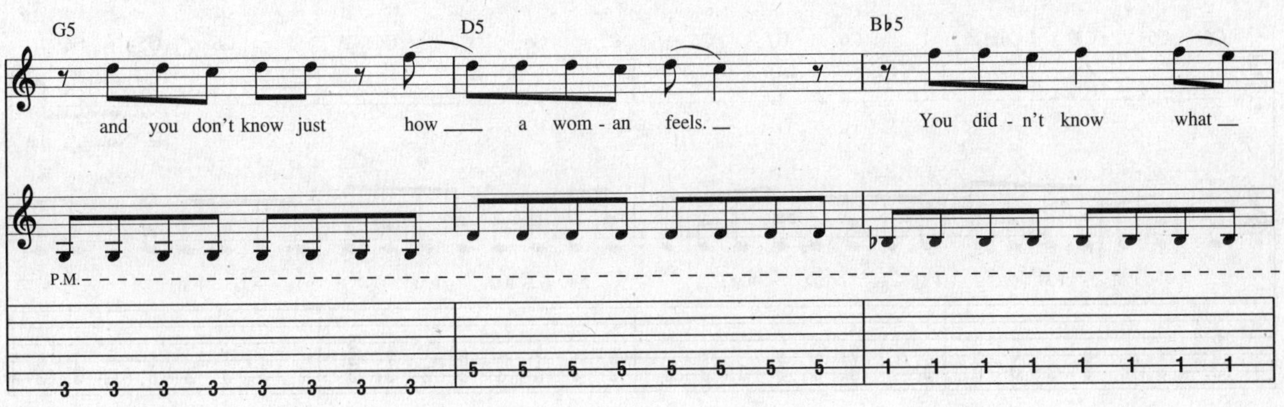
G5
D5
B♭5
and you don't know just how a wom - an feels.
You did - n't know what
P.M.
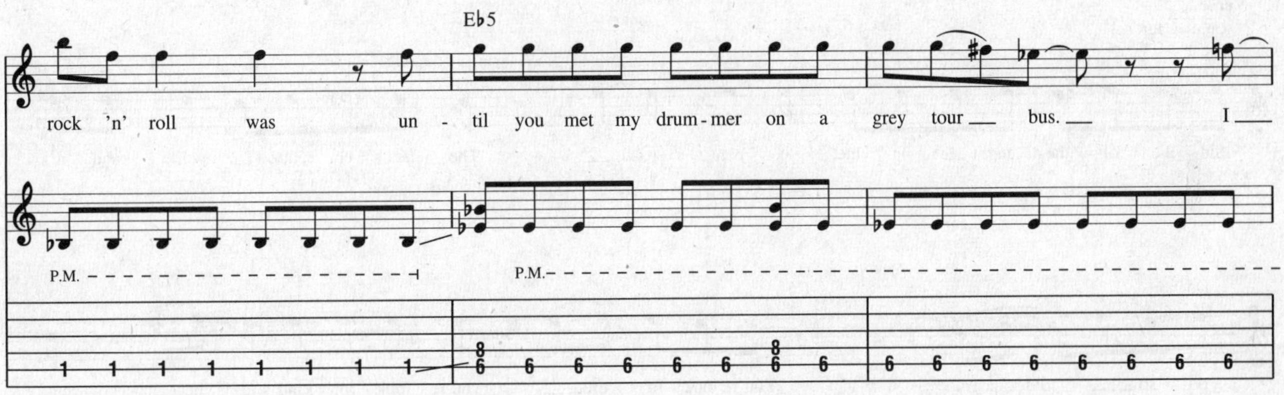
E♭5
rock 'n' roll was un - til you met my drum - mer on a grey tour bus. I
P.M.
P.M.

B♭5
E♭5
got there in the nick of time be - fore he got his hands a - cross
End Riff A
P.M.

Interlude

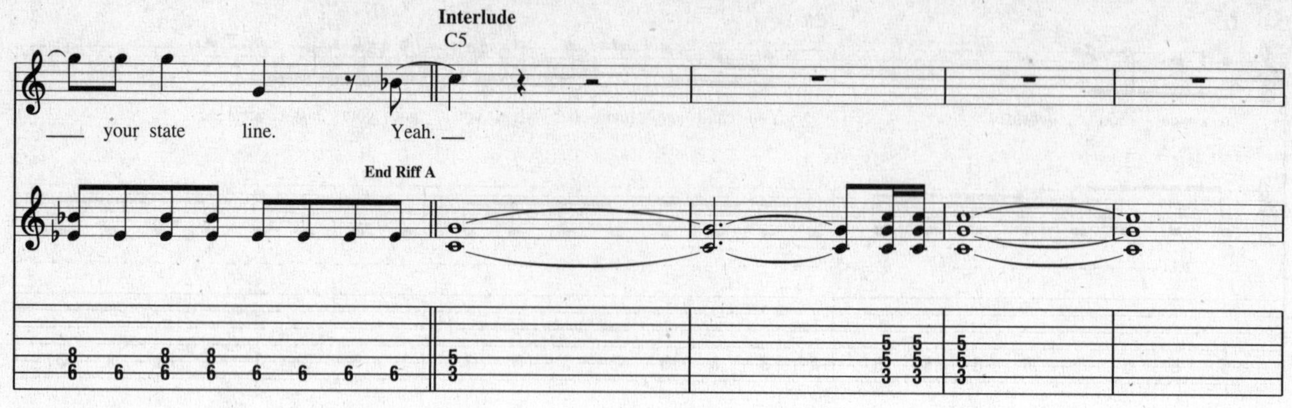

Verse

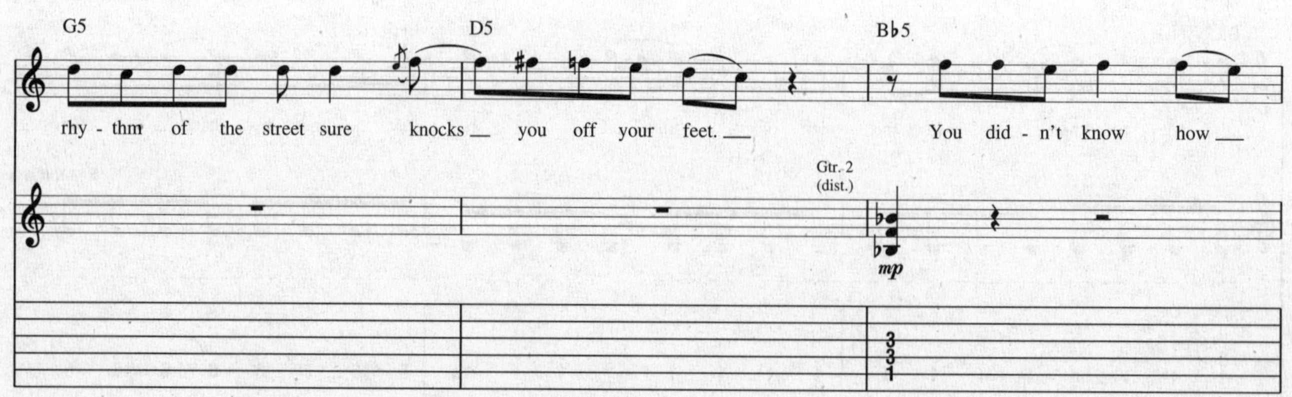

Eb5
rock 'n' roll looked un - til you caught your sis - ter with the guys from the group. Half -
Bb5
Eb5
- way home in the park - ing lot, by the look in her eye she was
Chorus
C5
giv - ing what she got.
(I said my, my, my.
I'm once bit - ten, twice
* Gtrs. 1 & 2
Rhy. Fig. 1
* Composite arrangement
F5 F6 F5 F6 F5 F6 F5 F6 C5
shy, babe.
My, my, my.
P.M.
P.M.
P.M.
F5 F6 F7 F6 F5 F6 F7 F5
I'm once bit - ten, twice shy, ba - by.
End Rhy. Fig. 1
P.M.
P.M.
P.M.
P.M.
P.M.

C5
F5
F6
F5
F6
F5
I'm once bit - ten, twice shy, ba - by.
My, my, my.)
P.M.
To Coda 1
F6
F5
F6
G5
3. Oh,
P.S.
Verse
Gtr. 1: w/ Riff A
Gtr. 2 tacet
C5
G5
wom - an you're a mess gon - na die in your sleep, there's blood on my amp and my
D5
C5
G5
Les Paul's beat. Can't keep you home, you're mes - sin' a - round. My best friend told me you're the
D5
2nd time, Gtr. 2: w/ Fill 1
B♭5
best lick in town.
You did - n't know that rock 'n' roll burned so
I did - n't know you had a rock 'n' roll re - cord un -
Fill 1
Gtr. 2

Eb5
Bb5
you bought a can - dle and you lived and you learned. You got the rhy - thm,
til I saw you're pic - ture on a - noth - er guy's jack - et. You told me I was the
Gtr. 2
mf
D.S. al Coda 1
To Coda 2
Eb5
you got the speed, ma - ma's lit - tle ba - by likes it short and sweet.
on - ly one but look at you now it's dark and is dawn, ah.
(I said oh
Coda 1
G5
Gtr. 2
Gtr. 1
w/ bar
-2 1/2
-2
-1
-1/2

Guitar Solo

Coda 2
Chorus
Gtr. 1: w/ Rhy. Fig. 1 (2 times)
C5
F5 F6 F5 F6 F5
I'm once bit - ten, twice shy, babe.
(My, my, my.
F6 F5 F6 C5
1.
F5 F6 F7 F6 F5
I'm once bit - ten, twice shy, ba - by.
My, my, my.)
F6 F7 F6
2.
F5 F6 F7 F6 F5 F6 F7 F6
shy.
Oh, so shy.
Guitar Solo
Gtr. 1 tacet
C5
F5
Gtr. 2
w/ wah-wah
C5
F5
C5
F5

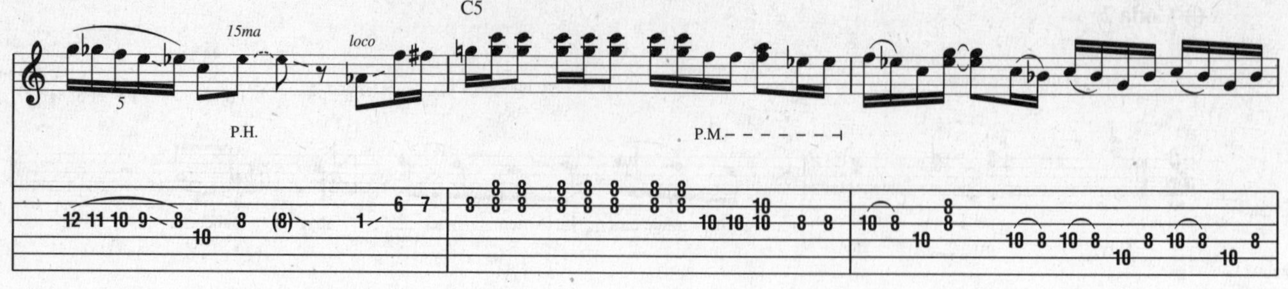
C5
15ma
loco
P.H.
P.M.

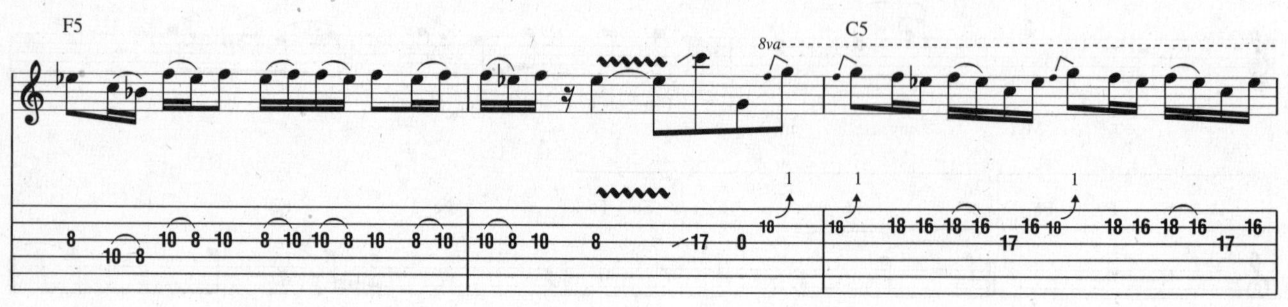
F5
8va
C5

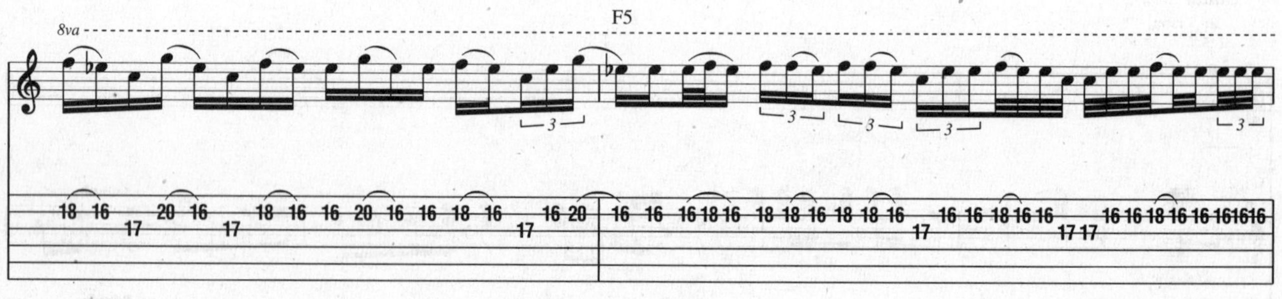
8va
F5

8va
C5

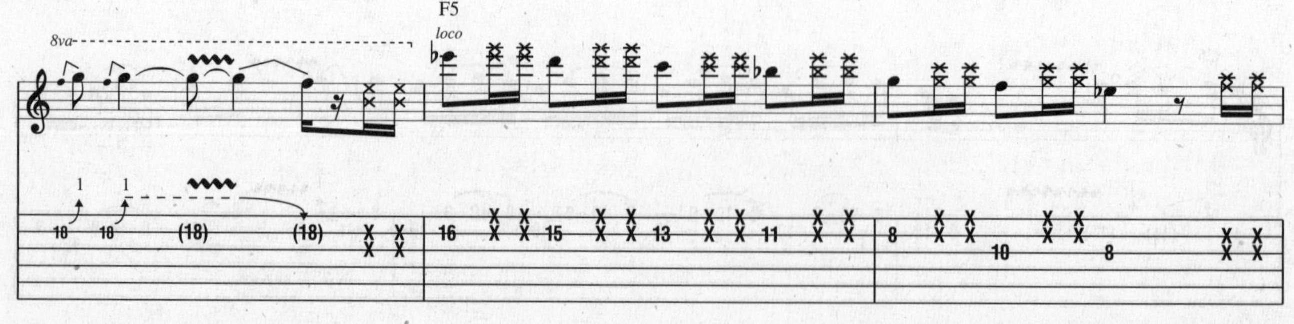
8va
F5
loco

C5
F5

Begin Fade
C5
F5
P.M.

C5
F5

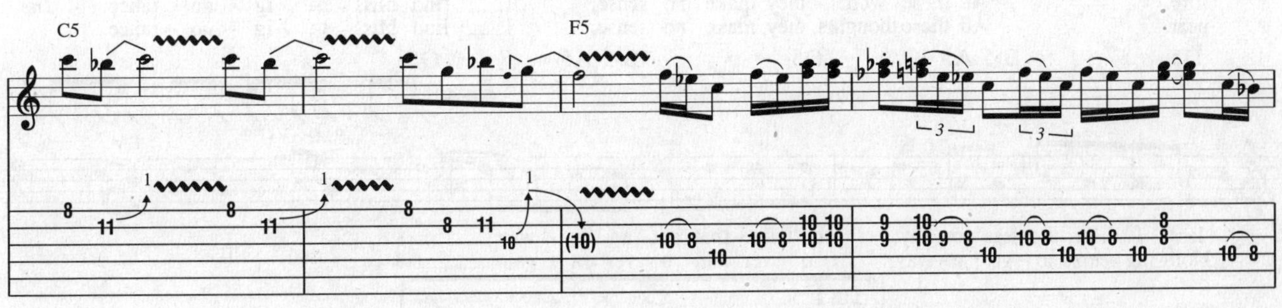
C5
F5

Fade out
C5
F5

One Step Closer

Words and Music by Rob Bourdon, Brad Delson, Joe Hahn, Mike Shinoda and Charles Bennington

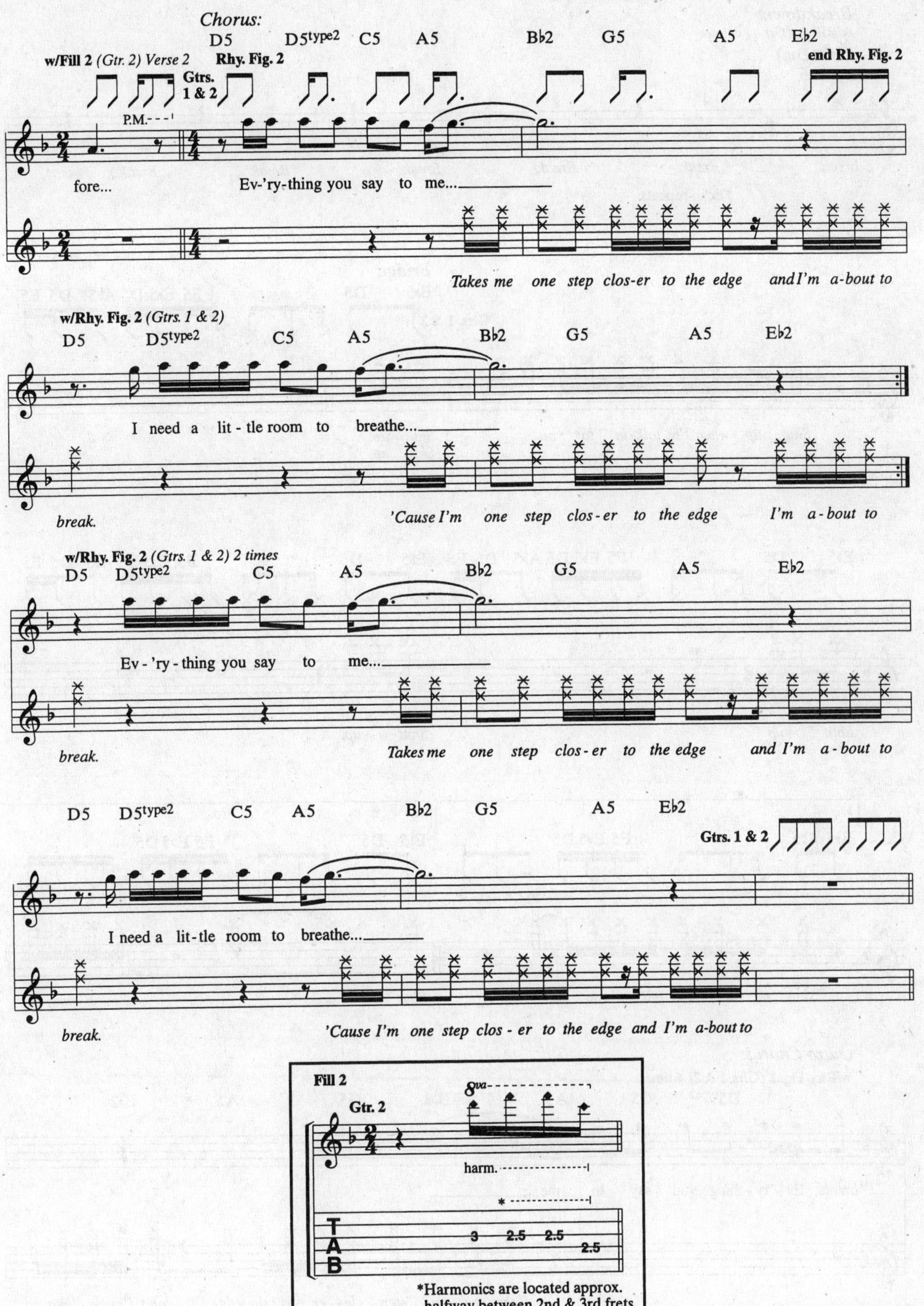
Chorus:
w/Fill 2 (Gtr. 2) Verse 2
Rhy. Fig. 2
Gtrs. 1 & 2
end Rhy. Fig. 2
D5 D5type2 C5 A5 Bb2 G5 A5 Eb2
P.M.
fore... Ev-'ry-thing you say to me...
Takes me one step clos-er to the edge and I'm a-bout to
w/Rhy. Fig. 2 (Gtrs. 1 & 2)
I need a lit-tle room to breathe...
break. 'Cause I'm one step clos-er to the edge I'm a-bout to
w/Rhy. Fig. 2 (Gtrs. 1 & 2) 2 times
Ev-'ry-thing you say to me...
break. Takes me one step clos-er to the edge and I'm a-bout to
Gtrs. 1 & 2
I need a lit-tle room to breathe...
break. 'Cause I'm one step clos-er to the edge and I'm a-bout to
Fill 2
Gtr. 2
8va
harm.
3 2.5 2.5 2.5
*Harmonics are located approx. halfway between 2nd & 3rd frets.

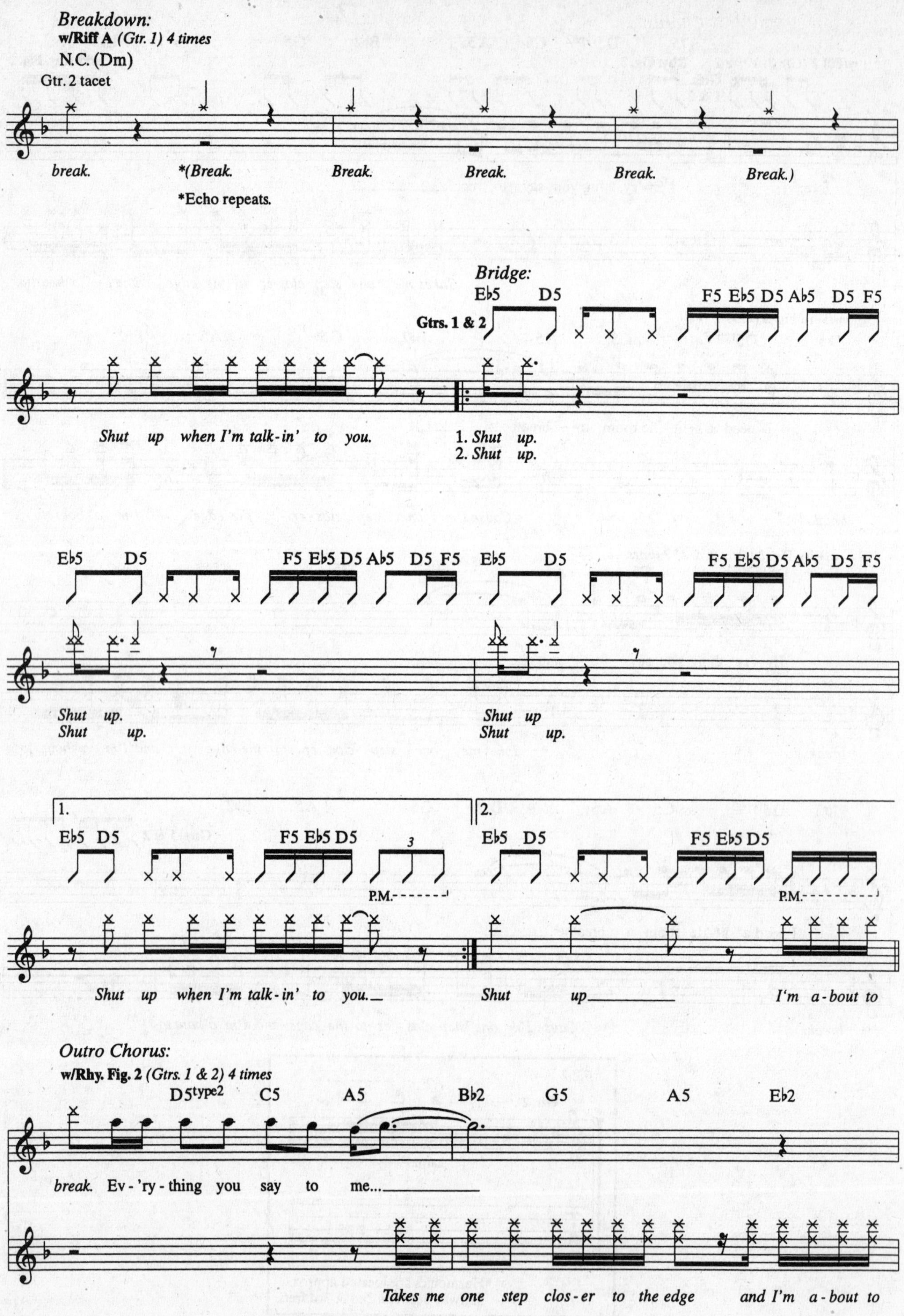

Breakdown:

w/Riff A *(Gtr. 1) 4 times*

N.C. (Dm)

Gtr. 2 tacet

*break. *(Break. Break. Break. Break. Break.)*

*Echo repeats.

Bridge:

E♭5 D5 F5 E♭5 D5 A♭5 D5 F5

Gtrs. 1 & 2

Shut up when I'm talk-in' to you. 1. *Shut up.* 2. *Shut up.*

E♭5 D5 F5 E♭5 D5 A♭5 D5 F5 E♭5 D5 F5 E♭5 D5 A♭5 D5 F5

Shut up. Shut up.
Shut up Shut up.

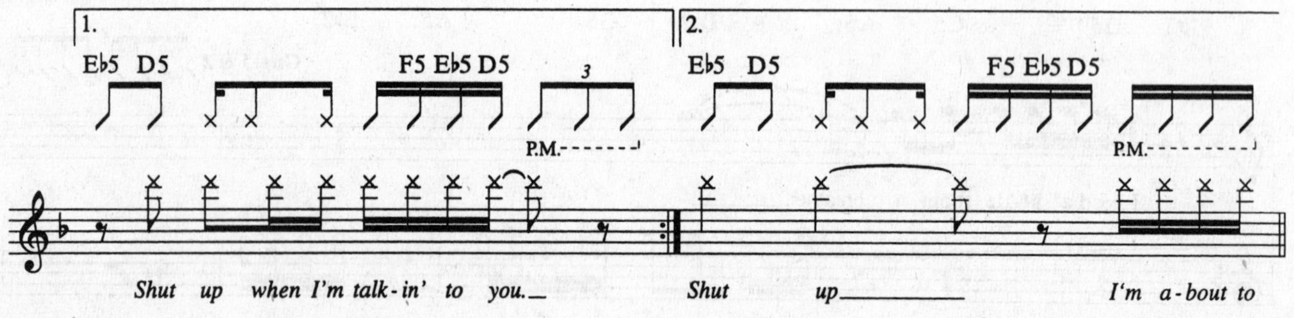

Outro Chorus:

w/Rhy. Fig. 2 *(Gtrs. 1 & 2) 4 times*

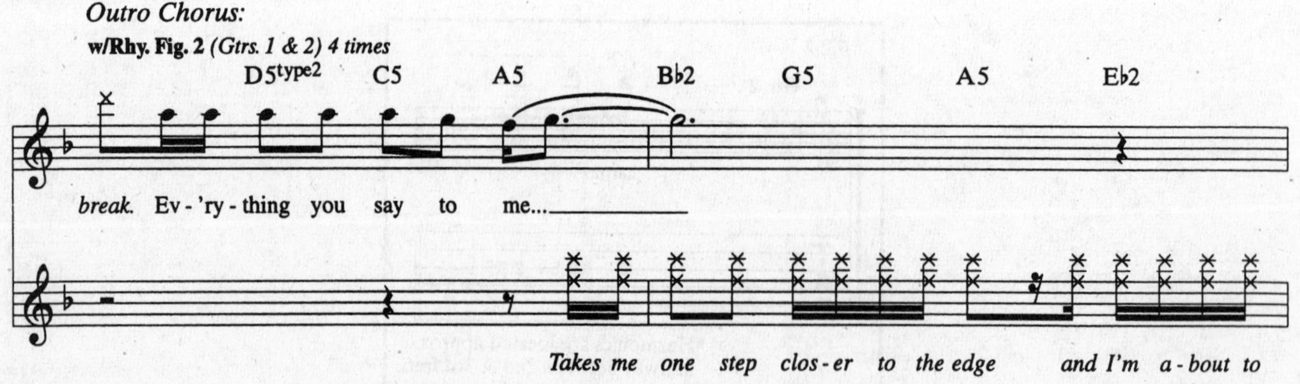

D5
D5type2
C5
A5
B♭2
G5
A5
E♭2
I need a lit - tle room to breathe...
break.
'Cause I'm one step clos - er to the edge; I'm a - bout to

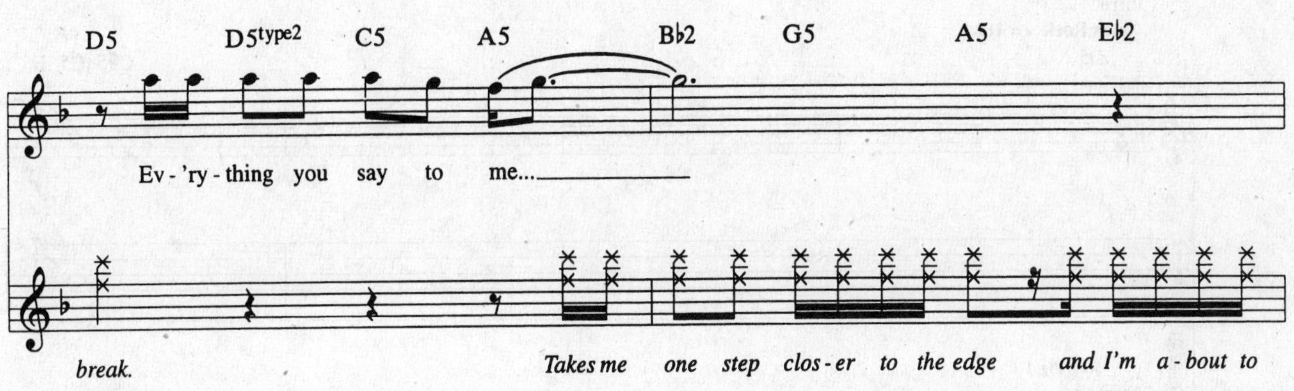
D5
D5type2
C5
A5
B♭2
G5
A5
E♭2
Ev - 'ry - thing you say to me...
break.
Takes me one step clos - er to the edge and I'm a - bout to

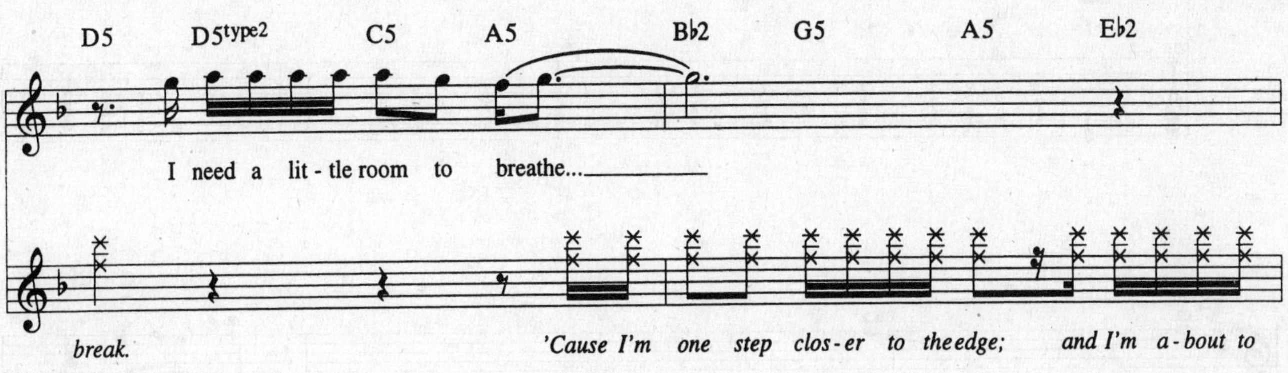
D5
D5type2
C5
A5
B♭2
G5
A5
E♭2
I need a lit - tle room to breathe...
break.
'Cause I'm one step clos - er to the edge; and I'm a - bout to

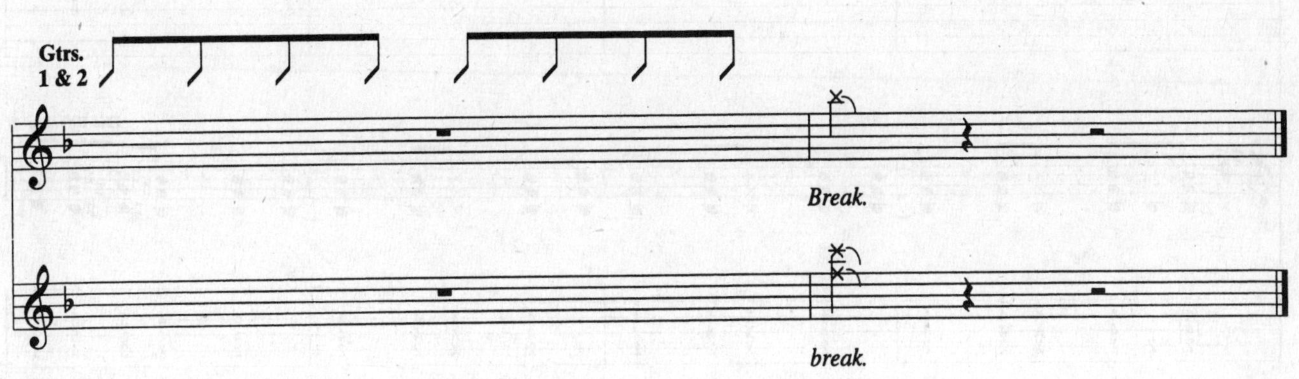
Gtrs. 1 & 2
Break.
break.

One Way or Another

Words and Music by Deborah Harry and Nigel Harrison

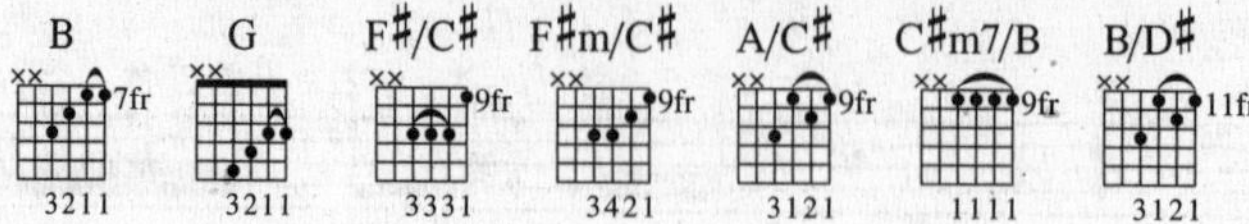

Gtr. 1: w/ Rhy. Fig. 1
D
C♯5 C5 B5
Rhy. Fig. 2
Gtr. 3 (clean)
f
w/ chorus
Riff A
Gtr. 2
B
C5 C♯5 D5
End Rhy. Fig. 2
End Riff A
Verse
Gtr. 1: w/ Rhy. Fig. 1 (1 3/4 times)
Gtr. 2: w/ Riff A
Gtr. 3: w/ Rhy. Fig. 2 (1 3/4 times)
D
C♯5 C5 B5
1. One way or an - oth - er, I'm gon - na find ya. I'm gon - na get ya, get ya, get ya, get ya.
B
C5 C♯5 D5
One way __ or an - oth - er, I'm gon - na win ya. I'm gon - na get ya, get ya, get ya, get ya.

D
One way, or an - oth - er, I'm gon - na see ya, I wan - na
Riff B
Gtr. 2
C♯5 C5 B5
B
meet ya, meet ya, meet ya, meet ya. One day, may - be next week, I'm gon - na
End Riff B
Riff C
B
Rhy. Fig. 3A
Gtr. 3
End Rhy. Fig. 3A
meet ya. I'm gon - na meet ya, I'll meet you.
Rhy. Fig. 3
Gtr. 1
End Rhy. Fig. 3
Gtr. 2
End Riff C

Bridge

Gtr. 3 tacet

G B5 C#5 B5 A5 F#5

Rhy. Fig. 4 End Rhy. Fig. 4

I will drive past ___ your house.

Riff D

Riff D1

G B5 C#5 B5 A5 F#5

And if the lights are ___ all down, I'll

G5 A5 B5 E5 F#5
see who's a - round.
End Riff D
1/2
End Riff D1
Verse
Gtr. 1: w/ Rhy. Fig. 1 (1 3/4 times)
Gtr. 2: w/ Riff B
Gtr. 3: w/ Rhy. Fig. 2 (1 3/4 times)
D5 D C#5 C5 B5
2. One way or an - oth - er, I'm gon - na find ya. I'm gon - na get ya, get ya, get ya, get ya.
Gtr. 2: w/ Riff A (last 4 meas.)
B C5 C#5 D5
One way or an - oth - er, I'm gon - na win ya. I'll get ya, I'll get ya.
Gtr. 2: w/ Riff B
D C#5 C5 B5
One way or an - oth - er, I'm gon - na see ya. I'm gon - na meet ya, meet ya, meet ya, meet ya.
Gtr. 2: w/ Riff C
Gtrs. 1 & 3: w/ Rhy. Figs. 3 & 3A
B
One day may - be next week, I'm gon - na meet ya. I'll meet ya, ah.
Bridge
Gtrs. 1 & 2: w/ Riffs D & D1
Gtr. 3: w/ Rhy. Fig. 4
G B5 C#5 B5 A5 F#5 G5
And If the lights are all out, I'll
B5 C#5 B5 A5 F#5 G5 A5 B5 E5
fol - low your bus down - town. See who's hang - in' 'round.

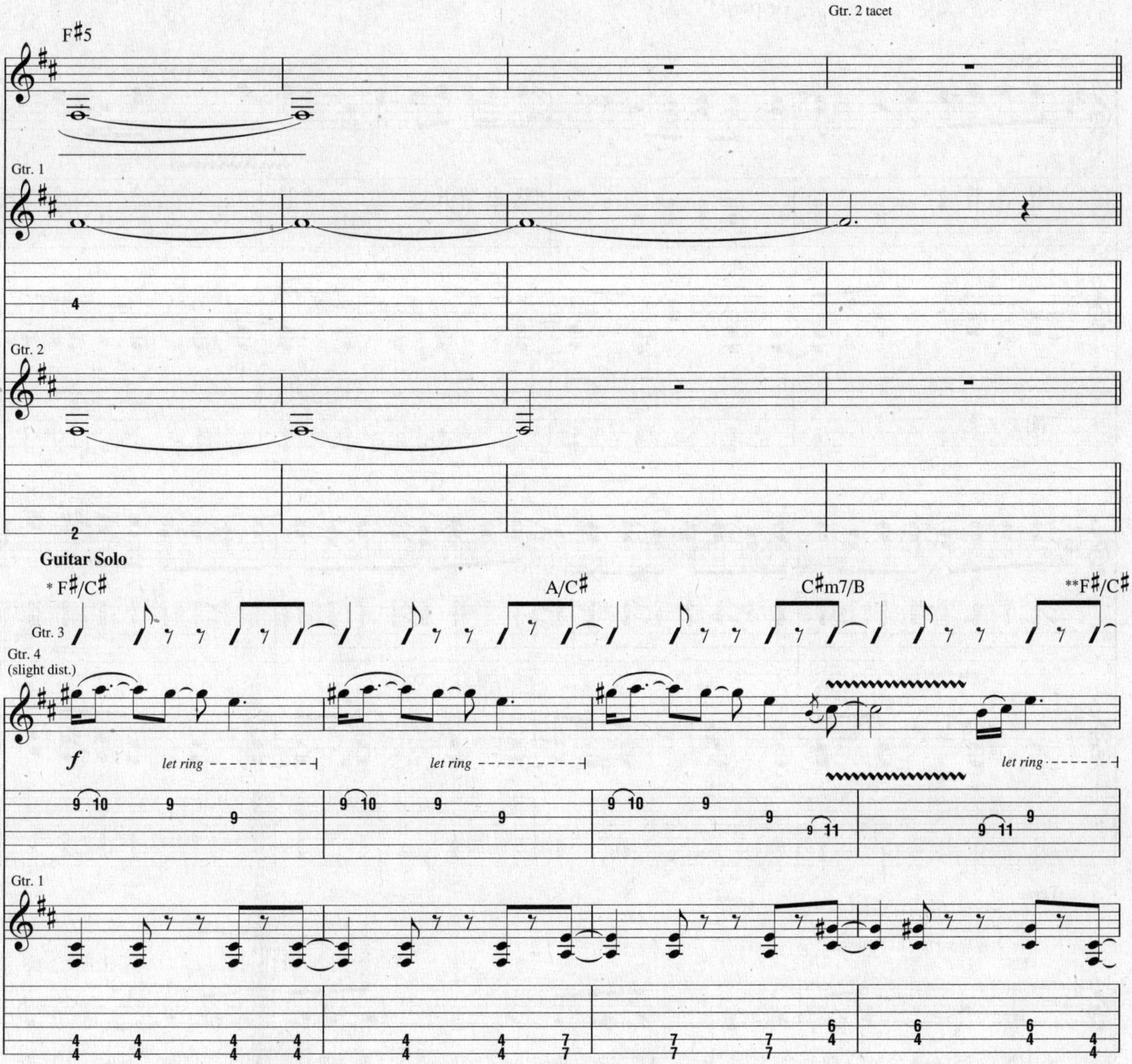

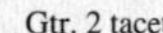

F♯5

Gtr. 1

Gtr. 2

Guitar Solo

*F♯/C♯ A/C♯ C♯m7/B **F♯/C♯

Gtr. 3

Gtr. 4
(slight dist.)

f

let ring

Gtr. 1

*Editors note: To avoid clash between A♮ (played by Gtr. 4) and A♯ (the Major 3rd in the F♯/C♯ chord) substitute F♯m/C♯.

**As before.

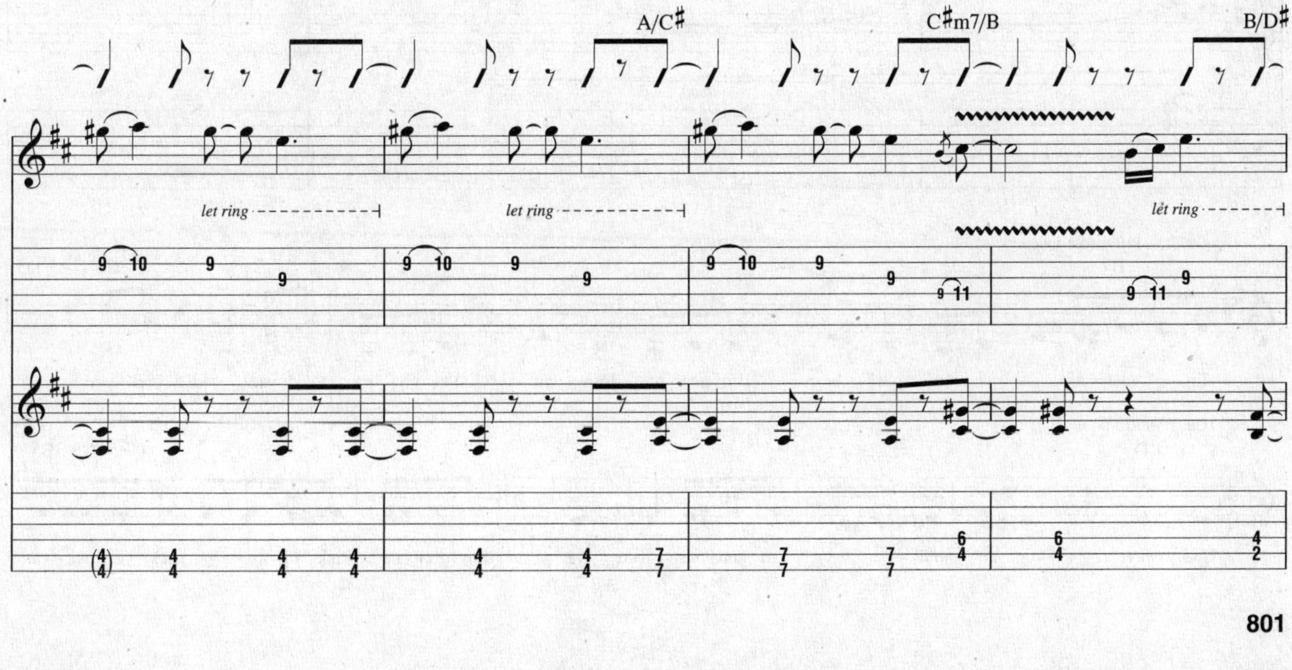

A/C♯ C♯m7/B B/D♯

let ring

Gtr. 3 tacet
E5
F♯5
A5
B5
C5 C♯5 D5
Verse
Gtr. 1: w/ Rhy. Fig. 1 (1 3/4 times)
Gtr. 2: w/ Riff B
Gtr. 3: w/ Rhy. Fig. 2 (1 3/4 times)
Gtr. 4 tacet
D5 D
C♯5 C5 B5
3. One way __ or an - oth - er, I'm gon - na lose ya. I'm gon - na give you the slip, a
Gtr. 4
Gtr. 2: w/ Riff A (last 4 meas.)
B
C5 C♯5 D5
slip o' the hip __ or an - oth - er. I'm gon - na lose ya. I'm gon - na trick ya, I'll trick ya.
Gtr. 2: w/ Riff B
D
C♯5 C5 B5
One way or an - oth - er. I'm gon - na lose ya. I'm gon - na trick ya, trick ya, trick ya, trick ya.

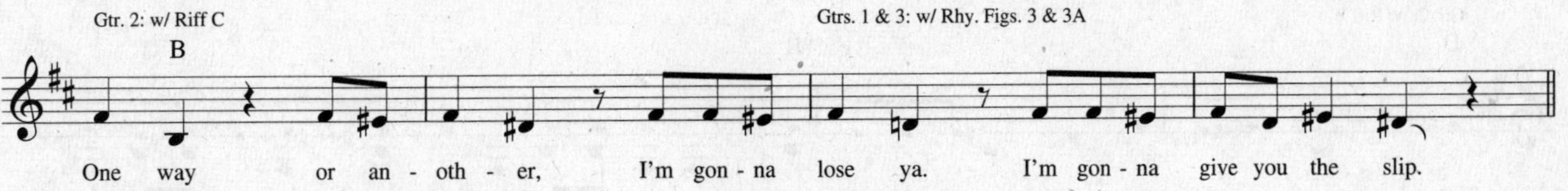

Interlude

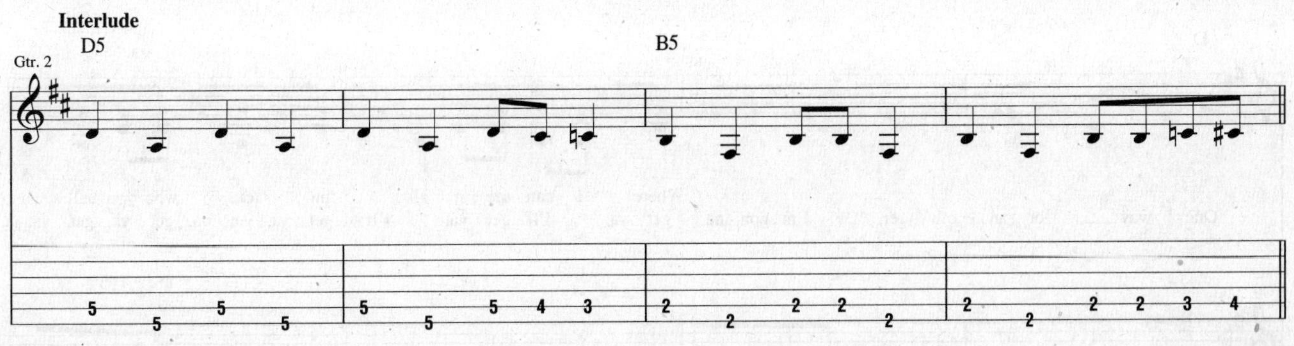

Outro

*Two synths. arr. for gtr.

Play 3 times & fade

Gtr. 5: w/ Riff F (till fade)

D7 B7

Where I can see it all, find out who you call.

One way___ or an - oth - er, I'm gon - na get ya. I'll get ya, I'll get ya, get ya, get ya, get ya.)

Panama

Words and Music by David Lee Roth, Edward Van Halen and Alex Van Halen

Tune down 1/2 step:
(low to high) E♭-A♭-D♭-G♭-B♭-E♭

Intro

Moderate Rock ♩ = 144

*E Esus4 B/E E Esus4 B/E D Dsus4 A

Gtr. 1 (dist.)

f

P.M. P.M. P.M. P.M. P.M. P.M. P.M.

*Chord symbols reflect basic harmony.

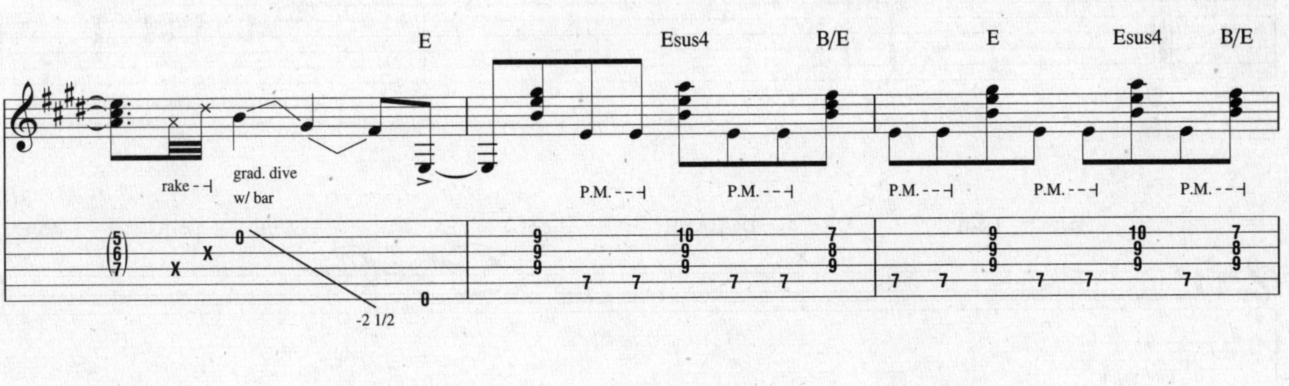

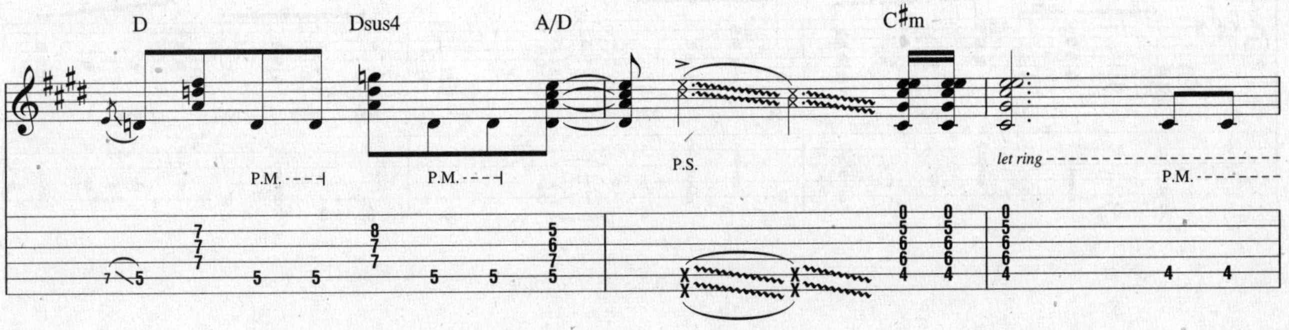

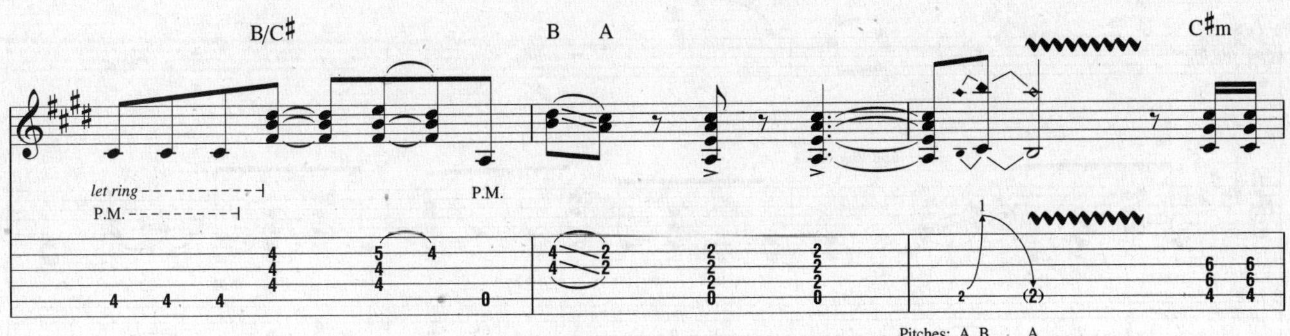

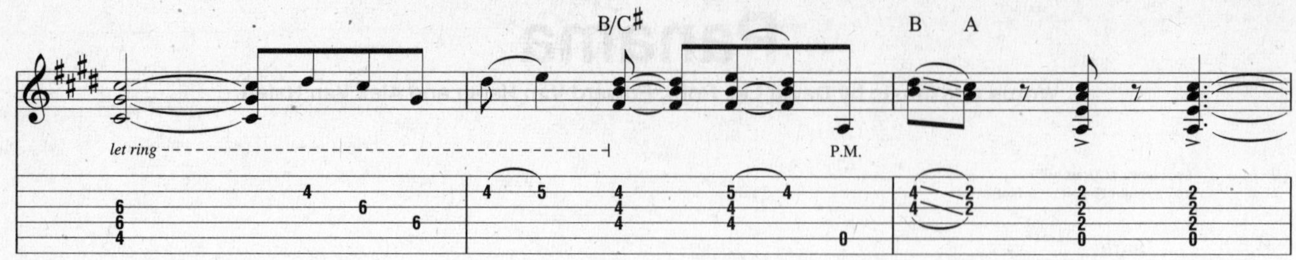

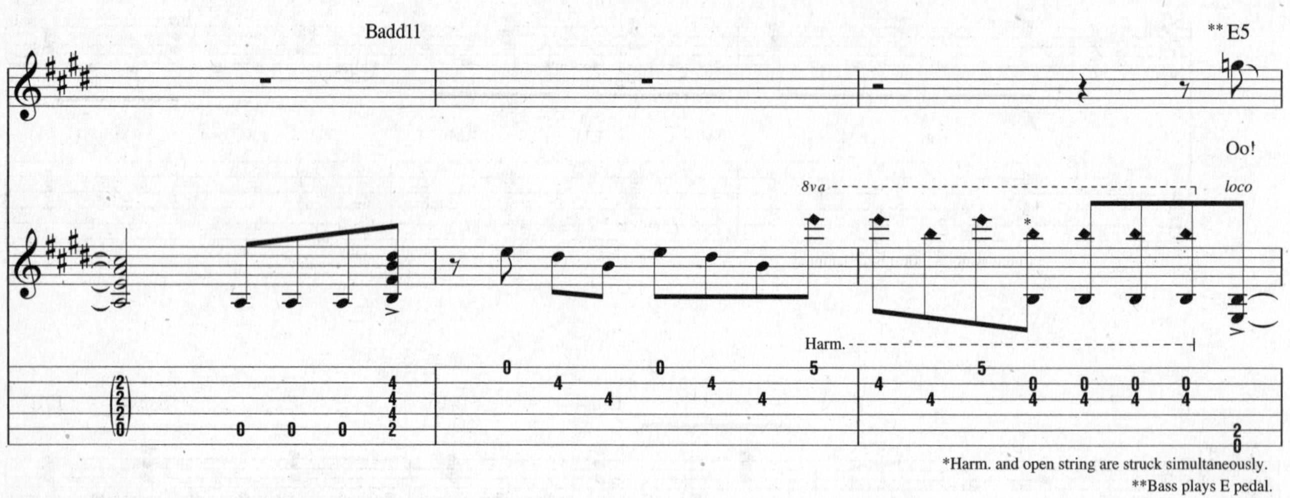

*Harm. and open string are struck simultaneously.

**Bass plays E pedal.

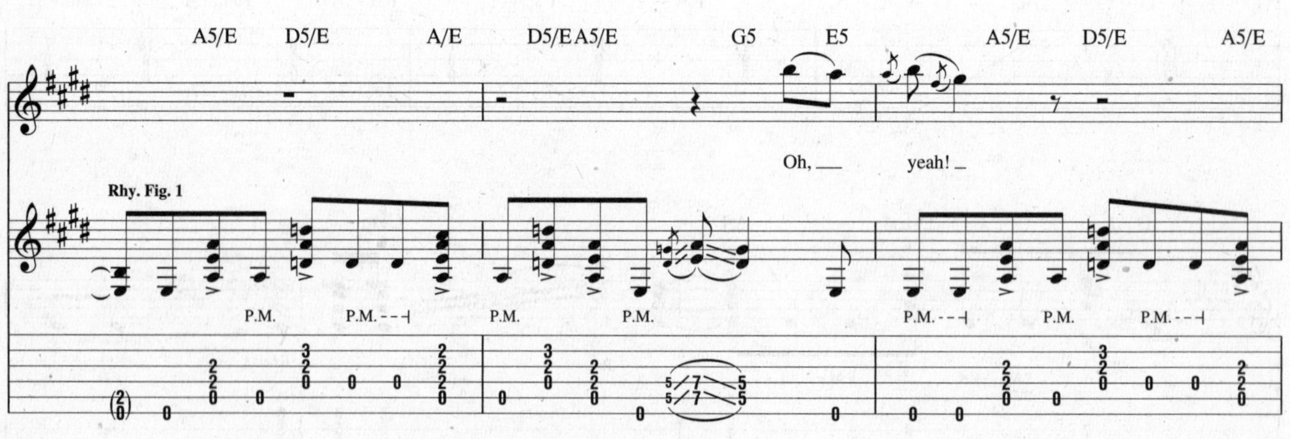

Verse
A5/E D5/E A5/E D5/E A5/E G5 D5/E E5
1. Jump back!
P.M. P.M. P.M. P.M.
mf
let ring
A/E E7sus4 D5/E
What's that sound? Here she comes, full blast and top down.
let ring
let ring
E5 A/E E7sus4
Hot shoe, burn-in' down the av-e-nue. Mod-el cit-i-zen,
let ring
let ring
Pre-Chorus
F#sus4 F#11
ze-ro dis-ci-pline. Don't you know she's com-in' home to me?
P.S.
let ring
let ring
let ring

C♯m7
N.C.
You'll lose her in the turn.
I'll get her!
let ring
P.S.
Badd11
E5
Pan - a - ma,
15ma
loco
8va
Harm.
P.M.
Chorus
A5/E D5/E A5/E D5/E A5/E G5 E5 A5/E D5/E A5/E
Pan - a - ma.
D5/E A5/E G5 E5 A5/E D5/E A5/E D5/E A5/E G5 E5
Pan - a - ma,
Pan - a - ma.

Verse
A5/E
D5/E
A5/E
D5/E
A5/E
G5
D5/E
E5
2. Ain't noth - in' like it, her
P.M.
let ring
A/E
E7sus4
D5/E
shin - y ma - chine, got the feel for the wheel, keep the mov - ing parts clean.
let ring
E5
A/E
E7sus4
Hot shoe, burn - in' down the av - e - nue, got an on - ramp
let ring
Pre-Chorus
F♯7sus4
F♯11
com - in' through my bed - room. Don't you know she's com - in' home to me?
let ring
P.S.
P.M.

C#m7
N.C.
C5
3
You'll lose her in the turn. I'll get her!
let ring

N.C.
Badd11
E5
Wuh oh!
Pan - a - ma,
15ma
loco
Harm.
P.M.

Chorus

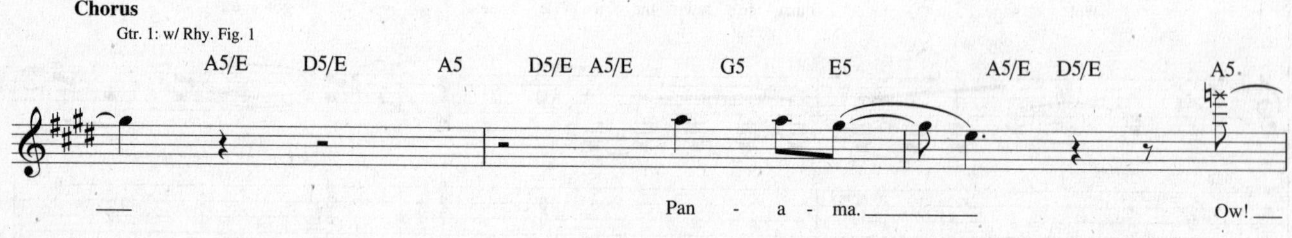
Gtr. 1: w/ Rhy. Fig. 1
A5/E
D5/E
A5
D5/E
A5/E
G5
E5
A5/E
D5/E
A5
Pan - a - ma.
Ow!

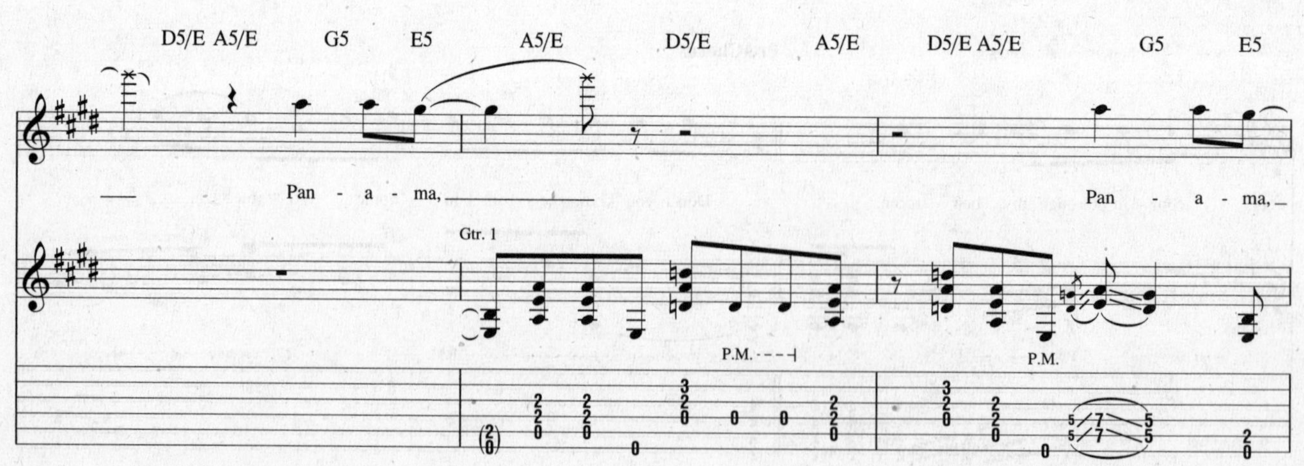
D5/E
A5/E
G5
E5
A5/E
D5/E
A5/E
D5/E
A5/E
G5
E5
Pan - a - ma,
Pan - a - ma,
Gtr. 1
P.M.

Guitar Solo
A5/E
D5/E
Csus2
G/B
Csus2
B
E
ah, oh, oh, oh, oh.
Woo!
P.M.
P.M.
let ring
B
E
w/ bar
B
E
hold bend
C
D
w/ bar
-2 1/2
*15ma
loco
P.H.
*Applies to P.H. only.
Interlude
Em
C/E
P.M.

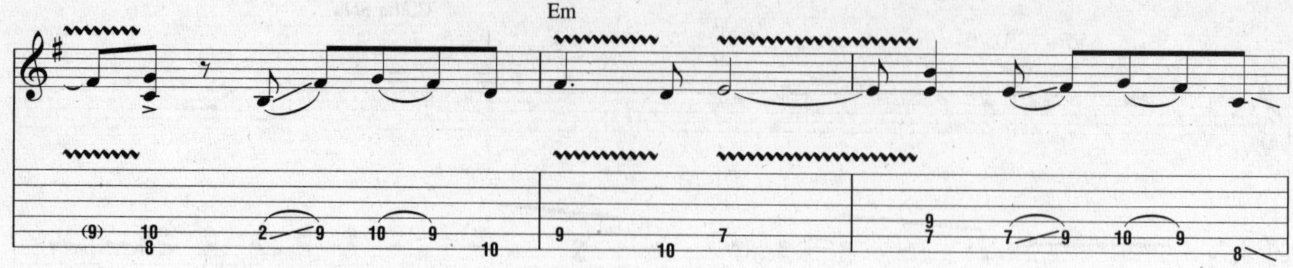
Em
(9) 10 8 2 9 10 9 10
9 10 7
9 7 7 9 10 9 8

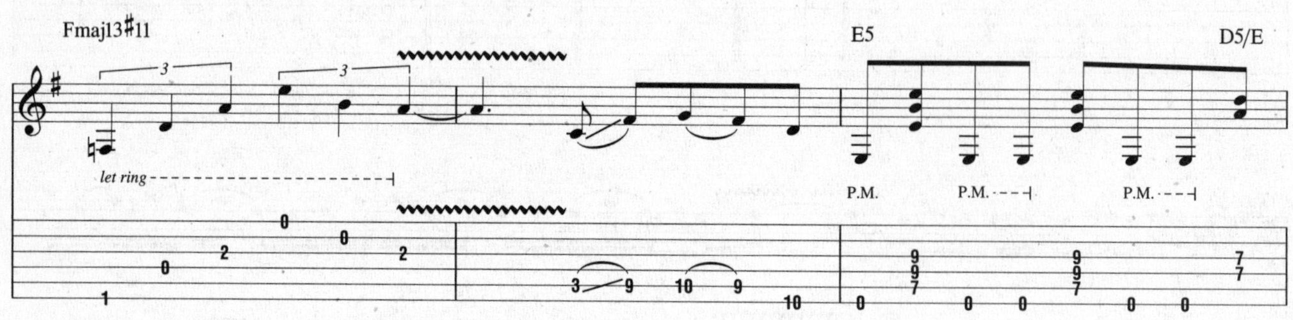
Fmaj13♯11
E5
D5/E
let ring
P.M.
P.M.
P.M.

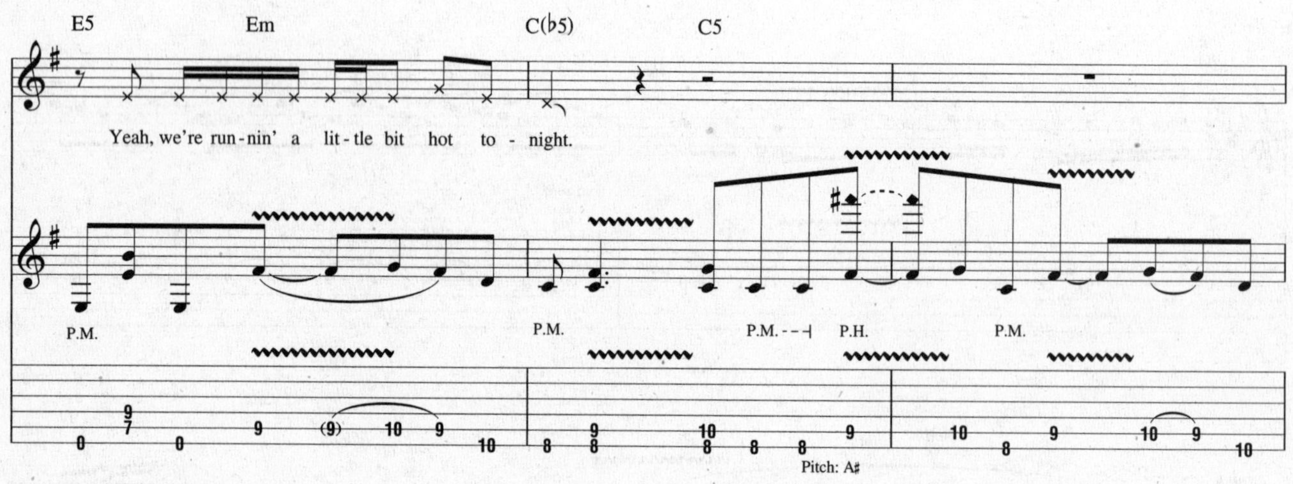
E5
Em
C(♭5)
C5
Yeah, we're run-nin' a lit-tle bit hot to-night.
P.M.
P.M.
P.M.
P.H.
P.M.
Pitch: A♯

Em
C(♭5)
C5
I can bare-ly see the road from the heat com-in' off it.
P.M.
P.M.
P.M.

E5

Ah, you reach down be - tween my legs,

P.M. P.M. P.M. P.M. P.M.

C7(♭5) C5 C(♭5) C5 E5 F

ease the seat back. She's blind - in'

P.M. P.M. P.M.

D/F♯ G5 E/G♯

I'm fly - in', right be - hind in the rear - view mir - ror now.

P.M. P.M. P.M.

A5 Gm/B♭ B

Got the feel - ing, pow - er steer - ing, pis - tons pop - pin', ain't

P.M. *let ring*

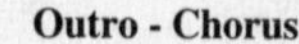
Outro - Chorus

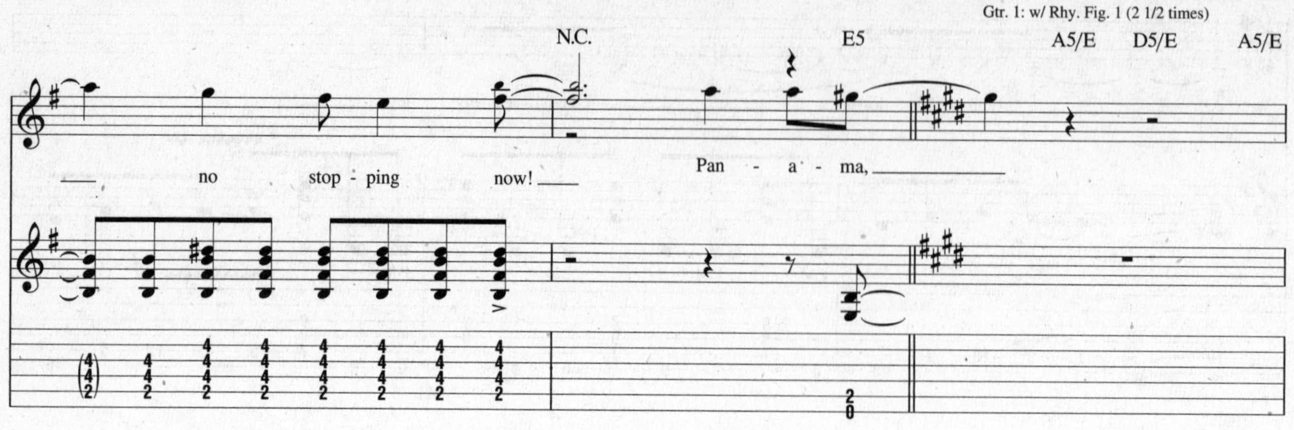
Gtr. 1: w/ Rhy. Fig. 1 (2 1/2 times)
N.C.
E5
A5/E
D5/E
A5/E
no
stop - ping
now!
Pan - a - ma,

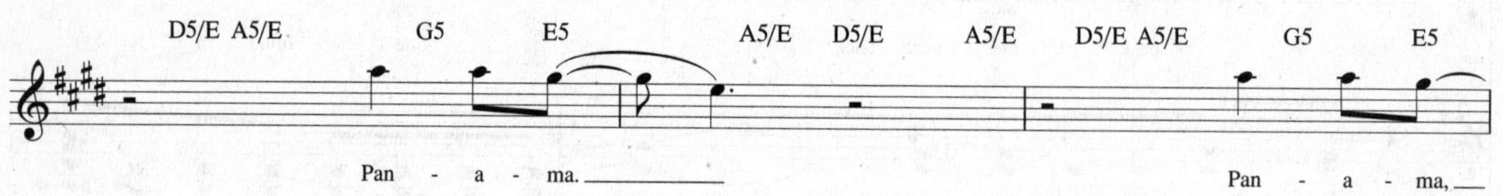
D5/E A5/E
G5
E5
A5/E
D5/E
A5/E
D5/E A5/E
G5
E5
Pan - a - ma.
Pan - a - ma,

A5/E
D5/E
A5/E
D5/E A5/E
G5/E
E5
A5/E
D5/E
A5/E
Pan - a - ma,
ah,
oh,
oh,
oh,

D5/E
A5/E
G5
E5
A5/E
D5/E
A5/E
D5/E
A5/E
G5
E5
oh.
Pan - a - ma,
Pan - a - ma,

Gtr. 1 tacet
A5/E
D5/E
A5/E
D5/E
A5/E
G5
N.C.
ah,
oh,
oh,
oh,
oh.
Pan - a - ma.
Gtr. 1
P.M.
P.M.

Peg

Words and Music by Walter Becker and Donald Fagen

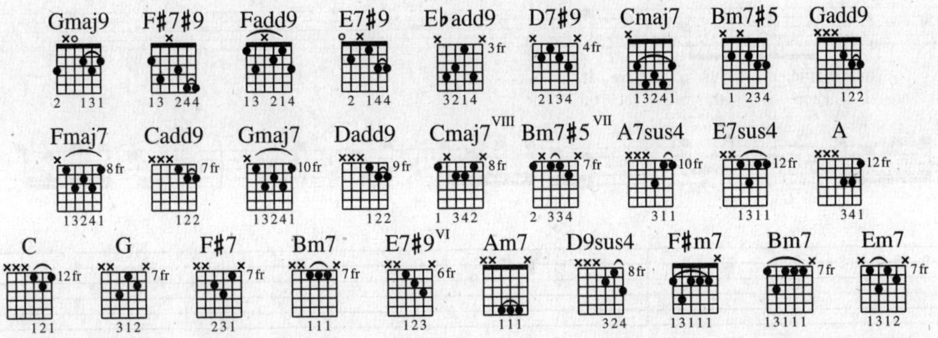

Gmaj9 F#7#9 Fadd9 E7#9 E♭add9 D7#9 Cmaj7 Bm7#5 Gadd9

Fmaj7 Cadd9 Gmaj7 Dadd9 Cmaj7 VIII Bm7#5 VII A7sus4 E7sus4 A

C G F#7 Bm7 E7#9 VI Am7 D9sus4 F#m7 Bm7 Em7

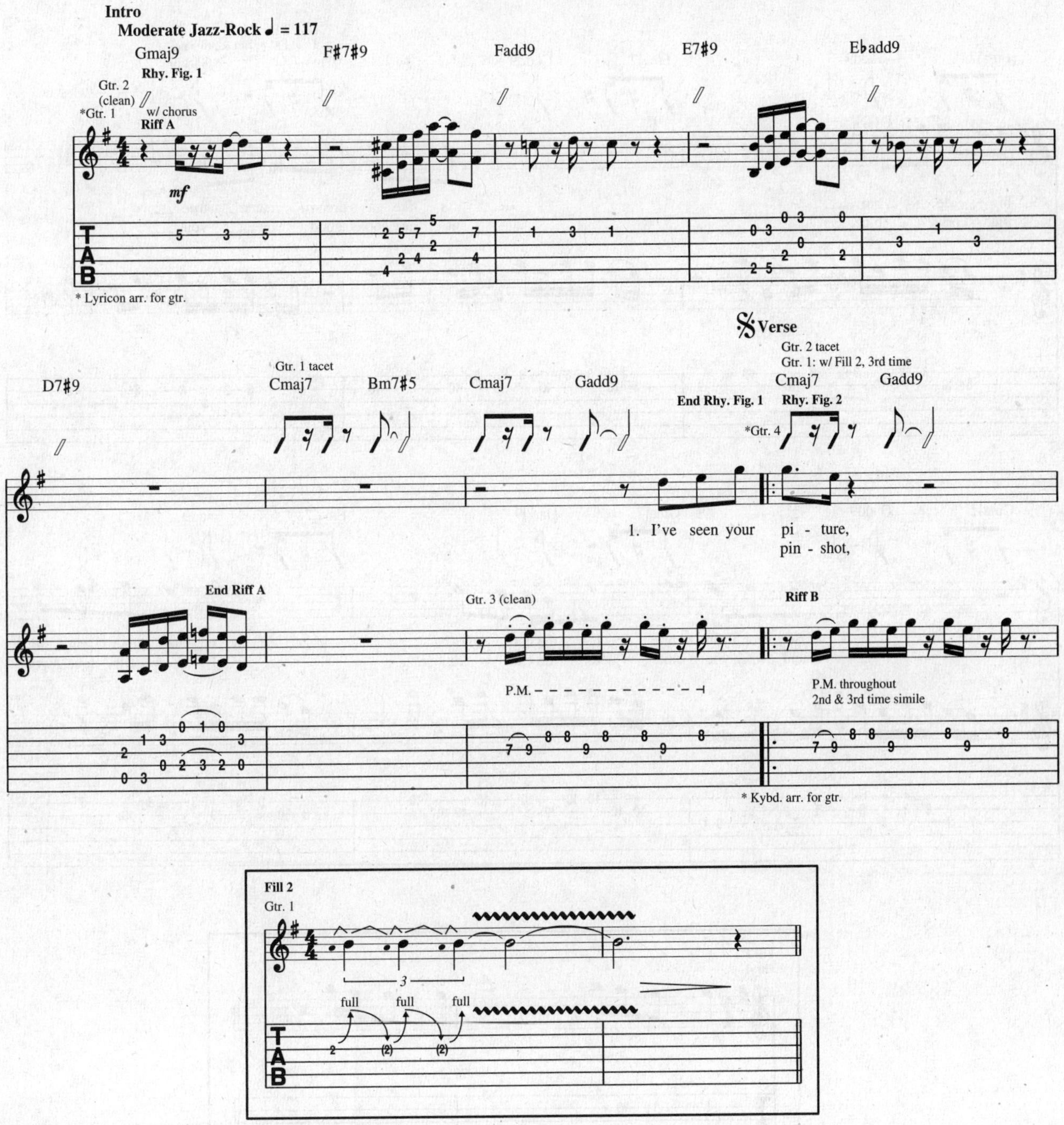

Intro

Moderate Jazz-Rock ♩ = 117

Gmaj9 F#7#9 Fadd9 E7#9 E♭add9

Rhy. Fig. 1

Gtr. 2 (clean)

*Gtr. 1 w/ chorus

Riff A

mf

* Lyricon arr. for gtr.

D7#9 Cmaj7 Bm7#5 Cmaj7 Gadd9

Gtr. 1 tacet

Verse

Gtr. 2 tacet

Gtr. 1: w/ Fill 2, 3rd time

Cmaj7 Gadd9

End Rhy. Fig. 1

Rhy. Fig. 2

*Gtr. 4

1. I've seen your pi - ture,

pin - shot,

End Riff A

Gtr. 3 (clean)

Riff B

P.M.

P.M. throughout

2nd & 3rd time simile

* Kybd. arr. for gtr.

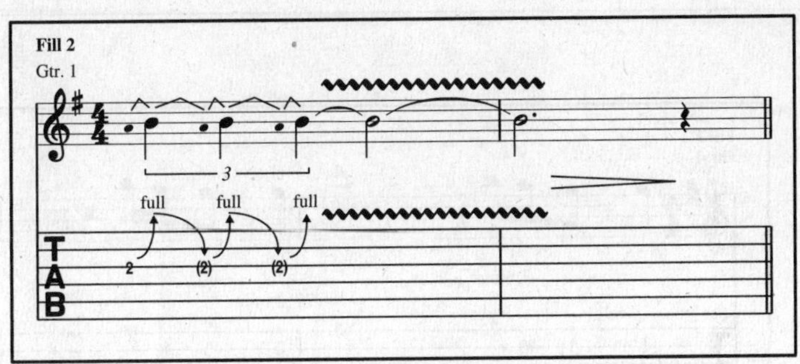

Gtr. 1: w/ Fill 1, 2nd & 3rd time
Cmaj7
Gadd9
Cmaj7
Gadd9
Cmaj7
Gadd9
your name in lights a - bove it.
I keep it with your let - ter.
This is your
Done up in
Fmaj7
Cadd9
Fmaj7
Cadd9
Gtr. 1: w/ Fill 1, 2nd & 3rd time
Cmaj7
Gadd9
big de - but,
blue - print - blue,
it's like a dream come - true.
it sure looks good on you,
Cmaj7
Gadd9
Gmaj7
Dadd9
Fmaj7
Cadd9
So won't you smile for the cam - 'ra?
and when you smile for the cam - 'ra,
I know they're gon - na
I know I'll love you
Fill 1
Gtr. 1

1.
2.
End Rhy. Fig. 2
Gtr. 3: w/ Fill 3, 2nd time
Cmaj7
Gadd9
love it,
bet - ter.
Peg.
2. I like your
End Riff B
(cont. in slash)
Chorus
Gtr. 4 tacet
Cmaj7 VIII Bm7♯5 VII
A7sus4
E7sus4
Rhy. Fig. 3
Gtr. 3
Peg, it will come back to you.
(Peg. Back to you.
To Coda
Gtr. 1: w/ Fill 4, 2nd time
A
C
G
F♯7
Bm7
E7♯9 VI
Am7
D9sus4
End Rhy. Fig. 3
(cont. in notatoion)
Then the shut - ter falls, you see it all in three D. It's your fav - 'rite for - eign
Ah, shut - ter falls all in three D. for - eign mo - vie.)
Gtr. 3 tacet
F♯m7
Em7
Gtr. 2
mo - vie.
P.M.
Fill 3
Fill 4
Gtr. 1

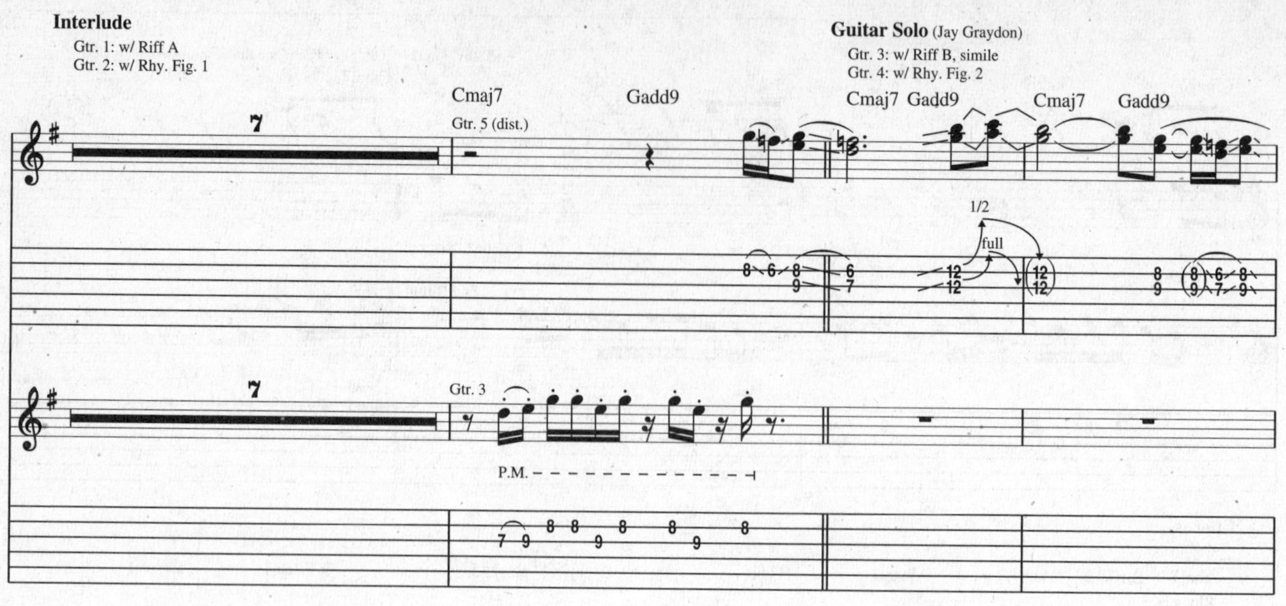
Interlude
Gtr. 1: w/ Riff A
Gtr. 2: w/ Rhy. Fig. 1
Guitar Solo (Jay Graydon)
Gtr. 3: w/ Riff B, simile
Gtr. 4: w/ Rhy. Fig. 2
Cmaj7
Gadd9
Gtr. 5 (dist.)
Gtr. 3
P.M.

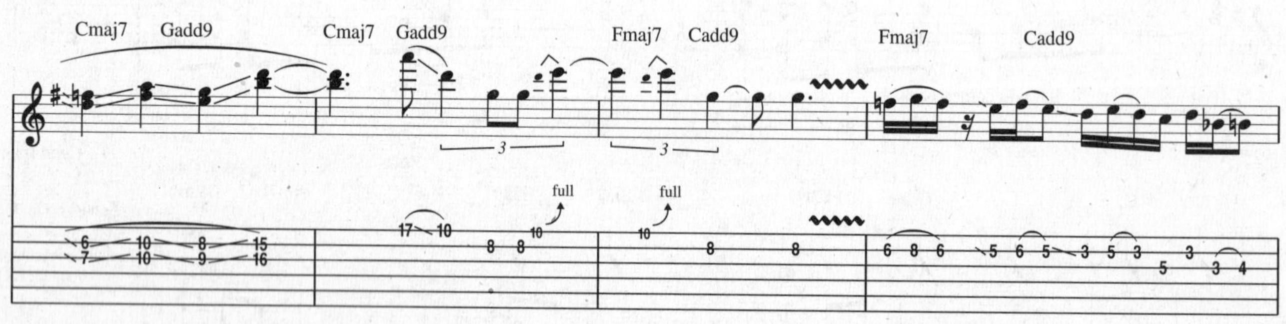
Cmaj7
Gadd9
Fmaj7
Cadd9

Cmaj7
Gadd9
Gmaj7
Dadd9

D.S. al Coda
(take 2nd lyrics/2nd ending)
Fmaj7
Cadd9
Cmaj7
Gadd9
3. I like your

Coda
Outro
Gtr. 3: w/ Rhy. Fig. 3, 4 times & fade
Cmaj7 Bm7♯5 A7sus4 E7sus4 Cmaj7 Bm7♯5
Voc. Fig. 1
mo - vie it will come back to you. Peg, it will come
(Peg. Back to you. Peg.
A7sus4 E7sus4 A C G F♯7 Bm7 E7♯9
back to you. then the shut - ter falls you see it all in three D.
Back to you. Ah, shut - ter falls all in three D.
w/ Voc. Fig. 1, 3 times
Am7 D9sus4 Cmaj7 Bm7♯5 Asus4 E7sus4 Cmaj7 Bm7♯5 Asus4 E7sus4
End Voc. Fig. 1
It's your fav 'rite for - eign
for - eign mo - vie.)
Gtr. 5 (dist.)
Bm7 E7♯9 Am7 D9sus4 Cmaj7 Bm7♯5 A7sus4 E7sus4 Cmaj7 Bm7♯5 A7sus4 E7sus4
full full full
Begin Fade
A C G F♯7 Bm7 E7♯9 Am7 D9sus4 Cmaj7 Bm♯5
Fade Out
A7sus4 E7sus4 Cmaj7 Bm7♯5 A7sus4 E7sus4 A C G F♯7
8va
loco
full full full full full full full

Photograph

Words and Music by Robert Lange, Lawrence Elliott, Stephen Clark, Peter Willis and Richard Savage

w/Rhy. Fig. 1 (Gtr. 1) 1st 2 bars only
A5 D5/A E5 B A5 D5/A
uh, pas-sion kill-er, you're too much. You're the on-
w/Rhy. Fig. 1 (Gtr. 1)
E5 B A Asus E5 Rhy. Fig. 2 open E
*Gtr. 2
P.M.
ly one I wan-na touch. I see your face ev-'ry-time
Rhy. Fig. 1A
*Doubled by another gtr.
end Rhy. Fig. 2 E5 open E E5
(P.M.)
w/Rhy. Fig. 2 (Gtr. 2)
I dream. On ev-'ry page, ev-'ry mag-a-zine. So wild,
Rhy. Fig. 2A open E E5 end Rhy. Fig. 2A
P.M.
so free, so far from me. You're all
Rhy. Fig. 1B end Rhy. Fig. 1B

E
B
A
A5
I want, my fan - ta - sy, yeah!
Gtrs. 1 & 2
Rhy. Fig. 2B
Pre-Chorus:
Rhy. Fig. 3A
Csus2
G
Asus
A
*Gtr. 3
Oh, look what you've done to this rock 'n' roll
Gtrs 1 & 2
Rhy. Fig. 3
*Keybd. arr. for gtr.
end Rhy. Fig. 3A
w/Rhy. Fig. 3 (Gtrs. 1 & 2) 1st 3 bars only
& Rhy. Fig. 3A (Gtr. 3)
Asus
A
Asus2
A
Csus2
G
clown. Oh, oh, look what you've
end Rhy. Fig. 3

Chorus:
Asus A Asus A Asus2 A G/B C
done. (Bkgd. voc.) Pho - to - graph.
Rhy. Fig. 4
hold throughout
D(11) Em(9) G/B C Em(9) D(11)
I don't want your... Pho - to - graph. I don't need your...
end Rhy. Fig. 4
2nd time To Coda I
3rd time To Coda II
G/B C D(11) Em(9) G/B C
Pho - to - graph. All I've got is a pho - to - graph.
Pho - to - graph.
N.C.
But it's not e - nough! I'd be your

Verse 2:
w/Rhy. Fig. 1 (Gtr. 1)
open
E
Gtr. 2
P.M.
lov - er, (if) you were there. Put your hurt on me, if you dare.
w/Rhy. Fig. 1 (Gtr. 1) 1st 2 bars only
Such a wom - an, you got style. You make ev -
w/Rhy. Fig. 1A (Gtr. 1)
A5
E5
open
E
w/Rhy. Fig. 1 (Gtr. 1)
& Rhy. Fig. 2 (Gtr. 2) 2 times
'ry man feel like a child, oh! You got some kind a hold
E5
open
E
E5
on me. You're all wrapped up in mys - ter - y. So wild
w/Rhy. Figs. 1B (Gtr. 1) & 2A (Gtr. 2)
open
E
E5
w/Rhy. Fig. 2B (Gtrs. 1& 2)
E B A A5
D.S. al Coda I
an' free, so far from me. You're all I want, my fan - ta - sy.
G/B C E5 D5
Coda I
Gtr. 2
- to - graph. You've gone straight to my
Pho - to - graph.
Gtrs. 1 & 2
Gtr. 1
hold
T
A
B

Interlude:
w/Rhy. Fig. 5 (Gtrs. 1 & 2) 2 times
N.C. E5
B
A5
D5/A
E5
B
A5
D5/A
head!
Gtrs. 1 & 2
Rhy. Fig. 5
Gtr. 3
trem. bar
(15ma)
fdbk.
E5
B
E
B
A
Asus[II]
Gtrs. 1 & 2
(8va)
hold bend
fdbk.
grad. release
Gtr. 4

Guitar Solo:
Gtrs. 1 & 2
Gtr. 3
E5 A B5 A A5 A A E5 B5 A
open
grad. release
A A5 E5 A B5 A A A E5
trem. bar
B5 A A5
D.S. 𝄋 al Coda II
Coda II
G/B C N.C. C5 C D E
- to - graph.
Pho - to - graph.
I wan-na touch you!
Ah!
mf
cresc.
f
P.M.

Out-Chorus:
w/Rhy. Fig. 4 (Gtrs. 1 & 2) till fade
G/B
C
D(11)
Em(9)
Oh,
oh.
Yeah,
pho - to - graph.
(Bkgd. voc.) Pho - to - graph.
Pho - to - graph.
w/4-bar Bkgd. vocal figure & lead vocal ad lib. (both till fade)
Gtr. 3
(15ma)
A.H.
8va
Begin fade
hold bend
Fade

Pornograffitti

Words and Music by Nuno Bettencourt and Gary Cherone

Rhy. Fig. 2
N.C.
(end Rhy. Fig. 2)
Verses 1 & 2:
1. Sex on the brain,
2. See additional lyrics.
Harm.
8va
Rhy. Fig. 3
*Substitute w/Fill 1 (2nd time)
pumped in my veins,
flow - ing from my head to my feet.
Fill 1
wah wah
*w/wah wah pedal

Sex on T. V., rotation heav - y you
and I are what we eat.
Sex when I'm all a - lone.
It calls me on the phone,
can't stop this ring-ing in my ear.
A.H.
(end Rhy. Fig. 3)
Substitute Fill 2 (2nd time)
Fill 2
*w/wah wah
1/2

Sex in ex - cess_ fill - ing all our sens - es_ keep say - in' there's noth-in' to_ fear._
A.H.
Bridge:
Can't you read the writ - ing on the
Rhy. Fig. 5
1/2
wall?
Can't you see the
ris - ing and the fall?
Oh, can't you see it?
(end Rhy. Fig. 5)

Chorus:
w/Rhy. Fig. 1
All I see__ por - no - graf - fit - ti.
All I hear__ por - no - graf - fit ti.
See no,
hear no.
All I speak__ por - no - graf - fit - ti.
All I fear__ por - no - graf - fit -
ti.
Speak no
To Coda
1.
A5
e - vil.
w/Rhy. Fig. 2
N.C.
Rhy. Fig. 6
(end Rhy. Fig. 6)
2.
e - vil.
w/Rhy. Fig. 1 (1st 3 bars only)
N.C.
All I see's__ por - no - graf - fit -
ti.
All I hear__ por - no - graf - fit - ti.
Speak no,
w/Fill 3
hear no.
Fill 3
A.H.
8va

w/Rhy. Fig. 1 (1st 3 bars only)
All I speak_ por - no - graf - fit - ti.
All I fear_ por - no - graf - fit - ti.
Speak no
e - vil.
Solo
E5
A.H.
8va
16va
w/trem. bar
w/flange
A5
G

B5
A5
C5
D5
D♯5
E5
w/trem. bar
1/2
w/Rhy. Fig. 3 (Gtr. II)
w/Rhy. Fig. 4
Rhy. Fig. 4
(Play 3 times.)
1/2

w/Rhy. Fig. 5
N.C.
8va
N.C.
pick slide
Say, say, say, say!
A.H.
1/2
Can't you hear the writ - ing on the wall?
D.S. al Coda
Coda
w/Rhy. Fig. 1
N.C.
e - vil.
All I see is por - no - graf - fit - ti.
All I hear por - no - graf - fit -
8va
*gliss w/pick
A7
See no, hear no.
ti.
All I speak por - no - graf - fit -
w/Rhy. Fig. 6
A5
ti.
All I fear por - no - graf - fit - ti.
Speak no e - vil.

Verse 2:
Sex in 3-D.
No evil eyes see too much of it and you'll go blind.
Sex education,
Misinformation,
Kiss me where the sun don't shine.

Bridge:
Sex, it all surrounds me,
Pornograffitti.
It's all so constitutional.
Sex is literate, read all about it,
But censor where you all can go.

Practice What You Preach

Words and Music by Eric Peterson, Luciano Clemente, Alex Skolnick, Gregory Christian and Charles Billy

A Introduction

* Half time feel for first 3 measures only

* Double time feel throughout

Guitar 1
E5 B♭ Am Gm E5 G5 B♭5
Guitar 2
E5 B♭5 Am Gm E5 B♭5
Fig.1
E5 G5 A5 G5 A5 G5 E5 G5 F5
Guitar 1 only
Guitar 2 enters
E5 G5 A5 G5 A5 G5 E5 G5 F♯5 B♭5 A5 G5 A5

E5 G5 A5 G5 A5 G5 E5 G5 F5
B Verse
G5 A5 G5 F5
You think your life's so grand, You don't be - lieve a word you say,
Fig.1 variation
G5 A5 G5 F5
your feet aren't on the ground you let your life just slip a - way.
Guitars play Fig.1
A5 G5 A5 G5 E5
Just so un - cer - tain of your bod - y and your soul.
Guitars play Fig.1
G5 A5 G5 A5 G5
The prom - is - es you make, your mind goes blank and then you lose con - trol.

C **Chorus**

D **Verse**

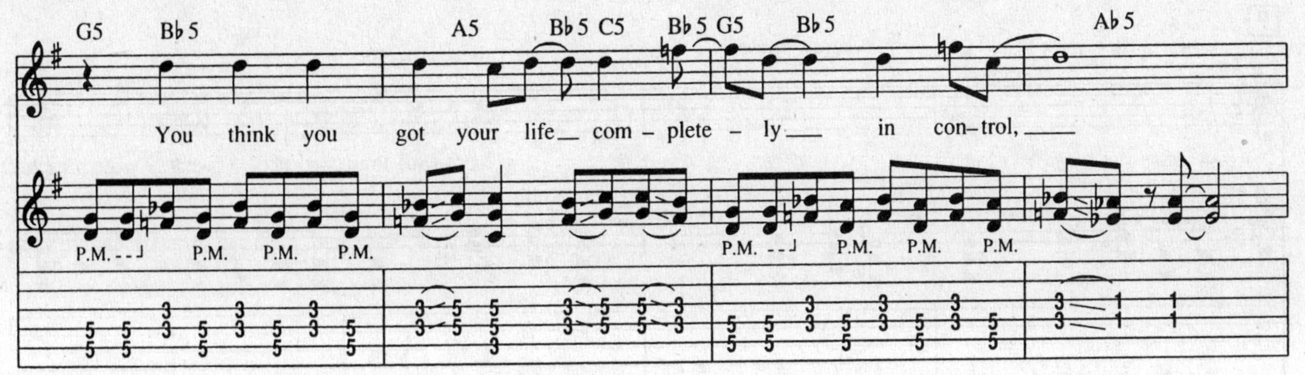
G5
Bb5
A5
Bb5 C5
Bb5 G5
Bb5
Ab5
You think you got your life_ com - plete - ly_ in con-trol,_
P.M.
P.M.
P.M.
P.M.
P.M.
P.M.
P.M.
P.M.

D.S. al Coda
G5
Bb5
C5
Bb5 C5 Bb5
G5
G5 F5
you've_ got a lot_ to learn,_ the bridge_ you burn,_ it's gon - na take_ it's toll.
P.M.
P.M.
P.M.
P.M.

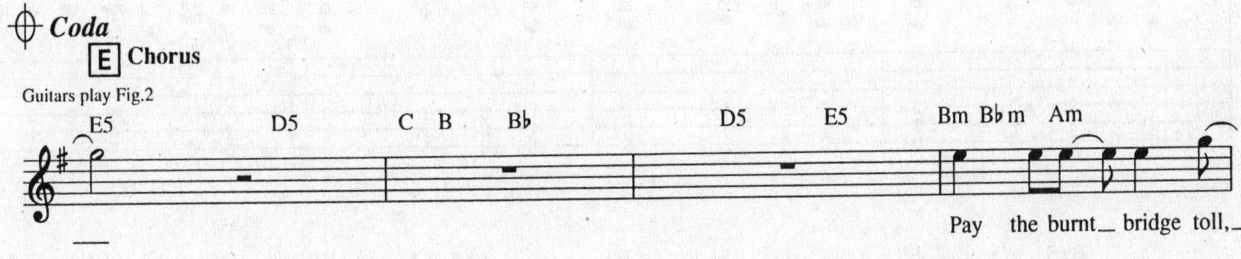
Coda
E Chorus
Guitars play Fig.2
E5
D5
C B
Bb
D5
E5
Bm Bbm Am
Pay the burnt_ bridge toll,_

Guitars play Fig.2
E5
D5
C B
Bb
D5
E5
Bm Bbm Am
So prac - tice what_ you preach,_

F
E5 B♭5 A5 E5 G5 F♯5 E5 B♭5 A5 E5
(So) Prac - tice what _ you preach._
B♭5 A5 E5 G5 F♯5 E5 B♭5 A5 E5 B♭5 E5
(Preach.)
Prac - tice what _ you preach._
B♭5 A5 E5 G5 F♯5 E5 B♭5 A5 E5 B♭5 E5
(So) Prac - tice what _ you preach._
B♭5 A5 E5 G5 F♯5 E5 B♭5 A5 E5 B♭5 E5
(Preach.)
Prac - tice what _ you preach._
(no vocal on D.S.)

Bb5
E5
Fine
G
Guitar Solo*
E5
Preach.
Guitar 1
Guitar 2
* half time
Guitar 2 continues simile
full
Guitar 1
A tempo (♩ = 180, double time feel)

Guitar 1
E5 A5 B5 C#5
D5 C#5 D5 C#5 B5 F#5
full full
E5 D5
8 va
1/2 1/2 1/2 1/2
8 va
C#5 A D5 C#5 D5 C#5
1/2 1/2 full
D5 C#5 G#5
8 va
full full full full full

A5
B5
D5 C#5
D5 C#5
D5 C#5
D5 C#5
B5
C#5 B5 D5
A5
8va
A5 G#5
A5 G#5
A5 G#5
A5 G#5
A5 G#5
A5 G#5
tr
A5 G#5
A5 G#5
Bb5
full
full

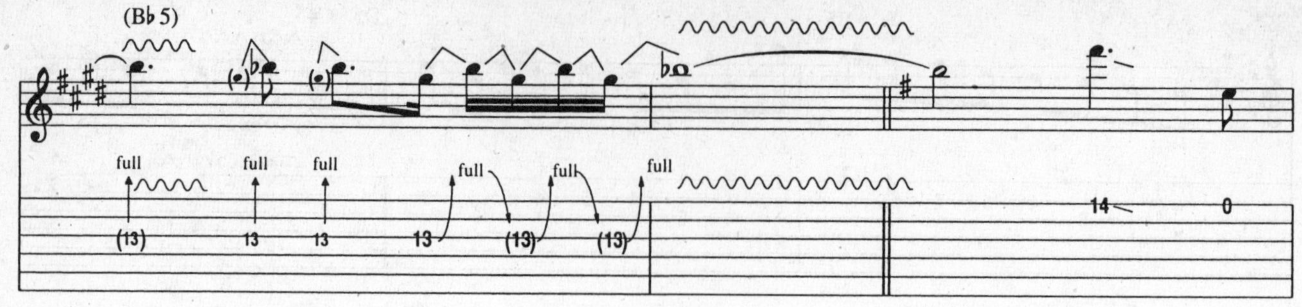
(B♭5)
full
full
full
full
full
full
13
(13)
14
0

E5
full

E5
G5
B5
w/bar
1/2

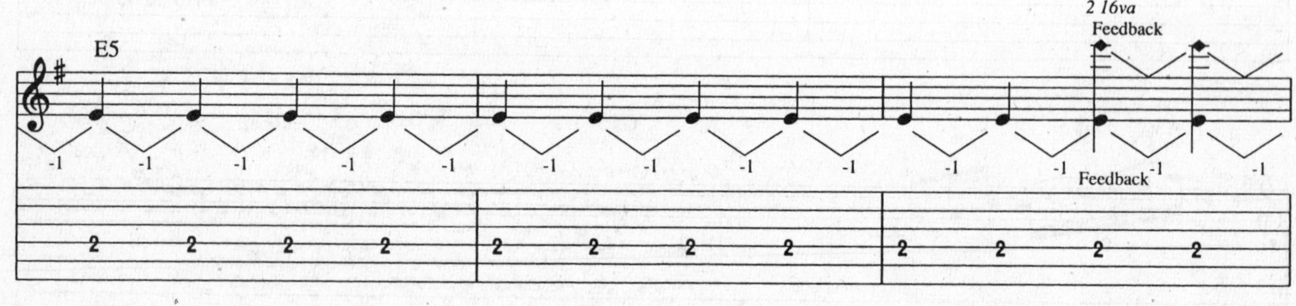
E5
2 16va
Feedback
Feedback

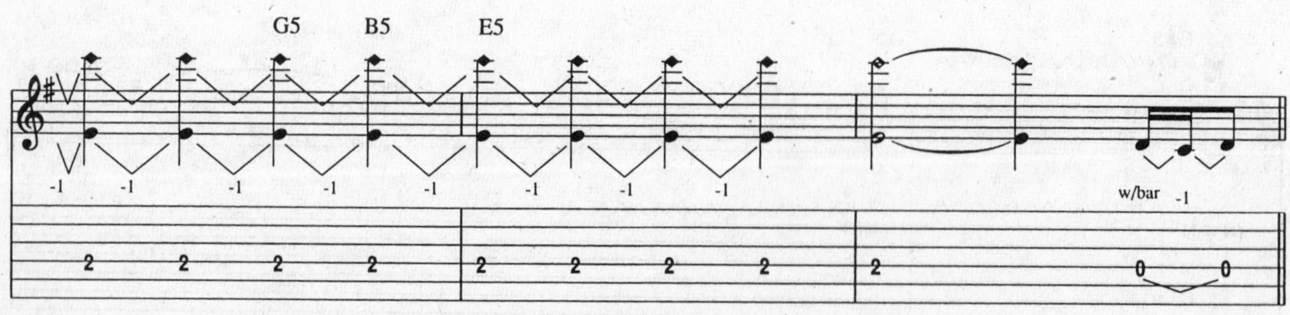
G5
B5
E5
w/bar

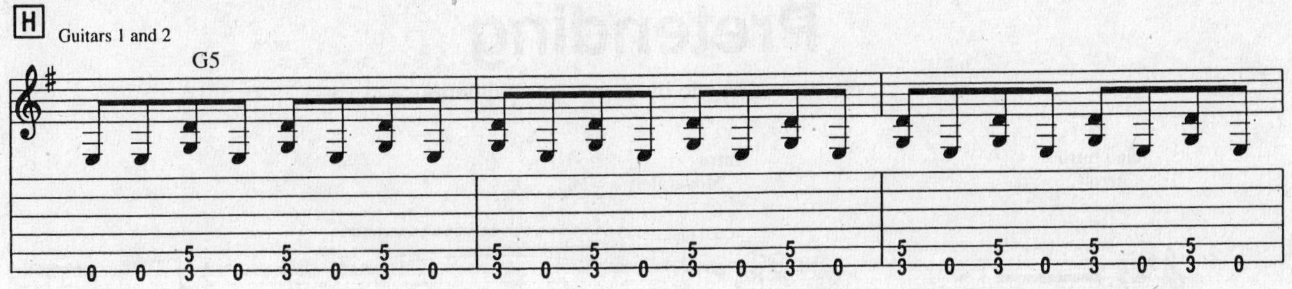
H
Guitars 1 and 2
G5

8va
Guitar 1
Guitar 2

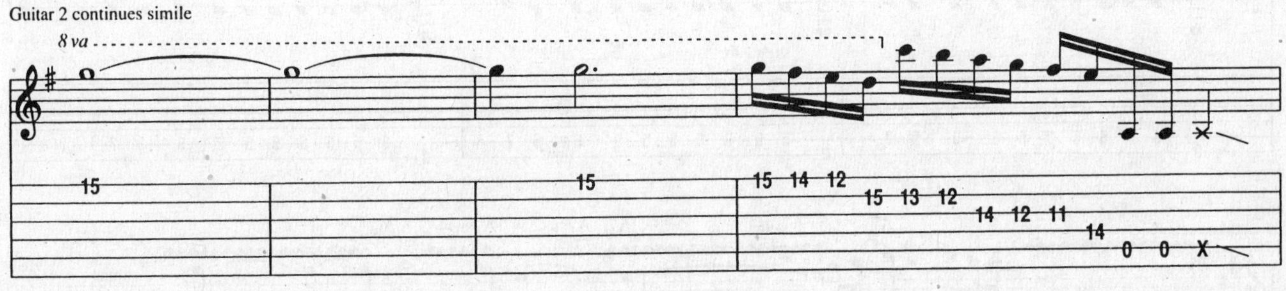
Guitar 2 continues simile
8va

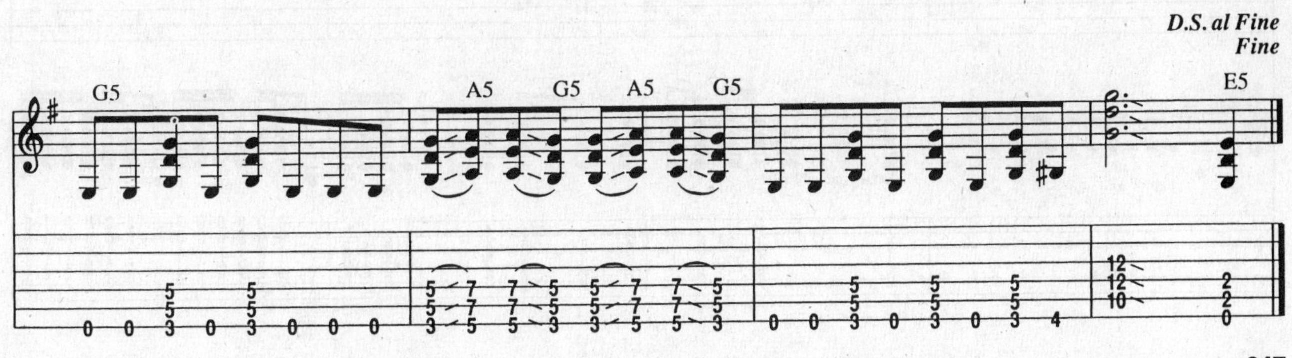
D.S. al Fine
Fine
G5
A5
G5
A5
G5
E5

Pretending

Words and Music by Jerry Lynn Williams

A7 A7sus2 A7 A7sus4 A7

Verse

E

1. How man-y times ___ must we tell the tale? ___

fdbk.

Rhy. Fig. 1

G/E

How man-y times ___ must we fall? ___

A7/E

Liv-in' in ___ lost ___

*T

T

*T=Thumb on ⑥

A7sus4/E
A7/E
E
mem-o-ry you just re-called.
let ring
fdbk.
End Rhy. Fig. 1
Verse
Gtr. 2: w/ Rhy. Fig. 1, 1st 7 meas.
E
G/E
2. Work-in' on the sound of the band, try'n' to get the mu - sic right.
Gtr. 1
full
A7/E
A7sus4/E
A7/E
E
Gtr. 2: w/ Fill 1
N.C.
Two go out work-ing, three stay home at night.
full
1/4
*vol. swell
Fill 1
Gtr. 2

Chorus
A
E
D
Gtr. 1: w/ Fill 2, 2nd time
That's when she said she was pre - tend - ing,
just like she knew the plan.
Gtr. 1
Gtr. 2
Rhy. Fig. 2
w/ Leslie effect
To Coda
Gtr. 2: w/ Rhy. Fill 1, 2nd time
That's when I knew she was pre - tend - ing,
pre - tend - ing to un - der - stand.
Pre -
End Rhy. Fig. 2
w/ pick & fingers
Fill 2
Gtr. 2
full
Rhy. Fill 1
Gtr. 2
P.M.

Gtr. 2: w/ Riff A, 2 times
E7
tend - ing, pre - tend - ing, pre -
Gtr. 1
full
full
A7
E7
tend - ing, pre - tend - ing.
full
full
Verse
Gtr. 2: w/ Rhy. Fig. 1
E
G/E
3. Sa-tis - fied, but lost in love, sit - u - a - tions change.
Harm.
D.S. al Coda
A7
A7sus4
A7
E
Gtr. 2: w/ Fill 1
N.C.
You're nev-er who you used to think you are, how strange.

Coda
Gtr. 2: w/ Riff A, 2 times
E7
tend - ing,
pre - tend - ing,
Gtr. 1
full
full
full
A7
pre - tend - ing,
pre -
1/4
full
full
full
E7
tend - ing.
(Pre - tend - ing, pre - tend - ing.)
Guitar Solo
Gtr. 2: w/ Rhy. Fig. 1
E
1/4
full
full
G/E
A7
full
hold bend
even release
full
full
A7sus4
A7
E
Verse
Gtr. 2: w/ Rhy. Fig. 1, 1st 7 meas.
E
4. I get lost in
full
full
1/2
full
1 1/2
1/2

G/E
A7
al - i - bis,
sad - ness can't
pre - vail.
Ev-'ry-bod-y
fdbk.
A7sus4
A7
E
Gtr. 2: w/ Fill 1
N.C.
Chorus
Gtr. 2: w/ Rhy. Fig. 2, simile
A
E
knows strong love can't
fail.
Don't be pre - tend - ing
1/4
D
A
E
D
A
E
a-bout how you feel.
Don't be pre-tend - ing
D
A
E
1.
D
2.
D
your love is real.
Don't be pre -
Pre -

Gtr. 2: w/ Riff A, 2 times
E7
tend - ing,
pre - tend - ing,
pre -
let ring
1/2
A7
E7
tend - ing,
pre - tend - ing, pre - tend - ing pre -
let ring
Outro-Guitar Solo
Gtr. 2: w/ Rhy. Fig. 1
Begin Fade
E
G/E
tend - ing.
let ring
1/4
A7
A7sus4
A7
E
Fade Out
full

Rock This Town

Words and Music by Brian Setzer

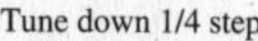

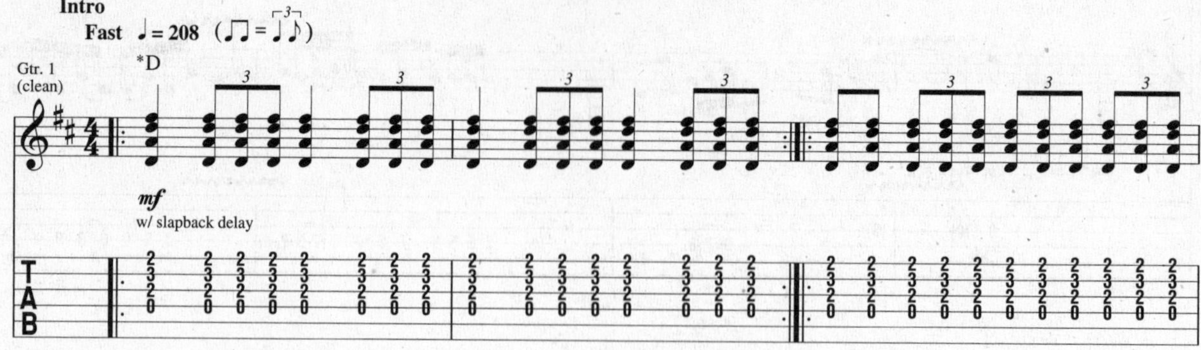

*Chord symbols reflect basic harmony.

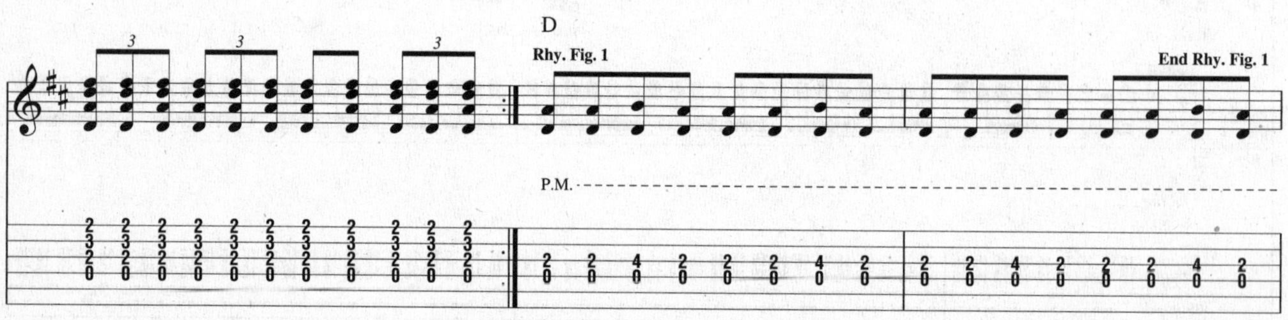

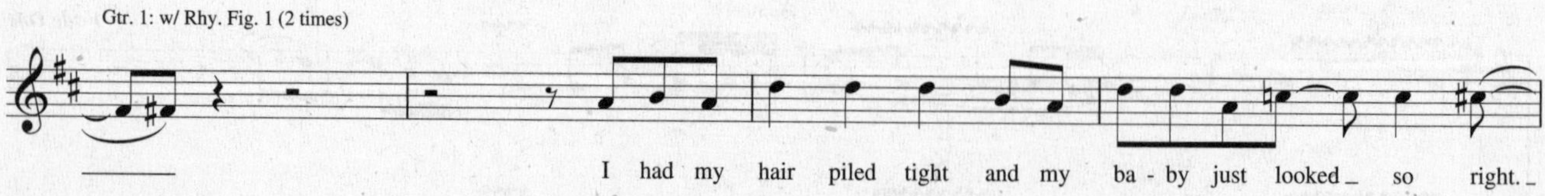

A
D
Well,
pick you up at ten, got - ta
Gtr. 1
let ring
D9
G
E7
have you home at two. Your ma - ma don't know what I got in store for you. But that's
let ring
Interlude
D
A
D
all right 'cause we're look - in' as cool as can be.
let ring
P.M.
P.M.

2. Well, we
P.M.
Verse
D
found a lit - tle place that real - ly did - n't look half bad.
P.M.
I had a whis - key on the rocks and change of a dol - lar for the
P.M.
A
juke - box.
Well,
D
I put a quar - ter right in -

Chorus

1st & 3rd times, Gtr. 1: w/ Rhy. Fig. 1 (2 times)
2nd time, Gtr. 1: w/ Riff A

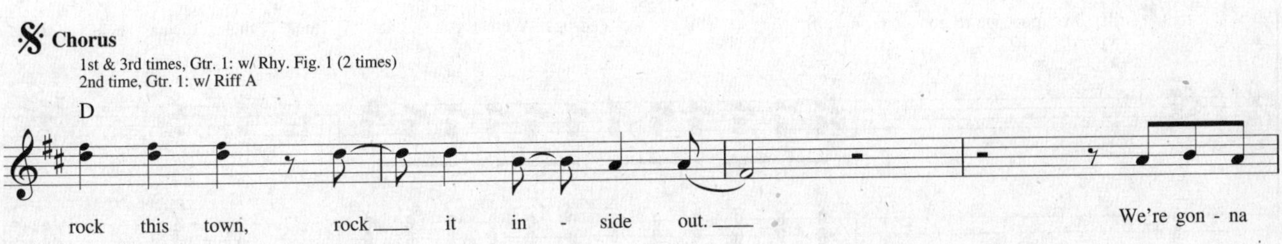

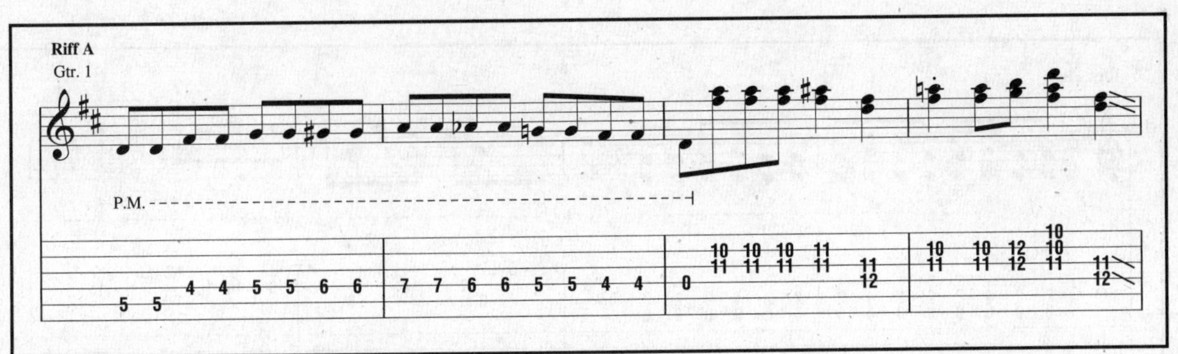

3rd time, Gtr. 1: w/ Rhy. Fig. 2

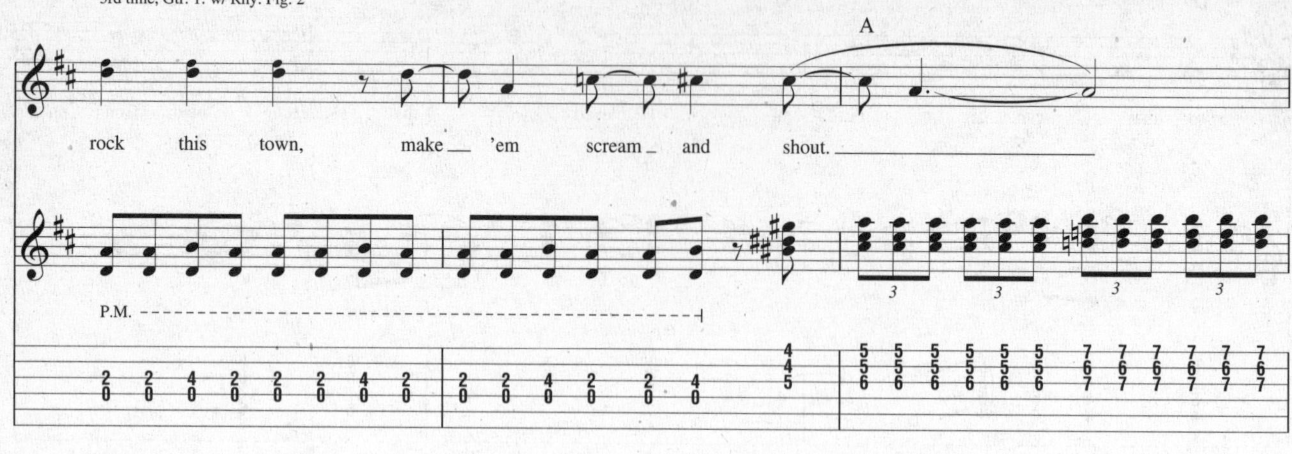

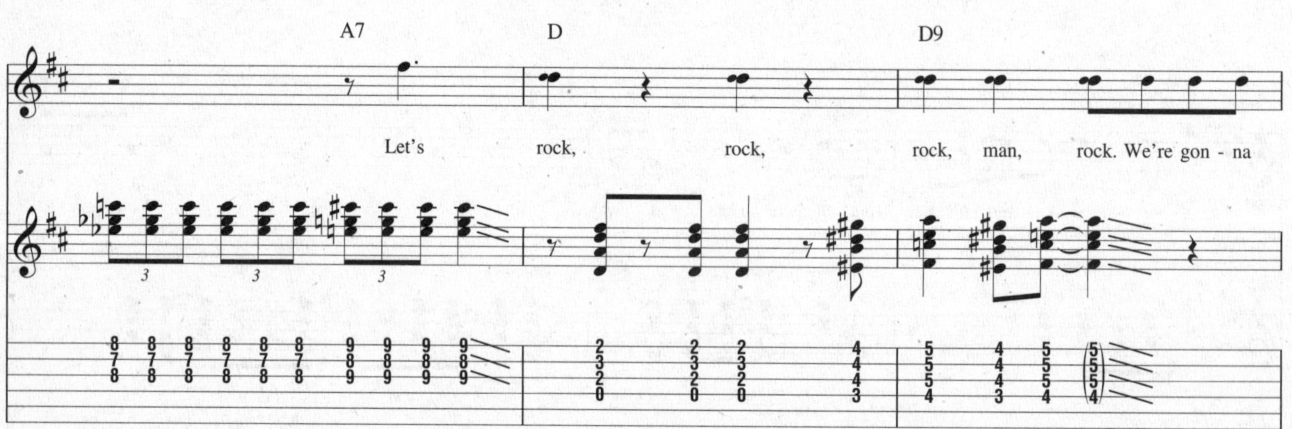

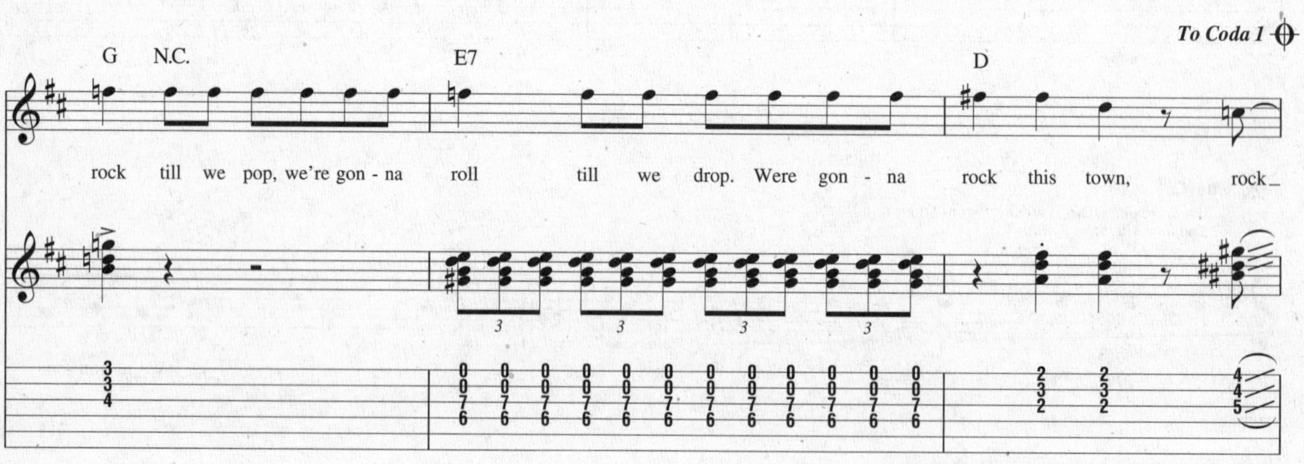

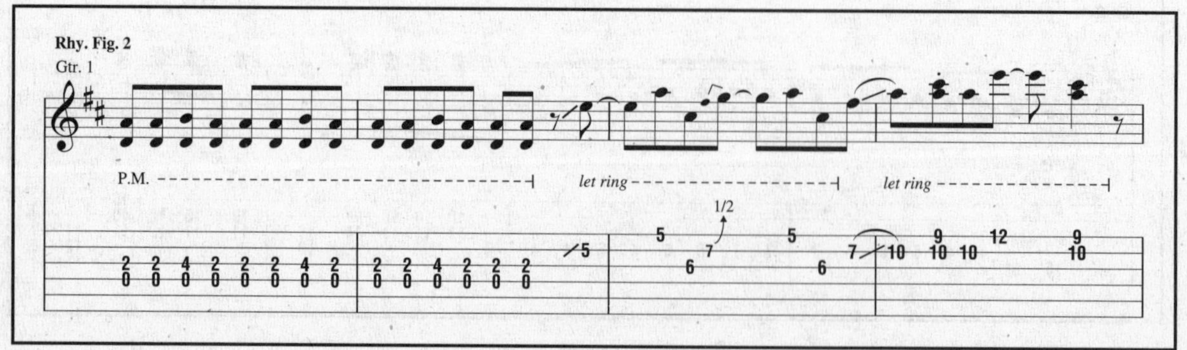

To Coda 2
Guitar Solo
A
D
D
it in - side out.
All right, rock it, boys!
Whoa!
Whoa.
A
D
Oh, rock it!
D7
G
E7
D

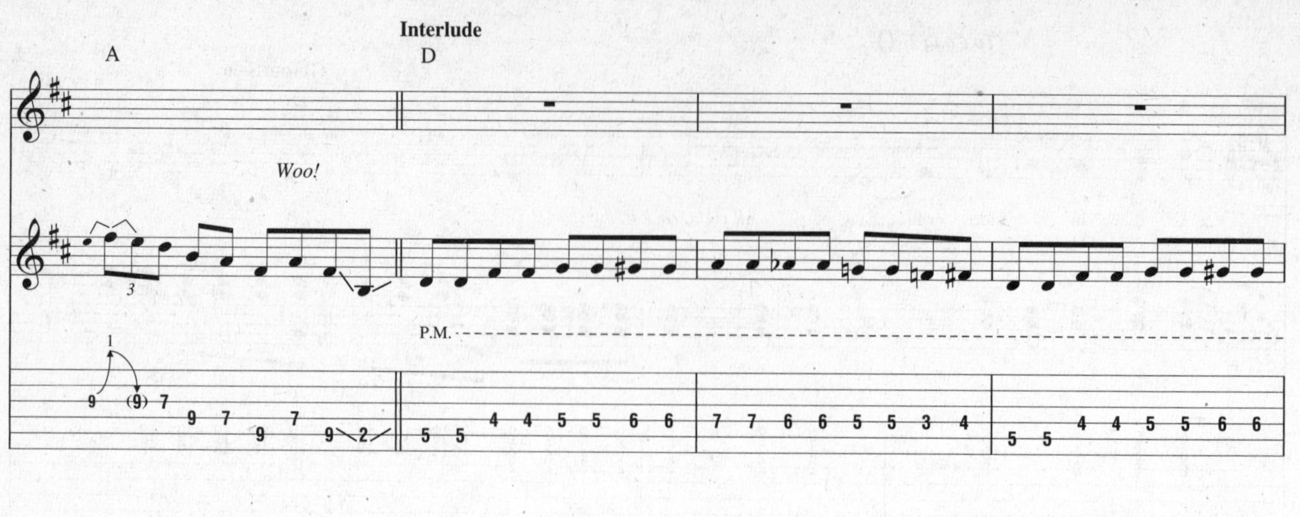
Interlude
A
D
Woo!
P.M.

P.M.

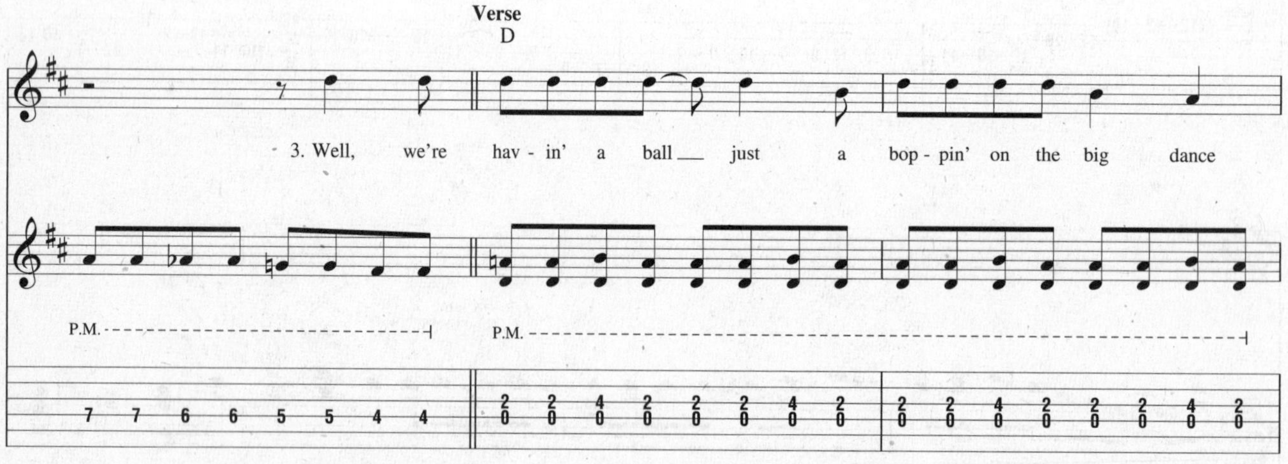
Verse
D
3. Well, we're hav - in' a ball just a bop - pin' on the big dance
P.M.
P.M.

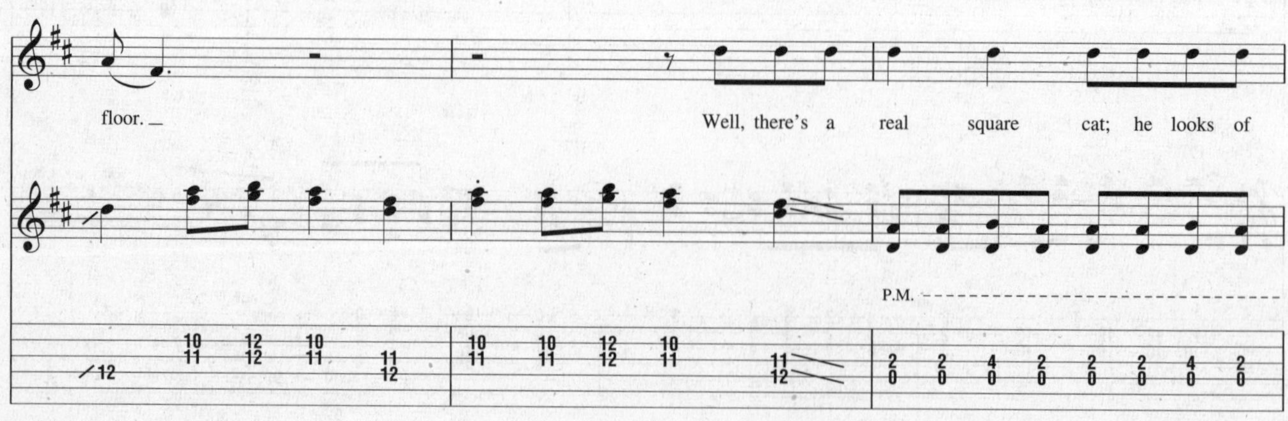
floor.
Well, there's a real square cat; he looks of
P.M.

A
D N.C.
nine - teen - sev - en - ty - four.
Well,
you look at me once,
you
P.M.
D9 N.C.
G N.C.
E7
look at me twice.
Look at me a - gain and there's a gon - na be a fight. We're gon - na
D.S. al Coda 1
D
A
Dsus2
rock this town, we're gon - na rip this place a - part.
We're gon - na
Coda 1
A7
D
this place a - part.
Woo!

*Chord symbols reflect implied harmony.

Interlude
D
1., 2., 3.
4.
D.S. al Coda 2
We're gon - na
P.M.
Coda 2
D
We're gon - na rock this town, rock
it in - side out.
it in - side out.
1.
2.
A
A
N.C.
Free time
8va
Woo!
w/ bar
N.C.

Rock'n Me

Words and Music by Steve Miller

Verse
N.C.
A5 A♯5 B5 B6 B5 B6 B5
1. Well, I've been look - in' real hard, and I'm
3. Don't get sus - pi - cious now don't
End Rhy. Fig. 1
Rhy. Fig. 2
P.M.
B6 B5 B6 B5 A5 A6 A5 A6 A5 A6 A5 A6 E5
try - in' to find a job, but it just keeps get - tin' tough - er ev - 'ry day. But I got
be sus - pi - cious, babe, you know you are a friend of mine. And you know
E6 E5 E6 E5 E6 E5 E6 E5 B5 B6 B5 B6 B5
to do my part, 'cause I know in my heart, I got to please my sweet mm, ba - by, yeah.
that it's true, that all the things that I do are gon - na come back to you in your sweet time.
Gtr. 1: w/ Rhy. Fig. 2
B6 B5 B6 B5 B6 B5 B6 B5 B6 B5 B6 B5
Well, I ain't su - per - sti - tious, and I don't get sus - pi - cious, but my
I went from Phoe - nix, Ar - i - zo - na, all the way to Ta - co - ma, Phil - a -
End Rhy. Fig. 2

A5 A6 A5 A6 A5 A6 A5 A6 E5 E6 E5 E6 E5
wom - an is a friend of mine. And I know that it's true that all the
del - phi - a, At - lan - ta, L. A. North - ern Cal - i - for - nia where the
To Coda
E6 E5 E6 E5 B5 B6 B5 B6 B5 B6 B5 B6 B5
things that I do will come back to me in my sweet - n time. So keep on
girls are warm, so I could hear my sweet, mm, ba - by say. Keep on a
Chorus
B5 B6 B5 B6 B5 B6 B7 B5 A5 A6 A5 A6 A5
rock - in' me, ba - by. Keep on a rock - in' me, ba - by.
Gtr. 1
A6 A7 A5 E5 E6 E5 E6 E5 E5
Keep on a rock - in' me, ba - by. Keep on a
P.M.
Verse
Gtr. 1: w/ Rhy. Fig. 2
B5 B6 B5 B6 B5 B6 B7 B6 B5 B6 B5 B6 B5
rock - in' me, ba - by. 2. I went from Phoe - nix, Ar - i - zo - na all the
P.M.

B6 B5 B6 B5 A5 A6 A5 A6 A5 A6 A5 A6 E6
way to Ta - co - ma, Phil - a - del - phi - a, At - lan - ta, L. A. North -
E6 E5 E6 E5 E6 E5 E6 E5 B5 B6 B5 B6 B5
- ern Cal - i - for - nia where the girls are warm, so I can be with my sweet ba - by, yeah.
Chorus
B6 B5 B6 B5 B6 B5 B6 B5 B6 B7 B6 A5
Keep on a rock - in' me, ba - by. Keep on a
Gtr. 1
P.M.
A6 A5 A6 A5 A6 A7 A6 E5 E6 E5 E6 E5
rock - in' me, ba - by. Keep on a rock - in' me, ba - by.
E6 E7 E5 B5 B6 B5 B6 B5 B6 B7 A5
Keep on a rock - in' me, ba - by. Ba - by, ba - by, ba - by, keep on

Gtr. 1: w/ Rhy. Fig. 1
B5 E5 B5 E B5 A5 B5 E5
rock - in', rock - in' me, ba - by. Keep on a rock - in', rock - in' me
D.S. al Coda
B5 E N.C. A5 A♯5
ba - by. Who, who, who, yeah.
(Ba - by. Who.)
Coda
Outro-Chorus
Gtr. 1: w/ Rhy. Fig. 2 (1st 6 meas.)
B5 B6 B5 B6 B5 B6 B5 B6 B5 A5 A6 A5 A6 A5
rock - in' me, ba - by. Keep on a rock - in' me, ba - by.
A6 A5 A6 E5 E6 E5 E6 E5 E6 E5 E6 E5
Keep on a rock - in' me, ba - by. Keep on a
Begin fade
B5 B6 B5 B6 B5 B6 B5 A5 B5 B6 B5 B6 B5 A♯5 B5 A♯5 B5
rock-in' me, rock-in' me, rock-in', ba-by, ba-by, ba-by. Keep on rock-in' me, ba - by. Keep on a
P.M.
P.M.
Fade out
A5 A6 A5 A6 A5 A6 A7 A6 E5 E6 E5 E6
rock - in' me, ba - by. Keep on a rock - in' me, ba - by.
P.M.

Rocky Mountain Way

Words and Music by Joe Walsh, Joe Vitale, Ken Passarelli and Rocke Grace

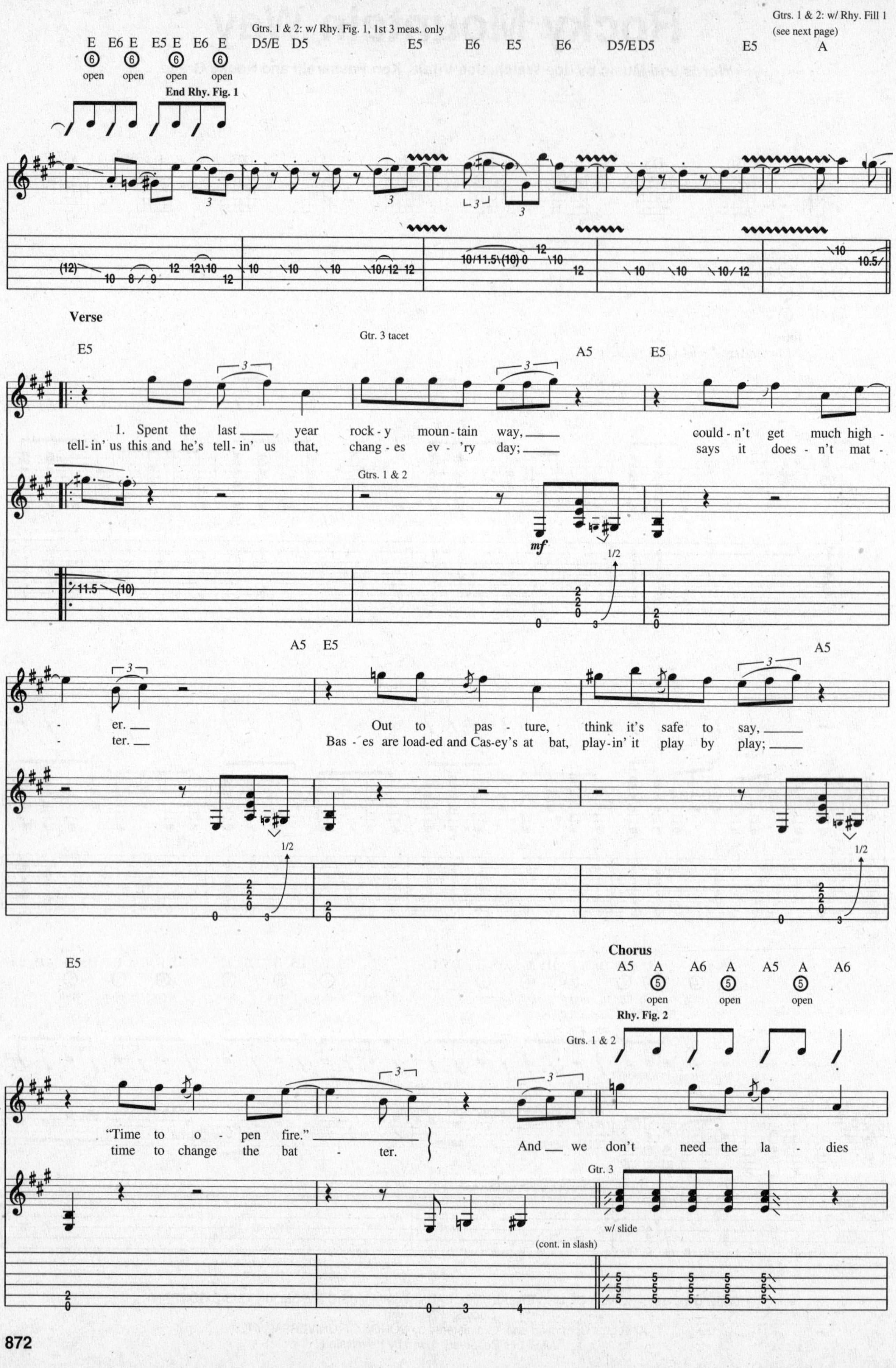

Gtrs. 1 & 2: w/ Rhy. Fig. 1, 1st 3 meas. only
Gtrs. 1 & 2: w/ Rhy. Fill 1
(see next page)
E E6 E E5 E E6 E D5/E D5 E5 E6 E5 E6 D5/E D5 E5 A
open open open open
End Rhy. Fig. 1
Verse
Gtr. 3 tacet
E5 A5 E5
1. Spent the last year rock-y moun-tain way,
tell-in' us this and he's tell-in' us that, chang-es ev-'ry day;
could-n't get much high-er.
says it does-n't mat-ter.
Gtrs. 1 & 2
mf
1/2
A5 E5 A5
Out to pas-ture, think it's safe to say,
Bas-es are load-ed and Cas-ey's at bat, play-in' it play by play;
E5
Chorus
A5 A A6 A A5 A A6
open open open
Rhy. Fig. 2
Gtrs. 1 & 2
"Time to o-pen fire."
time to change the bat-ter.
And we don't need the la-dies
Gtr. 3
w/ slide
(cont. in slash)

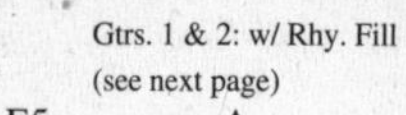

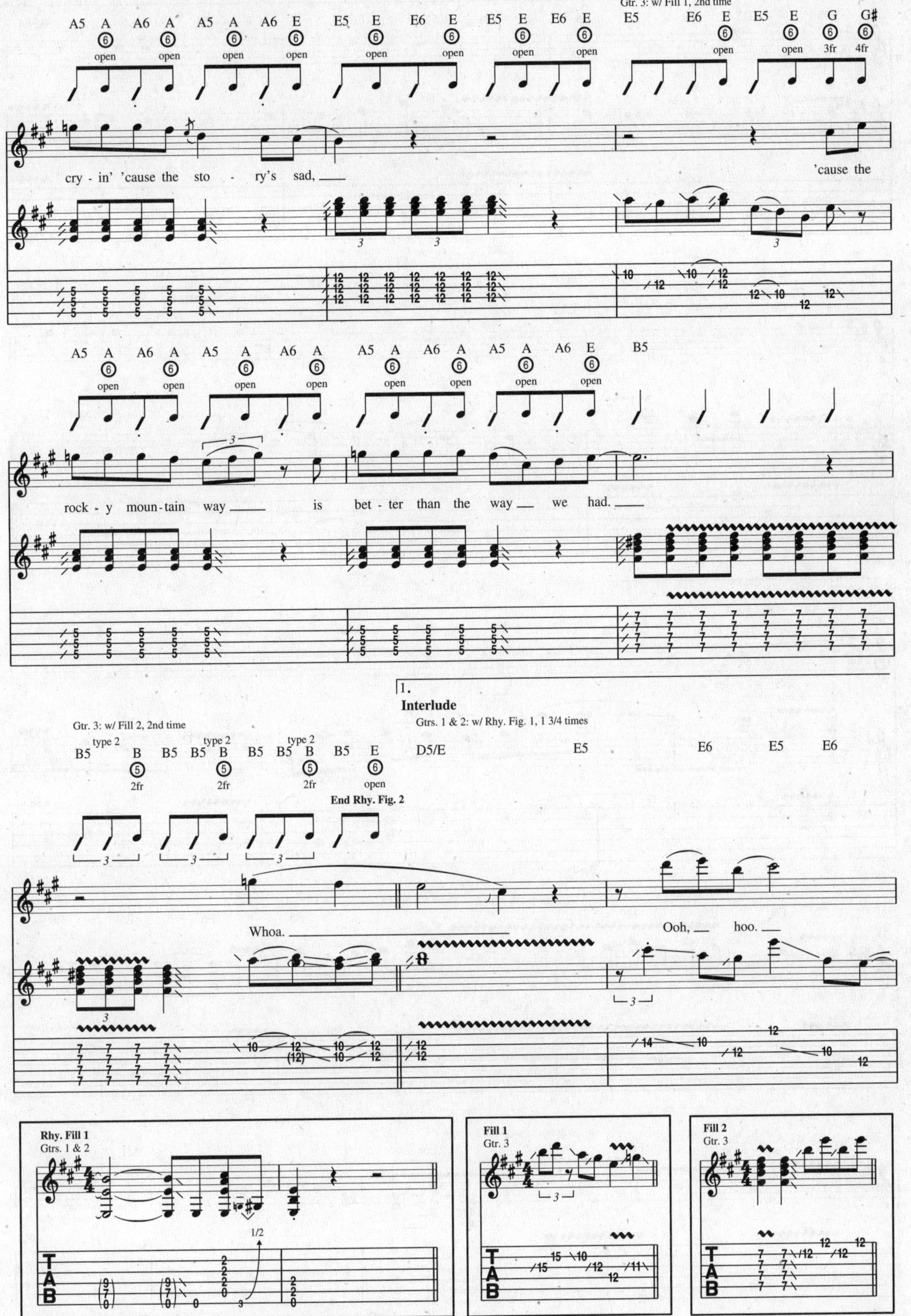
Gtr. 3: w/ Fill 1, 2nd time
A5 A A6 A A5 A A6 E E5 E E6 E E5 E E6 E E5 E6 E E5 E G G#
open open open open open open open open open open 3fr 4fr
cry - in' 'cause the sto - ry's sad,
'cause the
A5 A A6 A A5 A A6 A A5 A A6 A A5 A A6 E B5
rock - y mountain way is bet - ter than the way we had.
1.
Interlude
Gtr. 3: w/ Fill 2, 2nd time
Gtrs. 1 & 2: w/ Rhy. Fig. 1, 1 3/4 times
B5 type 2 B B5 B5 type 2 B B5 B5 type 2 B B5 E D5/E E5 E6 E5 E6
2fr 2fr 2fr open
End Rhy. Fig. 2
Whoa.
Ooh, hoo.
Rhy. Fill 1
Gtrs. 1 & 2
Fill 1
Gtr. 3
Fill 2
Gtr. 3

*Chord Symbols implied by kbd.

Guitar Solo
N.C.
Gtr. 4
w/ talk box
mf
Gtr. 5 (talk box)
Gtr. 4
divisi
full
E
open
E5
Gtr. 1
P.M.
8va
Gtrs. 4 & 5
Gtr. 5
Gtr. 4
divisi
1/2

E
6
open
E6 E E5 E6 E5 E6 E5
P.M.
loco
Gtrs. 4 & 5
full
1/2
E6 E5 E5 E6 E5 E6 E5
Gtr. 1: w/ Rhy. Fill 2
F#
10fr
B C#
15fr 17fr
Gtr. 3
(cont. in notation)
Guitar Solo
Gtrs. 1 & 2: w/ Rhy. Fig. 2
Gtrs. 4 & 5: w/ Rhy. Fill 3
Gtrs. 4 & 5 tacet
A5type2 A6 A5 A6 A5 A6 A5 A6 E5 E6 E5 E6 E5 E6 E5
8va
steady gliss.
A A6 A5 A6 A5 A6 A5 A6 B5
let ring
Rhy. Fill 2
Gtr. 1
Rhy. Fill 3
Gtrs. 4 & 5

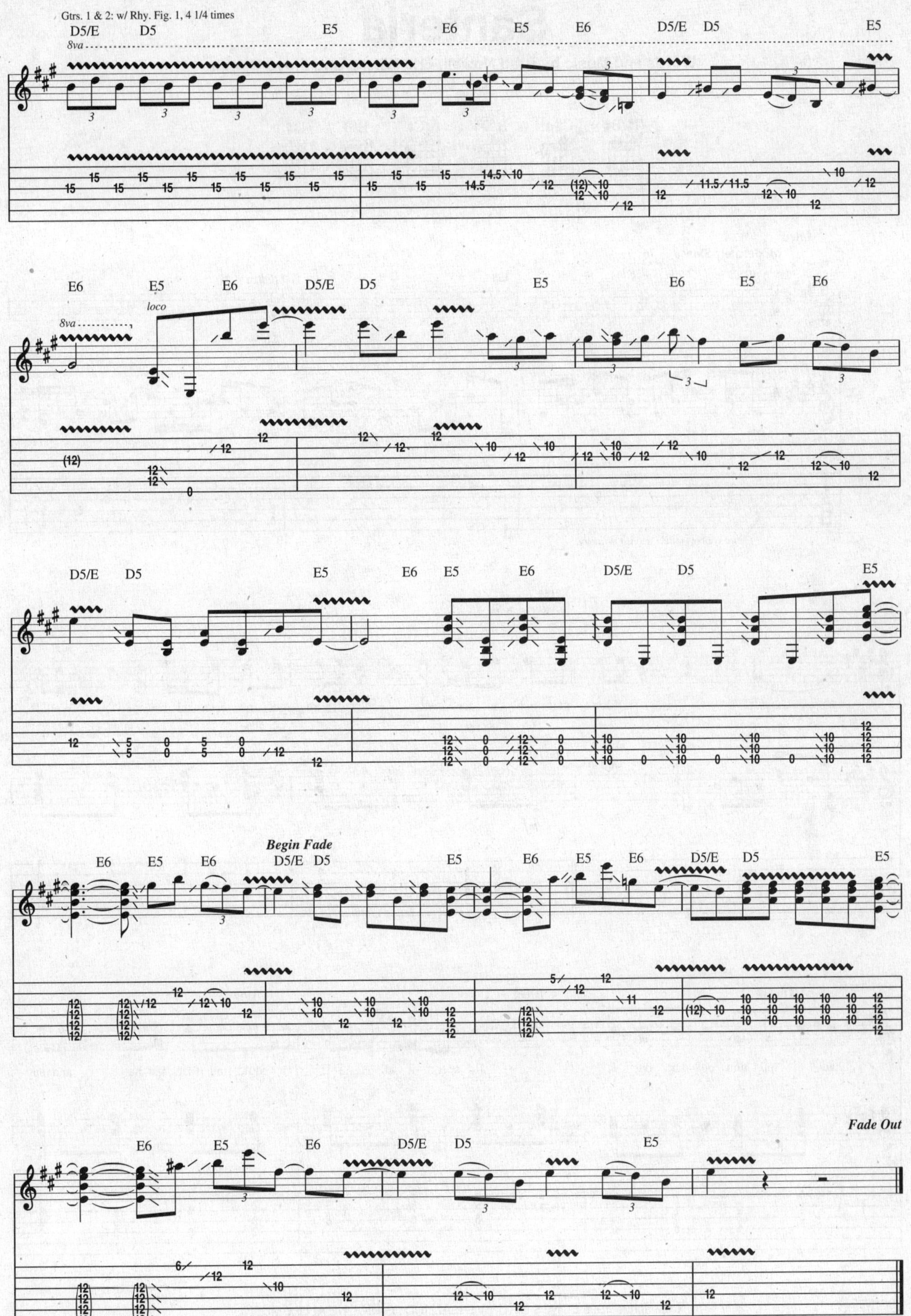
Gtrs. 1 & 2: w/ Rhy. Fig. 1, 4 1/4 times
D5/E
D5
E5
E6
8va
loco
Begin Fade
Fade Out

Santeria

Words and Music by Brad Nowell, Eric Wilson and Floyd Gaugh

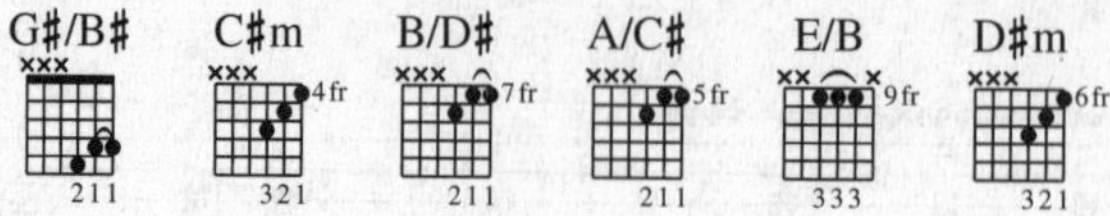

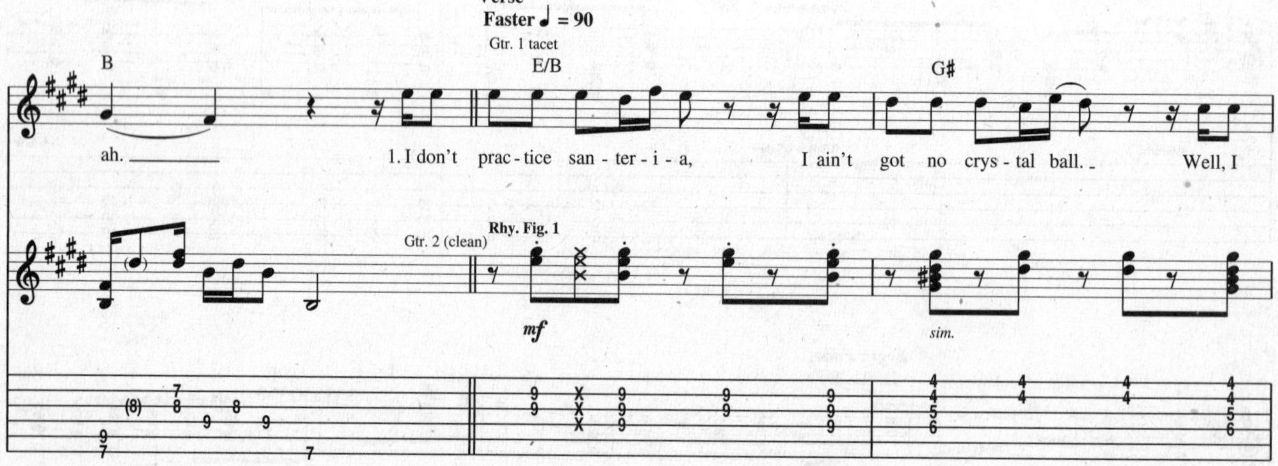

G#/B#
C#m
B/D#
A/C#
End Rhy. Fig. 1
Gtr. 2
San - cho that she's found, well I'd pop a cap in San - cho and I'd slap her down.
Gtr. 3 (clean)
Riff A
mf
Chorus
A/C#
Rhy. Fig. 2
B/D#
E/B
D#m
C#m
A/C#
B
E/B
(cont. in notation)
But I real - ly wan - na know, ah, ba - by, mm. All I real - ly wan - na say
let ring throughout
D#m/A# C#m/G# A/E
B/F#
E/B D#m
C#m
A/C#
B/D#
E/B
I can't de - fine. Well, it's love that I need. 2. Oh, my soul will have to
Gtr. 2
End Rhy. Fig. 2
Gtr. 3
End Riff A

Verse
Gtr. 2: w/ Rhy. Fig. 1, simile
Gtr. 3 tacet
E/B
G#
C#m/G#
wait 'til I get back, find a hei-na of my own. Dad-dy's gon-na love one and
knows what is good for him he best go run and hide. Dad-dy's got a new for-ty-
Gtr. 3
B/D#
E/B
G#/B#
all. I feel the break, feel the break, feel the break and I got to live it out,
five and I won't think twice to stick that bar-rel straight down San-cho's throat. Be-
Chorus
Gtr. 3: w/ Riff A, simile
Gtr. 2: w/ Rhy. Fig. 2, simile
C#m
B/D#
A/C#
B/D#
oh, yeah, huh. Well, I swear that I, well I real-ly wan-na know,
lieve me when I say that I got some-thing for his punk ass. What I real-ly wan-na know,
E/B
D#m
C#m
A/C#
B
E/B
D#m/A#
C#m/G#
A/E
ah, ba-by. All I real-ly wan-na say I can't de-fine.
ah, ba-by. Oo, what I real-ly wan-na say is there's just
To Coda
B/F#
E/B
D#m
C#m
A/C#
B/D#
E/B
Got love, make it go. Well, my soul will have to...
one way back and I'll make it. Yeah, my soul will have to
Guitar Solo
Gtr. 2: w/ Rhy. Fig. 1, simile
Gtr. 3 tacet
E/B
G#
C#m/G#
Gtr. 1
full
1/2
1/2
Gtr. 3

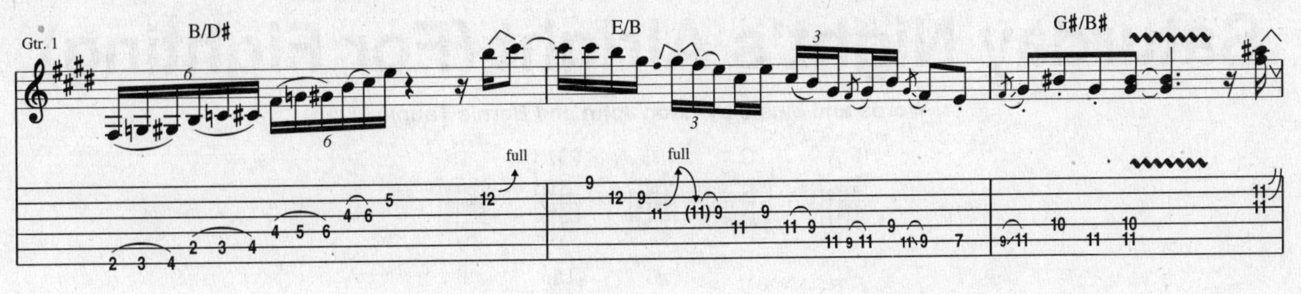
Gtr. 1
B/D♯
E/B
G♯/B♯
full
full

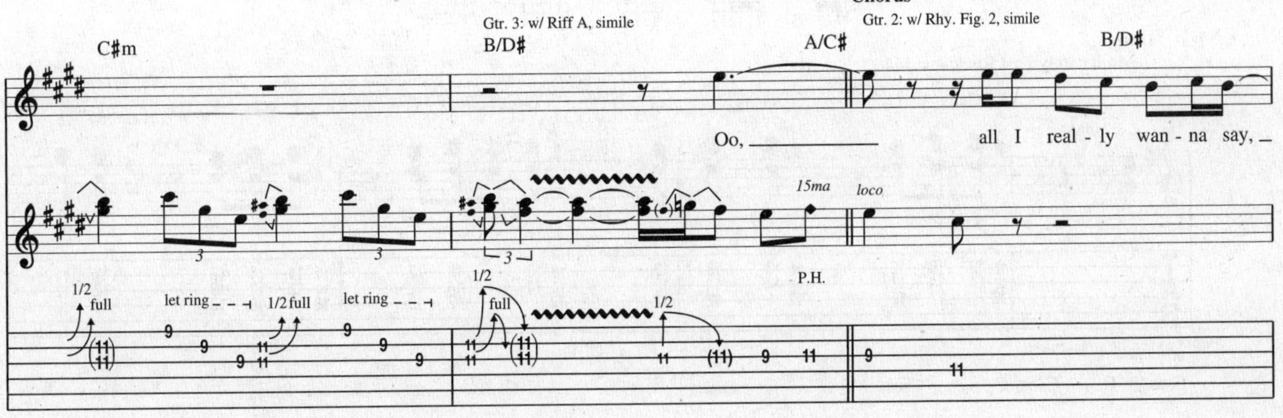
Chorus
C♯m
Gtr. 3: w/ Riff A, simile
B/D♯
A/C♯
Gtr. 2: w/ Rhy. Fig. 2, simile
B/D♯
Oo,
all I real - ly wan - na say,
15ma
loco
P.H.
1/2 full
let ring
1/2 full
let ring
1/2 full
1/2

Gtr. 1 tacet
E/B
D♯m
C♯m
A/C♯
B
E/B
D♯m/A♯ C♯m/G♯
A/E
ah, ba - by.
What I real - ly wan - na say
is
I've got

D.S. al Coda
B/F♯
E/B
D♯m
C♯m
A/C♯
B/D♯
E/B
mine
and I'll make it.
Oo, yes I'm
com - ing up.
3. Tell San - chi - to that if he

Coda
E
D♯5
C♯
B
A5
B
E7
rit.
wait.
Gtr. 2
rit.
w/ bar
Gtr. 3
rit.

Saturday Night's Alright (For Fighting)

Words and Music by Elton John and Bernie Taupin

G
na rock. Wan - na get a bel - ly full of beer. My
what I need. I can sink a lit - tle drink and shout out "She's with me!" A
End Rhy. Fig. 1
Gtr. 1
Gtr. 2
mf
Gtr. 1: w/ Rhy. Fig. 1
Gtr. 2 tacet
F
old man's a drunk - er than a bar - rel full of mon - keys and my ol' la - dy she don't care.
cou - ple of the sounds that I real - ly like are the sounds of a switch-blade and a
C
G
My sis - ter looks cute in her britch - es and boots.
mo - tor bike. I'm a ju - ve - nile prod - uct of the work - ing class. A Whose
Gtr. 2
simile on repeat
Dm
Dm7
hand-ful of grease in her hair.
best friend floats in the bot - tom of a glass. Oh.
Oh.
Gtrs. 1 & 2
P.M.
(Gtr. 2, cont. in slash)

Pre-Chorus
F/A C
Rhy. Fig. 2
Gtr. 2
Bb Eb/G Bb Eb/G Bb
Don't give us none of your ag - gra - va - tion we've had it with your dis - ci - pline.
Rhy. Fig. 2A
Gtr. 1
Eb/G Bb Eb/G Bb F
C
Woah. Sat - ur - day night's al - right for fight - ing. Get
F/A C F/A C
Gtr. 3: w/ Fill 1
F/A C
End Rhy. Fig. 2
Gtr. 2: w/ Rhy. Fig. 2, simile
F C
a lit - tle ac - tion in. Get a - bout as oiled as a
End Rhy. Fig. 2A
Fill 1
Gtr. 3 (slight dist.)
1/4

Bb
Eb/G
Bb
Eb/G
Bb
Eb/G
Bb
Eb/G
Bb
F
die - sel train. Gon - na set this dance a - light. 'Cause
C
F/A
C
F/A
C
Sat - ur - day night's the night I like. Sat - ur - day night's al - right.
To Coda 1
To Coda 2
Gtr. 2: w/ Rhy. Fill 1, 2nd & 3rd times
F/A C
G
Eb/G
Bb
Eb/G
Bb
F/A C
Gtr. 2
(cont. in notation 2nd & 3rd times)
Al - right, al - right. Oo.
Rhy. Fill 1
C
Gtr. 2

D.S. al Coda 1
Dm
F
G
Dm
F
G
2. Well they're

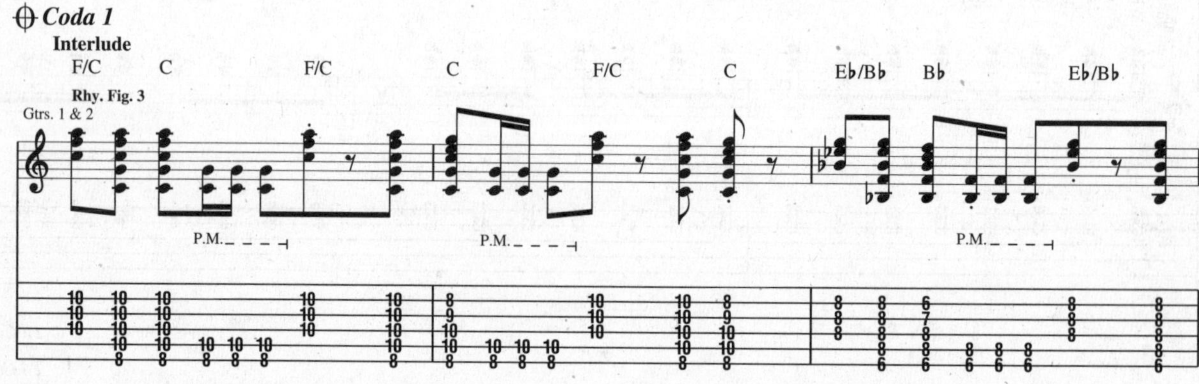
Coda 1
Interlude
F/C
C
F/C
C
F/C
C
Eb/Bb
Bb
Eb/Bb
Rhy. Fig. 3
Gtrs. 1 & 2
P.M.
P.M.
P.M.

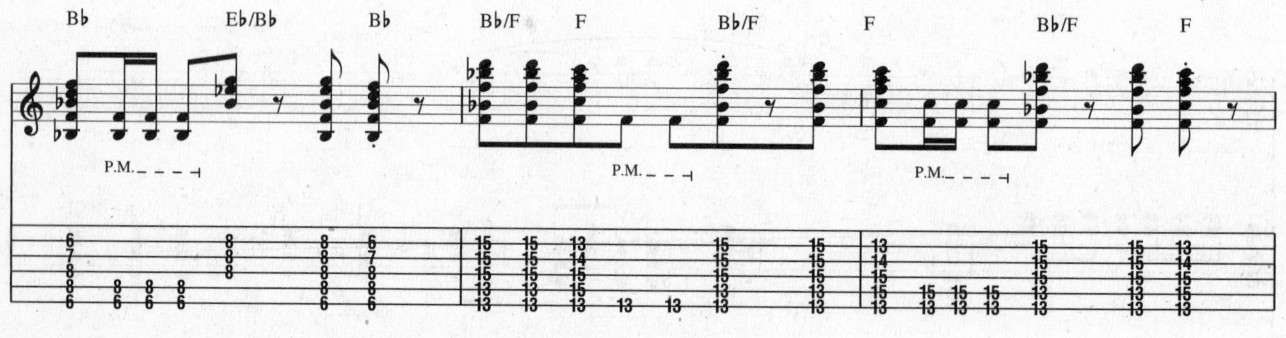
Bb
Eb/Bb
Bb
Bb/F
F
Bb/F
F
Bb/F
F
P.M.
P.M.
P.M.

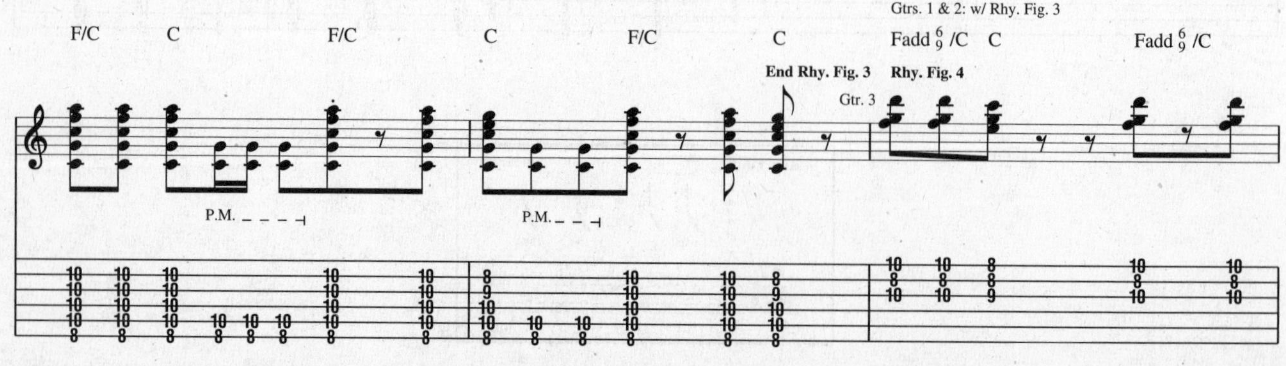
F/C
C
F/C
C
F/C
C
Gtrs. 1 & 2: w/ Rhy. Fig. 3
Fadd 6/9 /C
C
Fadd 6/9 /C
End Rhy. Fig. 3
Rhy. Fig. 4
Gtr. 3
P.M.
P.M.

C
Fadd6/9/C
C
Eb6/Bb
Bb
Eb6/Bb
Bb
Eb6/Bb
Bb
Bb6/F
F
Bb6/F
F
Bb6/F
F
Fadd9/C
C
Fadd9/C
C
Fadd9/C
C
Gtr. 3 tacet
D5
D.S.S. al Coda 2
Dm7
Woah.
End Rhy. Fig. 4
Gtrs. 1 & 2
Coda 2
Interlude
F/C
C
F/C
C
F/C
C
Eb/Bb
Bb
Eb/Bb
Bb
Eb/Bb
Bb
Gtrs. 1 & 2
P.M.
P.M.
P.M.
P.M.
Bb/F
F
Bb/F
F
Bb/F
F
F/C
C
F/C
C
F/C
C

Chorus

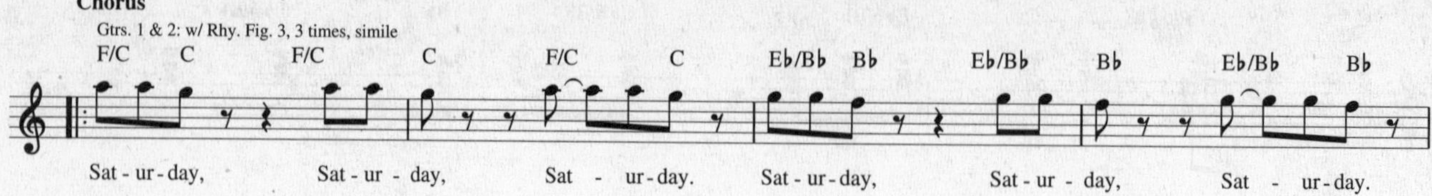

Outro

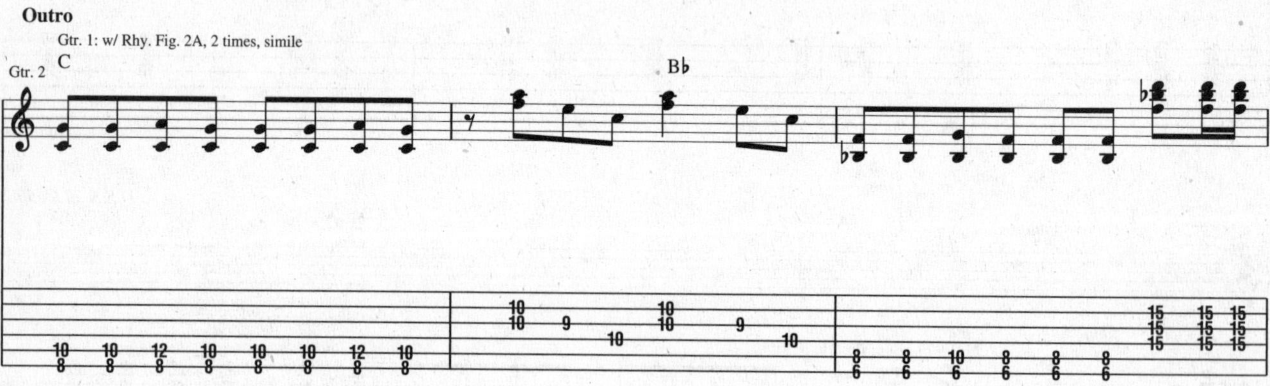

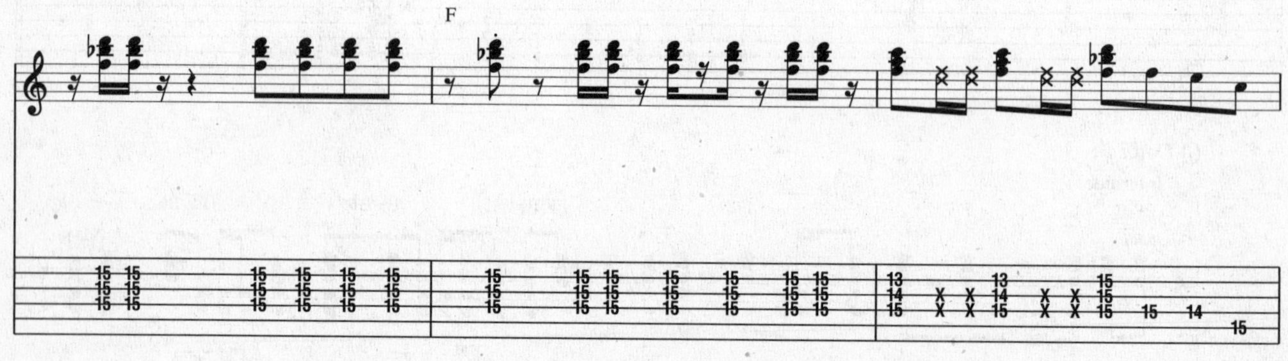

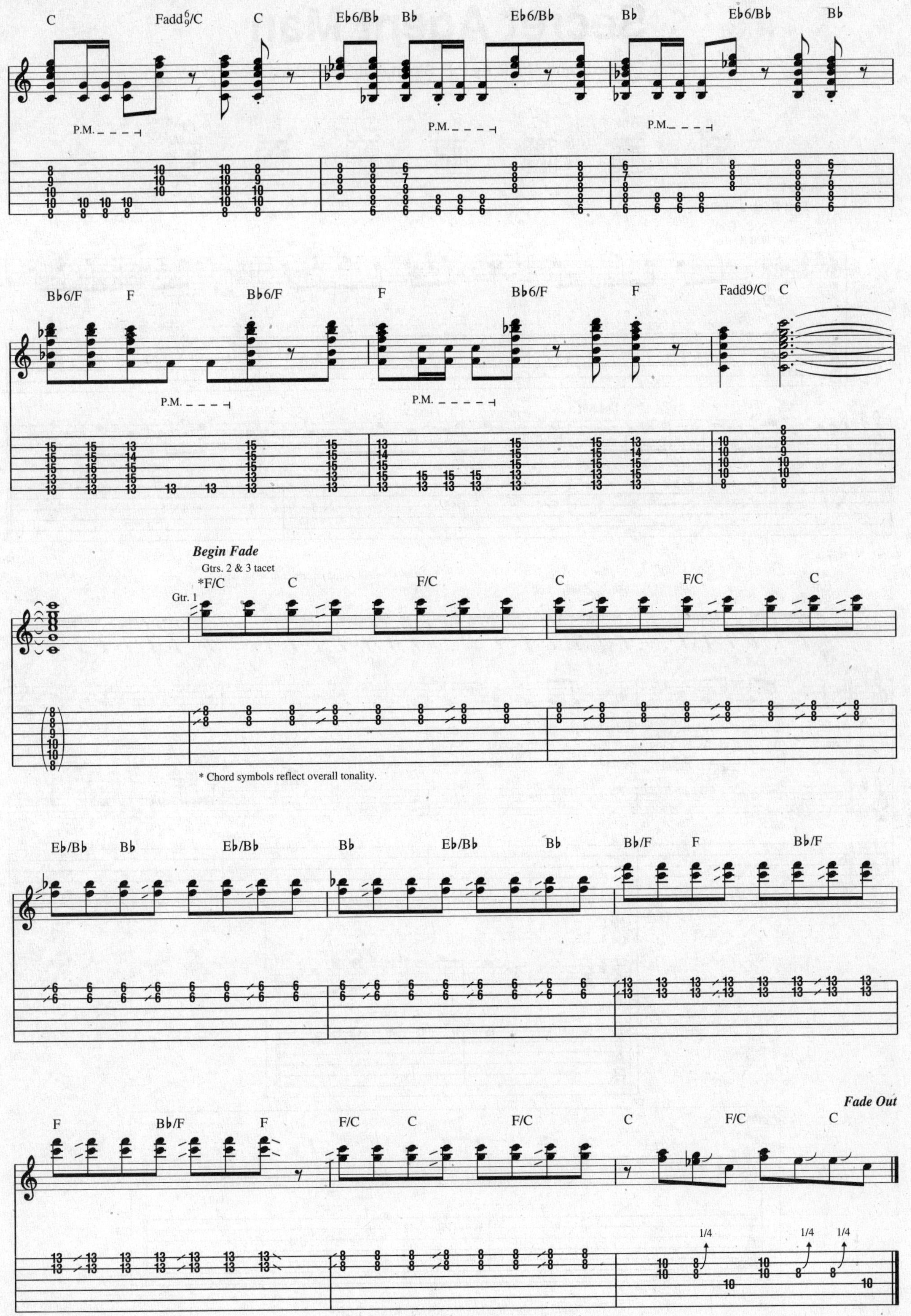

* Chord symbols reflect overall tonality.

Secret Agent Man

Words and Music by P.F. Sloan and Steve Barri

Gtr. 1: w/ Fill 2, 2nd time; w/ Fill 6, 3rd time
B7
ev - 'ry - one he meets, he stays a stran - ger.
pret - ty face can hide an e - vil mind.
lay - in' in the Bom - bay al - ley next day.
12
Gtr. 1: w/ Fill 3, 2nd time; w/ Fill 7, 3rd time
Em
With ev - 'ry move he makes, an -
Ah, be care - ful what you say, or you will
Oh, no you let the wrong words slip while kiss -
full hold bend
full
full
14 12 12 14 (14) 12 14
2 0 2 2 0
Fill 2
Gtr. 1
10 12 10 12 10 8
Fill 3
Gtr. 1
full
2 0 2 2 2 0
Fill 6
Gtr. 1
16 15 16 14 12 14 14 16
Fill 7
Gtr. 1
mp
1/2
2 2 0 0 2 4 0 2 2 2 0

Gtr. 1: w/ Fill 4, 2nd time

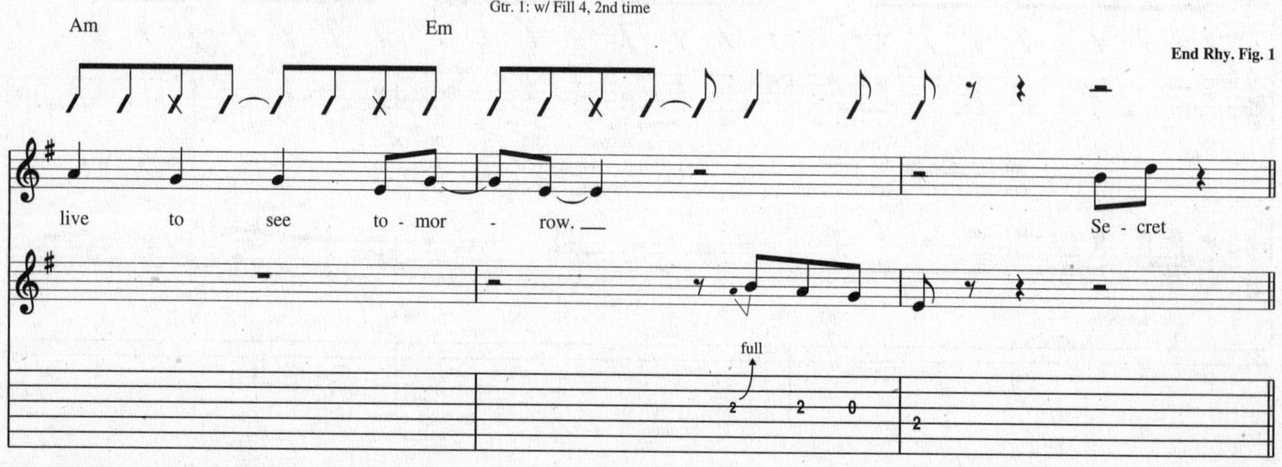

𝄋 Chorus

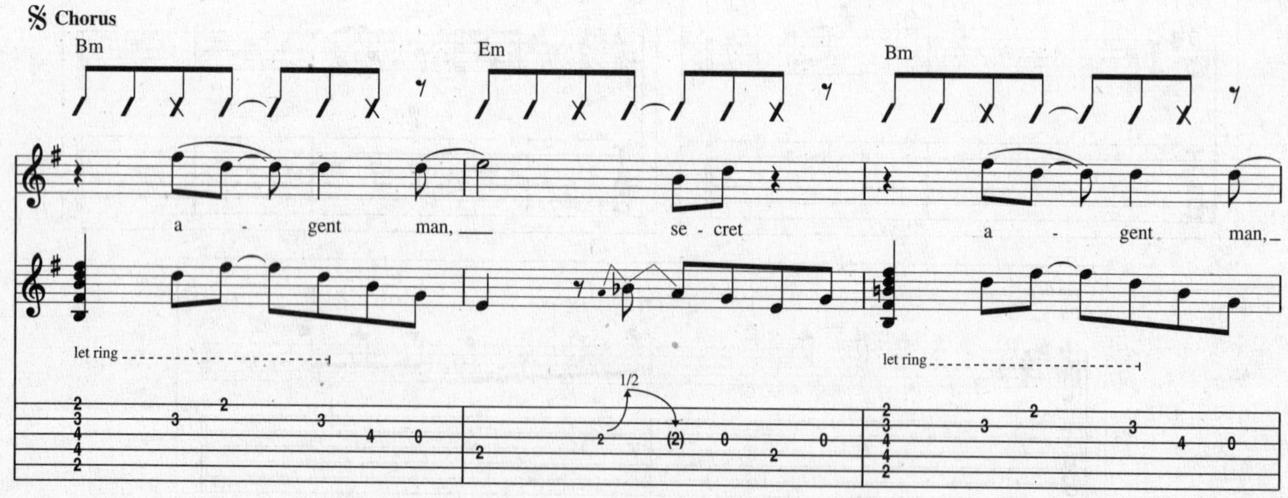

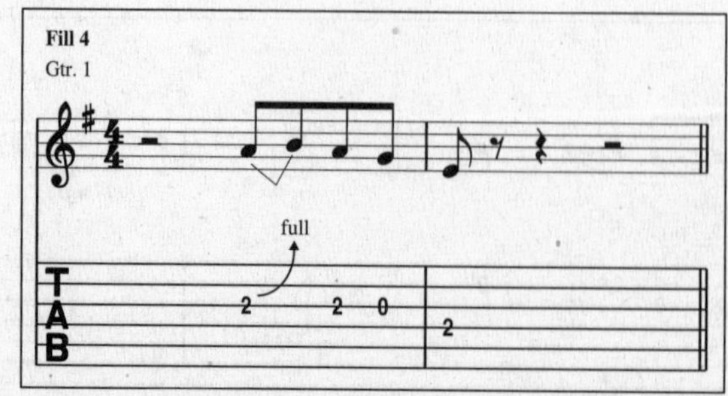

Em
C7
B7type2
they've giv - en you a num - ber and tak - en 'way your name.
full
let ring
4th time, To Coda
1.
2.
Gtr. 1: w/ Riff A
Gtr. 2 tacet
N.C.(Em)
2. Be -
Guitar Solo
Gtr. 2: w/ Rhy. Fig. 1
Em
Am
Gtr. 1
1/2
B7
1/4

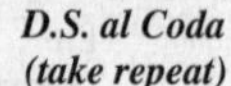
D.S. al Coda
(take repeat)

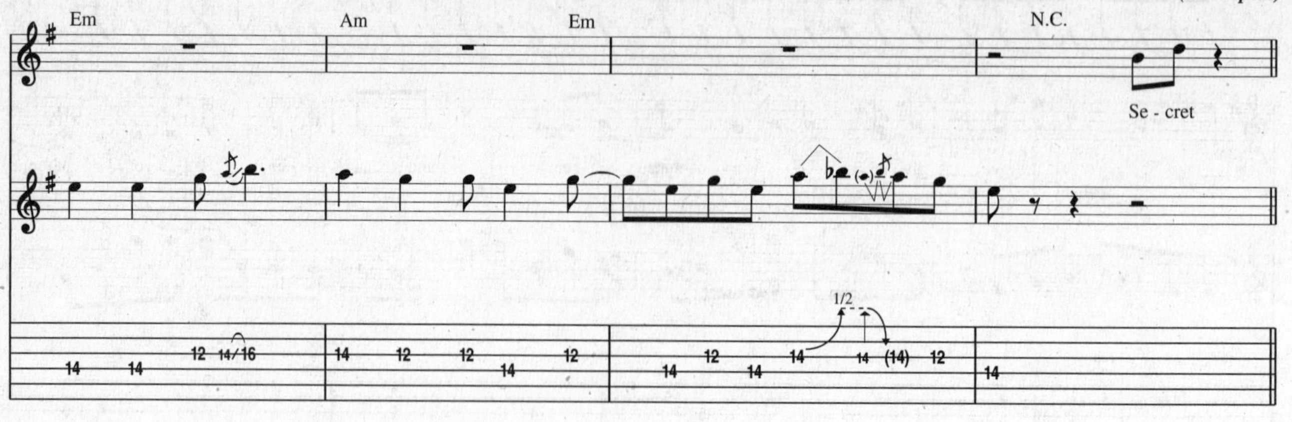
Em
Am
Em
N.C.
Se - cret
1/2

𝄌 Coda

N.C.(Em)
let ring

Gtr. 2
Emtype2
Se - cret a - gent man.

Seven Bridges Road

Words and Music by Stephen T. Young

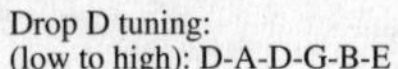

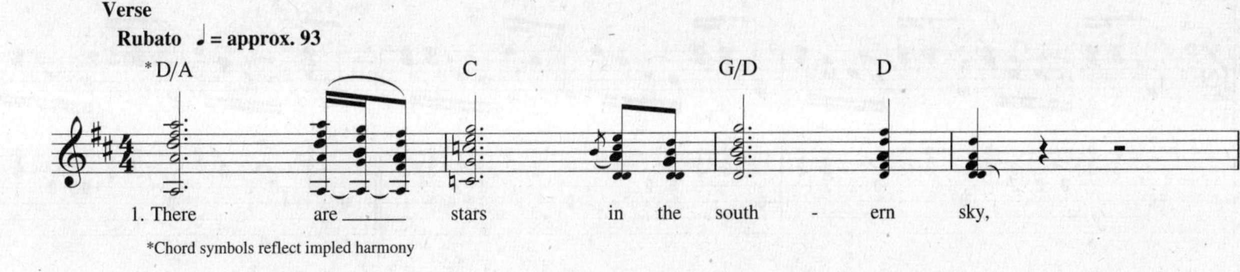

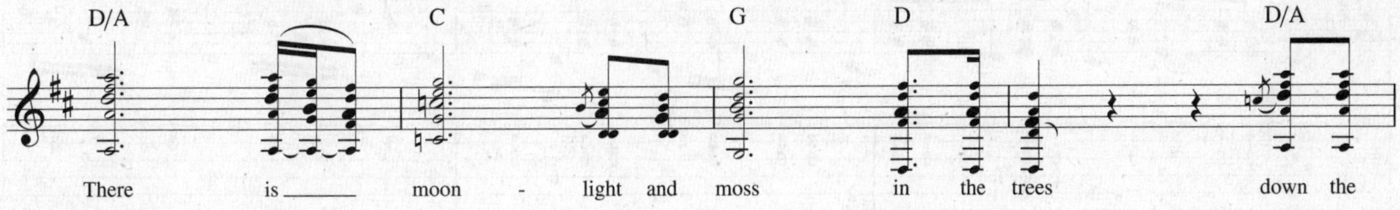

**Two gtrs. (6 & 12-str. acous.) arr. for one.

D
Verse
D
2. Now I have
Rhy. Fig. 1
C
G/B
D
loved you like a ba - by,
End Rhy. Fig. 1
Gtr. 1: w/ Rhy. Fig. 1
C
G/B
D
like some lone - some child.
Gtr. 1: w/ Rhy. Fig. 1 (2 times)
C
And I have loved
Gtr. 1
G/B
D
you in a tame way, and I have

C
G/B
D
loved
wild.
Some -
Gtr. 1
Bridge
C
D
times
there's
a part
of me
C
has to
turn
from
here
and
1/4
D
C
go.
Run - nin'
like
a child

D
from these warm stars down the
C
G/B
D5
Sev - en Bridg - es Road.
Verse
Rubato ♩ = approx. 90
Gtr. 1 tacet
D
C
G/D
D/A
3. There are stars in the south - ern sky, and if
C
G
D
ev - er you de - cide you should go,
D/A
C
G/D
D/A
there is a taste of time sweet and hon - ey down the
C
G
D
N.C.
Sev - en Bridg - es Road.

Sharp Dressed Man

Words and Music by Billy F Gibbons, Dusty Hill and Frank Beard

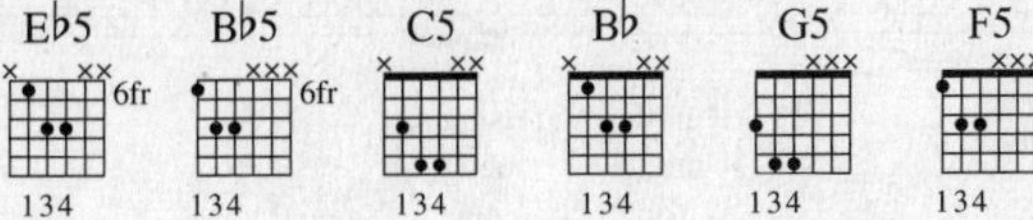

Gtr. 3: Open G tuning:
(low to high) D-G-D-G-B-D

Intro

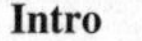

Moderately fast ♩ = 124

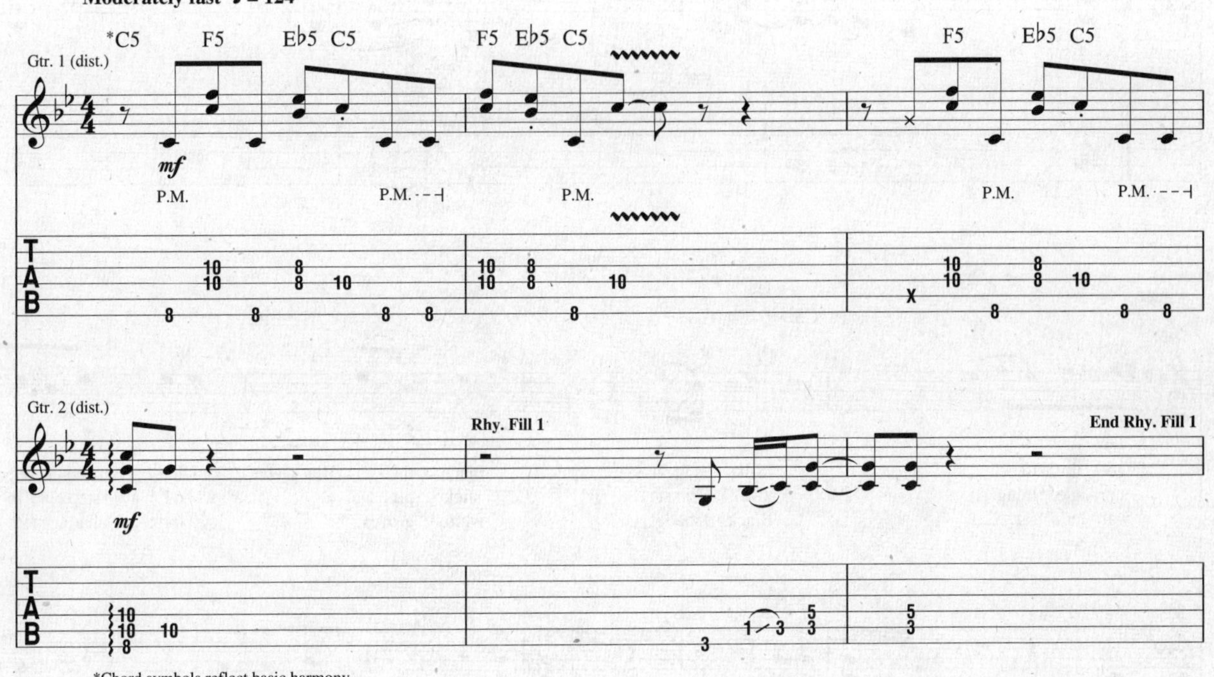

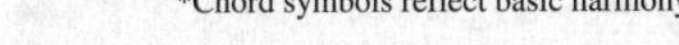
*Chord symbols reflect basic harmony.

Gtr. 2: w/ Rhy. Fill 1 (4 1/2 times)

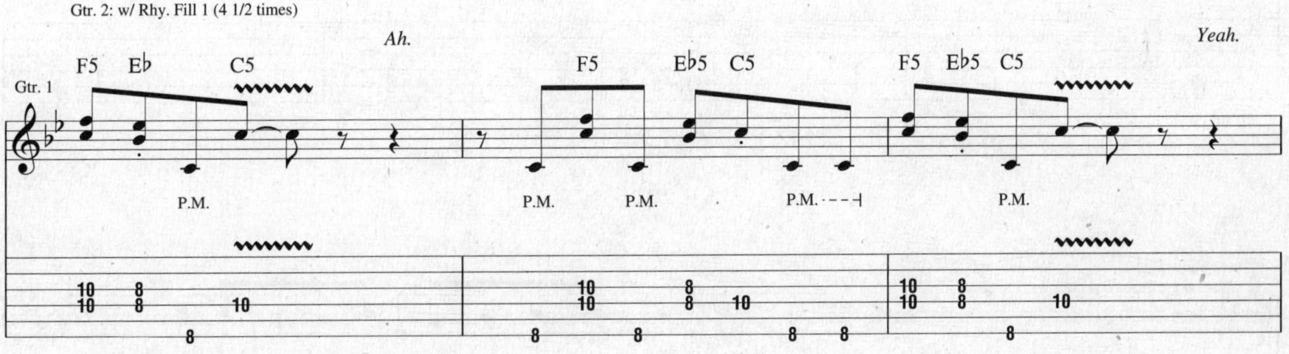

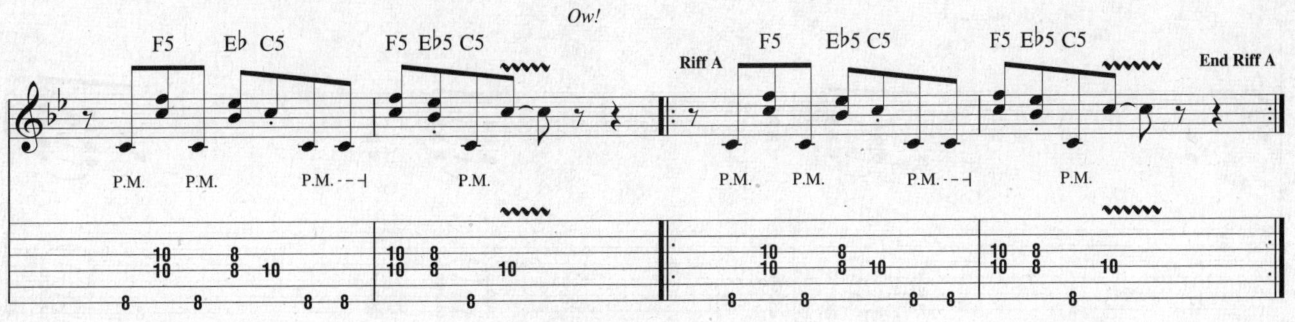

Verse
Gtr. 1 tacet
C5
B♭5
F5
1. Clean shirt, new shoes, and I don't know where I am go - in' to. Silk suit, black tie, (Black tie.) I don't need a rea - son why.
2. Gold watch, dia - mond ring, I ain't miss - in' not a sin - gle thing. Cuff links, stick pin, when I step out I'm gon - na do you in.
3. Top coat, top hat, an' I don't wor - ry 'cause my wal - let's fat. Black shades, white gloves, look - in' sharp, look - in' for love.
Gtr. 2
G5
F5 G5
B♭5 C5
They come run - nin' just as fast as they can, 'cause

1.
To Coda
Interlude
Gtr. 1: w/ Riff A (2 times)
N.C.
E♭5 B♭5
C5 F5 E♭ C5 F5 E♭ C5
ev - 'ry girl __ cra - zy 'bout a sharp dressed man. _
Rhy. Fill 2
(2nd time, cont. in slashes)
F5 E♭ C5 F5 E♭ C5
2.
E♭5 B♭5
Gtr. 2
sharp dressed man. ______ Uh huh.
End Rhy. Fill 2
Gtr. 3 (dist.)
mf
w/ slide
w/ pick & finger
Guitar Solo
C5
Gtrs. 1 & 2: w/ Rhy. Fig. 1 (8 1/2 times)
Rhy. Fig. 1
End Rhy. Fig. 1
Gtrs. 1 & 2

steady gliss.
Yeah, baby.
B♭5
G5
F5
Gtrs. 1 & 2
let ring
w/o slide
1/4
C5
F5
let ring
1/4
1/2
let ring

Interlude

Gtr. 1: w/ Riff A (4 times)
Gtrs. 2 & 3 tacet

Gtr. 2: w/ Rhy. Fill 2 (3 1/2 times)

C5 F5 E♭5 C5 | F5 E♭5 C5 | F5 E♭5 C5 | F5 E♭5 C5

How, how.

D.S. al Coda

F5 E♭5 C5 | F5 E♭5 C5 | F5 E♭5 C5 | F5 E♭5 C5

Coda

Outro-Guitar Solo

Gtr. 2: w/ Rhy. Fill 2 (9 times)

E♭5 B♭5 | C5

sharp dressed man. *Spoken: Uh huh. You can't lose when you dress like I do. That's right. I'm*

Gtr. 4 (dist.)

mf
w/ pick & finger

P.H. P.H.

Gtr. 2

Gtr. 1: w/ Rhy. Fig. 2 (8 times)
fine.
Gtr. 4
P.H. semi-harm.
Gtr. 1
Rhy. Fig. 2
End Rhy. Fig. 2
Gtr. 4

1/4
1/4

F5
Gtr. 4
P.M.
1/4
1/4
Gtr. 2
Rhy. Fill 3
Gtr. 1
Gtr. 2
divisi
End Rhy. Fill 3

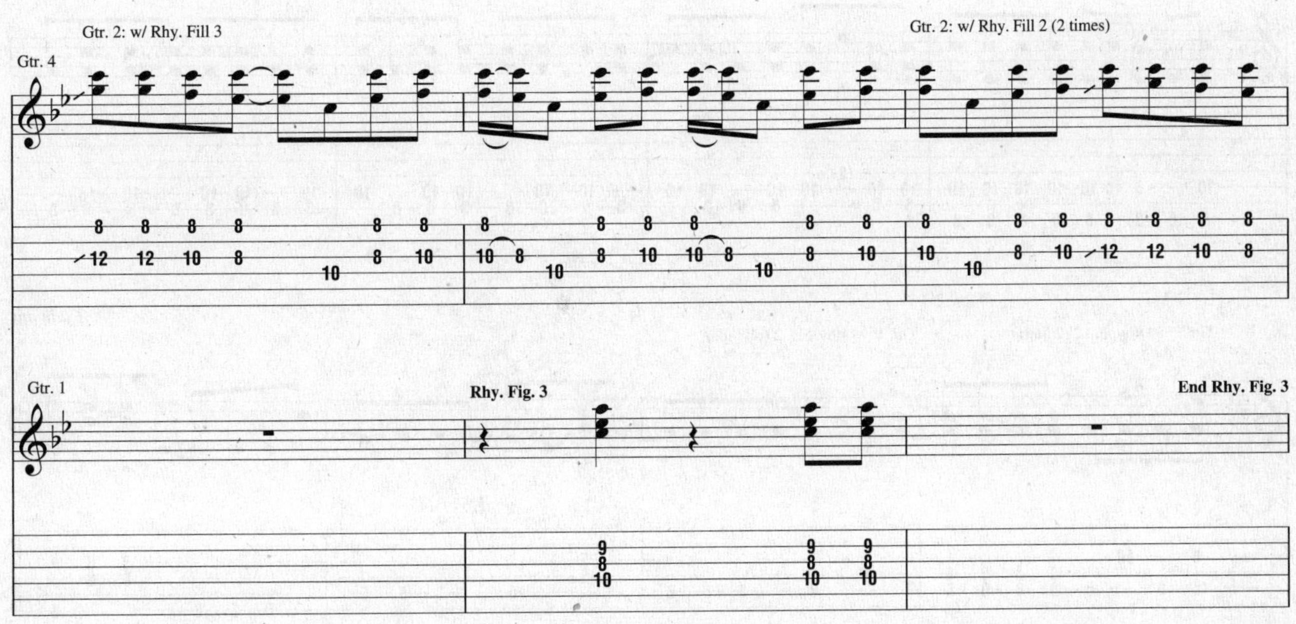
Gtr. 2: w/ Rhy. Fill 3
Gtr. 2: w/ Rhy. Fill 2 (2 times)
Gtr. 4
Gtr. 1
Rhy. Fig. 3
End Rhy. Fig. 3

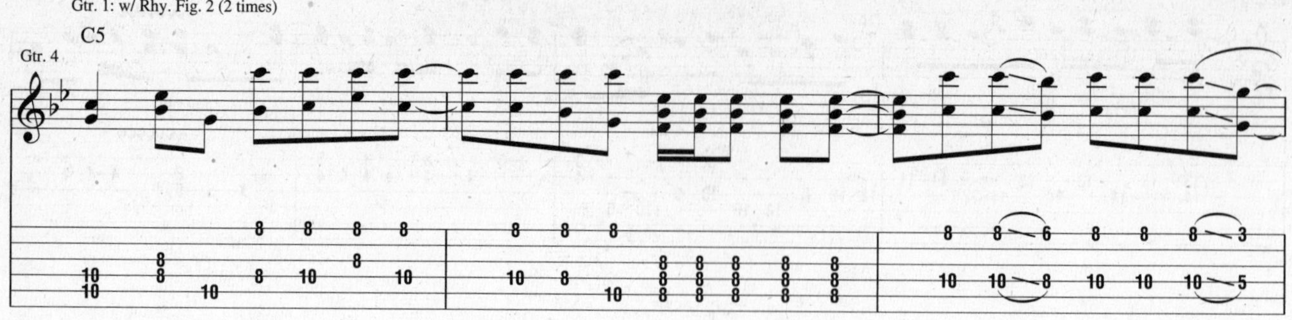
Gtr. 1: w/ Rhy. Fig. 2 (2 times)
C5
Gtr. 4

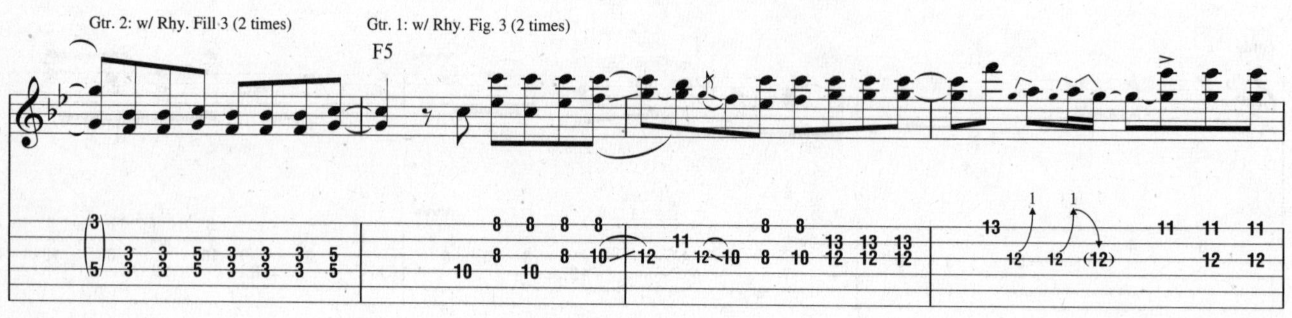
Gtr. 2: w/ Rhy. Fill 3 (2 times)
Gtr. 1: w/ Rhy. Fig. 3 (2 times)
F5

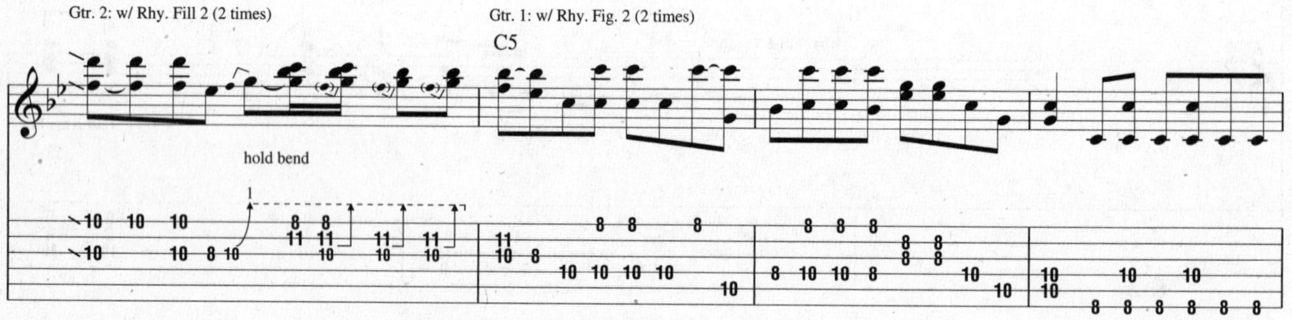
Gtr. 2: w/ Rhy. Fill 2 (2 times)
Gtr. 1: w/ Rhy. Fig. 2 (2 times)
C5
hold bend

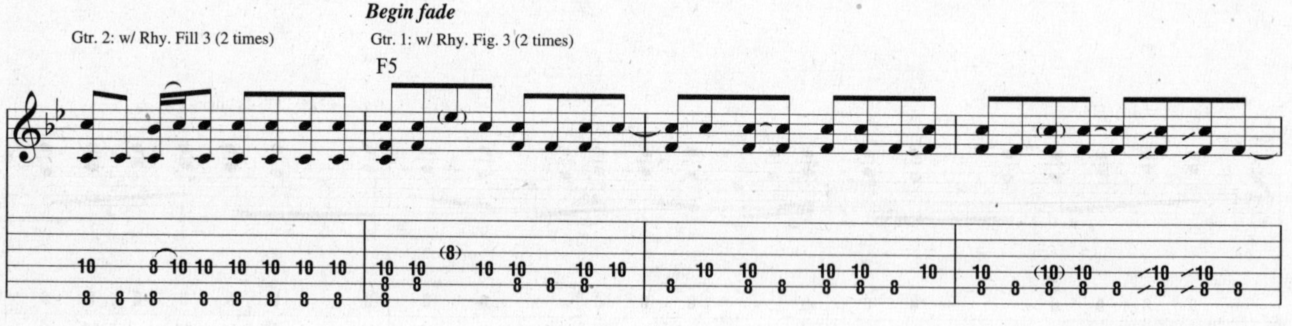
Begin fade
Gtr. 2: w/ Rhy. Fill 3 (2 times)
Gtr. 1: w/ Rhy. Fig. 3 (2 times)
F5

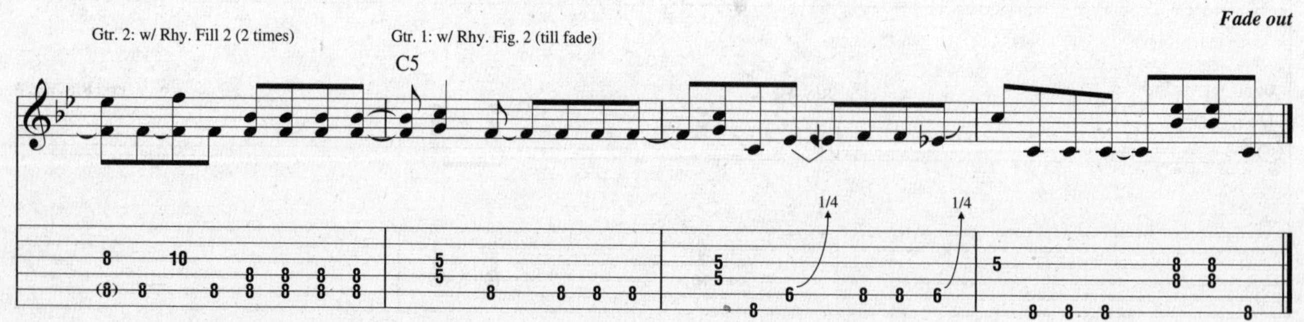
Fade out
Gtr. 2: w/ Rhy. Fill 2 (2 times)
Gtr. 1: w/ Rhy. Fig. 2 (till fade)
C5

Shimmer

Words and Music by Carl Bell

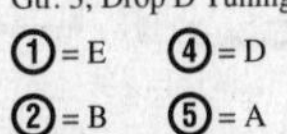

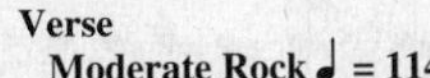

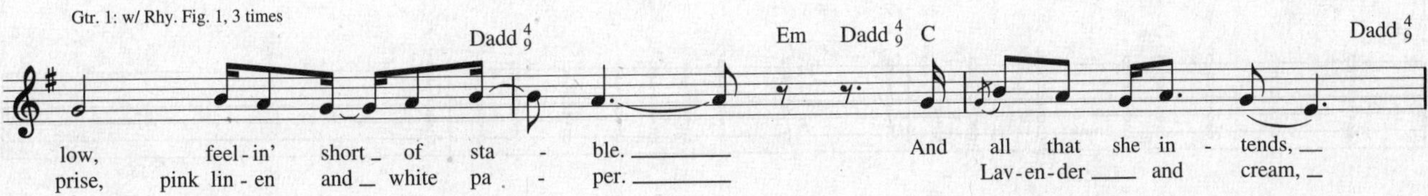

Gtr. 2: w/ Rhy. Fig. 3, 2nd time
Gtr. 4: w/ Fill 1, 2nd time

Gtr. 4: w/ Fill 2, 2nd time
Am G/B Cadd9
'Cause I have found all that shim - mers in this world is sure to fade
End Rhy. Fig. 3
Gtr. 1: w/ Rhy. Fig. 1, 2 times
C Dadd4/9 Em Dadd4/9 C Dadd4/9
a - way a - gain.
1.
Em Dadd4/9 C
2. She
2.
Dadd4/9 Em Dadd4/9
Gtrs. 1, 2 & 3: w/ Rhy. Fig. 2, 1st 2 meas., 3 times
C Dadd4/9 Em Dadd4/9
It's too far a - way for me to hold,
C Dadd4/9 Em Dadd4/9 C Dadd4/9 Em Dadd4/9
too far a - way. It's too far a - way for me to hold,
Interlude
C Dadd4/9 Em D D5 D5add#11 D
too far a - way, ah.
Gtrs. 1 & 2
let ring throughout
Gtr. 3
let ring throughout
Fill 2
Gtr. 4
TAB

D5
D5add#11
D
D5
D5add#11
It's
Outro-Chorus
Gtr. 1: w/ Rhy. Fig. 2, 1st 2 meas., 7 times
Gtr. 2: w/ Rhy. Fig. 2, 1st 2 meas.
Gtr. 3: w/ Rhy. Fig. 2, 1st 2 meas., 6 times
C
Dadd4/9
Em
Dadd4/9
too far a - way for me to hold,
C
Dadd4/9
Em
Dadd4/9
C
Dadd4/9
Em
too far a - way, ah. It's too far a - way
Rhy. Fig. 4
Gtr. 2
Gtr. 2: w/ Rhy. Fig. 4, 2 1/2 times
Dadd4/9
C
Dadd4/9
Em
for me to hold, too far a - way.
End Rhy. Fig. 4

Dadd4/9 C Dadd4/9 Em
It's too far a - way
Gtr. 4
Dadd4/9 C Dadd4/9 Em
for me to hold, far a - way,
Riff A
End Riff A
Gtr. 4: w/ Riff A, 2 1/2 times, simile
Dadd4/9 C Dadd4/9 Em Dadd4/9
ah. It's too far a - way for me to hold,
Gtr. 3
C Dadd4/9 Em Dadd4/9 Cadd9
too far a - way. Guess I'll let it go.
rit.
Gtr. 3
Gtr. 4
divisi
* Gtr. 3 tabbed to left of slash.
Gtr. 1
Gtrs. 1 & 2

Should I Stay or Should I Go

Words and Music by Mick Jones and Joe Strummer

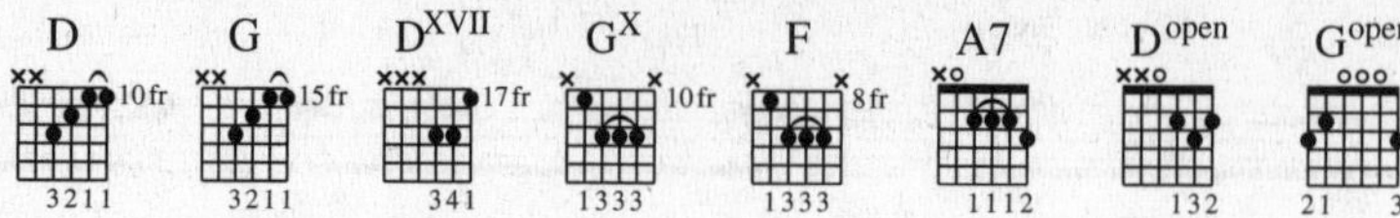

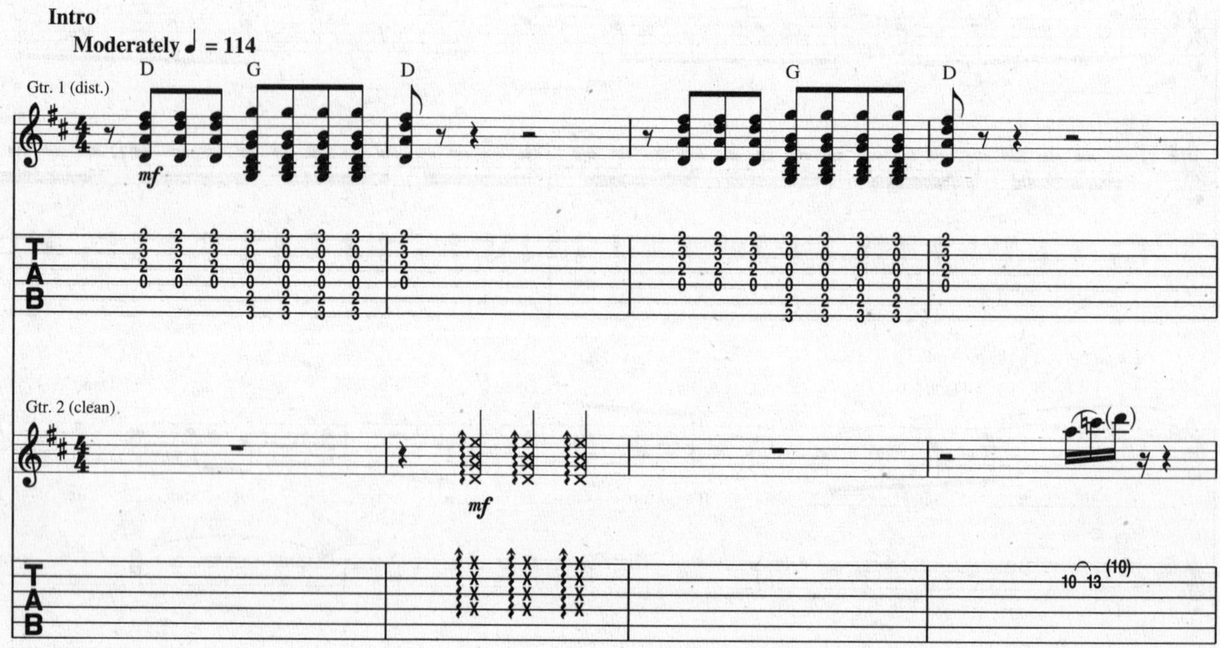

Verse
Gtr. 1: w Rhy. Fill 1, 4th time
D G D G D
know: should I stay or should I go? If you say that you are
tease. You're hap-py when I'm on my knees. One day is fine and next it's
3., 4. See Additional Lyrics

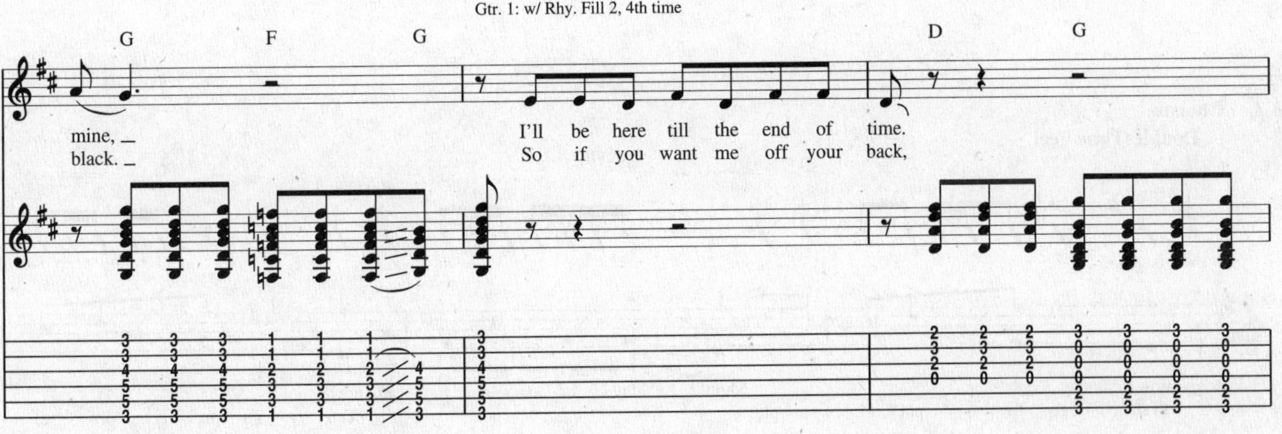

Gtr. 1: w/ Rhy. Fill 2, 4th time
G F G D G
mine, I'll be here till the end of time.
black. So if you want me off your back,

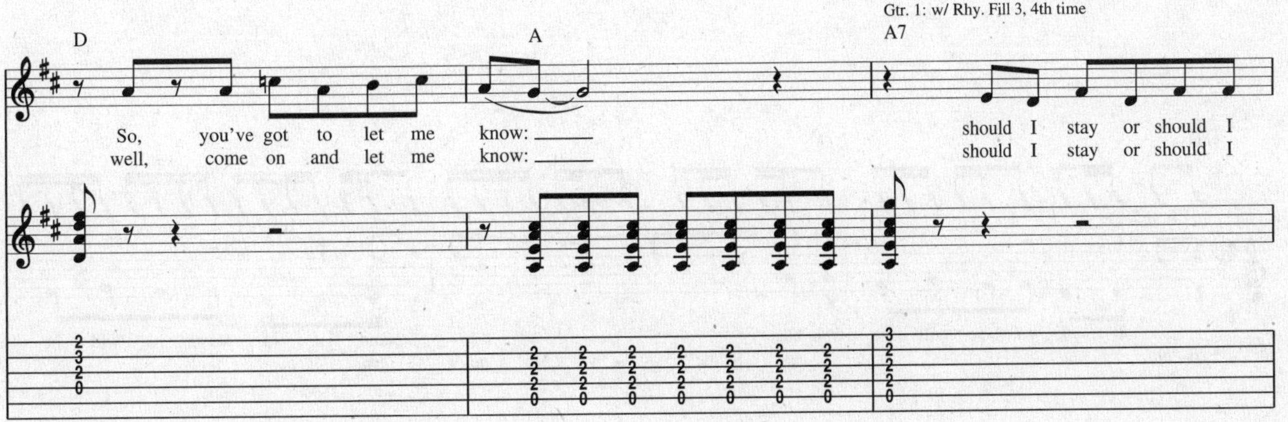

Gtr. 1: w/ Rhy. Fill 3, 4th time
D A A7
So, you've got to let me know: should I stay or should I
well, come on and let me know: should I stay or should I

Rhy. Fill 1
Gtr. 1
grad. bend
1/2

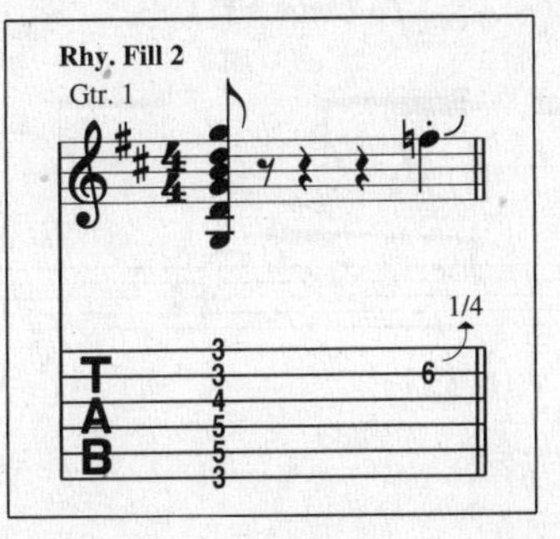

Rhy. Fill 2
Gtr. 1
1/4

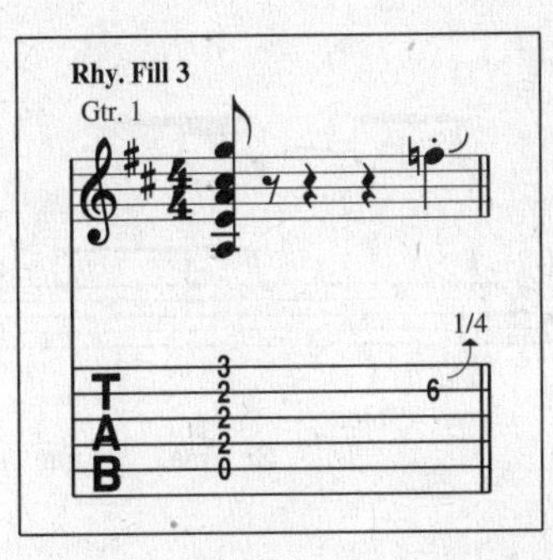

Rhy. Fill 3
Gtr. 1
1/4

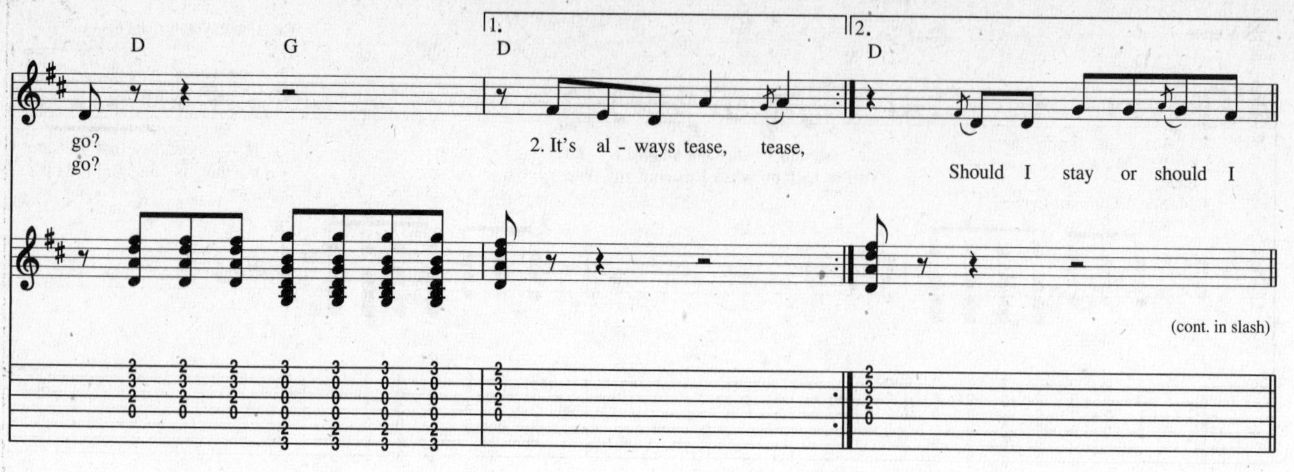
1.
2.
D
G
D
D
go?
go?
2. It's al - ways tease, tease,
Should I stay or should I
(cont. in slash)

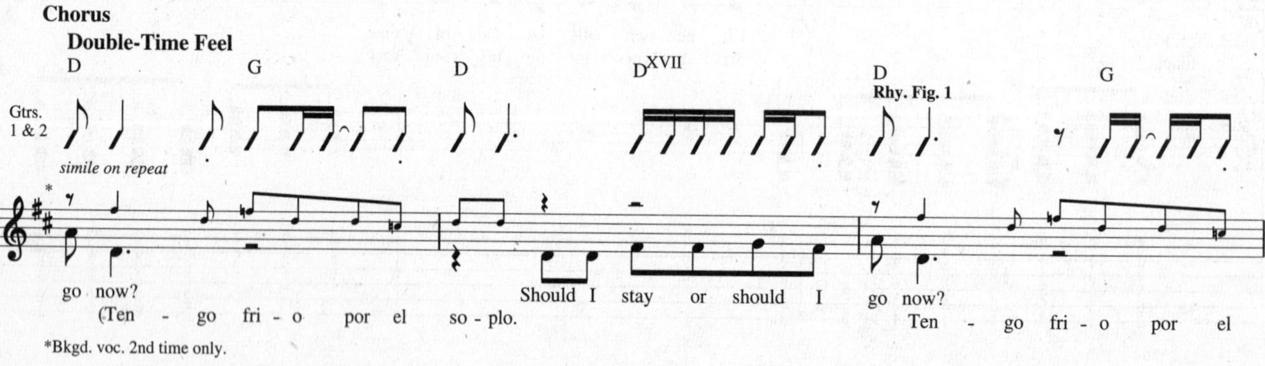
Chorus
Double-Time Feel
D
G
D
D XVII
D
Rhy. Fig. 1
G
Gtrs. 1 & 2
simile on repeat
go now?
(Ten - go fri - o por el so - plo.
Should I stay or should I go now?
Ten - go fri - o por el
*Bkgd. voc. 2nd time only.

D
G X
F
G X
If I go, there will be trou - ble,
so - plo.
Si me voy - va a ser pe - li - gro.
and if I stay, it will be

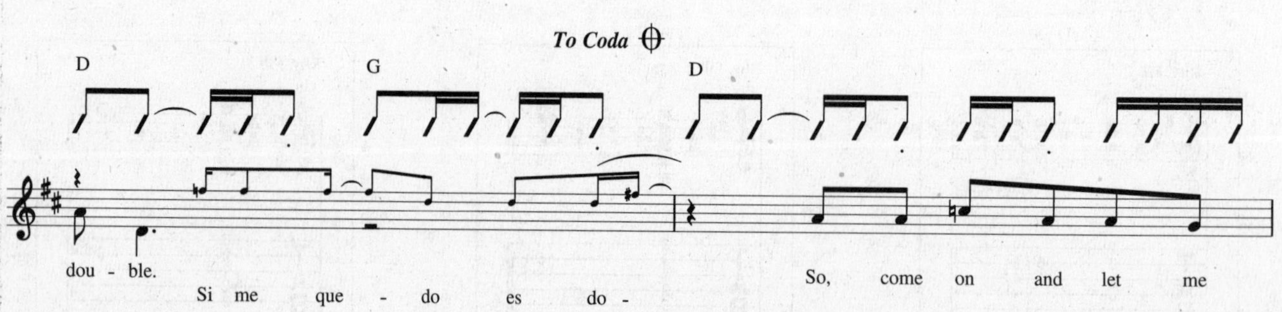
To Coda
D
G
D
dou - ble.
Si me que - do es do -
So, come on and let me

D.S. al Coda
(take repeat)

End Double-Time Feel

End Rhy. Fig. 1

A7 D^open G^open D^open

know. ____ 3. This in - de - ci - sion's bug - gin'

𝄌 *Coda*

D A7

So, you've got to let me know: ____ should I cool it or should I

- ble. Me ti - en - es que de - cir.

Outro-Chorus

Gtrs. 1 & 2: w/ Rhy. Fig. 1, simile

D G D D G

blow? Should I stay or should I go now?

De - bo ir o pon - go so - lo.) (Ten - go fri - o por el

D G F G

If I go, there will be trou - ble, and if I stay, it will be

so - plo. Si me voy __ va a ser pe - li - gro.

Additional Lyrics

3. This indecision's buggin' me. *(Indecisión me molesta.)*
If you don't want me, set me free. *(Si no me quieres líbrame.)*
Exactly who I'm s'pose to be? *(Dígame que tengo ser.)*
Don't you know which clothes even fit me? *(Sabes que ropa me queda?)*
Come on and let me know: *(Me tienes que decir.)*
Should I cool it or should I blow? *(Me debo ir o quedarme?)*

4. *Instrumental (w/ Voc. ad lib.)*

Somebody Told Me

Words and Music by Brandon Flowers, Dave Keuning, Mark Stoermer and Ronnie Vannucci

Tune down 1/2 step:
(low to high) E♭-A♭-D♭-G♭-B♭-E♭

Intro
Moderately ♩ = 138

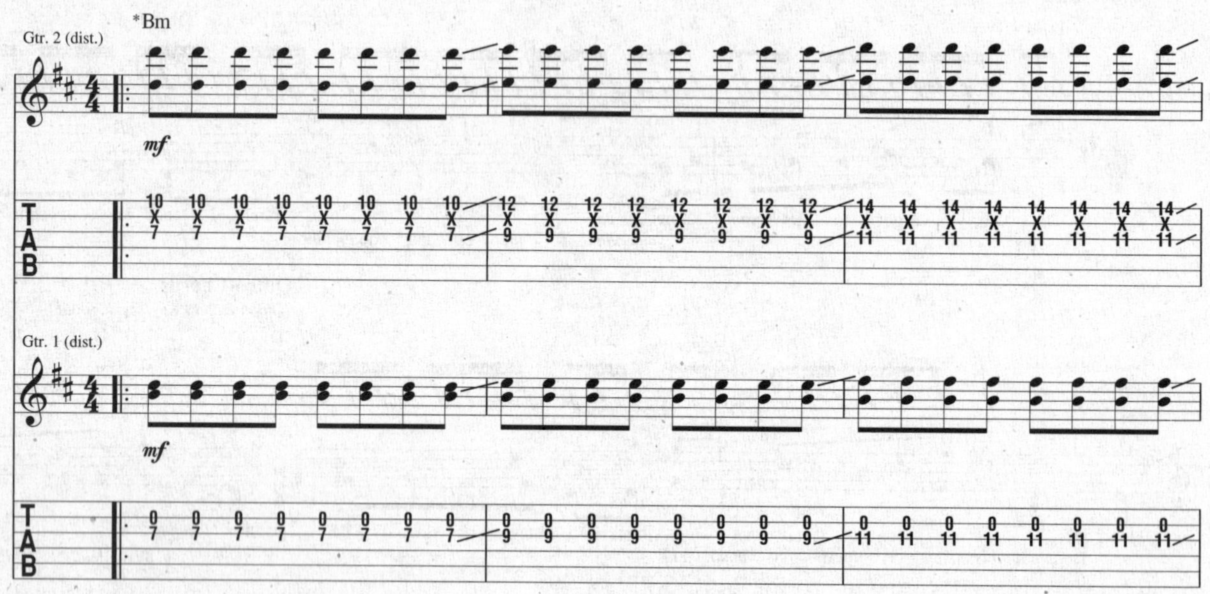

*Chord symbols reflect overall harmony.

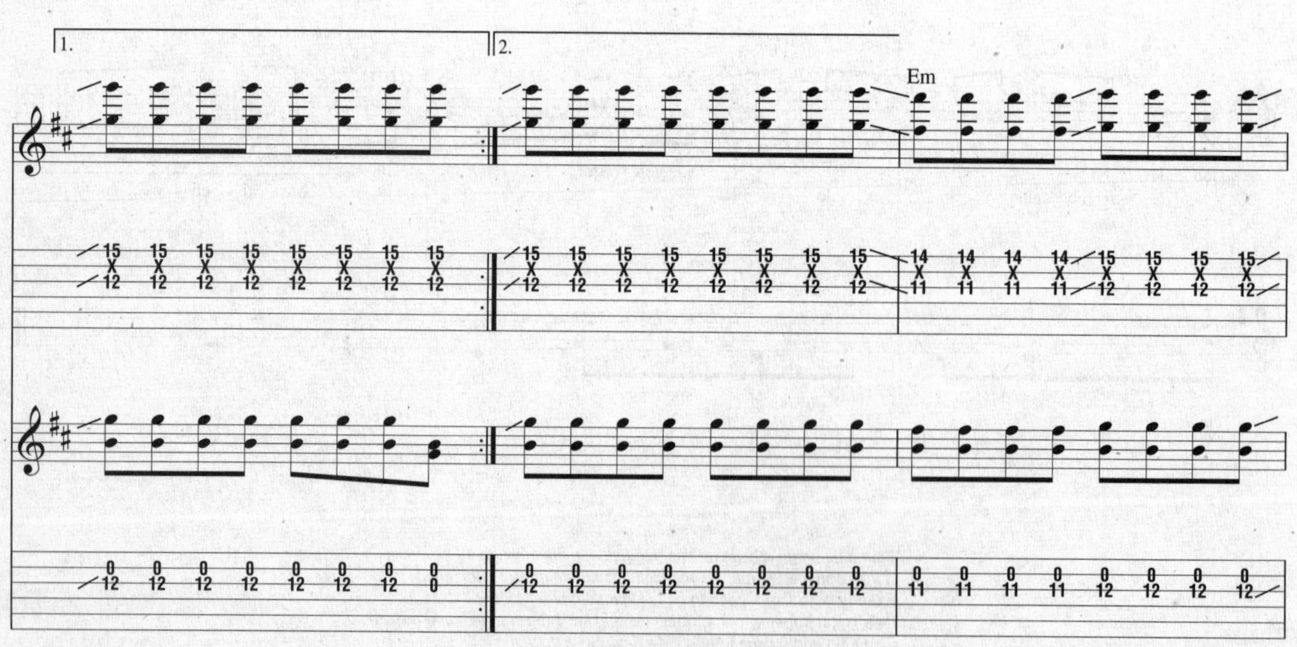

Bm

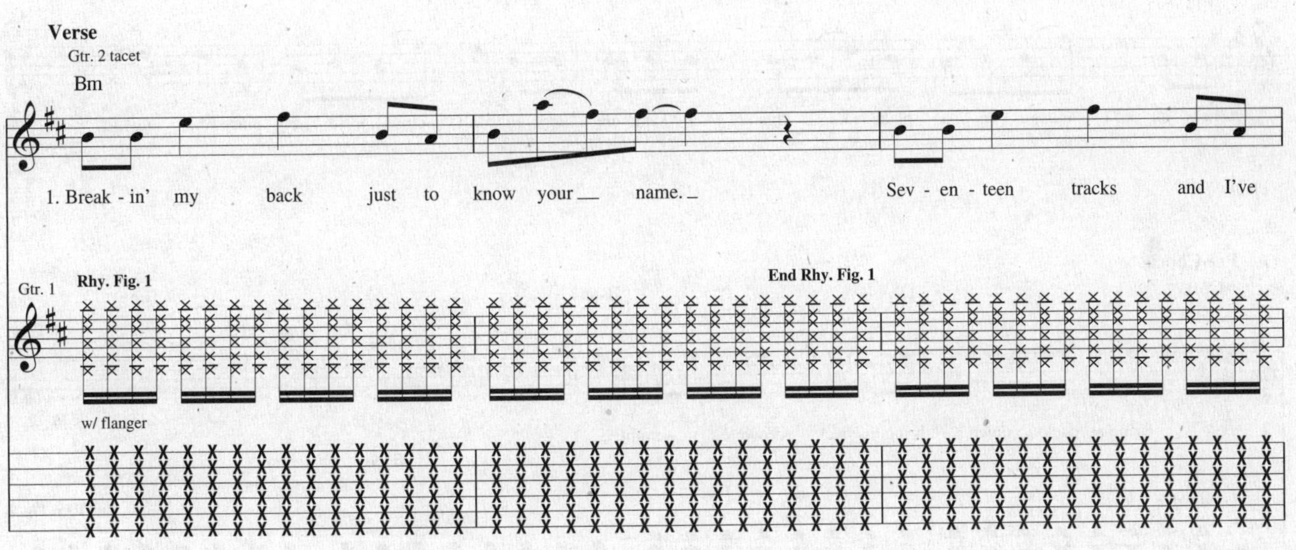
Verse
Gtr. 2 tacet
Bm
1. Break - in' my back just to know your name.
Sev - en - teen tracks and I've
Gtr. 1
Rhy. Fig. 1
End Rhy. Fig. 1
w/ flanger

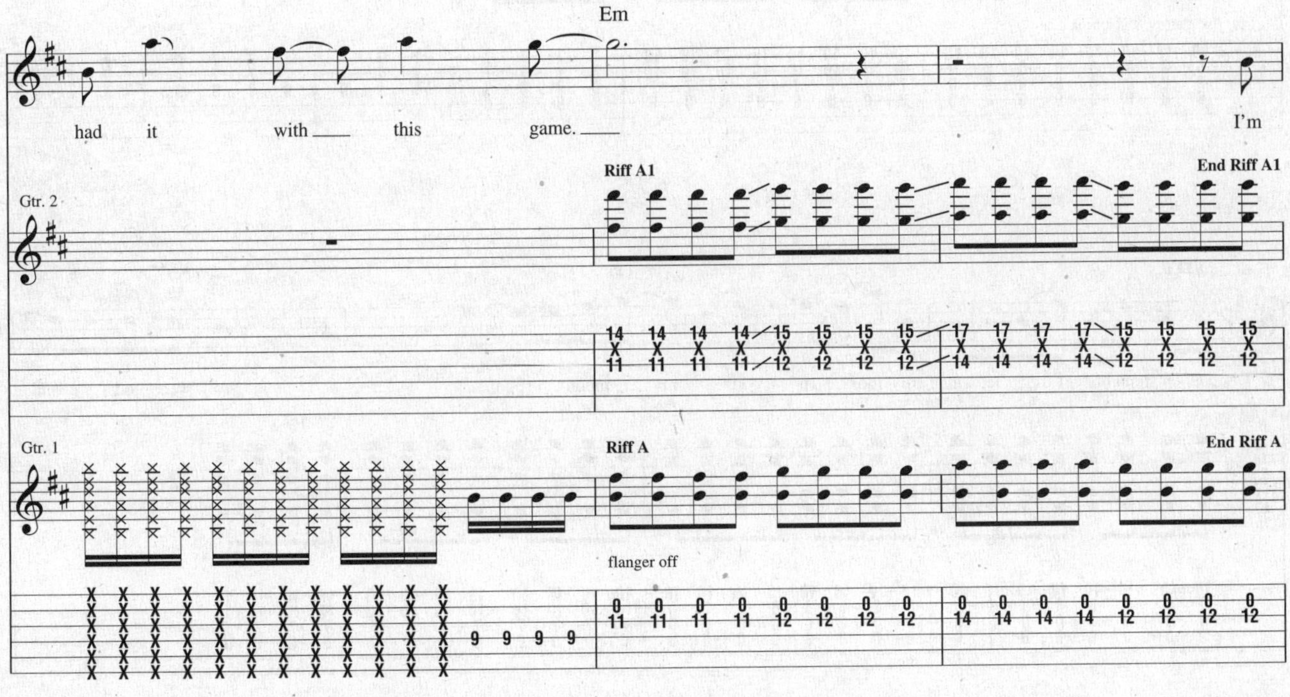
Em
had it with this game.
I'm
Gtr. 2
Riff A1
End Riff A1
Gtr. 1
Riff A
End Riff A
flanger off

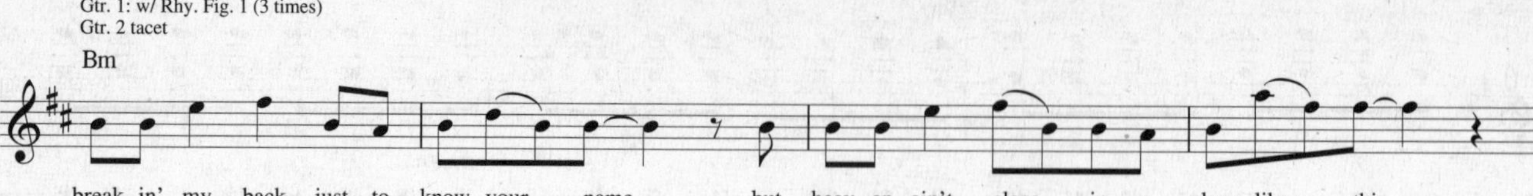
Gtr. 1: w/ Rhy. Fig. 1 (3 times)
Gtr. 2 tacet
Bm
break - in' my back just to know your name, but heav - en ain't close in a place like this.

Gtrs. 1 & 2: w/ Riffs A & A1
Em
An - y - thing goes, but don't blink, you might miss. 'Cause

Gtr. 1: w/ Rhy. Fig. 1 (2 times)
Bm
heav - en ain't close in a place like this. I said, uh, heav - en ain't close in a place like this.

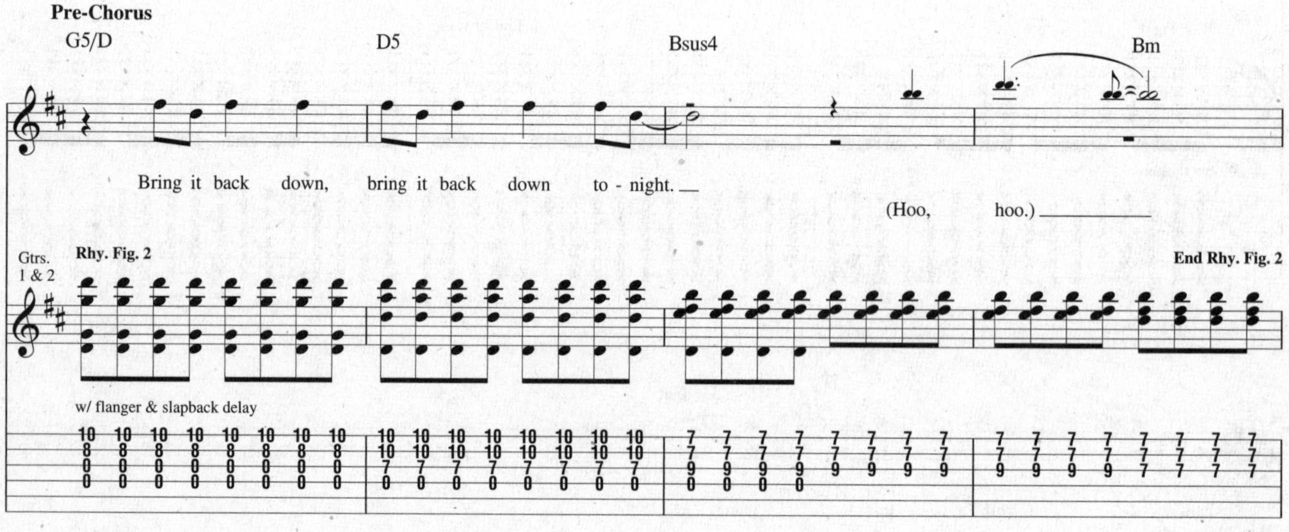
Pre-Chorus
G5/D
D5
Bsus4
Bm
Bring it back down, bring it back down to - night.
(Hoo, hoo.)
Gtrs. 1 & 2
Rhy. Fig. 2
End Rhy. Fig. 2
w/ flanger & slapback delay

G5/D
D5
N.C.
Nev - er thought I'd let a ru - mor ru - in my moon - light. Well, some - bod - y told

Chorus
Bm
G
A
me you had a boy - friend who looked like a girl - friend that I had in Feb -
Rhy. Fig. 3
flanger & delay off

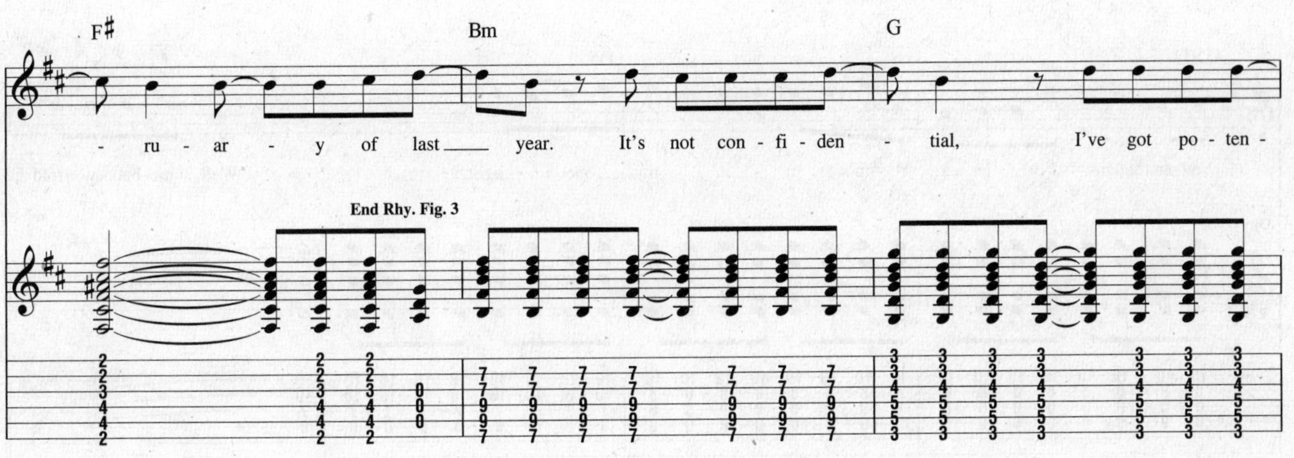
F♯
Bm
G
- ru - ar - y of last year. It's not con - fi - den - tial, I've got po - ten -
End Rhy. Fig. 3

A
Gtr. 2 tacet
N.C.
Verse
Gtr. 1: w/ Rhy. Fig. 1 (2 times)
Bm
- tial. 2. Read - y, let's roll on to some - thin' new.

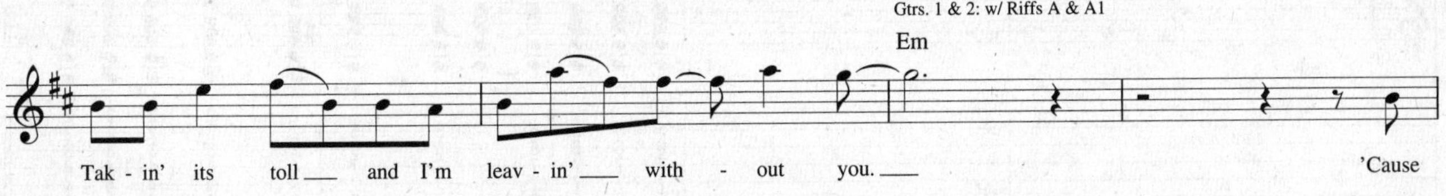
Gtrs. 1 & 2: w/ Riffs A & A1
Em
Tak - in' its toll and I'm leav - in' with - out you. 'Cause

Pre-Chorus

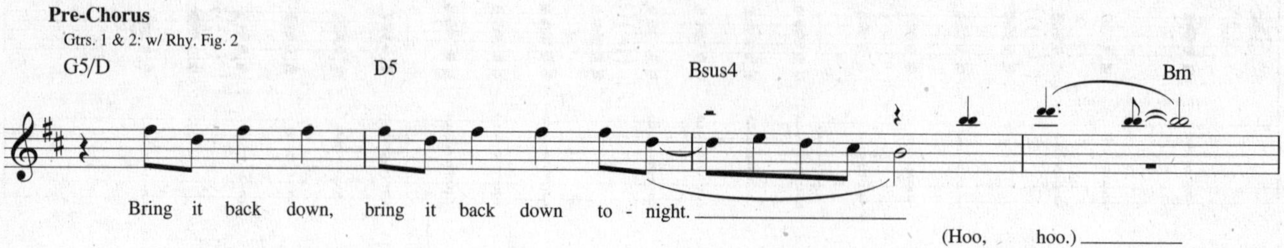

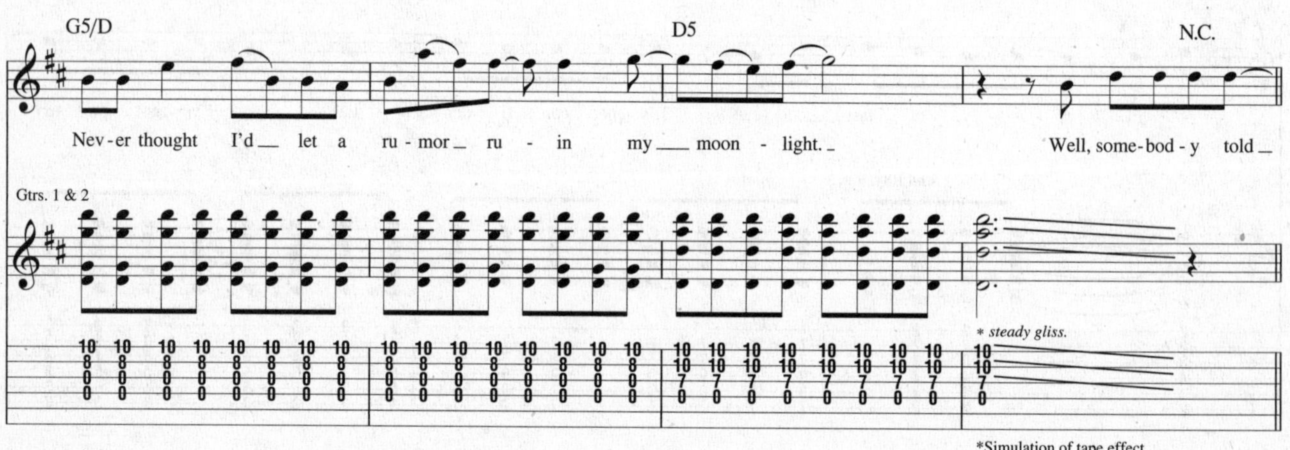

*Simulation of tape effect.

Chorus

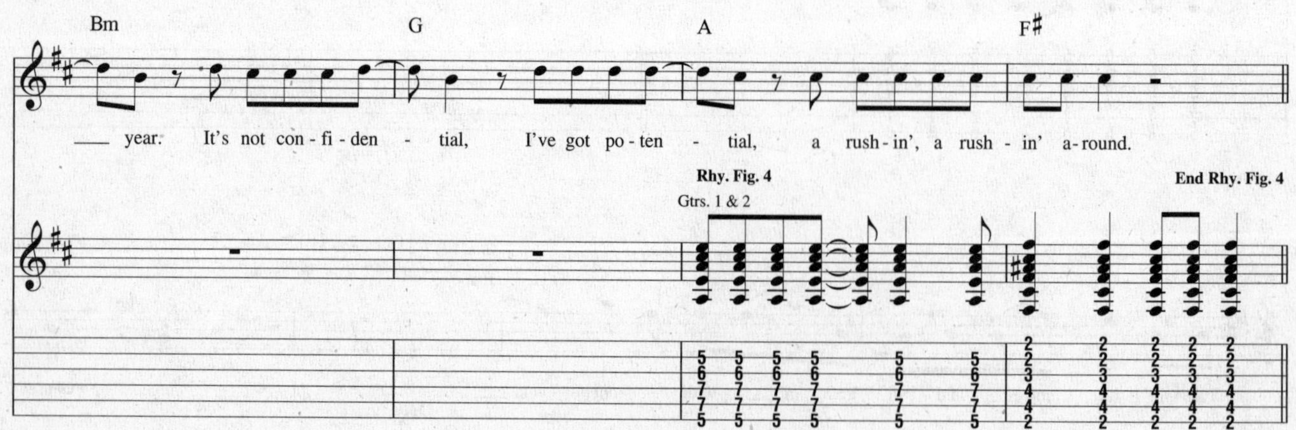

Bridge
Gtrs. 1 & 2 tacet
G
A
E5
Pace your - self from me.
(From me.
I said,
Gtr. 3
(slight dist.)
mf
D
E5
G
may - be, ba - by please.
Please.
But, I just don't
Bm
A
G
know now
May - be, ba - by.)
when
F#5
A
N.C.
all I wan-na do is try.
Well, some-bod - y told
*w/ delay
delay off
*Set for eighth-note regeneration w/ 5 repeats.

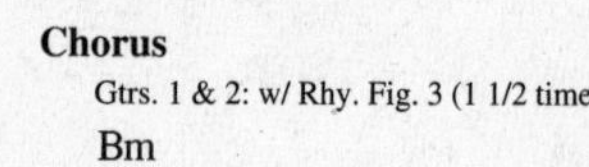
Chorus
Gtrs. 1 & 2: w/ Rhy. Fig. 3 (1 1/2 times)

Bm
G
A
me you had a boy - friend who looked like a girl - friend that I had in Feb -

F♯
Bm
G
- ru - ar - y of last year. It's not con - fi - den - tial, I've got po - ten -

1.
2.
Gtrs. 1 & 2: w/ Rhy. Fig. 4
A
F♯
Gtrs. 1 & 2: w/ Rhy. Fig. 4
A
- tial, a rush - in', a rush - in' a - round. Now some - bod - y told - tial, a rush - in', a rush -

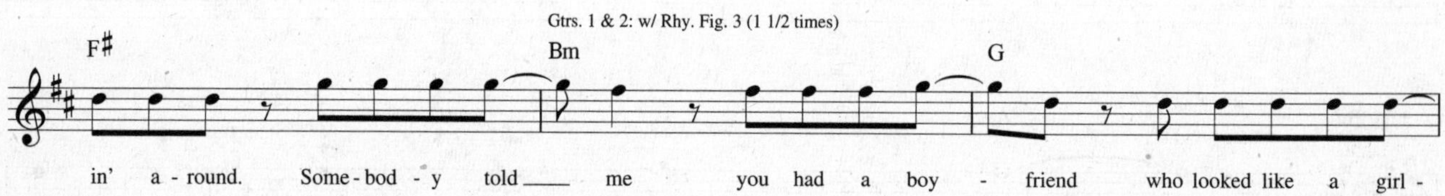
Gtrs. 1 & 2: w/ Rhy. Fig. 3 (1 1/2 times)
F♯
Bm
G
in' a - round. Some - bod - y told me you had a boy - friend who looked like a girl -

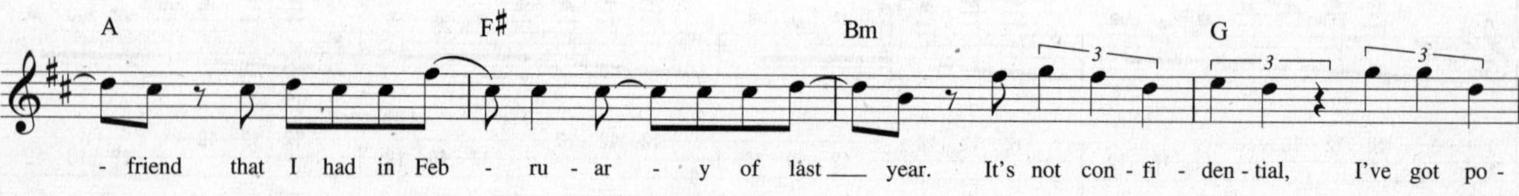
A
F♯
Bm
G
3
3
3
- friend that I had in Feb - ru - ar - y of last year. It's not con - fi - den - tial, I've got po -

Gtrs. 1 & 2: w/ Rhy. Fig. 4
A
F♯
Bm
N.C.
ten - tial, a rush - in', a rush - in' a - round.
Gtrs. 1 & 2
7 7 9 9 7
7 7 9 9 7

Space Lord

Words and Music by Dave Wyndorf

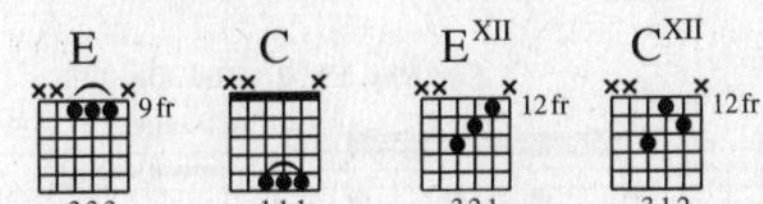

Tune Down Two Whole Steps:
① = C ④ = B♭
② = G ⑤ = F
③ = E♭ ⑥ = C

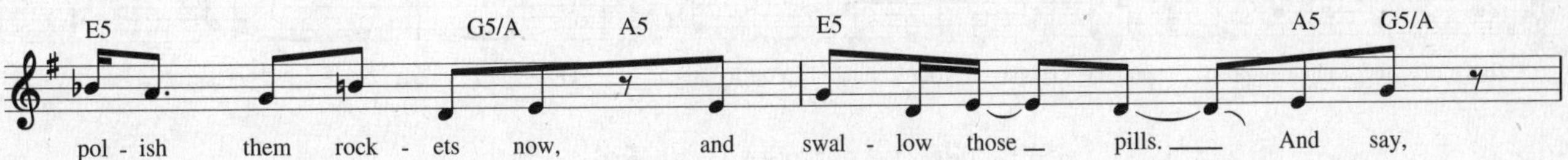

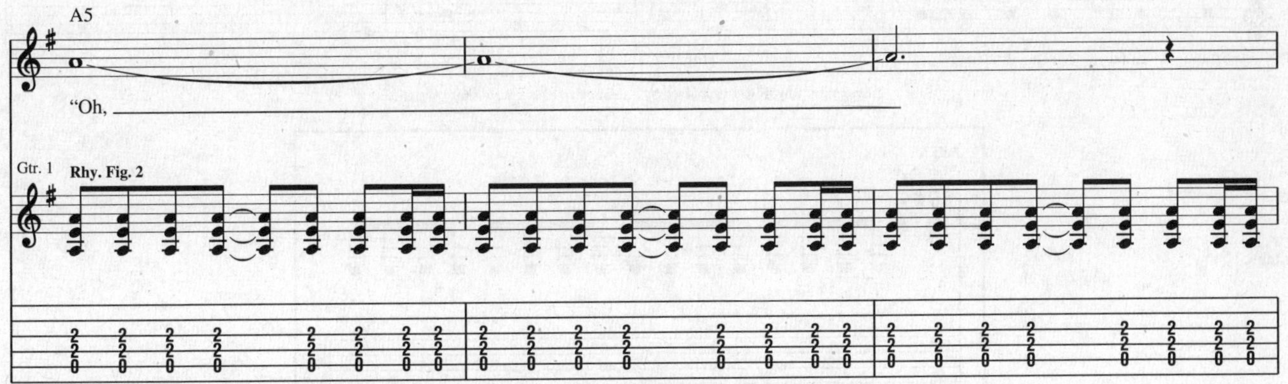

Gtr. 1: w/ Rhy. Fig. 1, 2 times
E5
G5/A
A5
G5/A
Space
Lord
Moth - er - fuck - er."
Huh!
End Rhy. Fig. 2
Rhy. Fig. 3
Gtr. 2 (elec.)
mf w/ clean tone
E5
G5/A A5
G5/A E5
G5/A A5 G5/A E5
G5/A A5
G5/A
Uh, huh.
Mm.
2. There's a
End Rhy. Fig. 3
Verse
Gtrs. 1 & 2: w/ Rhy. Figs. 1 & 3, 4 times
* E5
G5/A A5
E5
A5 G5/A
E5
G5/A A5
car in the field now in a col - umn of flame, with two doors to choose, but on - ly
3. See Additional Lyrics
* Chord symbols reflect overall tonality.
Gtr. 5: w/ Riff A, 12 times, 2nd time
E5
A5 G5/A
E5
G5/A A5
E5
A5 G5/A
one bears your name. You been drink - in' my blood while I been lick - in' your wounds. Well, I
Gtrs. 1 & 2: w/ Rhy. Fig. 2
E5
G5/A A5
E5
A5 G5/A
A5
shave off the pitch now, and the scope of your tune. You'll sing, "Oh,
* Gtrs. 1 & 2: w/ Rhy. Figs. 1 & 3, 2 times
E5
G5/A A5
E5
A5 G5/A
E5
G5/A A5
E5
A5 G5/A
Space Lord Moth - er - fuck - er."
Huh!
Yeah.
* On repeat, Rhy. Fig. 1 is doubled by a semi-clean elec. gtr. w/ slight variations.
Riff A
* Gtr. 5
mf
P.M.
* Synth. arr. for gtr.

Chorus
Gtrs. 1 & 2 tacet
Gtrs. 3 & 4: w/ Rhy. Fig. 4, 3 times
I left my throne a mil - lion miles a - way. I drink from your tit and sing the
* Gtrs. 3 & 4 (elec.)
Rhy. Fig. 4
End Rhy. Fig. 4
w/ dist.
* composite arrangement.
** Lead voc. doubled one octave lower during Chorus.
blues ev - 'ry day. They'll give me the strength to split this world in two, yeah. I
Gtrs. 1 & 2: w/ Rhy. Figs. 1 & 3, 2 times
ate all the rest and now I've got - ta eat you. Well, I say...
Gtrs. 3 & 4: w/ Rhy. Fig. 4, 2 times
got - ta eat you. Well, I say, "Oh,
Space Lord Moth - er - fuck - er. Oh, Space Lord Moth - er - fuck - er."
Voc. ad lib.
Gtr. 5: w/ Riff A, till fade
Verse
Rhy. Fig. 5A
End Rhy. Fig. 5A
Gtr. 4
play 4 times
4. I lost my soul when I fell to Earth.
Gtr. 3
Rhy. Fig. 5
End Rhy. Fig. 5
full

Gtrs. 3 & 4: w/ Rhy. Figs. 5 & 5A, 3 times

E C E

My plan - ets call ___ me to the void of my birth. ___ The time ___ has come

C E C

for me to kill this game. ___ Now o - pen wide ___ and ___ say ___ my ___ name. ___

Gtrs. 3 & 4: w/ Rhy. Fig. 4, 4 times

E D E G D E D E G D E D E G D E D E G D

___ Space Lord Moth - er - fuck - er. Oh, ___ Space Lord Moth - er - fuck - er.

E D E G D E D E G D E D E G D E D E G D

Voc. Fig. 1 **End Voc. Fig. 1**

Oh, ___ Space Lord Moth - er - fuck - er. Oh, ___ Space Lord Moth - er - fuck - er.

Guitar Solo

Lead Voc.: w/ Voc. Fig. 1, 7 1/2 times
Gtrs. 3 & 4: w/ Rhy. Fig. 4, 15 times

E D E G D E D E G D E D E G D E D E G D E D E G D

Gtr. 6

f

* w/ wah-wah

5 7 | 8 10 12 | 12 10 8 7 | 7 8 7 7 3 | 0 5

* Rock wah erractically throughout solo.

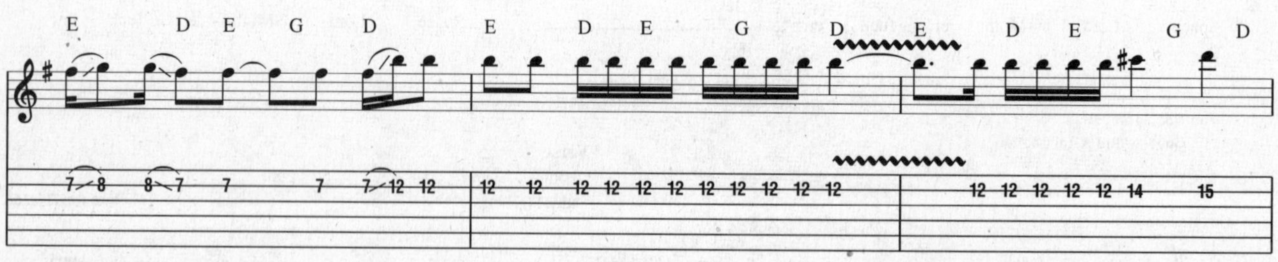

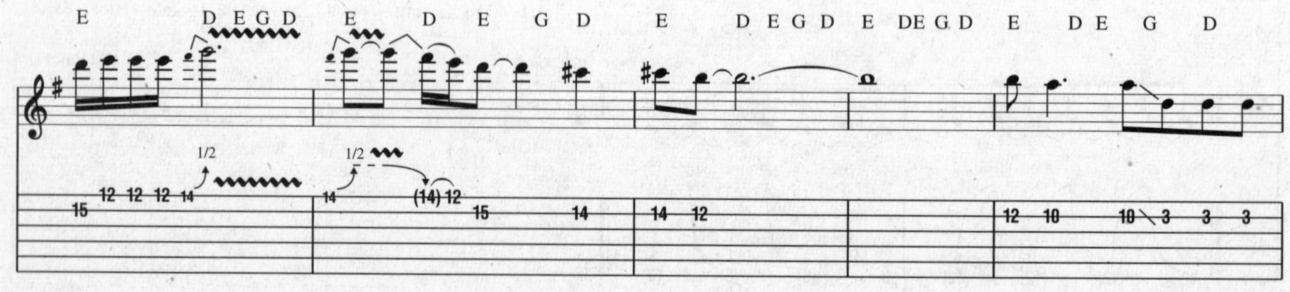

Additional Lyrics

3. Milking my nightmares and using my name.
You're stabbing my cortex when you know I'm insane.
I'm squeezed out in hump-drive and I'm drowning in love.
Encompass immortal position above,
And say, "Oh, Space Lord Motherfucker."

Stay

Words and Music by Lisa Loeb

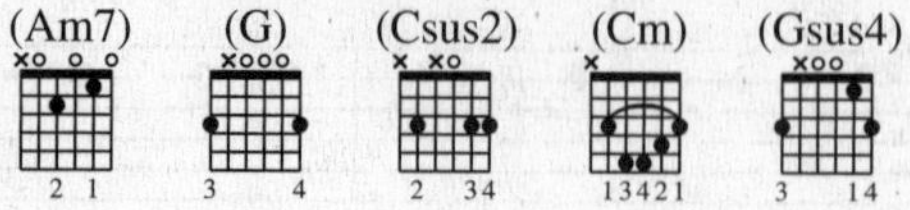

(Am7) (G) (Csus2) (Cm) (Gsus4)

Capo VI

Intro

Slow Folk Rock ♩ = 84

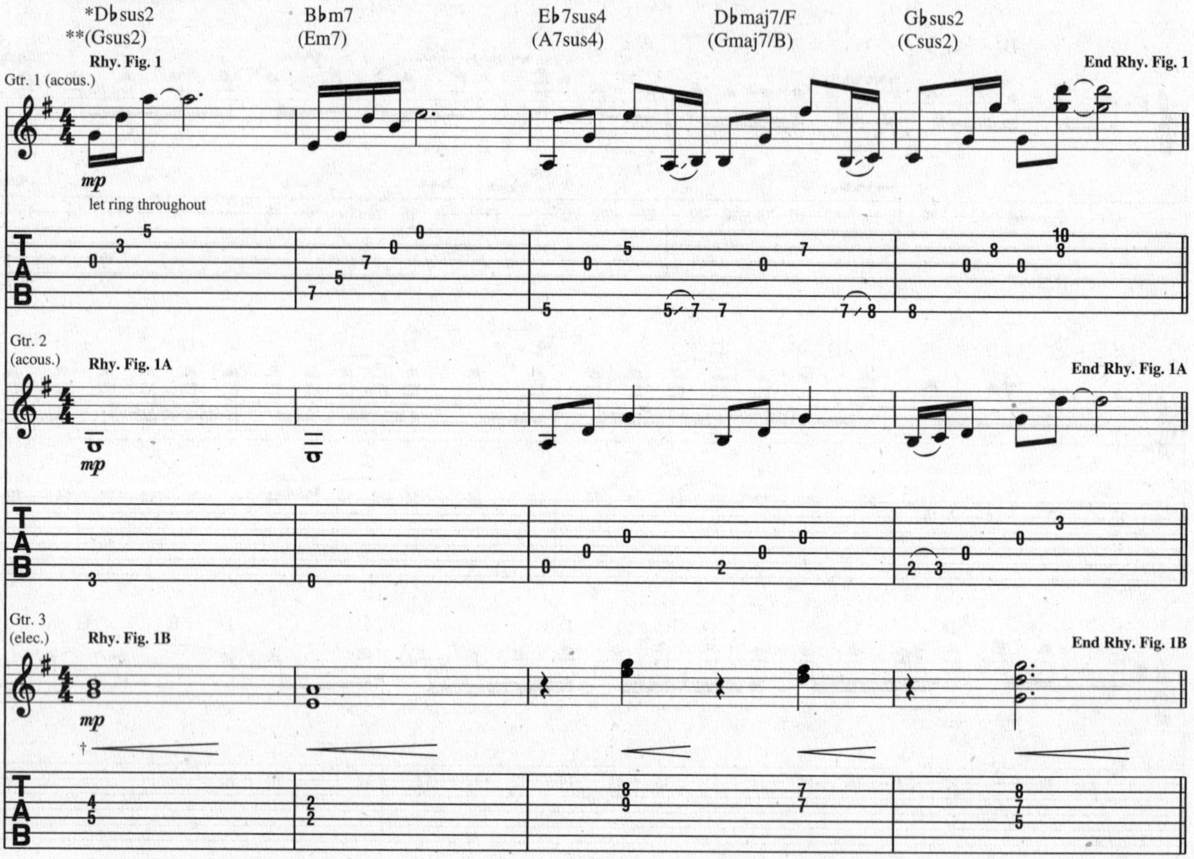

*D♭sus2 **(Gsus2) | B♭m7 (Em7) | E♭7sus4 (A7sus4) | D♭maj7/F (Gmaj7/B) | G♭sus2 (Csus2)

Rhy. Fig. 1 — End Rhy. Fig. 1

Gtr. 1 (acous.)

mp

let ring throughout

Gtr. 2 (acous.) Rhy. Fig. 1A — End Rhy. Fig. 1A

mp

Gtr. 3 (elec.) Rhy. Fig. 1B — End Rhy. Fig. 1B

mp

*Chord symbols reflect basic tonality.

**Symbols in parentheses reflect chord names respective to capoed guitar. Symbols above reflect actual sounding chord. Capoed fret is "0" in TAB.

†vol. swells

Verse

Gtrs. 1 & 2: w/ Rhy. Figs. 1 & 1A, 2 times
Gtr. 3: w/ Rhy. Fig. 1B, simile

Ebm7
(Am7)
Db
(G)
Dbsus4
(Gsus4)
And I thought what I felt was sim - ple,
and I thought that I don't be - long.
Rhy. Fig. 2
End Rhy. Fig. 2
*Gtrs. 1, 2 & 3
mp
*composite arrangement
And now that I am leav - ing,
now I know that I did some-thing wrong 'cause I
Gtr. 3
let ring
Gtrs. 1 & 2
Gtr. 1
Gtr. 2
divisi
(Gtr. 1 cont. in slash)
(Csus2)
(Cm)
(cont. in notation)
missed you.
Yeah, yeah,
I missed you.
Gtr. 2

Verse
D♭sus2
(Gsus2)
B♭m7
(Em7)
E♭7sus4
(A7sus4)
D♭maj7/F
(Gmaj7/B)
2. And you say
I on-ly hear what I want to. I don't lis-ten hard, don't pay at-ten-tion to the
(Don't.
Gtr. 1
Gtr. 2
Gtr. 3
G♭sus2
(Csus2)
D♭5
(G5)
E♭7sus4
(A7sus4)
D♭maj7/F
(Gmaj7/B)
dis-tance that you're run-ning to an-y-one, an-y-where. I don't un-der-stand if you real-ly care. I'm
Don't.

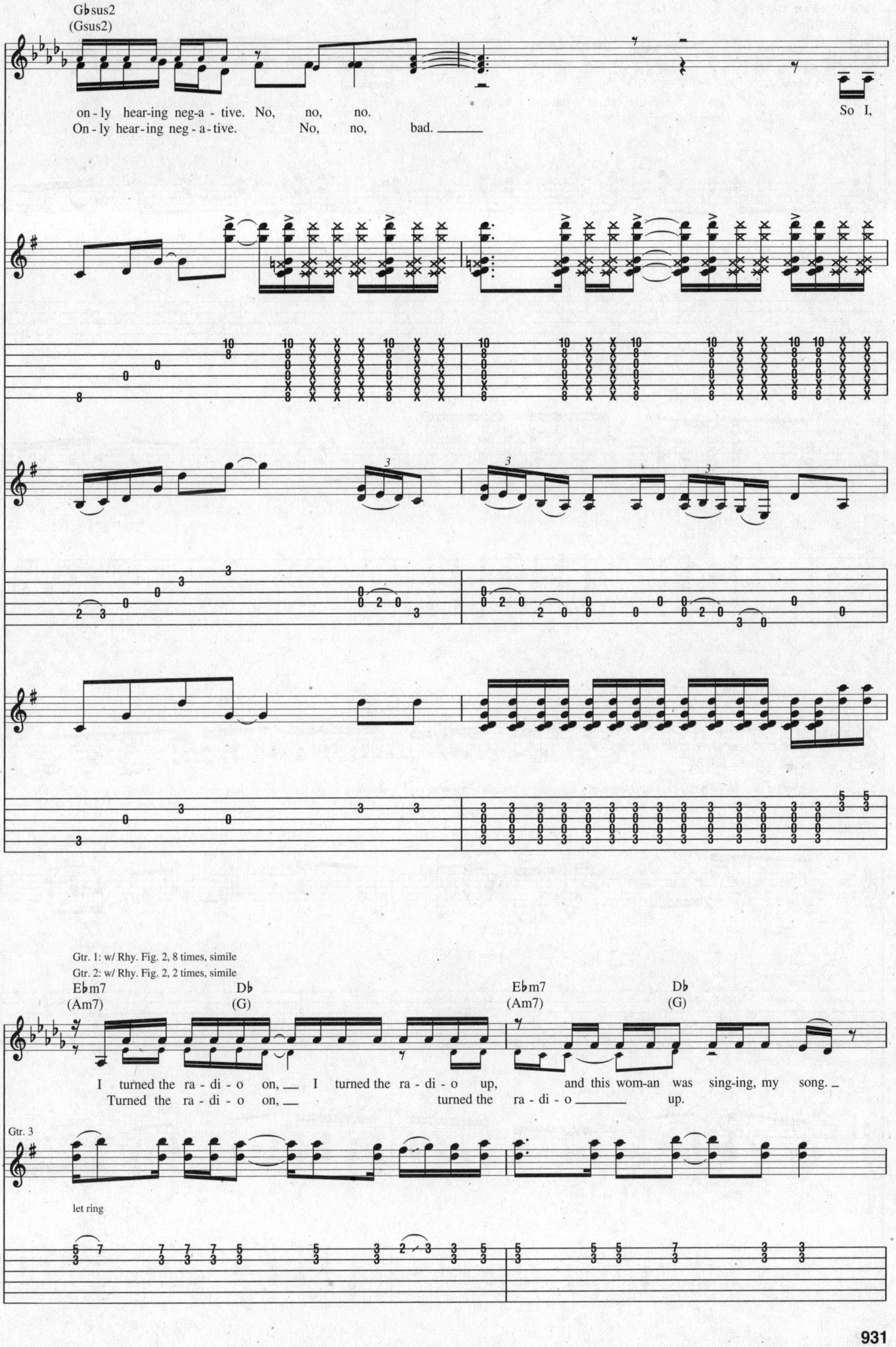

G♭sus2
(Gsus2)

on-ly hear-ing neg-a - tive. No, no, no. So I,
On-ly hear-ing neg - a - tive. No, no, bad. ____

E♭m7
(Am7)
D♭
(G)
Lov-er's in love and the oth-er's run a - way,
lov - er is cry - ing 'cause the oth - er won't stay.
Lov-er's in love.
Lov - er is cry-ing.
Gtr. 3
Gtr. 2
Some of us hov - er when we weep for the oth - er who was dy - ing since the day they were born. Well, well,
Some.)

Ebm7 (Am7) Db (G) Ebm7 (Am7) Db (G)

this is not ___ that. I think that I'm throw-ing, but I'm ___ thrown. ___ And I

Eb7sus4 (A7sus4) Gbsus2 (Csus2)

thought I'd live for-ev-er, but now I'm not so sure. You try to tell me that I'm clev-er, but that won't take me an-y-how ___

(Na, na,

Rhy. Fig. 3

End Rhy. Fig. 3

Gtr. 1

*Gtrs. 2 & 3 Rhy. Fig. 3A

End Rhy. Fig. 3A

let ring

Harm.

*composite arrangement

E♭sus4
(Asus4)
D♭maj7/F
(Gmaj7/B)
G♭sus2
(Csus2)
or an - y - where with you.
na. An - y - where.)
Verse
Gtrs. 1 & 3: w/ Rhy. Fig. 2, 4 times, simile
E♭m7
(Am7)
D♭
(G)
3. You said that I was na - ive, and I thought that I was strong, oh.
(You said that I was na - ive.
Gtr. 2
let ring
I thought, "Hey, I can leave, I can leave." Oh, but now I know that I was wrong 'cause I
I can leave, I can leave.)

(Csus2)
(Cm)
Gtrs. 1 & 3
missed you.
Yeah,
Gtr. 2
decresc.
Gtrs. 1 & 3: w/ Rhy. Fig. 2, 2 times, simile
Ebm7
(Am7)
Db
(G)
missed you.
You said, "You
Gtrs. 1 & 2: w/ Rhy. Figs. 3 & 3A, simile
Eb7sus4
(A7sus4)
Gbsus2
(Csus2)
caught me 'cause you want me, and one day you'll let me go." You try to give a-way a keep-er or keep me 'cause you know you're just so
Gtr. 3

E♭7sus4
(A7sus4)
D♭maj7/F
(Gmaj7/B)
G♭sus2
(Csus2)
scared to lose.
And you say,
Gtr. 1
Gtr. 2
let ring
Gtr. 3
Outro
Gtrs. 1 & 2: w/ Rhy. Fig. 1 & 1A, 2 times
D♭sus2
(Gsus2)
B♭m7
(Em7)
E♭7sus4
(A7sus4)
D♭maj7/F
(Gmaj7/B)
G♭sus2
(Csus2)
"Stay."
Gtr. 3
*Vol. swell
D♭sus2
(Gsus2)
B♭m7
(Em7)
E♭7sus4
(A7sus4)
D♭maj7/F
(Gmaj7/B)
G♭sus2
(Csus2)
rit.
You say,
I on-ly hear what I want to.
*Gtrs. 1 & 2 hold
last notes w/ fermata.

Stupid Girl

Words and Music by Joe Strummer, Mick Jones, Duke Erikson, Shirley Manson, Steve Marker and Butch Vig

Chorus
Gtr. 2: w/ Rhy. Fill 1
F#
B
You stu - pid girl.
Gtr. 5 (dist.)
mf
Riff B
End Riff B
Gtr. 1
divisi
Rhy. Fig. 1
End Rhy. Fig. 1
1/2
Gtr. 1: w/ Rhy. Fig. 1, 2 times
Gtr. 5: w/ Riff B, 2 times
To Coda 1
To Coda 2
1., 3. All you had, you wast - ed.
2. Can't be - lieve you fake it.
All you had, you wast - ed.
Can't be - lieve you fake
Interlude
Gtr. 1: w/ Rhy. Fig. 1, 4 times
Gtr. 2: w/ Rhy. Fill 1
Gtr. 3: w/ Riff A, 2 times
Gtr. 6
Rhy. Fig. 2
play 3 times
End Rhy. Fig. 2
Verse
Gtr. 1: w/ Rhy. Fig. 1
Gtr. 6 tacet
2. What drives you on, (echo repeat) it can drive you mad. (echo repeat) A
mil - lion lies to sell your - self is all you ev - er had.
D.S. al Coda 1
Coda 1
it.
Interlude
Gtrs. 1 & 6: w/ Rhy. Figs. 1 & 2, 4 times
Gtr. 3: w/ Riff A, 2 times
Gtr. 5: w/ Riff B, 4 times
play 4 times
* Gtr. 7
Riff C
End Riff C
* Kybd. arr. for gtr.
Rhy. Fill 1
Gtr. 2
play 6 times

Guitar Solo

Gtrs. 1 & 6: w/ Rhy. Figs. 1 & 2, 4 times
Gtrs. 5 & 7: w/ Riff B, 4 times

F# B F# B

Gtr. 3 — Riff D — End Riff D

mf w/ dist.
w/ slide

steady gliss.

10—12 0 2—3 0 2—3 | 10—12 0 2—3 0 2—3

Coda 2

Gtr. 1: w/ Rhy. Fig. 1, 8 times
Gtr. 2: w/ Rhy. Fill 1, 2 times
Gtr. 5: w/ Riff B, 8 times

B F# B F# B

You stu-pid girl. ___ You stu-pid girl. ___

Gtr. 7 — Riff E — End Riff E

9 7 7 6 | 9 7 7 6 | 9 7 7 6

Gtr. 7: w/ Riff E, 2 3/4 times

F# B F# B

Can't be - lieve you fake ___ it. I can't be - lieve ___ you fake ___ it.

Gtr. 3: w/ Riff A, 2 times
Gtr. 6: w/ Rhy. Fig. 2, 4 times

F# B F# B

You stu - pid girl. ___ You stu - pid girl. ___

F# B F# B

Can't be - lieve you fake ___ it. Can't be - lieve ___ you fake ___ it.

Outro

Gtrs. 1 & 6: w/ Rhy. Figs. 1 & 2, 4 times
Gtr. 3: w/ Riff D, 2 times
Gtr. 5: w/ Riff B, 4 times

F# B F# B F# B F# B F#5

Gtrs. 1 & 6

You stu-pid girl.

Gtr. 2

P.S. P.S. P.S. P.S.

Sweet Home Alabama

Words and Music by Ronnie Van Zant, Ed King and Gary Rossington

G
D
Csus2
G
Sing-in' songs a - bout - the south - land.
D
Csus2
G
Interlude
N.C.(D)
(C)
I miss ole 'Bam - ee once a - gain - and I think it's a sin, - yes.
Gtr. 2
Riff A1
End Rhy. Fig. 1
Gtr. 1
(G)
End Riff A1
(D)
(C)
(G)
let ring
let ring
let ring
* w/ bar
harm.
slight vib. w/ bar
Harm.
*Depress and release trem. bar at each beat indicated
Verse
Gtr. 1: w/ Rhy. Fig. 1
Gtr. 2: w/ Riff A, 1 3/4 times
D
Csus2
G
D
Csus2
2. Well, I heard Mist-er Young sing a - bout - her.
(Ooh, ooh, ooh.
Well, I heard old Neil - put 'er down. -
Ooh, ooh,

G D Csus2 G D Csus2

Well, I hope Neil Young will re-mem - ber, a south-ern man _ don't need him a -

ooh. Ooh, ooh, ooh. South-ern man don't need him a -

Chorus

Gtr. 2: w/ Riff B

Rhy. Fig. 2A

Gtr. 2

D5 D6 D5 C5 C6 C5 G5 G6 G5 Csus2

round, an-y-how. Sweet _ home Al - a-bam - a,

round.)

Gtr. 1

Riff B1 End Riff B1 Rhy. Fig. 2

let ring

D5 D6D5 C5 C6C5 G5 C5 D5 D6 D5 C5 C6 C5

where the skies are so blue. _ Sweet _ home Al - a -

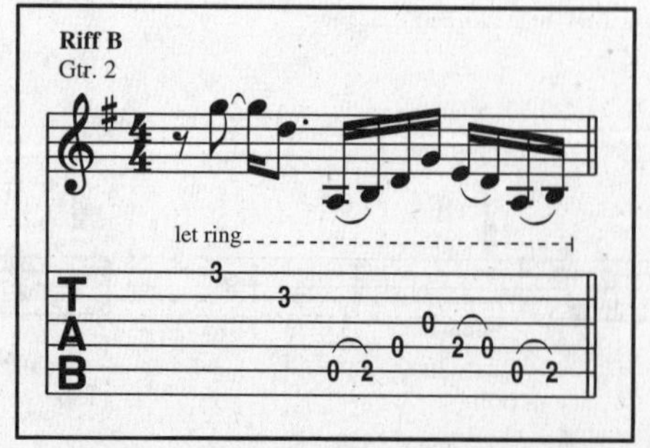

Gtr. 2: w/ Fill 1
G5 G6 G5 Csus2 D5 D6 D5 C5 C6 C5 G5 F/C C
End Rhy. Fig. 2A
bam - a, Lord, I'm com-in' home to you.
End Rhy. Fig. 2
Guitar Solo
Gtr. 1: w/ Rhy. Fig. 3, 2 times
D Csus2 G D Csus2
Gtr. 2
P.H.
full
Verse
Gtr. 2: w/ Riff A, 1st meas. only
Gtr. 2: w/ Riff C
G D Csus2 G F/C C
3. In Bir-ming - ham they love the gov - 'nor, boo, boo,
let ring
Fill 1
Gtr. 2
mf
f
full
Rhy. Fig. 3
Gtr. 1
let ring

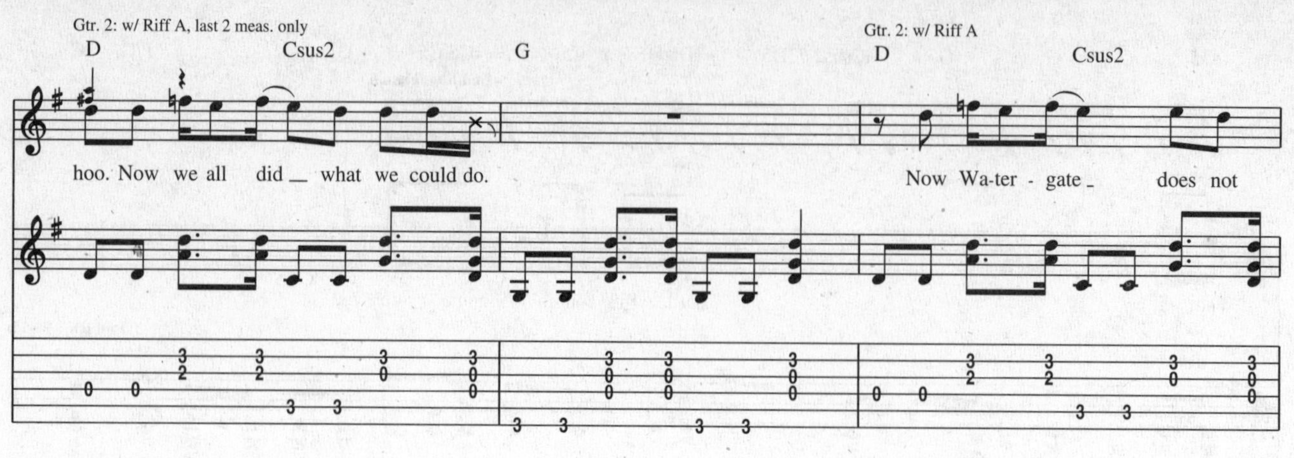

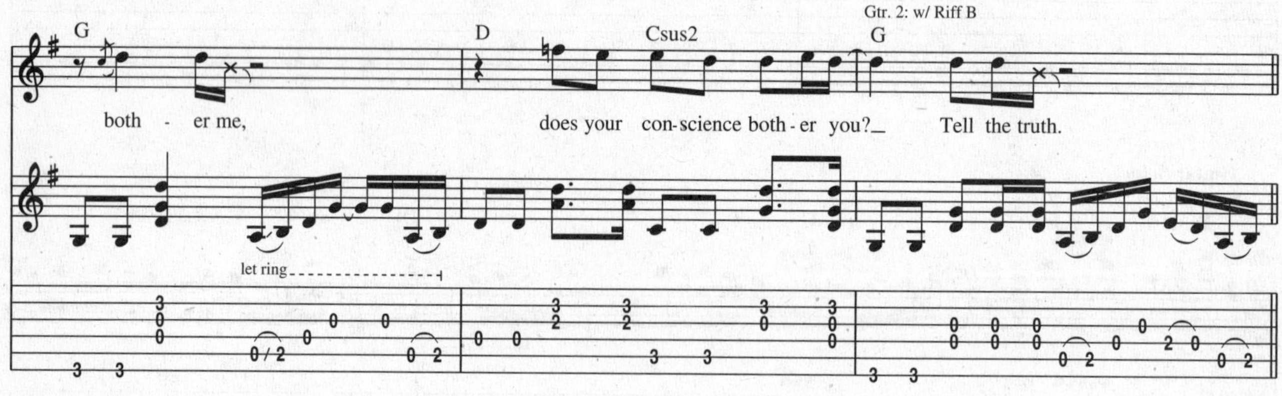

Chorus

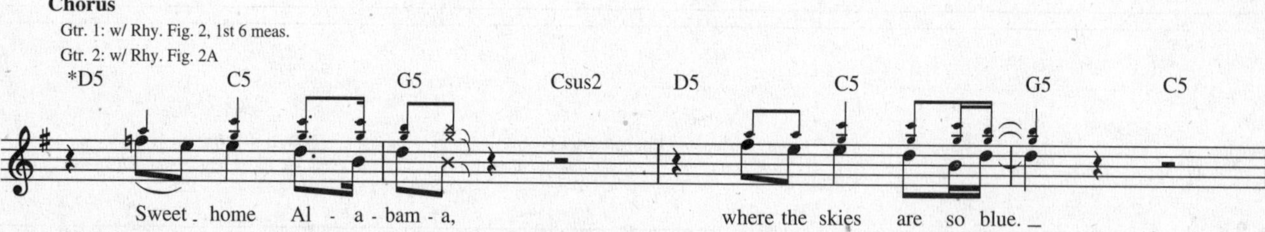

*Only the primary chords are notated here; "6th" chords are implied by the rhythm figure.

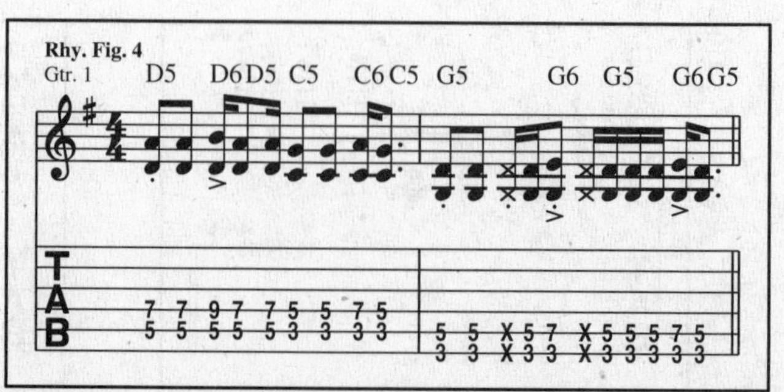

Guitar Solo

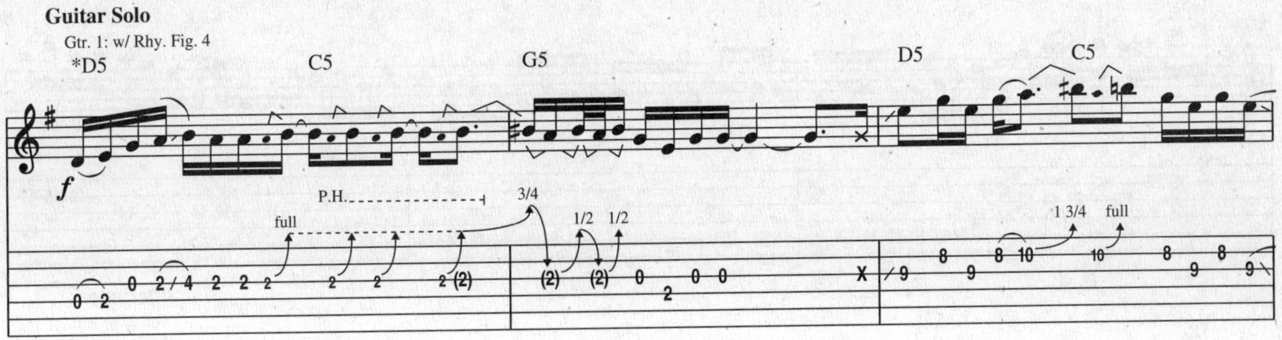
Gtr. 1: w/ Rhy. Fig. 4
*D5
C5
G5
D5
C5
f
P.H.
full
3/4
1/2
1/2
1 3/4
full

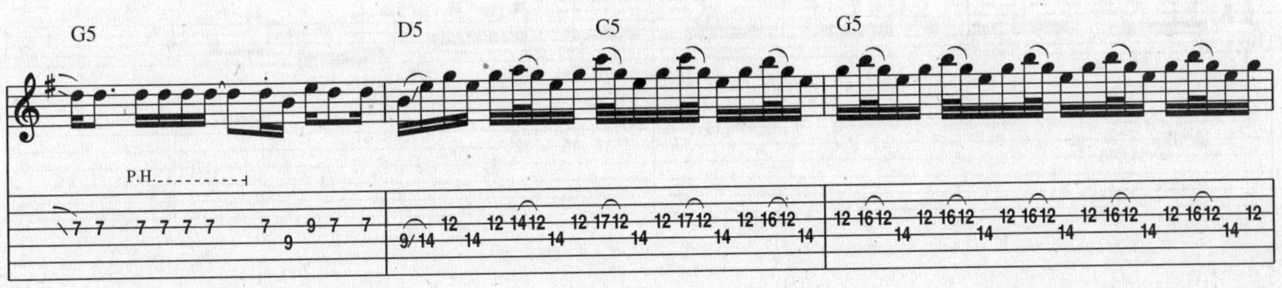
G5
D5
C5
G5
P.H.

w/ Bkgd. Voc. Fig. 1, 4 times
D5
C5
G5
D5
C5

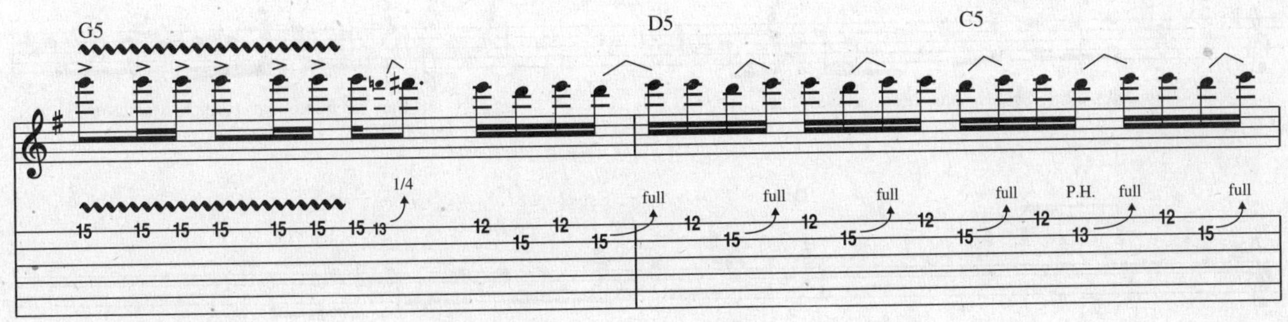
G5
D5
C5
1/4
full
full
full
full
P.H.
full
full

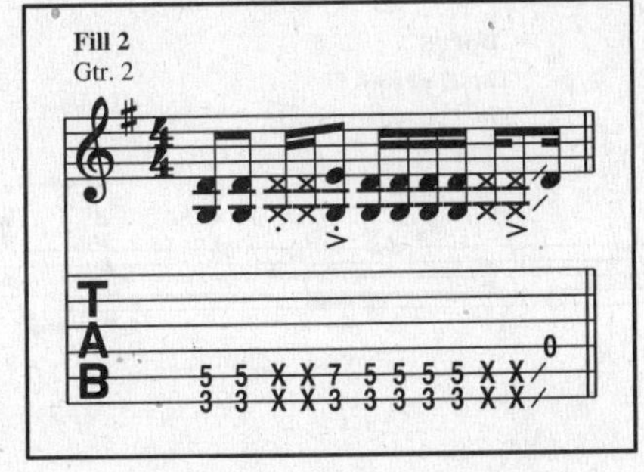
Fill 2
Gtr. 2
T
A
B

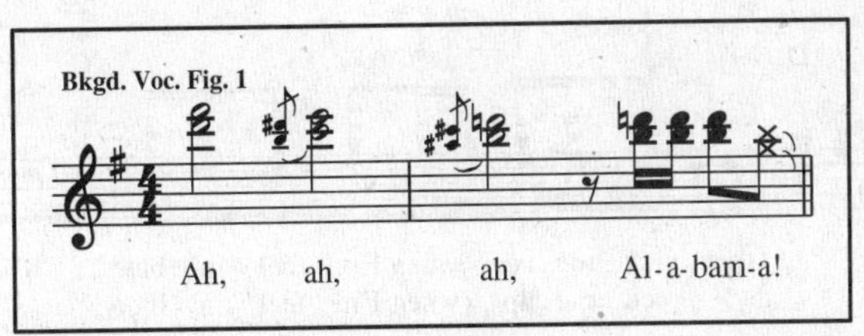
Bkgd. Voc. Fig. 1
Ah,
ah,
ah,
Al-a-bam-a!

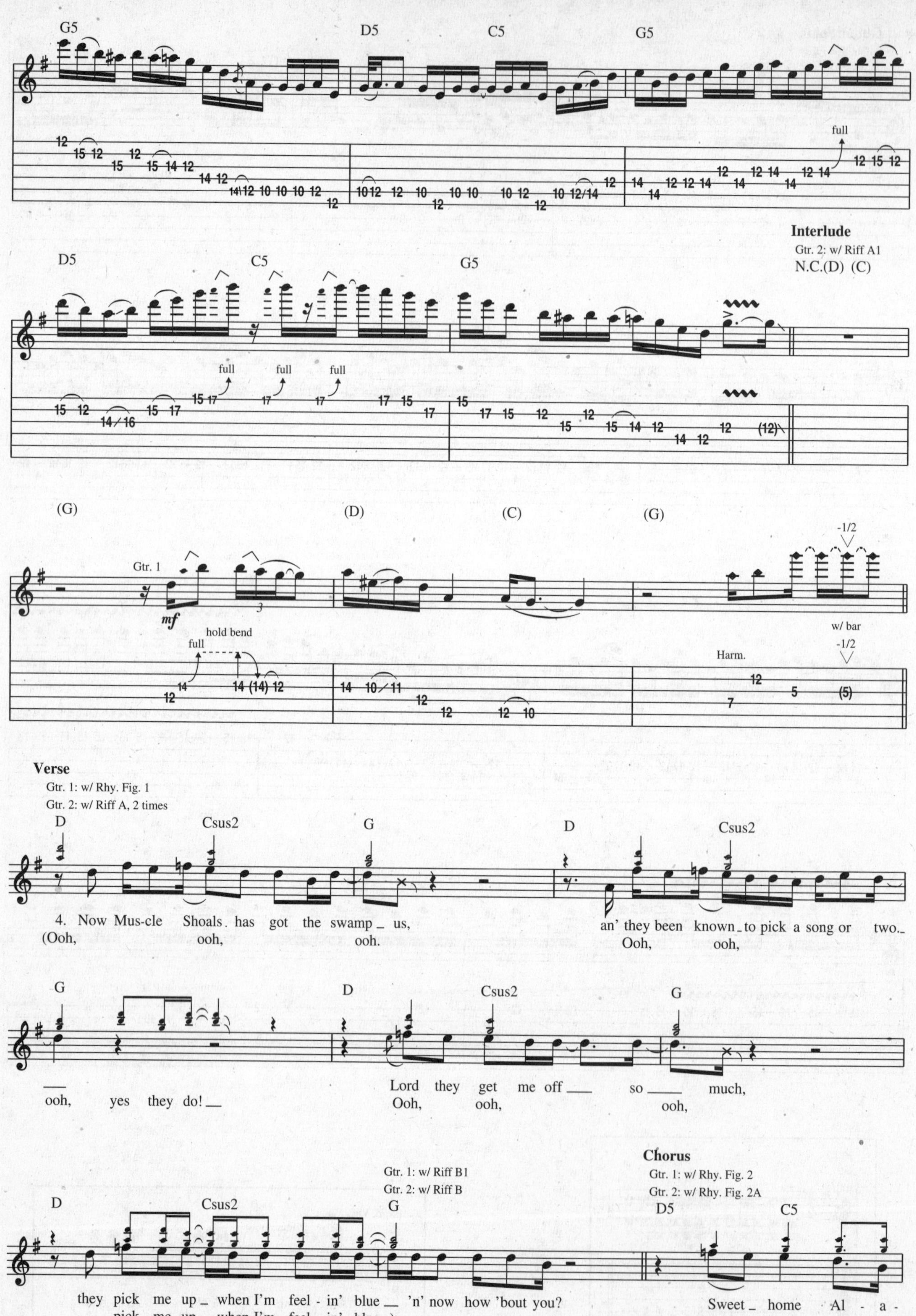

G5 D5 C5 G5
full
D5 C5 G5
full full full
Interlude
Gr. 2: w/ Riff A1
N.C.(D) (C)
(G) (D) (C) (G)
Gtr. 1
mf
hold bend
full
Harm.
w/ bar
-1/2
Verse
Gtr. 1: w/ Rhy. Fig. 1
Gtr. 2: w/ Riff A, 2 times
D Csus2 G D Csus2
4. Now Mus-cle Shoals has got the swamp _ us, an' they been known to pick a song or two. _
(Ooh, ooh, ooh. Ooh, ooh,
G D Csus2 G
Lord they get me off ___ so ___ much,
ooh, yes they do! _ Ooh, ooh, ooh,
Gtr. 1: w/ Riff B1
Gtr. 2: w/ Riff B
D Csus2 G
they pick me up _ when I'm feel - in' blue __ 'n' now how 'bout you?
pick me up _ when I'm feel - in' blue._)
Chorus
Gtr. 1: w/ Rhy. Fig. 2
Gtr. 2: w/ Rhy. Fig. 2A
D5 C5
Sweet _ home Al - a -

G5 Csus2 D5 C5 G5 C5
bam - a, where the skies are so blue.

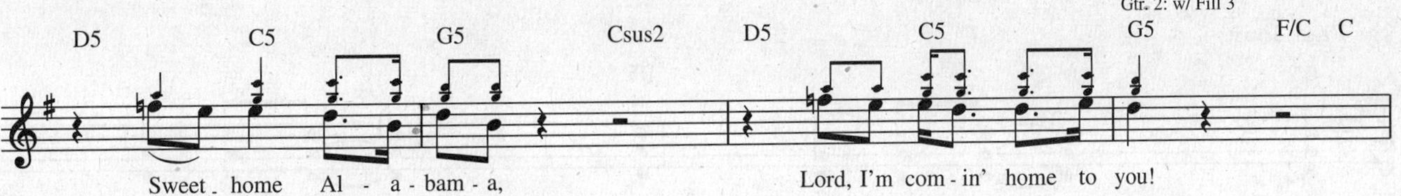
Gtr. 2: w/ Fill 3
D5 C5 G5 Csus2 D5 C5 G5 F/C C
Sweet home Al - a - bam - a, Lord, I'm com - in' home to you!

Gtr. 1: w/ Rhy. Fig. 2
Gtr. 2: w/ Rhy. Fig. 2A
D5 C5 G5 Csus2 D5 C5 G5 C5
Sweet home Al - a - bam - a, oh sweet home! Where the skies are so blue, and the gov - 'nor's true.

Gtrs. 1 & 2: w/ Rhy. Fig. 4
D5 C5 G5 Csus2 D5 C5 G5
Sweet home Al - a - bam - a, oh yeah. Lord, I'm com in' - home to you. Yeah.
(Oo! Oo! Oo!)

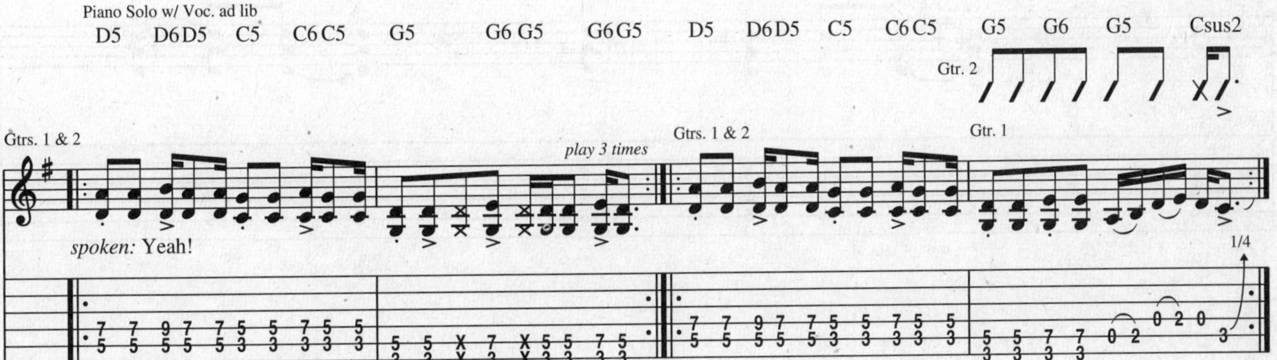
Play 6 times and Fade
Piano Solo w/ Voc. ad lib
D5 D6 D5 C5 C6 C5 G5 G6 G5 G6 G5 D5 D6 D5 C5 C6 C5 G5 G6 G5 Csus2
Gtr. 2
Gtrs. 1 & 2
play 3 times
Gtrs. 1 & 2
Gtr. 1
spoken: Yeah!
1/4

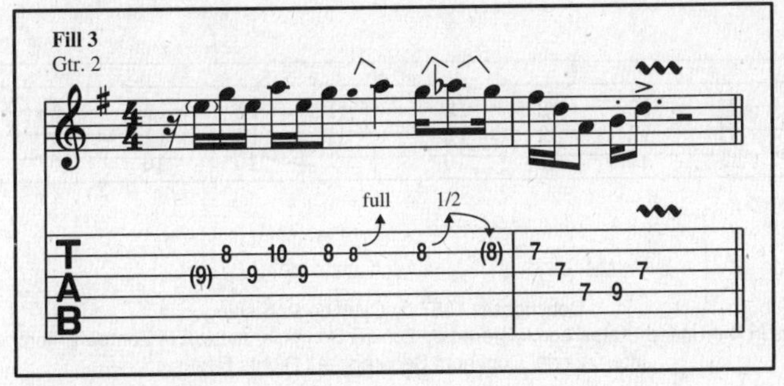
Fill 3
Gtr. 2
full
1/2

Talk Dirty to Me

Words and Music by Bobby Dall, Brett Michaels, Bruce Johannesson and Rikki Rockett

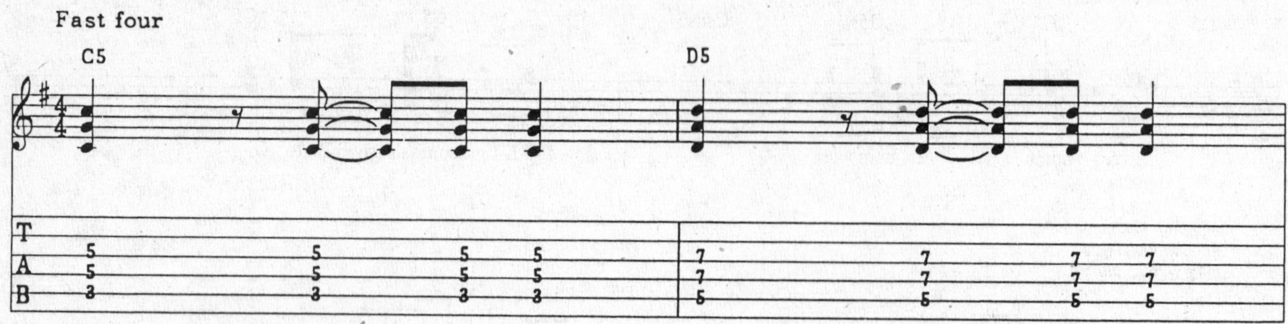

You know I
G5
nev - er,
I nev - er seen you look so good.
You nev - er act the way you should,
D5
But I like it.
And I

D5
know you like it too,
C5
the way that I want you.
G5
I got - - ta have
D5
you. Oh yes I do. You know I

G5
nev - er,
I nev - er ev - er stay out late
D5
You know that I can hard - ly wait
just to see
you.
And I

C5
know you can - - - not
wait, oh wait to see me too.
G5
I got - - ta touch
D5
you. 'cause ba - - by we'll be

C5
D5
at the drive - - - in
F♯5
G5
in the old man's Ford
be - hind them bush - es,
till I'm scream-in' for more.

C5
D5
Down the base - - ment,
Em5
C5
To Double Coda
A5
lock the cellar door, and ba - - by,
D5
F#5 G5
To Coda
F#5 G5
talk dirt -y to me.
You know I
G5
call you. I call you on the tel - e - - phone,

I'm on - - ly hop - in' that you're home
D5
so I can hear
you.
When you
C5
say those words to me

G5
and whis - - per so soft - - ly
D5
I got - - ta hear
D.S. al Coda
you. 'cause ba - - by we'll be
Coda
F♯5
G5
D5

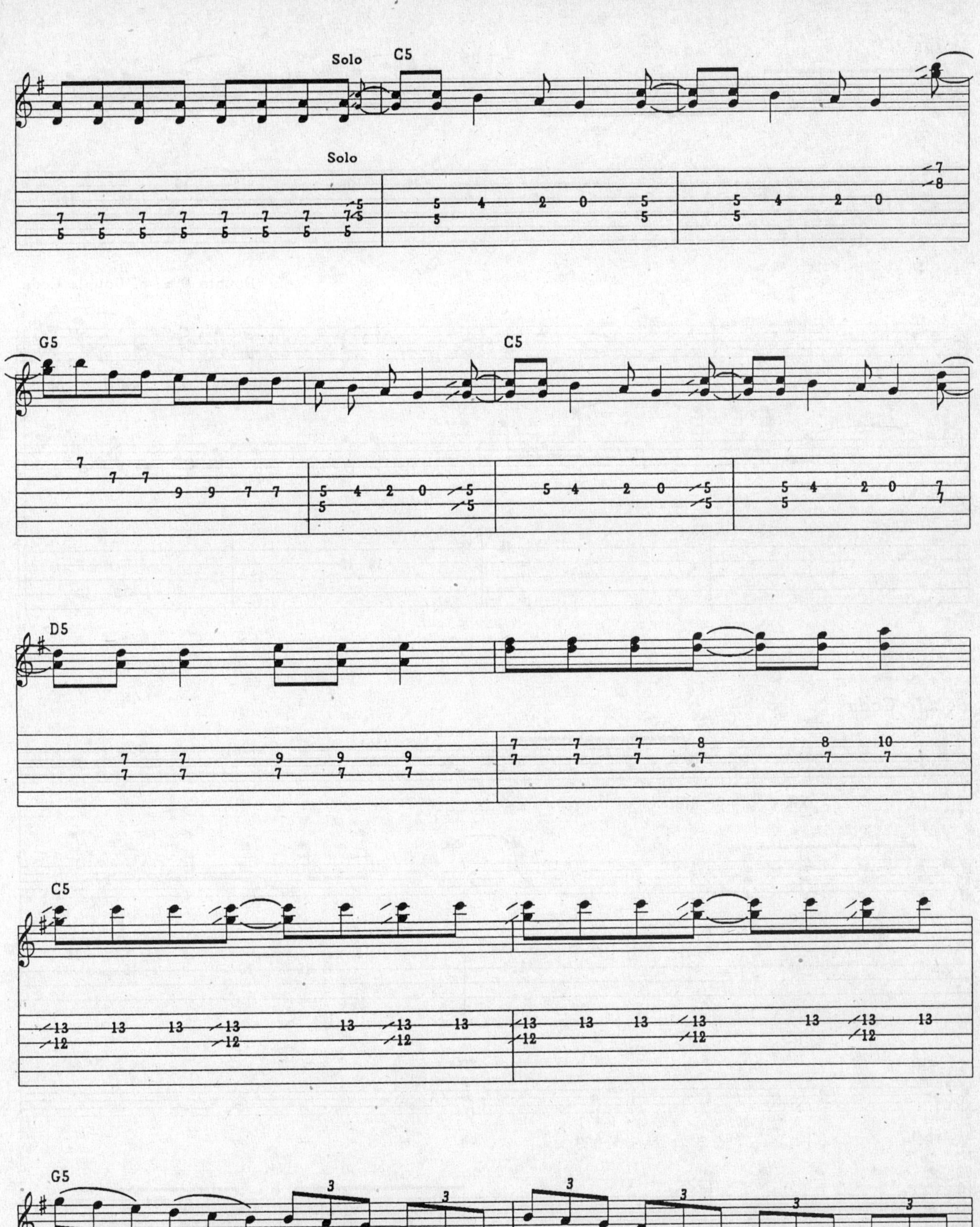
Solo
C5
Solo
G5
C5
D5
C5
G5

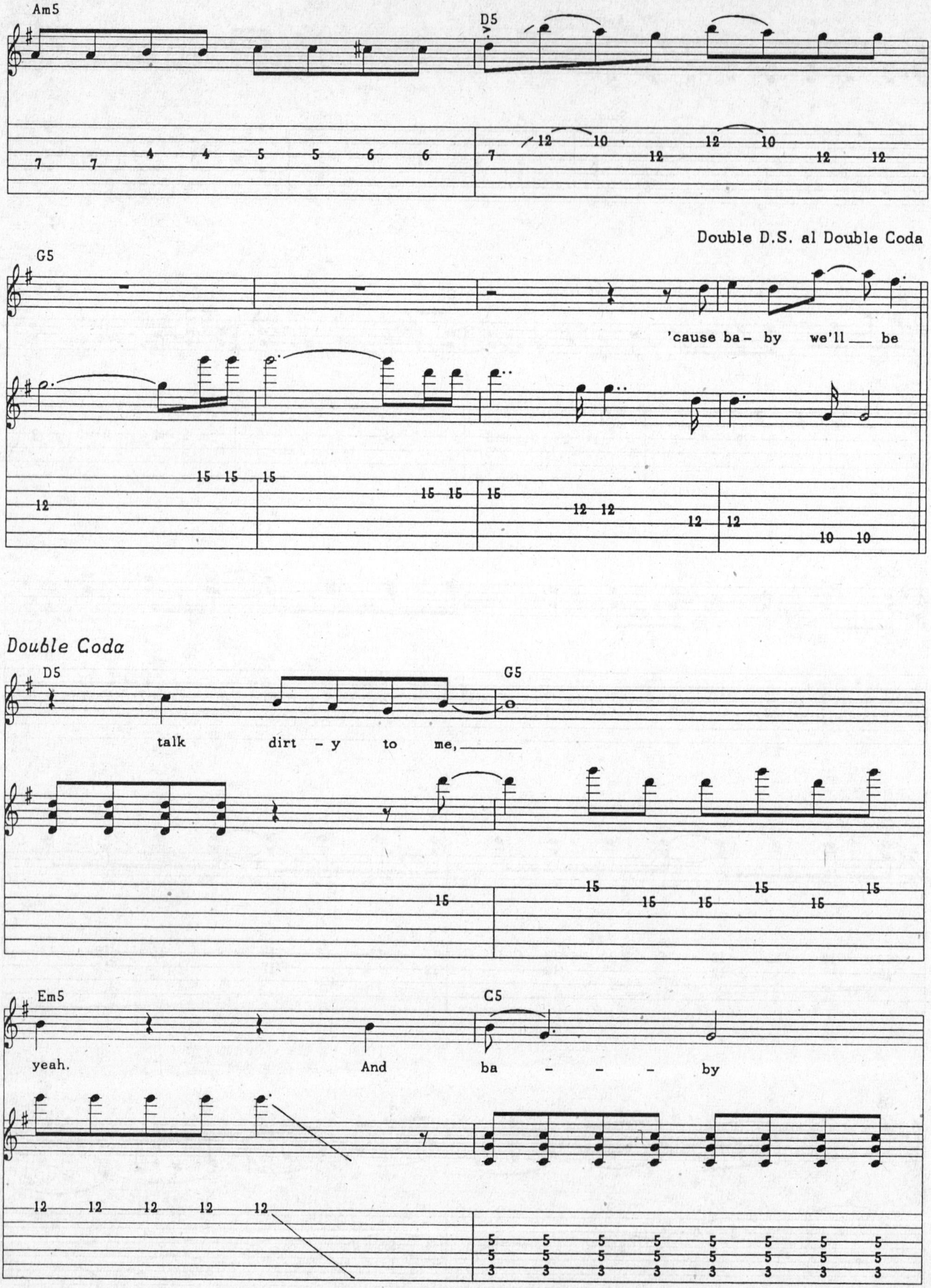

Double D.S. al Double Coda

Double Coda

D5 G5

talk dirt - y to me, ___

Em5 C5

yeah. And ba - - - by

D5
talk dirt - y to me,
yeah, yeah, yeah, yeah.
8va
C5
D5
And ba - by
talk dirt - y to me.
F#5
G5
Freely
8va
1½

Texas Flood

Words and Music by Larry Davis and Joseph W. Scott

Tune Down 1/2 Step:
①=E♭ ④=D♭
②=B♭ ⑤=A♭
③=G♭ ⑥=E♭

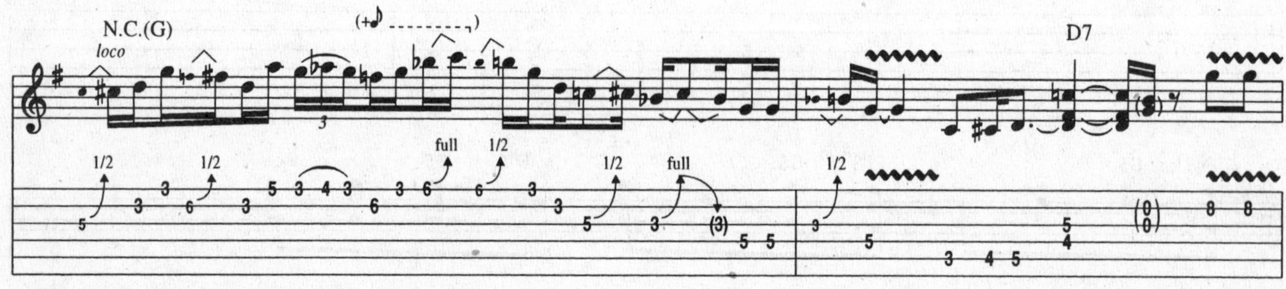

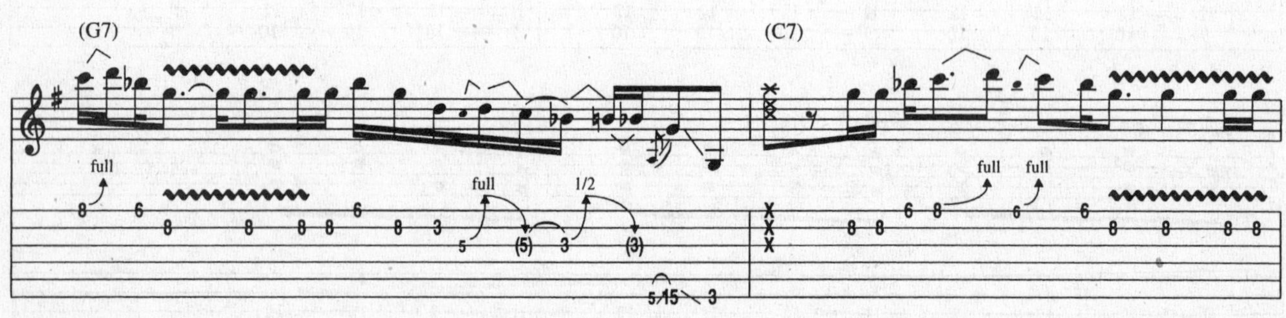

loco
(G7)
full
1/2
1/2
full
full
1 1/2
2
(D7)
full
full
1/4
full
(C7)
(G7)
(C7)
grad. bend
1/2
3/4
full
grad. bend
full
full
1/2
1/2
grad. bend
1/2
(G7)
D7
Verse
N.C.(G)
G6
1. Well, it's flood-in' down in Tex - as.
rake
*T T
*T = thumb
C9
N.C.
(G7)
All of the tel - e-phone lines are down.
1/4
grad. bend
full
full
full

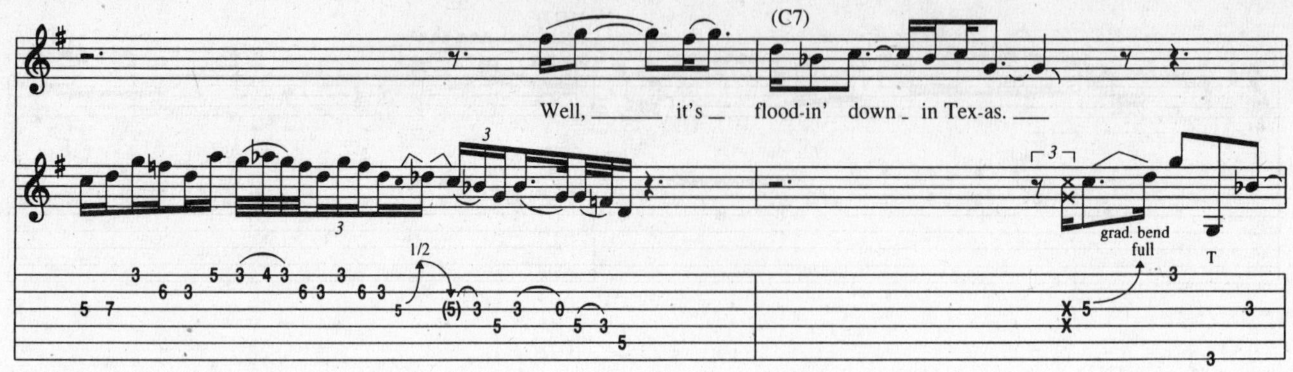
(C7)
Well, it's flood-in' down in Tex-as.
1/2
grad. bend
full
T

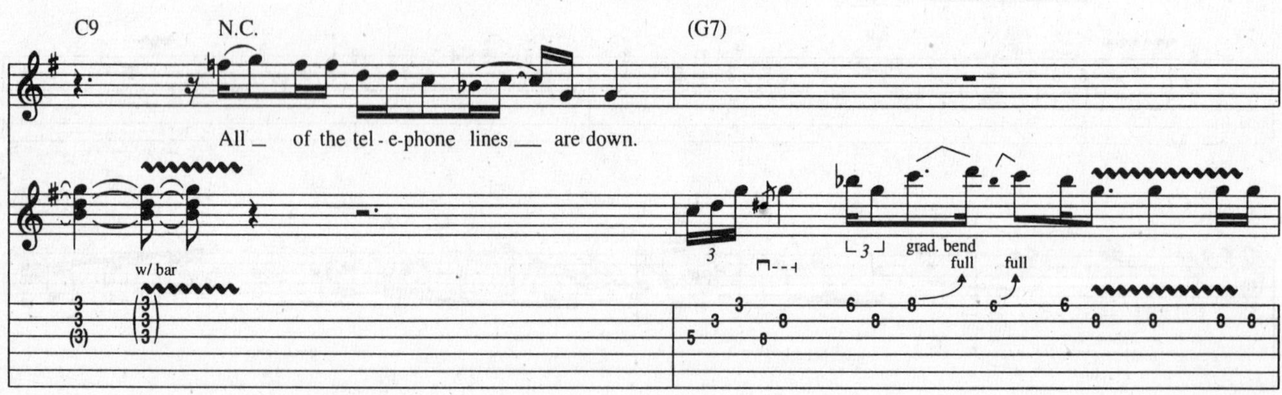
C9
N.C.
(G7)
All of the tel-e-phone lines are down.
w/ bar
grad. bend
full
full

(D7)
D9
Yeah, I been try-in' to call my ba-by.
8va
loco

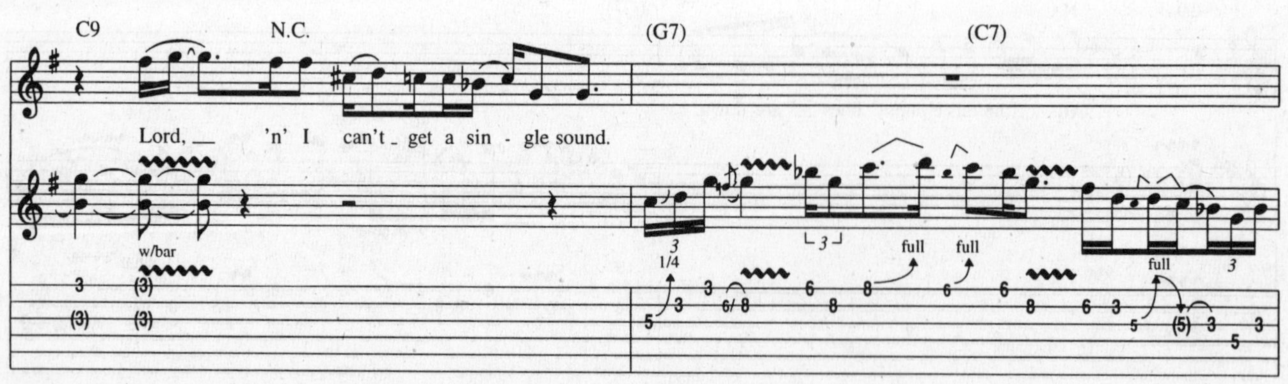
C9
N.C.
(G7)
(C7)
Lord, 'n' I can't get a sin-gle sound.
w/bar
1/4
full
full
full

Verse
(G7)
D7
N.C.(G7)
C9
2. Well, dark clouds are roll - in',
full
let ring
man, I'm stand-in' out in the rain.
N.C.
(G7)
w/ bar
full
(C7)
C9
Well, dark clouds are roll - in',
1/4
man, an' I'm stand-in' out in the rain.
N.C.
(G7)
1/4
full

(D7)
Yeah, flood water keep a-roll - in',
8va
loco
C9
N.C.
(G7)
(C7)
man, it's a-bout to drive poor me in-sane.
w/ bar
Guitar Solo
(G7)
(D7)
N.C.(G7)
(C7)
(G7)
(C7)
(G7)

(D7)
grad. bends
(C7)
grad. bends
(G7)
(C7)
(G7)
(D7)
(G7)
(C7)
(G7)
rake
(C7)
full
hold bend

(G7)
8va
loco
full
1/2
1/4
1/4
full
full
let ring
(D7)
(C7)
full
1/2
(G7)
(C7)
(G7)
D7
3. Well, I'm
full
Verse
(G7)
C9
N.C.
(G7)
leav-in' you ba-by.
Lord, now I'm go-in' back home to stay.
full
full
1/2
(C7)
Well, I'm leav-in' you ba - by.
full
full

(G7)
Lord, 'n' I'm go-in' back home to stay.
full
full 1/2
full
full 1/2

(D7)
D9
D♭9
Well, back home there's no floods or tor - na - does,
full
1/4
full
full

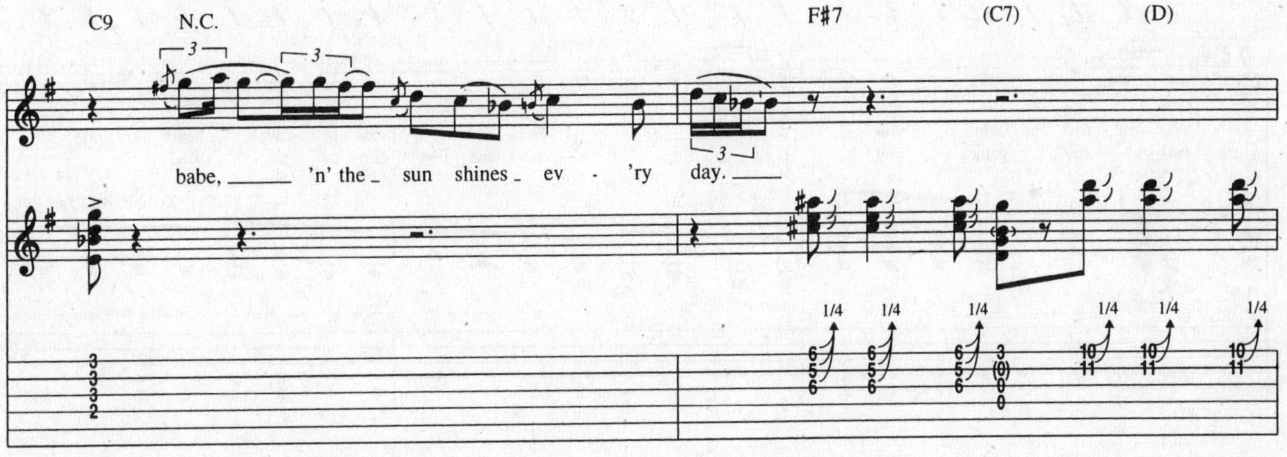
C9
N.C.
F#7
(C7)
(D)
babe, 'n' the sun shines ev - 'ry day.
1/4

Free Time
Gm
N.C.(G#)
G9
N.C.
G9
rit.
1/4
1/2
w/ bar

That Thing You Do!

from the Original Motion Picture Soundtrack THAT THING YOU DO!

Words and Music by Adam Schlesinger

Gtr. 1: w/ Riff A, simile
E A B E A B
1. you don't mean to be cruel. You nev - er e - ven
2., 3. we could be hap - py, can't you see, if you'd on - ly let me
Gtr. 2
C♯m F♯ D B
knew a - bout the heart - ache I've been go - ing through. Well, I
be the one to hold you and keep you here with me. 'Cause I 'Cause it
Gtrs. 1 & 2
C♯m F♯ E E7
1., 2. try and try to for - get you, girl, but it's just so hard to
3. hurts me so just to see you go a - round with some - one
To Coda
A Am E Am
do ev - 'ry time you do that thing you do.
new, and if I know you, you're

E
1.
B7
2.
Bridge
A5
C#5
I don't ask a - lot, girl, but I know one thing's for sure.
(I don't ask a - lot, girl.)
P.M.
F#5
(Know one thing's for sure.)
It's the love I have - n't got, girl, and I
B
C
B7
just can't take it an - y - more.
Whoa!

Guitar Solo
Gtr. 2: w/ Rhy. Fig. 1
E
A
B
E
A
B
Gtr. 1
mf
full
full
D.S. al Coda
C#m
F#
F#m
Am
B7
3. 'Cause
full
Coda
Am
E
Am
do - in' that thing,
ev - 'ry day just
do - in' that
thing,
Gtr. 3
full
Gtr. 1
E
Gtr. 3 tacet
B7
A
Am
N.C.
Emaj7
I can't take you
do - in' that thing you do.

This Love

Words and Music by Adam Levine and Jesse Carmichael

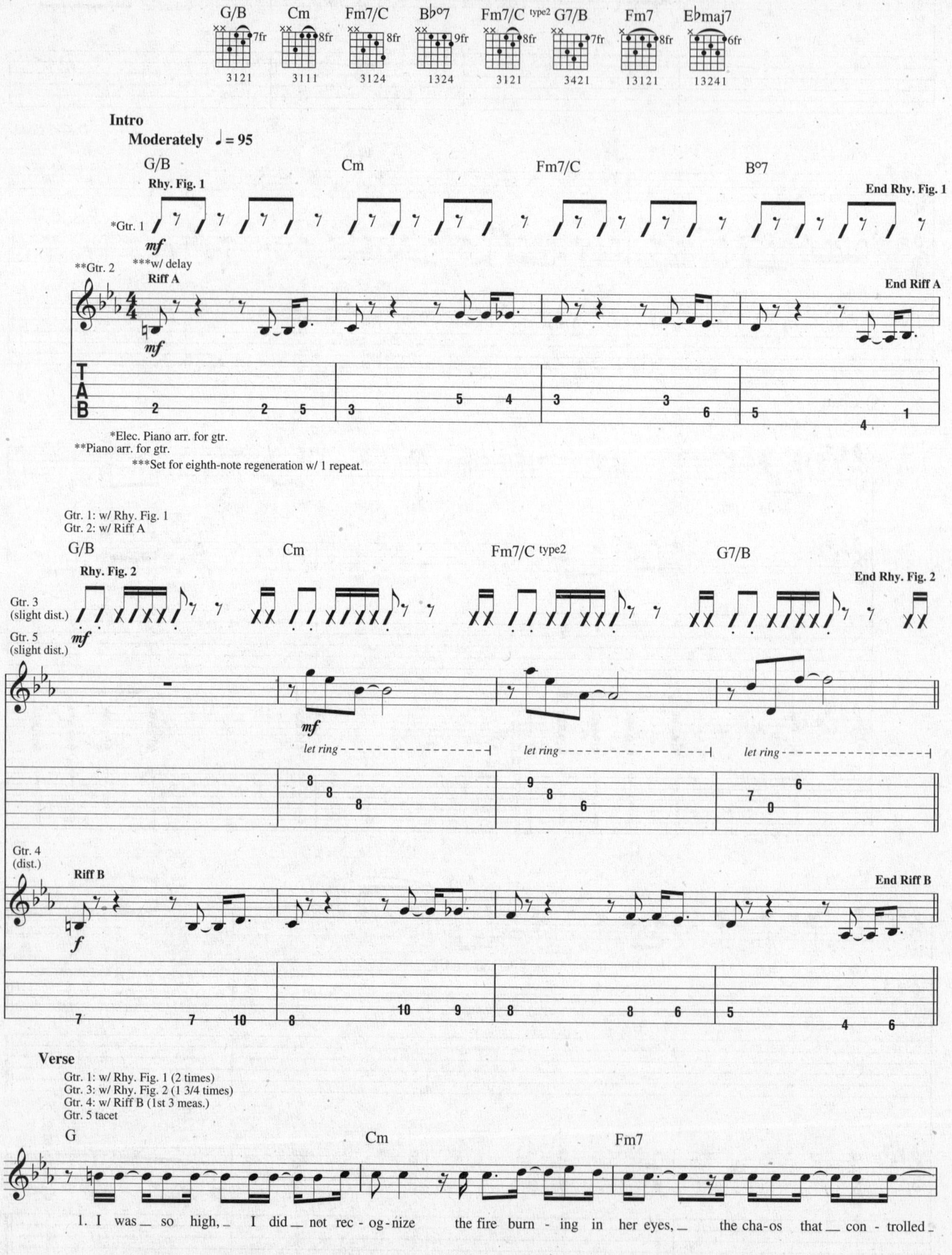

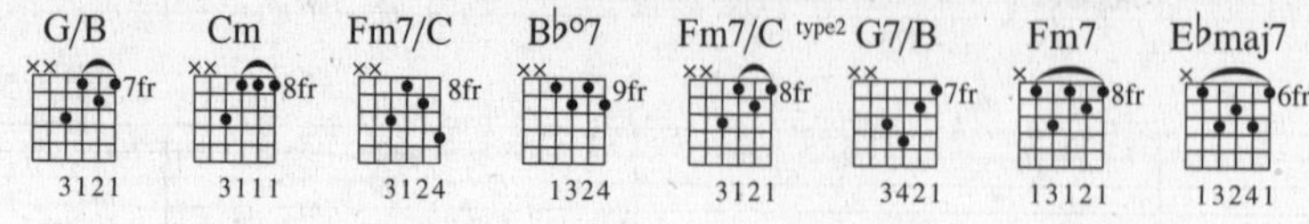

Intro

Moderately ♩ = 95

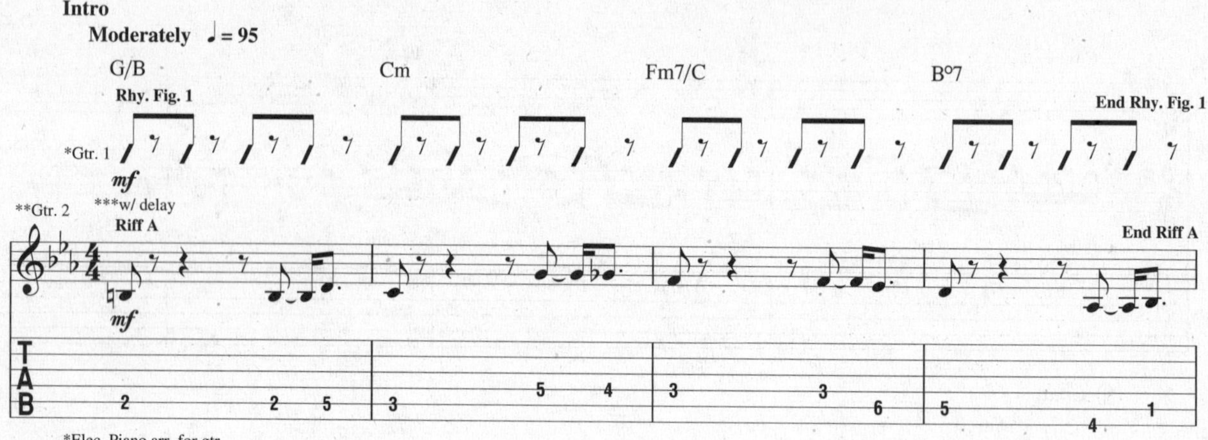

*Elec. Piano arr. for gtr.

**Piano arr. for gtr.

***Set for eighth-note regeneration w/ 1 repeat.

Gtr. 1: w/ Rhy. Fig. 1
Gtr. 2: w/ Riff A

G/B | Cm | Fm7/C type2 | G7/B

Rhy. Fig. 2 — End Rhy. Fig. 2

Gtr. 3 (slight dist.)

mf

Gtr. 5 (slight dist.)

mf

let ring

Gtr. 4 (dist.)

Riff B — End Riff B

f

Verse

Gtr. 1: w/ Rhy. Fig. 1 (2 times)
Gtr. 3: w/ Rhy. Fig. 2 (1 3/4 times)
Gtr. 4: w/ Riff B (1st 3 meas.)
Gtr. 5 tacet

G | Cm | Fm7

1. I was_ so high,_ I did_ not rec - og - nize the fire burn - ing in her eyes,_ the cha-os that_ con - trolled_

G7♭9
G
my mind.
Whis - pered, "Good - bye," as she got on
Gtr. 4
Cm
Fm7
G7/B
Gtr. 3
a plane, nev-er to re - turn a - gain, but al - ways in my heart,
ho.
Gtr. 5
let ring
*Gtr. 6 (clean)
divisi
mf
**w/ delay
**Set for eighth-note regeneration w/ 1 repeat.
Chorus
Gtrs. 3, 4 & 5 tacet
B♭
E♭6
This love has tak - en its toll on me.
Rhy. Fig. 3
Gtr. 6
Gtr. 7 (dist.)
Riff C
mp
***w/ delay
***Set for eighth-note regeneration w/ 1 repeat.

Cm Fm7 B♭ E♭6

She said, "Good - bye," too man - y times be - fore.

let ring - - -┤

Cm Fm7 B♭ E♭6

And her heart is break - ing in front ___ of me, ___ and

let ring - - -┤

Interlude
Gtr. 3: w/ Rhy. Fig. 2
Cm
F
Fm7/C
G/B
I have no choice 'cause I won't say, "Good-bye," an-y-more.
Whoa,
Gtr. 6
End Rhy. Fig. 3
Gtr. 7
End Riff C
Gtr. 4
To Coda
Gtrs. 6 & 7 tacet
Cm
Fm7
G7
whoa,
whoa,
whoa.
Gtr. 4
Verse
G/B
Gtr. 3: w/ Rhy. Fig. 2 (last 3 meas.)
Gtr. 4: w/ Riff B (last 3 meas.)
Cm
Fm7
Gtr. 3
2. I tried my best to feed her ap-pe-tite, to keep her com-ing ev-'ry night, so hard to keep her sat-
Gtr. 4
Gtr. 8
End Riff D
*Gtr. 8
divisi
Riff D
mf
*Hammond organ arr. for gtr.

Gtr. 3: w/ Rhy. Fig. 2 (1st 3 meas.)
Gtr. 4; w/ Riff B (1st 2 meas.)
Gtr. 8: w/ Riff D
G7
G
Cm
is - fied. Oh. Kept play - ing love like it was just a game, pre - tend - ing to feel
Fm7
G7/B
D.S. al Coda
Gtr. 3
the same, then turn a - round and leave a - gain. A, but, oh.
Gtr. 6
Gtr. 4
divisi
*String noise
Coda
Bridge
Gtr. 4 tacet
G7
Fm7
E♭maj7
Gtr. 6
whoa. I'll fix these bro - ken things, re - pair your bro - ken wings,
Gtr. 9 (clean)
let ring throughout
mp
Gtr. 4
Gtr. 7
divisi
G/B
Cm
and make sure ev - 'ry - thing's al - right. Oo, oo.
Female: (It's al - right, it's al - right.)

Fm7
E♭maj7
My pres - sure on your hips,
ah, sink - ing my fin - ger - tips in - to
G7/B
ev - 'ry inch of you be-cause I know that's what you want me to do.
Outro-Chorus
Gtr. 6: w/ Rhy. Fig. 3 (till fade)
Gtr. 7: w/ Riff C
Gtr. 9 tacet
Cm
Fm7
B♭
E♭6
This love has tak - en its toll on me.
She said, "Good - bye," too man - y times be - fore.
Her heart is
breaking - ing in front of me,
and I have no choice 'cause
F

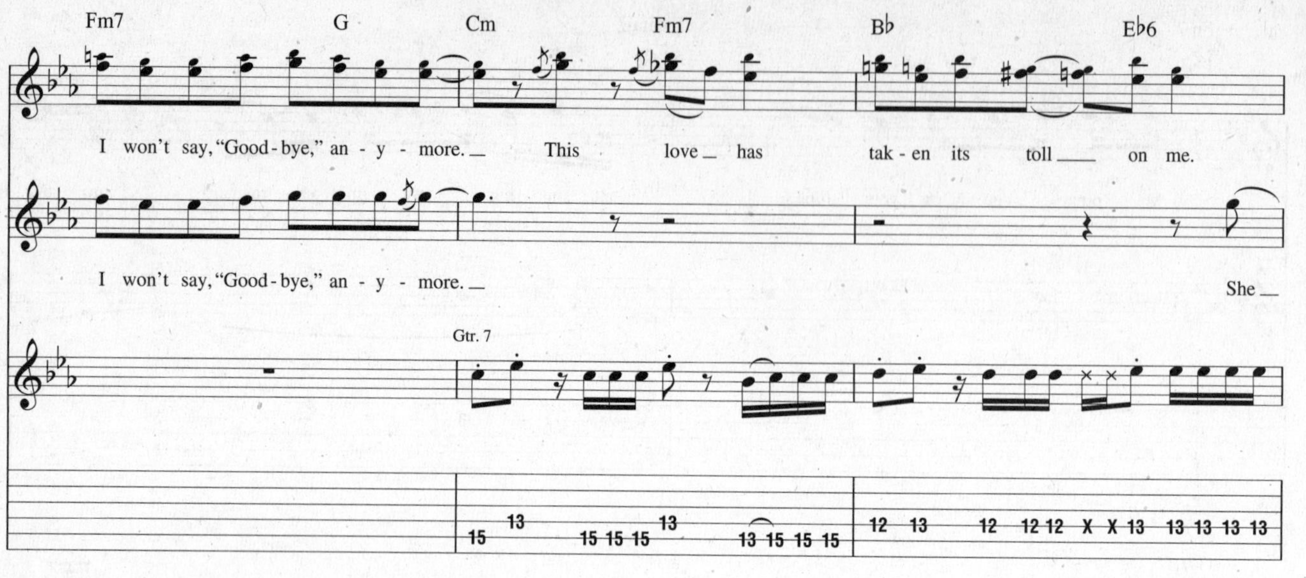
Fm7 G Cm Fm7 B♭ E♭6
I won't say, "Good-bye," an - y - more. This love has tak-en its toll on me.
I won't say, "Good-bye," an - y - more. She
Gtr. 7
15 13 15 15 15 13 13 15 15 15
12 13 12 12 12 X X 13 13 13 13 13
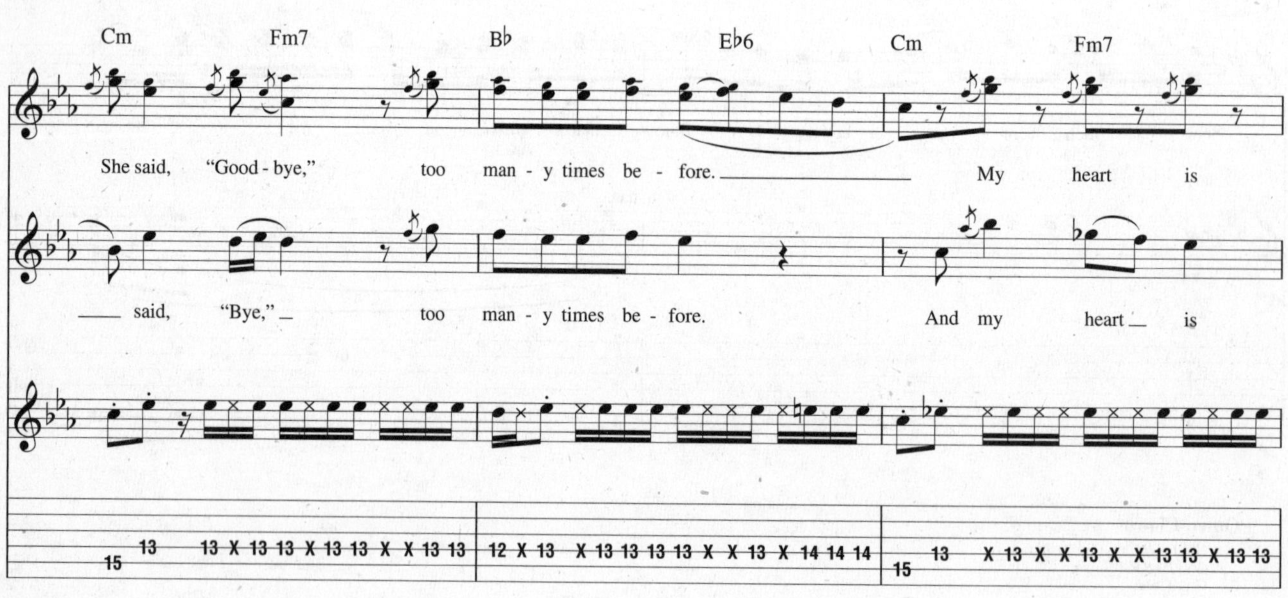
Cm Fm7 B♭ E♭6 Cm Fm7
She said, "Good-bye," too man - y times be - fore. My heart is
said, "Bye," too man - y times be - fore. And my heart is
15 13 13 X 13 13 X 13 13 X X 13 13
12 X 13 X 13 13 13 13 X X 13 X 14 14 14
15 13 X 13 X 13 X 13 X X 13 13 X 13 13
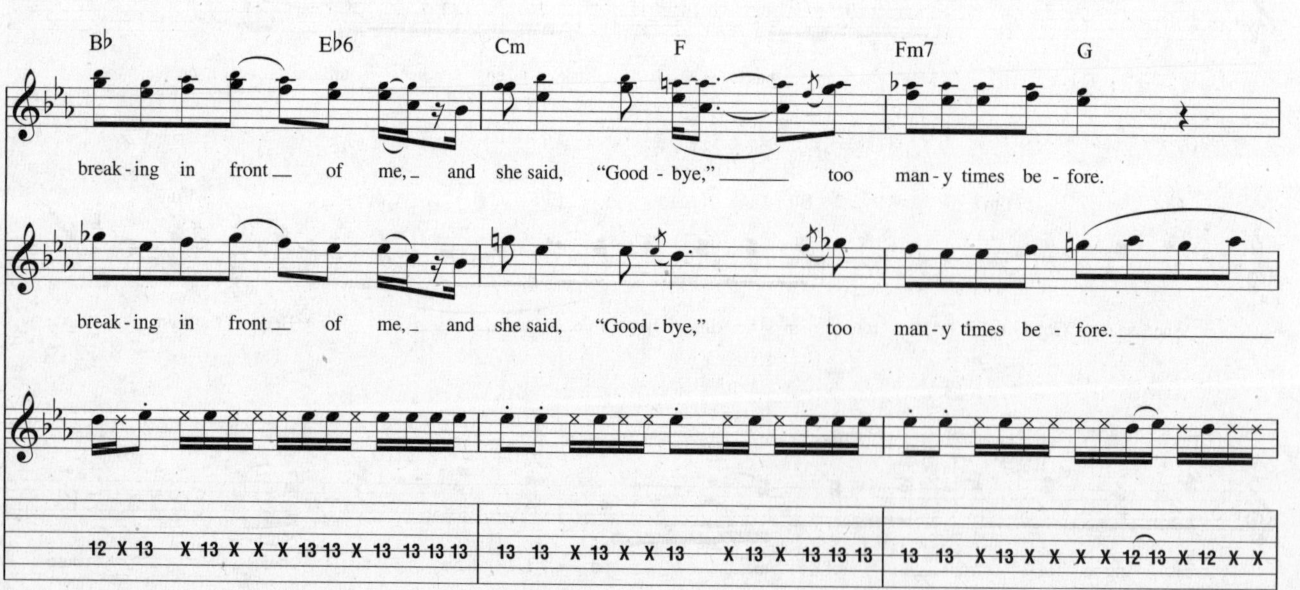
B♭ E♭6 Cm F Fm7 G
break-ing in front of me, and she said, "Good - bye," too man-y times be - fore.
break-ing in front of me, and she said, "Good - bye," too man-y times be - fore.
12 X 13 X 13 X X X 13 13 X 13 13 13 13
13 13 X 13 X X 13 X 13 X 13 13 13
13 13 X 13 X X X X 12 13 X 12 X X

Begin fade
Cm
Fm7
Bb
Eb6
Cm
Fm7
This love has tak-en its toll on me. She said, "Good-bye," too
Oh, yeah, yeah, yeah.
15 13 13 X 13 13 X 13 13 X X 13 13
12 13 X 15 X 13 13 X 13 14 14 14
15 13 13 13 X 13 13 X X 13 13 13 13

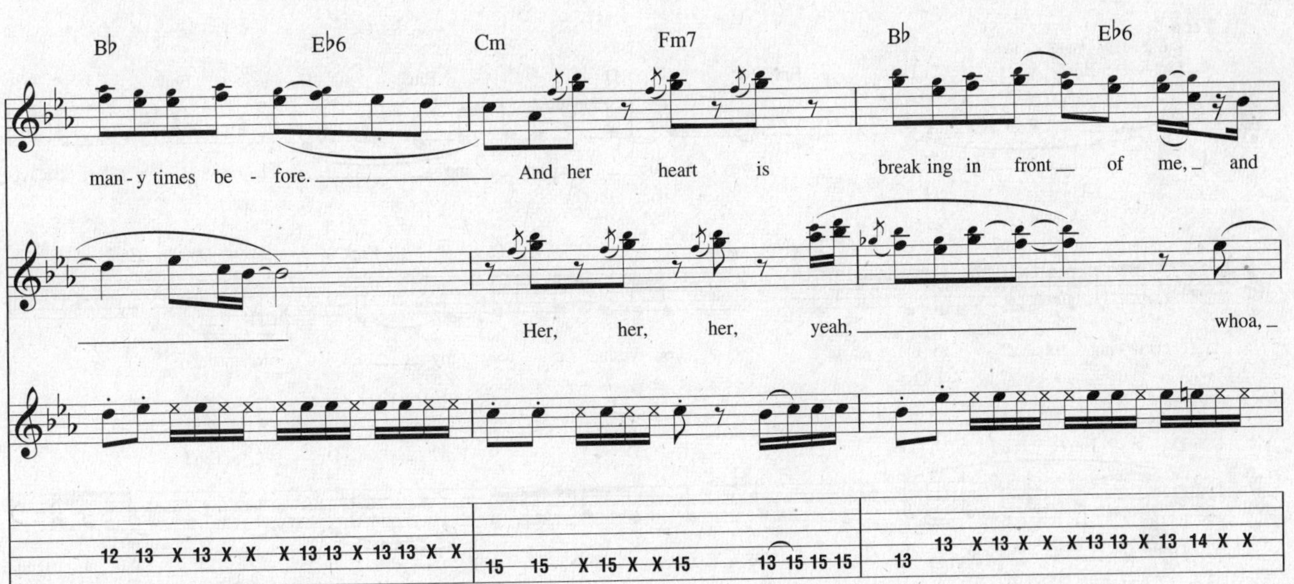
Bb
Eb6
Cm
Fm7
Bb
Eb6
man-y times be - fore. And her heart is break ing in front of me, and
Her, her, her, yeah, whoa,
12 13 X 13 X X X 13 13 X 13 13 X X
15 15 X 15 X X 15 13 15 15 15
13 13 X 13 X X X 13 13 X 13 14 X X

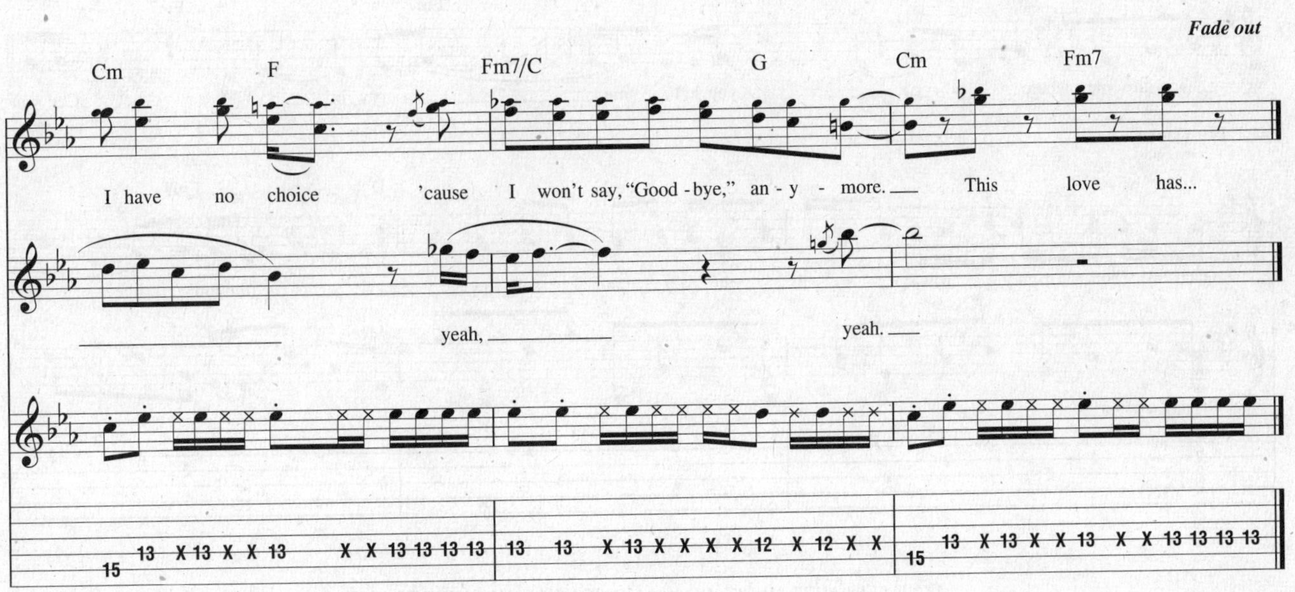
Fade out
Cm
F
Fm7/C
G
Cm
Fm7
I have no choice 'cause I won't say, "Good-bye," an-y - more. This love has...
yeah, yeah.
15 13 X 13 X X 13 X X 13 13 13 13
13 13 X 13 X X X X 12 X 12 X X
15 13 X 13 X 13 X X 13 13 13 13

Time

Words and Music by Darius Carlos Rucker, Everett Dean Felber, Mark William Bryan and James George Sonefeld

D
Em7
Asus4
A
'Cause to-mor-row's just an-oth-er day,
and I don't be-lieve in
End Rhy. Fig. 2
Interlude
drums enter
Gtr. 1: w/ Rhy. Fig. 1, 2 times
*D
time.
Gtr. 2 (acous.)
Rhy. Fig. 3
End Rhy. Fig. 3
let ring throughout
**Gtr. 3
Riff A
End Riff A
w/ clean tone
let ring
*combined tonality
**Bass arr. for gtr.
Verse
Gtrs. 1 & 2: w/ Rhy. Figs. 1 & 3, 4 times
Gtr. 3: w/ Riff A, 2 times
3. Time, I don't un-der-stand.
Chil-dren
kil-lin' in the street, dy-in' for the col-or of a rag.
Gtr. 4 (dist.)

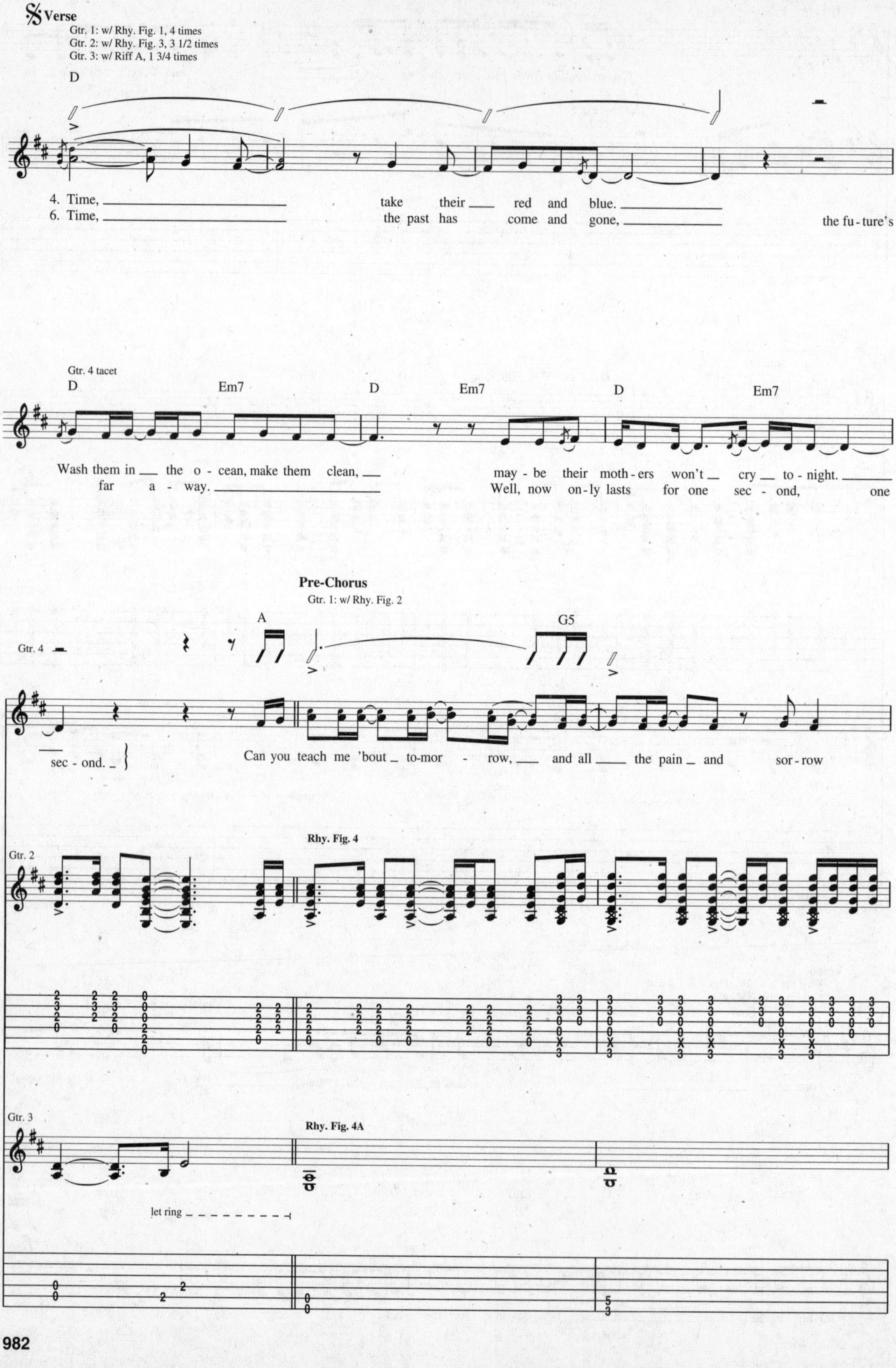

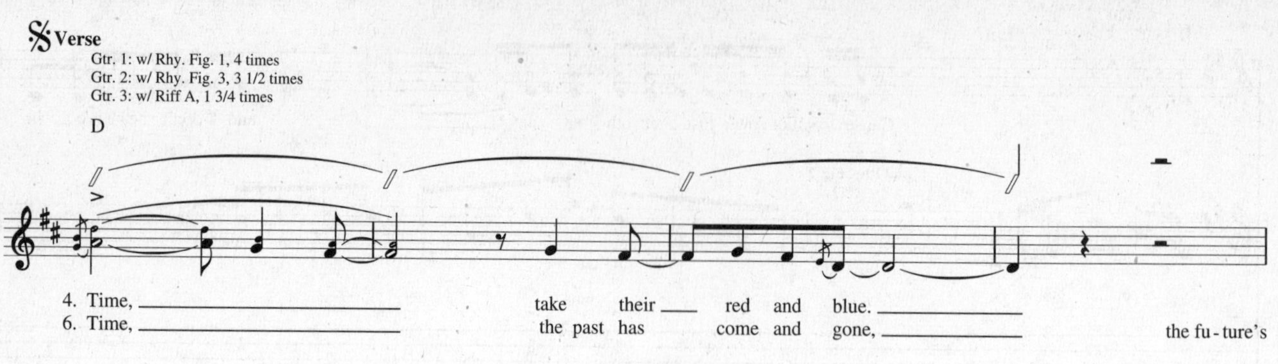

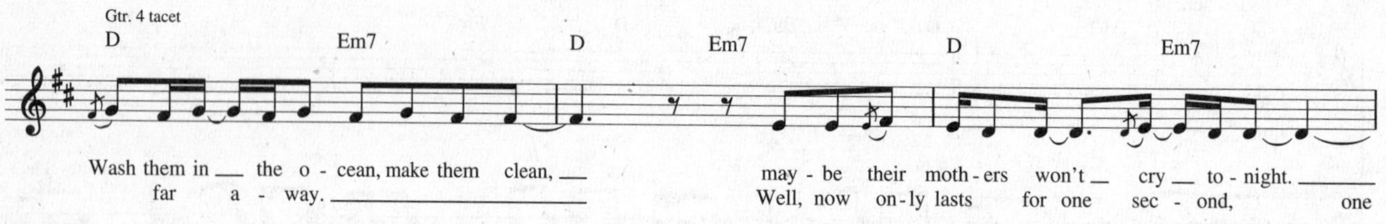

Pre-Chorus

Gtr. 1: w/ Rhy. Fig. 2

A G5

Gtr. 4

sec - ond. Can you teach me 'bout to-mor - row, and all the pain and sor - row

Gtr. 2

Rhy. Fig. 4

Gtr. 3

Rhy. Fig. 4A

let ring

D
Gtr. 1: w/ Rhy. Fill 1
Em7
Asus4
A
run-nin' free?
'Cause to-mor-row's just an-oth-er day,
and I don't be-lieve in
End Rhy. Fig. 4
End Rhy. Fig. 4A
let ring
Chorus
Gtr. 3: w/ Riff A
Gtr. 4
time is wast - in', is walk - in'. You ain't no friend of mine.
(Time time, time, time,
Gtr. 1
Rhy. Fig. 5
Gtr. 2
Rhy. Fig. 5A
Rhy. Fill 1
Gtr. 1

To Coda
Em7
D
Em7
I don't know where I'm go-in'.
time, time, time, time,
I think I'm out of my mind
End Rhy. Fig. 5
End Rhy. Fig. 5A
Gtr. 2: w/ Rhy. Fig. 4, 1st 4 meas.
Gtr. 3: w/ Rhy. Fig. 4A, 1st 5 meas.
A
G5
D
Gtr. 4
time.)
think-ing a - bout time.
Gtr. 1
Rhy. Fig. 6
End Rhy. Fig. 6

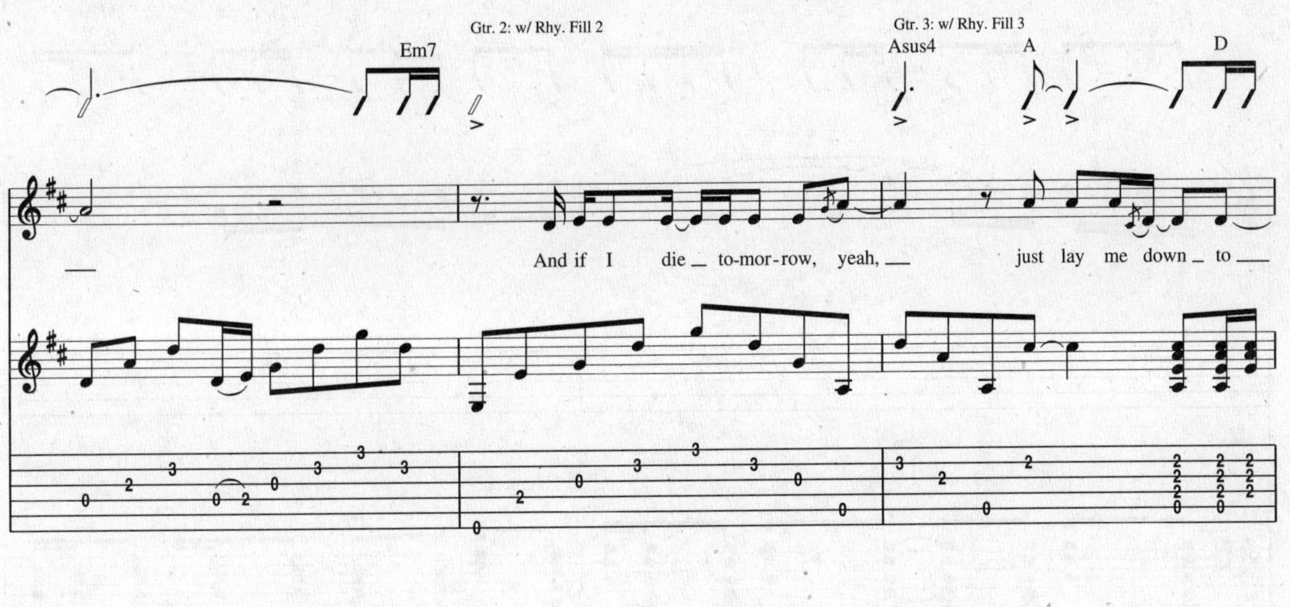

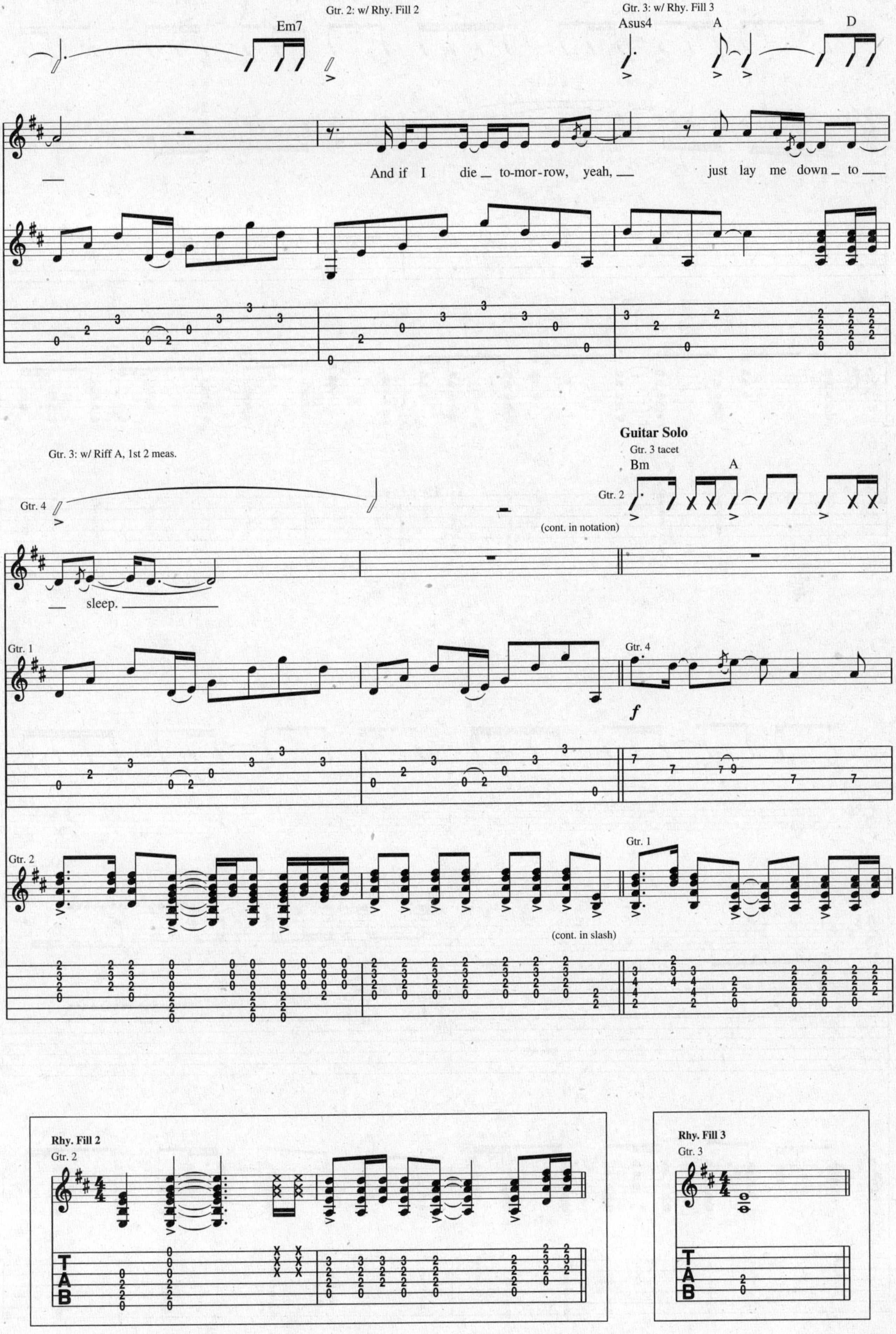

Gtr. 3: w/ Riff A, 1st 2 meas.

Guitar Solo

Gtr. 3 tacet

Bm A

Gtr. 4

Gtr. 2

(cont. in notation)

sleep.

Gtr. 1

Gtr. 4

f

Gtr. 2

Gtr. 1

(cont. in slash)

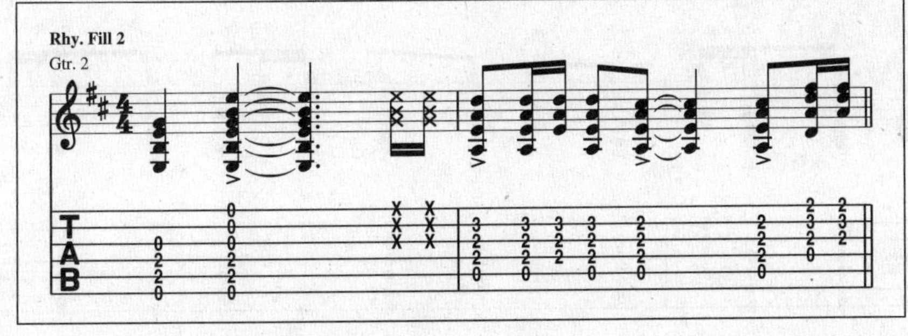

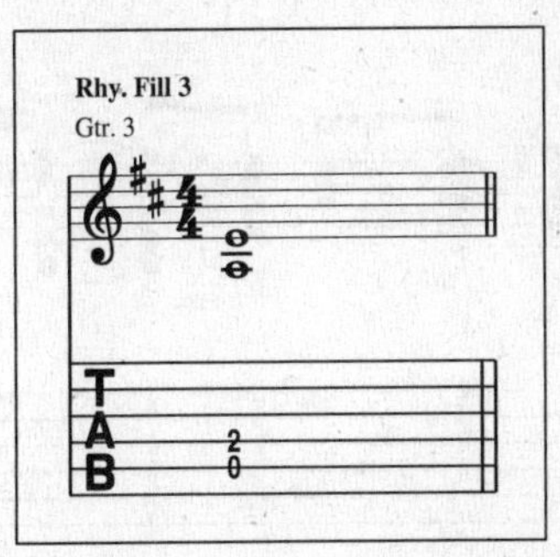

G5
Bm
A
D
G5
A
G5
Oh.
let ring
full
hold bend
full

A
G5
A
G5
No, no.
Chorus
Gtrs. 1 & 2: w/ Rhy. Figs. 5 & 5A
Gtr. 3: w/ Riff A
D
Em7
D
Em7
Time is wast - in', is walk - in'. You ain't no friend of mine.
(Time, time, time, time,
Gtr. 4
let ring
Gtr. 1: w/ Rhy. Fig. 6
Gtrs. 2 & 3: w/ Rhy. Figs. 4 & 4A, 1st 2 meas.
D
Em7
D
Em7
A
I don't know where I'm go-in'. I think I'm out of my mind
time, time, time, time, time.
let ring

Gtr. 1: w/ Rhy. Fig. 1, 1 1/2 times
Gtr. 2: w/ Rhy. Fig. 5A
Gtr. 3: w/ Riff A
G5
D
Em7
D
Em7
D
Em7
think-in' a - bout time.
(cont. in slash)

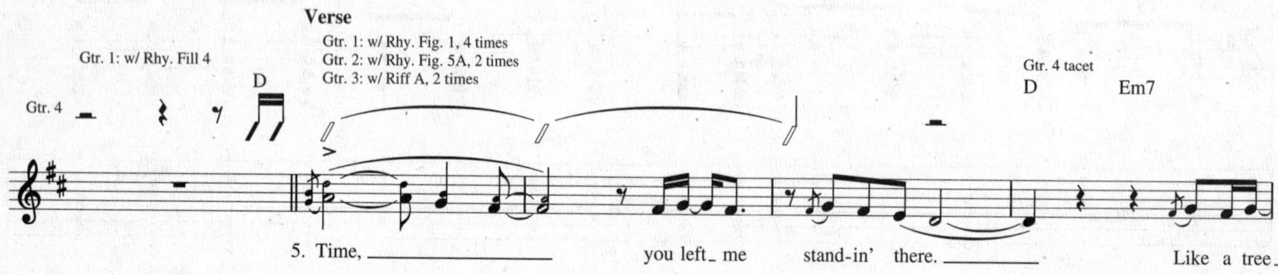
Verse
Gtr. 1: w/ Rhy. Fill 4
Gtr. 1: w/ Rhy. Fig. 1, 4 times
Gtr. 2: w/ Rhy. Fig. 5A, 2 times
Gtr. 3: w/ Riff A, 2 times
Gtr. 4
D
Gtr. 4 tacet
D
Em7
5. Time, you left me stand-in' there. Like a tree

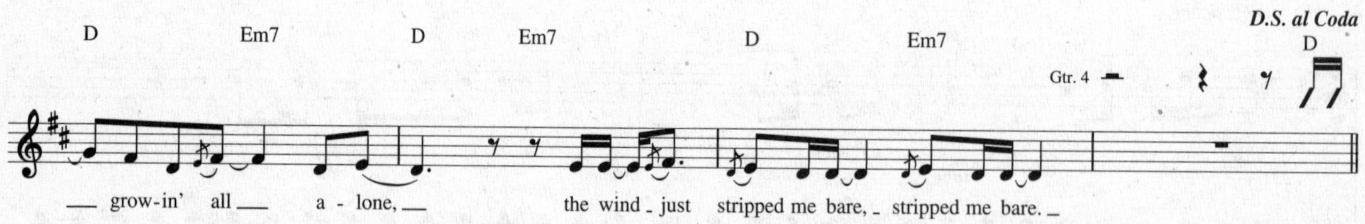
D.S. al Coda
D
Em7
D
Em7
D
Em7
Gtr. 4
D
grow-in' all a - lone, the wind just stripped me bare, stripped me bare.

Coda
Gtrs. 1 & 2: w/ Rhy. Figs. 5 & 5A, simile
Gtr. 3: w/ Riff A
D
Em7
D
Em7
D
Gtr. 4
Walk - in', wast - in', you ain't no friend of mine.
(time, time, time, time,

Rhy. Fill 4
Gtr. 1
let ring
TAB

Gtr. 1: w/ Rhy. Fig. 6
Gtrs. 2 & 3: w/ Rhy. Figs. 4 & 4A, 1st 2 meas.
Em7
D
Em7
A
G5
I don't know where I'm go - in', lost. No, no, no.
time, time, time, time.)
Time with-out cour-age, and time
Gtr. 1: w/ Rhy. Fig. 1
Gtr. 2: w/ Rhy. Fig. 5A, 1st 2 meas.
Gtr 3: w/ Riff A, 1st 2 meas.
D
with - out fear is just wast - ed, wast - ed, wast - ed time.
Outro
Gtrs. 3 & 4 tacet
Asus4
A
D
Em7
D
Em7
Gtr. 4
rit.
Oh.
Ooh.
Gtr. 1
rit.
Gtrs. 2 & 3
Gtr. 2
rit.
Gtrs. 1 & 2: w/ Rhy. Fig. 1, 2 1/2 times
D
Em7
D
Em7
D
Em7
Time,
D
Em7
D
Em7
D
Gtrs. 1 & 2
why you pun - ish me?

(So) Tired of Waiting for You

Words and Music by Ray Davies

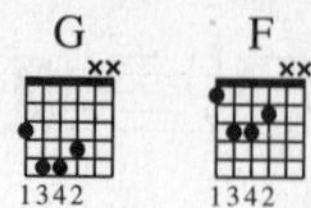

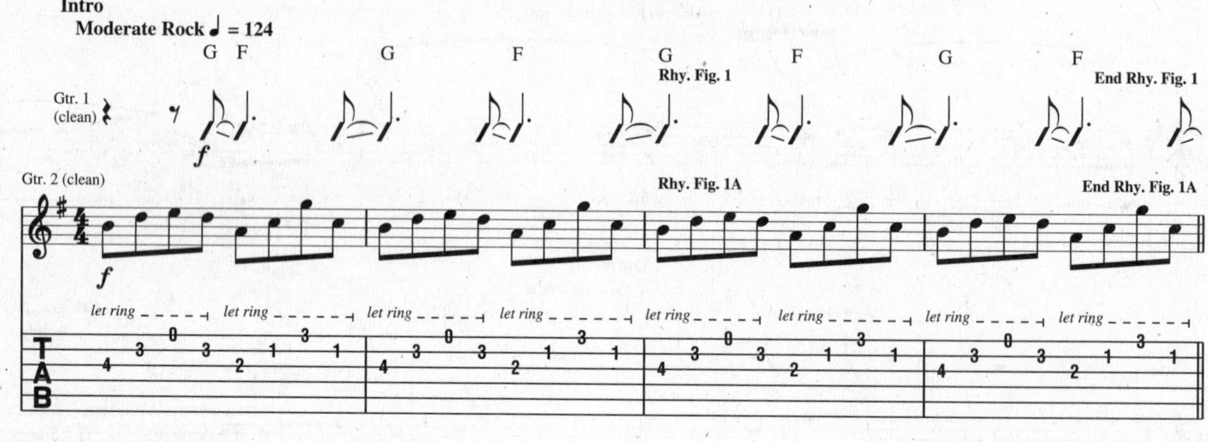

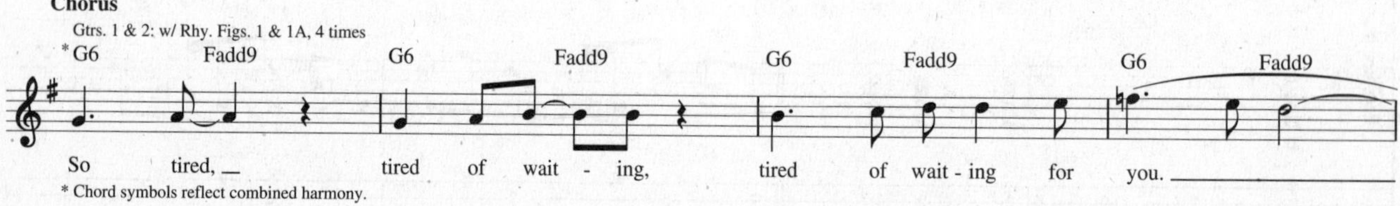

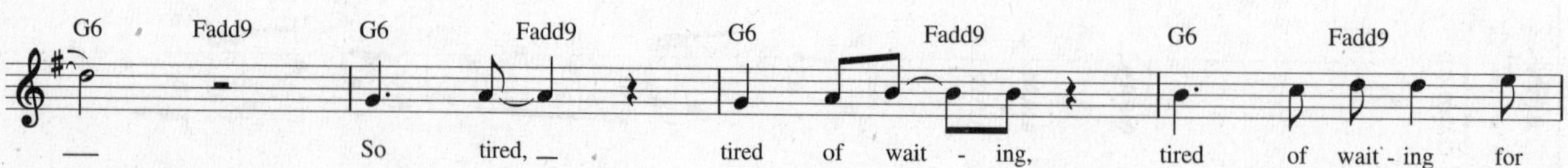

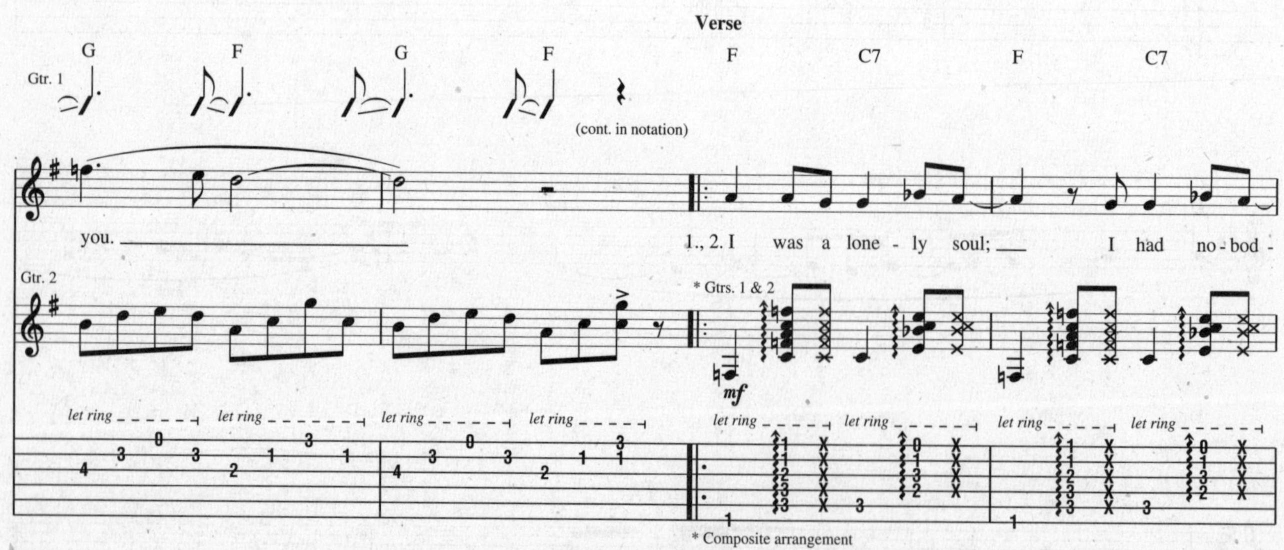

F C7 F F#5 G N.C.(D7) G N.C.(D7)
- y till I met you. But you keep a me wait - ing all of the time.
let ring

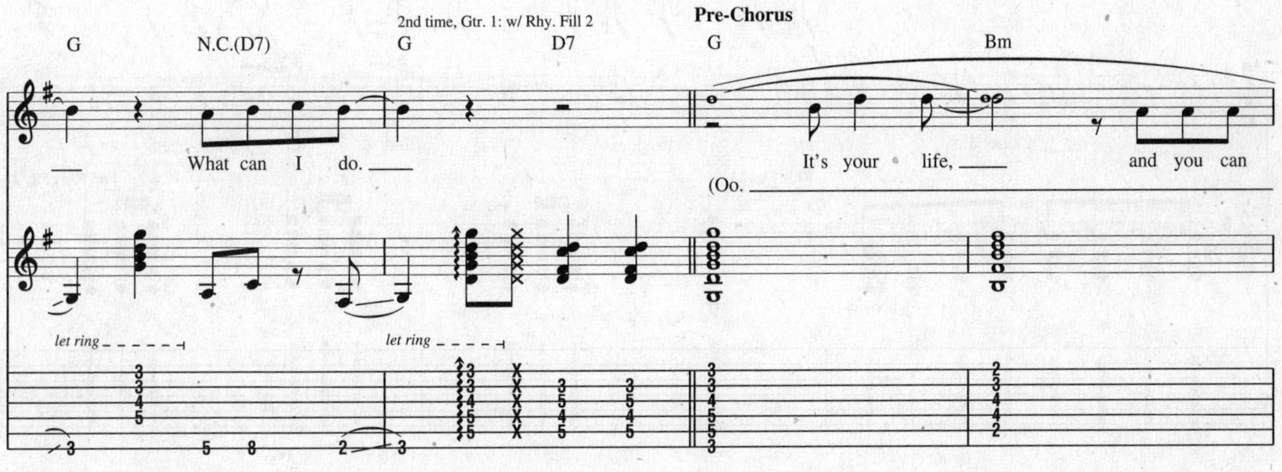
2nd time, Gtr. 1: w/ Rhy. Fill 2
Pre-Chorus
G N.C.(D7) G D7 G Bm
What can I do. It's your life, and you can
(Oo.
let ring

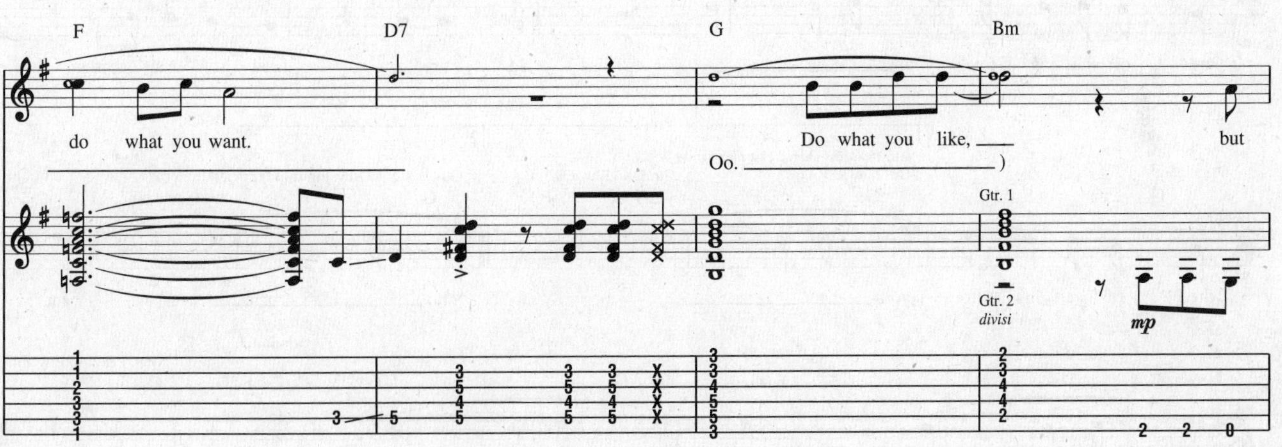
F D7 G Bm
do what you want. Do what you like, but
Oo.)
Gtr. 1
Gtr. 2
divisi
mp

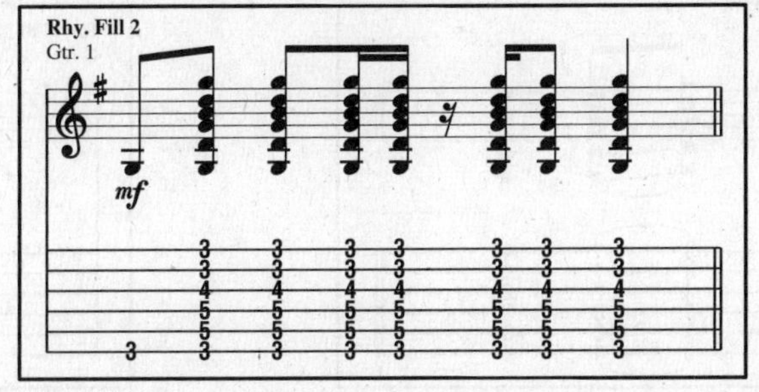
Rhy. Fill 2
Gtr. 1
mf

F D7/A F
please don't keep a me wait - ing. Please don't keep a me wait -
Gtrs. 1 & 2
grad. cresc.
Chorus
D7/A N.C. F F G F G F
Rhy. Fig. 2
Gtr. 1
End Rhy. Fig. 2
- ing. 'Cause I'm so tired, tired of wait - ing,
Rhy. Fig. 2A
Gtr. 2
End Rhy. Fig. 2A
(Gtr. 1, cont. in slashes)
Gtrs. 1 & 2: w/ Rhy. Figs. 2 & 2A (3 times)
F G F G F G F G F G F
tired of wait-ing for you. So tired, tired of wait - ing,
1.
2.
Gtr. 1: w/ Rhy. Fig. 2 (1st meas.)
Gtr. 2: w/ Rhy. Fig. 2
Gtr. 1: w/ Rhy. Fill 1
Gtrs. 1 & 2: w/ Rhy. Fig. 2 (3 1/2 times)
G F G F G F G F G F
tired of wait-ing for you. you, for
Gtrs. 1 & 2: w/ Rhy. Fill 3
G F G F G F G F G
you, for you.
Rhy. Fill 1
Gtr. 1
Rhy. Fill 3
Gtrs. 1 & 2

Too Rolling Stoned

Words and Music by Robin Trower

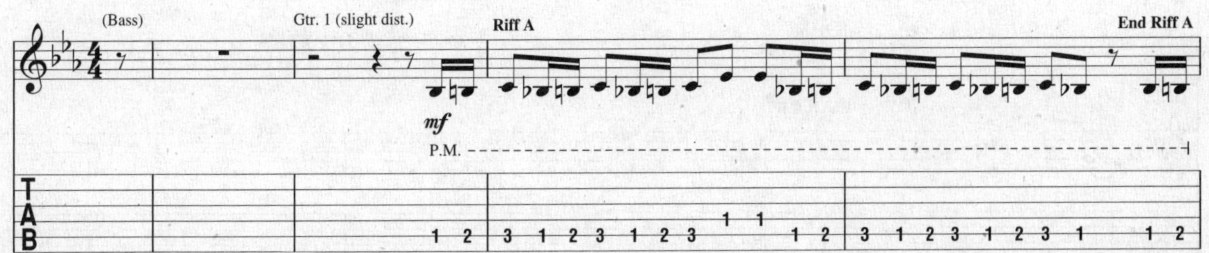

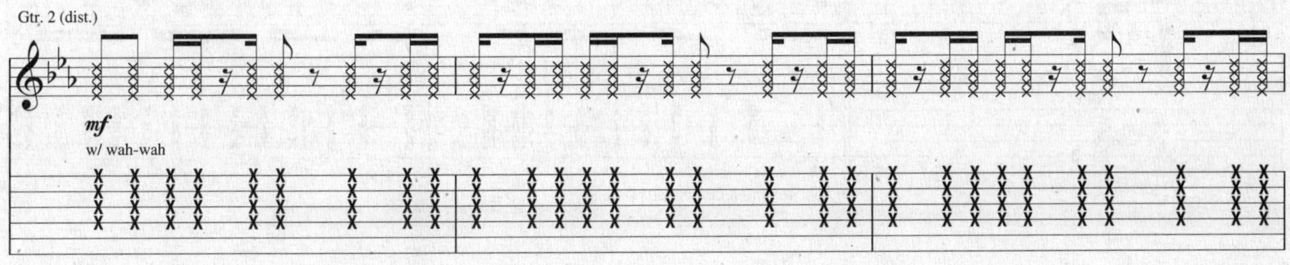

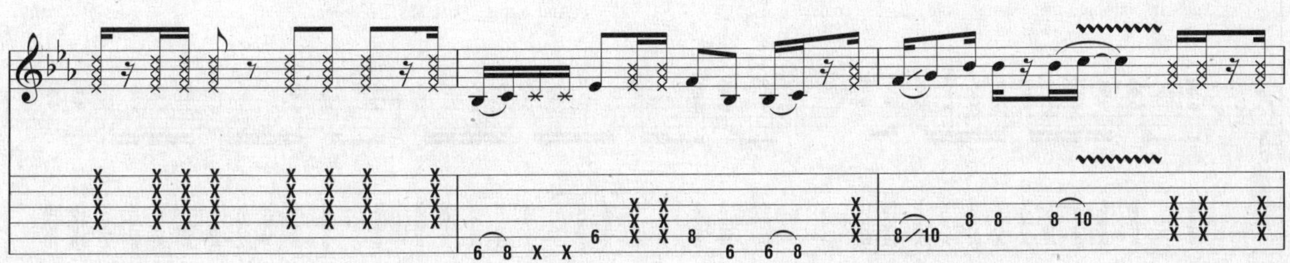

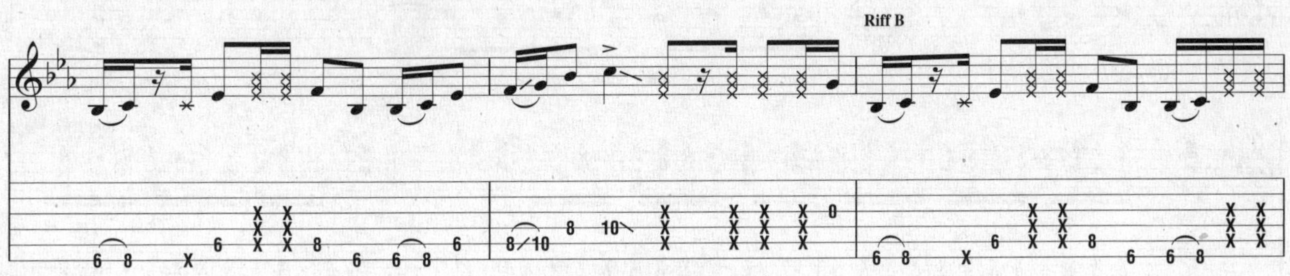

Verse
Gtr. 2 tacet
*Cm7
F/C
Cm7
1. Oh, a stitch in time just a-bout saved me from
Gtr. 2
End Riff B
Gtr. 1
Fill 1
End Fill 1
Rhy. Fig. 1
P.M.
*Chord symbols reflect overall harmony.
go-in' through the same old moves. And this cat has nine, he still
Gtr. 1
suf-fers, he's go-in' through the same old grooves. But that
End Rhy. Fig. 1

Chorus
E♭ B♭ F E♭ B♭ C
stone just keeps on roll - in', bring - in' me some real bad news.
Voc. Fig. 1
(Stone just keeps on roll - in', bring me real bad news.
Rhy. Fig. 2
Gtr. 1: w/ Riff A (1 1/2 times)
Gtr. 2: w/ Riff B
E♭ B♭ F N.C.
Tak - ers get the hon - ey, giv - ers sing the blues.
End Voc. Fig. 1
Tak - ers get the hon - ey.)
End Rhy. Fig. 2
Verse
Gtr. 1: w/ Fill 1
Gtr. 1: w/ Rhy. Fig. 1
Cm7 F/C Cm7
2. Too man - y crooks, yeah, spoil such a good thing, I
F/C Cm7 F/C
know I laughed out loud but that was then. Ain't it fun - ny, a fool and his

Chorus

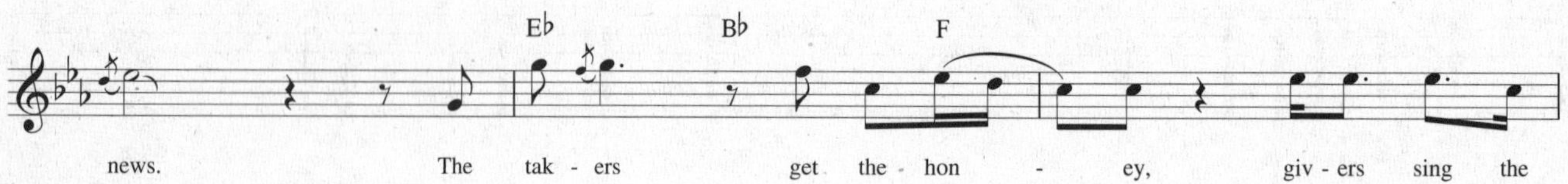

Interlude

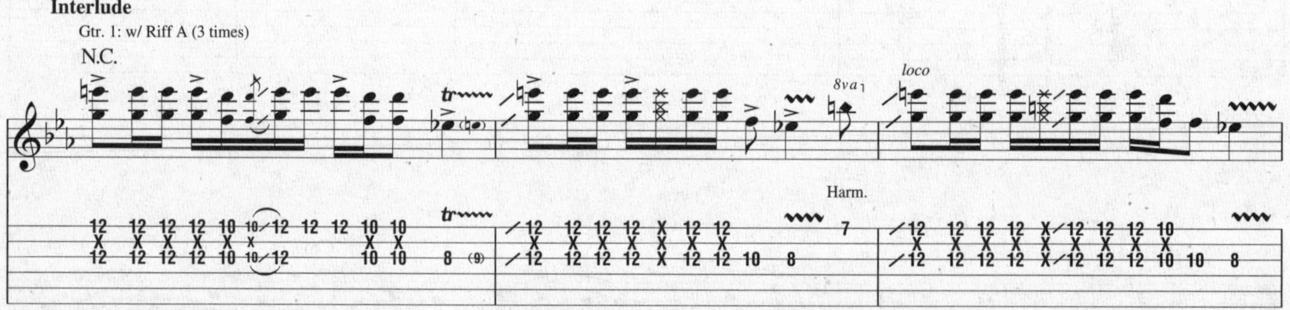

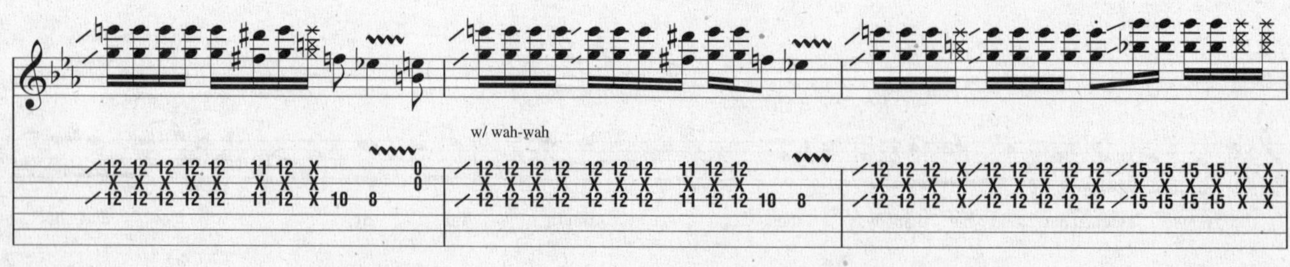

Gtr. 1: w/ Fill 3
Gtr. 2
Gtr. 1
P.M.

Guitar Solo

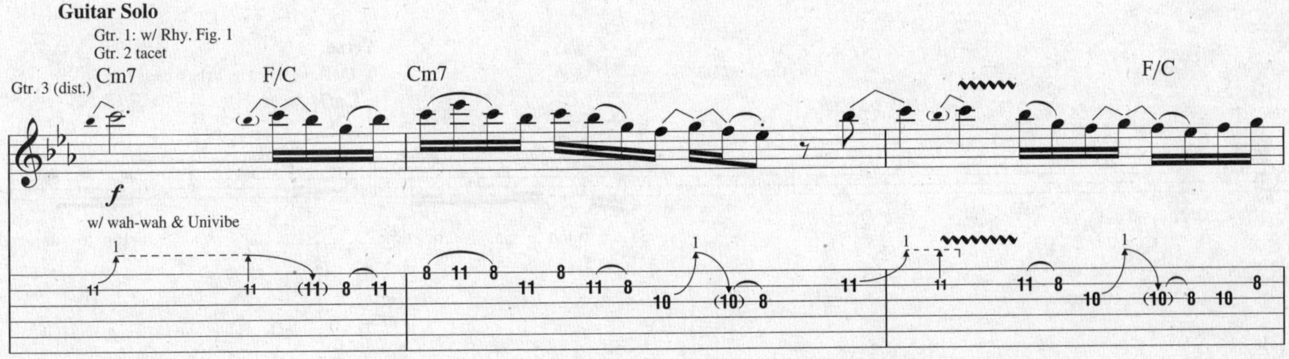
Gtr. 1: w/ Rhy. Fig. 1
Gtr. 2 tacet
Gtr. 3 (dist.)
Cm7
F/C
Cm7
F/C
f
w/ wah-wah & Univibe

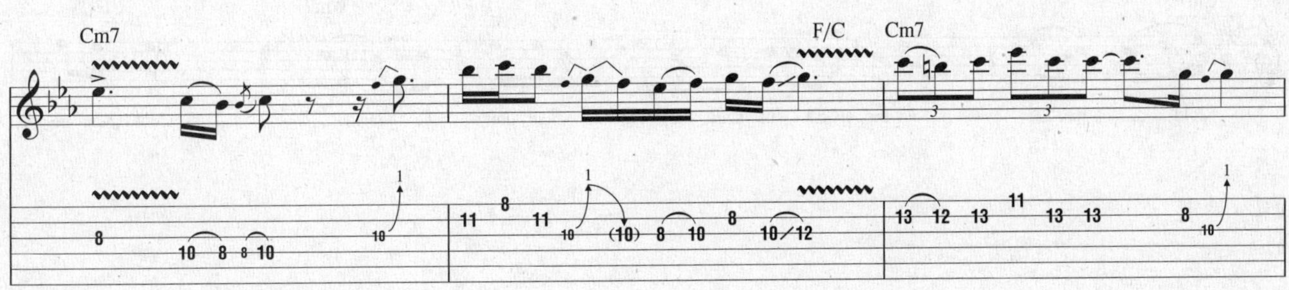
Cm7
F/C
Cm7

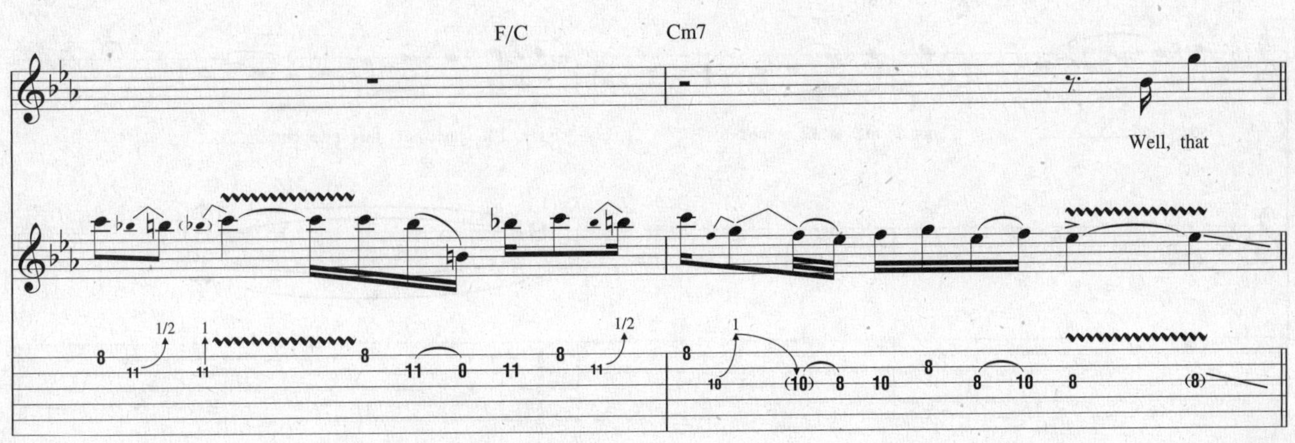
F/C
Cm7
Well, that

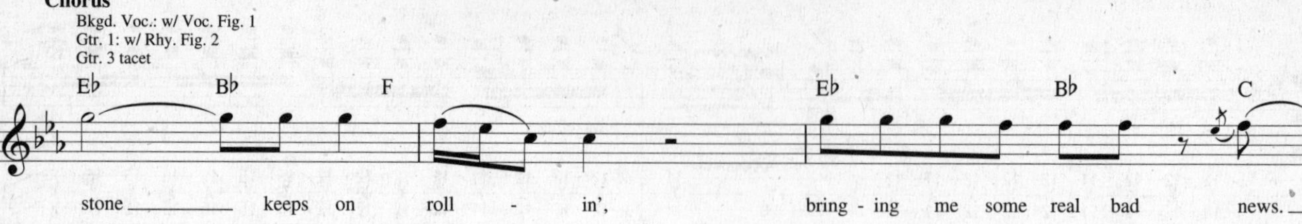
Chorus
Bkgd. Voc.: w/ Voc. Fig. 1
Gtr. 1: w/ Rhy. Fig. 2
Gtr. 3 tacet
E♭
B♭
F
E♭
B♭
C
stone keeps on roll - in', bring - ing me some real bad news.

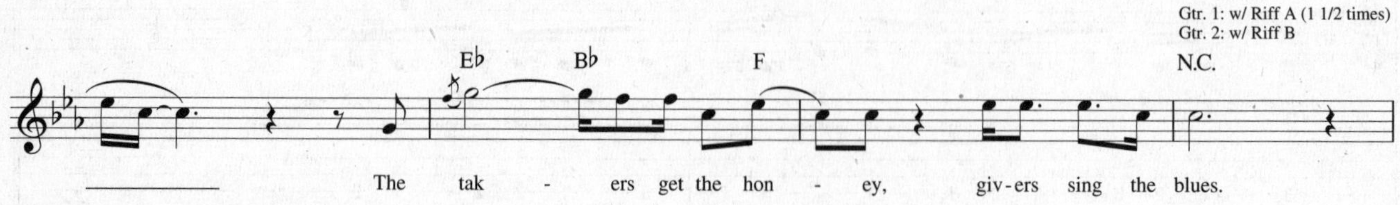
Gtr. 1: w/ Riff A (1 1/2 times)
Gtr. 2: w/ Riff B
E♭
B♭
F
N.C.
The tak - ers get the hon - ey, giv-ers sing the blues.

Verse
Gtr. 1: w/ Fill 1
Gtr. 1: w/ Rhy. Fig. 1 (1st 6 meas.)
Cm7
F/C
3. A stitch in, in time helps to un -

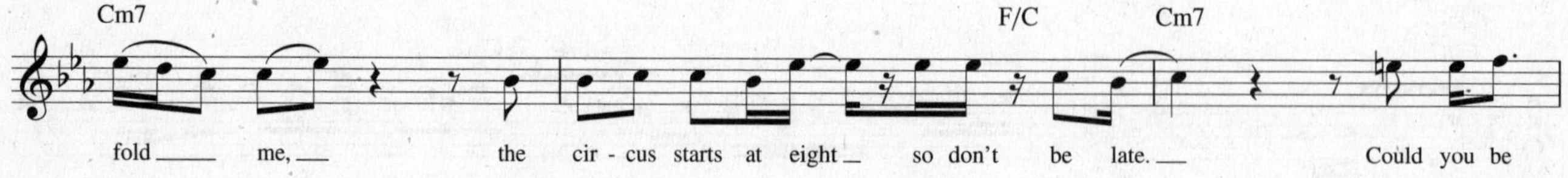
Cm7
F/C
Cm7
fold me, the cir - cus starts at eight so don't be late. Could you be

Free time
F/C
Cm7
so kind not to wake me? I think I'll just sit this one out.
Gtr. 1

Bridge
Slower ♩= 84
*Cm7
Gtr. 1: w/ Riff C (11 times)
But I'm too roll - in' stoned,
Riff C
End Riff C
mf
w/ Univibe
P.M.
P.M.
*Chord symbol reflects basic harmony.
I'm too roll - in' stoned. Yeah!
Like a roll - in' stone. Yes, yes, just like a roll - in'
stone. Roll - in', roll - in', roll - in', roll - in' stone, yeah.
Too roll - in' stoned! Hmm. Hmm.
Oh, just like a roll - in' stone!
Well, like a roll - in' stone! Hmm.

Outro-Guitar Solo

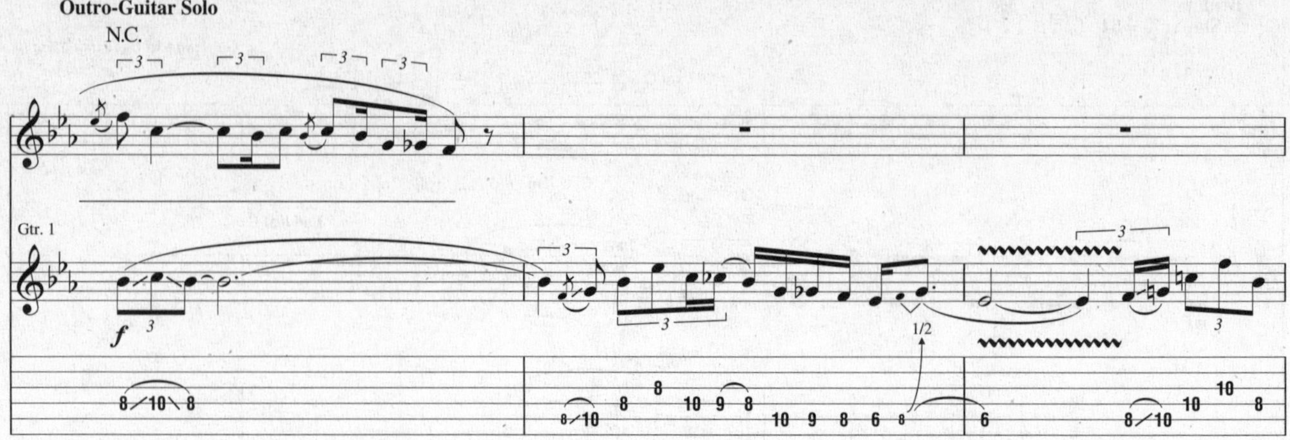

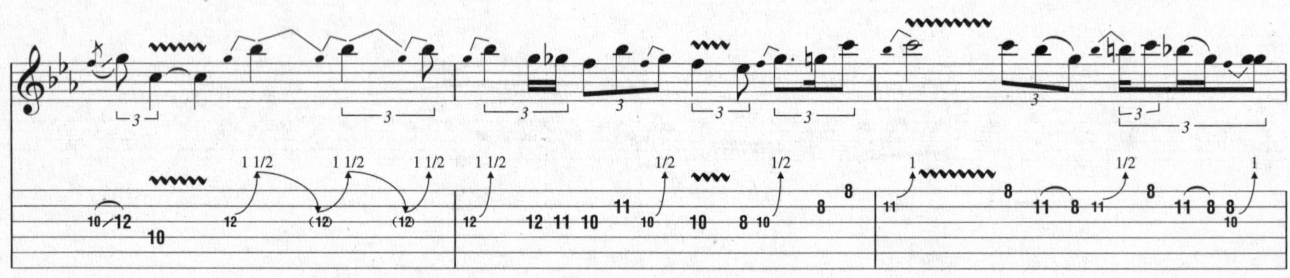

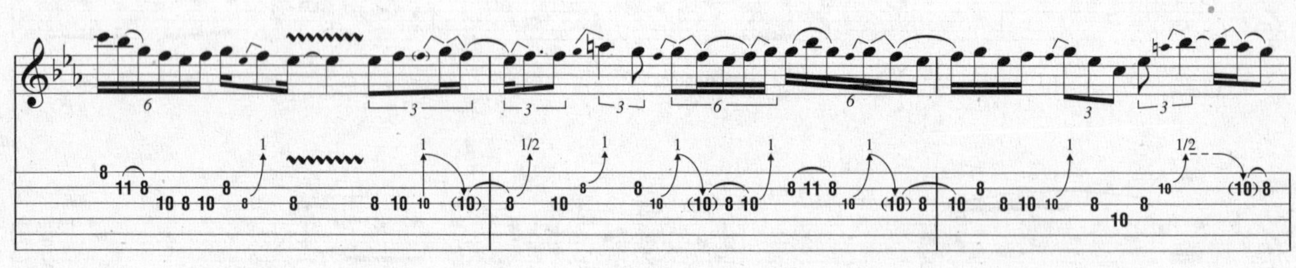

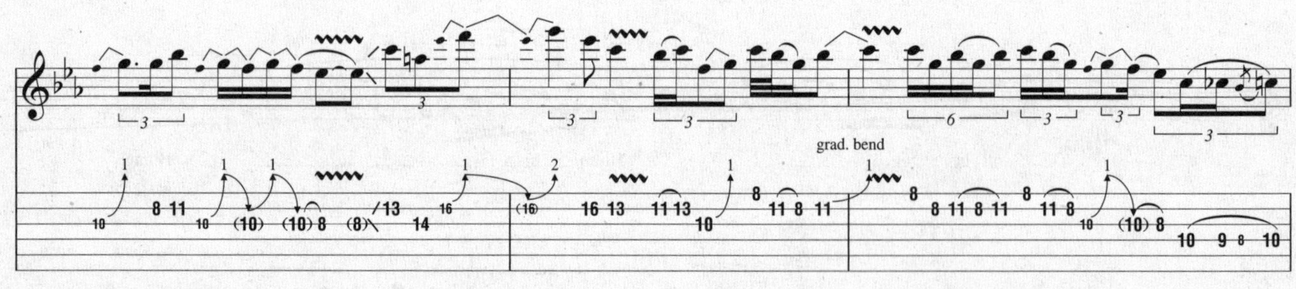

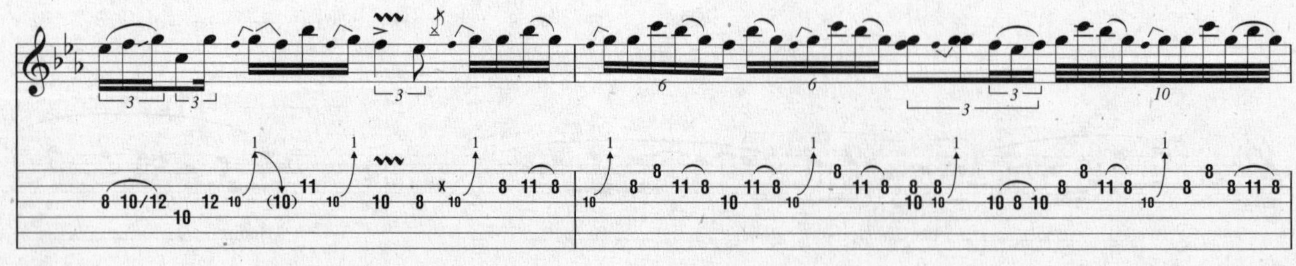

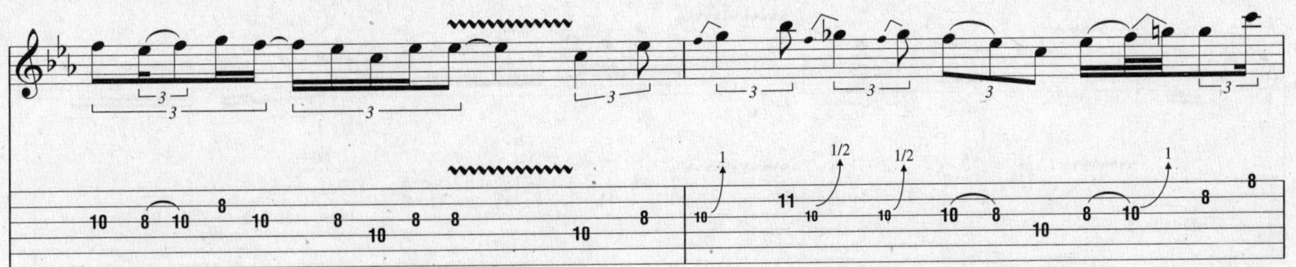

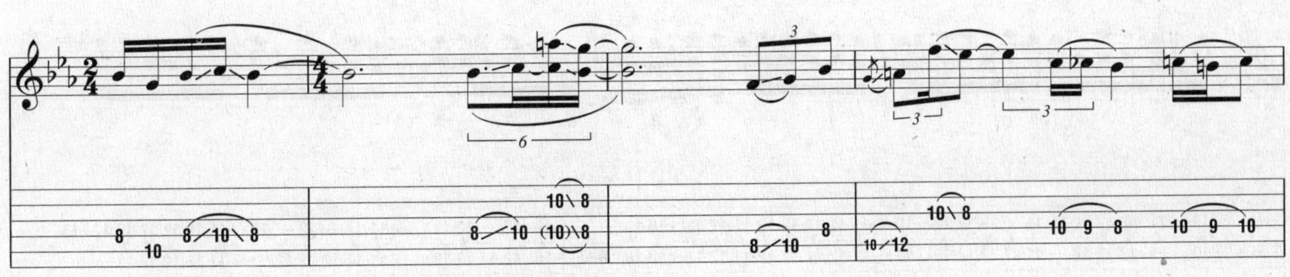

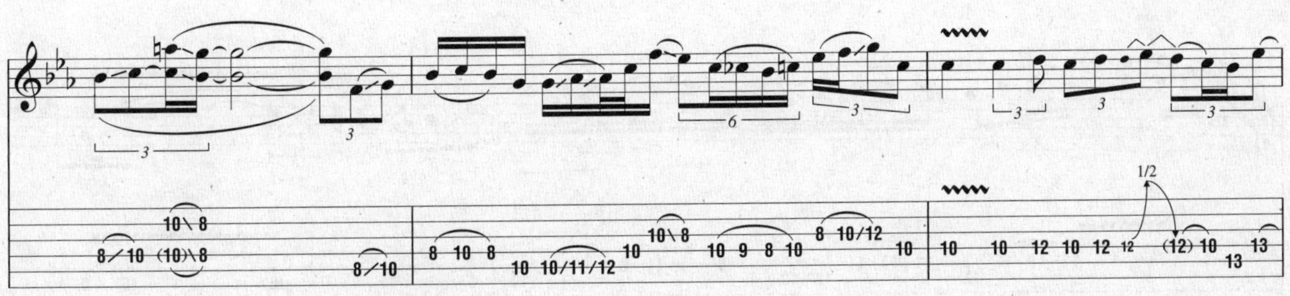

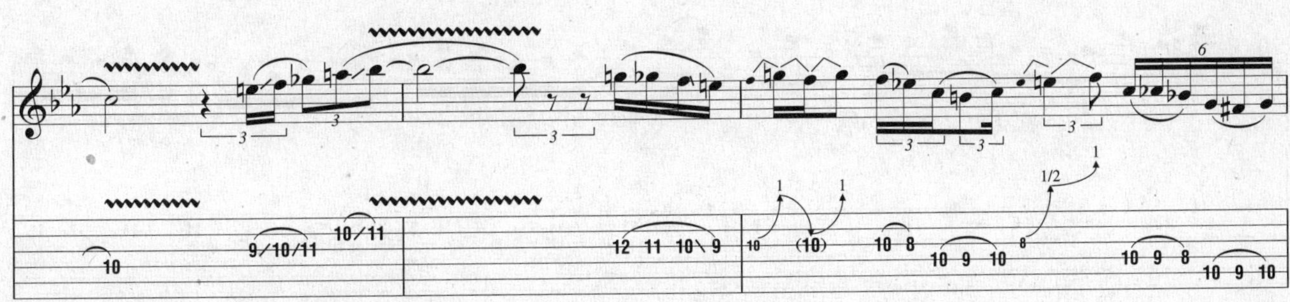

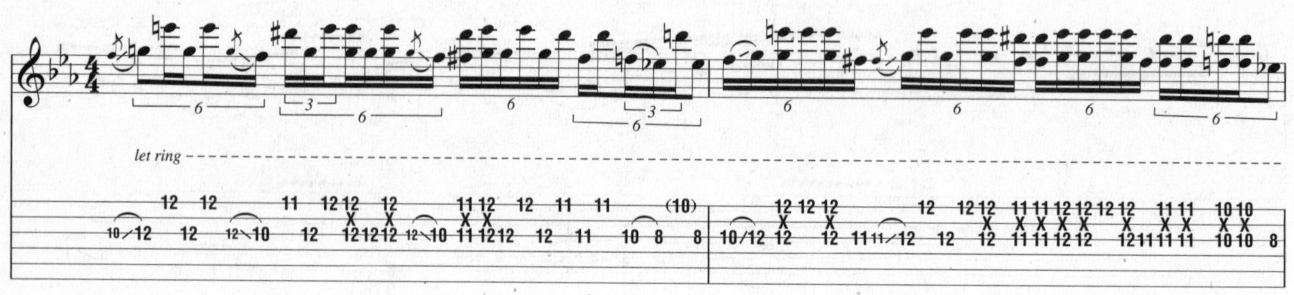
let ring

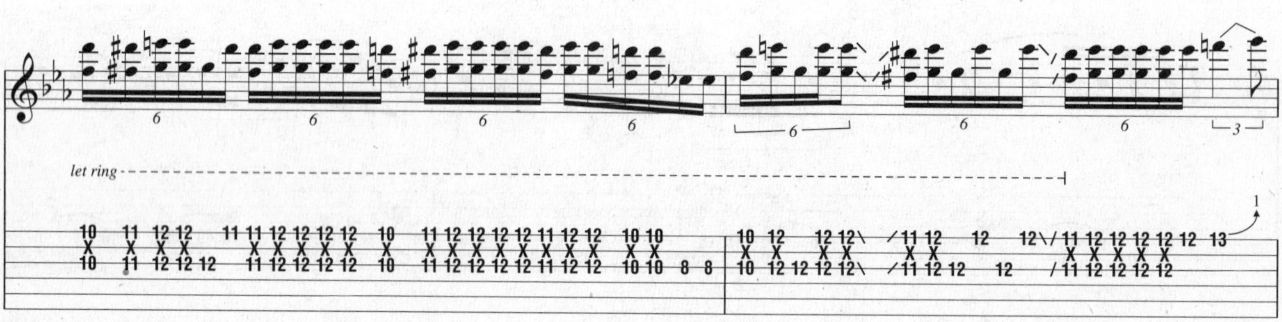
let ring

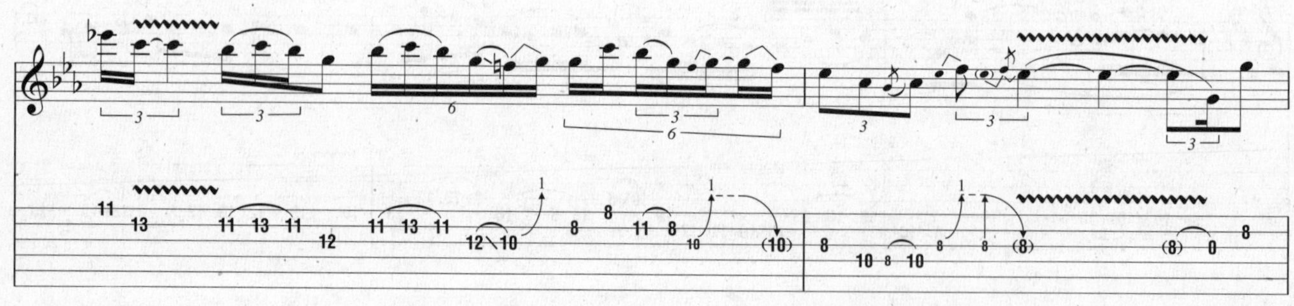

let ring

w/ bar

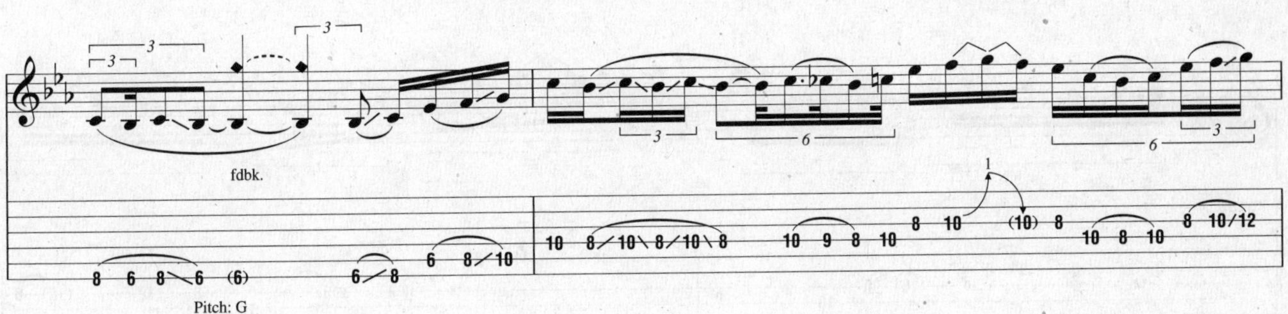
fdbk.
Pitch: G

let ring

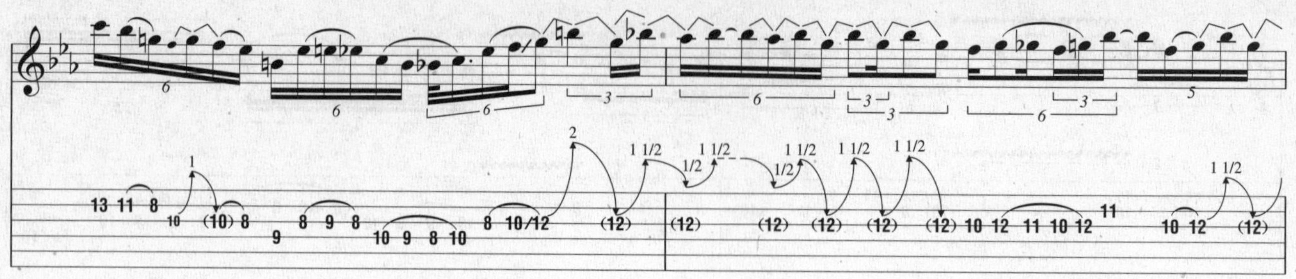
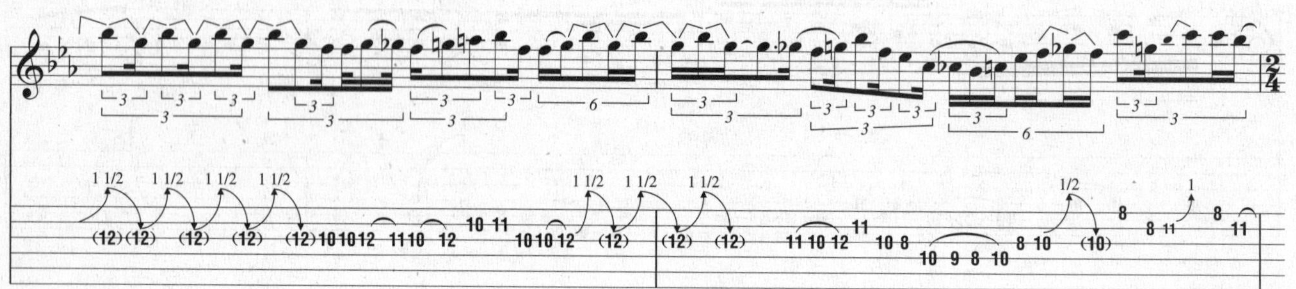

hold bend
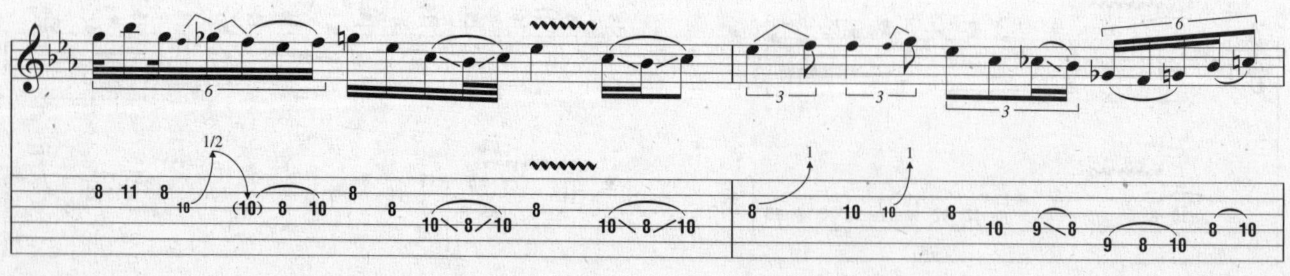

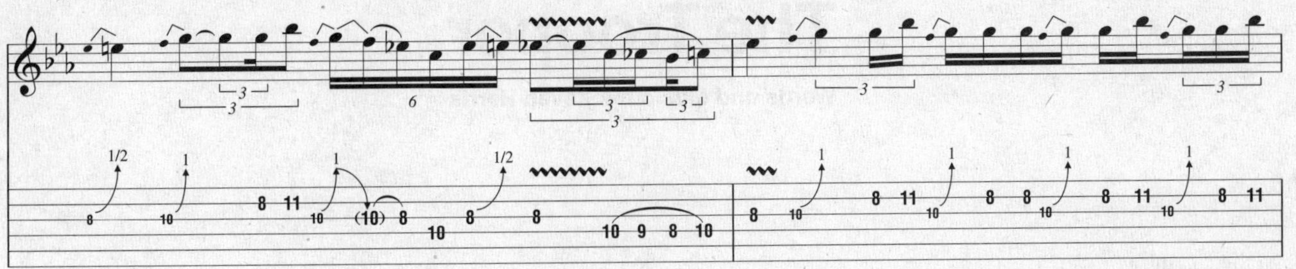

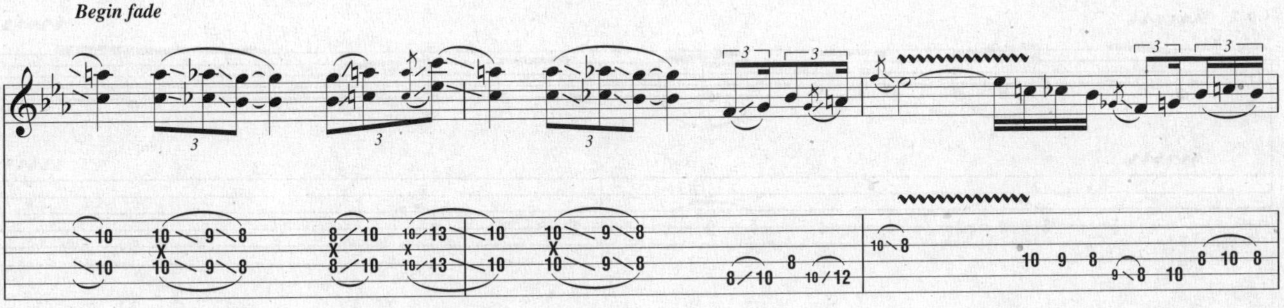
Begin fade

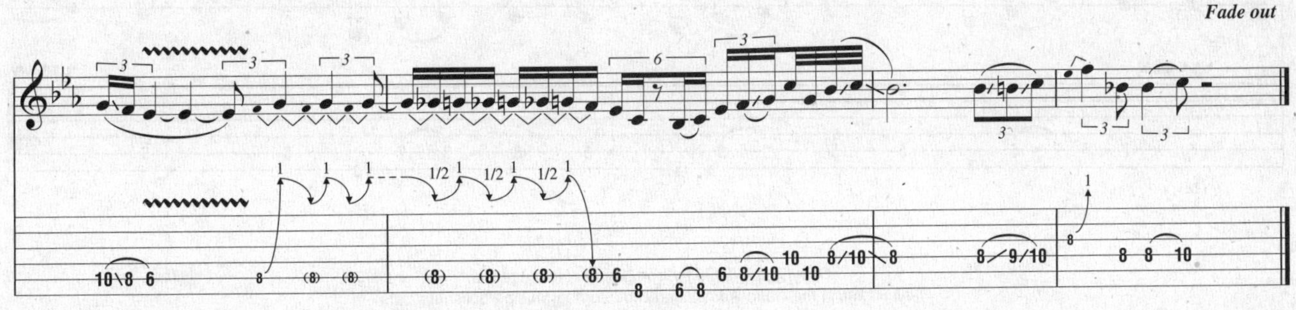
Fade out

The Trooper

Words and Music by Steven Harris

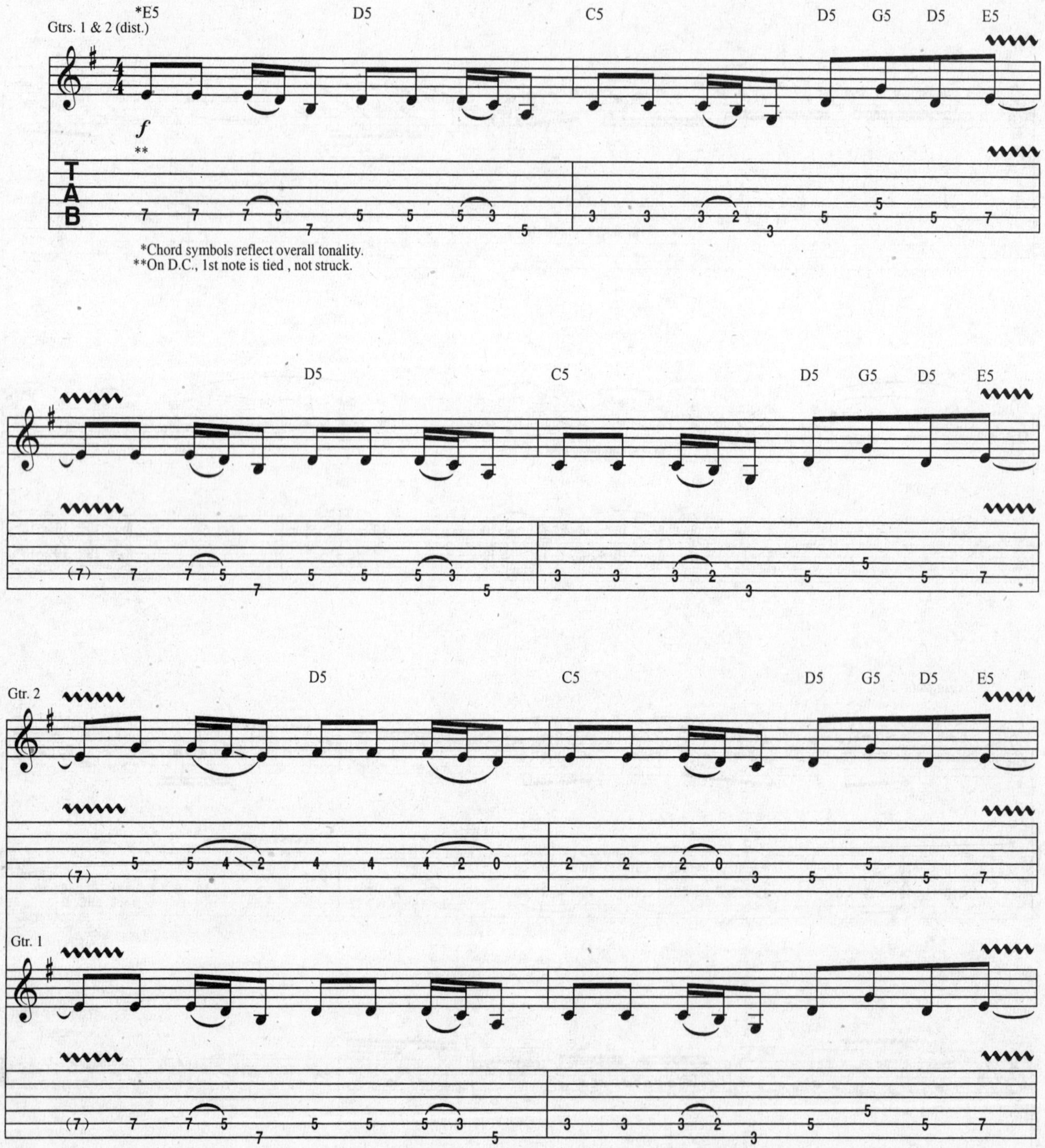

Intro

*Chord symbols reflect overall tonality.
**On D.C., 1st note is tied , not struck.

D5 C5 D5 G5 D5 E5

Gtr. 2

D5 C5 D5 G5 D5 E5

Gtr. 1

*D5, 2nd & 3rd times

D5 G5 D5 E5
D5 G5 D5 E5
D5 G5 D5 C5
D5 G5 D5 *E5
D5 G5 D5 E5
*D5, 2nd & 3rd times
*Ties refer to 2nd & 3rd times only.

Verse

Gtrs. 1 & 2: w/Rhy. Fig. 1, 1⅓ times, 2nd & 3rd times
E5
D5 G5 D5 E5
1. You'll take my life but I'll take yours, too.
2. The horse, he sweats with fear; we break to run.
3. We get so close, near e - nough to fight
Gtrs. 1 & 2
D5 G5 D5 C5
You'll fire your mus - ket but I'll run you through.
The might - y roar of the Rus - sian guns.
when a Rus - sian gets me in his sights.
D5 G5 D5 E5
So when you're wait - ing for the next at - tack,
And as we race to - wards the hu - man wall,
He pulls the trig - ger and I feel the blow,

D5 G5 D5 E5
you'd bet - ter stand, there's no turn - ing back.
the screams of pain as my com - rades fall.
a burst of rounds takes my horse be - low.
D5 G5 D5 E5
The bu - gle sounds, the charge be - gins,
We hur - dle bod - ies that lay on the ground,
And as I lay there gaz - ing at the sky,
Rhy. Fig. 1
P.M.
D5 G5 D5 C5
but on this bat - tle - field no one wins.
and the Rus - sians fire an - oth - er round.
my bod - y's numb and my throat is dry.
P.M.
D5 G5 D5 E5
The smell of ac - rid smoke and hors - es' breath
We get so near yet so far a - way.
And as I lay for - got - ten and a - lone,
End Rhy. Fig. 1
P.M.

D5
as I plunge on in - to cer - tain death.
We won't live to fight an - oth - er day.
with - out a tear I draw my part - ing groan.
Oh.
P.M.
E5
D5
Oh.
1., 3.
2nd time, D.C. al Coda
D5 G5 D5 E5

2.
Guitar Solo
D5
G5
D5
E5
Gtr. 3 (dist.)
full
Gtrs. 1 & 2
P.M.
B5
C5
D5
E5
grad. bend
Rhy. Fig. 2

B5
C5
D5
8va
full
End Rhy. Fig. 2
P.M.
Gtrs. 1 & 2: w/Rhy. Fig. 2, 1½ times
E5
D5
B5
8va
Gtr. 3
full
C5
D5
E5
D5
8va
Gtr. 3
full
8va
Gtr. 4 (dist.)
f
1/2

B5
C5
D5
A5
Gtr. 3
loco
full
full
Gtr. 4
loco
Gtrs. 1 & 2
P.M.
Gtr. 3 tacet
G5
Gtr. 4
tr
tr
full
Gtrs. 1 & 2
P.M.

E5
F5
G5
P.M.
A5
G5
Rhy. Fig. 3
full
E5
F5
G5
full
full
End Rhy. Fig. 3

Gtrs. 1 & 2: w/Rhy. Fig. 3, 1¾ times
A5
G5
Gtr. 4
full
full
3

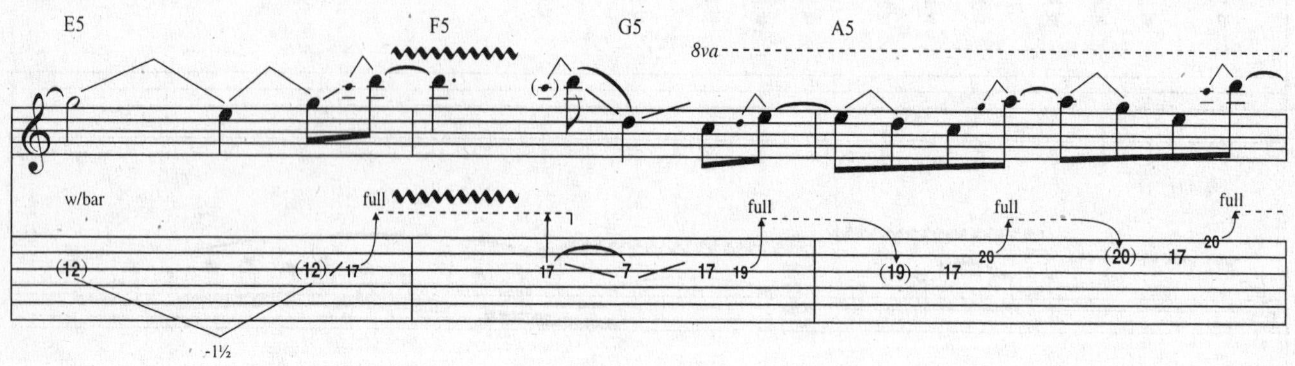
E5
F5
G5
A5
8va
w/bar
full
full
full
full
-1½

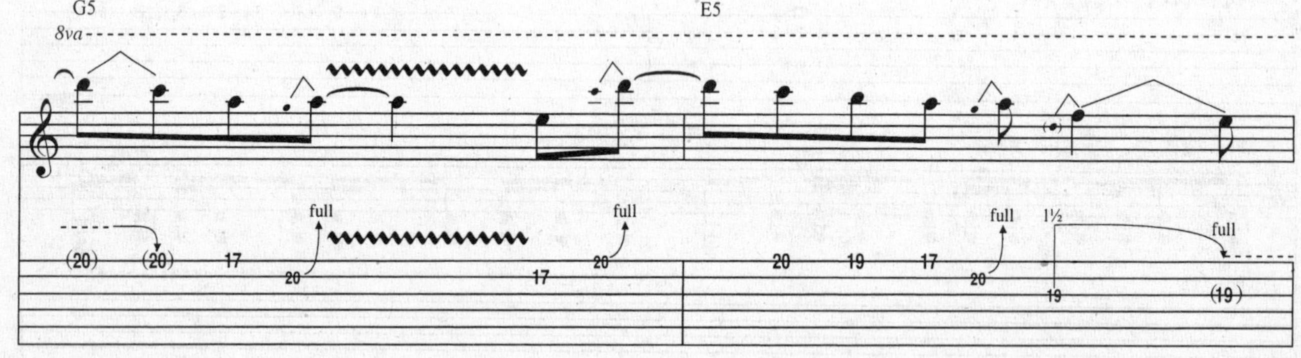
G5
E5
8va
full
full
full
1½
full

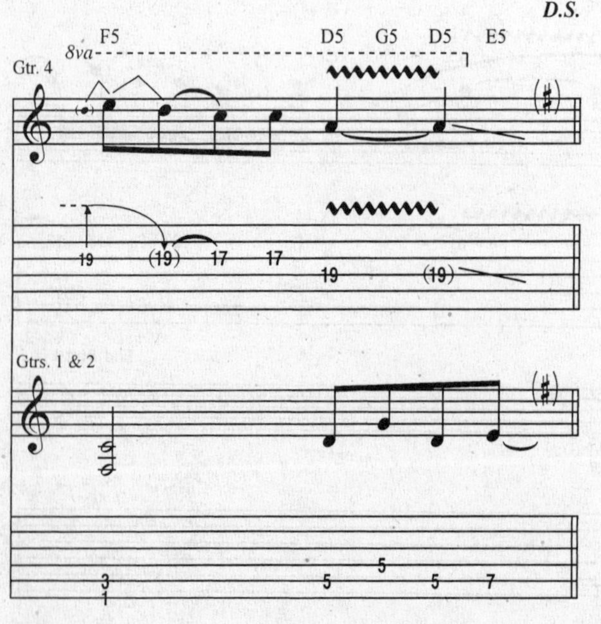
D.S.
F5
D5
G5
D5
E5
8va
Gtr. 4
Gtrs. 1 & 2

Coda
C5
D5
G5
D5
E5

Turn Me Loose

Words and Music by Paul Dean and Duke Reno

Verse
G5
1. I was born to run, I was born to dream. The
came a - round, tried to tie me down. I
Riff A
P.M.

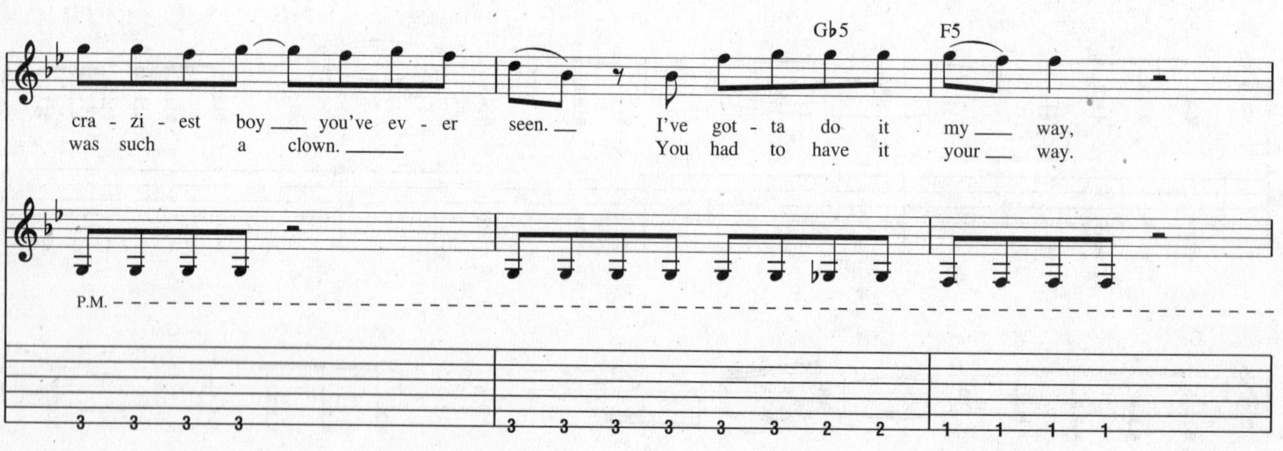
G♭5
F5
cra - zi - est boy you've ev - er seen. I've got - ta do it my way,
was such a clown. You had to have it your way.
P.M.

F♯5
G5
N.C.
or no way at all.
or no way at all.
And I was
But I've had
End Riff A
P.M.

Gtr. 1: w/ Riff A
G5
here to please, I'm e - ven on my knees mak - ing
all I can take, I can't take it no more. I'm gon - na

G♭5
F5
love to ev - er I please.
I've got - ta do it my way,
pack my bags and fly
it my ' way,
F♯5
G5
N.C.
or no way at all.
or no way at all.
2. And then you
So why don't you
Chorus
2nd time, Bkgd. Voc.: w/ Voc. Fig. 2
G5
Voc. Fig. 1
G♭5
turn me loose?
Turn me loose.
Turn me loose.
I've got - ta do it
Gtr. 1
Riff B
P.M.
F5
End Voc. Fig. 1
F♯5
G5
N.C.
my way,
or no way at all.
Why don't you
End Riff B
P.M.
Gtr. 1: w/ Riff B
Bkgd. Voc.: w/ Voc. Fig. 1
2nd time, Bkgd. Voc.: w/ Voc. Fig. 2
G5
turn me loose?
Turn me loose.
Turn me loose.
To Coda
F5
F♯5
G5
I've got to do it my way.
I wan - na fly.

Interlude
E5
N.C.
E5
Gtr. 1
P.M.
N.C.
E5
Eadd♯5
3. I'm
let ring
Verse
Gtr. 1: w/ Riff A (2 times)
G5
here to please, I'm e - ven on my knees mak - ing love to ev - er I please.
Voc. Fig. 2
(Ooh, ooh, ooh,
G♭5
F5
F♯5
I've got - ta do it my way, I've got - ta do it
ooh.)
End Voc. Fig. 2
G5
N.C.
Bkgd. Voc.: w/ Voc. Fig. 2
G5
my way. And when you come a - round, you tried to

Gb5
tie me down, I was such a clown. You had to have it
D.S. al Coda
F5
F#5
G5
N.C.
your way, well I'm say - in' no way. So why don't you
Coda
G5
E5
F5
F#5
Interlude
G5
Gm7
Oh, yeah.
Gtr. 1
P.M.
G5
Gm7
G5
Gm7
G5
Gm7
F5
F5add9
F5
F#5
G5
Gm7
P.M.
P.M.
Guitar Solo
G5
P.M.
semi-harm.
let ring

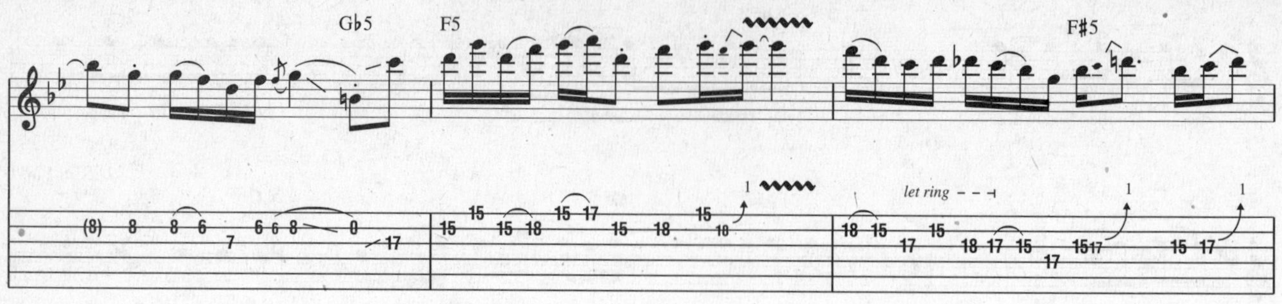

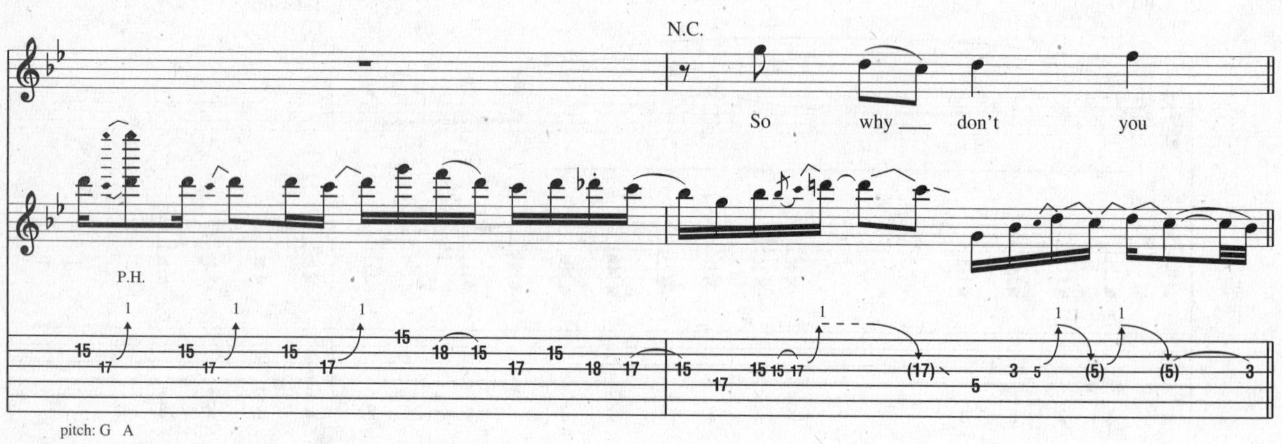

Outro-Chorus

Bkgd. Voc.: w/ Voc. Fig. 1

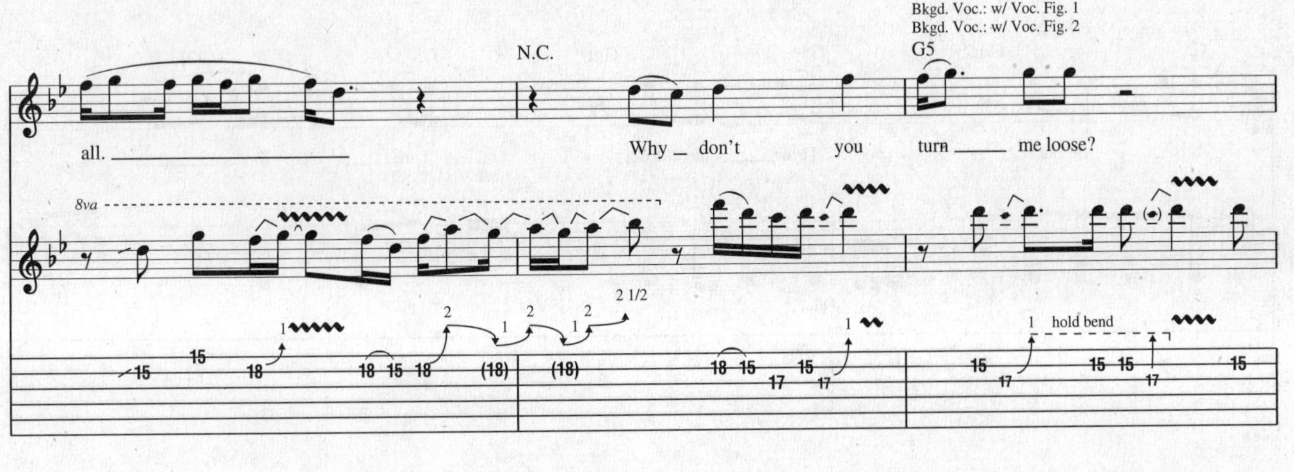
N.C.
Bkgd. Voc.: w/ Voc. Fig. 1
Bkgd. Voc.: w/ Voc. Fig. 2
G5
all.
Why don't you turn me loose?
8va
hold bend

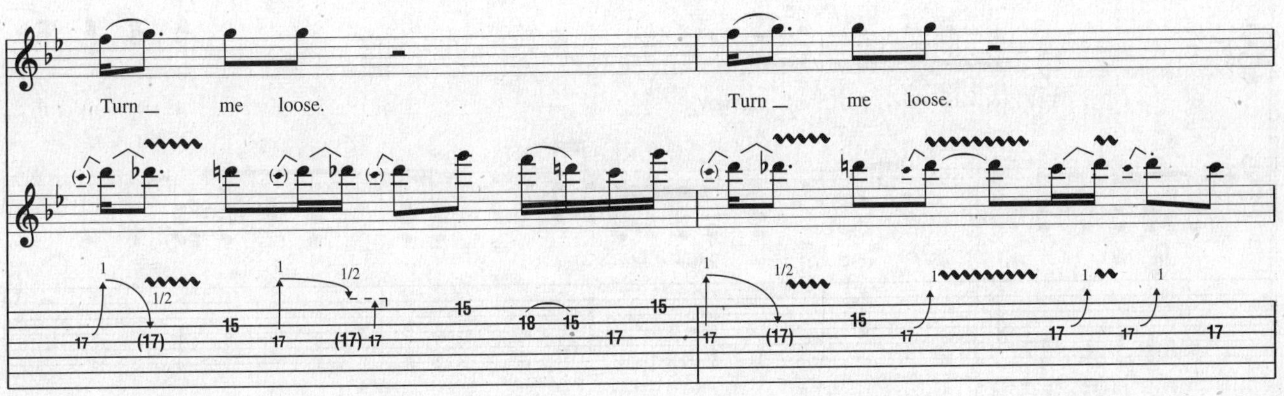
Turn me loose.
Turn me loose.

G♭6
F5
F♯5
I've got-ta do it my way.
I've got-ta do it
P.H.
semi-harm.

G5
N.C.
my way.
Why don't you

Bkgd. Voc.: w/ Voc. Fig. 1
Bkgd. Voc.: w/ Voc. Fig. 2
G5
Gm7
G5
Gm7
G5
Gm7
turn _ me loose?
Turn ___ me loose.
Turn ___ me loose. ______
P.M. - -
P.M. - -
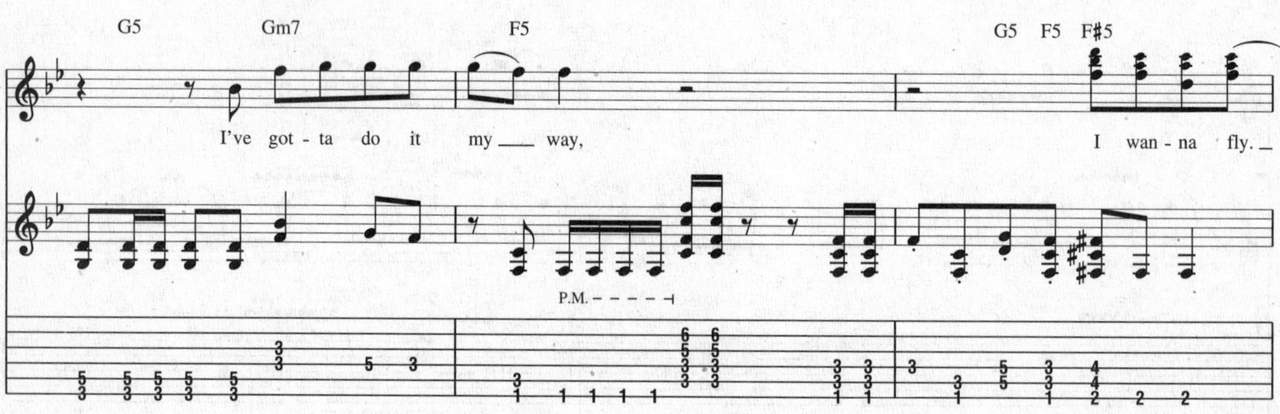
G5
Gm7
F5
G5 F5 F#5
I've got - ta do it my ___ way,
I wan - na fly. _
P.M. - - - - -
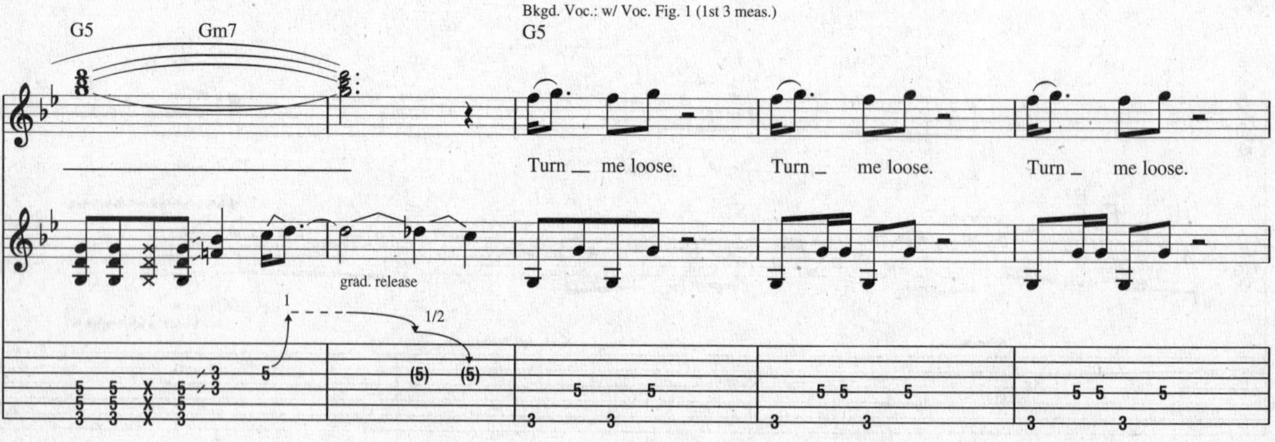
G5
Gm7
Bkgd. Voc.: w/ Voc. Fig. 1 (1st 3 meas.)
G5
Turn _ me loose.
Turn _ me loose.
Turn _ me loose.
grad. release
1
1/2

Bkgd. Voc.: w/ Voc. Fig. 1 (1st 3 meas.)
G♭5
F5
F#5
Bkgd. Voc.: w/ Voc. Fig. 1 (1st meas.)
G5
Turn _ me loose.
Turn _ me loose. _
Turn me loose. _
Turn _ me loose. _

Turn the Page

Words and Music by Bob Seger

1st Verse
Em
long and lone - some high - way, east of O - ma - ha, you can
H
H
H
H
D
lis - ten to the en - gine, moan - in' out his one-note song. You
H
H
H
H

A

think a - bout the wom - an, or the girl you knew the night be - fore.

Em

But your

thoughts will soon be wan - d'rin', the way they al - ways do. When you're
f w/o slide
P.M.
P.M.
sl.
sl.
f dist. tone
H
P
D
rid - in' six - teen ho - urs, there's noth - in' much to do. And you
H

A

don't feel much like rid - in', you just wish the trip — was through.

w/slide

H P P H H P

Em

Here I am, —

H H

Chorus

D5 E5

on the road a - gain. There I am,

w/o slide

*Rhy. Fig. 1

P.M. P.M. P.M. P.M. P.M.

*Play all guitar parts w/slight variations ad lib when recalled (throughout).

D5 E5

up on the stage. Here I go,

P.M. P.M. P.M. P.M. P.M. P.M.

D5 A

play-in' star a-gain. There I go,

H P

H P

P.M. P.M. P.M.

sl.

sl.

C5 D5 Em

turn the page. 2. As we

w/slide

(end Rhy. Fig. 1)

H H sl.

H H sl.

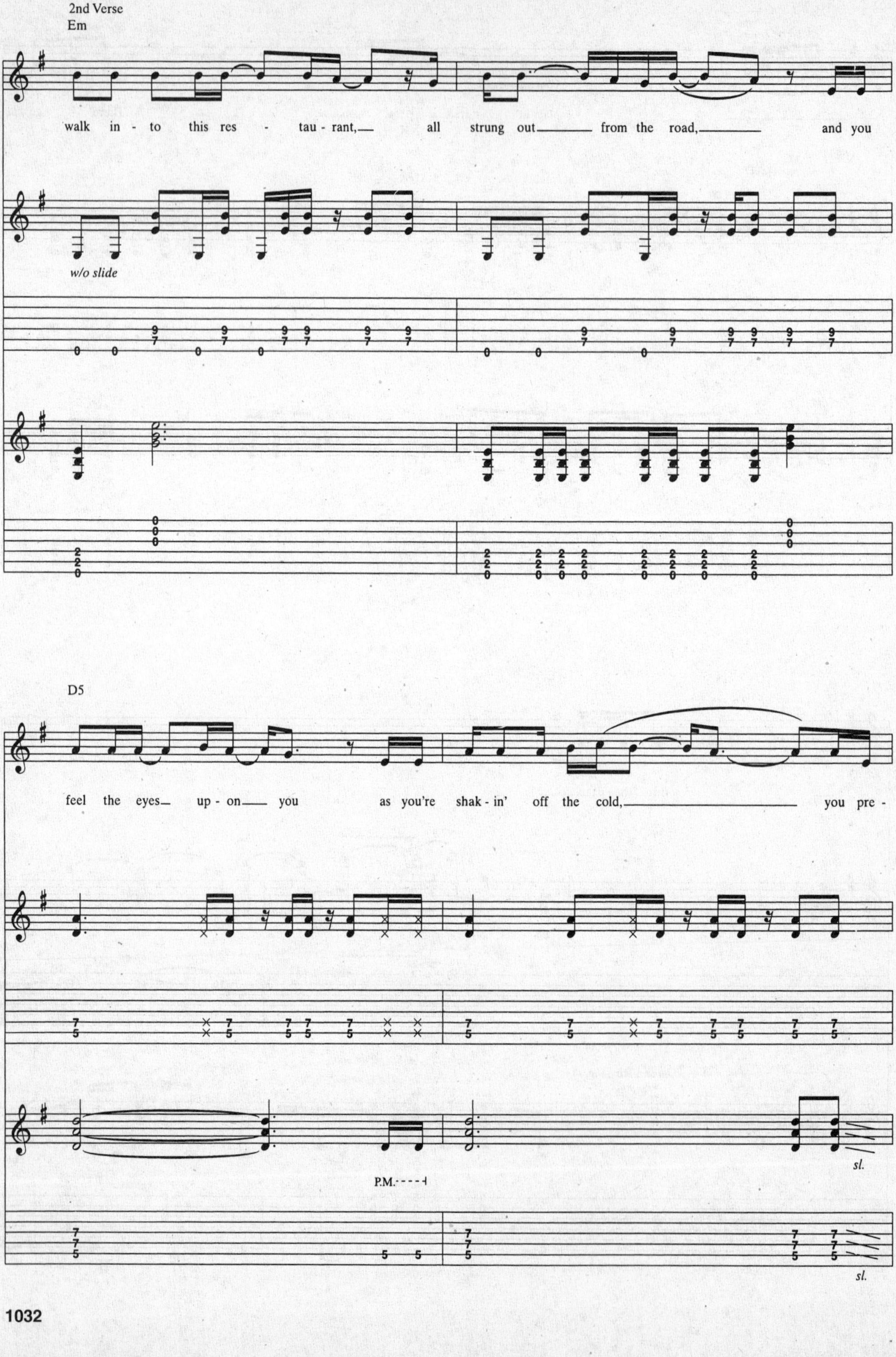

D5

feel the eyes up - on you as you're shak - in' off the cold, you pre -

P.M.

sl.

sl.

A5
tend it does - n't both - er you, but you just want to ex - plode.
P
w/slide
P
15
P
P.M.
P
Em
Yeah, most
14
(14) 15 14
10
12
12
H
H
P
H
H
P

times you can't hear 'em talk, oth - er times___ you can.___ All the

D

same old cli - chés,___ "Is it wom - an, is it man?"___ And you

P.M.

A

al - ways seem out - num - bered, you don't dare make a stand.

P P w/slide

H H P H P

Em

Make your stand. Oh, here I am,

sl. H H H H sl.

Chorus
w/Rhy. Fig. 1
D5
E5
on the road a - gain.
There I am,
(Gtr. II)
w/o slide
D5
E5
up on the stage.
Here I go,
w/slide
D5
A
C5
D5
I'm play - in' star a - gain.
There I go,
turn the page.
w/o slide
w/slide

E5

Woh, oh.

(Gtr. II)

Gtr. I

H H H

sl.

3rd Verse

E5

3. Out there in the spot - light, you're a mil - lion miles a - way. Ev - 'ry

w/o slide P.M. P.M. sl. P.M. P.M. P.M. P.M. sl.

P.M. P.M. P P.M. P.M. P.M.

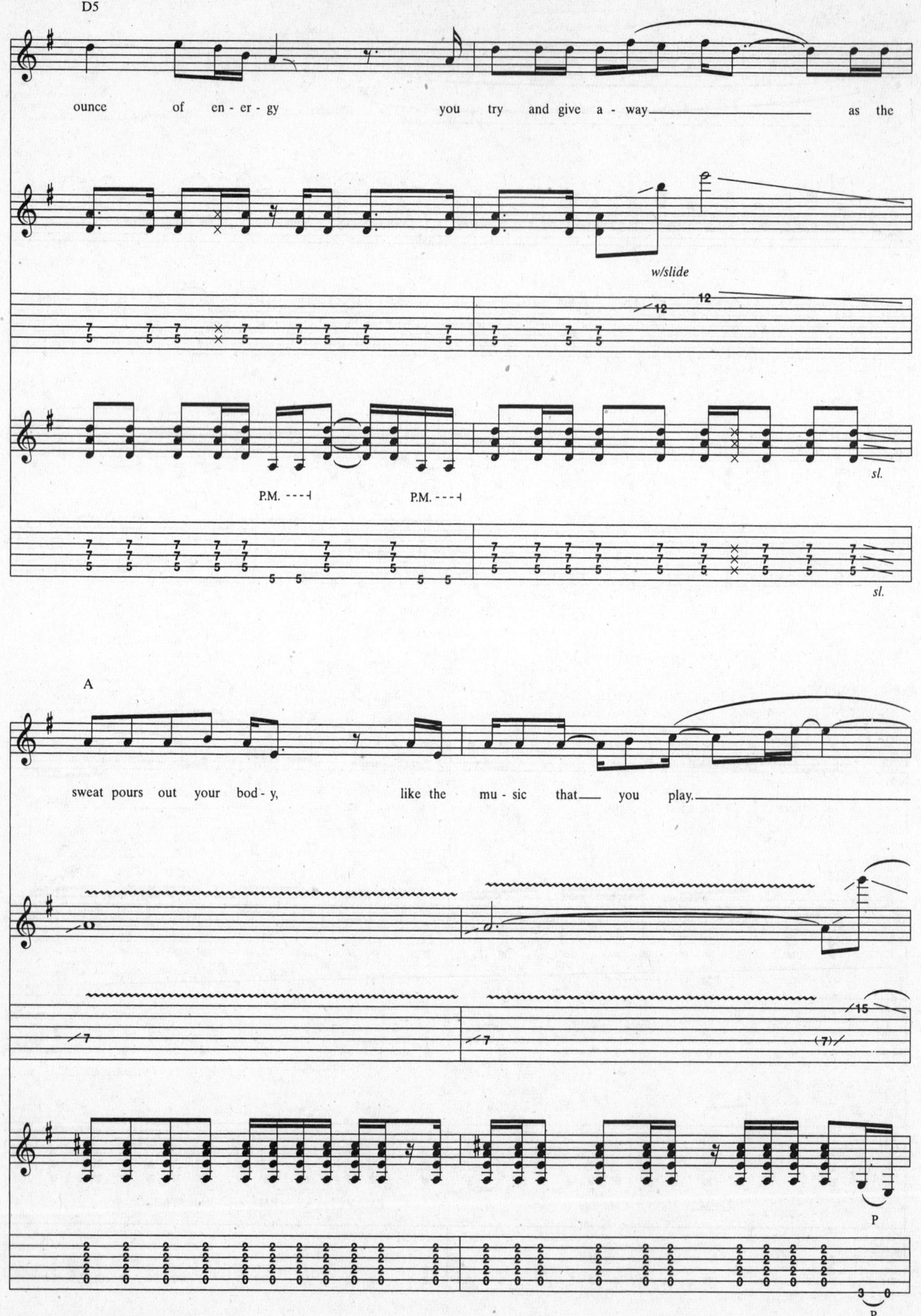
D5
ounce of en - er - gy you try and give a - way as the
w/slide
P.M.
P.M.
sl.
sl.
A
sweat pours out your bod - y, like the mu - sic that you play.
P
P

Em
(Gtr. II out)
P
P
E5
Lat - er in the eve - ning, as you lie a - wake in bed with the
(Gtr. I)
(Gtr. I out)
*(D5)
ech - oes of the am - pli - fi - ers ring - in' in your head, you
*Chords implied by bass (next 6 bars).
(A5)
smoke the day's last cig - a - rette, re - mem - b'rin' what she said,

what ___ she said.

Gtr. I

1/2

1/2

Interlude

D5 E5

Gtr. II

w/o slide

Rhy. Fig. 2

Harm.

1/2

sl. H *sl.* P

D5 E5

sl. H H *sl.* P P

1/2

D5 E5

sl. H H *sl.* H

P.M.

1/2

C5
D5
(cont. in notation)
E5
Oh,
yeah.
(end Rhy. Fig. 2)
Gtr. II
Guitar solo
w/Rhy. Fig. 2
D5
Gtr. III
dist. tone
Rhy. Fig. 3 (Gtr. II)
(end Rhy. Fig. 3)
w/Rhy. Fig. 3 (2 times)
D5
(Gtr. III)
E5

D5
E5
1/2
Full
sl.
H
C5
Yeah, here I am,
(Gtr. III)
Gtr. III
(Gtr. III out)
P
Gtr. I
(flanger off)
Gtr. II
P.M.
Chorus
w/Rhy. Fig. 1
on the road a - gain.
There I am
w/slide
w/wah

D5
E5
up on the stage.
Here I go,
D5
A
play-in' star a-gain.
Yeah, there I go,
C5
D5
E5
turn the page.
Yeah, there I go,
(wah off)
w/o slide
H
P.M.
Gtr. I

C5
D5
E5
turn that page.
There I go,
P.M.
sl.
C5
D5
yeah,
yeah.
There I go,

Em
yeah, yeah.
*Gtr. III
P.M.
H
Gtr. II
*w/slide
1/2
P
Outro
w/Rhy. Fig. 2 (1st 6 bars only)
w/Rhy. Fig. 3 (3 times)
D5
E5
D5
There I go, yeah.
Gtr. III
E5
D5
E5
Here I go, yeah.
There I go,

(cont. in notation)

①15fr.

C5 D5 G

Gtr. II

rit. 3 w/slide

woh, woh. There I go.

A.H. (15ma)

(Gtr. III) (Gtr. III out)

w/wah rit.

A.H.

A.H. pitches: D F♯

Gtr. I

H

P.M. rit. H sl.

H

H sl.

E5

w/fdbk. ad lib

(Spoken:) I'm gone.

Gtr. II

H

H

Gtr. I

25 or 6 to 4

Words and Music by Robert Lamm

Am
Am7/G
F#m7♭5
Fmaj7
E
Flash - ing lights a - gainst the sky.
Giv - ing up, I close my eyes.
Chorus
Half-Time Feel
Gtrs. 2 & 3 tacet
F
C
Sit - ting cross - leg on the floor.
Gtr. 4 (elec.)
mf
w/ dist.
G
End Half-Time Feel
Twen-ty - five or six to four.
Interlude
Gtr. 2: w/ Rhy. Fig. 1, 2 times, simile
1/2
full

F#m7b5
Fmaj7
E
full
1/2

Verse
Gtr. 2: w/ Rhy. Fig. 1, 4 times, simile
Gtr. 3: w/ Riff B, 4 times
Am
Am7/G
F#m7b5
Fmaj7
E
2. Star-in' blind - ly in - to space.
1/2

Am
Am7/G
F#m7b5
Fmaj7
E
Get-ting up to splash my face.
full

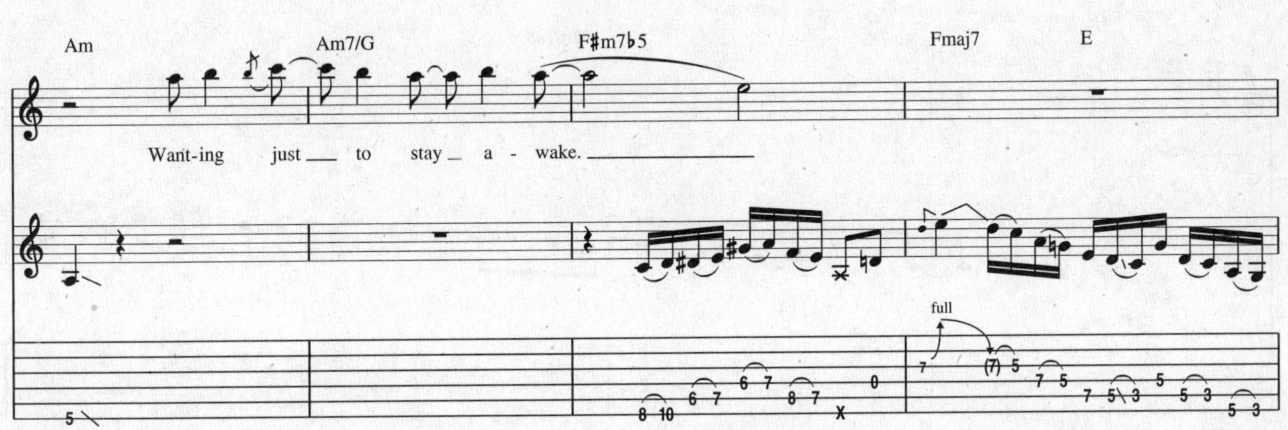
Am
Am7/G
F#m7b5
Fmaj7
E
Want-ing just to stay a - wake.
full

Am
Am7/G
F♯m7♭5
Fmaj7
E
Won-d'rin' how much I can take.
Oo.
1 1/2
1 3/4
full
Chorus
Half-Time Feel
Gtrs. 2 & 3 tacet
F
C
Should I try to do some more?
G
F
End Half-Time Feel
Twen-ty - five or six to four.
(four.)
Oh,
Guitar Solo
Gtr. 2: w/ Rhy. Fig. 1, 12 times, simile
Am
Am7/G
F♯m7♭5
Fmaj7
E
yeah!

Am
Am7/G
F#m7♭5
Fmaj7
E
Am
Am7/G
F#m7♭5
Fmaj7
E
Am
Am7/G
F#m7♭5
Fmaj7
E
full
Am
Am7/G
F#m7♭5
full
Fmaj7
E
Am
Am7/G
full

F♯m7♭5
Fmaj7
E
Am
Am7/G
F♯m7♭5
Fmaj7
E
Am
Am7/G
F♯m7♭5
Fmaj7
E
Am
* w /wah-wah
* + = closed (toe down) o = open (toe up)
Am7/G
sim.
F♯m7♭5
Fmaj7
E
Am
Am7/G
F♯m7♭5

Fmaj7
E
Am
Am7/G
F#m7b5
full
1/2
full
Fmaj7
E
Am
8va
Am7/G
F#m7b5
wah-wah off
1 1/2
full
3/4
full
full
full
full
full
full
Interlude
Gtrs. 1 & 2: w/ Riffs A & A1, 2 times
Fmaj7
E
N.C.(A5)
(G5)
(F#5)
(F5)
E5
8va
loco
1 1/4
full
N.C.(A5)
(G5)
(F#5)
(F5)
E5
Gtr. 2: w/ Rhy. Fig. 1, 2 times, simile
Gtr. 4
Am
Am7/G
F#m7b5
Fmaj7
E
full
Gtr. 1
Riff C
End Riff C

Gtr. 1: w/ Riff C
Gtr. 4
Am
Am7/G
F#m7b5
Fmaj7
E
full
Verse
Gtr. 1: w/ Riff C, 4 times
Gtr. 2: w/ Rhy. Fig. 1, 4 times, simile
Gtr. 3: w/ Riff B, 4 times
3. Feel - ing like I ought to sleep.
Spin - ning room is sink - ing deep.
Search-ing for some - thing to say.

F#m7♭5
Fmaj7
E
Am
Am7/G
Wait - ing for the break of day.
w/ pick & finger
full
Chorus
Half-Time Feel
Gtrs. 1, 2 & 3 tacet
F
Oo.
Twen - ty - five
full
C
or six to four.
w/ pick & finger
G
F
End Half-Time Feel
Twen - ty - five or six to four.
(four.
Al -

Outro-Guitar Solo

Gtrs. 1 & 2: w/ Riffs A & A1, 2 times, simile

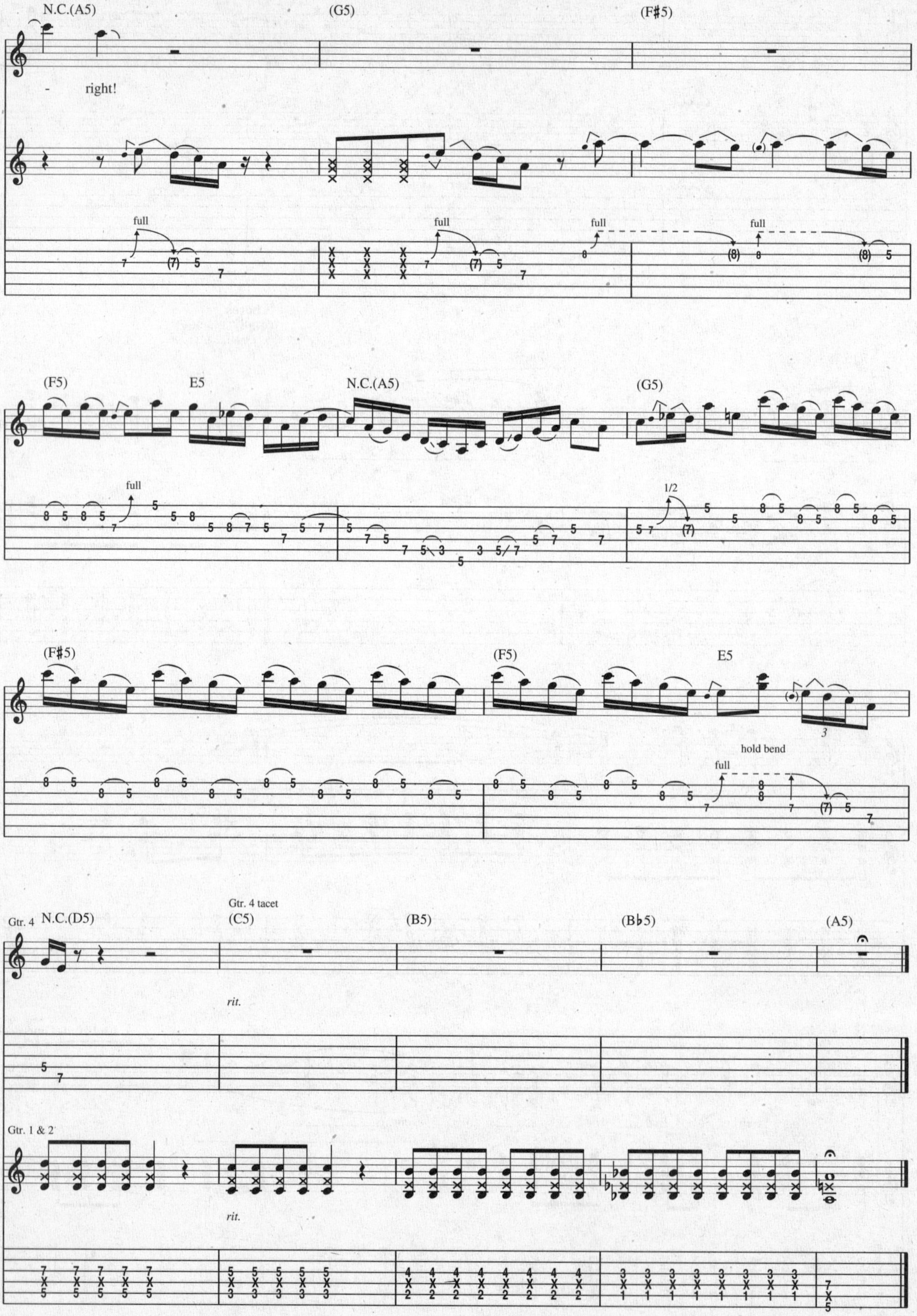

N.C.(A5) (G5) (F#5)

- right!

full full full full

(F5) E5 N.C.(A5) (G5)

full 1/2

(F#5) (F5) E5

full hold bend

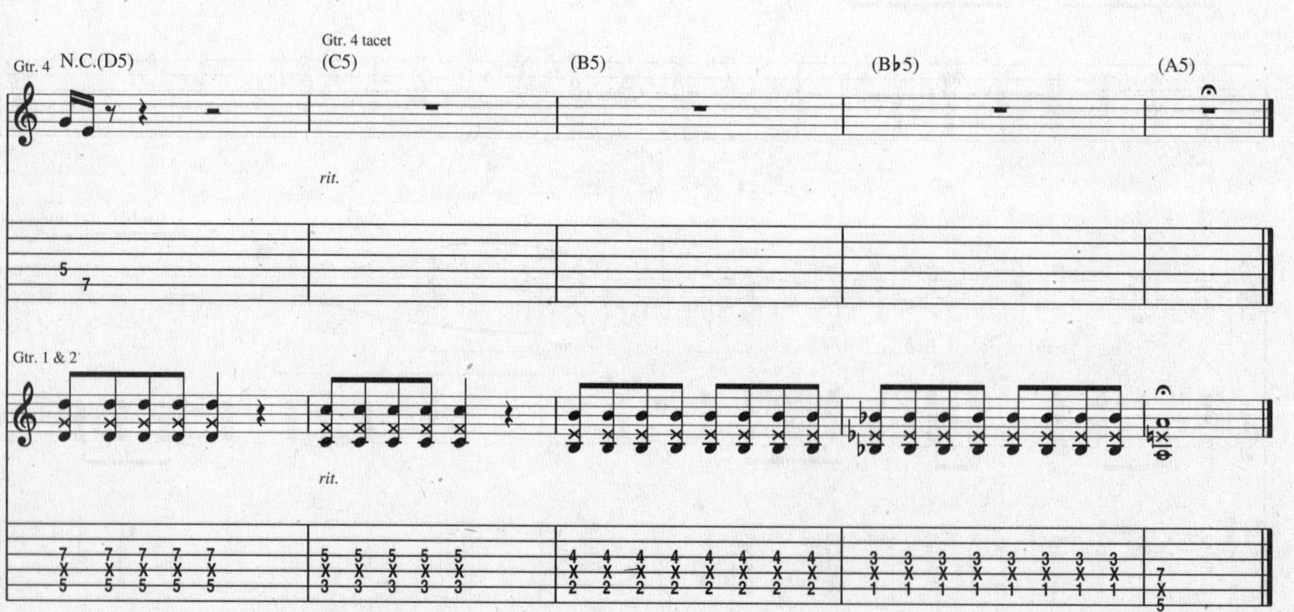

Up All Night

Words and Music by Mark Slaughter and Dana Strum

Verse
D5/E
E7
D5/E
E7
1. When eve - nin' comes
2. See additional lyrics
I am a - live.
I love to prowl a - round in the streets.
P.M.
let ring
P.M.
P.M.

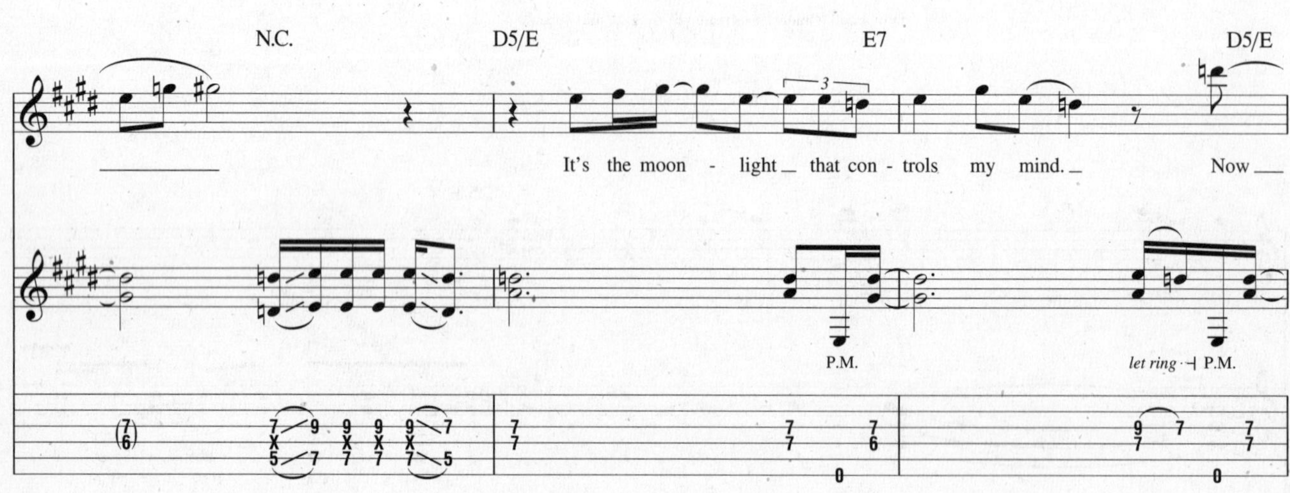
N.C.
D5/E
E7
D5/E
It's the moon - light that con - trols my mind.
Now
P.M.
let ring
P.M.

E7
N.C.
Pre-Chorus
F5
C5
G5
I've got the pow - er to speak,
yeah.
P.M.
let ring

F5
C5
G5
Watch - in' the cit - y lights.
(A - wake from dusk to dawn.
Stars are shin - in' down.
let ring

F5
C5
G5
F5
C5
G5
They'll be shin - in' down on you and I.
And I'll hold you till the morn - in' light.
And when morn - ing comes.)
let ring

Chorus
A5
Dsus2
G5
N.C.
Ev - 'ry - bod - y sing it now.
Up all night, sleep all day.
let ring
1/4
1/4

To Coda
A5
Dsus2
G5
N.C.
Up all night, sleep all day. That's right.
1/4
1/4

Interlude

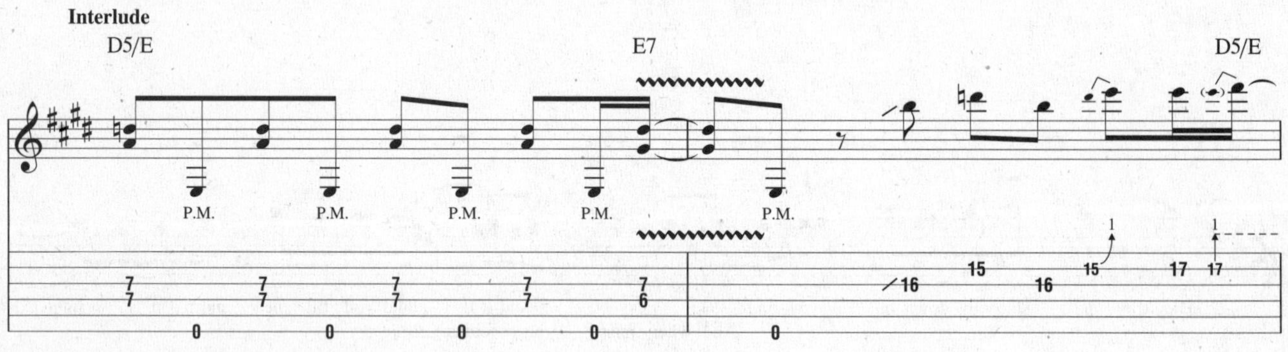
D5/E
E7
D5/E
P.M.
P.M.
P.M.
P.M.
P.M.

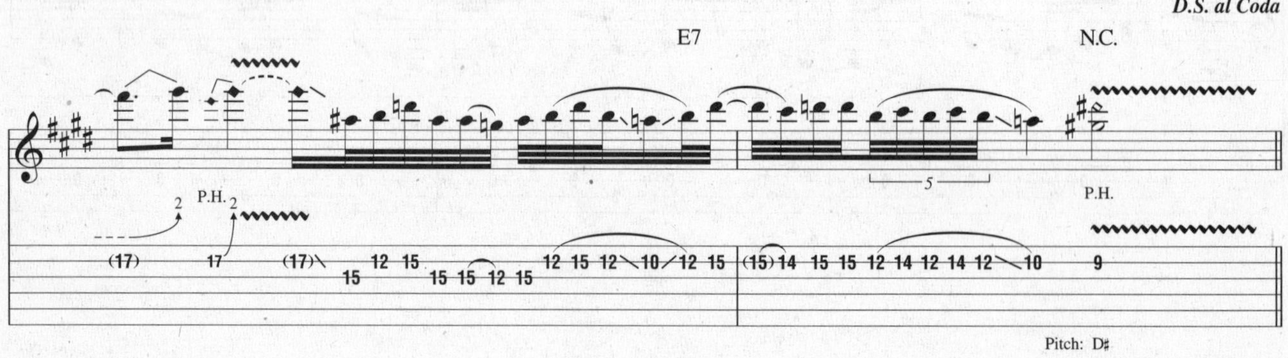
D.S. al Coda
E7
N.C.
P.H.
P.H.
Pitch: D♯

Coda
A5
Dsus2
G5
N.C.
A5
Dsus2
Up all night, sleep all day. Come on, come on. Up all night. Oh,
1/4
1/4

G5

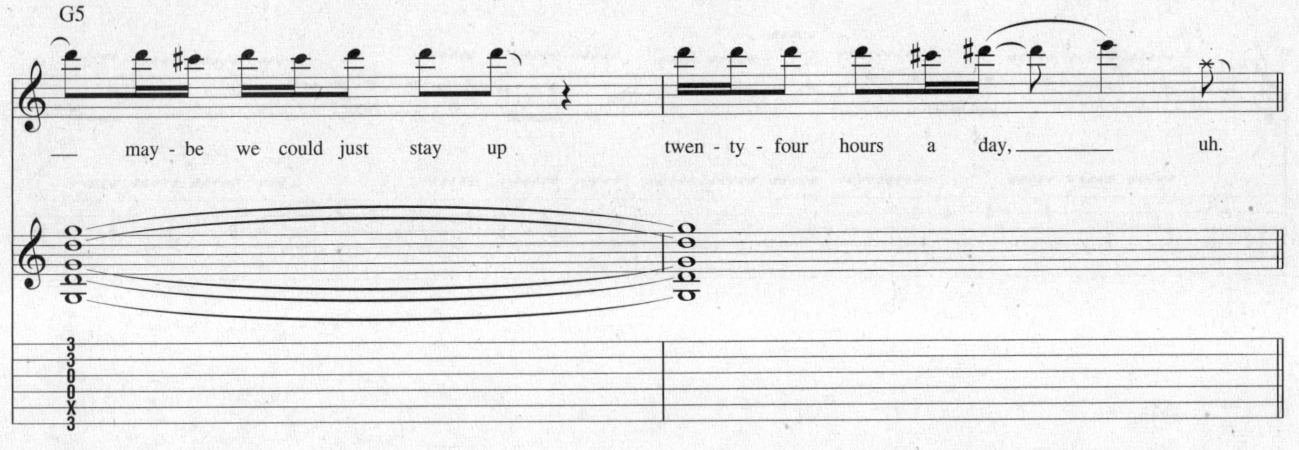

Interlude

N.C.

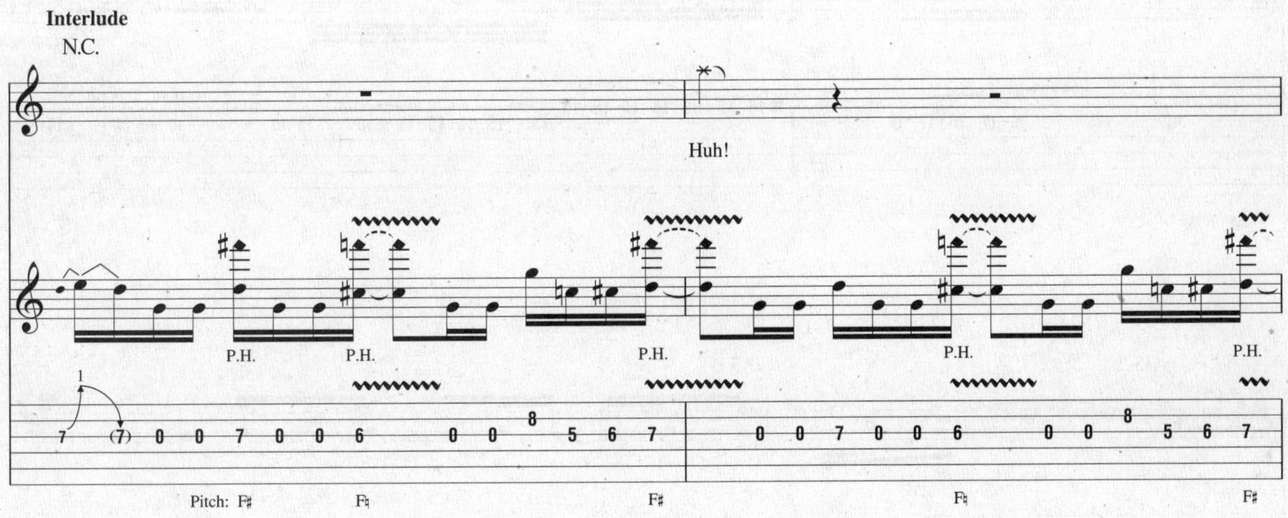

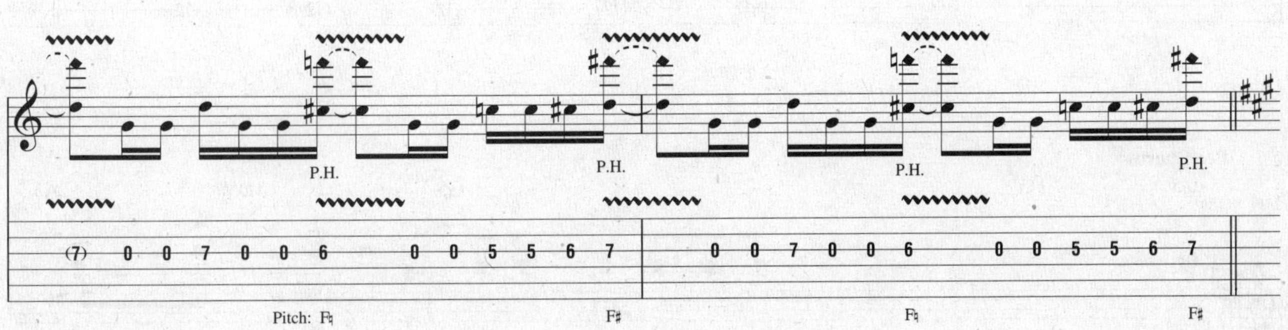

Guitar Solo

F♯m Fmaj7♯11 G6

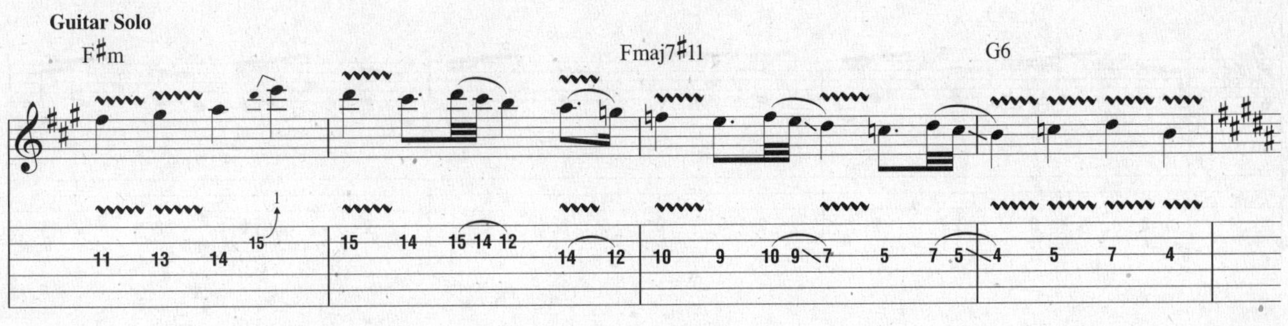

B5
A5
P.H.
1/2

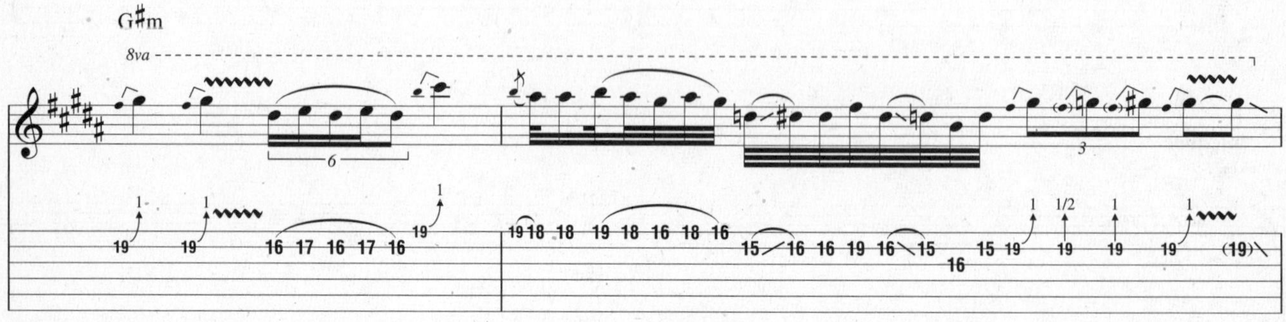
G♯m
8va

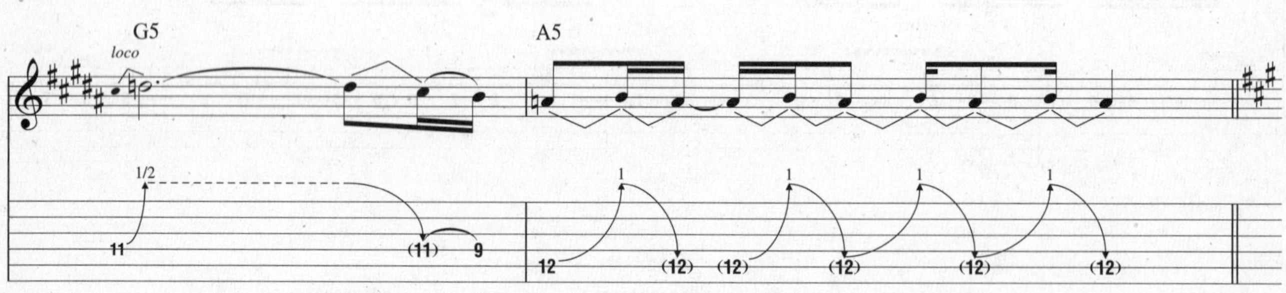
G5
loco
A5
1/2

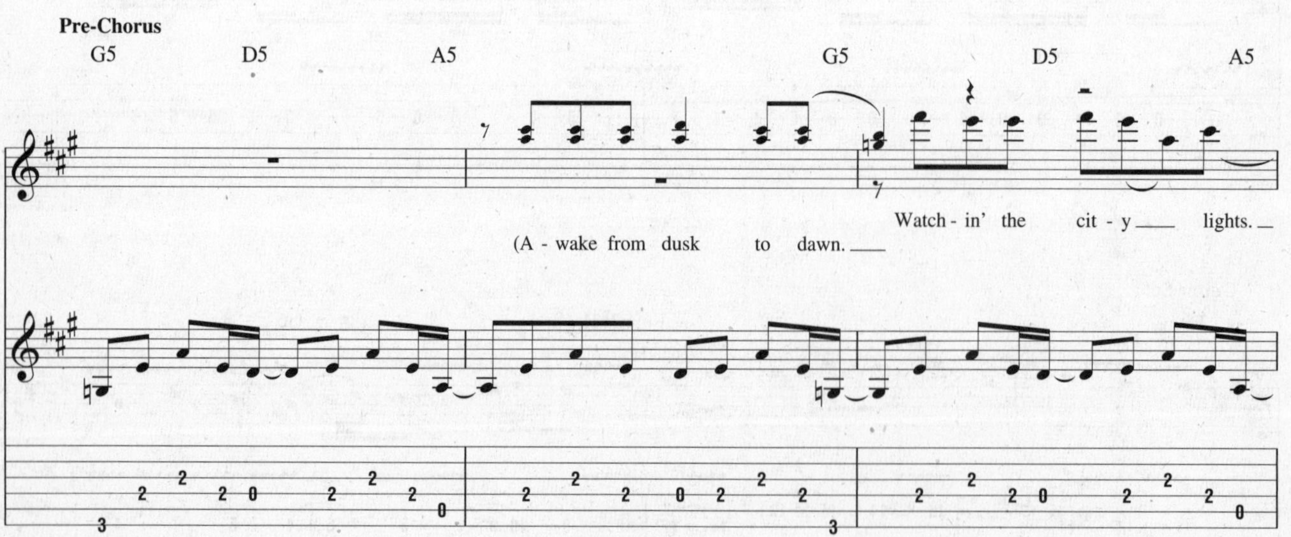
Pre-Chorus
G5
D5
A5
G5
D5
A5
Watch - in' the cit - y lights.
(A - wake from dusk to dawn.

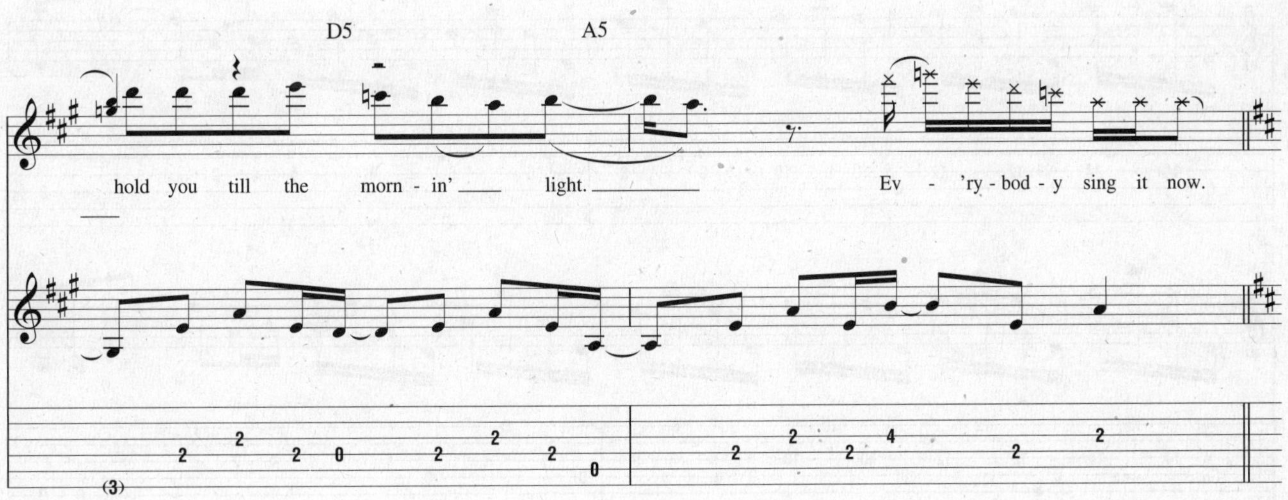

Additional Lyrics

2. Drivin' down the boulevard, all alone.
The neon signs are callin' your name.
Find me in the corner havin' the time of my life.
You'd think you'd want to do the same.

Wanted Dead or Alive

Words and Music by Jon Bon Jovi and Richie Sambora

Verse
F E D
D5
C5
G5
*Gtr. 3
1. It's all the same, on - ly the names will change.
times I sleep, some-times it's not for days. The
walk these streets, a load - ed six string on my back. I
Rhy. Fig. 1
*Play 3rd time only.
**Play simile 2nd & 3rd times.

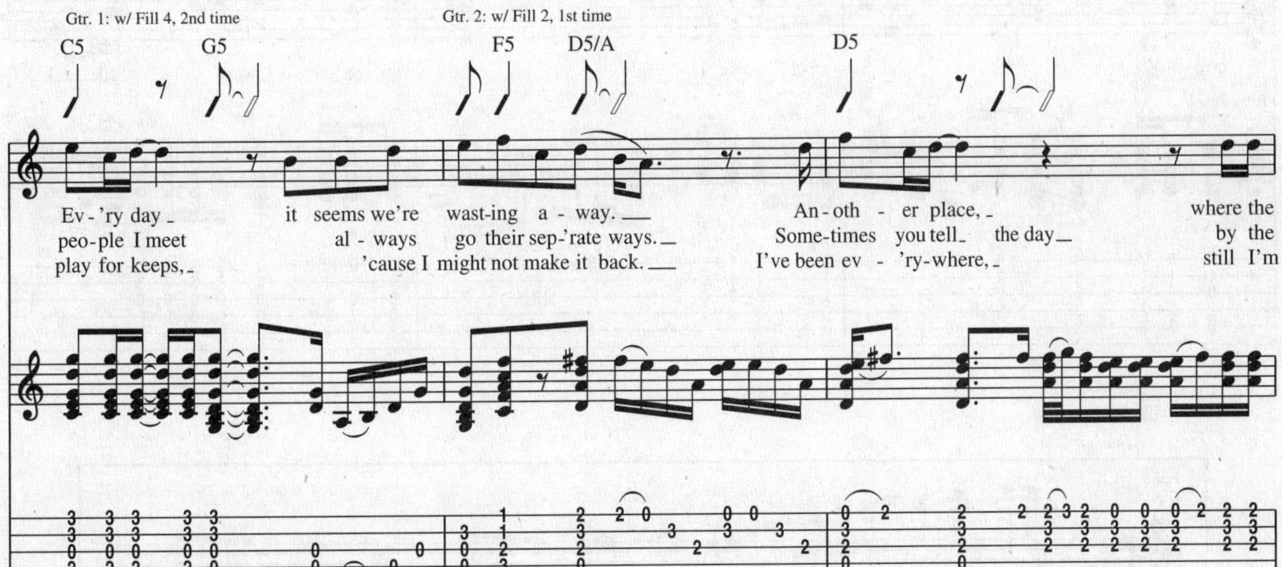
Gtr. 1: w/ Fill 4, 2nd time
Gtr. 2: w/ Fill 2, 1st time
C5
G5
F5
D5/A
D5
Ev - 'ry day it seems we're wast-ing a - way. An - oth - er place, where the
peo-ple I meet al - ways go their sep-'rate ways. Some-times you tell the day by the
play for keeps, 'cause I might not make it back. I've been ev - 'ry-where, still I'm

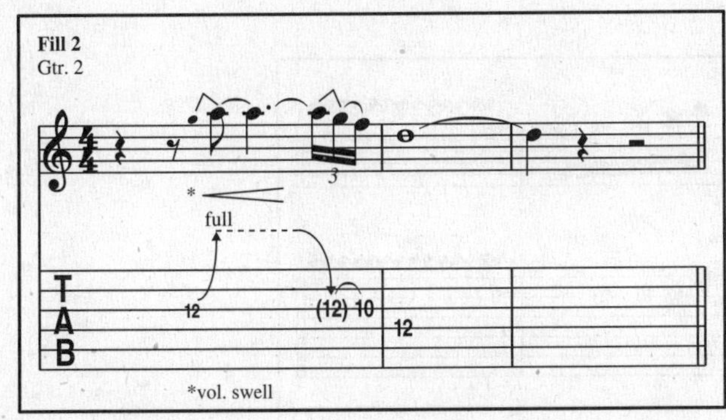
Fill 2
Gtr. 2
full
*vol. swell

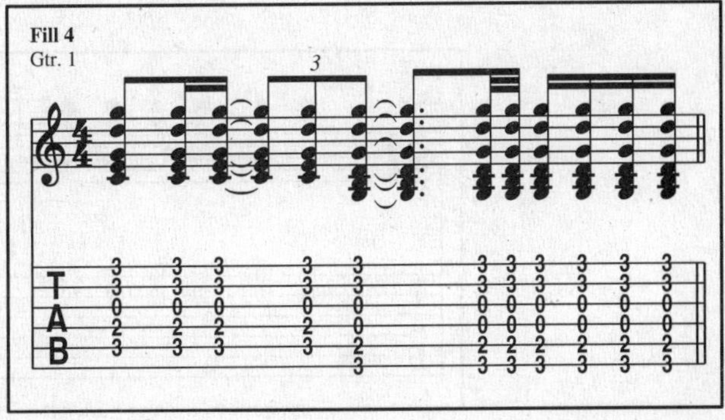
Fill 4
Gtr. 1

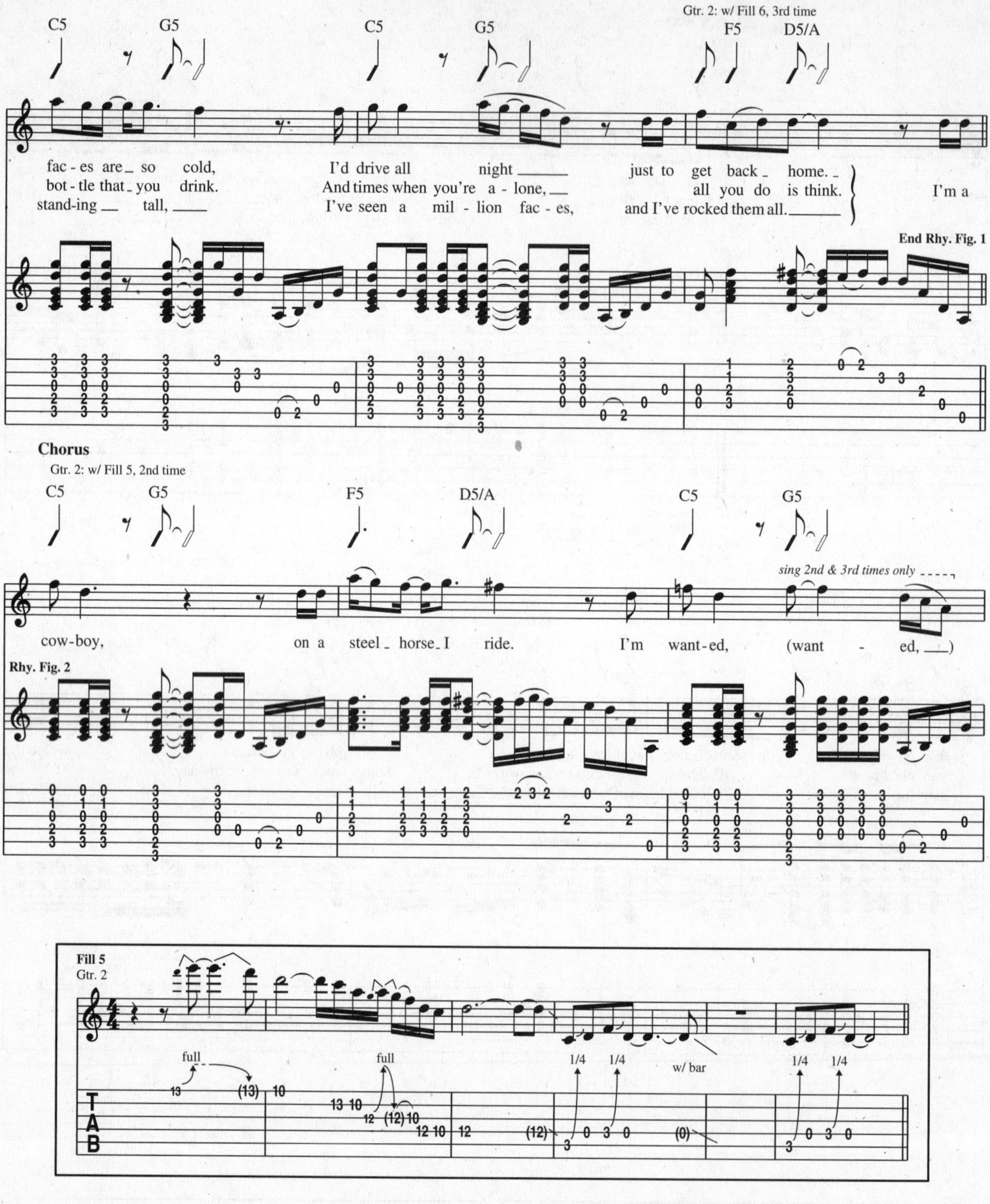

Gtr. 2: w/ Fill 6, 3rd time

C5 G5 C5 G5 F5 D5/A

fac - es are so cold, I'd drive all night just to get back home.
bot - tle that you drink. And times when you're a - lone, all you do is think. I'm a
stand-ing tall, I've seen a mil - lion fac - es, and I've rocked them all.

End Rhy. Fig. 1

Chorus

Gtr. 2: w/ Fill 5, 2nd time

C5 G5 F5 D5/A C5 G5

sing 2nd & 3rd times only

cow-boy, on a steel horse I ride. I'm want-ed, (want - ed,)

Rhy. Fig. 2

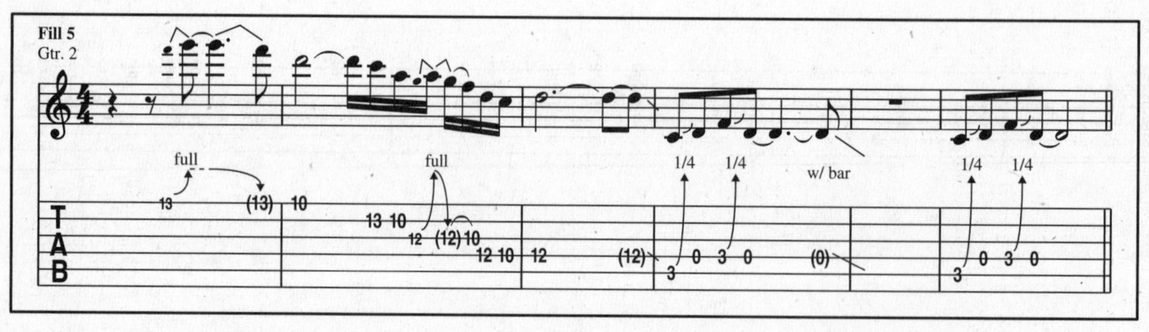

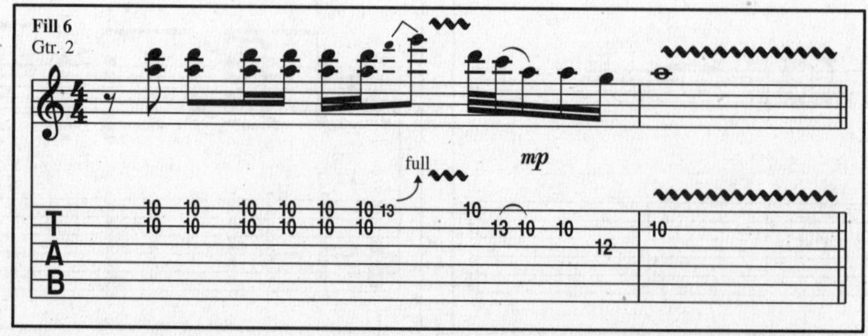

To Coda
C5 D5 F5VIII D5
C
G5
N.C.
D
(cont. in notation)
sing 2nd time only
dead or a - live. ('Cause I'm a) Want - ed, (want - ed.) dead or a - live.
End Rhy. Fig. 2
*Upper harmony tacet 1st time.
**Sing 3rd time only.
Gtr. 2: w/ Fill 3, 1st time
Guitar Solo
Gtr. 1: w/ Rhy. Fig. 1, simile
D5
2. Some - Al - right.
Gtr. 1
Gtr. 3 (dist.)
mf
Gtr. 2
Fill 3
Gtr. 2
full

C5
G5
C5
G5
F5
D5
P.H.
full
pitch: C♯ D C♯
pitch: A
C5
G5
C5
G5
8va
loco
P.H.
1/4
pitch: E♭
pitch: D D E D C
pitch: D E D C
pitch: D E D F
P.M.
Chorus
Gtr. 1: w/ Rhy. Fig. 2, 1st 3 meas., simile
Gtr. 2 tacet
F5
D5
C5
G5
F5
D5
Oh, I'm a cow - boy, on a steel _ horse _ I ride. I'm

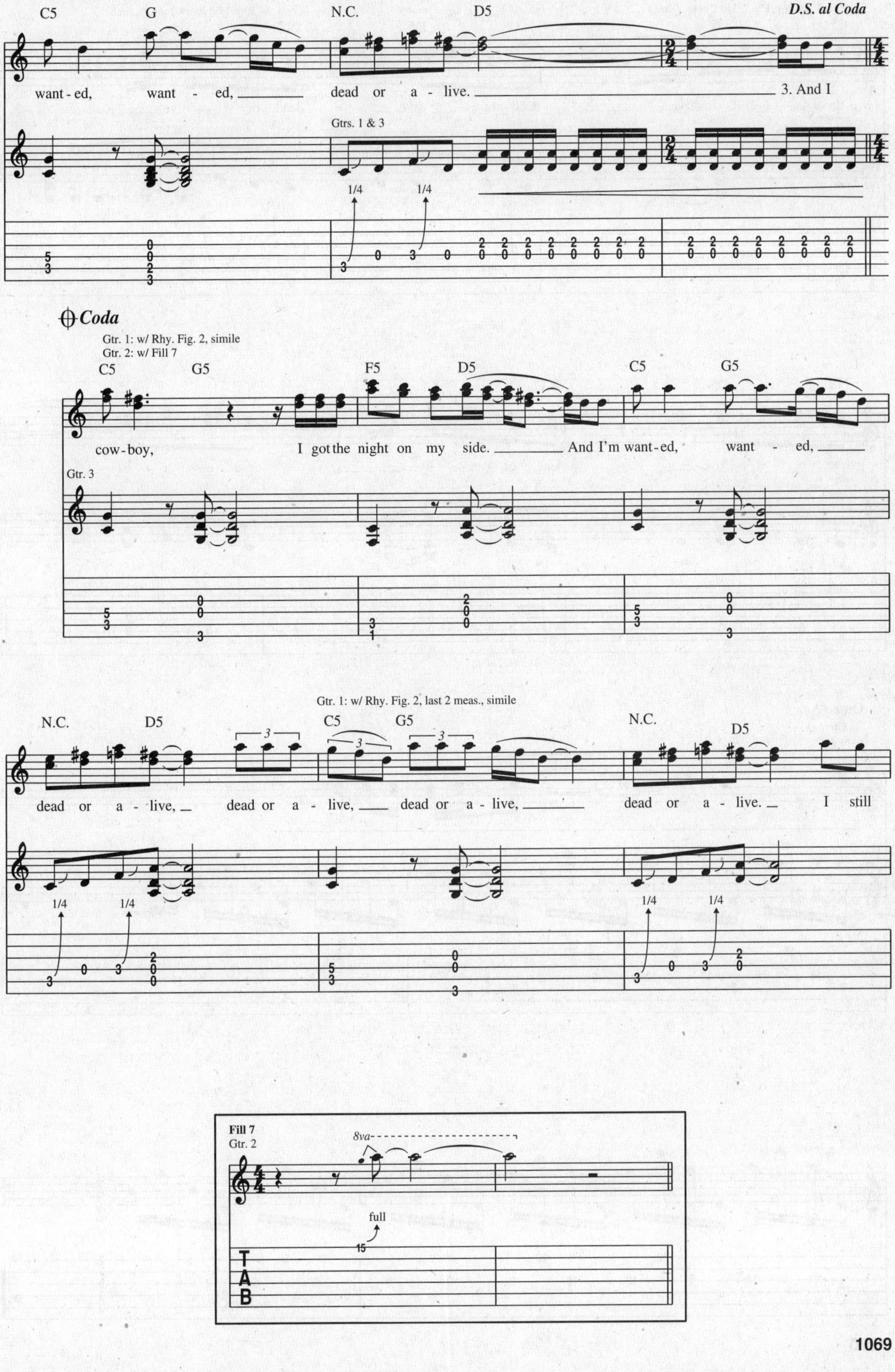

C5 G N.C. D5 *D.S. al Coda*

want-ed, want - ed, dead or a - live. 3. And I

Gtrs. 1 & 3

1/4 1/4

Coda

Gtr. 1: w/ Rhy. Fig. 2, simile
Gtr. 2: w/ Fill 7

C5 G5 F5 D5 C5 G5

cow-boy, I got the night on my side. And I'm want-ed, want - ed,

Gtr. 3

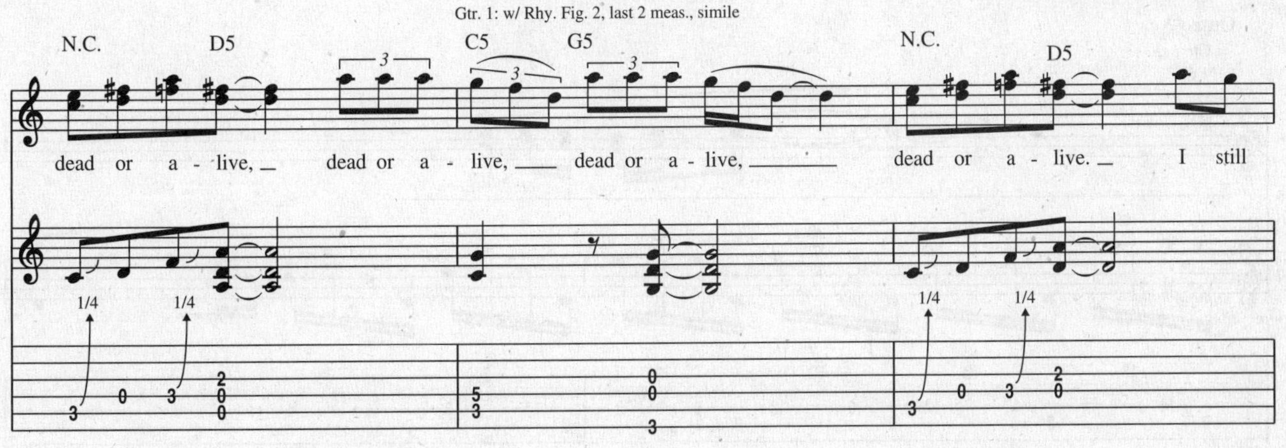

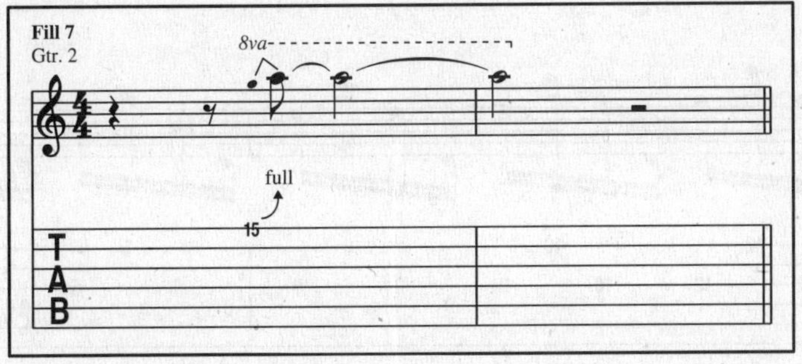

Gtr. 1: w/ Rhy. Fig. 2, last 2 meas., simile
C5
G5
N.C.
D5
Gtr. 1: w/ Rhy. Fig. 2, last 2 meas., simile
N.C.
G5
drive, I still drive, dead or a - live, dead or a - live,
1/4
1/4
1/4
1/4

N.C.
D5
N.C.
G5
N.C.
D5
dead or a - live, dead or a - live, dead or a - live.
Gtrs. 1 & 3
1/4
1/4
1/4
1/4
1/4
1/4

Outro
Gtr. 3 tacet
N.C.
Gtr. 1

D/A
rit.

The Warrior

Words and Music by Nick Gilder and Holly Knight

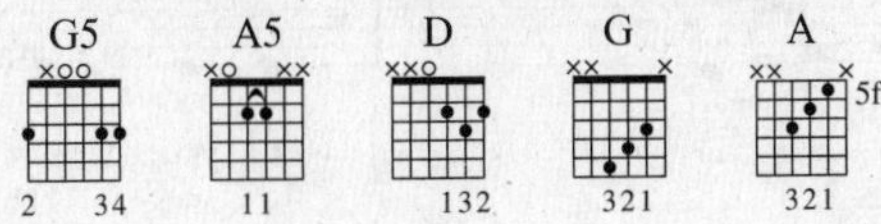

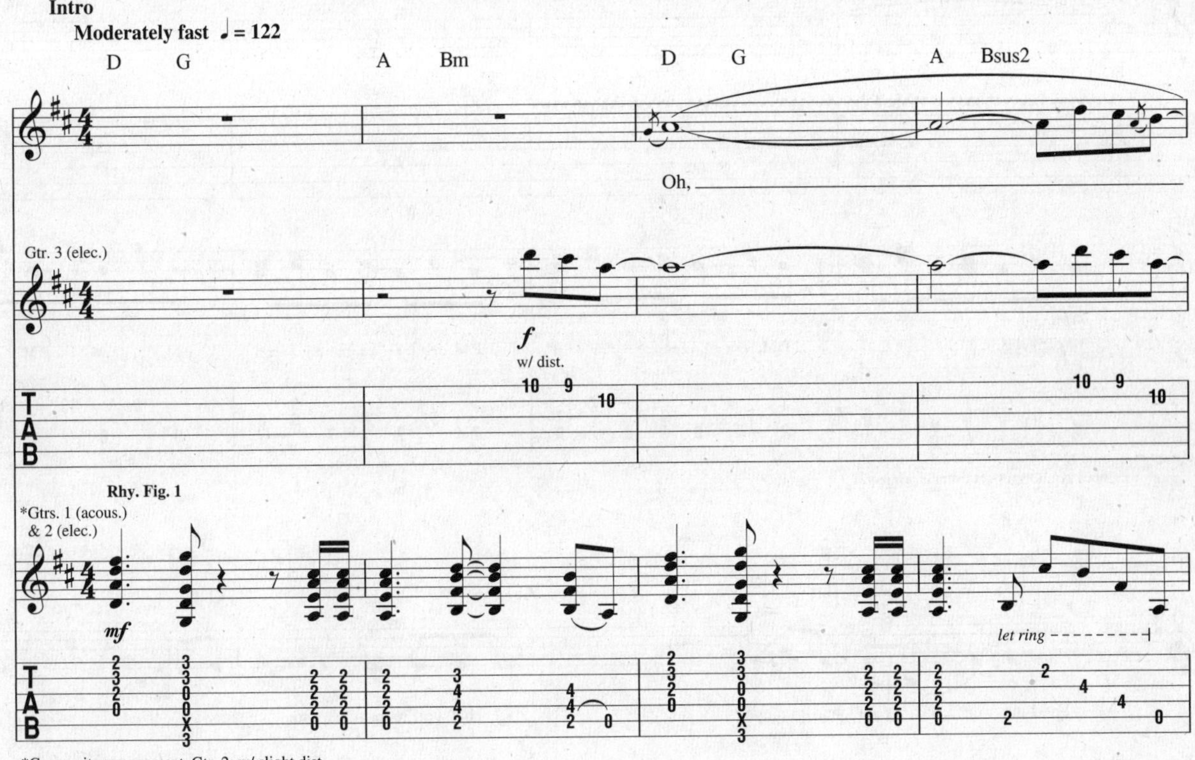

*Composite arrangement. Gtr. 2: w/ slight dist.

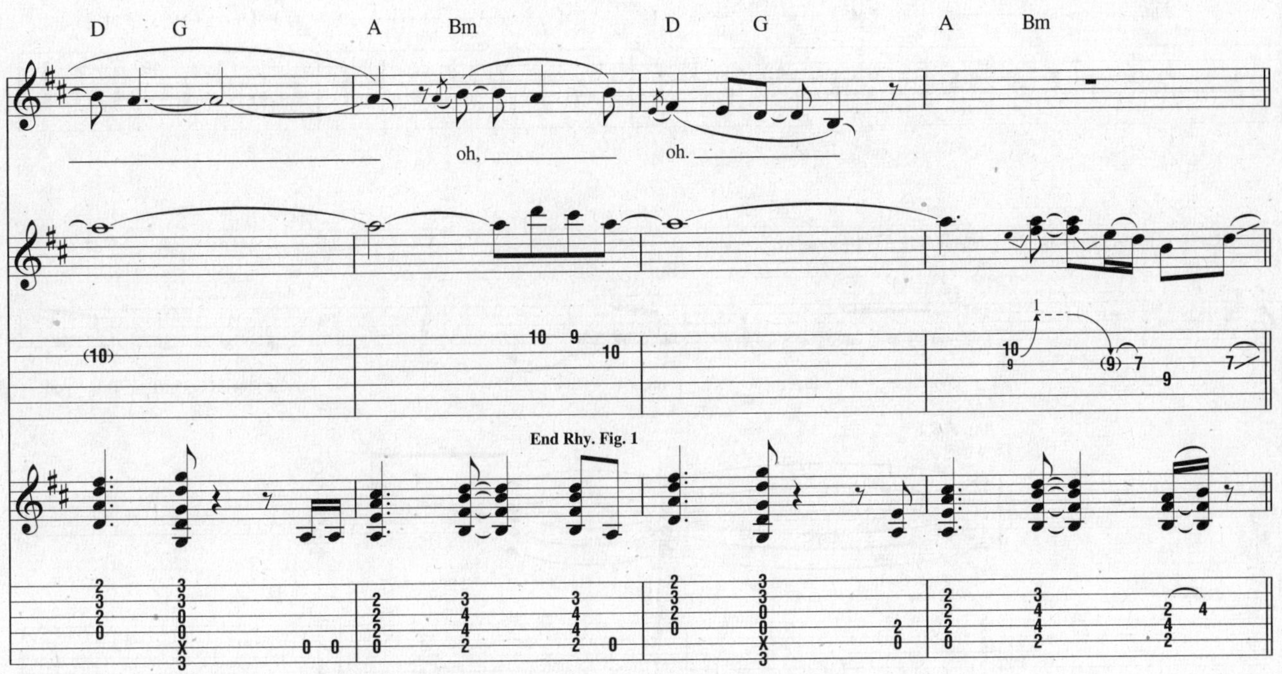

Verse

*Chord symbols reflect overall harmony.

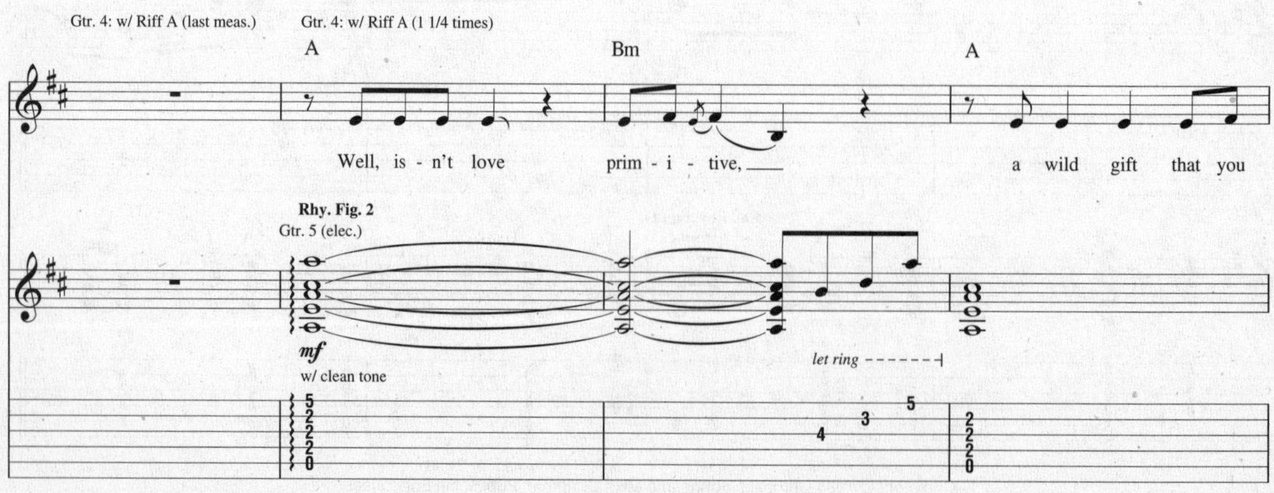

Gtr. 5 tacet
G A B G5
⑥ 7fr
Rhy. Fig. 2
Gtr. 2
wan - na give? Break out of cap - tiv - i - ty, and fol - low me ster - e - o
Rhy. Fig. 2A
Gtr. 4
P.M.
let ring
Gtr. 5
A5 G5 D
End Rhy. Fig. 2
jun - gle child. Love is the kill, your heart's still wild.
Gtr. 4
End Rhy. Fig. 2A
Gtr. 1
divisi
Chorus
Gtrs. 1 & 2: w/ Rhy. Fig. 1
D G A Bm D G A Bsus2
Shoot-in' at the walls of heart - ache, bang, bang! I am the war - ri - or.
Riff B
End Riff B
P.M.
*Gang vocals, next 9 meas.

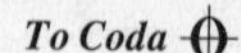
To Coda

Gtr. 4 tacet
D G A Bm Asus4 A D/F♯ G
Well, I am the war - ri - or, and heart to heart you win if you sur - vive.
Gtrs. 1 & 2
P.M.
P.M.
T
T = Thumb on 6th string.

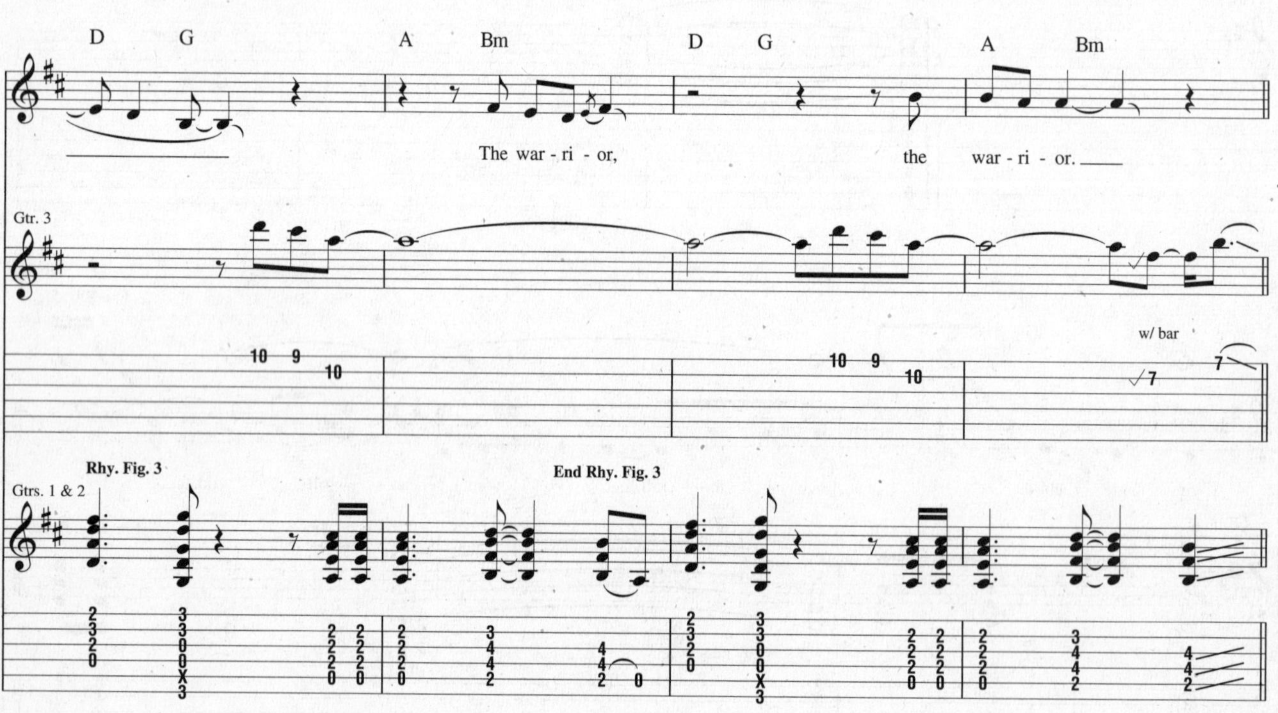
D G A Bm D G A Bm
The war - ri - or, the war - ri - or.
Gtr. 3
w/ bar
Rhy. Fig. 3
End Rhy. Fig. 3
Gtrs. 1 & 2

Verse
Gtrs. 1 & 2 tacet
Gtr. 4: w/ Riff A (2 times)
Gtr. 3 tacet
A Bm A G
2. You talk, talk, talk to me. Your eyes touch me phys - i - c'ly.
Gtr. 3

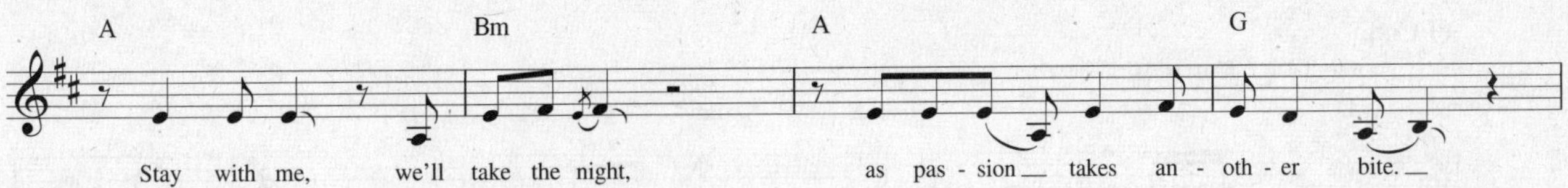
A
Bm
A
G
Stay with me, we'll take the night, as pas - sion takes an - oth - er bite.

Gtr. 4: w/ Riff A (last meas.)
Gtr. 4: w/ Riff A (1 1/4 times)
A
Bm
A
Gang vocals: Oh, oh.
Who's the hunt - er, who's the game?
I feel the beat
Gtr. 5
let ring

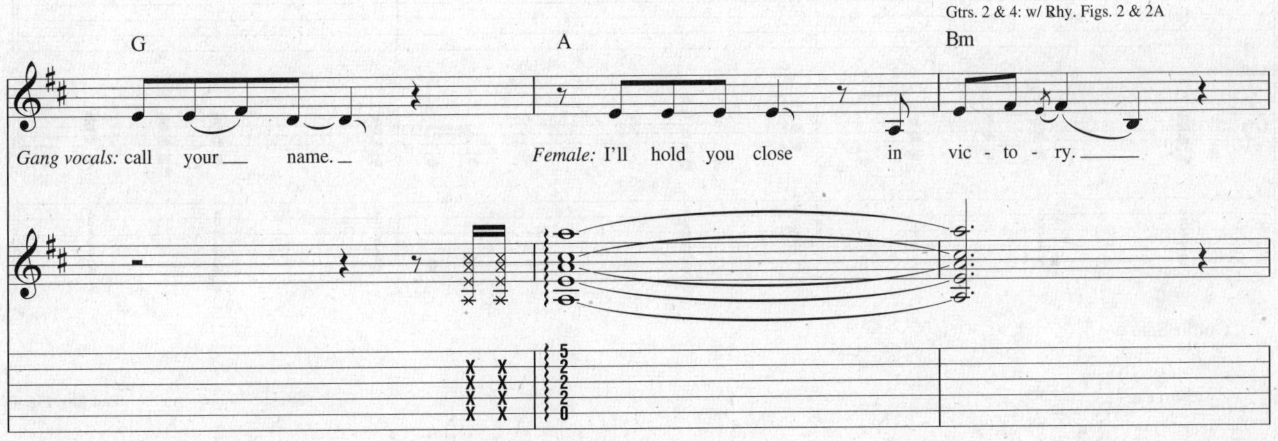
Gtrs. 2 & 4: w/ Rhy. Figs. 2 & 2A
G
A
Bm
Gang vocals: call your name.
Female: I'll hold you close in vic - to - ry.

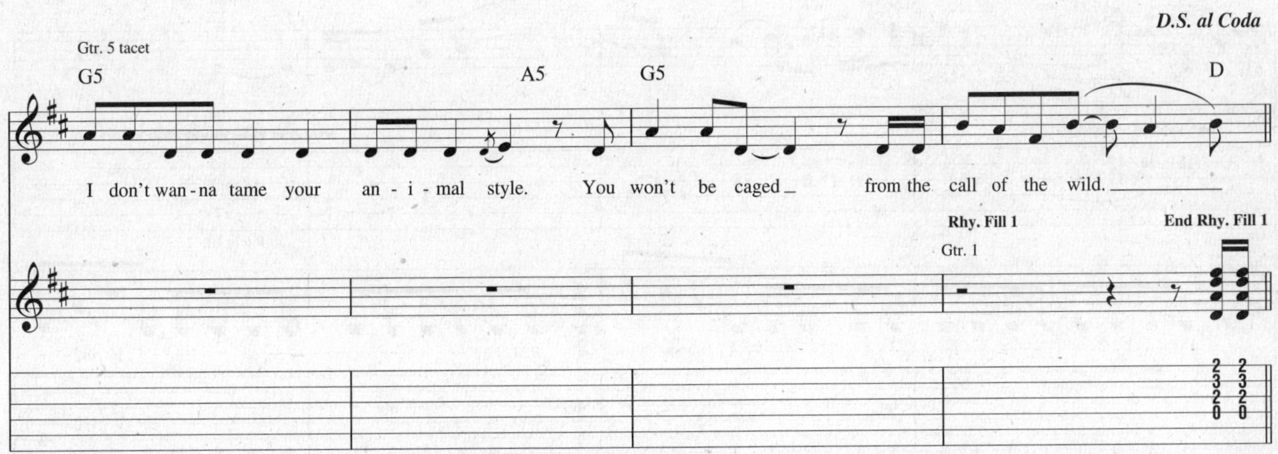
D.S. al Coda
Gtr. 5 tacet
G5
A5
G5
D
I don't wan - na tame your an - i - mal style. You won't be caged from the call of the wild.
Rhy. Fill 1
End Rhy. Fill 1
Gtr. 1

Coda
Gtrs. 1 & 2: w/ Rhy. Fig. 3 (1 1/2 times)
D G A Bm D G
Female: The war - ri - or, the
Gtr. 3
A Bm D G A Bm
war - ri - or. I am the war - ri - or.
fdbk.
Gtrs. 1 & 2
Guitar Solo
Gtr. 1 tacet
Gtr. 3 tacet
G A G A
Rhy. Fig. 4
End Rhy. Fig. 4
Gtr. 6 (elec.)
mf
w/ clean tone & chorus
Gtr. 7
Gtr. 7 (elec.) divisi
f
w/ dist.
fdbk.
Gtr. 2
Pitch: G♯
P.M.
let ring

Gtr. 6: w/ Rhy. Fig. 4 (3 times)
G
A/G
G
A/G
Gtr. 7
w/ bar
Gtr. 2
P.M.
P.M.
let ring
G
A/G
G
A/G
let ring
let ring
P.M.
P.M.
P.M.
P.M.
P.M.
G
A/G
G
A/G
w/ bar
P.M.
P.M.
P.M.
P.M.
P.M.
P.M.
P.M.

Outro-Chorus
Gtr. 7 tacet
D5 G5 A5 Bsus2 D5 G5 A5 Bsus2
Shoot-in' at the walls of heart - ache, the war - ri - or.
Voc. Fig. 1
Gang vocals: (Shoot-in' at the walls of heart - ache.)
Gtr. 7
Gtr. 4
P.M.
Gtr. 2
P.M.
D5 G5 A5 Bsus2 Asus4 A D/F♯ G
I am the war - ri - or. And heart to heart, you win,
End Voc. Fig. 1
P.M.
let ring

Gtr. 1: w/ Rhy. Fill 1
Gtrs. 1 & 2: w/ Rhy. Figs. 1 & 1A (1st 4 meas.) (till fade)
Gtr. 4: w/ Riff B (till fade)
Asus4
A
D/F♯
G
D
G
A
Bm
heart to heart you win, if you sur - vive. The war - ri - or,
Gtr. 4
Gtr. 3
fdbk.
Gtr. 2
P.M.
Bkgd. Voc.: w/ Voc. Fig. 1
Bsus2
the war - ri - or. Shoot - in' at the walls of heart - ache, bang, bang!
I am the war - ri - or. Yes, I am the war - ri - or.

Bkgd. Voc.: w/ Voc. Fig. 1 (2 times)
D G A Bsus2 D G A Bm
Vic - to - ry is mine. The war - ri - or.
fdbk.
10 9
10
(10)
10 9
10
(12)

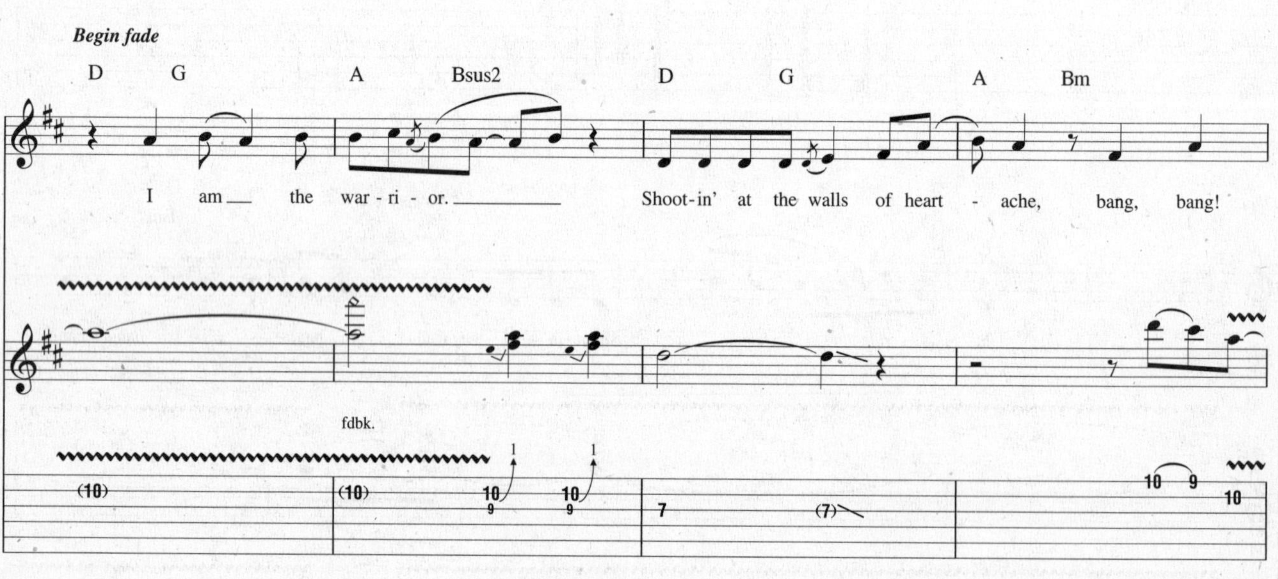
Begin fade
D G A Bsus2 D G A Bm
I am the war - ri - or. Shoot-in' at the walls of heart - ache, bang, bang!
fdbk.
1
1
(10)
(10)
10
9
10
9
7
(7)
10 9
10

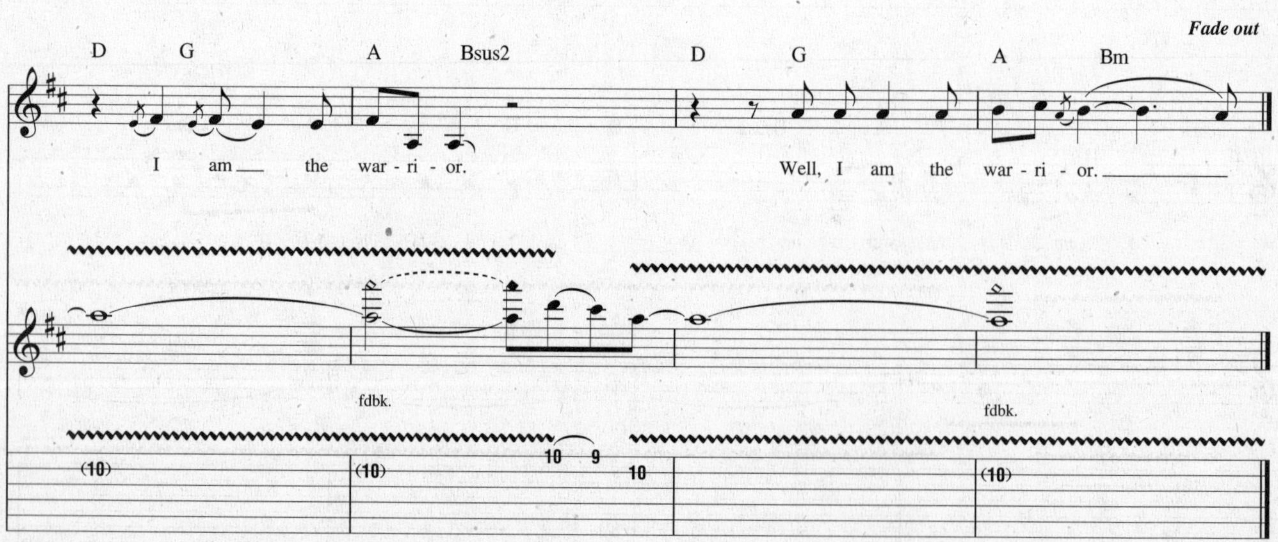
Fade out
D G A Bsus2 D G A Bm
I am the war - ri - or. Well, I am the war - ri - or.
fdbk.
fdbk.
(10)
(10)
10 9
10
(10)

We Built This City

Words and Music by Bernie Taupin, Martin Page, Dennis Lambert, and Peter Wolf

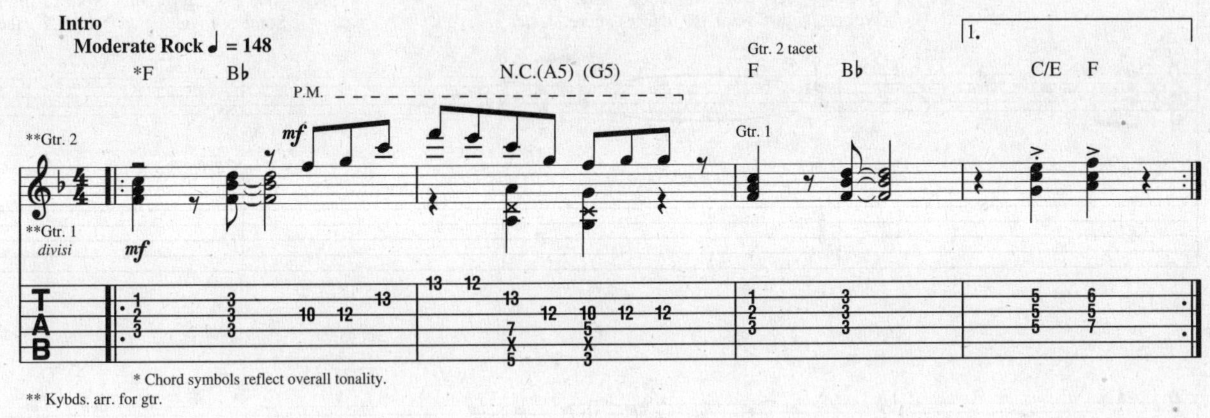

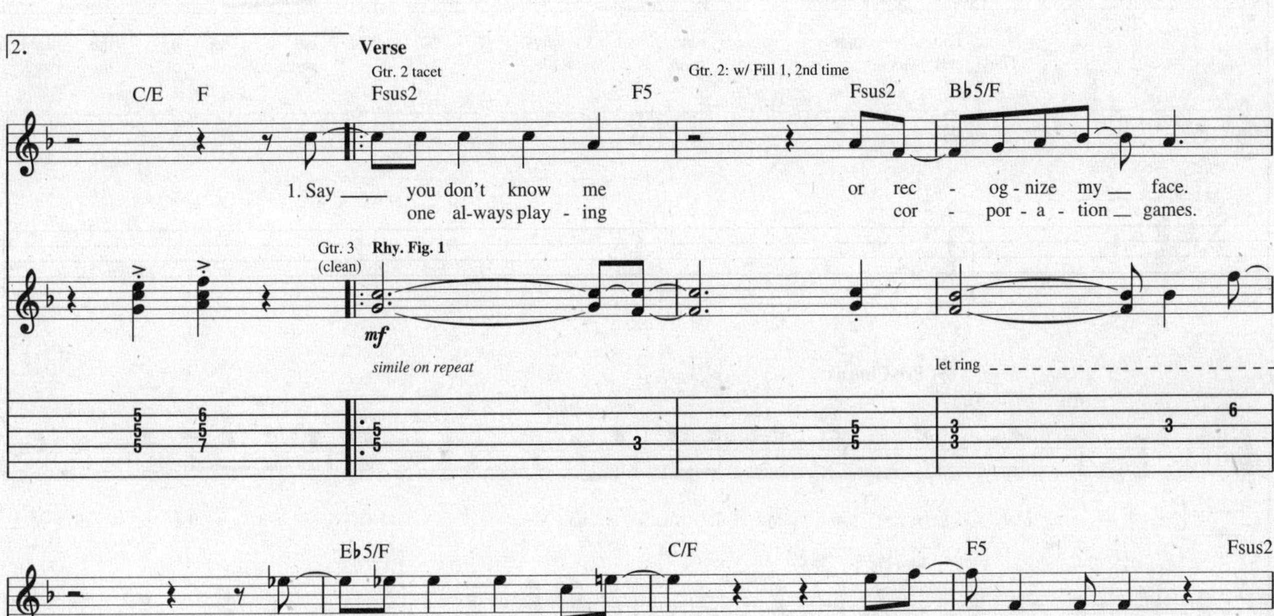

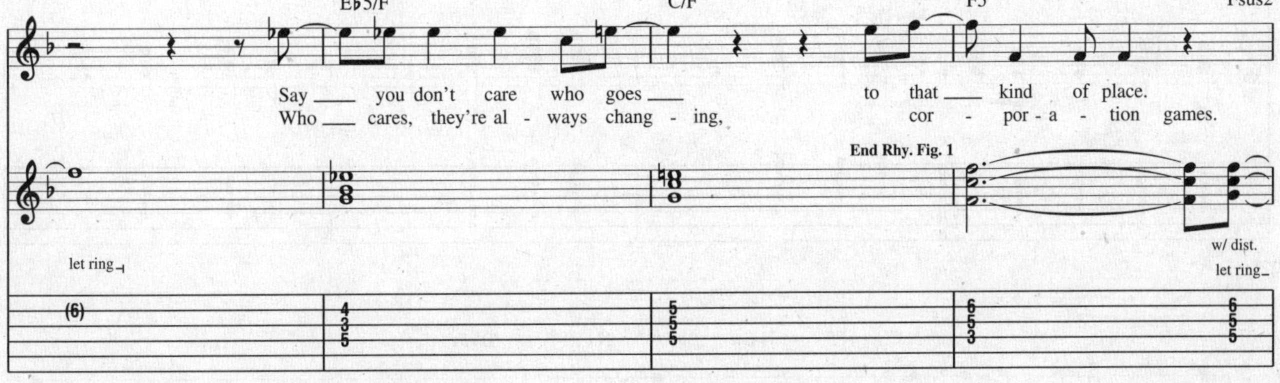

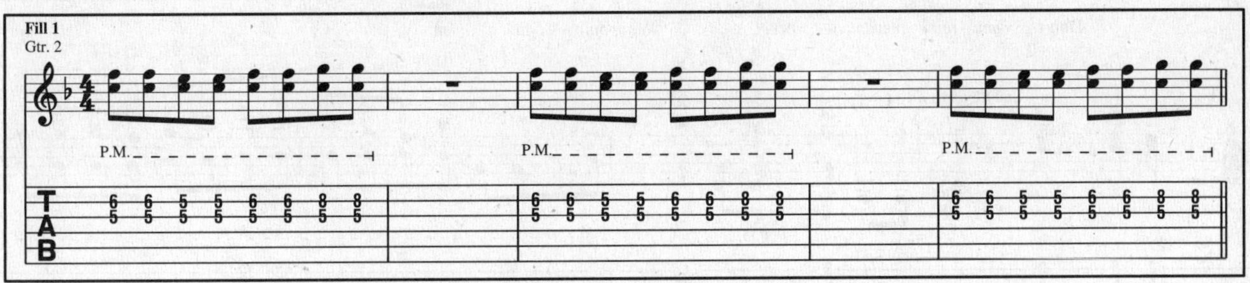

* Gtr. 2 notated to left of slashes.

Chorus
Gtr. 2 tacet
(F) (Bb5) (F) (C/E) (Dm)
built this cit - y on rock and roll.
N.C.
We built this cit - y,
Gtr. 3
P.M.
Bb5 N.C. Bb5 N.C. (F/A) N.C. Bb5 N.C.
we built this cit - y on rock and roll. Built this cit - y,
To Coda
1.
Bb5 N.C. Bb5 N.C. Bb5 N.C. (F/A) C5 F/A Bb5
we built this cit - y on rock and roll.
Interlude
Gtr. 3 tacet
F Bb N.C.
Gtr. 2 tacet
F Bb C/E F
2.
C5 F/A Bb5
2. Some rock and roll.
Gtr. 2
Gtr. 1
divisi
Gtrs. 1 & 3

Interlude
Half-Time Feel
Gtr. 3 tacet
C/B♭
B♭
N.C.
End Half-Time Feel
It's just an -
Gtr. 4 (dist.)
1/2
1/2
full
full
Gtr. 3
Gtr. 2
Gtr. 2 divisi
Bridge
N.C.
Gtr. 4 tacet
C/E
F
N.C.
C/E
F
oth - er Sun - day in a ti - red old street. Po - lice have
Gtr. 4
Gtrs. 2 & 3
*Gtrs. 2 & 3 divisi
P.M.
* composite arrangement
N.C.
C/E
F
N.C.
C/E
F
got the choke - hold. Oh. Then we just lost the beat.
Harm.
Harm.
Harm.
Harm.
Harm.
Harm.
Harm.
P.M.

Verse
Gtr. 3 tacet
C/E F N.C.
Gtr. 3: w/ Rhy. Fig. 1, simile
Fsus2
Gtr. 2: w/ Fill 1
F5
3. Who counts the mon - ey un -
Gtr. 2
Gtr. 3
divisi
Gtr. 4
P.M.
Bb5/F
Eb/F
- der - neath the bar?
Who rides the wreck - ing ball
Rhy. Fig. 3
C/F
Gtr. 3: w/ Rhy. Fill 1
Gtr. 4: w/ Rhy. Fig. 3, 2 1/2 times
F5
in two - part gui - tars?
Don't
End Rhy. Fig. 3
Gtr. 5 (dist.)
Gtr. 6 (dist.) divisi
mf
*P.M.
* P.M. refers to both gtrs.
Gtrs. 5 & 6 tacet
Fsus2
Gtr. 2: w/ Fill 1
F5
Fsus2
Bb5/F
tell us you need us, 'cos we're the ship of fools
Rhy. Fill 1
Gtr. 3

Interlude
Gtr. 3: w/ Rhy. Fig. 2
Eb5/F C/F F5 F C/E Dm Dm
look - ing for A - mer - i - ca, com - ing through your schools.
Gtr. 2
8va
mp
Bb/D F/C C N.C. F5 N.C. Bb5
Don't you re - mem - ber,
*Gtrs. 1 & 3 divisi
P.M.
* composite arrangement
Gtr. 3 tacet
N.C.(F5) (Bb5) N.C. (F5) (Bb5) N.C. F C/E
D.S. al Coda
...mem - ber, ...mem - ber?
Mar -
Gtr. 1 divisi
Coda
C/G F/A Bb/F Bb5 N.C. Bb5 N.C. Bb5 N.C. Bb5 N.C.
rock and roll. Built this cit - y,
(Oo.
We

(F/A)
N.C.
B♭5
N.C.
B♭5 N.C.
B♭5 N.C.
B♭5 N.C.
built this cit - y on rock and roll. Built this cit - y, we
P.M.
(F/A)
C5
F/A
B♭5
built this cit - y on rock and roll.
P.M.
Outro
Gtr. 3 tacet
B♭
C/B♭
F/B♭
C/B♭
B♭
F/B♭
C/B♭
Built this cit - y.
(We built, we built this cit - y. We built, we built this cit - y.
Gtr. 4
w/ bar
Rhy. Fig. 4
w/ fingers
End Rhy. Fig. 4
Gtr. 2
Gtr. 1
divisi
P.M.
Rhy. Fig. 4A
End Rhy. Fig. 4A

Gtrs. 1 & 2: w/ Rhy. Figs. 4 & 4A, till fade
B♭
C/B♭
F/B♭
C/B♭
B♭
We built, we built this cit - y. Built this cit - y. We built, we
1/2
full
w/ bar
Begin Fade
F/B♭
C/B♭
B♭
C/B♭
built this cit - y. We built, we built this cit - y.
8va
F/B♭
C/B♭
B♭
F/B♭
C/E
B♭
C/B♭
Built this cit - y We built, we built this cit - y. We built, we
8va
-1
loco
w/ bar
w/ bar
w/ bar
-1 1/2
Fade Out
F/B♭
C/B♭
B♭
F/B♭
C/B♭
built this cit - y. Built this cit - y. We built, we built this cit - y.)
w/ bar
w/ bar

We're Ready

Words and Music by Tom Scholz

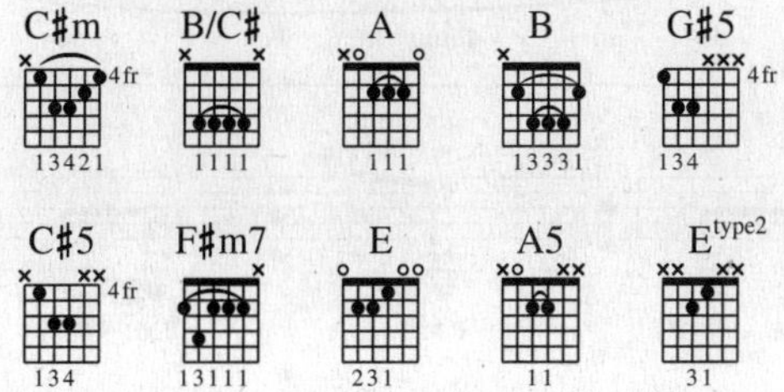

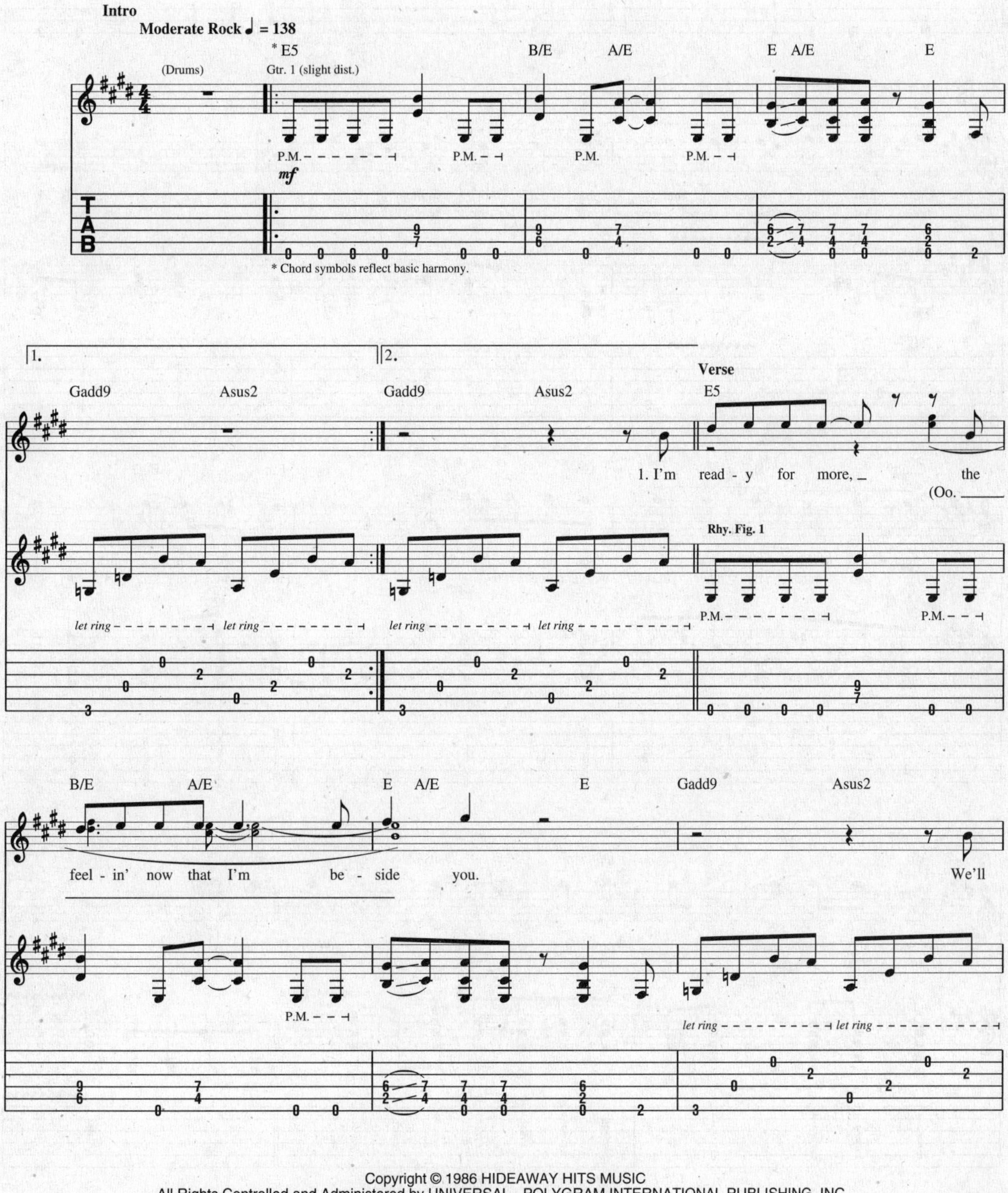

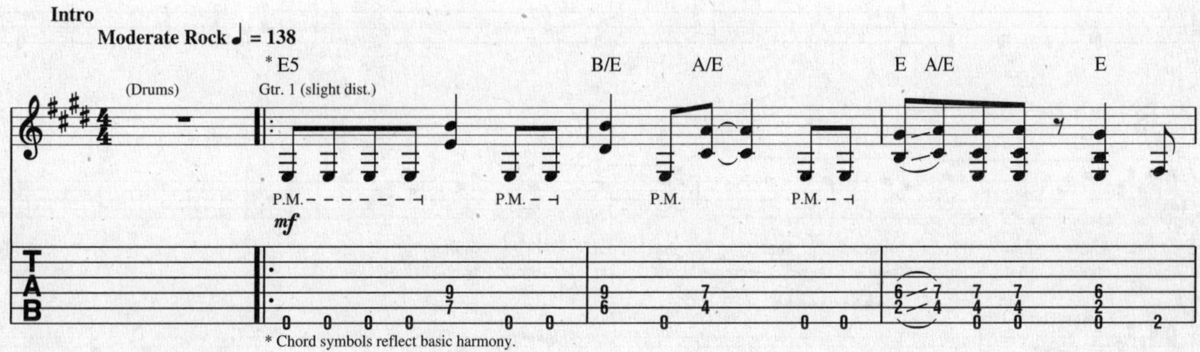

1. 2.

Verse

Gadd9 Asus2 Gadd9 Asus2 E5

1. I'm read - y for more, the

(Oo.

Rhy. Fig. 1

let ring let ring let ring let ring P.M. P.M.

B/E A/E E A/E E Gadd9 Asus2

feel - in' now that I'm be - side you. We'll

P.M. let ring let ring

E5 B/E A/E E A/E E
o - pen the door, do an - y - thing that we de - cide to. And I
Oo.)
Gtr. 1
End Rhy. Fig. 1
P.M.
Gtr. 2 (dist.)
divisi
Rhy. Fill 1
End Rhy. Fill 1
Gtr. 1 tacet
G D5 A
know that there's some - thing that's just out of sight. And I
feel that it's time we were off on our way. We can
Gtr. 2
Rhy. Fig. 2
let ring
Cadd9 D5 G5 Em Em7
feel like I'm fi - nal - ly see - ing the light. Hold - in' on, girl, I
go so much far - ther than we've come to - day. Hold - in' on, girl, and
let ring
mf
Chorus
Am D5 Dsus4 D E5 A5
know it's right, I know it's right. We're read - y!
come what may, come what may, we're read - y!
End Rhy. Fig. 2
let ring
P.M.
f

To Coda
Verse
Gtr. 1: w/ Rhy. Fig. 1
E5 B5 A5 E A5 E5 B5 E5
Hey! Yeah!
2. You and I,
(Oo.
P.M.
Gtr. 2 tacet
B/E A/E E A/E E Gadd9 Asus2
oo, will find a rea - son to
Gtr. 2: w/ Rhy. Fill 1
D.S. al Coda
E5 B/E A/E E A/E E
sim - pli - fy a change of sea - son. And I
sim - pli - fy a change of sea - son.)
Coda
E5 B5 A5 Esus4 E A5 E5 B5 A5
We're read - y. We're
Gtr. 2
E A5 E5 B5/E
Guitar Solo
C♯m
Rhy. Fig. 3
read - y. We're read - y. Come on!
Yeah!
Gtr. 3 (dist.)
Gtr. 2 divisi
Gtr. 3
(Gtr. 2 cont. in slashes)
1/2

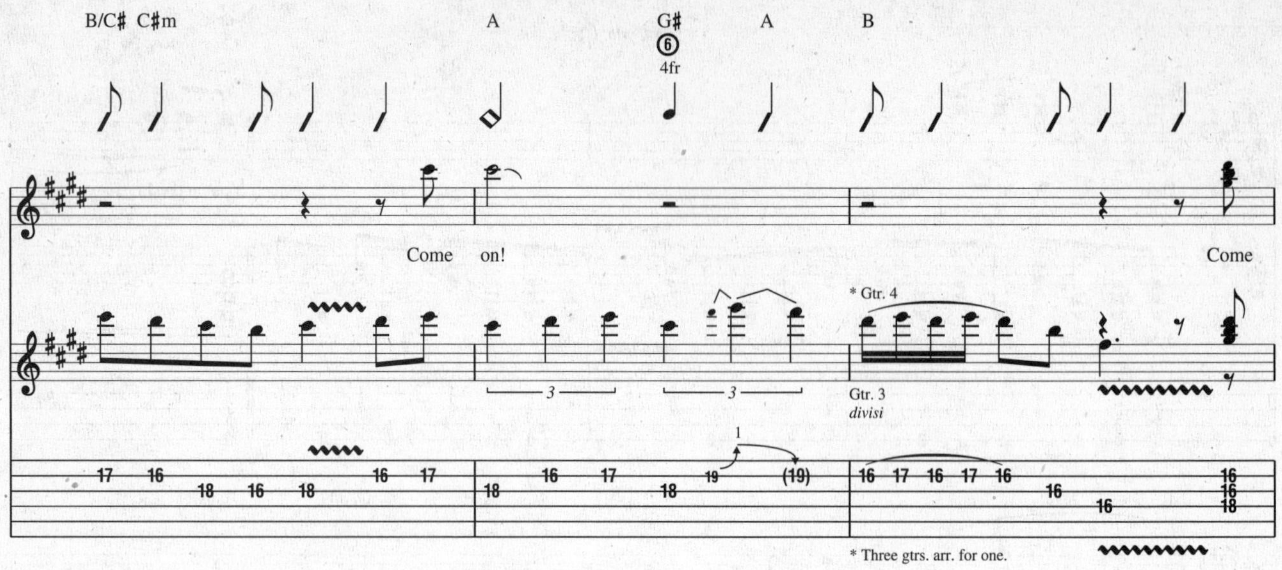

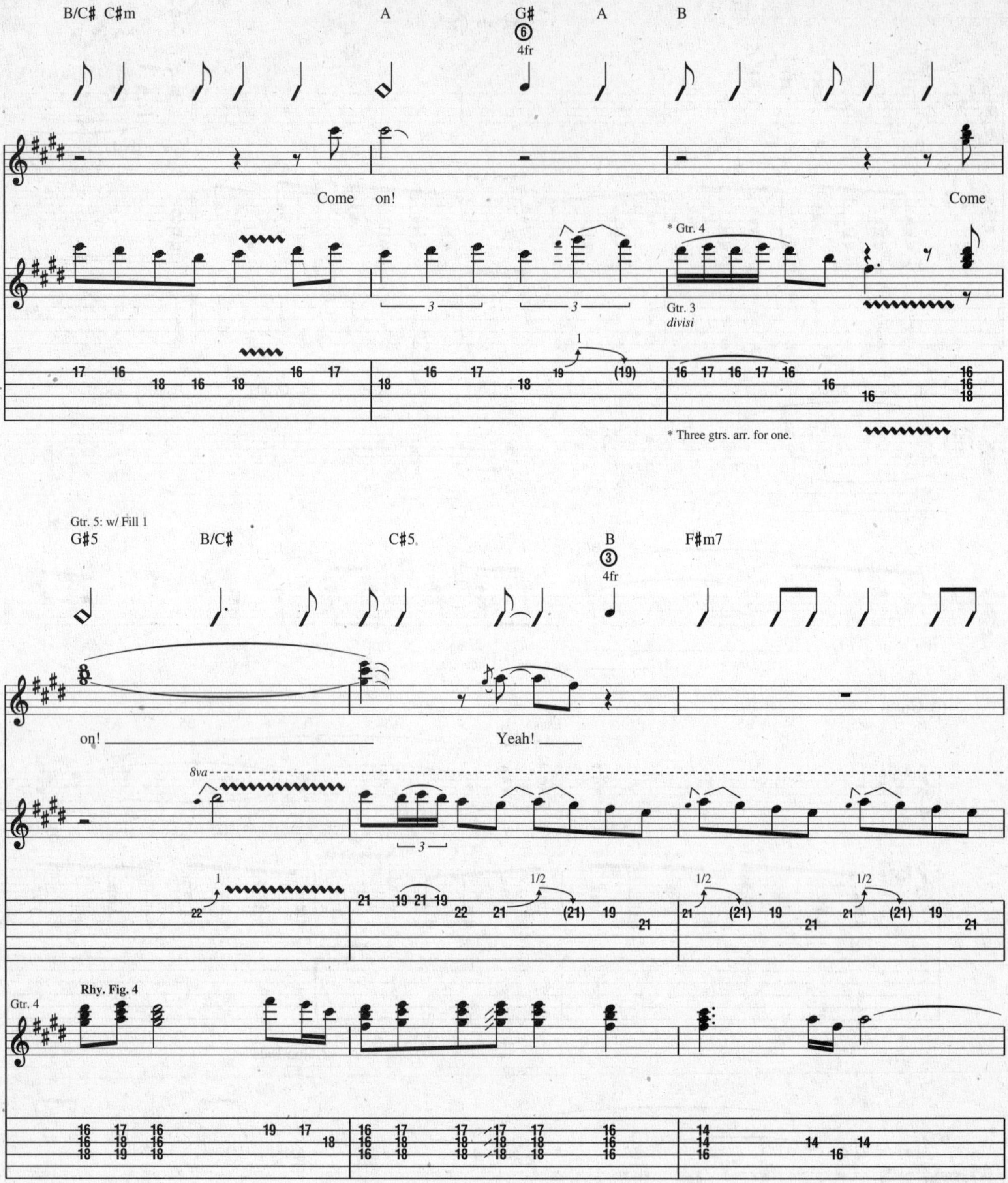

Gtr. 5: w/ Fill 1

G♯5 B/C♯ C♯5 B F♯m7

3

4fr

on! Yeah!

8va

Gtr. 4

Rhy. Fig. 4

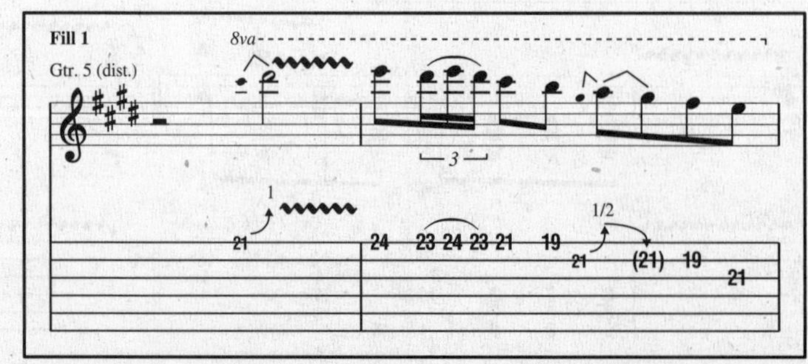

E
B
F#
A
B
We can
8va
Gtr. 5
Gtr. 3
divisi
Gtr. 4
End Rhy. Fig. 4
Gtrs. 3, 4 & 5 tacet
A5
Gtr. 2 tacet
Asus2
End Rhy. Fig. 3
find a way.
Gtr. 6 (clean)
let ring throughout
(cont. in slashes)
Etype2
Gtr. 6
Gtr. 6 tacet
B/E
A/E
E
A/E
E
A5
A/B
3. We're
Gtr. 1
P.M.
let ring
let ring

Verse
Gtr. 1: w/ Rhy. Fig. 1
E5 B/E A/E E A/E E Gadd9 Asus2
read - y now, catch - in' a wave to ride on.
(Oo.
Gtr. 2: w/ Rhy. Fill 1
Gtr. 2: w/ Rhy. Fig. 2
E5 B/E A/E E A/E E G D
Stead - y now, head - in' where we de - cide on. And I know that there's some - thing that's
Oo.)
A Cadd9 D G
just out of sight. And I feel like we're try - in' to do some - thing right.
Em Em7 Am D5 Dsus4 D
Come on, make it if we hold on tight, hold on tight. We're
Chorus
E5 A5 E5 B5 A5 E A5 E5 B5
read - y! Yeah, yeah! We're
Gtr. 2
P.M.
E5 A5 E5 B5 A5 E A5 E5 B5 D
read - y! Yeah, yeah! We're read - y! Hoo, hoo. We're
P.M.

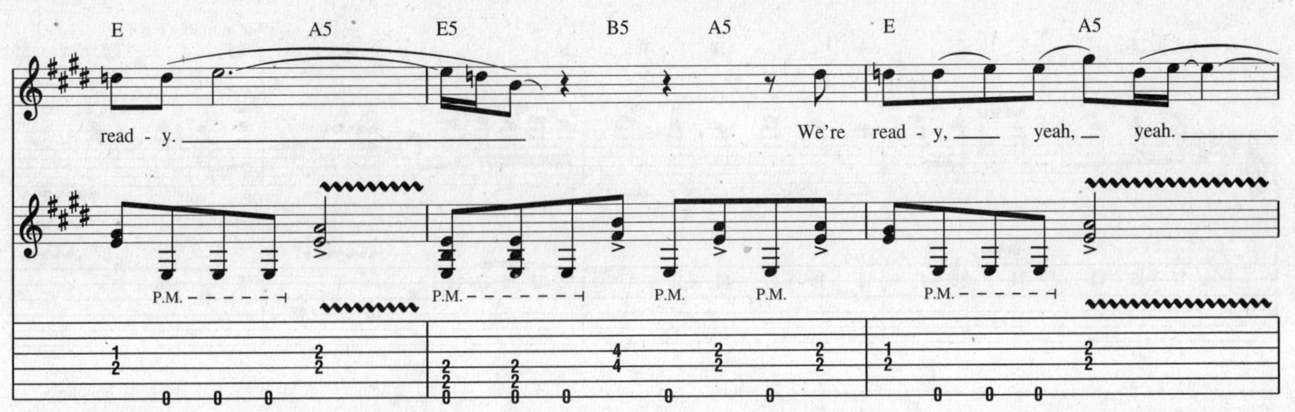
E
A5
E5
B5
A5
E
A5
read - y.
We're read - y,
yeah,
yeah.
P.M.
P.M.
P.M.

Gtr. 3: w/ Fill 2
E
B5
E
A5
E5
B5
A5
We're read - y,
hey,
yeah!
We're
P.M.
P.M.
P.M.

Guitar Solo

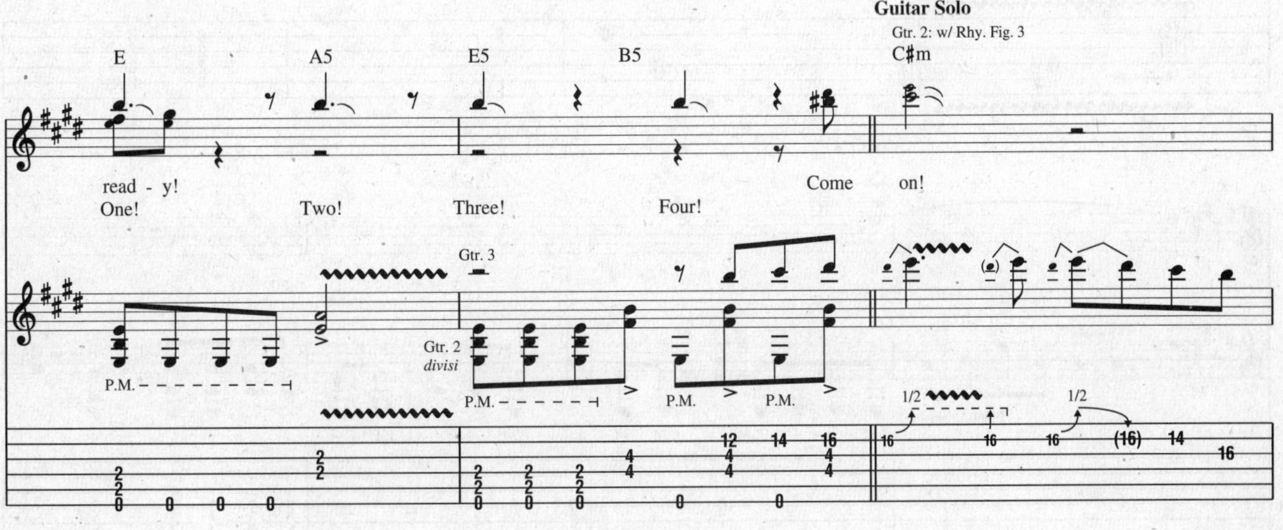
Gtr. 2: w/ Rhy. Fig. 3
E
A5
E5
B5
C♯m
read - y!
One!
Two!
Three!
Four!
Come on!
Gtr. 3
Gtr. 2
divisi
P.M.
1/2

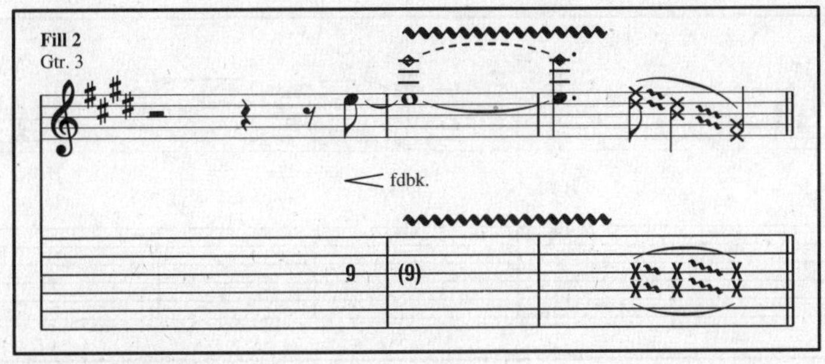
Fill 2
Gtr. 3
fdbk.

Gtr. 4: w/ Rhy. Fig. 4
B/C♯ C♯m
A
G♯
A
B
G♯5
F♯5/G♯
G♯5
8va
Gtr. 5
Gtr. 3
divisi
B/C♯ C♯5
F♯m7
E
B
F♯
Gtrs. 3 & 5 tacet
Gtr. 3: w/ Fill 3
A
B
A5
Asus2
We can find a way.
Gtr. 6
E type2
Gtr. 6 tacet
B/E
A/E
E
A/E
E
Gtr. 1
(cont. in slashes)
P.M.
Fill 3
Gtr. 3
Harm.
fdbk.
pitch: B

A5 A/B E5 B/E A/E E A/E E
We're read - y now, oo, we're read - y now.
P.M. P.M. P.M. P.M.
let ring let ring
Free time
Gtr. 1 tacet
Gadd9 Asus4 E5 B/E A/E Aadd9
rit.
We're read - y now, oo.
Gtr. 1
Gtr. 6
Gtr. 6
divisi
P.M. rit. P.M.
let ring let ring
Begin fade
Fade out

What's My Age Again?

Words and Music by Tom De Longe and Mark Hoppus

B5 F#5 C#5 D#5 B5
and are still more a - mused by T - V shows. What the hell is A. D. D.? My
and you still act like you're in fresh - man year. What the hell is wrong with me? My
To Coda
Gtr. 1: w/ Riff A
F#5 C#5 D#5 C#5 Bmaj7 F#
friends say I should act my age. What's my age a - gain? What's my age a - gain?
friends say I should act my age.
End Rhy. Fig. 1
Verse
F#/C# D#m B5 F#5 C#5 D#5 B5 F#5
2. Then la - ter on, on the drive home, I called her mom
P.M.
C#5 D#5 B5 F#5 C#5 D#5
from a pay phone. I said I was the cops, and your hus - band's in jail.
P.M.

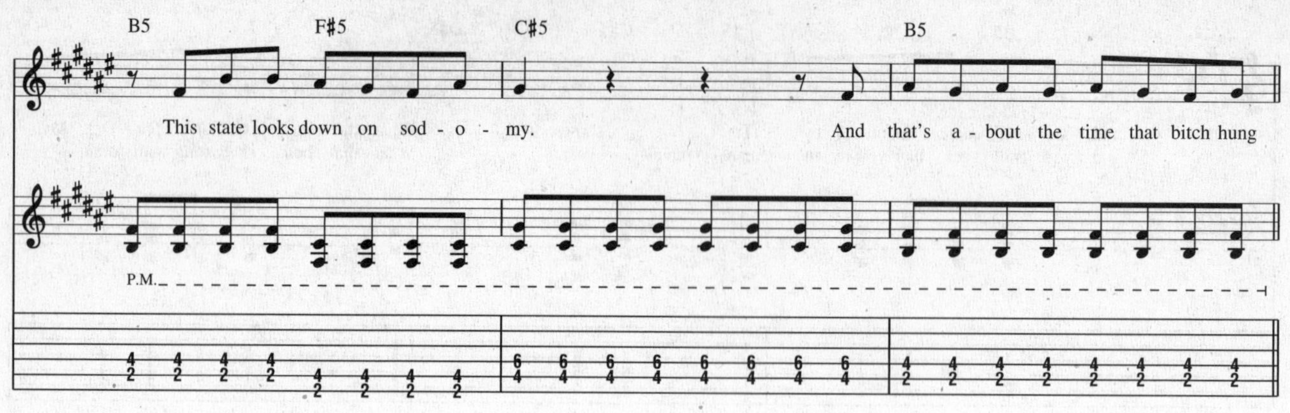

Chorus

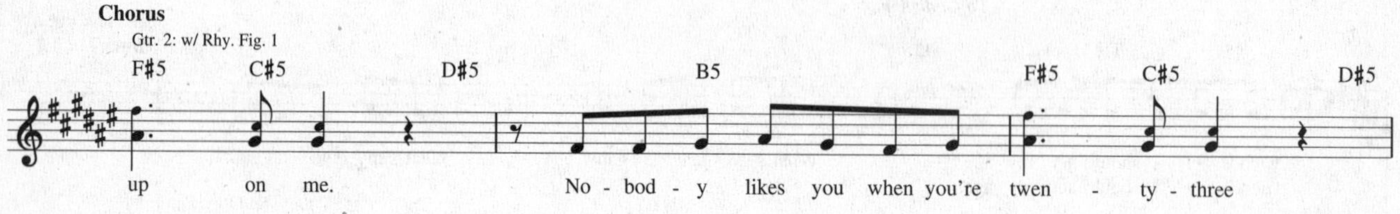

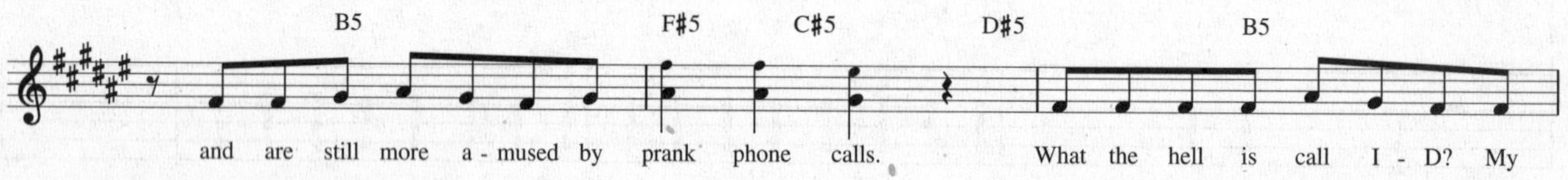

Interlude

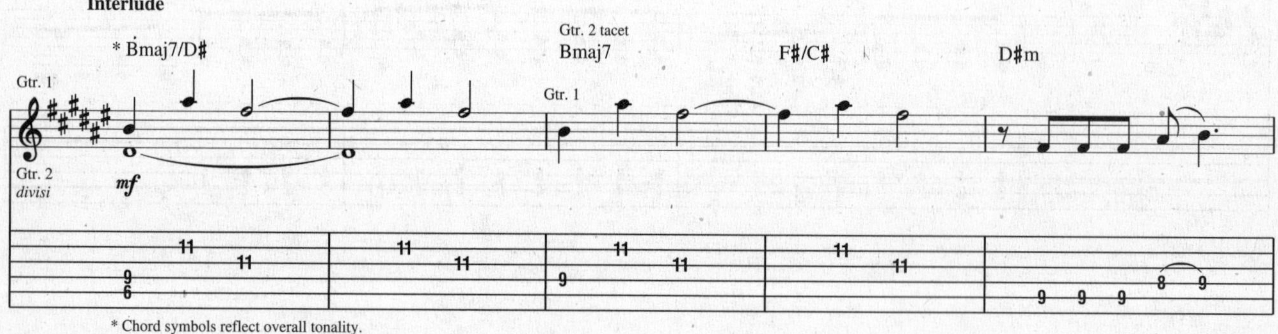

* Chord symbols reflect overall tonality.

F#/C# Bmaj7 F#/C# D#m

F#/C#
Bmaj7
F#/C#
D#m

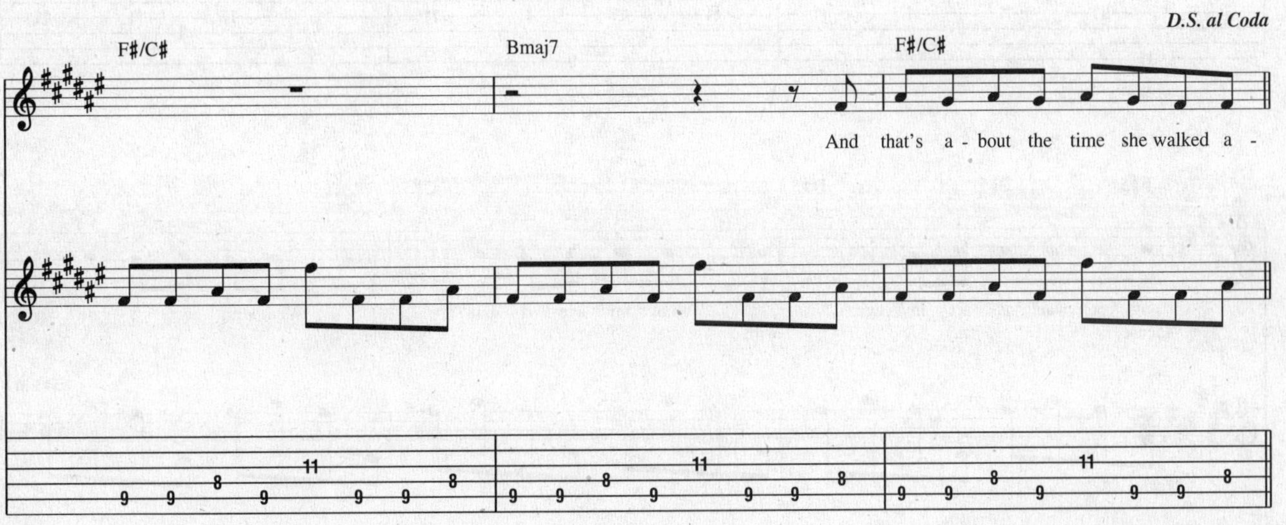
D.S. al Coda
F#/C#
Bmaj7
F#/C#
And that's a - bout the time she walked a -

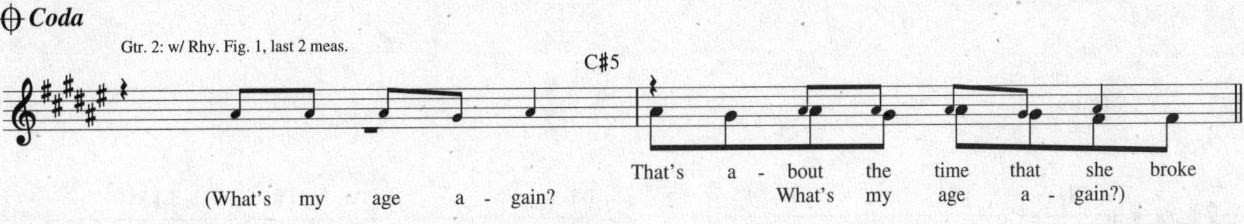
Coda
Gtr. 2: w/ Rhy. Fig. 1, last 2 meas.
C#5
That's a - bout the time that she broke
(What's my age a - gain? What's my age a - gain?)

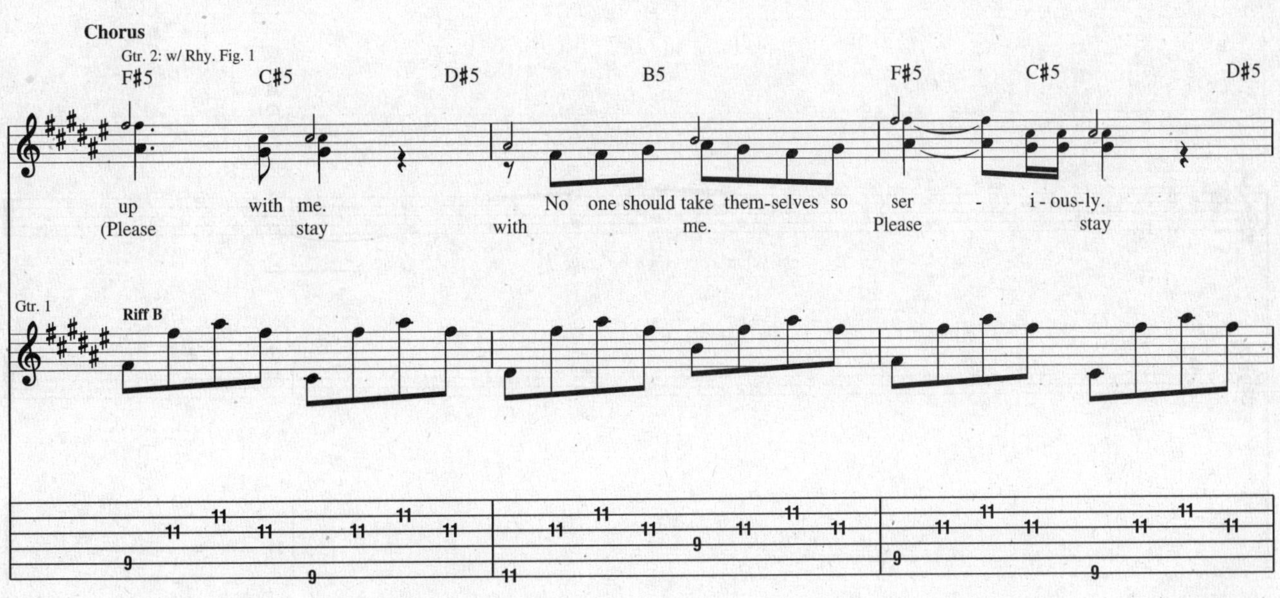
Chorus
Gtr. 2: w/ Rhy. Fig. 1
F#5
C#5
D#5
B5
F#5
C#5
D#5
up with me. No one should take them-selves so ser - i - ous-ly.
(Please stay with me. Please stay
Gtr. 1
Riff B

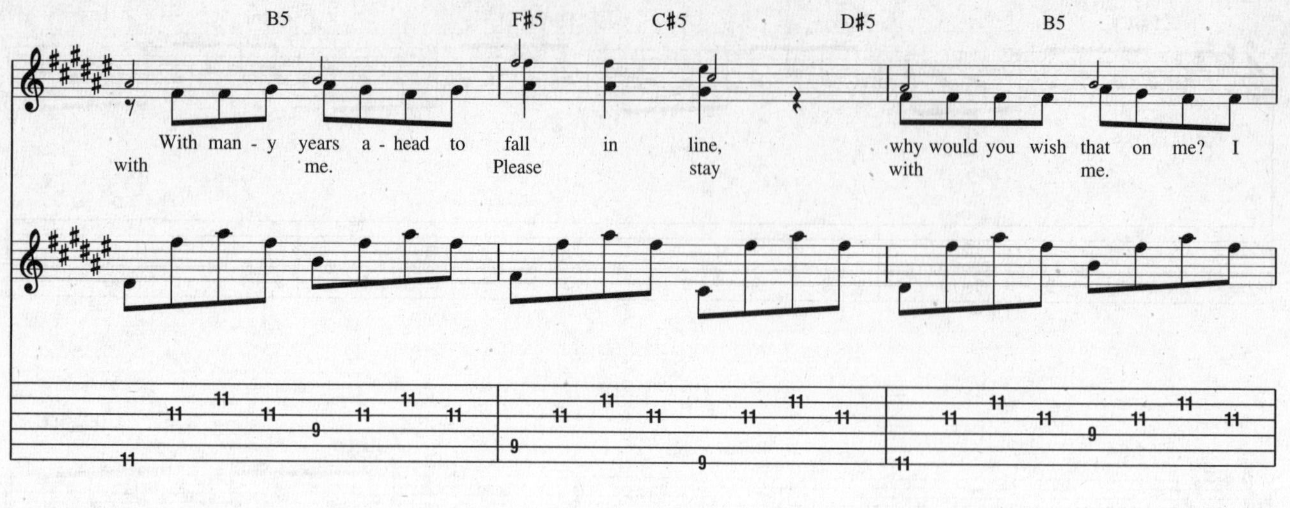

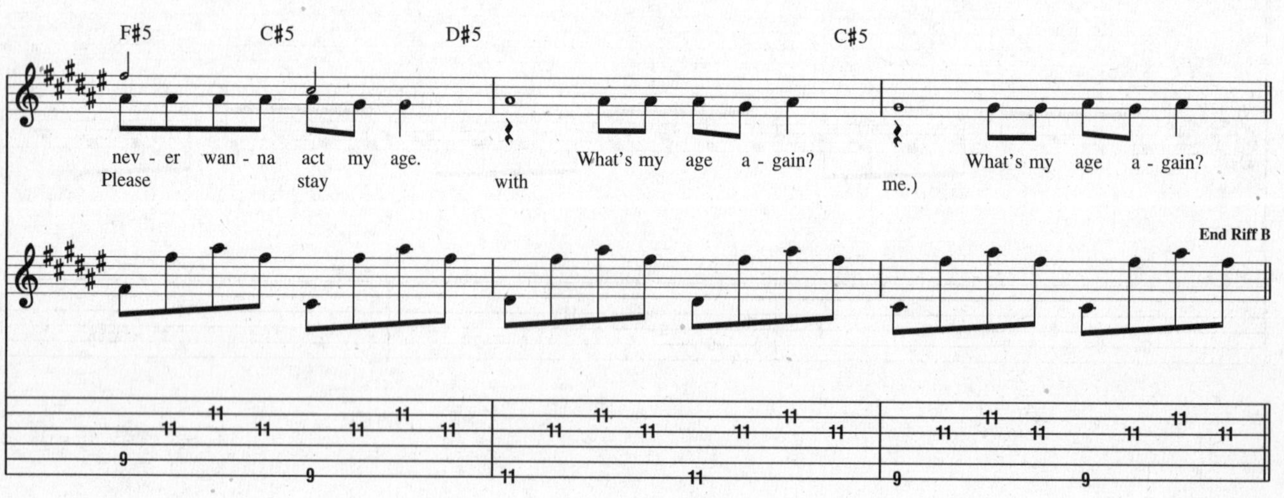

Outro

Gtr. 1: w/ Riff B
Gtr. 2: w/ Rhy. Fig. 1

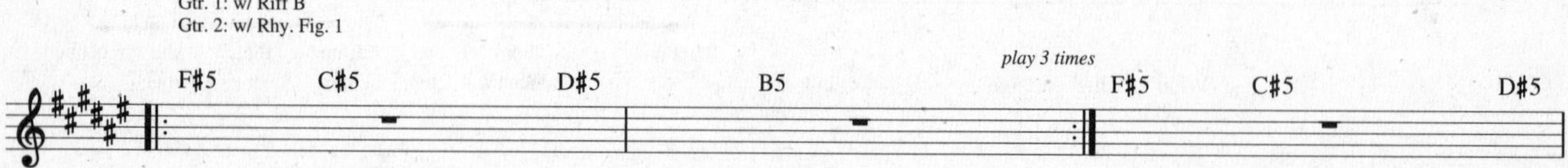

Whip It

Words and Music by Mark Mothersbaugh and Gerald Casale

Gtr. 2: w/ Riff D (2 times)

E5 D5 A5 E5 D5 A5

cream sits out too long, you ___ must whip it. When some-thing's go - ing wrong you ___ must whip it.

Chorus

C5 G5 D5 C5

Spoken: Now whip it in - to shape. Shape it up. Get straight.

Rhy. Fig. 1

Gtr. 3 *8va*

End Rhy. Fig. 1

19 19 19 19 19 19 19 19 19 19 19 19 19 19 19 19
17 18 17 18 17 18 17 18 17 18 17 18 17 18 17 18

Gtrs. 1 & 2

Riff E

End Riff E

P.M. P.M. P.M. P.M. P.M.

5 5 3 | 5 5 3 | 7 7 5 3 | 5 5 3

Gtrs. 1 & 2: w/ Riff E

Gtr. 3: w/ Rhy. Fig. 1 (1 1/2 times)

G5 D5

Go for - ward. Move a - head. Try to de - tect it.

To Coda 𝄌

C5

It's not too late to whip it. Whip it good.

Gtrs. 1 & 2

Rhy. Fill 1

End Rhy. Fill 1

P.M. P.M.

5 5 3 | 5 5 3 15

Verse

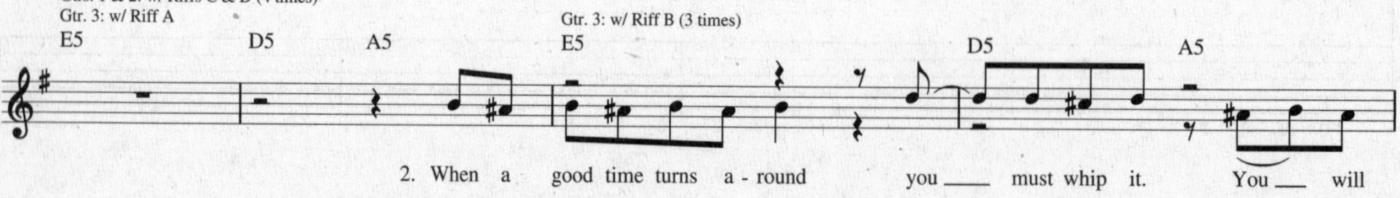

E5
D5
A5
E5
D5
A5
nev - er live it down un - less you whip it. No one gets a - way un - til they whip it.
Bridge
Gtr. 3 tacet
E5
G5
C5
E5
G5
1.
D5
Spoken: I say whip it.
Whip it good.
Gtrs. 1 & 2
2.
Interlude
D.S. al Coda
D5
E5
Gtrs. 1 & 2: w/ Riff F (7 times)
Play 6 times
Whip it good.
Gtr. 3
Riff F
End Riff F
P.M.
Coda
Gtrs. 1 & 2: w/ Riff E (2 times)
Gtr. 3: w/ Rhy. Fig. 1 (2 1/2 times)
G5
D5
C5
to whip it in - to shape. Shape it up. Get straight. Go for - ward.
G5
D5
C5
Gtrs. 1 & 2: w/ Rhy. Fill 1
Move a - head. Try to de - tect it. It's not too late to whip it. Whip it good.
Outro
Gtr. 3: w/ Riff A
E5
Gtrs. 1 & 2
Gtr. 1
Gtr. 2
divisi
D5
A5
Gtrs. 1 & 2
Gtr. 3: w/ Riff B (1st. meas.)
E5
P.M.
P.M.
P.M.

White Rabbit

Words and Music by Grace Slick

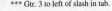

* Two gtrs. arr. for one through the remainder of the song.
** 1st time only.
*** Gtr. 3 to left of slash in tab.

1.
G
A
an - y - thing at all. Go ask Al - ice.
giv - en you the call. And call
mf
C
D
A
when she's ten feet tall.
2. And if
let ring
2.
A
C
D
A
Al - ice when she was just small.
Bridge
E
Gtr. 4 (clean)
mp
When the men on the chess board get up and

A
E[VII]
tell you where to go.
And you have just had some kind of
A
mush-room and your mind is mov-ing low.
3. Go ask
Verse
F#5
Al - ice.
I think she'll know.

When log - ic and pro - por - tion have
G5
F#5
fal - len us all be dead. And the white knight is talk - ing
G5
back - wards and the red queen's off with her head. Re -
(cont. in notation)

Chorus
A
C
D
A
mem - ber
what the dor - mouse
said,
Gtr. 3
let ring throughout
Gtr. 4
E
A
E
"Feed your
head.
Feed your
A
head."

White Wedding

Words and Music by Billy Idol

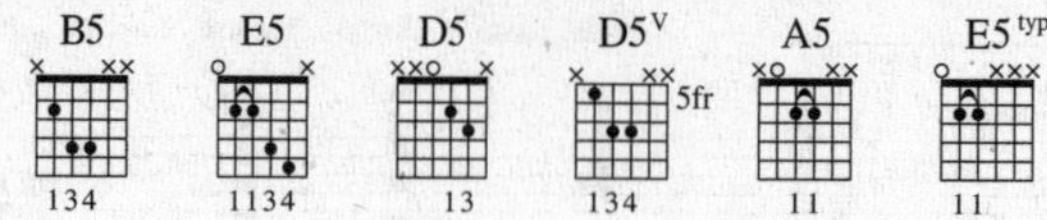

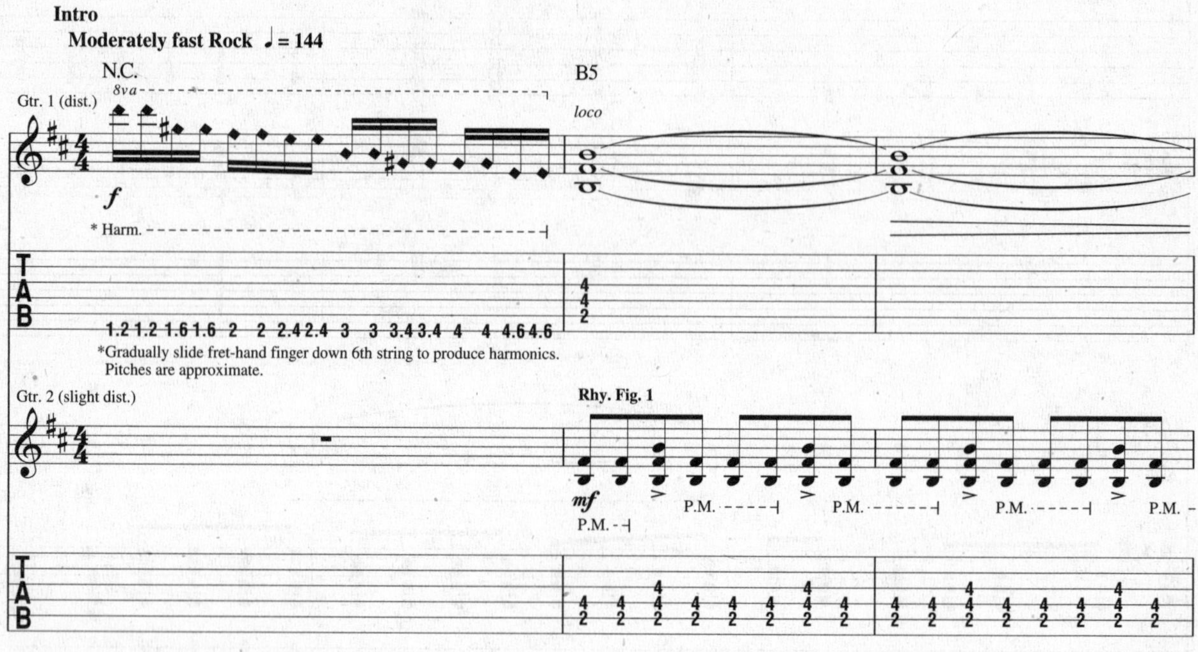

B5

E5

Rhy. Fig. 2

Gtr. 1

Gtr. 3 (clean)

f

(cont. in slashes)

f

w/ chorus

let ring

Rhy. Fig. 2B

Gtr. 4 (dist.)

Gtr. 2

End Rhy. Fig. 1

Rhy. Fig. 2A

P.M.

D5
B5
let ring
mf
P.M.
D5
E5
B5
Gtr. 2: w/ Rhy. Fig. 1
End Rhy. Fig. 2
Rhy. Fig. 2B
fdbk.
End Rhy. Fig. 2A
P.M.

Verse
Gtrs. 1 & 3 tacet
2nd & 3rd times, Gtr. 5: w/ Riff A (7 times)
Gtr. 4 tacet
B5
Gtr. 1
dim.
1. Hey, lit - tle sis - ter, what have you done?
2. Hey, lit - tle sis - ter, who is it you're with?
3. Hey, lit - tle sis - ter, what have you done?
Rhy. Fig. 3
Gtr. 3
Gtr. 2
dim.
P.M.

2nd & 3rd times, Bkgd. Voc: w/ Voc. Fill 1
A5
E5
Gtr. 2: w/ Rhy. Fig. 3
B5
Oh.
Hey, lit - tle sis - ter, who's
Hey, lit - tle sis - ter, what's
Hey, lit - tle sis - ter, who's
End Rhy. Fig. 3
P.M.

Riff A
Gtr. 5 (dist.)
f

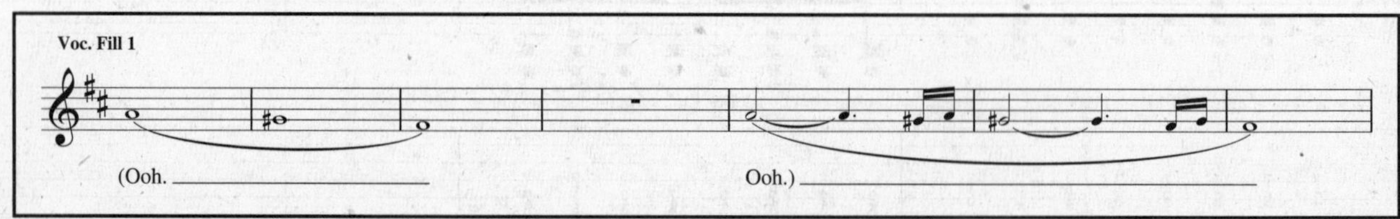
Voc. Fill 1
(Ooh.
Ooh.)

3rd time, Bkgd. Voc.: w/ Voc. Fill 2

A5 E5

— the on - ly one? —
— your fas - ci - na(tion)? —
— the on - ly one? —

3rd time, Bkgd. Voc.: w/ Voc. Fill 3

B5 A5

Hey, lit - tle sis - ter, who's — your su - per - man? Hey, lit - tle sis - ter, who's —
Hey, lit - tle sis - ter, shot - gun, oh, — yeah. Hey, lit - tle sis - ter, who's —
I've been a - way for so — long. I've been a - way for so —

Gtr. 2

P.M.

4	4	4	4	4	4	4	4	4	4	4	4	4	4	4	4	2	2	2	2	2	2	2	2
2	2	2	2	2	2	2	2	2	2	2	2	2	2	2	2	0	0	0	0	0	0	0	0

B5

— the one — you want? Hey, lit - tle sis - ter, shot - gun!
— your su - per - man? Hey, lit - tle sis - ter, shot - gun! It's a
— long. I let you go for so — long.

P.M.

2	2	2	2	2	2	2	2	4	4	4	4	4	4	4	4	4	4	4	4	4	4	4	4
0	0	0	0	0	0	0	0	2	2	2	2	2	2	2	2	2	2	2	2	2	2	2	2

Voc. Fill 2

(On - ly one, on - ly one, on - ly one, on - ly one.)

Chorus
2nd & 3rd times, Gtr. 5: w/ Riff A (4 times)
A5
E5 type2
B5
Gtr. 1
nice day to start a - gain. It's a
Gtr. 2
Rhy. Fig. 4
End Rhy. Fig. 4
P.M.
To Coda
E5 type2
D5
B5
nice day for a white wed - ding. It's a
P.M.
1.
E5
D5
Rhy. Fig. 5
End Rhy. Fig. 5
Gtr. 1
dim.
nice day to start a - gain.
Gtr. 3
Rhy. Fig. 6
End Rhy. Fig. 6
dim.
Gtr. 2
Rhy. Fig. 5A
End Rhy. Fig. 5A
P.M.
P.M.

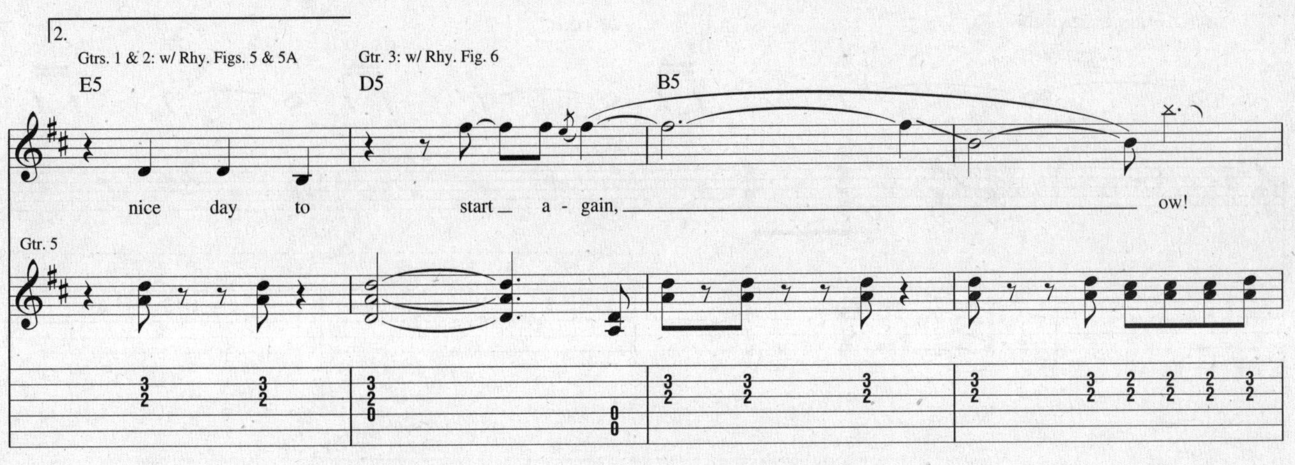
2.
Gtrs. 1 & 2: w/ Rhy. Figs. 5 & 5A
Gtr. 3: w/ Rhy. Fig. 6
E5
D5
B5
nice day to start a - gain, ow!
Gtr. 5

Gtr. 2: w/ Rhy. Fig. 1 (1st 2 meas.)
Interlude
Gtrs. 1, 2 & 4: w/ Rhy. Figs. 2, 2A & 2B
Gtr. 5 tacet
B5
Riff B
E5
End Riff B
Gtr. 3
let ring

D5
B5
let ring
D5
E5
B5

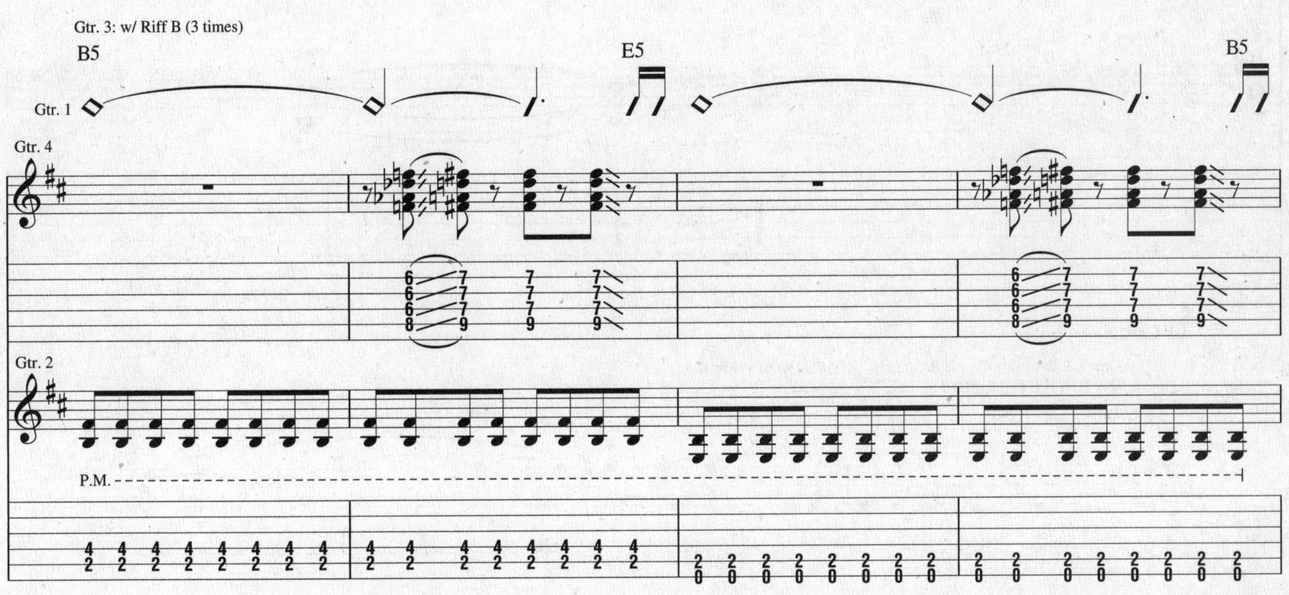
Gtr. 3: w/ Riff B (3 times)
B5
E5
B5
Gtr. 1
Gtr. 4
Gtr. 2
P.M.

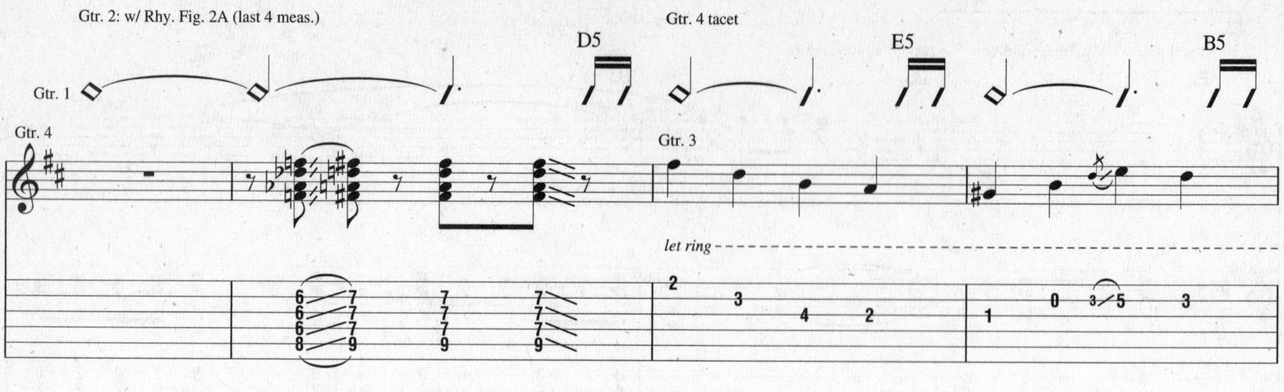
Gtr. 2: w/ Rhy. Fig. 2A (last 4 meas.)
Gtr. 4 tacet
D5
E5
B5
Gtr. 1
Gtr. 4
Gtr. 3
let ring

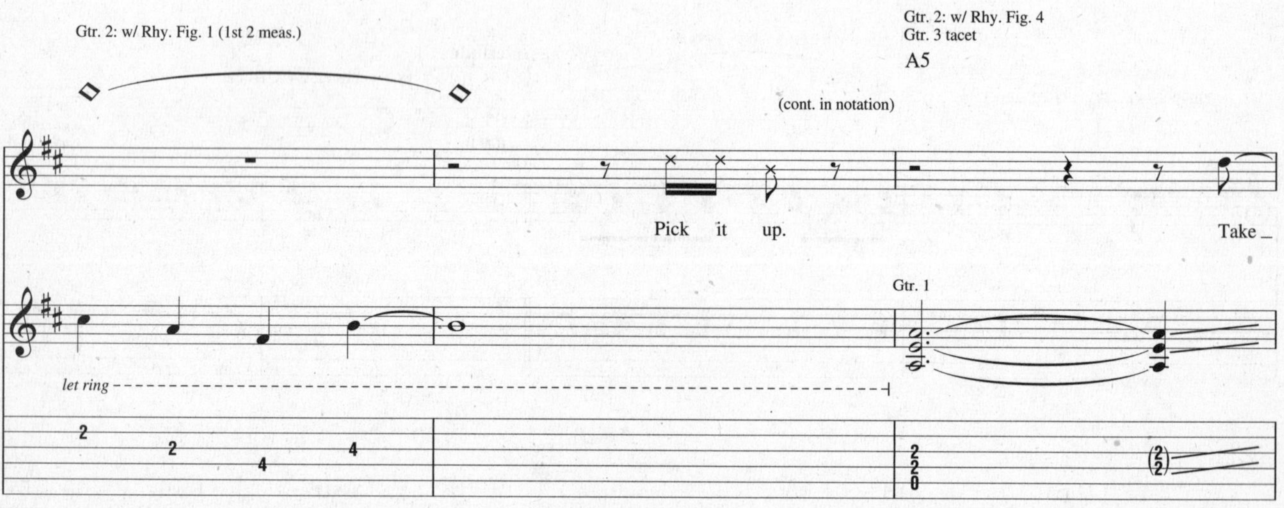
Gtr. 2: w/ Rhy. Fig. 1 (1st 2 meas.)
Gtr. 2: w/ Rhy. Fig. 4
Gtr. 3 tacet
A5
(cont. in notation)
Pick it up.
Take
let ring
Gtr. 1

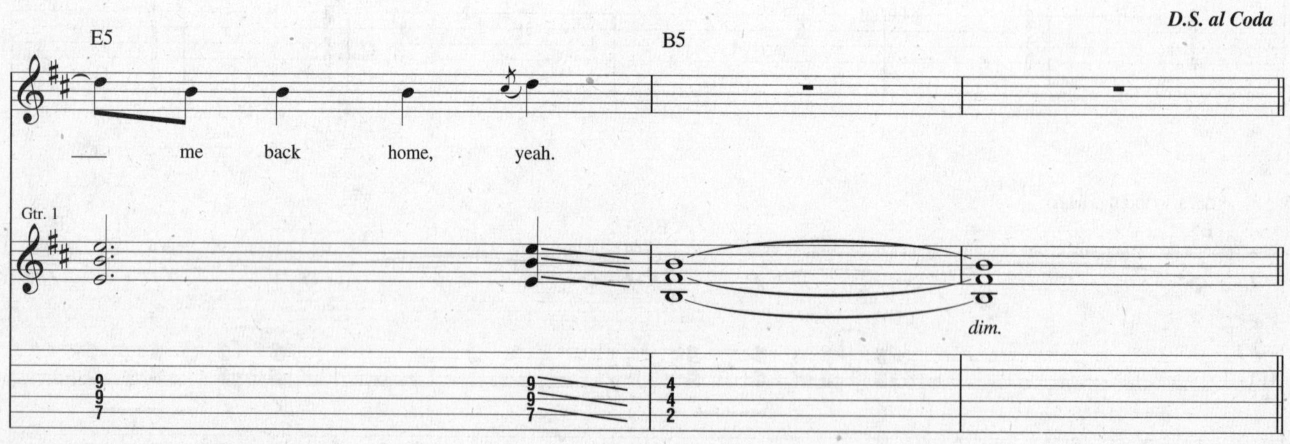
D.S. al Coda
E5
B5
me back home, yeah.
Gtr. 1
dim.

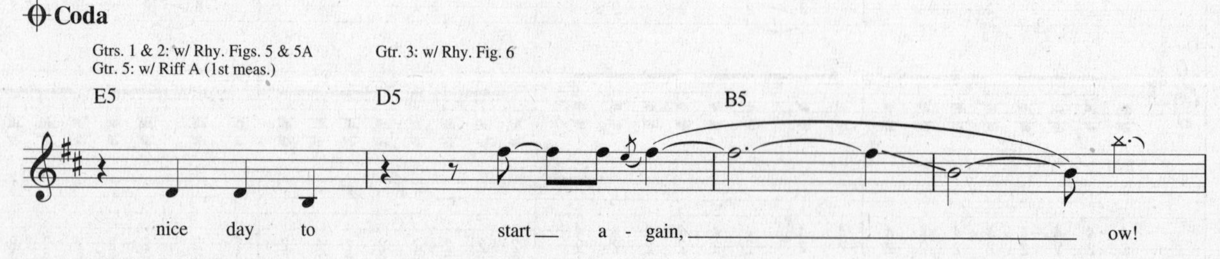
Coda
Gtrs. 1 & 2: w/ Rhy. Figs. 5 & 5A
Gtr. 5: w/ Riff A (1st meas.)
Gtr. 3: w/ Rhy. Fig. 6
E5
D5
B5
nice day to start a - gain, ow!

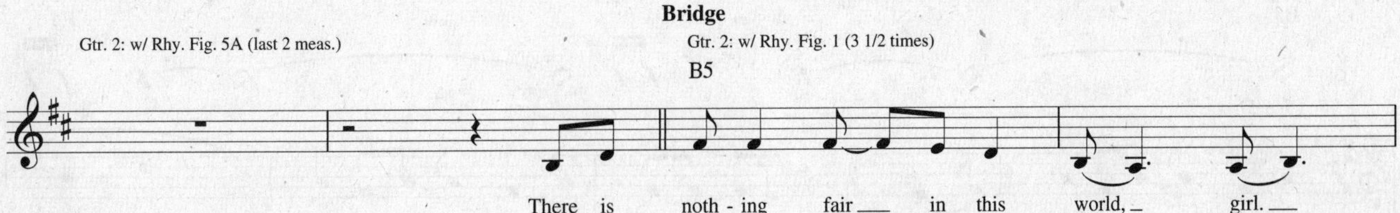
Bridge
Gtr. 2: w/ Rhy. Fig. 5A (last 2 meas.)
Gtr. 2: w/ Rhy. Fig. 1 (3 1/2 times)
B5
There is noth - ing fair in this world, girl.

Bm
There is noth - ing safe in this world.
Gtr. 6 (dist.)
mf
1
1/2
*Vol. swell
Gtr. 3
mf

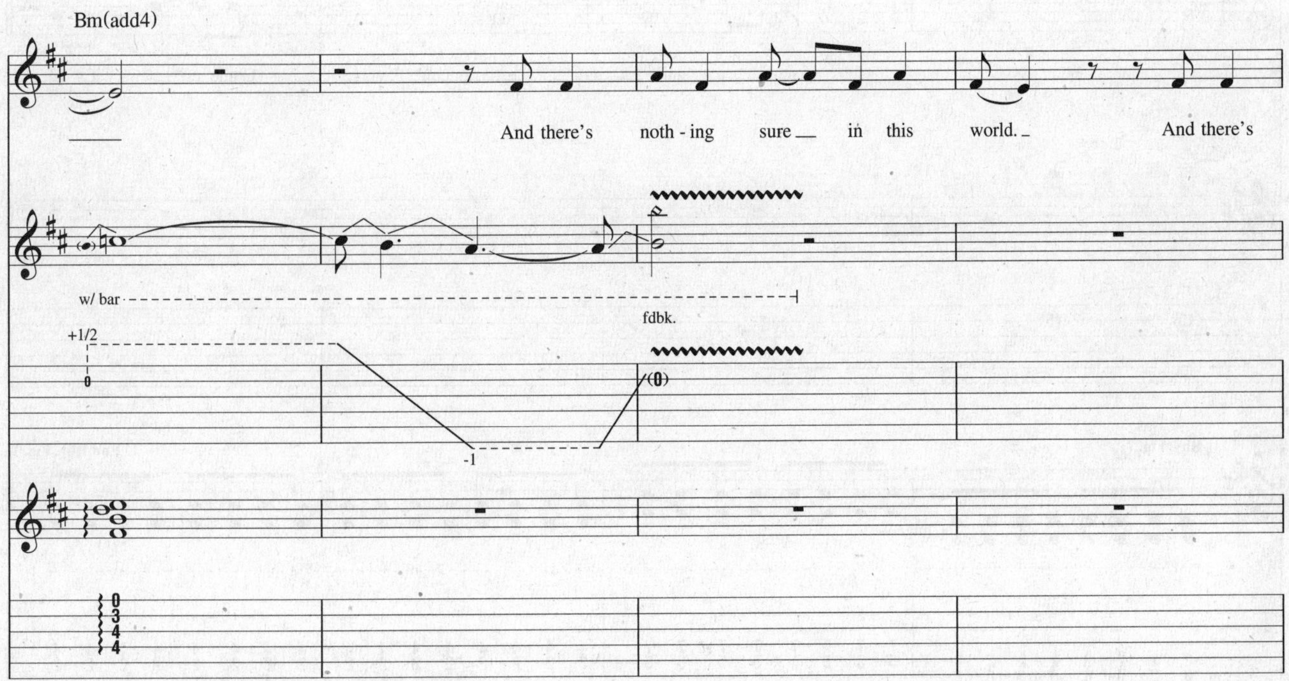
Bm(add4)
And there's noth - ing sure in this world. And there's
w/ bar
fdbk.
+1/2
-1

B5 E5

Gtr. 1

f

noth - ing pure __ in this world. __ And if __ there's some - thing left __ in this world, ______

Gtr. 6

w/ bar

Gtr. 3

Gtr. 3 tacet
Gtr. 5: w/ Riff A (2 times)

D5 Gtr. 6 tacet B5 D5

__ start __ a - gain. ______ Come on, __ it's a __

Gtr. 6

Gtr. 2

Rhy. Fig. 7 End Rhy. Fig. 7

P.M.

Outro-Chorus

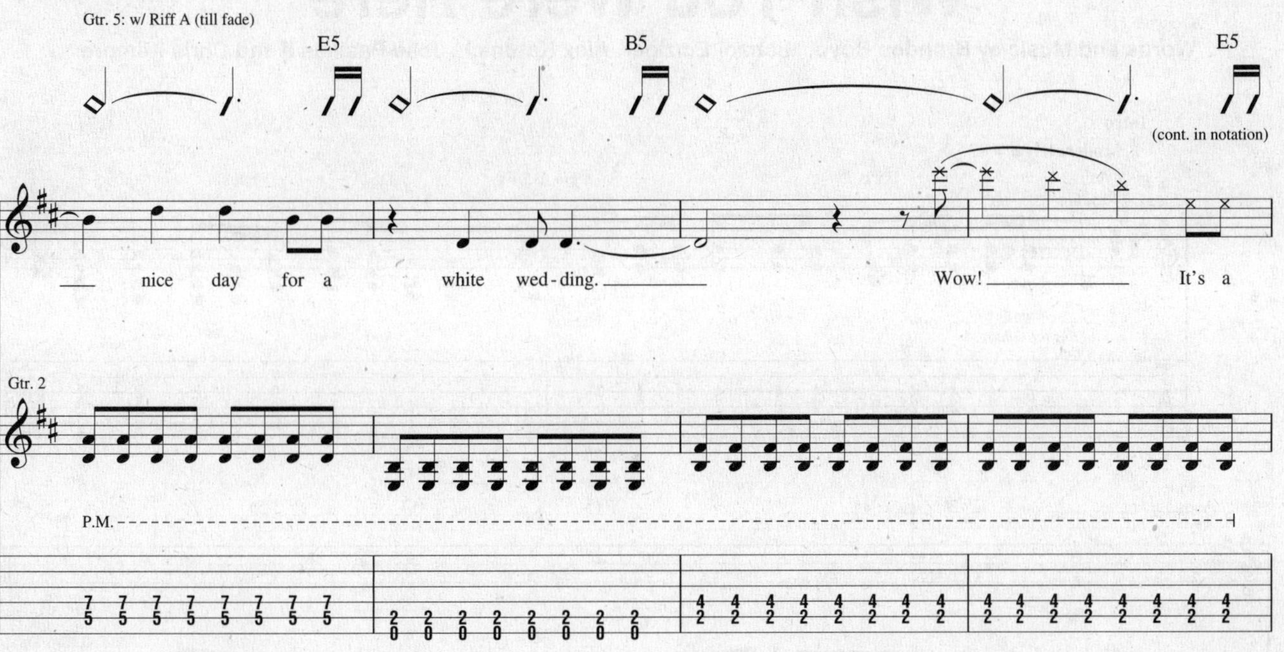

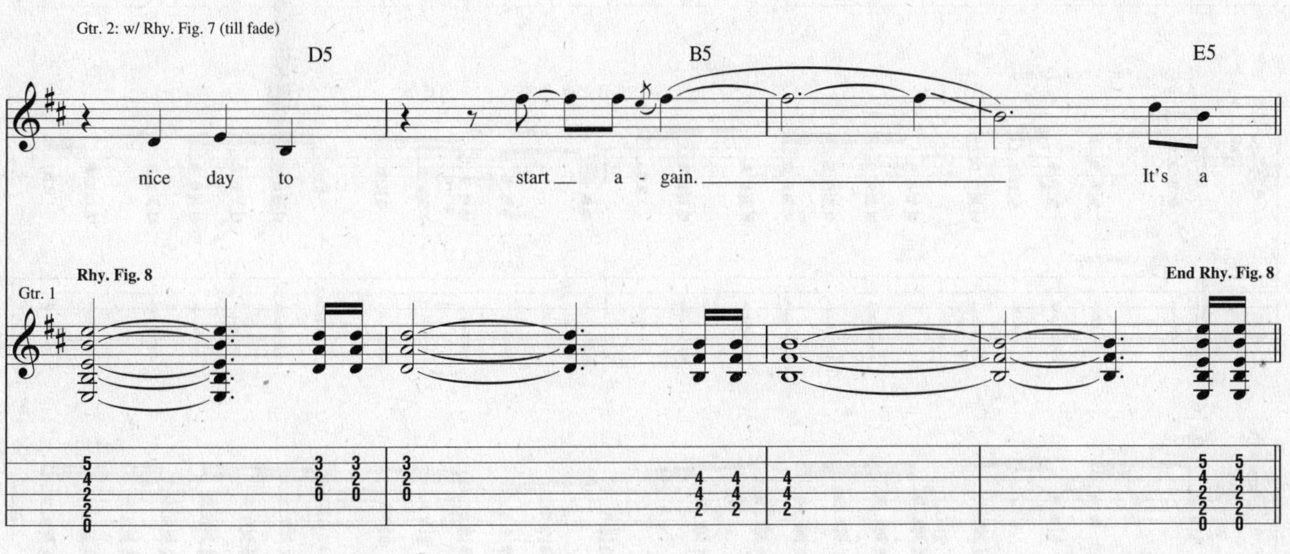

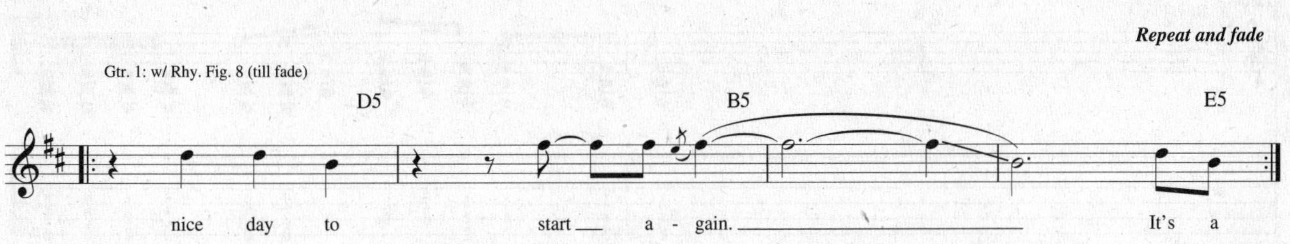

Wish You Were Here

Words and Music by Brandon Boyd, Michael Einziger, Alex Katunich, Jose Pasillas II and Chris Kilmore

*Chord symbols reflect overall harmony.

Verse

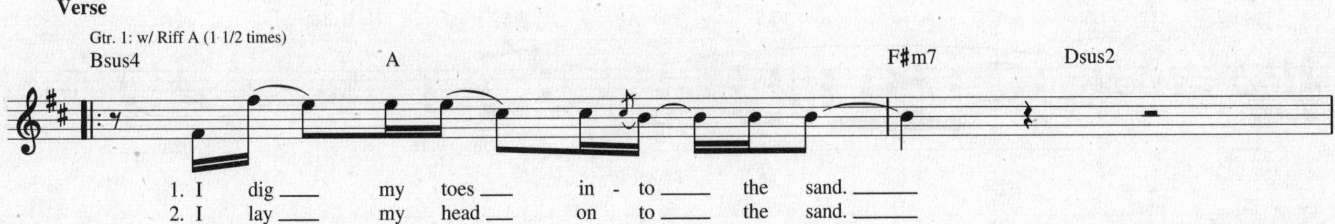

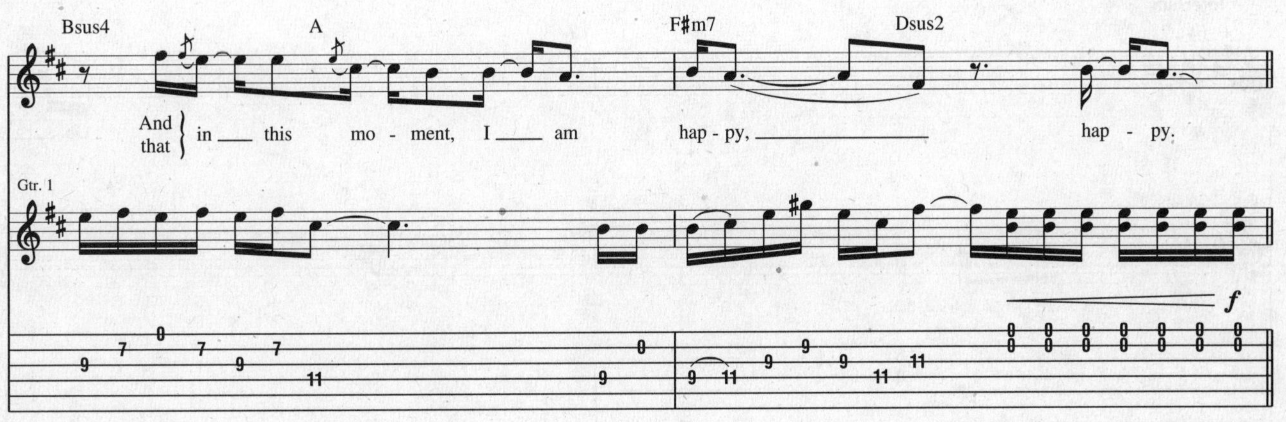

Chorus

1.
To Coda
F♯5
A5
E5
Asus2
E5
B5/F♯
D5/A
E5
wish you were here.
I
wish you were here.

Interlude
Gtr. 3: w/ Rhy. Fig. 3
Gtr. 1: w/ Riff A
Asus2
E5
F♯5
A5
E5
Bsus4
A
I
wish you were
here.
F♯m7
Dsus2
Bsus4
A
F♯m7
Dsus2
2.
Asus2
E5
I

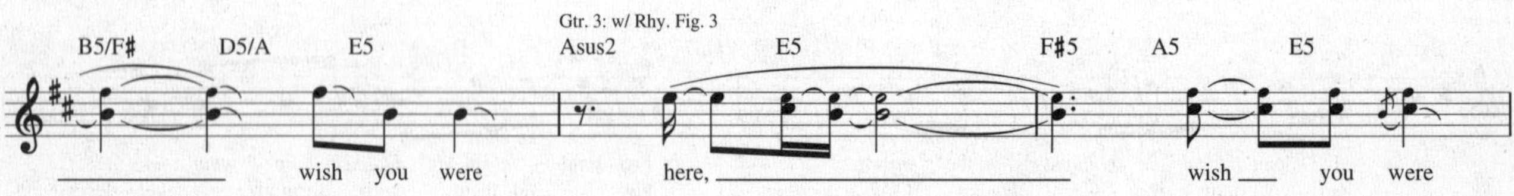
Gtr. 3: w/ Rhy. Fig. 3
B5/F♯
D5/A
E5
Asus2
E5
F♯5
A5
E5
wish you were
here,
wish you were

Interlude
F♯m7
G6
here.
Oh,
Gtr. 4 (elec.)
mf w/ dist. & heavy flanger
let ring throughout
Gtr. 1

F♯m7
G6
yeah, oh.

Bridge

F♯m7
G6
The world's a rol - ler coast - er, and I am not strapped in.

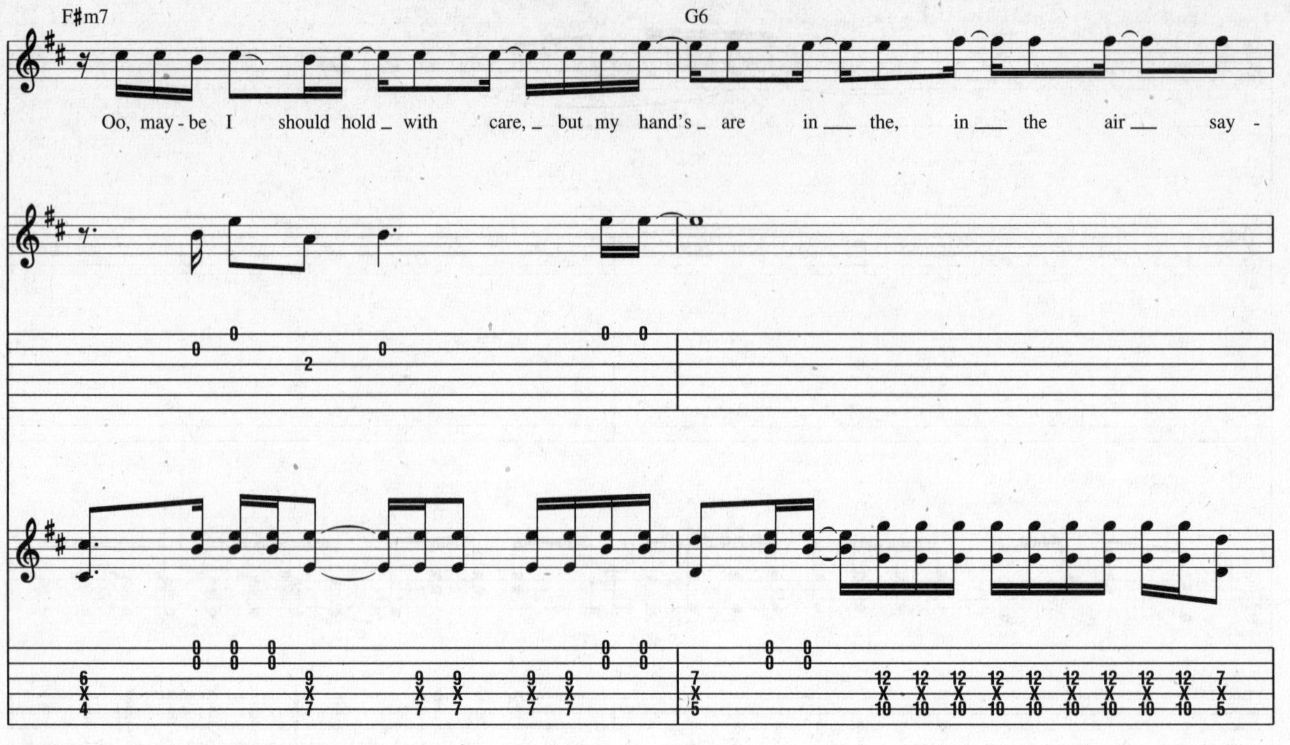
F♯m7
G6
Oo, may - be I should hold _ with care, _ but my hand's _ are in ___ the, in ___ the air ___ say -

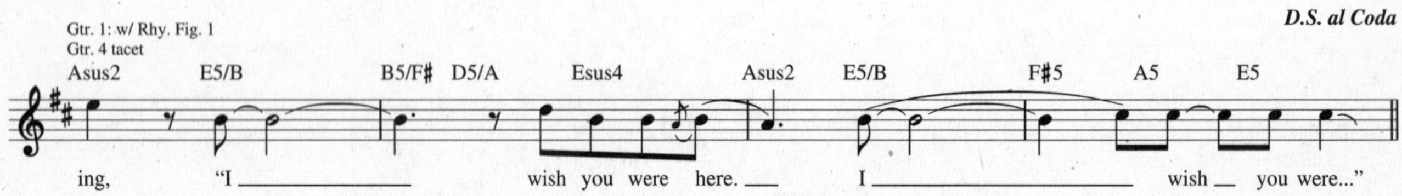
D.S. al Coda
Gtr. 1: w/ Rhy. Fig. 1
Gtr. 4 tacet
Asus2
E5/B
B5/F♯
D5/A
Esus4
Asus2
E5/B
F♯5
A5
E5
ing, "I ___ wish you were here. ___ I ___ wish _ you were..."

Coda
Gtrs. 1 & 2: w/ Rhy. Fig. 2
Asus2
E5
B5/F♯
D5/A
E5
___ I ___ wish you were

Gtr. 3: w/ Rhy. Fig. 3
Asus2
E5
F♯5
A5
E5
Asus2
here, ___ wish ___ you were here.
Gtrs. 1 & 2

Yankee Rose

Words by David Lee Roth
Music by Steve Vai

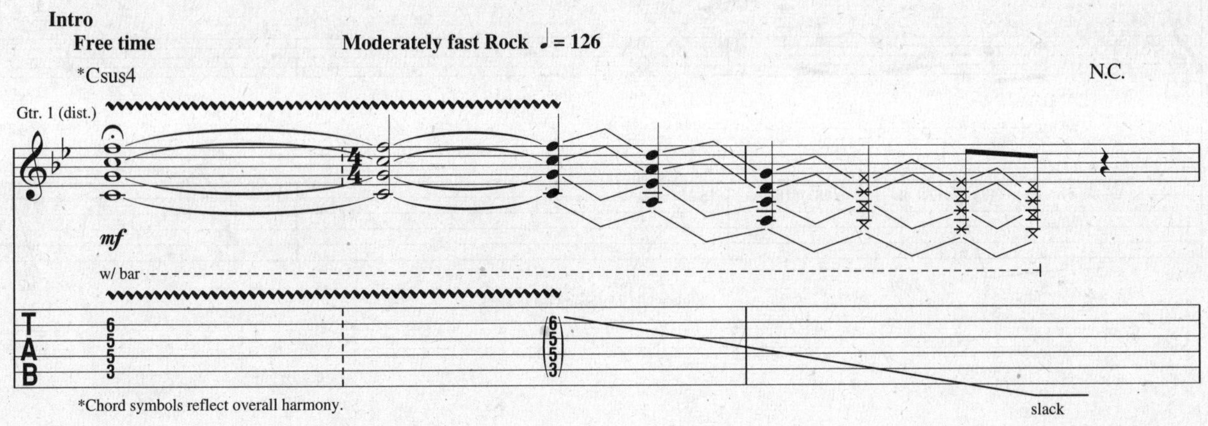

*Chord symbols reflect overall harmony.

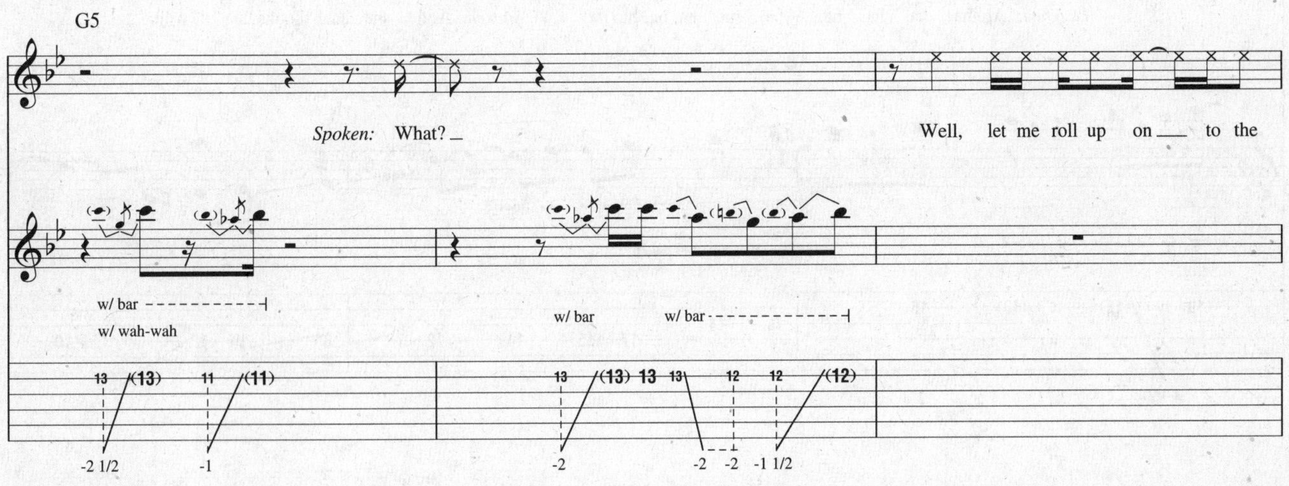

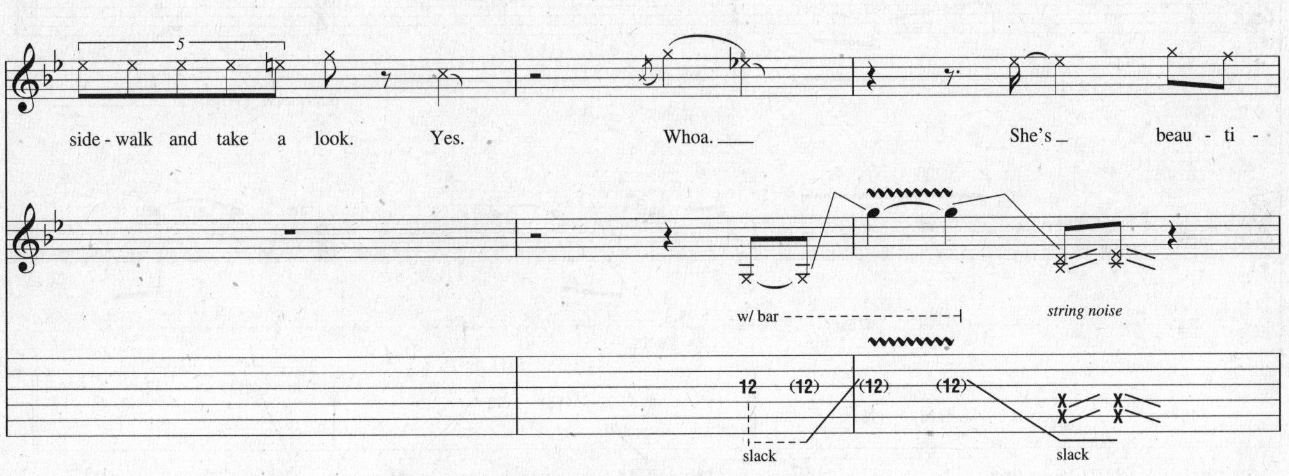

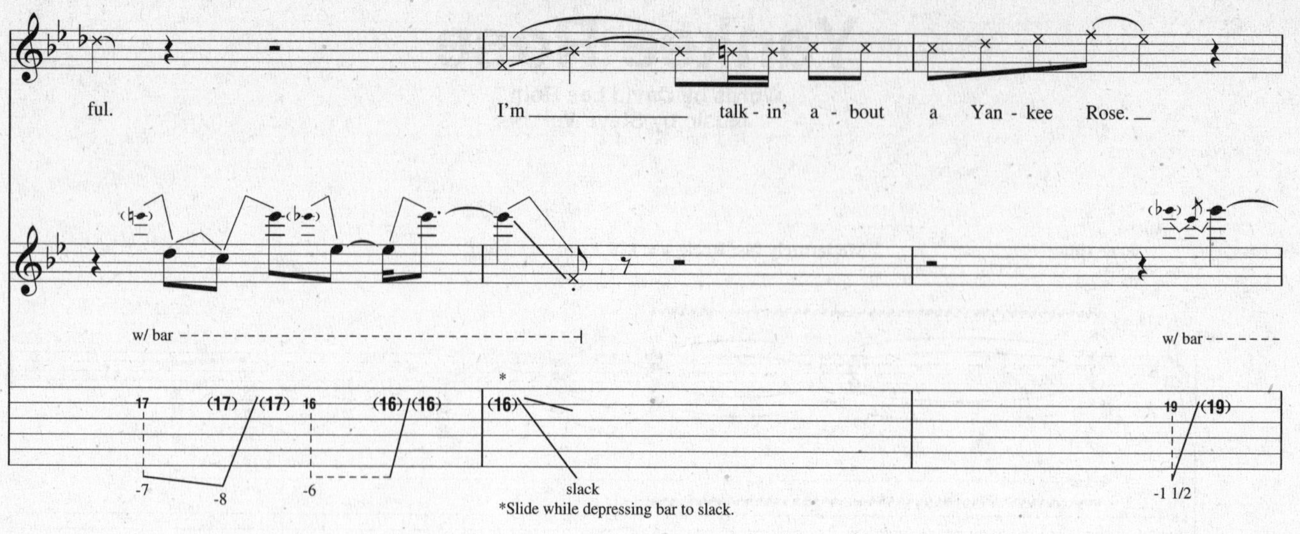
ful.
I'm talk - in' a - bout a Yan - kee Rose.
w/ bar
17 (17) (17) 16 (16) (16)
-7 -8 -6
(16)
slack
*Slide while depressing bar to slack.
19 (19)
-1 1/2

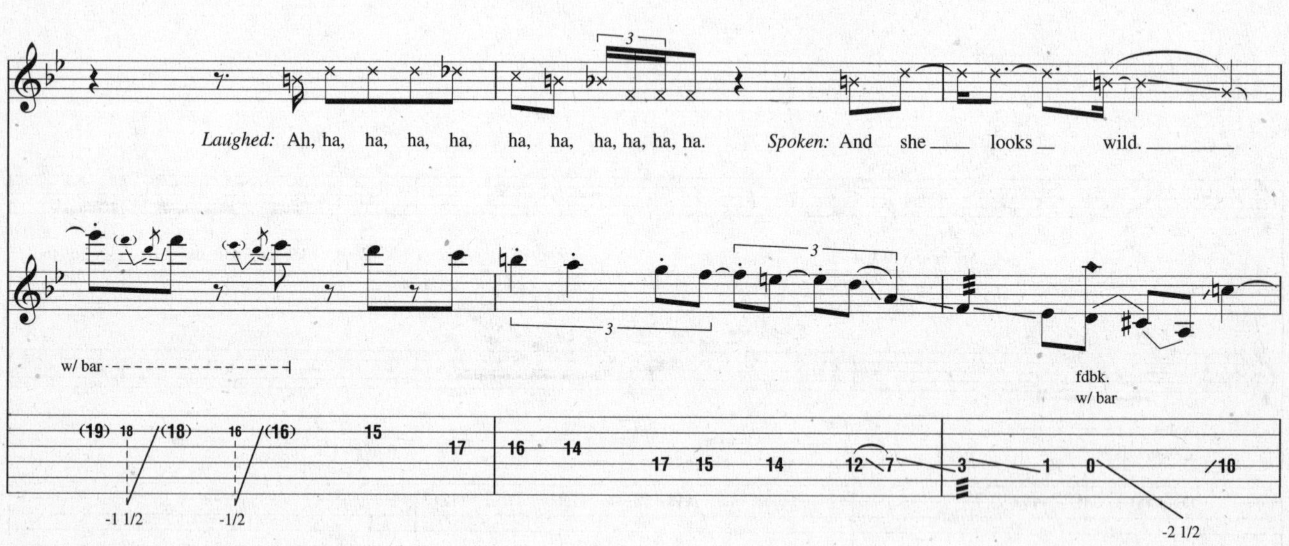
Laughed: Ah, ha, ha, ha, ha, ha, ha, ha, ha, ha, ha.
Spoken: And she looks wild.
w/ bar
(19) 18 (18) 16 (16) 15 17
-1 1/2 -1/2
16 14 17 15 14 12 7
3 1 0 10
fdbk.
w/ bar
-2 1/2

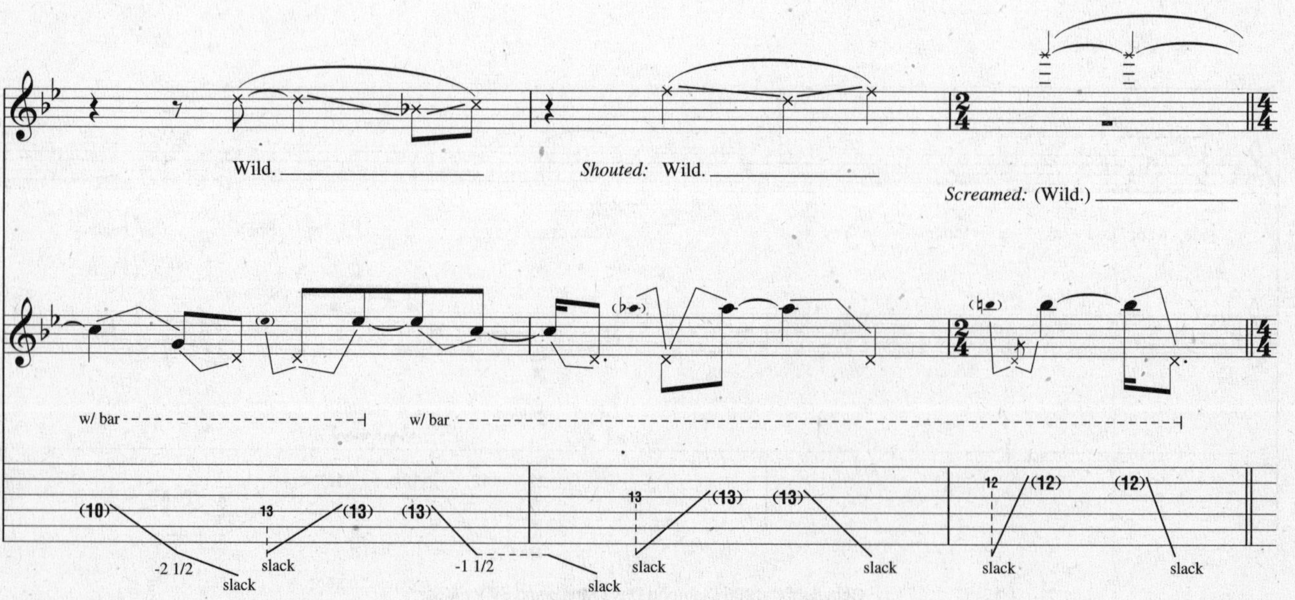
Wild.
Shouted: Wild.
Screamed: (Wild.)
w/ bar
w/ bar
(10) 13 (13) (13)
-2 1/2 slack slack -1 1/2 slack
13 (13) (13)
slack slack
12 (12) (12)
slack slack

Verse
G5
E5 F5 F♯5 G7sus4
1. Are you read - y for the new sen - sa - tion? Well, here's the shot heard
walks, watch the sparks will fly. Fire crack - in' on the
*Gtrs. 1 & 2 Riff A
wah-wah off
P.M.
let ring
*Gtr. 2 (dist.) mf
**Bkgd. Voc., 1st time only.
B♭
'round the world. All you back - room boys sa - lute when her flag un - furls.
Fourth of Ju - ly. No sad songs to - night, some-thing's in the air.
End Riff A
let ring
P.M. P.M.
let ring
1/4 1/2 3/4 1
Gtr. 1: w/ Riff A
Gtr. 2: w/ Riff A (1st 3 meas.)
2nd time, Gtr. 2: w/ Riff A
2nd time, Gtrs. 1 & 2: w/ Fill 1
G5
Well, guess who's back in
Spoken: You can feel it, can't ya? Screamed: Whoa. A real state of
w/ bar
Harm.
w/ bar
slack Pitch: D
-1 -1 1/2 -1 -1 1/2
Fill 1
Gtrs. 1 & 2
8va
loco
†Harm.
string noise
w/ bar
slack -1 1/2
Pitch: F
†Harmonic located two-thirds the distance between the 2nd & 3rd frets.

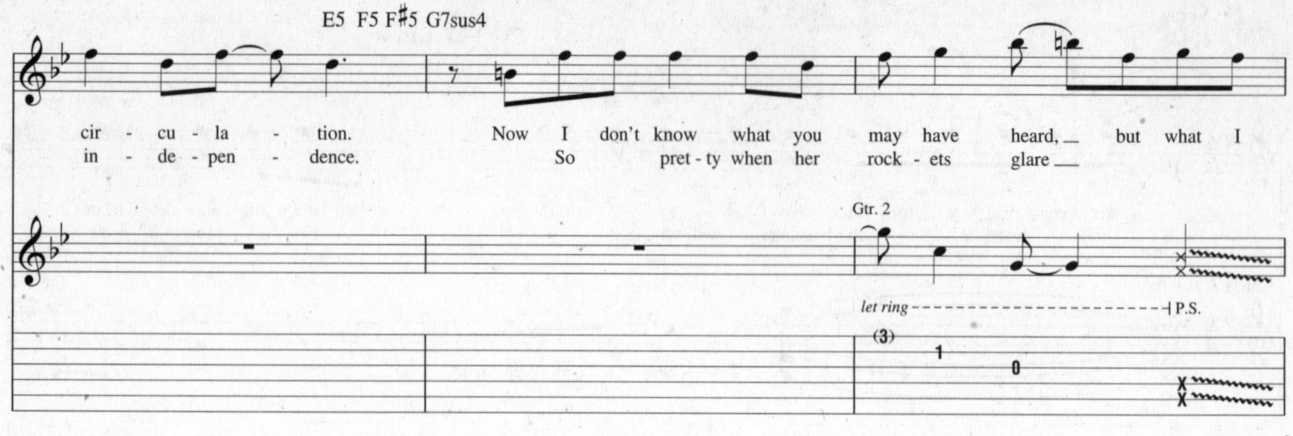

**Bend notes sharp by pressing harder w/ left hand.

Fill 2

Gtrs. 1 & 2

let ring

1/4 1/2 3/4 1

w/ bar w/ bar w/ bar w/ bar

slack

*Vibrato bar scoops to slack (next 2 meas.).

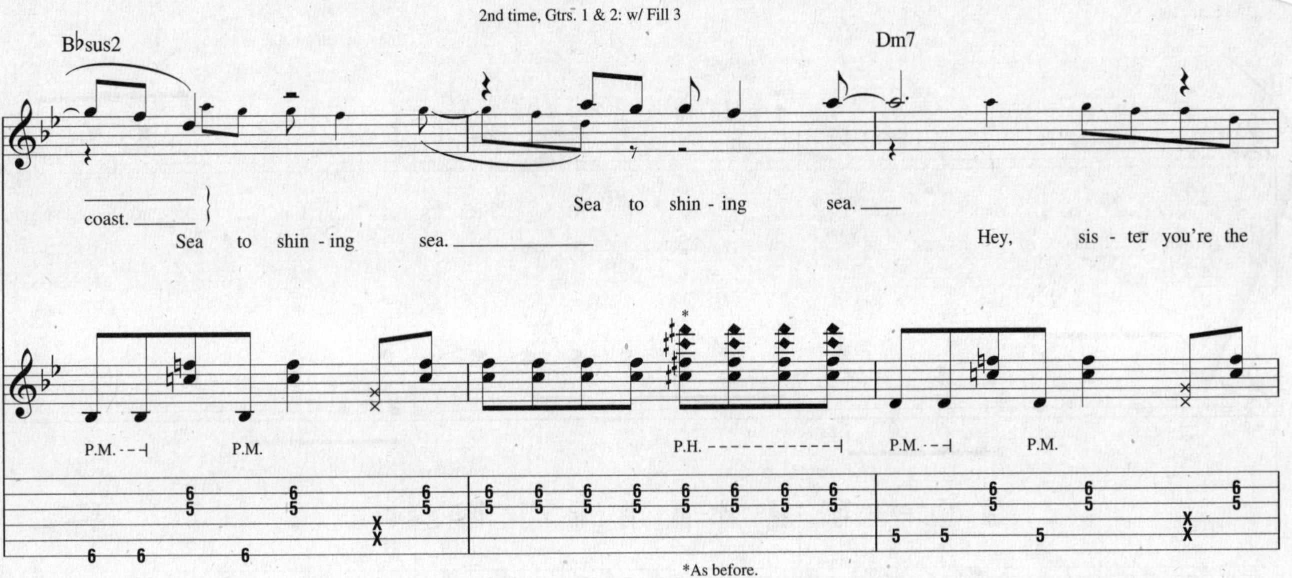
2nd time, Gtrs. 1 & 2: w/ Fill 3
B♭sus2
Dm7
coast.
Sea to shin - ing sea.
Sea to shin - ing sea.
Hey, sis - ter you're the
P.M.
P.H.
*As before.

2nd time, Gtrs. 1 & 2: w/ Fill 4
B♭sus2
E5 B♭5 F5 G5
per - fect toast.)
That's
Make
a toast.
Show me your.
Gtrs. 1 & 2
Gtr. 1
Gtr. 2
P.H.
P.M.
*As before.

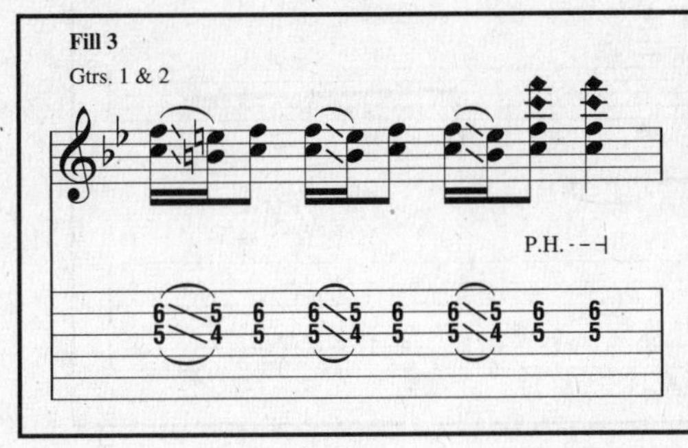
Fill 3
Gtrs. 1 & 2
P.H.

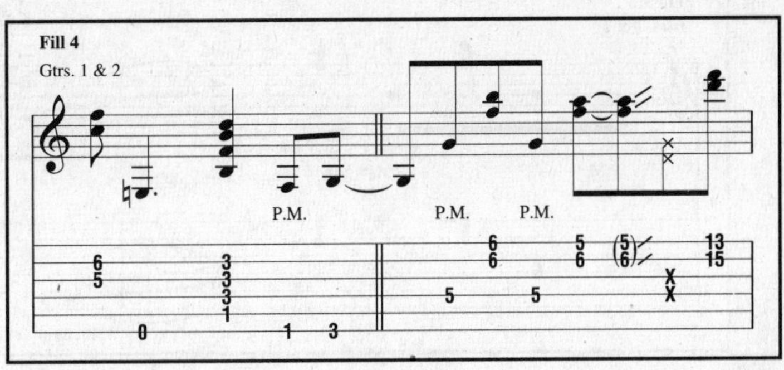
Fill 4
Gtrs. 1 & 2
P.M.

Chorus
Gm7
2nd time, Gtrs. 1 & 2: w/ Fill 5
And your. Al - right. I'm talk - in' 'bout the
(Bright lights, {your} cit - y lights.
Gtrs. 1 & 2
P.M.
steady gliss.
To Coda
D5 C5 B♭5 C5 B♭5 G5 E5 B♭5 Gm7
Yan - kee Rose. {Your} And your. Al - right.
Bright lights, cit - y lights.)
P.H.
Pitches: G A G
Fill 5
P.S.

D.S. al Coda

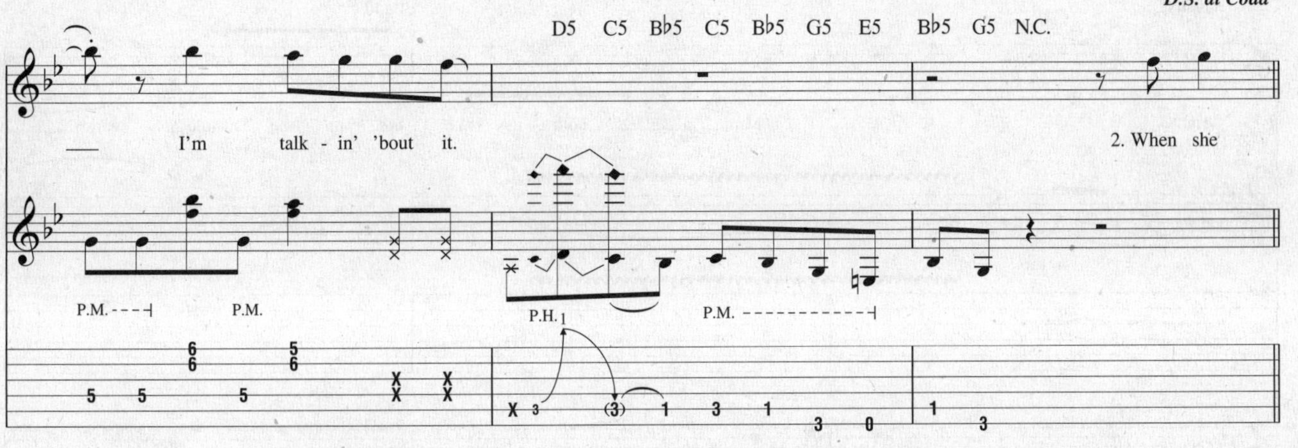
D5 C5 B♭5 C5 B♭5 G5 E5 B♭5 G5 N.C.
I'm talk - in' 'bout it.
2. When she
P.M.
P.M.
P.H.
P.M.

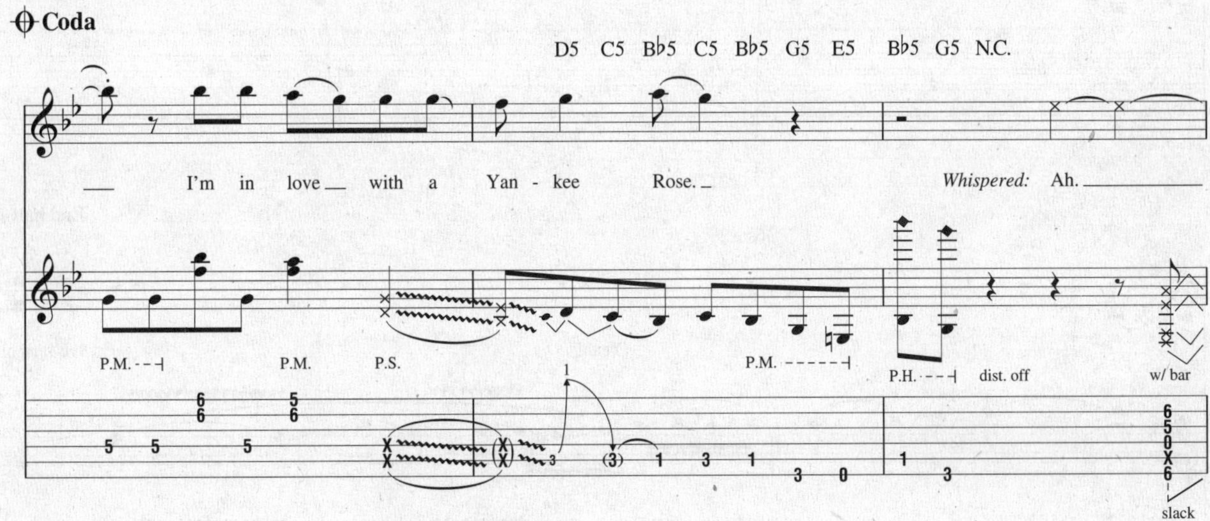
Coda
D5 C5 B♭5 C5 B♭5 G5 E5 B♭5 G5 N.C.
I'm in love with a Yan - kee Rose.
Whispered: Ah.
P.M.
P.M.
P.S.
P.M.
P.H.
dist. off
w/ bar
slack

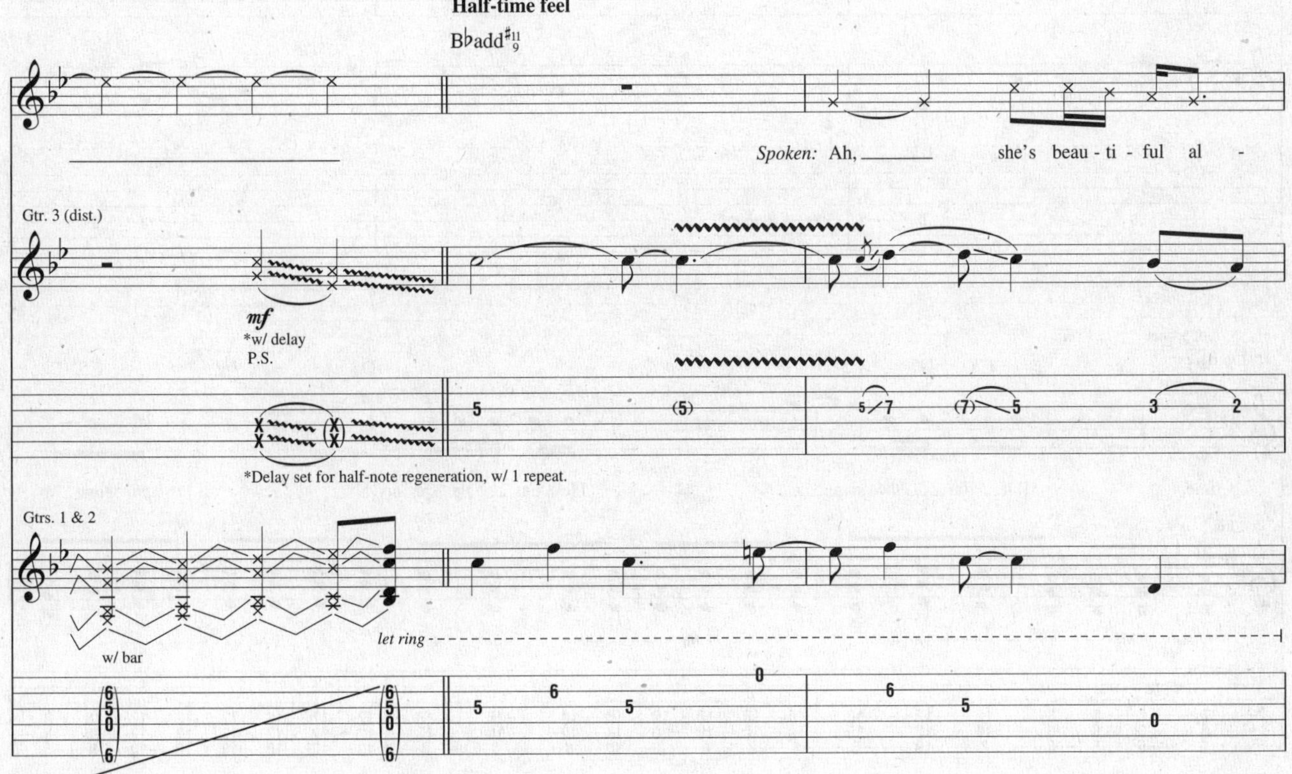
Bridge
Half-time feel
B♭add♯11 9
Spoken: Ah, she's beau - ti - ful al -
Gtr. 3 (dist.)
mf
*w/ delay
P.S.
*Delay set for half-note regeneration, w/ 1 repeat.
Gtrs. 1 & 2
w/ bar
let ring

G6sus2
B♭add#11/9
right.
Mm,
noth - in' like her in the whole world.
w/ bar
-1/2
let ring

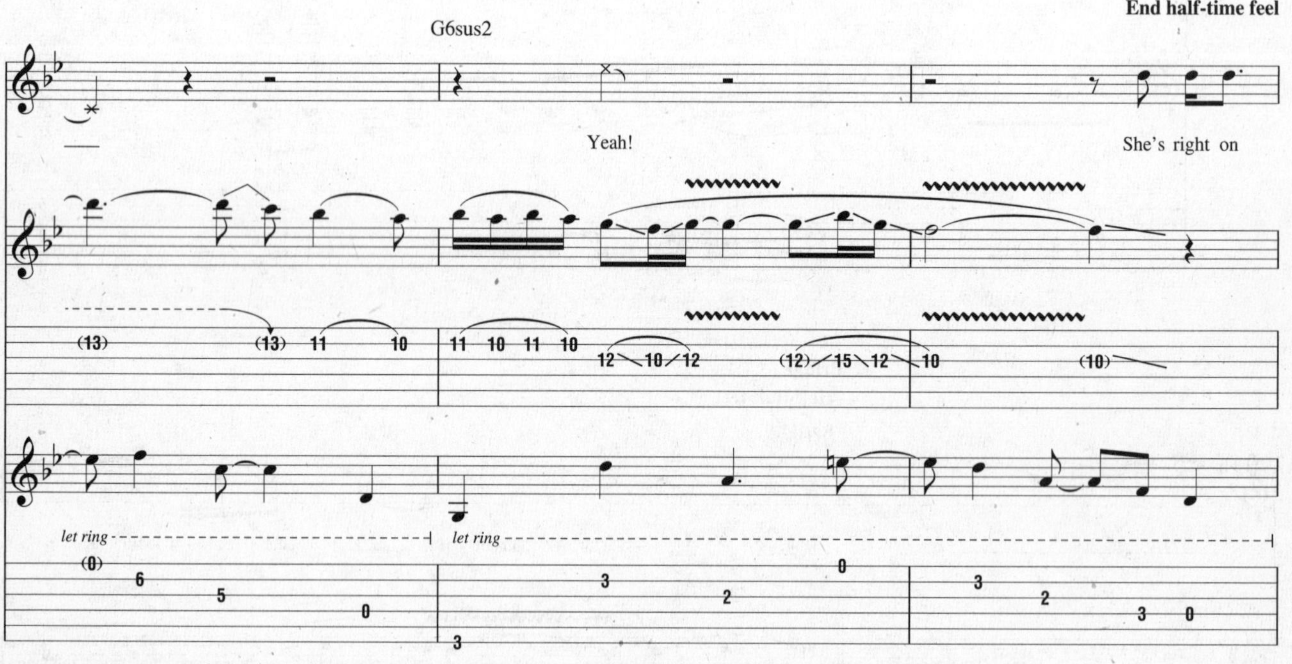
G6sus2
End half-time feel
Yeah!
She's right on
let ring

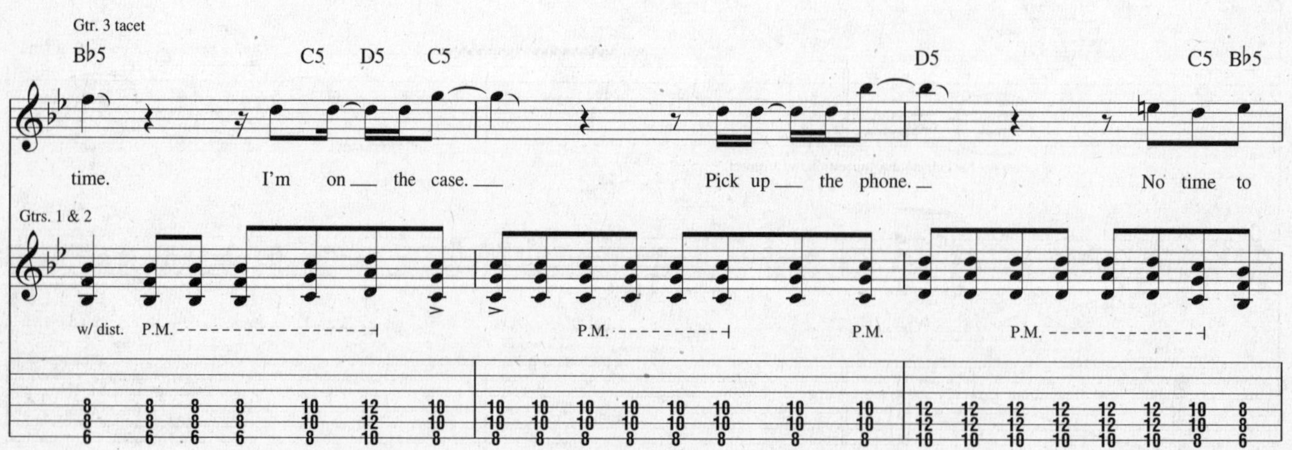
Gtr. 3 tacet
B♭5
C5
D5
C5
D5
C5
B♭5
time.
I'm on the case.
Pick up the phone.
No time to
Gtrs. 1 & 2
w/ dist.
P.M.

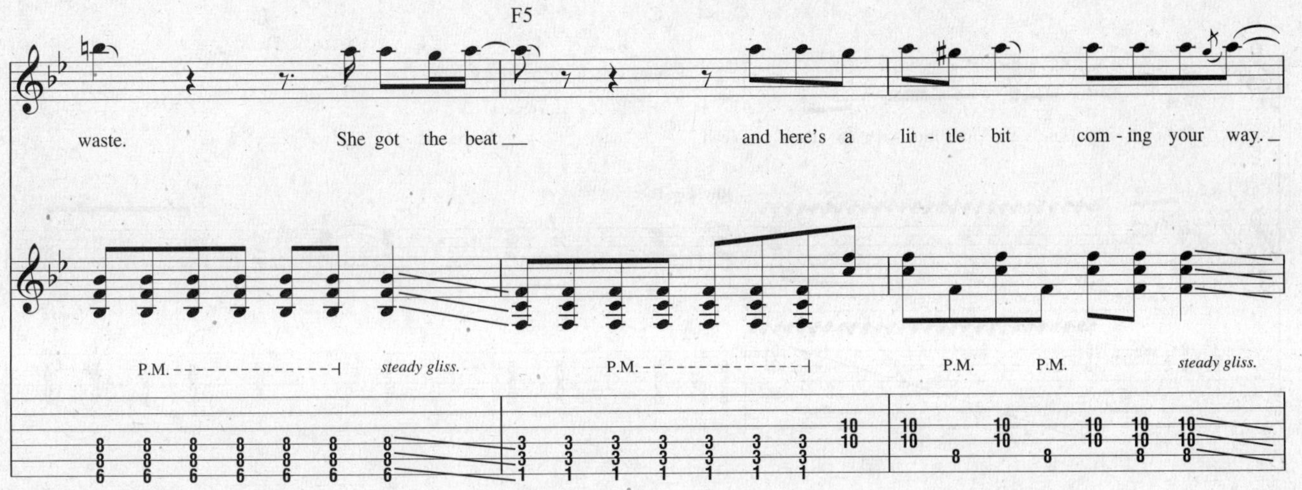
F5
waste. She got the beat
and here's a lit - tle bit com - ing your way.
P.M.
steady gliss.
P.M.
P.M. P.M.
steady gliss.

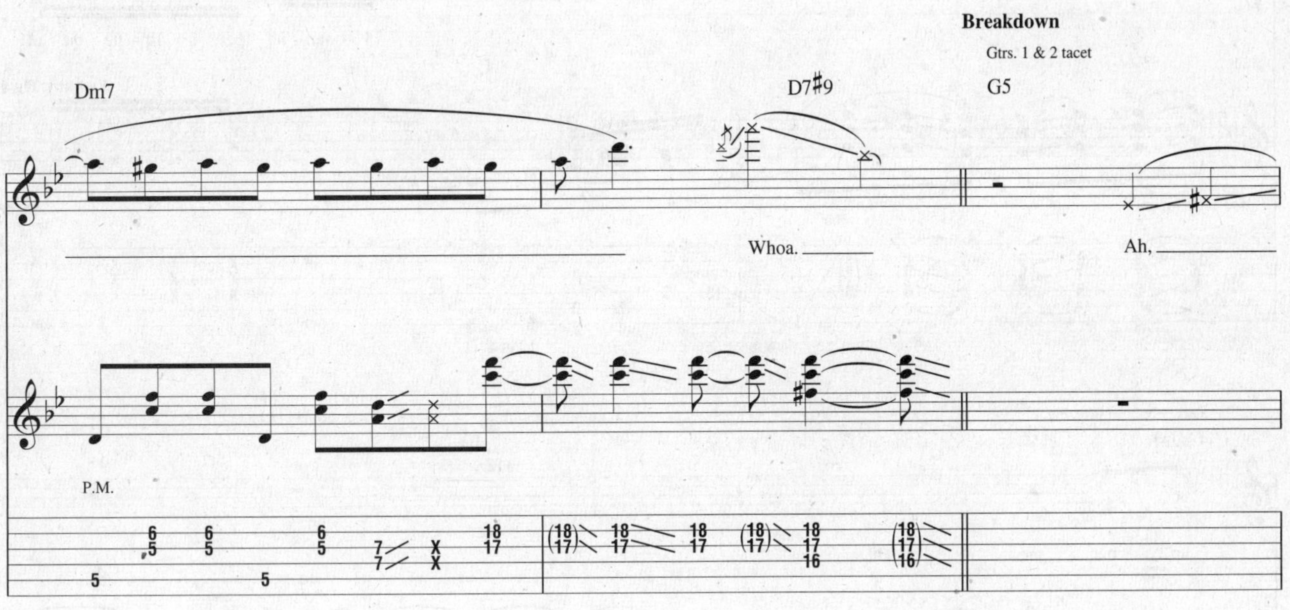
Breakdown
Gtrs. 1 & 2 tacet
Dm7
D7♯9
G5
Whoa.
Ah,
P.M.

raise them up, now. Let's see who sa - lutes, ba - by.

Yeah. Yeah. Yeah. Yeah. Yeah. Lit - tle bit, lit - tle bit, lit - tle bit high - er.

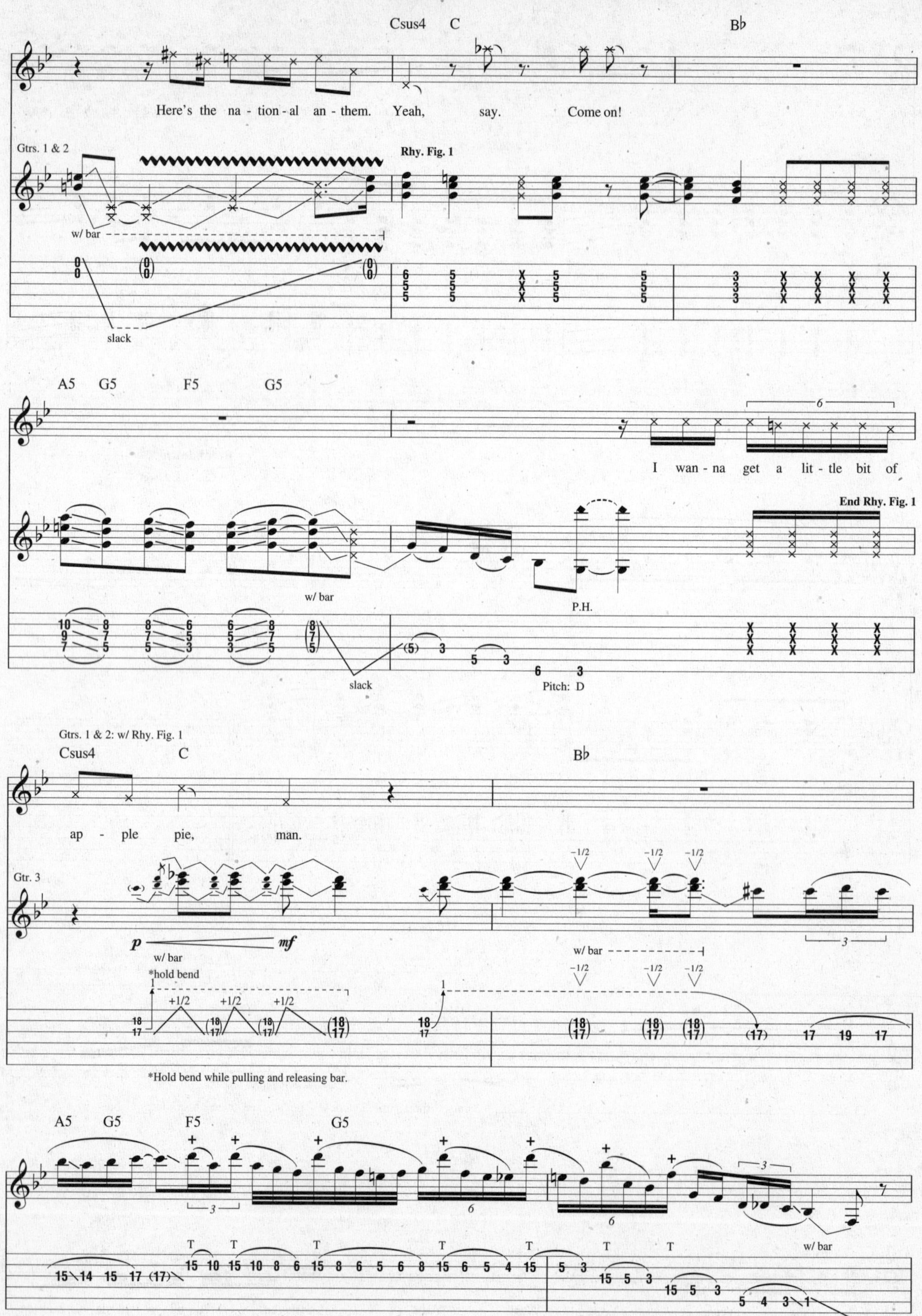
Csus4 C
B♭
Here's the na - tion - al an - them. Yeah, say. Come on!
Gtrs. 1 & 2
Rhy. Fig. 1
w/ bar
slack
A5 G5 F5 G5
I wan - na get a lit - tle bit of
End Rhy. Fig. 1
w/ bar
P.H.
slack
Pitch: D
Gtrs. 1 & 2: w/ Rhy. Fig. 1
Csus4 C
B♭
ap - ple pie, man.
Gtr. 3
p
mf
w/ bar
*hold bend
w/ bar
*Hold bend while pulling and releasing bar.
A5 G5 F5 G5
w/ bar

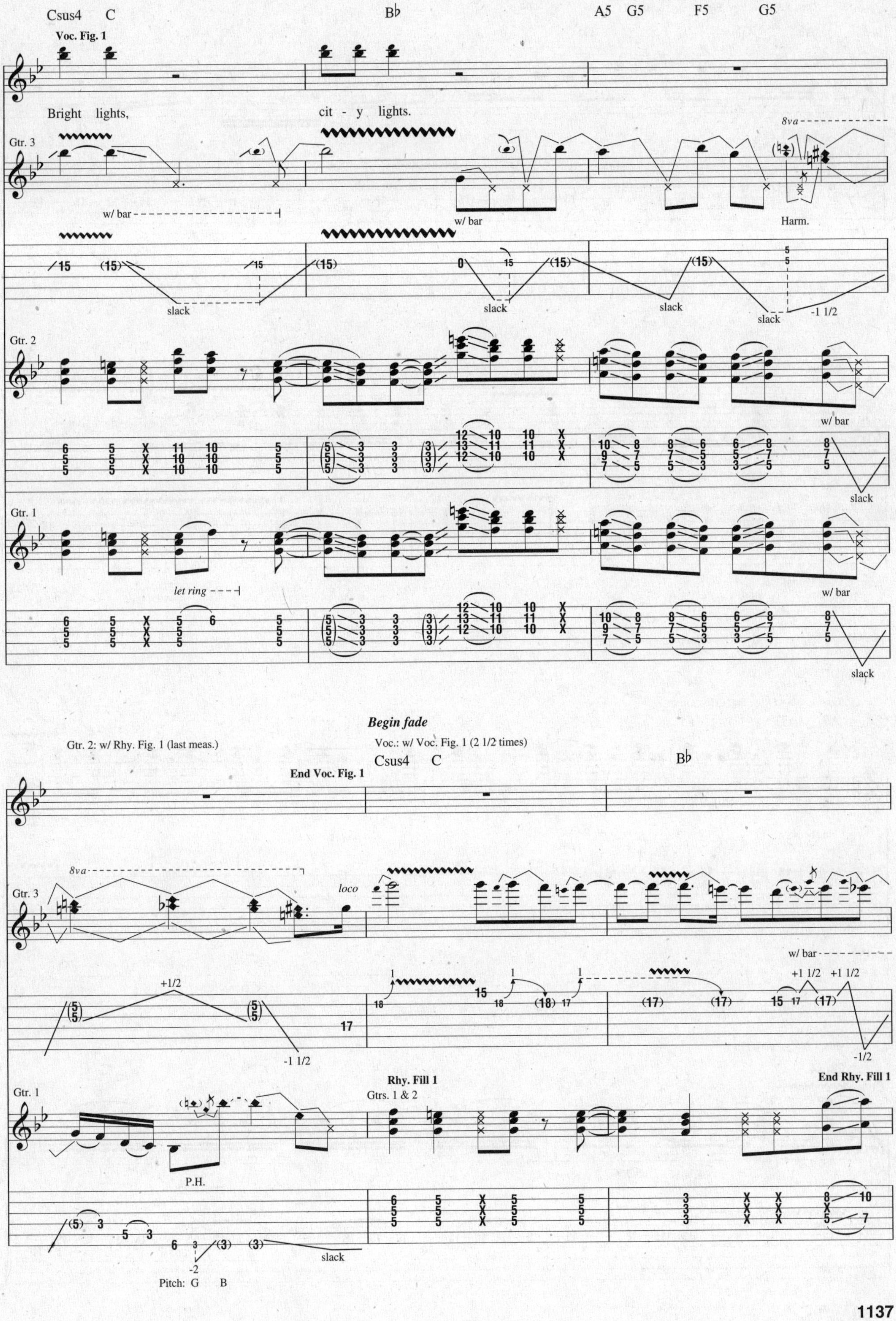

Csus4 C Bb A5 G5 F5 G5

Voc. Fig. 1

Bright lights, cit - y lights.

Gtr. 3

w/ bar

w/ bar

8va

Harm.

slack

slack

slack

slack

-1 1/2

Gtr. 2

w/ bar

slack

Gtr. 1

let ring

w/ bar

slack

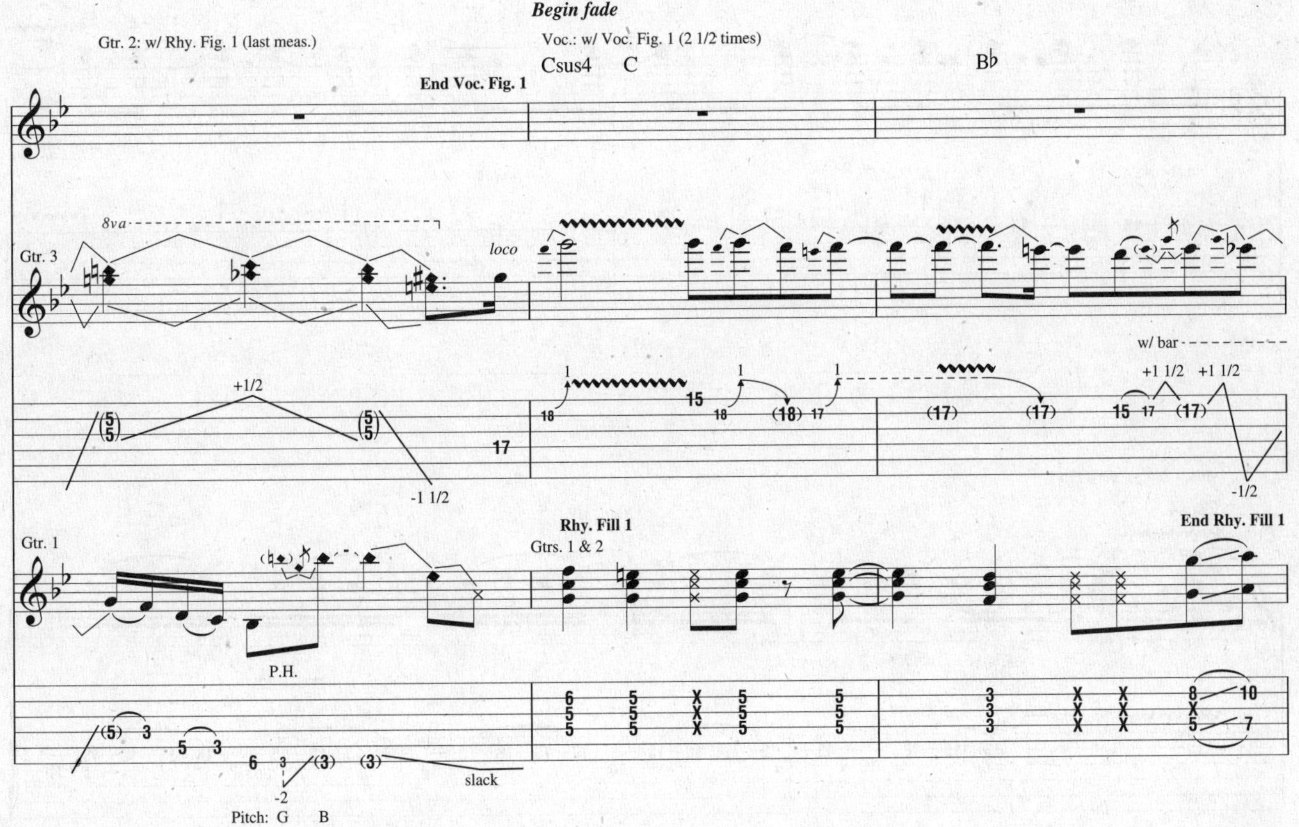

Gtrs. 1 & 2: w/ Rhy. Fig. 1 (last 2 meas.)
A5
G5
F5
G5
Gtr. 3
w/ bar
+1 1/2
-1/2

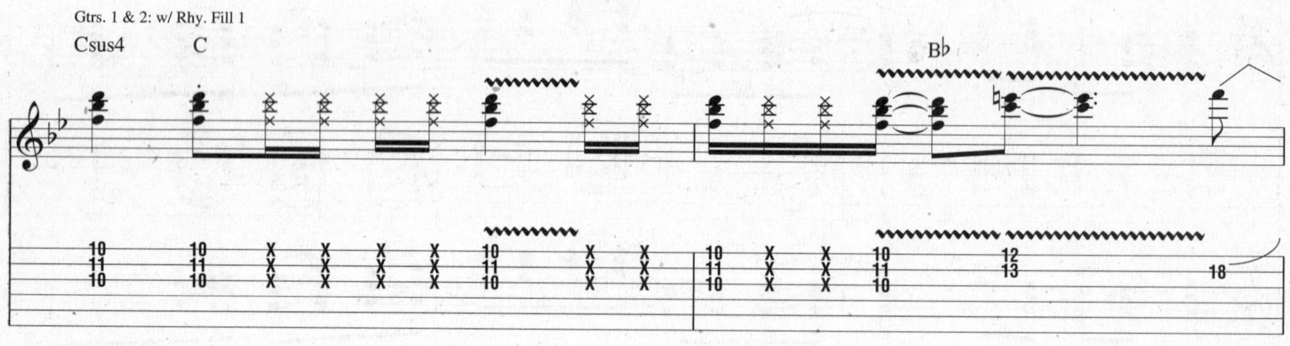
Gtrs. 1 & 2: w/ Rhy. Fill 1
Csus4
C
B♭

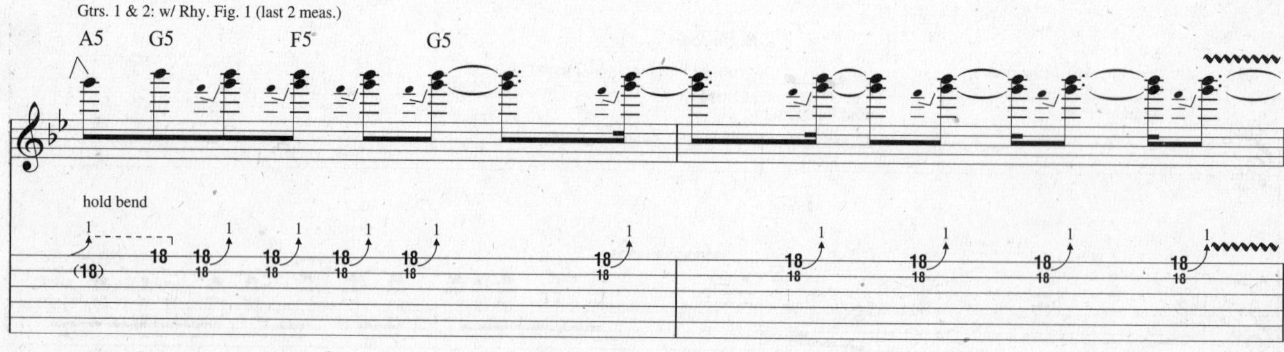
Gtrs. 1 & 2: w/ Rhy. Fig. 1 (last 2 meas.)
A5
G5
F5
G5
hold bend

Fade out

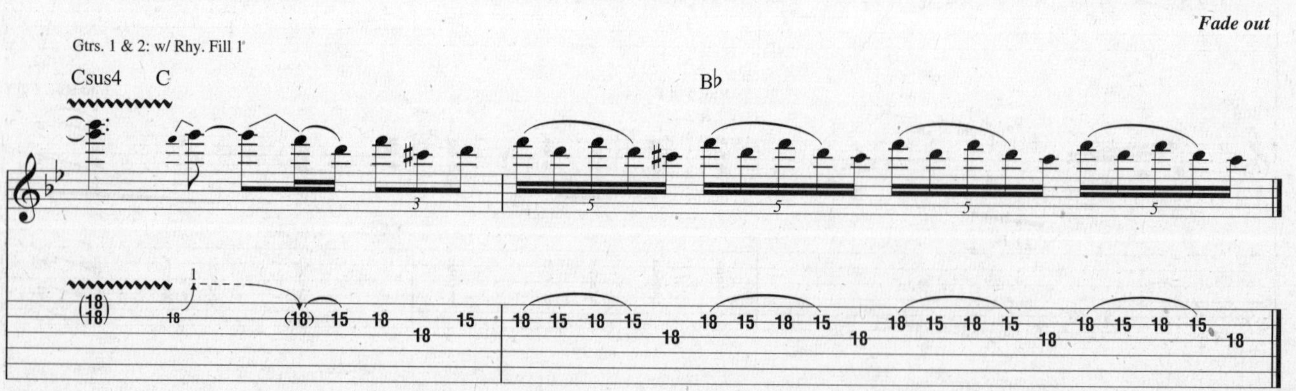
Gtrs. 1 & 2: w/ Rhy. Fill 1
Csus4
C
B♭

Ziggy Stardust

Words and Music by David Bowie

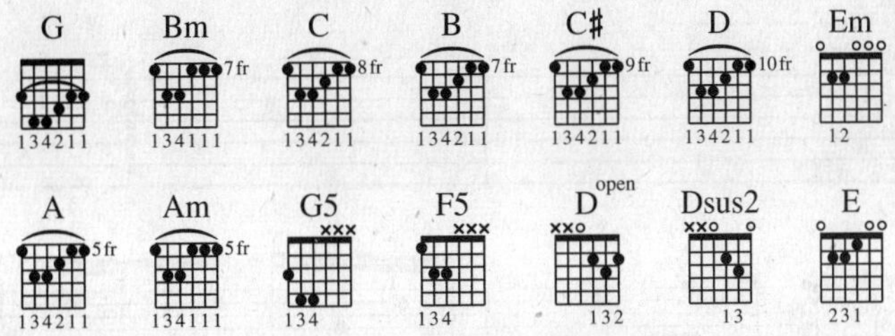

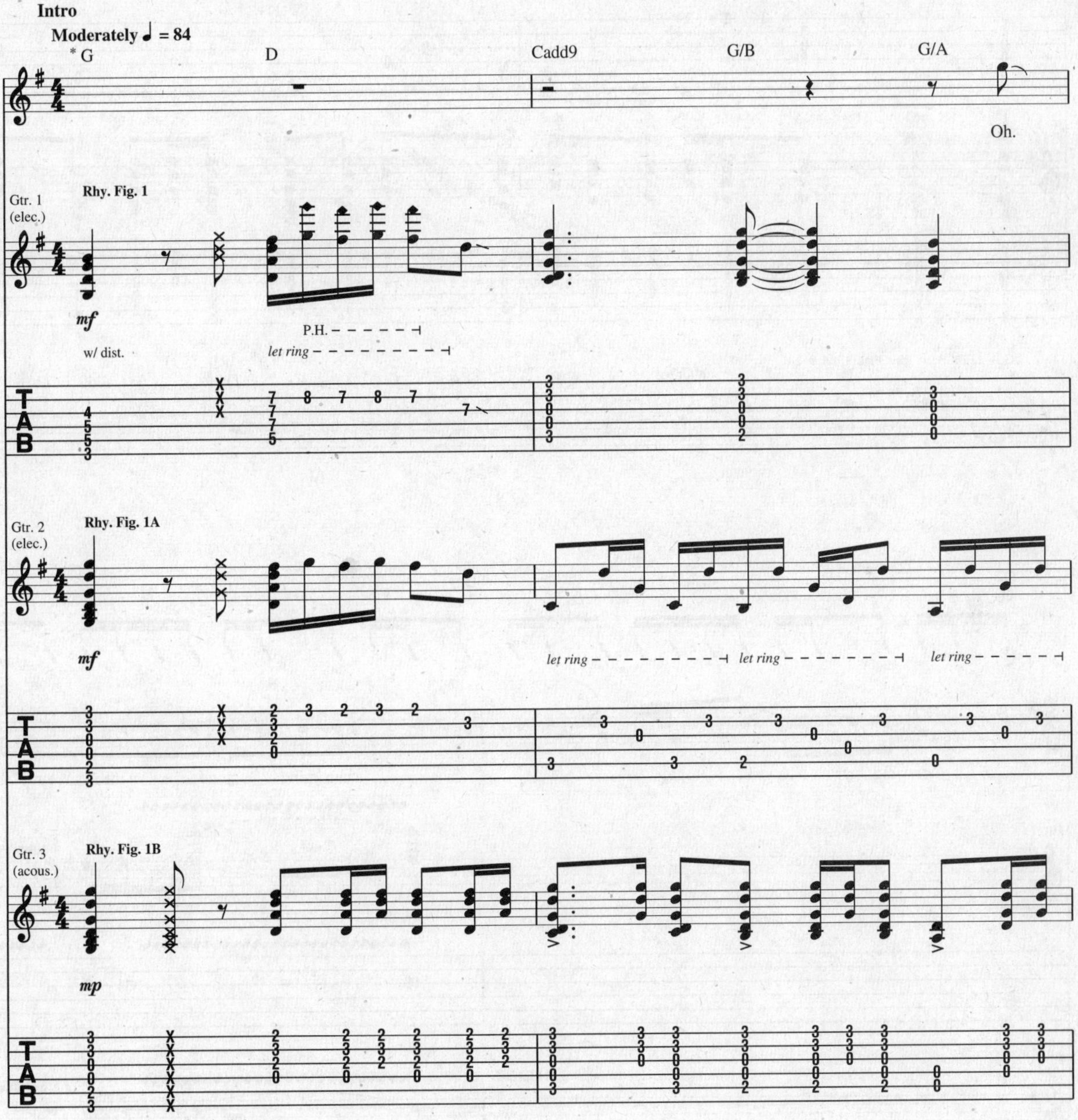

Intro

Moderately ♩ = 84

*G D Cadd9 G/B G/A

Oh.

Gtr. 1 (elec.)

Rhy. Fig. 1

mf

w/ dist.

P.H.

let ring

Gtr. 2 (elec.)

Rhy. Fig. 1A

mf

let ring *let ring* *let ring*

Gtr. 3 (acous.)

Rhy. Fig. 1B

mp

* Chord symbols reflect basic harmony.

End Rhy. Fig. 1
G
D
Cadd9
G/B
G/A
P.H.
let ring
End Rhy. Fig. 1A
let ring
let ring
let ring
End Rhy. Fig. 1B
Gtrs. 1, 2 & 3: w/ Rhy. Figs. 1, 1A & 1B
Oh,
yeah.
Ah.
Verse
Rhy. Fig. 2
Gtr. 3
Bm
1. Now Zig - gy played gui - tar, jam - ming good with Weird and
Gtr. 1
P.H.
Gtr. 4
(elec.)
mf
w/ dist.

C B C C♯ D

Gil - ly and the Spi - ders from Mars. He played it left - hand

1/4

1/4

* Composite arrangement

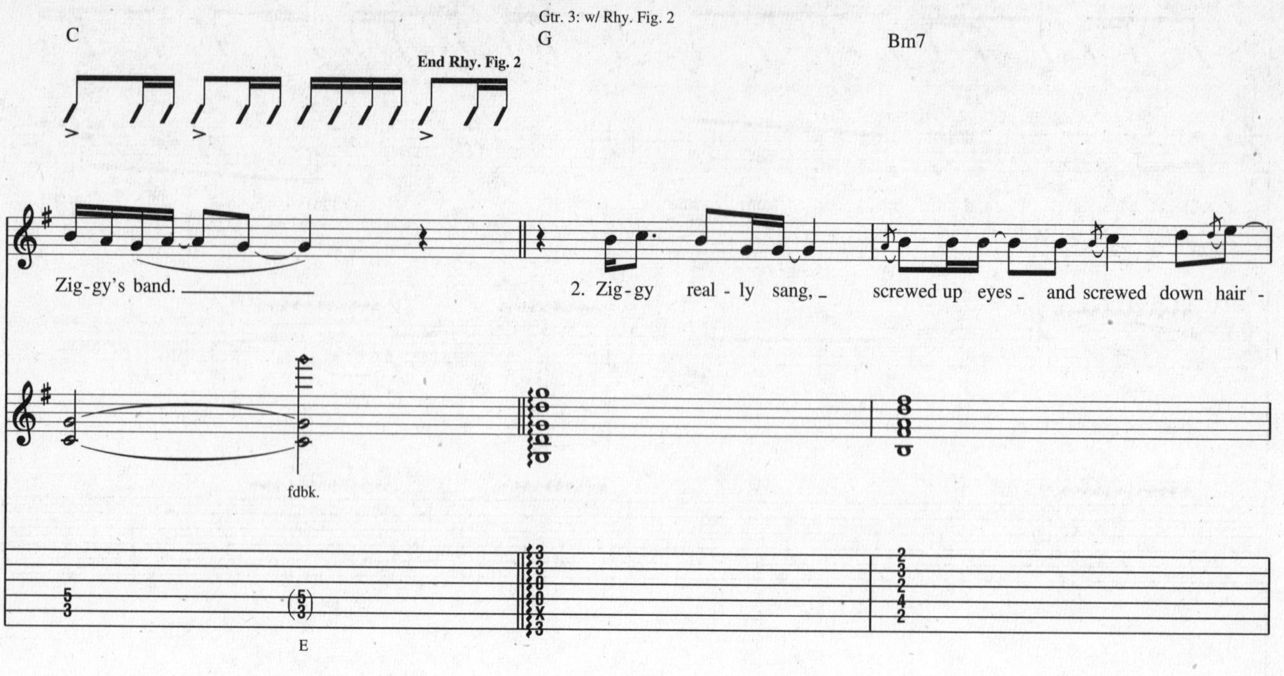
Verse
Gtr. 3: w/ Rhy. Fig. 2
C
G
Bm7
End Rhy. Fig. 2
Zig-gy's band.
2. Zig-gy real - ly sang,
screwed up eyes
and screwed down hair -
fdbk.
E

C
B C C♯ D
G
- do like some cat from Ja - pan.
He could lick 'em by smil - ing
he could leave 'em to hang.

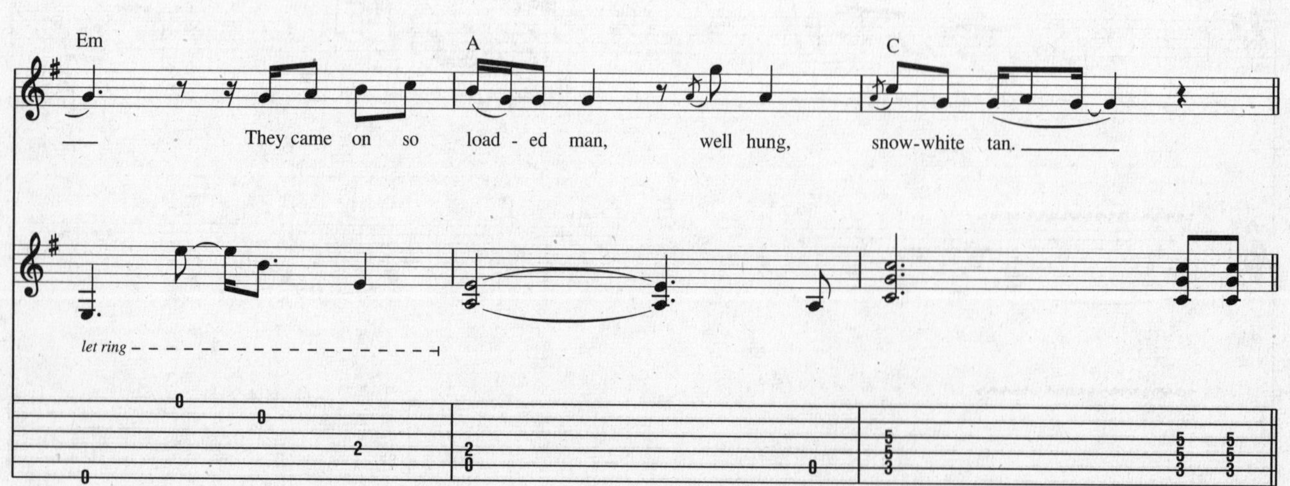
Em
A
C
They came on so load - ed man, well hung, snow-white tan.
let ring

Chorus

Am G5 F5 E F5 E F5 E F5 G5

Rhy. Fig. 3A — Gtr. 3 — open — End Rhy. Fig. 3A

1. So where were the Spi - ers
2. Mak-ing love with his e - go,

Gtrs. 1 & 2 — Rhy. Fig. 3 — End Rhy. Fig. 3

Gtrs. 1, 2 & 3: w/ Rhy. Figs. 3 & 3A (2 times)

Am G5 F5 E F5 E F5 E F5 G5 Am G5

while the fly tried to break our balls? Just the beer light to guide
Zig-gy sucked up in-to his mind. Oh. Like a lep-er mes-si-

F5 E F5 E F5 E F5 G5 D[open] Dsus2D[open] E

Gtr. 3

us. So we bitched a-bout his fans and should we crush his sweet hands? Oh.
-ah. When the kids had killed the man, I had to break up the band.

Gtr. 1

Gtr. 2

Interlude
Gtrs. 1, 2 & 3:
w/ Rhy. Figs. 1, 1A & 1B
To Coda
G D Cadd9 G/B G/A G D Cadd9 G/B G/A
Mmm.
Oh,
Verse
Gtr. 3: w/ Rhy. Fig. 2
G Bm7 C B C C♯
3. Zig-gy played for time, jiv - ing us that we were voo - doo. The kids were just crass,
Gtr. 1
Gtr. 4
divisi
* Gtr. 1 to the left of slash in tab.
Gtr. 2
let ring throughout
D G Em
Gtr. 4 tacet
he was the nazz with God giv - en ass. He took it all
Gtrs. 1 & 4
Gtr. 1
1/4
Gtr. 2

D.S. al Coda

A
C
too far
but boy could he play gui - tar.
Coda
Free Time
Gtrs. 1, 2 & 3: w/ Rhy. Figs. 1, 1A & 1B (1st 3 meas.)
G
D
Cadd9 G/B
G/A
G
D
Cadd9
yeah.
Ooo.
Zig - gy played gui -
Gtrs. 1, 2 & 3
rit.
G
tar.
Gtr. 1
Harm.
P.H.
Gtrs. 2 & 3

Zombie

Lyrics and Music by Dolores O'Riordan

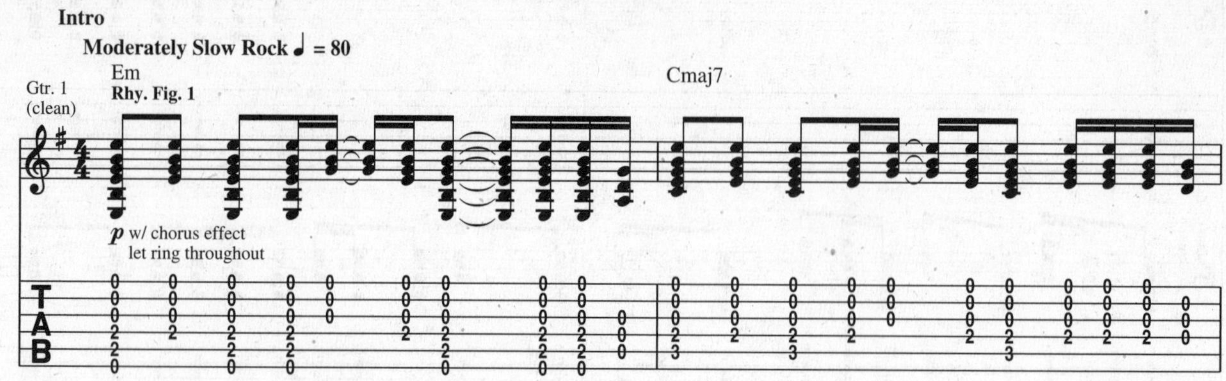

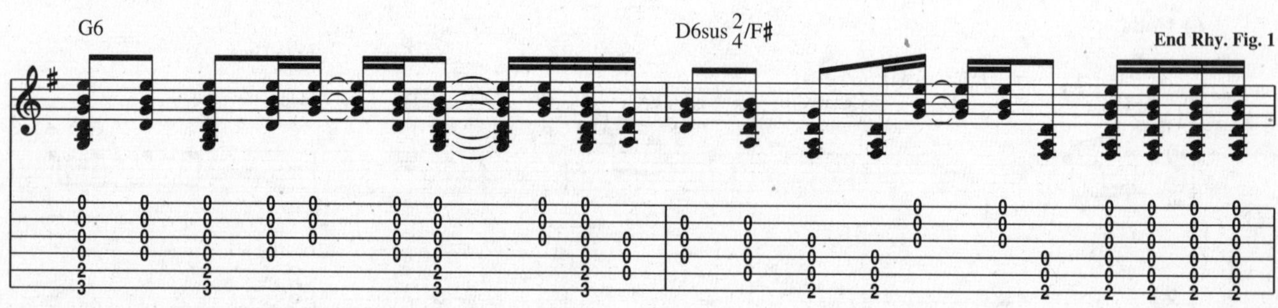

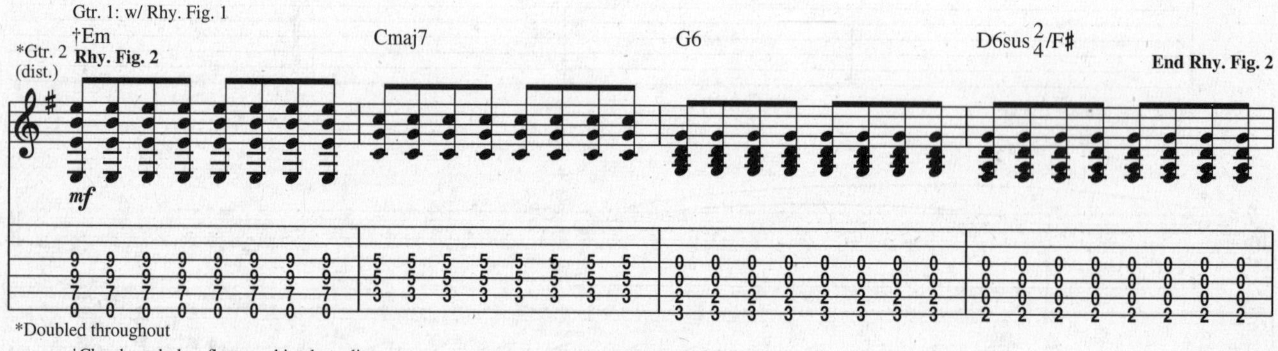

*Doubled throughout

†Chord symbols reflect combined tonality.

Gtr. 2
Em
C
Gtr. 2 tacet
Gtr. 3 G
(dist.)
Dsus 2/4 /F#
mf
Gtr. 1
Verse
Gtr. 3: w/ Fill 1
*Em
Cmaj7
G6
Dsus 2/4 /F#
Em
1. An-oth - er head hangs low - ly, child is slow - ly tak - en.
2. An-oth - er moth - er's brak - in' heart is tak - ing o - ver.
Gtr. 1
*Chord symbols represent combined tonality of gtr. and bass.
Cmaj7
G6
And the vio - lence caused such si - lence, who are we mis - tak -
When the vio - lence caus - es si - lence, we must be mis - tak -
Fill 1
Gtr. 3
T
A
B

Dsus 2/4/F#
Em
Cmaj7
en? But you see, it's not me, it's not my fam - i - ly. In your head,
en. It's the same old theme since nine - teen - six - teen. In your head,
G6
Dsus 2/4/F#
Em
in your head they are fight - ing with their tanks, and their bombs and their bombs
in your head they're still fight - ing with their tanks, and their bombs and their bombs
Cmaj7
G6
Dsus 2/4/F#
and their guns. In your head. in your head they are cry - ing
and their guns. In your head. in your head they are dy - ing in your
Chorus
Gtr. 1 tacet
Gtr. 2: w/ Rhy. Fig. 2, 3 times, simile
E5
C5
G
head, in your head, zom - bie, zom - bie, zom - bie,
Dsus4/F#
E5
C5
hey, hey. What's in your head, in your head, zom - bie,

G
Dsus4/F#
1.
E5
zom - bie, zom - bie? Hey, hey, hey, oh, doo, doo, doo, doo,
C5
G
Dsus4/F#
doo, doo, doo, doo, doo, doo, doo, doo, doo, doo, doo, doo.
2.
E5
C5
G
Dsus4/F#
oh, oh, oh, oh, oh, oh, hey, oh, ya, ya.
Gtr. 2: w/ Rhy. Fig. 2
Guitar Solo
Gtr. 2
Gtr. 2 tacet
Gtr. 1
Gtr. 3

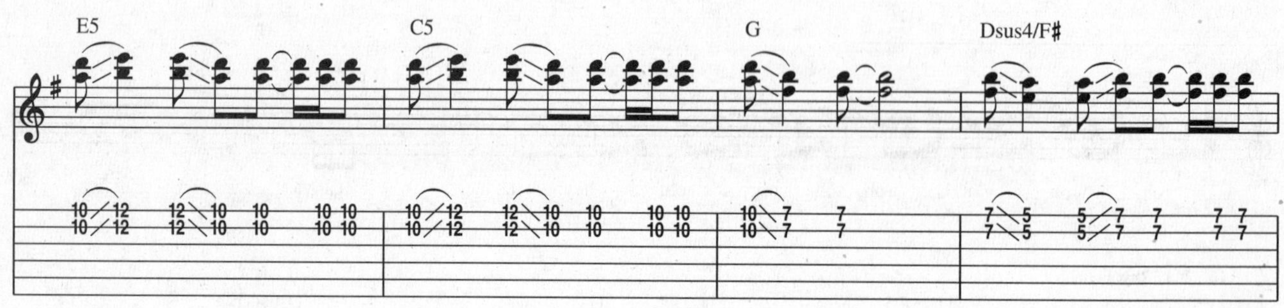

Outro

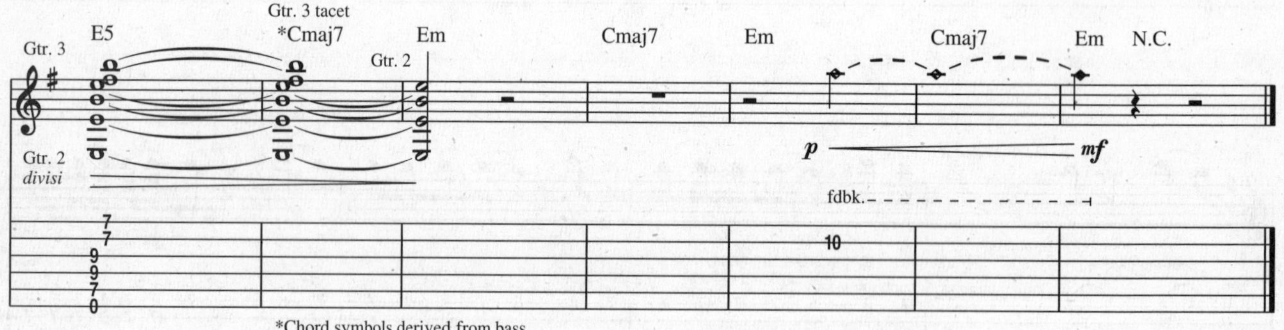

*Chord symbols derived from bass.

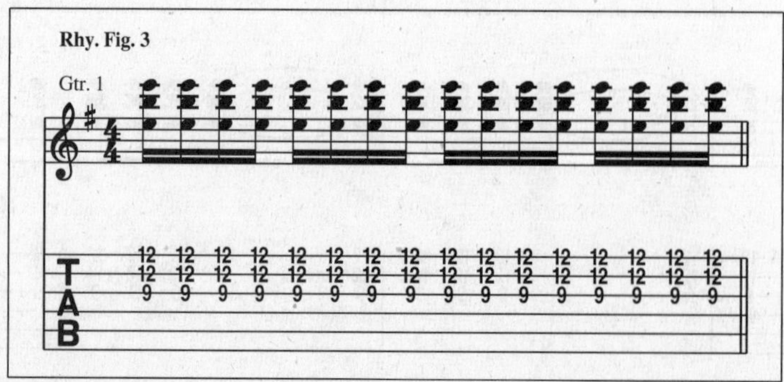

Guitar Notation Legend

Guitar Music can be notated three different ways: on a *musical staff*, in *tablature*, and in *rhythm slashes*.

RHYTHM SLASHES are written above the staff. Strum chords in the rhythm indicated. Use the chord diagrams found at the top of the first page of the transcription for the appropriate chord voicings. Round noteheads indicate single notes.

THE MUSICAL STAFF shows pitches and rhythms and is divided by bar lines into measures. Pitches are named after the first seven letters of the alphabet.

TABLATURE graphically represents the guitar fingerboard. Each horizontal line represents a a string, and each number represents a fret.

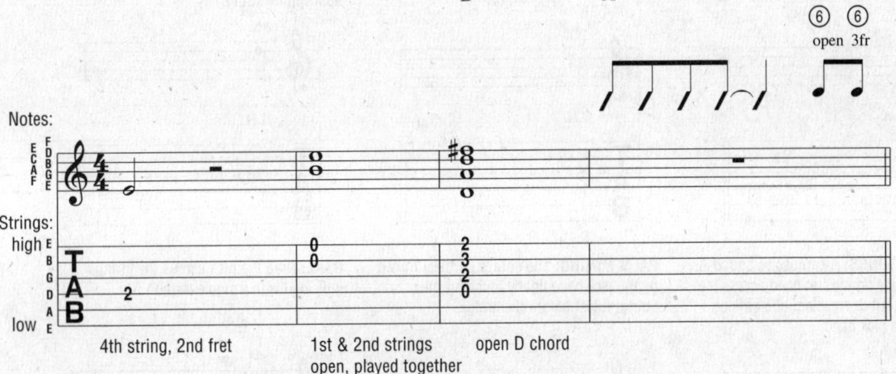

Definitions for Special Guitar Notation

HALF-STEP BEND: Strike the note and bend up 1/2 step.

WHOLE-STEP BEND: Strike the note and bend up one step.

GRACE NOTE BEND: Strike the note and immediately bend up as indicated.

SLIGHT (MICROTONE) BEND: Strike the note and bend up 1/4 step.

BEND AND RELEASE: Strike the note and bend up as indicated, then release back to the original note. Only the first note is struck.

PRE-BEND: Bend the note as indicated, then strike it.

PRE-BEND AND RELEASE: Bend the note as indicated. Strike it and release the bend back to the original note.

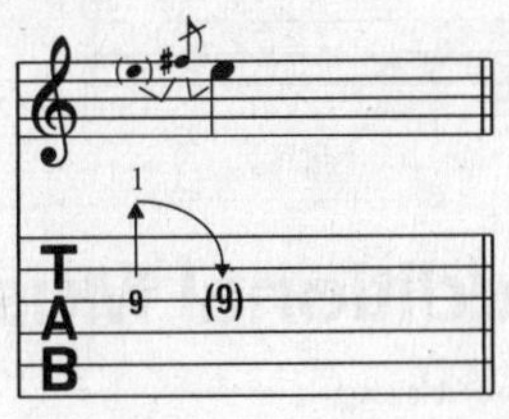

UNISON BEND: Strike the two notes simultaneously and bend the lower note up to the pitch of the higher.

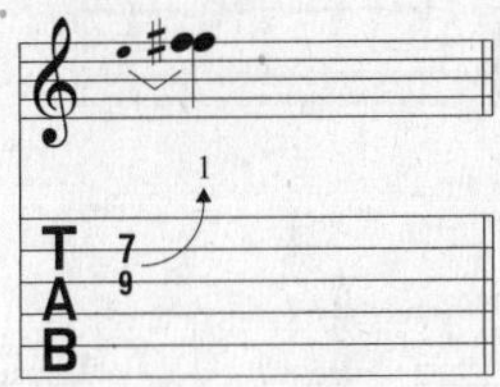

VIBRATO: The string is vibrated by rapidly bending and releasing the note with the fretting hand.

WIDE VIBRATO: The pitch is varied to a greater degree by vibrating with the fretting hand.

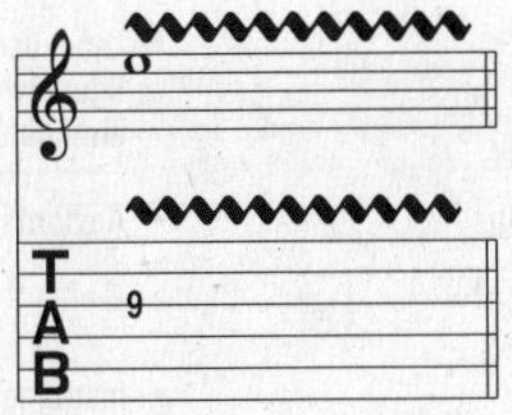

HAMMER-ON: Strike the first (lower) note with one finger, then sound the higher note (on the same string) with another finger by fretting it without picking.

PULL-OFF: Place both fingers on the notes to be sounded. Strike the first note and without picking, pull the finger off to sound the second (lower) note.

LEGATO SLIDE: Strike the first note and then slide the same fret-hand finger up or down to the second note. The second note is not struck.

SHIFT SLIDE: Same as legato slide, except the second note is struck.

TRILL: Very rapidly alternate between the notes indicated by continuously hammering on and pulling off.

TAPPING: Hammer ("tap") the fret indicated with the pick-hand index or middle finger and pull off to the note fretted by the fret hand.

NATURAL HARMONIC: Strike the note while the fret-hand lightly touches the string directly over the fret indicated.

PINCH HARMONIC: The note is fretted normally and a harmonic is produced by adding the edge of the thumb or the tip of the index finger of the pick hand to the normal pick attack.

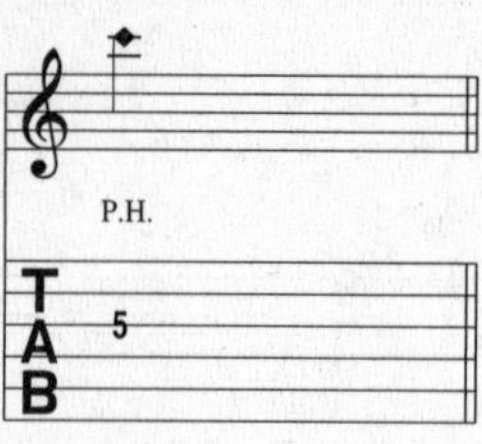

HARP HARMONIC: The note is fretted normally and a harmonic is produced by gently resting the pick hand's index finger directly above the indicated fret (in parentheses) while the pick hand's thumb or pick assists by plucking the appropriate string.

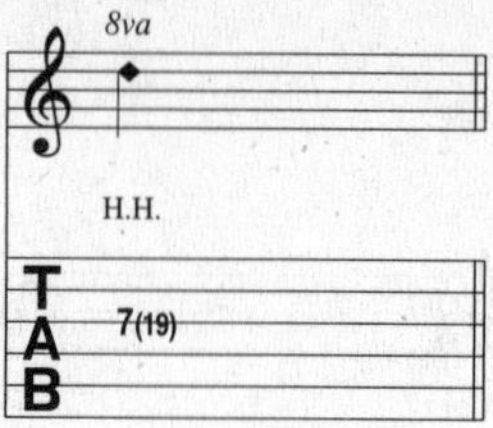

PICK SCRAPE: The edge of the pick is rubbed down (or up) the string, producing a scratchy sound.

MUFFLED STRINGS: A percussive sound is produced by laying the fret hand across the string(s) without depressing, and striking them with the pick hand.

PALM MUTING: The note is partially muted by the pick hand lightly touching the string(s) just before the bridge.

RAKE: Drag the pick across the strings indicated with a single motion.

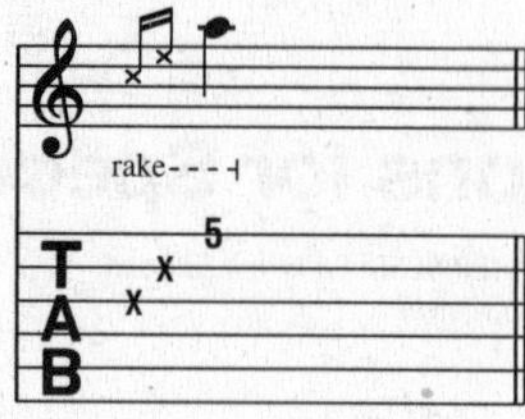

TREMOLO PICKING: The note is picked as rapidly and continuously as possible.

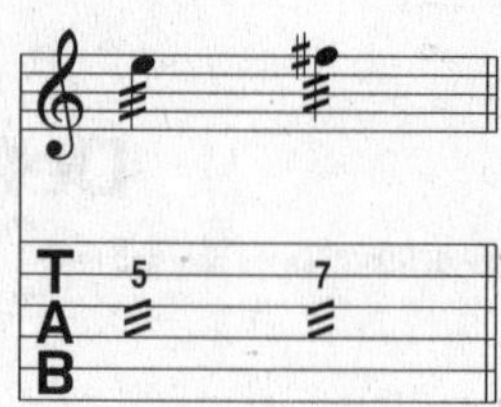

ARPEGGIATE: Play the notes of the chord indicated by quickly rolling them from bottom to top.

VIBRATO BAR DIVE AND RETURN: The pitch of the note or chord is dropped a specified number of steps (in rhythm) then returned to the original pitch.

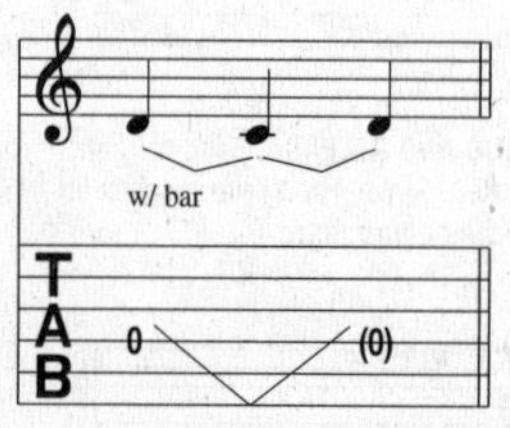

VIBRATO BAR SCOOP: Depress the bar just before striking the note, then quickly release the bar.

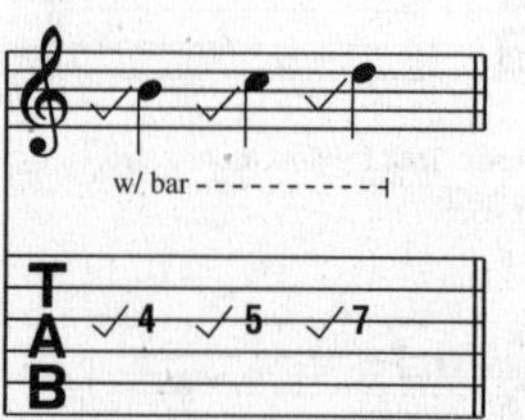

VIBRATO BAR DIP: Strike the note and then immediately drop a specified number of steps, then release back to the original pitch.

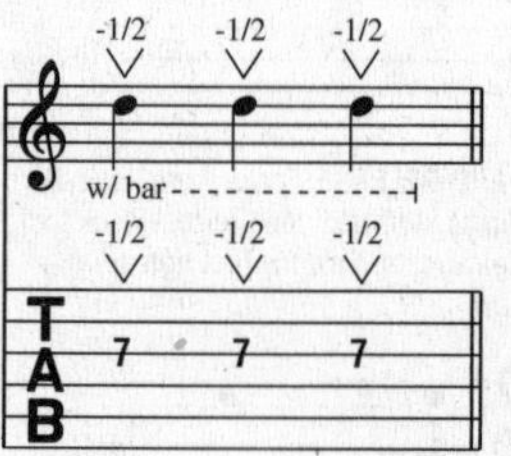

Additional Musical Definitions

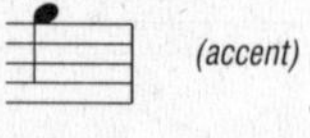 *(accent)* • Accentuate note (play it louder)

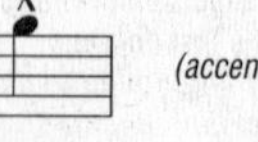 *(accent)* • Accentuate note with great intensity

 *(staccato)* • Play the note short

⊓ • Downstroke

V • Upstroke

D.S. al Coda • Go back to the sign (𝄋), then play until the measure marked "***To Coda,***" then skip to the section labelled "**Coda.**"

D.C. al Fine • Go back to the beginning of the song and play until the measure marked "***Fine***" (end).

Rhy. Fig. • Label used to recall a recurring accompaniment pattern (usually chordal).

Riff • Label used to recall composed, melodic lines (usually single notes) which recur.

Fill • Label used to identify a brief melodic figure which is to be inserted into the arrangement.

Rhy. Fill • A chordal version of a Fill.

tacet • Instrument is silent (drops out).

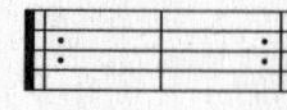 • Repeat measures between signs.

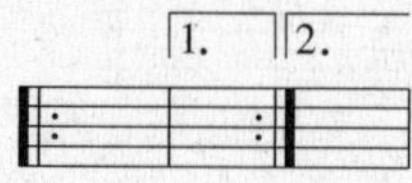

• When a repeated section has different endings, play the first ending only the first time and the second ending only the second time.

NOTE: Tablature numbers in parentheses mean:
1. The note is being sustained over a system (note in standard notation is tied), or
2. The note is sustained, but a new articulation (such as a hammer-on, pull-off, slide or vibrato begins), or
3. The note is a barely audible "ghost" note (note in standard notation is also in parentheses).